AUSCHWITZ CHRONICLE

1939 – 1945

DANUTA CZECH

AN OWL BOOK
HENRY HOLT AND COMPANY   NEW YORK

Henry Holt and Company, Inc.
Publishers since 1866
115 West 18th Street
New York, New York 10011

Henry Holt® is a registered
trademark of Henry Holt and Company, Inc.

Library of Congress Cataloging-in-Publication Data
Czech, Danuta.
[Kalendarium der Ereignisse im Konzentrationslager Auschwitz-
Birkenau, 1939–1945. English]
Auschwitz chronicle, 1939–1945 / Danuta Czech.—1st American ed.
p. cm.
Translation of: Kalendarium der Ereignisse im Konzentrationslager
Auschwitz-Birkenau, 1939–1945.
Includes bibliographical references and index.
1. Auschwitz (Poland: Concentration camp). 2. Holocaust, Jewish
(1939–1945). I. Title.
D805.P7C87   1989   89-35351
940.53'174386—dc20   CIP

ISBN 0-8050-0938-8
ISBN 0-8050-5238-0 (An Owl Book: pbk.)

Henry Holt books are available for special promotions and
premiums. For details contact: Director, Special Markets.

Originally published in Germany in 1989 by Rowohlt Verlag under the title
*Kalendarium der Ereignisse im Konzentrationslager
Auschwitz-Birkenau 1939–1945,* translated from the Polish
*Kalendarium wydarzeń w obozie Koncentracyjnym
Auschwitz-Birkenau 1939–1945.*

First published in the United States in 1990 by
Henry Holt and Company, Inc.

First Owl Book Edition—1997

Designed by Kate Nichols
Maps on pages 3, 4, and 5 drawn by Jurgen Pieplow.

Printed in the United States of America
All first editions are printed on acid-free paper.∞

1 3 5 7 9 10 8 6 4 2
1 3 5 7 9 10 8 6 4 2 (pbk.)

CONTENTS

PREFACE

In order to preserve the historical context, in translating from Polish, German place names have been used whenever they were commonly used at the time, but the Polish name appears in parentheses at the first mention. Names of places associated with National Socialism are used for the many auxiliary camps of Auschwitz Concentration Camp.

It is interesting to note that in the Nazi bureaucracy the names of things such as camp sections, work units, headquarters, and the like, kept changing. This stems from both the continuously expanding bureaucracy of the death camps and the use of euphemisms to keep the murderous events secret from the public. One example makes this clear.

On March 26, 1942, when the first transport of female prisoners from Ravensbrück Concentration Camp reaches Auschwitz, a "women's section" is formed, which remains subordinate to Ravensbrück. About four months later, on July 10, 1942, the RSHA (Reichssicherheitshauptamt–Reich Central Security Office) informs all headquarters that the "Women's Section, Ravensbrück Concentration Camp" now is called "Auschwitz Concentration Camp, Women's Section, Auschwitz East, Upper Silesia." After the transfer of the women's section to Birkenau on August 5, 1942, the place name "Auschwitz East" was changed to "Birkenau." On March 30, 1943, the Commandant of Auschwitz, Rudolf Höss, changed the name to "Women's Camp" to hide the fact that it was a women's concentration camp. Finally, on November 27, 1944, this camp was dubbed "Auschwitz Concentration Camp, Birkenau Auxiliary Camp, Women's Camp."

In the Index of Names, if only a last name is listed it generally means the prisoner's first name could not be ascertained. SS members, especially from the lower ranks, whose first names are not known have their rank indicated in parentheses.

In the original Polish manuscript, which is based on Polish sources (e.g., documents of the camp resistance), Polish spellings were used for Russian and Czech first names. These spellings have been retained where there is uncertainty about the original spelling.

Part of the previously unpublished photographic material in this volume is based on originals whose technical quality is generally rather poor. Despite all efforts, this is visible in reproduction.

Regarding the source references in the text, the original abbreviations for archives have been retained to facilitate direct access to these sources. The Bibliography includes a list of abbreviations of names of archives and terms used in the footnotes, source notes, and bibliographic entries.

The Appendix also contains a glossary of camp terms and other relevant expressions, a bibliography, the Index of Names, and "Sketches of the Perpetrators." The latter makes no claim to completeness but rather attempts to show through typical examples the diverse origins of the perpetrators of criminal acts under the auspices of the Third Reich, who did, however, agree on one thing: the rightness of their course of action.

Henry Holt and Company joins Rowohlt Verlag in thanking the Auschwitz Memorial for making the publication of this book possible. Thanks are also due to Barbara Harshav, Martha Humphreys, and Stephen Shearier for translation, and to Kate Scott for extensive editorial assistance.

INTRODUCTION

Historical study of the Auschwitz-Birkenau concentration and death camp is vitally dependent on the sources available. A historian who wishes to reconstruct the history of the concentration camp encounters serious problems, since most of the sources necessary for such a reconstruction were deliberately destroyed by the authorities of the Third Reich to get rid of incriminating evidence of their crimes. In Auschwitz, this process began in the summer of 1944, when the transport lists of Jews deported to Auschwitz were burned. The second round of destroying evidence took place in January 1945, when during the evacuation and dissolution of Auschwitz and its auxiliary camps, documents were burned all over the camps. A small portion of the camp documents was transferred to Gross-Rosen Concentration Camp, only to be destroyed later. Finally, just before the liberation of the camp, the remaining death factories were destroyed and the warehouse containing the property stolen from the victims of the destruction was burned down. Nevertheless, the SS did not manage to kill approximately 7,000 inmates who were so extremely debilitated they could no longer be evacuated on a forced march and so were left behind in Auschwitz-Birkenau and its auxiliary camps.

On January 27, 1945, Auschwitz was liberated. Soviet soldiers had finally reached the complex of concentration camps in Auschwitz-Birkenau and Monowitz. Although the most important task now was to help the survivors, in the first weeks after liberating the camp the Soviet military authorities and the Polish authorities also tried to obtain a general idea of the crimes committed there and to secure evidence; thus, they compiled the first comprehensive collection of documents and this formed the basis for all subsequent research.

The 7,000 liberated prisoners were eyewitnesses of the crimes committed there. The liberators found several hundred corpses of prisoners whom the SS had executed at the last minute as well as of those who had died from extreme exhaustion; they also discovered the ruins of the crematoriums; pits with the ashes of human beings; camp buildings and some documents; prisoners who, risking their lives, hid during the last weeks before the liberation and thus were saved from the destruction.

The survival of even some of the camp documents is due to the fact that the circulation of correspondence and reports within the camps themselves and between the camps and their governing authorities as well as with other German authorities and institutions (e.g., businesses that used prisoners as forced laborers) was very extensive. In the normal routine of the separate sections of the camp, hundreds of documents of varying importance and value were produced in such quantities that they could not all be destroyed.

After a few days, Soviet military units continued their advance westward, leaving Oświęcim, but the following day, two Soviet field hospitals were set up in the camp, and in early February 1945 in buildings of the former main camp a Polish Red Cross hospital was established under the direction of the Kraków physician Dr. Józef Bellert.

A few days after the liberation, Soviet military authorities in cooperation with the Polish authorities in the region began investigating crimes committed within the territory of the former concentration camp. The very first inquiry was begun by the public prosecutor's office of the first Ukrainian Front. Its work, the "investigation of the crimes of the German-Fascist aggressors," was directed by a Special Soviet Official Committee represented by D. J. Kudriavcev and S. G. Kuzmin. On February 4, 1945, the first official inspection of the grounds and buildings of the liberated camp and the ruins of the mass extermination facility took place. Moreover, several committees of experts were formed to investigate specific objects and installations and to clarify what means and methods the SS had used to destroy the prisoners in Auschwitz.

The work of the Soviet commissions resulted in a list of liberated prisoners, medical opinions on their health, photodocumentation of all the sections of the camp, protocols of the testimony of former prisoners, and a documentary film showing the former camp after the liberation, the work of the investigating committee, and the burial of several hundred prisoners.

On March 29, 1945, the presidium of the Polish National Council appointed the High Commission for the Investigation of German Crimes in Poland as a special office of the Ministry of Justice (renamed in the 1950s the High Commission for the Investigation of Nazi Crimes in Poland), which began its investigations on the site of the former camp. The long and exhaustive investigations were carried out by the District Commission for the Investigation of German Crimes in Kraków and supervised by a member of the High Commission, Judge Jan Sehn. He spared no effort to secure all the camp documents that could be found, going so far as to sift through the garbage left behind. The investigation, including comprehensive local inspections of everything pertaining to the vast Auschwitz complex, lasted somewhat longer than a year. Moreover, special technical commissions were formed to investigate the crematoriums, gas chambers, and pits where the bodies of gassed victims were burned. All the documents, plans, and maps that had accidentally escaped destruction or removal were investigated in detail.

Several hundred former prisoners were summoned as witnesses, as were members of the civilian population living in the vicinity of the camp. All investigations were conducted as legal proceedings, according to the relevant provisions of the Polish Criminal Code.

This commission's work resulted in additional protocols of site inspections and in the securing of documents of the former concentration camp; documentary photographs were made of individual objects in the camp. Voluminous interrogation protocols of statements of former prisoners, including several hundred members of the Special Squad,* were also recorded.

These materials were used as evidence in two trials held in the Supreme People's Court of Poland: that of the first Commandant of Auschwitz, Rudolf Höss, and the Kraków Auschwitz Trial of 40 members of the Auschwitz SS garrison.**

Workers in the clinic set up by the Polish Red Cross also established an information service for former prisoners in the Polish Red Cross hospital and were able to save some camp documents. These documents were first used to collect information on missing former prisoners; later, after abstracts were made from them, they were turned over to the District Commission in Kraków. This material was subsequently acquired by the

---

*Prisoner labor squad whose task was to operate the crematoriums and burn corpses in the vicinity of the crematorium.
**Compare Kazimierz Smolén, "Bestrafung der Verbrecher von Auschwitz" (Punishment of the Criminals of Auschwitz), in Józef Buszko, Danuta Czech, Tadeusz Iwaszko, Franciszo Piper, Barabara Jarosz, Andrzej Strzelecki, Kazimierz Smolén, eds., Auschwitz: Geschichte und Wirklichkeit des Vernichtungslagers (Auschwitz: History and Reality of the Extermination Camp), Reinbek/Hamburg, 1980, pp. 181–211.

information office of the Polish Red Cross in Warsaw; today it is part of the collection of the State Museum in Oświęcim.* The approximately 40,000 negatives of photographs of prisoners made by the Identification Service of the Political Department (the camp Gestapo) went first to the Polish Red Cross in Kraków and were turned over to the State Auschwitz Museum in Oświęcim in 1954 when the latter took over the research work concerning former prisoners.

On July 2, 1947, the Polish *Sejm* (parliament) passed legislation establishing a state museum in Oświęcim-Brzezinka to commemorate the ordeal of the Polish people and others in Auschwitz. Preparation for the museum had already begun in early 1946. The organizers included a large group of former prisoners who obtained objects of the camp and made them accessible to the thousands of visitors from Poland and other countries who wanted to see with their own eyes what crimes had taken place here, and who wanted to honor the victims. In fulfillment of its mission, the museum collects, secures, and prepares all transmitted sources on the history of Auschwitz Concentration Camp, preserves the collections and objects from the camp, and makes them available to visitors. The museum is under the Ministry of Culture and Art of the Republic of Poland and is funded by the ministry's budget.

The museum's first years were devoted primarily to funding an appropriate organizational form, conceptualizing its work, acquiring extant collections and objects of the camp, and developing a long-term agenda. In 1956, a research plan was worked out, and I was assigned to assemble a "Chronicle of Events in Auschwitz Concentration Camp," a project encouraged by the director of the museum, Kazimierz Smoleń, a former prisoner of Auschwitz.

When I began to prepare the "Chronicle," I had access to 21 volumes of documents from the trial of Rudolf Höss and seven volumes of documents from the Kraków trial of 40 members of the Auschwitz SS garrison. The Höss trial documents included photocopies and hand copies of documents from individual offices at Auschwitz and the protocols of interrogations and statements of former prisoners (for example, the detailed statement of Dr. Otto Wolken, based on clandestine notes and records he made during his imprisonment in the quarantine camp in Section B-IIa in Birkenau). I also had photocopies and originals of various camp documents in German which were then in the Documentation Department of the Museum (the archive was established later as an independent institution), namely, admissions lists for the period January 7, 1941, to December 22, 1941, and several others from 1942; the Camp Occupancy Register for the period January 19, 1942, to August 19, 1942; some documents of the offices of the Labor Deployment Department; the card index of Soviet prisoners of war for the period October 6 to October 19, 1941; the Death Register of the Russian prisoner-of-war camp for the period October 7, 1941, to February 28, 1942; the two volumes of the Bunker Register of Block 11 for the period January 9, 1941, to February 1, 1944 (the first an original, the second a copy smuggled out of the camp and sent to Kraków by members of the resistance movement); the register of the Penal Company for the period July 8, 1943, to November 22, 1944; the Morgue Register for October 7, 1941 to August 31, 1943, naturally with some gaps, in which daily entries recorded the numbers of prisoners who died or were murdered; and copies of pages from these books made clandestinely by prisoners, smuggled out of the camp, and sent to Kraków. In addition, I had the registers of the Gypsy camp, containing accounts of the men and women imprisoned there for the period February 26, 1943, to July 21, 1944, which were stolen by Polish prisoner functionaries and buried in the Gypsy camp and are the only surviving documents from the office of the Gypsy Family Camp in Birkenau; orders from headquarters, the regiment, and the garrison, obtained individually for 1942

*The Germans use "Oświęcim" for the contemporary town and "Auschwitz" or "the town of Auschwitz" for historical references.

and for the period February 14, 1943, to November 1, 1944; the quarantine lists for Section B-IIa in Birkenau for the period October 21, 1943, to July 28, 1944; and fragmentary documents on, for example, the number of inmates in separate sections of the prisoners' infirmary, requests for troop vehicles, travel orders, etc.

Along with these documents, I used photocopies of documents clandestinely copied by members of the camp resistance movement; these were secret messages, accounts and reports that had been passed on to Teresa Lasocka, an active member of the Kraków underground organization Pomoc Więźniom Obozów Koncentracyjnych (Assistance for Concentration Camp Prisoners). These documents were labeled "Material of the Resistance Movement in the Camp."

This collection included several lists made in September 1944 in a few days by prisoners working in the Admissions Unit of the Political Department registering incoming transports and smuggled out of the camp: These lists contained names of men and women admitted to the camp as registered prisoners, the date of the transport's arrival, the date of admission, the prisoner number, the transport's place of origin or the RSHA* office that had sent the prisoner to Auschwitz. The lists were kept by the mother of Kazimierz Smoleń, who had copied them.

These lists were crucial in establishing when the transports began and the number of new prisoners. They formed one of the basic documents for the "Chronicle."

The available sources—original documents, resistance movement documents, statements of former prisoners, and trial materials—were subjected to a strict source check and were compared with other appropriate documents. A contribution to this checking process was made by the statements and memoirs of Rudolf Höss, who had willingly talked about Auschwitz while in detention and, during his investigative detention in Kraków, had voluntarily written down his autobiography and his thoughts about Auschwitz and related subjects. These materials form an important supplement and facilitate the reading of camp documents, which use many pseudonyms and abbreviations.

The "Chronicle" was examined by Kazimierz Smoleń, director of the Auschwitz Memorial, and by Dr. Włradyslaw Bieda, lecturer at the School of Economics. As the work progressed it was published by the Auschwitz Memorial, from 1958 to 1963, in Nos. 2, 3, 4, 6, and 7 of Zeszyty Oświęcimskie (Annals of Auschwitz), and from 1954 to 1964 in Nos. 2, 3, 4, 6, 7 and 8 of the journal's German edition, Hefte von Auschwitz.

The most urgent task in 1957 was to collect and safeguard in the archives of the Memorial the basic sources necessary to initiate and continue the study of the history of Auschwitz. Contact with various institutions and authorities as well as with organizations of former prisoners outside Poland and a search for additional sources in Polish and foreign archives made it possible for the Archive of the Memorial to collect several thousand microfilms of various documents. The basic documents of several trials against Nazi criminals were also put on film (the trial of Höss, the former Commandant of Auschwitz; the trial of Gerhard Maurer, the head of the SS Economic and Administrative Office (Wirtschafts- und Verwaltungshauptamt—WVHA); the Kraków Auschwitz Trial of 1947; and the Nuremberg Doctors' trial, Case 1).

Starting in 1962, the museum received from the High Commission for the Investigation of Nazi Crimes in Poland the documents that had been collected in Auschwitz by the Kraków District Commission in the first two years after the war.

Other important documents were discovered by the museum staff while doing research in the registries and archives of industrial firms that had operated auxiliary camps of Auschwitz and of factories that had used forced laborers. The most voluminous of these are the documents found in the Brzeszcze-Jawiszowice mine, in two mines in Jaworzno, and in the "Fürstengrube" colliery.

---

*Reichssicherheitshauptamt, the Reich Central Security Office, which organized many of the transports of Jews.

In the course of research on the camp resistance movement and outside resistance groups that worked with them, several hundred original secret messages were discovered that inmates had written to members of the underground organization outside the camp. Most of these concerned help given in the form of food but some also dealt with organizing escapes.

The archive of the Auschwitz Memorial has only 5½ feet of shelf space of original documents from the offices of the camp. But it is the possessor of most of the surviving documents relating to Auschwitz Concentration Camp in original, microfilm, or photocopy. Nevertheless, archives outside Poland have access to documents that are still unavailable to us.

The archive obtained some of the documents of the SS Central Building Administration (Zentralbauverwaltung), amounting to 16½ feet. Some of the most valuable documents of this group are the plans for the expansion of Auschwitz I ("Mexico") and the construction of Auschwitz II (Birkenau), and the plans and sections of the construction journal for the gas chambers and crematoriums erected in Birkenau.* The remaining records from the former SS and Police Hygiene Institute occupy barely 5½ feet of shelf space. These are primarily ledgers and orders for laboratory experiments listing the names of the people affected. The entries make it possible to clarify statements of many prisoners and members of the SS garrison. Particularly valuable are the experimental results noted in special registers (auxiliary registers) on, for example, the quality of the food distributed to the inmates or the products of the camp butcher shop.**

There is much valuable information in materials gathered by the camp's underground movement. About 2,000 documents relate to the camp resistance movement.

Several more or less organized groups of prisoners worked secretly in the camp to collect incriminating evidence against the SS. This was done by prisoners working at various levels of the camp administration—the prisoners' office, the prisoners' infirmary, the Labor Deployment Department, and even the Political Department. These people risked their lives to make clandestine copies of letters, reports, and statistics. All the material that could be collected in this way was channeled out of the camp and used by the Polish resistance groups. They were also passed on to the Allied reconnaissance offices and published in the underground press.

Some of the most valuable of these are the records made secretly by the members of the Special Squads (Sonderkommandos) and concealed near the crematoriums. They were discovered between 1945 and 1981 and are now published and accessible.

Of different character but also important are a number of autobiographies by SS Men: Höss's memoirs; the account written by Pery Broad, a functionary of the Political Department, the camp Gestapo; and the diary of Johann Kremer, Camp Doctor at Auschwitz for several months, which was included in the documentation of the trial of Rudolf Höss. The Memorial has also published these documents, making them generally available.

For three decades now, former prisoners of Auschwitz have been urged to write down their recollections, and oral accounts have been recorded and transcribed. These autobiographical materials are collected to fill the gaps in the source material and to interpret better the partially preserved and deliberately falsified documents of the camp. So far, the archive of the Memorial has collected 943 memoirs (about 20,000 pages) and 2,744 accounts, most of them transcribed by the staff of the Memorial (about 17,000 pages).

Thus, three decades after the first publication of the "Chronicle," the Archive of the

*Tadeusz Iwaszko, "The Sources for the History of Auschwitz Concentration Camp and Their Value for Research," unpublished typescript in the archive of the Auschwitz Memorial.
**Ibid.

Auschwitz Memorial possesses considerably expanded resources. This extensive documentary foundation and the knowledge acquired through almost three decades of research on the history of Auschwitz have enabled the author to take up once again work on the "Chronicle of Events in Auschwitz Concentration Camp."

The author is grateful to the book collector Klaus Kunz, who is also knowledgeable on the subject of the "Chronicle," for his suggestion to rewrite the "Chronicle" for publication in the Federal Republic of Germany.

For the new edition it was possible to expand the "Chronicle" considerably. In view of the deliberate destruction of documents by the SS, it is impossible to reconstruct the entire past of Auschwitz Concentration Camp. We must not exclude the possibility that more sources will become available in the future, allowing us to further clarify questions on the history of the camp. The Archive of the State Museum in Oświęcim will gratefully accept all relevant information.

The "Chronicle" has been an important resource for collecting evidence against former members of the SS in Auschwitz and other camps and continues to play this role. As its author, I gave expert testimony in the trial of Robert Mulka, who oversaw the gas chambers and the production of Zyklon B at Auschwitz, and others, in the first Frankfurt Auschwitz Trial, from December 20, 1963, to August 1965 in the Frankfurt District Court. I also served as an expert witness in the trial of the members of the Security Police (Sicherheitspolizei—Sipo) and the Gestapo of Białystok in Bielefeld 1967-68 and in March 1988 in Siegen in the trial of the former Block Leader in the Gypsy camp in Birkenau, Ernst-August König.

The High Commission for the Investigation of Nazi Crimes in Poland has sent hundreds of microfilmed documents on crimes committed in Auschwitz to legal authorities in other countries, particularly prosecutors and courts of the Federal Republic of Germany. During the trials of former SS members in the Federal Republic of Germany, the Memorial made the former camp available to the investigating authorities so that site visits could be made. The first took place on December 14, 1964, the last so far in June 1987.

The Auschwitz Memorial makes its archives, photographic materials, and special collections available not only to legal authorities but also to institutions and private individuals from Poland and other countries for scientific, journalistic, and other purposes.

Thus, the "Chronicle," now published for the second time, has had direct significance for historical research on the camp as well as for the criminal prosecution of the perpetrators. Its meaning, however, goes beyond this—and hence its value for a broader readership. In this revision, I have deliberately introduced several hundred names of inmates—the partially reconstructed file of people deported to Auschwitz contains countless more—for not numbers but only real, specific human beings can touch the feelings and imagination of other human beings.

The "Chronicle" is not only a framework for research into the camp's history and the fate of the prisoners and an aid for criminal investigations, it is also an epitaph, a memorial book for those who suffered and struggled in Auschwitz-Birkenau and its auxiliary camps, for those who did not survive Auschwitz, who died nameless—I am thinking especially of those who were killed in the gas chambers immediately after their arrival, without even being registered. It is my hope that the "Chronicle" will be recognized as such an epitaph.

Danuta Czech

FOREWORD
by Walter Laqueur

The town of Auschwitz (Oświęcim) is located on the outskirts of the Upper Silesian industrial region, near the Vistula River, approximately 18 miles southeast of Kattowitz (Katowice). Residence of a prince, and a duchy during the Middle Ages, Auschwitz initially belonged to the Piasts, then belonged to the Czechs, then again to Poland, which lost it to Austria in 1772 and didn't get it back again until 1918. After the invasion and occupation of western Poland by German military forces under the National Socialist government in 1939, Upper Silesia was incorporated into the Greater German Empire (Grossdeutsches Reich).

Soon afterward, the proposal was worked out among the higher SS leadership to establish a concentration camp in Auschwitz. For this purpose, two investigative commissions were sent to the area; and they reported that neither the old (Austro-Hungarian) army barracks nor the factory buildings of the Polish national tobacco monopoly were suited to accommodate a large number of prisoners. Still, the site satisfied many of the requirements for the planned concentration camp, unlike other locations under consideration at that time.

Auschwitz was situated at the juncture of a major traffic network, so it was possible to transport large numbers of people there without difficulty. At the same time, the camp could easily be shielded from the Polish population living in the vicinity; to accomplish this, "only 2,000" people had to be evacuated. On April 27, 1940, SS Commander in Chief Himmler issued an order effectively establishing Auschwitz Concentration Camp (Auschwitz C.C.). The original so-called main camp was small; an initial transport of 728 political prisoners who arrived there on June 14, 1940, formed its nucleus. The fact that the appointed Commandant, Rudolf Höss, the adjutant and Chief of Camp Supervision of Sachsenhausen, was an experienced SS man whose rank was comparable to Eichmann's, indicated that the new camp soon would increase in size and significance.

Birkenau (Brzezinka), just under two miles from the original camp, was established in the winter of 1941–42. Eventually, Auschwitz III (Monowitz) was added. Ultimately the "interest zone" of Auschwitz Concentration Camp covered almost 25 square miles, including the newly constructed factories such as I. G. Farben's "Buna Works," the German Armaments Works, and the German Earth and Stone Works.

Although millions of people came to Auschwitz, it is doubtful that more than 120,000–150,000 ever lived there at any one time. Even housing this number was a challenge for the camp administrators and was made possible only "thanks to [their] utmost efforts," as it was expressed in the language of that time. Stable barracks were built (of a design and size designated OKH—type 2609). This model was intended for stabling 52 horses, but owing to the "efficiency" of the administration 800 men (or women and children) were crammed into the barracks, six, eight, or more on one plank-bed.

Auschwitz was not a typical concentration camp: within the Greater German Reich* there were 20 such camps (with 160 associated "affiliates"). Auschwitz was the largest of the extermination camps; other significantly smaller extermination camps were Sobibor, Belzec, Treblinka, and Majdanek. An official of the English Foreign Ministry wrote in a brief memorandum before the end of the war that Auschwitz had evidently been the worst of all these camps. Although this was secondhand information, those who had made Auschwitz possible were of the same opinion. Doctor Johann Paul Kremer, an SS volunteer from Münster and an enthusiastic Nazi who had come to Auschwitz as a man in his fifties to conduct medical experiments, wrote in his diary on September 5, 1942, that after being present at a "special operation," he would altogether have to agree with a colleague (Lieutenant Colonel Thilo) that they found themselves at the *anus mundi*, the asshole of the world. This "special operation" involved the gassing of a group of completely emaciated women, so-called Muslims, who were required to undress outdoors before being herded into the gas chambers.

Nobody knows exactly how many people perished in Auschwitz; the estimates range between one and four million. Even Korherr, the SS statistician who in the spring of 1943 had been directed by Himmler to write a report, had to settle for estimates. People had been murdered faster than records could be kept. Undoubtedly, though, the number was greater than in the other extermination camps. Only 404,222 people, their specific number tattooed on the forearm, were entered in the Camp Occupancy Register. But this total means little, for "selection" occurred immediately upon the arrival of the mass transports, and the elderly, the weak, children, the ill, many women—frequently 90 percent or more—were herded directly into the gas chambers without being entered in the register at all. Probably the Commandant's daily operation reports to the Reich Security Central Office (RSHA) included the numbers of all people who were sent to Auschwitz by rail. But these reports were strictly secret and were destroyed so that no evidence would remain.

The first selection among weak and sick prisoners took place on May 4, 1942; 1,200 prisoners who had arrived in the previous months were declared "unfit for work." On May 12, 1942, for the first time a transport of 1,500 people was brought from the nearby town of Sosnowitz (Sosnowice) directly into the gas chambers. While the other extermination camps served mainly for the killing of Polish Jews (especially as part of the so-called "Operation Reinhardt"), transports came to Auschwitz from all the countries of Europe. It was the most "international" of all death factories: The stream of Jews from France and Slovakia began at the end of March 1942. The first trains from Holland arrived on July 17, 1942, in the presence of Himmler, who observed the selection and killing of the victims. The Commander in Chief of the SS visited camps unwillingly and seldom, but believed it was his duty to provide his subordinates with a "good example." After the gassing, he had a snack (with ladies) with the gauleiter** of Upper Silesia, Bracht, who lived in a villa in the vicinity of Kattowitz.

Transports from Belgium arrived in August 1942, from Yugoslavia that same month, from Czechoslovakia in December, followed by trains from Germany, Greece in March 1943, Italy in October 1943, and Latvia and Austria in November 1943. The last large transports occurred in May 1944 after the invasion of Hungary by the Wehrmacht, and in the ensuing months.

---

*Encompassing Germany within its prewar borders and annexed territories in Austria, Czechoslovakia, and Poland. —ED.
**The head of a Nazi Party administrative district, or *Gau*. —ED.

But Auschwitz was by no means only an extermination camp for European Jews: There were Polish and Russian prisoners of war, political prisoners (with red triangles on their arms), religious sectarians (with purple marks), criminal felons from Germany (green triangles), homosexuals (pink triangles), and Gypsies (*Zigeuner*) who were required to wear the letter Z. There were even "reeducation prisoners," who did not wear a triangle, just the letter E. Ultimately, there were thousands of prisoners from other concentration camps and the Theresienstadt (Terezín) ghetto in Czechoslovakia.

While the Jews were systematically murdered, the survival chances of the other prisoners were somewhat better—but not much. Thus, for example, of a total of 13,000 Russian prisoners of war brought to Auschwitz, only 92 were alive when the camp was shut down. That fate of these Russian prisoners shows that it was not possible to think of active resistance and mass uprising in Auschwitz. If young Russians with military training and discipline were not capable of putting up resistance, what could be expected of those who were neither young nor healthy and also were unable to fight?

Although the greatest number of people died in the gas chambers, there were many other ways to die. Thousands starved, froze to death, or died of untreated illnesses. Many committed suicide, others died in escape attempts, were given lethal injections, were shot, hanged, beaten to death, or died as victims of medical experiments.

The gas chambers were in operation for two years and ten months. In late November 1944, the order came from Berlin to destroy the gas chambers and crematoriums. But the bureaucratic forces of the Final Solution remained active up to the last moment. Although thousands of prisoners had already been marched off toward the West and parts of the storehouses set afire, a new group of Jews arrived on January 5, 1945, from Berlin. To the officials in Berlin, the final solution was not quite over and the war not yet completely lost. On January 17, 1945, evacuation of the camp was completed. When units of the Red Army entered Auschwitz ten days later, 7,600 prisoners were still alive. The Russian soldiers also found 348,820 men's suits and 836,515 women's dresses that in the haste of evacuation had not been disposed of.

When did the outside world find out about Auschwitz? The first news arrived early and from many sources. Of course every SS man who served in Auschwitz (and there were 6,000) had to swear that under no circumstances would he ever disclose what he had seen in the extermination camp. But not everyone complied, and information about the camp continued to seep out. Photographs were taken, although this too was strictly forbidden: photographs of the camp gate with its sign, ARBEIT MACHT FREI, and of the railway ramps on which the selections took place, have been widely published. Photos exist of the women's camp in Birkenau and of the sorting of seized valuables.

Furthermore, SS people were by no means the only ones stationed in Auschwitz. There were the directors and technicians of I. G. Farben and other factories, there were the trainmen who brought the trains to the camp ramp—and what went on in the camp was not unknown to the residents in the vicinity. Several hundred prisoners were set free, and 200 succeeded in escaping—most of them in the last two years of the war. Finally, there are the photos of Auschwitz made by the United States Air Force; furthermore, the English radio monitoring personnel in Bletchley Park, who had broken the code of the SS and the police, knew by 1942 what was going on in Auschwitz. Although they didn't have complete figures and could not know precise details, it didn't require much fantasy to form an approximate picture, when reports were monitored day after day of 4,000 people arriving in the evening, of whom less than 1,000 were still alive the following morning.

Thus, millions of people had already heard of Auschwitz during the war. Perhaps they did not know the name, but they knew that somewhere in the East, not far from the German border, millions of people were being murdered. They probably didn't know how slowly or quickly it happened, whether victims were shot or gassed or starved to death. But the fact that they had vanished could not be doubted. Even so, the full extent of what Auschwitz meant was not understood in Germany or abroad.

In Germany the annihilation of the Jews was kept secret. Of course, the Führer himself had threatened the destruction of the Jews even before the outbreak of the war, and gradually they vanished from the towns where they lived. It was obvious to anyone with eyes and ears, but people did not want to know further details.

Thus, it was not surprising that after the war the majority of Germans did not want to believe that there had ever been such a thing as Auschwitz, that most of them only unwillingly gave any credence to the information coming out. Today, some still refuse to accept Auschwitz. For them Auschwitz remains a wildly exaggerated or freely invented horror story used by the victorious powers as propaganda to saddle the German people with a bad conscience for all eternity.

Psychologically this reaction is understandable: There are always people who assert the opposite of what others say. And the truth about Auschwitz exceeded by far the average citizen's faculty of imagination.

Thus began the "relativization" of Auschwitz: When Churchill wrote, in July 1944, to his foreign minister, Anthony Eden, that there was no longer any doubt that the mass murder of the European Jews was probably the greatest and most terrible crime in the history of the world, this assessment was downplayed with the observation that Churchill had always been an enemy of the Krauts anyway—justice could not be expected from such a man. After all, the British had incarcerated women and children in concentration camps during the Boer War, millions had died in Stalin's collectivization and purges, and Genghis Khan and Tamerlane also did not go down in world history as humanitarians. Even if it had come to "regrettable excesses and outrages" (which was not even certain, for after all the corpus delicti had vanished), others had also committed crimes, which some Germans now balanced against their own misdeeds.

These doubters also did not find convincing the words of the Commandant of Auschwitz, who had written in his memoirs that terrible crimes against humanity had been committed in the camp and that he only wished the disclosure of these crimes would forever prevent a repetition. Rudolf Höss wrote these words in captivity, and one knows, after all, that such coerced confessions should not be taken very seriously. But how was it possible to explain Dr. Johann Kremer's diary entry of September 2, 1942, that he had participated in a "special operation" for the first time and that by comparison, Dante's *Inferno* was a comedy? (The incident involved the arrival of a train from the Drancy camp in France; of the 957 Jews, 928 were murdered immediately after their arrival.)

For anyone who wanted to know the truth about Auschwitz, there was undoubtedly more than enough evidence from unassailable witnesses. But the truth was shocking, horrifying, and there is something in human nature that does not like to accept such news. Even if the information was true, people told themselves, an individual couldn't do anything about it—not during the war, for we were in a state of emergency, and definitely not after the war, for the Jews and the other victims were now dead. Nobody would be helped by having these dreadful stories repeated and discussed ad infinitum.

But in foreign countries, too, and among foreign Jews, the entire truth about Auschwitz was grasped only during the last year of the war. There were various reasons for this. The Allied governments and secret services were in possession of much information, but they considered Auschwitz a secondary problem. The main issue, the urgent task, was to win the war as soon as possible. The argument was repeatedly made that the defeat of the Nazi regime would also bring an end to the massacre of the Jews. It seemed senseless to threaten Hitler and his accomplices with punishment; they had burned their bridges anyway. And many Jews were disinclined to accept the entire dreadful truth. This was the twentieth century, and the Germans were the people of Bach and Beethoven, Kant,

Goethe, and Schiller—a culture in which most European Jews, even in the East, had been reared. People told themselves that even though the situation of the Jews in the camps was undoubtedly terrible, and although many had already died, in the end perhaps most of them would survive. Everyone knew that in the First World War, both sides had conducted horror propaganda, and so they hoped that the worst stories would prove to be exaggerated. Only after early 1944, when the long and detailed report of Rudolf Vrba and Alfred Wetzler, two Slovak Jews who had succeeded in escaping from Auschwitz, became known in Switzerland, did it become clear that the reality far exceeded the worst fears.

What happened to the people who were liberated from Auschwitz? Many survived the liberation of the camp for only a few days or weeks. Irrevocably weakened and ill, many died from the after-effects of torture. The few who survived were marked forever by their experiences in Auschwitz, and the camp's liberation did not mean the end of their life-and-death struggle. The majority emigrated during the postwar years to what was then Palestine; many emigrated to the United States; and some went to Canada and England.

In Poland the first trials against the Auschwitz murderers occurred in 1947 in Warsaw and Kraków. Rudolf Höss was executed on the grounds of the camp. In Poland a total of 617 people were convicted as accomplices, of whom 24 were sentenced to death. In addition, Auschwitz trials were held by the American, English, French, Russian, and Czechoslovak military authorities; but a 1951 decree of the states of the Federal Republic of Germany suspended all sentences imposed by the Allied authorities. The German Auschwitz trials began in Münster in 1960 and continued for two decades in Frankfurt. Some of the accused—among them, the camp physician, Dr. Carl Clauberg—died in prison. Others, such as Dr. Josef Mengele, managed to escape from justice. Still others, such as Mengele's colleague, Dr. Horst Schumann, escaped but were extradited sooner or later by their host countries.

Investigations against former Auschwitz functionaries were also conducted in Austria, but did not result in any indictments.

Since the end of the war a great deal of Auschwitz-related material has been published, including testimonials of great literary value, such as Primo Levi's autobiographical accounts and memoirs of prisoners who survived Auschwitz as members of the women's orchestra. The Polish government saw to it that a museum and research center was erected on the grounds of the former camp. In the Soviet Union, however, Auschwitz and everything connected with it was until recently a taboo topic, not written about and seldom discussed. The subject of Auschwitz has inspired philosophers and theologians, writers, filmmakers, and composers. But there were also those who felt that what happened there was so incomprehensible that neither everyday language nor academic terminology could make any contribution to the emotional and intellectual explanation of the phenomenon. Among the historians, particularly in the Federal Republic of Germany, the dispute between the "intentionalists" and "functionalists" was not only about Auschwitz but about the whole Final Solution. The intentionalists regarded the murder of millions of Jews and non-Jews as the logical consequence of the Nazi ideology, while the functionalists believed that neither Hitler nor his underlings had a clear conception of how the Reich could be made "free of Jews" (*Judenfrei*). They maintained that the Final Solution came into being only after the invasion of the Soviet Union, if not coincidentally, in any case gradually and haphazardly. It was not a very important debate, from the standpoint of the victims or from any meaningful historical perspective. Ultimately, the argument hinged on whether mass murder had been decided upon in the year 1940 or 1941 and whether Hitler had issued a direct command and had been involved in how it was actually carried out. These discussions did little to clarify the issue, because there were so few written documents: The most important orders had been conveyed orally. This is nothing new in human history: The greater the crime, the less likely it is that the perpetrators will leave any traces.

Dr. Danuta Czech, the former head of the research department of the Auschwitz Memorial, worked for years on compiling the Auschwitz Chronicle from files and documents, from accounts of the camp's resistance movement, and from witnesses' statements and subsequent research. This history reconstructs the perpetrators and victims and presents an oppressive chronicle of destruction and suffering, day by day and month by month for 4½ years.

To kill a single human being, no particularly complicated preparations are necessary, and certainly not file-generating government offices with their plans, reports, bills, and engagement reports. Auschwitz, however, was a mass extermination facility, hence the necessity for official agencies both on-site as well as in Berlin and elsewhere which almost always bore long and complicated names such as Headquarters for Industrial Management, Security Police Administration, Central Resettlement Headquarters, just to mention a few examples.

The history of Auschwitz begins with the visit of Höss and five of his advisers from the Reich Central Security Office (RSHA). Thirty professional criminals from German camps—all Germans—are put in charge of setting up the camp. They are dependable, they create order; one of them becomes the "Camp Senior," the others are made Capos. But an extermination camp of this size cannot be run by a Commandant and a few dozen criminals, so after a few weeks First and Second "Protective Custody" Commanders* are appointed, and someone is put in charge of food and lodging. What food! What lodgings!

A large camp has the same problems as a town, even if the task of the town fathers is not seeing to the well-being of citizens but killing the residents. From the very first day there are difficulties: Höss, having been ordered to set up a concentration camp, is not even supplied the necessary barbed wire, which he must acquire by having it stolen. Then a crematorium with five three-muffle ovens for reducing corpses to ash is ordered from the firm of Topf and Sons in Erfurt. The plans look good, but the wrong iron parts are delivered to Auschwitz by mistake and have to be taken away and replaced by new ones. Records exist documenting all these events, down to the necessity of replacing the iron urns for the ashes of the privileged deceased with porcelain ones—it was necessary to conserve iron during the war. Even the dead Jews cause the camp management further difficulties: Fishermen in the neighborhood complain about the poisoning of fish, which in their opinion is the result of toxins from corpses.

Even with the living there are problems. Who will pay the travel expenses of prisoners who are in the labor force in the outlying camps? The German National Railways has submitted a prime-cost calculation: Perhaps this expense can be offset by the value of the human hair supplied to industry for about twenty-five cents per pound, or by gold fillings? There are jurisdictional disputes. The SS is charged with killing as many Jews as possible, as quickly as possible, but the armaments industry needs laborers; and so there is a new twist in racial politics: "Extermination through Work." Occasionally corpses are exchanged for live prisoners, who are then worked for a few weeks or months in Monowitz or one of the other factories.

All these events, along with the outbreaks of typhus fever, executions, and escape attempts, find their way into the files. Most frequent, though, are the monotonous reports—how many people were delivered on a particular day, how old were they, which country did they come from, what number were they given (if they were not herded into the gas chambers immediately). Not that these statistics are of great importance, for the

---

*"Protective custody" (Schutzhaft) is a euphemism for unlimited preemptive detention and incarceration, hence the original term for concentration camps, "Schutzhaftlager." —ED.

end is always the same. But a bureaucratic system must record events and announce plan fulfillment and invent alibis if complications occur.

It is interesting to observe how an attempt is made to maintain secrecy even in official documents. Thus a travel permit to Dessau is issued not, say, to obtain Zyklon B, which is manufactured there, but for the purpose of buying "materials for resettlement of Jews." On another occasion there is a trip to Lodz "to inspect field ovens." A non-Jewish prisoner is condemned to death because, while performing labor outside the camp, he related what was happening in the gas chambers and thus "harmed the reputation of the Reich." And this at a time when the secret had been out for a long time. But the logic of Auschwitz was not the logic of the outside world. Thus Dr. Ernst Robert Grawitz, the Reich physician of the SS and head of the main medical office of the camp, witnesses the gassing of Jews and the subsequent cremation of corpses. In his report Grawitz, who is also chairman of the German Red Cross, states that the medical supervision by the camp doctors is insufficient, the sick are inadequately cared for, and the general state of health of the prisoners is not good. Grawitz is only following to the letter the directives of the RSHA, that prisoners are to be a source of labor.

An extermination camp of this size is a complicated institution with countless offices for typists, a construction office, bursars. For example, on the fifth day of each month accounts covering deliveries of human hair had to be complete. One great advantage of officialese is that it is neutral and aseptic. It conceals nothing, but it reduces the most terrible things to one-dimensional "operations," bloodless statistics, pain-free and odorless diagrams.

No death scream reaches our ears from this prose, no whiff of decomposition remains. In these documents can be found all and nothing about the inferno—unless one pauses from time to time and asks what these documents actually mean. Whoever does this will probably have to stop reading for a while. The "Chronicle" cannot be read like any other book.

AUSCHWITZ CHRONICLE

1939 – 1945

1 9 3 9

On August 22, 1939, a few days before the German attack on Poland and the outbreak of World War II, Hitler addressed the commanding general of the Wehrmacht at his Berchtesgaden retreat, the Berghof, on the Obersalzberg:

> Our strength is our speed and our brutality. Genghis Khan drove many women and children to death, deliberately and joyously. History sees him as a great founder of a state. What weak western European civilization says about me doesn't matter. I have given the order—and I will have anyone shot who expresses even one word of criticism—that the aim of the war is not to reach definite lines but rather the physical destruction of the enemy. So, I have assembled my Death's Head Formations, for the time being only in the East, with the command to send man, woman and child of Polish origin and language to death, ruthlessly and mercilessly. This is the only way we can win the living space we need. . . . Poland will be depopulated and settled with Germans.

Cf. Documents on German Foreign Policy 1918–1945, Series D, Baden-Baden 1956, vol. VII, p. 171f, note 1.

The attack on Poland represents only one stage in the German imperial endeavor; more attacks quickly follow. On April 9, 1940, Denmark and Norway become victims of the Nazi policy of aggression, followed by Holland, Belgium, Luxembourg, and France in May 1940. As Hitler and his dedicated party machinery plan the conquest of Europe to subordinate it to the Third Reich, they look not only to the economic exploitation of the conquered territories but also to the acquisition of new living space. This is especially true of the East, which is to be annexed to the Greater German Reich after the extermination of millions of Slavs living there. The fate of these peoples is determined: Their extermination, indeed their biological annihilation, is decided. They are thus to be excluded from the ranks of civilized states. Plans for these people's systematic extermination are worked out.

Plans regarding Poland are:

1. Men and material goods of the so-called General Government* should be intensively exploited to reinforce the German war machine, to reduce Poland to poverty, and hence to change it to the condition of a vassal state. Scattered German settlements are to be interspersed in the most fertile areas of Poland with the goal of surrounding the Polish population and accelerating the process of Germanization.
2. The territories incorporated into the Reich, including the so-called Reichsgau (Administrative Region) Wartheland, are to be relentlessly Germanized. The Polish population in these territories that is unfit for Germanization is to be expelled to the General Government or deported to Germany as forced labor. Deportation plans target the entire Polish intelligentsia and "other unreliable elements," as well as all Jews.
3. "Especially active Polish elements" are to be deported to concentration camps.

According to the final plans of the National Socialists, 85 percent of the Poles are to be driven out of their homeland, most of them to be settled in Siberia.

The realization of this program requires an immense institutionalized apparatus of terror. This apparatus exists in the machinery of the Third Reich, in which a system of concentration camps is established. Eventually it is taken over by Himmler's SS (Schutzstaffel) organization. From 1942 on, the official, personnel, administrative, and financial and economic administration and supervision of the concentration camps in the Reich devolves on Branch D of the SS Economic and Administrative Central Office (Wirtschafts- und Verwaltungshauptamt—WVHA). The Reich Central Security Office (Reichssicherheitshauptamt—RSHA) of the SS, on the other hand, organizes the transports of prisoners and decides their fate. The annihilation function of the concentration camp is the result of the directives of these two central offices of the SS administration, led by Heinrich Himmler, Commander in Chief of the SS and German Police in the Reich Ministry of the Interior.

The concentration camps are official state institutions financed by the state budget and administered and operated by the SS.

The German Wehrmacht that marches into Poland in September 1939 is followed immediately by mobile units of the Security Police (Sicherheitspolizei—Sipo) and the Security Service (Sicherheitsdienst—SD) of the SS. Their terrorist measures include shooting hostages and making mass arrests according to already prepared lists of political and social figures in precarious positions, representatives of the Polish intelligentsia, clergy, and Jews.

Just a few months after the occupation of Poland, the existing prisons, especially those in Upper Silesia and the General Govern-

---

*"What was left of Poland after Russia seized her share in the east and Germany formally annexed her former provinces and some additional territory in the west was designated by a decree of the Führer of October 12 [1939] as the General Government of Poland and Hans Frank appointed as its Governor General . . ." (William L. Shirer, *The Rise and Fall of the Third Reich*, New York, 1960, p. 661).

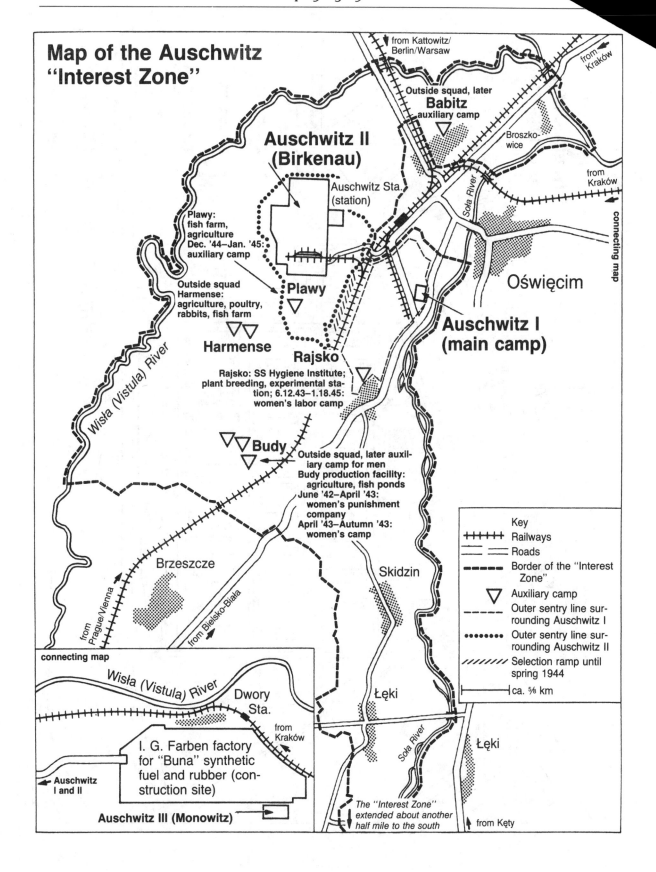

Map of the Auschwitz "Interest Zone"

from Kattowitz/Berlin/Warsaw

from Kraków

Outside squad, later
Babitz
auxiliary camp

Broszko-wice

Auschwitz II
(Birkenau)

Auschwitz Sta.
(station)

from Kraków

Sola River

connecting map

Plawy:
fish farm,
agriculture
Dec. '44–Jan. '45:
auxiliary camp

Oświęcim

Outside squad
Harmense:
agriculture, poultry,
rabbits, fish farm

Plawy
▽

Auschwitz I
(main camp)

Wisła (Vistula) River

Harmense
▽ ▽

Rajsko
▽

Rajsko: SS Hygiene Institute;
plant breeding, experimental station; 6.12.43–1.18.45:
women's labor camp

▽ ▽ **Budy**
▽

Outside squad, later auxiliary camp for men
Budy production facility:
agriculture, fish ponds
June '42–April '43:
women's punishment
company
April '43–Autumn '43:
women's camp

Brzeszcze

Skidzin

from Prague/Vienna

from Bielsko-Biała

Key

┼┼┼┼┼	Railways
═══	Roads
▬ ▬ ▬	Border of the "Interest Zone"
▽	Auxiliary camp
– – –	Outer sentry line surrounding Auschwitz I
••••••	Outer sentry line surrounding Auschwitz II
//////	Selection ramp until spring 1944
⊢———⊣	ca. ⅝ km

connecting map

Wisła (Vistula) River

Dwory
Sta.

from Kraków

I. G. Farben factory
for "Buna" synthetic
fuel and rubber (con-
struction site)

◄– Auschwitz
I and II

Auschwitz III (Monowitz) ►

Łęki

Łęki

Sola River

The "Interest Zone"
extended about another
half mile to the south

from Kęty

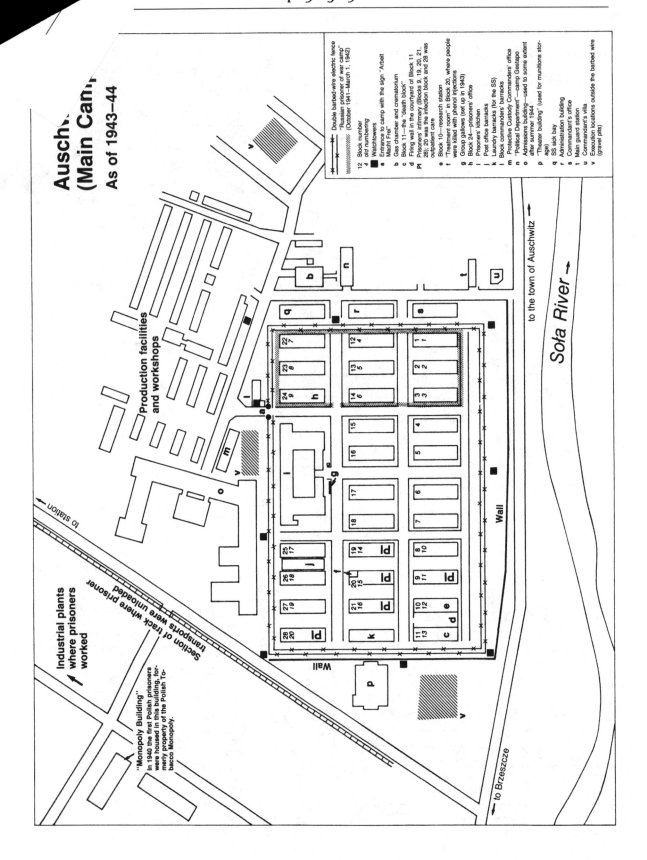

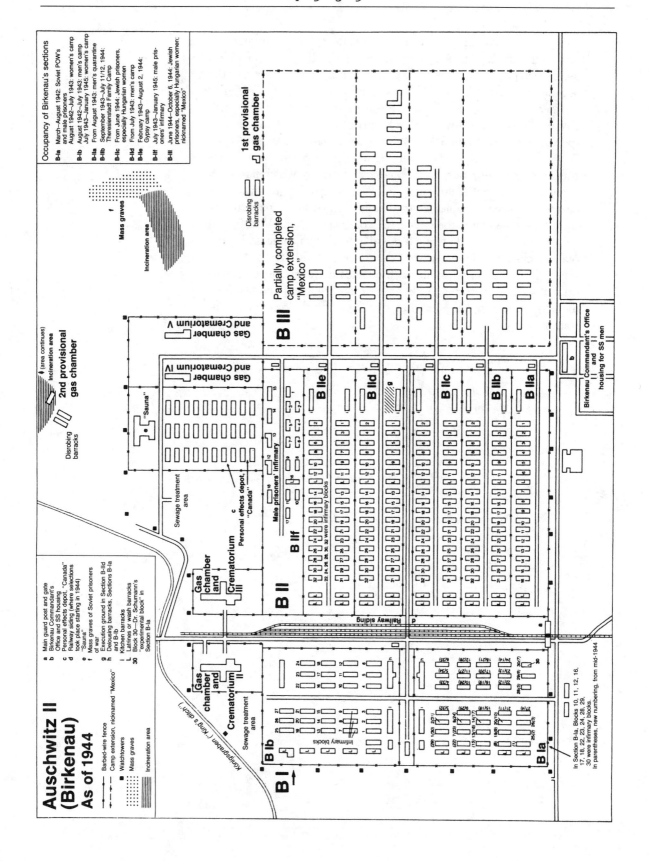

ment, are no longer able to accommodate the large number of prisoners. Hence, in December 1939, in the Breslau (Wrocław) headquarters of the superior SS and police commander for the Southeast region, SS Major General Erich von dem Bach-Zelewski, the idea comes up of building a concentration camp near the Polish city of Auschwitz (Oświęcim). The proposal comes from the inspector of the Sipo and SD in Breslau, SS Brigadier General Arpad Wigand. He describes Auschwitz as a suitable place for a future concentration camp because of the barracks there, which had been taken over by the Wehrmacht in 1939. Wigand thinks that the barracks can be occupied immediately by prisoners, particularly since they are outside the city at the confluence of the Vistula and Soła rivers. This should make it possible to build a camp and eventually facilitate isolating it from the outside world. The favorable railroad connection with Silesia, the General Government, Czechoslovakia, and Austria is another important argument and becomes the decisive factor in the selection of the site for the future concentration camp.

1 9 4 0

From January to April 1940, representatives of the SS, the Security Police (Sipo), and the Security Service (SD) make several visits to the site of Auschwitz, weigh the pros and cons of the location, and begin negotiations with the Wehrmacht concerning turning over the barracks to the SS.

JANUARY

On orders of the inspector of concentration camps, SS Brigadier General Richard Glücks, a commission arrives in Auschwitz headed by the Protective Custody Commander of Sachsenhausen concentration camp, SS Major Walter Eisfeld, to investigate the property proposed by the Sipo and SD Inspector in Breslau, SS Brigadier General Arpad Wigand, for a concentration camp. As a result of their inspection, the commission declares that the barracks in Auschwitz are not suitable for the construction of a camp.

APMO, Höss Trial, vol. 21, p. 26.

JANUARY 25

The head of the SS main office informs SS Commander in Chief Himmler that according to the report of SS Major General Erich von dem Bach-Zelewski, "A camp is soon to be erected near Auschwitz which is considered a kind of official concentration camp."

APMO, D-RF-3/RSHA/117a, p. 59, General Orders of the RHSA.

FEBRUARY 1

To reach a final decision on the location of the planned camp, SS Commander in Chief Himmler orders the inspection of the following: the police prison in Welzheim and the transit camp in Kislau (both in the Southwest Superior SS and Police Command), the camp in Frauenberg near Admont (in the Alps Superior SS and Police Command), and the camps in Sosnowitz and Auschwitz (both in the Southeast Superior Police Command).

Ibid., p. 55.

FEBRUARY 21

SS Brigadier General Glücks informs Himmler that the inspection has shown that the former Polish artillery barracks in Auschwitz are suitable for a quarantine camp after the "removal of some sanitary and structural deficiencies." As soon as the negotiations with the Wehrmacht ordered by the head of the Sipo concerning the transfer of the property are concluded, the quarantine camp should begin operations at once.

Ibid., pp. 55–57.

APRIL 8

On the basis of the negotiations, Luftwaffe General Halm gives his approval to lease the Auschwitz barracks and to draft an agreement concerning their transfer to the control of the SS.

WAP Kattowitz, RK 2905, folio 119; see also Alfred Konieczny, "Bemerkungen über die Anfänge des Konzentrationslagers Auschwitz" (Remarks on the beginnings of Auschwitz Concentration Camp, hereafter cited as Konieczny, "Remarks"), *Hefte von Auschwitz* (Auschwitz Journals), no. 12, 1970, p. 27 (hereafter cited as *HvA*).

APRIL 9

Germany attacks Denmark and Norway.

APRIL 18–19

In connection with the final negotiations between the Wehrmacht and the SS, a commission meets once again in Auschwitz under the direction of SS Captain Rudolf Höss, successor to Eisfeld as Protective Custody Commander at Sachsenhausen. On the way, the commission meets in Breslau with Inspector Wigand of the Sipo and SD in Breslau. He gives the commission a detailed report of his plan to construct a quarantine transit camp in Auschwitz for Polish prisoners. The prisoners are to be sent ultimately to concentration camps within the German Reich. According to Wigand's plans, this camp is to accept 10,000 inmates.

APMO, Höss Trial, vol. 21, p. 27; D-RF-3/RSHA/117a, pp. 55–57, General Orders of the RSHA.

APRIL 27

On the basis of the report of Höss's inspection, Himmler orders Concentration Camps Inspector Glücks to establish a concentration camp in the artillery barracks in Auschwitz and to have it enlarged by prisoners.

APMO, Höss Trial, vol. 21, p. 27; the date is established by the declaration of the defendant Rudolf Höss during the judicial investigation. According to this statement, eight days after the delivery of the report, Himmler gave the order to construct a camp in Auschwitz.

APRIL 29

Concentration Camps Inspector Glücks appoints SS Captain Rudolf Höss to the command of the future concentration camp in Auschwitz.

Ibid. The date is established by Rudolf Höss's statement during the investigation, that Glücks assigned him the function of commandant in late April, after Himmler ordered the establishment of a camp in Auschwitz.

APRIL 30

In Auschwitz, Höss meets with five SS men to supervise clearing the sites of the former barracks to prepare them to accept prisoners as quickly as possible.

Ibid.

From May to the end of December 1940, clearing and organizational work is done. The camp must be ready to accept thousands of Polish prisoners as soon as possible. In his autobiography, written while he was in prison under investigation in Kraków, Höss states, "My task was not an easy one. In the shortest possible time I had to construct a transit camp for ten thousand prisoners, using the existing complex of buildings, which, though well constructed, had been completely neglected and were swarming with vermin. From the point of view of hygiene practically everything was lacking. I had been told in Oranienburg, before setting off, that I could not expect much help, and that I would have to rely largely on my own resources. In Poland I would find everything that had been unobtainable in Germany for years!

"It is much easier to build a completely new concentration camp than to make one quickly out of a conglomeration of buildings and barracks built for a different purpose, which require a large amount of alteration. . . ." Höss continues: "In order to get the camp started I had already had to negotiate with various economic offices, and with the local and district authorities. My executive officer was a complete nitwit and I was thus forced to take matters out of his hands and to organize the entire provisioning of troops and prisoners myself. Whether it was a question of bread or meat or potatoes, it was I who had to go and find them. Yes, I even had to take straw out to the [camp's] farms. . . . I had to drive as far as Zakopane and Rabka to acquire cooking pots for the prisoners' kitchen, and to the Sudetenland for bedsteads and straw mattresses. . . . In Berlin they were still quarreling about the responsibility for the development of Auschwitz, for according to the agreement the whole thing was an army affair and had only been handed over to the SS for the duration of the war."

Rudolf Höss, *Kommandant in Auschwitz: Autobiographische Aufzeichnunger des Rudolf Höss* (Commandant in Auschwitz: The autobiography of Rudolf Höss), Munich, 1963, pp. 91–94.

MAY

Höss gets a transfer of 300 Jews from the mayor of Auschwitz to clear the area of the future camp. They are sent by the local Jewish community organization and work until the beginning of June cleaning the barracks and the area around them.

APMO, Höss Trial, vol. 21, p. 27; vol. 5, p. 138; Statements of Former Prisoner Karol Lehrer.

MAY 4

Höss is officially named Commandant of Auschwitz.

Jan Sehn, Introduction to *Wspomnienia Rudolfa Hössa* (Polish ed. of Höss, *Commandant in Auschwitz*), Warsaw, 1956, p. 16.

MAY 10

Germany attacks Belgium, Holland, Luxembourg and subsequently France.

MAY 14

The chief of police notifies the governor in Kattowitz that the Gestapo (Geheime Staatspolizei—secret state police) is trying to turn the former refugee camp near the future concentration camp, which

WAP Kattowitz, RK 2900, folio 25; cf. also Konieczny, "Remarks," p. 35.

can accommodate approximately 30,000 people,* into a prison camp.

MAY 20

The Roll Call Leader (Rapportführer), Staff Sergeant Gerhard Palitzsch, who has been assigned to Commandant Rudolf Höss by Concentration Camp Inspector Glücks during the construction of the Auschwitz camp, brings 30 German common criminals to Auschwitz who have been selected on Höss's recommendation from among the prisoners of Sachsenhausen. They are Bruno Brodniewitsch (No. 1), Otto Küsel (No. 2), Artur Balke (No. 3), Fritz Biesgen (No. 4), Hans Bock (No. 5), Bernard Bonitz (No. 6), Karl Benna (No. 7), Arno Böhm (No. 8), name missing (No. 9), Michael (Miki) Galas (No. 10), Erich Grönke (No. 11), Arnold Hartwig (No. 12), Hans Henning (No. 13), Winant Jansen (No. 14), Dietrich Jüchter (No. 15), Bruno Kellert (Kehlert) (No. 16), Max Küserow (No. 17), Konrad Lang (No. 18), Johannes Lachenich (No. 19), Willi Meyer (No. 20), Berthold Missun (No. 21), August Müller (No. 22), Kurt Müller (No. 23), Kurt Pachala (No. 24), Herbert Roman (Romann) (No. 25), Johann Siegruth (No. 26), Paul Schikowski (No. 27), Otto Stiel (Stiell or Still) (No. 28), Albin Vogel (Vogl or Voigt) (No. 29), Leo Wietschorek (Witschorek) (No. 30).

They are appointed so-called Prisoner Functionaries and form an extension of the SS machinery, since they have direct, often brutal supervision of prisoners in the camp and in the labor squads. The criminal Prisoner Functionaries model their behavior on that of the SS Men, which leads to the abandonment of all scruples vis-à-vis the prisoners under their control. Bruno Brodniewitsch (No. 1) becomes Camp Senior, the others become Block Seniors, Capos, etc.

At the same time, 15 SS men of the SS cavalry are transferred from Kraków to Auschwitz as guards.

APMO, Höss Trial, vol. 21, p. 27; numerical and alphabetical card index of former prisoners of Auschwitz; compare Stanisław Kłodziński, "Rola kryminalistów niemieckich w poczatkach obozu oświęciemskiego" (The Role of German Criminals in the Origins of Auschwitz Concentration Camp), *Przegląd Lekarski* (Medical Overview) (1974): 113–126 (hereafter cited as *PL*).

MAY 29

Forty prisoners from Dachau, a so-called outside squad, led by SS Sergeant Beck, are brought to Auschwitz. The squad consists of one German prisoner, the Capo, and 39 Polish prisoners, young men, most of them gymnasium students from Lodz. The squad brings a cart of barbed wire to fence off the future camp. The prisoners are housed in the kitchen barracks of the former military camp and are employed in building the first temporary fence around the camp. They have no freedom of movement and are forbidden to establish contact with the Jews and civilian workers in the camp employed by Höss in renovation and construction.

APMO, Accounts, vol. 115, Account of Former Dachau Prisoner Edward Flakiewicz.

*The shacks near the barracks are populated by Poles who came from the Olsa territory after World War I. The shacks, which house entire families, 1,200 people altogether, are designated a refugee camp.

The entrance of Auschwitz-Birkenau, through which the trains pulled up to the ramp.

The gate of the Auschwitz main camp, with the sign LABOR MAKES FREE.

JUNE 6

State Councillor Schmidt from the county prefecture in Bielitz (Bielsko) reports to the governor in Kattowitz that he has been informed by the "camp commander of the future camp in Auschwitz that the shacks directly next to the camp, where some 1,200 Poles live, must be cleared since this site is also to be included in the camp." Schmidt agrees to accommodate 400 persons in the district of Wadowice. Since this concerns a camp of supraregional significance, he proposes evacuating the remaining 800 inhabitants to other districts.

WAP Kattowitz, RK 2910, folio 4.

JUNE 8

A commission that includes a deputy of the governor; the commander of the regular police (Ordnungspolizei—Orpo) of Kattowitz, Major von Coelln; the county prefect of Bielitz; and the Commandant of Auschwitz visit the colony of huts in front of the camp, where some 1,200 people live, and decide the following:

Ibid., folio 6.

1. An official of the criminal police department of Kattowitz will examine the personal data of the inhabitants of the huts and ascertain immediately which persons can be considered for preventive detention and are to be transferred to the camp of Sosnowitz.
2. The county prefect of Bielitz is to contact the labor office at once to transport as many people as possible to Germany for forced labor. Families should not be separated if possible.
3. Those persons still remaining in the district of Bielitz are to be distributed among other districts. Approximately 600 persons at the most are to be transferred to the district of Saybusch (Żywiec). The districts of Ilkenau (Olkusz) and Krenau (Chrzanów) are exempt since they have been engaged in the evacuation of the Jews in recent weeks.

JUNE 10

At the company J. A. Topf and Sons in Erfurt, a machine factory and a heating technology construction business, the technical model for a coke-heated oven to incinerate bodies in Auschwitz is made. The model is designated D-57253. It is commissioned by the central office of the SS Department of Budget and Buildings (Haushalt und Bauten) for the SS Office of New Construction at Auschwitz C.C.* According to the technical draft, the oven has two combustion points and is called a double-muffle incinerator.

APMO, IZ-13/89, Various Documents of the Third Reich, pp. 241–244. Original in the Archives of the Federal Republic of Germany, Coblenz (hereafter cited as BA Koblenz).

Italy declares war on France and Great Britain.

JUNE 12

Paris is declared an open city.

*The SS probably already assumes there will be an especially high death rate among the Polish prisoners in the newly constructed concentration camp since they order a double-muffle incinerator from J. A. Topf and Sons even before the first prisoners are sent to this camp.

JUNE 14

German troops march into Paris. The victory parade takes place on the Champs Elysées.

For this occasion occupied Poland is bedecked with banners and swastikas. Polish prisoners transported from Tarnów to Auschwitz see the decorated Kraków railroad station and find out about the Germans' entry into Paris from the loudspeakers.

Wiesław Kielar, *Anus Mundi: Fünf Jahre Auschwitz* (Anus Mundi: Five Years of Auschwitz), Frankfurt/Main, 1979, p. 15.

The first Polish inmates, 728 men, are sent to Auschwitz from the prison in Tarnów by the Kraków Sipo and SD commander. The prisoners are given Nos. 31–758 and are quarantined in the building of the former Polish tobacco monopoly* near the siding and separated from the rest of the buildings by barbed wire. This transport contains many young, healthy men fit for military service, arrested on the southern borders of Poland attempting to cross the border to reach the newly formed Polish army in France. In addition, among them are the organizers of this border crossing, underground fighters, politicians, representatives of the Polish intelligentsia, clergymen, and Jews arrested in the spring of 1940 in Operation A-B, ordered by General Governor Hans Frank.

APMO, D-RO/123; List of Male Transports, vol. 20; the list contains the arrival date of the transport, the camp numbers of the new prisoners, and where the specific transport came from, in German. The list covers prisoners with Nos. 1–199541 for the period May 20, 1940, to September 18, 1944. This document (which received the classification NO KW-2824 at Nuremberg), based on the lists of incoming prisoners in the Admissions Office of the Political Department (camp Gestapo) of Auschwitz, was made illicitly by the prisoners who worked there and clandestinely sent out of the camp in 1944. It is the most important source of information concerning prisoner transports and hence is not cited specifically hereafter.

At the same time, 100 SS men, officers, and noncommissioned officers of various ranks arrive to reinforce the camp personnel and assume administrative functions in the camp.

The 40 inmates employed in the construction of the camp fence are sent back to Dachau. As they depart, they see the train with Polish prisoners from Tarnów on the siding. The prisoners from Dachau are not happy to leave Auschwitz since they count on the help of their fellow countrymen here. On hearing this SS Sergeant Beck informs them they have no reason to regret since that camp will be hell on earth.

APMO, Accounts, vol. 115, Account of Former Dachau Prisoner Edward Flakiewicz.

With blows, kicks, and shouts, the detainees from Tarnów are driven into the cellar, where they undergo the admissions procedure. They are robbed of their personal belongings, shorn of their hair, taken to the baths for disinfection, registered, and marked with numbers. As soon as they get their clothes back they are taken to the courtyard, where they have to line up in rows of five for the first roll call. The First Camp Commander, SS Captain Karl Fritzsch, greets them with the following speech translated into Polish by two inmates selected as interpreters: "You have not come to a sanatorium here but to a German concentration camp and the only way out is through the chimney of the crematorium. If there's anybody who doesn't like it, he can walk into the wire right away. If there are any Jews in a transport, they have no right to live longer than two weeks, priests for a month, and the rest for three months."

Kielar, *Anus Mundi*, p. 17. The text of this speech is also contained in APMO, Materiały Obozowego Rychu Oporu (Materials of the Camp Resistance Movement), vol. VII, p. 464 (hereafter cited as Mat.RO).

*This building is destined for the future SS guards. The prisoners are lodged there only temporarily, since the barracks blocks are not yet cleared and have no equipment.

JUNE 15

The prisoners admitted to Auschwitz the previous day are under quarantine. This is how the SS tries to terrorize the prisoners and break them physically and emotionally. Every day after morning roll call they are forced into the courtyard, where they remain the entire day. When the SS men and the foremen order "Down," "Up," "Jump," etc., the inmates must exercise, shrouded in clouds of dust. In the pauses between exercises, the inmates learn German marching songs, entrance and exit formations and taking off and putting on their caps on command. Throughout this process, they are brutally beaten and tortured by the SS men and the German foremen.

APMO, Höss Trial, vol. 2, pp. 49, 161–163; vol. 4, p. 126; vol. 7, p. 145. Accounts of Former Auschwitz Prisoners.

JUNE 18

County Prefect Schmidt of Bielitz informs the governor in Kattowitz that in the night 38 families secretly left the huts and even dismantled some of the shacks they had previously lived in because news of the proposed liquidation of the settlement had reached those affected.

WAP Kattowitz, RK 2910, folio 10.

JUNE 19

On orders from County Prefect Schmidt the evacuation of the colony of huts bordering the camp begins. The local labor office, supported by the local police, participates. 500 inhabitants are arrested, 250 of whom are deported to Germany for forced labor. 30 persons unfit for work and children under 14 remain temporarily in the colony, as well as members of eight families employed by the SS camp and some 15 families whose members work in the nearby coal mine of Brzeszcze. But all these people are also soon to be evacuated so that there will be no more obstacles to the final seizure of the area by Auschwitz C. C.

Ibid., folio 11f.

JUNE 20

On orders of the head of the Kraków Sipo and SD the second transport of 313 Polish political detainees is sent from the prison in Wiśnicz Nowy. The inmates are given Nos. 759–1071 and are lodged in Block 2 of the camp. The famous sculptor and painter Xawery Dunikowski, born December 24, 1875, in Kraków, receives No. 774.

JUNE 22

On orders from Stapo (Staatspolizei—state police) headquarters in Kattowitz, the first transport of Polish political prisoners from Silesia is sent from the police prison in Sosnowitz.* The 23 men in this transport receive Nos. 1072–1094.

Konieczny, "Remarks," pp. 23–37.

The signing of the German-French armistice agreement.

*At the end of March 1940, a camp for prisoners is built in Sosnowitz in the machine shops of the former Schön textile factory, in the Erster-Mai-Strasse; the camp is variously designated as a transit camp, a refugee camp, or a prison camp. The SS

JUNE 24

On orders from Stapo headquarters in Kattowitz, 27 political prisoners are sent to the camp from the police prison in Sosnowitz; they are given Nos. 1095–1121.

JUNE 25

A plan is made to have a block serve as a prisoners' infirmary.

On orders from Stapo headquarters in Kattowitz, 100 political prisoners are sent from the police prison in Sosnowitz and given Nos. 1122–1221.

APMO, Documents of the Central Construction Administration (hereafter cited as: Docs. ZBL), BW 20/18, Prisoners' Infirmary, Ground-Floor Plan, Building No. 20.

JUNE 26

On orders from Stapo headquarters in Kattowitz, 42 political prisoners are sent from the police prison in Sosnowitz and given Nos. 1222–1263.

JUNE 27

On orders from the Stapo central office in Kattowitz, 19 political prisoners are sent from the police prison in Sosnowitz and are given Nos. 1264–1282.

JULY 1

The following SS men have administrative positions in the Auschwitz C. C.:*

APMO, D-RF-3, RSHA/117/2, p. 166, RSHA General Orders.

Special Commando Sosnowitz, accompanied by SS Major Rudolph, supervises the camp. Until March 1940, Jews are concentrated in this camp.

*In his autobiography, Höss makes a very negative judgment of the SS men and officers under his command:

> Over the years the teaching of Eicke, Koch, and Loritz had penetrated so deeply into the minds of the "old hands," had become so much a part of their flesh and blood, that even the best-willed of them simply could not behave otherwise than in the way to which they had become accustomed during long service in the concentration camps. The "beginners" were quick to learn from the "old hands," but the lessons they learned were unfortunately not the best. All my endeavors to obtain at least a few good and competent officers and noncommissioned officers for Auschwitz from the Inspector of Concentration Camps were to no avail. Glücks simply would not cooperate. —It was the same with the prisoners who were to act as supervisors of the others. . . . From the very beginning the camp was dominated by theories that were later to produce the most evil and sinister consequences. . . . It will be understood that my many and diverse duties left me but little time for the camp and the prisoners themselves. I had to leave them entirely in the hands of individuals such as Fritzsch, Meier, Seidler, and Palitzsch, distasteful persons in every respect, and I had to do this even though I was well aware that they would not run the camp as I wished and intended.

In contrast to what Höss writes in his autobiography, he allowed the SS staff under his control and the German common criminals unlimited despotism: terror, brutality, and even killing prisoners for fun (Höss, *Commandant in Auschwitz*, pp. 92, 93, 96).

1. Camp Commandant: Rudolf Höss, SS captain, SS No. 193616, detailed from Sachsenhausen C.C.
2. Adjutant: Josef Kramer, SS first lieutenant, SS No. 32217, transferred from Mauthausen C.C.
3. First Camp Commander: Karl Fritsch, SS first lieutenant, SS No. 7287, transferred from Dachau C.C.
4. Second Camp Commander: Franz Xaver Maier, SS second lieutenant, SS No. 69600, transferred from the SS Death's Head Division
5. Director of Administration: Max Meyer, SS first lieutenant, SS No. 289455, detailed from the Concentration Camps Inspectorate
6. Bursar: Herbert Minkos, SS technical sergeant, SS No. 293112, transferred from Buchenwald C.C.
7. Senior Food Clerk: Willi Rieck, SS second lieutenant, SS No. 63900, transferred from Dachau C.C.
8. Housing administration: Otto Reinicke, SS technical sergeant, SS No. 156653, transferred from Flossenbürg C.C.
9. Camp Doctor: Max Popiersch, SS captain, SS No. 176467
10. Camp Doctor: Robert Neumann, SS first lieutenant, SS No. 203348
11. Director of the Political Department (camp Gestapo): Maximilian Grabner, SS second lieutenant, appointed to the post by the Kattowitz Gestapo.

JULY

Start of construction of the foundations of the double-muffle incinerator.* The plan for the foundations of the oven for incinerating corpses is included in the technical drawing of oven model D-57753 ordered from Topf and Sons in Erfurt. Prisoners are deployed in this work.

APMO, Höss Trial, vol. 4, p. 73; vol. 21, p. 130; IZ-13/89, Various Documents of the Third Reich, pp. 241–244 (Original in BA Koblenz).

JULY 3

Concentration Camps Inspector Richard Glücks addresses a letter to the Commandants of the concentration camps reminding them that "the prisoners discharged from the concentration camp are not to become the subject of discussion among the population."** It is generally known that a few prisoners were released, after collapsing while changing trains at the railroad station because of their extreme physical weakness, so that they had to be turned over to the social welfare services and spend a long time in the hospital.†

APMO, IZ-13/89, Various Documents of the Third Reich, p. 256 (original in BA Koblenz).

---

*The former weapons bunker is designated as the shop for the crematorium oven and as the morgue. This is to the left of the entrance to the camp, opposite the one-story building assigned to the SS.
**The copy of the order of May 11, 1939, for Commanders of the SS Death's Head Banners and Commandants concerning the release of protective custody prisoners who are under medical care is attached to the aforementioned letter. It is forbidden to release prisoners who have not received a positive medical report on their health (*Ibid.*, p. 257).
†This order is not observed. Many prisoners released from the camp die in hospitals from total physical exhaustion, despite special medical treatment. Thus, for example,

Such releases are a disgrace to the camp. In the future, such cases are to be prevented.

JULY 6

Polish prisoner Tadeusz Wiejowski, born May 4, 1914, in Kolaczyce near Kraków, escapes from the camp. This is the first escape from Auschwitz. The escape is discovered during evening roll call. A punishment roll call is ordered that lasts from 6:00 in the evening of July 6 until 2:00 in the afternoon on July 7—20 hours. The entire time, SS men walk around among the standing prisoners, hitting them with sticks or kicking them. The escapee is not caught.

APMO, Höss Trial, vol. 4, pp. 75, 152, 153; vol. 12, p. 10.

Sixty prisoners newly arrived in a transport from the police prison at Sosnowitz and marked with Nos. 1283–1342 also take part in the punishment roll call occasioned by the escape of Tadeusz Wiejowski.

Adam Kozłowiecki, *Ucisk i strapienie* (Anguish and Grief), Kraków, 1967, pp. 141–142.

During this first punishment roll call, the first public flogging, on the stand made in the camp carpentry shop, takes place. Flogging is administered to prisoners interrogated by the SS functionaries of the Political Section on suspicion of helping Tadeusz Wiejowski escape and maintaining contacts with the civilian workers employed in the camp. Flogging is carried out by the Roll Call Leader, Gerhard Palitzsch,* with a stick four centimeters in diameter.

JULY 7

At night, after several hours of standing in the punishment roll call, the Jew David Wingoczewski is the first prisoner to die in Auschwitz. He was sent to the camp on June 20 from the prison in Wiśncz Nowy with signs of brutal torture, advanced tuberculosis of the lungs, rectal prolapse, and advanced gangrene.

APMO, Accounts, vol. 67, p. 50, Account of Former Prisoner Kazimierz Szczerbowski.

JULY 8

On the basis of the investigation by the camp Gestapo concerning the escape of Tadeusz Wiejowski, five civilian workers employed as electricians in the camp are arrested. They are suspected of facilitating his escape. They are lodged in the camp detention center, called a bunker by the prisoners, in the basement of Block 11; at

APMO, Accounts, vol. 170, pp. 9–17; Account of Former Prisoner Eugeniusz Gerard Hejka; Höss Trial, vol. 2, p. 51; vol. 3, p. 34.

---

it is reported in secret documents of the delegation of the Polish government in exile: "The young people are least capable of resistance. At the beginning of April, a 20-year-old lad came from Auschwitz to Warsaw. He died two weeks later. The autopsy showed a bruised liver, a severed kidney, a few broken ribs and tuberculosis of the lungs." (CA KCPZPR 202/III-8, Documents of the Delegation of the Polish Government in Exile, p. 21, Appendix 7, Report on the period April 16–30, 1941; cf. "Obóz koncentracyjny Oświęcim w świetle akt Delegatury Rządu R. P. na Kraj" (Auschwitz Concentration Camp in Light of the Documents of the Polish Government in Exile), *Zeszyty Oświęcimskie*, Polish-language edition of *Hefte von Auschwitz*, Special Issue 1 (1968): 6 (hereafter cited as ZO).
*Formally, a flogging consists of 25 blows, but this rule is not followed. The whipped prisoner has to count the blows himself aloud and in German. If he makes a mistake, the punishment is repeated from the beginning.

this time, it is called Block 13. The following civilian workers are involved: Bolesław Bicz, Emil Kowalowski, Stanisław Mrzygłód, Józef Muszyński, and Józef Patek.* After interrogation and torture, 11 more prisoners are locked in the bunker. They are charged with making contact with civilian workers employed in the camp and helping in the escape of inmate Tadeusz Wiejowski. Among the prisoners locked in the bunker of Block 11, who are then assigned to the Penal Company, are Jerzy Olek, Rudolf Gregor, Jerzy Urbański, Władysław Szczudlik, Karol Jurek, Paweł Zbieszczyk, Tadeusz Kukulski, Stanisław Bargiel, Leopold Gonia, Eugeniusz Gerard Hejka, and Zdzisław Wiesiołek.**

The residents of Legiony Street, Krótka Street, and Polna Street in the Zasole quarter are summoned by the city administration to appear in Birkenau, at the Wysoglad Hall at 10 o'clock in the morning in order to make their houses available to the SS. The assembled people are surrounded by SS men who have come with three trucks. During the assembly the SS men begin shooting inside and outside the hall. More than a dozen families are sent to the Sudetenland as forced laborers while the rest are allowed to return to their houses. The houses of the evacuated residents are assigned to members of the SS camp guard unit.

APMO, Höss Trial, vol. 12, pp. 42, 48.

Auschwitz is mentioned for the first time in the monthly statistical report concerning the number of prisoners and prisoner transports in the sphere of influence of the Breslau Superior SS and Police.

APMO, D-AuI-1/2, Monthly Report of the Gestapo in Silesia, pp. 55–57.

JULY 10

The first outside squad is formed, made up of 30 prisoners. Prisoner Michael Galas (No. 10), called Miki, assumes the function of capo. This unit is lodged in Sośnica in Gleiwitz (Gliwice) for three to four weeks. The prisoners are used to demolish a former camp for Polish prisoners of war. They tear up the barbed-wire fence, which is then used to build the fence around Auschwitz.†

APMO, Accounts, vol. 74, p. 166; vol. 27, p. 103; Accounts of Former Prisoners Bogumił Antoniewicz and Artur Rablin; Irena Strzelecka, "Pierwsi Polacy w Kl Auschwitz" (The First Poles in Auschwitz), ZO, no. 18 (1983): 50.

JULY 12

Commandant Höss sends a letter to the Inspector of Concentration camps Richard Glücks in Oranienburg, reporting that on July 11 at about 10:30 P.M. the sentry on duty at Post Number 3 near the quarantine camp, SS man Domenus, noticed three persons ap-

APMO, D-AuI-1/1, pp. 19–20, pp. 24ff.; The Escape of Tadeusz Wiejowski.

*During the search, objects are found on the civilian workers which proved they had helped the inmates. These include letters from inmates to their families which were not yet sent.
**Included among them are the writers of those letters; for example, Gerard Hejka (No. 608).
†Höss writes: "The Concentration Camps Inspectorate refused to help in this matter. So the urgently needed barbed wire just had to be pilfered. Whenever I found old field fortifications I ordered them to be dismantled and the pillboxes broken up, and thus I acquired the steel they contained. Whenever I came across installations containing material I urgently needed, I simply had it taken away at once without worrying about the formalities." (Höss, Commandant in Auschwitz, p. 121.)

proaching the camp. He commanded them to halt and fired three shots at them. The unknown persons escaped in the dark; the search of the grounds was unsuccessful. In the third point of the letter, Höss emphasizes that this was an attempt to get into the camp to free prisoners. In the last two paragraphs he adds that the local population is fanatically Polish and ready for any operation against the hated SS men. Every prisoner who succeeds in escaping could expect immediate help as soon as he reached the nearest Polish farm. Hence, Höss proposes initiating security measures. In another letter to SS and Police Commander von dem Bach-Zelewski, he says that suspicious persons were noticed in the area around the camp at night.

JULY 18

A transport of 12 prisoners from Kattowitz* is given Nos. 1343–1354.

65 prisoners sent to the camp from Kraków's Montelupich Prison by the head of the Kraków Sipo and SD receive Nos. 1355–1419. These prisoners are "greeted" with a flogging of 25 blows;** this beating takes place in front of Block 16. One of those who carry out the flogging is the Roll Call Leader Gerhard Palitzsch.

APMO, Höss Trial, vol. 55, pp. 229ff., 236ff.

The superior SS and Police commander in Breslau, SS Major General Erich von dem Bach-Zelewski, tours Auschwitz with the Director of the Board of Agriculture, SS Lieutenant Colonel Müller, and the Deputy Commander of the Southeast SD district, SS Lieutenant Colonel Somann. After being informed about the circumstances of the escape of prisoner Tadeusz Wiejowski and the alleged attempt to break into the camp to free prisoners on July 11, von dem Bach-Zelewski orders the following: immediate execution of civilians connected with the escape of Tadeusz Wiejowski; execution of all persons found on the camp grounds within the barbed wire; and an operation involving the police and the SD to clear the entire area around the camp within a radius of three miles of all suspicious and work-shy elements. This creates a pretext for more evacuation of the surrounding populace.

APMO, D-AuI-1/1, pp. 26ff., The Escape of Tadeusz Wiejowski.

---

*It appears from the log kept by the commanding officer on duty, which was kept in the main guardhouse, that prisoners whose names were registered in the list of transports sent from Kattowitz by order of the officials of the Stapo or Kripo headquarters came not only from Kattowitz but also from other locations in the Kattowitz District, e.g., Bielitz (Bielsko), Beuthen (Bytom), Sosnowitz, Teschen (Cieszyn), etc.

**According to the testimony of former prisoners, this was the revenge of the SS men for the escape of Stanisław Marusarz, a famous Polish ski jumper, from Montelupich Prison in Kraków. The escape took place on July 8, 1940, when three prisoners escaped from death cell No. 87: Stanisław Marusarz, Aleksander Bugajski, alias "Halny," and Sadowski. The fourth escapee, the 18-year-old Jabłoński, was wounded by a shot at the window (Włodzimierz Wnuk, *Walka podziemna na szczytach* (The Underground Struggle at Its Height), Poznań, 1948, pp. 144–145; Tadeusz Wroński, *Kronika okupowanego Krakowa* (Chronicle of Occupied Kraków), Kraków, 1974, p. 106).

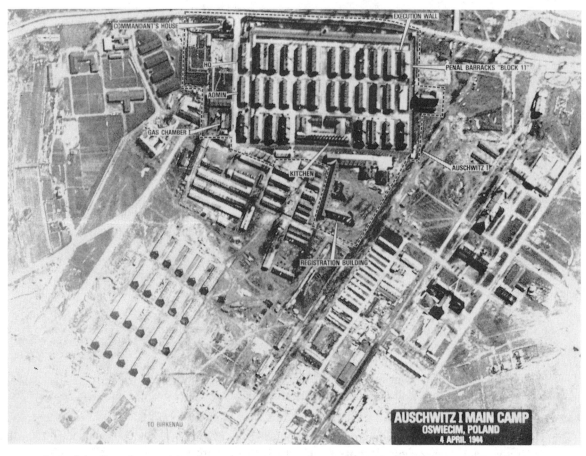

One of the first photos of Auschwitz by U.S. air reconnaissance, taken on April 4, 1944.

JULY 19

Rudolf Höss informs Concentration Camps Inspector Richard Glücks of the content of the order issued by von dem Bach-Zelewski during his visit.

Ibid.

Referring to a conversation with SS Major General von dem Bach-Zelewski during his visit, Höss proposes to execute the five Polish civilian workers and the 11 Polish political prisoners who are supposed to have helped Tadeusz Wiejowski escape.

Ibid., pp. 21–23.

JULY 21

During evening roll call, the prisoners are informed that they can write letters to their families and get from them 15 Reichsmarks a month, which they can spend in the camp canteen.*

Kozlowiecki, *Affliction and Anguish*, p. 152.

*The escape of Tadeusz Wiejowski and the contacts revealed with the civilian workers employed in the camp who secretly supply food, cigarettes, stationery, and money to the inmates, prompt the camp administration to issue this order.

General view of Auschwitz and Birkenau, taken by the U.S. Air Force on June 23, 1944.

JULY 22

One of the first maps of the area around the camp is made: a sketch of the northern portion.

APMO, Docs. CCA, BW 2/2.

JULY 24

Rudolf Höss receives a letter dated July 22, 1940 (No. 383/40), from SS Major General von dem Bach-Zelewski in which the latter confirms his oral order of July 18 and agrees to the execution of the civilian workers employed in the camp who supplied inmate Tadeusz Wiejowski with civilian clothing and food, thus making his escape possible.

APMO, D-AuI-I/I, pp. 15ff., The Escape of Tadeusz Wiejowski.

Höss also receives the copy of the letter dated July 22, 1940 (No. 384/40g), from SS Major General von dem Bach-Zelewski to the Sipo and Orpo inspector in Breslau in which he concurs with the Commandant's order of an operation to guarantee the security of the camp. The use of firearms against Poles in the area to be cleared is allowed. Women and children who happen to be found are to be imprisoned and sent to the Gestapo in Kattowitz for investiga-

Ibid., pp. 11ff.

tion. Von dem Bach-Zelewski also demands a detailed report on the result of the operation.

Rudolf Höss sends the copy of the letter to Concentration Camps Inspector Richard Glücks with a request for information about the time the evacuation operation is to begin and for a statement of the date of the executions ordered by von dem Bach-Zelewski.

Ibid., pp. 10, 13–14, 17ff.

JULY 25

Prisoners write the first letters from the camps to their families on plain stationery for the time being, as the printed forms for that purpose have not yet arrived.* One of the prisoners in quarantine has the necessary sum of money available in the camp depository and buys stationery and stamps for all of them. The contents of the letters are dictated and may not be changed. The words "I am healthy and happy" elicit the greatest resistance.**

APMO, D-AuI-I/I/7031, Camp Letters; Kozlowiecki, *Affliction and Anguish*, p. 152.

J. A. Topf and Sons Company in Erfurt, which is building crematoriums, receives more orders from concentration camps in the Reich for the construction of incinerators for burning corpses. The company offers temporary installations since it cannot keep up with the orders. Thus, on July 25, 1940, in a reply to a letter from the Mauthausen New Construction Administration, the company announces that the mobile plant for the incineration of corpses, intended originally for Flossenbürg C.C., could be delivered to the Gusen camp after the completion of the construction work and indication of the precise address. At the same time, Topf and Sons notes that the motors of these plants are designed for a 380-volt alternating current. A clearly marked technical diagram (D-56655) of the construction and size of the oven is attached to the letter. The company also mentions that it has delivered the same oven to Dachau. They continue that the abovementioned camp did not use this oven because of a lack of oil needed for heating. Hence, if the incineration plant was needed in Gusen, it could be taken over from Dachau and J. A. Topf and Sons would build a new cremation plant for Dachau that would be heated with coke. The letter concludes with the assertion that the company cordially awaits an answer and once again offers its services.

APMO, IZ-13/89, Various Documents of the Third Reich, pp. 236ff. (Original in BA Koblenz).

JULY 29

A prisoner sent from the Kattowitz district receives No. 1420.

August 1940 is marked by increasing terrorization of the prisoners by the SS. Along with the various kinds of harassment used by the

---

*The first official letter written to his family from the camp by Bronisław Czech (No. 349), an excellent Polish skier and an Olympic athlete known throughout Europe, bears the date July 25, 1940.
**According to the camp regulations, a prisoner may send and receive two letters a month. The correspondence is in German. The letters are written on a specially printed form. The content is limited to 15 lines. The letters are censored by the postal censorship administration in the Commandant's Office.

SS men and the Prisoner Functionaries, regular camp punishments are introduced by the camp administration. These are carried out on the basis of a written punishment report by SS men for a misdemeanor as soon as it is confirmed by the Commandant or the Camp Commander. After the regularly imposed flogging and punishment roll call already introduced in July, the punishments of being tied to a stake and assignment to a penal company are initiated in August. At the introduction of these punishments, however, the prisoners are neither informed of the effective camp order nor instructed in the offenses against the normal regulations. In addition, the obligation to run while working is introduced.

A Penal Company is formed that includes both those prisoners whose time in the company is imposed as a sentence as well as all prisoners of Jewish origin and all priests. Isolated from the other inmates, the Penal Company is lodged in a room on the first floor of Block 3 (at that time Block 5). Soon after, the Penal Company is moved to the ground floor of Block 11 (at that time Block 13), which the prisoners call the death block.*

AUGUST 2

Rudolf Höss receives an answer from Concentration Camps Inspector Richard Glücks to his letter of July 19 concerning von dem Bach-Zelewski's order. Glücks orders Höss to halt the executions and to send a precise description of the attempted assault on the camp as well as of the escape of inmate Tadeusz Wiejowski, made by the appropriate Stapo office in Kattowitz, to the Gestapo in Berlin, for the attention of SS Brigadier General Müller. The latter would endeavor to get a decision from the SS Commander in Chief in this matter.

APMO, AuI-1/1, p. 9, The Escape of Tadeusz Wiejowski.

18 inmates, sent from Kattowitz, are given Nos. 1421–1438.

AUGUST 3

After a telephone conversation with the director of Kattowitz Stapo on August 2, the director of the Political Department in Auschwitz sends an extensive, five-page letter to the Gestapo in Berlin, for the attention of SS Brigadier General Müller. It describes the charges made in connection with the escape of prisoner Tadeusz Wiejowski against the five civilian workers and 11 prisoners after an investigation carried out in the camp. The workers were charged with helping the prisoners, providing them with food and cigarettes and smuggling letters out. The prisoners were charged with asking for help and preparing to escape. The alleged attempts of five Poles to break into the camp on the night of July 11 is described in the letter

Ibid., pp. 4–8.

*Prisoners are assigned to the Penal Company for various alleged misdemeanors. Some are regular punishments, which can last from a month to a year; but most are imposed "until further notice." Aside from isolation, the prisoners in the Penal Company have more difficult living conditions and have to perform harder work than other prisoners. (Teresa Cegłowska, "Strafkompanien im KL Auschwitz" [Penal Companies in Auschwitz], HvA, no. 17 (1985): 157–203).

Der Höhere SS- und Polizeiführer
bei dem Oberpräsidenten in Schlesien
und beim Reichsstatthalter im Sudetengau
im Wehrkreis VIII

I. Nr. 383/40 (g)

Breslau 18, den 22. Juli 1940.
Oberschellstraße 14

Geheim!

An den

Kommandanten des Konzentrationslagers Auschwitz

SS-Hauptsturmführer H ö ß

in _A u s c h w i t z_

nachrichtlich:

1. An den
   Inspekteur der Sicherheitspolizei
   in Breslau

2. An den
   Leiter der Staatspolizeistelle Kattowitz
   in Kattowitz.

Wie mir von Ihnen gemeldet wurde, ist am 6.7.1940 der polnische Schutzhäftling Wiejowski,Thadeus aus dem dortigen Konzentrationslager entwichen. Nach dem bisherigen Ermittelungsergebnis steht fest daß die Flucht durch 5 Zivilarbeiter, die im Lager tätig waren, durch Beschaffung von Zivilkleidung und Lebensmitteln sowie Kassiber weiterleitung ermöglicht wurde.

Die Tatsache, daß bereits in der Nacht vom 11. zum 12.7.1940 von außen her ein Befreiungsversuch unternommen wurde und daß in der näheren Umgebung des Lagers, besonders nachts, verdächtige Personen bemerkt wurden, gebietet ein energisches Durchgreifen um Weiterungen, die sich aus dieser Lage ergeben könnten, von vornherein auszuschließen.

Ich ordne daher an, daß die fünf polnischen Zivilarbeiter und zwar:

1. B i o z	Boleslaus	geb. 1.4.1900 in Bielitz wohnh.in Auschwitz, Klutschnikowicestr. 43,
2. M u s c i n s k i	Josef	geb. 25.11.13 in Gruschow wohnh. in Babitze 333,
3. K o w a l o w s k i	Emil	geb. 5.6.1911 in Birkenau wohnh. in Birkenau,Koleowastr. 198,
4. P a t e k	Josef	geb.13.12.1913 in Godzienszenta wohnh. in Birkenau 321,
5. M r z y g l o d	Stanislaus	geb. 18.4.1914 in Auschwitz wohnh. in Babitz Nr.309

unverzüglich

Letter from SS Major General von dem Bach-Zelewski to Commandant Höss, ordering the execution of five civilians for helping a prisoner escape.

- 2 -

unverzüglich durch ein von Ihnen zu stellendes Exekutions-
kommando zu erschießen sind."
Ich stelle anheim, die Exekution so durchzuführen; daß sie eine
Warnung für diejenigen wird, die sich mit ähnlichen Gedanken
tragen."

SS - Gruppenführer.

as an attempt to free the aforementioned five arrested and detained civilian workers and 11 prisoners.

AUGUST 6

Three prisoners sent from Kattowitz are given Nos. 1439–1441.

AUGUST 9

43 prisoners sent from Kattowitz receive Nos. 1442–1484.

AUGUST 10

One prisoner sent from Kattowitz is given No. 1485.

AUGUST 13

27 prisoners sent from Kattowitz receive Nos. 1486–1512.

AUGUST 15

The first transport of prisoners from Warsaw, sent by the Warsaw Sipo and SD Commander enters Auschwitz C.C. In the transport are 513 prisoners from the Gestapo prison in Pawiak and 1153 inmates arrested in street raids. They are given Nos. 1513–1899 and 1901–3179. The Pawiak detainees include lawyers, doctors, officers of the Polish Army, leaders of social and community life, politicians, and priests. They are lodged in Blocks 12, 13, 14, 22, and 23 (then numbered 4, 5, 6, 7, and 8).

Regina Domańska, *Pawiak: Więzienie Gestapo, Kronika 1939–1944* (Pawiak: A Gestapo Prison, Chronicle 1939–1944), Warsaw, 1978, p. 79.

One prisoner sent from Kattowitz is given No. 1900.

AUGUST 20

One prisoner sent from Kattowitz is given No. 3180.

AUGUST 22

The administration of Auschwitz sends a letter to Katarzyna Wiejowska, residing in Kołaczyce, asking if the administration might send her the personal belongings of Tadeusz Wiejowski, who had died in that camp on July 7—i.e., in reality had escaped on July 6.*

APMO, D-AuI-1/1, p. 28, The Escape of Tadeusz Wiejowski.

AUGUST 23

Five inmates, sent from Kattowitz, are marked with numbers 3181–3185.

---

*After his escape, Tadeusz Wiejowski hides for a year in Kołaczyce. In autumn 1941, he is arrested again and sent to prison in Jaslo and finally shot in one of the abandoned oil wells near Gorlice. (APMO, Accounts, vol. 21, p. 145; vol. 57, pp. 2–8).

AUGUST 24

Two prisoners sent from Kattowitz are given Nos. 3186 and 3187.

AUGUST 28

SS Commander in Chief Himmler orders the following classification of concentration camps:

APMO, IZ-13/89, Various Documents of the Third Reich, p. 11 (Original in BA Koblenz).

1. Class I: Dachau and Sachsenhausen for detainees arrested on lesser charges and who are definitely capable of improvement, and for special cases and those in solitary confinement;
2. Class Ia: Dachau for all old and ablebodied prisoners who can still be used in gardening and growing medicinal herbs;
3. Class II: Auschwitz, Buchenwald, Natzweiler, Flossenbürg, Stutthof, Neuengamme, and Lublin for those charged with serious crimes but who are nevertheless still capable of rehabilitation and improvement;
4. Class III: Mauthausen-Gusen and Gross-Rosen for those detained on serious charges, and for previously convicted and asocial prisoners incapable of rehabilitation.

At the same time, Himmler indicates that old prisoners from Class Ia who are not able-bodied are not to receive medical treatment. They are to remain in their assigned camp sections.* Auschwitz is later reclassified.**

AUGUST 29

100 German political, criminal, and asocial detainees are transferred from Sachsenhausen. They are to take over the camp functions such as the posts of Block Seniors and Capos. They are given Nos. 3188–3287. One of them is Ernst Krankemann (No. 3210), who is appointed Capo of the Penal Company.†

One prisoner sent from Kattowitz receives No. 3288.

AUGUST 30

438 inmates sent to Auschwitz by the Sipo and SD chief for the Kraków District receive Nos. 3289–3698, 3701–3727, and 3730. They include 413 inmates from the prison in Tarnów and 25 inmates from Montelupich Prison in Kraków.

*In Auschwitz, prisoners who are old and sick and incapable of working are not exempt from labor; they die of exhaustion or are killed.
**Cf. entry for Jan. 2, 1941.
†Under his supervision, the prisoners of the Penal Company are harnessed to a road roller about two yards in diameter and begin tamping down the streets and parade grounds of the camp. Krankemann murders many prisoners. One of the methods he uses to kill is choking, strangling a prisoner who has been thrown to the floor by standing on a stick on his neck. In other cases, he lands kicks with his boots on the breast or has prisoners pressed into the rolled ground (APMO, Accounts, vol. 49., p. 132, Account of Former Prisoner Jan Bielecki).

Birkenau after the liberation of the camp in the winter of 1945, taken from a Soviet airplane.

Two new prisoners receive Nos. 3699 and 3700.

SEPTEMBER

A double-muffle incinerator is put in operation in the camp crematorium. Prisoners are assigned to service in the crematorium; one of them is Wacław Lipa (No. 2520).*

APMO, D-Mau-3a/14139, Prisoner Card Index of Mauthausen Concentration Camp.

SEPTEMBER 3

Two prisoners sent from Kattowitz receive Nos. 3728 and 3729.

SEPTEMBER 5

Eight prisoners sent from Kattowitz receive Nos. 3731–3738.

SEPTEMBER 6

19 prisoners sent from Kattowitz receive Nos. 3739–3751.

*Wacław Lipka (No. 2520), a mechanic by trade, is sent to the camp from Warsaw on August 15, 1940. From September 1940 on, he is employed as a stoker in Crematorium I. On July 19, 1943, he is transferred to Birkenau, where he is a foreman of the stokers in the crematorium from October 15, 1943 on. On January 5, 1945, with five other prisoners, the so-called bearers of secrets, he is transferred to Mauthausen, and there, on April 3, 1945, he is shot.

SEPTEMBER 7

15 prisoners sent from Kattowitz receive Nos. 3758–3772.

SEPTEMBER 10

One prisoner sent from Kattowitz receives No. 3773.

SEPTEMBER 11

One prisoner sent from Oppeln receives No. 3774.

SEPTEMBER 12

Two prisoners sent from Kattowitz receive Nos. 3775 and 3776.

SEPTEMBER 16

One prisoner transferred from Sachsenhausen is given No. 3777.

SEPTEMBER 19

Seven prisoners sent from Kattowitz receive Nos. 3778–3784.

SEPTEMBER 20

36 prisoners sent from Kattowitz receive Nos. 3785–3820.

SEPTEMBER 22

1,705 prisoners are sent to Auschwitz from Warsaw by the Sipo and SD commander for the Warsaw District. The transport contains 1139 men arrested in street roundups and 566 men from Pawiak Prison. They receive Nos. 3821–4959 and 4961–5526. No. 3904 is given to Stanisław Dębski, real name Stanisław Dubois, a young, active member of the Polish Socialist Party (Polska Partia Socjalistyczna—PPS). No. 4007 is given to Konstanty Jagiełło, also a member of PPS and active in the Red Scouts. The previously arrested Socialists in the camp rally around them and the basic structure of the PPS clandestine resistance organization in the camp is formed. No. 4859 is given to prisoner Tomasz Serafiński, real name Witold Pilecki, chief of staff of the underground organization of the Secret Polish Army (Tajna Armia Polska—TAP). With the consent of his immediate superior, Pilecki has voluntarily joined a group of people who were to be arrested during a street roundup in Warsaw in order to get into Auschwitz C.C. and organize a resistance group, encourage prisoners to undertake mutual aid, and seek ways of contacting the outside world.

Józef Garliński, *Oświęcim walczący* (Fighting Auschwitz), London, 1974, pp. 40, 49ff.

SEPTEMBER 23

Three prisoners sent from the Kattowitz District receive Nos. 5527–5529.

After evening roll call, the corpses of five prisoners newly arrived in a transport from Warsaw are taken to the crematorium. On their first day of quarantine they have been tortured to death by SS men by means of athletic exercises.

Stanisław Kowalski, *Numer 4410 opowiada (Number 4410 Speaks)*, Milwaukee, 1985, pp. 139–142.

SEPTEMBER 25

Three prisoners sent from Kattowitz are given Nos. 5530–5532.

SEPTEMBER 28

36 prisoners sent from Oppeln receive Nos. 5534–5569.

Two prisoners sent from Kattowitz are given Nos. 5570 and 5571.

SEPTEMBER 29

Four prisoners transferred from Sachsenhausen are given Nos. 5572–5575.

SEPTEMBER 30

Three prisoners sent from Kattowitz receive Nos. 5576–5578.

OCTOBER 1

One prisoner sent from Breslau receives No. 5579.

One prisoner sent from Hohensalza (Inowrocław) receives No. 5580.

One prisoner sent from the Kattowitz District receives No. 5581.

OCTOBER 2

One prisoner sent from the Kattowitz District receives No. 5582.

OCTOBER 4

Two prisoners sent from Kattowitz receive Nos. 5583 and 5584.

OCTOBER 5

17 prisoners sent from Kattowitz receive Nos. 5585–5601.

OCTOBER 7

One prisoner sent from Oppeln is given No. 4960, which had not previously been given out.

One prisoner sent from Kattowitz receives No. 5533, which had not previously been given out.

OCTOBER 8

342 prisoners are sent to Auschwitz by the Sipo and SD commander for the Kraków District. 312 prisoners come from the prison in Tarnów and 30 from Montelupich Prison in Kraków; they receive Nos. 5602–5890, 5894–5945, and 5950.

Seven prisoners sent from Lodz receive Nos. 5891–5893 and 5946–5949.

Concentration Camps Inspector Richard Glücks is informed by the RSHA that the SS Commander in Chief has made the following decision: The five civilian workers arrested in connection with the escape of prisoner Tadeusz Wiejowski are to be punished with a triple flogging (each flogging was 25 blows), and a five-year term in a Class III concentration camp; the 11 prisoners are to be punished with a single flogging and a transfer to a Class II concentration camp for three years.

APMO, D-AuI-1/1, p. 3, The Escape of Tadeusz Wiejowski.

As a result, the five civilian workers arrested because of Tadeusz Wiejowski's escape and locked in the bunker of Block 11 on July 8 are registered as prisoners. They receive Nos. 5951–5955. Bolesław Bicz receives No. 5954.

OCTOBER 9

Two prisoners sent from Kattowitz are marked with Nos. 5956 and 5957.

OCTOBER 10

14 prisoners sent from Kattowitz receive Nos. 5958–5971.

OCTOBER 11

A prisoner sent from Troppau (Opawa) receives No. 5972.

OCTOBER 12

A prisoner sent from Kattowitz receives No. 5973.

OCTOBER 14

The first transport with 64 prisoners from the prison in the Lublin fort is sent to Auschwitz by order of the Sipo and SD Commander for the Lublin District. They receive Nos. 5974–6037.

Ibid., p. 2.

Concentration Camps Inspector Glücks instructs Höss to transfer the five imprisoned former civilian workers to Mauthausen after the flogging and to transfer the 11 prisoners involved in assisting Wiejowski's escape to Flossenbürg.

OCTOBER 15

A prisoner sent from Kattowitz receives No. 6038.

OCTOBER 16

On the order of the SS Commander in Chief the 11 prisoners accused of assisting in the escape and who are to be punished by flogging and transferred to Flossenbürg are released from the Penal Company and locked in the bunker of Block 11.

APMO, Accounts, vol. 170, pp. 1–12, Account of Former Prisoner Eugeniusz Gerard Hejka.

OCTOBER 17

One prisoner sent from Ratibor receives No. 6039.

OCTOBER 18

Four prisoners sent from Kattowitz receive Nos. 6040–6043.

OCTOBER 19

Two prisoners sent from Kattowitz are given Nos. 6044 and 6045.

OCTOBER 20

Two prisoners sent from Kattowitz are given Nos. 6046 and 6047.

OCTOBER 28

During noon roll call, one prisoner is discovered to be missing. As a result, a punishment roll call is ordered. The inmates stand at attention in sleet from noon until 9:00 P.M. in cotton overalls, without coats, hats, sweaters, or shoes. The roll call is called off when a prisoner is found who had taken shelter from the sleet and had died. After this roll call, over 120 dead, unconscious, and sick men have to be carried from the roll-call area.

APMO, Höss Trial, vol. 4, p. 24; vol. 8, p. 102; Kozłowiecki, *Affliction and Anguish*, pp. 206ff.

OCTOBER 29

Two prisoners sent from Lodz are given Nos. 6048 and 6049.

Two prisoners sent from Kattowitz are given Nos. 6050 and 6051.

OCTOBER 30

One prisoner sent from Kattowitz receives No. 6052.

NOVEMBER 1

In their correspondence with the Mauthausen New Building Administration concerning the construction of an additional double-muffle incinerator, Type D-57253, Auschwitz model, for the camp in

APMO, IZ-13/89, Various Documents of the Third Reich, pp. 239ff. (Original in BA Koblenz).

Gusen, Topf and Sons confirms the opinion of their lead engineer, Prüfer, that two bodies an hour can be burned in the proposed oven.

The Head of the Sipo and SD in Berlin, Reinhard Heydrich, referring to the decision of the SS Commander in Chief, orders his subordinates at headquarters in Breslau and Kattowitz to carry out the execution of the 40 Poles Himmler selected from the four lists presented to him. The executions take place secretly, by shooting, and are in retaliation for alleged violence and assaults on police officials in Kattowitz.

APMO, D-AuI-1/50, Execution of November 22, 1940; Order of the Head of the Sipo and SD (IV D 2b, No. 4019/40g-162), of Nov. 1, 1940.

11 prisoners involved in the escape of Tadeusz Wiejowski and accused of contacts with civilian workers in the camp are taken out of the bunker for roll call. After Camp Commander SS First Lieutenant Karl Fritzsch reads them the death sentence, he says that Himmler has decided to punish them with a one-time flogging of 25 blows and transfer for three years to the stone quarries of Flossenbürg Concentration Camp. After the public administration of the flogging, these 11 prisoners are taken back to the bunker.

APMO, Accounts, vol. 170, pp. 9–12, Account of Former Prisoner Eugeniusz Gerard Hejka.

Six prisoners sent with a group transport receive Nos. 6053–6058.

NOVEMBER 3

The Camp Commander addresses a request to the camp administration for the distribution of 1,120 pairs of shoes.* Basically, this means that 825 inmates have been using their own almost completely worn-out shoes, 122 inmates wear camp sandals, and 172 inmates wear wooden shoes that absolutely must be changed. Moreover, in the prisoners' infirmary there are four prisoners who do not have any shoes.

APMO, D-AuI-3a, Various Documents.

NOVEMBER 6

15 prisoners sent from Kattowitz receive Nos. 6059–6073.

NOVEMBER 8

One prisoner sent from Kattowitz is given No. 6074.

Two prisoners sent from Lodz are given Nos. 6075 and 6078.

Two prisoners sent from Kattowitz are given Nos. 6076 and 6077.

The 11 prisoners involved in the escape of Tadeusz Wiejowski are sent from Auschwitz to Flossenbürg in a penal transport.

APMO, Accounts, vol. 170, pp. 9–12, Report of Former Prisoner Eugeniusz Gerard Hejka; Höss Trial, vol. 12, p. 14; Mat.RO, vol. VII, p. 474.

*These are probably shoes for prisoners employed in work squads outside the camp, since the occupancy of the camp at this time is more than 5,000 inmates.

The first transport with 69 prisoners from the prison in Radom arrives in Auschwitz, sent by order of the Sipo and SD Commander for the Radom District. They receive Nos. 6079–6147.

NOVEMBER 9

28 prisoners sent to Auschwitz from Montelupich Prison in Kraków by order of the Sipo and SD commander for the Kraków District receive Nos. 6148–6175.

NOVEMBER 12

62 prisoners sent to Auschwitz from the prison in Tarnów by order of the Sipo and SD commander for the District of Kraków receive Nos. 6176–6237.

14 prisoners sent from Kattowitz receive Nos. 6238–6251.

NOVEMBER 13

One prisoner sent from Lublin receives No. 6252.

NOVEMBER 14

Commandant Höss informs the Concentration Camps Inspector Richard Glücks in writing that the prisoners intended for Flossenbürg C.C. have been sent off with a group transport and will arrive on November 18.

APMO, D-AuI-1, p. 1, The Escape of Tadeusz Wiejowski.

NOVEMBER 15

13 prisoners sent with a general transport receive Nos. 6253–6265.

NOVEMBER 18

The Sipo and SD inspector in Breslau, SS Lieutenant Colonel Somann, informs the Stapo Chief and the chief of police in Kattowitz that the Superior SS and Police Commander in Breslau, SS Major General von dem Bach-Zelewski, following the order of Sipo and SD Head Reinhard Heydrich, of November 1, 1940, has ordered the execution of 40 Poles in retaliation for the alleged violence in Kattowitz. Somann recommends coordinating the precise date of the execution with the Commandant of Auschwitz. He proposes December 21 or 22, since he can be present at the execution on those days.

APMO, D-AuI-1/51, The Execution of November 22, 1940.

NOVEMBER 18–19

Political prisoner Leon Majcher, born June 28, 1912, in Lodz and residing in Skarżysko-Kamienna, escapes from Auschwitz. A punishment roll call is ordered in the camp. The search operation is unsuccessful.

APMO, IZ-8/Gestapo Lodz/3/88/224.

NOVEMBER 19

A prisoner sent from Kattowitz is given No. 6266.

NOVEMBER 22

A prisoner sent from Kattowitz is given No. 6267.

Five prisoners sent with a group transport receive Nos. 6268–6272.

The Adjutant of the Auschwitz commandant's office, SS First Lieutenant Josef Kramer, confirms in writing the acceptance of 40 Poles marked as BV prisoners sent by the Criminal Police (Kriminalpolizei—Kripo) of Kattowitz for execution in Auschwitz.

APMO, D-AuI-1/5, The Execution of November 22, 1940.

At 11 A.M., the prisoners are brought from their work posts back to the camp. Rumors of an execution that have been circulating for a few days turn out to be true; the prisoners are eyewitnesses to this execution. After lunch they are taken back to work.

Kozlowiecki, *Affliction and Anguish*, p. 210.

The first execution by shooting takes place in the camp. Those executed are the 40 Poles Himmler selected from the four lists presented by the local Stapo in retaliation for the alleged violence and assault on police officials in Kattowitz. Himmler orders the execution to be carried out without the public's knowledge. The list of the condemned is sent with instructions of the SS Commander in Chief* on November 1 in the form of an order through the Head of the Sipo and SD in Berlin, Heydrich, to the Superior SS and Police Commander in Breslau, von dem Bach-Zelewski. The latter gives an additional order to the head of the Gestapo in Kattowitz, Senior State Councillor Dr. Emmanuel Schäfer. Because of the order to carry out the execution in secret, the site of Auschwitz C.C. is selected. The condemned are admitted to Auschwitz on November 22 at 11:45 A.M. from the Kripo headquarters in Kattowitz. The execution is performed at 12 o'clock; it takes 20 minutes and is directed by SS First Lieutenant Karl Fritzsch, the Camp Commander. SS Second Lieutenant Täger is the commander of the execution squad, consisting of 20 SS Men from the Auschwitz Death's Head Guard Company. Two SS Men shoot each of the condemned individually.

APMO, D-AuI-1/5, 6, 8–9, 10–13, 50–56, The Execution of November 22, 1940.

40 separate protocols are made of the execution of the 40 Poles. Under the category of cause of death, a shot in the heart is registered and confirmed with the signature of the Camp Doctor, SS Captain Max Popiersch. Commandant Rudolf Höss also signs the protocols, which are stamped "Commandant's Office, Auschwitz."

APMO, D-AuI-1/10–49, The Execution of November 22, 1940.

Commandant Rudolf Höss makes a brief, written report to the concentration camps inspector concerning the execution of the 40 Poles

APMO, D-AuI-1/7, The Execution of November 22, 1940.

*The SS Commander in Chief condemns eight Poles whose names are not given on the list to life imprisonment in a Class III concentration camp.

ordered by the Head of the Sipo and SD, Heydrich, on November 1. At the same time, he informs him that the corpses of those who were shot are to be incinerated in the camp crematorium* and that a special report is being prepared for the SS Commander in Chief. A list of names and the 40 execution protocols are attached to the letter.

During evening roll call, Camp Commander Karl Fritzsch warns all prisoners against attempts to escape. He threatens that, in case of a successful escape, several residents from the escapee's hometown will be shot. He informs the prisoners that 40 inhabitants of the hometown of prisoner Majcher, who escaped from the camp, have to be shot that very day.**

Kozlowiecki, *Affliction and Anguish*, p. 210.

Referring to a previous conversation, Commandant Höss orders the Camp Commander in writing to make out death certificates by December 1, 1940, for the 40 Poles who were shot.†

APMO, D-AuI-1/4, The Execution of November 22, 1940.

NOVEMBER 23

300 prisoners sent from Pawiak Prison in Warsaw by order of the Sipo and SD Commander for the Warsaw District receive Nos. 6273–6572.

APMO, IZ-13/89, Various Documents of the Third Reich, pp. 247ff. (Original in the BA Koblenz).

Topf and Sons takes pains over the orders for incinerators for the concentration camps. In a letter to the Mauthausen New Building Administration, the company asks for a quick order confirmation because it hopes at this time to get an order from Auschwitz for a second coke-heated double-muffle incinerator for the cremation of corpses, like the one it has built in Gusen.

NOVEMBER 25

Commandant Höss receives a teletype message from the Concentration Camps Inspectorate with instructions to send immediately a copy of the November 1 order from the head of the Sipo and SD concerning the execution of 40 Poles. The message also asks if the RSHA has received a report and the execution protocols.

APMO, D-AuI-1/1–3, The Execution of November 22, 1940.

Commandant replies to the Concentration Camps Inspectorate with a teletype message that a report and the protocols of the execution of the 40 Poles has been sent to the RSHA by the Superior Commander of the SS and Police in Breslau.

Ibid.

---

*The deployment of the crematorium in the camp is mentioned officially for the first time in this letter.
**Leon Majcher escapes from the camp on the night of November 18–19. The Poles who were shot on November 22 were from his hometown.
†Probably in response to a request by the family, the registry in Auschwitz issues a death certificate for one of the shot Poles on August 8, 1942. It states that Bruno Felix Gruschka, Catholic, died on November 22, 1940, at 12 o'clock in Auschwitz on Kasernenstrasse. The deceased was born May 18, 1908, in Laurahütte. The death certificate is signed by SS Technical Sergeant Quakernack (APMO, D-AuI-2/3254, p. 21, The Execution of November 22, 1940).

NOVEMBER 26

The Commandant's office in Auschwitz sends the Concentration Camps Inspectorate a copy of the order of the Sipo and SD of November 1, 1940, concerning the execution.

Ibid.

NOVEMBER 27

27 prisoners sent from Kattowitz receive Nos. 6573–6599.

NOVEMBER 28

54 prisoners sent by the Kraków Sipo and SD receive Nos. 6600–6653.

13 prisoners are transferred from Auschwitz to Mauthausen.

APMO, Mat.RO, vol. VII, p. 474.

NOVEMBER 29

10 prisoners sent from Kattowitz receive Nos. 6654–6663.

26 prisoners sent with a group transport receive Nos. 6664–6689.

Between 11:00 and 11:30 A.M., the criminal prisoner Willi Meyer, a German born on July 4, 1909, in Elberfeld, escapes in Kattowitz. On May 20, 1940, he was transferred by Roll Call Leader Gerhard Palitzsch from Sachsenhausen with the first group of 30 German criminals to Auschwitz. He was No. 20 and was the Capo of a tailoring squad. In a telegram on the escape of the prisoner sent to the personal staff of the SS Commander in Chief, to Branch D of the WHVA in Oranienburg, to the Reich Criminal Police (Reichskriminalpolizeiamt—RKPA) in Potsdam, to Gestapo, Kripo, and Border Police headquarters, and to other concerned departments, Commandant Höss states that prisoner Willi Meyer, under the supervision of Roll Call Leader Palitzsch, had been in a Kattowitz hospital for outpatient treatment. He escaped because the supervisor did not know that the outpatient clinic had two doors.*

APMO, IZ-8/Gestapo Lodz/3/88/227.

NOVEMBER

At the end of November, Commandant Höss and the head of Office D-III of the Office of Administration and Economy (VWHA), SS Major Heinrich Vogel, who is responsible for the administration of agricultural, forest, and aquaculture facilities, including those in Auschwitz, submit a report to Himmler investigating the possibil-

APMO, Höss Trial, vol. 21, p. 32; Höss, *Commandant in Auschwitz*, pp. 95, 178.

---

*In Höss's characterization of Gerhard Palitzsch in the Kraków investigation of November 1946, he says that Palitzsch, along with the Second Protective Custody Commander Franz Xaver Maier and the criminal prisoner had carried on an extensive trade in Auschwitz in gold, jewelry, and illegally confiscated items. Höss learned of this from Meyer, who was arrested again in 1944 when Palitzsch was already on trial in the SS court. Meyer had threatened Palitzsch and two other junior officers of the camp administration that he would reveal the swindle. That's why Palitzsch helped him escape.

The electric barbed-wire fence around Birkenau; in the background the kitchen buildings.

ities of agricultural development in the area around Auschwitz. On the basis of this report, Himmler decides to create an SS farm district around the Auschwitz camp, in the third zone, which encompasses the villages of Babitz (Babice), Broschkowitz (Broszkowice), Birkenau (Brzezinka), Budy, Harmense (Harmęże), Plawy, and Rajsko.* In this farm district, an experimental agricultural station for the East is to be built with laboratories, a plant-breeding station in Rajsko, as well as cattle-, poultry-, and fish-breeding facilities. The poor living conditions of the prisoners and the deficiencies in the camp do not interest Himmler.

DECEMBER

In early December, during a noon roll call, one prisoner is discovered missing. It later turns out that he fell asleep in the straw in the camp storage depot. The roll call lasts from 12:00 to 1:00; finally the prisoners are sent to work without lunch. Almost a tenth of the unit employed in the camp warehouse, about 2,000 prisoners,

APMO, Höss Trial, vol. 7, pp. 107ff., Report of Former Prisoner Jan Kaszyński.

*The evacuation of these villages takes place in 1941. The entire cleared area, called the Auschwitz Interest Zone, encompasses some 25 square miles and includes a district office. This is headed by the Commandant as commissioner. He is responsible for all administrative and police as well as civilian matters, for which the district office has its own registry office, Registry Office Auschwitz II (Jan Sehn, *Obóz koncentracyjny Oświęcim-Brzezinka* [Auschwitz-Birkenau Concentration Camp], Warsaw, 1957, pp. 18ff).

die before evening roll call as a result of the abuse of the SS men and the Capos. The bodies are removed in carts. The Capos kill the prisoner who fell asleep in the straw.

DECEMBER 3

14 prisoners sent with a group transport receive Nos. 6690–6703.

Nine inmates sent from Kattowitz receive Nos. 6705–6713.

DECEMBER 4

103 prisoners sent by the Tarnów Sipo and SD receive Nos. 6714–6816.

DECEMBER 5

56 prisoners sent on a group transport receive Nos. 6817–6872.

DECEMBER 6

68 prisoners are transferred from Auschwitz to Dachau.

APMO, Mat.RO, vol. VII, p. 474.

Five prisoners sent with a group transport receive Nos. 6873–6877.

DECEMBER 10

At 8:45 A.M., a prisoner on an outside squad is shot attempting to escape.

APMO, Höss Trial, vol. 12, p. 216, Guard Register.

A prisoner sent from Kattowitz is given No. 6704.

DECEMBER 12

Seven prisoners sent in a group transport receive Nos. 6878–6884.

DECEMBER 15

500 prisoners transferred from Dachau to Auschwitz receive the Nos. 6885–7384.

DECEMBER 16

Eight prisoners sent from Kattowitz receive Nos. 7385–7392.

DECEMBER 18

78 prisoners sent from Kattowitz receive Nos. 7393–7470.

30 prisoners sent from Kattowitz receive Nos. 7471–7500.

240 prisoners sent from Kattowitz with a general transport receive Nos. 7501–7740.

DECEMBER 19

Three prisoners sent from Kattowitz and Kraków receive Nos. 7741–7743.

42 prisoners sent by the Kraków Sipo and SD receive Nos. 7744–7785.

The Archbishop of Kraków, Prince Adam Sapieha, sends a letter to the parish office in Auschwitz, addressed to the Commandant of Auschwitz Concentration Camp, requesting permission to read a Holy Mass at Christmas for the Catholic prisoners.

APMO, Materials, vol. 25, Chronicle of the Auschwitz Parish.

After receiving the Archbishop's letter, the priests of Auschwitz parish, Władysław Gross and Rudolf Schmidt, proceed to the Commandant to present the letter. He receives the two priests but does not give permission for a religious celebration because the rules of the concentration camp do not provide for religious observance. Nevertheless, Höss does allow approximately 6,000 food packages weighing about two pounds each to be sent to all prisoners on Christmas Eve. The packages are to be sent by mail, without addresses. Immediately money and food contributions begin to be collected among the neighboring population. Packages are put together from these contributions and from the funds granted for this purpose by Archbishop Sapieha and are mailed to the camp. Many prisoners get them only after the new year.

Ibid.

DECEMBER 20

19 prisoners sent with a group transport receive Nos. 7786–7804.

DECEMBER 21

11 prisoners sent with a group transport receive Nos. 7805–7815.

DECEMBER 23

One prisoner sent from Bielitz receives No. 7816.

36 prisoners sent by the Sipo and SD from the prison in Tarnów receive Nos. 7817–7852.

DECEMBER 27

20 prisoners sent from the prison in Tarnów by the Sipo and SD receive Nos. 7859–7878.

DECEMBER 28

Six prisoners sent with a general transport receive Nos. 7853–7858.

Prisoners working on the expansion of the kitchen buildings in Auschwitz I in the fall of 1943.

SS headquarters in Birkenau under construction; in the background, SS barracks.

DECEMBER 31

One prisoner sent from Kattowitz is given No. 7879. This is the last number to be assigned in 1940.*

The prisoners are employed in construction and renovation. They build supply installations, which are necessary for the functioning of the concentration camp. The construction office is created at the time the camp is established in June 1940; it is originally named the SS New Construction Administration—Auschwitz. Until October 1941, it is directed by SS Second Lieutenant Schlachter, described by Höss as "a provincial architect from Württemberg, a limited mind with little energy." One of the first prisoner labor squads is Building Office–Building Administration. Supervised and directed by SS Men, the prisoners in this squad are involved in working out camp plans and the drafting of technical plans for new buildings, etc. They also lay out sites for future buildings and streets. They survey the camp and its surrounding area and make precise maps and plans of the camp that relate to the changes in the future character of Auschwitz.

The following camp workshops are set up: a carpentry shop, a locksmith shop, an electrical and plumbing shop, a roofing shop, a painting shop, a forge, and a crew to make concrete. The prisoner labor squads working in these shops have a stable personnel structure; in 1940, there are not yet very many of them. The remaining prisoners work in squads made up of hundreds laboring in gravel pits, excavation, and transportation. The size of these units changes according to the requirements. In 1940 all inmates work at building the camp except for those who take care of the SS and the prisoners, e.g., in the camp kitchen, the prisoners' infirmary, the SS kitchen, the SS sick bay and in the SS departmental offices such as the Admissions Office of the Political Department.

In 1940, the hardest work was leveling the roll-call area, paving the streets (especially under the supervision of Capo Krankemann), working the gravel pits, demolishing the houses and farms of the residents evacuated from the town of Zasole, and transporting construction material to the so-called factory yard and the lumber yard. This work is carried out in the most primitive manner, almost without machines or other technological means. While doing this work, which is beyond their strength, the underfed and utterly exhausted prisoners are beaten, abused, and killed.

Although the camp is still in the construction stage, plans are made for a farm district and agricultural activities near it. Plowed fields, livestock, and fish breeding are to be attached to it. The camp does not lack a labor force since new transports are sent daily.

---

*There is no documentary information about the number of prisoners in the camp. Therefore, it is not known how many are killed in the camp and how many die from hunger, cold, bad sanitary conditions, overwork, and abuse. Höss's permission to send 6,000 packages to the camp for Christmas Eve allows us to infer that there were about 6,000 prisoners in Auschwitz in December 1940.

1 9 4 1

JANUARY

In early January, Dr. Otto Ambros, a member of the board of the I. G. Farben company and responsible for the entire Buna Division, and Head Engineer Biedenkopf, visit the State Planning Office in Kattowitz to look at maps and charts of various sites in Upper Silesia in order to select an appropriate site for the construction of four Buna factories to produce 30,000 tons of synthetic rubber a year. The region around Auschwitz seems favorable since the confluence of three rivers means that water and raw materials (lime, coal, and salt) are available in the area. The high population density in this region and the presence of a concentration camp are also important, since this assures the necessary labor force for the construction of the plant. After a visit through the region, Dr. Ambros selects the town of Dwory near Auschwitz as a favorable site for the factory. It had previously been the site of a Polish estate whose owner fled when the district was annexed to the Reich.

Reimund Schnabel, *Macht ohne Moral: Eine Dokumentation über die SS* (Power Without Morality: A Documentation of the SS), Frankfurt, 1957, p. 229; Testimony of Otto Ambros before the Nuremberg Military Tribunal in the I. G. Farben Case.

JANUARY 2

In an edict of January 2, 1941, Reinhard Heydrich, head of the RSHA, announces that SS Commander in Chief Heinrich Himmler has agreed to the classification of the concentration camps in three categories based on the personality of the prisoners and the level of danger they represent for the state.* The classifications are:

APMO, D-RF-3/RSHA/118/9, vol. 10, p. 607, Edict Collection of the Reichskriminalpolizeiamt (cited hereafter as: Edict Collection RKPA).

1. Class I: Dachau, Sachsenhausen and Auschwitz I** are designed for "less serious prisoners definitely capable of improvement";
2. Class II: Buchenwald, Flossenbürg, Neuengamme, and Auschwitz II† (which does not yet even exist!) are designed

---

*Compare entry of August 28, 1940.
**For the first time, the title "Auschwitz I Concentration Camp" is formally used to refer to the original camp.
†This proves that by the end of 1940 plans must have been made for the establishment of a second camp (Auschwitz II) in Auschwitz. This camp is considered, in advance, a Class II camp.

for "prisoners charged with serious crimes but nevertheless capable of rehabilitation and improvement";

3. Class III: Mauthausen is designed for "prisoners charged with serious crimes" and especially for "previously convicteds" and "asocials."

JANUARY 3

One prisoner sent from Troppau is given No. 7880.

At 7:10 A.M. an escaping prisoner who has climbed up the camp fence is shot and killed by SS Men Beier and Culemann.

APMO, Höss Trial, vol. 12, p. 216, Guard Register.

JANUARY 6

A few prisoners who have received musical instruments from home gather in Block 24 and begin to rehearse in a room on the ground floor. This is the beginning of what will later be the camp orchestra, which, after getting permission to rehearse, plays at the departure in the morning and return of the prisoner labor squads and also gives concerts for prisoners and for the Commandant near his villa. Permission for the establishment of the orchestra is given for propaganda purposes, to be able to demonstrate that prisoners are practicing their professions, as well as for practical reasons—to facilitate the orderly departure of the thousands of prisoners to work.

APMO, Höss Trial, vol. 15, p. 51, Account of Former Prisoner Franciszek Nierychło.

JANUARY 7

509 prisoners sent by the Sipo and SD from Pawiak Prison in Warsaw receive Nos. 7881–8389. One of these prisoners is Norbert Barlicki,* the former Polish Minister of the Interior and mayor of Lodz, an experienced politician of the PPS, who joins the clandestine resistance movement in the camp. No. 8230 is given to Jan Mosdorf, one of the leaders of the National Radical Camp (Obóz Narodowo Radykalny—ONR), who also begins conspiratorial activity in the camp. This transport also includes Juliusz Kempler (No. 2045) and Stanisław Palka (No. 4122),** who are being returned to Auschwitz after having been transferred from Auschwitz to Pawiak Prison.

APMO, D-AuI-2/I, p. 3, Admissions List. A list of names of prisoners brought to Auschwitz. This source refers to transports from January 7, 1941, to December 23, 1941, and will not be cited again in further entries on the admission of prisoners.

97 prisoners sent from Radom† by the Sipo and SD receive Nos. 8390–8486.

JANUARY 9

The clerk in Block 11, Franciszek Brol (No. 1159), makes the first entries in the secret notebook he kept on prisoners in the bunker

APMO, D-AuI-3/1/2, Bunker Register, 2 volumes. The first entries are made on January 9, 1941, and the last on February 2, 1944.

*He dies in the camp on September 27, 1941.
**Probably the Warsaw Gestapo needed them for eyewitness testimony or for confrontations.
†The Sipo and SD transports to Auschwitz consist solely of political prisoners.

The Admissions Building in the Auschwitz main camp.

of Block 11, those locked in under camp arrest. This is called the Bunker Register.*

121 prisoners sent by the Radom Sipo and SD receive Nos. 8487–8607.

525 prisoners sent from Lublin by the Sipo and SD receive Nos. 8608–9132.

JANUARY 10

169 prisoners from the prison in Tarnów and 102 from Monte-lupich Prison in Kraków are sent by the Kraków District Sipo and SD and receive Nos. 9133–9403. No. 9362 is given to Tadeusz Orzelski, a contact man for the clandestine PPS and the Association for Armed Struggle (Związek Walki Zbrojnej—ZWZ); he has been arrested while forging 10 passports to be used by the couriers of the underground movement.

Tadeusz Wroński, *Chronicle*, p. 120.

*The record of the prisoners locked up in the bunker of Block 11 is officially kept, chaotically and imprecisely, by the Block Leader, an SS man. The block clerk, on the other hand, keeps a record of attendance of the rest of the prisoners lodged on the ground floor or the first floor; he is obliged to give the total number of prisoners at camp roll calls. Inconsistencies in the number of prisoners prolong the roll calls and have unfavorable consequences for the prisoners. This leads the clerk to keep his own unofficial register. The Bunker Register is later accepted by the SS men.

JANUARY 11

61 prisoners sent by the Gestapo in Lodz receive Nos. 9404–9464.

JANUARY 12

At 8:20 A.M., next to Watchtower A, SS men Kehn and Bilss shoot a prisoner trying to escape over the barbed-wire fence of the camp.*

APMO, Höss Trial, vol. 12, p. 117, quoted from the Guard Register.

JANUARY 14

A prisoner sent from Kattowitz is given No. 9465.

JANUARY 15

At 9:30 A.M., the Commandant gives his approval for a sick woman and her mother, who want to see the body of a deceased prisoner, to be allowed in by the sentry. At noon the women leave the camp.

Ibid., p. 217.

JANUARY 16

26 prisoners sent from Kraków receive Nos. 9466–9491.

JANUARY 17

A prisoner sent from Kattowitz is given No. 9492.

JANUARY 18

Two prisoners sent with a group transport from Hamburg and Pahlshof receive Nos. 9493 and 9494.

JANUARY 22

Two prisoners sent from Kattowitz are given Nos. 9495 and 9496.

JANUARY 23

657 prisoners are transferred from Auschwitz to Flossenbürg.

APMO, Mat.RO, vol. VII, p. 474; Kraków Auschwitz Trial, vol. 3, p. 111.

JANUARY 24

23 prisoners sent with a group transport receive Nos. 9497–9519.

At 5:30 P.M. Maria Tümel is brought by the Birkenau police for interrogation by the SS Camp Guard.

APMO, Höss Trial, vol. 12, p. 217, quoted from the Guard Register.

JANUARY 25

20 prisoners sent from Kattowitz receive Nos. 9520–9539.

*The time of day suggests this was a suicide, not an escape attempt.

JANUARY 29

Two prisoners sent from Kattowitz are given Nos. 9540 and 9541.

JANUARY 31

29 prisoners sent with a group transport receive Nos. 9542–9570.

FEBRUARY 1

593 prisoners sent from Pawiak Prison by the Sipo and SD receive Nos. 9571–10163. The transport includes 383 prisoners arrested on January 12, 1941, in Warsaw, most of whom were interrogated by the Gestapo. The other 210 were arrested for illegal possession of weapons and contacts with illegal organizations.

Domańska, *Pawiak*, p. 126.

One prisoner sent from Kattowitz is given No. 10164.

FEBRUARY 5

23 prisoners sent from Lodz receive Nos. 10165–10187.

FEBRUARY 6

Nine prisoners sent from Kattowitz receive Nos. 10188–10196.

FEBRUARY 7

15 prisoners sent from Kattowitz receive Nos. 10197–10211.

FEBRUARY 8

26 prisoners sent with a group transport receive Nos. 10212–10237.

FEBRUARY 10

A special commission of the personal staff of the SS Commander in Chief comes to Auschwitz. Under the direction of Commandant Höss, this commission works out the main guidelines concerning the territory of the so-called Interest Zone and the number of people to be resettled. One of the commission members is SS Lieutenant Colonel Dr. Arlt.

Tadeusz Iwaszko, "Häftlings-fluchten aus dem KL Auschwitz" (Escapes from Auschwitz), *HvA*, no. 7 (1964):5–6; Memorandum of Dr. Arlt and Dr. Korn on their trip to Auschwitz and Chełmek.

FEBRUARY 11

Nine prisoners sent from Kattowitz receive Nos. 10238–10246.

FEBRUARY 12

24 prisoners sent from Kattowitz receive Nos. 10247–10270. Władysaw Prochot (No. 3675), who has been interrogated by the

APMO, D-AuI-2/1, p. 57, Admissions List.

Gestapo or taken for a confrontation, is transferred back with this group.

FEBRUARY 13

31 prisoners are sent from Kattowitz by the Gestapo and receive Nos. 10271–10301.

FEBRUARY 14

35 prisoners sent with a group transport* by Gestapo offices in Nuremberg, Berlin, Görlitz, Posen, Lodz, and Kattowitz receive Nos. 10302–10336.

Ibid., pp. 60ff.

In the camp, a prisoner is readmitted who was already marked with No. 1222 on June 26, 1940.

FEBRUARY 18

Two prisoners sent from Kattowitz receive Nos. 10337 and 10338.

Reich Marshal and Commissioner for the Four-Year-Plan Hermann Göring issues "population-political" guidelines concerning a state secret, the construction of the Buna factory in Auschwitz. To achieve the fastest possible pace of work, to ensure complete employment and to be able to accommodate the first workers in Auschwitz by early April, Göring requests the following measures from Himmler: the quick evacuation of the Jews from Auschwitz and the surrounding area to free up living space for the workers employed in the construction of the Buna factory; for the time being to let the Poles from Auschwitz and the surrounding area stay in their homes, since they are considered potential construction workers until the completion of the factory; the allocation of as many skilled and unskilled workers as possible from Auschwitz C.C. for the construction of the Buna factory. Göring works on the premise that the manpower

APMO, Maurer Trial, vol. 7, pp. 12ff. (NO-1240).

---

*In a group transport, there are prisoners from various prisons. Up to 56 prisoners are conveyed in one prison car. The German Railroad owns 64 such cars, which are attached to regular trains; they cover fixed distances, so-called loops. These loops run through the entire Reich, the Government General in central Poland, and Austria, as well as the protectorate of Bohemia and Moravia. There are 17 loops, on each of which prison cars make up to seven runs every day of the week except Sunday. According to the timetable valid from October 6, 1941, Auschwitz is the destination on Fridays of the fourth southern loop, in the first circuit. The route and timetable read: From Beuthen (5:43 A.M.) to Kattowitz–Trzebinia–Kraków–Auschwitz (arrival: 7:46 P.M.) back through Kattowitz to Beuthen (arrival 10:42 P.M.). Beuthen is the departure point for this circuit, where prisoners are brought from the other loops; there, prisoners destined for Auschwitz are loaded. In Beuthen, Gestapo and Kripo prisoners from Kattowitz are also loaded onto every transport. (*Kursbuch für die Gefangenenwagen, gültig vom 6. Oktober 1941 an, mit einem Anhang: Nummernplan und Übersichtszeichnungen der eingesetzten Gefangenenwagen* [Timetable for Prisoner Cars, valid from October 6, 1941, with an Appendix: Numbering System and a Summary of Drawings of Prisoner Cars in Use, Dokumente zur Eisenbahngeschichte 10] [Documents on the History of the Railroad, vol. 10], reprint, Mainz, 1979).

Office of the Central Construction Administration of Auschwitz and Birkenau.

requirement for the construction and installation will be between 8,000 and 12,000 laborers, depending on the pace of the work.

FEBRUARY 19

29 prisoners sent with a group transport receive Nos. 10339–10358.

FEBRUARY 21

55 prisoners sent from Montelupich Prison in Kraków by the Sipo and SD receive Nos. 10359–10413.

28 prisoners sent with a group transport receive Nos. 10414–10441.

FEBRUARY 25

290 prisoners sent from Radom by the Sipo and SD receive Nos. 10442–10731.

60 prisoners sent by the Kraków District Sipo and SD from the prison in Tarnów receive Nos. 10732–10794.

Three prisoners sent from Kattowitz receive Nos. 10792–10794.

The SS guard staff in Auschwitz is reinforced by one company, to four.

APMO, D-AuI-3a/1, Monthly Report of Field Office I/5, Folder 14, Report of Heinrich Schwarz of March 17, 1941.

In the bunker of Block 11, Jan Kalus (No. 1135), the first prisoner to be locked up in the bunker on February 19, 1941, dies.

APMO, D-AuI-3/1, Bunker Register, p. 1.

FEBRUARY 26

81 prisoners sent by the Kraków District Sipo and SD from the prison in Tarnów receive Nos. 10795–10875.

Three prisoners sent from Kattowitz receive Nos. 10876–10878.

At 11:45 P.M. prisoner No. 7190 is "shot while escaping."

APMO, Höss Trial, vol. 12, p. 217, Guard Register.

The SS Commander in Chief issues the order to evacuate the Jews from Auschwitz as soon as possible and to secure their houses for the construction workers of the Buna factory; Polish skilled and unskilled laborers from Auschwitz and vicinity who could be employed in the construction of the Buna factory are not to be evacuated.

APMO, Maurer Trial, vol. 7, p. 26 (NO-11086).

FEBRUARY 28

22 prisoners sent with a group transport receive Nos. 10879–10900.

Eight prisoners are transferred from Auschwitz to Mauthausen.

APMO, Mat.RO, vol. VII, p. 474.

In the office of the SS Commander in Chief Heinrich Himmler, the agenda for his visit to Auschwitz is determined. Participants are Himmler; SS General Karl Wolff, Himmler's chief of staff and appointed by him to be an SS liaison with the I. G. Farben company; SS Major Vogel; and SS Second Lieutenant von Thermann. The schedule is takeoff from Berlin's Tempelhof Airport at 11:00 A.M.; arrival in Gleiwitz at 1:00 P.M.; lunch in Gleiwitz and then departure by car; arrival in Auschwitz at 4:00 P.M. and the survey of the concentration camp; departure by car to Breslau at 5:30 P.M.; arrival in Breslau at 7:00 P.M.; finally, an evening invitation from SS Major General von dem Bach-Zelewski for his birthday. Overnight in the Hotel Monopol.

APMO, IZ-13/89, Various Documents of the Third Reich, p. 297 (Original in BA Koblenz).

MARCH 1

SS Commander in Chief Heinrich Himmler carries out his first inspection of Auschwitz. Along with the officials of his office, he is accompanied by Gauleiter and Governor of Upper Silesia, SS Brigadier General Fritz Bracht; the Superior SS and Police Commander in Breslau, SS Lieutenant General Ernst Schmauser; SS Brigadier General Glücks; and governors and leading representatives of I. G. Farben. After a detailed camp inspection and examination of the Interest Zone, Himmler issues the following orders to the Commandant:

APMO, D-AuI-3a, Folder 14, Report of Himmler's Visit by Heinrich Schwarz of March 17, 1941; Höss Trial, vol. 21, pp. 33ff; Höss, *Commandant in Auschwitz*, pp. 179ff.

1. to expand Auschwitz C. C. to hold 30,000 prisoners
2. to build a camp for 100,000 prisoners of war on the site of the village of Birkenau
3. to make 10,000 prisoners available to I. G. Farben for the construction of the industrial plant in Dwory near Auschwitz

SS Commander in Chief Heinrich Himmler (first row, left), Senior Engineer Faust (with hat), and the first commandant, Rudolf Höss, during an inspection of the industrial installations at Auschwitz.

4. to cultivate the whole area agriculturally

5. to expand the camp workshops

Himmler also indicates that armaments-production facilities are to be built in the vicinity of the camp, which will give the SS a leading role in providing weapons to the German Army.

The first plan of the Auschwitz Interest Zone is drawn up, which includes the camp in Birkenau.

APMO, D-AuI-3a, Docs. ZBL, BW 2/9.

Two prisoners sent from Kattowitz are given Nos. 10901 and 10902.

MARCH 2

The SS guard troops in Auschwitz are reinforced by one company and now number five guard companies.

APMO, D-AuI-3a/1, Folder 14, Report of March 17, 1941, by Heinrich Schwarz.

MARCH 4

The "plenipotentiary for special questions of chemical production," Professor Dr. Carl Krauch, notifies I. G. Farben that, at his suggestion and by order of Reich Marshal Göring of February 26, the following orders have been issued by the SS Commander in Chief: evacuation of the Jews from Auschwitz, and a prohibition against evacuating Polish construction workers from Auschwitz and vicinity. The SS Commander in Chief has recommended the concentration camps inspector and the Head of the WVHA to establish contacts with the builder of the Buna factory and to offer assistance from Auschwitz. The SS Commander in Chief has named the chief of his personal staff, SS General Karl Wolff, as liaison between himself and the Buna factory in Auschwitz.

APMO, Maurer Trial, vol. 7, pp. 25ff. (NO-11086).

MARCH 5

43 prisoners sent by the Gestapo from Oppeln receive Nos. 10903–10945.

Concentration Camps Inspector Richard Glücks conveys to Commandant Höss the order of the SS Commander in Chief issued after his inspection of the camp on March 1, 1941. According to the order, during the war, all officers and noncommissioned officers of the Waffen SS (Armed SS) who are qualified for service in the concentration camp are to be accepted. Glücks also informs the Commandant of the planned construction of an SS village in Auschwitz.

APMO, D-RF-3/RSHA/117/1, p. 91, General Orders of the RSHA.

MARCH 6

One prisoner sent from Kattowitz is given No. 10946.

MARCH 7

On written orders of the head of Office D-III of the WVHA, Vogel, Professor Dr. Engineer Zunker of Breslau has been conducting investigations of water and pond conditions over the entire Auschwitz Interest Zone since February 15, 1941, in the presence of Commandant Höss. The purpose is to assess the potential for livestock and fish-breeding operations.

APMO, Höss Trial, vol. 12, p. 210; vol. 21, p. 34.

19 prisoners sent with a general transport receive Nos. 10947–10965.

MARCH 8

In a 15-minute period the inhabitants of the village of Pławy are evacuated on this Saturday, without previous warning. The residents are brought in lorries and oxcarts to the assembly hall of the Praga company in Auschwitz, where they remain until the next day. On Sunday, they are transferred to Gorlice in the General Government. Miners living in Pławy are resettled with their families in Brzeszcze and Jawischowitz on March 10 and 11.

APMO, D-AuI-3a/1, Folder 14, Report of Heinrich Schwarz of March 17, 1941.

MARCH 9

Two prisoners sent from the Kattowitz District receive Nos. 10966 and 10967.

The evacuation of the Jews from the town of Auschwitz begins. They are resettled in Krenau (Chrazanów). Dr. Otto Ambros, board member of I. G. Farben, is present at the evacuation; he is shaken by this sight.

Schnabel, *Power Without Morality*, p. 231.

MARCH 14

25 prisoners sent with a group transport receive Nos. 10968–10992.

In the gravel pit next to the so-called theater building, 72 Polish prisoners selected by the Political Department are shot. They include a professor from Kraków University, Adam Zdzisław Heydel (No. 10564), and his brother, Woljciech Heydel (No. 10568). Both were sent to the camp from the prison in Radom by the Sipo and SD.

APMO, Accounts, vol. 67, p. 63, Account of Former Prisoner Kazimierz Szczerbowski; D-AuI-2/3601, Death Certificate in the Name of Adam Heydel; D-AuI-2/28, Death Certificate for Wojciech Heydel. Both documents give March 14, 1941, as the date of death.

MARCH 17

In a monthly report prepared by order of the Budget and Buildings Central Office, the head of Labor Deployment, SS Second Lieutenant Heinrich Schwarz, informs the office of the Chief of Police and the SS in the Ministry of the Interior that a room 10 feet long for potato peeling and vegetable preparation has been added to the prisoners' kitchen, and that on February 10 refrigerators for storing meat and fat have arrived. At the end of February, they received the first delivery of 1,000 bedsteads for equipping the hospital and two convalescent blocks. In two blocks, 350 three-tiered beds have been set up. In the prisoners' infirmary and the two convalescent blocks, there are two wardrobes in every room but 60 are still needed. Schwarz also states:

APMO, D-AuI-3a, Folder 14, Report of Heinrich Schwarz of March 17, 1941.

1. The planned Auschwitz building for the German Armaments Works (Deutsche Ausrüstungswerke GMBH—DAW) Ltd. is being expanded and renovated. Heating and hot-water facilities are to be installed within the next few days.

2. The additional story of the ground-floor building in the camp was progressing only slowly since the necessary quantity of windows and other wooden elements like doors, floors, and sills are lacking.

3. Because of the large number of transports into Auschwitz in February, there were 1,350 new prisoners. The necessity of lodging these inmates in the blocks has led to a decision to transfer various workshops out of the camp to the factory yard and to other areas occupied by the Waffen SS.

4. The manufacture of wooden spoons has been discontinued because of a lack of wood. Their number amounted to 2,450 pieces. Another 1,025 pieces are to be manufactured.

5. Because of the evacuation, all residents of the towns of Auschwitz, Birkenau, Harmense, Bór, Pławy, Babitz, Broschkowitz, Klutschnikowitz, Stare Stawy, Rajsko, Budy, Jawischowitz, Skidzin, and Dankowice are to be registered separately by nationality. Two transports, of 800 Poles and 250 Jews, have already been sent to the General Government. Since the evacuation operation of the Polish and Jewish population in the General Government has been discontinued, a new situation has emerged. In the interests of the expansion, draining, and cultivation of the entire site around the camp, internal resettlement is to take place. This work is to be carried out under the supervision and direction of the Commandant of Auschwitz Concentration Camp and the staff appointed for this purpose.

MARCH 18

35 prisoners sent from Kattowitz receive Nos. 10993–11027.

MARCH 20

Two prisoners sent from the Kattowitz District receive Nos. 11028 and 11029.

In Berlin, a conversation takes place. The participants are Dr. Engineer Heinrich Bütefisch of I. G. Farben; SS General Karl Wolff, the liaison man for SS Commander in Chief Himmler; SS Major General Georg Lörner of the Budget and Buildings Main Office; and Concentration Camps Inspector SS Brigadier General Richard Glücks. The discussion concerns the level of support by the Auschwitz camp of the construction of I. G. Farben's new chemical factory in Dwory near Auschwitz.

APMO, Maurer Trial, vol. 7, p. 15 (NO-15148).

MARCH 21

58 prisoners sent with a group transport receive Nos. 11030–11087.

MARCH 24

Three prisoners sent from the Kattowitz District receive Nos. 11088–11090.

Ibid., pp. 30ff. (NO-11115).

The participants of the first working meeting, in Ludwigshafen, concerning the construction of the Buna factory are Dr. von Staden, Dr. Eyman, Chief Engineers Faust, Santo, Dr. Dürrfeld, and Dr. Mach, and Certified Engineer Heidebröck. The following points are established:

1. The SS command succeeded in obtaining approval from the SS Budget and Buildings Main Office for transferring skilled laborers from concentration camps in Germany to Auschwitz.
2. All free labor in Auschwitz* is to be taken over completely.
3. The camp administration (Höss) takes charge of guarding the building site.
4. There is the possibility of building crafts shops within the camp.
5. The camp leadership will feed those who work on the construction site—as much as possible.
6. The police borders are to be expanded so that the construction site falls within the sentry lines.

Dr. Otto Ambros opens and leads the meeting. April 1, 1941, is set as the date for the next meeting.

*This concerns free workmen from the city and the vicinity.

MARCH 25

Two prisoners sent from Kattowitz receive Nos. 11091 and 11092.

MARCH 26

Professor Dr. Engineer Zunker, who investigated the water and ponds in the Auschwitz Interest Zone on March 7, states in a written report that the water brought into the camp is not even fit to rinse your mouth.

APMO, Höss Trial, vol. 12, p. 211.

14 prisoners sent from Kattowitz receive Nos. 11093–11106.

MARCH 27

Three prisoners sent from Kattowitz receive Nos. 11107–11109.

In the Commandant's Office in Auschwitz a conversation takes place among Commandant Höss, Head Engineers Faust, Flöter, and Murr, Dr. Dürrfeld of I. G. Farben and SS Major Kraus of the SS administrative office. The following points are agreed on:

APMO, Maurer Trial, vol. 7, pp. 15–20.

1. That Auschwitz C.C. is to make 1,000 inmates available as skilled and unskilled labor for the construction of the Buna factory in Dwory near Auschwitz in 1941.
2. That Auschwitz Concentration Camp is to make an additional 3,000 inmates available in 1941. This number is to be expanded to 8,000 as the need arises.
3. The number of inmates available in the next year is to rise to 30,000. Hence, a large number of Capos will be needed. These foremen, BV-prisoners, will have to be transferred to Auschwitz from other camps.
4. The prisoners are to be transported by railroad to the work site. The camp is to erect a railroad bridge for this purpose over the Soła River.
5. The prisoners' daily work hours are to be 11 hours in summer and nine hours in winter.
6. I. G. Farben is to pay 4 Reichsmarks a day for a skilled worker and 3 Reichsmarks a day for an unskilled worker.*

MARCH 29

12 prisoners sent with a group transport receive Nos. 11110–11121.

APRIL 1

In an hour's time the complete evacuation is carried out by the SS of the remaining resident population in the second camp zone,

APMO, Höss Trial, vol. 12, pp. 43, 45–47.

---

*The prisoners receive no pay for their labor. The bills issued by the camp administration to I. G. Farben show that the daily payment for the prisoners' labor is paid to the Commandant's Office. It is then transferred to the Reich from the camp account or from the account of the WVHA.

Kurzstrasse, Feldstrasse, and Bahnhofsstrasse. The residents, who received no previous information about the evacuation, are chased out of their houses onto the streets with the commands "Get out!" and "At once!" On the same day, prisoners on a demolition squad begin tearing down the cleared houses* and using the building material in the construction of the camp.

19 prisoners sent from Kattowitz by the Gestapo receive Nos. 11122–11140.

During the next working meeting in Ludwigshafen concerning the construction of the Buna factory, Head Engineer Dr. Dürrfeld reports on his conversation with the Commandant of Auschwitz, Rudolf Höss. Höss told Dürrfeld that he is prepared to make 1,000 to 1,500 prisoners available in 1941 and 3,000 to 4,000 in 1942 as unskilled labor. The prisoners will work in groups of 20 under the supervision of Capos. Höss has asked I. G. Farben to help him obtain steel and wood for the construction of camp barracks. At the same time, he had proposed to sell gravel to I. G. Farben for 4.50 Reichsmarks (RM) per cubic yard. Auschwitz C.C. possesses three excavators and can deliver to the site 400 cubic yards of gravel via a field-railway over the Soła River every day. Dr. Dürrfeld decides that the price is reasonable. He informs the meeting that the SS has taken over 20,000 acres between the Vistula and Soła rivers. Höss will erect a dam there to protect the camp area from flooding. He intends to have a sewage plant built on the Vistula for sewage purification. The next meeting is set for April 7, 1941.

APMO, Maurer Trial, vol. 7, pp. 32–34 (NO-11116).

APRIL 2

38 prisoners sent from Kattowitz receive Nos. 11141–11178.

APRIL 4

23 prisoners sent in a group transport receive Nos. 11179–11201.

APRIL 5

A prisoner sent from Kattowitz is given No. 11924.

933 prisoners are sent to Auschwitz by the commander of the Kraków Sipo and SD, including 536 prisoners from the prison in Tarnów and 397 from Montelupich Prison in Kraków. They receive the following numbers: 11202–11536, 11538–11923, 11925–12134, 13678–13683, 13685–13688, and 13692–13694.

536 prisoners are sent from the prison in Radom by the Sipo and SD commander for the Radom District. They receive Nos. 12125–

---

*123 houses are torn down or destroyed. In Feldstrasse and Bahnhofsstrasse, six residences are left. The demolition of the houses is to ease police operations in case of the escape of prisoners from the camp.

12351, 12887–12962, 12964–13192, 13194–13195, 13216, and 14944.

APRIL 6

1,021 prisoners from Pawiak Prison are sent to the camp by the Sipo and SD commander in Warsaw and receive Nos. 11537, 12352–12354, 12356–12886, 13193, 13196–13215, 13217–13677, 13684, and 13689–13691. This transport includes actors from Warsaw theaters arrested in retaliation for the shooting of film actor Igo Sym on March 7, 1941. Igo Sym was an ethnic German who collaborated with the Gestapo and the Propaganda Office of the Warsaw District. The arrested actors include Bronisław Dardziński, Tadeusz Hertman Kański, Stefan Jaracz, Zbigniew Nowakowski (Sawan), and Leon Schiller.

Domańska, *Pawiak*, pp. 136, 143.

1249 prisoners sent from the prison in Lublin castle by the Sipo and SD Commander in Lublin receive Nos. 13695–14943. Some of the prisoners are suffering from typhus. A typhus epidemic breaks out in the camp. For this reason, Block 12 (later Block 10) is temporarily reserved as an infection ward.

Germany attacks Yugoslavia and Greece.

APRIL 7

Two prisoners sent from Kattowitz receive Nos. 14945 and 14946.

In accordance with the decision made at a conference of representatives from the WVHA and I. G. Farben on March 27, 1941, that took place in the Commandant's Office in Auschwitz, prisoners begin construction of the Buna factory. They have to travel to the construction site and back, about 5 miles each way, on foot.

Schnabel, *Power Without Morality*, p. 236; Letter of Oswald Pohl to Fritz Kranefuss of January 15, 1944.

APRIL 9

98 prisoners sent with a general transport receive Nos. 14947–15044.

APRIL 11

41 prisoners arriving on a general transport receive Nos. 15045–15085.

In the bunker of Block 11, Polish prisoner Józef Stock (No. 10801), who was locked up in the bunker on April 9, dies.

APMO, D-AuI-3/1, Bunker Register, p. 7.

APRIL 12

On Holy Saturday the evacuation of the villages of Rajsko, Birkenau, Budy, Babitz, Broschkowitz, and Harmense is completed. The operation has been going on since April 7 without previous

APMO, Materials, vol. 25; Chronicle of the Auschwitz Parish.

warning under the supervision of the SS. The evacuated residents are robbed of all their property. Auschwitz Concentration Camp takes over the area between the Vistula and the Soła rivers.

APRIL 15

The Army high command (Oberkommando des Heeres—OKH) appeals to the Reich Finance Minister concerning the ceding of the barracks camp of Auschwitz in Upper Silesia to the SS. The letter states that the barracks camp is hardly suitable for the purposes of the Wehrmacht for various reasons. In fact, the Inspector of the Sipo feels that the transfer of this camp to the SD serves crucial political and official interests since it is in the vicinity of the capital, on the edge of the Upper Silesian industrial area, and on the border of the General Government, and thus is especially appropriate for the concentration camp. The letter states that the Army High Command is prepared to make the transfer and requests permission.*

APMO, IZ-13/89, Various Documents of the Third Reich, pp. 1–3 (original in BA Koblenz).

APRIL 16

Surrender of Yugoslavia. The government and the underage king, Peter II, go into exile.

Five prisoners brought with a group transport receive Nos. 15086–15090.

APRIL 17

Five prisoners sent from Kattowitz receive Nos. 12355, 12963, 13693, 15091, and 15092.

The Director of the Political Department at Auschwitz, SS Second Lieutenant and Criminal Clerk Maximilian Grabner, informs the Gestapo post in Posen, with reference to the order of the Concentration Camps Inspector of April 9, 1941, that according to the order of the SS Commander in Chief the urns with the ashes of Polish prisoners who have died in Auschwitz from now on are no longer to be sent to their families and the cemeteries.**

APMO, IZ-8/Gestapo Lodz/88/574,626

APRIL 18

27 prisoners sent with a group transport receive Nos. 15093–15119. They have been sent by the Gestapo and Kripo headquarters

---

*On April 8, 1940, the SS receives permission to lease the barracks. In connection with the plans of the SS Commander in Chief to form an SS agricultural district and an SS village around the camp, the high command of the army is prepared, on application of the SS, to transfer the barracks buildings, called a barracks camp, to the SS, no doubt gratis. This is indeed linked with the plans for an extension of the camp since a base is to be laid on fourteen razed buildings, and eight new one-story houses are to be built on the previous parade grounds, the former racetrack.

**Because of the demonstrative nature of the burials, sending urns with the ashes of Polish prisoners who die in the concentration camps of the Third Reich is discontinued and prohibited. Often several burials of deceased prisoners of the same concentration camp take place at the same time, arousing curiosity and interest among the German citizens who have settled in the Polish cities.

in Breslau, Oppeln, Kattowitz, Lodz, Posen, Reichenberg, Stettin (Szezecin), and Schwerin. One prisoner is sent from Buchenwald.

APRIL 21

Prisoner Franciszek Brudek receives No. 15120.

APRIL 22

31 prisoners sent from Kattowitz by the Gestapo receive Nos. 15121–15151.

APRIL 23

The Greek generals sign an unconditional surrender.

For the first time, with the cooperation of Camp Commander Karl Fritzsch and a few SS Men, Commandant Höss chooses 10 prisoners from Block 2 as hostages and condemns them to starve to death in retaliation for the escape of a prisoner. The selected prisoners include the Polish political prisoners Marian Batko (No. 11795) from Kraków, a physics teacher at the humanistic Odrowąż Gymnasium in Königshütte (Chrozów), who voluntarily stepped out of the line during the selection in place of another, very young inmate;* Wincenty Rejowski (No. 3301); Antoni Sufin Suliga (No. 7883); Stefan Otulak (No. 7904); Tadeusz Kustra (No. 12906); Jan Schefler (No. 11860); Franciszek Bobla (No. 1075); Stanisław Opasiak (No. 9638); Adam Giermakowski (No. 12889); and Józef Nocko (No. 12929). They are locked up together in a cell in the cellar of Block 11 and receive nothing to eat or drink. The dark cell is opened a few days later and the bodies of the deceased prisoners are taken out. On April 27, Marian Batko is the first to die; the rest die by May 26, 1941.

APMO, D-AuI-3/1, Bunker Register, pp. 9–11; Franciszek Brol, Gerard Włoch, Jan Pilecki, "Das Bunkerbuch des Blocks 11 im Nazi-Kontzentrationslager Auschwitz" (The Bunker Register of Block 11 in the Nazi Concentration Camp Auschwitz), *HvA*, no. 1, 1959, p. 33; Kowalski, *Number 4410*, p. 179.

APRIL 24

The Polish prisoner Jan Hajduga (No. 7758), locked in the bunker of Block 11 on April 19, 1941, dies.

APMO, D-AuI-3/1, Bunker Register, p. 8.

1,002 prisoners are transferred from Auschwitz to Neuengamme.

APMO, Mat.RO, vol. VII, p. 474.

APRIL 25

30 prisoners sent with a general transport receive Nos. 15152–15181.

*Prisoner Mieczysław Pronobis (No. 9313), born on October 17, 1924, reported this act after the war to his family and friends and stated that he was selected. Paralyzed with fear, he didn't leave the line of prisoners, and in his place an old man, who was very debilitated, allegedly a high-school teacher, whose name he did not know, came forward.

The extensive evacuation in the first half of April of the residents of the Zasole quarter and the villages of Pławy, Rajsko, Birkenau, Budy, Babitz, Broschkowitz, and Harmense increase the Auschwitz interest zone to 9,880 acres. Aside from residential and industrial buildings, which have been torn down, the livestock, machines, and agricultural equipment remaining in the cleared area enable the camp command to cultivate the area. In accordance with Himmler's order to create a farm district around the camp, fish and poultry farming are begun in spring 1941 in Harmense, and a market garden is established in Rajsko, as well as cultivation of horse, pig, and poultry raising and tillage in Babitz, Budy, Pławy and Birkenau. The agricultural labor squad formed in 1940 is expanded and assigned to the individual farms.

MAY 2

204 prisoners sent by the Gestapo from the prison in Lodz receive Nos. 15182–15385.

24 prisoners sent with a general transport receive Nos. 15386–15409.

36 prisoners are transferred from Auschwitz to Dachau.   Ibid.

MAY 5

Three prisoners sent from Lublin by the Sipo and SD receive Nos. 15410–15412.

MAY 6

A prisoner sent from Kraków by the Sipo and SD receives No. 15413.

Two prisoners sent from Kattowitz by the Gestapo receive Nos. 15414 and 15415.

MAY 8

48 prisoners sent from Kraków by the Sipo and SD receive Nos. 15416–15463.

77 prisoners transferred to Auschwitz from Buchenwald, Dachau, and Mauthausen receive Nos. 15464–15540. In the transport from Mauthausen are 20 German common criminals, prisoners who assume positions as Capos and are to supervise prisoners employed in the construction of the Buna factory.   APMO, D-Mau, Folder 11, p. 3845.

MAY 9

The Army high command receives permission from the Ministry of Finance to turn over the Auschwitz barracks camp to the SS Commander in Chief.*

APMO-IZ-13/89, Various Documents of the Third Reich, pp. 1–3 (original in BA Koblenz).

29 prisoners sent with a general transport receive Nos. 15541–15569.

MAY 12

Three prisoners sent from Kattowitz receive Nos. 15570–15572.

The Director of Administration, Section IV, of Auschwitz C.C. informs the Gestapo in Lodz that, after deducting postage of .61 RM, he is sending 235.38 RM to be remitted to the families of prisoners who have died in the camp. The money is the property of the following 13 deceased prisoners: Zygmunt Spitz (No. 5946), 8.65 RM; Stefan Antczak (No. 5947), 11.02 RM; Majloch Reichmann (No. 6701), 3.25 RM; Jerzy Kasałudzki (No. 6970), 47.25 RM; Franciszek Pawłowski (No. 6980), 17.85 RM; Brunon Krapp (No. 7011), 58.89 RM; Władyslaw Blaszczyk (No. 7034), 2.45 RM; Henryk Śliwiński (No. 7048), 2.65 RM; Czesław Jarosz (No. 7063), 9.25 RM; Teofil Rzadka (No. 7221), 9.30 RM; Roman Chruścielewski (No. 7268), 38.05 RM; Stanisław Sobczak (No. 7294), 23.98 RM; Wenzel Wendrzychowski (No. 9415), 3.65 RM.

APMO, IZ-8/Gestapo Lodz 88/628.

The Gestapo transports prisoner Tadeusz Orzelski, the contact man between the clandestine PPS and the Association for Armed Struggle (Związek Walki Zbrojnej—ZWZ) in the district of Kraków for a confrontation with the underground fighters arrested in Kraków; these are mainly illegal members of the ZWZ and the secretary of the clandestine workers' district committee, Józef Cyrankiewicz,** who will later be brought to Auschwitz. The confrontation does not take place because Tadeusz Orzelski is seriously ill and is put in St. Lazarus Hospital under Gestapo guard. Nevertheless, he is liberated on June 11, 1941, by PPS members. He survives the occupation in Międzylesie near Warsaw under the pseudonym "Oremus."

Wroński, Chronicle, pp. 120, 150, 155, 158ff.

MAY 14

15 prisoners sent with a group transport receive Nos. 15573–15587.

---

*This can be seen from notations attached to the letter of April 15, 1941. On the basis of this decision, the construction of eight one-story buildings is begun. Prisoners are employed in this work.
**Cyrankiewicz became the general secretary of the PPS in 1945, premier of Poland in 1947, vice premier from 1952 to 1954, and again premier from 1954 to 1970.

A selection on the ramp. The people at the back in the line on the left will be taken directly to the gas chambers.

MAY 15

A prisoner sent from Kattowitz is given No. 15588.

The Director of Administration of Auschwitz informs the Gestapo in Lodz that after deducting postage of .41 RM, he is sending 91.85 RM to be remitted to the families of six deceased prisoners. The money is the property of Zenon Matysiak (No. 7113), Czesław Jozwik (No. 7225/7545),* Piotr Gąsiorkiewicz (No. 7334), Kazimierz Kaczarek (No. 7384), Dawid Majorowicz (No. 9425/5154),* and Franciszek Piasecki (No. 10167).

APMO, IZ-8/Gestapo Lodz/88/ 630–634.

MAY 16

27 prisoners sent in a group transport receive Nos. 15589–15615.

MAY 17

A prisoner sent from Kattowitz is given No. 15616.

*Two numbers were given by mistake.

On the way to the crematorium.

MAY 20

A prisoner sent from Kattowitz is given No. 15617.

MAY 21

27 prisoners transferred to Auschwitz by Stapo and Kripo* headquarters from prisons in Posen, Lodz, Liegnitz (Legnica), and Kattowitz receive Nos. 15618–15644.

MAY 22

109 prisoners transferred in a general transport by the Stapo and Kripo** from prisons in Königsberg, Danzig (Gdańsk), Bromberg (Bydgoszcz), Zichenau (Ciechanów), Hohensalza, Tilsit, and Breslau receive Nos. 15645–15753.

Five prisoners sent from Kattowitz receive Nos. 15754–15758.

*The Kripo transferred criminals and asocial prisoners, predominantly of German origin, to Auschwitz, where many of them assumed positions as Capos.
**Most prisoners sent by the Stapo from prisons within the Reich are Polish and Jewish political prisoners.

Partial view of Birkenau.

MAY 23

20 prisoners transferred in a group transport by the Stapo and Kripo from Buchenwald, Breslau, Troppau, Oppeln, Schwerin, and Kattowitz receive Nos. 15759–15778.*

216 prisoners sent by the Sipo and SD from the prison in Radom receive Nos. 15779–15994.

MAY 24

487 prisoners sent by the Sipo and SD from the prison in Lublin castle receive Nos. 15995–16481.

MAY 26

149 prisoners sent by the Gestapo from the prison in Oppeln receive Nos. 16482–16630.

MAY 28

13 prisoners sent in a group transport by the Stapo and Kripo from Königsberg, Tilsit, Zichenau, Bromberg, and Stettin receive Nos. 16631–16643.

The Administrative Director of Auschwitz informs the Gestapo in Lodz that after deducting postage of .41 RM he is sending 51.34 RM to be remitted to the families of four deceased prisoners, Tadeusz Pabijaniak (No. 7125), Franciszek Trzaskaliński (No. 7182), Tadeusz Tomczyński (No. 7194), and Mieczysław Nowakowski (No. 7329).

APMO, IZ-8/Gestapo Lodz/88/635.

*The transport includes 17 German prisoners classified as professional criminals, asocials, and homosexuals and three Polish political prisoners.

MAY 29

304 prisoners sent by the Sipo and SD from Pawiak Prison in Warsaw receive Nos. 16644–16830 and 16832–16948. Aside from Poles, the transport includes German political prisoner Adolf Rusiński (No. 16792) and Turkish political prisoner Jakob Sehid (No. 16858). Father Maksymilian Rajmund Kolbe arrives with this transport; he was arrested in the Franciscan monastery in Niepokalanów and locked up in Pawiak Prison on February 17 with other monks of the order. In Auschwitz C.C. he is given No. 16670.

After interrogation by the Gestapo, three prisoners are returned to Auschwitz from Warsaw with the transport. These are Stanisław Dębski (Dubois) (No. 3904), Mieczysław Hrabyk (No. 1116) and Kazimierz Protrzebowski (No. 4729).

SS Reich Doctor, SS General Professor Dr. Ernst Robert Grawitz, sends to SS Commander in Chief Himmler a proposal originated by Professor Dr. Carl Clauberg to establish a research center in or near Königshütte. In this institute Clauberg wants to carry out experiments to work out a new method for sterilization without an operation.* For this research a women's concentration camp for about 10 women must be attached to the institute.

Schnabel, *Power Without Morality*, pp. 263, 266.

MAY 30

SS Reich Doctor Grawitz sends Himmler a list of medical specialists who have been instructed in Professor Dr. Clauberg's method of treating female infertility: Professor Dr. von Wolff, Professor Dr. Erhardt and Professor Dr. Günther.

Ibid., pp. 266ff.

25 prisoners sent by the Stapo and Kripo in a general transport receive Nos. 16949–16973.

*Clauberg's specialty is curing infertility in women. Himmler, on the other hand, is interested in the development of a cheap and fast method of sterilization to be used against enemies of the Third Reich like Russians, Poles, and Jews. Thus the capacity to reproduce is to be limited while maintaining the ability to work.

MAY 31

At 8:30 P.M., the body of a prisoner is pulled out of the Soła River and taken to the crematorium.

APMO, D-AuI-1/2a, FvD (records of commanding officer on duty [Führer vom Dienst]), p. 16.

JUNE 3

Four prisoners sent from Kattowitz receive Nos. 16831, 16974, 16975, and 16976.

JUNE 5

66 prisoners from the prison in Tarnów and two prisoners from Kraków, sent by the Sipo and SD, receive Nos. 16977–17044.

JUNE 6

The first transport of Czechoslovakian prisoners is sent from Brünn (Brno). It contains 60 people sent to Auschwitz by the Gestapo. They receive Nos. 17045–17104.

38 prisoners sent with a group transport by the Gestapo and Kripo from Posen, Lodz, Oppeln, Breslau, Kattowitz, Bromberg, and Liegnitz receive Nos. 17106–17143.

JUNE 7

A prisoner sent from Kattowitz by the Gestapo is given No. 17144.

JUNE 8

37 prisoners sent by the Gestapo and Kripo from Vienna, Prague, Danzig, Zichenau, and Kattowitz receive Nos. 17145–17181.

JUNE 9

48 prisoners sent by the SD and the Gestapo from Montelupich Prison in Kraków receive Nos. 17182–17229.

JUNE 12

A prisoner sent from Kattowitz is given No. 17230.

JUNE 13

14 prisoners sent with a group transport receive Nos. 17231–17244.

JUNE 14

One prisoner sent by the Gestapo from Kattowitz is marked with No. 17150.

JUNE 16

Three prisoners from Bielitz, sent by the Kattowitz Gestapo, receive Nos. 17245–17247.

The Polish prisoner Antoni Jeliński, born February 20, 1908, sent by the Sipo and SD from Warsaw on August 15, 1941, escapes in the afternoon from one of the outside squads.

APMO, IZ-8/Gestapo Lodz/88/237.

JUNE 17

At 9:45 A.M., prisoner Leon Zollowski (No. 9889) is shot while escaping. A civilian is shot during the pursuit of the escapee and is brought to the hospital in Kattowitz.

APMO, D-AuI-1/2a, FvD, p. 26.

Commandant Höss selects 10 prisoners from Block 2 and condemns them to starve to death in retaliation for the escape of Antoni Jedliński.* The condemned are Bolesław Piński (No. 16761), Aleksander Paszkowski (No. 13953), Roman Orzel (No. 12922), Wasyl Fediuszko (No. 7354), Witales Łoposki (No. 9608), Wojciech Szczepanek (No. 13939), Franciszek Juszczyk (No. 12322), Antoni Grzesiak (No. 11858), Stanisław Wysocki (No. 13220), Jan Pajor (No. 11852). These prisoners starve to death between June 19 and June 27, 1941, in the bunker of Block 11.

APMO, D-AuI-3/1, Bunker Register, pp. 15ff; Brol et al. "Bunker Register of Block 11," p. 33.

The Director of Administration of Auschwitz informs the Lodz Gestapo that, after deducting postage of .41 RM, he is sending 94.69 RM to be remitted to the families of the following three deceased prisoners: Johann Florczyk (No. 6910), Gierazon Lichtenstein (No. 7023) and Kazimierz Ciepły (No. 9452).

APMO, IZ-8/Gestapo Lodz/88/636.

JUNE 18

Five prisoners sent by the Gestapo from the prison in Kattowitz receive Nos. 17248–17252. Prisoners No. 7091, 7399, and 7459 are returned to Auschwitz and are reinterrogated.

JUNE 19

At 5:30 P.M. Polish prisoner Edward Grzywacz is locked in the bunker of Block 11. He dies the same day.

APMO, D-AuI-3/1, Bunker Register, p. 16.

JUNE 20

17 prisoners sent by the Stapo and Kripo with a group transport receive Nos. 17253–17269.

Four prisoners are transferred from Auschwitz to Mauthausen. One of them is Bolesław Bicz, who is suspected of helping prisoner Tadeusz Wiejowski escape on July 6, 1940.

*The documents show two spellings for Jeliński.

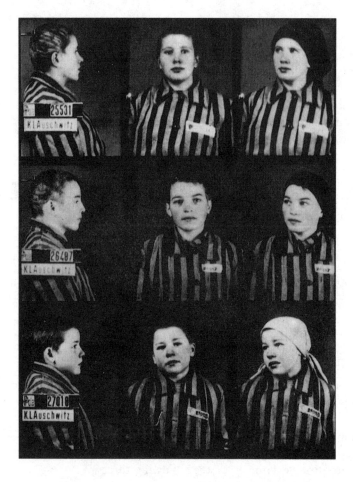

From prisoner files.

Antoni Jeliński, who escaped on June 16, 1941, is caught. But this does not result in the release of the 11 hostages locked in the bunker of Block 11 on June 17, 1941.

APMO, D-AuI-1/2a, p. 155, Bulletin of the Gestapo in Silesia of June 20, 1941.

JUNE 21

Bolesław Buczek (No. 7479) is readmitted after another interrogation by the Gestapo in Kattowitz.

At 11:00 P.M., a civilian with a horse-drawn cart is arrested by the SS Camp Patrol. The civilian is locked in the bunker and the horse and wagon are taken to the stables.

APMO, D-AuI-1/2, FvD, p. 31.

JUNE 22

Polish prisoner Helmut Wegner (No. 6752) is admitted after another interrogation by the Warsaw Sipo and SD.

The German Wehrmacht attacks the Soviet Union. British Prime Minister Winston S. Churchill declares in a radio address: "The Russian danger is, therefore, our danger, and the danger of the United States, just as the cause of any Russian fighting for his hearth

Winston S. Churchill, The Second World War, vol. 3: *The Grand Alliance*, Boston, 1950, p. 373.

and home is the cause of free men and free peoples in every quarter of the globe."

JUNE 23

60 prisoners sent by the Gestapo from Oppeln receive Nos. 17270–17329. The transport includes 43 Poles and 13 Jews.

JUNE 24

Commandant Höss chooses 10 hostages from among the prisoners in Block 2 in retaliation for another prisoner's escape and condemns them to starve to death in the bunker of Block 11. The following Polish prisoners are condemned: Albert Bies (No. 14033), Piotr Prozorowski (No. 12195), Marcin Domino (No. 14440), Włodzimierz Krat (No. 8749), Władysław Głąb (No. 14243), Stanisław Markiewicz (No. 12116), Marian Sośniczka (No. 16626), Stanisław Ungier (No. 12959), Roman Hejduk (No. 17207), Feliks Królik (No. 16741). On June 30 the bunker is opened and their death ascertained.

APMO, D-AuI-3/1, Bunker Register, pp. 16ff; Brol et al., "Bunker Register of Block 11," p. 33.

JUNE 25

Two prisoners sent by the Gestapo from Kattowitz receive Nos. 17330 and 17331.

JUNE 26

50 prisoners sent by the Sipo and SD from Montelupich Prison in Kraków receive Nos. 17332–17381. The former mayor of Kraków, Dr. Bolesław Czuchajowski, receives No. 17365.

JUNE 27

Polish inmate Julian Zych (No. 5866) is sent to the bunker in Block 11, where he dies the same day.

APMO, D-AuI-3/1, Bunker Register, p. 18.

14 prisoners sent by the Stapo and Kripo with a group transport from Kattowitz, Beuthen, Oppeln, and Troppau receive Nos. 17382–17395.

JUNE 28

A prisoner sent from the Kattowitz District by the Gestapo receives No. 17396.

JUNE 29

48 prisoners sent by the Gestapo with a group transport from Vienna, Linz, Prague, Zichenau, Danzig, Bromberg, Posen, Lodz, Königsberg, and Dachau C.C. receive Nos. 17397–17441.

JUNE 30

Three prisoners from Teschen, sent by the Gestapo from the Kattowitz District, receive Nos. 17445–17447.

258 prisoners sent from the prison in Radom by the Sipo and SD receive Nos. 17448–17705.

JULY 1

At 2:00 P.M. SS Private Klossen of the 3rd Company shoots prisoner Józef Wawrzyniak (No. 15674) "while [he was] escaping."

APMO, D-AuI-1/2, FvD, p. 36.

JULY 2

15 prisoners sent with a group transport by the Stapo and Kripo receive Nos. 17706–17720.

JULY 3

80 Polish political prisoners sent to Auschwitz by the Sipo and SD from Kraków with various transports are shot. The execution takes place in the gravel pit near the theater building. Among those who are shot are some sick prisoners from Block 15, including Kropatsch. In this group also are the former mayor of Kraków, Dr. Bolesław Czuchajowski (No. 17365), and Karol Karwat (No. 17349), father of Jerzy Karwat.* Prisoners locked in the bunker of Block 11 on June 30 are probably shot with this group, i.e., Leon Jarosz (No. 14600), Roman Popławski (No. 16945), Stefan Tomczyk (No. 16277), Czesław Wilkowski (No. 16000), and Józef Syguda (No. 16539).

APMO, Accounts, vol. 20, p. 151, Account of Former Prisoner Tadeusz Paczula; Höss Trial, vol. 2, p. 108, Account of Former Prisoner Oskar Stuhr; D-AuI-3/1, Bunker Register, p. 19.

JULY 4

92 prisoners sent with a group transport receive Nos. 17721–17812. They have been sent by the Gestapo from Zichenau, Plock, Posen, Danzig, Bromberg, Hohensalza, Lodz, Tilsit, and Sachsenhausen C.C.

JULY 5

Two prisoners sent by the Gestapo from Bielitz receive Nos. 17813 and 17814.

JULY 6

30 prisoners sent by the Stapo and Kripo from Lodz, Troppau, Stettin, and Breslau receive Nos. 17815–17844.

*Compare entry for September 22, 1941.

JULY 8

Nine prisoners, sent with a group transport by the Stapo and Kripo from Breslau, Schwerin, Troppau, and Kattowitz receive Nos. 17845–17853.

JULY 9

Ten prisoners sent from Kattowitz by Gestapo and Kripo headquarters receive Nos. 17854–17863.

JULY 10

The Director of Administration of Auschwitz informs the Gestapo in Lodz that, after deducting postage of .41 RM, he is sending 56.75 RM to be remitted to the families of the following six deceased prisoners: Kazimierz Kowrotkiewicz (No. 7105), Ignacy Chojnowski (No. 9418), Henryk Pelczyński (No. 10165), Juliusz Knycz (No. 15003), Marian Jeżyk (No. 15245), Paweł Spławski (No. 15333).

APMO, IZ-8/Gestapo Lodz/88/639.

JULY 11

182 prisoners sent by the Sipo and SD from Montelupich Prison in Kraków receive Nos. 17864–18045. There are 171 Jews in the transport.

39 prisoners sent with a group transport receive Nos. 18046–18084. In the transport are 34 Czech and five German and Polish prisoners sent by Stapo and Kripo offices from Brünn, Frankfurt am Main, Schwerin, Kattowitz, and Oppeln.

JULY 12

At 10:20 A.M., 15 prisoners arrive with a group transport. They receive Nos. 18085–18099.

APMO, D-AuI-1/2, FvD, p. 44.

JULY 13

36 prisoners sent by the Gestapo from Oppeln receive Nos. 18100–18135.

JULY 14

J. A. Topf and Sons reply to the letter of July 9, 1941, with operating instructions in triplicate to the SS Commander in Chief and Chief of Police, the Budget and Buildings Main Office, and the Mauthausen SS Construction Administration. The letter requests that the operating instructions be posted in a visible place in the crematorium. The letter also states: "In the coke-heated T-double-muffle incinerator, 10 to 35 bodies can be incinerated in about 10 hours. The quantity mentioned above can be incinerated daily without any

Trial of the Major War Criminals Before the International Military Tribunal Nuremberg, 1948, Bd 26, pp. 267ff. (710-PS).

Crematorium III in Birkenau.

problem, without overworking the oven. It is not harmful to operate the incinerators day and night, if required, since the fire clay lasts longer when an even temperature is maintained."*

24 prisoners sent by the Gestapo from Oppeln receive Nos. 18136–18159.

The Traffic Minister and General Director of the German Railroad, Dr. Dorpmüller, issues an order (21 Bfsv 413) about special trains to every central office in the East, South, and West, as well as to the Office of Railways and the Office of Eastern Railways in Kraków and the General Government. It is obligatory that the following special trains be made available, as they are vital to the war effort and to save lives:

APMO, IZ-13/89, Various Documents of the Third Reich, pp. 23, 35 (original in BA Koblenz).

1. Trains reserved for the transport of prisoners either in or out of concentration camps by the Sipo and SD Chief of Staff or by the Gestapo.
2. Trains ordered by the public utility, Transport for the Ill, Ltd., Berlin, for the transport of the mentally ill because of transfer or evacuation of an institution.**

*These comments also refer to the incinerators in Auschwitz, which are of the same construction.

**In October 1939, Hitler issues an order concerning the use of "euthanasia" in cases of incurable disease. The order is backdated to September 1, 1939. This operation is marked with the code name T4. The mentally ill selected for euthanasia

JULY 16

For the first time 16 so-called "reeducation" prisoners are sent to Auschwitz by the Kattowitz Gestapo. They are given consecutive Nos. 18160–18175. In the camp documents their numbers begin with "Erz" (Erziehung, or education) or "EH" (Erziehungshäfling). On the camp clothing, the number starts with the letter E.*

APMO, D-AuI-2/3, Admissions List, p. 268.

Concentration Camps Inspector Richard Glücks warns the Commandant that the number of successful escape attempts from the camp has increased, primarily by Poles and, in one case, a so-called Red Spanish fighter. Glücks thinks that the reason prisoners do everything to escape is the war being fought in the East. Therefore, the SS Commander in Chief has decided that every Commandant is responsible for making it impossible for prisoners to escape. He recommends instructing all SS personnel, stand-by Kommandos, and guard companies accordingly. In case of a successful escape, if the SS men are found to be at fault, the one guilty of dereliction of duty shall be punished very severely.

APMO, IZ-13/89, Various Documents of the Third Reich, p. 253.

JULY 17

Two prisoners sent from the Kattowitz District receive Nos. 18176 and 18177.

Sipo and SD Chief SS Lieutenant General Reinhard Heydrich, in accordance with Hitler's guidelines of March 30, 1941, and the guidelines worked out by the Army high command for the treatment of political commissars of June 6, 1941, issues an order to shoot all Russian prisoners of war who are or might be a danger to National Socialism. This concerns all important party and state functionaries and especially so-called professional revolutionaries, all People's Commissars of the Red Army, government leaders, all members of the Russian intelligentsia, all Jews, and all persons characterized as agitators or fanatical Communists.

Tadeusz Cyprian, Jerzy Sawicki, *Materiały Norymberskie* (The Nuremberg Materials), Warsaw, 1948, p. 207.

JULY 18

95 prisoners, including 52 political prisoners, sent with a group transport by the Kraków Sipo and SD and the Stapo and Kripo

---

are transferred to special institutions, Hadamar in Hessen, Hartheim near Linz, Grafenek in Württemberg, Brandenburg on the Havel, and Sonnenstein in Pirna, where they are killed, most of them with carbon monoxide gas, or with poison administered orally or by injection. Those who have full authority for carrying out the euthanasia operation are Reich Administrator Philipp Bouhler and Dr. Karl Brandt. As for deciding which illnesses euthanasia is to be used for, a group of doctors is appointed that includes Dr. Horst Schumann.

*According to the regulations in effect in the Third Reich, "reeducation" prisoners are to be sent to special "labor training camps" (Arbeitserziehungslager—AEL) for 56 days. In Auschwitz these prisoners are subject to the severity of the concentration camp. Many of them die before the end of the punishment, which is often extended. On February 2, 1942, the numbers for reeducation prisoners are changed. From then on, they are marked with a special series of numbers beginning with the No. 1. The numbers they had been given between July 16, 1941 and February 1, 1942 are given to new admissions.

from Zichenau, Kattowitz, Königsberg, Stettin, Oppeln, and Breslau receive Nos. 18178–18272. In the transport are two Spanish political prisoners sent by the Bremen Stapo.

A few hundred Russian prisoners of war are admitted and put in Block 11. They are put to work excavating sand in the gravel pit behind the camp kitchen, next to the SS Block Leader's room. Within a few days the entire group is murdered during work. The SS Men kill them with shots from a short, small-caliber gun and the Capos beat them to death with shovels and picks.

APMO, Höss Trial, vol. 4, pp. 53–58; Kraków Auschwitz Trial, vol. 54, p. 207.

The Administrative Director of Auschwitz informs the Gestapo in Lodz that, after deducting postage of .61 RM, he is sending 111.59 RM to be remitted to the families of the following six deceased prisoners: Ignacy Taler (No. 6688), Józef Błaszczyk (No. 9438), Stanisław Grenda (No. 14976), Bolesław Gabała (No. 14997), Dezydery Muszyński (No. 15283), Adam Wielkopolski (No. 15368).

APMO, IZ-8/Gestapo Lodz/88/641.

JULY 22

27 prisoners sent in a group transport by the Stapo receive Nos. 18273–18300. In the transport is one German BV prisoner sent to the camp by Kripo headquarters.

JULY 23

11 rehabilitation prisoners sent by the Gestapo in Kattowitz receive Nos. 18301–18311.

Two prisoners from Bielitz sent by the Kattowitz Gestapo receive Nos. 18312 and 18313.

19 reeducation prisoners from Bielitz sent by the Kattowitz Gestapo receive Nos. 18314–18334.

JULY 24

At 8:15 P.M. 350 prisoners are admitted. They have been sent by the Sipo and SD from Pawiak Prison in Warsaw and receive Nos. 18335–18684. A Lithuanian Pole, Konstantin Daukantos, a priest, receives No. 18372.

APMO, D-AuI-1/2a, FvD, p. 50.

JULY 25

60 prisoners sent by the Kraków District Sipo and SD from the prison in Tarnów receive Nos. 18685–18744.

19 prisoners sent with a group transport by the Stapo and Kripo receive Nos. 18745–18763. In the transport are seven political prisoners—three Germans, three Poles, and a Czech—as well as 12 German criminal and asocial prisoners.

JULY 26

28 prisoners sent with a group transport by the Stapo and Kripo offices in Danzig, Königsberg, Bromberg, Zichenau, and Tilsit receive Nos. 18764–18791. A Lithuanian Polish prisoner, Anton Jasulaitis, receives No. 18790.

16 reeducation prisoners sent by the Kattowitz Stapo receive Nos. 18792–18807.

Five prisoners from Teschen sent by the Kattowitz Gestapo receive Nos. 18808–18812.

JULY 28

A special commission created on Himmler's orders arrives at Auschwitz to select prisoners within the framework of the "Euthanasia Program" for the incurably ill, extended in 1940 to Jews and in the middle of 1941 to prisoners of concentration camps. The committee inspects all invalids, cripples, and chronically ill who have been previously chosen by the camp administration under the pretext of shifting them to another camp for easier work. One member of this special doctors' committee is Dr. Horst Schumann, who has directed the Grafeneck Euthanasia Institute in Württemberg since August 1939 and, after its dissolution, served as director of a similar institution in Sonnenstein near Pirna. Most of the selected prisoners come from what was then called Block 15, the convalescent block, where sick and exhausted prisoners and those incapable of working are sent when an SS Doctor no longer wants to let them remain in the prisoners' infirmary. Some of these prisoners have registered voluntarily because of the rumor circulating in the camp that the inmates chosen for this transport are to be transferred to a sanatorium. Altogether, 573 inmates, most of them Poles, are chosen. At the last moment, two German BV prisoners who have participated eagerly with the SS men in killing prisoners are added to the transport: Johann Siegruth (No. 26), the one-armed head Capo of the lumber yard, and Ernst Krankemann (No. 3210), the Block Senior of Block 11 and Capo in the road construction labor squad.* Following Dr. Schumann's orders, the transport is sent to Sonnenstein under the direction of Roll Call Leader Franz Hössler. A report to Höss that Hössler makes after his return states that the prisoners were gassed in a bathroom where carbon monoxide gas was introduced through the showerheads.

APMO, Höss Trial, vol. 21, pp. 137, 138; vol. 4, p. 99; vol. 7, pp. 180, 183; vol. 8, p. 109; Witnesses' Accounts; Mat.RO, vol. VII, p. 474, a transport of 575 prisoners to Dresden is recorded; Memoirs, vol. 20, p. 153, Memoir of Former Prisoner Tomasz Paczuła; Kowalski, *Number 4410*, pp. 183ff., 200–203.

JULY 29

63 prisoners sent by the Kraków Sipo and SD from the prison in Tarnów receive Nos. 18813–18875.

*According to an alleged report by Hössler that reaches the prisoners, Krankemann is murdered during the trip and Siegruth commits suicide.

A prisoner from Pless (Pszczyna) sent by the Kattowitz Gestapo receives No. 18876.

The Director of Administration of Auschwitz informs the Gestapo in Lodz that, after deducting .61 RM for postage, he is sending 165.09 RM to be remitted to the families of 10 deceased prisoners.

APMO, IZ-8/Gestapo Lodz/88/643.

According to a contract among the management of the railroad in Oppeln, the I. G. Farben factory in Dwory near Auschwitz, and Commandant Höss, prisoners are to be taken to work and back to the camp by train. In the morning, prisoners are taken in freight cars from the siding in the camp to the siding of the I. G. Farben factory in Dwory and back to the camp after work. The train has 10 to 12 freight cars. In every car there are approximately 100 prisoners and a few SS men as supervisors.*

APMO, IZ-13/89, Various Documents of the Third Reich, pp. 44, 45.

The Commandant of Auschwitz is called to Berlin by the SS Commander in Chief. Without any witnesses, Himmler discusses the technical aspects of the so-called "Final Solution of the Jewish question" with him. As a result of the conversation, Höss receives from Himmler the order to carry out in Auschwitz the extermination of the Jews and to present construction plans for the extermination plants for killing people within four weeks. Himmler tells Höss that he will get more details from SS Major Adolf Eichmann of the RSHA, who will soon be coming to Auschwitz.**

APMO, Höss Trial, vol. 21, pp. 3ff., 23; Höss, *Commandant in Auschwitz*, pp. 157, 181.

In the afternoon, the Polish prisoner Zymunt Pilawski (No. 14156) escapes. The telegram informing all appropriate departments of the escape is signed by Camp Commander Fritzsch in the absence of Commandant Höss.

APMO, IZ-8/Gestapo Lodz/2/88/33; D-AuI-1/2, Bulletin, p. 5.

Camp Commander Fritzsch probably chooses 15 hostages—this number is written in the Bunker Register—from among the prisoners in Block 14 in retaliation for the escape. He condemns them to death by starvation in the bunker of Block 11. During the selection, a Polish prisoner who is a Franciscan monk and missionary, Maksymilian Rajmund Kolbe (No. 16670), steps out of line and asks Camp Commander Fritzsch to take him instead of the desperate selected prisoner Franciszek Gajowniczek (No. 5659). After a brief dispute with Father Kolbe, Fritzsch agrees to the substitution, especially when he finds out that Kolbe is a Catholic priest. The 15 selected prisoners are led off to Block 11. In the Bunker Register, the admission of the 15 prisoners is merely noted without listing names, numbers, day of admission, or day of death.

APMO, D-AuI-3/1a, Bunker Register, p. 21; Mat. 605/47a, Materials on Father Kolbe, Accounts of Former Prisoners Franciszek Gajowniczek, Mieczysław Kościelniak, and others.

*Until July 29, the so-called Buna squad, numbering approximately 1,000 prisoners, had walked to work and back to camp, altogether about nine miles.
**The date of July 29 for the meeting is probable on the basis of the document cited below, according to which Camp Commander Fritzsch selects hostages and signs documents in the absence of Höss.

JULY 30

11 prisoners sent by the Gestapo from Kattowitz receive Nos. 18877–18887. This transport includes prisoners returned from the Gestapo prison in Kattowitz who had already gotten Nos. 7440, 7441, and 7464.

Five reeducation prisoners sent by the Gestapo from Kattowitz receive Nos. 18888–18892.

306 prisoners sent by the Sipo and SD from Radom receive Nos. 18893–19198. This transport includes Stanisław Kowalski (No. 13018), a teacher, returned to the camp from Radom by the Gestapo.

APMO, D-AuI-2, Admissions List, p. 295.

658 prisoners sent by the Sipo and SD from the prison in Lublin castle receive the numbers 19199–19856. Prisoner Stefan Jakubczak (No. 14896), a teacher, is returned to the camp after another interrogation.

Ibid., p. 307.

JULY 29–31

During these three days, the Reich railroad carries 3,215 prisoners employed in the construction of the I. G. Farben factory and their SS Guards from Auschwitz to Dwory, near the building site of the Buna factory, and back.

APMO, IZ-13/89, Various Documents of the Third Reich, p. 45.

JULY 31

Reich Marshal Hermann Göring addresses the following order to Chief of the Sipo and SD SS Lieutenant General Reinhard Heydrich: "In addition to the task already assigned to you by edict of January 24, 1939, to find a favorable solution to the Jewish question in the form of emigration or evacuation as is most appropriate to the circumstances of the time, I now order you to take all necessary preparations concerning organizational, practical, and material considerations for a total solution of the Jewish question in the German sphere of influence in Europe. To the extent that this affects the responsibilities of other central authorities, they are to participate. I also order you to submit to me soon a complete draft of the organizational, practical, and material advance measures for carrying out the desired Final Solution of the Jewish question."

Trial of the Major War Criminals Before the International Military Tribunal, Nuremberg, 1948, Bd26, pp. 267ff. (710-PS).

AUGUST

The first experiments are undertaken in Auschwitz to kill prisoners with intravenous injections of perhydrol, benzine, ether, evipan, and phenol. The experiments are conducted in a special room in Block 21 on sick inmates. Every morning, all those who have been murdered are removed. The experiments show that the fastest way to kill is with an injection of phenol to the heart. After that, killings with a phenol injection are moved from Block 20 to a so-called

APMO, Höss Trial, vol. 4, pp. 161–163; vol. 7, p. 90; vol. 6, pp. 17, 176; Friedrich Karl Kaul, Ärzte in Auschwitz (Doctors in Auschwitz), Berlin, 1968; Stanisław Kłodzinski, "Esesmani z oświęcimskiej 'sluzby zdrowis'" (The SS Men of the "Health Service" in Auschwitz),

treatment room. Sometimes prisoners are also killed in the anteroom of the morgue in Block 28. This is a continuation of the euthanasia operation which started on July 28, 1941, and to which 575 prisoners have fallen victim. The selection of the inmates who are ill and no longer able to work is carried out by the following SS Doctors: Siegfried Schwela, Oskar Dienstbach, Franz Bodmann, Kurt Uhlenbrock, Friedrich Entress, Heinz Thilo, Bruno Kitt, Josef Mengele, among others. The phenol injections are usually given by SS Medical Officers Josef Klehr and Herbert Scherpe and by the trained prisoners Hans Bock, Capo of the infirmary and later Block Senior of the prisoners' infirmary; Mieczysław Pańszczyk; Alfred Stössel; Mieczysław Szymkowiak; Feliks Walentynowicz; and Leon Landau.

in *Okupacja i medycyna*, Vol. I (The Occupation and Medicine, Vol. I), Kraków, 1971; Tadeusz Paczuła, "Organizacja i administracja szpitala obozowego KL Auschwitz I" (The Organization and Administration of the Prisoners' Infirmary in Auschwitz I), *PZ*, no. 1a (1962): 64–68.

Adolf Eichmann comes to Auschwitz to inform Höss of the details connected with Himmler's decision to select this camp as the site for the Final Solution of the Jewish question, i.e., the extermination of the Jews. Eichmann agrees with Höss that the mass extermination can only be carried out by gas since shooting such a large number of people, including women and children, would be too great a strain for the SS men. Höss writes in his autobiography:

> We left the matter unresolved. Eichmann decided to try and find a gas that was in ready supply and would not entail special installations for its use, and to inform me when he had done so. We decided that a peasant farmstead situated in the northwest corner of what later became Section III in Birkenau would be the most suitable. It was isolated and screened by woods and hedges, and it was also not far from the railroad. The bodies could be placed in long, deep pits dug in the nearby meadows. We had not at that time thought of burning the corpses. We calculated that after gasproofing the premises then available, it would be possible to kill about 800 people simultaneously with a suitable gas. . . . Eichmann returned to Berlin to report our conversation to the SS Commander in Chief. A few days later I sent to the SS Commander in Chief by courier a detailed site plan and description of the installation.

Höss, *Commandant in Auschwitz*, pp. 206–207.

AUGUST 1

At 8:15 A.M., Jewish prisoner Froim Miodownik (No. 18518) is shot "while escaping."

APMO, D-AuI-1/2a, FvD, p. 53.

Five prisoners sent with a group transport by the Stapo and Kripo in Kattowitz, Oppeln, and Prague receive Nos. 19857–19861.

33 reeducation prisoners from Bielitz, sent by the Kattowitz Gestapo, receive Nos. 19862–19894.

AUGUST 5

Two prisoners sent by the Gestapo from Pless and Kattowitz receive Nos. 19895 and 19896.

AUGUST 6

27 reeducation prisoners sent by the Kattowitz Gestapo receive Nos. 19897–19923.

AUGUST 7

Polish prisoner Roman Sanowski (No. 13474) escapes from the Penal Company.

APMO, D-AuI-3/1, Bunker Register, p. 22.

Most likely in connection with the escape of Roman Sanowski, prisoners are selected from the Penal Company and locked in the bunker of Block 11. These include Tales Naftali (No. 18724) and eight Jews whose names are not recorded. Eight more inmates from Block 12 are also lodged in the bunker. In the Bunker Book the deaths of these inmates are registered but not their names or date of death.

AUGUST 8

Tales Naftali and eight Jews sent to the bunker the day before are sent to the prisoners' infirmary. Since, at that time, Jews in the Penal Company are not accepted for treatment in the infirmary, these are probably sent there to be given phenol injections.

Ibid.; Brol et al., "Bunker Register of Block 11," p. 30.

34 prisoners sent with a group transport by the Stapo and Kripo receive Nos. 19924–19957. In the transport are 19 Polish prisoners, given Nos. 19924–19942, sent by the field station in Bielitz.

AUGUST 9

47 prisoners sent with a group transport by the Stapo and Kripo in Lodz, Posen, Zichenau, Bromberg, and Tilset receive Nos. 19958–20004. Lithuanian prisoner Michael Wilkuwitis receives No. 20004.

Escaped prisoner Roman Sanowski (No. 13474) is captured, brought back to the camp at 2:30 P.M., and then locked in the bunker of Block 11.

APMO, D-AuI-3/1, Bunker Register, p. 23.

Block 13, called the Death Block by the prisoners, receives the number 11. This is seen from the entry of the block clerk who keeps the Bunker Register. In the fourth column he enters the number of the block from which the prisoner locked in the bunker comes. On this day, under the name of Roman Sanowski, he notes for the first time "Bl 11 SK."* He makes the same entry on August 10 and 15.

Ibid.

---

*The change of block numbering occurs at the beginning of August, probably on August 9, and is connected with the building of eight new blocks on the assembly area, which is in the middle of the camp, opposite the camp kitchen. In the first row the new blocks are numbered 4, 5, 6, and 7 and in the second row, 15, 16, 17, and 18. Block 18 is completed in August, Blocks 4, 5, and 7 in November 1941. The rest of the blocks are finished in the first half of 1942.

AUGUST 12

Five reeducation prisoners from Teschen, sent by the Kattowitz Gestapo, receive Nos. 20005–20009.

38 prisoners sent by the Kraków Sipo and SD receive Nos. 20010–20047. After more interrogation by the Kraków Gestapo, the following prisoners are readmitted to the camp: Józef Bednarczyk (No. 3536), Michal Ciastoń (No. 3632), Jan Nowak (No. 3633), Józef Góra (No. 3634) and Stanisław Michalewicz (No. 9185).

APMO, D-AuI-2, Admissions List, p. 315.

AUGUST 14

After spending two weeks in the bunker of Block 11 and surviving—his fellow sufferers all died—the priest Maksymilian Rajmund Kolbe is killed with a phenol injection by Hans Bock (No. 5). Hans Bock is the Block Senior in the prisoners' infirmary.

APMO, D-AuI-2/3574, Death Certificates; Mat. 605/47a, Accounts of Former Prisoners Brunon Borgowiec and Maksymilian Chlebik.

13 prisoners sent by the Stapo and Kripo with a group transport receive Nos. 20049–20060 and 20077.

17 reeducation prisoners sent from Kattowitz by the Stapo receive Nos. 20061–20076 and 20048.

Concentration Camps Inspector Richard Glücks informs the Commandant that orders for urns should be sent early to the Inspectorate's because the firms of Grosskopf Ludwig and Co. of Ilmenau and J. A. Topf and Sons, which fill the orders, need more time for their manufacture and delivery.*

APMO, IZ-13/89, Various Documents of the Third Reich, p. 225.

AUGUST 15

The executions of inmates carried out by the SS in the gravel pit next to the camp kitchen and the so-called theater building are confirmed in the status report for the period April 1 to August 15, 1941, in the documents of the Polish Government in Exile, which state:

CA KCPZPR, 202/II-6, Documents of the Delegation of the Polish Government in Exile, p. 5.

> The camp: Most Poles continue to be detained in Auschwitz and die there. The mortality rate is of course lower now than in the cold of winter. Then, several prisoners on average died daily, and the maximum mortality rate was on October 28, 1940, when 86 deaths were counted. The camp can hold 40,000 inmates; at the moment about 12,000 inmates are lodged there, including 1,000 Germans. The cumulative number is 17,000, so it is calculated that 4,000 to 5,000 inmates have already died, i.e., been tortured to death, and about 300 shot. According to the comments of those who have returned, there are different causes of death: exhaustion from work, lack of fat in the diet,

*The families of German prisoners who die in the camp continue to receive urns with the ashes of the deceased.

vitamin deficiency, diarrhea, infections from various injuries, severe internal and external injuries as a result of beatings, but especially inner breakdown to which the above listed causes and the entire system lead. This results in a severe lowering of physical resistance. The shootings began in the winter and included a few or several inmates. Sometimes a shooting is the execution of a sentence that has already been passed in camp. At noon roll call, the numbers of inmates are called who must stand next to the camp office until evening with their faces to the wall of Block 9. After work and evening roll call, they are executed. They go through a kind of dug-out corridor and are shot there. Those who are only wounded are shot with revolvers by SS noncommissioned officers. The dead are stripped and their numbers are painted on their chests.

AUGUST 19

Six prisoners sent by the Kattowitz Gestapo receive Nos. 20078–20083.

AUGUST 20

Roman Sanowski, locked in the bunker of Block 11 because of his escape attempt, is killed.

APMO, D-AuI-3/1, Bunker Register, p. 23.

26 prisoners sent from Kraków by the Sipo and SD receive Nos. 20084–20109. After interrogation by the Gestapo in Kraków, Edward Steczowicz (No. 12093) is brought back to the camp.

Three prisoners sent from Oppeln by the Gestapo receive Nos. 20110–20112.

AUGUST 21

28 reeducation and one political prisoner from Bielitz sent by the Kattowitz Gestapo receive Nos. 20113–20140 and 20141.

AUGUST 22

29 prisoners sent by the Stapo and Kripo with a group transport from Oppeln, Breslau, Tilsit, Stettin, Posen, Königsberg, and Bromberg, receive Nos. 20142–20170.

AUGUST 23

19 prisoners sent by the Stapo and Kripo with a group transport from Bromberg, Lodz, Zichenau, Hohensalza, and Königsberg receive Nos. 20171–20189.

A prisoner for rehabilitation from Bielitz sent by the Kattowitz Gestapo receives No. 20190.

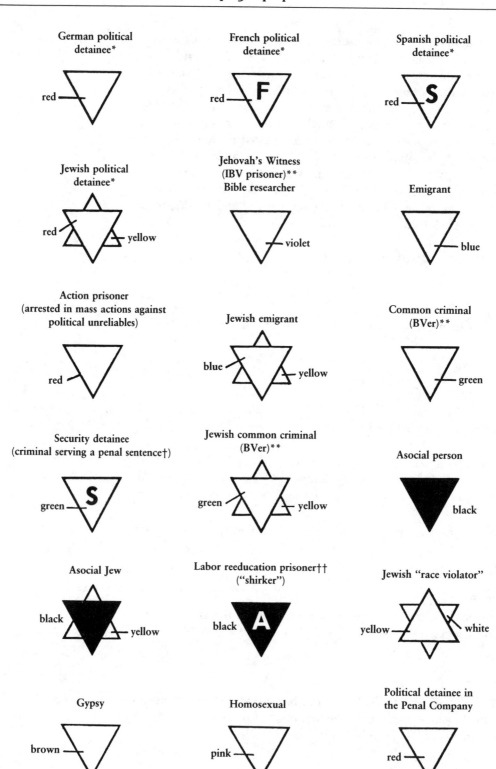

Prisoners' identification badges.

*"Schutzhaftling," literally one in "protective custody." This actually meant incarceration for an indefinite period of time, with no charges being brought.

**See Glossary p. 827.

†S stands for *Strafhaft*, "penal sentence."

††A stands for *Arbeitserziehungshäftling*, "labor reeducation prisoner."

AUGUST 25

63 prisoners sent by the Gestapo from Oppeln receive Nos. 20191–20253.

AUGUST 26

15 prisoners sent by the Gestapo from Oppeln receive Nos. 20254–20268.

APMO, D-AuI-2/4a, Admissions List, p. 327.

One reeducation prisoner from Bielitz sent by the Kattowitz Gestapo receives No. 20269.*

AUGUST 29

21 prisoners sent with a group transport by the Stapo and Kripo from Vienna, Brünn, Prague, Troppau, Breslau, Schwerin, Frankfurt an der Oder, and Kattowitz receive Nos. 20270–20290.

AUGUST 30

39 prisoners sent with a group transport receive Nos. 20291–20329. The inmates are sent by the Stapo headquarters in Lodz, Hohensalza, Bromberg, Zichenau, Posen, and Allenstein and by the Kripo offices in Danzig, Königsberg, Posen, and Tilsit. Ludwik Banach from Bromberg, who receives number 20317, is sent to the Penal Company immediately by Camp Commander Fritzsch.

APMO, Kraków Auschwitz Trial, vol. 55, pp. 79–81.

AUGUST 1–31

During the 26 workdays in August, the German Railroad transports 28,995 prisoners working at the Buna factory and the SS men who guard them from Auschwitz to Dwory and back. An average of 1,115 inmates and SS men a day are transported.

APMO, IZ-13/89, Various Documents of the Third Reich, p. 45.

AUGUST**

Rudolf Höss takes part in a conference of the Jewish Section, IV-B-4, of the RSHA in Berlin, whose director is Adolf Eichmann. At this conference, problems concerning the planned extermination of the Jews in Auschwitz are discussed. Eichmann's deputies in the individual regions report on the state of the operation and on difficulties in carrying it out, e.g., accommodations for prisoners, availability of trains for transports, scheduling, etc.

Höss, *Commandant in Auschwitz*, pp. 158ff.

*In 1942, under the new numbering system for reeducation prisoners, this prisoner's number is not withdrawn. In the meantime, his reason for imprisonment has been changed and he is classified as a political prisoner.
**Höss writes in his memoirs that this discussion took place at the end of November: "I didn't hear anything about the start-up of the operation. And Eichmann hadn't obtained any suitable gas." The discussion must have taken place before the gas Zyklon B was used in Auschwitz, thus the end of August.

The ovens of the twin crematoriums II and III under construction; left, prisoners at work.

AUGUST*

In Höss's absence, Camp Commander SS Captain Karl Fritzsch uses the gas Zyklon B to kill Russian POW's.**   Ibid.

SEPTEMBER 1

22 reeducation prisoners from Bielitz sent by the Kattowitz Gestapo receive Nos. 20330–20351.

*This most likely happens at the end of August because Höss is present at the next killing of the Russian POW's and the Polish prisoners in the cellar of Block 11.

**Following Hitler's order of March 30, 1941 and the guidelines worked out by the High Command of the Armed Forces for the treatment of political commissars of June 6, 1941 (NO-1076), and on the basis of the operational order No. 8 issued by the Head of the RSHA Heydrich on July 17, 1941, small groups of political functionaries are sent to Auschwitz by the Gestapo in August. They are selected in the POW camp to be liquidated. The time of the admission and the size of this group cannot be ascertained because of the lack of documents. In his autobiography, Rudolf Höss writes: "In accordance with a secret order issued by Hitler, these Russian *politruks* and political commissars were searched out in all the prisoner-of-war camps by special Gestapo commandos. When identified, they were transferred to the nearest concentration camp for liquidation. . . . The political officials of the Red Army thus identified were brought to Auschwitz for liquidation. The first, smaller transports were shot by execution commandos. While I was away on duty, my deputy, Fritzsch, the Protective Custody Commander, first tried gas for these killings. It was a preparation of prussic acid, called Zyklon B, which was used in the camp as an insecticide and of which there was always a stock on hand. On my return, Fritzsch reported this to me, and the gas was used again for the next

Polish prisoner Jan Nowaczek (No. 8488) escapes from the Penal Company deployed for excavating sand in the gravel quarry next to the so-called theater building. He is dressed in an SS uniform and has a pistol.

APMO, D-AuI-1/2, p. 9, Bulletin of the Gestapo in Upper Silesia of September 15, 1941; Kraków Auschwitz Trial, vol. 55, p. 101, Statement of Former Prisoner Ludwik Banach.

Because of Nowaczek's escape, 19 prisoners who worked in his labor squad are sent to the bunker of Block 11. One of the prisoners in the bunker is Ludwik Banach (No. 20317), who has been put into the Penal Company on the day of his admission to the camp, August 30.

APMO, Kraków Auschwitz Trial, vol. 55, p. 101, Statement of Former Prisoner Ludwik Banach.

SEPTEMBER 2

Camp Commander Karl Fritzsch selects 10 of the 19 prisoners sent to the bunker of Block 11 the previous day in retaliation for the escape of Jan Nowaczek, locks them up again in the bunker as hostages, and condemns them to death. Nine prisoners are sent back to the Penal Company. One of these is Ludwik Banach. In the afternoon, Fritzsch instructs several prisoners in the Penal Company, including those released from the bunker, to clear out all the living quarters on the ground floor and first floor of Block 11 and to take the plank beds with the straw sacks to the attic. That day, the condemned prisoners and those in the Penal Company leave Block 11 and after work are sent to Block 5a, which is still under construction.

Ibid.

SEPTEMBER 3*

After the success of the experiment of killing the small group of Russian prisoners of war with gas, ordered by Karl Fritzsch a few days earlier, the camp administration decides to repeat the experiment in the cellar of Block 11. This no doubt has to do with the news that the Gestapo is planning to send a large transport of officers, People's Commissars, and Russian prisoners of war for liquidation. In this connection, Camp Doctor SS Captain Dr. Siegfried Schwela orders a selection in the prisoners' infirmary, in which about 250 inmates are selected. The attendants are instructed to take the selected prisoners to the bunker of Block 11 and to bring

APMO, Höss Trial, vol. 2, p. 97; vol. 4, pp. 21, 34, 99, 128; vol. 54, p. 207; Vol. 78, p. 1, Statements of Former Prisoners.

---

transport." In the notes titled by Höss "The Solution to the Jewish Question in Auschwitz Concentration Camp," he writes the following: "In the autumn of 1941 a secret order was issued instructing the Gestapo to weed out the Russian *politruks*, commissars, and certain political officials from the prisoner-of-war camps, and to transfer them to the nearest concentration camps for liquidation. Small transports of these prisoners were continually arriving in Auschwitz and they were shot in the gravel pit near the Tobacco Monopoly buildings or in the courtyard of Block 11. When I was absent on duty, my deputy, Captain Fritzsch, on his own initiative used gas for killing those Russian prisoners of war. He crammed the underground detention cells with Russians and, protected by a gas mask, discharged Zyklon B gas into the cells, killing the victims instantly" (Höss, *Commandant in Auschwitz*, pp. 125ff., 159). Höss mentions neither the number of the murdered Russian prisoners of war nor the place where Zyklon B is used.
*The date comes from an analysis of the statements of former prisoners and of the Bunker Register, in which between August 31 and September 5 no entries occur regarding admission of prisoners into the bunker.

a few of them there on stretchers. In the bunker they are crammed together in a few cells. The cellar windows are blocked up with earth. Then about 600 Russian POW's, officers, and people's commissars are driven into the cellar. They have been chosen in the camp's prisoner-of-war section by special Gestapo commandos. As soon as they are pushed into the cells and the SS men have thrown in the Zyklon B gas, the doors are locked and sealed.* This operation takes place after evening roll call, after announcement of a so-called camp curfew, during which prisoners are forbidden to leave the blocks and move around in the camp.

SEPTEMBER 4

In the morning Roll Call Leader Gerhard Palitzsch, protected by a gas mask, opens the doors and discovers that one of the POW's is still alive. More Zyklon B is poured and the doors are closed once more.

APMO, Höss Trial, vol. 2, pp. 21, 97; Statements of Former Prisoners Jan Krokowski and Michał Kula.

70 prisoners sent by the Sipo and SD from Pawiak Prison in Warsaw receive Nos. 20352–20421. Included are 20 monks of the Capuchin monastery in Warsaw.

Three prisoners from Rybnik sent by the Kattowitz Gestapo receive Nos. 20422–20424.

66 Czechs and Czech Jews sent by the Brünn Gestapo receive Nos. 20425–20490.

In the afternoon all the doors of the bunker in Block 11 are opened and unsealed after it is ascertained that the second dose of Zyklon B has killed the Russian POW's and the Polish prisoners. There is a wait until the gas has evaporated. After evening roll call, another camp curfew is ordered.

APMO, Höss Trial, vol. 2, p. 97; Statements of Former Prisoner Michał Kula; Kielar, *Anus Mundi*, p. 92.

In the evening Roll Call Leader Palitzsch summons 20 prisoners from the Penal Company in Block 5a as well as all the hospital orderlies and two prisoners, Eugeniusz Obojski and Teofil Bansiuk, who are to be put to work as corpse bearers. They are given two carts to transport the bodies to the morgue and the crematorium. All are taken to the courtyard of Block 11. They are told in advance that they have been put on a special work detail and are not to tell anyone what they see, under penalty of death. At the same time they are promised that after performing this work they will receive larger portions of food.

APMO, Höss Trial, vol. 4, p. 21; vol. 54, pp. 208ff; vol. 55, pp. 101ff.; Statement of Former Prisoners; Kielar, *Anus Mundi*, pp. 92–94.

In the courtyard of Block 11, SS officers Fritzsch, Maier, and Palitzsch, the Camp Doctor Schwela, and SS men who occupy positions

*In his autobiography Rudolf Höss writes: "The gassing was carried out in the detention cells of Block 11. Protected by a gas mask, I watched the killing myself. In the crowded cells death came instantaneously the moment the Zyklon B was thrown in. A short, almost smothered cry, and it was all over" (Höss, *Commandant in Auschwitz*, p. 126).

as Block Leaders are already there. Prisoners Obojski and Bansiuk receive gas masks and go with Palitzsch and the SS men, who also wear gas masks, to the cellar of Block 11. They return from the cellar without gas masks to show that the gas has evaporated. The prisoners are divided into four groups. One group, with gas masks, hauls the bodies of the murdered men out of the cellar to the ground floor; the second group strips the bodies; the third group carries the bodies to the courtyard of Block 11, where they are loaded onto the trucks by the fourth group. The Russian prisoners of war are dressed in uniforms; in the pockets are documents, family photos, money, various trinkets, and cigarettes. In the courtyard, under the supervision of the SS men, seven dentists extract gold crowns and teeth from the corpses. The prisoners pull the cart loaded with the bodies of the prisoners of war and the Polish prisoners from the courtyard of Block 11 to the crematorium, accompanied by Obojski and Bansiuk and under the supervision of the SS men. Among the murdered are also the bodies of the 10 inmates who were locked in the bunker and condemned to death by Fritzsch on September 1 in retaliation for the escape of Jan Nowaczek. The bodies of the prisoners selected in the hospital are in underwear. The hauling, stripping, searching, and transporting of the bodies lasts until dawn and is not finished.

SEPTEMBER 5

19 prisoners sent with a group transport by the Stapo and Kripo from Breslau, Oppeln, Schwerin, Stettin, Vienna, Troppau, and Kattowitz receive Nos. 20491–20509.

Five reeducation prisoners from Gleiwitz sent by the Kattowitz Gestapo receive Nos. 20510–20514.

After evening roll call, a camp curfew is ordered. The same prisoners who were detailed the night before march into the courtyard of Block 11 to complete the transporting of the bodies to the crematorium. There, the corpses are laid in a big, long hall* which is already half full. The crematorium unit cannot keep up with the cremation of the corpses. It is a few more days before all the bodies are incinerated.**

Kielar, *Anus Mundi*, pp. 95–98.

In the Bunker Book, the death of the civilian Władysław Maślak, born on February 2, 1920, in Kurnik, is noted. He was put in the bunker of Block 11 on August 10, 1941. No doubt he has been gassed in the bunker with the other prisoners.

APMO, D-AuI-3/1, Bunker Register, p. 24.

*The morgue is later changed into a gas chamber. Prisoners are also shot there.
**The news of the death of about 600 Russian POW's and some 250 Polish prisoners by gas leaks out. On November 17, 1941, in *Informator bieżący*, the underground bulletin of the high command of the Federation for Armed Struggle, a notice about it appears. "The night of September 5 to September 6" is given as the date, i.e., the day on which the transport of the bodies to the crematorium is completed (CA KC PZPR, 202/III-7, Documents of the Delegation of the Polish Government in Exile, p. 12).

The deaths of three prisoners put in the bunker of Block 11 on the same day, is noted in the Bunker Book. These are Fritz Renner (No. 11179), born December 21, 1899, in Breslau, and Bruno Grosmann (No. 15083), born January 17, 1881, in Breslau, both of Block 14; and Roman Drost (No. 10992), born December 10, 1899, in Słupno, of Block 18a.*

Ibid.

SEPTEMBER 6

Two prisoners from Bielitz, sent by the Kattowitz Gestapo, receive Nos. 20515 and 20516. In the Camp Register, next to the name of prisoner No. 20516 is the note "Personal data currently unknown."

APMO, D-AuI-2/4, Admissions List, p. 337.

Three reeducation prisoners from Bielitz sent by the Kattowitz Gestapo receive Nos. 20517–20519.

SEPTEMBER 8

The Penal Company is brought back to Block 11 after the block has been cleaned and ventilated.

APMO, Höss Trial, vol. 55, p. 81.

SEPTEMBER 9

Prisoner No. 20516 is put in the bunker of Block 11 with the note "feebleminded."** He is sent to the bunker on suspicion that he is simulating mental illness.

APMO, D-AuI-3/1, Bunker Register, p. 24.

Seven reeducation prisoners sent by the Kattowitz Gestapo receive Nos. 20520–20526.

Five reeducation prisoners are given Nos. 20527, 20528, and 20530–20532, and one political prisoner receives No. 20529. These prisoners come from Bielitz and are sent by the Kattowitz Gestapo.

SEPTEMBER 11

39 prisoners sent by the Gestapo and Kripo from Lodz receive Nos. 20533–20571. The transport includes 34 political prisoners, three asocials, and two criminals.

Prisoners Józef Kościelniak (No. 17421), Stefan Smulski (No. 17497), Bolesław Marcula (No. 17632), and Marceli Wójcik (No. 17305) are sent to the bunker of Block 11 because they are suspected of making preparations for an escape. The next day, they are assigned to the Penal Company.

Ibid., p. 25.

---

*The reason these prisoners are sent to the bunker is not known. It is possible that they die in the bunker of poisoning. The bunker was not yet properly ventilated and not sufficiently cleaned of chloral which is poured out on the floor for disinfection purposes.
**Compare the entry for September 6, 1941.

SEPTEMBER 12

114 prisoners sent by the Sipo and SD from Pawiak Prison in Warsaw receive Nos. 20572–20685.

15 reeducation prisoners sent by the Stapo from Sosnowitz, Gleiwitz, Pless, and Beuthen receive Nos. 20686–20695 and 20710–21714.*

19 prisoners sent by the Stapo and Kripo with a group transport receive Nos. 20696–20709 and 20715–20719.

SEPTEMBER 13

28 prisoners sent by the Stapo and Kripo with a group transport from Lodz, Danzig, Königsberg, Hohensalza, Bromberg, Tilsit, and Kattowitz receive Nos. 20720–20746 and 20751.

Four reeducation prisoners from Bielitz sent by the Stapo receive Nos. 20747–20750.

SEPTEMBER 15

In the Gestapo Register in Upper Silesia it is noted that prisoner Józef Gawl, born July 4, 1923, in Kurdwanów near Kraków, has escaped from Auschwitz. The date of the escape is not given. On July 23, 1941, he was sent to the camp from Bielitz as a reeducation prisoner by the Kattowitz Gestapo. | APMO, D-AuI-1/2, Bulletin, p. 9.

190 prisoners sent by the Sipo and SD from the prison in Radom receive Nos. 20752–20941.

In the morning prisoner Karol Schornstein (No. 6273), born June 4, 1908, in Serajewo, escapes from a labor squad at the Buna factory, riding a bicycle and wearing a civilian cap. | APMO, IZ-8/Gestapo Lodz/3/88/238.

The area to the left of the camp gate with the inscription WORK MAKES FREE is fenced off with electric barbed wire. The separate part comprises nine blocks, Numbers 1, 2, 3, 12, 13, 14, 22, 23, and 24. Between Blocks 14 and 24 is the entrance gate, over which the inscription RUSSIAN PRISONER-OF-WAR LABOR CAMP is posted. | APMO, Höss Trial, vol. 4, pp. 71, 122; vol. 7, p. 219; Jerzy Adam Brandhuber, "Die sowjetischen Kriegsgefangenen im Konzentrationslager Auschwitz" (The Russian Prisoners of War in Auschwitz), HvA, no. 4 (1961): 18.

SEPTEMBER 16

16 prisoners previously housed in Blocks 21a and 22 are sent to the bunker of Block 11, very likely because of the escape of Karol Schornstein. On September 22 these prisoners are sent to the Penal Company. | APMO, D-AuI-3/1a, Bunker Register, pp. 27ff.

Prisoner Tadeusz Szafran (No. 321), sent to the bunker from the Penal Company on September 10 because of an escape attempt, dies. | Ibid., p. 24.

*Nos. 20687, 20689, 20693, and 20714 are not withdrawn in 1942. Probably the reason for arrest of these prisoners changes.

900 Russian POWs are killed with gas. This takes place in the morgue of the crematorium because the use of the cellar in Block 11 would be too complicated.*

SEPTEMBER 17

Eight reeducation prisoners and one political prisoner sent by the Kattowitz Stapo receive Nos. 20943–20950 and 20942.

SEPTEMBER 18

36 prisoners sent from Kattowitz by the Sipo and SD receive Nos. 20915–20986.

SEPTEMBER 19

Ten reeducation prisoners sent by the Kattowitz Stapo receive Nos. 20987–20992 and 21008–21011.

22 prisoners sent with a group transport by the Stapo and Kripo from Kattowitz, Breslau, Troppau, Oppeln, Linz, Prague, and Essen receive Nos. 20993–21007 and 21012–21018.

SEPTEMBER 20

32 reeducation prisoners from Bielitz sent by the Kattowitz Gestapo receive Nos. 21019–21050.

SEPTEMBER 22

Mentally ill prisoner No. 20516, put in the bunker on September 9, is moved to the infirmary, where he dies the same day. Probably he is killed with a phenol injection.

APMO, D-AuI-3/1a, Bunker Register, p. 24; Brol et al., "The Bunker Register of Block 11," p. 33.

Three prisoners from Bielitz sent by the Kattowitz Stapo receive Nos. 21051–21053.

*This probably happened in September, for Höss writes in his autobiography, "During this first experience of gassing people, I did not fully realize what was happening, perhaps because I was too impressed by the whole procedure. I have a clearer recollection of the gassing of nine hundred Russians, which took place shortly afterward in the Old Crematorium, since the use of Block 11 for this purpose caused too much trouble. While the transport was detraining, holes were pierced in the earth and concrete ceiling of the mortuary. The Russians were ordered to undress in an anteroom; they then quietly entered the mortuary, for they had been told they were to be deloused. The whole transport exactly filled the mortuary to capacity. The doors were then sealed and the gas shaken down through the holes in the roof. I do not know how long this killing took. For a little while a humming sound could be heard. When the powder was thrown in, there were cries of 'Gas!' then a great bellowing and the trapped prisoners hurled themselves against both the doors. But the doors held. They were opened several hours later, so that the place might be aired. It was then that I saw, for the first time, gassed bodies in the mass. . . . I must even admit that this gassing calmed me, for the mass extermination of the Jews had to start soon, and at that time neither Eichmann nor I had any idea how these killings were to be carried out in the expected mass. . . . Now we had discovered the gas and also the method." (Höss, *Commandant in Auschwitz*, pp. 126ff).

No. 21054 is given to Jerzy Karwat, born August 28, 1923, sent by Sipo and SD from Montelupich Prison in Kraków. Karwat is bound hand and foot with heavy chains that are unfastened by order of the Gestapo in the camp locksmith's shop. Karwat is immediately locked up in the bunker, where he dies on October 15, 1941.*

APMO, D-AuI-3/1a, Bunker Register, p. 29; Brol et al., "Bunker Register of Block 11," pp. 33, 34.

SEPTEMBER 23

No. 21055 is given to a reeducation prisoner sent by the Kattowitz Gestapo.

14 prisoners are sent from Block 18 to the bunker of Block 11. The reason is not given. They all die between September 26 and October 15.

APMO, D-AuI-3/1a, Bunker Register, pp. 29–31.

SEPTEMBER 24

Concentration Camps Inspector Richard Glücks allows the families of prisoners to send a single shipment of underwear and a pullover.

APMO, D-RF-3/RSHA/118/3, p. 280, Edict Collection RKPA.

After a conversation between the Waffen SS Deputy Director of Construction in Auschwitz, SS Technical Sergeant Urbanczek and Head Engineer Prüfer of J. A. Topf and Sons, the company sends operating instructions in triplicate for the Topf incinerator and the Topf induced-draft plant in Kamin. The company also requests that the operating instructions be posted in the oven area under a protective glass cover to ensure the proper operation of the incineration facility.

APMO, D-AuI, Docs. ZBL, BW 11.

SEPTEMBER 25

At Topf and Sons, the technical sketch (No. D 59042) for the third incinerator for the Auschwitz crematorium is drawn.

Ibid.

SEPTEMBER 26

62 prisoners sent in a group transport by the Stapo and Kripo from Kattowitz, Bromberg, Brünn, Vienna, Graz, Linz, Breslau, Lodz, Prague, Posen, Königsberg, Troppau, and Schneidemühl and by the Sipo and SD from Lublin receive Nos. 21056–21114, 21116,

---

*On the night of May 20–21, 1941, Jerzy Karwat, a member of an illegal organization, shoots and wounds Gestapo agents and then escapes while being arrested in his parents' house in Kraków. Three Gestapo agents are wounded. The Gestapo thereupon arrests his parents, Paulina and Karol. Jerzy Karwat is caught near Ojców and put in Montelupich Prison in Kraków. Despite inhuman torture, he does not betray anyone. On the night of July 21–22, he tries to escape from Montelupich. After being again captured, he is put in a dark cell, where he spends 46 days with his mother, who asks to be locked up with him. His father is sent to Auschwitz on June 26, 1941 (No. 17353), where he is probably shot on July 3, 1941. At the beginning of September, the mother Paulina is transported to Ravensbrück Concentration Camp (Wroński, *Chronicle*, pp. 155, 163, 170; Antonia Piątkowska, *Wspomnienia oświęcimskie* [Auschwitz Memoirs], Kraków, 1977, pp. 36–38).

21118, and 21122. The first Yugoslavian prisoner, who receives No. 21092, comes with this transport. There are also five reeducation prisoners from Kattowitz who receive Nos. 21115, 21117 and 21119–21121.

SEPTEMBER 28

Eight Polish prisoners sent by the Stapo and Kripo receive Nos. 21123–21130.

22 Yugoslavian prisoners, the first from the annexed area of Carinthia, are sent by the Sipo and SD and receive Nos. 21131–21152.

SEPTEMBER 1–30

During the 26 working days in September, the German Railroad transports 34,594 prisoners working on the construction of the Buna factory and the SS men who guard them from the camp and back. The average number transported per day is 1,330.

APMO, IZ-13/89, Various Documents of the Third Reich, p. 45.

OCTOBER 1

Two reeducation prisoners sent from Kattowitz receive Nos. 21153 and 21154.

140 prisoners sent by the Sipo and SD from the prison in Radom receive Nos. 21155–21294.

Following an order of the head of Office II in the Budget and Buildings Main Office, SS Major General Dr. Engineer Heinz Kammler, SS Major Karl Bischoff arrives in Auschwitz to become the Director of the Special Construction Administration newly formed for the construction of a Waffen SS prisoner-of-war camp in Auschwitz.

APMO, D-AuI-3a, Folder 17, p. 292.

The head of Office I in the Budget and Buildings Main Office, SS Major General Georg Lörner, proposes to the Finance Minister to buy a mill belonging to Krzikalla and Co. for the Waffen SS in Auschwitz. The price is 119,500 RM. Lörner justifies the purchase with the observation that it lies within the Auschwitz Interest Zone, which was evacuated long ago because of the national political tasks of the camp. In connection with the planned establishment of an SS agricultural district, the utility of a mill must be considered.

APMO, IZ-13/89, Various Documents of the Third Reich, p. 6 (Original in BA Koblenz).

OCTOBER 2

Field Marshal Fedor von Bock, who commands 77 divisions, including 14 tank divisions and eight motorized divisions, advances toward Moscow.

OCTOBER 3

30 prisoners sent by the Stapo and Kripo in a group transport from Lodz, Breslau, Stettin, Oppeln, Vienna, Troppau, Frankfurt/Oder

Klagenfurt, Prague, and Posen receive Nos. 21295–21316, 21319–21325, and 21329.

30 prisoners sent by the Kattowitz Stapo from Beuthen, Hindenburg (Zabrze), Gleiwitz, and Bielitz receive Nos. 21317, 21318, 21326–21328, and 21330–21354.

OCTOBER 4

One political and eight reeducation prisoners sent by the Kattowitz Stapo receive Nos. 21362, 21355–21361, and 21363.

OCTOBER 5

29 prisoners, including 26 political prisoners, sent by the Stapo and Kripo in a group transport from Posen, Lodz, Prague, and Stettin receive Nos. 21364–21392.

OCTOBER 6

The timetable for prison cars* to transport prisoners from various prisons to their destinations goes into effect. According to this schedule, the prison car attached to Train 553 at 5:43 on Friday in Beuthen travels the route Beuthen—Kattowitz—Trzebinia—Kraków—Auschwitz (arrival 5:46 P.M., departure 8:17)—Kattowitz—Beuthen. On Saturday it leaves Beuthen at 6:51 A.M. and reaches Breslau at 8:21 P.M.

Timetable for Prisoner Cars.

Two political and two reeducation prisoners sent by the Kattowitz Stapo receive Nos. 21393, 21394, 21395, and 21396.

OCTOBER 7

2,014 Russian prisoners of war are sent from the prisoner-of-war camp, Stalag 308,** in Neuhammer am Quais (Sowiętoszów nad Kwisa). Before entering the camp, prisoners must be disinfected. They have to strip naked and dive into a vat of cold disinfectant fluid. This procedure takes place at the so-called lumberyard. From there they are driven naked in groups of 100 to the unheated blocks in the fenced-off part of the camp. Only a few days later are they given their uniforms, linen, and blankets, which have been disinfected. Five prisoners of war die on the day of admission.

APMO, Höss Trial, vol. 4, pp. 71, 128; vol. 7, p. 219; D-AuI-3/1–7646, Index of the Russian Prisoners of War.

*The schedule gives information about which station a transfer is designated for, where the prison cars are cleaned, and which trains they are attached to. The police officials provide the guards and transport managers. They also determine from which prisons and how many prisoners are to be on board, to whom they have to be transferred and in which institutions prisoners must wait for further transport to the destination.
**Acronym for Stammlager, "main camp." Stalags were German prison camps for noncommissioned officers and enlisted men. —ED.

The bodies of 31 prisoners are brought to the morgue* in the cellar of Block 28—which was Block 20 in 1940 and now belongs to the infirmary—and entered in the Morgue Register.** Afterward they will be brought to the crematorium. A special squad, known as the corpse bearers, works in the morgue.

APMO, D-AuI-5/3, Morgue Register, p. 1.

OCTOBER 8–9

2,145 Russian prisoners of war from Stalag 308 in Neuhammer are admitted and the process of taking down their personal data is begun. This takes place on the ground floor of Block 24, where the Admissions Office of the Political Department is located. Prisoners chosen for this job are those who generally work as translators in the camp because of their knowledge of German and Russian. Others already work in the Admissions office of the Political Section. A few days earlier, the latter have had to learn Russian numbers and whatever basic words are necessary to fill out the personal forms. The prisoners of war are taken to the admissions process naked. At the same time as the admission of the prisoners of war, the demolition of the farms in Birkenau and the construction of a new prisoner-of-war camp is begun.†

APMO, Höss Trial, vol. 4, p. 64; D-AuI-3/1..7646, Card Index of Russian Prisoners of War; Brandhuber, "Russian POWs," p. 18.

OCTOBER 10

Seven reeducation prisoners sent by the Kattowitz Stapo from Sosnowitz, Beuthen, and Oppeln receive Nos. 21397–21403.

12 prisoners sent by the Stapo and Kripo in a group transport from Oppeln, Breslau, Vienna, Karlsruhe, Linz, Troppau, and Kattowitz receive Nos. 21404–21415.

---

*The morgue possesses several crates to transport corpses to the crematorium and a few stretchers on which the corpses of prisoners are carried from the residential and infirmary blocks. The wooden stretchers are replaced with metal litters when the shootings begin so as to be able to wash the traces of blood off more easily. At first the prisoners carried the corpses in the crates on their backs, but then they receive wagons they pull themselves. Only the bodies of prisoners and sometimes of civilians interrogated by the Political Department are brought to the morgue. After mass executions, the bodies of the hostages and prisoners are brought directly from the site of the execution to the crematorium.

**The Morgue Register covers the period October 7, 1941 to August 31, 1943. The entries are made by the individual body bearers. The following data are noted daily: the current number, the prisoner number, and the place of admission, i.e., usually the number of the residential or infirmary block, Block 11, or the abbreviation for the Penal Company (SK—Strafkompanie), the gravel pit (KG—Kiesgrube), the Political Department (PA—Politische Abteilung) or the Russian Camp (RL—Russisches Lager). The last refers to prisoners who were put in the camp of the Russian POWs and died there. Many entries are made in code. Some cannot be deciphered since the prisoners who wrote them die in the camp. The entry "27w" probably means that the prisoner was killed by phenol injection in the lavatory of Block 28 or in the waiting room of the morgue of Block 28 where the corpse bearers gathered and were also given phenol injections. The entry "27w" is under the current number entry during the period October 7, 1941 to January 10, 1942; later "28w" is entered.

†Höss states that, at that time, SS Lieutenant General Hans Kammler had come to Auschwitz Concentration Camp and declared that a camp for 200,000 prisoners of war, and not for 100,000 as planned in March, is to be built (APMO, Höss Trial, vol. 21, p. 35).

During the day, 61 corpses are brought to the morgue. Next to the numbers of 15 prisoners the code "27w" is noted, indicating that these were killed with a phenol injection.

APMO, D-AuI-5/3, Morgue Register, pp. 4ff.

OCTOBER 11

58 prisoners sent by the Stapo and Kripo in a group transport from Danzig, Königsberg, Zichenau, Bromberg, Hohensalza, Tilsit, and Graudenz (Grudziądz) receive Nos. 21416–21473.

OCTOBER 13

The Finance Minister entrusts the proceedings concerning the mill takeover by the Auschwitz camp to the Minister for Food and Agriculture with a request for a comment.*

APMO, IZ-13/89, Various Documents of the Third Reich, p. 7.

In the Death Register of Russian POWs,** 64 deaths are noted.

APMO, D-AuI-5/1, Russian Prisoner-of-War Camp Auschwitz, Death Register, Infirmary.

OCTOBER 14

29 corpses are sent to the morgue. Next to the numbers of six inmates, who were brought in one after another, is the code "27w."

APMO, D-AuI-5/3, Morgue Register, p. 9.

One Czech political prisoner and two reeducation prisoners from Teschen, sent by the Kattowitz Stapo, receive Nos. 21474, 21475, and 21476.

60 prisoners sent by the Sipo and SD from the prison in the castle in Lublin receive Nos. 21477–21536.

900 Russian prisoners of war are sent from Stalag 308 in Neuhammer.

Alfred Przyblski (No. 471), employed in the building office, is ordered to make a site plan for a prisoner-of-war camp in Birkenau. It is marked "Plan for the Prisoner-of-War Camp in Auschwitz O/S [Oberschlesien—Upper Silesia]." The camp is designed for 100,000 prisoners of war.

APMO, D-AuI, Docs. ZBL, Site Plan for the Prisoner-of-War Camp in Auschwitz, O.S., of October 14, 1941.

OCTOBER 15

31 corpses are sent to the morgue.

APMO, D-AuI-5/3, Morgue Register, p. 10.

*The comment must have been positive since the camp administration takes over the mill operation and replaces its equipment. The mill is operated by prisoners under SS supervision.
**The Death Register contains seven categories: the current number, the number of the prisoner of war, the block number, the date of death, the hour of death, last name, first name, date of birth, cause of death. Under this last category the alleged illness is entered in Latin or German or, instead, reads "transferred." The entry "transferred" also means death. In the Death Register, 72 various illnesses are stated as the cause of death (APMO, Höss Trial, vol. 10, pp. 135–137, analysis of the Death Register of the Russian prisoners of war, which was carried out during investigation procedures against the former Commandant of Auschwitz, Höss).

Next to ten sequential prisoner numbers the code "27w" is entered.

The plan for the prisoner-of-war camp in Birkenau is approved by Construction Director SS Major Karl Bischoff and signed by Commandant Rudolf Höss. According to the plan, the site is to be divided by the main street of the camp. A railroad platform is planned to run alongside the street. To the left of the street and platform will be a quarantine camp, to the right, Administrative Sections I and II. The whole site forms a rectangle surrounded by a barbed-wire fence and watchtowers. The dimensions of this rectangle are 787 by 1236 yards. The plan calls for a total of 174 masonry residence barracks in the three sections.*

APMO, D-AuI, Docs. ZBL, Site Plan for Prisoner-of-War Camp, Auschwitz, O.S., of October 14, 1941.

18 reeducation prisoners sent by the Kattowitz Stapo receive Nos. 21537–21554.

OCTOBER 16

Following the telephone order of Office III of the Budget and Buildings Main Office, the Construction Administration of Waffen SS and Police of Mauthausen orders from J. A. Topf and Sons a double-snout incinerator, Auschwitz model. The company is obligated to deliver the plant immediately.

APMO, IZ-13/89, Various Documents of the Third Reich, p. 238 (Original in BA Koblenz).

119 prisoners sent by the Sipo and SD from the prison in Radom receive Nos. 21555–21673.

108 prisoners sent by the Sipo and SD from Pawiak Prison in Warsaw receive Nos. 21674–21781.

No. 21782 is given to a reeducation prisoner and No. 21783 to a political prisoner. Both are sent from Pless by the Kattowitz Stapo.

34 reeducation prisoners sent from Bielitz by the Stapo receive Nos. 21784–21817.

In the prisoners' infirmary 21 prisoners are killed with phenol injections. In the Morgue Register, the entry "27w" appears next to these prisoners' numbers.

APMO, D-RO/90K, 1/B.**

OCTOBER 17

One reeducation prisoner sent from Beuthen by the Kattowitz Stapo receives No. 21818.

APMO, D-AuI-5/3, Morgue Register, p. 13.

*This plan is only partially realized. The next plan, of August 15, 1942, already foresees accommodating 200,000 prisoners.
**This is a list of prisoners who died or were killed by shooting and injections. The list was made in Auschwitz and, with the help of the resistance movement, was sent illicitly to Kraków. It is a copy of the Morgue Register. The numbers of 21 prisoners who were brought in one after another are put together in brackets and the note "injection" is added. Next to these numbers is the code "27w." Thus we can assume that previous entries marked with the same code concern prisoners who were also killed with phenol injections.

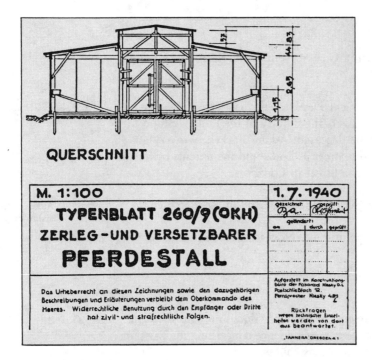

QUERSCHNITT

M. 1:100   1.7.1940

TYPENBLATT 260/9 (OKH)
ZERLEG - UND VERSETZBARER
PFERDESTALL

Cross section of the "stable" type of barracks, which was used by the German Army to house horses.

17 prisoners sent in a group transport by the Stapo from Oppeln, Vienna, and Graz and by the Kripo from Kattowitz, Oppeln, and Breslau receive Nos. 21819–21835. In the transport are five Yugoslav political prisoners sent from Graz.

28 prisoners sent by the Sipo and SD from Kraków receive Nos. 21836–21863.

32 corpses are sent to the morgue. Next to 20 numbers is the code "27w."

The administration of Auschwitz receives a letter from the Lodz Gestapo with the request for the home addresses of deceased prisoners Wawrzyniec Binczyk and Karol Tokarski. The Lodz Gestapo has no personal files on these inmates and therefore cannot inform the families that they are to come and get the packages of the prisoners' belongings, clothing, and personal objects, which have been sent to Auschwitz C.C.

APMO, IZ-8/Gestapo Lodz/3a/88/646.

OCTOBER 18

53 corpses are sent to the morgue. Next to 26 numbers the code "27w" is entered.

APMO, D-AuI-5/3, Morgue Register, pp. 14ff.

OCTOBER 19

1955 Russian POWs are sent from Stalag 308 in Neuhammer.

APMO, D-AuI-3/1–7646, Card Index of Russian POWs.

OCTOBER 20

One German prisoner from Gleiwitz sent by the Kattowitz Gestapo receives No. 21864.

The director of the Political Department, SS Second Lieutenant Maximilian Grabner, answers the inquiry of the Lodz Gestapo for the home addresses of the deceased: Adam Binczyk, Wawrzyniec's brother, lives at 98 Śląska Street in Lodz, and the parents of Karol Tokarski live at 51 Bratnia Street in Lodz.

APMO, IZ-8/Gestapo Lodz/3a/88/647.

986 Russian POWs are sent from Stalag 308 in Neuhammer.

APMO, D-AuI-3/1–7646, Card Index of Russian POWs.

27 corpses are sent to the morgue. Next to the numbers of nine is the code "27w."

APMO, D-AuI-5/3, Morgue Register, p. 17.

OCTOBER 21

Concentration Camps Inspector Richard Glücks informs the Commandant that in the future correspondence concerning the Russian prisoners of war is to be coded as follows:

APMO, D-RF-3/RSHA/117/6, p. 65, General Orders of the RSHA.

1. 14 b 18 on general correspondence and reports of changes
2. 14 f 7 for cases of death by natural causes
3. 14 f 8 for suicides and accidents
4. 14 f 9 for shootings during escapes
5. 14 f 10 for injuries from weapon use
6. 14 f 14 for executions

The previous file code "Az.: 14" is to be replaced by the above codes.

31 corpses are sent to the morgue. Next to the numbers of 17 prisoners is the code "27w."

APMO, D-AuI-5/3, Morgue Register, p. 18.

OCTOBER 22

48 prisoners sent by the Sipo and SD for the Kraków District from the prison in Reichshof (Rzeszów) receive Nos. 21865–21912.

OCTOBER 23

46 deaths of Russian POWs are recorded in the Death Register.

Three political prisoners receive Nos. 21912–21915. 11 reeducation prisoners from Rybnik and Pless sent by the Kattowitz Stapo receive Nos. 21916–21926.

In the afternoon, Polish prisoner Jan Dygas (No. 15873) escapes from an outside squad.

APMO, IZ-8/8/Gestapo Lodz/3/88/242.

OCTOBER 24

95 deaths are recorded in the Death Register of the Russian POWs.

Shoes in the personal effects warehouse, nicknamed "Canada."

Four reeducation prisoners from Sosnowitz sent by the Kattowitz Stapo receive Nos. 21927–21930.

32 corpses are sent to the morgue. Next to the numbers of 18 prisoners is the code "27w."

APMO, D-AuI-5/3, Morgue Register, p. 24.

12 prisoners sent by the Stapo and Kripo in a group transport from Kattowitz, Breslau, Oppeln, and Troppau receive Nos. 21931–21942.

103 prisoners sent by the Sipo and SD from the prison in Radom receive Nos. 21943–22045.

47 Czechs and Czech Jews sent from Brünn by the Gestapo receive Nos. 22046–22092.

60 prisoners sent by the Sipo and SD from the prison in the castle in Lublin receive Nos. 22093–22152.

Two prisoners sent from Radom by the Sipo and SD receive Nos. 22153 and 22154.

OCTOBER 25

132 prisoners sent by the Sipo and SD from Warsaw receive Nos. 22155–22286.

1,908 Russian POWs are sent from Stalag 308 in Neuhammer.

APMO, D-AuI-3/1–7646, Card File of Russian POWs.

18 prisoners sent in a group transport by the Stapo from Lodz, Graudenz, Zichenau, Bromberg, and Danzig and by the Kripo from Stettin and Königsberg receive Nos. 22287–22304.

OCTOBER 27

In retaliation for the escape of a prisoner from Block 18a, 10 hostages are selected from the prisoners in that block and condemned to starve to death in the bunker of Block 11. The following Polish inmates are selected: Henryk Kozłecki (No. 11278), Jan Skierniewski (No. 21157) who is 70 years old, Władysław Maciag (No. 20908), Józef Tomczak (No. 21373), Stanisław Kocek (No. 21173), Stefan Kiśniewicz (No. 16189), Zdzisław Witamborski (No. 13882), Franciszek Roller (No. 21086), Pawel Olszówka (No. 21062), and Wacław Kieszkowski (No. 14634). Six of these die of hunger between October 31 and November 10, 1941. Skierniewski, Tomczak, and Roller are shot on November 11, 1941. Henryk Kozłecki is released from the bunker into the camp on October 29. This is the only instance of a release from the bunker of an inmate condemned to starve to death.*

APMO, D-AuI-3/1a, Bunker Register, pp. 34ff.

34 corpses are sent to the morgue. Next to the numbers of 19 prisoners is the code "27w."

APMO, D-AuI-5/2, Morgue Register, p. 28.

87 deaths are entered in the Death Register of the Russian POWs.

OCTOBER 28

68 corpses are sent to the morgue. Next to the numbers of 20 prisoners is the code "27w." The entry "11" and a cross appears next to the numbers of 30 inmates. This probably means that those prisoners were shot.

Ibid., pp. 29–30.

24 reeducation prisoners sent from Kattowitz and Beilitz by the Stapo receive Nos. 22305–22328.

Four prisoners from Beilitz sent by the Kattowitz Stapo receive Nos. 22329–22332.

90 deaths are entered in the Death Register of the Russian POWs.

11 prisoners sent by the Gestapo from Oppeln receive Nos. 22333–22343.

161 deaths are entered in the Death Register of the Russian POWs.

*Former prisoner Stanisław Kowalski describes such a case, attributing the release of the prisoner, without mentioning his name, to the three-time intervention of the Head Capo of the carpentry shop, Reinhold, with the Political Department (Kowalski, *Number 4410*, pp. 286ff.).

Women who have been designated "able-bodied" at the selection.

OCTOBER 30

187 deaths are entered in the Death Register of the Russian POWs.

OCTOBER 31

15 prisoners sent by the Kattowitz Gestapo receive Nos. 22344–22358.

12 reeducation prisoners from Sosnowitz, Gleiwtiz, and Rybnik sent by the Kattowitz Gestapo receive Nos. 22359–22364 and 22388–22393.

167 deaths are entered in the Death Register of the Russian POWs.

27 prisoners sent in a group transport by the Stapo from Vienna, Breslau, Oppeln, Brünn, Frankfurt an der Oder, Graz, and Prague, and by the Kripo from Breslau, Kattowitz, and Oppeln receive Nos. 22365–22387 and 22394–22397. German common criminal Bruno Graf (No. 3268), born March 4, 1906, in Berlin, is sent back to the camp in this transport. In the camp, he had the position of Capo in the shoemaking labor squad; he was caught trying to escape

APMO, D-AuI-3/1a, Bunker Register, p. 36.

and sent back to the camp by the Stapo office in Vienna. He is put in the bunker of Block 11.*

OCTOBER 1–31

During the 26 working days in October, the German Railroad transports 34,111 prisoners working on the construction of the Buna factory and the SS Men who guard them from the camp and back. The average number transported per day is 1,312.

APMO, IZ-13/89, Various Documents of the Third Reich, p. 45.

OCTOBER 7–31

In Auschwitz 1,255 Russian POWs died; they die in droves. The ill are killed with phenol injections, those still alive are beaten to death with sticks. Not a day passes without a death.**

APMO, D-AuI-5/1, POW Camp, Auschwitz, Death Register, Infirmary.

The numbers of 873 inmates are listed in the Morgue Register. They have died from hunger, exhausting work, illness, physical abuse, or were shot or given a phenol injection.†

APMO, D-AuI-5/3, Morgue Register, pp. 1–34.

NOVEMBER

A special Gestapo commission comes to Auschwitz from Kattowitz. It consists of three people and is led by the head of the Kattowitz Gestapo, Dr. Rudolf Mildner. The commission, which proceeds according to the operational order of July 17, 1941, divides the Russian POWs into the following groups:

APMO, Höss Trial, vol. 7, pp. 219ff., Account of Former Prisoner Kazimierz Smoleń; Kazimierz Smoleń, "Sprawa No. 13" (Case No. 13), *Wolni ludzie* (Free Men), no. 11, June 1948.

1. Fanatic Communists—approximately 300
2. Group A: politically suspect—approximately 700
3. Group B: not politically suspect—approximately 8000
4. Group C: suitable for habilitation—approximately 30

The group of so-called fanatical Communists is marked in the card index and by tattoo with the letters "AU." The prisoners of war so designated are sent to the cellar of Block 24 and are intended to be liquidated in the near future along with those of Group A, the "politically suspect." The commission's work lasts about a month.

NOVEMBER 1

253 deaths are entered in the Death Register of the Russian POWs.

*He spends over two months in the bunker. On January 9, 1942, he is sent to the Penal Company, where he steals margarine. He is locked up in the bunker again on Jaunary 7, 1943, and condemned to death by starvation. Bruno Graf dies on February 5, 1943, after spending almost a month in the standing cell (Brol, et al., "The Bunker Register of Block 11," p. 34).
**The number of the dead is calculated by the entries in the Death Register.
†This figure is based on the entries in the Morgue Register. Nevertheless, the 873 dead prisoners do not include those who were shot en masse and whose bodies were taken directly to the crematorium.

78 prisoner numbers are listed in the Morgue Register. In addition, five numbers are entered with the note that there was no available death certificate.

APMO, D-AuI-5/3, Morgue Register, pp. 35–38.

NOVEMBER 2

213 deaths are entered in the Death Register of the Russian POWs.

NOVEMBER 3

A prisoner from Bielitz sent by the Kattowitz Stapo receives No. 22398.

The Central Construction Administration of the Waffen SS and Police in Auschwitz comes into being through the amalgamation of the SS New Construction Administration of Auschwitz, which has existed since June 1940, with the Special Construction Administration, formed on October 1, 1941, for the construction of a prisoner-of-war camp for the Waffen SS and Police in Auschwitz. The director of the Central Construction Administration is SS Major Karl Bischoff. It takes over responsibility for new construction and expansion of the camp in Auschwitz and Birkenau and all related matters. It drafts building plans and oversees their execution, using prisoner labor but also employing various construction companies for special jobs. Aside from their own laborers, these companies also employ prisoners from Auschwitz.

APMO, D-AuI-3/a, Folder 17, pp. 289, 292; Franciszek Piper, *Zatrudnienie więźniów KL Auschwitz* (Labor Deployment of Prisoners in Auschwitz), Oświęcim, 1981, pp. 134ff.

80 corpses are sent to the morgue. From the entries in the Morgue Register, it appears that 33 prisoners were probably shot; 18 of them had previously been sent to the Penal Company.

APMO, D-AuI-5/3, Morgue Register, pp. 41–43.

278 deaths are entered in the Death Register of the Russian POWs. The high mortality rate can probably be traced to the activity of the special Gestapo commission from Kattowitz.

NOVEMBER 4

20 prisoners sent by the Sipo and SD from Montelupich Prison in Kraków receive Nos. 22399–22418.

14 reeducation prisoners sent by the Kattowitz Stapo receive Nos. 22419–22432.

69 corpses are sent to the morgue. The bodies of Numbers 11463 and 20463 are assigned for autopsy.*

Ibid., pp. 44–46.

352 deaths are entered in the Death Register of the Russian POWs. These probably include the 300 POWs classified as fanatical Com-

Brandhuber, "Russian POWs," p. 25.

*The autopsy room is in the crematorium. The autopsy is performed by the Czech prisoner Georg Zemanek.

munists by the special Gestapo commission and shot that day in the courtyard of Block 11.

NOVEMBER 5

19 prisoners sent by the Sipo and SD for the Kraków District receive Nos. 22433–22451.

122 deaths are entered in the Death Register of the Russian POWs.

NOVEMBER 6

No. 22452 is given to a reeducation prisoner; Nos. 22453 and 22454 are given to two political prisoners sent by the Kattowitz Stapo.

55 prisoners sent by the Sipo and SD from Montelupich Prison in Kraków receive Nos. 22455–22509.

52 deaths are entered in the Death Register of the Russian POWs.

NOVEMBER 7

23 prisoners sent in a group transport by the Stapo and Kripo from Prague, Breslau, Oppeln, Troppau, and Kattowitz receive Nos. 22510–22532.

140 deaths are entered in the Death Register of the Russian POWs.

56 corpses are sent to the morgue.

APMO, D-AuI-5/3, Morgue Register, pp. 50ff.

NOVEMBER 8

23 prisoners sent in a collective transport by the Stapo and Kripo from Lodz, Tilsit, Zichenau, Königsberg, and Vienna receive Nos. 22533–22555. The transport includes German political and criminal prisoners, Polish and Jewish political prisoners, and one Lithuanian.

41 corpses are sent to the morgue. The entries in the Morgue Register indicate that 13 prisoners were probably shot.

Ibid., p. 52.

85 deaths are entered in the Death Register of the Russian POWs.

NOVEMBER 9

One reeducation prisoner sent by the Kattowitz Stapo receives No. 22556.

91 deaths are entered in the Death Register of the Russian POWs.

NOVEMBER 10

51 corpses are sent to the morgue. Next to the numbers of 13 prisoners is the code "27w."

Ibid., pp. 55–56.

75 deaths are entered in the Death Register of the Russian POWs.

NOVEMBER 11

On the Polish national holiday, the first series executions in Auschwitz using small-caliber weapons fired point-blank at the base of the neck takes place. The executions are performed in the courtyard of Block 11, at the execution wall, also called the death wall. Those condemned to death are led to the wall one by one.* They are naked and their hands are tied behind their backs. Before the execution, the prisoner's number is written on his chest if he is killed with a shot at the base of the neck or on the leg if he is shot by an execution squad. The Commandant, the Camp Commander, and the SS Camp Doctor are present at the execution. The prisoners are shot by Roll Call Leader Gerhard Palitzsch.

APMO, Prisoner Kraków Auschwitz Trial, vol. 55, pp. 102–103, Statement of Former Prisoner Ludwik Banach; D-AuI-3/1a, Bunker Register, pp. 33–40; D-AuI-5/3, Morgue Register, pp. 57ff; Mat.RO, vol. IV, pp. 249–251.

Altogether 151 inmates are shot on this date. They include: 80 Poles who have been sent from Myslowitz (Mysłowice) and put in the bunker of Block 11 until their execution;** the following 27 prisoners, who have been kept in the bunker of Block 11 from October 10 to November 2, 1941, for various offenses:† Franciszek Cichoradzki (No. 17794), Jan Skierniewski (No. 21157), Józef Tomczak (No. 21373), Franciszek Roller (No. 21086), Stanisław Pyza (No. 22259), Stanisław Lipiński (No. 22036), Franciszek Hejkie (No. 21843), Herbert Hildebrandt (No. 20495), Max Sonntag (No. 15097), Jan Tomczyk (No. 16278), Witold Kurpik (No. 17159), Stanisław Bandura (No. 12312), Adam Chwistek (No. 18691), Adam Korzeniowski (No. 16184), Stefan Rutkowski (No. 19359), Teofil Sujecki (No. 18627), Kazimierz Zakowski (No. 3057), Jan Danilowicz (No. 19663), Edward Jakóbek (No. 16543), Stefan Gaszyna (No. 21161), Mieczysław Stolarski (No. 20776), Mieczysław Zieliński (No. 6765), Zbigniew Goliszewski (No. 13496), Otto Domagala (No. 18763), Józef Kula (No. 20021), Mieczysław Hamerski (No. 11820), Antoni Walasik (No. 17126); the following 44 prisoners are listed by the Political Department:‡

*At this time, executions are carried out individually because the executioner has to load his gun after every shot. In 1942, the small-caliber weapon is improved and a cartridge drum for 10 to 15 cartridges is incorporated so that the executioner can fire repeatedly. (APMO, Kraków Auschwitz Trial, vol. 55, p. 103).
**Prisoner Ludwik Banach, employed as a janitor in Block 11 at that time, secretly watches the execution.
†This is probably one of the first selections that were later carried out regularly by the SS camp administration in the bunker of Block 11. During the selection, the prisoners housed in the bunker are condemned to death, sent to the Penal Company, or released into the camp. On November 11, 1941, 33 prisoners are in the bunker. Four are left behind in the bunker, one is sent to the Penal Company, another is released into the camp, and 27 are condemned to be shot to death. After the shooting, the 27 corpses are sent to the morgue and their numbers are entered in the Morgue Register.
‡An illegally made list of names of 44 prisoners shot on November 11, 1941, contains their dates of birth and the addresses of the families. The corpses of these prisoners are taken directly to the crematorium.

Bronisław Ujdak (No. 9141), Józef Lepianka (No. 9152), Piotr Borek (No. 9168), Lech Strusiewicz (No. 9176), Jerzy Walaszcyk (No. 9177), Henryk Brymianowski (No. 9179), Mieczysław Oleś (No. 9188), Eugeniusz Weber (No. 9193), Michał Weber (No. 9195), Jan Górnikowski (No. 9198), Mieczysław Dadal (No. 9202), Jan Ruszel (No. 9203), Julian Blaskowitz (No. 9207), Marian Gremiuch (No. 9209), Tadeusz Lech (No. 9235), Władysław Zarychta (No. 9241), Stefan Przybylo (No. 9251), Józef Moskalik (No. 9255), Stanisław Pittio (No. 9261), Stefan Radyk (No. 9269), Jan Wilczak (No. 9272), Franciszek Zarzeka (No. 9342), Jan Kantor (No. 9363), Franciszek Hrebiczek (No. 9481), Józef Zydek (No. 10776), Antoni Kadernuszka (No. 10788), Jan Jędrzejowski (No. 11508), Stanisław Berek (No. 11512), Zbigniew Butscher (No. 11515), Stanisław Wąsowicz (No. 11516), Kazimierz Sikora (No. 11521), Antoni Marek (No. 11530), Wiktor Koliński (No. 11755), Aleksander Niedziela (No. 11758), Karol Postawa (No. 11761), Stefan Pawlik (No. 11842), Jan Wielebnowski (No. 11978), Czesław Ogłódek (No. 11983), Jan Ogłódek (No. 11984), Julian Mikoś (No. 12035), Witold Pruski (No. 12077), Władysław Żytkowicz (No. 12082), Bronisław Żurek (No. 12089), Ludwik Stankiewicz (No. 12095).

In the afternoon the German political prisoner Oskar Weihs (No. 20964), born December 1, 1918, in Neustadt/Pfalz, escapes. He works on street construction near the railroad station and takes off his camp clothing before the escape. Oskar Weihs is a musician and painter who was sent to the camp on September 18, 1941, by the Sipo and SD in Kraków.

APMO, IZ-8/Gestapo Lodz/3 88/244, 245.

88 deaths are entered in the Death Register of the Russian POWs.

NOVEMBER 12

No. 22557 is given to a political prisoner; Nos. 22558–22571 are given to 14 reeducation prisoners sent by the Kattowitz Stapo.

19 prisoners sent by the Prague Stapo receive Nos. 22572–22590. In the transport are nine Jews, one German, and nine Czechs.

167 deaths are entered in the Death Register of the Russian POWs.

NOVEMBER 13

A political prisoner receives number 22594; Nos. 22591–22593 are assigned to three reeducation prisoners from Teschen sent by the Kattowitz Stapo.

60 prisoners sent by the Sipo and SD from the prison in Lublin receive Nos. 22595–22654.

Three prisoners sent by the Oppeln Stapo receive Nos. 22655–22657.

284 deaths are entered in the Death Register of the Russian POWs.

NOVEMBER 14

78 corpses are sent to the morgue.

APMO, D-AuI-5/3, Morgue Register, pp. 65–67.

27 reeducation prisoners from Bielitz, Beuthen, and Gleiwitz sent by the Kattowitz Stapo receive Nos. 22658–22684.

Two Jewish prisoners sent by the Gestapo from Breslau receive Nos. 22685 and 22686.

No. 22687 is given to a German criminal prisoner sent by the Oppeln Kripo.

14 reeducation prisoners and one asocial prisoner* sent by the Kattowitz Kripo receive Nos. 22688–22701 and 22702.

255 deaths are entered in the Death Register of the Russian POWs.

NOVEMBER 15

Four political prisoners, three Poles and one German, sent from Vienna by the Gestapo, receive Nos. 22703–22706.

Six Yugoslav political prisoners sent by the Graz Stapo receive Nos. 22707–22712.

Seven prisoners sent by the local Krenau police authorities receive Nos. 22713–22719.

55 corpses are sent to the morgue. The entries in the Morgue Register indicate that eight prisoners were probably shot.

Ibid., pp. 68ff.

201 deaths are entered in the Death Register of the Russian POWs. The high mortality rate among these prisoners in November is connected not only with the hard labor of constructing the Birkenau camp, the insufficient food rations and constant torture, but also with the presence of the special Gestapo commission from Kattowitz, which has been active in the camp for about a month.

Brandhuber, "Russian POWs," pp. 21–25.

About 75 Russian POWs are sent from Stalag 308 in Neuhammer.

APMO, D-AuI-3/1–7646, Card Index of the Russian POWs.

The next stage of the German offensive on Moscow begins.

NOVEMBER 16

On Sunday, Holy Mass is held secretly on the first floor of Block 4, in the corner of the hall in a narrow, dark aisle between double-decker beds.

APMO, Accounts, vol. 86, p. 87, Account of Former Prisoner Konrad Szweda, a Clergyman;

*A professional musician.

88 deaths are entered in the Death Register of the Russian POWs.

Konrad Szweda, "Katakumby XX wieku" (Catacombs of the Twentieth Century), in *Gośę Niedzielny* (The Sunday Guest), September 22, 1946.

NOVEMBER 17

97 deaths are entered in the Death Register of the Russian POWs.

NOVEMBER 18

Ten reeducation prisoners sent by the Kattowitz Stapo receive Nos. 22720–22729.

Three prisoners sent by the police authorities in Krenau receive Nos. 22730–22732.

81 deaths are entered in the Death Register of the Russian POWs.

NOVEMBER 19

Five reeducation prisoners sent by the police authorities in Krenau receive Nos. 22733–22737.

81 deaths are entered in the Death Register of the Russian POWs.

Mechanic Mähr of J. A. Topf and Sons comes to Auschwitz to pour the foundations for the third incinerator in the crematorium and to repair the two ovens that are in operation but need servicing. Mähr begins work the day he arrives.

APMO, D-AuI, Docs. ZBL, BW/ 11.

NOVEMBER 20

Because of the work on the foundation of the new third incinerator and the servicing of the two old crematorium ovens, the Commandant of Auschwitz halts the incineration of the corpses in the crematorium and orders that the corpses of inmates and prisoners of war be put in the mass grave in Birkenau.

APMO, D-AuI-1/a FvD, p. 77; Höss, *Commandant in Auschwitz*, p. 161.

One Jewish and one reeducation prisoner sent from Gleiwitz by the Kattowitz Stapo receive Nos. 22738 and 22739.

60 prisoners sent by the Sipo and SD from the prison in Lublin receive Nos. 22740–22799.

157 prisoners sent by the Sipo and SD from Pawiak Prison in Warsaw receive Nos. 22800–22956. During loading in Warsaw there are 174 inmates in the transport; 16 of them have escaped en route.

Domańska, *Pawiak*, pp. 181ff.

140 prisoners sent by the Sipo and SD from Radom receive Nos. 22957–23096.

62 deaths are entered in the Death Register of the Russian POWs.

NOVEMBER 21

Four reeducation prisoners sent from Sosnowitz by the Kattowitz Stapo receive Nos. 23097–23100.

A reeducation prisoner sent by the Stapo from Breslau receives No. 23101.

Seven reeducation prisoners and one criminal sent by the Kattowitz Kripo receive Nos. 23102–23108 and 23109.

Nine prisoners sent in a group transport by the Stapo and Kripo from Prague, Oppeln, Breslau, Stettin, Beuthen, and Gleiwitz receive Nos. 23110–23118.

Seven reeducation prisoners sent from Pless by the Kattowitz Stapo receive Nos. 23119–23125.

54 Czech prisoners sent from Brünn by the Stapo receive Nos. 23126–23178. 21 Jews are in the transport.

82 deaths are entered in the Death Register of the Russian POWs.

NOVEMBER 22

18 prisoners sent from Posen by the Gestapo receive Nos. 23180–23197.

Four prisoners sent from Vienna by the Gestapo receive Nos. 23198–23201. They are two Poles, one Czech, and one Austrian. In the camp the Austrian is marked as an ethnic German with the letter D.

Nine Yugoslavian prisoners sent by the Sipo and SD from Veldes (Bled) receive Nos. 23202–23210.

Three prisoners sent by the Stapo from Linz, Graz, and Troppau receive Nos. 23211–23213.

58 deaths are entered in the Death Register of the Russian POWs.

Polish prisoner Feliks Nakielski (No. 16004) escapes from Auschwitz.

APMO, D-AuI-123, Commandant's Office Order No. 33/41, Dec. 4, 1941.

NOVEMBER 23

The German Panzer Divisions are 16 miles from Moscow, after occupying the cities of Klin and Solnečnogorsk.

On the Soła River, SS men Fritz Rott and Johann Kamphus capture a prisoner who escaped from the camp the day before. They receive a commendation.

Ibid.

88 deaths are entered in the Death Register of the Russian POWs.

NOVEMBER 24

Feliks Nakielski (No. 16004), caught trying to escape the day before, is put in the bunker of Block 11. On December 2, 1941, he is sent to the Penal Company.

APMO, D-AuI-3/1a, Bunker Register, p. 42.

11 reeducation prisoners sent by the Kattowitz Stapo and the police from Ilkenau and Bolesławiec receive Nos. 23214–23224.

51 deaths are entered in the Death Register of the Russian POWs.

NOVEMBER 25

Three reeducation prisoners sent by the Stapo from Bielitz and Oppeln receive Nos. 23225–23227.

Six reeducation prisoners sent by the Kattowitz Kripo receive Nos. 23228–23233.

Four prisoners sent by the Kattowitz Kripo receive Nos. 23234–23237.

42 deaths are entered in the Death Register of the Russian POWs.

NOVEMBER 26

115 prisoners sent by the Sipo and SD from the prison in Radom receive Nos. 23238–23352.

65 deaths are entered in the Death Register of the Russian POWs.

NOVEMBER 27

42 reeducation prisoners sent by the Kattowitz Gestapo receive Nos. 23353–23396.

123 prisoners sent in a group transport by the Stapo and Kripo from Posen, Lodz, Bromberg, Zichenau, Hohensalza, Danzig, Stettin, Graudenz, Tilsit, and Königsberg receive Nos. 23397–23520.

70 prisoners sent by the Sipo and SD from the prison in Lublin receive Nos. 23521–23590.

57 deaths are entered in the Death Register of the Russian POWs.

NOVEMBER 28

Two reeducation prisoners sent by the Stapo from Oppeln and Kattowitz receive Nos. 23591 and 23592.

Nos. 23593–23597 are given to five reeducation prisoners. Two Germans, one asocial and one criminal, sent by the Kattowitz Kripo, are assigned Nos. 23598 and 23599.

24 prisoners sent in a group transport by the Stapo and Kripo from Oppeln, Breslau, Prague, Schwerin, Klagenfurt, Frankfurt an der Oder, and Berlin as well as by the Sipo and SD for the occupied Netherlands in The Hague receive Nos. 23600–23623. The transport includes one Polish prisoner transferred to Auschwitz from Buchenwald and two Dutch political prisoners (Nos. 23610 and 23611).

APMO, D-AuI-2/3, Admissions List, pp. 440ff.

Seven reeducation prisoners sent by the Kattowitz Kripo, the Labor Office in Krenau, and the police in Neu-Dachs (Jaworzno) receive Nos. 23624–23630.

48 deaths are entered in the Death Register of the Russian POWs.

NOVEMBER 29

A reeducation prisoner sent by the Kattowitz Kripo is given No. 23631.

74 deaths are entered in the Death Register of the Russian POWs.

The Inspector of Concentration Camps and the Plenipotentiary for Labor Deployment informs the Commandants of the concentration camps that Russian POWs may be used for work if the need arises. At the meetings of November 10 and 11, 1941, a brief presentation on the number of prisoners and the payment structure was given. In this connection, an order is issued to make the same reports regarding Russian POWs as have been obligatory for other prisoners since October 27, 1941, as follows:

APMO, IZ-13/89, Various Documents of the Third Reich, p. 259.

1. Manpower report (on the first and fifteenth of the month)
2. Transport vouchers
3 The number of skilled laborers
4. Deployment in the camp by profession

At 5:00 P.M., the absence of a prisoner employed in the labor squad in the DAW factory is discovered. The sentry line is reinforced and a search operation is begun. At 6:00 P.M. the search is halted because of darkness.

APMO, D-AuI-1/2a, FvD, p. 86.

NOVEMBER 30

At 8:00 A.M. the SS sentries in the outer sentry line are reinforced. At 10:30 A.M. Henryk Linowski (No. 20384), who escaped the previous day from the DAW labor squad, is captured and sent to the bunker of Block 11. He dies in the bunker on Feburary 17, 1942.

Ibid., p. 87; D-AuI-3/1a, Bunker Register, p. 43.

56 deaths are entered in the Death Register of the Russian POWs.

NOVEMBER 1-30

During the 26 working days in November, the German Railroad transported 33,028 prisoners working on the construction of the Buna factory and their SS guards from Auschwitz and back. The average number of persons transported per day is 1,270.

3,726 Russian POWs have died in Auschwitz, a result of the work of the special commission of the Kattowitz Gestapo, acting on the operational order of June 17, 1941, and of inhuman treatment especially in the construction of the Birkenau camp.*

APMO, D-AuI-5/1, Russian POW Camp Auschwitz, Death Register; Höss Trial, vol. 8, pp. 20, 79, 81.

Numbers of 1,358 prisoners are listed in the Morgue Register who have died of hunger, overwork, illness, torture, shootings, and phenol injections.**

APMO, D-AuI-5/3, Morgue Register, pp. 35-91.

DECEMBER 1

Three reeducation prisoners sent from Teschen by the Kattowitz Stapo receive Nos. 23632-23634.

Five Jewish prisoners sent from Oppeln by the Stapo receive Nos. 23635-23639.

15 reeducation prisoners sent by the Kattowitz Stapo receive Nos. 23640-23654.

A reeducation prisoner sent from Trzynietz (Trinec), Czechoslovakia, by the Gendarmerie receives No. 23655.†

At 8:45 A.M. SS man Thran doing sentry duty on Watchtower C shoots a prisoner who crossed into the forbidden zone alongside the camp fence.

APMO, D-AuI-1/2a, FvD, p. 87.

The prisoner who was shot probably was No. 18360, since next to this number in the Morgue Register appears the note "shot."

APMO, D-ÁuI-5/3, Morgue Register, p. 92.

DECEMBER 2

A reeducation prisoner sent by the Kattowitz Kripo, Saybusch gendarmerie post, receives No. 23656.

DECEMBER 3

J. A. Topf and Sons' mechanic, Mähr, finishes servicing the two crematorium ovens and working on the third oven for incinerating bodies in the crematorium building.

APMO, D-AuI, CCA, BW 11

---

*The number of the dead is based on the entries in the Death Register.
**The number of deaths is based on the entries in the Morgue Register. Not counted in the 1,358 deceased prisoners are the hostages killed and the prisoners who were shot but not previously lodged in the bunker of Block 11.
†In Poland, the Gendarmerie were policemen operating in the countryside on the county level. As Chief of the German Police, Himmler had authority over them in German-occupied Poland.—ED.

Two reeducation prisoners sent by the Kattowitz Kripo from the Janowitz and Jawischowitz Gendarmerie stations receive Nos. 23657 and 23658.

Polish prisoner Jan Kubiak (No. 17806), caught trying to escape, is sent to the bunker of Block 11. He dies in the bunker on February 6, 1942.

APMO, D-AuI-3/1a, Bunker Register, p. 43.

DECEMBER 4

26 reeducation prisoners sent from Bielitz by the Kattowitz Stapo receive Nos. 23659–23684.

Reeducation Prisoner No. 20348, from Bielitz, is sent to the camp a second time. He was sent the first time on September 1, 1941.

Five reeducation prisoners sent by the Labor Office from Krenau receive Nos. 23685–23689.

DECEMBER 5

22 reeducation prisoners sent from Sosnowitz, Gleiwitz, and Beuthen by the Kattowitz Stapo receive Nos. 23690–23708 and 23710, 23727, and 23728.

20 prisoners sent in a group transport by the Stapo and Kripo from Breslau, Köslin, Oppeln, Karlsbad, Reichenberg, Prague, and Kattowitz receive Nos. 23709, 23711–23726 and 23729–23732.

DECEMBER 6

The German offensive is halted at Moscow. Soviet soldiers begin a counteroffensive.

80 prisoners sent in a group transport by the Stapo and Kripo from Bromberg, Allenstein, Königsberg, Graudenz, Stettin, Schneidemühl, Zichenau, and Danzig receive Nos. 23733–23780.

64 prisoners sent from Oppeln by the Gestapo receive Nos. 23781–23844.

Two reeducation prisoners sent from Krenau by the Labor Office receive Nos. 23845 and 23846.

One reeducation prisoner sent by the Labor Office from Krenau receives No. 23847.

13 prisoners sent by the Stapo from Breslau, Vienna, Graz, Prague, and Schneidemühl receive Nos. 23848–23860. Four Yugoslav prisoners are in the transport.

Seven Yugoslav prisoners sent by the Sipo and SD from Veldes receive Nos. 23861–23867.

No. 23868 is assigned to a reeducation prisoner sent by the Gendarmerie in Kęty.

DECEMBER 7

The corpses of 21 prisoners are sent to the morgue. Entries in the Morgue Register show that five, Nos. 23616, 15653, 19374, 21057, and 20254, were killed with phenol injections in Block 19.

APMO, D-AuI-5/3, Morgue Register, p. 99.

Without declaring war, Japanese armed forces attack the largest American naval base, Pearl Harbor.

DECEMBER 8

Japan declares war on the United States, Great Britain, Australia, and Canada.

Two prisoners, Nos. 20815 and 18846, are killed with phenol injections.

Ibid., p. 100.

Three reeducation prisoners sent from Ilkenau by the police authorities receive Nos. 23869–23871.

Five reeducation prisoners sent from Bolesławiec by the police authorities receive Nos. 23872–23876.

The poultry and fish farm begun in the spring on the site of the evacuated village of Harmense, where an outside squad had been working, is one of the first auxiliary camps of Auschwitz to be established; 50 inmates are housed there. The director of the farm is SS Corporal Glaue. An angora rabbit operation is also moved there that was previously located in the vicinity of the camp, in a storage area between farm buildings.*

Anna Zięba, "Die Geflügelfarm Harmense" (Harmense Poultry Farm), *HvA*, no. 11, 1971, pp. 39–42.

DECEMBER 9

35 reeducation prisoners from Kattowitz receive Nos. 23877–23911.

DECEMBER 10

The Concentration Camps Inspectorate instructs camp commandants, including Rudolf Höss, to be ready to fill out report forms to facilitate the work of the doctors' commissions. These commis-

Alexander Mitscherlich, Fred Mielk, eds., *Medizin ohne Menschlichkeit: Dokumente des Nürnberger Ärzteprozesses* (Medicine Without Humanity: Documents of the Nuremberg Doctors' Trials), Frankfurt/Main, 1978, pp. 214ff. (Doc. No. 1151-PS).

---

*The existing barracks within the storage area are outfitted as stalls for horses, cows, sheep, pigs, chickens, and rabbits. The livestock comes from the farms and was formerly the property of the evacuated farmers. It is entrusted to the animal husbandry squad.

sions have been appointed to select prisoners incapable of work in the concentration camps and to subject them to so-called Special Treatment "14 f 13," i.e., "euthanasia."*

18 reeducation prisoners sent by the Kattowitz Stapo receive Nos. 23912–23929.

One criminal and nine reeducation prisoners sent by the Kattowitz Kripo receive Nos. 23930–23939.

Nine prisoners are killed with phenol injections in the prisoners' infirmary. They carry Nos. 22366, 24470, 18853, 20873, 13534, 7966, 22584, 22148, and 20417.

APMO, D-AuI-5/2, Morgue Register, p. 102.

At 4:50 P.M. the absence of a prisoner from the Penal Company is discovered. The sentry line is reinforced and a search operation is begun.

APMO, D-AuI-1/2a, FvD, p. 87.

J. A. Topf and Sons appeals for the third time to the SS Construction Administration with a request for payment for half the sum they are owed on the order (No. 41D 1980/1) they received on September 25, 1941. The costs of constructing one incinerator are 3,650 RM. The company also mentions its letters of November 17 and November 27, 1941.

APMO, D-AuI, CCA, BW 11.

DECEMBER 11

Camp Doctor SS Second Lieutenant Friedrich Entress comes from Gross-Rosen C. C. and assumes the same position in Auschwitz.

Entress does not have a medical degree. Since he wants to continue his surgical education, he helps the prisoner doctors set up an operating room, at this time quite primitive, in Block 21. He often does selections among sick inmates and experiments on those suffering from typhus.

Klodziński, "SS Men of the 'Health Service,' " p. 341.

Jan Olbrycht, "Sprawy zdrowotne w obozie koncentracyjnym w Oświecimiu: Orzeczenie wygłoszone na rozprawie sądowej przed Najwyższym Trybunałem Narodowym w dniu 10 grudnis 1947" (Health Concerns in Auschwitz Concentration Camp: Statements Made During the Trial in the Supreme People's Court on December 10, 1947), P.L., no. 1a (1962): 41; Władysław Fejkiel, "Eksperymenty sanitariatu SS w Oświęcimiu" (Experiments by SS Medical Officers in Auschwitz), in Occupation and Medicine I, p. 41.

At 2:50 A.M., a prisoner is caught next to Gate 21 trying to break through the sentry line. He is locked in the bunker of Block 11. The man is Feliks Nakielski (No. 16004), who has attempted another escape, this time from the Penal Company.** He dies in the bunker on February 7, 1942.

Germany and Italy declare war on the United States.

Two reeducation prisoners sent from Łazy and Porombka (Porąbka) by the Gendarmerie stations receive Nos. 23940 and 23941.

APMO, D-AuI-1/2a, FvD, p. 88; D-AuI-3/1a, Bunker Register, p. 43. [Feliks Nakielski]

*In Auschwitz, no preparations are made in this connection and the committee of physicians is not expected to return. Selections among sick and incapacitated are carried out by individual SS Camp Doctors in the prisoners' infirmary and in the camp.
**Compare entry of November 24, 1941.

288 prisoners sent by the Sipo and SD from Radom receive Nos. 23942–24229.

DECEMBER 12

Two prisoners sent by the Auschwitz police authorities receive Nos. 24230 and 24231.

Eight reeducation prisoners sent by the Kattowitz Stapo and Kripo from Rybnik, Sosnowitz, and Beuthen receive Nos. 24233–24237, 24240, 24242, and 24243.

Three prisoners sent by the Kattowitz Stapo receive Nos. 24232, 24238, and 24239.

One prisoner sent by the Kattowitz Kripo receives No. 24241.

Four Yugoslav prisoners sent by the Graz Stapo receive Nos. 24244–24247.

18 prisoners sent in a group transport by the Stapo from Oppeln, Reichenberg, Dresden, Breslau, Frankfurt/Main, Danzin, Tilsit, and Prague and by the Kripo from Breslau receive Nos. 24248–24265.

102 prisoners, including 99 Jews, sent by the Sipo and SD from the prison in Tarnów receive Nos. 24266–24367.

Two reeducation prisoners sent by the Saybusch police receive Nos. 24368 and 24369.

101 Czech prisoners sent by the Gestapo from Brünn receive Nos. 24370–24470.

DECEMBER 13

One reeducation prisoner sent by the Krenau county prefecture receives No. 24471.

DECEMBER 14

A reeducation prisoner sent by the Teschen county prefecture receives No. 24472.

22 prisoners sent in a group transport by the Stapo from Zichenau, Graudenz, Tilsit, Hohensalza, Posen, and Prague and by the Kripo from Königsberg receive Nos. 24473–24494. The transport includes the Lithuanian diplomat Wenzel Szidzikauskas (No. 24477).

A reeducation prisoner sent from Osiek by the Gendarmerie post receives No. 24495.

DECEMBER 15

23 corpses are sent to the morgue. Next to eight numbers is the code "27w."

APMO, D-AuI-5/3, Morgue Register, p. 107.

The mechanic, Mähr, of J. A. Topf and Sons finishes setting up the third incinerator in Auschwitz.*

APMO, D-AuI, Docs. ZBL, BW 11.

100 prisoners sent by the Sipo and SD from Montelupich Prison in Kraków receive Nos. 24496–24595. There are two Gypsies among them.

Seven reeducation prisoners sent by the Kattowitz Stapo and the Gendarmerie posts in Tschechowitz (Czechowice) and Inwald receive Nos. 24596–24602.

DECEMBER 16

At 4:00 P.M., Polish political prisoner Stanisław Limanowski (No. 22984) of the Buna labor squad escapes from the camp. He was sent to the camp from Radom on November 20, 1941, by the Sipo and SD and worked in the Buna plants in the labor squad of the Schulz company.** The search is unsuccessful.

APMO, IZ-8/Gestapo Lodz/88/248; D-AuI-2a, FvD, p. 94.

DECEMBER 17

Two reeducation prisoners sent by the police authorities in Auschwitz receive Nos. 24603 and 24604.

A reeducation prisoner sent by the guard unit of I.G. Farben's Auschwitz plant receives No. 24605.

11 prisoners sent by the Kattowitz Stapo receive Nos. 24606–24616.

31 political prisoners sent by the Danzig Stapo receive Nos. 24617–24647. There are 29 Poles and two Germans in the transport.

Three reeducation prisoners sent from Krenau by the Labor Office receive Nos. 24648–24650.

Eight Jewish prisoners from the Penal Company die in Block 11.† They had been given Nos. 24203, 24239, 24263, 24270, 24302, 24314, 24567, and 24568.

APMO, D-AuI-5/3, Morgue Register, p. 109.

*This is indicated by the letter of January 8, 1942, from the Central Construction Administration to J. A. Topf and Sons that the bill of December 16, 1941 (No. 2363), for the sum of 3,650 RM, and of December 18, 1941, for the sum of 25,000 RM has been passed on to the comptroller's office of Office II in Berlin.
**I.G. Farben was a cartel with many member companies who pooled capital to erect factories, etc. —ED.
†The Jewish prisoners, sent in "protective custody" by the Sipo and SD from prisons in Kraków, Tarnów, Radom, Warsaw, Lublin, and other places, were selected out of the transport and sent to the Penal Company in Block 11. These prisoners were brought to Auschwitz between December 11 and 15, 1941.

DECEMBER 18

In Block 11, where the Penal Company is housed, 11 Jewish prisoners die. They are Chaim Ackermann (No. 22355), Rubin Opel (No. 22935), Herbert Guttman (No. 23618), Isaak Oppel (No. 24271), Juda Gutwein (No. 24290), Anschel Rausen (No. 24326), Gerson Ring (No. 24333), Richard Spira (No. 24441), Stanisław Borski (No. 24508), Moses Eichenstein (No. 24531), Olmer Rubin (No. 24574). *Ibid., p. 110.*

Two reeducation prisoners sent by the police authorities in Saybusch and Neu-Dachs receive Nos. 24651 and 24652.

96 prisoners sent by the Sipo and SD for the Kraków District receive Nos. 24563–24748.

Two reeducation prisoners sent by the Gendarmerie posts in Porombka and Spytkowitz (Spytkowice) receive Nos. 24749 and 24750.

46 reeducation prisoners sent by the Stapo, Kripo, and Gendarmerie post in the Kattowitz District receive Nos. 24751–24780, 24784–24787, 24790–24795, 24797–24801, and 24811.

15 prisoners sent in a group transport by the Stapo and Kripo from Oppeln, Kattowitz, Breslau, Schwerin, and Frankfurt/Oder receive Nos. 24781–24783, 24788, 24789, 24796, 24802–24810.

55 prisoners sent by the Sipo and SD from the prison in Lublin receive Nos. 24812–24866.

DECEMBER 19

Seven prisoners die in the gravel quarry. They were Nos. 21853, 24319, 24338, 24352, 24353, 24445, and 24616. They were probably shot while working. *Ibid., p. 112.*

DECEMBER 20

Four reeducation prisoners sent by Gendarmeries in Zator, Zwardon, Dziedzice, and Schwarzwaser (Czarna Woda) receive Nos. 24867–24870.

84 prisoners sent by the Gestapo from the prison in Kattowitz receive Nos. 24871–24954.

Five prisoners are shot at the execution wall in the courtyard of Block 11. Their numbers are 24274, 24277, 24554, 24616, and 24734. *Ibid.*

33 corpses are sent to the morgue. Next to 13 numbers is the code "27w." *Ibid.*

20 prisoners sent by the Sipo and SD from Radom receive Nos. 24955–24974.

Kaluga is liberated. During the last battle for Moscow, the German divisions are smashed and driven back 125 to 150 miles from Moscow, where the Russians recapture North Klin and Kalinin. In the battle for Moscow the soldiers of the Red Army hand the German Wehrmacht its first strategic defeat and explode the idea of Blitzkrieg in the East.

DECEMBER 21

Hitler personally takes command of the Army after the resignation of Field Marshal von Brauchitsch on December 19, 1941. Hitler blames him for the failure of the Blitzkrieg against the Soviet Union and for the first defeat of the German Wehrmacht on the Eastern Front.

22 prisoners sent in a group transport by the Stapo of Graz, Linz, Lodz, Prague, Reichenberg, Vienna, and Regensburg receive Nos. 24975–24996. The transport includes 14 Czechs, three Yugoslavs, two Germans, one Pole, and one Jew.

DECEMBER 22

Eight prisoners sent by the police authorities and Gendarmerie posts in Krenau, Auschwitz, Rajcza, and Przyborów receive Nos. 24997–25004.

DECEMBER 23

Six reeducation prisoners sent by the Stapo and Kripo office and the Gendarmerie posts in the Kattowitz District from Nikolai (Nikołów), Kattowitz, Ilkenau, and Pietrzykowice receive Nos. 25005–25010.

One Polish prisoner, a priest sent by the Zichenau Stapo, receives No. 25011.

APMO, D-AuI-2/5, Admissions List, p. 485.

DECEMBER 24

94 deaths are entered in the Death Register of the Russian POWs.

23 prisoner numbers are entered in the Morgue Register.

APMO, D-AuI-5/3, Morgue Register, p. 177.

DECEMBER 25

60 deaths are entered in the Death Register of the Russian POWs.

13 numbers are entered in the Morgue Register.

Ibid., p. 118.

DECEMBER 26

Six reeducation prisoners receive Nos. 25012–25017.

Three prisoners sent in a group transport receive Nos. 25018–25020.

DECEMBER 27

Six reeducation prisoners receive Nos. 25021–25026.

59 prisoners sent by the Sipo and SD from Kraków receive Nos. 25027–25085.

DECEMBER 29

Seven reeducation prisoners receive Nos. 25086–25092.

57 prisoners sent from Kraków by the Sipo and SD receive Nos. 25093–25149. This is the last transport to arrive in Auschwitz in 1941.

DECEMBER 30

At 6:00 P.M. the absence of a prisoner is discovered. As a result, an alert is ordered and the outer sentry line is reinforced. At 8:00 P.M., SS sentries bring Artur Preussing (No. 17112) to a halt between Watchtowers 15 and 16 with three shots and bring him into the camp. He is probably put in the bunker of Block 11, since his corpse is taken to the morgue on the morning of January 1, 1942, from this block.

APMO, D-AuI-1/2a, FvD, p. 108; D-AuI-5/3, Morgue Register, p. 123.

DECEMBER 1–31

During the 25 working days in December, the German Railroad transported 24,626 inmates working on the construction of the Buna factory and the SS men who guard them from the camp and back. The average number transported per day is 986 persons.

APMO, IZ-13/89, Various Documents of the Third Reich, p. 45.

1,912* Russian prisoners of war died at Auschwitz.

APMO, D-AuI-5/1, POW Camp Auschwitz, Death Register, Infirmary.
APMO, D-AuI-5/3, Morgue Register, pp. 92–123.

A total of 673 prisoners' numbers have been entered in the Morgue Register.

The year 1941 is marked by the expansion of Auschwitz Concentration Camp. In the Spring work is begun on adding a second story to 14 one-story buildings, pouring new foundations, and the construction of eight new, one-story blocks for prisoners in the roll-

*The number of the dead is based on the entries in the Death Register of the Russian POWs.

call area. Construction is finished in the first quarter of the next year.

In spring of 1941 the evacuation of the Polish population from the Interest Zone is completed. The agricultural work begun by the farmers before their evacuation is continued, and in this area, which encompasses 2,000 acres, agriculture as well as livestock, poultry, and fish breeding is carried on.

In October 1941, in addition to the admission of approximately 10,000 Russian prisoners of war, the construction of the camp for 100,000 prisoners of war in Birkenau is begun.

Auschwitz Concentration Camp, originally intended as a transit camp for inmates from the prisons of Upper Silesia and the General Government, is transformed into a concentration camp for the extermination of Poles and Russian prisoners of war. It is also a place for indirect extermination, through the inhuman conditions of life and the hard labor, and a place of direct extermination, through mass executions of Polish hostages, Russian POWs, and other prisoners who are killed by phenol injections and Zyklon B gas, a procedure tested on Polish prisoners and Russian POWs. This makes it easy for the Commandant of Auschwitz, Rudolf Höss, to carry out the task turned over to him by the SS Commander in Chief: to prepare for the mass extermination of Jews in his area. Höss chooses Birkenau as a suitable place for this purpose.

In 1941, 17,270 detainees and other prisoners and 9,997 Russian prisoners of war* are brought to Auschwitz. Between May 20, 1941, and December 31, 1941, a total of 35,146 prisoners are housed there. The number of prisoners as of December 31, 1941, is unknown; nevertheless, from later camp documents, it appears that this number could not have exceeded 11,500. Assuming that approximately 3,000 inmates were transferred to other concentration camps, a few hundred were released, and a few succeeded in escaping, we can state that approximately 20,000 prisoners and prisoners of war died that year.

---

*This figure comes from the numbers in the Card Index of Russian prisoners of war. Consecutive numbers in the regular series are assigned to them and tattooed on them during the registration in October 1941.

1 9 4 2

The Commandant of Auschwitz, Rudolf Höss, continues the program ordered by SS Commander in Chief Himmler. In Birkenau, the officially designated prisoner of war camp (Kriegsgefangenenlager—KGL) is built as a separate camp. At the same time, the Commandant begins to set in motion the mass extermination of the Jews. The first transports of several hundred Jews are sent from Upper Silesia by the Kattowitz Stapo and received by the SS at the railroad platform of the camp siding. The people are killed with Zyklon B gas in the morgue, converted for this purpose, of the crematorium. It is later numbered I and is also called the Old Crematorium.

Participants in these killing operations are the new First Protective Custody Commander, SS Captain Hans Aumeier;* Roll Call Leader Gerhard Palitzsch; the Director of the Political Department, SS Second Lieutenant Maximilian Grabner; and the gas specialist, SS Sergeant Adolf Theuer. In the spring, the killing of the Jews is moved to Birkenau. During his first visit to Auschwitz Adolf Eichmann has selected two farmhouses, the so-called "white cottage" and the "red cottage" in Birkenau, where gas chambers, called bunkers, are built. In early spring, Bunker 1 in the "red cottage" begins operations; starting in June, the mass extermination is carried on in the "white cottage," in Bunker 2. The corpses of those killed with gas are taken to mass graves. Primitive and hardly effective, the gas chambers are considered temporary, and by the middle of the year the construction of an extermination center in Birkenau is begun. It is planned to consist of two, later four, large crematoriums with gas chambers and related facilities.

In the spring a women's section is formed in Auschwitz, now officially designated a "main camp." Originally subordinate to the Commandant of Ravensbrück Concentration Camp, in midyear it is transferred to the Commandant of Auschwitz and is moved to Birkenau.

*The previous First Camp Commander, Karl Fritzsch, has been transferred to Flossenbürg C.C.

The pressure from industrial circles, because of the exhaustion of the labor reserves, and the SS's desire to expand some of its operations, suggests to the camp administration the possibility of selling the prisoners' labor to businesses and German enterprises and to set up auxiliary camps in the vicinity of these operations. Thus Auschwitz C.C. seeds auxiliary camps in Golleschau, Jawischowitz, Chełmek, and Monowitz.

The rapid increase in the number of prisoners, and Jews, substantially worsens the living and sanitary conditions in the camp. This deplorable state of affairs leads to the outbreak of a typhus epidemic, which claims masses of victims.

1942 is distinguished by an unusual level of terror. The mass executions of Polish prisoners in the main camp seem to be a kind of retaliation against the defenseless for the struggle of the resistance organization in the General Government of Poland.

JANUARY 1

SS Staff Sergeant Helmut Walter takes over the function of Staff Sergeant in the Commandant's Office.

D-AuI-1, Commandant's Office Order No. 1/42.

JANUARY 2

A prisoner sent from Kattowitz receives No. 25164.

Two reeducation prisoners are given Nos. 25165 and 25166.

18 prisoners sent in a group transport receive Nos. 25167–25184.

JANUARY 2–5

36 reeducation prisoners receive Nos. 25185–25220.

APMO, D-AuI, Docs. ZBL, BW 11.

JANUARY 5

J. A. Topf and Sons appeals again to the Central Construction Administration because of the unpaid balance for a double-muffle incinerator. They write that to their regret, in the matter of payment as per their letters, especially the last one of December 20, 1941, they remain without any news. Therefore, they would like to present once again their request for 3,650 RM, the 50 percent payment due at the time of the order, in accordance with the letter confirming the contract, dated September 25. They close with the hope that they receive payment in the near future and add, Heil Hitler!

JANUARY 6

22 prisoners sent in a group transport receive Nos. 25221–25242.

JANUARY 7

29 reeducation prisoners receive Nos. 25243–25271.

At 4:00 P.M., the absence of a prisoner from the Birkenau labor squad is discovered. The sentry line is reinforced and a search operation is begun.

APMO, D-AuI-1/2a, FvD, p. 125.

JANUARY 8

At 4:00 A.M. the prisoner who escaped from the Birkenau squad is caught and sent to the bunker of Block 11. This is Ryszard Bebel (No. 23062); he dies in the bunker on February 17, 1942.

Ibid., p. 126; D-AuI-3/1, Bunker Register, p. 46.

60 prisoners sent by the Sipo and SD from Kraków receive Nos. 25272–25331.

Three reeducation prisoners are given Nos. 25332–25334.

Four prisoners sent from Kattowitz receive Nos. 25335–25338.

Six reeducation prisoners receive Nos. 25339–25344.

The Central Construction Administration of Auschwitz replies to the letters of December 20, 1941, and January 5, 1942, from J. A. Topf and Sons that the invoices of December 16, 1941 (No. 2363) for the amount of 3,650 RM and of December 18, 1941, for a sum of 25,000 RM have been referred to the comptroller's office of Office II in Berlin.*

APMO, D-AuI, Docs. CCA, BW 11.

JANUARY 9

Three prisoners sent from Kattowitz receive Nos. 25345–25347.

One reeducation prisoner receives No. 25348.

14 prisoners sent in a group transport receive Nos. 25349–25362.

24 reeducation prisoners receive Nos. 25363–25386.

62 prisoners sent by the Sipo and SD from Pawiak Prison in Warsaw receive Nos. 25387–25448.

JANUARY 10

26 prisoners sent by the Sipo and SD from Kraków receive Nos. 25449–25474.

JANUARY 12.

25 prisoners sent by the Sipo and SD from Kraków receive Nos. 25475–25499.

*The sum of 3,650 RM probably represents the advance payment for the assembly, whereas the sum of 25,000 RM is the total price for the double-muffle incinerator installed in the crematorium of Auschwitz in December.

JANUARY 13

21 reeducation prisoners receive Nos. 25500–25520.

Polish political prisoner Mieczysław Mutka escapes Auschwitz Concentration Camp from the agricultural and animal husbandry labor squad in a stolen SS uniform. He was born July 7, 1919, and was sent by the Tarnów external service station field office of the Kraków Sipo and SD.

APMO, IZ-8/Gestapo Lodz/3/8/ 251/252.

25 prisoners sent by the Sipo and SD in Kraków receive Nos. 25521–25545.

JANUARY 14

Five reeducation prisoners are given Nos. 25546–25550.

JANUARY 15

135 prisoners sent by the Gestapo from Prague receive Nos. 25551–25685.

A reeducation prisoner receives No. 25686.

SS Sergeant Ulmer of the office of the Central Construction Administration of Auschwitz creates plans (façade and side) for a new type of crematorium. On the basis of these plans, numbered 936, 937, and 938, the construction of Crematorium II and later of Crematorium III in Birkenau will begin in the summer of 1942.

APMO, D-AuI, Docs. ZBL, POW Camp, BW 30/4, 5, 6.

JANUARY 16

Three prisoners sent from Kattowitz receive Nos. 25687–25689.

18 reeducation prisoners receive Nos. 25690–25707.

12 prisoners sent in a group transport receive Nos. 25708–25719.

At 4:50 P.M., SS Man Stadler, on guard at Watchtower L, shoots a Russian prisoner of war.

APMO, D-AuI-2a, FvD, p. 125.

Four reeducation prisoners receive Nos. 25720–25723.

Six prisoners sent in a group transport receive Nos. 25724–25729.

60 prisoners sent by the Sipo and SD from Pawiak Prison in Warsaw receive Nos. 25730–25789.

Four reeducation prisoners receive Nos. 25790–25793.

81 prisoners sent by the Gestapo from Brünn receive Nos. 25794–25874.

JANUARY 17

A reeducation prisoner receives No. 25875.

Polish prisoner Franciszek Batek (No. 22331), who was locked in the bunker of Block 11 on December 17, 1941, by order of the Political Department, commits suicide there.

APMO, D-AuI-3/1a, Bunker Register, p. 45.

The Political Department ascertains from its documents that political prisoner Antoni Mościński, sent to the camp on December 12, 1941, and assigned No. 24238, has been brought to the camp a second time. His first time was as a reeducation prisoner, and he was given No. 20714. He is now given the first number and his category changes from reeducation to political prisoner. No. 24238 is given to a new arrival.

APMO, D-AuI-2/5, Admissions List, p. 461.

JANUARY 18

Because of a considerable reduction of the number of Russian POWs, Block 22 in the POW camp is once again filled with other prisoners.*

APMO, Accounts, vol. 13, p. 164, Account of Former Prisoner Władysław Siwek.

JANUARY 19

38 prisoners are released from the camp.

A reeducation prisoner receives No. 25876.

SS Captain Hans Aumeier, transfered from Flossenbürg C.C., assumes the post of First Camp Commander in Auschwitz.

AGKBZH, DC-180, p. 2.

The occupancy of the camp at morning roll call is 11,703, including 1,510 Russian prisoners of war. In the course of the day, 14 prisoners, including two reeducation prisoners, and 20 Russian prisoners of war die. 38 prisoners are released from the camp and one is admitted. At evening roll call, the occupancy level is 11,632, including 1,490 Russian POWs.

APMO, D-AuI-3/1/1, Register,** pp. 1–3.

SS Corporal Ulmer of the SS Central Construction Administration of Auschwitz completes the drawings for a new type of cremato-

APMO, D-AuI, Docs. ZBL, POW Camp, BW 30/2.

---

*According to the Bunker Register, Block 22 is a residential block for prisoners after this date.
**The Occupancy Register, kept for the period from January 19 to August 19, 1942, includes the number of prisoners in the camp as of morning roll call, the number admitted during the day, the names and numbers of POWs who die in the camp, the names and numbers of prisoners who die in the camp, the names and numbers of prisoners released from the camp, escaped from the camp, or transferred to other camps (without giving the names of the destinations), and the number of prisoners and POWs at evening roll call.

rium; the draft is numbered 933. In summer 1942, Crematoriums II and III will be built according to these plans.

JANUARY 20

In a villa on Lake Wannsee in Berlin, a secret conference is held under the direction of the Chief of the Sipo and SD, Reinhard Heydrich, on the "Final Solution of the Jewish question." The substance of the meeting has been prepared by SS Lieutenant Colonel Adolf Eichmann. Along with Heydrich, the participants include the head of Office IV (Gestapo) of the RSHA, Heinrich Müller, and the Director of the Jewish Section (IV-B4) of the RSHA, Adolf Eichmann, as well as 13 state secretaries and undersecretaries of the various ministries and government offices and representatives of party authorities. They represent the Reich Ministry for the Occupied Eastern Territories, the Ministry of the Interior responsible for the four-year plan, the Ministry of Justice, the Office of the General Governor, the Foreign Ministry, the Party Chancellery, the Reich Chancellery, the Race and Settlement Administration, the RSHA, the Security Police (Sipo) and the Security Service (SD) in the General Government of Poland and the General District of Latvia, and the Office of the Reich Commissioner of the East.

Heydrich informs the gathering on the course of the measures taken so far concerning the "Final Solution" of the European Jewish question. He repeats that by order of the SS Commander in Chief the emigration of the Jews has been forbidden, and that with the approval of the Führer, instead of emigration, the deportation of the Jews to the East is to begin. In this connection, he notes the importance of practical experience with respect to the impending "Final Solution" of the Jewish question. The "Final Solution" of the European Jewish question concerns approximately 11 million Jews. Heydrich emphasizes that in the course of carrying out the "Final Solution," Europe is to be combed from West to East. In the European countries within the sphere of interest of the Third Reich, the experts of the Foreign Office are to cooperate with the regular officials of the Sipo and SD. The conference works out general guidelines for the cooperation of the separate ministries and offices in the execution of the Final Solution. The code "J" conceals the plan for the total annihilation of the Jews of Europe.*

Helmut Eschwege, ed., *Kennzeichnen J: Bilder, Dokumente, Berichte zur Geschichte der Verbrechen des Hitler faschismus an den deutschen Juden 1944–1945* (The Letter J: Photographs, Documents, Reports on the History of the Crime of Hitler's Fascism Against the German Jews 1944–1945), Eschwege, Berlin, 1966, pp. 225–235.

*The Wannsee Conference is the signal for the beginning of the destruction of the Jews in Auschwitz. Rudolf Höss writes of the Final Solution of the Jewish question in Auschwitz: "I cannot say on what date the extermination of the Jews began. Probably it was in September 1941, but it may not have been until January 1942. The Jews from Upper Silesia were the first to be dealt with. These Jews were arrested by the Kattowitz Stapo unit and taken in transports by train to a siding on the west side of the Auschwitz–Dziedzice stretch of the railroad line, where they were unloaded. So far as I can remember, these transports never consisted of more than 1,000 prisoners. On the platform, the Jews were handed over from the Stapo to a detachment from the camp and were brought by the Protective Custody Commander in two sections to the bunker, as the extermination building was then called. Their luggage was left on the platform, whence it was taken to the sorting area, called Canada, situated between the DAW and the lumber yard" (Höss, *Commandant in Auschwitz*, pp. 208–209).

JANUARY 21

As a result of hunger, hard labor, illness, and torture, 25 prisoners die in Auschwitz, among them 18 Poles (two of them reeducation prisoners), four Jews, two Czechs, and the German political prisoner Walter Miethe (No. 21933). 22 Russian POWs die in the prisoner-of-war camp.

APMO, D-AuI-3/1/1, Occupancy Register, pp. 6ff.

JANUARY 22

24 prisoners sent from Kraków by the Sipo and SD receive Nos. 25939–25952.

14 reeducation prisoners receive Nos. 25939–25952.

As a result of hunger, hard labor, illness, and abuse, 26 prisoners and 27 Russian prisoners of war die in Auschwitz.

Ibid., pp. 7–9.

JANUARY 23

17 prisoners, including nine reeducation prisoners, are transferred.

20 prisoners sent from Kraków by the Sipo and SD receive Nos. 25953–25972.

21 prisoners sent in a group transport receive Nos. 25973–25984 and 25995–26003.

24 reeducation prisoners receive Nos. 25985–25994 and 26004–26017.

As a result of hunger, hard labor, illness, and abuse, 21 prisoners and 24 Russian prisoners of war die in Auschwitz.

Ibid., pp. 9–10.

SS Corporal Ulmer of the SS Central Construction Administration has finished the drawings for the foundations for the new type of crematorium. In the plan (Drawing 932) are two large underground rooms; after the building is completed, one is to serve as a disrobing room, the other as a gas chamber where people will be killed with Zyklon B gas.

APMO, D-AuI, Doc. CCA, POW Camp, BW 30/1.

JANUARY 24

At 2:25 P.M., SS Men Emberger of Watchtower A and Wimmer of Watchtower B shoot a Russian prisoner of war while he is "escaping."

APMO, D-AuI-1/2a, FvD, p. 132.

As a result of hunger, hard labor, illness, and abuse, 33 prisoners and 13 Russian POWs die in Auschwitz; one of them is shot in an escape attempt.

APMO, D-AuI-3/1/1, Occupancy Register, pp. 11–13.

JANUARY 25

On Sunday, as a result of hard labor, illness, and abuse, 18 prisoners and 15 Russian POWs die in Auschwitz.

SS Commander in Chief Himmler informs Concentration Camps Inspector Glücks that in the next few weeks the concentration camp is to face serious tasks and that he will be informed of the details by SS Lieutenant General Oswald Pohl. Since no transports of Russian prisoners of war are expected in the near future, he will be sending 100,000 Jewish men and 50,000 Jewish women evacuated from Germany to the concentration camp within the next four weeks.

APMO, IZ-13/89, Various Documents of the Third Reich, p. 302.

JANUARY 26

As a result of hunger, hard labor, illness, and abuse, 31 prisoners and 10 Russian POWs die in Auschwitz.

APMO, D-AuI-3/1/1, Occupancy Register, pp. 14–18.

The Administrative Director of Auschwitz informs the Gestapo in Lodz that he is sending the sum of 2825.89 RM, the property of 69 inmates who died in the camp. He is adding a list of names and an accounting of the sums of money that belonged to the deceased prisoners.

APMO, IZ-8/Gestapo Lodz/3a/88/648–651.

JANUARY 27

As a result of hunger, hard labor, illness, and abuse, 31 prisoners and 13 Russian POWs die in Auschwitz. The deceased include 24 Poles (six of them reeducation prisoners), five Czechs, one Jew, and one German criminal prisoner.

APMO, D-AuI-3/3/1, Occupancy Register, pp. 16ff.

SS Commander in Chief Himmler sends a teletype message to the Head of Sipo and SD in Berlin, Heydrich, in which he writes that a delegate of Field Marshal Keitel will be visiting him. He has told the Field Marshal that the SS will take the Communists and Jews arrested en bloc in France by the Wehrmacht commander there. On this occasion, he has once again touched on the question raised by the Superior SS and Police Commander in France,* to which the Field Marshal has responded with complete understanding.

APMO, IZ-13/89, Various Documents of the Third Reich, p. 303.

JANUARY 28

As a result of hunger, hard labor, illness, and abuse, 46 prisoners and 14 Russian POWs die in Auschwitz.

APMO, D-AuI-3/1/1, Occupancy Register, pp. 18–21.

38 reeducation prisoners are released from Auschwitz.

JANUARY 29

As a result of hunger, hard labor, illness, and abuse, 34 prisoners and eight Russian POWs die in Auschwitz.

Ibid., pp. 21–23.

*This probably concerns the deportation of the Jews from France.

JANUARY 30

62 prisoners sent by the Sipo and SD from the Kraków District receive Nos. 26018–26079.

141 prisoners sent by the Sipo and SD from the prison in Radom receive Nos. 26080–26220.

21 Poles, including seven reeducation prisoners, are transferred out of Auschwitz.

As a result of hunger, hard labor, illness, and abuse, 29 prisoners and 13 Russian POWs die in Auschwitz.

Ibid., pp. 23–25.

JANUARY 31

68 prisoners sent from Brünn receive Nos. 26221–26288.

As a result of hunger, hard labor, illness, and abuse, 27 prisoners and 10 Russian POWs die in Auschwitz.

Ibid., pp. 23–25.

At evening roll call the occupancy level of Auschwitz is 11,449, including 1,305 Russian POWs.

Ibid., p. 25.

JANUARY 1–31

1,107 Russian POWs have died in Auschwitz.*

APMO, D-AuI-5/1, Russian POW Camp, Auschwitz, Death Register, Infirmary.
APMO, D-AuI-5/3, Morgue Register, pp. 124–156.

A total of 669 prisoner numbers are entered in the Morgue Register; the corpses are taken to the crematorium for incineration.

FEBRUARY 1

The Economic and Administrative Office of the SS (Wirtschafts- und Verwaltungshauptamt—WVHA), one of the 12 main divisions of the Reich SS command structure, is created from the reorganization and linking of three departments: Budget and Buildings (Haushalt und Bauten), Administration and Economy (Verwaltung und Wirschaft), and Administration (Verwaltung).

International Military Tribunal, Nuremberg, Doc. No. NO-495.

26 prisoners sent in a group transport receive Nos. 26289–26314.

As a result of hunger, hard labor, illness, and abuse, 15 prisoners and six Russian POWs die in Auschwitz.

APMO, D-AuI, 3/1/1, Occupancy Register, p. 26.

During the morning roll call, the occupancy level of Auschwitz is 11,472, including 1,305 Russian POWs.

*The death count is calculated on the basis of the entries in the Death Register.

Commandant Höss decides to introduce a special number series for reeducation prisoners. These prisoners' previously received general numbers will be replaced with new numbers, begining with "EH 1." This number series applies not only to current prisoners but also to released or deceased prisoners. 1,137 new numbers are assigned.*

FEBRUARY 2

A prisoner sent from Kattowitz receives No.18160.**

APMO, D-RO/123, Mat.RO, vol. XX (NO-KW-2824).

As a result of hunger, hard labor, illness, and abuse, 35 prisoners and seven Russian POWs die in Auschwitz.

APMO, D-AuI-3/1/1, Occupancy Register, pp. 26ff.

FEBRUARY 3

170 prisoners sent from Pawiak Prison in Warsaw by the Sipo and SD receive Nos. 18161–18175, 18301–18334, 18792–18807, 18888–18892, 19862–19894, 19897–19923, 20005–20009, 20061–20076, 20113–20131.

As a result of hunger, hard labor, illness, and abuse, 35 prisoners and 12 Russian POWs die in Auschwitz.

Ibid., pp. 28–29.

Polish inmate Bogusław von Skrzetuski (No. 23403), born August 12, 1897, is transferred to another camp or prison for further interrogation.

Ibid., p. 30.

FEBRUARY 4

As a result of hunger, hard labor, illness, and abuse, 23 prisoners and five Russian POWs die in Auschwitz.

Ibid., pp. 29–31.

Polish prisoner Tadeusz Kalisiński (No. 26074), born March 28, 1923, is captured while escaping and sent to the bunker of Block 11. He dies in the bunker on February 27, 1942.

APMO, D-AuI-3/1a, Bunker Register, p. 47; D-AuI-5/12, Morgue Register, p. 200.

FEBRUARY 5

A prisoner sent from Kattowitz receives No. 20132.

29 reeducation prisoners are released from the camp.

As a result of hunger, hard labor, illness, and abuse, 41 prisoners die in Auschwitz. They include 34 Poles (including five reeducation prisoners), four Jews, three Czechs, and eight Russian POWs.

APMO, D-AuI-3/1/1, Occupancy Register, pp. 31–36.

*From July 16, 1941, to January 31, 1942, about 1,140 reeducation prisoners are sent to Auschwitz.
**Prisoners sent to the camp in February from various prisons by the Sipo and SD and by the Stapo and Kripo receive numbers from the general series that were formerly assigned to reeducation prisoners. This can be seen from the list of male transports which was made clandestinely in 1944 in Auschwitz.

FEBRUARY 6

Eight prisoners sent in a group transport receive Nos. 20133–20140.

A prisoner sent from Troppau receives No. 20190.

Two prisoners sent from Graz and Berlin receive Nos. 20330 and 20331.

Two Polish inmates are transferred.*   Ibid., p. 36.

As a result of hunger, hard labor, illness, and abuse, 39 prisoners   Ibid., pp. 36–38.
and 18 Russian POWs die in Auschwitz.

FEBRUARY 7

As a result of hunger, hard labor, illness, and abuse, 49 prisoners   Ibid., pp. 38–40.
and 14 Russian POWs die in Auschwitz.

FEBRUARY 8

34 prisoners sent in a group transport receive Nos. 20332–20351
and 20510–20523.

96 Russian prisoners of war are sent from a prisoner-of-war camp   Ibid., p. 43.
to Auschwitz.

As a result of hunger, hard labor, illness, and abuse, 41 prisoners   Ibid., pp. 41ff.
and eight Russian POWs die in Auschwitz.

FEBRUARY 9

As a result of hunger, hard labor, illness, and abuse, 48 prisoners   Ibid., pp. 43–45.
and 25 Russian POWs die in Auschwitz.

FEBRUARY 10

23 prisoners sent from Kraków by the Sipo and SD receive Nos. 20524–20528, 20530–20532, 20686, 20288, 20690–20692, 20694, 20695, 20710–20713, and 20747–20750.

67 prisoners are released from Auschwitz.

Five prisoners are transferred.

*The entry in the Occupancy Register about the transfer of two prisoners is not equivalent to transfer to another camp or being sent back to prison for further interrogation. The entry simply means that two prisoners have departed. It often happens that the transferred prisoner is removed according to a judgment of the police court-martial of the responsible Gestapo office to a place designated for enforcement of the sentence.

As a result of hunger, hard labor, illness, and abuse, 34 prisoners die in Auschwitz, including 26 Poles, four Czechs, three Jews, one Yugoslav, and 13 Russian POWs.

Ibid., pp. 45, 48ff.

FEBRUARY 11

81 prisoners sent from Brünn receive Nos. 20943–20950, 20987–20992, 21008–21011, 21019–21050, 21055, 21117, 21119–21121, 21153, 21154, 21317, 21318, 21326–21328, and 21330–21348.

As a result of hunger, hard labor, illness, and abuse, 22 prisoners and 14 Russian POWs die in Auschwitz.

Ibid., pp. 50ff.

FEBRUARY 12

60 prisoners sent by the Sipo and SD from Pawiak Prison in Warsaw receive Nos. 21349–21361, 21363, 21395–21403, 21475, 21476, 21537–21554, 21782, and 21784–21799.

22 prisoners sent from Kraków by the Sipo and SD receive Nos. 21800–21818 and 21916–21918.

Concentration Camps Inspector Glücks informs the camp commandants of the number of prisoners to be employed in cleaning and maintaining order in the concentration camps, reduced to a maximum of one-tenth the number of able-bodied inmates in the camp.* He emphasizes further that in addition to the allowed tenth of healthy prisoners, certain suitable prisoners could be used for cleaning and clearing up.

Schnabel, *Power Without Morality*, pp. 210ff.

As a result of hunger, hard labor, illness, and abuse, 46 prisoners and 15 Russian POWs die in Auschwitz.

APMO, D-AuI-3/1/1, Occupancy Register, pp. 52ff.

FEBRUARY 13

11 prisoners are transferred.

64 prisoners sent by the Kattowitz Stapo receive Nos. 21919–21930, 22305–22328, 22359–22364, 22388–22393, 22419–22432, 22452, and 22556.

28 prisoners sent in a group transport receive Nos. 22558–22571, 22591–22593, and 22658–22668.

As a result of hunger, hard labor, illness, and abuse, 30 prisoners and 11 Russian POWs die in Auschwitz.

Ibid., pp. 54–56.

*This order is to facilitate the intensified deployment of prisoners in the armaments industry, which the SS plans to expand in the vicinity or on the site of the concentration camps.

The main camp after the liberation in 1945.

FEBRUARY 14

As a result of hunger, hard labor, illness, and abuse, 36 prisoners and seven Russian POWs die in Auschwitz.

Ibid., pp. 56ff.

FEBRUARY 15

The first transport of Jews who have been arrested by the Stapo and destined for death in Auschwitz arrives from Beuthen. They are unloaded on the platform of the camp siding. They have to leave their bags on the platform. The standby squad takes charge of the deportees from the Stapo and leads them to the gas chamber in the camp crematorium. There they are killed with Zyklon B gas.*

Höss, *Commandant in Auschwitz*, p. 160; Pery Broad, "KZ Auschwitz: Erinnerungen eines SS-Mannes der Politischen Abteilung in dem Konzentrationslager Auschwitz" (Memoirs of an SS Man in the Political Department of Auschwitz Concentration Camp), *HvA*, no. 9 (1966): pp. 30ff.

As a result of hunger, hard labor, illness, and abuse, 28 prisoners and nine Russian POWs die in Auschwitz.

APMO, D-AuI-3/1/1, Occupancy Register, pp. 57–59.

*In the first edition of the *Calendar* (*HvA*, no. 3, 1960), it was assumed, according to Höss's memoirs, that the gassing of the Jews of Upper Silesia began at the end of January 1942 and was carried out in Bunker 1 in Birkenau. This change of date to February 15 comes from information attained by Martin Broszat from the International Red Cross Search Service in Arolsen. From the memoirs of Pery Broad, an official of the Political Department in Auschwitz, it appears that the gassing of the Jews was begun in 1942 in the gas chamber of Crematorium I. The corpses of the gassed Jews are also incinerated there. This seems more probable, since burial of the corpses in the meadow near Bunker 1 in Birkenau would have caused great difficulties in the winter months.

FEBRUARY 16

As a result of hunger, hard labor, illness, and abuse, 39 prisoners and one Russian POW die in Auschwitz.

Ibid., pp. 59–60.

FEBRUARY 17

Two prisoners sent from Kattowitz receive nos. 22669 and 22670.

As a result of hunger, hard labor, illness, and abuse, 52 prisoners and 40 Russian POWs die in Auschwitz.

Ibid., pp. 60–63.

FEBRUARY 18

35 reeducation prisoners are released from the camp.

Four Polish prisoners who are doctors are transferred to Lublin (Majdanek) C.C. These are Edward Nowak (No. 447), Romuald Sztoba (No. 10997), Stanisław Wrona-Merski (No. 13842) and Jan Nowak (No. 17380).

APMO, Kraków Auschwitz Trial, vol. 61, p. 161; D-AuI-3/1/1, Occupancy Register, p. 65.

As a result of hunger, hard labor, illness, and abuse, 48 prisoners and 53 Russian POWs die in Auschwitz.

APMO, D-AuI-3/1/1, Occupancy Register, pp. 63, 65–67.

FEBRUARY 19

A prisoner sent from Kattowitz receives No. 22671.

19 Polish prisoners are transferred.

As a result of hunger, hard labor, illness, and abuse, 40 prisoners and 65 Russian POWs die in Auschwitz.

Ibid., pp. 67–70.

FEBRUARY 20

Nine prisoners sent in a group transport are given Nos. 22672–22680.

21 prisoners sent from the prison in Tarnów by the Sipo and SD for the Kraków District receive Nos. 22681–22684, 22688–22701, and 22713–22715.

171 prisoners sent from Radom by the Sipo and SD are assigned Nos. 22716–22737, 22739, 22797–23108, 23119–23125, 23214–23233, 23353–23396, 23591–23597, 23624–23634, and 23640–23686.

23 prisoners are transferred.

As a result of hunger, hard labor, illness, and abuse, 36 prisoners and 36 Russian prisoners of war die in Auschwitz.

Ibid., pp. 71–73.

FEBRUARY 21

24 prisoners sent from the prison in Tarnów by the Sipo and SD for the Kraków District receive Nos. 23687–23708, 23727, and 23728.

113 prisoners sent from Radom by the Sipo and SD receive Nos. 23845–23847, 23868–23929, 23931–23941, 24233–24237, 24240, 24242, 24243, 24368, 24369, 24471, 24472, 24495, 24596–24605, 24648–24652, and 24749–24756.

As a result of hunger, hard labor, illness, and abuse, 37 prisoners and one Russian POW die in Auschwitz.

Ibid., pp. 74ff.

FEBRUARY 22

As a result of hunger, hard labor, illness, and abuse, 36 prisoners and five Russian POWs die in Auschwitz.

Ibid., pp. 76ff.

FEBRUARY 23

24 prisoners sent from Kraków by the Sipo and SD receive Nos. 24757–24780.

As a result of hunger, hard labor, illness, and abuse, 34 prisoners die in Auschwitz Concentration Camp.

Ibid., pp. 78ff.

FEBRUARY 24

67 prisoners sent from Pawiak Prison in Warsaw by the Sipo and SD receive Nos. 24784–24787, 24790–24795, 24798–24801, 24867–24870, 24997–25010, 25012–25017, 25021–25026, 25086–25092, 25150–25163, and 25165.

27 prisoners from Kraków by the Sipo and SD receive Nos. 25166 and 25185–25210.

Five prisoners in the agriculture labor squad are locked in the bunker of Block 11 for maintaining contacts with the civilian population. They are Romuald Krzywosiński (No. 6529), Ignacy Stefanek (No. 14036), Bogusław Ohrt (No. 367), Kazimierz Kluźniak (No. 1544), and Michal Kubiak (No. 15262). All are sent to the Penal Company on February 28.

APMO, D-AuI-3/1, Bunker Register, p. 48.

As a result of hunger, hard labor, illness, and abuse, 42 prisoners and one Russian POW die in Auschwitz.

APMO, D-AuI-3/1/1, Occupancy Register, pp. 79–81.

FEBRUARY 25

26 inmates sent from Kraków by the Sipo and SD receive Nos. 25211–25220 and 25243–25258.

As a result of hunger, hard labor, illness, and abuse, 37 prisoners and three Russian POWs die in Auschwitz.

Ibid., pp. 81ff.

FEBRUARY 26

47 prisoners sent by the Kattowitz Stapo receive Nos. 25259–25271, 25332–25334, 25339–25344, 25348, and 25363–25386.

28 inmates sent from Kraków by the Sipo and SD receive Nos. 25500–25520, 25546–25550, 25686, and 25690.

26 prisoners, including 13 reeducation prisoners, are released from the camp.

Ibid., pp. 83–85.

As a result of hunger, hard labor, illness, and abuse, 34 prisoners and two Russian POWs die in Auschwitz.

FEBRUARY 27

Russian POW No. 9914 is released from the camp.

Ibid., p. 87.

Reeducation Prisoner No. 810 is released from the camp.

30 prisoners sent in a group transport receive Nos. 25691–25707, 25720–25723, and 25875–25879.

A prisoner sent from Oppeln receives No. 25904.

As a result of hunger, hard labor, illness, and abuse, 43 prisoners and one Russian POW die in Auschwitz.

Ibid., pp. 85–87.

FEBRUARY 28

The management of the German Railroad appeals to the Reich Ministry of Transportation to confirm the bill for the conveyance of inmates of Auschwitz and the SS men guarding them to the railroad platform of the I. G. Farben factory in Dwory. The letter states that the Commandant of Auschwitz requisitioned freight cars to transport the inmates and supervisors. The transporting began in July 1941. There was room for 100 inmates in each car. I. G. Farben was told that a monthly bill of lading may not be made without the approval of the Reich Ministry of Transportation. To calculate the costs for conveyance, the number of prisoners and supervisors transported daily is established and the charges are based on the price of a third-class monthly ticket for up to ten kilometers (six miles). Up until the end of December 1941, a total

APMO, IZ-13/98, Various Documents of the Third Reich, pp. 44–46.

of 158,569 trips by inmates and SS men were made. The total cost of the conveyance is therefore 45,636.80 RM.*

As a result of hunger, hard labor, illness, and abuse, 49 prisoners and 35 Russian prisoners of war die in Auschwitz.

APMO, D-AuI-3/1/1, Occupancy Register, pp. 87–89.

On the night of February 28–March 1, 40 Russian POWs die in Auschwitz.

Ibid., p. 90.

FEBRUARY 1–28

455 Russian POWs have died in Auschwitz.

Ibid., pp. 25–90.

1,060 other prisoners have died in Auschwitz.**

Ibid.

MARCH 1

At morning roll call, the camp occupancy level is 11,132, including 945 Russian POWs.

Ibid., p. 90.

On this Sunday, the Russian POW camp is dissolved. The 945 POWs who still remain and some of the inmates of the main camp are transferred to the Birkenau camp, which is still under construction. The two camps, Auschwitz and Birkenau, form one administrative unit. Both camps use the same Occupancy Register. The Death Register of the Russian POWs is discontinued.†

Ibid., p. 91; D-AuI-5/1, Russian POW Camp Auschwitz, Death Register, Infirmary.

27 prisoners die in Auschwitz Concentration Camp.

APMO, D-AuI-3/1/1, Occupancy Register, pp. 90ff.

MARCH 2

The disinfection of the residence blocks, begun in February in the cleared camp of the Russian POWs, is completed. Prisoners are immediately housed in these blocks.††

APMO, D-AuI-5/1, Morgue Register, p. 4.

24 prisoners sent from Kraków by the Sipo and SD receive Nos. 25905–25914 and 25939–25952.

*Monthly transportation costs in 1941 were as follows:

Month	Number Transported	Cost in Reichsmarks
July	3215	906.40
August	28,995	8,236.80
September	34,594	10,146.40
October	34,111	9,680.00
November	33,028	9,680.00
December	24,626	6,987.20

**The mortality rate is based on the entries in the Occupancy Register.
†The last entry in the Death Register is dated February 28, 1942. The 40 prisoners of war who die between February 28 and March 1, probably during the transfer to Birkenau, are not listed.
††From March 2, 1942, Blocks 2, 3, 13, 22a and 23, from which corpses of inmates are brought to the morgue, are specified in the Morgue Register. In earlier entries, the numbers of the blocks occupied by the prisoners of war do not appear.

23 reeducation prisoners are released from the camp.

The transfer of nine prisoners is entered in the Camp Occupancy Register. One of them is Polish political prisoner Edward Rochacz (No. 15838), executed on the same day to carry out the sentence of the Special Police Court in Radom.*

Jewish prisoner Samuel Grünhut (No. 25208), born May 12, 1894, in Tarnów, is lodged in the bunker of Block 11. On the same day, he hangs himself.

APMO, D-AuI-3/1a, Bunker Register, p. 49.

29 prisoners and 35 Russian POWs die in Auschwitz-Birkenau.

APMO, D-AuI-3/1/1, Occupancy Register, pp. 91–94.

MARCH 3

19 prisoners sent from Kraków by the Sipo and SD receive Nos. 25985–25994 and 26004–26012.

Six prisoners sent from Posen receive Nos. 21115 and 26013–26017.

69 prisoners sent in a group transport receive Nos. 26315–26383.

51 prisoners and 39 Russian POWs die in Auschwitz Birkenau.

Ibid., pp. 94–97.

By order of SS Commander in Chief Himmler, the Concentration Camps Inspectorate is incorporated as Branch D into the Economic and Administrative Office (WVHA), formed on February 1, 1942.

APMO, D-RF-3/RSHA/17a, RSHA General Orders, p. 16.

MARCH 4

51 prisoners are released from the camp.

Two prisoners sent from Kattowitz receive Nos. 26384 and 26385.

59 prisoners and 36 Russian POWs die in Auschwitz-Birkenau. Next to the numbers of 18 prisoners whose corpses are sent to the morgue the Corpse Bearer has entered an additional "X," which most likely means death by phenol injection.

APMO, D-AuI-5/1, Morgue Register, pp. 5ff.; D-AuI-3/1/1, Occupancy Register, pp. 97–101.

MARCH 5

27 prisoners sent from the prison in Tarnów by the Sipo and SD receive Nos. 26386–26412.

Two prisoners sent from Kattowitz receive Nos. 26413 and 26414.

60 prisoners and 48 Russian prisoners of war die in Auschwitz-Birkenau. Next to the numbers of eight prisoners whose corpses

APMO, D-AuI-5/1, Morgue Register, pp. 7ff.; D-AuI-3/1/1, Occupancy Register, pp. 102–104.

*According to the property inventory he dies on March 2, 1942. His mother is informed that the sentence of the Special Police Court in Radom was carried out that day. (Correspondence with the family.)

are sent to the morgue the corpse bearer has entered "X," and next to four a cross, " + ." The cross very likely indicates prisoners who were shot.

MARCH 6

73 prisoners sent from Brünn receive Nos. 26415–26487.

Ten prisoners are transferred.

72 prisoners sent in a group transport receive Nos. 26488–26559.

Polish political prisoner Władysław Jaworek (No. 16616), captured while escaping, is put into the bunker of Block 11. He dies there on March 8, 1942.

APMO, D-AuI-3/1a, Bunker Register, p. 50.

65 prisoners and 48 Russian prisoners of war die in Auschwitz-Birkenau. Next to the numbers of 16 prisoners whose corpses are brought to the morgue the corpse bearer has entered an "X." This most likely refers to prisoners selected by SS doctors and killed with phenol injections.

APMO, D-AuI-5/1, Morgue Register, pp. 9ff.; D-AuI-3/1/1, Occupancy Register, pp. 105–107.

MARCH 7

69 prisoners sent from Pawiak Prison in Warsaw by the Sipo and SD receive Nos. 26560–26628.

60 prisoners and 40 Russian POWs die in Auschwitz-Birkenau. Next to numbers of 10 prisoners whose corpses are brought to the morgue the corpse bearer has entered an "X" and next to six a cross, " + ."

APMO, D-AuI-5/1a, Bunker Register, pp. 11ff.; D-AuI-3/1/1, Occupancy Register, pp. 108–111.

MARCH 8

41 prisoners, including 28 Poles, six Jews, six Czechs, German political prisoner Friedrich Kössler (No. 22581), born June 25, 1912, and 36 Russian POWs die in Auschwitz-Birkenau. Next to the numbers of nine prisoners is an "X."

APMO, D-AuI-5/1, Bunker Register, pp. 13ff.; AuI-3/1/1, Occupancy Register, pp. 111–113.

Two Polish political prisoners, Leon Mańczak (No. 26413) and Edward Heller (No. 26414), die in the bunker of Block 11. Both were sent to the camp from Kattowitz on March 5 and put into the bunker of Block 11 the next day.

APMO, D-AuI-3/1a, Bunker Register, pp. 49ff.

After the temporary fence separating the nine blocks of the Russian prisoner-of-war camp from the other blocks is torn down, the construction of a high concrete wall the lengths of Blocks 1 to 10 is begun. Prisoners from the camp workshops are deployed in building the wall. The rumor circulates in the camp that female inmates are to be housed in the separate part.

Kielar, *Anus Mundi*, p. 142; APMO, Accounts, vol. 13, p. 15, Account of Former Prisoner Władysław Siewek.

MARCH 9

28 prisoners sent from Kattowitz by the Stapo receive Nos. 26629–26656.

Eight prisoners are transferred.

44 prisoners die in Auschwitz-Birkenau. Next to numbers of 10 prisoners in the Morgue Register is an "X."

APMO, D-AuI-3/1/1, Occupancy Register, pp. 113–115.

MARCH 10

The railroad department of the Reich Ministry of Transportation authorizes the managers of the German Railroad in Oppeln to make a new calculation of the cost of conveying prisoners and their SS supervisors from Auschwitz to Dwory.

APMO, IZ-13/89, Various Documents of the Third Reich, pp. 45ff.

29 prisoners sent by the Kattowitz Stapo receive Nos. 26657–26685.

24 reeducation prisoners are released from the camp.

47 prisoners die in Auschwitz-Birkenau. Next to the numbers of eight prisoners in the Morgue Register is an "X" and next to four other numbers a cross, "+."

APMO, D-AuI-5/1, Morgue Register, pp. 17ff.; D-AuI-3/1/1, Occupancy Register, pp. 116–119.

MARCH 11

16 prisoners sent in a group transport receive Nos. 26686–26701.

50 prisoners and two Russian prisoners of war die in Auschwitz-Birkenau.

APMO, D-AuI-5/1, Morgue Register, pp. 19ff.; D-AuI-3/1/1, Occupancy Register, pp. 119–121.
APMO, I. G. Farben Weekly Report, p. 114, Report No. 42 of March 9–15, 1942.

Representatives of I. G. Farben visit the camp in Birkenau, which consists of primitive barracks with no equipment other than plank-beds. Although the Russian prisoners of war lodged there make a pitiful impression on them, they declare the camp habitable and set the condition that the POWs must be lodged in this camp if they are to be employed in the I. G. Farben factory.

MARCH 12

Four Jews sent by the Kattowitz Stapo receive Nos. 26702–26705.

30 prisoners, including 29 Poles and the German criminal prisoner Otto Stiel (No. 28), are released from the camp. Otto Stiel was transferred on May 20, 1940, in the first transport to Auschwitz, of 30 criminal prisoners from Sachsenhausen C.C.

APMO, D-AuI-3/1/1, Occupancy Register, pp. 120–121.

Following the order of the SS Commander in Chief, SS Lieutenant Colonel Dr. Joachim Caesar takes over the direction of the Agricultural Department of Auschwitz. He is given a great deal of

APMO, D-AuI-1/78, Commandant's Office Order 5/42.

power; the authority of the Camp Commandant with respect to the Agricultural Department is not determined by the WVHA.

71 prisoners and four Russian prisoners of war die in Auschwitz-Birkenau. Next to three numbers in the Morgue Record is an "X" and next to eight other numbers is a cross, "+."

APMO, D-AuI-3/1/1, Occupancy Register, pp. 121–125.

MARCH 13

62 prisoners sent from Pawiak Prison in Warsaw by the Sipo and SD receive Nos. 26706–26767.

86 prisoners sent in a group transport receive Nos. 26768–26853.

1,200 convalescents and patients whose rapid recovery to the point of being able to work seems questionable are transferred to Birkenau and lodged in Barrack Number 4, later Number 7, the so-called isolation ward of Section B-Ib. The sick are unloaded in the courtyard of the barrack and are beaten to death with rods by SS men. The corpses of the murdered men are brought back to Auschwitz and incinerated in the crematorium.

APMO, Höss Trial, vol. 4, p. 88, Account of Former Prisoner Stefan Wolny; D-AuI-5/2, Morgue Register, pp. 159ff.; D-AuI-5/3, Infirmary Register of Block 28, pp. 485–494; Czesław Ostańkowicz, "Isolation Ward, 'Last' Block," HvA, no. 16 (1978): 159ff.

Seven prisoners, including one reeducation prisoner, are transferred.

48 prisoners and eight Russian POWs die in Auschwitz-Birkenau.

APMO, D-AuI-3/1/1, Occupancy Register, pp. 125, 127.

SS Commander in Chief Himmler visits General Governor of Poland, Hans Frank, in Kraków. Topics touched on include the plans for the area of Zamość as a settlement district for German colonists. The SS Commander in Chief assigns the Higher SS and Police Commander for the General Government, SS General Friedrich Krüger, to take steps so that the settlement operation in the General Government can begin.

Wroński, Chronicle, p. 192.

MARCH 14

32 prisoners and Russian POWs die in Auschwitz-Birkenau.

APMO, D-AuI-3/1/1, Occupancy Register, pp. 127–129.

MARCH 15

On this Sunday, before noon roll call in Birkenau, 131 prisoners are killed by drunken SS men. After noon roll call, an additional 147 prisoners and 103 Russian POWs are tortured to death. In Sick Blocks 20, 21, and 28 in the main camp,* 28 inmates die. Altogether, 306 prisoners die, including 198 Poles, 68 Jews, 20 Czechs, eight Germans, two Yugoslavs, and 103 Russian POWs.**

Ibid., pp. 129–140.

*After the construction of Birkenau, the original camp at Auschwitz was called the main camp.
**Drunken SS men carried out such operations in Birkenau on a few of the following Sundays. The carts on which food was conveyed from the main camp to Birkenau returned loaded with the corpses of the murdered men.

The I. G. Farben plant in Auschwitz, where synthetic rubber and gasoline would be produced.

MARCH 16

Following Himmler's order of March 3, the Concentration Camps Inspectorate is incorporated into the WVHA formed on February 1, 1942, where it continues its activities as Branch D and is still directed by SS Lieutenant General Glücks. Branch D consists of the following offices:

APMO, D-RF-3/RSHA/117a, p. 16, RSHA General Orders.

D-I: The central office, responsible for matters concerning prisoners, communications, camp security, sentry duty, motor vehicles, weapons, and training of the SS; the director of this office is SS Lieutenant Colonel Arthur Liebehenschel.

D-II: Is responsible for the deployment of prisoner labor; the director of this office is SS Colonel Gerhard Maurer.

D-III: Is responsible for sanitation and hygiene in the camps; the director of this office is SS Colonel Dr. Enno Lolling.

D-IV: Is responsible for the administration of the concentration camps; the director of this office is SS Major Willi Burger.

During a meeting with the office director for the Ministry of Armaments and Munitions, Karl Otto Saur, a memorandum is made noting that on the basis of a discussion in the Führer's headquarters, the concentration camps are to be deployed to a great extent in the armaments industry. Further, a large influx of prisoners is expected at the end of the month. Craftsmen and those of related professions

APMO, Pohl Trial, vol. 11, pp. 168ff. (NO-569).

will be classified and assigned to the camps that take over munitions production.

18 prisoner numbers are entered in the Morgue Register of the main camp. Next to two numbers is a cross.

APMO, D-AuI-5/1, Morgue Register, p. 27.

MARCH 17

23 reeducation prisoners are released from the camp.

69 prisoners sent in a group transport receive Nos. 26855–26922.

As a result of the conditions in the camp and the various forms of extermination, 111 prisoners die, 22 of them in the main camp: 77 Poles, 17 Czechs, 13 Jews, two Germans, one Lithuanian, and one stateless prisoner.

APMO, D-AuI-3/1/1, Occupancy Register, pp. 142–147.

MARCH 18

Two Jewish prisoners, Robert Mangel (No. 25262) and Marek Libermann (No. 25263), are transferred.* They were sent to Auschwitz by the Kattowitz Stapo on February 26, 1942.

Ibid., p. 148.

As a result of the conditions in the camp and the various forms of extermination, 117 prisoners and seven Russian POWs die in Auschwitz-Birkenau: 70 Poles, 34 Jews, 10 Czechs, and three Germans.

Ibid., pp. 147–152.

MARCH 19

64 Polish prisoners and one reeducation prisoner are released.

Ibid., pp. 152–155.

Six prisoners, three Poles and three Jews, are transferred.

48 prisoners and three Russian POWs die in Auschwitz-Birkenau.

Ibid., pp. 155–157.

144 women are sent from the prison in Myslowitz. They are taken to Block 27, the dressing rooms. Then they are brought to Block 11, where Camp Commander Aumeier, Roll Call Leader Palitzsch, and an official of the Political Department also go. The women are shot in the courtyard of Block 11 at the execution wall. Before the execution, the women must strip naked. The executions are witnessed by corpse bearers Eugeniusz Obojski and Teofil Banasiuk, who are taken to the courtyard of Block 11 to carry away the corpses.**

APMO, Accounts, vol. 13, p. 165, Account of Former Prisoner Władysław Siwek; Kielar, *Anus Mundi*, pp. 123–125.

*The destination is unknown. Perhaps they are taken by the Gestapo in connection with a current investigation.
**This execution makes a strong impression on the prisoners, since this is the first time the prisoners deployed in the camp and working on the construction of the concrete wall have seen such a large group of women in the camp.

MARCH 20

Gas chambers are put into operation in a farmhouse in Birkenau renovated for this purpose; this is the so-called Bunker Number 1. The house is in the northwest corner of the later Section B-III in Birkenau. The transport of Polish Jews sent by the Gestapo from Upper Silesia are taken from the unloading platform at the freight depot in Auschwitz directly to the gas chambers or taken without undergoing a selection. The corpses of the murdered people are buried in mass graves in the nearby meadow.* After each operation, the prisoners used in the burial are killed in the prisoners' infirmary with a phenol injection. Although the SS men responsible for the operations are sworn to strict secrecy, these operations become known to many prisoners.**

State Auschwitz Museum (SAM), *KL Auschwitz in den Augen der SS* (Auschwitz in the Eyes of the SS: Höss, Broad, Kremer), Oświęcim, 1973, pp. 93, 110ff., 173, 179.

126 prisoners sent in a group transport receive Nos. 26923–27048.

14 prisoners, including six reeducation prisoners, are transferred.

12 Jewish prisoners sent by the Kattowitz Stapo to Auschwitz on March 13, 1942, are transferred.

51 prisoners and four Russian prisoners of war die in Auschwitz-Birkenau.

APMO, D-AuI-3/1/2, Occupancy Register, pp. 157–159.

MARCH 21

A prisoner sent from Vienna receives No. 27049.

Ibid., pp. 160–165.

116 prisoners and six Russian POWs die in Auschwitz-Birkenau: 80 Poles, 18 Czechs, 10 Jews, and eight Germans.

---

*Höss talks twice about the beginning of the extermination operation of the Jews from Upper Silesia, giving different dates: December 1941 or January 1942 and spring 1942. The extermination of the Jews was probably begun on February 15, 1942. At first the Jews are killed by gas in Crematorium 1 in Auschwitz. The process is described in detail by Pery Broad. In spring 1942, the killing by gas is carried out also in Birkenau, in Bunker 1, after gas chambers are erected there. Höss's descriptions of the course of extermination of the Jews of Upper Silesia refers to the gas chamber in Bunker 1; the killing could have taken place there by the spring since it would have been possible to bury corpses in the meadow near the bunker.

**In his memoirs, former prisoner Wiesław Kielar writes: "In spring—always at night—came transports of Jews, which were not brought into the camp but to a farm in the woods of Birkenau. The house there was arranged so that a large number of people could be killed there at the same time. They were taken over a siding of the Auschwitz railroad. After a transport was gassed in the gas chamber of the harmless-looking farmhouse, a small group of young, strong Jews, perhaps 20 men, who remained alive, had to take the corpses of their fellow sufferers out of the gas chambers and bury them in pits in a meadow next to the house. When the traces of the crime were thus removed, the men were brought to us in the infirmary and stood in a line in front of the clinic. . . . The Jews were told that after the exhausting work, they were to get strengthening injections. They were at the infirmary, that couldn't rouse any mistrust.

"Klehr, in a white doctor's smock, received them individually in his 'treatment room,' where he carefully locked the door behind every patient. At the same time, Obojski and Teofil [the corpse bearers—D.C.] entered the room, put the 'sleeping' patient on the stretcher, covered him with a blanket and carried him inside the block" (Kielar, *Anus Mundi*, p. 118).

MARCH 22

On this Sunday, drunken SS men abuse the prisoners in Birkenau so that before the noon roll call 106 prisoners die and between noon roll call and morning roll call the next day, another 97 die of exhaustion. Altogether, 219 prisoners and five Russian POWs lose their lives in the main camp and in Birkenau.

Ibid., pp. 165–172; Ostańko-wicz, "Isolation Ward," pp. 163–166.

MARCH 23

52 prisoners sent from Kraków by the Sipo and SD receive Nos. 27050–27101.

18 prisoners sent by the Kattowitz Stapo receive Nos. 27102–27119.

Jewish prisoner Chaim Rosenbaum (No. 26961) is transferred.

APMO, D-AuI-3/1/2, Occupancy Register, p. 173.

As a result of the massacres of the SS men the day before, another 103 prisoners and 24 Russian prisoners of war lose their lives.

The corpses of 18 prisoners are taken from the prisoners' infirmary blocks to the morgue; 14 of them probably have been killed with phenol injections.

APMO, D-AuI-5/1, Morgue Register, p. 34.

MARCH 24

50 Jewish prisoners sent from the ghetto in Kraków by the Sipo and SD receive Nos. 27120–27169.

34 prisoners die in Auschwitz-Birkenau.

APMO, D-AuI-3/1/2, Occupancy Register, pp. 178ff.

MARCH 25

48 prisoners sent from Kraków by the Sipo and SD receive Nos. 27170–27217.

Five prisoners sent in a group transport receive Nos. 27218–27222.

46 prisoners and seven Russian POWs die in Auschwitz-Birkenau.

Ibid., pp. 180ff.

MARCH 26

The Head of the Sipo and SD Heydrich instructs Reich Marshal Hermann Göring, responsible for the Four-Year Plan, that Russian POWs taken during the expected spring offensive are to be used for labor.*

APMO, D-RF-3-RSHA118/6, p. 442, RKPA Edicts.

*The changed attitude of the German authorities concerning the treatment of Russian POWs has to do with the economic bottleneck caused by the conscription of soldiers. Between May 1939 and May 1942, the number of employed decreases from 39.4 million to 35.5 million.

12 reeducation prisoners are released from the camp.

60 prisoners sent from Kraków by the Sipo and SD receive Nos. 27224–27283.

A prisoner from Oppeln receives No. 27284.

The first transport of female prisoners is transferred from Ravensbrück to Auschwitz. They are the first prisoners in the women's section, subordinate to the Commandant of Ravensbrück for the time being. In the transport are 999 German women classified as asocial, criminal, and a few as political prisoners. They receive Nos. 1–999 and are lodged in the part of the main camp separated by the wall along Blocks 1 to 10. German criminal and asocial female prisoners, the founders of the women's camp as it were, are to take over the functions of Block Seniors and capos.* The director of the camp is SS Chief Supervisor** Johanna Langefeldt.†

999 Jewish women from Poprad in Slovakia are sent to the women's section of Auschwitz. This is the first registered transport sent to the camp by Section IV-B4†† of the RSHA. The director of Section IV-B 4, responsible for Jewish affairs, is SS First Lieutenant Adolf Eichmann. The Jewish women get the uniforms that belonged to the murdered Russian POWs.

APMO, D-RO/123, List of Female Transports to Auschwitz, vol. 20. The list contains, in German: Arrival dates of the transports, numbers issued, and the name of the place the transport came from. It includes female prisoners Nos. 1–75697 for the period March 26, 1942 to February 26, 1944. The list is made clandestinely by prisoners employed in the Admissions Office of the Political Department, using the arrivals list of women sent to Auschwitz-Birkenau. It is secretly smuggled out of the camp in 1944. This document (numbered NOKW-2824 at Nuremberg) forms the major source of information on all women's transports and will not be cited in further entries. APMO, Höss Trial, vol. 4, pp. 104, 106, 130; vol. 16, p. 53.

**In his memoirs, Höss judges them very negatively. He writes: "The 'green' [i.e., criminal] female prisoners were of a special sort. I believe that Ravensbrück was combed through to find the 'best' for Auschwitz. They far surpassed their male equivalents in toughness, squalor, vindictiveness, and depravity. Most were prostitutes with many convictions, and some were truly repulsive creatures. Needless to say, these dreadful women gave full vent to their evil desires on the prisoners under them, which was unavoidable. The Reichsführer SS regarded them as particularly suitable to act as Capos over the Jewish women, when he visited Auschwitz in 1942." (Höss, *Commandant in Auschwitz*, p. 149.)
**The function of SS Head Supervisor is equivalent to Camp Commander in the men's camp.
†Rudolf Höss judges the female SS Head Supervisor just as negatively. He writes in his autobiography: "The female Head Supervisor of the period, Frau Langefeldt, was in no way capable of coping with the situation, yet she refused to accept any instructions given her by the Protective Custody Commander. . . . Hardly a day passed without discrepancies in the prisoner totals. The Supervisors ran hither and thither in all this confusion like a lot of flustered hens. . . . When the Reichsführer SS visited the camp in July 1942 I reported all this to him, in the presence of the female Head Supervisor, and I told him that Frau Langefeldt was and always would be completely incapable of commanding and organizing the women's camp at Auschwitz as this should be done. I requested that she be once again subordinated to the First Protective Custody Commander. The Reichsführer SS absolutely refused to allow this. . . . As was only to be expected, the morals of these women were, almost without exception, extremely low. Many of them appeared before the SS tribunal charged with theft in connection with Operation Reinhard [the code name given to the operation of collecting and processing the clothing, valuables and other belongings, including gold fillings from teeth and women's hair, taken from the slaughtered Jews—D.C.]. But these were only the few who happened to be caught. In spite of the most fearful punishments, stealing went on, and the supervisors continued to use the prisoners as go-betweens for this purpose" (Höss, *Commandant in Auschwitz*, pp. 149, 152, 153–154).
††Until July 1942, transports sent to Auschwitz by the RSHA did not undergo any additional selection, since this was already done when the transport was assembled. Young, healthy people are sent in these transports.

SS Staff Sergeant Willi Gehring takes over as supervisor of Commandant's Office arrests in Block 11.* Previously he worked in the camp administration. Prisoners sent to the block are those who have been sentenced to arrest by the SS authorities, for example, those suspected of illegal contacts with civilians or of planning an escape, or those caught while escaping.

APMO, D-AuI-1/3, Commandant's Office Order 6/42.

Seven Polish inmates are transferred out of the camp. These are Konstanty Borowski (No. 21802), Aleksander Kiciński (No. 21808), Jan Kleszek (No. 21810), Józef Kuniec (No. 21812), Wojciech Salitra (No. 21816), Stanisław Balowski (No. 25954) and Stanisław Ruskiewicz (No. 25964).

APMO, D-AuI-3/1/2, Occupancy Register, pp. 183ff.

Commandant Rudolf Höss informs the responsible departments, i.e., the personal staff of the SS-Commander-in-Chief, the WVHA, the Reich Criminal Police Headquarters (Reich Kriminalpolizeiamt—RKPA), the Gestapo, Kripo headquarters as well as the border police commissioner that a female prisoner escaped in the night of March 25–26 from a transport of 1,000 prisoners from Ravensbrück. The prisoner is Elfriede Martens, who succeeded in escaping in the area of Oppeln; she was wearing the typical, striped camp clothing.

APMO, IZ-8/Gestapo Lodz/88/15,2, Telegram About the Escape.

113 prisoners and seven Russian prisoners of war die in Auschwitz-Birkenau.

APMO, D-AuI-3/1/2, Occupancy Register, pp. 182–187.

MARCH 27

In a supplementary telegram to the departments concerned with escapes, it is stated that the escaped Elfriede Martens, born February 7, 1908, in Düsseldorf, was sent to Ravensbrück on August 16, 1941, for subversive activity. In addition to German, she speaks French, English, and Dutch. Her father, Gottfried Schüller, lives in Munich.

APMO, IZ-8/Gestapo Lodz/88/15,2, Telegram About the Escape.

20 prisoners sent in a group transport receive Nos. 27285–27304.

55 prisoners sent from Kraków by the Sipo and SD receive Nos. 27305–27359.

A prisoner is given No. 27360.

15 prisoners including four reeducation prisoners are transferred.

39 prisoners and six Russian prisoners of war die in Auschwitz-Birkenau.

APMO, D-AuI-3/1/2, Occupancy Register, pp. 187–189.

By order of the Political Department, Polish prisoner Józef Dusza (No. 26698) is locked in the bunker of Block 11. He is shot on April 7, 1942.

APMO, D-AuI-3/1a, Bunker Register, p. 52.

*The Arrest Supervisor participates in the executions in the courtyard of Block 11.

Because of the appearance of a case of typhus in the Birkenau camp, a disinfection is ordered there. There is no water in the primitive barracks; the floors consist of stamped clay. Under these conditions, it is impossible for the prisoners to take care of personal hygiene and lice increase. For the disinfection, the prisoners in the isolation block have to submerge naked in a tub and a vat of lysol solution placed in the courtyard especially for this procedure.*

Ostańkowicz, "Isolation Ward," pp. 168ff.

MARCH 28

A prisoner is given No. 27223.

55 prisoners sent by the Sipo and SD from the prison in Tarnów receive Nos. 27361–27415.

61 prisoners sent by the Sipo and SD from Radom receive Nos. 27416–27476.

798 Jewish women from Brünn, sent by the RSHA, receive Nos. 1999–2796.

63 prisoners die in Auschwitz-Birkenau.

APMO, D-AuI-3/1/2, Occupancy Register, pp. 189–192.

In the night, political prisoner Franz Doschek (No. 18271) escapes from the work group for the officers' mess in an SS uniform on a stolen bicycle. He was imprisoned on June 6, 1935, in Hirschberg (Jelenia Góra) for subversive activity and sentenced to six years of prison. He was sent to Auschwitz by the Leignitz Stapo on July 18, 1941.

APMO, IZ-8/Gestapo Lodz/3/88, pp. 254–256; D-AuI-3/1/2, Occupancy Register, p. 198.

MARCH 29

On this Sunday, 151 prisoners die in Auschwitz-Birkenau. In Birkenau alone, SS men murder 133 prisoners and 26 Russian POWs. Among those murdered are 121 Poles, 13 Czechs, 11 Jews, and six Germans.**

APMO, D-AuI-3/1/2, Occupancy Register, pp. 192–198.

The total number of male prisoners who have died so far in the camp is 11,025.

APMO, Höss Trial, vol. 4, p. 82, Account of Former Prisoner Wilibald Pajak.†

MARCH 30

Three Polish prisoners are transferred out of the camp. They are Mirosław Radwan-Przypkowski (No. 13110), Jan Goździk (No. 22011), and Bolesław Sochański (No. 22014).

APMO, D-AuI-3/1/2, Occupancy Register, p. 198.

---

*The lice are not rendered harmless by these measures and the spreading typhoid epidemic is not checked. On the contrary, the "bath" accelerates the high mortality rate among the prisoners in Birkenau.
**The figures refer to the mortality rate of the male prisoners in Auschwitz-Birkenau. The documents on the women's camp are destroyed by the SS in the evacuation of the camp in January 1945.
†Prisoner Wilibald Pajak is employed in the Political Department in the "Death Section."

56 prisoners sent by the Sipo and SD from Kraków receive Nos. 27477–27532.

1,112 Jews sent in a transport of the RSHA from the Compiègne camp in France receive Nos. 27533–28644. They come from various European countries and were arrested in Paris on May 14, August 20, and December 12, 1941. Some were kept in the Drancy camp and others in Compiègne. This is the first mass transport of Jews from France who enter Auschwitz and are not subject to any selection.*

APMO, Höss Trial, vol. 1, pp. 3–28, Account of Former Prisoner Stanisław Jankowski, aka Alter Feinsilber.

95 prisoners in Birkenau and 12 prisoners in the main camp die.

APMO, D-AuI-3/1/2, Occupancy Register, pp. 198–203.

MARCH 31

Office D-I of the WVHA instructs the Commandants of concentration camps to introduce a work day of at least 11 hours. A lesser labor deployment can be allowed only in case of required security measures.

APMO, Kraków Auschwitz Trial, vol. 49, p. 196.

The Commandant of Auschwitz informs the WVHA and other responsible offices that prisoner Elfried Martens, who escaped from a transport on March 26, has been captured in Munich.

APMO, IZ-8/Gestapo Lodz/2/88/18.

63 prisoners and 34 Russian POWs die in Auschwitz-Birkenau.

APMO, D-AuI-3/1/2, Occupancy Register, pp. 203–206.

A prisoner sent from Kattowitz receives No. 28645.

MARCH 1–31

580 Russian POWs have died in Auschwitz-Birkenau.**

Ibid., pp. 90–206.

411 reeducation prisoners are sent to Auschwitz-Birkenau.†

As a result of the conditions prevailing in the camp and the various forms of extermination, 2,397 prisoners, including 73 reeducation prisoners, die in Auschwitz-Birkenau.††

Ibid.

APRIL 1

48 prisoners are released from the camp.

---

*According to the prisoner Alter Feinsilber, a member of the Special Squad who goes under the name Stanisław Jankowski, there are 1,118 prisoners in this transport. On the trip, which lasts a few days, they receive nothing to drink. A few die. (Serge Klarsfeld, *Memorial to the Jews Deported from France 1942–1944*, New York, 1983. All previous statements concerning the transports of Jews sent to Auschwitz from France by the RSHA are compared with and corrected according to details in Serge Klarsfeld's work.)
**The number of dead is calculated on the basis of entries in the Occupancy Register.
†The number comes from the difference between the assigned numbers between 25905 and 28645 and the total number of prisoners sent to the camp, who are listed in the Occupancy Register.
††The number of deaths is calculated on the basis of the entries in the Occupancy Register. The number of female prisoners who died at this time is not known.

15 prisoners sent in a group transport receive Nos. 28646–28660.

At morning roll call the occupancy level in the men's camp of Auschwitz-Birkenau is 10,629, including 365 Russian POWs.

Ibid., p. 206.

78 prisoners sent from Brünn receive Nos. 28661–28738.

72 prisoners and 19 Russian POWs die in Auschwitz-Birkenau.

Ibid., pp. 208–211.

APRIL 2

The head of the Central Construction Administration, Karl Bischoff, answers the letter of J. A. Topf and Sons of March 12, 1942, concerning the installation of the ventilation and exhaust systems for the planned crematorium at Birkenau. He writes that the desired direction of the ventilation and exhaust canals is marked on the plans. He requests that in carrying out or modifying the project the duct and drain plans shown in Drawing D be adhered to. Roof ventilation and exhaust is to be in the form of a walled chimney. Because of the urgency of the building project, a quick settlement is requested.

APMO, Docs. CCA, BW 11/1.

Five IBV prisoners, members of the sect of International Bible Researchers (Internationale Bibelforschungvereinigung), are transferred out of the camp.

15 Russian POWs are sent to the camp.

30 prisoners sent from Kraków by the Sipo and SD receive Nos. 28739–28768.

A prisoner receives No. 28769.

Two prisoners sent from Oppeln receive Nos. 28770 and 28771.

965 Jewish women sent by the RSHA receive Nos. 2797–3761.

35 prisoners and 13 Russian POWs die in Auschwitz.

APMO, D-AuI-3/1/2, Occupancy Register, pp. 211–213.

APRIL 3

27 reeducation prisoners are released from the camp.

15 reeducation prisoners are transferred to another camp.

30 prisoners sent from Kraków by the Sipo and SD receive Nos. 28772–28801.

12 prisoners sent in a group transport receive Nos. 28802–28813.

One female prisoner sent from Munich receives No. 3762.

997 Jewish women sent by the RSHA from Slovakia receive Nos. 3763–3812 and 3814–4760.

On Good Friday, 11 Polish prisoners are shot at the execution wall of Block 11. They are Marian Bienek (No. 11395), Jan Murek (No. 11754), Władysław Sobas (No. 11871), Bronisław Jaron (No. 11877), August Lewkowicz (No. 11889), Zdzisław Gdowski (No. 11892), Michał Marciniak (No. 11894), Zygfryd Małyszczyk (No. 11895), Bogumił Tuss (No. 12033), Franciszek Łopatecki (No. 21201), and Stanisław Sobon (No. 23015).

Ibid., pp. 216ff.

13 Russian POWs and 58 prisoners, 11 of whom have been shot, die in Auschwitz-Birkenau.

Ibid., pp. 213–217.

APRIL 4

A reeducation prisoner is released from the camp.

Branch D of the WVHA informs the Commandants of the concentration camps of the order of the SS Commander in Chief that the aggravated punishment of flogging has to take place on the bare buttocks of both male and female inmates.

Schnabel, *Power Without Morality*, p. 190.

27 prisoners in the main camp and 41 in Birkenau Camp, a total of 68, lose their lives.

APMO, D-AuI-3/1/2, Occupancy Register, pp. 217–220.

APRIL 5

On Easter Sunday, 89 prisoners and 31 Russian prisoners of war die in Auschwitz-Birkenau.

Ibid., pp. 220–224.

APRIL 6

44 prisoners die in Auschwitz-Birkenau.

Ibid., pp. 224–226.

APRIL 7

51 prisoners and seven Russian POWs die in Auschwitz-Birkenau.

Ibid., pp. 226–228.

Three prisoners are sent from Birkenau to the bunker of Block 11. They are Aleksander Buczyński* (No. 12754), Stanisław Stachańczyk (No. 641) and Józef Chaszewski (No. 1367). On May 18, they are released from the bunker and put in the Penal Company.

APMO, D-AuI-3/1a, Bunker Register, p. 56.

APRIL 8

45 prisoners and four Russian POWs die in Auschwitz-Birkenau.

APMO, D-AuI-3/1/2, Occupancy Register, pp. 228–230.

*On June 16 Aleksander Buczyński tries to escape from the Penal Company. He is captured while escaping and locked in the bunker once again. He dies there on July 14, 1942.

APRIL 9

51 prisoners sent in a group transport receive Nos. 28814–28864.

43 prisoners and four Russian POWs die in Auschwitz-Birkenau.   Ibid., pp. 230–232.

APRIL 10

Nine prisoners, including seven reeducation prisoners, are transferred to other camps.

35 prisoners sent in a group transport receive Nos. 28865–28899.

47 prisoners and six Russian POWs die in Auschwitz-Birkenau.   Ibid., pp. 232–234.

APRIL 11

Three prisoners sent from Kattowitz receive Nos. 28900–28902.

Two Polish prisoners, Wiktor Bartosz (No. 24872) and Edward Litwicki (No. 28883), are transferred.

47 prisoners die in Auschwitz-Birkenau.   Ibid., pp. 235ff.

APRIL 12

On this Sunday, 83 prisoners and nine Russian POWs die in Auschwitz-Birkenau.   Ibid., pp. 237–240.

APRIL 13

634 Jewish men and 443 Jewish women, sent from Slovakia by the RSHA, receive Nos. 28903–29536 and 4761–5203.

60 prisoners sent from Kraków by the Sipo and SD receive Nos. 29537–29596.

58 prisoners and 12 Russian POWs die in Auschwitz-Birkenau.   Ibid., pp. 240–242.

APRIL 14

45 Polish prisoners are released from the camp.

Three prisoners sent in a group transport receive Nos. 29597–29599.

57 prisoners sent from Kraków by the Sipo and SD receive Nos. 29600–29656.

84 prisoners and nine Russian POWs die in Auschwitz-Birkenau.   Ibid., pp. 245–247.

Polish prisoner Kazimierz Polończyk (No. 11664), born February 12, 1912, sent to the camp by the Sipo and SD for the Kraków District on April 5, escapes from the camp. The search operation remains unsuccessful.*

APMO, IZ-8/Gestapo Lodz/3/88/258; D-AuI-3/1/2, Occupancy Register, p. 252.

APRIL 15

An IBV prisoner, No. 21918, is transferred.

Two prisoners from Kattowitz receive Nos. 29657 and 29658.

30 prisoners sent from Kraków by the Sipo and SD receive Nos. 29659–29688.

The Commandant of Auschwitz, Rudolf Höss, reorganizes the former labor deployment office, which has been subordinate to Section III, the protective custody command, and makes it into the independent Department IIIa, Labor Deployment. He names the Second Protective Custody Commander, SS First Lieutenant Heinrich Schwarz, as director of the section. The new department retains SS Technical Sergeant Franz Hössler, SS Corporal Wilhelm Emmerich, SS Corporal Göbbert, and SS Corporal Heinrich Schoppe as Labor Managers.

APMO, D-AuI-1/80, Commandant's Office Special Order No. 1/42.

Commandant Höss orders that male and female prisoners are not to work on Sundays except for those deployed in livestock breeding, in the kitchen, and possibly in urgent repair work.

Ibid.

88 prisoners and 10 Russian POWs die in Auschwitz-Birkenau.

APMO, D-AuI-3/1/2, Occupancy Register, pp. 248–251.

APRIL 16

15 reeducation prisoners are released from the camp.

A prisoner sent from Kattowitz receives No. 29690.

58 prisoners sent from the prison in Tarnów by the Sipo and SD for the District of Kraków receive Nos. 29691–29748.

67 prisoners and 16 Russian POWs die in Auschwitz-Birkenau.

Ibid., pp. 251–255.

APRIL 17

A prisoner sent from Kattowitz receives No. 29689.

58 prisoners sent from Kraków by the Sipo and SD receive Nos. 29749–29806.

25 prisoners sent in a group transport receive Nos. 29807–29831.

*The next day, an entry about the escape of a prisoner is made in the Occupancy Register.

The Trafo (Transformatorenstation diente zur Regelung des Eisenbahnverkehrs auf dem Nebengleis—switching station for regulating the sidetracking of railroad traffic) in Birkenau under construction.

973 Jews* sent from Slovakia by the RSHA are given Nos. 29832–30804.

APMO, Höss Trial, vol. 6, p. 114.

132 prisoners sent from Lublin by the Sipo and SD receive Nos. 30805–30936.

27 Jewish women sent by the RSHA from Slovakia receive Nos. 5204–5230.

Two female prisoners sent from Oppeln receive Nos. 5231 and 5232.

13 prisoners, including one reeducation prisoner, are transferred.

45 prisoners and seven Russian POWs die in Auschwitz-Birkenau.

APMO, D-AuI-3/1/2, Occupancy Register, pp. 256ff.

APRIL 18

461 prisoners sent by the Sipo and SD from Pawiak Prison in Warsaw receive Nos. 30937–31397.

20 prisoners sent by the Sipo and SD for the District of Kraków receive Nos. 31398–31417.

76 prisoners die in Auschwitz-Birkenau.

Ibid., pp. 258–260.

APRIL 19

464 Jewish men** and 536 Jewish women sent by the RSHA from Slovakia receive Nos. 31418–31881 and 5233–5768.

APMO, Höss Trial, vol. 6, p. 114.

79 prisoners and eight Russian POWs die on this Sunday in Auschwitz-Birkenau.

Ibid., pp. 261–264.

APRIL 20

200 convalescents are taken from Block 20 of the prisoners' infirmary to Birkenau and lodged in the isolation ward of Section B-Ib. At this time, there are approximately 200 Russian prisoners of war in this block from a group of 945 Russian POWs brought here on March 1 and another 40 prisoners from a group of 1,200 sick and physically weak brought there since March 13, 1942. As daily rations, three and sometimes even five prisoners receive one quart of soup among them; they seldom get bread. They receive no medical care and are not employed in any work. During the day they stand in front of the barracks; every other night, they are forced to stand.

APMO, Höss Trial, vol. 17, p. 39; Ostańkowiecz, "Isolation Ward," pp. 170ff.

*On August 15, 1942, only 88 of these deportees are still alive; i.e., within 17 weeks, 885 people die.
**On August 15, 1942, only 10 of them are still alive; i.e., within 16 weeks, almost all of these men are dead.

The mortality rate among them is very high since they are often abused and murdered by drunken SS men.

34 prisoners die in Auschwitz-Birkenau.

APMO, D-AuI-3/1/2, Occupancy Register, pp. 264ff.

APRIL 21

50 prisoners sent by the Sipo and SD from Pawiak Prison in Warsaw receive Nos. 31882–31931.

10 prisoners sent in a group transport receive Nos. 31932–31941.

49 prisoners and 10 Russian POWs die in Auschwitz-Birkenau.

Ibid., pp. 266–268.

APRIL 22

Five reeducation prisoners are released from the camp.

Polish prisoner Stanisław Lenart (No. 16907) escapes from the camp.

APMO, D-AuI-1/3a, FvD, p. 16.

61 prisoners and six Russian POWs die in Auschwitz-Birkenau.

APMO, D-AuI-3/1/2, Occupancy Register, pp. 268–270.

APRIL 23

Polish prisoner Władysław Jaskold-Gabszewicz (No. 309) is released from the camp.

543 Jewish men* and 457 Jewish women sent by the RSHA from Slovakia receive Nos. 31942–32484 and 5769–6225.

APMO, Höss Trial, vol. 6, p. 117.

84 prisoners and two Russian POWs die in Auschwitz-Birkenau.

APMO, D-AuI-3/1/2, Occupancy Register, pp. 271–274.

APRIL 23–24

In the WVHA in Berlin, a meeting of concentration camp Commandants and directors of companies that employ concentration camp inmates is held to clarify guidelines for the deployment and organization of prisoner labor.

Schnabel, *Power Without Morality*, pp. 204–207.

APRIL 24

16 prisoners, including 13 reeducation prisoners, are transferred.

At 2:30 A.M., Polish prisoner Stanisław Lenart, who escaped on March 22, is captured by a supervisor in the military bakery. He is brought to the camp immediately and locked in the bunker of Block 11. The alarm for the standby squad, consisting of four noncommissioned officers and 60 SS men who are searching the

APMO, D-AuI-1/3a, FvD, p. 16; D-AuI-3/1a, Bunker Register, p. 58.

*On August 15, 1942, only 41 of them are still alive; i.e., within 16 weeks, 502 men die.

area around the camp is lifted. Stanisław Lenart is sent to the Penal Company on May 7.

Four prisoners sent from Kattowitz receive Nos. 32485–32488.

Wroński, *Chronicle*, p. 198.

98 prisoners sent by the Sipo and SD from Montelupich Prison in Kraków receive Nos. 32489–32586. These inmates were arrested in the Kraków Artists' Café at 3 Łobzowska Street on April 16, 1942. The 198 detainees include artists, painters, actors, etc. They are arrested in retaliation for the attack on a high-level SS commander at the Kraków airport.

62 prisoners sent in a group transport receive Nos. 32587–32648.

442 Jewish men* and 558 Jewish women, sent in a transport from Slovakia by the RSHA, receive Nos. 32649–33090 and 6226–6783.

APMO, Höss Trial, vol. 6, p. 115.

91 prisoners and five Russian POWs die in Auschwitz-Birkenau.

APMO, D-AuI-3/1/2, Occupancy Register, pp. 274–278.

APRIL 25

100 prisoners sent by the Sipo and SD from Montelupich Prison in Kraków receive Nos. 33091–33190. This is the rest of the group arrested in the Artists' Café on April 16, 1942.**

Prisoner Stanisław Wisłocki (No. 32571) is transferred out of the camp. He was arrested on April 16, 1942, in the Artists' Café in Kraków and sent to Auschwitz the previous day with the group of 98 detainees.

Ibid., p. 282.

85 prisoners and one Russian POW die in Auschwitz-Birkenau.

Ibid., pp. 278–282.

APRIL 26

On this Sunday 11 prisoners selected from the prisoners' infirmary in the main camp are killed with phenol injections. Altogether, 73 prisoners and three Russian POWs die in Auschwitz-Birkenau.

APMO, D-AuI-5/1, Morgue Register, p. 70; D-AuI-3/1/2, Occupancy Register, pp. 282–285.

APRIL 27

14 prisoners sent from Kattowitz receive Nos. 33191–33204.

The first transport of female Polish political prisoners arrives at Auschwitz. In the transport are 127 women, including 58 from the prison in Tarnów and 69 from Montelupich Prison in Kraków, sent to the camp by the Sipo and SD for the Kraków District. They receive Nos. 6784–6910. After a bath in a basin of dirty water,

Piątkowska, *Auschwitz Memoirs*, pp. 47ff.

*On August 15, 1942, only 23 of them are still alive; i.e., within 16 weeks, 419 men die.
**See entry for April 24, 1942.

they are given striped summer clothes, dirty underwear, and wooden shoes. Late at night, they are brought by force to Block 8, where there are no pallets, no straw, and no blankets. The next day they must clear the reeds from a pit filled with water, 2½ miles from the camp. Each group of 10 Polish women gets a German woman with a black patch, the mark for asocial prisoners. They are supervised by armed SS men; and every SS man has a German shepherd dog.

71 prisoners and two Russian POWs die in Auschwitz-Birkenau. Nine of these inmates are killed with phenol injections in the prisoners' infirmary of the main camp.

APMO, D-AuI-3/1/2, Occupancy Register, pp. 285–288; D-AuI-5/1, Morgue Register, p. 71.

APRIL 28

Seven Polish prisoners are released from the camp.

24 prisoners sent from Kattowitz receive Nos. 33205–33228.

31 prisoners sent from Kraków by the Sipo and SD receive Nos. 33229–33259.

As a result of camp conditions and the various forms of extermination, 101 prisoners and two Russian POWs die in Auschwitz-Birkenau.

APMO, D-AuI-3/1/2, Occupancy Register, pp. 288–292.

APRIL 29

Prisoner Jan Nowaczek, who escaped from the Penal Company on September 1, 1941, is sent to the bunker of Block 11. After an interrogation by the Political Department, which determines the stages of his escape, he is sent back to the Penal Company on June 1, 1942.

APMO, D-AuI-3/1a, Bunker Register, p. 59.

26 prisoners sent in a group transport receive Nos. 33260–33285.

423 Jewish men* and 300 Jewish women, sent in a transport from Slovakia by the RSHA, receive Nos. 32286–33708 and 7108–7407.

APMO, Höss Trial, vol. 6, p. 115.

287 male and 197 female prisoners sent to Auschwitz from Prague receive Nos. 33709–33995 and 6911–7107.

One reeducation prisoner is released from the camp.

95 prisoners and two Russian POWs die in Auschwitz-Birkenau.

APMO, D-AuI-3/1/2, Occupancy Register, pp. 292–296.

APRIL 30

The head of the WVHA, Oswald Pohl, announces the guidelines for the deployment and organization of prisoner labor; these are

International Military Tribunal, Nuremberg, Doc. No. NO-R-129; in more detail in Piper, *Labor Deployment*, pp. 32–46, 76–85.

*On August 15, 1942, only 20 of them are still alive; i.e., within 15 weeks, 403 of the deported men die.

the result of the meeting of Commandants and plant managers held on April 23 and 24. The order, which is to take effect on May 1, specifies that the Commandant himself has exclusive responsibility for the deployment of the labor force. The deployment of labor is to utilize the prisoners' labor potential until it is utterly exhausted, in order to maximize performance. Orders for labor will be handled centrally and assigned by the head of Division D. The Camp Commandants may neither accept labor assignments independently from a third party nor carry on negotiations in this matter.

At 1:40 A.M., the SS men on guard at Watchtowers C and D fire nine shots at a prisoner who is approaching the fence of the main camp. Wacław Chojnacki (No. 19992) is shot.

APMO, D-AuI-1/3a, FvD, p. 22; D-AuI-5/1, Morgue Register, p. 77; D-AuI-3/1/2, Occupancy Register, p. 301.

606 prisoners sent by the Sipo and SD from Radom receive Nos. 33996–34601.

Two prisoners arrested on April 16, 1942, in the Artists' Café in Kraków and sent to Auschwitz on April 25 are released from the camp. They are Ferdynand Boruszczak (No. 33098) and Juliusz Kydryński (No. 33142).

APMO, D-AuI-3/1/2, Occupancy Register, p. 299.

65 prisoners and two Russian POWs die in Auschwitz-Birkenau.

Ibid., pp. 296–299.

At 8:40 P.M., the absence of a prisoner is discovered in the camp in Birkenau. At 8:55 a standby squad consisting of 32 SS men begins the search operation.

APMO, D-AuI-3a, FvD, p. 22.

APRIL 1–30

6,388 prisoners, including 432 reeducation prisoners, were sent to Auschwitz-Birkenau.

APMO, D-AuI-3/1/2, Occupancy Register, pp. 206–299.

193 Russian POWs died in Auschwitz-Birkenau.

Ibid.

618 prisoners in the main camp and 1,381 in Birkenau died. Altogether, 1,999 prisoners, including 135 reeducation prisoners, died in Auschwitz-Birkenau.*

Ibid.; D-AuI-3/1, Morgue Register, pp. 45–76.

MAY 1

The occupancy level at morning roll call in the men's camp of Auschwitz-Birkenau is 14,624, including 186 Russian POWs.

APMO, D-Au-I-3/1/2, Occupancy Register, p. 299.

At 5:00 A.M. the SS standby squad searching for the missing prisoner is recalled, since he has been discovered in the latrine barracks.

APMO, D-AuI-1/3a, FvD, p. 23.

---

*The numbers are calculated on the basis of the entries contained in the sources cited above. The numbers refer to male prisoners. Data is lacking concerning the female prisoners.

27 reeducation prisoners are released from the camp.

100 prisoners sent in a group transport receive Nos. 34602–34701.

24 female prisoners sent from Kraków by the Sipo and SD receive Nos. 7408–7431.

Two female prisoners sent from Troppau receive Nos. 7432 and 7433.

Polish prisoner Juliusz Studnicki (No. 33179), born July 17, 1906, is released from the camp. He was arrested on April 16, 1942, in the Artists' Café in Kraków and sent to Auschwitz on April 25, 1942.

The head of the WVHA, Oswald Pohl, appoints the Commandants of the concentration camps as directors of the SS enterprises within their spheres of influence; they receive an appropriate stipend.

APMO, D-AuI-1/1/83, Commandant's Office-Special Order, May 8, 1942; Höss Trial, vol. 23, p. 41.

88 prisoners and one Russian POW die in Auschwitz-Birkenau.

APMO, D-AuI-3/1/2, Occupancy Register, pp. 299–303.

MAY 2

73 prisoners die in Auschwitz-Birkenau, 15 of them in the main camp

Ibid., pp. 304–306.

MAY 3

A civilian is captured in the camp area and put under arrest.

APMO, D-AuI-1/3a, FvD, p. 26.

101 prisoners and two Russian POWs die in Auschwitz-Birkenau, nine of them in the main camp.

APMO, D-AuI-3/1/2, Occupancy Register, pp. 307–311.

102 prisoners are transferred to Mauthausen C.C.

Ibid., pp. 314–318.

MAY 4

In Birkenau the first selection takes place among the prisoners. An SS Medical Officer (Sanitätsdienstgrad) carried out the selection in the isolation ward. The selected prisoners are loaded onto a truck and taken to the bunker put into operation the previous spring, and there they are killed with gas. After this selection, the isolation barracks is surrounded with a wall. Inmates who are exhausted, sick, and incapable of work are transferred to this barracks from other parts of the Birkenau men's camp. The isolation ward is always overcrowded. From time to time, trucks drive up and take away up to 90 percent of the people. The number in this barracks is about 1,200 inmates.

APMO, Höss Trial, vol. 17, p. 100; Ostańkowicz, "Isolation Ward," pp. 175ff.

89 prisoners and one Russian POW die in Auschwitz-Birkenau, 31 of them in the main camp.

APMO, D-AuI-3/1/2, Occupancy Register, pp. 311–314.

MAY 5

In the Camp Occupancy Register it is noted that two Polish prisoners have escaped from the camp:* Piotr Gieras (No. 9395), born November 15, 1904; and Antoni Malawski (No. 14441), born December 30, 1904.

An SS Camp Doctor orders 6½ pounds of phenol from the camp pharmacy. This is used in the prisoners' infirmary to kill prisoners with phenol injections in the heart.

APMO, D-AuI-5/1, Pharmaceutical Order, p. 381.

98 prisoners sent from Kraków by the Sipo and SD receive Nos. 34702–34799.

21 prisoners sent in a group transport receive No. 34800–34820.

Nine prisoners arrested on April 16, 1942, in the Kraków Artists' Café and sent to Auschwitz are transferred out of the camp. They are Bolesław Angelus (No. 32489), Stanisław Konogrodzki (No. 32522), Gustaw Kurdziel (No. 32529), Rudolf Ostachowicz (No. 32549), Jan Siwiec (No. 32564), Jan Gumowski (No. 33122), Antoni Kostarczyk (No. 33134), Adam Mossakowski (No. 33152), and Józef Pokorny (No. 33163).

APMO, D-AuI-3/1/3, Occupancy Register, p. 319.

87 prisoners die in Auschwitz-Birkenau, 43 of them in the main camp.

Ibid., pp. 318–322.

MAY 6

26 prisoners sent by the Sipo and SD from Kraków receive Nos. 34821–34846.

21 male prisoners sent from Kattowitz receive Nos. 34847–34867; 15 female prisoners are marked with Nos. 7434–7448.

24 reeducation prisoners are released from the camp.

144 prisoners die in Auschwitz-Birkenau, 28 of them in the main camp.

Ibid., pp. 323–329.

MAY 7

89 prisoners and three Russian POWs die in Auschwitz-Birkenau, 23 of them in the main camp.

Ibid., pp. 329–332.

At evening roll call in the men's camp, the absence of one prisoner is discovered. At 8:30 P.M. the standby alert is ordered. At 9:30, the alert is called off because the prisoner has been captured.**

APMO, D-AuI-1/3, FvD, p. 30.

---

*The escape took place at least three days before, since prisoners who escape from the camp are listed only when the SS Standby Squad is called off. This takes three days.
**The prisoner is probably killed in the course of the capture, since he is not sent to the bunker of Block 11.

MAY 8

31 prisoners, including 22 reeducation prisoners, are transferred.

36 prisoners sent in a group transport receive Nos. 34868–34903.

Commandant Höss issues a special order informing the members of the SS garrison of Auschwitz that he has been named director of SS enterprises in the area under his control by the head of the WVHA, Oswald Pohl.

APMO, D-AuI-1, Commandant's Office Special Order, May 8, 1942.

Jewish prisoner Simon Cohen (No. 27905) is shot "while escaping."*

APMO, D-AuI-5/1, Morgue Register, p. 85.

135 prisoners and three Russian POWs die in Auschwitz-Birkenau.

APMO, D-AuI-3/1/3, Occupancy Register, pp. 332–339.

MAY 9

The prisoners in the Penal Company are transferred from Block 11 in the main camp to Birkenau and put first in Barracks 2 and then in Barracks 1 of the men's camp of Section B-Ib.**

APMO, D-AuI-3/1, Penal Company Register; Cegłowska, *Penal Companies in Auschwitz*, p. 163.

61 prisoners and two Russian POWs die in Auschwitz-Birkenau, 16 of them in the main camp.

APMO, D-AuI-3/1/3, Occupancy Register, pp. 239–241.

---

*The quotation marks indicate that the prisoner broke down psychologically and, since he did not see any chance of surviving, decided to take his own life. He can achieve this by:

1. Passing through the SS sentry line during work. In such cases, the prisoner is immediately shot by the SS guard. The camp administration indicates this as shooting "while escaping"; that happens during the day. In such cases, an official protocol is drawn up and corpse bearers take the corpse to the morgue.
2. Passing through a forbidden zone within the camp on the way "into the wire." The camp fence is electrically charged, and touching the barbed wire is fatal. The SS guards in the watchtowers immediately shoot prisoners who approach the camp fence. In such cases, the camp administration also indicates this as shooting a prisoner "while escaping." Prisoners usually go "into the wire" after evening roll call or at night. Shooting a prisoner while he is passing through a forbidden zone or at the camp fence is entered in the register of the officer on duty (Führer vom Dienst, FvD).

SS sentries also indicate as shot "while escaping" those cases in which they themselves force the prisoner to pass through the sentry line in order to shoot him. For example, they throw the prisoner's cap behind the sentry line and order him to get it. Many SS men do this for amusement, but most do it to get a commendation or to receive a few days' special leave for vigilance and preventing an escape. These cases are confirmed by countless orders of the Commandant's Office, garrison orders, reports and memoirs of former prisoners, as well as entries in the Morgue Register.

**The isolation of the prisoners in the Penal Company is achieved by enclosing the courtyard between barracks Nos. 1 and 2 with a wall. The prisoners of the Penal Company work in Birkenau digging a drainage ditch called the Royal Ditch to divert rainwater and groundwater from the site of the camp. After they finish their work for the day, after evening roll call, they are divided up for additional work, for example, excavations, carrying stones, etc. The prisoners of the Penal Company have no right to free time. They also receive smaller food rations and may not send or receive any letters. In the first weeks, the function of Block and Squad Leader is filled by SS Corporal Sternberg. His successor in June 1942 is SS Master Sergeant Otto Moll.

MAY 10

The spreading typhus epidemic in Auschwitz also threatens the SS Guards. Garrison Doctor SS Captain Dr. Siegfried Schwela dies of typhus. SS Captain Dr. Franz Bodmann, formerly SS Camp Doctor in the women's camp at Auschwitz, replaces him.

Kaul, *Doctors in Auschwitz*, p. 334; APMO, Höss Trial, vol. 4, p. 177, Account of Former Prisoner Władysław Tondos.

49 prisoners and six Russian POWs die in Auschwitz-Birkenau, 12 of them in the main camp.

APMO, D-AuI-3/1/3, pp. 341–343.

MAY 11

Six prisoners, including four IBV prisoners, are transferred.

60 prisoners from the prison in Tarnów and 61 from Montelupich Prison in Kraków, sent by the Sipo and SD for the Kraków District, receive Nos. 34904–35024.

62 prisoners die in Auschwitz-Birkenau, 24 of them in the main camp.

Ibid., pp. 343–346.

MAY 5–11

In the gas chamber of Bunker 1, approximately 5,200 Polish Jews from the ghettos of Dombrowa (Dąbrowa Górnicza), Bendsburg (Bedzin), Warthenau (Zawiercie), and Gleiwitz (Gliwice) die.

Martin Gilbert, *Endlösung: Die Vertreibung und Vernichtung der Juden—Ein Atlas* (Final Solution: The Expulsion and Destruction of the Jews; originally published in the U.S. as *Atlas of the Holocaust*—see Bibliography), Reinbek/Hamburg, 1982, pp. 100, 102.

MAY 12

56 prisoners, including 34 Poles, 18 Czechs, two Dutch, and two Germans, are released from the camp. One of them is Michael Galas (No. 10), sent to Auschwitz from Sachsenhausen with the first transport of Germans on May 20, 1940.

APMO, D-AuI-3/1/3, Occupancy Register, pp. 346–348. [56 Prisoners released]

Five female prisoners transferred from Ravensbrück receive Nos. 7449–7453. The transferred women include Engineers Wanda Dutczyńska and Maria Raczyńska and Emilia Goszkowska, M.A. and Janina Kukowska, M. A. Their transfer is connected with the newly founded plant breeding station by the director of the Agricultural Department in Auschwitz, SS Lieutenant Colonel Dr. Joachim Caesar. There, experiments with caoutchouc-producing plants are carried out. Caesar has ordered prisoners from Ravensbrück who have qualifications in biology, chemistry, agriculture, and gardening.

Anna Zięba, "Das Nebenlager Rajsko." (The Auxiliary Camp Rajsko), *HvA*, no. 9 (1966): 75–95.

A prisoner sent from Kattowitz to the camp on April 16, 1942, receives No. 35025.

A prisoner sent from Kattowitz receives No. 35026.

In the courtyard of Block 11, four Polish prisoners sent by the Sipo and SD from Radom with the transports of April 5, 1941, and October 4, 1941, are shot at the execution wall. They are Artur

APMO, Accounts, vol. 13, p. 166, Account of Former Prisoner Władysław Siwek.

Crematorium II under construction.

Paraszewski (No. 12252), born April 11, 1921; Stefan Szczęsny (No. 12253), born August 22, 1903; Stanisław Gajda (No. 12254), born October 22, 1920; and Feliks Potęga (No. 22044), born May 30, 1892.*

In Bunker 1 in Birkenau, 1,500 Jewish men, women, and children sent from Sosnowitz are killed with Zyklon B gas.

At 4:45 A.M. the SS head guard on duty finds the body of a Jewish woman hanging on the electrical wire of the camp fence between Watchtowers B and C of the women's section.

At 1:55 P.M. the Slovak Jew Jakob Spitz is shot (No. 31565) "while escaping" by the SS man on duty at Watchtower Number 12 in Birkenau.

At 3:00 P.M. the SS men on duty at Watchtowers 22 and 23 in Birkenau take 10 shots at and kill a prisoner. The murdered man shot "while escaping" is German asocial prisoner Johann Fleischmann (No. 3209).

At 4:45 P.M. Jewish prisoner Jozef Landau (No. 34742) is shot "while escaping" by the SS man on duty at Watchtower 12 in Birkenau.

Natan Eliasz Szternfinkiel, *Zagłada Żydów Sosnowca (The Extermination of the Jews of Sosnowitz)*, Katowice, 1946, p. 34.

APMO, Höss Trial, vol. 12, p. 218, quoted from the Guard Register. [Jewish woman]

Ibid.; APMO, D-AuI-3/1/3, Occupancy Register, p. 349; D-AuI-5/1, Morgue Register, p. 89.

APMO, D-AuI-1/3, FvD, p. 35; D-AuI-5/1, Morgue Register, p. 89; D-AuI-3/1/3, Occupancy Register, p. 350.

APMO, Höss Trial, vol. 12, p. 218, quoted from the Guard Register; D-AuI-5/1, Morgue Register, p. 89; D-AuI-3/1/3, Occupancy Register, p. 350.

*Their names are entered in the Morgue Register because in 1942 the corpses of shot prisoners are taken directly to the crematorium. In the Occupancy Register their names are listed among the prisoners who died the next day (APMO, D-AuI-3/1/3, Occupancy Register, p. 353).

Prisoner Henryk Kaczorek (No. 16725), caught attempting to escape, is put in the bunker of Block 11. On May 14 he is transferred to Birkenau and sent to the Penal Company.

APMO, D-AuI-3/1a, Bunker Register, p. 61.

The management of the German Railroad in Oppeln provides for the Ministry of Transportation in Berlin a prime cost calculation of the transporting of prisoners of Auschwitz and their SS supervisors to the construction site of the I. G. Farben factory in Dwory near Auschwitz. It states that the two-way transport of one prisoner costs 0.29 RM; hence the charge for transporting 158,569 prisoners and SS guards between July and December 1941 amounts to 45,985.01 RM. According to the previous calculation, the charge for transportation was still 45,636.80 RM; so the difference in the cost is 348.21 RM. Because of the small difference, the management of the German Railroad in Oppeln requests permission to make a simpler calculation on the basis of the fee for a monthly card.

APMO, II.Z-13/89, Various Documents of the Third Reich, pp. 46–49.

Since it is necessary to renovate the chimney and the engine housing of the crematorium, the incineration of corpses is halted. The prisoners' corpses are collected in the morgue of the main camp.

APMO, D-AuI-5/1, Morgue Register, p. 92; Docs. ZBL, BW 11/2.

108 prisoners and two Russian POWs die in Auschwitz-Birkenau.

APMO, D-AuI-3/1/3, Occupancy Register, pp. 348–352.

MAY 13

A prisoner from Kattowitz receives No. 35027.

49 prisoners sent from the prison in Tarnów by the Sipo and SD for the Kraków District receive Nos. 35028–35076.

286 prisoners sent from Lublin by the Sipo and SD receive Nos. 35077–35362.

Four prisoners in the surveying unit of the agriculture squad are sent to the bunker of Block 11. They are suspected of maintaining contacts with the civilian population.* They are Tadeusz Kokesz (No. 10745), Roman Dobosz (No. 19595), Józef Danilel (No. 19380), and Józef Kret (No. 20020).

APMO, D-AuI-3/1a, Bunker Register, p. 61.

The Gestapo in Kraków sends a telegram to the Political Department of Auschwitz concerning the prisoners sent from the Montelupich Prison in Kraków on April 24 and 25. Those given Nos. 32489–32586 and 33091–33190 were arrested as hostages for the attack on the SS Commander at Kraków airport, Rakowitz. The telegram contains the command to liquidate the prisoners mentioned.

APMO, Höss Trial, vol. 4, p. 80, Account of Former Prisoner Tadeusz Wasowicz.

*The prisoners who do surveying work in the 25-square-mile Interest Zone of the camp are liaisons between the outside world and the clandestine organizations in the camp. It is through them that news of what is happening in the camp begins to seep out. Thus medicine, injections, food, and news come into the camp from outside. The camp administration suspects the agriculture labor squad of maintaining illegal contacts with the civilian population and it is often checked. Prisoners caught picking up the food that is left for them are locked in the bunker and sent to the Penal Company.

The administration of Auschwitz sends an order (No. 451) to the Central Construction Administration for the following:

1. The repair of the chimney* and the engine housing of the crematorium.
2. Mounting an iron door**

APMO, D-AuI, Docs. ZBL, BW 11/2.

89 prisoners die in Auschwitz-Birkenau.

APMO, D-AuI-3/1/3, Occupancy Register, pp. 353–356.

MAY 14

298 prisoners sent by the Lodz Gestapo receive Nos. 35363–35660.

67 prisoners die in Auschwitz-Birkenau.

Ibid., pp. 356–359.

Five prisoners—three bricklayers and two assistants—begin to repair the chimney and the engine housing in the crematorium under the supervision of the Head Capo, Prisoner Number 17401.

APMO, D-AuI, Docs. ZBL, BW 11.

MAY 15

27 prisoners sent in a group transport receive Nos. 35661–35687.

One female prisoner sent from Chemnitz receives No. 7454.

35 prisoners, including 35 reeducation prisoners, are transferred.

65 prisoners die in Auschwitz-Birkenau.

APMO, D-AuI-3/1/3, Occupancy Register, pp. 360–363.

MAY 16

At 1:45 A.M., the SS guard on duty at Watchtower F in the main camp shoots three times at a running prisoner. The prisoner is not hit.

APMO, D-AuI-1/3a, FvD, p. 38.

At 8:55 P.M., two Polish prisoners, Wincenty Gawron (No. 11237) and Stefan Bielecki (No. 12692), born February 20, 1908, in Tschenstochau, escape from the auxiliary camp Harmense. The search operation, in which 60 SS men take part, is unsuccessful.

APMO, D-AuI-1/3a, FvD, p. 39; IZ-8/Gestapo Lodz 3/88/266–286; D-AuI-3/1/3, Occupancy Register, p. 373.

After the conclusion of the servicing, the crematorium is started up. The corpse bearers bring 103 corpses from the main camp that have been collected in the cellar of Block 28 for incineration.

APMO, Au-5/1, Morgue Register, p. 92.

Czech prisoner Miroslaus Pavelka (No. 33808) escapes from the camp.

APMO, D-AuI-3/1/3, Occupancy Register, p. 373.

*Because of the excessive work load of 24-hour incineration of corpses in the three double-muffle incinerators, the chimney burst.
**On May 19, the head of the Central Construction Administration notes on the order: "Lubitz to do immediately and enter on the bill."

96 prisoners die in Auschwitz-Birkenau. Ibid., pp. 363–366.

MAY 17

91 prisoners and one Russian POW die in Auschwitz-Birkenau. Ibid., pp. 367–370.

MAY 18

70 prisoners sent by the Sipo and SD from Montelupich Prison in Kraków receive Nos. 35688–35757.

Three prisoners are transferred.

78 prisoners die in Auschwitz-Birkenau. Ibid., pp. 370–373.

MAY 19

29 prisoners sent by the Sipo and SD from Kraków receive Nos. 35758–35786.

One female prisoner sent from Kattowitz receives No. 7455.

Prisoner Leopold Almasi (No. 32695), a Slovak Jew, is shot "while escaping." APMO, D-AuI-5/1, Morgue Register, p. 96; D-AuI-3/1/3, Occupancy Register, p. 375.

16 reeducation prisoners are released from the camp.

Four Polish prisoners sent from Kraków by the Sipo and SD on March 26 are transferred. They are Tomasz Gołda (No. 27279), Teobald Handke (No. 27281), Henryk Kozień (No. 27282), and Józef Krzysztoforski (No. 27283).

The release of 47 Slovak Jewish prisoners is noted in the Occupancy Register.* The names and numbers of the allegedly released prisoners are not indicated. APMO, D-AuI-3/173, Occupancy Register, p. 378.

99 prisoners and five Russian POWs die in Auschwitz-Birkenau. Ibid., pp. 374–378.

During evening roll call the absence of one prisoner is discovered. Standby alert is lifted at midnight after the escapee is captured. APMO, D-AuI-1/3a, FvD, p. 42.

Commandant Höss orders all civilian workers employed in the camp to be strictly checked to prevent them from supplying civilian clothing to prisoners planning escapes from the camp. APMO, D-Au-1/84, Commandant's Office Order No. 9/42.

MAY 20

Reeducation prisoner Michał Łysień (No. EH-2026) is shot "while escaping." APMO, D-AuI-5/1, Morgue Register, p. 98; D-AuI-3/1/3, Occupancy Register, p. 379.

A female prisoner sent from Oppeln receives No. 7456.

*Jewish prisoners are not released from the camp. These were probably transferred out of the camp for execution.

Two prisoners sent from Oppeln receive Nos. 35787 and 35788.

237 male and 13 female prisoners sent by the Gestapo from Prague receive Nos. 35789–36025 and 7457–7469.

84 prisoners and one Russian POW lose their lives in Auschwitz-Birkenau.

APMO, D-AuI-3/1/3, Occupancy Register, pp. 378–381.

Prisoner No. 17401, the Head Capo of the bricklayers, reports on the repairs carried out and states that the chimney flue in the crematorium of the main camp has been fixed and a wall pulled down in the motor housing, the ceiling reinforced, and the interior wall plastered. Five laborers—three bricklayers and two assistants—worked on it. The work was done on May 14 and 15. A day's shift was 11 hours; the prisoners worked a total of 110 hours on the job.

APMO, D-AuI, Docs. ZBL, BW/11.

MAY 21

22 prisoners including eight reeducation prisoners are released from the camp.

114 prisoners and one Russian POW die in Auschwitz-Birkenau.

APMO, D-AuI-3/1/3, Occupancy Register, pp. 382–387.

MAY 22

42 prisoners including 39 reeducation prisoners are transferred.

Nine female prisoners sent by the Sipo and SD from Helcl Prison in Kraków receive Nos. 7470–7478.

106 prisoners sent in a group transport receive Nos. 36026–36131.

1,000 Slovak Jews transferred from Lublin (Majdanek) to Auschwitz* receive Nos. 36132–37131.

APMO, Höss Trial, vol. 6, p. 115.

114 prisoners lose their lives in Auschwitz-Birkenau.

APMO, D-AuI-3/1/3, Occupancy Register, pp. 388–392.

MAY 23

106 prisoners and one Russian POW die in Auschwitz-Birkenau.

Ibid., pp. 393–397.

MAY 24

Two Slovak Jews, Martin Weiss (No. 30715) and Zoltan Hochfelder (No. 33319) are shot "while escaping."

APMO, D-AuI-5/1, Morgue Register, p. 102; D-AuI-3/1/3, Occupancy Register, p. 398.

99 prisoners and one Russian POW die in Auschwitz-Birkenau.

APMO, D-AuI-3/1/3, Occupancy Register, pp. 397–401.

*By August 15, only 53 of them are still alive; within 12 weeks, 947 of the transferred prisoners, almost all of them, die.

MAY 25

Numerous cases of typhus are discovered in the prisoners' infirmary.

APMO, D-AuI-5/2-HKB, Infirmary Register of Block 28, p. 130.

94 prisoners die in Auschwitz-Birkenau.

APMO, D-AuI-3/1/3, Occupancy Register, pp. 401–404.

MAY 26

Prisoner Isaak Herskovic (No. 30256), a Slovak Jew, is shot "while escaping."

APMO, D-AuI-5/1, Morgue Register, p. 104; D-AuI-3/1/3, Occupancy Register, p. 405.

The director of the Political Department signs an application to transfer the corpses of four men executed by hanging; they are brought to the crematorium of Auschwitz from Zabrzeg near Dziedzitz.

APMO, Höss Trial, vol. 12, p. 56, Appendix 18.

112 prisoners and one Russian POW die in Auschwitz-Birkenau.

APMO, D-AuI-3/1/3, Occupancy Register, pp. 404–409.

MAY 27

In the main camp the numbers are called of approximately 400 prisoners sent to Auschwitz by the Sipo and SD for the Kraków District and Warsaw from 1940 to 1941. Guarded by SS men, these prisoners are taken to Birkenau and sent to the Penal Company.

APMO, Höss Trial, vol. 4, p. 79, Account of Former Prisoner Tadeusz Wąsowicz; Kraków Auschwitz Trial, vol. 7, pp. 60ff., Account of Former Prisoner Tadeusz Chruścicki; Józef Kret, "Ein Tag in der Strafkompanie" (A Day in the Penal Company), HvA, no. 1 (1959): 87.

168 prisoners are shot at the execution wall in the courtyard of Block 11. They belong to the group of painters, artists, and actors who were arrested on April 16, 1942, in the Artists' Café in Kraków and sent to Auschwitz on April 24 and 25. In the camp, they were given Nos. 32489–32586 and 33091–33190. The prisoners are taken to the courtyard four at a time and shot. The Block Senior utters the following sentence: "For the murder of the head of the Luftwaffe in Kraków, you are condemned to death." Then they are killed with individual shots from a small-caliber weapon. Present at the execution are the Director of the Political Department, Maximilian Grabner, Protective Custody Commander Hans Aumeier, and the Labor Deployment Director, Heinrich Schwarz.

APMO, Höss Trial, vol. 4, p. 80, Account of Former Prisoner Tadeusz Wąsowicz; D-AuI-3/1/3, Occupancy Register, pp. 410–416; Kret,* "Penal Company," p. 104. [168 executed]

60 prisoners sent from the prison in Tarnów by the Sipo and SD for the Kraków District receive Nos. 37133–37192.

Two Polish prisoners, Stanisław Unger (No. 5147) and Stanisław Kozioł (No. EH-2273), are shot "while escaping."

APMO, D-AuI-5/1, Morgue Register, p. 106; D-AuI-3/1/3, Occupancy Register, pp. 409, 416.

278 prisoners and one Russian POW die in Auschwitz-Birkenau.**

APMO, D-AuI-3/1/3, Occupancy Register, pp. 409–419.

*Kret, who is housed at the time on the courtyard side of the bunker, where the execution takes place, hears the words of the Block Senior, the conversation of the SS officers, and with a fellow sufferer, counts the number of shots fired.
**This number includes the prisoners shot on this day.

At 4:00 P.M., prisoner Daniel Wincenty (No. 33804), a Gypsy, born August 15, 1919, in Smerzna, escapes from the Buna plant squad.

APMO, D-AuI-1/3a, FvD, p. 48; IZ-8/Gestapo Lodz/3/88/269ff.; D-AuI-3/1/3, Occupancy Register, p. 425.

MAY 28

54 female prisoners sent from the prison in Tarnów by the Sipo and SD for the Kraków District receive Nos. 7479–7532.

Jewish prisoner Isaak Singer (No. 30100) is shot "while escaping."

APMO, D-AuI-3/1/3, Occupancy Register, p. 419; D-AuI-3/1, Morgue Register, p. 107.

20 prisoners are transferred from the bunker of Block 11 to the Penal Company in Birkenau. Among them are four prisoners from the agriculture squad who were locked in the bunker on May 13 because of forbidden contacts with the civilian population.

APMO, D-AuI-3/1a, Bunker Register, p. 61; Kret, "Penal Company," pp. 89ff. [20 transferred]

92 prisoners die in Auschwitz-Birkenau.

APMO, D-AuI-3/1/3, Occupancy Register, pp. 419–428.

MAY 29

44 prisoners sent in a group transport receive Nos. 37193–37236.

26 prisoners, including 20 reeducation prisoners, are transferred.

87 prisoners and two Russian POWs die in Auschwitz-Birkenau.

Ibid., pp. 425–428.

MAY 30

Two female prisoners sent from Breslau receive Nos. 7533 and 7534.

51 female prisoners sent from Kraków by the Sipo and SD receive Nos. 7535–7585.

61 prisoners and two Russian POWs die in Auschwitz-Birkenau.

Ibid., pp. 428–431.

Professor Dr. Clauberg appeals to SS Commander in Chief Himmler concerning carrying out the sterilization experiments on female prisoners. In his letter, he asks for help with the procurement of the necessary equipment.

Schnabel, *Power Without Morality*, pp. 269–271.

MAY 31

51 prisoners die in Auschwitz-Birkenau.

APMO, D-AuI-3/1/3, Occupancy Register, pp. 431–433.

MAY 1–31

369 reeducation prisoners are sent to Auschwitz.*

*The figure is arrived at by comparing the total numbers from the general number series given to prisoners in other groups according to the list of male transports and the entries for the number of new arrivals contained in the Occupancy Register.

32 Russian POWs die in Auschwitz-Birkenau.*

Ibid., pp. 304–433.

2,950 prisoners, including 120 reeducation prisoners, die in Auschwitz-Birkenau.**

Ibid.

JUNE 1

At morning roll call the occupancy level in the men's camp of Auschwitz-Birkenau is 14,188, including 154 Russian POWs.

Ibid., p. 433.

Four prisoners sent from Kattowitz receive Nos. 37237–37240.

Five prisoners sent on April 11, 1942, from Oppeln,† receive Nos. 37241–37245.

A prisoner sent from Kraków receives No. 37246.

A report on the repair work on Crematorium I in the main camp states that the repairs required 500 bricks, 770 pounds of cement, two 5-yard iron girders (NP 12), 50 fire-clay bricks, and 110 pounds of mortar.

APMO, D-AuI, Docs. ZBL, BW/11.

103 prisoners and one Russian POW die in Auschwitz-Birkenau.

APMO, D-AuI-3/1/1, Occupancy Register, pp. 433–437.

JUNE 2

In Bunker 1 in Birkenau, men, women, and children sent from Ilkenau are killed with Zyklon B gas.

Szternfinkiel, *Jews of Sosnowitz*, p. 35.

47 prisoners are released from the camp. They include 33 Czechs, 13 Poles, including two reeducation prisoners, as well as the German BV prisoner Paul Schikowski (No. 27), born June 26, 1896, who was sent from Sachsenhausen in the first group of 30 criminal prisoners.

APMO, D-AuI-3/1/3, Occupancy Register, p. 437.

129 prisoners die in Auschwitz-Birkenau, including two from the Buna factory squad, Emmanuel Spitzstein (No. 31871), a Slovak Jew, and Czech BV prisoner Karl Hein (No. 33715).††

Ibid., pp. 439–442.

*This figure is based on the entries in the Occupancy Register.
**This number is based on the entries in the Occupancy Register. Not included are the female prisoners, the Polish hostages, and members of clandestine organizations from Upper Silesia—who are shot or gassed—as well as the Jews, who are killed in Bunker Number 1 with gas. None of these groups are included in the camp registers.
†It is very likely that after admission to the camp they were put in Block 11, where since April 11 they have been waiting for the decision concerning their fate by the office or the police court that sent them.
††For the first time the word "Buna" is entered in the Morgue Register of the main camp next to the number. This means that these prisoners either had a work-related accident or were shot "while escaping." In such cases, an official of the Political Department, a medical officer, and the corpse bearers go to the scene of the accident in an ambulance. After the coroner's inquest and the completion of a protocol, the corpse of the dead man is transported to the camp and taken to the morgue next to the prisoners' infirmary.

JUNE 3

Polish prisoner Jan Basta (No. 11801), caught trying to escape, is sent to the bunker of Block 11. He is shot on July 31, 1942.

APMO, D-AuI-3/1a, Bunker Register, p. 65.

68 prisoners sent from Montelupich Prison in Kraków by the Sipo and SD receive Nos. 37247–37314.

58 prisoners, Polish priests and monks, are transferred from Auschwitz to Dachau.

APMO, D-AuI-3/1/3, Occupancy Register, pp. 442–444; IV-8520-175/3028/74, Correspondence.

38 reeducation prisoners are released from the camp.

The Head of Office D-II of the WVHA, which regulates the deployment of prisoner labor, SS Lieutenant Colonel Gerhard Maurer, says in a letter to the Commandants of the concentration camps that the practice of several camps of employing inmates only for half days on Saturdays and not at all on Sundays indicates a misunderstanding of the rule "to completely exhaust the prisoners' productive capacity." He orders the Commandants to discuss the issue of labor deployment with the local plant managers and to report to him by June 15, 1942, wherever this necessary work time cannot be logged.*

Schnabel, *Power Without Morality*, p. 215, Document 69.

85 prisoners die in Auschwitz-Birkenau.

APMO, D-AuI-3/1/3-4, Occupancy Register, pp. 445–449.

JUNE 4

73 prisoners sent from Bromberg receive Nos. 37315–37387.

500 prisoners are transferred to Buchenwald.

Ibid., pp. 449–467.

Three Slovak Jews are shot "while escaping." They are Josef Spitz (No. 30223), Franz Hauser (No. 31647), and Moritz Citron (No. 33603).

APMO, D-AuI-5/1, Morgue Register, p. 114; D-AuI-3/1/4, Occupancy Register, p. 468.

Czech prisoner Rudolf Knežek (No. 35960) is shot in Birkenau "while escaping."

Ibid.

The Political Department recalls 12 Polish prisoners sent to the Penal Company on May 27, 1942, back to the main camp. They are put in Block 11 and shot at the execution wall. They are Mirosław Mirowski (No. 12401), Włodzimierz Makaliński (No. 12710), Bolesław Penta (No. 13337), Tadeusz Łącki (No. 16818), Franciszek Jarzyna (No. 16859), Hieronim Klepacki (No. 16897), Jarema Fediw (No. 18390), Stefan Kunka (No. 18484), Stanisław Malinszewski (No. 18504), Stanisław Mucha (No. 18526), Stanisław Paderewski (No. 18554), and Witko Skiepko (No. 18615).

APMO, D-AuI-3/1/4, Occupancy Register, p. 467; Józef Kret, *Ostarni krąg* (The Last Circle), Kraków, 1973, pp. 77–141.

82 prisoners die in Auschwitz-Birkenau. 12 of them are executed and four are shot "while escaping."

APMO, D-AuI-3/1/4, Occupancy Register, pp. 467–470.

*This order cancels the commandant's order of April 15, 1942, forbidding work on Sunday.

The camp orchestra played as prisoners departed for their work details and on their return. The SS wanted to ensure that the thousands of prisoners would parade by in an orderly fashion so they could be counted.

JUNE 5

47 prisoners sent in a group transport receive Nos. 37388–37434.

11 female prisoners sent from Kattowitz receive Nos. 7586–7596.

Five female prisoners sent in a group transport receive Nos. 7597–7601.

24 prisoners, including 21 reeducation prisoners, are transferred out of the camp.

Two Slovak Jews in the Buna squad, Moritz Regner (No. 36247) and Ferdinand Kellermann (No. 36434), and Polish prisoner Józef Wolański (No. 31371) die.

APMO, D-AuI-5/1, Morgue Register, p. 115; D-AuI-3/1/3, Occupancy Register, p. 472.

The Capo, Martin Richter (No. 3232), a German asocial prisoner, born September 1, 1908, in Radeburg, and a Pole, Jan Poloczek (No. 1065), escape from the labor squad of the Schulz Company in the Buna plant. At 10:00 P.M. the leader of the search unit, Miller, reports that the search operation has been unsuccessful.

APMO, D-AuI-1/3a, FvD, p. 53; Accounts, vol. 106, pp. 108–111, Account of Former Prisoner Jerzy Strzelecki.

92 prisoners die in Auschwitz-Birkenau.

APMO, D-AuI-3/1/4, Occupancy Register, pp. 471–474.

JUNE 6

731 prisoners sent by the Sipo and SD from Radom receive Nos. 37435–38165.*

*In the register of the commander on duty, it says that the transport from Radom arrived at 2:00 A.M. and numbered 732 prisoners.

11 prisoners sent in a group transport receive Nos. 38166–38176.

The Political Department recalls nine prisoners to the main camp from the Penal Company in Birkenau. They are taken to Block 11 and shot at the execution wall. The executed Polish inmates are Stanisław Czech (No. 11227), Franciszek Czerniak (No. 11235), Władymir Goliński (No. 11248), Władysław Joniec (No. 11257), Władysław Jarosz (No. 11258), Zbigniew Kotoswki (No. 11264), Aleksander Radomski (No. 12547), Zygmunt Kalinowski (No. 18799), and Feliks Konca (No. 22841).

APMO, D-AuI-3/1/4, Occupancy Register, p. 475; Józef Kret, *Last Circle*, pp. 77–141.

Five female prisoners sent in a group transport receive Nos. 7602–7606. The Yugoslav Stefania Štibler, who is employed in the camp office, receives No. 7602. She will later be active in the camp resistance movement.

The names and numbers of four prisoners who have escaped from the camp are entered in the Occupancy Register. Aside from Martin Richter and Jan Poloczek, listed the day before, they are Aleks Krzyżewski (No. 12570), born February 18, 1912, in Dabrowka, and Stanisław Szymański (No. 13405).

168 prisoners die in Auschwitz-Birkenau; nine of them are executed.

APMO, D-AuI-3/1/4, Occupancy Register, pp. 475–478.

JUNE 7

1,000 Jews of various nationalities* sent to Auschwitz by the RSHA from the Compiègne camp in France receive Nos. 38177–39176.**

APMO, Höss Trial, vol. 6, p. 115.

58 prisoners die in Auschwitz-Birkenau.

APMO, D-AuI-3/1/4, Occupancy Register, pp. 478–480.

JUNE 8

Two prisoners, the Pole Wiktor Banasik (No. EH-2116) and the Slovak Jew Ladysław Lilienthal (No. 29878), are shot "while escaping."

APMO, D-AuI-5/1, Morgue Register, p. 118; D-AuI-3/1/4, Occupancy Register, p. 481.

87 prisoners die in Auschwitz-Birkenau.

APMO, D-AuI-3/1/4, Occupancy Register, pp. 481–484.

JUNE 9

1,000 prisoners are transferred to Mauthausen C.C.

Ibid., pp. 484–520.

13 prisoners sent in a group transport receive Nos. 39177–39189.

Three Jewish prisoners are shot "while escaping." They are Abraham Chaskel (No. 35670), Benjamin Weiss (No. 36628), and Mordka Marber (No. 38762).

APMO, D-AuI-5/1, Morgue Register, p. 119.

*571 Jews of Polish descent are among those sent. This is the second transport of the RSHA from France.
**On August 15, 1942, only 217 of them are still alive; i.e., within 10 weeks, 783 men die.

92 prisoners die in Auschwitz-Birkenau.

APMO, D-AuI-3/1/4, Occupancy Register, pp. 520–523.

JUNE 10

By order of the Camp Commander, Jewish prisoner Zelman Diament (No. 28568) is put in the bunker of Block 11. He commits suicide the same day.

APMO, D-AuI-3/1a, Bunker Register, p. 66.

Two female prisoners sent in a group transport receive Nos. 7607 and 7608.

82 prisoners die in Auschwitz-Birkenau.

APMO, D-AuI-3/1/4, Occupancy Register, pp. 524–527.

APMO, IZ-8/Gestapo Lodz 3/ 272–280; D-AuI-3/1/4, Occupancy Register, pp. 528ff., 536ff; Kret, *Last Circle*, pp. 77–141.

Some of the Polish political prisoners sent in May to the Penal Company in Birkenau and who are threatened with execution decide to escape from the work site together. The escape is planned to take place at the whistle signaling the end of work. But because of the pouring rain the supervisor of the squad, SS Technical Sergeant Otto Moll, blows the whistle to order a break. This causes confusion, 50 prisoners trying to escape while several are held back by the Capos. The pursuit of the escaping prisoners is ordered and the rest are taken back to the camp. In the pursuit, two prisoners, Tadeusz Pejsik (No. 12549) and Henryk Pajączkowski (No. 22867), are caught and brought to Block 11 of the main camp.

The prisoners in the Penal Company have to line up in the courtyard between Barracks 1 and 2 for roll call. The 13 Polish prisoners shot during the pursuit are brought into the courtyard through the gate: Mieczysław Kawecki (No. 3673), Julian Dębiec (No. 9180), Bolesław Pejsik (No. 12540), Stanisław Maringe (No. 12691), Mieczysław Jaworski (No. 13353), Edward Rogaliński (No. 13407), Bogusław Szubarga (No. 13576), Henryk Lachowicz (No. 16809), Antoni Urban (No. 18647), Władysław Pruszyński (No. 19905), Jerzy Neymann (No. 22293), Władysław Skurczyński (No. 22876), and Adam Paluch (No. 27064). After the search operation is halted, nine prisoners who succeeded in escaping are missing. The escapees are August Kowalcyzk (No. 6804), Jerzy Łachecki (No. 12541), Jan Laskowski (No. 12543), Zenon Piernikowski (No. 12544), Aleksander Buczyński (No. 12754), Józef Traczyk (No. 13323), Tadeusz Chróścicki (No. 16655), Józef Pamrow (No. 22858) and Eugeniusz Stoczewski (No. 22883).

JUNE 11

After morning roll call, more than 100 prisoners marked with a black dot and several marked with a red dot are taken to work at the Königsgraben pit. About 320 prisoners marked with a red dot have to stand with bent knees and outstretched arms in the courtyard of the Penal Company. At 10:00 A.M., Protective Custody Commander Hans Aumeier enters with a few SS men; he orders the 320 prisoners to point out the instigators of the disturbances. Receiving no answer, Aumeier personally shoots 17 prisoners. SS

APMO, Höss Trial, vol, 4, pp. 32, 79; vol. 8, p. 97; Kraków Auschwitz Trial, vol. 7, pp. 60ff., Accounts of Former Prisoners.

Technical Sergeant Hössler shoots three more prisoners. In the afternoon, a few more prisoners with a red dot are brought from the prisoners' infirmary in Birkenau and put with the others. They must undress and take off their shoes. Their hands are tied behind their backs with barbed wire. After the SS guards, led by Gerhard Palitzch, have arrived, the group of about 320 prisoners is taken to Bunker 1 and gassed. In addition, 20 prisoners of the Penal Company are shot on this date.*

62 prisoners sent by the Sipo and SD from Montelupich Prison in Kraków receive Nos. 39101–39251.

One prisoner sent from Kattowitz receives No. 39252.

103 prisoners sent by the Gestapo from Brünn receive Nos. 39253–39355.

Three Jewish prisoners are shot "while escaping": Bernard Kluger (No. 38660), Leo Rochlin (No. 38901) and Aizek Roset (No. 38911).

APMO, D-AuI-5/1, Morgue Register, p. 121; D-AuI-3/1/4, Occupancy Register, p. 528.

The Occupancy Register indicates that a total of 103 male prisoners died in Auschwitz-Birkenau. This does not include the prisoners in the Penal Company shot or gassed.**

APMO, D-AuI-3/1/4, Occupancy Register, pp. 527–533.

JUNE 12

18 prisoners, including seven reeducation prisoners, are transferred out of the camp.

64 prisoners sent in a group transport receive Nos. 39356–39419.

One prisoner sent from Kattowitz on June 9, 1942, receives No. 39420.

*The names and numbers of the prisoners killed on this day are listed in the Occupancy Register on following days.
**Like the other concentration camp Commandants, the Commandant of Auschwitz is required to send a report of the number of deceased prisoners to Branch D. But because of the high mortality rate, the Commandant's Office wants to avoid provoking interest on the part of civilian authorities and the German public on the one hand, and abroad via the news that gets out through illegal means, on the other. The high mortality rate results from the intensified terror and the introduction of various forms of extermination like phenol injections, shooting, and killing with poison gas. Also, the Commandant's Office wants to avoid undesirable inspections and visits from outsiders. Therefore, in 1941, the Commandant's Office informs the offices in the prisoners' infirmaries to make out on a few successive days, i.e., in installments, death certificates for illness ending in death with the details of the course of the disease and the cause of death. For all who are killed, death certificates with fictitious descriptions of disease are made in the office of the prisoners' infirmary. As cause of death, one of several illnesses stipulated by the Camp Doctor may be chosen. To wipe out the traces of the crimes, the names of the prisoners killed in mass executions are crossed out in the Occupancy Register on a few successive days. Despite the intensified terror in June and the next few months, the Occupancy Register does not indicate the actual higher number of victims. The number of victims is not indicated on the individual days but rather in the monthly totals.

10 female prisoners sent in a group transport receive Nos. 7609–7618.

Two Jewish prisoners, Armand Klein (No. 31785) and Max Grünwald (No. 36374), are shot "while escaping."

APMO, D-AuI-5/1, Morgue Register, p. 122; D-AuI-3/1/4, Occupancy Register, pp. 532ff.

Three Jewish prisoners die in the Buna plant squad: Aladar Deucht (No. 36866), Juda Grünberg (No. 38530), and Jules Tavlitzki (No. 39060).

Ibid.

At morning roll call, the numbers of 60 prisoners sent to Auschwitz in 1941–1942 by the Gestapo from Sosnowitz, Kattowitz, and Kraków are called. Guarded by SS Men, the prisoners are taken to Block 11. They are shot at the execution wall in retaliation for the activity of clandestine organizations in Upper Silesia.* Those shot include Józef Białecki (No. 1087), Teodor Krawczyk (No. 1127), Antoni Kawka (No. 1151), Antoni Mierzejewski (No. 1168), Alfons Czajor (No. 1193), Ryszard Czajor (No. 1194), Alojz Pniok (No. 132), Marian Świercz (No. 1330), Stanisław Ostrowski (No. 5940), Władysław Tempka (No. 5941),** Wacław Chiemiński (No. 10295), Stanisław Knapik (No. 10296), Edward Kasperrczyk (No. 11000), Zbigniew Malota (No. 11002), Stanisław Gutkiewicz (No. 11003), Wacław Jacyna (No. 15136), Mieczysław Kozarski (No. 15139), Kazimierz Wajdziński (No. 17353), Stanisław Maślanka (No. 26781), Paweł Przywara (No. 26791), Paweł Waluda (No. 27104), Stefan Losa (No. 27106).

APMO, Höss Trial, vol. 4, pp. 51, 143, Accounts of Former Prisoners Paweł Dubiel and Erwin Olszówka; D-AuI-3/1/3, Occupancy Register, pp. 537ff., 541, 543.

JUNE 13

Six Jews are shot "while escaping": Johann Sternberg (No. 36862), Nathan Levin (No. 38718), Dawid Levy (No. 38271), Josef Kraischmann (No. 38687), Hermann Rosenberg (No. 38907), and Israel Wodnicki (No. 39126).

APMO, D-AuI-5/1, Morgue Register, p. 124; D-AuI-3/1/4, Occupancy Register, p. 538.

Two female prisoners sent from Kattowitz receive Nos. 7619 and 7620.

Between 3:00 and 5:00 P.M. three Polish prisoners escape from a labor squad mowing meadows on the Soła River. They are Marian Mykala (No. 1363), born February 14, 1920, in Prochowitz, Zygmunt Piotrowski (No. 15303), born October 12, 1919, in Opatowok, and Franciszek Sykosz (No. 15402), born September 3, 1919, in Kattowitz.† In the telegram reporting the escape to the responsible authorities, the Commandant states that the prisoners overpowered the SS guard, stole his weapon, and killed him. In retaliation for the killing of the SS man, several inhabitants of the town of Auschwitz are arrested and shot in Auschwitz C.C.

APMO, IZ-8/Gestapo Lodz/3/88/282–285; Accounts, vol. 70, p. 13, Account of Anna Zięba.

*The shot prisoners are entered in the Occupancy Register as "deceased" between June 13 and 15.
**The death certificate of Prisoner No. 5941, Władysław Tempka, signed by Camp Doctor Friedrich Entress, states that the prisoner was sent to the prisoners' infirmary on June 12, 1942, for pneumonia and it was impossible to save him.
†The names of the escaped prisoners are entered in the Occupancy Register on June 14.

JUNE 14

The two prisoners Aleksander Buczyński (No. 12754) and Eugeniusz Stoczewski (No. 22883), who escaped from the Penal Company on June 10, 1942, are captured about 15 miles from Auschwitz C.C. They are returned to the camp and sent to the bunker of Block 11.

APMO, IZ-8/Gestapo Lodz/2, Telegram About the Capture of Prisoners of June 18, 1942; D-AuI-3/1a, Bunker Register, p. 67.

At morning roll call, the numbers of more than 200 Polish prisoners are called who had been sent to Auschwitz from 1940 to 1942 by the Sipo and SD for the Warsaw, Radom, and Kraków Districts and by the Stapo of Kattowitz, Litzmannstadt, Posen, etc. Guarded by SS men, they are taken to Block 11 and shot at the execution wall. Some of those shot are Michał Grzyb (No. 3315), Franciszek Grzymala (No. 12714), Jan Deresiewicz (No. 13242), Józef Krajewski (No. 13512), Bolesław Domański (No. 16715), Stanisław Branicki (No. 16891), Zygmunt Beczek (No. 18165), Leonard Jarocki (No. 18792), Władysław Lada (No. 19869), Mieczysław Witkoś (No. 5032), Adam Pisz (No. 5936), Stanisław Czajer (No. 10300), Zdisław Grudziński (No. 15150), August Bara (No. 21921), Władysław Minkiewicz (No. 23290), Zbigniew Rudzki (No. 27318), Jan Libucha (No. 10743), Kazimierz Kisielewski (No. 11372), Karol Switalski (No. 11443), Fryderyk Szadziński (No. 11552), Tadeusz Szadziński (No. 11553), Stanisław Sitt (No. 11561), Tadeusz Figiel (No. 11563), Jan Mazek (No. 12433), Tadeusz Kowalski (No. 12581), Kazimierz Piasecki (No. 10283), Jan Żmuda (No. 11435), Tadeusz Now (No. 11451), Wilhelm Türschmied (No. 11461), Jan Suchodolski (No. 11492), Jan Augustynik (No. 15144), Józef Szymański (No. 21115), Emil Sroka (No. 27266), Stanisław Madej (No. 19874), and Kazimierz Gosk (No. 20088).

APMO, D-AuI-3/1/4, Occupancy Register, pp. 543–545 (75 names of prisoners from transports from Warsaw), pp. 547, 549–555, 557–558 (130 names of prisoners sent in transports from Upper Silesia, Radom, Kraków, and Tarnów June 14–17, 1942.

JUNE 15

132 prisoners sent by the Sipo and SD for the District of Kraków receive Nos. 39421–39552. There are 67 prisoners from the prison in Tarnów and 65 from Montelupich Prison in Kraków.

Two Jewish prisoners, Izydor Tauber (No. 33394) and Isaak Abrachkopf (No. 38180), are shot "while escaping."

APMO, D-AuI-5/1, Morgue Register, p. 127; D-AuI-3/1/4, Occupancy Register, p. 548.

Slovak Jew Martin Schlesinger (No. 36649) dies in the Buna plant squad.

APMO, D-AuI-5/1, Morgue Register, p. 127; D-AuI-3/1/4, Occupancy Register, p. 549.

JUNE 16

67 prisoners, including 59 reeducation prisoners, are released from the camp.

Two Jewish prisoners, Albert Timfold (No. 36810) and Erich Kirchenberg (No. 38646), are shot during the day "while escaping."

APMO, D-AuI-5/1, Morgue Register, p. 128; D-AuI-3/1/4, Occupancy Register, p. 556.

At 5:30 P.M., Head of Branch D Richard Glücks enters Auschwitz Concentration Camp.

APMO, Höss Trial, vol. 12, p. 218.

The "sauna" in Birkenau.

During evening roll call in the main camp, the absence of two prisoners from the lumberyard squad is discovered. At 8:10 P.M., the search operation ends successfully.

APMO, D-AuI-1/3a, FvD, p. 58.

Feliks Żurek (No. 21242), captured while escaping, is sent to the bunker of Block 11. He is shot on July 31, 1942.

APMO, D-AuI-3/1a, Bunker Register, p. 67.

During the night, four Jews and two Czech BV are shot "while escaping." They are Jacques Porecki (No. 22038), Adalbert Neumann (No. 29087), Jonas Benedikt (No. 29378), Samuel Garnter (No. 30047); and Josef Hula (No. 33962) and Vlastimil Koutny (No. 33967).

APMO, D-AuI-5/1, Morgue Register, p. 129; D-AuI-3/1/4, Occupancy Register, pp. 558ff.

JUNE 17

At 3:35 A.M., the SS guard on duty at Watchtower B in the main camp reports that the corpse of a female prisoner is hanging on the barbed-wire fence of the women's camp.

APMO, D-AuI-1/3a, FvD, p. 58.

123 prisoners sent by the Sipo and SD for the District of Kraków receive Nos. 39553–39675. There are 58 prisoners from the prison in Tarnów and 65 from Montelupich Prison in Kraków.

Five prisoners sent from Kattowitz receive Nos. 39676–39690.

139 prisoners sent by the Gestapo from Prague receive Nos. 39691–39829.

Six female prisoners sent from Kattowitz receive Nos. 7621–7626.

45 female prisoners sent by the Gestapo from Prague receive Nos. 7627–7671.

120 Poles selected by the Political Department are shot at the execution wall in the courtyard of Block 11. The political prisoners were sent to Auschwitz by the Sipo and SD from Radom, Warsaw, Kraków, Tarnów, and Lublin between 1941 and April 1942. Among them are Bartłomiej Kondrat (No. 14747), Edward Rabczyński (No. 22869), Stanisław Rabczyński (No. 22870), Jerzy Pracki (No. 23697), Ignacy Wilk (No. 23704), Józef Witek (No.

APMO, D-AuI-3/1/5, Occupancy Register, pp. 563–570.

23705), Józef Galica (No. 24765), Karol Głód (No. 24766), Leon Filipowicz (No. 27052), Franciszek Franczysty (No. 27053), Lucjan Kryński (No. 25000), Stanisław Lipiński (No. 25004), Stanisław Grzesik (No. 28740), Stefan Pieczonka (No. 28741), Edward Popiel (No. 28743), Franciszek Bilaoń (No. 29680), Edmond Chrześcik (No. 29681), Władysław Adamczuk (No. 30805), Wacław Drygiel (No. 30813), and Władysław Drozd (No. 30814).*

The number of prisoners with typhus increases in Auschwitz. Every day the SS Camp Doctor, who decides on admissions to the prisoners' infirmary, selects some prisoners who register and stipulates that they be killed with phenol injections.**

APMO, Höss Trial, vol. 4, pp. 175–177, Account of Former Prisoner Dr. Władysław Tondos.

15 prisoners who had registered in the outpatient clinic of the main camp are killed with phenol injections.

APMO, D-AuI-5/1, Morgue Register, p. 130.

In Bunker 1 in Birkenau, about 2,000 men, women, and children are killed with Zyklon B gas. They were sent from the ghetto of Sosnowitz.

Szternfinkiel, *Jews of Sosnowitz*, p. 35.

JUNE 18

Eight Jewish prisoners are shot "while escaping": Isaak Chapiro (No. 39022), Armin Blaufeder (No. 31696), Moritz Lowenrosen (No. 36510), Lenzer Sztorchau (No. 39043), Hermann Apollo (No. 39190), Josef Fried (No. 36284), Moritz Lustbader (No. 36874), Elias Horowitz (No. 38589).

APMO, D-AuI-5/1, Morgue Register, pp. 132ff.; D-AuI-3/1/5, Occupancy Register, pp. 567, 569, 572.

Asocial prisoner Johann Ondraz (No. 36022) is shot "while escaping."

APMO, D-AuI-5/1, Morgue Register, p.133; D-AuI-3/1/5, Occupancy Register, p. 572.

The Polish Government in Exile in London receives news of what is going on in Auschwitz. It is reported that "in various places in the country, numerous reports of the death of Auschwitz prisoners are cropping up simultaneously. News then follows soon after of the shootings of several hundred prisoners because of alleged preparations for an uprising in the camp."

CA KC PZPR, 202/I-31, Documents of the Delegation of the Polish Government in Exile, p.6.

JUNE 19

20 prisoners, including 19 reeducation prisoners, are transferred.

58 prisoners sent by the Sipo and SD from Montelupich Prison in Kraków receive Nos. 39830–39887.

35 prisoners sent in a group transport receive Nos. 39888–39922.

Six female prisoners sent in a group transport receive Nos. 7672–7677.

*The prisoners who are shot are entered as "deceased" between June 17 and 19, 1942.
**The number of selected prisoners will later amount to several hundred.

Prisoners in the "sauna."

During the day, three Jewish prisoners are shot "while escaping": Adolf Lichtenstein (No. 32655), Julius Vogel (No. 36712), and Ludwig Morgenbesser (No. 34760).

APMO, D-AuI-5/1, Morgue Register, p. 134; D-AuI-3/1/5, Occupancy Register, p. 575.

In the night, five prisoners are shot "while escaping." These are the Jew Jakob Hirsch (No. 30760), the Czech Franz Kelnar (No. 33806), BV prisoner Josef John (No. 35790), BV prisoner Josef Boula (No. 35921), and one asocial prisoner, Johann Ružil (No. 35991).

Ibid.

One female prisoner sent from Radom receives No. 3813.

In the courtyard of Block 11, 50 Poles selected by the Political Department are shot at the execution wall. These are political prisoners sent to Auschwitz between June 1940 and April 1942 by the Sipo and SD from Kraków, Tarnów, Radom, and Warsaw. They include Mieczysław Drzewiecki (No. 10742), Marceli Kwiecień (No. 11294), Stanisław Król (No. 18892), Zygmunt Jaworski (No. 18924), Jan Jankowski (No. 200), Franciszek Bielawski (No. 3585), Klemens Kaczorowski (No. 6940), Henryk Bessert (No. 6946), Tadeusz Kobyłecki (No. 18804), Zygmunt Kulesza (No. 20379), Marian Piwoński (No. 24693), Wacław Ratyński (No. 25025), Bohdan Zawadzki (No. 31388), Stefan Mikulski (No. 31907), Jan Olechowski (No. 29743), Leon Rydz (No. 30902), Jerzy Kalicki (No. 31088), Jan Ponowski (No. 31250).*

APMO, D-AuI-3/1/5, Occupancy Register, pp. 573ff., 579, 584ff.

JUNE 20

In Bunker 1 in Birkenau, approximately 2,000 Jewish men, women, and children are gassed. They came from the ghetto of Sosnowitz.

Szternfinkiel, *Jews of Sosnowitz*, p. 35.

*The prisoners who are shot are entered as "deceased" between June 17 and 19, 1942.

404 male* and 255 female Jewish prisoners sent by the RSHA from Slovakia receive Nos. 39923–40326 and 7678–7932.

APMO, Höss Trial, vol. 6, p. 115.

25 female prisoners transferred to Auschwitz from Ravensbrück receive Nos. 7933–7957.**

During the day, four Jewish prisoners are shot "while escaping": Nikolaus Goldstein (No. 33563), Isidor Fischer (No. 36365), Julius Trauer (No. 36854), and Jakob Deutsch (No. 38360).

APMO, D-AuI-5/1, Morgue Register, p. 136; D-AuI-3/1/5, Occupancy Register, p. 580.

In the night the Jewish prisoner Chaim Geminder (No. 34713) is shot "while escaping."

APMO, D-AuI-5/1, Morgue Register, p. 137; D-AuI-3/1/5, Occupancy Register, p. 583.

Between 3:00 and 4:00 P.M., four Polish prisoners working in the garage of the troops' supply depot (Truppenwirtschaftslager—TWL) escape from Auschwitz. They are Kazimierz Piechowski (No. 918), Józef Lempart (No. 3419), Stanisław Gustaw Jaster (No. 6438), and Eugeniusz Bendera (No. 8502). Three of them wear SS uniforms, one the uniform and visored cap of an SS Staff Sergeant, and the other two steel helmets and rifles. The fourth is chained like a prisoner. They leave the camp from the garage in a Steyer Model 220 automobile with the license number SS-20868. 50 miles from the camp they leave the car concealed in a pit in the Sucha Forest near Saybusch. After the successful escape, they send the Camp Commandant a letter ironically asking forgiveness for stealing an automobile from him.

APMO, D-AuI-1/3a, FvD, p. 64; IZ-8/Gestapo Lodz/3/88/288–291; D-AuI-3/1/5, Occupancy Register, p. 589; Höss Trial, vol. 8, p. 103, Accounts of Former Prisoners Kazimierz Piechowski, Józef Lampart, Eugeniusz Bendera.

Commandant Höss informs the personal staff of the SS Commander in Chief and the other responsible authorities that he has learned from the Warsaw Sipo and SD that prisoner Zymunt Pilawski, who escaped from Auschwitz on July 29, 1941, has been arrested again.

APMO, IZ-Gestapo Lodz 2/88/35.

JUNE 21

Eight prisoners sent from Kraków receive Nos. 40327–40334.

304 prisoners sent by the Sipo and SD from Lublin receive Nos. 40335–40638.

At 5:20 P.M. the commander of the SS guard receives information that one prisoner is missing from the Harmense auxiliary camp. At 8:40 P.M., the successful search operation is ended and the alert called off.

APMO, D-AuI-1/3, FvD, p. 65.

JUNE 22

The Commandant's Office of Auschwitz is informed that at 9:20 a transport of 1,000 Jews left le Bourget–Drancy in France for Auschwitz.

APMO, D-RF-3/2, Inventory No. 22003.

*By August 15, 1942, only 45 of them are still alive; i.e., within eight weeks, 359 men die.
**The transport also includes the female prisoners who were transferred to Auschwitz at the request of SS Lieutenant Colonel Caesar as a qualified labor force for the plant-breeding station in Rajsko.

25 male prisoners and one female prisoner sent from Oppeln are marked with Nos. 40636–40663 and 7958.

In the night, three Jewish prisoners are shot "while escaping": Dawid Brockmann (No. 38286), Josef Schweitzer (No. 38958), and Ladislaus Schiller (No. 39600).

APMO, D-AuI-5/1, Morgue Register, pp. 139ff.; D-AuI-3/1/5, Occupancy Register, p. 594.

JUNE 23

The German BV prisoner Kurt Pachala (No. 24) is locked in the bunker of Block 11. He was the Capo of the troops' supply depot. Pachala is suspected of having helped the four prisoners who escaped in the auto on June 20, 1942.

APMO, D-AuI-3/1a, Bunker Register, p. 69.

58 prisoners, including 31 reeducation prisoners, are released from the camp.

17 prisoners sent from Kattowitz receive Nos. 40664–40680.

In the night two Jewish prisoners, Josef Cohen (No. 38330) and Israel Zaks (No. 39140), are shot "while escaping."

APMO, D-AuI-5/1, Morgue Register, p. 142; D-AuI-3/1/5, Occupancy Register, p. 603.

At 4:20 A.M. Jewish prisoner Aleksander Farkas (No. 36455) is shot by SS guard Jarosiewicz on duty at Watchtower E "while escaping."

APMO, D-AuI-1/3a, FvD, p. 66; D-AuI-3/1/5, Occupancy Register, p. 598.

In Bunker 1 in Birkenau, 566 people are killed with Zyklon B gas. They were sent from a mental hospital in Kobierzyn* near Kraków.

APMO, Kraków Auschwitz Trial, vol. 38, p. 56; Wroński, p. 211; *Biuletyn Głównej Komisij Badania Zbrodni Hitlerowskich w Polsce* (Bulletin of the High Commission for the Investigation of Nazi Crimes in Poland), Vol. 3, Warsaw, 1947, p. 102 (hereafter cited as Bulletin of the High Commission).

JUNE 24

The Polish woman Janina Nowak (No. 7615), sent to Auschwitz in a group transport on June 12, 1942, escapes from a labor squad raking hay near the Soła River. After the escape is discovered, the unit of 200 Polish women is taken to the camp for a punishment roll call. Höss, Aumeier, Grabner, and Palitzsch come to the women's camp. The Political Department begins an investigation to learn the particulars of the escape. The female prisoners are threatened that some of them will be killed. After a few hours, a telephone order comes from Berlin to send the female prisoners to the Penal Company. At the same time, it is ordered that the hair of non-Jewish female prisoners is to be cut off.

APMO, IZ-8/Gestapo Lodz/2/88/19; Memoirs, vol. 69, p. 8, Memoirs of the Former Prisoner Wanda Tarasiewicz; Piatkowska, *Memoirs*, p. 52.

Two female prisoners sent in a group transport receive Nos. 7959 and 7960.

*Before the liquidation of the mental hospital in Kobierzyn, the Polish doctors are killed, on June 18, 1942; on the following days, all the nurses and the hospital chaplain are killed. The patients are treated by German doctors. The liquidation begins on June 23 and is carried out by the SS and the Gestapo. During the liquidation, 30 patients are shot either in the nearby cemetery or in their beds. 20 Jews brought from Skawina to dig the graves are also shot. After the patients are killed, a hospital for the SS, an agricultural station, and a bureau of the Hitler Youth are set up in the buildings of the mental hospital.

933 Jewish men* and 66 Jewish women sent by the RSHA from the Drancy camp in France receive Nos. 40681–41613 and 7961–8026.

APMO, Höss Trial, vol. 6, p. 115.

Ten prisoners sent from Kattowitz receive Nos. 41614–41623.

In the night, four Jewish prisoners are shot "while escaping": Ladislaus Fischer (No. 31767), Jonas Wajener (No. 39092), Desider Smuk (No. 39935), and Armin Haasz (No. 40010).

APMO, D-AuI-5/1, Morgue Register, p. 144; D-AuI-3/1/5, Occupancy Register, p. 609.

Three Polish prisoners—Piotr Kopyt (No. 37524), Antoni Żabicki (No. 37609), and Adalbert Piwowarczyk (No. 37941)—escape from the camp. They were sent to Auschwitz from Radom by order of the Sipo and SD. During the pursuit, Adalbert Piwowarczyk is shot.

APMO, IZ-8/Gestapo Lodz/3/88/292; D-AuI-3/1/5, Occupancy Register, p. 610; D-AuI-5/1, Morgue Register, p. 145.

JUNE 25

The Penal Company for women is set up in the town of Budy, about 4½ miles from the main camp. 200 female Polish prisoners** sent to Auschwitz on April 27 and May 28 are sent to the Penal Company. They are housed in the former school building, which is surrounded by a double barbed-wire fence. The women live in the attic and the cellar of the school building in an auxiliary barracks. In the room there is only straw and wood shavings. The female prisoners of the Penal Company are used for hard labor, for example, cleaning the fish ponds, cutting reeds, digging drainage ditches, etc. The first director of the penal camp in Budy is SS Supervisor Elfriede Runge.† The camp is guarded by 25 SS men with guard dogs.

APMO, Höss Trial, vol. 21, p. 42; Accounts, vol. 66, pp. 103, 147, Account of Former Prisoners Marta Wijas-Bielecka and Jadwiga Kopeć.

The Commandant's office of Auschwitz is informed that a transport of 1,000 Jews left Pithiviers in France at 6:15 A.M. for Auschwitz.

APMO, D-RF-3/3, Inventory No. 22004.

24 female prisoners sent in a group transport receive Nos. 8027–8050.

Jewish prisoner Emanuel Dvidovic (No. 30472) is shot "while escaping."

APMO, D-AuI-5/1, Morgue Register, p. 145; D-AuI-3/1/5, Occupancy Register, p. 610.

Prisoner Zygmunt Pilawski (No. 14156) is sent back to the camp and locked in the bunker of Block 11. Pilawski escaped from the camp on July 29, 1941. He is shot on July 31, 1942.

APMO, D-AuI-3/1a, Bunker Register, p. 70.

Five Russian POWs are sent to Auschwitz.††

APMO, D-AuI-3/1/5, Occupancy Register, pp. 589, 594, 598, 603, 605, 609.

*By August 15, 1942, only 186 men are still alive; i.e., within seven and a half weeks, 747 deportees die.
**A few days later, about 200 Slovak and French Jewish women and German female prisoners who fill the role of Capos are also sent to the Penal Company.
†In October, she is replaced by SS Supervisor Elisabeth Hasse.
††The number of Russian POWs on June 25, 1942, is 154, but between June 22 and 24 is 149.

40 prisoners are shot in the courtyard of Block 11 at the execution wall. They include 18 Czechs with the Nos. 33678, 35822, 35829, 35855, 35860, 35876, 35881, 35896, 35898, 35901, 35904, 35906, 35913, 35916, 35978, 35989, 36014, and 36018. Also included are 10 Poles sent to the camp between 1940 and 1941 by the Sipo and SD for the District of Kraków who had Nos. 595, 3488, 9167, 9171, 10765, 12075, 13680, 22713, 23691, and 23698. Also included are 12 Poles sent from Kattowitz on June 23, 1942, and given Nos. 40664, 40665, 40666, 40667, 40668, 40669, 40670, 40671, 40672, 40673, 40674, and 40675. A few of these prisoners are brought from the prisoners' infirmary.*

APMO, D-AuI-5/3, Prisoners' Infirmary Register of Block 28, p. 151.

JUNE 26

20 prisoners sent by the Sipo and SD from Montelupich Prison in Kraków receive Nos. 41624–41643.

65 prisoners sent by the Sipo and SD from Pawiak Prison in Warsaw receive Nos. 41644–41708.

64 prisoners sent in a group transport receive Nos. 41709–41772.

38 prisoners, including 29 reeducation prisoners, are transferred.

During the day, two Jewish prisoners—Josef Rodrigue (No. 41373) and Marcel Meyer (No. 41538)—are shot "while escaping."

APMO, D-AuI-5/1, Morgue Register, p. 146; D-AuI-3/1/5, Occupancy Register, p. 617.

In the night, four Jewish prisoners are shot "while escaping." They are Leopold Weiss (No. 36729), Albert Stern (No. 36794), Wladislaus Weiss (No. 40138), and Jakob Frydmann (No. 40824).

APMO, D-AuI-5/1, Morgue Register, p. 146; D-AuI-3/1/5, Occupancy Register, p. 621.

JUNE 27

1,000 Jews** arrive in a transport of the RSHA from the Pithiviers Camp and receive Nos. 41773–42772. Among them are 937 Jews of Polish origin.

APMO, Höss Trial, vol. 6, p. 115.

Jewish prisoners Szulim Zyltmann (No. 41255), Mordka Bortuoi (No. 41613), and Nathan Hersen (No. 40889) are shot "while escaping."

APMO, D-AuI-5/1, Morgue Register, p. 148; D-AuI-3/1/5, Occupancy Register, pp. 622, 264.

Two Polish inmates, Eryk Nowak (No. 41709) and Antoni Walczak (No. 41737), sent the previous day in a group transport, are shot.

Ibid.

Reeducation prisoner Henryk Surma (No. EH-2714) is released from the camp.

*"Transferred" is entered next to the names and numbers of these prisoners. The same day they are listed in the Occupancy Register among the deceased (APMO, D-AuI-3/1/5, Occupancy Register, pp. 612, 614ff).
**By August 15, 1942, only 557 of them are still alive. Within seven weeks almost half the deportees have died.

JUNE 28

The Commandant's Office of Auschwitz is informed that the fifth transport with 1,038 Jews left Beaune-la-Rolande in France at 5:20 A.M. for Auschwitz.

APMO, D-RF-3/4, Inventory Number 22005.

At 2:30 A.M., a female prisoner is shot by SS man Peitz "while escaping."

APMO, D-AuI-1/3a, FvD, p. 72.

JUNE 29

Four prisoners sent from Kattowitz receive Nos. 42773–42776.

Polish prisoner Antoni Mroczek (No. 37648) is shot "while escaping."

APMO, D-AuI-5/1, Morgue Register, p. 150; D-AuI-3/1/5, Occupancy Register, p. 627.

In the night, 15 Jewish prisoners are shot "while escaping." They are Josef Knöpflmacher (No. 40228), Chaim Fouks (No. 40813), Georg Freudenstein (No. 40816), Boris Kolmanowitch (No. 40909), Jacques Kotschouk (No. 40932), Abraham Blotkin (No. 41047), Sergius Rabinovitsch (No. 41059), Elie Rechszaft (No. 41066), Moise Vormas (No. 41213), Weiman Orlowski (No. 41353), Robert Bilis (No. 41455), Ili Mitrany (No. 41541), James Steinberg (No. 41578), and Israel Trefler (No. 39070).

APMO, D-AuI-5/1, Morgue Register, pp. 150ff.; D-AuI-3/1/5, Manpower Register, pp. 629ff.

At evening roll call, the absence of one prisoner is discovered. Guard Companies 2, 3, and 4 reinforce the outer sentry line. The prisoner is captured by two SS Men shortly before 3:00 A.M., brought back to the camp, and handed over to Protective Custody Commander Aumeier. The alert is lifted. This probably concerns Ukrainian prisoner Hryc Hłusak (No. 37421).

APMO, D-AuI-1/3, FvD, p. 73.

Cyryl Ratajski, pseudonym "Wrzos," the delegate of the Polish Government in Exile, writes in a radiogram to the Polish government in London: "In Auschwitz, 200 persons were shot in retaliation for Heydrich.* Moreover, on June 8, 160 persons were shot for the murder of a Gestapo supervisor.** At present, there are 14,000 people there, including about 3,000 women. The 70-year-old sculptor, Ludwik Puget, was shot in Auschwitz." The report was based on data from inside the camp itself and from the interest zone, which reached the outside world through underground channels.

CA KC PZPR 202/I-31, Documents of the Delegation of the Polish Government in Exile, p. 22.

JUNE 30

The Ukrainian political prisoner, Hryc Hłusak (No. 37421), captured in the morning, is locked in the bunker of Block 11. He is

APMO, D-AuI-3/1a, Bunker Register, p. 71.

*The execution of 200 Polish political prisoners on June 14 may have been retaliation for the killing of the Head of the Sipo and SD, SS General Reinhard Heydrich, on June 5, 1942, in Prague by members of the Czech resistance movement.
**This refers to the execution of May 27, when 168 prisoners were shot as hostages in retaliation for the alleged killing of a high SS officer. One of those executed was Ludwik Puget (No. 33164), born June 21, 1877.

released from the bunker on July 10, 1942, and probably sent to the Penal Company.

1,004 Jewish men* and 34 Jewish women arrive in the fifth transport of the RSHA from Beaune-la-Rolande Camp in France. They receive Nos. 42777–43780 and 8051–8084. There are 752 Jews of Polish origin in the transport.

APMO, Höss Trial, vol. 6, p. 115.

52 male and 26 female prisoners sent in a group transport are given Nos. 43781–43832 and 8085–8110.

400 Jews** transferred to Auschwitz Camp from the Lublin (Majdanek) C.C. receive Nos. 43833–44232.

Ibid.

19 prisoners are transferred.

Between 1:00 and 2:00 P.M., Polish political prisoner Aleksander Pietrzak (No. 30894), escapes. Born May 1, 1918, he was sent to Auschwitz on April 17, 1942, by the Sipo and SD from Lublin. He escapes from the Buna plant squad in civilian clothing and throws away his camp uniform clothes.

APMO, IZ-8/Gestapo Lodz/3/88/295ff; D-AuI-3/1/5, Occupancy Register, p. 636.

In the night, Jewish prisoner Nassim Eskenasi (No. 40789) is shot "while escaping."

APMO, D-AuI-5/1, Morgue Register, p. 152.

In connection with the announced delivery of additional transports of Jews to Auschwitz by the RSHA for extermination, more gas chambers are built in a farmhouse similar to Bunker Number 1. It is west of the later site of Crematoriums IV and V and is designated Bunker Number 2.† Next to it, three barracks are built to serve as undressing rooms for people condemned to be gassed.

Höss, Commandant in Auschwitz, pp. 127ff., 158–161.

JUNE 1–30

Five Russian POWs die in Auschwitz-Birkenau.

APMO, D-AuI-3/1/3/4/5, Occupancy Register, pp. 433–636.

341 reeducation prisoners are sent to Auschwitz.††

2,289 Jews, 1,203 Poles, including 100 reeducation prisoners, 149 Czechs, 49 Germans, and one Gypsy die in Auschwitz-Birkenau. A total of 3,683 prisoners have lost their lives. Most of the 2,289 Jewish prisoners were killed in the gas chamber. After intensive

Ibid.

*By August 15, 1942, 703 of them are still alive; i.e., in 6½ weeks, 301 men, about a third of the deportees, die.
**On August 15, 1942, i.e., 6½ weeks later, only 208 of them are still alive. About half of the deportees, 192, die.
†Prisoner Franciszek Gulba witnesses the killing of a transport of women in the gas chamber of Bunker 2 even before the road is laid. Gulba works in one of the labor squads building the road (APMO, Accounts, vol. 70, pp. 50–52, Account of Former Prisoner Franciszek Gulba).
††The figure is based on the difference between the number of numbers assigned to prisoners of other groups from the general number series, according to the lists of male transports, and the number of new arrivals listed in the Occupancy Register.

exploitation of their labor, they are declared incapable of working by SS Doctors during the selections carried out in Birkenau. Most of the 1,203 Polish prisoners are executed, over 500 prisoners are shot, and over 300 are gassed.*

JULY 1

At morning roll call the occupancy of Auschwitz-Birkenau is 15,925, including 154 Russian POWs.

Ibid., p. 636.

The Central Construction Administration of the Waffen SS and Police in Auschwitz contacts the companies that have already carried out building contracts in Auschwitz C.C. It asks Huta Hoch- und Tiefbau AG (Huta Surface and Underground Engineering) and Lenz Industrial Construction Company of Silesia, located in Kattowitz, to submit proposals to build new crematoriums in the camp. The companies are to undertake construction, whereas the plant for the incineration of the corpses and the gas chambers are to be delivered and installed by J. A. Topf and Sons, Erfurt.

APMO, D-Z Bau/6, Docs. CCA.

111 male prisoners are given Nos. 44233–44343; 73 female prisoners sent from Kattowitz by the Gestapo receive Nos. 8111–8183. The men are workers in the Paris coal mine, now called the General Zawadzki mine, in Dombrowa. They are sent with their sons. The female prisoners are the mothers, wives, and daughters of these men.

APMO, IV-8521/141/68, Questionnaire for the coal mine "General Zawadzki" in Dąbrowa Górnicza; Memoirs, vol. 62, p. 21, Memoirs of Former Prisoner Tadeusz Ostrega (No. 44330).

In the night, nine Jewish prisoners are shot "while escaping." They are Aleksander Iwanowsky (No. 33419), Julius Jakubovic (No. 36954), Hersz Finkelstein (No. 38427), Israel Stern (No. 40007), Josef Kern (No. 40914), Salomon Sichem (No. 41128), Isaak Warszawski (No. 41207), Moritz Benasajac (No. 41262), and Wolf Schuster (No. 41394).

APMO, D-AuI-5/1, Morgue Register, p. 153; D-AuI-3/1/5, Occupancy Register, p. 639.

JULY 2

330 prisoners sent by the Sipo and SD from the prison in Radom receive Nos. 44344–44673.

202 female prisoners receive Nos. 8184–8385.

26 prisoners, including 20 reeducation prisoners, are released from the camp.

Two Jewish prisoners, Juda Trewgoda (No. 41198) and Alois Koksz (No. 43944), are shot "while escaping."

APMO, D-AuI-5/1, Morgue Register, p. 154; D-AuI-3/1/5, Occupancy Register, p. 641.

*The figures are based on the Occupancy Register. Not included in these totals are female prisoners, hostages, and members of the resistance movement who were brought to Auschwitz to be executed, as well as those Jews who were taken directly to the gas chambers and were not registered.

In the Buna plant squad, 11 Jewish prisoners die while working. They are Adalbert Weiss (No. 40161), Wilhelm Schloss (No. 40309), Moritz Abrannovitch (No. 40685), Samuel Fridmann (No. 40817), Abram Grinberg (No. 40864), Felix Nirenstein (No. 41025), Wally Schaffier (No. 41110), Moritz Waserstein (No. 41219), Moses Daum (No. 41274), Mordka Wengerow (No. 41417), and Luzian Dreyfus (No. 41478).

APMO, D-AuI-5/1, Morgue Register, pp. 154ff.; D-AuI-3/1/5, Occupancy Register, p. 643.

10 Polish prisoners sent by the Gestapo from Kattowitz on April 27 and May 6 are executed at the execution wall in the courtyard of Block 11. They are Karol Turczak (No. 33192), Jan Drożdż (No. 33193), Stefan Janik (No. 33194), Emil Mentel (No. 33197), Michał Jakubiec (No. 33198), Józef Kufel (No. 34852), Michał Zuziak (No. 34853), Wincenty Biegun (No. 34855), Władysław Matlak (No. 34856), and Jan Moczek (No. 34857).

APMO, D-AuI-3/1/5, Occupancy Register, p. 644.

JULY 3

18 Polish prisoners, including one reeducation prisoner, are transferred.

53 male prisoners are marked with Nos. 44674–44726; three female prisoners receive Nos. 8386–8388. They are sent in a group transport.

In the prisoners' infirmary, Block 28 of the main camp, German BV prisoner Leo Witschorek (No. 30) dies of typhus. He was the Block Senior in the men's camp in Birkenau and was described by the prisoners as the worst executioner among the prisoner functionaries in the camp.

Ibid., p. 646; Klodziński, "German Criminals," p. 125.

A typhus epidemic breaks out in Auschwitz-Birkenau. 56 numbers, including those of 24 prisoners in the Buna plant squad, are entered in the Morgue Register. They were probably killed with phenol injections after registering with the SS Doctor in the infirmary admissions room. In the men's camps of Auschwitz and Birkenau, 184 deceased prisoners are listed.*

APMO, D-AuI-5/1, Morgue Register, pp. 156–158; D-AuI-3/1/5, Occupancy Register, pp. 465–650.

JULY 4

For the first time, the camp administration carries out a selection** among the Jews sent to the camp; these are in an RSHA transport

APMO, Höss Trial, vol. 6, p. 115.

---

*The typhus epidemic also broke out in the women's camp. The lack of documents prevents certainty regarding the mortality rate of the female prisoners. To stop the spread of the epidemic, similar methods were used here as in the other camps: An SS Doctor carried out selections that resulted in sick prisoners being killed with phenol injections.
**The selections take place on the unloading platform while the SS Standby Squad surrounds the train. The debarking people are placed in two groups, men and women. Then they come to an SS Doctor accompanied by other SS officials like the Camp Commander, the Roll Call Leader, officials of the Political Department, etc. On the basis of his impression, the SS Doctor decides whether the person is able-bodied or not. Young, healthy, and strong men and women are led off to the camp in groups. Old people, children, mothers with children, and pregnant women are told that they are to be driven to the camp. Then they are taken to the bunker in Birkenau and killed in the gas chambers.

from Slovakia. During the selection, 264 men* from the transport are chosen as able-bodied and admitted to the camp as registered prisoners. They receive Nos. 44727–44990. In addition, 108 women are selected and given Nos. 8389–8496. The rest of the people are taken to the bunker and killed with gas.

The so-called Sonderkommando (Special Squad) is formed, consisting of several dozen Jewish prisoners. They must dig pits near the bunker and bury those who are killed in the gas chambers. The squad is housed in the barracks in the men's camp in Birkenau. It is completely isolated from the other prisoners.

CA KC PZPR 202/I-31, Documents of the Delegation of the Polish Government in Exile, p. 27.

JULY 5

31 male and eight female prisoners sent in a group transport receive Nos. 44991–45021 and 8497–8504.

A female prisoner sent to the camp the previous day receives No. 8508.

JULY 6

60 prisoners sent by the Sipo and SD from the prison in Tarnów receive Nos. 45022–45081.

JULY 7

700 prisoners are transferred to Mauthausen C.C.

Seven male and two female prisoners sent from Kattowitz receive Nos. 45082–45088, 8506, and 8507.

57 prisoners sent by the Sipo and SD from the prison in Tarnów receive Nos. 45089–45145.

Polish prisoner Władysław Jura (No. 38112), born November 11, 1915, in Tomaschow, escapes from the Budy auxiliary camp after he has taken off his camp clothing. The escape is noted at 4:00 P.M.

APMO, IZ-8/Gestapo Lodz/3/88/298; D-AuI-3/1/5, Occupancy Register, p. 688.

The SS Commander in Chief discusses the sterilization of Jewish women with SS Brigadier General Professor Dr. Gebhardt, SS Major General Glücks, and SS Brigadier General Professor Dr. Clauberg. Himmler informs Dr. Clauberg that Auschwitz is at his disposal for experiments on animals and humans. The SS Commander in Chief says he wants a report on the results of the experiments in order to begin the practical use of sterilization of Jewish women. Moreover, in consultation with Prof. Dr. Hohlfelder, a specialist in X rays, the extent to which sterilization in men can be achieved with X rays is to be tested.

Schnabel, *Power Without Morality*, p. 272, Doc. 102.

*On August 15, 1942, only 69 of them are still alive; i.e., within six weeks, more than two-thirds of the men die.

"Able-bodied" men after the selection.

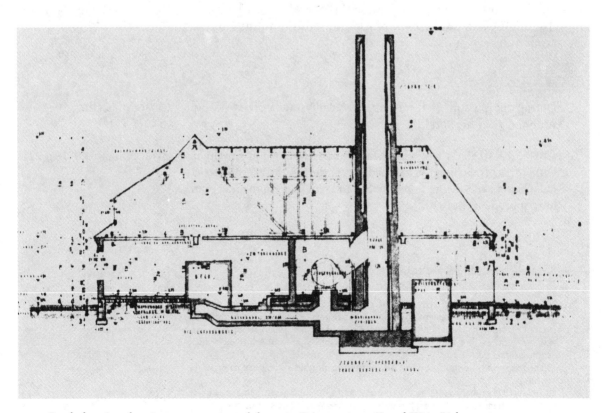

Draft drawing showing cross section of the twin Crematoriums II and III in Birkenau.

JULY 8

Probably for the first time, a public hanging is carried out in Auschwitz. Two Polish political prisoners, Tadeusz Pejsik (No. 12549) and Henryk Pajączkowski (No. 22867), are executed. They were caught escaping from the Penal Company on July 10, 1942, and sent to the bunker of Block 11 the same day.

APMO, Höss Trial, vol. 39, p. 5; Account of Former Prisoner Edward Błotnicki; D-AuI-3/1a, Bunker Register, p. 66; D-AuI-3/1/5, Occupancy Register, p. 691; D-AuI-5/1/2, Morgue Register, p. 166; Kazimierz Tymiński, *Uspokoić sen* (To Quiet Sleep), Kattowitz, 1985, pp. 54–57.

10 inmates sent from Kattowitz receive Nos. 45146–45155.

A prisoner sent from Troppau receives No. 45156.

1170 non-Jewish and Jewish prisoners from Paris, sent to Auschwitz by the RSHA, receive Nos. 45157–46326. They include French Communists and members of other leftist parties as well as people of various nationalities imprisoned as part of the Night and Fog Operation (Nacht und Nebel—NN).* In the camp, they are identified with green badges, the identification badge of common criminals. This is to hinder contact with other political prisoners.

APMO, Höss Trial, vol. 4, p. 130; vol. 7, p. 219.

55 prisoners sent by the Sipo and SD for the District of Kraków from the prison in Tarnów receive Nos. 46327–46381.

Two male and two female prisoners sent from Kattowitz receive numbers 46382, 46383, 8508, and 8509. Three female prisoners transferred from Ravensbrück C.C. receive Nos. 8510–8512.

Polish prisoners Władysław Borkowski (No. 495), Antoni Cymer (No. 2235), and Bronisław Macoch (No. 16557) escape from the camp.

APMO, D-AuI-3/1/5, Occupancy Register, pp. 692ff.

JULY 9

During the pursuit of the escapees, Władysław Borkowski and Antoni Cymer are shot.**

APMO, D-AuI-5/1/2, Morgue Register, p. 168.

At 10:50 A.M. SS General Heinrich Schmauser arrives at Auschwitz with an escort. Schmauser† is the head of the Southeastern District, i.e., Silesia, and is the Superior SS and Police Commander with headquarters in Breslau.

APMO, D-AuI-1/3, FvD, p. 82.

JULY 10

Six Polish prisoners are transferred.

---

*This code name conceals actions of the Sipo against members of resistance movements in the occupied Western countries. NN prisoners remain in the camps until the end of the war. Their families are not informed of their whereabouts and they may not write to their families or friends. Their families are not informed of their deaths either.
**The corpses of the shot prisoners are sent to the morgue in the main camp in the afternoon.
†Schmauser is probably supposed to inform the Commandant of the intended visit of SS Commander in Chief Himmler to the camp and especially of the planned course of Jewish extermination.

Two reeducation prisoners are released.

77 male and 29 female prisoners sent in a group transport receive Nos. 46384–46462 and 8513–8541. The female prisoners were previously held in Helcl Prison in Kraków.

SS Lieutenant Colonel Rudolf Brandt of the personal staff of SS Commander in Chief Himmler sends a letter to Professor Dr. Clauberg informing him that after discussions with the head of the WVHA, SS General Pohl, and the Camp Doctor of the women's camp in Ravensbrück, Himmler has expressed a wish that Clauberg go to Ravensbrück to carry out the sterilization of Jewish women there using his procedure. Brandt also writes that it is important for the SS Commander in Chief to know approximately how much time is needed for the sterilization of 1,000 Jewish women.

Schnabel, Power Without Morality, p. 268, Doc. 99.

The RSHA informs the Gestapo that a separate section for female prisoners has been formed in Auschwitz, whose official name is "Auschwitz Concentration Camp—Women's Section, Auschwitz East, Upper Silesia, Post Office 2."*

APMO, Rund-Edict of the RSHA, July 10, 1942, IV-C2, No. 42187.

SS Major Willi Burger becomes Administrative Director of Auschwitz Concentration Camp. The former Administrative Director, Rudolf Wagner, is assigned to the SS Death's Head Division on July 15, 1942.

APMO, D-AuI-1/87, Commandant's Office Order 12/42.

149 names of "deceased" inmates are entered in the Occupancy Register. The high mortality rate is attributed primarily to the typhus epidemic.

APMO, D-AuI-3/1/5, Occupancy Register, pp. 698–703.

Forced by the typhus epidemic, Commandant Höss orders the SS men and their dependents confined to camp, thus limiting their freedom of movement. Höss forbids leaving the interest zone of the camp and entering and shopping in the town of Auschwitz, which is threatened by the epidemic.**

JULY 11

SS Lieutenant Colonel Brandt writes a memorandum about the discussion of July 7, 1942, with the SS Commander in Chief about the establishment of an experimental station for Professor Dr. Clauberg in Auschwitz.

Schnabel, Power Without Morality, pp. 271ff.; Doc. 101.

Head of Branch D of the WVHA Glücks informs the Commandants of the concentration camps, including Rudolf Höss, that according

APMO, IZ-13/89, Various Documents of the Third Reich, p. 212 (Original in BA Koblenz).

*Thus, the women's camp is no longer under the Commandant's Office of Ravensbrück but under the Commandant's Office of Auschwitz (APMO, Kraków Auschwitz Trial, vol. 57, p. 77, Statement of Defendant Maria Mandel).
**Garrison Order No. 17/42 of July 10, 1942, did not survive. Number, date, and content are nevertheless known. They can be reconstructed from the partial repetition in Garrison Order No. 26/42 of September 30, 1942, which was preserved (APMO, D-AuI-1).

to information of the RSHA packets of prisoners' clothing have been sent from the concentration camps to the Gestapo, especially in Brünn. In some cases, damage was discovered on the items caused by shots or bloodstains. Some of the packets were damaged on arrival, so that outsiders could see them. Soon RSHA will issue an order regulating sending the belongings of deceased prisoners. Until a general regulation for the confiscation of property is in effect, sending the belongings and clothing of executed prisoners is to be discontinued immediately.

30 female prisoners sent by the Sipo and SD from Helcl Prison in Kraków receive Nos. 8542–8571.

Four female prisoners sent from Kattowitz receive Nos. 8572–8575.

Jews from Slovakia arrive in a transport of the RSHA. After the selection, 182 men* and 148 women are admitted to the camp. The men receive Nos. 46463–46644 and the women 8576–8723. The rest of the deportees are killed in the gas chambers.

APMO, Höss Trial, vol. 6, p. 115.

Six prisoners sent from Kattowitz receive Nos. 46645–46650.

JULY 12

Polish prisoner Juliusz Hampel (No. 24610) is transferred.

127 prisoners die in Auschwitz-Birkenau, most of them from typhus.

APMO-D-AuI-3/1/5, Occupancy Register, pp. 706–710.

JULY 13

The Huta Engineering Company submits a bid with a cost estimate for the construction of a crematorium in Birkenau of 133,756.65 RM.

APMO, D-Z-Bau/6, Docs. CCA.

In the register of the prisoners' infirmary in Block 28 of the main camp, several cases of typhus are listed.**

APMO, D-AuI-5/3, Prisoners' Infirmary Register of Block 28.

Polish prisoner Kazimierz Leśnik (No. 39500), who was captured while escaping, is sent to the bunker of Block 11. He dies in the bunker on July 17.

APMO, D-AuI-3/1a, Bunker Register, p. 72; D-AuI-3/1/5, Occupancy Register, p. 731.

70 prisoners sent by the Sipo and SD from Montelupich Prison in Kraków receive Nos. 46651–46720. Dr. Jan Olbrycht receives No. 46688.†

*By August 15, 1942, i.e., after five weeks, 64 men are still alive, and 118 have died, almost two-thirds.
**Many register in the infirmary admissions room, where they are divided into two groups by an SS Doctor. He leads one group into the prisoners' infirmary and the other to the treatment room of Block 20, where they are killed with phenol injections.
†In 1947, he is called as an authority in the area of treatment and health, hygiene and nutrition in Auschwitz-Birkenau at the trial of the members of the SS of Auschwitz-Birkenau. He presents his expert opinion at the trial on December 10, 1947, before the Supreme National Court in Kraków.

217 prisoners sent by the Sipo and SD from Radom receive Nos. 46721–46937.

One female prisoner sent from Kattowitz receives No. 8724.

JULY 14

Two Polish political prisoners, Aleksander Buczyński (No. 12754) and Eugeniusz Stoczewski (No. 22883), who escaped from the Penal Company on June 10, 1942, are executed in Auschwitz. They were captured on June 14, 1942, and locked in the bunker of Block 11.

APMO, IZ-8/Gestapo Lodz/2-62, 133/3-272, 278; D-AuI-3/1a, Bunker Register, p. 67; D-AuI-3/1/5, Occupancy Register, p. 717.

In the courtyard of Block 11 the seven Polish political prisoners called out the day before by the Political Department are shot. They are Antoni Cieślak (No. 14149), Jerzy Jurkowski (No. 16650), Alojzy Przegiętka (No. 16754), Adolf Rusiński (No. 16792), Józef Wieczorek (No. 18656), Władysław Matyjaszek (No. 19533), and Józef Jakielek (No. 33126).

APMO, D-AuI-3/1/5, Occupancy Register, p. 717.

One female prisoner transferred from Ravensbrück receives No. 8725.

JULY 15

In connection with the decision to employ prisoners from Auschwitz in the cement factory in Golleschau* of Golleschau Portland Cement, Inc., which is under Office W-II of the WVHA, a squad of 12 prisoners** is sent to the cement factory. An auxiliary camp of Auschwitz is set up there and the prisoners are to furnish the designated areas.

Jerzy Frąckiewicz, "Das Nebenlager Golleschau" (The Golleschau Auxiliary Camp), *HvA*, no. 9 (1966), 57–71.

The Lenz company refuses to build a crematorium in Birkenau because of the lack of labor. As a result, the Central Construction Administration of the Waffen SS and the Auschwitz Police ask Huta Engineering to begin construction immediately, in accordance with their offer of July 13.

APMO-D-Z-Bau/6, Docs. ZBL, Inventory No. 27954.

22 prisoners sent from Lodz receive Nos. 46938–46959.

One prisoner sent from Kattowitz receives No. 46960.

Greek prisoner Emmanuel Kukjainis (No. 19109), born June 8, 1897, is released from the camp.

*Golleschau (Goleszów) is on the railroad line connecting Bielietz with Teschen. The distance to Auschwitz is almost 40 miles, hence the necessity of setting up an auxiliary camp there.
**Michał Kruczek (No. 218), Paweł Balura (No. 1329), Aleksander Masłowicz (No. 4915), Piotr Maroszek (No. 6433), Stefan Garbacki (No. 11226), Zygmunt Dusza (No. 18191), Tadeusz Zimnowlocki (No. 18682), Alojzy Dombau (No. 22459), Jerzy Kosarowski (No. 38159), Jan Grajek (No. 39199), Józef Śliwa (No. 39239), Ignacy Fraczkowski (No. 39563).

Two Polish prisoners, Stefan Wazdrąg (No. 39872) and Władysław Kaminski (No. 46665), are transferred.

APMO, D-AuI-3/1/5, Occupancy Register, pp. 718–723.

146 prisoners die in Auschwitz-Birkenau.

JULY 16

127 prisoners sent by the Sipo and SD from Pawiak Prison in Warsaw receive Nos. 46961–47087.

19 female prisoners sent from Lodz receive Nos. 8726–8744.

One female prisoner sent from Kattowitz receives No. 8745.

Commandant Rudolf Höss informs the SS personnel in the garrison that SS First Lieutenant Schöttl has taken over the Buna plant labor squad. He is responsible for security and transport of the squad.

APMO, D-AuI-1/87, Commandant's Office Order 12/42.

Because of the typhus epidemic, Commandant Höss forbids swimming, washing, and watering animals in the Vistula and Soła rivers.

Ibid.

50 Polish prisoners summoned the day before to register in the office after morning roll call are shot in the courtyard of Block 11. They include Stanisław Stankiewicz (No. 34358), Henryk Sejpt (No. 34482), Stefan Szymczak (No. 34484), Antoni Malinowski (No. 39387), Stanisław Czyzycki (No. 39471), Zygmunt Lewicki (No. 39502), Władysław Lezański (No. 39503), Tadeusz Oszust (No. 14004), Wacław Okoniewski (No. 14539), Jan Okoniewski (No. 14541), Edward Szczerbowski (No. 21052), Jerzy Pogdziński (No. 23312), Włodzimierz Szadkowski (No. 31322), Władysław Szczepański (No. 31323) and Edmund Szymański (No. 31329).

APMO, D-AuI-3/1/5, Occupancy Register, pp. 724–731.

JULY 17

55 female prisoners sent in a group transport receive Nos. 8746–8800.

In two transports of the RSHA, 2,000 Jews arrive from Westerbork and Amersfoort camps in Holland. 1,303 men and boys and 697 women and girls arrive. After the selection, 1,251 men and 300 women are admitted to the camp. The men receive Nos. 47088–47687, the women, Nos. 8801–8999 and 9027–9127. The other 449 deportees are killed in the gas chambers.

APMO, Höss Trial, vol. 6, p. 115.

155 prisoners sent in a group transport receive Nos. 47688–47842.

A female prisoner sent from Kattowitz is given No. 9000.

25 female Jewish prisoners receive Nos. 9001–9025.

SS Commander in Chief Himmler carries out a second inspection in Auschwitz. The Gauleiter of Upper Silesia, Bracht, SS General

Höss, *Commandant in Auschwitz*, pp. 233–236.

Schmauser, and SS Lieutenant General Kammler also take part. On the first day, Höss explains the arrangement and position of the camp using maps. In the Construction Administration, Kammler explains the projects either planned or under construction with the help of maps, blueprints, and models. Finally, Himmler and his escort tour the whole Interest Zone: the farms and soil improvement projects, the dam construction, the laboratories, and the plant breeding in Rajsko, the cattle breeding and nursery. Inspecting Birkenau, Himmler observes the prisoners at work, tours accommodations, kitchens, and infirmaries and sees the emaciated victims of the epidemic. After touring Birkenau, he takes part in the killing of one of the newly entered transports of Jews. He attends the unloading, the selection of the able-bodied, the killing by gas in Bunker 2, and the clearing of the bunker. At this time, the corpses are not yet being burned but are piled up in pits and buried. Then Himmler tours the Buna plant and the installation of a sewage gas plant. In the evening there is a reception for the guests and all SS officers of the Auschwitz garrison. After the reception, Himmler goes with Höss, Schmauser, Kammler and the Director of Agriculture Caesar to a reception at the home of Gauleiter Bracht in Kattowitz, to which, at Himmler's request, Mrs. Höss also comes.

JULY 18

With Schmauser, Himmler visits the kitchens, the women's camp (which then includes Blocks 1–10), the workshops, the stables, the personal effects camp (so-called Canada), and the DAW plant as well as the butcher shop and the bakery. He sees the prisoners and makes precise inquiries about each prisoner category and the current occupancy level. In the women's camp he is shown the effect of a whipping. Himmler must personally approve the flogging of women. He is also present at the roll call. There, SS Head Supervisor Langefeldt applies for the release of a few German female prisoners who have been imprisoned for a long time in the concentration camp. Himmler consents to the release.* After the tour, a final discussion takes place in Höss's office. In Schmauser's presence, Himmler says the Sipo operations he has ordered must not be stopped for any reason, least of all because of the lack of accommodations and so forth which was presented to him. He orders Höss to proceed faster with the construction of the Birkenau camp, to kill the Jewish prisoners who are unfit for work, to prepare for the building of armaments plants, and to pursue the agricultural experiments intensively. In recognition for his work and performance, Höss is promoted to SS Lieutenant Colonel.

Jews from Slovakia enter in a transport of the RSHA. After the selection, 327 men are admitted to the camp and given Nos. 48494–48820. 178 women receive Nos. 9160–9337. The rest of the people are killed in the gas chambers.

Ibid., pp. 237–238; APMO, Höss Trial, vol. 6, p. 85; Julia Skodowa, *Tri roky bez mena* (Three Years Without a Name), Bratislava, 1962, p. 35.

*The approved release does not take place immediately. One of the women proposed for release, Luise Maurer, does not leave the camp until the end of 1943 (APMO, Accounts, vol. 66, p. 172, Account of Former Prisoner Luise Maurer).

36 prisoners sent by the Sipo and SD from Kraków receive Nos. 48821–48856.

23 male and 32 female prisoners sent in a group transport receive Nos. 48857–48879 and 9128–9159.

The Jew Michen Bino (No. 41607), born September 15, 1895, hangs himself. He was locked in the bunker of Block 11 on July 13 by order of the Political Department.

APMO, D-AuI-3/1a, Bunker Register, p. 73.

Jewish women arrive with a transport of the RSHA. After the selection, 212 women are admitted to the camp as prisoners. They receive Nos. 9338–9549.

JULY 19

The Commandant's Office of Auschwitz is informed that a transport with 1,000 Jews, including 121 women, left le Bourget–Drancy at 9:05 A.M. for Auschwitz.

APMO, D-RF-3/6, Inventory No. 22007.

809 Jewish men and 119 Jewish women are sent with the sixth transport of the RSHA from Pithiviers Camp in France. They receive Nos. 48880–49688 and 9550–9668.

23 female prisoners sent in a group transport receive Nos. 9669–9691.

As a result of the typhus epidemic and various methods of extermination, 135 male prisoners die in Auschwitz-Birkenau.

APMO, D-AuI-3/1/5, Occupancy Register, pp. 736–741.

JULY 20

At 4:20 A.M., the SS Guard in Watchtower D in the main camp shoots Jewish prisoner Szlama Garfinkel (No. 42042).

APMO, D-AuI-1/3a, FvD, vol. 91.

At 4:50 A.M., Jewish prisoner Rudolf Fried (No. 42023) is shot by the SS guard in Watchtower D in the main camp.*

Ibid.

70 prisoners sent by the Sipo and SD from Kraków receive Nos. 49689–49758.

As a result of the typhus epidemic and the various methods of extermination, 150 male prisoners die in Auschwitz-Birkenau.

APMO, D-AuI-3/1/5, Occupancy Register, pp. 741–746.

JULY 21

Four prisoners sent from Kattowitz receive Nos. 49759–49762.

*These prisoners probably decided to commit suicide by going "to the wire." They are shot when the SS guard notices them.

14 male and nine female prisoners sent from Oppeln receive Nos. 49763–49776 and 9692–9700.

Two female prisoners sent from Kattowitz receive Nos. 9701 and 9702.

879 Jewish men and 121 Jewish women arrive with the seventh RSHA transport from Drancy. After the selection, 504 men, who receive Nos. 49777–50280, and 121 women, given Nos. 9703–9823, are admitted to the camp as prisoners. The other 375 people are killed in the gas chambers. There are 386 Jews of Polish origin in this transport.

112 prisoners sent from Radom by the Sipo and SD receive Nos. 50281–50392.

Two prisoners sent from Oppeln receive Nos. 50393 and 50394.

Six prisoners sent from Kattowitz receive Nos. 50395–50400.

The Commandant's Office is informed that a transport of 824 people, including 430 women, left Angers-St.-Laud in France at 11:35 P.M. for Auschwitz.

APMO, D-RF-3/7, Inventory No. 22008.

Two female German prisoners escape from the Penal Company in Budy. They were sent to Auschwitz from Ravensbrück on March 26, 1942. They are Greta Jaskulski (No. 253),* born February 8, 1919, in Kriefkohl; and Hildegard Heine,** born March 15, 1917, in Berlin.

APMO, IZ-8/Gestapo Lodz/3/88/301–306.

As a result of the typhus epidemic and the various methods of extermination, 128 male prisoners die in Auschwitz-Birkenau.

APMO, D-AuI-3/1/6, Occupancy Register, pp. 745–750.

JULY 22

Two prisoners sent from Kattowitz receive Nos. 50401 and 50402.

56 female political prisoners sent from Yugoslav Maribor in Slovenia receive Nos. 9824–9879.

931 Jews arrive from Westerbork Camp in an RSHA transport. After the selection, 479 men and 297 women are admitted to the camp as inmates. The men are given Nos. 50403–50881, the women, 9880–10176. The other 155 deportees are killed in the gas chambers.

The Commandant's Office is informed that a transport with 996 Jews left le Bourget–Drancy at 8:55 A.M. for Auschwitz.

APMO, D-RF-3/8, Inventory No. 22009.

*She is captured in Hamburg, according to the telegram of the Gestapo of September 9, 1942, and transferred back to Auschwitz.
**She is captured in Berlin on September 14, 1942.

Four Polish prisoners from Kattowitz, sent to Auschwitz on June 29, 1942, are shot. They are Władysław Drabek (No. 42773), Franciszek Drabek (No. 42774), Jan Igawa (No. 42775) and Józef Gawęda (No. 42776).

APMO, D-AuI-3/6, Occupancy Register, p. 753.

As a result of the typhus epidemic and the various methods of extermination, 139 male prisoners die in Auschwitz-Birkenau.

Ibid., pp. 750–755.

JULY 23

As 5:15 A.M., Jewish prisoner Abraham Warszawski (No. 42679) is shot by the SS Guard in Watchtower D of the main camp.

APMO, D-AuI-1/3a, FvD, p. 94.

At 6:00 A.M., Jewish prisoner Hans Redlich (No. 43798) is shot by the SS Guard in Watchtower D of the main camp.

Ibid.

Three prisoners sent from Kattowitz receive Nos. 50882–50884.

In Garrison Order No. 19/42, Commandant Höss orders a total camp curfew. The SS men and their families are forbidden to leave the area inside the outer sentry line. SS families living outside the outer sentry line may not enter the camp area. Official passports are introduced allowing the SS men to go back and forth from their homes to their posts via the most direct route. Linen is to be cleaned and changed at least once a week. SS men may not visit their families. An immediate travel ban is imposed on all SS dependents, officers, noncommissioned officers, civilian officials, and workers. In case of official travel, SS men must report to the SS clinic for bathing and release before the trip. It is forbidden to enter the headquarters of the Waffen SS.* Civilian workers are to go back and forth to work on designated roads under the supervision of the SS. At 3:00 P.M. on Mondays and Fridays, a medical examination for families is to be carried out in the school building on the Soła River. Permission of a doctor must be obtained for official or private trips to Kattowitz.**

APMO, D-AuI, Garrison Order 19/42 of July 23, 1942.

130 prisoners sent by the Sipo and SD from Lublin receive Nos. 50885–51014.

827 Jews arrive with the eighth RSHA transport from Angers St. Laud. After the selection 411 men and 390 women are admitted to the camp. The men are given Nos. 51015–51425, the women, Nos. 10177–10566. The other 26 deportees are killed in the gas chambers. There are 337 Jews of Polish origin in the transport.

---

*A hotel next to the railroad station in Auschwitz.
**For prisoners, the camp arrest means that releases and transfers to other camps are postponed until the arrest is lifted. The Buna factory squad is forbidden to go to work in the I. G. Farben factory. The precise date of this order is unknown. According to reports of former prisoners, it takes place at the end of July and is later the reason for the construction of an auxiliary camp in Monowitz, close to the Buna works, which are under construction.

In the courtyard of Block 11, 14 Polish political prisoners are shot. The day before, they were summoned by the Political Department to register. They are Stanisław Arct (No. 12654), Tadeusz Filipiak (No. 13654), Stefan Wiśniewski (No. 13663), Jan Chabros (No. 14060), Władysław Majek (No. 14273), Jan Kryszczuk (No. 14632), Marian Pietrzyk (No. 14732), Bogusław Pietrzyk (No. 14733), Marian Kowalczyk (No. 16930), Władysław Lubawski (No. 18495), Wacław Kamiński (No. 19678), Stansław Wilkożek (No. 19680), Stefan Dymel (No. 21510), and Jan Bartnik (No. 22762).

APMO, D-AuI-3/1/6, Occupancy Register, p. 759.

As a result of the typhus epidemic and the various methods of extermination, 140 prisoners die in Auschwitz-Birkenau.

Ibid., pp. 755–760.

JULY 24

60 prisoners sent from Kraków by the Sipo and SD receive Nos. 51426–51485.

18 male and four female prisoners sent in a group transport receive Nos. 51486–51503 and 10567–10570.

615 Jewish male prisoners are marked with Nos. 51504–52118; 385 female Jewish prisoners receive Nos. 10664–11049. They are sent to Auschwitz with the ninth RSHA transport from Drancy. There are 596 Jews of Polish origin in the transport.

The Commandant's Office is informed that a transport with 1,000 Jews left le Bourget–Drancy for Auschwitz at 8:55 A.M.

APMO, D-RF-3/9, Inventory No. 20010.

Two Polish prisoners, Józef Musielak (No. 512) and Albin Borowicz (No. 6756), escape from the auxiliary camp Rajsko. Musielak was sent to Auschwitz from Kraków by the Sipo and SD on June 14, 1940, because of his attempt to cross the Hungarian border. Borowicz was sent to Auschwitz by the Sipo and SD because of deliberate assistance to the Polish resistance movement. The prisoners worked as dairymen on the farm of the auxiliary camp Rajsko.

APMO, IZ-8/Gestapo Lodz/3/88/308; D-AuI-3/1/6, Occupancy Register, p. 773.

As a result of the typhus epidemic and the various methods of extermination, 184 male prisoners die in Auschwitz-Birkenau.

APMO, D-AuI-3/1/6, Occupancy Register, pp. 760–767.

JULY 25

Jews from Slovakia arrive with an RSHA transport. After the selection, 192 men and 93 women are admitted to the camp as inmates. The men are given Nos. 52119–52310 and the women, Nos. 10571–10663. The other deportees are killed in the gas chambers.

200 young, educated French Jewesses, considered Communists by the SS men, are sent to the Penal Company in Budy. In this group are also a few Polish women whose husbands emigrated to France in search of work.

Piątkowska, *Memoirs*, p. 57.

Five prisoners sent in a group transport receive Nos. 52311–52315.

34 prisoners sent from Kraków by the Sipo and SD receive Nos. 52316–52349.

17 prisoners sent from Kattowitz receive Nos. 52350–52366.

Two female prisoners sent from Oppeln receive Nos. 11050 and 11051.

An RSHA transport of 1,000 Jews from Westerbork Camp arrives. In it are 577 men and boys and 427 women and girls. After the selection, 516 men and 293 women are admitted to the camp. The men are given Nos. 52367–52882, the women, Nos. 11052–11344. The other 191 people are killed in the gas chambers.

In the courtyard of Block 11 five Polish political prisoners are shot at the execution wall. The day before, they were summoned by the Political Department to register. They are Józef Hess (No. 40676), Wojciech Cader (No. 40679), Paweł Kania (No. 40680), Franciszek Pytlik (No. 45082) and Józef Zon (No. 45086).

APMO, D-AuI-3/1/6, Occupancy Register, p. 773.

At evening roll call, the absence of one prisoner is discovered. The search operation remains unsuccessful.

APMO, D-AuI-1/3, FvD, p. 95.

As a result of the spreading typhus epidemic and the various methods of extermination, 234 male prisoners die in Auschwitz-Birkenau; the next day, another 99 die.

APMO, D-AuI-3/1/6, Occupancy Register, pp. 767–774, 778.

JULY 26

370 male and 630 female Jewish prisoners are given Nos. 52883–53252 and 11345–11974. They are sent with the tenth RSHA transport from Drancy. There are 551 Jews of Polish origin in the transport.

JULY 27

The standby alert is called off and the missing prisoner is entered as an escapee. He is Simon Jacobs (No. 48177), a Dutch Jew.

Ibid., p. 784.

68 male and 35 female prisoners sent by the Sipo and SD for the Kraków District from the prison in Tarnów receive Nos. 53253–53320 and 11975–12009.

German political prisoner Dr. Diethelm Scheer (No. 11111) is released from the camp but remains as a civilian worker and continues to direct an ichthyology laboratory in the fish-breeding plant in the auxiliary camp Harmense.

Ibid., p. 783; Zięba, "Harmense," pp. 48–52.

The Commandant's Office is informed that a transport with 1,000 Jews left le Bourget–Drancy for Auschwitz at 10:30 A.M.

APMO, D-RF-3/10, Inventory No. 22011.

As a result of the typhus epidemic and the various means of extermination, 191 male prisoners die in Auschwitz-Birkenau.

APMO, D-AuI-3/1/6, Occupancy Register, pp. 778–784.

JULY 28

Four prisoners sent from Kattowitz receive Nos. 53321–53324.

1,010 Jews arrive with an RSHA transport from Westerbork. There are 542 men and boys in the transport and 468 women and girls. After the selection, 473 men and 315 women are admitted to the camp as inmates. The men are given Nos. 53325–53797, the women, Nos. 12010–12324. The other 222 deportees are killed in the gas chambers.

At 2:30 A.M., a female prisoner is shot by SS man Peitz "while escaping."

APMO, Höss Trial, vol. 12, p. 218, quoted from the Guard Register.

The Commandant's Office is informed by the Sipo and SD in Kraków that Jan Laskowski (No. 12543), who escaped from the Penal Company on June 10, 1942, has been captured in Tarnów and will be sent back to Auschwitz in the next transport.

APMO, IZ-8/Gestapo Lodz/2-182, 3a-589.

The Commandant's Office informs the appropriate authorities that Józef Traczyk, who escaped from the Penal Company on June 10, 1942, has been recaptured.

APMO, IZ-8/Gestapo Lodz/3a-586.

During the day, 10 Jewish prisoners are shot by SS men "while escaping." They are Calel Roza (No. 28414), Zoltan Weltman (No. 30109), Szulim Frankel (No. 30357), Adolf Blich (No. 30397), Ezriel Bodner (No. 31692), Moses Ratner (No. 38887), Dawid Rosenbaum (No. 38905), Egon Meuzer (No. 39970), Salomon Mizrahi (No. 41005), and Jean Doktor (No. 46316).

APMO, D-AuI-5/1, Morgue Register, p. 169; D-AuI-3/1/6, Occupancy Register, pp. 785–787, 790.

An SS Doctor carries out a selection in the prisoners' infirmary, Block 20. He chooses 86 prisoners who, in his opinion, cannot be expected to make a rapid recovery; they are killed the same day with phenol injections.

APMO, Mat.RO, vol. VI, p. 14.

As a result of the typhus epidemic and the various means of extermination, 228 male prisoners die in Auschwitz-Birkenau.

APMO, D-AuI-3/1/6, Occupancy Register, pp. 785–792.

JULY 29

15 female prisoners sent in a group transport receive Nos. 12325–12339.

31 prisoners sent from Troppau receive Nos. 53798–53828.

In the eleventh RSHA transport from le Bourget–Drancy, 248 Jewish men receive Nos. 53829–54076; 742 Jewish women receive Nos. 12340–13081. There are 595 Jews of Polish origin in this transport.

The Commandant's Office obtains approval from the WVHA to send a truck to Dessau to fetch gas for the disinfection of the camp.*

APMO, Höss Trial, vol. 12, p. 166, Appendix 110.

As a result of the typhus epidemic and the various means of extermination, 116 male prisoners die in Auschwitz-Birkenau.

APMO, D-AuI-3/1/6, Occupancy Register, pp. 792–796.

Simon Jacobs (No. 48177), who escaped from the camp on July 25, is captured. He is locked in the bunker of Block 11 and sent on July 31 to the Penal Company in Birkenau, where he dies on August 3, 1942.

APMO, D-AuI-3/1/b, Bunker Register, p. 76; D-AuI-3/1/6, Occupancy Register, p. 813.

At 5:10 A.M., Jewish prisoner Albert Müller (No. 42343) is shot "while escaping."

APMO, Höss Trial, vol. 12, p. 219; D-AuI-5/1, Morgue Register, p. 174; D-AuI-3/1/6, Occupancy Register, p. 795.

The Commandant's Office is informed that a transport with 1,000 Jews left le Bourget–Drancy for Auschwitz at 8:55 A.M.

APMO, D-RF-3/11, Inventory No. 22012. [transport]

Three female prisoners, the Pole Alicja Zarytkiewicz (No. 7585**) and two Germans, escape from the Penal Company in Budy. The two Germans are Paulina Górska, born May 13, 1912, in Urbanowice, sent to Ravensbrück on August 9, 1941, and transferred to Auschwitz on March 26, 1942; and Erika Krause (No. 858), born May 29, 1918, in Dembowo, sent to Ravensbrück on February 4, 1942, and transferred to Auschwitz on March 26, 1942.†

APMO, IZ-8/Gestapo Lodz/3/ 311–314, Telegrams About the Escape.

Eduard Schulte, a German industrialist and antifascist from Breslau, visits Zurich and informs the Allies that during Himmler's visit to Auschwitz in July, he attended the killing of 499 Jews by gas, which took place in so-called Bunker Number 2. This is the first precise information the Allies receive from a German source about the extermination of the Jews carried out in the gas chambers of Auschwitz. Nevertheless, the Allies do not use the information appropriately; it is not accompanied by any retaliatory operation to prevent the Nazis from continuing with the extermination of the European Jews, which has begun.

Walter Laqueur and Richard Breitman, *Der Mann, der das Schweigen brach: Wie die Welt vom Holocaust erfuhr* (The Man Who Broke the Silence: How the World Learned of the Holocaust), Frankfurt/Main, 1986.

At evening roll call, the absence of one prisoner from the DAW plant is discovered and an alert ordered. The search operation remains unsuccessful until 6:15 A.M.

APMO, D-AuI-1/3, FvD, p. 99.

JULY 30

Escaped Czech prisoner Franciszek Stary (No. 39751) is captured. He is sent to the bunker of Block 11, where he hangs himself the next day.††

APMO, D-AuI-3/1b, Bunker Register, p. 74; D-AuI-5/1, Morgue Register, p. 178.

---

*Zyklon B gas is used both for killing in the gas chambers and for disinfecting the blocks.
**Alicja Zarytkiewicz goes to Kraków and fights in a partisan division.
†Erika Krause is captured and sent back to Auschwitz. On August 30, 1944, she is transferred to Ravensbrück.
††The suicides committed in the bunker of Block 11 can be explained by the prisoners' fear that they cannot stay alert during the torture and abuse during the interrogation by Political Department functionaries and might unwillingly betray people who had helped them; and also by the torture itself or the fear of impending torture.

110 female prisoners sent from Radom by the Sipo and SD receive Nos. 13082–13191.

Polish political prisoners Hugo Ćwierk (No. 18090), Marian Gieszczykiewicz (No. 39197), professor of bacteriology at the Jagiellonen University in Kraków, Eugeniusz Jurkowski (No. 39205), and Jerzy Karwaj (No. 39220) are ordered to register in the office after morning roll call.

APMO, Höss Trial, vol. 4, pp. 163ff, Account of Former Prisoner Stanisław Głowa.

At 10:50 P.M. the SS man on guard in Watchtower F in the main camp shoots a prisoner who approached the camp fence.

APMO, D-AuI-1/3a, FvD, p. 100.

As a result of the typhus epidemic and the various means of extermination, 107 male prisoners die in Auschwitz-Birkenau.

APMO, D-AuI-3/1/6, Occupancy Register, pp. 797–800.

JULY 31

After evening roll call, seven prisoners are shot at the execution wall in the courtyard of Block 11. Those shot are three prisoners captured after their escape and sent to the bunker—Jan Basta (No. 11801), Zygmunt Pilawski (No. 14156),* and Feliks Zurek (No. 21242)—and the prisoners summoned to register the previous day. Professor Dr. Marian Gieszczykiewicz has not registered, as his comrades in the prisoners' infirmary restrained him, and he pretended illness. At 9:00 A.M. Roll Call Leader Palitzsch issues an order to bring Gieszczykiewicz to the bunker of Block 11, regardless of his physical condition. They put the completely healthy professor on a stretcher and cover him with a blanket. The two prisoner orderlies, Stanisław Głowa and Klein, carry him to the courtyard of Block 11. Roll Call Leader Palitzsch pulls back the blanket, checks the number, and kills Professor Gieszczykiewicz with two shots to the head.**

APMO, Höss Trial, vol. 4, pp. 163ff, Account of Former Prisoner Stanisław Głowa; D-AuI-3/1/6, Occupancy Register, pp. 800ff.; D-AuI-3/1a, Bunker Register, pp. 65, 67, 70.

76 male and 53 female prisoners sent to Auschwitz in a group transport receive Nos. 54077–54152 and 13192–13244.

1,001 Jews arrive in the twelfth RSHA transport from Drancy. There are 270 men and 730 women in the transport. After the selection, all the men and 514 women are admitted to the camp as prisoners. The men receive Nos. 54153–54422 and the women, 13320–13833. The other 216 women are killed in the gas chambers. There are 622 Jews of Polish origin in the transport.

The Commandant's Office is informed that a transport of 1,049 Jews left Pithiviers for Auschwitz at 6:15 A.M.

APMO, D-RF-3/12, Inventory No. 22013.

*Zygmunt Pilawski escaped on July 29, 1941, and was sent back to Auschwitz on June 25, 1942.
**In the medical findings of the death certificate signed by SS Camp Doctor Friedrich Entress and addressed to the Commandant's Office, it is stated that prisoner Marian Gieszczykiewicz died of weakening resulting from intestinal catarrh (APMO, Dpr.-HD/37, p. 57).

Janusz Skrzetuski-Pogonowski (No. 253), who works in the surveying squad, confirms with name and number the receipt of a parcel from a secret assistance organization that is intended for the prisoners' infirmary. The parcel contains about 1,000 ampules of various medicines, Coramina, Digipuratum, calcium, glucose, etc.*

APMO, Mat.RO, vol. 1, p. 5.

As a result of the typhus epidemic and the various forms of extermination, 145 male prisoners die in Auschwitz-Birkenau.

APMO, D-AuI-3/1/6, Occupancy Register, pp. 800–805.

JULY 1–31

10,311 detainees are sent to Auschwitz. 10,190 prisoners are given numbers from the general series 44233–54422. The other 121 inmates are either reeducation prisoners or those sent back to the camp after interrogation by the Gestapo or after escaping from the camp and being sent back again to the bunker of Block 11.**

As a result of the difficult conditions of life, the typhus epidemic, and the various forms of extermination such as shooting and selection of prisoners in the camp and the prisoners' infirmary (where those not expected to make a quick recovery and regain their "able-bodied" status are selected and killed in the gas chambers or with phenol injections), 4,124 inmates die in Auschwitz-Birkenau. These include 2,903 Jews, 977 Poles (including 125 reeducation prisoners), 190 Czechs, 41 Germans, five Russians (including one POW), three Yugoslavs, three French, one Bulgarian, and one Gypsy.†

APMO, D-AuI-3/1/5–6, Occupancy Register, pp. 636–805.

AUGUST 1

At morning roll call, the occupancy level of Auschwitz-Birkenau is 21,421 male prisoners, including 153 Russian POWs.††

APMO, D-AuI-3/1/6, Occupancy Register, p. 805.

An RSHA transport of Jews from Slovakia arrives. After the selection, 165 men receive Nos. 54423–54587, 75 women, Nos. 13254–13319; they are admitted to the camp as inmates. The rest of the deportees are killed in the gas chambers.

An RSHA transport of 1,007 Jews from Westerbork arrives with 540 men and boys and 467 women and girls. After the selection,

---

*The medicines officially available for the treatment of sick prisoners are either too little or ineffective in the difficult living conditions in the camp. Much more than two-thirds of the medicines used in the prisoners' infirmary of the main camp are provided by illegally supplied drugs. Some are obtained by inmates who work in outside squads. Concealing goods is very dangerous for the prisoners and many are killed for it.
**The figures are based on the entries in the Occupancy Register and the lists of male transports.
†Based on the data in the Occupancy Register. This number does not include Jews killed in the gas chamber, who are brought directly from the loading platform to the bunker without being entered in the camp register.
††The occupancy of the women's camp is not known; since the relevant documents are missing, it cannot be established.

490 men and 317 women are admitted to the camp as inmates; they receive Nos. 54588–55077 and 13834–14150. The other 200 deportees are killed in the gas chambers.

The Head of Branch B of the WVHA, Lorner, explains in a letter (No. BI320-1-Ha-E) to Office D-IV, the concentration camps administration, that it is agreed that on the day of an execution, the execution squad is to receive an additional ration of 100 grams of meat, a fifth of a liter of liquor, and five cigarettes per person.*

APMO, Dpr.-Hd/12, p. 58, Appendix 20.

The Sipo Sergeant assigned to Auschwitz, Josef Bailer, becomes head of the guard dog squadron.**

APMO, D-AuI-1/88, Commandant's Office Order No. 13/42.

The corpses of 60 male and five female† prisoners are sent to the morgue from the main camp.

APMO, D-AuI-5/1, Morgue Register, pp. 181ff.

As a result of the typhus epidemic and the various forms of extermination, 129 prisoners die in Auschwitz-Birkenau.

APMO, D-AuI-3/1/6, Occupancy Register, pp. 805–810.

Höss informs the staff of the Commandant's Office of an order of the higher SS authorities of July 15, 1942, forbidding photographing executions.

APMO, D-AuI-1/88, Commandant's Office Order No. 13/42.

AUGUST 2

Five prisoners sent in a group transport receive Nos. 55078–55082. Five female prisoners sent from Prague receive Nos. 14151–14155.

The thirteenth RSHA transport from Pithiviers arrives. 693 Jewish men receive Nos. 55083–55775; 359 Jewish women receive Nos. 14156–14514.††

100 prisoners are transferred to the Golleschau cement factory and form an auxiliary camp there. The prisoners work in quarries, in the cement factory itself, and in the provisioning of the auxiliary

Frąkiewicz, "Golleschau," pp. 57–60; APMO, Höss Trial, vol. 21, p. 39; D-AuI-5/1, p. 188, Morgue Register of the Main Camp. The name Golleschau is mentioned here for the first time on August 4, 1942, next to the name of the deceased prisoner Elia Rozenwurzel (No. 43486), born April 16, 1904, in Warsaw. Rozenwurzel was sent to Auschwitz with the fifth RSHA transport from France.

---

*SS men who participate in the selection and gassing probably receive an additional ration on the basis of this order. A functionary of the Political Department, Pery Broad, writes: "Every SS man gets a coupon for a special ration and liquor. A fifth of a liter for every transport. No wonder that alcohol flows from the staff of the Commandant's Office" (Broad, "Memoirs," p. 35).

**In his autobiography, Höss writes "dog squadron" or "guard dog squadron." The guard dog squadron is used to oversee female prisoners working outside the camp, to bring transports from the unloading platform to the camp, and to search for escaped prisoners. According to Höss's report, there are extreme difficulties with the dog squadron (Höss, *Commandant in Auschwitz*, pp. 156–158).

†For the first time, female prisoners are entered in the Morgue Register without numbers, as for example "u. 5 F.K.L.," meaning "and five women in the women's camp" (Frauenkonzentrationslager).

††Berta Falk, who works in the auxiliary camp Rajsko in the plant-breeding squad, receives No. 14184. There, a plant related to the dandelion, *Taraxacum officinale*, is cultivated, from whose roots a rubberlike substance is extracted. Berta Falk writes the doctoral thesis for the second wife of SS Lieutenant Colonel Caesar, the Director of Agriculture in Auschwitz. Caesar's first wife died of typhus.

camp. The commander of the auxiliary camp is SS Staff Sergeant Picklapp. The guard consists of 40 SS men.*

As a result of the typhus epidemic and the various forms of extermination in Auschwitz-Birkenau, 112 male prisoners die. In the Morgue Register the corpse of one woman is listed FKL (Frauenkonzentrationslager), without a number, along with the corpse of a civilian worker.

APMO, D-AuI-3/1/6, Occupancy Register, pp. 810–813; D-AuI-5/1/2, Morgue Register, p. 184.

AUGUST 3

The SS Camp Doctor carries out a selection in the prisoners' infirmary. He selects 193 prisoners recuperating from typhus. They are taken to Birkenau and killed in the gas chambers.**

APMO, Höss Trial, vol. 7, p. 155; D-AuI-5/3, Prisoners' Infirmary Register of Block 28, pp. 172–178; D-AuI-3/1/6, Occupancy Register.

48 prisoners sent by the Sipo and SD for the District of Kraków receive Nos. 55776–55823.

Two prisoners sent from Kattowitz receive Nos. 55824 and 55825.

The Commandant's Office is informed that a transport of 1,034 Jews left Pithiviers for Auschwitz at 6:15 A.M.

APMO, D-RF-3/13, Inventory No. 22014.

As a result of the typhus epidemic and various forms of extermination, 142 prisoners die in Auschwitz-Birkenau.

APMO, D-AuI-3/1/6, Occupancy Register, pp. 814–818.

AUGUST 1–3

In the gas chambers of Bunkers 1 and 2, almost 5,000 Jewish men, women, and children from Bendsburg are killed. They were deported to Auschwitz for extermination by the RSHA.

Gilbert, *Final Solution*, p. 112.

AUGUST 4

39 prisoners receive Nos. 55826–55864; one female prisoner sent from Kattowitz receives the free No. 9026.

43 prisoners, transferred to Auschwitz from Flossenbürg, receive Nos. 55865–55909.

Two female Czech prisoners, Anna Přihoda (No. 7457),† born April 9, 1906, and Maria Poček (No. 7636),†† born September 24, 1919, escape from the Penal Company in Budy on the night of August 3–4.

APMO, IZ-8/Gestapo Lodz/2-68–71.

---

*The number of prisoners employed in the cement factory by 1942 reaches 350, rises to 450 in 1943, and surpasses 1,000 in 1944.
**In the Prisoners' Infirmary register of Block 28, "moved to Birkenau" is entered next to the names of the 193 sick prisoners. In the Occupancy Register, on the other hand, the names of these prisoners are entered in the list of the deceased, the entries divided among three successive days. 30 of them are entered on August 10, 100 on August 11, and 63 on August 12.
†She is caught and sent back to Auschwitz, where she dies on November 27, 1943.
††She is caught and sent back to Auschwitz, where she dies in 1942.

Polish prisoner Zygmunt Slowik (No. 52346) escapes from the agriculture squad. He is arrested on October 13, 1942, in Sandomierz and sent to the prison in Lublin.

APMO, IZ-8/Gestapo Lodz/2-98, pp. 100ff.

As a result of the typhus epidemic and various forms of extermination, 138 prisoners die in Auschwitz.

APMO, D-AuI-3/1/6, Occupancy Register, pp. 819–823.

1,013 Jews arrive in an RSHA transport from Westerbork that includes 520 men and boys and 493 women and girls. After the selection, 429 men and 268 women are admitted to the camp as inmates. The women receive Nos. 14515–14782. The other 316 deportees are killed in the gas chambers.

AUGUST 5

Five prisoners sent from Prague receive Nos. 55910–55914.

A prisoner sent from Kattowitz receives No. 55915.

429 Jews sent from Westerbork the day before with an RSHA transport and classified as able-bodied receive Nos. 55916–56344.

66 prisoners sent to the camp by the Lublin Sipo and SD receive Nos. 56345–56410.

In connection with the decision of the Commandant's Office to move the women's camp out of the main camp to Birkenau, where several dozen barracks have already been put up in Section B-Ia, the move is begun by putting Jewish women arriving in RSHA transports there. At first this leads to confusion in the distribution of numbers to female prisoners, since some of the transports are still getting identification numbers in the main camp, while others are already numbered in Birkenau. This leads to a delay before female prisoners receive numbers that run in order.

52 Jewish men and 982 Jewish women arrive with the fourteenth RSHA transport from Pithiviers. After the selection, 22 men, who receive Nos. 56411–56432, and 542 women, who are numbered after the registration of the deported Belgian Jewish women, are admitted to the camp. The other 470 people are killed in the gas chambers.

998 persons arrive with the first RSHA transport from Malines Camp in Belgium. There are 570 men and boys and 428 women and girls in this transport.* After the selection, 426 men, who

*The figures quoted in this work for the number of Belgian Jews sent to Auschwitz by all the RSHA transports are based on the work of Serge Klarsfeld and Maxime Steinberg (Serge Klarsfeld and Maxime Steinberg, *Mémorial de la Déportation des Juifs de Belgique* [*Memorial of the Deportation of the Jews of Belgium*], printed in Belgium, 1982).

receive Nos. 56433–56858, and 318 women, who receive Nos. 14784–15101, are admitted to the camp as inmates.

542 women sent from Pithiviers Camp in France with the fourteenth RSHA transport and classified as able-bodied receive Nos. 15102–15267 and 15269–15644.

Jewish prisoner Samuel Tempel (No. 41409) is shot "while escaping."

APMO, D-AuI-5/1, Morgue Register, p. 189; D-AuI-3/1/6, Occupancy Register, p. 825.

The Commandant's Office is informed that a transport with 1,014 Jews left Beaune-la-Rolande for Auschwitz at 5:25 A.M.

APMO, D-RF-3/14, Inventory No. 22015.

As a result of the typhus epidemic and various forms of extermination, 125 prisoners die in Auschwitz-Birkenau.

APMO, D-AuI-3/1/6, Occupancy Register, pp. 823–828.

AUGUST 6

In the early morning hours, Polish prisoner Teresa Gawet, born October 15, 1914, escapes from the camp. She was sent to Auschwitz from Radom on July 30, 1942, by the Sipo and SD.

APMO, IZ-8/Gestapo Lodz/3-315.

German prisoner Frieda Wiese, born December 9, 1918, in Rankwitz, escapes from the Penal Company in Budy.

APMO, IZ-8/Gestapo Lodz/2-76–77.

A start has been made to move the female prisoners out of the main camp to Birkenau. After morning roll call, the women are lined up in work columns and taken to Camp B-Ia in Birkenau.

APMO, Depositions, vol. 14, pp. 70, 74, 88.

20 prisoners sent from Kattowitz receive Nos. 56859–56878.

Polish prisoner Franciszek Majchert (No. 51468) is shot "while escaping."

APMO, D-AuI-5/1, Morgue Register, p. 191; D-AuI-3/1/6, Occupancy Register, p. 830.

The WVHA issues an order to the Commandants of the concentration camps "that the shorn human hair obtained in all concentration camps is to be utilized." Men's hair is to be made into industrial felt and spun into yarn; women's hair cut off and combed is to be made into hair-yarn socks for submarine crews and hair-felt stockings for the German Railroad. The Commandants are also instructed to register "amounts of hair collected monthly, separated according to male and female hair ... on the fifth of every month."

Jewish Historical Institute of Warsaw, *Faschismus, Getto, Massenmord: Dokumentation über Ausrottung und Widerstand der Juden in Polen während des Zweiten Weltkrieges* (Fascism, Ghetto, Mass Murder: Documentation of the Extermination and Resistance of the Jews in Poland During the Second World War), 2d. ed., Berlin, 1961, p. 402.

126 male prisoners die in Auschwitz.

APMO, D-AuI-3/1/6, Occupancy Register, pp. 828–832.

AUGUST 7

224 male and 28 female prisoners sent in a group transport receive Nos. 56879–57102 and 15645–15672.

Five Russian POWs are sent to Auschwitz.

Jewish prisoner Majer Lyszkiewicz (No. 40897) hangs himself in the main camp.

APMO, D-AuI-5/1, Morgue Register, p. 194; D-AuI-3/1/6, Occupancy Register, p. 835.

20 Polish prisoners are shot at the execution wall in the courtyard of Block 11.

APMO, D-AuI-3/1/6, Occupancy Register, pp. 832ff.

The corpses of seven women are listed in the Morgue Register.

APMO, D-AuI-5/1/2, Morgue Register, p. 192.

The fifteenth RSHA transport arrives from Beaune-la-Rolande in France with 1,014 Jews. There are 588 men and boys and 426 women and girls in the transport. After the selection, 214 men, who receive Nos. 57103–57316, and 96 women are admitted to the camp as inmates. The rest of the deportees are killed in the gas chambers.

148 prisoners die in Auschwitz-Birkenau.

APMO, D-AuI-3/1/6, Occupancy Register, pp. 832–837.

AUGUST 8

63 prisoners sent to the camp by the Sipo and SD of the Kraków District receive Nos. 57317–57379.

25 prisoners sent from Kattowitz receive Nos. 57380–57404.

38 female prisoners sent in a group transport receive Nos. 15673–15710.

96 Jewesses receive Nos. 15711–15806. They were selected the previous day from the RSHA transport from France.

Five female prisoners sent from Kattowitz receive Nos. 15807–15811.

987 Jews arrive with an RSHA transport from Westerbork. There are 510 men and boys and 477 women and girls in the transport. After the selection, 315 men receive Nos. 57405–57719 and 149 women receive Nos. 15812–15960 and are admitted to the camp as inmates. There are several Catholic Jews, as well as nuns and monks in the transport. These include Dr. of Philosophy Edith Theresia Hedwig Stein, called Sister Theresia Benedicta of the Cross, from the Carmelite Convent in Echt, who was born in Breslau October 21, 1891. Like the other nuns and monks, she is deported to Auschwitz in the clothing of her order. After the selection, she is killed in the gas chambers with the other deportees.

Robert M. W. Kempner, *Edith Stein und Anne Frank: Zwei von Hunderttausend* (Edith Stein and Anne Frank: Two Out of One Hundred Thousand), Freiburg, 1968, pp. 97–116.

The SS Camp Doctor carries out a selection among those who are ill with typhus in Block 20. He chooses 41 prisoners who are killed with phenol injections the same day.

APMO, Mat.RO, vol. 6, p. 15; D-AuI-5/1, Morgue Register, pp. 195–197.

AUGUST 9

Frieda Wiese, who escaped from the Penal Company in Budy on August 6, 1942, is imprisoned and sent back to the camp. The search operation is called off.

APMO, IZ-8/Gestapo Lodz/2-78.

1,069 Jews arrive with the sixteenth RSHA transport from Pithiviers and Beaune–La Rolande Camps in France. There are 209 men and boys and 860 women and girls in the transport. After the selection, 63 men and 211 women are admitted to the camp as inmates and receive Nos. 57720–57782 and 15961–16171. The other 794 people are killed in the gas chambers.

AUGUST 10

Ten male prisoners and one female prisoner sent from Kattowitz receive Nos. 57783–57792 and 16172.

The Commandant's Office is informed that a transport with 1,000 Jews left le Bourget–Drancy for Auschwitz at 8:55 A.M.

APMO, D-RF-3/16, Inventory No. 20017.

118 male and 333 female prisoners brought to Auschwitz from Yugoslavian Celje in Slovenia receive Nos. 57793–57910 and 16173–16505.

The SS Camp Doctor carries out a selection among the patients in the prisoners' infirmary, Block 20. He selects 75 prisoners, who are killed with phenol injections the same day.*

APMO, Mat.RO, vol. VI, pp. 16 A, B; D-AuI-5/1, Morgue Register, pp. 201–204.

The move of the women's camp from the main camp to Section B-Ia in Birkenau is completed. A selection is carried out in the prisoners' infirmary. The seriously ill female prisoners are brought to the gas chambers in Birkenau. Female prisoners who can walk are led on foot to Camp B-Ia.

APMO, Memoirs, vol. 75, pp. 266ff., Memoirs of Former Prisoner Helena Siemaszkiewicz.

AUGUST 11

Five Russian POWs are sent to Auschwitz.

APMO, D-AuI-3/1/6, Occupancy Register, pp. 895, 866. This is indicated by the number of Russian POWs.

559 Jews arrive from Holland with an RSHA transport from Westerbork. There are 288 men and boys and 271 women and girls in the transport. After the selection, 164 men and 131 women are admitted to the camp as inmates and receive Nos. 57911–58074 and 16506–16636. The other 264 deportees are killed in the gas chambers.

Polish prisoner Zbigniew Dąbrowski (No. 45114), born February 7, 1922, is shot in the courtyard of Block 11. He was sent to Auschwitz by the Sipo and SD for the Kraków District on July 7, 1942.

APMO, D-AuI-5/1, Morgue Register, p. 205; D-AuI-3/1/6, Occupancy Register, p. 865.

The SS Camp Doctor carries out a selection among the patients in the prisoners' infirmary, Block 20. He chooses 79 prisoners, who are killed with phenol injections the same day.**

APMO, Mat.RO, vol. VI, pp. 16C, 16D.

---

*In the Morgue Register of the main camp, the names of 129 prisoners are listed (APMO, D-AuI-5/1, Morgue Register, pp. 200–204).
**The numbers of 143 prisoners are entered in the Morgue Register of the main camp (APMO, D-AuI-5/1, Morgue Register, pp. 203–209).

To create discord among prisoners of various nationalities, Office D-I instructs the Commandants of the concentration camps to use prisoners to carry out floggings.

APMO, Maurer Trial, vol. 10, p. 92 (PS-2189).

AUGUST 12

After moving the female prisoners to Camp B-Ia in Birkenau,* the disinfection of the empty Blocks 1–10 in the main camp is begun. Zyklon B gas is used for this purpose. Before the disinfection is begun, a passage is made in the wall that previously separated the women's camp from the men's camp.

APMO, Höss Trial, vol. 25, p. 31; vol. 24, p. 25, Statements of Former Prisoners Michał Kula and Feliks Myłyk.

11 prisoners sent from Kattowitz receive Nos. 58075–58085.

1,006 Jews arrive in a RSHA transport from Drancy. There are 525 women and 475 men in the transport, including 400 old people. Almost all of them were born in Germany. After the selection, 140 men and 100 women are admitted to the camp and receive Nos. 58086–58225 and 16337–16736. The other 766 deportees are killed in the gas chambers.

The SS Camp Doctor carries out a selection among the patients in the prisoners' infirmary, Block 20. He chooses 50 prisoners, who are killed with phenol injections the same day.

APMO, Mat.RO, vol. VI, pp. 16C, 16D.

Jewish prisoner Gejza Landesmann (No. 44846) is shot during the night "while escaping."

APMO, D-AuI-5/1, Morgue Register, p. 213; D-AuI-3/1/6, Occupancy Register, p. 876.

Commandant Höss makes the SS Garrison Doctor responsible for accidents to SS men caused by gas, especially those resulting from opening rooms treated with gas without wearing a gas mask. He calculates that a distance of 16 yards from the gassed room must be maintained, taking into account the direction of the wind. The gas presently used is especially dangerous because it is almost odorless.**

APMO, D-AuI-1/1/90, Commandant's Office Special Order, August 12, 1942.

AUGUST 13

Jewish prisoner Jekusil Gurfinkiel (No. 43071) is shot "while escaping."

APMO, D-AuI-5/1, Morgue Register, p. 214; D-AuI-3/1/6, Occupancy Register, p. 881.

999 Jews from Belgium arrive with the second RSHA transport from Malines Camp. There are 407 men and 79 boys and 445 women and 68 girls in the transport. After the selection, 290 men and 228 women are admitted to the camp as inmates and receive

*The numbers of 108 prisoners and the corpses of 12 women, without numbers, are entered in the Morgue Register of the main camp. (APMO, D-AuI-5/1, Morgue Register, pp. 210–213).
**Höss issues this special order when the symptoms of a slight poisoning with hydrogen cyanide appear in an SS man. Since gassing of the rooms with Zyklon B is discussed in this order, this accident probably happened in the disinfection of the blocks left by the women inmates in the main camp.

Nos. 58226–58515 and 16737–16964. The other 481 deportees are killed in the gas chambers.

15 male and three female prisoners sent from Kattowitz receive Nos. 58516–58530 and 16965–16967.

A Russian POW is sent to Auschwitz.

The SS Camp Doctor carries out a selection among the patients in the prisoners' infirmary, Block 20. He selects 60 prisoners, who are killed with phenol injections the same day.

APMO, Mat.RO, vol. IV, pp. 16C, 16D.

The numbers of 119 prisoners are entered in the Morgue Register of the main camp.

APMO, D-AuI-5/1, Morgue Register, pp. 214–218.

47 prisoners sent from Troppau receive Nos. 58531–58577.

55 male and 101 female prisoners sent in a group transport receive Nos. 58578–58632 and 16968–17068.

152 prisoners sent from Prague receive Nos. 58633–58784.

1,007 Jews from France, predominantly old people, arrive with the eighteenth RSHA transport from Drancy. After the selection, 233 men and 62 women are admitted to the camp as inmates and receive Nos. 58785–59017 and 17069–17130. The other 712 deportees are killed in the gas chambers.

60 Polish political prisoners are shot at the execution wall in the courtyard of Block 11. They had received orders the day before to register in the office. Those shot include Stanisław Chmiel (No. 340), Jerzy Stanisław Szymański (No. 5288), Józef Zak (No. 5519), Kazimierz Julski (No. 16926), Henryk Sawicz (No. 22940), Teodor Sklorz (No. 26772), Ryszard Brodawski (No. 30965), Stanisław Andrzejak (No. 35363), Antoni Barasiński (No. 35368), Teodor Bogacki (No. 35374), Wiesław Borkowski (No. 35375), Franciszek Drebniczak (No. 35400), Jan Dudczak (No. 35403), Józef Sajdak (No. 35376), and Michał Krakowiak (No. 37528).

APMO, D-AuI-3/1/6, Occupancy Register, pp. 888–891.

16 female prisoners sent by the Sipo and SD for the Kraków District receive Nos. 17131–17146.

The SS Camp Doctor carries out a selection among the patients in the prisoners' infirmary, Block 20. He chooses 58 prisoners, who are killed with phenol injections the same day.

APMO, Mat.RO, vol. VI, pp. 17A, 17B.

269 deaths are entered in the Occupancy Register of Auschwitz-Berkenau.

APMO, D-AuI-3/1/6, Occupancy Register, pp. 888–897.

Medical Officer SS Staff Sergeant Josef Klehr orders 4½ pounds of phenol for the camp pharmacy to be used for killing prisoners with injections to the heart.

APMO, D-AuI-5/1, Pharmaceutical Order, p. 412.

The Camp Doctor of the women's concentration camp in Birkenau (Frauenkonzentrationslager—FKL) orders the following medicines for the camp pharmacy: benzine, adhesive bandages, coal tablets, Cuprex, Tannalbin, and 30 percent hydrogen.*

APMO, D-AuI-5/1, Pharmaceutical Order, p. 411.

AUGUST 15

An auxiliary camp is opened in the Brzeszcze-Jawischowitz coal mine in Jawischowitz (Jawiszowice), belonging to the Upper Silesian mine administration of the Hermann Göring Reich Works. 150 prisoners transferred from Auschwitz are lodged in the camp built in the first half of 1942, originally for foreign labor, i.e., Russian POWs. The prisoners are employed in the mines. The first director of the auxiliary camp is Sergeant Wilhelm Kowol. The guard unit of the Jawischowitz A.C. (Auxiliary Camp) in 1942 consists of 30 SS men. Administratively the auxiliary camp is under the control of the Commandant's Office of Auschwitz. By the end of 1942, about 700 prisoners are lodged in the auxiliary camp. For the first time in the history of Nazi concentration camps, prisoners are used underground.

APMO, Höss Trial, vol. 21, p. 38; Schnabel, *Power Without Morality*, p. 236, Document 82; Andrzej Strzelecki, "Das Nebenlager Jawischowitz" (The Auxiliary Camp Jawischowitz), *HvA*, no. 15 (1975): 183–250.

About 2,000 Jewish men, women, and children arrive from Sosnowitz with an RSHA transport. After the selection, 27 men and 75 women are admitted to the camp and receive Nos. 59018–59044 and 17147–17221. The other 1,898 people are killed in the gas chambers.

Szternfinkiel, *Jews of Sosnowitz*, pp. 36–39.

Ten prisoners sent to the camp by the Sipo and SD for the Kraków District receive Nos. 59045–59054.

505 Jews from Holland arrive in a RSHA transport from Westerbork. There are 238 men and boys and 267 women and girls in the transport. After the selection, 98 men and 79 women are admitted to the camp and receive Nos. 59055–59152 and 17238–17316. The other 328 people are killed in the gas chambers.

64 prisoners sent to the camp by the Sipo and SD from Lublin receive Nos. 59153–59216.

Jewish prisoner Karl Biederer (No. 41827) is shot "while escaping."

APMO, D-AuI-5/1, Morgue Register, p. 223; D-AuI-3/1/6, Occupancy Register, p. 903. APMO, Mat.RO, vol. VI, pp. 17A, 17B.

The SS Camp Doctor carries out a selection among the patients in the prisoners' infirmary, Block 20. He selects 38 prisoners, who are killed with phenol injections the same day.

The corpses of two prisoners are sent to the morgue of the main camp from the Golleschau A.C. The dead men are Moses Symkviz (No. 43550) and Icek Wajnstajn (No. 52084).

APMO, D-AuI-5/1, Morgue Register, p. 225; D-AuI-3/1/6, Occupancy Register, p. 903.

*The staff in the infirmary, the so-called sick bay, of the women's concentration camp, which is also gripped by the typhus epidemic, has access to such supplies.

286 male prisoners die in Auschwitz-Birkenau.

APMO, D-AuI-3/1/6, Occupancy Register, pp. 897–906.

In the office of the Waffen SS Central Construction Administration in Auschwitz, plans for a new type of crematorium are worked out for the new Crematoriums IV and V, to be built at Birkenau. The plans carry the number 1,678. Gas chambers are planned in each of these crematoriums.

APMO, D-ZBau, BW 30/22, Documents of the POW Camp Building Office.

The Head of the Central Construction Administration, SS Major Bischoff, approves an additional construction project for the Birkenau camp that is intended to house 200,000 POWs. In connection with the decision to carry out the mass extermination of the Jews in Auschwitz and simultaneously use Auschwitz as a reservoir of the labor of Jewish prisoners selected from the transports, to be employed for the benefit of German industry, it is necessary to change the previous plan and create space for a temporary housing of the prisoners as well as to erect appropriate extermination facilities. Of the previous plan, only Section I remains, encompassing the women's camp in Section B-Ib and a men's camp in Section B-Ia. The second section (B-II) is to be to the right of these camps, and next to these the third section (B-III)—later called "Mexico" by the prisoners. The fourth section (B-IV), destined not to be constructed, is planned to be to the left of Section B-I. Between Sections B-I and B-II is the main street of the camp, where a railroad siding is planned for Section B-II. Except for the already built camp areas housing male and some female prisoners, the new sections are to consist of six camps each, separated from one another by fences with their own entrance gates and guard rooms for the SS men. Each of these sections is to hold 60,000 people; only the first section is planned to accommodate 20,000 people. The entire camp is to occupy a rectangular site of 790 × 2660 yards. Two crematoriums with gas chambers are planned for two rectangular sites at the western side of the camp, to be built on the extension of the main street of the camp and the railroad siding. In fact, four crematoriums with gas chambers are built and the construction of an additional crematorium is planned. Altogether, the plan encompasses 600 new buildings: residential, warehouse, and office barracks, bathing facilities, laundry buildings, latrines, guard rooms, etc.

In an area of 432 acres, the following buildings are constructed: four large crematoriums with gas chambers; a delousing and bathing facility, the so-called "sauna"; about 300 barracks for housing, administration, offices, latrines, and laundry; a personal effects camp consisting of about 30 barracks for stolen property, which is called "Canada II" by the prisoners and SS men; a railroad siding with an unloading platform and a barbed-wire fence, 8 miles of drainage ditches and several miles of streets and roads.

APMO, POW Camp Building Office, Plan of August 15, 1942.

After the evening roll call in the women's Penal Company in Budy, all Polish prisoners must step forward; they are subsequently brought to the newly built camp in Section B-Ia of Birkenau. The transfer of the female prisoners out of the Penal Company to the

APMO, Depositions, vol. 67, p. 154, Account of Former Prisoner Monika Galica; Piątkowska, Memoirs, p. 59.

Prisoners working on the construction of Crematorium II.

women's concentration camp in Birkenau is equivalent with release from the Penal Company to the camp. 137 of the 200 Polish women sent to the Penal Company on June 25, 1942, return to Birkenau. The rest die while serving out their punishment.

AUGUST 16

About 2,000 Jewish men, women, and children, including old people and those without any occupation, arrive with a transport of the RSHA. All of them are killed in the gas chambers.

Szternfinkiel, *Jews of Sosnowitz,* pp. 36–39.

Three male and 16 female prisoners sent in a group transport receive Nos. 59217–59219 and 17222–17237.

Nine prisoners sent by the Sipo and SD for the Kraków District receive Nos. 59220–59228.

261 male prisoners die in Auschwitz.

APMO, D-AuI-3/1/6, Occupancy Register, pp. 907–915.

991 Jews arrive from Drancy with the nineteenth RSHA transport from France. Children under 12 are also in the transport. After the selection, 115 men are admitted to the camp and receive

On the ramp, shortly after the arrival of a trainload of deportees. In the middle, prisoners being used as prefects.

Nos. 59229–59343. The other 876 people are killed in the gas chambers.

AUGUST 17

Another RSHA transport from Sosnowitz of 2,000 Jewish men, women, and children is killed in the gas chambers.

Szternfinkiel, *Jews of Sosnowitz,* pp. 36–39.

SS Captain Dr. Kurt Uhlenbrock succeeds Siegfried Schwela, who died in May 1942, as SS Garrison Doctor. The SS Medical Office in Berlin assigns him to Auschwitz to fight the typhus epidemic. Uhlenbrock carries out this function until June 9, 1942.*

Kaul, *Doctors in Auschwitz,* pp. 86–88.

1,000 Jews from the Malines camp arrive in the third RSHA transport from Belgium, which includes 342 men and 86 boys and 486 women and 86 girls. After the selection, 157 men and 205 women are admitted to the camp as inmates and given Nos. 59344–59500 and 17317–17521. The other 638 people are killed in the gas chambers.

87 male and 24 female prisoners sent by the Sipo and SD for the Kraków District receive Nos. 59512–59598 and 17522–17544.

*Uhlenbrock stays in Auschwitz until October 2, 1942, for he is himself stricken with typhus.

Two male and seven female prisoners sent from Oppeln receive Nos. 59599–59600 and 17545–17551.

The corpse of prisoner Benjamin Kleiner (No. 49532) is brought to the morgue from the roll-call area.

APMO, D-AuI-5/1, Morgue Register, p. 229.

249 deaths are listed in the Occupancy Register.

APMO, D-AuI-3/1/6, Occupancy Register, pp. 915–923.

AUGUST 18

Polish prisoner Piotr Szalas (No. 52327) is shot "while escaping."

APMO, D-AuI-5/1, Morgue Register, p. 232; D-AuI-3/1/6, Occupancy Register, p. 932.

A fourth RSHA transport from Sosnowitz arrives with 2,000 Jewish men, women, and children, who are killed in the gas chambers of Bunkers 1 and 2.

Szternfinkiel, *Jews of Sosnowitz*, pp. 36–39. [RSHA transport]

The SS Camp Doctor carries out a selection of the patients in the prisoners' infirmary, Block 20. He selects 82 prisoners, who are killed the same day with phenol injections.

APMO, Mat.RO, vol. VI, p. 17.

After morning roll call, 56 Polish prisoners register in the prisoner office. They were ordered there the day before by the Political Department. They are stood in rows of five, surrounded by Block Leaders, and taken to Block 11. There, Roll Call Leader Palitzsch shoots them at the execution wall. The condemned men come from Silesia and were sent to the camp in 1940 and 1941. Thus, the execution is thought to be in retaliation for the burning of six farms in Silesia at this time. The condemned men sing the Polish national anthem, "Poland Is Not Yet Lost," in Block 11. Some of those shot are Józef Bernat (No. 1162), Franciszek Durczak (No. 1246), Franciszek Białek (No. 1255), Zbigniew Bałut (No. 1260), Franciszek Bereza (No. 1284), Józef Biernacki (No. 1287), Zygmunt Dychala (No. 1291), Jerzy Murkowski (No. 1300), Józef Badura (No. 1472), Tadeusz Konopnicki (No. 3721), Jan Rudawski (No. 4961), Jakób Bunas (No. 7592), Jan Buhl (No. 7685), Jerzy Brem (No. 10190), Erwin Duda (No. 10194), Zbiegniew Bolechowski (No. 10966), Bolesław Barczyk (No. 21922), Stanisław Bartochowski (No. 21923), Jan Bednarek (No. 21925), August Bijak (No. 21929), and Józef Cichoń (No. 22309).

APMO, Höss Trial, vol. 4, pp. 4–5; vol. 55, p. 155, Statements of Former Prisoners Tadeusz Balut and Kazimierz Smoleń; D-AuI-3/1/6, Occupancy Register, pp. 937ff. Some of the names of the shot prisoners are entered in the Occupancy Register under August 19, 1942. The continuation of the Occupancy Register has not survived.

Shortly before registering in the office, Zbigniew Bałut (No. 1260) is able to write a secret message with a letter of farewell to his parents, which is smuggled out and sent on by a civilian worker, Adam Kaczyński, employed by force in the camp. The text of the secret message reads as follows: "August 18, 1942. My Dear ones! I write the last words to you! I devote this last moment to you, my most loved ones. But do not torment yourselves, for all this is for our homeland, Poland. Be well, my dears! May God protect you. May God unite me with you again someday. Zbyszek."

APMO, Inventory No. 155581.

Three prisoners receive numbers 59601–59603.

Destined for the gas chamber.

An RSHA transport of Jews comes from Yugoslavia. After the selection, 87 men and 69 women are admitted to the camp and given Nos. 59604–59690 and 17552–17620.

An RSHA transport with 506 Jews comes from Westerbork in Holland. There are 364 men and boys in the transport and 142 women and girls. After the selection, 319 men and 40 women are admitted to the camp and receive Nos. 59691–60009 and 17621–17660. The other 147 deportees are killed in the gas chambers.

According to the Occupancy Register, 390 prisoners die in the main camp and in section B-Ib.

APMO, D-AuI-3/1/6, Occupancy Register, pp. 923–936.

AUGUST 19

The representative of J. A. Topf and Sons of Erfurt, Head Engineer Prüfer, arrives at Auschwitz to conduct discussions with the Central Construction Administration about the construction of the crematorium ovens for incinerating corpses. In the course of the discussion, it is decided that a mechanic, Holik, will come from Buchenwald on August 26 or 27 at the latest and another mechanic, Koch, will arrive within 14 days. The assembly of five triple-muffle crematorium ovens is to begin immediately. Walling in the ovens and constructing the chimney is to be done by the Köhler Company of Myslowitz according to the plans and specifications of J. A. Topf and Sons.

APMO, D-ZBau/5, Docs. CCA, Inventory No. 29752.

Two prisoners, the Jew Lobel Feiler (No. 41987) and the Yugoslav Wilhelm Ramszak (No. 57851) are shot "while escaping."

APMO, D-AuI-5/1, Morgue Register, p. 238.

33 male and 18 female prisoners sent to the camp by the Sipo and SD for the Kraków District receive Nos. 60010–60042 and 17661–17678.

69 prisoners sent by the Sipo and SD of Warsaw from Pawiak Prison receive Nos. 60043–60111.

The Commandant's Office is informed that a transport with 1,000 Jews left le Bourget–Drancy for Auschwitz at 8:55 A.M.

APMO, D-RF-30/20, Inventory No. 22021.

The SS Camp Doctor carries out a selection among the patients in the prisoners' infirmary, Block 20. He selects 67 prisoners, who are killed the same day with phenol injections.

APMO, Mat.RO, vol. VI, pp. 17C, 17D, 18A.

997 Jews, including a number of families with children, arrive with the twentieth RSHA transport from France, from Drancy. 341 children between two and 10 years of age and 323 girls up to the age of 16 arrive with the transport. After the selection, 65 men and 35 women of this transport are admitted to the camp and given Nos. 60113–60177 and 17679–17713. The other 897 people are killed in the gas chambers.

According to the Occupancy Register, 220 prisoners die in Auschwitz in the course of the day.

APMO, D-AuI-3/1/6, Occupancy Register, pp. 936–943.

AUGUST 1–19

4,113 male prisoners die in Auschwitz-Birkenau.* These include 2,941 Jews, 859 Poles (including 120 reeducation prisoners), 140 French arrested within the framework of the Night and Fog (Nacht und Nebel—NN) operation,** 133 Czechs, 20 Germans (10 of them political prisoners), 11 Russians, eight Yugoslavs, and one Lithuanian.

AUGUST 19

At evening roll call in Auschwitz-Birkenau, the occupancy level, including the prisoners in the main camp, Section B-Ib in Birkenau,

Ibid., p. 943.

---

*This figure includes all the male prisoners who die as a result of conditions in the camp, who are selected by the SS Camp Doctor because they suffer from typhus and are killed with an injection, or are killed in the gas chamber in Birkenau or shot. No data exists on the number of female prisoners or on the killing of the Jews deported to the camp and murdered in the gas chambers. The figures are based on the Occupancy Register of Auschwitz-Birkenau. The last entry in the surviving register is on August 19, 1942.

**The purpose of the *Nacht and Nebel Erlass*, the Night and Fog Decree, issued by Hitler himself on December 7, 1941, "was to seize persons [in the conquered territories in the West] 'endangering German security' who were not to be immediately executed and make them vanish without a trace into the night and fog of the unknown in Germany. No information was to be given their families as to their fate even when, as invariably occurred, it was merely a question of the place of burial . . ." (Shirer, *Rise and Fall of the Third Reich*, p. 957).

and the auxiliary camps of Jawischowitz and Golleschau, is 22,925 men prisoners, including 163 Russian POWs.*

The head of WVHA Office D-I, Liebehenschel, informs the Commandants of the concentration camps that information is reaching the RSHA from various sources that, in several cases, concentration camp prisoners have been punished by the courts for severe abuse of fellow prisoners, in one case with fatal results. Such cases are to be reported to the prosecutor's office for further investigation. Should such abuse of prisoners happen again, it could have a negative influence on the courts' perception of conditions in the concentration camps. Commandants are also ordered to use all the means at their disposal to prevent abuses of this sort from happening again so that the prosecutors' offices will have no occasion to be involved with matters of this kind and to hear such cases.**

APMO, IZ-13/89, Various Documents of the Third Reich, p. 254 (original in BA Koblenz).

AUGUST 20

The owner of the Köhler Company of Myslowitz and SS 1st Lieutenant Janisch of the Central Construction Administration in Auschwitz go to the construction site of one of the crematoriums in Birkenau to discuss details concerning the construction of the masonry for the five triple-snout crematorium ovens and the chimney.

APMO, D-ZBau/5, Docs. ZBL, Inventory No. 29752.

One prisoner sent from Kattowitz receives No. 60112.

998 Jews from the Malines Camp arrive with the fourth RSHA transport from Belgium, 337 men and 161 boys and 374 women and 126 girls. After the selection, 104 men and 71 women are admitted to the camp and given Nos. 60178–60281 and 17714–17784. The other 823 deportees are killed in the gas chambers.

45 male and 11 female prisoners sent from Kattowitz receive Nos. 60282–60326 and 17785–17795.

21 male and 61 female prisoners sent from Yugoslavia by the Gestapo of Celje in Slovenia receive Nos. 60327–60347 and 17796–17856.

17 Austrian and German political prisoners transferred from Dachau to Auschwitz receive Nos. 60348–60364. This transport includes Hermann Langbein (No. 60355), Karl Lill (No. 60356), and Ludwig Wörl (No. 60363), who soon become active in the camp resistance organization.

*This is the last entry in the surviving Occupancy Register.
**The order comes too late and results in no change in camp conditions. In Auschwitz, prisoners are constantly abused by fellow prisoners, predominantly by German criminal prisoners, who are encouraged in this by the SS, incited to it, and are never punished. A great many prisoners die or commit suicide because they are abused by fellow prisoners, primarily German criminals employed in the camp as block seniors, Capos, etc. The same conditions also prevail in the women's camp.

The SS Camp Doctor carries out a selection among the patients in the prisoners' infirmary, Block 20. He selects 59 prisoners, who are killed the same day with phenol injections.

APMO, Mat.RO, pp. 18A, B; D-AuI-5/1, Morgue Register, pp. 240–242.

AUGUST 21

At the execution wall in the courtyard of Block 11, Polish political prisoner No. 3904 is shot. He had been sent to the concentration camp by the Sipo and SS of Warsaw on August 14, 1940, under the name of Stanisław Debski and identified by the Gestapo as Stanisław Dubois in 1942. The publicist and Socialist politician Dubois had been a delegate to the Polish Sejm (parliament) from 1928 to 1930 and belonged to the leadership of the camp resistance movement.

Encyklopedia II Wojny Świato-wej (*Encyclopedia of World War II*), Warsaw, 1975, p. 122.

42 male and 18 female prisoners sent in a group transport receive Nos. 60365–60406 and 17857–17874.

64 prisoners sent in a group transport receive Nos. 60407–60470.

1,000 Jews arrive from Drancy with the twenty-first RSHA transport from France. In the transport are many families—grandparents, parents, and 373 children below the age of 13. After the selection, 138 men and 45 women are admitted to the camp and given Nos. 60471–60608 and 17875–17919. The other 817 deportees are killed in the gas chambers.

The SS Camp Doctor carries out a selection among the patients in Block 13. He chooses 50 prisoners, who are killed the same day with phenol injections.

APMO, Mat.RO, vol. VI, p. 18A, 18B; D-AuI-5/1, Morgue Register, pp. 245ff.

The Commandant's Office is informed that a transport with 1,000 Jews has left le Bourget–Drancy at 10:00 A.M. for Auschwitz.

APMO, D-RF-3/21, Inventory No. 22022.

A Dutch Jew, Franz Leimann (No. 52497), is caught escaping and locked in the bunker of Block 11. On September 2, he is released from the bunker and transferred to the Penal Company in Birkenau.

APMO, D-AuI-3/1b, Bunker Register, p. 76.

The Dutch Jew with the number 47185, sent to the camp on July 17, 1942, is shot "while escaping."

APMO, D-AuI-5/1, Morgue Register, p. 246.

The corpses of 111 prisoners are sent to the morgue of the main camp.

Ibid., pp. 244–247.

AUGUST 22

Jews from Yugoslavia arrive with an RSHA transport. After the selection, 110 men and 86 women are admitted to the camp and given Nos. 60609–60718 and 17920–18005.*

*It is not known how many people arrived with this transport or how many of them were killed in the gas chambers.

34 prisoners sent to the camp by the Sipo and SD for the Kraków District receive Nos. 60719–60752.

19 prisoners sent from Kattowitz receive Nos. 60753–60771.

A prisoner sent from Oppeln receives No. 60772.

1,008 Jews arrive in a RSHA transport from Westerbork, 493 men and boys and 515 women and girls. After the selection, 411 men and 217 women are admitted to the camp and receive Nos. 60774–61184 and 18006–18222. The other 380 deportees are killed in the gas chambers.

The female prisoners employed in the Political Department as office staff and in the SS tailor shop and women arrested for belonging to the IBV prisoners who work as house servants for the families of SS men are moved out of Camp B-Ia in Birkenau to the staff buildings of Auschwitz. This is to prevent the SS members and their families from being infected with typhus by the female prisoners with whom they are in daily contact.

Škodowa, *Three Years*, pp. 55–57.

The SS Camp Doctor carries out a selection among the patients in the prisoners' infirmary, Block 20. He selects 92 prisoners, who are killed the same day with phenol injections.

APMO, Mat.RO, vol. VI, pp. 18C, 18D.

The corpses of 136 prisoners are sent to the morgue of the main camp.

APMO, D-AuI-5/1/6, Morgue Register, pp. 248–252.

AUGUST 23

A prisoner sent from Stettin receives No. 60773.

A beginning is made to move male prisoners into the disinfected and cleared blocks formerly occupied by women. The prisoners housed there leave this part of the camp for roll call and their labor squads via a passageway made in the wall which separated the women's camp from the men's camp at the street between Blocks 3 and 4.*

12 female prisoners sent in a group transport receive Nos. 18223–18234.

1,000 Jews from Drancy arrive with the twenty-second RSHA transport from France. 544 children below the age of 14 are among them. After the selection 90 men and 18 women are admitted to the camp and receive Nos. 61185–61274 and 18235–18252. The other 892 deportees are sent to the gas chambers.

*Under the dates of August 23–29, 1942, it is entered in the Morgue Register that the corpses of male prisoners are taken out of Blocks 3a, 9, 6a, 10, 7a, 5, and 8a. This indicates that male prisoners must already be housed there.

A prisoner transferred from Neuengamme receives No. 61275.

AUGUST 24

SS guards capture three Russians at 1:55 A.M. in Neu Berun (Nowy Bierun), not far from Auschwitz. The captured men have sketches of the area in their possession, which is considered proof of an attempt to escape.

APMO, Höss Trial, vol. 12, p. 219, quoted from the Guard Register.

A prisoner transferred from Gross-Rosen receives No. 61276.

The SS Camp Doctor carries out a selection among the patients in the prisoner infirmary, Block 20. He selects 35 patients, who are killed the same day with phenol injections.

APMO, D-AuI-5/1, Morgue Register, pp. 255ff.

AUGUST 25

50 female prisoners sent from Pawiak Prison by the Sipo and SD of Warsaw receive Nos. 18253–18302.

519 Jews arrive from Westerbork in an RSHA transport from Holland of 351 men and boys and 168 women and girls. After the selection, 231 men and 38 women are admitted to the camp as inmates and receive Nos. 61277–61507 and 18303–18340. The other 250 deportees are killed in the gas chambers.

The Jewess Lea Prin (No. 17725), sent to Auschwitz from Malines in an RSHA transport on August 20, 1942, is shot "while escaping."

APMO, Microfilm No. 1027/7, Report of an SS man.

The SS Camp Doctor carries out a selection among the patients in the prisoners' infirmary in Blocks 13, 20, 21, and 28. He selects 80 prisoners, who are killed the same day with phenol injections.

APMO, Mat.RO, vol. VI, pp. 19A, 19B.

The corpses of 152 prisoners are sent to the morgue of the main camp from the blocks of the prisoners' infirmary.

APMO, D-AuI-5/1, Morgue Register, pp. 258–262.

AUGUST 26

The Commandant's Office receives a travel permit from the WVHA to send a truck to Dessau to fetch material for "special treatment" (Sonderbehandlung—SB).*

APMO, Höss Trial, vol. 12, p. 167, Exhibit 111; reproduced in HvA, no. 3 (1960): 121.

Jews from Yugoslavia arrive with an RSHA transport. After the selection, 71 men and 88 women are admitted to the camp as prisoners and receive Nos. 61508–61578 and 18341–18428.

51 male and 16 female prisoners sent from Kattowitz receive Nos. 61579–61629 and 18429–18444.

*"Special treatment" is an SS euphemism for liquidation, i.e., killing by poison gas or phenol. The "material" meant here is Zyklon B gas.

32 prisoners transferred from Sachsenhausen receive Nos. 61630–61661.

1,000 Jews arrive from Drancy with the twenty-third RSHA transport from France, which includes 518 children below the age of 14, many without their parents. After the selection, 92 men are admitted to the camp and receive Nos. 61662–61753. The other 908 deportees are killed in the gas chambers.

The Commandant's Office is notified that a transport with 1,000 Jews has left le Bourget–Drancy for Auschwitz at 8:55 A.M.

APMO, D-RF-3/23, Inventory No. 22024.

AUGUST 27

Jews arrive with an RSHA transport. After the selection, 82 men are admitted to the camp and receive Nos. 61754–61835.*

Two prisoners transferred from Mauthausen C.C. receive Nos. 61836 and 61837.

19 male and four female prisoners sent from Kattowitz receive Nos. 61838–61856 and 18445–18448.

66 prisoners sent to the camp by the Sipo and SD for the Kraków District from Montelupich Prison receive Nos. 61857–61922.

15 prisoners sent from Kattowitz receive Nos. 61923–61937.

995 Jews arrive from Malines Camp with the fifth RSHA transport from Belgium, of 363 men and 123 boys and 400 women and 109 girls. After the selection, 101 men and 114 women are admitted to the camp and receive Nos. 61938–62038 and 18449–18562.

AUGUST 28

30 male and four female prisoners sent to the camp by the Sipo and SD for the Kraków District receive Nos. 62039–62068 and 18563–18566.

24 male and 29 female prisoners sent in a group transport receive Nos. 62069–62092 and 18567–18595.

1,000 Jews from Drancy arrive with the twenty-fourth RSHA transport from France, which includes 320 children below the age of 12. A first selection of this transport is probably carried out at the railroad junction of Cosel (Kózle),** where 200 able-bodied men

---

*This probably refers to a transport of 723 Jews from Luxembourg sent to Auschwitz in August 1942 (Martin Gilbert, *Final Solution*, pp. 109, 133).
**In his *Memorial to the Jews Deported from France 1942–1944*, Serge Klarsfeld says that Transports 24–35, 37, 38, and 44 underwent the first selection in Cosel. The boys and healthy Jews chosen were sent to Blechhammer, Johannisdorf, Kochanowitz, Oderberg, Gogolin, Ottmuch and other forced labor camps. Some of them belong to the 3,056 Jewish prisoners taken over by the Commandant's Office of Auschwitz on April 1, 1944, from the Jewish forced labor camp Blechhammer and given Nos. 176512–179567. The research conducted by Serge Klarsfeld is incorporated in this work.

are selected and exchanged for unfit or dead prisoners.* A second selection takes place at the unloading platform in Auschwitz, called the Jew Platform. 27 men and 36 women are admitted to the camp and receive Nos. 62093–62119 and 18609–18644. The other 737 deportees are killed in the gas chambers.

The Commandant's Office is notified that a transport with 1,000 Jews has left le Bourget–Drancy for Auschwitz at 8:55 A.M.

In Golleschau A.C. two Jewish prisoners, Nos. 60952 and 61061, are shot. They were sent to Auschwitz from Westerbork on August 22, 1942, with an RSHA transport.

APMO, D-AuI-5/1, Morgue Register, p. 268.

AUGUST 29

44 male and 13 female prisoners sent to the camp by the Sipo and SD for the Kraków District receive Nos. 62120–62168 and 18596–18603.

On the pretext of fighting typhus in Auschwitz, Garrison Doctor Uhlenbrock orders a selection among sick and convalescent prisoners. The selected are to be killed in the gas chambers in order to destroy the carriers of typhus, both the lice and the patients. The prisoner doctors in the prisoners' infirmary of the main camp receive instructions to release the convalescent to the camp that day. The news spreads among the staff that a major delousing operation is to be carried out the next day in which the sick prisoners are to be brought to Birkenau. From previous experience, the prisoners know that this means a transport to the gas chamber.

Kielar, *Anus Mundi*, pp. 155ff.

All the sick and recovering prisoners are gathered in the corridors and staircases leading to the closed courtyard between Blocks 20 and 21 of the main camp. SS Camp Doctor Entress and Medical Officer Klehr carry out the selection. The Block Senior reads out a list of prisoner numbers and the Camp Doctor indicates to them where they are to stand. A small group, consisting mostly of the staff of the prisoners' infirmary, has to stand at the wall of Block 21. The sick and convalescent prisoners take a position at the wall

APMO, Höss Trial, vol. 2, p. 155; vol. 4, p. 177; vol. 7, pp. 17, 116, 156, 175, Statements of Former Prisoners; Mat.RO, vol. 1, p. 6, Kielar, *Anus Mundi*, pp. 155–160. Wiesław Kielar is one of the few prisoners who succeeded in surviving this selection.

---

*After the incorporation of Upper Silesia into the German Reich, at Himmler's order, SS Major General Albrecht Schmelt (later governor in Oppeln) forms labor camps in a series of factories in Upper Silesian cities where the Jews who live there are housed. Some of these camps are dissolved in accordance with Himmler's "extermination order"; some of them nevertheless survive because of constant, important objections of the Wehrmacht. In his autobiographical notes, Höss writes of the Schmelt Organization: "In the summer of 1942, at the urging of the Armaments Ministry, Schmelt had received permission from the SS Commander-in-Chief to withdraw 10,000 Jews from the transports from the west to stock the labor camps working on the most important munitions projects. The sorting took place in Cosel, Upper Silesia, by a director of labor deployment of D-II and Schmelt. Later, on his own hook and without my knowledge and without permission from the RSHA, Schmelt continually stopped the transports in Upper Silesia and exchanged unfit and often even dead Jews for healthy, able-bodied Jews. Because of this, there were considerable difficulties, delays in trains, escapes, etc., until my complaints caused the Supreme SS and Police Commander SS Lieutenant General Schmauser to put an end to this practice" (APMO, Höss Trial, vol. 21, p. 181).

of Block 20. Then the trucks drive up on which the sick prisoners are loaded, after another check of the list. The trucks take some of the prisoners to the gas chambers in Birkenau and return to fetch the next inmates. Altogether, Camp Doctor Entress selects 746 prisoners from the infection block and they are killed in the gas chambers the same day. During the selection, a few prisoners are able to hide in a trench between Blocks 20 and 21.

AUGUST 30

608 Jews arrive from Westerbork with an RSHA transport from Holland. None of them is admitted to the camp.*

Kempner, Edith Stein and Anne Frank, p. 76.

Jews arrive from Yugoslavia with an RSHA transport. After the selection 45 men and 31 women are admitted to the camp and receive Nos. 62164–62208 and 18645–18675. It is not known how many deportees are killed in the gas chambers.

43 male and 73 female prisoners sent to the camp by the Gestapo in Maribor, Slovenia, receive Nos. 62209–62251 and 18676–18748.

SS First Lieutenant Johann Paul Kremer, M.D., Ph.D. and Associate Professor of anatomy at the University of Münster, arrives in Auschwitz. He is assigned to the camp to replace a sick SS Camp Doctor. Dr. Kremer keeps a diary in which he records the most important events of the day.** Thus, on the day of his arrival, he notes: "Am here because of several contagious-disease (typhus, malaria, diarrhea) quarantines in the camp. Receive strict instructions about secrecy† from Garrison Doctor Captain Uhlenbrock and am lodged in the Waffen SS headquarters in a hotel room (26)."

SAM, Auschwitz in the Eyes of the SS, pp. 214ff.

AUGUST 31

1,000 Jews arrive from Drancy with the twenty-fifth RSHA transport from France. In the transport are 280 children under the age of 14. The adults include 253 men from 18 to 20 years old. A first selection is probably carried out in Cosel. After the selection in Auschwitz, only 71 women are admitted to the camp and receive Nos. 18749–18819. If we assume that 253 men were taken in the first selection in Cosel,†† then 676 people died in the gas chambers.

---

*Kempner reports that all the people who came with this transport were killed in the gas chambers. The Schmelt organization possibly took some of the men beforehand.

**Kremer is prosecuted in the Kraków Auschwitz Trial of 1947. His diary is appended to the trial documents. During the proceedings, he gives detailed explanations of the meaning of some of the entries in the diary (APMO, Dpr.-ZOd/59, pp. 13–26).

†This order refers to the preservation of secrecy.

††Two prisoners in this transport are Tobiasz Schiff (No. 160275), born April 25, 1925, who will be sent to Auschwitz on November 2, 1943, with an RSHA transport from Schoppinitz (Szopienice); and Abraham Korn (No. 177769), born April 25, 1911, inmate of Auschwitz from April 1, 1944, i.e., after the incorporation of Blechhammer work camp into the camp. This means that these men were taken off the transport on August 30 and 31 but were considered prisoners of Auschwitz only later.

1,000 Jews from Malines arrive with the sixth RSHA transport from Belgium. There are 322 men and 90 boys in the transport and 489 women and 89 girls,* none of whom are admitted to the camp. About 200 men were probably taken in Cosel for the work camps in Upper Silesia, while the remaining 800 people in Auschwitz are sent directly from the unloading platform to the gas chambers.

At 6:05 A.M., SS Man Hunka, on duty at Watchtower 4 in Birkenau, shoots Jewish prisoner No. 42482.

APMO, Höss Trial, vol. 12, p. 219.

Political prisoner Maria Stromec, sent to Auschwitz from Celje in Yugoslavia with a transport on August 10, 1942, escapes from the camp.

APMO, IZ-8/Gestapo Lodz/2/110–113.

Polish political prisoner Władysław Pronobis (No. 60405), born August 9, 1914 in the town of Auschwitz, sent to Auschwitz C.C. by the Kattowitz Stapo on August 21, 1942, escapes from the camp.

APMO, IZ-8/Gestapo Lodz/2-64.

Disinfection of the prisoner blocks in the main camp is begun. The prisoners in the blocks that are to be disinfected are lodged in Blocks 1–10, previously occupied by female prisoners and meanwhile disinfected. Zyklon B gas is used for the disinfection.

APMO, Depositions, vol. 13, p. 169, Account of Former Prisoner Władysław Siwek.

The newly arrived SS Camp Doctor, Dr. Kremer, is the first to receive a vaccination against typhus.

SAM, Auschwitz in the Eyes of the SS, Kremer's Diary, p. 215.

The killing of 746 sick and recovering prisoners in Block 20, the infection block of the prisoners' infirmary, has not stopped the typhus epidemic. The corpses of 35 prisoners are sent to the morgue; 23 of them come from Block 20.

APMO, D-AuI-5/1, Morgue Register, p. 272.

SEPTEMBER 1

SS Camp Doctor Kremer takes part in the disinfection and delousing of a block with Zyklon B gas.

SAM, Auschwitz in the Eyes of the SS, Kremer's Diary, p. 215.

61 male and seven female prisoners sent from Kattowitz receive Nos. 62252–62312 and 18820–18826.

18 male and 13 female prisoners sent from Prague receive Nos. 62313–62330 and 18854–18866.

Two prisoners sent from Breslau receive Nos. 62331 and 62332.

514 prisoners transferred from prison by the Sipo and SD of Radom receive Nos. 62333–62846.

560 Jews arrive from Westerbork with a RSHA transport from Holland. None of the people arriving in this transport is admitted to the camp.**

Kempner, Edith Stein and Anne Frank, p. 76.

*Klarsfeld and Steinberg, Memorial, statistical section.
**The men are probably selected in Cosel and sent to labor camps.

R 2

isoners transferred to Auschwitz from Flossenbürg receive Nos. 62847–62896.

The corpses of three prisoners, marked with Nos. 59454, 59666, and 60919, are sent to the morgue of the main camp from Golleschau A.C.

APMO, D-AuI-5/1, Morgue Register, p. 273.

Two prisoners, Nos. 59928 and 57935, are shot "while escaping."

Ibid., pp. 273ff.

The SS Camp Doctor carries out a selection among the sick prisoners in the prisoners' infirmary, Block 28. He selects 12 patients, who are killed the same day with phenol injections.

Ibid., p. 274.

1,000 Jews arrive from Drancy with the twenty-sixth RSHA transport from France. There are 545 men and boys and 455 women and girls in the transport. A first selection is carried out in Cosel. After the selection on the unloading platform at Auschwitz, 12 men and 27 women are admitted to the camp and receive Nos. 62897–62908 and 18827–18853. If we assume that the Schmelt Organization took about 200 men, then about 761 people are killed in the gas chambers.

SS Camp Doctor Kremer writes in his diary: "Present for the first time at a special operation, outside at three o'clock in the morning. In comparison with this, Dante's Inferno seems almost like a comedy. Not for nothing is Auschwitz called the camp of extermination!"

Auschwitz in the Eyes of the SS, Kremer's Diary, p. 215.

SEPTEMBER 3

1,000 Jews arrive from Malines camp in the seventh RSHA transport from Belgium. There are 269 men and 179 boys and 387 women and 169 girls in the transport. A first selection was probably carried out in Cosel. After the selection at the unloading platform in Auschwitz, 10 men and 86 women are admitted to the camp and receive Nos. 62909–62918 and 18867–18952. If we assume that the Schmelt Organization in Cosel took about 200 men, then about 709 people are killed in the gas chambers.

12 male and three female prisoners sent from Kattowitz receive Nos. 62919–62930 and 18953–18955.

Prisoner No. 59680 is shot "while escaping."

APMO, D-AuI-5/1, Morgue Register, p. 275.

The corpses of two prisoners, marked with numbers 57811 and 57858, are sent to the morgue of the main camp from the Golleschau A.C.

Ibid.

In an order of the Commandant's Office, Commandant Höss commends SS Corporals Kelm and Reichenbacher for finding and hand-

APMO, D-AuI-1/91, Commandant's Office Order No. 16/42.

ing over 400 American dollars, 90 English pounds and 4,000 French francs.*

SEPTEMBER 4

Jewish prisoner Otto Roniger, born in Vienna on May 29, 1902, escapes from Auschwitz.

APMO, IZ-8/Gestapo Lodz/2-114.

34 prisoners sent from Montelupich Prison by the Sipo and SD for the Kraków District receive Nos. 62931–62964. Józef Cyrankiewicz receives No. 62933 and Tadeusz Hołuj, No. 62937. After being sent to the camp, both of them join the left-oriented resistance groups in the camp. The Polish group will be led by Cyrankiewicz. Some of those who work with him in the main camp are Tadeusz Hołuj, Ludwik Rajewski (No. 4217), Stanisław Kłodziński (No. 20019), Tadeusz Wąsowicz (No. 20035), Adam Kuryłowicz (No. 18487), Konstanty Jagiełło (No. 4507), and Lucjan Motyka (No. 136678).

90 male and 47 female prisoners sent in a group transport receive Nos. 62965–63054 and 18956–19002.

1,000 Jewish men, women, and children arrive from Drancy in the twenty-seventh RSHA transport from France. The transport undergoes a first selection in Cosel. The second selection takes place on the unloading platform in Auschwitz. 10 men and 113 women are admitted to the camp and receive Nos. 63055–63064 and 19003–19115. If one assumes that the Schmelt Organization took about 200 men, then about 677 people are killed in the gas chambers of Birkenau.

SEPTEMBER 5

One female prisoner sent from Kattowitz receives No. 19116.

The SS Camp Doctor carries out a selection among the female prisoners in Block 27 of the prisoners' infirmary in the women's camp of Birkenau. He selects all the sick Jewesses, about 800 women. They are killed in the gas chamber the same day.** Dr. Kremer, who is present at the selection and gassing, writes in his diary: "Noon today at a special operation at the FKL. 'Moslems':

APMO, Höss Trial, vol. 16, p. 55; SAM, Auschwitz in the Eyes of the SS, Kremer's Diary, pp. 217ff.

*This money was no doubt found in the personal effects camp, Canada, or on the unloading platform during the search through the clothing and property of the people who were killed.
**In the protocol of the hearing of July 18, 1947, in Kraków, Kremer explains his entry thus: "I remember that I once took part in a daily gassing of such a group of women. How big the group was, I can't say. When I came to the vicinity of the bunker, they were sitting on the ground. Since they were in worn-out camp clothing, they were not allowed in the undressing barracks but rather undressed out in the open. From the behavior of these women, I concluded that they were clear about the fate that awaited them, since they were pleading with the SS Men around them and crying; nevertheless, they were all driven into the gas chamber and gassed" (Kraków Auschwitz Trial, vol. 59, p. 20; quoted from *Auschwitz in the Eyes of the SS*, p. 217).

the most ghastly of the ghastly. Master Sergeant Thilo, Troop Doctor, is right when he said to me today that we are here at the *anus mundi* [anus of the world]."

SEPTEMBER 5

714 Jewish men, women, and children from Westerbork arrive in an RSHA transport from Holland. After the selection, 53 women are admitted to the camp and receive Nos. 19117–19169. The other 661 deportees are killed in the gas chambers. Dr. Kremer is present and writes in his diary: "This evening at 8 o'clock again at a special operation from Holland.* Because of the special ration that comes with it, consisting of a fifth of a liter of liquor, five cigarettes, 100 grams of sausage, and bread, the men are eager for such operations."

SAM, *Auschwitz in the Eyes of the SS*, Kremer's Diary, p. 218.

Two prisoners, Nos. 57672 and 57890, are shot "while escaping."

APMO, D-AuI-5/1, Morgue Register, p. 277.

Prisoner No. 53321, sent from Kattowitz on July 28, 1942, is shot "while escaping," crossing the outer sentry line.

Ibid.

SEPTEMBER 6

The SS Camp Doctor carries out a selection among the prisoners in the infirmary, Block 13, the so-called Jewish infirmary.** He selects nine prisoners, who are killed the same day with phenol injections.

Ibid., p. 278.

SS Lieutenant Colonel Dr. Eduard Wirths is assigned to Auschwitz to take over the function of Garrison Doctor.†

1,013 Jewish men, women, and children arrive from Drancy in the twenty-eighth RSHA transport from France. A first selection of the transport took place in Cosel. After the second selection on the unloading platform in Auschwitz, 16 men and 38 women are admitted to the camp as prisoners and receive Nos. 63065–63080 and 19170–19207. If one assumes that the Schmelt Organization took about 200 men, about 759 people die in the gas chambers of Birkenau. Dr. Kremer is present at the gassing and writes in his diary, "Evening at 8 o'clock, out again for a special operation."

SAM, *Auschwitz in the Eyes of the SS*, Kremer's Diary, p. 219.

Two female prisoners sent from Kattowitz receive Nos. 19208 and 19209.

---

*In the protocol of the hearing of July 18, 1947, Kremer states the following: "An SS doctor was always present at these gassings. They made a fixed rotation of service. Among the physicians in my time I recall the following names: Thilo, Kitt, Uhlenborck, Wirths, Meyer, and Entress" (APMO, Dpr. ZOd/59; *Auschwitz in the Eyes of the SS*, p. 218).

**During the typhus epidemic, Jewish prisoners are lodged in this locked block and not given medical treatment; hence the mortality rate in this block is very high.

†Kremer writes in his diary, "Today, Sunday, excellent lunch: tomato soup, half a chicken with potatoes and red cabbage (20 grams of fat), a sweet and marvellous vanilla ice cream. After the meal, greeting the new Garrison Doctor, Lieutenant Colonel Wirths" (SAM, *Auschwitz in the Eyes of the SS*, p. 218).

SEPTEMBER 7

The SS Camp Doctor carries out a selection in the infirmary, Block 28. He selects 33 patients, who are killed the same day with phenol injections.

APMO, D-AuI-5/1, Morgue Register, pp. 279ff.; Mat.RO, vol. VI, p. 20A.

SS Camp Doctor Kremer has himself inoculated a second time against typhus.

SAM, *Auschwitz in the Eyes of the SS*, p. 219.

Seven prisoners sent from Kattowitz receive Nos. 63081–63087.

Because of the typhus epidemic in the camp, Protective Custody Commander Aumeier forbids SS dependents to enter the town of Auschwitz. He also reminds them of the strict prohibition against entering the area of the camp.

APMO, D-AuI-1, Commandant's Office Special Order, Sept. 7, 1942.

SEPTEMBER 8

A prisoner sent from Kattowitz receives No. 63088.

930 Jewish men, women, and children arrive from Westerbork in an RSHA transport from Holland. A first selection of this transport was probably carried out in Cosel. After the selection at Auschwitz, six men and 26 women are admitted to the camp and receive Nos. 63089–63094 and 19210–19235. If one assumes that the Schmelt Organization in Cosel took about 200 men, then about 698 people die in the gas chambers.

Prisoner No. 58663 is shot "while escaping."

APMO, D-AuI-5/1, Morgue Register, p. 282.

The corpses of 62 prisoners are sent to the morgue of the main camp.

Ibid., pp. 282ff.

SEPTEMBER 9

18 male and seven female prisoners sent from Kattowitz receive Nos. 63095–63112 and 19236–19242.

51 prisoners sent by the Warsaw Sipo and SD from Pawiak Prison receive Nos. 63113–63163.

1,000 Jewish men, women, and children arrive from Drancy in the twenty-ninth RSHA transport from France. A first selection is held in Cosel and 200 men are probably chosen for the Schmelt Organization. After the selection in Auschwitz, 59 men and 52 women are admitted to the camp and receive Nos. 63164–63222 and 19243–19294. The other 689 people are killed in the gas chambers. SS Camp Doctor Kremer, who takes part in the operation, writes in his diary: "Evening, attended a special operation (4th time)."

SAM, *Auschwitz in the Eyes of the SS*, p. 219.

SS Camp Doctor Kremer is present at the flogging of eight prisoners.

Ibid.

Camp Doctor Kremer is present at the shooting of Polish prisoner Tadeusz Kulka (No. 17166). He was sent to the camp in a group transport on June 8, 1941.

Ibid.

The Commandant's Office ends the search operation for Maria Stromec, who escaped from the camp on August 31, 1942, after she is captured.

APMO, IZ-8/Gestapo Lodz/2-110–112.

The Commandant's Office ends the search operation for Otto Roninger, who escaped on September 4, 1942, and is captured in the vicinity of the camp.

APMO, IZ-8/Gestapo Lodz/2-116, 117.

SEPTEMBER 10

1,000 Jews arrive from Malines Camp with the eighth RSHA transport from Belgium. In the transport are 376 men and 124 boys and 386 women and 114 girls. A first selection was carried out in Cosel, where about 200 men were chosen for the Schmelt Organization. After the selection in Auschwitz, 21 men and 64 women are admitted to the camp and receive Nos. 63223–63243 and 19295–19358. The other 715 people are killed in the gas chambers. SS Camp Doctor Kremer takes part in the selection and the gassing.*

Two inmates sent from Kattowitz the day before receive Nos. 63244 and 63245.

One female prisoner transferred from Ravensbrück receives No. 19359.

Political prisoner Franz Doschek (No. 18271), who escaped from the camp on March 28, 1942, is captured and locked in the bunker of Block 11. He is released from the bunker to the camp on December 12, 1942, and is probably shot.

SEPTEMBER 11

148 male and 54 female prisoners sent in a group transport receive Nos. 63246–63393 and 19360–19413.

APMO, D-AuI-3/1b, Bunker Register, p. 78.

76 prisoners sent by the Lublin Sipo and SD from the castle in Lublin, receive Nos. 63394–63469.

1,000 Jewish men, women and children arrive with the thirtieth RSHA transport from France. A first selection took place in Cosel, where 200 men were probably chosen for the Schmelt Organization. After the selection in Auschwitz, 23 men and 68 women are admitted to the camp and receive Nos. 63471–63493 and 19414–19481. The other 709 deportees are killed in the gas chambers.

---

*In his diary, he writes, "Morning present at a special operation (5th time)" (SAM, *Auschwitz in the Eyes of the SS,* pp. 220ff.).

The medical officer on duty, SS Staff Sergeant Klehr, kills the Dutch Jew Heiman Kohen (No. 52425) with a poker in the corridor of Block 20 of the prisoners' infirmary. He sends the body of the murdered man to the morgue in the cellar of Block 28. Finally, he orders a death registration made out stating that Kohen died a natural death.

APMO, Höss Trial, vol. 4, p. 166, Statement of Former Prisoner Stanisław Głowa; D-AuI-5/1, Morgue Register, p. 288.

The head of Office D-III in the WVHA—responsible for sanitation and camp hygiene—Lieutenant Colonel Enno Lolling, arrives in the camp for an inspection.

SAM, *Auschwitz in the Eyes of the SS*, p. 221.

SS Private First Class Hans Luger, SS Private Adolf Taube, and SS Private Martin Birli receive commendations from Commandant Höss because they have turned over large amounts of discovered money and foreign exchange.

APMO, Commandant's Office Order No. 17/42.

SEPTEMBER 12

Nine prisoners sent in a group transport receive Nos. 63494–63502.

874 Jewish men, women, and children arrive from Westerbork with an RSHA transport from Holland. A first selection took place in Cosel, where 200 men were probably chosen for the Schmelt Organization. After the selection in Auschwitz, 26 men and 34 women are admitted to the camp and receive Nos. 63503–63528 and 19482–19515. The remaining 614 deportees are killed in the gas chambers.

14 female prisoners sent in a group transport receive Nos. 19516–19529.

1,000 Jewish men, women, and children arrive with the thirty-first RSHA transport from France. A first selection took place in Cosel, where 300 men were probably chosen for the Schmelt Organization. After the selection in Auschwitz, two men and 78 women are admitted to the camp and receive Nos. 63529 and 63530 and 19530–19607. The remaining 620 deportees are killed in the gas chambers.

SEPTEMBER 14

1,000 Jews arrive from Malines with the ninth RSHA transport from Belgium. There are 399 men and 108 boys in the transport and 373 women and 120 girls. A first selection took place in Cosel, where about 250 men were probably chosen for the Schmelt Organization. After the selection in Auschwitz, 45 men and 105 women are admitted to the camp and receive Nos. 63531–63575 and 19608–19712. The remaining 600 people are killed in the gas chambers.

SS Camp Doctor Kremer receives the third and last inoculation against typhus.

SAM, *Auschwitz in the Eyes of the SS*, p. 221.

The bodies of two prisoners, Nos. 49245 and 60778, from the Golleschau A.C., and the body of prisoner 63055 from Jawischowitz A.C. are sent to the morgue of the main camp.

APMO, D-AuI-5/1, Morgue Register, p. 294.

The Commandant's Office receives five trucks from the WVHA to carry out a special operation. This euphemism refers to exterminating Jews.

APMO, Kraków Auschwitz Trial, Dpr. ZO/38, p. 113.

SEPTEMBER 15

79 male and seven female prisoners sent from Kattowitz receive Nos. 63576–63651 and 19713–19719.

98 prisoners sent from Radom by the Sipo and SD receive Nos. 63652–63749.

75 prisoners sent by the Warsaw Sipo and SD from Pawiak Prison receive Nos. 63750–63824.

The Commandant's Office receives signed permission from Richard Glücks, Head of Branch D of the WVHA, for an automobile trip to Lodz, dated September 16, 1942. The purpose of the trip is to inspect an experimental facility for field ovens to be used in connection with Operation Reinhardt.*

APMO, Höss Trial, vol. 12, p. 168; vol. 38, p. 114, Appendix 59.

Polish prisoner Janina Kukowska, M.A. (No. 7453), dies of typhus in the women's camp. She worked with other female prisoners as a botanist in the plant breeding station in Rajsko. Agriculture Director Caesar, fearing that the other women employed in the laboratory, who come in contact with SS personnel at work, might spread typhus in their work area, obtains permission to lodge them in the camp staff building.

Zięba, "Rajsko," p. 84; APMO, D-RO/10, List of Polish Women Who Died in Auschwitz.

SEPTEMBER 16

Commandant Höss, SS Second Lieutenant Hössler,** and SS Second Lieutenant Dejaco, who is employed in the Central Construction Administration, go to Kulmhof (Chełmno),† where SS Colonel

APMO, Central Construction Administration/KGL, BW 30/25/6, Memorandum of September 17, 1942, on the Official Trip to Litzmannstadt (Lodz) (No. 4467), reproduced in *HvA*, no. 3, 1960, p. 122; SAM, *Auschwitz in the Eyes of the SS*, pp. 166ff.

*A euphemism for the seizure and processing of all the clothing, personal belongings, and items of value obtained from the Jews killed in the gas chambers. In this document, the "experimental facility for field ovens" means the facility for the incineration of corpses.
**As Pery Broad recounts, " . . . the fisheries complained that the fish in the largest fish ponds in the area of Birkenau . . . died. Experts saw the cause of this phenomenon in the poisoning of the groundwater by cadaveric poisons. . . . The summer sun burned on the ground of Birkenau, the corpses, not decomposed but only rotting, began to stir, and a dark-red mass seethed out of the bursting crust of the earth and spread an indescribable stench. . . . Therefore, Franz Hössler . . . was assigned to dig up the bodies and have them burned, preserving as much secrecy as possible" (SAM, *Auschwitz in the Eyes of the SS*, p. 170).
†The death camp of Kulmhof is in operation from December 1941 to April 7, 1943, and from June 26 to July 14, 1944. The victims are killed there in specially built vehicles with the carbon monoxide gas of the motors. The corpses are burned in primitive field ovens. About 310,000 people are murdered in Kulmhof, most of them Jews from the so-called Reichsgau Wartheland and Jews and Gypsies deported from the Lodz ghetto.

Blobel* demonstrates the machinery for incinerating bodies. The purpose of the inspection is to find a process to empty the mass graves in Birkenau, burn the bodies, and get rid of the ashes so that all traces of the crime can be wiped out.

902 Jewish men, women, and children arrive from Westerbork with an RSHA transport from Holland. A first selection took place in Cosel, where about 200 men were probably chosen by the Schmelt Organization. After the selection on the unloading platform in Auschwitz, 47 men and 29 women are admitted to the camp and receive Nos. 63825–63871 and 19720–19748. The remaining 626 people are killed in the gas chambers.

20 female prisoners sent from Kattowitz on August 10, 1942, receive Nos. 19749–19768. Until the day of their registration, these women are probably held prisoner in the bunker of Block 11 while they wait for the Gestapo to decide on their fate.

27 male and three female prisoners sent from Kattowitz receive Nos. 63470, 63872–63897, and 19769–19771.

1,000 Jewish men, women, and children arrive with the thirty-second RSHA transport from France. A first selection took place in Cosel, where about 250 men were chosen for various work camps. After the selection on the unloading platform of Auschwitz, 56 men and 49 women are admitted to the camp and receive Nos. 63898–63953 and 19772–19820. The remaining 745 people are killed in the gas chambers.

The SS Camp Doctor carries out a selection in the prisoners' infirmary, Block 28. He selects 23 sick prisoners, who are killed with phenol injections the same day.

APMO, Mat.RO, vol. VI, p. 20C.

SEPTEMBER 17

Jewish prisoner Ernest Elster (No. 58834), born January 16, 1904, in Lemberg (Lwiw), in the Ukraine, is captured in an escape attempt and locked in the bunker of Block 11. On October 3, 1942, he is released from the bunker and transferred to the Penal Company.

APMO, D-AuI-3/1b, Bunker Register, p. 78.

51 prisoners sent from Troppau receive Nos. 63954–64004.

1,048 Jews arrive from Malines with the tenth RSHA transport from Belgium. There are 383 men, 151 boys, 401 women, and 113 girls in the transport. After the selection on the unloading platform of Auschwitz, 230 men and 101 women are admitted to the camp

*Until January 1942, Blobel was head of Special Commando 4a, which was part of Mobile Strike Squad (Einsatzgruppe) C deployed in the occupied areas of the Soviet Union (in Kiev and Poltawa). From June 1942 on, Blobel has the function of removing the traces of earlier mass murder operations from Polish and Soviet territory.

Pit for incinerating corpses.

and receive Nos. 64005–64234 and 19821–19921. Mala Zimet-baum,* born January 26, 1918, in Brzesko, receives No. 19880. The remaining 717 deportees are killed in the gas chambers.

Five female prisoners sent from Troppau receive Nos. 19922–19926.

Prisoner No. 60120 shot "while escaping."

APMO, D-AuI-5/1, Morgue Register, p. 299.

The SS Camp Doctor carries out a selection in the prisoners' infirmary. He selects 98 sick prisoners, who are killed with phenol injections the same day.

APMO, Mat.RO, vol. VI, pp. 20C, 20D.

The bodies of 147 prisoners are sent to the morgue of the main camp.

APMO, D-AuI-5/1, Morgue Register, pp. 299–303.

SS Camp Doctor Kremer accompanies Camp Doctor Georg Mayer on a visit to the women's camp at Birkenau.

SAM, *Auschwitz in the Eyes of the SS*, pp. 220ff.

SEPTEMBER 18

Six male and 22 female prisoners sent in a group transport receive Nos. 64235–64240.

*On June 24, 1944, she escapes from the camp with Edward Galiński (No. 531).

70 prisoners sent by the Sipo and SD for the Kraków District receive Nos. 64241–64310.

85 male and 31 female prisoners sent in a group transport receive Nos. 64311–64395 and 19949–19979.

1,003 Jewish men, women, and children arrive with the thirty-third RSHA transport from France. A first selection took place in Cosel, where about 300 men were probably transferred to various work camps. After the selection in Auschwitz, 147 women are admitted to the camp and receive Nos. 19980–20216. The remaining 556 deportees are killed in the gas chambers.

The SS Camp Doctor carries out a selection in the prisoners' infirmary. He selects 16 prisoners, who are killed with phenol injections the same day.

APMO, Mat.RO, vol. VI, pp. 21A, 21B.

SS Commander in Chief Himmler and the newly appointed Minister of Justice, Otto Thierack, come to an agreement on the following:

APMO, Pohl Trial, vol. 12, p. 37 (654-PS); quoted from International Military Tribunal, Nuremberg, Doc. No. 654-PS (hereafter cited as IMG).

> Release of asocial elements from court-imposed sentences to the SS Commander in Chief for extermination by labor. According to the decision of the Minister of Justice, criminals serving sentences, Jews, Gypsies, Russians, Ukrainians, Poles with more than a three-year sentence, Czechs or Germans with more than eight-year sentences are extradited without exception. . . .
>
> It is agreed that, in consideration of the intended goals of our nation's leaders for the purification of the East, in the future, Jews, Poles, Gypsies, Russians, and Ukrainians are no longer to be sentenced by regular judges, whenever a punishment is at issue, but rather will be handled by the SS Commander in Chief.

SEPTEMBER 19

Jews from Slovakia arrive with an RSHA transport. After the selection, 206 men and 71 women are admitted to the camp and receive Nos. 64396–64601 and 20127–20197. The remaining deportees are killed in the gas chambers.

16 male and 19 female prisoners sent to the camp by the Sipo and SD for the Kraków District receive Nos. 64602–64617 and 20198–20216.

Prisoner No. 57640 is shot "while escaping."

APMO, D-AuI-5/1, Morgue Register, p. 306.

The SS Camp Doctor carries out a selection in the Infection Block 20 of the prisoners' infirmary. He selects 31 sick prisoners, who are killed with phenol injections the same day.

APMO, Mat.RO, vol. VI, p. 21A.

SEPTEMBER 20

1,002 Jewish men, women, and children arrive from Westerbork with an RSHA transport from Holland. A first selection took place in Cosel, where about 200 men were probably chosen for various labor camps. After the selection in Auschwitz, 101 men and 111 women are admitted to the camp as prisoners and receive Nos. 64618–64718 and 20217–20327. The remaining 590 deportees are killed in the gas chambers.

1,000 Jewish men, women, and children arrive from Drancy with the thirty-fourth RSHA transport from France. A first selection took place in Cosel, where about 200 men were probably chosen for various work camps. After the selection in Auschwitz, 31 men and 110 women* are sent to the camp and receive Nos. 64710–64749 and 20328–20436. The remaining 659 people are killed in the gas chambers.

SEPTEMBER 21

Burning the corpses of the dead in the open is begun in Birkenau. At first the bodies are burned on wood piles on which 2,000 bodies are stacked at a time, and later in pits with earlier buried and again uncovered bodies. To burn the bodies faster, they are first drenched with oil residue and then with wood alcohol. The pits burn ceaselessly, day and night.

SAM, *Auschwitz in the Eyes of the SS*, Comments by Höss, p. 115.

18 prisoners sent from Kattowitz receive Nos. 64750–64767.

Two prisoners, Nos. 51367 and 60580, are shot "while escaping."

APMO, D-AuI-5/1, Morgue Register, pp. 309ff.

The bodies of 75 prisoners are sent to the morgue of the main camp.

Ibid., pp. 309–311.

SEPTEMBER 22

Three Polish prisoners, Alfons Kiprowski (No. 801), born October 9, 1921; political prisoner Piotr Jaglicz, born June 29, 1922; and Adam Szumlak (No. EH-1954), born June 16, 1920, escape from the camp.

APMO, IZ-8/Gestapo Lodz/3/88/319.

11 male prisoners and one female prisoner sent from Kattowitz receive Nos. 64768–64778 and 20438.

75 prisoners sent by the Warsaw Sipo and SD from Pawiak Prison receive Nos. 64779–64853.

On Wagon 320224, the Central Construction Administration sends to Mauthausen the parts for a coke-heated double-muffle oven for the incineration of bodies. The shipment was destined for Mauthausen and mistakenly sent by J. A. Topf and Sons to Auschwitz.

APMO, IZ-13/89, Various Documents of the Third Reich, p. 249.

68 prisoners sent from Lublin by the Sipo and SD receive Nos. 64854–64921.

*According to Klarsfeld, *Memorial*, p. xxvi.

713 Jewish men, women, and children arrive from Westerbork with an RSHA transport from Holland. After the selection 133 men and 50 women are admitted to the camp and receive Nos. 64922–65054 and 20439–20488. The remaining 530 people are killed in the gas chambers.

Two prisoners, Nos. 49932 and 59674, are shot "while escaping."

APMO, D-AuI-5/1, Morgue Register, p. 312.

The SS Camp Doctor carries out a selection in the prisoners' infirmary, Block 28. He selects 24 sick prisoners, who are killed with phenol injections the same day.

APMO, Mat.RO, vol. VI, p. 21B.

SEPTEMBER 23

Jews from Slovakia arrive with an RSHA transport. After the selection, 294 men and 67 women are admitted and receive Nos. 65055–65348 and 20489–20555. The rest of the people are killed in the gas chambers.

Seven male and ten female prisoners sent from Kattowitz receive Nos. 65349–65355 and 20556–20565.

1,000 Jewish men, women, and children from Pithiviers arrive with the thirty-fifth RSHA transport from France. A first selection took place in Cosel, where about 150 men were chosen for the Schmelt Organization. After the selection in Auschwitz, 65 men and 144 women are admitted to the camp and given Nos. 65356–65420 and 20566–20709. The remaining 641 deportees are killed in the gas chambers.*

SS General Pohl, Head of the WVHA, and his escort arrive in Auschwitz. It is the occasion for a ceremonial dinner at the Commandant's home.**

The SS Camp Doctor carries out a selection in the prisoners' infirmary, Block 28. He selects 16 sick prisoners, who are killed with phenol injections the same day.

Ibid., p. 210.

The Commandant's Office is notified that a transport with about 1,000 Jews left le Bourget–Drancy for Auschwitz at 8:55 A.M. It is also informed that the brother of former French Prime Minister Leon Blum is in this transport.

APMO, D-RF-3/35, Inventory No. 22036; reproduced in *HvA*, no. 3, 1960, p. 123.

Commandant Höss discontinues the search for Władysław Pronobis, who escaped from the camp on August 31, 1942, and informs

APMO, IZ-8/Gestapo Lodz/2-88/66.

---

*SS Camp Physician Kremer takes part in the selections of the Jews from Slovakia and from Pithiviers Camp in France, which took place on the platform, as well as in the gassing in the bunker. In his diary, he notes: "Tonight at the 6th and 7th special operation" (SAM, *Auschwitz in the Eyes of the SS*, Kremer's Diary, pp. 220–222).
**Kremer writes, "There was baked pike, as much as everybody wanted, real coffee, excellent beer, and sandwiches" (Ibid., p. 222).

the relevant headquarters that the escapee has been captured and is being interrogated in the criminal police station in the town of Auschwitz, since he has meanwhile committed a holdup and a break-in.

SEPTEMBER 24

A prisoner sent from Kattowitz receives No. 65421.

A prisoner sent from Vienna on July 18, 1942, receives No. 65422. He has probably been imprisoned in the bunker of Block 11 until now as a civilian prisoner.

Polish prisoner Klemens Grecko, sent to Auschwitz by the Sipo and SD for the Kraków District on August 27, 1942, escapes from the camp.

APMO, IZ-8/Gestapo Lodz/3/88/317.

SEPTEMBER 25

36 male and 23 female prisoners sent in a group transport receive Nos. 65423–65458 and 20710–20722.

1,000 Jewish men, women, and children arrive from Drancy with the thirty-sixth RSHA transport from France. After the selection, 399 men and 126 women are admitted to the camp and receive Nos. 65460–65858 and 20723–20848. The remaining 475 deportees are killed in the gas chambers.

SS Chief Doctor and Head of the Sanitation Central Office, SS General Dr. Ernst Robert Grawitz, inspects the camp.* During his visit, he inspects the overcrowded infirmaries, the morgue, and the temporary sewage plant in Birkenau. He is present at a gassing of Jews and the subsequent burning of the bodies in the pits. He sees that the medical supervision by the SS Camp Doctors is unsatisfactory and that the patients do not receive adequate care and also notes the generally bad health of the prisoners.

APMO, Höss Trial, vol. 7, p. 61; SAM, *Auschwitz in the Eyes of the SS*, Kremer's Diary, p. 222.

The SS Camp Doctor carries out a selection in the prisoners' infirmary, Block 28. He chooses 48 sick prisoners, who are killed with phenol injections the same day.

APMO, Mat.RO, vol. VI, pp. 21C, 21D.

Political prisoner Filip Litwin (No. 60314), who is captured trying to escape on October 3, 1942, is released from the bunker of Block 11 and transferred to the Penal Company in Birkenau.

APMO, D-AuI-3/1b, Bunker Register, p. 79.

Polish political prisoner Józef Bobicki (No. 62931), born December 10, 1913, in Kraków, sent to Auschwitz by the Sipo and SD for the Kraków District on September 4, 1942, escapes from the camp.

APMO, IZ-8/Gestapo Lodz/3/88/321.

*Grawitz is also the executive president of the German Red Cross.

The Commandant's Office is notified that a transport with 1,000 Jews left le Bourget–Drancy for Auschwitz at 8:55 A.M. A special car with 3,000 woolen blankets is attached to this transport. It is also informed that Nathan Tannenzopf, who became famous because of a major film scandal in France and whose French citizenship was revoked by the authorities, is in this transport.

APMO, D-RF-3/36, Inventory No. 22037.

SEPTEMBER 26

42 male and 14 female prisoners sent in a group transport receive Nos. 65859–65900 and 20849–20862.

928 Jewish men, women, and children arrive from Westerbork in an RSHA transport from Holland. After the selection, 129 men and 50 women are admitted to the camp and receive Nos. 65901–66029 and 20863–20912. The remaining 749 deportees are killed in the gas chambers.

Three prisoners, Nos. 50161, 62245, and 41845, are shot "while escaping."

APMO, D-AuI-5/1, Morgue Register, pp. 322ff.

The Head of Branch A of the WVHA, SS Brigadier General August Frank, orders the Commandants of Lublin and Auschwitz, with regard to the property of the killed Jewish population, to deposit all cash in German Reichsbank notes in the Reichsbank in Berlin-Schöneberg; and to turn over all foreign exchange, precious metals, and jewelry to the WVHA. Watches of every kind, alarm clocks, and fountain pens are to be repaired by the WVHA, cleaned, and then sent to the troops at the front. The clothing, linens, fabrics, and personal and household utensils of those who are killed are to be turned over to the office of the German People's Fund (Volksdeutsche Mittelstelle) in exchange for cash.

APMO, Kraków Auschwitz Trial, vol. 37, p. 127; Pohl Trial, vol. 18, pp. 108–110 (NO-724); Jewish Historical Institute (Warsaw), *Fascism, Ghetto, Mass Murder*, pp. 404–406.

SEPTEMBER 27

1,004 Jewish men, women, and children arrive from Drancy with the thirty-seventh RSHA transport from France. A first selection took place in Cosel, where 175 men were taken. 40 men and 91 women are then admitted to Auschwitz and receive Nos. 66030–66069 and 20913–21003. The remaining 698 deportees are killed in the gas chambers.

30 female prisoners receive Nos. 21004–21033.

SEPTEMBER 28

1,742 Jews arrive from Malines with the eleventh RSHA transport from Belgium. There are 383 men, 151 boys, 401 women, and 113 girls. After the selection, 286 men and 58 women are admitted to the camp and receive Nos. 66070–66355 and 21034–21091. The remaining 1,398 people are killed in the gas chambers.

German prisoner Friede Alt, born April 14, 1910, in Siersleben, imprisoned in Ravensbrück since September 10, 1941, and transferred to Auschwitz on March 26, 1942, escapes from the camp.

APMO, IZ-8/Gestapo Lodz/2/88/95.

SEPTEMBER 29

The Commandant's Office ends the search operation, since Friede Alt has been captured and brought back to the camp.

APMO, IZ-Gestapo Lodz/2/88/97.

Polish prisoner Władysław Pronobis (No. 60405), who escaped from the camp on August 31, 1942, is locked in the bunker. On October 10, 1942, he is released from the bunker and probably transferred to the Penal Company.

APMO, D-AuI-3/1b, Bunker Register, p. 79.

20 female prisoners sent from Pawiak Prison by the Sipo and SD of Warsaw receive Nos. 21092–21111.

12 male and four female prisoners sent from Kattowitz receive Nos. 65459, 66356–66366, and 21112–21115.

148 prisoners sent from Radom by the Sipo and SD receive Nos. 66367–66514.

904 Jewish men, women, and children arrive with the thirty-eighth RSHA transport from France. A first selection took place in Cosel, where about 100 men were probably taken for Blechhammer Labor Camp. After the selection in Auschwitz, 123 men and 48 women are admitted to the camp and given Nos. 66515–66637 and 21116–21163. The remaining 633 people are killed in the gas chambers.

SEPTEMBER 30

20 prisoners sent from Kattowitz receive Nos. 66638–66657.

55 male and 13 female prisoners sent to the camp by the Sipo and SD for the Kraków District receive Nos. 66658–66712 and 21164–21176.

10 female prisoners sent from Kattowitz receive Nos. 21177–21286.

610 Jewish men, women, and children arrive from Westerbork in an RSHA transport from Holland. After the selection, 37 men and 119 women are admitted to the camp and given Nos. 66713–66749 and 21187–21305. The remaining 454 people are killed in the gas chambers. SS Camp Doctor Kremer and Protective Custody Commander Aumeier take part in the selection and subsequent gassing.

Auschwitz in the Eyes of the SS, p. 223.

80 prisoners sent to the camp from Pawiak Prison by the Sipo and SD of Warsaw receive Nos. 66750–66829.

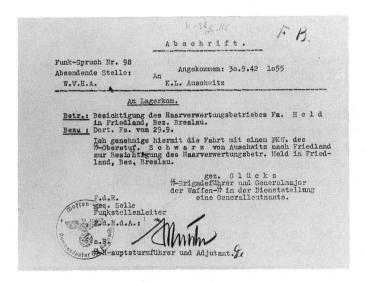

Armed SS Brigadier General Richard Glücks issues a travel permit for the inspection of the Held hair-processing plant.

Two prisoners, Nos. 59247 and 59642, are shot "while escaping." APMO, D-AuI-5/1, Morgue Register, p. 331.

The SS Camp Doctor carries out a selection in the prisoners' infirmary. He selects 84 sick prisoners, who are taken to Birkenau and killed in the gas chamber. APMO, D-AuI-5/1, Prisoners' Infirmary, Register of Block 28, pp. 221–223.

Because of the typhus epidemic raging in Auschwitz-Birkenau, Commandant Höss forbids SS personnel and their families to consume raw fruits and vegetables or raw milk. He reminds them that it is forbidden to enter the town of Auschwitz and buy groceries there. APMO, D-AuI-1, Garrison Order 26/42.

Commandant Höss reminds the SS personnel that it is forbidden to take labor squads along the railroad tracks. APMO, D-AuI-1/94, Commandant's Office Order 19/42.

The Commandant's Office receives permission from the WVHA for an automobile trip to Friedland, near Breslau, where SS First Lieutenant Schwarz is to inspect the Held company and get information on the processing of human hair. The trip is authorized by Head of Branch D Richard Glücks.* APMO, Kraków Auschwitz Trial, vol. 38, p. 115, Appendix 60; Schnabel, *Power Without Morality*, p. 262, Doc. 94.

Commandant Rudolf Höss allows female IBV prisoners to be employed as officers' orderlies instead of SS men, since there are not enough SS men available for guarding prisoners at work. APMO, D-AuI-1/94, Commandant's Office Order No. 19/42.

OCTOBER 1

A prisoner sent from Kattowitz receives No. 66830.

A selection is carried out in the women's camp, Section B-Ia, in Birkenau. 2,000 prisoners are selected and killed in the gas chamber the same day. APMO, Höss Trial, vol. 16, p. 55.

---

*Not only do the prisoners have their hair shorn, but those who are killed with poison gas are also shaved. The Commandants of the concentration camps sell this hair, which is processed into such items as felt and mattresses, to German companies for .25 RM per pound (Schnabel, *Power Without Morality*, pp. 262ff, Doc. 95).

OCTOBER 2

152 male and 67 female prisoners sent in a group transport receive Nos. 66831–66982 and 21306–21372.

210 Jews are sent from Drancy with the thirty-ninth RSHA transport from France. In the transport are 103 men and three boys and 100 women and four girls. After the selection, 34 men and 22 women are admitted to the camp and receive Nos. 66983–67016 and 21373–21394. The remaining 154 deportees are killed in the gas chambers.

The WVHA authorizes a travel permit to the Commandant's Office for a five-ton truck with a trailer to drive to Dessau and back to fetch "material for Jewish resettlement." This is a euphemism for the poison gas Zyklon B.

Ibid., vol. 12, p. 170.

A selection is carried out in the women's camp, Section B-Ia in Birkenau. 2,012 prisoners are chosen and killed in the gas chambers.

Ibid., vol. 16, p. 55.

OCTOBER 3

A prisoner sent from Kattowitz receives No. 67017.

1,014 Jewish men, women, and children are sent from Westerbork with an RSHA transport from Holland. A first selection took place in Cosel, where about 300 men were taken for the labor camps in Silesia. At the selection on the unloading platform in Auschwitz, 29 men and 33 women are admitted to the camp and receive Nos. 67018–67046 and 21395–21427. The remaining 652 people are killed in the gas chambers.

At another selection in the women's camp in Birkenau, 1,800 female prisoners are selected. They are killed in the gas chambers.

Ibid.; APMO, Kraków Auschwitz Trial, vol. VII, pp. 123ff.

SS Camp Doctor Kremer writes in his diary: "Today fresh living material from the human liver and spleen as well as pancreas fixed,* along with lice from typhus patients fixed in pure alcohol. In Auschwitz, whole streets are struck down with typhus. So today I had the first serum injection against abdominal typhus administered to me. First Lieutenant Schwarz is sick with typhus."

Auschwitz in the Eyes of the SS, Kremer's Diary, pp. 223ff.

---

*At his interrogation on July 30, 1947, in Kraków, Kremer explained that he had "long been interested in the changes in human organisms resulting from hunger," and had introduced this interest to Wirths, "who explained to me that I could take fresh living material for these investigations from prisoners killed by phenol injections." After the selection of a particular prisoner designated by Kremer, the person is brought in again and laid, still alive, on the dissection table. "I stepped up to the table and asked the patient about various details, which were essential for my investigations. . . . After getting this information, a medic approached the patient and killed him with an injection in the heart." Then Kremer removed the "fresh living material."

OCTOBER 4

In Fort Wawel in Kraków, in the headquarters of General Governor Hans Frank, a discussion takes place concerning the evacuation of the Poles from the Zamość region. Heinrich Himmler takes part in the talk.

Wroński, *Chronicle*, p.

At 12:30 A.M., the SS standby squad is called to take charge of a transport. This probably concerns guarding a transport of 1,800 female prisoners who are taken to the gas chambers.

APMO, D-AuI-1/31, FvD, p. 103.

Polish political prisoner Feliks Arendarski (No. 20801), born May 17, 1907, in Medrow, sent from Radom to Auschwitz by the Sipo and SD on September 15, 1941, escapes from the camp.

APMO, IZ-8/Gestapo Lodz/3/88/ 329.

OCTOBER 5

23 prisoners sent from Prague receive Nos. 67047–67069.

In connection with the transfer of about 1,600 Jewish prisoners from various concentration camps in Germany to Auschwitz, Office D-II of the WVHA calls on the Commandant of Auschwitz to provide Polish, Ukrainian, or other prisoners in exchange.

Dokumenty i materiały czásow okupaciji niemieckiej w Polsce (Documents and material on the German Occupation of Poland), vol. I, Obozy (*Oświęcim*) (Camp), Lodz, 1946, p. 73 (hereafter cited as *Dokumenty i materiały*).

At night, a massacre takes place among the French Jewesses in the Penal Company in Budy. About 90 women are beaten to death with clubs, rifle butts, and axes; others are thrown out of upper-story windows and die. The perpetrators are SS guards and German prisoner functionaries sent to the camp as criminals or for prostitution. Commandant Höss is informed at 5:00 A.M. that the alleged revolt has been successfully defeated. After a cursory inspection of the site, he returns to the Commandant's Office and turns the issue over to the Political Department, which is to carry out an investigation. Höss records the murder of the French Jewesses as the "bloodbath of Budy."*

OCTOBER 6

During the morning, the SS Identification Service of the Political Department and SS medical orderlies enter the Penal Company in Budy. The Identification Service photographs the bodies of the prisoners lying on top of one another and those who tried to get away from the massacre hanging on the barbed wire.** The SS medical orderlies drag the wounded and still living inmates individually into

---

*On the basis of the inquiries made by the Political Department, Pery Broad, a functionary of the Political Department, describes in detail how the massacre in Budy occurred; Höss and Kremer also mention it (*Auschwitz in the Eyes of the SS*, pp. 77ff, 227, 162–168).
**Pery Broad writes: "Later, in the developing room, under the strictest supervision, only one print is made of each picture. The plates had to be destroyed in the presence of the Commandant. The pictures were put at his disposal" (*Ibid.*, Broad's Memoirs, p. 166).

a cleared room and kill them with an injection in the heart of 2 cubic centimeters of phenol.

622 female prisoners transferred from Ravensbrück to Auschwitz receive Nos. 21428–22049. There are 522 Jewesses among the arrivals. This transport also includes 18 female prisoners trained in poultry breeding in Ravensbrück who are to work in the Harmense A.C. in the poultry farm. During the admissions procedure, these prisoners observe a truck passing by with the corpses of the murdered women from the Penal Company in Budy.*

Four male prisoners and one female sent from Kattowitz receive Nos. 67070–67073 and 22050.

47 female prisoners sent from Radom by the Sipo and SD receive Nos. 22051–22097.

SS Camp Doctor Entress has a motorcycle accident. Dr. Kremer substitutes for Entress in the selection for admission to the main camp.

Auschwitz in the Eyes of the SS, Kremer's Diary, p. 224.

At roll call in the men's camp, B-Ib, in Birkenau, it is discovered that one prisoner is missing. The standby squad begins a search operation led by SS Second Lieutenant Miller.

APMO, D-AuI-1/3a, FvD, p. 106.

OCTOBER 7

2,012 Jewish men, women, and children arrive from Westerbork in an RSHA transport from Holland. A first selection took place in Cosel, where about 500 men were probably taken for various labor camps. After the selection on the unloading platform in Auschwitz, 40 men and 58 women are admitted to the camp and receive Nos. 67074–67113 and 22098–22155. Some 1,414 deported men, women, and children, as well as female prisoners selected from the camp, are killed in the gas chambers.**

Nos. 22156–22223 are given to 68 female prisoners sent by the Lublin Sipo and SD.

Commandant Höss lifts the camp ban for the Auschwitz interest zone and determines that SS personnel may move around within an area bordered on the north and west by the Vistula River, on the east by the Soła, and on the south by the town of Brzeszcze and may not go beyond. Crossing the bridge to Neu Berun and over the Vistula to Wola and Jedlina is forbidden. The camp ban on the town of Auschwitz and all the other instructions of the Commandant's Office Order 19/42 of July 23, 1942, also remain in effect.

APMO, D-AuI-1, Garrison Special Order, October 7, 1942.

*This event is witnessed by the Polish political prisoner Antonina Kozubek (No. 21994) (APMO, Depositions, vol. 45, p. 29).
**SS Camp Doctor Kremer writes in his diary: "Present at the 9th special action (outsiders and Moslems)." Extremely emaciated women are called Moslems in the camp. (SAM, *Auschwitz in the Eyes of the SS,* Kremer's Diary, p. 224.)

OCTOBER 8

The Commandant's Office receives permission from the WVHA for a truck to travel to Breslau and back to get an X-ray machine.*

APMO, Kraków Auschwitz Trial, vol. 38, p. 118.

The female Head Supervisors in Auschwitz and Ravensbrück are exchanged. Following a quarrel with Höss, Head Supervisor Johanna Langefeldt returns to Ravensbrück and resumes her former position. The women's camp in Birkenau is taken over by SS Head Supervisor Maria Mandel, born January 10, 1919, in Münzkirchen, Upper Austria. Mandel already has several years experience as she has been supervisor in Lichtenburg Concentration Camp since October 15, 1938, and in Ravensbrück since May 15, 1939.

APMO, Dpr.-ZOd/56, pp. 104–114.

Prisoner No. 66363 escapes from the water supply labor squad. The standby squad calls off the search at 6:40 P.M. without finding the escapee.

APMO, D-AuI-1/31, FvD, p. 108.

The deputy for the Head of the WVHA, SS Major General Frank, writes the SS Commander in Chief that the Office of Medical Affairs and Camp Hygiene has so far collected 110 pounds of gold from the teeth of deceased prisoners for dental purposes and that SS Brigadier General Blaschke has determined that this supply will last for five years. Frank suggests that additional shipments of gold from the concentration camps be delivered to the Reichsbank.

Schnabel, *Power Without Morality*, p. 254, Doc. 91.

OCTOBER 9

17 male and four female prisoners sent from Kattowitz receive Nos. 67115–67131 and 22224–22227.

52 male and ten female prisoners sent to the camp by the Sipo and SD for the Kraków District receive Nos. 67132–67183 and 22228–22237.

41 male and 24 female prisoners sent in a group transport receive Nos. 67184–67224 and 22237–22261.

48 prisoners sent from Radom by the Sipo and SD receive Nos. 67225–67272.

OCTOBER 10

In connection with the outbreak of typhus, Commandant Höss orders a general disinfection of the rooms in the SS buildings, the bathing facilities, the washrooms and latrines, and all other installations and clothing.

APMO, D-AuI-1, Garrison Order No. 28/42.

*This X-ray machine, installed in Block 30 of the women's camp in Birkenau, is to be set up as an X-ray ward. The X-ray ward is built to investigate the sterilization of men and women by X rays.

88 male and 20 female prisoners sent from Prague receive Nos. 67273–67360 and 22262–22281.

One prisoner sent from Kattowitz receives No. 67361.

In the afternoon, three prisoners escape from the men's camp in Birkenau, the German BV prisoner Johannes Lechenich (No. 19), the Capo of the production squad, and the Poles Kazimierz Nowakowski and Fryderyk Klytta. The search operation of the standby squad is directed by SS Second Lieutenant Miller. Only the escapees' camp clothing is found.

APMO, IZ-8/Gestapo Lodz/3/88/ 323; D-AuI-1/3a, FvD, p. 110.

The Director of Labor Deployment, Department IIIa of Auschwitz C.C., informs the WVHA in an answer to a letter of October 5, 1942, "that a transfer of Polish prisoners to other camps is impossible because of a lack of skilled workers among the incoming Jewish prisoners." "A transfer of the Polish prisoners would inevitably bring the whole construction process of this camp to a standstill." There is no objection to the transfer of Jews to Auschwitz, since they are most urgently needed there.

APMO, D-AuI-3a/9, Labor Deployment, Letters and Telegrams, quoted from *Documents and Materials*, vol. I, p. 74.

SS Camp Doctor Kremer writes in his diary: "Fresh living material from liver, spleen, and pancreas removed and preserved."

SAM, *Auschwitz in the Eyes of the SS*, p. 224.

OCTOBER 11

1,703 Jewish men, women, and children arrive from Westerbork in an RSHA transport from Holland. After the selection on the unloading platform in Auschwitz, 334 men and 108 women are admitted to the camp and receive Nos. 67362–67705 and 22282–22389. The remaining 1,251 people are killed in the gas chambers. The operation takes place in the night of October 11–12. SS Camp Doctor Kremer writes in his diary: "present at night at a special operation from Holland (1600 people). Ghastly scenes in front of the last bunker! That was the 10th special operation. (Hössler!)"*

Ibid., p. 225.

OCTOBER 12

20 male and seven female prisoners sent in a group transport receive Nos. 67706–67725 and 22390–22396.

At 7:40 P.M., the SS standby squad is called to the unloading platform. The twelfth and thirteenth RSHA transports from Belgium bring 995 and 675 Jews, respectively, from Malines Camp. Altogether, there are 1,674 people, 534 men and 237 boys and 653 women and 250 girls. After the selection, 28 men and 88 women

APMO, D-AuI-1/3, FvD, p. 112.

---

*In the protocol of the investigation of July 18, 1947, in Kraków, Kremer explained that the operation was carried out by SS Officer Hössler, who had taken the trouble to drive the whole group into a single bunker. He succeeded in this except for one man whom he could not possibly cram into the bunker. Hössler shot this man with his pistol (APMO, Dpr.-ZOd/59/1, pp. 13–26; quoted from SAM, *Auschwitz in the Eyes of the SS*, p. 225, Note 54).

are admitted to the camp and receive Nos. 67726–67753 and 22397–22484. The remaining 1,558 deportees are killed in the gas chambers.

OCTOBER 13

SS Captain Dr. Helmuth Vetter comes to Auschwitz. From 1941 to 1944, Vetter carries out pharmacological experiments on prisoners of Auschwitz, Dachau, and Mauthausen concentration camps, in order to test the effects of medicines and preparations.*

SAM, *Auschwitz in the Eyes of the SS*, Kremer's Diary, p. 226.

SS Lieutenant Colonel and Director of Agriculture Joachim Caesar contracts typhus. His wife has died of typhus a few days earlier.

Ibid.

SS Camp Doctor Kremer attends a flogging and the shooting of seven Polish civilians.

Ibid.

Five male and eight female prisoners sent from Kattowitz receive Nos. 67754–67758 and 22485–22492.

In connection with the typhus epidemic, Commandant Höss orders that families of SS Men in the camp area must be immunized against typhus. Employees and laborers are instructed to enter the main camp only through the main guard post. Entering Birkenau through other entrances than the main guard post is forbidden. The SS garrison is warned that anyone who dares to go 11 feet (10 meters) over the prescribed roads can be shot.

APMO, D-AuI-1, Garrison Order 29/42.

OCTOBER 14

43 male and 19 female prisoners sent from Lodz receive Nos. 67759–67801 and 22493–22511.

50 female prisoners sent to the camp by the Warsaw Sipo and SD from Pawiak Prison receive Nos. 22512–22561.

1,711 Jewish men, women, and children arrive from Westerbork with an RSHA transport from Holland. After the selection, 351 men and 69 women are admitted to the camp and receive Nos. 67802–68152 and 22562–22630. The remaining 1,291 people are killed in the gas chambers.

The Commandant's Office is notified that 405 Jewish inmates are to be transferred from Buchenwald to Auschwitz on October 16, 1942. The transport is accompanied by 18 SS personnel from the

APMO, IZ-13/89, Various Documents of the Third Reich, p. 214.

*Vetter is an employee of the I. G. Farben company. The medical preparations are marked, for example, B-1012, B-1034 or 3582 (Jan Mikulski, "Pharmakalogische Experimente in Konzentrationslager Auschwitz-Birkenau" [Pharmacological Experiments in Auschwitz-Birkenau], *HvA*, no. 10 [1967]: 3–18; Schnabel, *Power Without Morality*, pp. 308–315, Doc. 114–118).

garrison and by 88 SS men from the Commandant's Office of Buchenwald C.C.

OCTOBER 15

One female prisoner sent from Kattowitz receives No. 22631.

German prisoner Augusta Würtz (No. 19370), born February 4, 1920, in Frauenkirchen and sent to Auschwitz on September 11, 1942, in a group transport, escapes from the camp. She is captured in Klagenfurt and sent back to Auschwitz on February 18, 1943.

APMO, IZ-8/Gestapo Lodz/2/88/194, 196.

SS Camp Doctor Kremer writes in his diary: "Fresh living material from the liver, spleen, and pancreas removed from a heteromorph."

SAM, *Auschwitz in the Eyes of the SS*, Kremer's Diary, p. 226.

OCTOBER 16

156 male and 37 female prisoners sent in a group transport receive Nos. 68153–68308 and 22632–22668.

Two Polish prisoners, Władysław Janas, born August 15, 1900, in Swoszowice; and Mieczysław Dziób (No. 64258),* born May 22, 1922, in Piaski Wielkie, sent to the camp by the Sipo and SD for the Kraków District on September 18, 1942, escape from the camp.

APMO, IZ-8/Gestapo Lodz/2/88/327.

Six German female prisoner functionaries who participated in the murder of the French Jewesses in the Penal Company in Budy are locked in the bunker of Block 11. The Political Department continues its investigation of the murders and promises the female prisoners to transfer them to the Buna plant squad if they give truthful statements.

APMO, Depositions, vol. 13, pp. 102ff., Account of Former Prisoner Eleonora Hodys, who was also imprisoned in Block 11 at this time.

OCTOBER 17

Three prisoners sent from Kattowitz receive Nos. 67114, 68309, 68310.

11 prisoners are shot in the courtyard of Block 11 in the presence of SS Camp Doctor Kremer. He is also present at the flogging of a prisoner.

SAM, *Auschwitz in the Eyes of the SS*, Kremer's Diary, p. 226.

SS Camp Physician Kremer notes in his diary: "Fresh living material from liver, spleen, and pancreas taken after an injection of Pilocarpine."

Ibid.

The SS standby squad takes charge of unloading a transport with 1,710 Jews from Holland at 8:45 A.M.**

APMO, D-AuI-1/3, FvD, p. 115.

*Mieczysław Dziób is arrested again and sent to the bunker of Block 11 on September 27, 1943, and is shot two days later.
**This is the only entry in the surviving Guard Register in which the number of deported people and the country of origin of the transport are listed.

OCTOBER 18

1,710 Jewish men, women, and children arrive. After the selection, 116 women are admitted to the camp and receive Nos. 22669–22784. The remaining 1,594 deportees are killed in the gas chambers. SS Camp Doctor Kremer participates in the gassing. In his diary he writes: "Present in raw, cold weather, today Sunday morning at the 11th special operation (Dutch people). Horrible scenes with three women, who beseech us for bare survival."*

Auschwitz in the Eyes of the SS, Kremer's Diary, pp. 226ff.

OCTOBER 19

Commandant Höss orders the closing of the Birkenau area to civilians. The Birkenau area may be entered only by holders of a special pass who come on official business.**

APMO, D-AuI-1/97, Commandant's Office Order of October that was not fully transmitted.

At 5:30 A.M. it is discovered that Jewish prisoner No. 68044 is hanging on the barbed wire fence between Watchtowers B and C and is critically injured.

APMO, D-AuI-1/3, FvD, p. 116.

29 male and 12 female prisoners sent in a group transport receive Nos. 68311–68339 and 22785–22796.

At 10:00 P.M. the SS standby squad is sent to the railroad station under the direction of SS Second Lieutenant Josten to accept a transport of 405 Jews transferred from Buchenwald. 404 prisoners are admitted to the camp and receive Nos. 68340–68743.†

Ibid., p. 117; APMO, Höss Trial, vol. 5, p. 148.

OCTOBER 20

28 male and four female prisoners sent from Kattowitz receive Nos. 68744–68771 and 22797–22800.

66 prisoners sent to the camp by the Sipo and SD of Lublin receive Nos. 68772–68837.

---

*In the protocol of the investigation of July 18, 1947, in Kraków, Kremer explains: "Three women from Holland didn't want to go to the gas chamber and begged for their lives. They were young and healthy women and yet their pleas weren't heard; instead, the SS men participating in the operation shot them right on the spot" (APMO, Dpr.-ZOd/59, pp. 13–26; quoted from SAM, *Auschwitz in the Eyes of the SS*, Kremer's Diary, pp. 226ff., Note 59).
**This order is probably connected with Hössler's being assigned to get rid of the traces of the crimes—to dig up and burn the bodies in the mass graves, which have not decomposed and, in fact, even surface again. For this work Hössler forms a new Special Squad of several hundred Jews of various nationalities. It is divided into groups working in two shifts. Anyone who recoils from doing this work is shot on the spot. Hössler chooses about 20 SS men as sentries who must sign a special declaration that they will maintain silence about their activity under threat of the death penalty. Because of the stench from the opened graves, the SS Men guard the prisoners from a distance; they receive a special daily allotment in the SS kitchen consisting of a liter of milk, sausage, cigarettes, and liquor. The prisoners in the Special Squad, on the other hand, are lodged in a barracks isolated from the other prisoners' barracks by a wooden fence. No one may even approach this place unless they have a special pass, but the clouds of smoke and the stench of burning bodies confirms the rumor circulating about the burning of bodies (SAM, *Auschwitz in the Eyes of the SS*, pp. 166ff; Höss, *Commandant in Auschwitz*, pp. 210ff.).
†The prisoners of this transport are to be employed in the Buna plant.

165 prisoners sent to the camp from Radom by the Sipo and SD receive Nos. 68838–69002.

OCTOBER 21

70 Jewish prisoners transferred from Dachau to Auschwitz receive Nos. 69003–69072.

At 6:30 A.M. a prisoner is shot "while escaping" by the SS sentry on duty at Watchtower G of the main camp.

APMO, D-AuI-1/3a, FvD, p. 118.

At 8:30 A.M. the SS standby squad is sent to the unloading platform to take charge of a transport of Jews.

Ibid.

Jews from Slovakia arrive in an RSHA transport. After the selection, 121 men and 78 women are admitted to the camp and receive Nos. 69073–69193 and 22801–22878. The remaining people are killed in the gas chambers.

18 male and eight female prisoners sent from Kattowitz receive Nos. 69194–69211 and 22879–22886.

1,327 Jewish men, women, and children arrive from Westerbork with an RSHA transport from Holland. After the selection, 497 men are admitted to the camp and receive Nos. 69212–69708. The remaining 830 deportees are killed in the gas chambers.

OCTOBER 23

69 male and 19 female prisoners sent in a group transport receive Nos. 69709–69777 and 22887–22905.

At 3:30 P.M., two female prisoners escape from a labor squad working in the village of Babitz. The SS standby squad, led by SS Second Lieutenant Josten, returns at 7:30 P.M. The search operation remains unsuccessful.

Ibid., p. 121.

OCTOBER 24

30 Jewish prisoners transferred to Auschwitz from Natzweiler Camp in Alsace receive Nos. 69778–69807.

On orders from the Political Department, medical officer Josef Klehr kills six German female prisoner functionaries with injections for their participation in the murder of the Jewish women in the Penal Company in Budy on October 5, 1942. One of the women is Elfriede Schmidt, whom Pery Broad calls the "Axe Queen." The execution is carried out in the autopsy room of Block 28, the prisoners' in-

SAM, *Auschwitz in the Eyes of the SS*, Broad's Memoirs, p. 167; Kremer's Diary, p. 227.

firmary, in the presence of SS Camp Doctor Kremer, who is to certify death. The women are killed by Klehr in a sitting position.*

German prisoner Lucie Liduner, born June 28, 1913, in Gera, Thuringia, escapes from the camp.**

APMO, IZ-8/Gestapo Lodz/2/88/134, 135.

32 Jewish prisoners transferred from Mauthausen to Auschwitz receive Nos. 69808–69839.

12 Jewish prisoners transferred from Flossenbürg to Auschwitz receive Nos. 69840–69851.

26 prisoners sent in a group transport receive Nos. 69852–69877.

The SS standby squad is informed at 12:30 P.M. that a prisoner has left the construction site of the sewage plant in Birkenau. At 5:45, the standby squad returns with the captured prisoner. He is brought to the camp and locked in the bunker of Block 11. He is Polish asocial prisoner Antoni Cios (No. 60785). He is released from the bunker on November 17, 1942, and shot.

APMO, D-AuI-1/3a, FvD, p. 122; D-AuI-3/1b, Bunker Register, p. 81; D-AuI-5/4, Morgue Register, p. 17.

Prisoner No. 64495 is condemned to the standing cell† for three days because he left work.

APMO, Höss Trial, vol. 12, p. 163, Exhibit 107.

In reply to a letter from the Construction Administration of the Waffen SS and Police of Gusen, an auxiliary camp of Mauthausen, J. A. Topf and Sons says it built a crematorium in Auschwitz with five three-muffle ovens for the incineration of corpses. In the summer, the iron parts for the second crematorium oven in Gusen were mistakenly sent to Auschwitz, along with iron parts for the crematorium there. This error was discovered in August. The foreman of J. A. Topf and Sons, Wilhelm Koch, who built the oven in Auschwitz, has located the iron parts for Gusen and has already sent the shipment.

APMO, Various Documents of the Third Reich, p. 251.

---

*Obviously, this is not a formal sentence but rather an internal instruction, since the family members receive notifications that these prisoners died from natural causes. The reason for this instruction is that there were close contacts between these women and SS sentries and that the participation of the SS in the massacre became known. Thus, the important thing is to remove witnesses of the participation of SS men in this crime. As Pery Broad reports, the sentry commander is simply admonished and the sentries may not enter the camp again in the future. Höss admits that the guilty parties can no longer be determined, so he orders no more punishment measures and simply has the sentry commander and the SS Head Supervisor transferred. Höss does not consider this incident worthy of remembering; he does not know that Dr. Kremer will note it in his diary and Pery Broad will report on it.
**On November 9, 1942, the Commandant's Office ends the search operation, since the escapee has been arrested by the Kripo in Görlitz.
†The punishment consists of being locked for several successive nights in a standing cell. The standing cell has a surface area of about one square yard; there is one in the cellar of Block 11 of the main camp and one in Barracks 2 of the men's camp, BI-b, in Birkenau. Several (at least four) prisoners are locked in every cell. The entrance is at floor level so that one must crawl inside. The cells are closed with iron grates and wooden doors and have no windows; air enters only through a four-square-inch opening. In the morning the prisoners are released from this cell and taken to work. In this cell, the prisoners can neither move nor sit and are in danger of suffocating.

On the return of the labor squads working outside the outer sentry line, it is discovered that one prisoner is missing. All the guards that were leading the labor squads back to the camp are employed in the search operation, which is unsuccessful. At 8:00 P.M., the guards on the outer sentry line are called back. An SS Technical Sergeant on his bicycle near the DAW sees the escaped prisoner and shoots at him twice. An immediate, thorough search of the adjoining area is unsuccessful. At 9:30 the search operation is called off.

APMO, D-AuI-1/3a, FvD, p. 122.

The responsible headquarters are notified by telegram that the escaped prisoner is a Polish Jew, Adolf Zwerdling, a political prisoner (No. 57379) sent to Auschwitz by the Sipo and SD for the Kraków District on August 8, 1942.

APMO, IZ-8/Gestapo Lodz/2/72–74.

OCTOBER 25

Adolf Zwerdling, who escaped from the camp the day before, is captured and locked in the bunker of Block 11.* The search is called off.

APMO, IZ-8/Gestapo Lodz/2/73, 75; D-AuI-3/1b, Bunker Register, p. 81.

11 female prisoners sent in a group transport receive Nos. 22906–22916.

A prisoner sent from Oppeln receives No. 69878.

454 Jewish prisoners transferred to Auschwitz from Sachsenhausen receive Nos. 69879–70332.

At 11:30 A.M., the SS standby squad is assigned to the unloading platform to take charge of a transport of Jews.

APMO, D-AuI-1/3a, FvD, p. 123.

988 Jewish men, women, and children arrive with a RSHA transport from Holland. After the selection, 21 men and 32 women are admitted to the camp and receive Nos. 70333–70353 and 22917–22948. The remaining 935 people are killed in the gas chambers.

OCTOBER 26

J. A. Topf and Sons considers their crematorium oven a technical innovation and applies for a patent at the Reich Patent Office.

Kaul, *Doctors in Auschwitz*, p. 63.

At 6:30 A.M. two prisoners leave the animal husbandry squad. They are captured by the squad leader of the disinfection room, which is in the vicinity of the personal effects warehouse, Canada I, and brought to the camp.

APMO, D-AuI-1/3a, FvD, p. 123.

The fourteenth and fifteenth RSHA transports from Belgium bring 995 and 476 Jews, respectively, from Malines Camp. In the four-

---

*Adolf Zwerdling is shot on December 17, 1942.

teenth transport are 320 men and 120 boys and 425 women and 130 girls. In the fifteenth transport are 314 men and 28 boys and 91 women and 43 girls. After the selection, 460 men and 116 women from both transports are admitted to the camp and are given Nos. 70354–70813 and 22949–23064. The remaining 895 people are killed in the gas chambers.

Five prisoners sent in a group transport receive Nos. 70814–70818.

One female prisoner sent from Breslau receives No. 23065.

At 5:00 P.M. the dog squadron and the SS standby squad begin to search for an escaped prisoner. The unsuccessful search operation is called off at 7:10. The alarm is lifted at 8:30 after two SS men capture the prisoner in the vicinity of the civilian workers' camp for the Huta firm.

Ibid., p. 124.

OCTOBER 27

17 male and four female prisoners sent from Kattowitz receive Nos. 70819–70835 and 23066–23069.

841 Jewish men, women, and children arrive from Westerbork with an RSHA transport from Holland. After the selection, 224 men and 205 women are admitted to the camp and receive Nos. 70836–71059 and 23070–23274.

In the main camp, 280 Polish prisoners are ordered to report to Block 3 the next day after morning roll call.

OCTOBER 28

After morning roll call and the departure of the labor squads, the 280 Polish prisoners gathered in Block 3 are led to Block 11 under heavy SS guard and shot. In addition, in the morning, several prisoners employed as attendants in the prisoners' infirmary are summoned by the Political Department, taken to Block 11, and put with the other inmates who are to be shot. These include Dr. Henryk Suchnicki and Leon Kukiełka. When they find themselves in the group of condemned, they begin to revolt and to try to escape from Block 11. Some of the prisoners are shot in the courtyard of Block 11, others die during the revolt from wounds incurred in the vestibule of Block 11. Before the execution, one prisoner gives prisoner Eugeniusz Obojski, who is summoned to the execution as a stretcher bearer, a secret message for his family which he has had time to write. The secret message is discovered and Obojski is removed.

The shot prisoners had been sent to the camp from Radom and Lublin by the Sipo and SD. Their shooting is thought to be in retaliation for acts of sabotage and partisan operations in the region of Lublin.

APMO, Höss Trial, vol. 3, p. 55; vol. 4, pp. 5, 165; vol. 7, pp. 19, 156.

At around noon, Roll Call Leader Palitzsch comes to Block 20 of the prisoner hospital and gets the charts of the five prisoners held back by the prisoner attendants, who did not obey the summons to the Political Department. They are Maks Weber (No. 39610), a lawyer, Mieczysław Krupisz (No. 13909), and Dąbrowski. After an order to close the block, the five prisoners are taken to the so-called treatment room on the ground floor and killed with phenol injections.

Ibid., vol. 4, p. 166.

The first RSHA transport from Czechoslovakia arrives with 1,866 Jewish men, women, and children from the Theresienstadt (Terezín) ghetto. After the selection, 215 men and 32 women are admitted to the camp and receive Nos. 71060–71274 and 23275–23306. The remaining 1,619 are killed in the gas chambers.

APMO, D-RF-3/84, Transport "By" of October 26, 1942; Kraków Auschwitz Trial, vol. 3, p. 197.

OCTOBER 29

On instructions of the Political Department, Polish political prisoner Eugeniusz Obojski (No. 194) is locked in the bunker of Block 11. The day before, a secret message was found on him, which he got from one of those condemned to be shot. Obojski worked as a stretcher bearer in the morgue and was called to every execution to bring the corpses of shot prisoners and civilians to the crematorium.

APMO, D-AuI-3/1b, Bunker Register, p. 81; Kielar, *Anus Mundi* (Kielar finds warm and friendly words for Eugeniusz Obojski).

SS Commander in Chief Heinrich Himmler permits the prisoners to receive a food package the size of a daily ration from their families.

APMO, D-RF-9, WVHA, 8, p. 52, Edict Collection.

The standby squad is sent to the railroad platform at 8:15 P.M. to take charge of a transport of prisoners from Dachau.

APMO, D-AuI-1/3a, FvD, p. 127.

486 of 499 arrivals receive Nos. 71275–71760. These include German, Polish, Czech, Ukrainian, and Jewish prisoners transferred from Dachau. They are to work in the chemical plant of the I. G. Farben Company in Auschwitz. 13 of the newly arrived prisoners were probably in Auschwitz previously and therefore did not receive new numbers.

OCTOBER 30

80 prisoners sent from Radom by the Sipo and SD receive Nos. 71761–71840.

186 prisoners transferred from Ravensbrück receive Nos. 71841–72026.

84 male and 19 female prisoners sent in a group transport receive Nos. 72027–72110 and 23307–23325.

Jews transferred to Auschwitz from concentration camps inside Germany are taken to the roll-call area of the main camp and there

APMO, Höss Trial, vol. 5, p. 149.

One of two kitchen barracks in Birkenau. To the right, a water tank.

undergo a selection by the labor manager. After the selection, those who are weak and unfit for work are taken to the gas chamber in Birkenau with other prisoners selected from the camp. The approximately 800 prisoners regarded as able-bodied are to be relocated in a new auxiliary camp built near the I. G. Farben works.

Approximately 800 male prisoners are relocated out of the main camp to the newly built auxiliary camp near the construction site of the I. G. Farben works in the village of Monowitz (Monowice), which has been cleared of its inhabitants. I. G. Farben has had the auxiliary camp built, since no prisoners could be employed there from the end of August to the end of November, because Auschwitz was closed on account of the typhus epidemic. The auxiliary camp is called Buna and is under the control of Auschwitz C.C. In the early days, a few prisoners are still working on erecting additional barracks, building lavatories and latrines, and paving roads, while others are already building the Buna plant.

Ibid.; APMO, Depositions, vol. 116, pp. 126–136, Account of Former Prisoner Leon Stasiak; D-AuIII-3a, Graphic Representation of the Occupancy Level of the Buna Auxiliary Camp for the period October 1–December 31, 1942.

Department IIIa of the camp, responsible for labor deployment, notifies Office D-II of the WVHA that the 499 prisoners transferred from Dachau are in very bad physical condition and none of them is suitable for work in the Buna plant. Barely a third of them can be employed in other work and these only after a two-week recovery time. 50 of the arrivals could be employed in their profession; 162 have no profession, and 287 of the transferees are farm workers. 186 prisoners transferred from Ravensbrück were in a better phys-

APMO, D-AuI-3a/11, Labor Deployment.

ical condition than those from Dachau; 128 of them are employed in their professions and only 58 of them have no profession.

OCTOBER 31

Because of the danger of another epidemic visits to all sick SS personnel and their families are forbidden. The order is signed for Höss by Protective Custody Commander SS Captain Aumeier.

APMO, D-AuI-1, Garrison Order 31/42.

33 female prisoners sent in a group transport receive Nos. 23326–23358.

34 male and 10 female prisoners sent to the camp by the Sipo and SD for the Kraków District receive Nos. 72111–72144 and 23359–23368.

16 male and eight female prisoners sent from Kattowitz receive Nos. 72145–72160 and 23369–23376.

Polish political prisoner Bogusław Wrana (No. 67357), born January 11, 1920, escapes from Auschwitz. His absence is discovered at 6:00 P.M. The search operation is unsuccessful.

APMO, D-AuI-1/3a, FvD, p. 129; IZ-8/Gestapo Lodz/2/88/198.

NOVEMBER 1

At 1:30 A.M. a transport arrives with Jews from Holland. The SS standby squad, whose members come from the 4th Company, is sent to the unloading ramp. The transport contains 659 people, who are all killed in the gas chambers after the selection.

APMO, D-AuI-1/3a, FvD, p. 129; Kempner, *Edith Stein and Anne Frank*, p. 76.

The twenty-second RSHA transport arrives from Berlin with 1,014 people, primarily women and old people. After the selection, 37 women are admitted to the camp and receive Nos. 23377–23413. The remaining 977 deportees are killed in the gas chambers.

APMO, D-RF-3/121/Gestapo Berlin/Auschwitz Transports, vol. 1, pp. 44–87.

NOVEMBER 2

Approximately 150 prisoners, most of them Jews, are relocated to the newly built auxiliary camp Chełmek. They are to clean and deepen a pond that is planned as a reservoir for the "Bata" shoe factory, taken over by the Ota-Silesian Shoe Works. They are housed in Chełmek-Paprotnik, a former wooden locomotive hangar to which a morgue had been added. The area around the hangar is fenced with barbed wire. The commander is first SS Staff Sergeant Josef Schillinger and later SS Corporal Wilhelm Emmerich. The prisoners are guarded by six SS men. The new auxiliary camp of Chełmek is under the supervision of Auschwitz C.C.*

APMO, D-AuI-1/94, Commandant's Office Special Order, November 2, 1942; Emeryka Iwaszko, "Das Aussenkommando Chełmek" (The Outside Squad Chełmek), *HvA*, no. 12 (1970): 45–54.

Dr. Horst Schumann arrives in Auschwitz to develop by experimentation a method by which several men and women can be

---

*The Chełmek outside squad is dissolved on December 9, 1942.

sterilized without large expenditures of time and money. In Barracks No. 30 of the women's camp in Birkenau, Section B-Ia, an experimental station is set up where he tests X rays as a method of sterilization. He also performs castrations, first in Block 21 and later in Block 10 of the main camp.

The SS Camp Doctor carries out a selection in the prisoners' infirmary, Block 20. He selects 49 prisoners, who are killed with phenol injections the same day.

APMO, D-AuI-4/5, Morgue Register, p. 3; Mat.RO, vol. VI, p. 22.

15 prisoners sent in a group transport receive Nos. 72161–72175.

One female prisoner sent from Breslau receives No. 23414.

Prisoner No. 66293 is shot "while escaping."

APMO, D-Au-4/5, Morgue Register, p. 4.

Polish prisoner Kazimierz Kawski (No. 18849), born March 18, 1919, escapes from Auschwitz. The telegram about the escape states that the prisoner is wearing a blue jacket and a black hat and has a blue camp identification card in the name of Milos Vucelic, born April 7, 1917, and has 180 RM on him.

APMO, IZ-8/Gestapo Lodz/3/88/ 331/332.

Jewish prisoner Leopold Fenster from Slovakia, born July 11, 1924, in Stara Lubovna, escapes from Auschwitz.

APMO, IZ-8/Gestapo Lodz/3/88/ 329.

NOVEMBER 3

70 prisoners sent from Lublin by the Sipo and SD receive Nos. 72176–72245.

1,696 Jews arrive from Malines in Belgium with two RSHA transports. In the sixteenth transport are 683 men and 21 boys and 89 women and 29 girls. In the seventeenth transport are 622 men and 51 boys and 165 women and 36 girls. After the selection, 702 men and 75 women from both transports are admitted to the camp and receive Nos. 72246–72947 and 23415–23489. The remaining 919 people are killed in the gas chambers.

Polish political prisoner Heinz Radomski (No. 14185) is captured trying to escape from Section B-Ib in Birkenau and a pistol is found on him. He is locked in the bunker of Block 11, where he remains imprisoned for 260 days, since the Political Department hopes to get important information from him. On July 24, 1943, he is shot in the washroom of Block 11.

APMO, D-AuI-3/1b, Bunker Register, p. 82; Brol et al., "Bunker Register of Block 11," p. 32.

80 male and 18 female prisoners sent from Brünn receive Nos. 72948–73027 and 23490–23507.

The SS Camp Doctor makes a selection in the prisoner infirmary. He selects 23 prisoners, who are killed with phenol injections the same day.

APMO, Mat.RO, vol. VI, p. 22D.

NOVEMBER 4

Luise Palitzsch, wife of the Roll Call Leader, dies of typhus.

20 male and 26 female prisoners sent in a group transport receive Nos. 73028–73047 and 23508–23533.

954 Jewish men, women, and children arrive from Westerbork in Holland with an RSHA transport. After the selection, 50 women are admitted to the camp and receive Nos. 23534–23583. The remaining 904 are killed in the gas chambers.

NOVEMBER 5

It is discovered that two prisoners from the district heating plant squad are missing. The standby squad is ordered to reinforce the outer sentry line and assigned to the search operation, which is called off without success at 9:00 P.M.

APMO, D-AuI-1/31, FvD, p. 132.

The Czech asocial prisoner Jaroslav Studeny (No. 67311), born August 3, 1921, in Obitschdorf, escapes from Auschwitz.

APMO, D-AuI-1/2b, p. 254, Bulletin of the Gestapo of Silesia.

NOVEMBER 6

Prisoner No. 67396 is shot in an attempt to escape.

APMO, D-AuI-5/4, Morgue Register, p. 7.

171 male and 41 female prisoners sent in a group transport receive Nos. 73048–73218 and 23584–23624.

1,000 Jewish men, women, and children arrive in the fortieth RSHA transport from France. After the selection, 269 men and 92 women are admitted to the camp and receive Nos. 73219–73487 and 23625–23716.

During roll call it is discovered that two prisoners are missing. One is found by the standby squad during the search operation.

APMO, D-AuI-1/3, FvD, p. 133.

In the afternoon it is discovered in Birkenau that one prisoner is missing. A dozen Russian POWs (Russische Kriegsgefangene— RKG) are to comb the area of Section B-II, which is under construction, for the missing prisoner. As they leave the grounds of Section B-Ib, the Russian POWs, who have prepared for such an occasion, undertake a mass escape, shouting hurrah. The darkness closing in and the large number of escapees make it possible for many of the POWs to break through the outer sentry line.

APMO, Positions, vol. 29, pp. 8–10, Account of Former Russian Prisoner of War Andrei Pogožev.

NOVEMBER 7

In a letter to the Auschwitz Commandant's Office, SS Captain Bischoff, the Head of the SS Central Construction Administration, indicates that the productivity of the labor squad, consisting of a hundred women, employed for four days digging the waterpipe

APMO, D-AuI-3a/12, Labor Deployment.

ditches from the pump to the X-ray station in the women's camp*
is so low that no progress can be perceived. The waterpipes from
the guard house to the X-ray station are temporarily installed with
above-ground tubing and the water might freeze in the tubing at
any minute. Consequently, the digging must be completed as fast
as possible so that the X-ray station can work. For technical reasons,
the solution thus far is only provisional. For this reason, a more
able-bodied labor force is to be sent to the squad, and the administration of the women's camp should make every effort to accelerate the work.

42 prisoners sent from Radom by the Sipo and SD receive Nos.
73488–73529.

A prisoner sent from Kattowitz receives No. 73530.

17 female prisoners sent in a group transport receive Nos. 23717–
23733.

2,000 Jewish men, women, and children arrive with an RSHA transport from the Zichenau ghetto in the so-called Administrative District of Zichenau (Ciechanow). After the selection, 465 men and
229 women are admitted to the camp and receive Nos. 73531–
73995 and 23734–23962. The remaining 1,306 people are killed
in the gas chambers.

APMO, Höss Trial, vol. 1, p.
133.

465 Jewish men, women, and children arrive from Westerbork in
Holland with an RSHA transport. At the selection, all those unfit
to work are classified and led to the gas bunker.

Kempner, *Edith Stein and Anne
Frank*, p. 76.

The corpses of eight male prisoners from the Chełmek auxiliary
camp (A.C.) are sent to the morgue of the main camp. The prisoners
have the Nos. 64650, 65740, 67532, 69392, 67543, 69600, 69695,
and 72165.

APMO, D-AuI-4/5, Morgue
Register, p. 8.

At 5:45 A.M. the commander on duty receives a report that one
male prisoner is missing in Harmense A.C. The standby squad is
sent for immediately.

APMO, D-AuI-1/3, FvD, p. 133.

In the morning, Polish prisoner Szymon Kuras, born March 2, 1903,
sent to the camp by the Sipo and SD for the Kraków District on
June 15, 1942, escapes from the camp. This is probably the prisoner
missing from Harmense A.C.

Around noon, Polish prisoner Aleksander Baum, born April 18,
1918, sent to the camp by the Sipo and SD from Radom on October
20, escapes from the camp.

APMO, IZ-8/Gestapo Lodz/3/88/
342.

*In this station, Dr. Horst Schumann performs his sterilization experiments with
X rays. The experiments are carried out on selected male and female prisoners.

Two prisoners, Isaak Grün (No. 60883), a Jew born April 6, 1921, in Holland; and Władysław Puszycki (No. 64840), a Pole, are captured in an attempt to escape and locked in the bunker of Block 11. Both are released from the bunker on November 17, 1942, and shot the same day.

APMO, D-AuI-3/1b, Bunker Register, p. 83; D-AuI-5/4, Morgue Register, p. 17.

At 3:30 P.M., the absence of a prisoner is discovered. The search operation remains unsuccessful.

APMO, D-AuI-1/3, FvD, p. 134.

NOVEMBER 8

The missing prisoner of the previous day is captured and sent to the bunker of Block 11. It is the Czech asocial prisoner Józef Róziczka (No. 63707), born October 19, 1924. He is released from the bunker on November 17, 1942, and shot the same day.

APMO, D-AuI-3/1b, Bunker Register, p. 83; D-AuI-5/4, Morgue Register, p. 17.

1,000 Jews arrive with an RSHA transport from the ghettos in the so-called Administrative District of Zichenau. At the selection, the entire transport is sent to the gas chambers. SS Camp Doctor Kremer participates in the special operation.*

25 prisoners receive Nos. 73996–74020. They are Jewish watchmakers transferred from Lublin (Majdenek) C.C. to Auschwitz and are later sent to Sachsenhausen.

APMO, Höss Trial, vol. 12, p. 160, Appendix 104.

1,000 Jewish men, women, and children arrive from Drancy with the forty-second RSHA from France. After the selection, 145 men and 82 women are admitted to the camp and receive Nos. 74021–74165 and 23963–24044. The remaining 773 deportees are killed in the gas chambers.**

1,000 Jewish men, women, and children arrive with an RSHA transport from the ghetto in the Białystok District. After the selection, all of them are sent to the gas chambers. This is the fourteenth special operation Dr. Kremer participates in.†

NOVEMBER 9

33 prisoners sent in a group transport receive Nos. 74166–74198.

One female prisoner sent from Kattowitz receives No. 24045.

1,000 Jewish men, women, and children arrive with an RSHA transport from the ghetto in the Białystok District. After the selection, 190 men and 104 women are admitted to the camp and receive

---

*This is the twelfth special operation attended by Dr. Kremer (SAM, *Auschwitz in the Eyes of the SS*, Kremer's Diary, p. 232).
**This is the thirteenth special action in which Dr. Kremer participates (Ibid.).
†After three special operations, Kremer writes in his diary: "In the evening a pleasant get-together, invited by Captain Wirths. There was Bulgarian red wine and Croatian plum schnapps" (Ibid.).

Nos. 74199–74388 and 24046–24149. The remaining 706 deportees are killed in the gas chambers.

Three female prisoners sent in a group transport receive Nos. 24150–24152.

Prisoner No. 65276 is shot "while escaping."

APMO, D-AuI-5/4, Morgue Register, p. 9.

NOVEMBER 10

Dr. Kremer states that the first snow has fallen and there was an overnight frost.

SAM, *Auschwitz in the Eyes of the SS*, Kremer's Diary, p. 232.

NOVEMBER 11

36 prisoners sent from Prague receive Nos. 74389–74424.

At 3:00 A.M., 75 female prisoners are delivered to the camp from Radom by the Sipo and SD. They receive Nos. 24153–24227.

APMO, D-AuI-1/3, FvD, p. 135.

26 female prisoners sent in a group transport receive Nos. 24228–24253.

The standby squad is called to the unloading platform to take charge of the forty-fourth RSHA transport from France of Jews from Drancy. These Jews are predominantly of Greek origin. A first selection of 1,000 persons included in the transport took place in Cosel, where 150 men were probably taken for the Schmelt Organization. After the selection on the unloading platform in Auschwitz, 100 women are admitted to the camp and receive Nos. 24254–24353. The remaining 750 people are killed in the gas chambers.

Ibid., p. 136; Klarsfeld, *Memorial*, pp. 344–346.

In the late afternoon, Polish prisoner Stanisław Mazur, born September 12, 1910, sent to the camp by the Sipo and SD from Radom on September 29, 1942, escapes from the camp.

APMO, IZ-8/Gestapo Lodz/3/88/334.

The corpses of 96 prisoners are sent to the morgue in the main camp. The typhus epidemic remains rampant in the men's and women's camps.

APMO, D-AuI-5/4, Morgue Register, pp. 11ff.

NOVEMBER 12

758 Jewish men, women, and children arrive from Westerbork with an RSHA transport from Holland. After the selection, three men and 48 women are admitted to the camp and receive Nos. 74425–74427 and 24354–24401. The remaining 707 people are killed in the gas chambers.

71 male and 24 female prisoners, sent to the camp by the Lodz Gestapo, receive Nos. 74428–74498 and 24402–24425.

45 male and ten female prisoners sent to the camp by the Sipo and SD for the Kraków District receive Nos. 74499–74543 and 24426–24435.

NOVEMBER 13

The standby squad is sent to the unloading platform at 7:30 A.M. to receive a transport and bring it into the camp.

APMO, D-AuI-1/3, FvD, p. 137.

76 male and 52 female prisoners sent to the camp by the Sipo and SD from Pawiak Prison receive Nos. 74544–74619 and 24436–24487. They are brought to the camp by the standby squad.

13 male and two female prisoners sent in a group transport receive Nos. 74620–74632, 24488, and 24489.

745 Jewish men, women, and children arrive from Drancy with the forty-fifth RSHA transport from France. After the selection, 112 men and 34 women are admitted to the camp and given Nos. 74633–74744 and 24490–24523. The remaining 599 are killed in the gas chambers.

Dr. Kremer removes "fresh living material (liver, spleen & pancreas)" from a corpse sent to him, a badly atrophied prisoner, No. 68030. Before he is killed, Kremer has him photographed. It is the Jew Hans de Yong, born February 18, 1924, in Frankfurt, and sent to Auschwitz from Westerbork on October 14, 1942, with an RSHA transport from Holland.

SAM, *Auschwitz in the Eyes of the SS*, Kremer's Diary, p. 232.

Polish prisoner Ignacy Korzeński (No. 72120) escapes from the men's camp in Birkenau.

APMO, IZ-8/Gestapo Lodz/2/88/186.

NOVEMBER 14

Prisoner No. 69656 is shot at 5:40 A.M. by the SS sentry on duty at Watchtower B of the main camp "while escaping."

APMO, D-AuI-5/4, Morgue Register, p. 14; D-AuI-1/3, FvD, p. 138.

The standby squad is ordered to the unloading ramp at 1:45 A.M. to take charge of a transport.

APMO, D-AuI-1/3, FvD, p. 138.

2,500 Jewish men, women, and children arrive with an RSHA transport from the ghetto of the Zichenau District. After the selection, 633 men and 135 women are admitted to the camp and receive Nos. 74745–75377 and 24524–24658. The remaining 1,732 are killed in the gas chambers.

1,500 Jewish men, women, and children arrive with an RSHA transport from the ghetto in the Białystok District. After the selection, 282 men and 379 women are admitted to the camp and receive Nos. 75378–78659 and 24659–25037. The remaining 839 deportees are killed in the gas chambers.

71 male and two female prisoners sent to the camp by the Sipo and SD for the Kraków District receive Nos. 75660–75730, 25038, and 25039.

The SS Camp Doctor makes a selection in the prisoners' infirmary. He selects 110 prisoners, who are taken to Birkenau and killed in the gas chambers.

APMO, D-AuI-5/3, Prisoners' Infirmary Register of Block 28, pp. 225–228.

NOVEMBER 15

Fiodor Jarmolenko (No. 68181), who escaped from the camp on November 11, 1942, is captured and locked in the bunker of Block 11. He is released from the bunker on November 17, 1942, and shot the same day.

APMO, D-AuI-3/1b, Bunker Register, p. 84; D-AuI-5/4, Morgue Register, p. 17.

Polish prisoner Czesław Morus (No. 62384) is captured trying to escape. He is released from the bunker to the camp the next day.

APMO, D-AuI-3/1b, Bunker Register, p. 84.

NOVEMBER 16

Russian POW Alexander Kostiuchenko is hanged on the orders of the Kattowitz Gestapo.

APMO, Mat.RO, vol. VI, p. 33.

36 prisoners sent in a group transport receive Nos. 75731–75766.

Two female prisoners sent from Kattowitz receive Nos. 25040 and 25041.

NOVEMBER 17

The standby squad is ordered to the unloading platform at 3:00 A.M. to take charge of a transport from Pawiak Prison in Warsaw.

APMO, D-AuI-1/3, FvD, p. 141.

60 prisoners sent from Pawiak Prison by the Sipo and SD of Warsaw receive Nos. 75767–75826.

19 male prisoners and one female prisoner sent from Kattowitz receive Nos. 75827–75845 and 25042.

In the courtyard of Block 11, two Russian POWs with Nos. RKG-4290 and RKG-6122 and nine male prisoners previously imprisoned in the bunker are shot. The executed prisoners, caught trying to escape, are Antoni Cios (No. 60725), Isak Grün (No. 60883), Władysław Puszycki (No. 64840), Józef Różiczka (No. 67307) and Fiodor Jarmolenko (No. 68181), Zdzislaw Dudzik (No. 60050), Mikołaj Ilczenko (No. 68163), Iwan Atomoniuk (No. 73170), and Otto Saluzansky (No. 71273).

APMO, D-AuI-3/1b, Bunker Register, pp. 81, 83ff.; D-AuI-5/4, Morgue Register, p. 17.

Polish prisoner Ignacy Korzeński (No. 72120), captured trying to escape on November 13, 1942, is locked in the bunker by order of the Political Department. On November 25, Ignacy Korzeński is released to the camp and shot.

APMO, D-AuI-3/1b, Bunker Register, p. 85; IZ-8/Gestapo Lodz/2/88/188; D-AuI-5/4, Morgue Register, p. 25.

NOVEMBER 18

An RSHA transport arrives with Jews. After the selection, eight men and 22 women are admitted to the camp and receive Nos. 75846–75853 and 25043–25064.*

44 prisoners sent from Pawiak Prison by the Sipo and SD of Warsaw receive Nos. 75854–75871 and 75873–75898.

A prisoner sent from Kattowitz receives No. 75872.

53 prisoners sent by the Sipo and SD for the Kraków District receive Nos. 75899–75951.

Approximately 1,000 Jewish men, women, and children arrive from the ghetto of Grodno, in the Białystok District, with an RSHA transport. After the selection, 165 men and 65 women are admitted to the camp and receive Nos. 75952–76116 and 25065–25129. The remaining 770 are killed in the gas chambers.

NOVEMBER 19

64 prisoners sent from Pawiak Prison by the Sipo and SD of Warsaw receive Nos. 76117–76180.

12 male and five female prisoners sent from Kattowitz receive Nos. 76181–76192 and 25130–25134.

Approximately 1,500 Jewish men, women, and children arrive from the ghetto in the Zichenau District with an RSHA transport. After the selection, 532 men and 361 women are admitted to the camp and receive Nos. 76193–76724 and 25135–25495. The remaining 607 are killed in the gas chambers.

The SS Camp Doctor makes a selection in the prisoners' infirmary, in Blocks 20 and 28. He selects 65 sick prisoners, who are killed with phenol injections the same day.

APMO, Mat.RO, vol. VI, pp. 24A, 24B.

Germany's first decisive defeat takes place. The Red Army breaks through the German front north of Stalingrad and surrounds the left flank of the German Sixth Army.

NOVEMBER 20

The second powerful blow by the Red Army south of Stalingrad leads to the surrounding of the right flank of the German Sixth Army.

162 prisoners sent from Oppeln receive Nos. 76725–76886.

*This is probably a transport of 209 Jews from Norway, taken in October by ship to Stettin and sent from there by train to Auschwitz (Gilbert, *Final Solution*, p. 130).

80 prisoners sent from Pawiak Prison by the Sipo and SD of Warsaw receive Nos. 76887–76966.

67 prisoners sent from Radom by the Sipo and SD receive Nos. 76967–77033.

24 male and 125 female prisoners sent in a group transport receive Nos. 77034–77057 and 25496–25620.

52 prisoners sent from Brünn receive Nos. 77058–77109.

32 prisoners sent in a group transport receive Nos. 77110–77141.

The SS Camp Doctor makes a selection in the prisoners' infirmary. He selects 48 sick prisoners, who are killed with phenol injections the same day.

Ibid.

NOVEMBER 21

50 prisoners sent from Pawiak Prison by the Sipo and SD of Warsaw receive Nos. 77142–77191.

Two prisoners sent from Kattowitz receive Nos. 77192 and 77193.

At 8:00 P.M. the standby squad is ordered to the unloading platform to take charge of a transport of Jews.

APMO, D-AuI-1/3, FvD, p. 146.

726 Jewish men, women, and children arrive from Westerbork with an RSHA transport from Holland. After the selection, 47 men and 35 women are admitted to the camp and receive Nos. 77194–77240 and 25621–25655. The remaining 644 are killed in the gas chambers.

The bodies of 70 prisoners are sent to the morgue of the main camp. 11 of the dead are brought from the auxiliary camps:* one from Budy, seven from the auxiliary camp Buna, two from Chełmek, and one from Jawischowitz.

NOVEMBER 22

Tank columns of the Red Army attack both wings of the German front near Stalingrad and cut off all retreat routes for General Paulus's 6th Army.

Approximately 1,500 Jewish men, women, and children arrive from the ghettos in the Zichenau District in an RSHA transport. After the selection, 300 men and 132 women are admitted to the camp

---

*The corpses of prisoners from the auxiliary camps are sent to the morgue of the main camp daily, since the registration of deaths is done in the office of the prisoners' infirmary.

and receive Nos. 77241–77540 and 25656–25787. The remaining 1,068 people are killed in the gas chambers.

NOVEMBER 23

18 prisoners sent in a group transport receive Nos. 77541–77558.

Four female prisoners sent from Kattowitz receive Nos. 25788–25791.

NOVEMBER 24

Prisoner No. 69212 is shot "while escaping."

APMO, D-AuI-5/4, Morgue Register, p. 25.

62 prisoners sent to the camp by the Sipo and SD for the Kraków District receive Nos. 77559–77620.

One female prisoner sent from Kagenfurt, Austria, receives No. 25792.

The SS Camp Doctor makes a selection in the prisoners' infirmary in Block 20. He selects 28 sick prisoners, who are killed with phenol injections the same day.

Ibid.

NOVEMBER 25

45 prisoners sent from Kattowitz receive Nos. 77621–77665.

54 prisoners sent to the camp by the Sipo and SD for the Kraków District receive Nos. 77666–77719.

Approximately 2,000 Jewish men, women, and children arrive from the Grodno ghetto in an RSHA transport. After the selection, 305 men and 128 women are admitted to the camp and receive Nos. 77720–78024 and 25793–25920.

Six female prisoners sent from Kattowitz receive Nos. 25921–25926.

Four prisoners and one Russian POW are killed in Block 11. They are Adolf Hanan (No. 69994), sent to the bunker on November 12 by order of the Political Department; Ignacy Korzeński (No. 72120), captured trying to escape and sent to the bunker on November 17; Polish Jews Haim Wassermann (No. 49328) and Mordka Sonnenschein (No. 42746), both caught trying to escape from the Buna auxiliary camp and sent to the bunker on November 25; and the Russian POW No. RKG-8590, who was also put in the bunker on November 25 for helping the two Jewish prisoners escaping from the Buna A.C.*

APMO, D-AuI-3/1b, Bunker Register, p. 81; D-AuI-5/4, Morgue Register, p. 25.

*Next to these names, it is noted in the Bunker Register that they are released into the camp on this date. However, on the same day their numbers are entered in the Morgue Register.

The SS Camp Doctor makes a selection in the prisoners' infirmary, Block 28. He selects 27 prisoners who registered for admission and are killed with phenol injections the same day.

APMO, Mat.RO, vol. VI, pp. 24C, 24D.

The bodies of 84 prisoners are sent to the morgue of the main camp. 11 corpses come from the Chełmek A.C. and eight from the Birkenau squad.

APMO, D-AuI-5/4, Morgue Register, p. 26.

NOVEMBER 26

709 Jewish men, women, and children arrive from Westerbork in an RSHA transport from Holland. After the selection, only 42 women are admitted to the camp and receive Nos. 25927–25968. The remaining 667 people are killed in the gas chambers.

The SS Camp Doctor makes a selection in the prisoners' infirmary as well as in the Buna auxiliary camp. He chooses 73 prisoners from Blocks 28 and 20 and 13 from the Buna A.C. These prisoners are killed with phenol injections the same day.

APMO, Mat.RO, vol. VI, pp. 24C, 24D; D-AuI-5/4, Morgue Register, pp. 27ff.

The corpses of 115 prisoners are sent to the morgue of the main camp.

APMO, D-AuI-5/4, Morgue Register, pp. 27ff.

Commandant Höss ends a search operation and informs the RSHA and other responsible offices that Polish prisoner Zygmunt Słowik (No. 52346), who escaped on October 13, was arrested in Sandomierz and is to be sent back to the camp with the next group transport.

APMO, IZ-8/Gestapo Lodz/3/88/ 101, 102.

At 2:30 P.M., 60 female prisoners from the women's camp in Birkenau are taken to the Penal Company in Budy, guarded by three SS men.

APMO, D-AuI-1/3, FvD, p. 147.

NOVEMBER 27

At 3:30 A.M., 12 sentries of the standby squad are ordered to the railroad station to take charge of a transport from Warsaw.

Ibid.

63 male and 53 female prisoners sent from Pawiak Prison by the Sipo and SD of Warsaw receive Nos. 78025–78087 and 25969–26021.

70 prisoners sent to the camp by the Sipo and SD for the Kraków District receive Nos. 78088–78157.

39 male and 13 female prisoners sent in a group transport receive Nos. 78158–78196 and 26022–26034.

Two prisoners sent from Kattowitz receive Nos. 78197 and 78198.

53 prisoners sent from Kattowitz receive Nos. 78199–78251.

At 4:45 P.M., the commander of the guard receives a report from the main guard post that two female prisoners from the poultry farm are missing from Harmense A.C. By 5:50, the search has produced no result. The guards are recalled at 11:00 P.M. Two Czech prisoners have escaped: Anna Čapek, born September 5, 1900, in Vesly and sent to Auschwitz by the Brünn Stapo on November 6, 1942, and Aloisia Katz (née Dasko), born March 17, 1899, in Mostkowice and sent to Auschwitz by the Prague Gestapo on November 11, 1942.

Ibid., p. 148; APMO, IZ-8/Gestapo Lodz/2/88/49.

The SS Camp Doctor makes a selection in the prisoners' infirmary, Block 20. He selects 62 sick prisoners, who are killed with phenol injections the same day.

APMO, Mat.RO, vol. VI, p. 24D.

NOVEMBER 28

1,000 Jewish men, women, and children arrive from the Zichenau ghetto in an RSHA transport. After the selection, 325 men and 169 women are admitted to the camp and receive Nos. 78252–78576 and 26035–26203. The remaining 506 people are killed in the gas chambers.

BV prisoner Kazimierz Nadolski (No. 59050), born December 8, 1911, is locked in the bunker of Block 11. It is noted in the Bunker Register that he was released to the camp the same day. However, his number is listed in the Morgue Register on the same day. Nadolski probably dies during an interrogation in the Political Department.

APMO, D-AuI-3/1b, Bunker Register, p. 87; D-AuI-5/4, Morgue Register, p. 30, Position 29.

NOVEMBER 29

163 prisoners transferred from Buchenwald to Auschwitz receive Nos. 78577–78739.

One female prisoner sent from Oppeln receives No. 26204.

28 female prisoners transferred from Ravensbrück to Auschwitz receive Nos. 26205–26232.

NOVEMBER 30

17 male and three female prisoners sent to the camp from Lemberg receive Nos. 78740–78756 and 26233–26235.

92 prisoners sent in a group transport receive Nos. 78757–78848.

1,000 Jewish men, women, and children arrive from the Zichenau ghetto in an RSHA transport. After the selection, 130 men and 37 women are admitted to the camp and receive Nos. 78849–78978 and 26236–26272. The remaining 833 deportees are killed in the gas chambers.

The SS Camp Doctor makes a selection in the infirmary, Block 20. He selects 35 sick prisoners who are killed with phenol injections the same day.

APMO, Mat.RO, vol. VI, p. 25B.

The Head of the Budget Office in the WVHA informs the administrations of all concentration camps as well as Branch D that the manufacture of iron urns for the ashes of the dead is discontinued until the end of the war by order of the SS Commander in Chief because of the limited supplies of iron. From January 1943 on, the demand for urns of other materials is to be filled by the porcelain manufacturer Allach-Munich GmbH. The camp administrations are requested to estimate their expected demand for urns up to the end of 1945 and submit it to Office A-I/1 of the WVHA by December 10, 1942. Office A I/1 will then send a group order and distribute the urns.

APMO, IZ-13/89, Various Documents of the Third Reich, p. 226.

Until production begins in Allach, one could, if necessary, contact Professor Lauermann Studios KG in Detmold. The price of a 3½-quart urn is 2.70 RM. This price is open until the beginning of delivery and may go higher.

The Special Squad formed by Hössler to wipe out the traces of the crimes—empty the mass graves in Birkenau and burn the corpses—completes its work. As Commandant Höss reports, 107,000 corpses are buried in the mass graves. These were Jews killed with gas who were brought to Auschwitz in transports from Upper Silesia since the beginning of the transport operation and Jews who arrived with transports before September 21, 1942, i.e., before the incineration of corpses began. In addition, the corpses of the Russian POWs and of prisoners who died in the winter of 1941–42, when the crematorium in the main camp was not operational, and the corpses of prisoners who died in Bunkers Number 1 and 2 in Birkenau are also burned.

SAM, *Auschwitz in the Eyes of the SS*, pp. 114ff., 165–168.

NOVEMBER 1–30

The bodies of 103 prisoners from the Buna A.C., 33 from the Chełmek A.C., six from the Jawischowitz A.C., and one from Golleschau A.C. are sent to the morgue in the main camp.

APMO, D-AuI-5/4, Morgue Register, pp. 3–32.

DECEMBER 1

85 male and 14 female prisoners sent to the camp by the Sipo and SD for the Kraków District receive Nos. 78979–79063 and 26273–26286.

The occupancy level of the women's camp in Auschwitz-Birkenau is 8232.

APMO, Mat.RO, vol. 5a, p. 301.

532 Jewish men, women, and children arrive with the second RSHA transport from Bergen in Norway.* After the selection, 186 men are admitted to the camp and receive Nos. 79064–79249. The remaining 346 people are killed in the gas chambers.

The occupancy level of the men's camp in Auschwitz-Birkenau is 22,391; this number includes those in the auxiliary camps.

Ibid.

The SS Camp Doctor makes a selection in the prisoners' infirmary, Block 20. He selects 45 prisoners, who are killed with phenol injections the same day.

Ibid., vol. VI, p. 25B.

86 bodies are sent to the morgue of the main camp.

APMO, D-AuI-5/4, Morgue Register, p. 33.

DECEMBER 2

63 prisoners sent from Radom by the Sipo and SD receive Nos. 79250–79312.

826 Jewish men, women, and children arrive from Westerbork with an RSHA transport from Holland. After the selection, 77 men are admitted to the camp and receive Nos. 79313–79389. The remaining 749 deportees are killed in the gas chambers.

Approximately 1,000 Jewish men, women, and children arrive from the Grodno ghetto in an RSHA transport. After the selection, 178 men and 60 women are admitted to the camp and receive Nos. 79390–79567 and 26287–26346. The remaining 762 people are killed in the gas chambers.

Four male prisoners and one female prisoner sent from Kattowitz receive Nos. 79568–79571 and the free number 15268.

23 female prisoners sent in a group transport receive Nos. 26347–26369.

The SS Camp Doctor makes a selection in the prisoners' infirmary, Block 20. He selects 35 patients who are not expected to recover quickly. These inmates are killed with phenol injections the same day.

APMO, Mat.RO, vol. VI, pp. 24A, 24B.

The Head of Office D-I of the WVHA instructs the Commandants of the concentration camps that flogging is to be used only in ex-

APMO, D-RF-9, WVHA, 8/1, p. 2, Edict Collection.

---

*This transport reaches Stettin by ship and is sent from there to Auschwitz by train. In this transport is Professor Dr. Bertold Epstein, professor of pediatrics at the University of Prague, who emigrated to Norway after German troops occupied Prague. He receives No. 79104 and becomes a prisoner physician in the men's camp in Birkenau, in the Buna auxiliary camp and in the Gypsy camp. His wife dies in the gas chamber in Birkenau.

ceptional cases and only when other punishments have been un-successful.*

As deputy Commandant, P.C. Commander Aumeier ends a search operation and notifies the RSHA and other headquarters that prisoners Anna Čapek and Aloisia Katz, who escaped from the camp on November 27, have been captured and are to be brought back to Auschwitz.

APMO, IZ-8/Gestapo Lodz/2/88/51.

Simcha Jurlicht, a Polish Jew (No. 78394), born December 14, 1924, is captured attempting to escape and sent to the bunker of Block 11. He is shot on December 4, 1942.

APMO, D-AuI-3/1b, Bunker Register, p. 87.

DECEMBER 3

46 prisoners sent to the camp by the Sipo and SD for the Kraków District receive Nos. 79572–79617.

Approximately 1,000 Jewish men, women, and children arrive from the Płońsk ghetto with an RSHA transport. After the selection, 347 men are admitted to the camp and receive Nos. 79618–79964. The remaining 653 deportees are killed in the gas chambers.

24 male and 96 female prisoners sent in a group transport receive Nos. 79965–79988 and 26370–26465.

The standby squad begins a search for two escaped prisoners at 9:00 A.M.

APMO, D-AuI-1/3, FvD, p. 153.

At 12:00 noon, the standby squad sets out for the railroad station to take charge of a transport of 93 Gypsies. This transport is not noted in the list of arriving transports either on this day or the following day. The Gypsies are probably killed in the gas chambers.

Ibid., p. 154.

During the admission of the sick in the prisoners' infirmary, the SS Camp Doctor classifies 64 prisoners as untreatable. They are killed with phenol injections the same day.

APMO, D-AuI-5/4, Morgue Register, pp. 35ff.; Mat.RO, vol. VI, pp. 25C, 25D.

The bodies of 125 prisoners, 15 of them from the Chełmek A.C., are sent to the morgue of the main camp.

APMO, D-AuI-5/4, Morgue Register, pp. 35ff.

The approximately 300 Jewish prisoners in the special squad who dig up and burn the 107,000 bodies buried in mass graves are taken from Birkenau to the main camp by the SS. There they are led to

APMO, Höss Trial, vol. 1, p.17; vol. 4, p. 76; Kraków Auschwitz Trial, vol. 7, pp. 7, 113.

*The purpose of this order is to maintain the prisoners' capacity to work.

the gas chamber in Crematorium I and killed with gas. Thus the witnesses to the corpse burning are disposed of.*

Political inmate Bogusław Wrana (No. 67357), who escaped from the camp on October 31 and was captured, is sent back to Auschwitz and locked in the bunker of Block 11.**

APMO, D-AuI-5/4, Bunker Register, p. 89.

DECEMBER 4

At 4:50 A.M., Polish prisoner No. 75675 is discovered hanging fatally wounded on the wires of the electrically charged camp fence.† He was sent to Auschwitz by the Sipo and SD of Kraków and put in Block 9 of the main camp.

APMO, D-AuI-1/3, FvD, p. 154; D-AuI-5/4, Morgue Register, p. 37.

81 male and 40 female prisoners sent in a group transport receive Nos. 79989–80069 and 26466–26505.

The SS Camp Doctor makes a selection in the prisoners' infirmary, Block 20. He classifies 78 patients as no longer treatable. They are killed with phenol injections the same day.

APMO, Mat.RO, vol. VI, pp. 25C, 25D.

Five prisoners are killed in Block 11: Simach Jurlicht (No. 78394), captured in an attempt to escape on December 2 and sent to the bunker of Block 11; Wiktor Tipliński (No. 71727), born September 25, 1925, and Nikolai Noczaczienko (No. 71613), born August 7, 1922, both from the Buna A.C., who were sent to the bunker the day before probably after a failed attempt to escape; prisoner No. 71626, who probably took part in that escape attempt; and Władysław Kaczan (No. 77630), born March 12, 1923, sent to the bunker of Block 11 the previous day by order of the Camp Commander.

APMO, D-AuI-3/1b, Bunker Register, pp. 87ff.; D-AuI-5/4, Morgue Register, p. 37.

The bodies of 119 prisoners are sent to the morgue of the main camp.

APMO, D-AuI-5/4, Morgue Register, pp. 37ff.

The 163 prisoners†† transferred from Buchenwald to Auschwitz on November 29 are examined by a doctor. At the examination,

APMO, Kraków Auschwitz Trial, vol. 35, pp. 105–107; D-AuI-3a/16, Labor Deployment.

---

*Pery Broad writes that a bad feeling spread among the SS men who had gotten a good look at the gassing operation, and some even assumed that in order to preserve secrecy, they themselves would be the last to go to the gas chambers (SAM, *Auschwitz in the Eyes of the SS*, Broad's Memoirs, p. 184). The prisoners in the Special Squad were to be liquidated after every large operation by order of Adolf Eichmann (Ibid., Comments of Höss, p. 114). The only ones left alive are the specialists: the stokers, the mechanics, and the prisoner functionaries. The other prisoners are killed with injections of phenol at regular intervals, in small groups; especially members of the Special Squads who evince too much energy and who could resist SS men under the right circumstances. These as well as physically exhausted prisoners are sent to the prisoners' infirmary of the main camp, where SS Medical Officers Klehr and Scherpe kill them with injections of phenol (SAM, Inmitten des grauenvollen Verbrechens [Amid Unspeakable Crimes: Manuscripts of Members of the Special Squad], Special Issue I, *HvA*, Oświęcim, 1972, p. 52).
**He is probably shot on December 17, 1942.
†Called thus in the usage of the inmates; official camp documents record this as "escape attempt."
††18 of them died in the meantime.

it is discovered that only 100 are able-bodied; three more have to be sent to the prisoners' infirmary, and physical exhaustion is discovered in the remaining 22 transferees. Of the others, three have inflamed wounds and gangrenous legs, one is missing his left arm, one has a deformed hand, and three have wounds on their fingers caused by frostbite. Only 2 percent of those transferred to Auschwitz at this time are construction workers. Office D-II of the WVHA is notified of this on December 5.

DECEMBER 5

In the women's camp in Birkenau, the SS carries out a large-scale selection, which lasts the entire day. Afterward, approximately 2,000 young, healthy, and able-bodied women are brought to the gas chambers in the bunkers.*

Škodowa, *Three Years*, p. 79.

Because of the altered borders of the camp interest zone the Commandant corrects the order issued as a special garrison order for SS personnel on October 7, 1942, as follows:

APMO, D-AuI-1, Garrison Order 34/42.

1. The barracks street Rajsko—Auschwitz is open in the direction of the city only as far as the greenhouse.
2. The railroad tracks may not be used for taking walks.
3. Entering the Visitors' Residence (Fremdenhaus) is forbidden.
4. Loitering in and in front of the railroad station is forbidden. As before Waffen SS House can be visited by all SS personnel. Entering the city is strictly forbidden.

69 prisoners sent from Lublin by the Sipo and SD receive Nos. 80070–80138.

At 2:45 P.M. it is discovered that a prisoner from the sewage-gas squad is missing. The search is unsuccessful.

APMO, D-AuI-1/3, FvD, p. 156.

Józef Pych (Leo Balzer) (No. 62678), born January 6, 1910, in Glowezyn, escapes from the camp.

APMO, IZ-8/Gestapo Lodz/3/88/346, 349; Mat.RO, vol. VI, p. 292.

Russian prisoner Johann Leonowiec (No. 73190), born December 28, 1914, in Tumen, escapes. He was sent to the camp from the prison in Brünn.

APMO, IZ-8/Gestapo Lodz/2/88/143.

The SS Camp Doctor makes a selection in the prisoners' infirmary, Blocks 20 and 28. He classifies 60 sick prisoners as untreatable. They are killed with phenol injections the same day.

APMO, Mat.RO, vol. VI, pp. 25ff.

DECEMBER 6

58 prisoners sent to the camp from Lublin by the Sipo and SD receive Nos. 80139–80196.

APMO, D-AuI-1/3, FvD, p. 156.

*In their accounts, the surviving female prisoners remember that selection clearly because they connected the date with St. Nicholas Day, which is celebrated in many countries.

49 prisoners sent in a group transport receive Nos. 80197–80245.

Ibid.

At 2:45 A.M., the whole standby squad is ordered to the unloading platform to take charge of an RSHA transport of Jews.

Ibid.

811 Jewish men, women, and children arrive from Westerbork with an RSHA transport from Holland. After the selection, 16 men are admitted to the camp and receive Nos. 80246–80261. The remaining 795 people are killed in the gas chambers.

Approximately 2,500 Jewish men, women, and children arrive from the Mława ghetto in an RSHA transport. After the selection, 406 men are admitted to the camp and receive Nos. 80262–80667. The remaining 2,094 deportees are killed in the gas chambers.

A new Special Squad is formed to which several dozen Jewish prisoners, selected from Section B-Ib, are assigned. It is probably called Special Squad II; some of those assigned to it are Meilech (Milton) Buki (No. 80312) and Szlama Dragon (No. 80359), who will work in the Special Squad until the end. During the evacuation of the camp in January 1945, Szlama Dragon succeeds in escaping to the vicinity of Pless (Pszczyna). In the trial against Rudolf Höss, he appears as a witness and charges that the group of Jewish prisoners was sent to the Special Squad on December 9 and employed in incinerating corpses for several days thereafter. On the other hand, the camp documents indicate that the Special Squad must have already been in existence when prisoners who were working in it made attempts to escape on December 7 and 9.

APMO, Höss Trial, vol. 11, pp. 102–121.

Two Jewish prisoners, the brothers Arno Hirsch (No. 78898), born April 19, 1927, and Norbert Hirsch (No. 78897), born December 30, 1924, both in Treuburg, East Prussia, are captured trying to escape from Birkenau and locked in the bunker of Block 11.*

APMO, D-AuI-3/1b, Bunker Register, p. 89.

DECEMBER 7

Mieczysław Jurkiewicz (No. 19360) escapes from the camp.

APMO, Mat.RO, vol. VI, p. 292.

Six male and 37 female prisoners sent in a group transport receive Nos. 80668–80673.

Seven male and two female prisoners sent from Białystok receive Nos. 80674–80680 and 26543 and 26544.

Two Jewish prisoners with the Nos. 36816 and 38313 escape from Special Squad II in Birkenau.

APMO, D-AuI-1/3, FvD, p. 158.

*It is noted next to the names of these prisoners that they were released from the bunker on December 17, 1942. Next to the entry is the mark "Ü," for "überstellt," which might mean transfer to another prison by order of the Gestapo, transfer to the Penal Company, or shooting.

It turns out that the two escapees from the special squad are the Slovak Jew Ladislaus Knopp (No. 36816), born May 6, 1912, in Topolčany, and the Rumanian Jew Samuel Culea, born May 4, 1901, in Jassy. In the teletype message to the RSHA and other headquarters about the escape, P.C. Commander Aumeier admits that the prisoners escaped in the early morning and it is very important to capture them for official police reasons.

APMO, IZ-8/Gestapo Lodz/2/88/87.

Two prisoners sent from Kattowitz receive Nos. 80681 and 80682.

Eight male and two female prisoners sent to the camp by the Lemberg Gestapo receive Nos. 80683–80690 and 26545 and 26546.

During the takeover of a transport with 60 male and 31 female prisoners transferred by the Prague Kripo, it is discovered that one prisoner is missing, the Czech Gypsy Franz Denhel, born January 12, 1905. The search remains unsuccessful. The 59 male prisoners arriving with this transport receive Nos. 80691–80749. The 31 transferred women are not recorded in the camp registers on December 7 or the following days. They are probably Jewesses who are killed in the gas chambers.

APMO, IZ-8/Gestapo Lodz/3/88/350.

Asocial prisoner Ignatz Mrnka (No. 80735), born April 26, 1910, in Banova, escapes from the camp. Mrnka escapes right after being admitted to the camp and receiving a number. He belongs to the same transport from which Franz Denhel escaped. On January 12, 1943, he is arrested again, sent to Auschwitz, and shot. He is probably, like Denhel, a Gypsy, and therefore identified as an asocial prisoner.

APMO, IZ-8/Gestapo Lodz/2/88/56ff; D-AuI-3/1b, Bunker Register, p. 108.

DECEMBER 8

Georg Etelsen (No. 68240) is shot "trying to escape."

APMO, D-AuI-5/4, Morgue Register, p. 41.

The SS Camp Doctor carries out a selection in the prisoners' infirmary. He selects 94 sick prisoners with poor prospects for a quick recovery. They are sent to Birkenau and killed there with gas.

APMO, D-AuI-5/3, Prisoners' Infirmary Register of Block 28, pp. 232–235.

14 male and 12 female prisoners sent from Kattowitz receive Nos. 80750–80763 and 26547–26558.

Approximately 1,000 Jewish men, women, and children arrive from the Grodno ghetto in an RSHA transport. After the selection, 231 men are admitted to the camp and receive Nos. 80764–80994. The remaining 769 people are killed in the gas chambers.

Eight prisoners sent from Kattowitz receive Nos. 80995–81002.

89 prisoners sent to the camp from Radom by the Sipo and SD receive Nos. 81003–81091.

Three Jewish prisoners are sent from the Buna plant AC to the bunker of Block 11. They are Paul Laufer (No. 70934), born June 1, 1899, and Fritz van Gelder (No. 69350), born May 15, 1913, who both arrived in the camp with transports from Holland; and Heinz Fritsche (No. 68228), born May 15, 1912, who arrived in a group transport. They are shot after a selection in the bunker on December 17.

APMO, D-AuI-3/1b, Bunker Register, pp. 90ff.

DECEMBER 9

Several trucks are sent to Chełmek to transfer the prisoners in the Chełmek outside squad, which was dissolved,* to Auschwitz.

APMO, D-AuI-4, Transit Order No. 9, Dec. 9, 1942; E. Iwaszko, "Chełmek," p. 52.

The SS Camp Doctor makes a selection in the prisoners' infirmary, Block 28. He selects 64 sick prisoners who are not expected to be able to work any time soon. They are killed with phenol injections the same day.

APMO, Mat.RO, vol. VI, pp. 26A, 26B.

12 male and 59 female prisoners sent in a group transport receive Nos. 81092–81103 and 26559–26617.

APMO, D-AuI-1/3, FvD, p. 158.

At 12:25 P.M., the Guard Commander receives the report that six prisoners have escaped from the Special Squad. The search is unsuccessful and is called off at 5:00 P.M. because of a heavy fog.

Ibid.

The two Jewish prisoners, Nos. 36816 and 38313, who escaped from Special Squad II on December 7, are captured at 8:30 P.M. in Harmense and brought to the main guardhouse.

Ibid.

DECEMBER 10

The two Jewish prisoners, Ladislaus Knopp (No. 36816) and Samuel Culea (No. 38313), who escaped from the Special Squad on December 7, are locked in the bunker of Block 11 and released from the bunker to the camp the same day.

APMO, D-AuI-3/1b, Bunker Register, p. 91.

Two Jewish prisoners who escaped from the Special Squad the previous day are captured and sent to the bunker of Block 11. They are Bar Borenstein (No. 74858), born February 10, 1920; and Nojech Borenstein (No. 74859), born March 25, 1925, in Szreńsk. They were sent to the camp from the Zichenau ghetto in an RSHA transport on November 14, 1942. The two of them are probably executed publicly on December 17 in the presence of the Special Squad to terrorize the other prisoners.**

Ibid.

Asocial prisoner Wasil Damienko (No. 66876), born October 27, 1920, in Kiev, is captured while escaping and sent to the bunker of Block 11. He is probably shot on December 17 after a selection in the bunker.

Ibid.

*The reasons for this are unknown.
**Next to the names of the two prisoners and the entry "released" is the letter "Ü."

The SS Camp Doctor carries out a selection in the prisoners' infirmary, Block 20. He chooses 29 sick prisoners who are not expected to recover quickly. They are killed with phenol injections the same day.

APMO, D-AuI-5/4, Morgue Register, p. 44; Mat.RO, vol. VI, p. 26A.

120 prisoners sent to the camp from Lublin by the Sipo and SD receive Nos. 81104–81223.

927 Jewish men, women, and children arrive with an RSHA transport from Holland. After the selection, 39 men and three women are admitted to the camp and receive Nos. 81224–81262 and 26618–26620. The remaining 885 people are killed in the gas chambers.

1,060 Jewish men, women, and children arrive with an RSHA transport from Germany. After the selection, 137 men and 25 women are admitted to the camp and receive Nos. 81263–81399 and 26621–26645. The remaining 898 people are killed in the gas chambers.

Approximately 2,500 Jewish men, women, and children from Poland arrive from the transit camp Małkinia in an RSHA transport. After the selection, 524 men are admitted to the camp and receive Nos. 81400–81923. The remaining 1,976 people are killed in the gas chambers.

Among the prisoners admitted to the camp is Sałmen Lewenthal, who is later sent to the Special Squad; he later belongs to the squad's resistance group and is one of the organizers of the armed uprising of October 7, 1944. Sałmen Lewenthal leaves behind a manuscript that is discovered, considerably damaged, near the crematorium in October 1962. It is published by the Auschwitz State Museum in 1971.

Sałmen Lewental, "Handschrift" (Hand-written record), reproduced in SAM, *Amid Unspeakable Crimes*, pp. 131–189.

13 female prisoners sent in a group transport receive Nos. 26646–26658.

Three female Jewish prisoners receive Nos. 26659–26661.

DECEMBER 11

66 male and 94 female prisoners sent in a group transport receive Nos. 81924–81989 and 26662–26755. 30 female prisoners from Yugoslavia receive Nos. 26662–26692.

Prisoners Samuel Colea and Ladislaus Knopp are probably sent to the bunker of Block 11 after their interrogation and the discovery of their escape route; according to an entry in the Bunker Register, they are released to the camp on December 15. No doubt they are shot publicly by SS men on the work site of the Special Squad.

APMO, D-AuI-3/1b, Bunker Register, p. 92.

The SS Camp Doctor carries out a selection in the prisoners' infirmary, Block 28. He selects 38 prisoners not expected to recover their health and their ability to work soon. They are killed with phenol injections the same day.

APMO, Mat.RO, vol. VI, p. 26B.

Of the 524 male prisoners who received Nos. 81400–81923 and were selected the day before from the RSHA transport, several dozen healthy-looking men are chosen and assigned to the Special Squad. They are deployed the same day in clearing out the gas bunker and recognize among the dead their family members, friends, and acquaintances with whom they arrived. Under the blows of the armed SS men they carry the bodies of their relatives out of the bunkers.

SAM, *Amid Unspeakable Crimes*, p. 142.

DECEMBER 12

57 prisoners sent in a group transport receive Nos. 81990–82046.

24 female prisoners sent from Lublin to the camp by the Sipo and SD receive Nos. 26756–26779.

20 female prisoners sent in a group transport receive Nos. 26780–26799.

416 Polish Jewish men and six Polish Jewish women receive Nos. 82047–82462 and 26800–26805. They are selected from an RSHA transport that arrived the previous day from the transit camp Małkinia. The transport consisted of approximately 2,000 Jewish men, women, and children. After the selection of 422 men and women, the remaining 1,578 people are killed in the gas chambers.

A prisoner sent from Kattowitz receives the No. 82463.

28 male and four female prisoners sent from Hamburg receive Nos. 82464–82491 and 26806–26809.

The SS Camp Doctor carries out a selection in the prisoners' infirmary, Block 28. He chooses 34 prisoners who are not expected to recover soon. They are killed with phenol injections the same day.

APMO, Mat.RO, vol. VI, p. 26C.

DECEMBER 13

300 prisoners are transferred from the men's camp, Section B-Ib in Birkenau, to the Buna A.C. I. G. Farben has requisitioned them from the Commandant's Office as laborers in the Buna plant.

APMO, D-AuI-1/3, FvD, p. 161.

56 prisoners sent in a group transport receive Nos. 82492–82547.

The first RSHA transport arrives in Auschwitz from the camp of the so-called Central Resettlement Office (Umwandererzentrale— U.W.Z.) in Zamość with 314 Polish men and 318 Polish women. They have been deported within the framework of the plan to

Archiwum Głownej Komisji Badania Zbrodni Hitlowskich w Polsce (Archive of the High Commission for the Investigation of Nazi Crimes in Poland); hereafter cited as: AGKBZH,

evacuate Poles from the region of Zamość, which is planned as a settlement area for German colonists. On admission to the camp, the men and boys receive Nos. 82548–82859, 83910, and 83911;* the women and girls receive Nos. 26810–27032, 27034–27038, and 27040–27129. The transport is composed of 644 people; 14 of them were able to escape during the transport.

963/z, Report of the Transport of 644 Poles to the Labor Camp Auschwitz on December 10, 1942, by SS Second Lieutenant Heinrich Kinna of December 16, 1942; reproduced in Czesław Madajczyk, ed., *Zamojszczyzna Sonderlaboratorium SS* (The Region Zamość—Special Laboratory of the SS: A Collection of Polish and German Documents from the Nazi Occupation), Vols. 1 and 2, Warsaw, 1977, pp. 220–222.

DECEMBER 14

Six prisoners sent to the camp on December 10 receive Nos. 82860–82865.

757 Jews arrive with an RSHA transport from Holland. After the selection, 121 men are admitted to the camp and receive Nos. 82866–82986. The remaining 638 people are killed in the gas chambers.

Approximately 1,500 Jewish men, women, and children arrive with an RSHA transport from the Nowy Dwor Mazowiecki ghetto. After the selection, 580 men are admitted to the camp and receive Nos. 82987–83566. The remaining 920 people are killed in the gas chambers.

41 prisoners sent from Zichenau receive Nos. 83567–83607.

22 prisoners sent from Kattowitz receive Nos. 83608–83629.

Two female prisoners sent to the camp on December 10, 1942, receive Nos. 27130 and 27131.

19 prisoners sent in a group transport receive Nos. 27132–27150.

Jakub Hanczarenko (No. 62921) escapes from the camp.

APMO, Mat.RO, vol. IV, p. 292.

The SS Camp Doctor carries out a selection in the prisoners' infirmary, Block 28. He chooses 48 prisoners who are not expected to recover quickly; they are killed with phenol injections the same day.

Ibid.

In the afternoon, criminal prisoner Alois Zedek, born December 13, 1911, escapes from the camp. He was sent to Auschwitz on November 3, 1942, by the Brünn Kripo.

APMO, IZ-8/Gestapo Lodz/3/88/352.

During roll call, it is discovered that two prisoners are missing. The search is unsuccessful. The outer sentry line is recalled at 8:00 P.M. and reinforced again at 7:00 in the morning.

APMO, D-AuI-1/3, FvD, p. 163.

*These are two boys of eight and nine years old whose mothers wanted to keep the children with them and so pass them off as girls; they first receive Nos. 27033 and 27039 from the number series for women. This is discovered on December 17. Tadeusz Rycyk thereupon receives No. 83910 and Mieczysław Rycaj No. 83911. The two boys are killed with phenol injections on January 21, 1943.

The Polish prisoner Franciszek Dembiniok (No. 72953), born July 2, 1916, and Russian prisoner Auror Bodnar (No. 75827), born January 1, 1924, are captured while escaping and sent to the bunker of Block 11. The two of them are probably shot on December 17, 1942, after a selection in the bunker.

APMO, D-AuI-3/1b, Bunker Register, p. 92.

DECEMBER 15

Four prisoners sent from Kattowitz receive Nos. 83630–83632 and 83747.

114 inmates sent in a group transport receive Nos. 83633–83746.

19 female prisoners receive Nos. 27151–27169.

The SS Camp Doctor carries out a selection in the prisoners' infirmary, in Blocks 28 and 20. He selects 57 prisoners who are not expected to recover quickly. They are killed with phenol injections the same day.

APMO, Mat.RO, vol. IV, 26D, 26C; D-AuI-5/2, Morgue Register, p. 34.

The bodies of 76 prisoners are sent to the morgue of the main camp.

APMO, D-AuI-5/2, Morgue Register, p. 34.

A female prisoner escapes from the Penal Company in Budy. The search is unsuccessful. At 6:00 P.M. the standby squad is recalled because of fog and oncoming darkness.

APMO, D-AuI-1/3, FvD, p. 169.

DECEMBER 16

11 female prisoners sent in a group transport receive Nos. 27170–27180.

53 male and 26 female prisoners sent to the camp by the Sipo and SD for the Kraków District receive Nos. 83748–83800, 27181–27186, and 27188–27207.

20 male prisoners and one female prisoner sent from Kattowitz receive Nos. 83801–83820 and 27187.

83 male and 49 female prisoners sent to the camp from Radom by the Sipo and SD receive Nos. 83821–83903 and 27208–27256.

Poles evacuated from the region of Zamość arrive with the second RSHA transport from the camp of the UWZ. 38 male and 48 female prisoners receive Nos. 84441–84478, 27257–27274, and 27276–27305.

The Political Department discovers some evidence of the resistance movement in the main camp. On this day, the Clerk of Block 17, Polish political prisoner Zdzisław Wróblewski (No. 1029), a former officer of the 1st Light Cavalry Regiment, is found with illegal records and sent to the bunker. At the same time, weapons are found hidden in a shed next to the military supply camp, and on the floor of Block 17, a revolver is allegedly found. This is the

APMO, D-AuI-3/16, Bunker Register, pp. 95–97; Brol et al., "Bunker Register of Block 11," pp. 34ff.

pretext for the incarceration of 22 Polish prisoners, who are sent to the bunker of Block 11 between December 16 and 18. These are young men who worked in various labor squads (e.g., the personal effects warehouse, the clothing room, the lumberyard and as animal keepers and cleaners for the SS).

Wróblewski is locked in the bunker in handcuffs. Józef Krall is also chained and tortured during the interrogation. Most of the prisoners taken into custody and sent to the bunker between December 16 and 18 by order of the Camp Commander and the Political Department are shot in executions carried out in the camp on January 25 and February 4, 13, and 16.

The SS Camp Doctor carries out a selection in the prisoners' infirmary, Block 28. He selects 38 prisoners who are not expected to recover soon. They are killed with phenol injections the same day.

APMO, Mat.RO, vol. VI, p. 26D.

The Commandant's Office gets an explanation from Office D-II in the WVHA concerning the 163 prisoners transferred to Auschwitz on November 29. The explanation says that the prisoners were previously examined by the Second Camp Doctor, SS First Lieutenant Dr. Heinrich Plaza, who selected them for work and classified them as able-bodied. The bad state of health is surely a result of the transport, which took several days. The one-armed prisoner was accepted for the transport because he is a skilled worker and had declared that he was able-bodied. Consonant with an order of the Commandant of Buchenwald SS Lieutenant Colonel Pister, only healthy and able-bodied prisoners are to be transferred to other camps. This order was strictly followed by the Camp Physician.

APMO, D-AuI-3a/18, Labor Deployment.

Head of Office IV (Gestapo) of the RSHA SS Lieutenant General Heinrich Müller has worked out a plan for the deportation of 45,000 Jews to Auschwitz to supply the munitions factories with a larger labor force. According to this plan, 30,000 Jews from the Białystok District, 10,000 from the Theresienstadt ghetto, 3,000 from Holland, and 2,000 from Berlin are to be deported. Of these, only 10,000 to 15,000 are to be left alive after the selection. Literally, this means: "By the application of a suitable standard, a labor force of at least 10,000 to 15,000 arriving Jews is created." Since the German Railroad cannot supply special trains to the Wehrmacht for conveying transports from December 15, 1942, to January 10, 1943, because of the Christmas holiday traffic, the "resettlement" operation is to take place between January 11 and 31, 1943.

APMO, Maurer Trial, vol. 13, p. 155 (1472-PS); Eschwege, *The Letter J*, pp. 262ff.

This plan is passed on by letter to Himmler's field headquarters.

DECEMBER 17

Six prisoners sent from Kattowitz receive Nos. 83904–83909.

Approximately 2,000 Polish Jewish men, women, and children arrive from the ghetto of Płónsk in an RSHA transport. After the selection, 523 men and 257 women are admitted to the camp and receive Nos. 83912–84434 and 27306–27562. The remaining 1,220 people are killed in the gas chambers.

With reference to an order from the SS Commander in Chief of December 14, 1942, the head of the Gestapo instructs the offices under his command to transfer 35,000 able-bodied detainees to the concentration camps. He orders that the prisons be surveyed, that lists of the names of transferred prisoners be sent to Section IV-C2 of the RSHA, and that copies be sent to the Commandants of the relevant camps.

APMO, Pohł Trial, vol. 12, pp. 63–65 (NO-1063-PS).

Six prisoners sent from Oppeln receive Nos. 84435–84440.

DECEMBER 18

In a garrison order, Höss announces that Branch D of the WVHA has ordered that SS personnel who are taking holiday leave must have a medical examination and all their luggage must be disinfected. They must leave the camp area immediately after the disinfection; they can stay in the Waffen SS House until their departure.

APMO, D-AuI, Garrison Order 35/42.

216 male and 114 female prisoners sent in a group transport receive Nos. 84479–84694 and 27563–27676.

The SS Camp Doctor carries out a selection in the prisoners' infirmary, Block 28. He selects 64 sick prisoners who are not expected to recover soon, and who are killed with phenol injections the same day.

APMO, Mat.RO, vol. VI, pp. 27B, 27A.

Prisoner Kazimierz Jezierski (No. 21277), born February 15, 1900, in Lodz, escapes from the camp.

Ibid., vol. IV, p. 292.

DECEMBER 19

71 male and four female prisoners sent in a group transport receive Nos. 84695–84765 and 27677–27680.

The SS Camp Doctor carries out a selection in Block 20. He classifies 80 sick inmates as untreatable. They are killed with phenol injections the same day.

APMO, Ibid., vol. VI, p. 27B.

Two prisoners, Maxim Hunczenko (No. 54079), born August 29, 1919, and Piotr Didyk (No. 56868), born July 21, 1921, sent to Auschwitz by the Kattowitz Stapo on August 6, 1942, escape from the camp.

APMO, IZ-8/Gestapo Lodz/3/88/359.

Mikołaj Radczenko (No. 56866), born in 1921, and Aleksander Baszuk (No. 58531), born in 1924, escape from the camp.

Ibid., vol. IV, p. 292.

Czech political prisoner Heinrich Leiksner (No. 63339), born June 20, 1917, escapes from the camp.

APMO, IZ-8/Gestapo Lodz/2/88/147.

DECEMBER 20

24 male and 42 female prisoners sent in a group transport receive Nos. 84766–84789 and 27681–27722.

Two female prisoners who arrive from Kattowitz receive Nos. 27033 and 27039.

DECEMBER 21

25 prisoners sent from Pawiak Prison by the Sipo and SD of Warsaw receive Nos. 84790–84814.

A prisoner sent from Kattowitz receives No. 84815.

24 prisoners sent from The Hague receive Nos. 84816–84839.

The SS Camp Doctor carries out a selection in the prisoners' infirmary, Block 28. He selects 50 sick prisoners who won't recover quickly. They are killed with phenol injections the same day.

APMO, Mat.RO, vol. VI, p. 27C; D-AuI-5/2, Morgue Register, pp. 11ff.

DECEMBER 22

56 male and 51 female prisoners sent in a group transport receive Nos. 84840–84895 and 27723–27773.

Two Polish prisoners, Władysław Kos (No. 34553), born October 14, 1902, and Władysław Jaroszczak (No. 53276), born May 11, 1911, escape from the camp.

APMO, IZ-8/Gestapo Lodz/3/88/363; Mat.RO, vol. IV, p. 292.

The SS Camp Doctor carries out a selection in the prisoners' infirmary, Block 20. He selects 32 sick inmates who are not expected to recover quickly. They are killed with phenol injections the same day.

APMO, Mat.RO, vol. VI, p. 27D.

Three Jewish prisoners, Szlama Trzmiel (No. 81847), born October 9, 1919; Ismar Ruschin (No. 83716), born March 6, 1923, in Berlin; and Hainz Totschek (No. 83737), born May 8, 1924, in Hamburg, are caught trying to escape from Birkenau. They are shot on January 6, 1943.

APMO, D-AuI-3/b, Bunker Register, pp. 97ff.

DECEMBER 23

Four prisoners sent from Kattowitz receive Nos. 84896–84899.

59 male and five female prisoners sent from Brünn receive Nos. 84900–84958 and 27774–27778.

Two male and two female prisoners sent from Kattowitz on December 19 receive Nos. 84959, 84960, 27779, and 27780.

The SS Camp Doctor carries out a selection in Block 20. He classifies 30 sick prisoners as untreatable. They are killed with phenol injections the same day.

APMO, Mat.RO, vol. VI, p. 27C; D-AuI-5/2, Morgue Register, pp. 13ff.

The bodies of 56 prisoners are sent to the morgue of the main camp.

APMO, D-AuI-5/2, Morgue Register, pp. 13ff.

At 9:30 A.M. the political prisoner Wasyl Bolszakow (No. 78593), born January 30, 1921, in Hirson, escapes from the camp.

APMO, D-AuI-1/3, FvD, p. 172.

DECEMBER 24

Wasyl Bolszakow is captured and sent to the bunker of Block 11. On January 6, 1943, he is shot—in the Bunker Register it is noted that he was transferred to the infirmary (Krankenbau—KB).

APMO, D-AuI-3/1b, Bunker Register, p. 98.

The SS Camp Doctor carries out a selection in Block 20. He selects 37 sick prisoners not expected to make a quick recovery. They are killed with phenol injections the same day.

APMO, Mat.RO, vol. VI, pp. 27D, 27C.

The bodies of 68 prisoners are sent to the morgue of the main camp; six of the dead come from Golleschau A.C., three from Buna A.C., and one from Budy.

In the evening, the Polish female prisoners who live in the staff building put candles on a pine branch, which they have secretly brought into the room allocated to them. They light the candles and sing Christmas carols and wish each other freedom. Such quiet celebrations take place in several blocks and barracks of Auschwitz and its auxiliary camps. They sustain the inmates and feed their hope of surviving the camp.

Škodowa, *Three Years*, p. 81.

DECEMBER 25

14 male and eight female prisoners sent in a group transport receive Nos. 84961–84974 and 27781–27788.

Polish political prisoner Stefan Muczkowski (No. 75688) is brought to Block 20 severely beaten on the first day of Christmas. He dies there of his wounds the same day. Muczkowski was curator of the national museum in Kraków.

APMO, Höss Trial, vol. 4, p. 168; D-AuI-5/2, Morgue Register, p. 14, Position 9.

DECEMBER 26

42 male and 18 female prisoners sent in a group transport receive Nos. 84975–85016 and 27789–27806.

DECEMBER 27

Two prisoners sent from Kattowitz receive Nos. 85017 and 85018.

DECEMBER 28

Professor Dr. Clauberg begins his sterilization experiments on female prisoners in Barracks 28 of the women's camp of Birkenau. Several female prisoners are housed in Barracks 27 for Clauberg's

APMO, Höss Trial, vol. 7, pp. 75ff., Testimony of Former Prisoner Felicja Pleszowska.

exclusive use. From time to time he comes to the camp and performs several operations at the same time in which he injects a fluid into the women's uteruses, and subsequently takes X rays of them.

33 male and 57 female prisoners sent with a group transport receive Nos. 85019–85051 and 27807–27863.

Head of Branch D of WVHA Glücks delivers a secret edict to the Camp Doctors in which he interprets their functions more closely: the goal is to lower the mortality rate of the camp inmates. The text runs:

Schnabel, *Power Without Morality*, p. 223, Doc. 75.

> Enclosed for your information is a list of the current arrivals and departures in all the concentration camps. From this it can be seen that of 136,000 arrivals, approximately 70,000 dropped out because of death. With such a high death rate, the number of prisoners can never be brought to the level ordered by the SS Commander in Chief. The First Camp Doctors must employ all means available so that the mortality figures in the individual camps drop significantly. The best doctor in a concentration camp is not the one who believes that he must be conspicuous for inappropriate harshness but rather the one who maintains productivity at as high a level as possible through supervision and substitutions in the specific jobs.
>
> More than they have in the past, Camp Doctors must supervise the nutrition of the inmates and incorporate proposals for improvement in agreement with the Camp Commandants. These proposals must not merely remain on paper but must be inspected regularly by the Camp Doctors. Moreover, Camp Doctors have to take care that working conditions in the individual work sites are improved as much as possible. For this purpose, it is necessary for Camp Doctors to inspect working conditions at the work sites. The SS Commander in Chief has ordered that the mortality rate must be brought down. For this reason, the above is ordered, and a monthly report on measures taken and results is to be made to the Head of Office D-III, the first on February 1, 1943.

The bodies of 29 prisoners as well as seven from Buna A.C. are sent to the morgue of the main camp.

APMO, D-AuI-5/2, Morgue Register, p. 18.

DECEMBER 29

During roll call, it is discovered that six prisoners are missing. The 75 men of the SS standby squad comb the lumberyard and construction yard. The search is unsuccessful. At 9:45 P.M., an SS man with the dog squadron shoots prisoner No. 78631, one of the men missing from the lumberyard squad.*

APMO, D-AuI-1/3, FvD, p. 178; D-AuI-5/2, Morgue Register, p. 19, Position 41.

*The number of the shot prisoner, who fled from the main camp to Birkenau, is listed in the Morgue Register.

In the afternoon, four prisoners escape from the camp: the German Otto Küsel (No. 2) and the Poles Jan Baraś (No. 564), Mieczysław Januszewski (No. 711), and Dr. Bolesław Kuczbara (No. 4308). The prepared and planned escape takes the following course: Otto Küsel, who has the function of so-called labor manager in the camp and who is thus known to the SS men and has their trust, drives into the camp with a truck, up to Block 24. He loads four cabinets and leaves the camp without being checked by the SS Block Commander at the gate. Without being stopped, he crosses the entire production area of the camp. In an open field, he opens one of the cabinets and Mieczysław Januszewski climbs out in the uniform of an SS man, armed with a rifle, and sits next to Küsel in the truck as an SS guard. Arriving at the barrier, Januszewski shows the SS noncommissioned officer on duty a previously procured transit pass for a prisoner accompanied by a guard. After leaving the Interest Zone, prisoners Jan Baraś and Bolesław Kuczbara also climb out of the cabinets.* The escape was prepared with the support of the underground Polish Home Army (Armia Krajowa—AK) and Janina Kajtoch, a resident of the town of Oświęcim. A go-between brings the escapees to the family of Andrezj Harat in Libiąż, where they can recover before fleeing farther toward the General Government.

APMO, D-AuI-1/1, Telegram About Escapes, p. 9; IZ-8/Gestapo Lodz/3/88/369; Mat.RO, vol. IV, p. 292; T. Iwaszko, Inmate Escapes, *Escapes from Auschwitz*, p. 27, Jan Baraś's Account.

In the afternoon, Polish prisoner Franciszek Brzeziński (No. 76970), born in Rychwald in 1920, escapes from the camp.

APMO, IZ-8/Gestapo Lodz/3/88/365; Mat.RO, vol. IV, p. 292.

Polish reeducation prisoner Jan Telega (No. EH-3037), born November 14, 1920, in Śliwnica, escapes from the camp. He is captured on December 31, 1942, and transferred back to the camp. His name is not listed in the Bunker Register.

APMO, IZ-8/Gestapo Lodz/2/88/52–54; Mat.RO, vol. IV, p. 294.

DECEMBER 30

At 7:30 A.M., the Guard Commander receives a report that nine female prisoners have escaped from the women's Penal Company in Budy. The SS motorized unit go out to search for them, under SS Captain Otto.

APMO, D-AuI-1/3, FvD, p. 178.

The escaped women are the Russians Paraska Savenko, born in Yekaterinoslav in 1915; Vassa Loczvimenko, born August 16, 1919; Fedosia Chichankova, born August 6, 1900; Dora Gavreluk, born July 5, 1914 in Lomaczuk; Vera Gunskai, born December 27, 1919; Taissa Panova, born September 23, 1915; Nadia Netrebko, born August 17, 1924; Viera Bovscha, born October 30, 1924; and Lena Avtamienko, born February 18, 1923.**

APMO, IZ-8/Gestapo Sieradz/1, pp. 278ff.

*Otto Küsel is captured in Warsaw and sent back to Auschwitz on September 25, 1943. He is held in the bunker of Block 11 until November 1943. On February 9, 1944, he is transferred to Flossenbürg C.C. Jan Baraś (his real name is Komski) is caught in Kraków in January 1943 and sent back to Auschwitz but is not identified. Mieczysław Januszewski is imprisoned again and most likely commits suicide during the transport to the camp.
**Nothing is known about the fate of the escapees.

30 male and 42 female prisoners sent in a group transport receive Nos. 85052–85081 and 27864–27905.

76 prisoners sent by the Sipo and SD for the Kraków District receive Nos. 85082–85157.

39 prisoners sent from Kattowitz receive Nos. 85158–85196.

The SS Camp Doctor carries out a selection in the prisoners' infirmary, Block 21. He classifies 44 sick prisoners as untreatable. They are killed with phenol injections the same day.

APMO, Mat.RO, vol. VI, p. 28A; D-AuI-5/2, Morgue Register, p. 20.

DECEMBER 31

The Head of Section IV-C2 in the RSHA, Dr. Berndorf, sends a secret letter to the Head of the WVHA, Pohl, in which he informs him that in connection with an order of the SS Commander in Chief of December 14, 1942, Minister of Justice Thierack has given permission to send all "asocial elements," primarily Poles, to the concentration camps, to be transferred from various prisons. At the same time, he assumes that some of the 12,000 prisoners have already been sent to camps.

APMO, Maurer Trial, vol. 13, pp. 159ff. (NO-1523).

Jewish women employed in the SS sewing squad and housed in the headquarters building secretly organize an artistic evening.

Škodowa, *Three Years*, pp. 83ff.

The bodies of 40 prisoners, including 16 from Buna A.C., are sent to the morgue of the main camp.

APMO, D-AuI-5/2, Morgue Register, p. 21.

During roll call it is discovered that three prisoners are missing. The search is begun immediately. At 6:30 P.M., SS man Georg Lang of the 7th Company brings Henryk Bugajski (No. 17539) to the camp and puts him in the bunker. Bugajski is suspected of facilitating the escape. On January 6, 1943, he is released from the bunker.

APMO, D-AuI-1/3, FvD, p. 180; D-AuI-3/1b, Bunker Register, p. 101.

German political prisoner Ernst Müller (No. 58615), probably an Austrian, born September 2, 1919, in Vienna, and Russian political prisoner Mark Hvedorenko (No. 75772), born May 11, 1914, in Michałowka, are captured trying to escape and sent to the bunker of Block 11. Ernst Müller is released from the bunker on January 6, 1943; Mark Hvedorenko is shot.

APMO, D-AuI-3/1b, Bunker Register, p. 101.

At 10:00 P.M., SS man Grotard of the 2nd Company, on duty at Watchtower 23 in Birkenau, brings the Czech political prisoner Heinrich Leiksner (No. 63339), who escaped on December 19, to the main guard house. He is immediately sent to the bunker of Block 11 and is shot on January 6, 1943.

APMO, D-AuI-1/3, FvD, p. 180; D-AuI-3/1b, Bunker Register, p. 101; IZ-8/Gestapo Lodz/2/88/147, Telegram About the Capture of a Prisoner.

68 prisoners are sent from Kattowitz and receive Nos. 85197–85264. This is the last transport to Auschwitz in 1942.

By December 31, Dr. Horst Schumann has carried out about 200 sterilizations on young Jewish men. After several weeks and months, the sterilized inmates will be castrated.

APMO, Höss Trial, vol. 8, p. 11, Testimony of Former Prisoner M. Waligóra.

1 9 4 3

The Auschwitz concentration camp is further enlarged during 1943, and new extermination facilities are set up.

Auschwitz now fulfills several functions simultaneously. It is the location for the direct extermination of deported Jews as well as for indirect extermination through inhuman camp conditions, ceaseless exploitation of the labor force, and terror. At the same time, Auschwitz is a reservoir for cheap labor and also an experimental station for pseudomedical and pharmacological experiments by SS doctors.

Between March 22 and June 25, 1943, the Central Construction Administration completes work on four crematoriums and gas chambers and turns them over to the camp administration. In these gas chambers several thousand people, the majority of them Jews, will be murdered at one time with the poison gas Zyklon B immediately after their arrival in the camp. With these new facilities the tempo of the mass murders increases. The Jewish victims are brought in from transit camps set up by the SS and from ghettos in France, Holland, Belgium, Greece, Germany, Yugoslavia, Czechoslovakia, Poland, and Italy.

In Birkenau, construction is completed on the second section (B-II), which is divided into six separate housing camps, called Camps B-IIa, B-IIb, B-IIc, B-IId, B-IIe, and B-IIf; the personal effects camp, given the designation Camp B-IIg, is for storage of possessions taken from the murdered and incarcerated Jews (see map, p. 5). Sixteen housing barracks are set up in Camp B-IIa and 32 each in Camps B-IIb, B-IIc, B-IId, and B-IIe. These stable barracks of the kind designated OKH-type 260/9 were originally intended for 52 horses. In Birkenau, however, they house 400 or more prisoners. Camp B-IIe is the first to be filled with prisoners: Starting in February it becomes the so-called Gypsy Family Camp, where Gypsies are brought from the occupied countries of Europe. By the end of 1943 a total of 18,736 men, women, and children are imprisoned here.

In July 1943, the male prisoners housed in Camp B-Ib are transferred to Camp B-IId, where the able-bodied prisoners used in the separate labor squads are housed, as well as to Camp B-IIf, where a special prisoners' infirmary camp is set up for male prisoners. The isolation of the ill prisoners is intended to prevent infectious diseases from being transmitted to prisoners in the adjacent camp sections.

Camp B-Ib, until then housing male prisoners, is now taken to enlarge the women's camp. Housed there are the female prisoners in the so-called outside squads deployed outside the camp, but within the Interest Zone, to work mainly in the camp's agricultural enterprises.

In August 1943 a quarantine camp is set up in the B-IIa section for recently arrived prisoners. The several-week quarantine becomes a time for testing the prisoners' physical endurance as well as for training them in the conditions of existence in the camp and in camp drill. Anyone surviving this test is moved to Camp B-IId, for able-bodied prisoners, or into one of the auxiliary camps. In September 1943, a family camp is set up on the B-Ib section for Jews from the Theresienstadt ghetto in Czechoslovakia. The Jewish prisoners interned there are housed under seemingly better conditions and receive permission to write letters to their families or to acquaintances abroad, including those in neutral countries. These letters are intended to counteract the information that has managed to leak out of the camp "into the free world," that Auschwitz is an extermination camp for Jews.

The number of prisoners has decreased as a consequence of deaths resulting from the inhuman camp conditions, the endless outbreaks of typhus, the terror, the murder by phenol injections or Zyklon B, and mass executions. To offset this decrease, prisoners already incarcerated in jails as well as deported Jews are delivered to Auschwitz. Approximately one-third of the Jews survive the selections and are admitted to the camp as laborers.

The victory of the Red Army at Stalingrad; the material and personnel losses of the Wehrmacht; and the 50-day battle at Kursk in August 1943, in which the Third Reich loses another half million people, approximately 3,000 tanks, and more than 3,000 airplanes and where the Red Army forces gain a total strategic initiative, lead to an increased demand for labor by the armaments industry. This forces the SS to sell prisoner labor to the armaments companies and factories. The SS sets up auxiliary camps, which are under the control of Auschwitz C.C., at various factories, foundries, and coal mines in Silesia: at Eintrachthütte (Harmony Foundry) in Schwientochlowitz (Świętochłowice), Neu-Dachs in Jaworzno, Fürstengrube (Prince Mine) in Wessolla near Myslowitz, Janinagrube in Libiąż, Lagischa in Lagiszo as well as in Sosnowitz and Brünn. Manufacturing facilities of Friedrich Krupp AG for the production of fuses are set up on the grounds of Auschwitz. The factory of the Weichsel-Union-Metallwerke, which was evacuated from Zaporož'e, is taken over in October 1943. In December 1943, 1,223 prisoners, including 560 women, are employed in the production of fuses for artillery weapons. Likewise, in December 1943 40 female prisoners from the Birkenau women's camp are employed in the newly constructed factory of Siemens-Schuckert-Werke AG in Bobrek, near Auschwitz.

Prisoner labor is cheap, and the prisoners are easily exploited. Between 4 and 6 Reichsmarks are paid for one day's work by a prisoner who is a skilled laborer, and 3 to 4 Reichsmarks per day for unskilled labor. Payments for prisoner labor are remitted to the treasury of the Reich via one of the camp's bank accounts or an omnibus account of the SS Economic and Administrative Office (WVHA). The prisoners have no claims whatsoever to benefits; prisoners who are ill or unfit for further labor are exchanged for healthy prisoners.

Professor Dr. Carl Clauberg and Dr. Horst Schumann continue their experiments on prisoners—Clauberg on women, Schumann mainly on men, but also on women. The goal of these experiments is the development of a method for mass sterilization of the peoples condemned to biological extermination by the Nazis. Despite the negative results, the SS Camp Doctors Helmuth Vetter, Eduard Wirths, and Friedrich Entress, working on assignment and for pay for the firm of Bayer, a pharmaceuticals subsidiary of I. G. Farben, conduct experiments on people. They carry out pharmacological experiments on typhus and tuberculosis patients as well as on women deliberately infected for the purpose of testing new medications not yet on the market.

The prisoners of the Auschwitz-Birkenau C.C. not only are test subjects but also are killed for the sole purpose of providing internal organs to be used in comparison studies—anatomical and genetic "research," including on the hereditary disposition of twins. Thus is developed, among other things, a collection of Jewish skeletons at the Institute for Anatomy in Strasbourg, whose director is Professor Dr. August Hirt.

During 1943 more than 150,000 prisoners, including 86,088 men and 46,077 women as well as 9,008 male and 9,728 female Gypsies, are delivered to Auschwitz. Approximately 20,000 prisoners are transferred to other concentration camps.

As a result of the systematic enlargement of the camp, which is oriented toward the armaments industry's need for and interest in prisoner labor, Auschwitz reaches the size of a large industrial facility.

The Commandant, Rudolf Höss, is chief organizer and most zealous implementor of the SS apparatus's orders. He also functions as the SS garrison senior and director of all SS operations within the camp's Interest Zone. As he himself writes in his autobiography, he places power and hence the fates of hundreds of thousands of male and female prisoners in the hands of the Camp Commanders and the functionaries of the Political Department, which he himself rated very negatively in human terms.

The terror they practice leads to a strengthening of prisoners' resistance and to the consolidation and solidarization of various conspiratorial groups that unite and fight together against the SS apparatus of violence. One type of work done by the prisoners' resistance movement consists of informing "the world on the other side of the barbed wire" about the crimes committed in the camp by the SS. For this purpose, evidence of SS crimes is collected and smuggled out of the camp.

This work by resistance groups shows positive results even while Auschwitz is in operation. In November 1943, Höss is relieved of

In February 1943, prisoners at work on the construction of the cellar roof of the "disrobing area" that was part of Crematorium II.

his function as Commandant and the camp is divided into three parts: Auschwitz I, the original camp, is administrative headquarters for the other camps; Auschwitz II includes the camp in Birkenau with the auxiliary camps located near the agricultural operations; under the control of Auschwitz III, whose Commandant's Office is located in Monowitz, are all the auxiliary camps that have been set up near industrial facilities.

SS Commander in Chief Himmler personally tells Höss the reasons for this tripartite division, probably during his third visit to Auschwitz in the summer of 1943. Because of the disagreeable consequences of this change for Höss, he no longer recalls it or does not mention it in his autobiography. As Franz Hössler states in his testimony during the Bergen-Belsen Trial, Himmler visited the Birkenau camp during his stay in the summer of 1943. At the judicial inquiry on August 7, 1946, the former Auschwitz concentration camp prisoner Stanisław Dubiel (No. 6059), who worked as a gardener for Höss, states before the regional investigating judge, Jan Sehn, that "in a conversation conducted in the garden shortly before Höss was recalled as commandant, Himmler told Höss that he [Höss] must leave Auschwitz, as the English radio is reporting too much about the extermination of prisoners in Auschwitz. In the ensuing discussion, Höss said he was convinced he was performing a valuable service for his country with his activity in Ausch-

APMO, Dpr.-Hd/4, pp. 45–52.

witz. Immediately before he said this, Himmler had spoken about gassing people. I personally heard one part of this conversation, the rest was reported to me by the female Bible researchers who worked in the Höss household. . . ."

It is very likely that during this visit Himmler looks at the crematoriums and gas chambers completed in the first half of 1943, and inspects the experimental station for the sterilization of women or at least speaks with Dr. Clauberg—who has been waiting for this visit for several months. Himmler visits the Gypsy Family Camp and decides, after hearing a report from Höss, to have the Gypsies killed. The decision to exterminate the Gypsies indicates that Himmler reproached Höss not for gassing prisoners, but for not concealing the crimes well enough. Such information, which has been reaching the outside world from the insufficiently "insulated" camp, should be kept secret, especially in regard to Germany's satellite states and neutral countries.

The Head of the WVHA, Otto Pohl, also values very highly the accomplishments of Rudolf Höss as the organizer of Auschwitz and offers him the choice of two positions: as Commandant of Sachsenhausen C.C., or as Head of Office D-I in Branch D of the WVHA.

JANUARY 1

Nos. 27906–27925 are given to 20 female prisoners, and Nos. 85265–85303 to 39 male prisoners sent with a group transport.

The registry office in Auschwitz C.C. becomes independent and receives the designation Auschwitz II Registry Office. It is responsible for all matters of personal civil status within the Auschwitz Interest Zone.

APMO, D-AuI/98, Commandant's Office Order No. 3/43.

JANUARY 2

Nos. 27926–27967 are given to 42 female prisoners, and Nos. 85304–85321 to 18 male prisoners delivered in a group transport.

The corpses of 55 prisoners are delivered to the morgue of the main camp. Eight of the dead are from the Buna auxiliary camp and one, from the Jawischowitz A.C.

The standby alert is suspended at 3:00 P.M., following the capture of Jewish prisoner Israel Zylberman (No. 76720) and two Russian prisoners, Vasyl Yerochim (No. 71484) and Vasyl Kravchenko (No. 67199). The three prisoners are delivered to the bunkers of Block 11. They are executed on January 6, 1943.

APMO, D-AuI-1/3, FvD, p. 182; D-AuI-3/1b, Bunker Register, p. 101.

JANUARY 3

At 2:00 P.M. the SS standby squad is ordered to the Buna A.C. to bring prisoners sick with typhus to the Birkenau camp. The guard consists of three second lieutenants and 75 SS men.*

APMO, D-AuI-1/3, FvD, p. 183.

*It is not known how many prisoners are brought from the Buna auxiliary camp.

JANUARY 4

Nos. 85322–85405 are given to 84 prisoners sent from Kattowitz.

Nos. 27968–27978 are given to 11 female prisoners and Nos. 85406–85427 to 22 male prisoners delivered in a group transport.

The corpses of 58 prisoners are delivered to the morgue of the main camp. Three of the dead are from the Buna A.C.

APMO, D-AuI-5/2, Morgue Register, pp. 24ff.

JANUARY 5

Nos. 85428–85457 go to 30 prisoners sent in a group transport.

No. 27979 goes to a female prisoner sent from Kattowitz.

The SS Camp Doctor carries out a selection in the prison infirmary, Block 28 in the main camp, during which he selects 56 prisoners who are not expected to be able to work again soon. These prisoners are killed the same day with phenol injections.

Ibid., pp. 25–27.

The corpses of 87 prisoners are brought in to the morgue of the main camp.

Ibid.

JANUARY 6

After the morning roll call and the command "Form work squads!", the clothing depot, personal effects warehouse, and Identification Service squads are detained in the roll-call area. Protective Custody Commander Aumeier, SS Second Lieutenant Grabner, the Director of the Political Department, the Roll Call Leader, Staff Sergeant Palitzsch, and other SS members walk over to the prisoners in the squads. SS Second Lieutenant Lachmann repeatedly asks the detained prisoners, "Who is the colonel?" The prisoner Colonel Karol Kumuniecki (No. 8361) steps forward. Afterward, the prisoners are queried individually about their schooling and their professions and are finally divided into three groups. Palitzsch leads the first group of 15 prisoners to Block 11 but returns with them soon afterward, as it turns out that the bunkers in Block 11 are overflowing. Aumeier, Grabner, and other functionaries of the Political Department also go to Block 11 to carry out a selection there. Palitzsch has the prisoners brought to the roll-call area, gets his carbine, and goes back to Block 11. Later, the 15 prisoners selected are brought to Block 11 and put in the bunkers. These have now been "emptied," i.e., Palitzsch has carried out executions there in the meantime. The following prisoners from Block 7 are delivered to the bunker: Bronisław Motyke (No. 3546); the Block Senior, Jan Wróblewski (No. 557); the Block Scribe, Mieczysław Garbowiecki (No. 2239); Wik-

APMO, Höss Trial, vol. 4, p. 100; vol. 8, p. 111; Kraków Auschwitz Trial, vol. 78, p. 9; Mat.RO, vol. VII, p. 482; D-AuI-3/1b, Bunker Register, pp. 103–105.

---

to the Birkenau camp; with such a strong escort, though, it must be assumed that at least 300 prisoners are involved. They receive no treatment for their typhus. The sick prisoners are housed in Barracks 7, the isolation station, of the men's camp, BIb, in Birkenau and are later killed in the gas chambers.

tor Kurzawa (No. 67124); Kazimierz Koliński (No. 3135); Mie-
czysław Koliński (No. 68884); Paweł Nierada (No. 3760); Henryk
Suligórski (No. 8635); Eugeniusz Eberle (No. 40393); Tadeusz Bil-
iński (No. 830); Colonel Edward Gött-Getyński (No. 29693); Karol
Korotyński (No. 8629); Colonel Karol Kumuniecki (No. 8361);
Józef Lichtenberg (No. 988); and Wilhelm Szyma (No. 6038).*

The second group consists of Germans and ethnic Germans who
are being sent back to work. The very large third group, however,
is assigned to the gravel pit squad, which does the very hard labor
of digging up gravel.

Camp Commander and the functionaries of the Political Depart-
ment carry out a selection in the bunkers of Block 11, in the course
of which Palitzsch shoots 14 prisoners. Among them are Michał
Dejneka (No. 70834), Szlama Trzmiel (No. 81847), Ismar Ruschin
(No. 83716), Hainz Totschel (No. 83737), Władysław Rožek (No.
62638), Wasyl Bolszakow (No. 78593), Marek Hvedorenko
(No. 75772), Heinrich Leiksner (No. 63339), Israel Zylberman
(No. 76720), Vasyl Yerochim (No. 71484), Vasyl Kravchenko (No.
67199), Jan Zwiendurowski (No. 37710), Czesław Gawlikowski
(No. 74508), and Franciszek Kulma (No. 83769).**

APMO, D-AuI-3/1b, Bunker
Register, pp, 97–102.

Nos. 85458–85504 are given to 47 prisoners brought from Lublin.

No. 27981 is given to a female prisoner brought from Bielsko.

No. 85505 is given to a prisoner brought from Lublin.

Nos. 27982–28054 are given to 73 female prisoners assigned to
the camp by the Kraków Sipo and SD.

The SS Camp Doctor carries out a selection in the prisoners' infirmary, Block 28, during which he selects 35 prisoners not expected
to recover soon. These prisoners are killed the same day with phenol
injections.

APMO, D-AuI-5/2, Morgue
Register, pp. 27ff.

The Polish Jew Mordka Furmański (No. 79718), born in Płońsk
on September 1, 1920, is put in the bunker of Block 11 because of
an attempted escape from the Birkenau camp. He dies there on
January 14, 1943.

APMO, D-AuI-3/1b, Bunker
Register, p. 105.

The corpses of 78 prisoners are delivered to the morgue of the main
camp. Five of the dead are from the Golleschau A.C., four from
the Buna A.C., and one from the Jaschowitz A.C.

APMO, D-AuI-5/2, Morgue
Register, pp. 27ff.

*The prisoners who are delivered to the bunker are suspected of carrying on illegal
work in the camp. Bronisław Motyka and Jan Wróblewski are again released from
the bunker; the others are shot on January 25, 1943.
**The prisoners who were shot had been delivered to the bunker after escape
attempts or for assisting escapes, or are suspected of having planned an escape. The
executed are Poles, Russians, Jews, and one Czech. In the Bunker Register it is noted
that they had been placed in the prisoners' infirmary, and a cross is added to this
entry.

The Commandant's Office of Auschwitz receives an order from the WVHA declaring the administrations of the concentration camps to be the owners of the possessions of deceased Jewish, Polish, and Russian prisoners and POWs. Sums of money should be paid into Account 426 of Branch D (the department of the WVHA responsible for the concentration camps) at the Stadtsparkasse (municipal savings bank) of Oranienburg. The clothing should be used in the camp or passed on for further processing. In addition, the Commandant's Office is ordered to make a list of the valuables on hand and to send it to Branch D. The order supersedes previous regulations.

APMO, Höss Trial, vol. 12, p. 179, Exhibit 123.

JANUARY 7

Nos. 85506–85524 are given to 19 male prisoners and Nos. 28055–28068 to 14 female prisoners delivered in a group transport.

Approximately 2,000 Jews arrive from the Augustów ghetto in an RSHA transport. Following the selection, 296 men, who are assigned Nos. 85525–85820, and 215 women, assigned Nos. 28069–28283, are admitted to the camp as prisoners. The other approximately 1,489 people are killed in the gas chambers.

The Commandant's Office receives from the WVHA a travel permit for a truck to Dessau and back to pick up "material for disinfection," i.e., the gas Zyklon B.

Ibid., p. 171, Exhibit 115.

SS Brigadier General Glücks, Head of Branch D in the WVHA, arrives in Auschwitz at 5:30 P.M.

APMO, D-AuI-1/3, FvD, p. 187.

At 9:10 P.M. a prisoner in the main camp runs "into the wire," i.e., into the electrically charged camp fence, between Watchtowers C and D.

Ibid.

The corpses of 78 prisoners are delivered to the morgue of the main camp. Nine of the dead are from the Buna A.C. and three from Birkenau.*

APMO, D-AuI-5/2, Morgue Register, pp. 29ff.

JANUARY 8

The corpses of 53 prisoners are delivered to the morgue of the main camp; two of the dead are from the Buna A.C. and four from Birkenau.**

Ibid., pp. 30ff.

Nos. 85821–85927 are given to 107 male prisoners, and Nos. 28284–28340 to 57 female prisoners sent in a group transport. In

APMO, D-AuI-1/3, FvD, p. 188.

---

*Probably the incident involves Jewish prisoners from the transport from Grodno on December 8, 1942, who had been sent to the prisoners' infirmary of the main camp and killed there with phenol injections. Part of this transport had been assigned to the Special Squad.
**Probably they were assigned to the prisoners' infirmary of the main camp in order to be killed there with phenol injections. They came from the ghettos in the Zichenau District.

the transport are male and female prisoners from prisons in Berlin and Vienna.

The Minister of Justice, Dr. Otto Thierack, arrives at Auschwitz at 2:00 P.M.

APMO, Höss Trial, vol. 12, p. 220.

JANUARY 9

No. 85928 is given to a prisoner sent from Kattowitz.

During the morning, the Czech prisoner Georg Zahradka or Zacharatka (No. 75749) escapes from the main camp. The search begins at 12:00 noon; 150 SS Men and 200 Capos participate. With the onset of darkness, the search is suspended. At 12:00 midnight the prisoner is captured in the vicinity of Watchtower 26 by three SS Men, and is brought back to the camp and put in the bunker of Block 11. He is executed on January 14, 1943, following a selection in the bunker.

APMO, D-AuI-1/3, FvD, p. 189; D-AuI-3/1b, Bunker Register, p. 106.

The SS Camp Doctor carries out a selection in the prisoners' infirmary, Block 28, during which he selects 55 prisoners who are not expected to recover quickly. They are killed with phenol injections the same day.

APMO, D-AuI-5/2, Morgue Register, pp. 31ff.

JANUARY 10

Two prisoners, No. 68726 and No. 70901, are shot "while escaping."

Ibid.

JANUARY 11

Under the pretext that sabotage and partisan activity is increasing within the General Government, SS Commander in Chief Himmler orders that all proletarian elements, including men, women, and children, suspected of guerilla activity be arrested and assigned to the Auschwitz and Lublin concentration camps as well as to concentration camps within the Reich. The arrests should be so extensive that the proletarian sector of the population not yet included in the labor force within the General Government diminishes in number, thus making it possible to achieve a clear improvement in the guerilla war.

APMO, Maurer Trial, vol. 143, p. 161.

Nos. 85929–85932 are given to four male prisoners, and the number 27980 to a female prisoner sent from Kattowitz.

Nos. 28341–28422 are given to 82 female prisoners and Nos. 86229–86279 to 51 male prisoners sent in a group shipment.

Prisoners sent from Brünn are given Nos. 85933–86288.

The free No. 27275 is given to a female prisoner sent from Augsburg.

In the afternoon, the Gypsy Ignacy Mrnka (No. 80735) escapes from the camp.

APMO, IZ-8/Gestapo Lodz/2/88/56.

The head of Office D-II, SS Lieutenant Colonel Mauer, orders the Commandant of Auschwitz to suspend the quarantine imposed in the Buna A.C. Starting immediately, the prisoners who are planned to be used as laborers in the Buna factories following a three-week quarantine period, should be put to work immediately after their delivery to the Buna A.C.

APMO, D-AuI-3a/21, Labor Deployment.

The SS Camp Doctor carries out a selection in the prisoners' infirmary, Block 28, at which he selects 55 prisoners who are not expected to recover quickly. These prisoners are killed the same day with phenol injections.

APMO, D-AuI-5/2, Morgue Register, pp. 34ff.

The corpses of 114 prisoners are delivered to the morgue of the main camp. In the Morgue Registry is the notation "Wirths" at the entry for the corpse of prisoner No. 31882, who had been brought from Block 19. Most probably the Garrison Doctor was particularly interested in this corpse.

Ibid.

JANUARY 12

The prisoner Ignacy Mrnka is captured while escaping and put in the bunker of Block 11. He is shot on May 14, 1943, following a selection in the bunkers.

APMO, IZ-8/Gestapo Lodz/2/88/57; D-AuI-3/1b, Bunker Register, p. 108.

Nos. 86280–86267 are given to eight prisoners sent from Kattowitz.

Nos. 86288–86544 are given to 257 prisoners sent from Oppeln.

Nos. 86545–86548 are given to four male prisoners and Nos. 28423–28471 to 49 female prisoners sent in a group transport.

The SS Camp Doctor carries out a selection in the prisoners' infirmary, Block 28, during which he chooses 35 who are not expected to recover quickly. These prisoners are killed the same day with phenol injections.

APMO, D-AuI-5/2, Morgue Register, p. 37.

The corpses of 123 prisoners are delivered to the morgue of the main camp: 18 of the dead are from the Buna A.C. and eight from the Golleschau A.C.

Ibid., pp. 36–38.

JANUARY 13

Nos. 86549 and 86550 are assigned to two prisoners transferred from Neuengamme C.C.

Nos. 28472–28511 are assigned to 40 female prisoners sent in a group transport.

Nos. 86551–86566 go to 16 male prisoners and Nos. 28511–28523 to 12 female prisoners sent from Kattowitz.

1,000 Jewish men, women, and children arrive with an RSHA transport from Berlin. Following the selection, 127 men who are assigned Nos. 86567–86692 are admitted to the camp. The other 873 people are killed in the gas chambers.

750 Jews, 346 men and boys as well as 404 women and girls, arrive from Westerbork with an RSHA transport from Holland. Following the selection, 88 men, assigned Nos. 86694–86696, 86698–86715, 86717–86729, and 86731–86784, and 101 women, who are assigned Nos. 28524–28624, are admitted to the camp. The other 561 people are killed in the gas chambers.

Nos. 86697, 86716, and 86730 are assigned to three prisoners delivered from The Hague.

Approximately 2,000 Jewish men, women, and children arrive in an RSHA transport from the Zambrów ghetto. Following a selection, 148 men, Nos. 86785–86932, and 50 women, Nos. 28634–28683, are admitted to the camp. The other approximately 1,802 people are killed in the gas chambers.

The Polish political prisoner Jan Poloczek (No. 1065), is captured while escaping from the Birkenau camp and delivered to the bunker of Block 11. He is shot on February 9, 1943, following a selection in the bunkers.

APMO, D-AuI-3/1b, Bunker Register, p. 108.

The corpses of 103 prisoners are delivered to the morgue of the main camp; 13 of the dead are from the Buna A.C.

APMO, D-AuI-5/2, Morgue Register, pp. 38–40.

JANUARY 14

Nos. 86933–87098 are given to 166 male prisoners and Nos. 28625–28633 to nine female prisoners sent in a group transport.

Nos. 87099–87167 are assigned to 69 prisoners sent to the camp from the prison in Tarnów by the Sipo and SD.

The Polish prisoner Antoni Pawelak (No. 12620), born in Łuck on June 13, 1923, escapes from the camp.

APMO, IZ-8/Gestapo Lodz/3/88/373; D-AuI-1/10, Telegram About the Escape; Mat.RO, vol. IV, p. 292.

The German prisoner Kurt Pachala (No. 24) dies after 200 days of arrest in the bunker of Block 11.

APMO, D-AuI-3/1a, Bunker Register, p. 69; D-AuI-5/2, Morgue Register, p. 41.

Following a selection in the bunkers of Block 11, the prisoners Ivan Slezarov (No. 71688), Mordka Furmański (No. 79718), Jan Woźnica (No. 60107), Adam Doliński (No. 72113), Georg Zacharatka (No. 75749), and Ignacy Mrnka (No. 80735) are shot at the execution wall.

APMO, D-AuI-3/1b, Bunker Register, pp. 103, 105, 106, 108.

The SS Camp Doctor carries out a selection in the prisoners' infirmary, Block 28, during which he chooses 52 prisoners not expected to recover soon. They are killed the same day with phenol injections.

APMO, D-AuI-5/2, Morgue Register, p. 41.

The corpses of 92 prisoners are delivered to the morgue of the main camp.

Ibid., pp. 40–42.

JANUARY 15

Nos. 87379–87491 go to 113 male prisoners, and Nos. 28684–28726 as well as 28731–28882 are assigned to 135 female prisoners sent in a group transport.

Nos. 28727–28730 are assigned to four female prisoners sent to the camp from the Białystok Prison.

Nos. 28823–28837 and 28859–29339 are assigned to 496 female prisoners sent from Bromberg.

At 5:30 P.M. the entire standby squad is ordered to the unloading ramp to take over an RSHA transport from the Zambrów ghetto of approximately 2,000 Polish Jews—men, women, and children. Following the selection, 217 men, given Nos. 87492–87708, as well as 21 women, Nos. 28838–28858, are admitted to the camp. The other approximately 1,762 deportees are killed in the gas chambers.

JANUARY 16

At midnight the entire standby squad is ordered to the unloading ramp. Approximately 2,000 Jewish men, women, and children from Zambrów have arrived in an RSHA transport. Following the selection, 211 men, assigned Nos. 87168–87378, are admitted to the camp as prisoners. The other approximately 1,789 deportees are killed in the gas chambers.

Nos. 87709–88344 are assigned to 636 prisoners sent to the camp from the prison in Schieratz (Sieradz) by the Lodz Gestapo. In the transport were 685 men, of whom 49 have meanwhile died. The transport consisted of Poles, Byelorussians, Ukrainians, and Jews. On behalf of the Director of the Political Department, SS Private Sturmann signs for the receipt of 636 prisoners as well as one deceased person.

APMO, IZ-8/Gestapo Lodz/88/568–573, Correspondence About Handing Over a Transport.

No. 88345 is assigned to a prisoner sent from Kattowitz.

Nos. 88346–88494 are assigned to 149 prisoners sent from Brünn.

Nos. 88495–88510 are assigned to 16 prisoners sent from Kattowitz.

Nos. 88511–88580 are assigned to 70 prisoners sent to the camp by the Sipo and SD for the Kraków District.

Approximately 2,000 Polish Jewish men, women, and children arrive from the Łomża transit camp in a transport of the RSHA. Following the selection, 170 men, assigned Nos. 88581–88750, are admitted to the camp. The other approximately 1,830 people are killed in the gas chambers.

At 9:00 A.M. the standby squad dispatches six guards to bring the female prisoners from the women's camp, B-Ia, in Birkenau to the Penal Company in Budy.

APMO, D-AuI-1/3, FvD, p. 195.

At 12:30 P.M., 20 SS Men from the standby squad are detailed to bring prisoners from Auschwitz to the Jawischowitz A.C.

Ibid., p. 196.

The Special Commando Zeppelin of the Breslau Sipo and SD* notifies its unit in Auschwitz that two SS leaders, First Lieutenant Brummerloch and Second Lieutenant von Sadowski, would arrive in Auschwitz on January 18, 1943. They should be picked up at the train station and housed for one night.

APMO, IZ-13/89, Various Documents of the Third Reich, p. 50.

The corpses of 22 prisoners are delivered to the morgue of the main camp; four of the dead have been brought from the Buna A.C., one from the Jawischowitz A.C., and five from Birkenau. The dead prisoners from Birkenau bear Nos. 80554, 80774, 80783, 80909, and 81017.

APMO, D-AuI-5/2, Morgue Register, p. 43.

JANUARY 17

The camp management carries out a selection among the prisoners in the quarantine Blocks 2 and 8 of the main camp, during which approximately 500 prisoners are selected. They are brought to Birkenau the same day and killed in the gas chambers there.

Brandhuber, "Vergessene Erde" (Forgotten Ground), HvA, no. 5 (1962): 84ff.

Approximately 2,000 Jewish men, women, and children arrive from the Łomża transit camp in an RSHA transport. Following the selection, 255 men, assigned Nos. 88751–89005, are admitted to the camp. The other approximately 1,745 people are killed in the gas chambers.

Nos. 89006–89075 are assigned to 70 male prisoners and Nos. 29340–29369 to 30 female prisoners sent in a group transport.

JANUARY 18

Some 945 and 610 Jews arrive from Malines with the eighteenth and nineteenth RSHA transport from Belgium. Among them are

*The Commando Zeppelin, trained for reconnaissance and diversionary operations in the frontline area, is under the Security Service (SD) and is led by SS First Lieutenant Huhn. It includes Ukrainian nationalists, among others, whom Pery Broad mentions in his account (SAM, *Auschwitz in the Eyes of the SS*, pp. 168ff.).

588 men, 162 boys, 680 women, and 125 girls. Following the selection, 387 men, assigned Nos. 89076–89462, and 81 women, assigned Nos. 29370–29450, are admitted to the camp. The other 1,087 people are killed in the gas chambers.

Approximately 2,000 Polish Jews—men, women, and children—arrive from the Zambrów ghetto in an RSHA transport. Following the selection, 130 men, assigned Nos. 89463–89592 are admitted to the camp as prisoners. The other 1,870 people are killed in the gas chambers.

Nos. 89593–89844 are assigned to 252 prisoners sent in a group transport.

Under guard by the standby squad, 200 prisoners are brought from the men's camp, B-Ib in Birkenau, to the Buna A.C.

APMO, D-AuI-1/3, FvD, p. 198.

The corpses of 30 prisoners are delivered to the morgue of the main camp; five of the dead are from the adjacent Buna camp.

APMO, D-AuI-5/2, Morgue Register, p. 44.

JANUARY 19

Approximately 2,000 Polish Jews—men, women, and children—arrive from the Zambrów ghetto in an RSHA transport. Following the selection, 164 men, given Nos. 89845–90008, and 134 women, given Nos. 29451–29584, are admitted to the camp as prisoners. The other approximately 1,702 people are killed in the gas chambers.

1,372 people arrive from Kraków in an RSHA transport. In the group are 300 Jews from the Kraków ghetto as well as 569 male and 403 female prisoners from the prisons in Kraków. 619 men, including 50 Jewish prisoners, who get Nos. 90009–90627, and 403 women, who get Nos. 29625–30027, are admitted to the camp. 350 deported Jews are killed in the gas chambers. Among the Jewish prisoners who are admitted is Henryk Tauber (No. 90124).*

Nos. 90629–90741 are given to 113 male prisoners and Nos. 29585–29599 to 15 female prisoners sent in a group transport.

Nos. 90742–90811 are assigned to 70 prisoners sent to the camp by the Sipo and SD for the Kraków District.

The Commandant's Office of Auschwitz is instructed by the WVHA to carefully clean blood spots from dead prisoners' clothing that is sent to their relatives or to offices of the German government.

APMO, Höss Trial, vol. 12, p. 182, Exhibit 124.

---

*Henryk Tauber is later assigned to the Special Squad, where he works until the evacuation of the camp in 1945. During the evacuation of the camp, he manages to escape from a transport. In the trial against Rudolf Höss, Henryk Tauber testifies as witness for the prosecution (APMO, Dpr.-Hd/11a, pp. 122–150, Exhibit 18).

The corpses of 53 prisoners are delivered to the morgue of the main camp: Three of the dead are from Birkenau and one, from the Buna A.C.

APMO, D-AuI-5/2, Morgue Register, p. 45.

JANUARY 20

748 Jews arrive from Westerbork in an RSHA transport from Holland. 315 men and boys as well as 433 women and girls are in the transport. Following the selection, 10 men, assigned Nos. 90812–90821, as well as 25 women, who get Nos. 29600–29624, are admitted to the camp. The other 305 men and boys as well as 408 women and girls are killed in the gas chambers.

Approximately 2,000 Jewish men, women, and children arrive from the Grodno ghetto in an RSHA transport. Following the selection, 155 men, assigned Nos. 90822–90976, as well as 101 women, assigned Nos. 30035–30135, are admitted to the camp. The other approximately 1,744 people are killed in the gas chambers.

JANUARY 21

Nos. 90977–91046 are assigned to 70 male prisoners and Nos. 30028–30034 to seven female prisoners sent in a group transport.

100 prisoners delivered by the Kattowitz Gestapo are assigned Nos. 91047–91061, 91095–91114, 92213, and 92214, as well as 92285–92347.

A conference of the plant managers of I. G. Farben takes place in Auschwitz, in which the directors of the Leuna plants from Ludwigshafen, Auschwitz, and Troppau participate. During the conference, Head Engineer Dr. Walter Dürrfeld of the Buna plant states that 30 to 40 percent of the prisoners made available to him are employed in the construction of the camp or are patients in the infirmary. He points out that the erection of a fence around the plant grounds would make it possible to decrease the number of guard posts, as the ratio of guards to prisoners should be one to 40.

APMO, Maurer Trial, p. 78.

Approximately 2,000 Jewish men, women, and children arrive from the Grodno ghetto in an RSHA transport. Following the selection, 175 men, given Nos. 91115–91289, and 112 women, with Nos. 30136–30247, are admitted to the camp as prisoners. The other approximately 1,713 people are killed in the gas chambers.

Approximately 2,000 Jews from the Theresienstadt ghetto in Czechoslovakia arrive in an RSHA transport. 856 men and boys as well as 1,144 women and girls arrived with the shipment. After the selection, 254 men and 164 women are admitted to the camp. They are assigned Nos. 91290–91543 and 30248–30411. The other 602 men and boys as well as 980 women and girls are killed in the gas chambers.

APMO, D-RF-3/85, 86, pp. 1–52, List of Names from Theresienstadt; D-AuI-3a/65, Labor Deployment; Höss Trial, vol. 12, p. 161.

Nos. 92214–92284 are given to 70 prisoners sent to the camp by the Sipo and SD for the Kraków District.

Nos. 30412–30415 are assigned to four female prisoners.

The Polish political prisoner Czesl Nowak (No. 76812), born on May 21, 1922, is captured by two SS men from the dog squadron next to House 7 [a store for SS men] during an escape attempt and is put into the bunker of Block 11. Following a selection in the bunkers, he is shot on January 25, 1943.

APMO, D-AuI-1/3, FvD, p. 201; D-AuI-3/1b, Bunker Register, p. 112.

SS Roll Call Leader Palitzsch brings two boys eight and nine years old from the Birkenau camp to the prisoners' infirmary, Block 20. These are Mieczysław Rycaj (No. 83911) and Tadeusz Rycyk (No. 83910) who, on orders from Palitzsch, are killed the same day by phenol injections. The two boys come from the vicinity of Azmosc and had been deported with their mothers on December 13, 1942, with a transport to the camp.

APMO, Höss Trial, vol. 4, p. 163; Kraków Auschwitz Trial, vol. 37, p. 43; D-AuI-5/2, Morgue Register, p. 46, Items 7, 8.

JANUARY 22

Nos. 91062–91094 are assigned to 33 prisoners sent from Kattowitz.

Nos. 91544–92212 are assigned to 669 male prisoners and Nos. 30416–30697 to 264 female inmates of the prison in Radom who are sent to the camp by the Radom Sipo and SD.

Nos. 92348–92543 are given to 196 male prisoners and Nos. 30680–30770 to 91 female prisoners sent in a group transport.

Approximately 3,650 Jewish men, women, and children from the Grodno ghetto arrive in an RSHA transport. After the selection, 365 men, who get Nos. 92544–92908, as well as 229 women, who get Nos. 30771–30999, are admitted to the camp as prisoners. The other approximately 3,056 people are killed in the gas chambers.

APMO, Höss Trial, vol. 8, p. 14.

The Jewish prisoner Charlie Wolman (No. 25442), born in Warsaw on May 25, 1904, escapes from the Birkenau camp in the afternoon.

APMO, D-AuI-1/1, p. 22, Telegram About the Escape; IZ-8/Gestapo Lodz/3/88/379; Mat.RO, vol. IV, p. 292.

Likewise in the afternoon, the Polish prisoner Michał Witko (No. 16340), born on November 10, 1913, escapes from the Birkenau camp. He was sent to Auschwitz on suspicion of belonging to an underground organization in the Lublin region.

APMO, D-AuI-1/1, p. 24, Telegrams; IZ-8/Gestapo Lodz/3/88/377; Mat.RO, vol. IV, p. 292.

At 1:15 P.M., SS guards bring prisoners from Camp B-Ib in Birkenau to the Buna A.C., where they are to be used for labor.

APMO, D-AuI-1/3, FvD, p. 202.

The corpses of 45 prisoners are delivered to the morgue of the main camp.

APMO, D-AuI-5/2, Morgue Register, pp. 47ff.

JANUARY 23

The Commandant's Office is notified by Section IV-B4 of the RSHA that 2,000 Jews have been deported from Theresienstadt to Auschwitz on January 20 and another 2,000 on January 23; another train will leave on January 26 with 1,000 people.

APMO, Höss Trial, vol. 12, p. 161, Exhibit 105.

Approximately 2,000 Jewish men, women, and children arrive from the Grodno ghetto with an RSHA transport. After the selection, 235 men, given Nos. 92902–93143, as well as 191 women, Nos. 31000–31190, are admitted to the camp. The other 1,574 are killed in the gas chambers.

No. 93144 is assigned to a prisoner sent from Kattowitz during the morning.

Nos. 93145–93175 are assigned to 31 prisoners sent from Kattowitz.

Nos. 93176–93245 are assigned to 70 prisoners sent to the camp by the Sipo and SD for the Kraków District.

The two Polish prisoners, Michał Porzuczek (No. 91658) and Józef Błodziński (No. 91752), escape from the camp.

APMO, Mat.RO, vol. IV, p. 292.

The corpses of 32 prisoners are delivered to the morgue of the main camp; one of the dead is from the Jawischowitz A.C. and one from the Buna A.C.

APMO, D-AuI-5/2, Morgue Register, pp. 48ff.

Colonel Jan Karcz (No. 23569), former head of the Polish cavalry division, states in the presence of Protective Custody Commander Aumeier that he has spent six months in the Penal Company and requests being released into the camp. On Aumeier's orders, Karcz is delivered the same day to the bunker of Block 11 and is shot two days later.

APMO, Mat.RO, vol. VII, p. 463; Kraków Auschwitz Trial, vol. 3, p. 138; D-AuI-3/1b, Bunker Register, p. 113.

JANUARY 24

A prisoner gets the free No. 90628.

Nos. 93246–93296 are assigned to 51 prisoners sent in a group transport.

921 Jewish patients, including children, and medical personnel from the psychiatric hospital Apeldoornse Bosch arrive with an RSHA transport from Holland. After the selection, 16 men, assigned Nos. 93297–93312, and 36 women, Nos. 31191–31226, are admitted to the camp. The other 869 people are killed in the gas chambers.

Nos. 31227–31271 are given to 34 female prisoners sent in a group transport.

Approximately 2,000 Jewish men, women, and children arrive from the Grodno ghetto in an RSHA transport. After the selection, 166 men and 60 women are admitted to the camp and are assigned Nos. 93313–93478 and Nos. 31362–31421. The other approximately 1,774 people are killed in the gas chambers.

2,029 Jews are sent from the Theresienstadt ghetto in an RSHA transport. Included are 771 men and boys and 1,258 women and girls. After the selection, 147 men, assigned Nos. 93479–93625, and 80 women, assigned Nos. 31422–31501, are admitted to the camp as prisoners. The other 624 men and boys and 1,178 girls and women are killed in the gas chambers.

APMO, D-AuI-3a/65, Labor Deployment.

516 Jews arrive from Westerbork in an RSHA transport from Holland. The shipment includes 234 men and boys as well as 282 women and girls. Following the selection, 18 men, given Nos. 93626–93643, and two women, given Nos. 31502–31503, are admitted to the camp. The other 496 people are killed in the gas chambers.

The corpses of 21 prisoners are delivered to the morgue of the main camp.

APMO, D-AuI-5/2, Morgue Register, p. 49.

JANUARY 25

Nos. 31272–31361 go to 90 female prisoners sent from Kattowitz.

Nos. 93644–93683 go to 40 prisoners sent in a group transport.

Nos. 93684–93753 go to 70 prisoners from the prison in Tarnów, sent to the camp by the Sipo and SD for the Kraków District.

The corpses of 48 prisoners are delivered to the morgue of the main camp. Eight of the dead have been brought from the Golleschau A.C., five from the Buna A.C., and one from the Budy A.C.

Ibid., p. 50.

At 3:30 A.M. the Guard Commander in Birkenau reports that three prisoners have escaped from the men's camp. The search, in which 196 SS men from the 1st, 3rd, 4th, and 7th companies, as well as 30 SS men from the dog squadron, participate, remains unsuccessful.

APMO, D-AuI-1/3, FvD, p. 204.

Two prisoners, Izak Zarembski (No. 87685) and Nikolaus Michałczuk (No. 88334), are captured while escaping and delivered to the bunker of Block 11. They are shot the next day.

APMO, D-AuI-3/1b, Bunker Register, pp. 113ff.

Protective Custody Commander Aumeier, Roll Call Leader Palitzsch, Director of the Political Department Grabner, and functionaries of the Political Department who are responsible for the individual cases, carry out a selection in the bunkers of Block 11. During the selection, three prisoners are discharged to the camp, one prisoner is assigned to the Penal Company, and 53 prisoners

APMO, D-AuI-3/1b, Bunker Register, pp. 81–82, 94–96, 103–113.

who were put in the bunkers between October 29, 1942, and January 23, 1943, are to be shot. The prisoners to be shot were put in the bunkers by order of the Political Department or the Protective Custody Commander and are under suspicion of conducting illegal activities directed against the SS in the camp or of having prepared escapes. Among the condemned, however, are numerous eyewitnesses to the crimes the SS members have committed in the camp. Among the ones selected are noncommissioned officers, officers, higher officers, and members of the intelligentsia from the main camp and the Buna camp. The prisoners who are shot include Colonel Edward Gött-Getynski, Colonel Jan Karcz, Colonel Karol Kumuniecki, Cavalry Captain Włodzimierz Koliński, Wiktor Koliński, Mieczysław Garbowiecki, Karol Karotyński, Henryk Suligórski, Marian Studencki, Tadeusz Radwański, Heliodor Zaleśny, Zbigniew Ruszczyński, Henryk Stirer, Kazimierz Superson, as well as Bolesław Borczyk and Eugeniusz Obojski, who prior to being delivered to the bunker had worked as a corpse bearer and had been present at almost all executions.

In addition to the two prisoners captured in an escape attempt, the Political Department has 10 more prisoners put in the bunker of Block 11.

Ibid., pp. 113ff.

22 members of the Polish Home Army (Armia Krajowa—AK) of the Bielsko Inspectorate in the Silesia District, condemned to death by court-martial in Kattowitz, are brought from the prison in Myslowitz to Auschwitz and shot.* They include Mieczysław Jonkisz, Jan Urbaniec, Stanisław Góra, Jan Litwiński, Władysław Obażanowski and Stanislaw Baron from the Żywiec region; Adam Boryczko, Jan Staszewski, Józef Walas, Romuald Pacuł, Erwin Czaia, Jan Jaqosz, Ferdynand Dzień, Maria Dzień, Józefa Golonka, and Stanisław Pinczer, from the region of Bielsko-Biała; and Aloizy Banaś, Jan Barcik, Józef Jakuczek, Maksymilian Niezgoda, Jadwiga Dylik and Anna Kubisty from the staff of the Oświęcim area group. Marian Feliks, who likewise was condemned to death, dies of typhus fever in Myslowitz.

CA KC PZPR, 202/III-146, Documents of the Delegation of the Polish Government in Exile, pp. 38ff.

JANUARY 26

Of the 12 prisoners who were delivered in the morning to the bunkers of Block 11, nine are shot. Involved are the Jew Izaak Zarembski (No. 87685), the Poles Nikolaus Michałczuk (No. 88334), Walenty Barłóg (No. 74444), Tadeusz Skalski (No. 74351), Stanisław Bochenski (No. 74555), Rudolf Matheisel (No. 74523), a Jew, Günther Hellinger (No. 85063), two Poles, Stanisław Pardela (No. 91841) and Stanisław Zajewski (No. 91891).

APMO, D-AuI-3/1b, Bunker Register, pp. 113ff.

*The shooting probably occurs in the gas chamber of Crematorium I, since according to a report of the information service of the Silesia District of the AK, the executed were poisoned in the gas chambers. Pery Broad describes in detail how the shootings took their course (*Auschwitz in the Eyes of the SS*, pp. 157–162). The members of the Special Squads also report about it in their statements (APMO, Höss Trial, vol. I, pp. 4–28; vol. 11, pp. 122–150, Statements by Former Prisoners Stanisław Jankowski [a.k.a. Alter Feinsilber] and Henryk Tauber).

No. 93754 is assigned to a prisoner transferred from Mauthausen C.C.

Approximately 2,300 Jewish men, women, and children arrive from the ghettos in Sokółka and Jasionówka with an RSHA transport. After the selection, 161 men, assigned Nos. 93755–93915, and 32 women, assigned Nos. 31559–31590, are admitted to the camp as prisoners. The other approximately 2,107 deportees are killed in the gas chambers.

Nos. 93916–93952 are assigned to 37 male and Nos. 31504–31558 to 55 female prisoners sent in a group transport.

The Commandant receives an order from the Head of Office D-II to have a list of the Jewish prisoners who were deported from Theresienstadt on January 20, 23, and 26 drawn up and sent off. These prisoners are intended for deployment in the squads of the Auschwitz Central Construction Office and the Buna plants.

APMO, D-AuI-31/32, Labor Deployment.

Nos. 93953–93983 are assigned to 31 prisoners sent in a group transport.

The corpses of 36 prisoners are delivered to the morgue of the main camp.

APMO, D-AuI-5/2, Morgue Register, p. 51.

JANUARY 27

Nos. 31591 and 31593–31624 are assigned to 33 female prisoners sent in a group transport.

Nos. 31625–31854 are given to 230 female political prisoners from France who have been brought to Auschwitz from Romainville. Among the women are Danielle Casanova (No. 31655), Maie Politzer, Hélène Solomon-Langevin, Ivonne Blech, Henriette Schmidt, and Raymonde Salez.

APMO, Kraków Auschwitz Trial, vol. 7, p. 103.

Dr. Bruno Weber and Dr. König from the firm of Bayer, Group W-II, Leverkusen, write to a Camp Doctor, SS First Lieutenant Dr. Vetter, and recommend testing the tolerance among typhus fever patients for the nitroacridine preparation "3582." If no typhus patients are available, the effect of the preparation should be observed on diarrhea patients. The persons placing the order stress the importance of these experiments for armed forces purposes; they provide Vetter with additional supplies of the medication in tablet form and as granules, and indicate details concerning dosage and intake.*

Schnabel, *Power Without Morality*, pp. 311–313, Doc. 116.

Nos. 31855, 31856, and 31858–31869 are assigned to 14 female prisoners sent in a group transport.

*Dr. Vetter observes the effect of the preparation "3582" as well as of Rutenol on 50 typhus patients in the main camp.

993 Jews, 409 men and boys and 584 women and girls, from the Theresienstadt ghetto arrive in an RSHA transport. Following the selection, 212 men, assigned Nos. 93984–94195, and 72 women, given Nos. 31870–31941, are admitted to the camp. The other 708 people are killed in the gas chambers.

APMO, D-RF-3/87, pp. 1–61, Transport CS of Jan. 26, 1943.

The corpses of 44 prisoners are delivered to the morgue of the main camp; 12 of the dead are from the Buna A.C., one is from the Jawischowitz A.C., and six are from Birkenau.

APMO, D-AuI-5/2, Morgue Register, p. 52.

JANUARY 28

The German female prisoner Hermina Maria Pavlata, born in Aussig on October 21, 1920, who had been detained in Ravensbrück since October 18, 1941, and was transferred to Auschwitz on March 26, 1942, escapes from the camp.

APMO, D-AuI-1/1, Telegrams, p. 27.

Six female prisoners sent in a group transport receive Nos. 31942–31947.

Approximately 2,000 Jewish men, women, and children from the Golkovysk ghetto arrive with an RSHA transport. Following the selection, 280 men, given Nos. 94196–32026, are admitted to the camp. The other approximately 1,641 people are killed in the gas chambers.

62 female prisoners sent in a group transport receive Nos. 32027–32088.

Nos. 94476–94612 and 94614–95038 go to 562 prisoners sent by the Prague Gestapo.

No. 94613 goes to a Jewish prisoner.

The corpses of 69 prisoners are delivered to the morgue of the main camp; 10 of the dead are from the Buna A.C. and four are from Birkenau.

APMO, D-AuI-5/2, Morgue Register, pp. 53ff.

Nos. 32089–32603 are given to 515 prisoners sent to the camp from prisons in Tarnów and Kraków by the Sipo and SD for the Kraków District.

Nos. 95039–96515 go to 1,477 prisoners from the prisons in Kraków and Tarnów, sent to the camp by the Sipo and SD for the Kraków District; 1,022 of the prisoners in this shipment come from the prison in Tarnów.

Nos. 96540–96600 are assigned to 61 prisoners sent to the camp by the Kattowitz Gestapo.

The SS Special Commando Zeppelin in Breslau notifies its SS Special Unit Auschwitz that, in keeping with an RSHA order of December

APMO, IZ-13/89, Various Documents of the Third Reich, p. 52.

1, 1942, it is transferring the activists Yakov Semionov, born on September 30, 1916, and Vasili Gachkov, born on October 20, 1918, who are ill with third-degree tuberculosis, for "special treatment."*

JANUARY 29

Three female prisoners sent in a group transport receive Nos. 32605–32607.

96 female prisoners sent the previous day by the Prague Gestapo receive Nos. 32608–32703.

19 prisoners sent by the Kattowitz Gestapo receive Nos. 96521–96539.

The corpses of 58 prisoners are delivered to the morgue of the main camp; 17 of the dead are from the Buna A.C. and 16 are from Birkenau.

APMO, D-AuI-5/2, Morgue Register, pp. 54ff.

Nos. 96601–97209 are assigned to 609 male prisoners, and Nos. 32704–32730 to 27 female prisoners sent in a group transport.**

Head Engineer Prüfer from the firm of J. A. Topf and Sons arrives at Auschwitz to hold discussions with the Central Construction Office of the Waffen SS and Police—Auschwitz. He inspects the construction of Crematoriums II, III, IV, and V in Birkenau, confirming that Crematorium II can start up operations on February 15, 1943, but that Crematorium III will be ready for operation on April 17, 1943, at the earliest. The work on Crematorium IV should be completed on February 28, 1943, but the completion of Crematorium V will depend upon weather conditions.

APMO, D-Z Bau/8, Inventory No. 29757.

The SS Special Commando Zeppelin of the Sipo and SD in Auschwitz conveys to Grabner, Director of the Political Department, the request for "special treatment" of the two activists transferred there, Yakov Semionov and Vasili Gachkov, and for transmission of a report of execution.†

APMO, IZ-13/89, Various Documents of the Third Reich, p. 53 (original in BA Koblenz).

The RSHA orders that all Gypsies living within the Reich and in the occupied territories be taken into custody and sent to the concentration camps.

APMO, Materials/78, Inventory No. 31090; Hans-Joachim Döring, *Die Zigeuner im Nationalsozialistischen Staat* (Gypsies in the National Socialist State), Hamburg, 1964, pp. 214–218.

*"Special treatment" (*Sonderbehandlung*) means execution.
**In the wake of the agreement between Minister of Justice Thierack and SS Commander in Chief Himmler on September 18, 1942, to assign 35,000 able-bodied prisoners to the concentration camps, and the simultaneous deportations of 45,000 Jews from Theresienstadt, Berlin, the Białystok District, and Holland to Auschwitz, the numbers of prisoners increase so rapidly that it is evidently impossible for the concentration camp administration to register the large number of prisoners consecutively according to the day of their delivery to the camp.
†In Auschwitz, not only incurably ill members of the Special Commando Zeppelin were shot, but mainly those who were suspected of disloyalty or a hostile attitude toward the Third Reich. Pery Broad mentions this in his account (SAM, *Auschwitz in the Eyes of the SS*, p. 169).

[handwritten annotations] **B.31**

Abschrift

29. Januar 1943

Bftgb.Nr.:2225e/43/Bi/L.

Betr.: Krematorium II. Bauzustand.
Bezug: Fernschreiben des ⚡-WVHA Nr. 2648 vom 28.1.43.
Anlg.: 1 Prüfbericht

An
Amtsgruppenchef C,
⚡-Brigadeführer und Generalmajor
der Waffen-⚡ Dr. Ing. Kammler,
Berlin-Lichterfelde-West
Unter den Eichen 126-135

    Das Krematorium II wurde unter Einsatz aller verfügbaren Kräfte trotz unsagbarer Schwierigkeiten und Frostwetter bei Tag- und Nachtbetrieb bis auf bauliche Kleinigkeiten fertiggestellt. Die Öfen wurden im Beisein des Herrn Oberingenieur Prüfer der ausführenden Firma, Firma Topf u. Söhne, Erfurt, angefeuert und funktionieren tadellos. Die Eisenbetondecke des Leichenkellers konnte infolge Frosteinwirkung noch nicht ausgeschalt werden. Die ist jedoch unbedeutend, da der Vergasungskeller hierfür benützt werden kann.

    Die Firma Topf u. Söhne konnte infolge Waggonsperre die Be- und Entlüftungsanlage nicht wie von der Zentralbauleitung gefordert rechtzeitig anliefern. Nach Eintreffen der Be- und Entlüftungsanlage wird jedoch mit dem Einbau sofort begonnen, sodass voraussichtlich am 20.2.43 die Anlage vollständig betriebsfertig ist.

    Ein Bericht des Prüfingenieurs der Firma Topf u. Söhne, Erfurt, wird beigelegt.

        Der Leiter der Zentralbauleitung
        der Waffen-⚡ und Polizei Auschwitz

Verteiler:
1 ⚡-Ustuf Janisch u. Kirschneck
1 Registratur (Akt Krematorium)

               ⚡-Hauptsturmführer

F.d.R.d.A.:
[signature] 25
⚡-Ustuf.(F)

In January 1943, the head of the Central Construction Administration in Auschwitz informs Berlin of the virtual completion of Crematorium II in Birkenau and the imminent start-up of operations.

Crematorium II shortly before start-up. On the right, in front, the cellar with the gas chambers.

JANUARY 30

No. 31857 goes to a Polish woman sent from Dresden as a political prisoner.

Nos. 97253–97684 are assigned to 432 prisoners sent to the camp by the Lodz Gestapo.

The corpses of 40 prisoners are delivered to the morgue of the main camp. Nine of the dead are from the Golleschau A.C., eight are from the Buna A.C., and one is from the Jawischowitz A.C.

APMO, D-AuI-5/2, Morgue Register, pp. 55ff.

1,000 Jewish men, women and children arrive in an RSHA transport from Berlin. Following the selection, 140 men, given Nos. 97685–97824, and 140 women, given Nos. 32744–32883, are admitted to the camp as prisoners. The other 720 people are killed in the gas chambers.

2,612 Polish Jews—men, women, and 518 children under 10 years of age—arrive in Auschwitz on a special train, Number Pj99, from Oranczyce, ordered by the Białystok Sipo. The Jews had been brought from the ghettos in Volkovysk and Prużany to a collection point in Oranczyce next to the train station, where a special train was waiting that departed on January 29, 1943, at 45 minutes past midnight. After approximately 24 hours' travel in packed boxcars,

APMO, IZ-13/19; Raul Hilberg, *Sonderzügenach Auschwitz* (Special Trains to Auschwitz), Documents in Railroad History, vol. 18, Mainz, 1981, pp. 207–215.

they arrive at the unloading ramp of the freight depot of Auschwitz. Following the selection, 327 men, given Nos. 97825–98151, and 275 women, given Nos. 32604 and 32884–33157, are admitted to the camp as prisoners. The other 2,010 people, including the 518 children, are killed in the gas chambers.

1,000 Jewish men, women, and children from the Theresienstadt ghetto arrive in an RSHA transport. Following the selection, 122 men, assigned Nos. 98152–98273, and 95 women, assigned Nos. 33158–33252, are admitted to the camp. The other 783 people are killed in the gas chambers.

APMO, D-RF-3/88, Transport Ct. of Jan. 29, 1943; Hans-Günter Adler, *Theresienstadt 1941–1945: Das Anthitz einer Zwangsgemeinschaft* (Theresienstadt 1941–1945: The Face of an Involuntary Community—History, Sociology, Psychology), Tübingen, 1955, p. 51.

JANUARY 31

659 Jews from the Westerbork camp arrive in an RSHA transport from Holland. In the shipment are 240 men and boys and 419 women and girls. After the selection, 50 men, given Nos. 96516–96520 and 98274–98318, and 19 women, Nos. 33253–33271, are admitted to the camp. The other 590 people are killed in the gas chambers.

69 prisoners sent the previous day in a group transport receive Nos. 98319–98387.

The free Nos. 97210 to 97252 go to 43 prisoners delivered from Posen.

35 female prisoners sent the previous day in a group transport receive Nos. 33272–33306.

Nos. 98388–98515 are given to 128 male prisoners, and Nos. 32731–32743 to 13 female prisoners sent from Brünn.

A transport of 2,450 Polish Jews arrives on the special train No. Pj 101, which departed Oranczyce on January 30, 1943, at 2:10 A.M. In the transport are 145 children under four years of age and 312 children ranging in age from three to 10 years. After the selection, 249 men, given Nos. 98516–98764, and 32 women, given Nos. 33326–33357, are admitted to the camp as prisoners. The other 2,169 people, including 457 children, are killed in the gas chambers.

Nos. 98765–98777 are given to 13 prisoners sent from Kattowitz.

In the night, the Polish prisoner Henryk Wąsik (No. 17465), born in Radom on January 4, 1922, escapes from the camp. Wąsik had been sent to the camp on June 30, 1941, by the Sipo and SD of Radom for membership in an illegal Polish political organization. He worked in the kitchen for the SS members in the main camp.

APMO, D-AuI/18, Telegrams; IZ-8/Gestapo Lodz 3/88/386; Mat.RO, vol. IV, p. 292.

With the special train No Pj 103 from Oranczyce, an RSHA transport arrives from the ghetto in Pruzani with 2,834 Jews, including

230 children under four years of age and 520 children from four to ten years old. Following the selection, 313 men, assigned Nos. 98778–99087 and 99110–99112, and 180 women, given Nos. 33358–33537, are admitted to the camp. The other 2,341 people, including the 750 children, are killed in the gas chambers.

The corpses of 13 prisoners are delivered to the morgue of the main camp; one of the dead is from Jawischowitz A.C.

APMO, D-AuI-5/2, Morgue Register, p. 56.

FEBRUARY 1

Seven prisoners sent from Kattowitz receive Nos. 99113–99119.

19 female prisoners sent from the town of Auschwitz receive Nos. 33307–33325.

Nos. 33538–33542 are given to five female prisoners sent in a group transport.

Nos. 99120–99210 are assigned to 91 male prisoners, and Nos. 33543–33927 to 385 female prisoners sent in a group transport.

Because of the approaching deadline for completion of the crematoriums in Birkenau, the camp management decides to train a group of selected Jewish prisoners for the operation of the crematoriums in Birkenau in the crematorium already in operation in the main camp. Under the pretext that experts were needed for the camp workshops, 20 young and healthy Jewish prisoners are selected from Camp B-Ib in Birkenau. They must undergo medical examinations, and are found to be healthy. An SS squad brings them to the main camp, where they are housed in Bunker 7 of Block 11. Among the 20 Jews chosen is Henryk Tauber (No. 90124).

APMO, Höss Trial, vol. 11, p. 123, Statement of Former Prisoner Henryk Tauber.

The corpses of 46 prisoners are delivered to the morgue of the main camp; 10 of the dead are from the Birkenau camp.*

APMO, D-AuI-5/2, Morgue Register, p. 57.

FEBRUARY 2

The German military catastrophe at the Volga reaches its nadir with the capitulation of the Sixth Army under Field Marshal Paulus. The Battle of Stalingrad comes to an end, after which the strongest German army no longer exists. Field Marshal Paulus is taken prisoner in a shelter in Stalingrad. More than 100,000 German soldiers, including 20 German generals, become prisoners of war. The Red

---

*The entry "Birkenau" beside these prisoners' numbers in the Morgue Registry of the main camp probably means that they had been brought from Birkenau to the prisoners' infirmary of the main camp in order to be killed there with phenol injections. The killed prisoners probably belonged to the Special Squad, as the prisoners of this squad were as a rule killed after a period of time, and other prisoners took their place. In Birkenau the mortality is very high, and the corpses of prisoners are burned in ditches that are in operation as primitive crematoriums in the vicinity of Bunkers 1 and 2.

Army gains the strategic initiative and retains it until the complete defeat of the German armed forces.

At 4:00 A.M. the Guard Commander in Birkenau reports to the main guard house that a prisoner has been shot near Watchtower 20 "while escaping" and that another prisoner has fled between Watchtowers 17 and 18.

APMO, Dpr.-Hd/12, p. 220, quoted from the Guard Register.

It turns out that the Polish prisoner Stanisław Janik (No. 91596) has escaped. He is captured while fleeing and delivered to the bunker of Block 11, where he dies the following day.

APMO, D-AuI-3/1b, Bunker Register, p. 116.

Nos. 99088–99109 are given to 22 prisoners sent from Kattowitz.

Under heavy guard, the group of 20 Jewish prisoners is brought from Bunker 7 in Block 11 to Crematorium I. After a speech by the Squad Leader, the prisoners are immediately forced to help in the work of burning many corpses; these are lying in the corpse chambers and gas chambers, which also serve as locations for shootings. Two Jewish Czech prisoners who are dentists by profession are assigned to the squad. In contrast to the already existing squad that operates Crematorium I, called the Crematorium I Squad,* the new squad receives the designation Crematorium II Squad. As long as the squad is housed in the main camp, it is isolated from the other prisoners and is housed in Bunker 7 of Block 11.

APMO, Höss Trial, vol. 11, pp. 123, 126.

1,265 Polish Jews have arrived from the ghetto in Pruzana with Special Train Pj-105, which departed Oranczyce at 1:29 A.M. on February 1, 1943. In the shipment are 35 children under four years of age and 60 of four to 10 years of age. Following the selection, 294 men, who are assigned Nos. 99211–99504, and 105 women, Nos. 33928–34032, are admitted to the camp as prisoners. The other 866 people, including 95 children, are killed in the gas chambers.

Nos. 99505–99636 are given to 132 prisoners delivered in a group transport.

1,001 Jewish men, women, and children from the Theresienstadt ghetto arrive with an RSHA transport. Following the selection, 155 men, assigned Nos. 99537–99791, and 63 women, assigned Nos. 34033–34095, are admitted to the camp. The other 783 people are killed in the gas chambers.

APMO, D-RF-3/89, Transport Cu of Feb. 1, 1943; Adler, *Theresienstadt 1941–1945*, p. 51.

Nos. 34096–34103 are given to eight female prisoners sent in a group transport.

APMO, D-AuI-1/1/99, Commandant's Office Order 4/43.

---

*This squad consists of the Polish prisoners Mieczysław Morawa (No. 5730), the Capo; Jozef Ilcztuk (No. 14916), the scribe; and Wacław Lipka (No. 2520), the mechanic; as well as seven other Jewish prisoners. It is likewise housed in isolation in the bunkers of Block 11. Stanisław Jankowski (a.k.a Alter Feinsilber) is also a member of this squad.

Commandant Höss reminds the SS members of the ban on taking pictures within the camp area.

Commandant Höss declares the adjacent Budy camp for female prisoners to be off limits for SS members.

Ibid.

The corpses of 43 prisoners are delivered to the morgue of the main camp.

APMO, D-AuI-5/2, Morgue Register, p. 58.

FEBRUARY 3

Five prisoners from the surveying squad are delivered to the bunker of Block 11: Marian Włodek (No. 26585), Tadeusz Hrehorowicz (No. 31054), Władysław Horodelski (No. 14213), Witold Frydrychowicz (No. 63668), and Bolesław Ponsyliusz (No. 174). They are imprisoned in the bunker because an SS Guard reported that while doing some surveying work in Rajsko they met with a woman who left behind packages of food at agreed-on places. Following the conclusion of the investigations by the Political Department, they are shot on February 13, 1943.

APMO, D-AuI-3/1b, Bunker Register, p. 116; Höss Trial, vol. 4, pp. 37ff., Statement of Former Prisoner Wilhelm Wohlfarth.

Nos. 99792–99865 are assigned to 74 prisoners sent to the camp by the Sipo and SD in Lublin.

No. 99866 is given to a prisoner delivered from Kattowitz.

The corpses of 43 prisoners are delivered to the morgue of the main camp; one of the dead is from the Buna A.C., one from the Budy A.C., one from the Jawischowitz A.C., and two from the Golleschau A.C.

APMO, D-AuI-5/2, Morgue Register, p. 59.

FEBRUARY 4

890 Jews, 321 men and boys and 569 women and girls, from Westerbork arrive with an RSHA transport from Holland. Following the selection, 48 men, given Nos. 99867–99914, and 52 women, given Nos. 34126–34177, are admitted to the camp. The other 790 people, including invalids and children, are killed in the gas chambers.

Five female prisoners, who get Nos. 34178–34182, are sent from Kattowitz.

1,000 Jewish men, women, and children arrive with Special Train Da 15, an RSHA transport from Berlin. Following the selection, 181 men, given Nos. 99915–10095, and 106 women, give Nos. 34183–34288, are admitted to the camp. The other 713 people are killed in the gas chambers.

The corpses of 33 prisoners are delivered to the morgue of the main camp; five of the dead are from Birkenau.

Ibid., p. 60.

FEBRUARY 5

The German criminal prisoner Bruno Graf (No. 3268) dies of starvation in a standing cell in the cellar of Block 11. He had been delivered to the bunker on January 4, 1943, because after being assigned to the Penal Company after an escape attempt he had stolen margarine.

Ibid.; APMO, D-AuI-3/1b, Bunker Register, p. 105; Brol et al., "Bunker Register of Block 11," p. 34.

The prisoners Michael Kavać (No. 86277), born in Huszt, Ukraine, on March 8, 1920, and Markus Coerant (No. 86712), born in Amsterdam on June 7, 1922, are captured while escaping and delivered to the bunker of Block 11.

APMO, D-AuI-3/1b, Bunker Register, p. 117.

A transport of Poles and Jews who had been evacuated from the Zamość region has arrived with Special Train Po 65, which departed from Zamość on February 3, 1943, at 11:00 A.M. Included are 1,000 people. Following the selection, 282 men, given Nos. 100096–100337, and 301 women, given Nos. 34289–34589, are admitted to the camp. The other 417 people are killed in the gas chambers.

Hilberg, *Special Trains*, pp. 209, 212; CA KC PZPR, 202/I, Documents of the Delegation of the Polish Government in Exile, p. 23.

Nos. 100378–100440 are given to 63 prisoners sent to the camp by the Sipo and SD for the Kraków District.

Nos. 100441–100497 are given to 57 male prisoners and Nos. 34590–34632 to 43 female prisoners sent in a group transport.

In the afternoon, the two Polish prisoners Zygmunt Gut (No. 91776), born on November 15, 1921, and Henryk Juszkiewicz (No. 91791), born on March 20, 1921, escape. They had been sent to the camp from Radom on January 22, 1943, by the Sipo and SD.

APMO, IZ-8/Gestapo Lodz/3/88/388; Mat.RO, vol. IV, p. 292.

Office D-I of the WVHA recommends to the concentration camp Commandants that they give civilian clothing from the stored possessions of the Polish and Russian prisoners to newly arrived prisoners.*

APMO, D-RF-9, WVHA, 8/1, Edict Collection.

Office D-II of the WVHA orders the Commandant to transfer the prisoner doctor Bronisław Zieliński (No. 88039) to the Herzogenbusch concentration camp, and to transfer the two prisoner doctors Jan Konieczny (No. 90336) and Antoni Kłopotowski (No. 91608) to Neuengamme.**

APMO, D-AuI-3a/40, Labor Deployment.

*The mass deportations of prisoners to the concentration camps lead to problems in supplying prisoners with camp clothing, the so-called striped suits.
**As can be inferred from a notation on the order, the prisoners are not transferred. Antoni Kłopotowski died on January 25, 1943, Jan Konieczny on February 23, 1943; their numbers are not mentioned in the Morgue Registry of the main camp, so it can be assumed that they died in Birkenau. Bronisław Zieliński dies on February 28, 1943, in Block 20 of the prisoners' infirmary; his number is noted under this date in the Morgue Registry of the main camp (APMO, D-AuI-3a/40, p. 155, Labor Deployment; D-AuI-5/2, Morgue Registry, p. 82).

The corpses of 42 prisoners are delivered to the morgue of the main camp.

APMO, D-AuI-5/2, Morgue Register, pp. 60ff.

FEBRUARY 6

Nos. 100498–100522 are given to 25 male prisoners and Nos. 34633–34727 to 95 female prisoners sent in a group transport. In this transport are 33 Yugoslavs from Maribor Prison, including Jožica Hodnikova, given No. 34634.

Jožica Veble-Hodnikova, *Preživela sem taborišče smrti* (I Survived the Death Camp), Liubliana, 1960, pp. 12, 18.

2,000 Jewish men, women, and children arrive in an RSHA transport from the ghetto in Białystok. Following the selection, 85 men, given Nos. 100523–100607, and 47 women, given Nos. 34728–34774, are admitted to the camp. The other 1,868 deportees are killed in the gas chambers.

The camp management orders a general roll call in the women's camp in Birkenau, to begin at 3:30 A.M. All female prisoners are herded onto the field in front of the women's camp, where they are detained on the open, snow-covered grounds, inadequately clad and without food, until 5:00 P.M. They must return to the camp at a run. At the camp gate stand female SS Supervisors and SS men, who goad the returning prisoners with cudgels. Those who are unable to run because of age, weakness, or disease are selected and led to Block 25, where they wait for shipment to the gas chambers. In women's Camp B-Ib, Block 25 is considered the waiting block for the route to the gas chambers.

This block is also called death block and has the same function as Block 7, the isolation station in Men's Camp B-Ib in Birkenau. As soon as the female prisoners are back in the camp, a squad made up of the stronger women is formed, which must gather up the corpses of the prisoners who met their death from being beaten by the female SS Supervisors and SS men on the grounds outside the camp. The corpses are brought to the court of Block 25; approximately 1,000 women have died during the roll call.

Committee of the Antifascist Resistance Fighters in the German Democratic Republic, *SS im Einsatz: Eine Dokumentation über die Verbrechen der SS* (The SS in Action: A Documentation of the Crimes of the SS), Berlin, 1957, pp. 274ff.; excerpts from the trail transcripts of the International Military Tribunal, Nuremberg, statement of Claude Vaillant-Couturier on Jan. 25, 1946, in Internationaler Militärgerichtshof Nürnberg, *Der Prozess gegen die Hauptkriegsverbrecher vor dem Internationalen Militärgerichtshof* (The Trial of the Principal War Criminals Before the International Military Tribunal), Vol. 6, Nuremberg, 1947–1949, pp. 232ff. (hereafter cited as IMG).

The corpses of 34 prisoners are delivered to the morgue of the main camp; six of the dead are from the Golleschau A.C., and five from the Buna A.C.

D-AuI-5/2, Morgue Register, pp. 61ff.

The Jewish prisoner Feliks Hofstaetter (No. 66104), born on August 27, 1908, in Duisburg, escapes from the camp.

APMO, IZ-8/Gestapo Lodz/2/88/58–61.

Four Polish prisoners, including Władyław Biskup (No. 74501) and Jan Agrestowski (No. 74545), are assigned to the Crematorium II Squad, which is being trained at Crematorium I in the main camp.

APMO, D-Mau-3a, Prisoner's Personal Information Card.

The Director of the Political Department, Grabner, signs a communication informing the SS Special Commando Zeppelin of the Sipo and SD in Auschwitz that the activists Semionov and Gachkov, who had been transferred to Auschwitz, have been executed. The

APMO, IZ-13/89, Various Documents of the Third Reich, p. 54 (original in BA Koblenz).

communication uses the camouflage designation, "lodged separately," which means that they have been killed.

FEBRUARY 7

The Guard Commander reports at 4:45 A.M. that in Birkenau two escaping prisoners have been shot and that one prisoner was successful in escaping.

APMO, Dpr.-Hd/12, p. 220.

The escaped prisoner is Stanisław Dobrogoszcz (No. 91908), born in Bendin on November 23, 1921.

APMO, IZ-8/Gestapo Lodz/3/88/ 395; Mat.RO, vol. IV, p. 292.

2,000 Polish Jews—men, women, and children—arrive in an RSHA transport from the ghetto in Białystok. Following the selection, 123 men, given Nos. 100608–100730, are admitted to the camp. The other 1,827 deportees are killed in the gas chambers.

Hilberg, *Theresienstadt 1941– 1945*, p. 211.

Nos. 34775–34778 are given to four female prisoners sent in a group transport.

The corpses of 22 prisoners are delivered to the morgue of the main camp.

APMO, D-AuI-5/2, Morgue Register, p. 62.

Scientists from the Weigl Institute in Lemberg (Lvov) and their family members are sent to the camp, including the doctor and microbiologist Dr. Ludwik Fleck, Dr. Jakób Seeman, Dr. Bernhard Umschweif, and Dr. Owsiej Abramowicz. They are housed with their wives and children in Block 20 of the prisoners' infirmary in the main camp, and must work in the newly formed SS Hygiene Institute, which for the time being is located in Block 10 of the main camp.

APMO Höss Trial, vol. 26, pp. 187ff.

The Director of the Central Construction Office informs the Commandant that he cannot complete the planned construction work deadline if he does not get an adequate number of skilled workers. Of the 500 masons and 300 carpenters requested for this day, who are necessary for the enlarging of the Birkenau camp,* not a single prisoner has been made available.

APMO, D-AuI-3a/280, Labor Deployment.

FEBRUARY 8

On the command of the SS Camp Doctor Vetter, the prisoner Dr. Władysław Fejkiel (No. 5647) makes a written report about his observations of a group of typhus fever patients who have been treated with the preparation "3582," made by I. G. Farben. He reports that 50 patients who had been treated with this preparation tolerated it very poorly. 15 patients, or 30 percent, had died, 2.6 percent of these after the conclusion of the treatment and 8 percent during the treatment. Six of the patients who did not survive died

APMO, photocopy of the document, and a statement by former prisoner Władysław Fejkiel that is attached to the document.

*The only masonry completed in Birkenau up to this point are the four crematoriums combined with gas chambers.

from weakness of the heart muscle, six from toxic consumption, two from brain complications, and one from a fever whose cause could not be determined.

Dr. Władysław Fejkiel reports that the preparation "3582," tried out on typhus fever patients by Dr. Vetter, has yielded no concrete therapeutic results.

2,000 Jewish men, women, and children arrive in an RSHA transport from the ghetto in Białystok. Following the selection, 75 men, given Nos. 100731–100805, and 95 women, given Nos. 34779–34873, are admitted to the camp. The other 1,830 deportees are killed in the gas chambers.

Hilberg, *Theresienstadt 1941–1945*, p. 211.

Nos. 100805–100836 go to 31 male prisoners and Nos. 34874–34892 to 19 female prisoners sent in a group transport.

The corpses of 59 prisoners are delivered to the morgue of the main camp; 30 of the dead are from Birkenau,* six from the Golleschau A.C.

APMO, D-AuI-5/2, Morgue Register, pp. 63ff.

Under the authority of an order of the Head of Branch D of the WVHA, Glücks, Commandant Höss again orders a quarantine of the camp as well as a ban on leave for the SS members of the garrison, because of the spread of the typhus fever epidemic, which is prevalent even outside the interest zone of Auschwitz. Höss advises the garrison that the special measures issued in the commandant's office orders of July 23 and September 24, 1942, are again in effect. The civilian workers employed by the construction office are threatened with being handed over to the special court if they fail to comply with the hygiene and health regulations.**

APMO, D-AuI-1, Garrison Order 2/43.

FEBRUARY 9

The Jewish prisoner Haske Szwarzhas (No. 83414), as well as Stanisław Skaraczyński (No. 88230) and Jósef Sott (No. 88233) are put in the bunker of Block 11 on suspicion of attempting an escape. The three prisoners are shot the same day at the execution wall in the courtyard of Block 11. By order of the Camp Commandant, the prisoners who were captured while escaping and then brought to the bunker, Jan Poloczek (No. 1065), Michael Kavač (No. 86227), Markus Coerant (No. 86712), and the Jewish prisoner Syskin Kempiński (No. 60493) are also shot on this day.

APMO, D-AuI-3/1b Bunker Register, pp. 108, 115, 117ff.

---

*As is clear from the prisoners' numbers, 22 of the 30 corpses were of prisoners who arrived in transport from the Theresienstadt ghetto on January 21, 1943. The numbers are 91361, 91362, 91369, 91370, 91373, 91382, 91385, 91389, 91397, 91478, 91479, 91488, 91492, 91498, 91501, 91502, 91504, 91507, 91511, 91516, 91518, and 91530.

**The mass killing of prisoners infected with typhus as well as the delousings and disinfections that are carried out in the prisoners' quarters, in which the sanitary and hygienic conditions remain unchanged, do not have the success expected by the SS and cannot prevent a further spread of the epidemic. Although SS personnel and members of their families have been vaccinated against typhus and take the recommended hygienic precautions, there are cases of typhus even among them, and they spread the disease outside the camp.

Two female prisoners sent from Oppeln are given Nos. 34893–34894.

Three prisoners sent in a group transport receive Nos. 100837–100839.

Nos. 100840–100850 are given to 11 prisoners transferred from Stutthof concentration camp.

No. 100851 is given to a prisoner sent from Kattowitz.

The corpses of 42 prisoners are delivered to the morgue of the main camp; seven of the dead are from the Buna A.C. and four from Birkenau.

APMO, D-AuI-5/2, Morgue Register, pp. 64ff.

FEBRUARY 10

The Jewish prisoner Feliks Hofstaetter (No. 66104), who had fled from the camp the previous day, is captured, brought back to Auschwitz, and delivered to the bunker of Block 11. He dies in the bunker the same day.

APMO, D-AuI-3/1b, Bunker Register, p. 118; IZ-8/Gestapo Lodz/2/88/61.

Nos. 34104–34125 are given to 22 female reeducation prisoners whose reason for arrest is changed and who remain incarcerated as political prisoners.

Clad as a civilian worker, the political prisoner Kazimierz Halon (No. 20687), who was registered in the camp under the name of Kazimierz Wrona, escapes from the camp in the afternoon. The escape is coordinated with the underground P.P.S. group in Brzeszcze, which is led by Edward Hałoń, who works in the vicinity of the camp and whose alias is "Boruta." It leads to an intensification of contacts between the P.P.S. group in Brzeszcze and the conspiratorial resistance group in the camp.

APMO, D-AuI-1, Telegrams, p. 36; IZ-8/Gestapo Lodz/3/88/397; Mat.RO, vol. IV, p. 292; Barbara Jarosz, "Widerstandsbewegung im Lager und in der Umgebung" (Resistance Movement in the Camp and Its Environs), in Józef Buszko, Danuta Czech, Tadeusz Iwaszko, Franciszo Piper, Barbara Jarosz, Andrzej Strzelecki, and Kazimierz Smolén, eds., *Auschwitz: Geschichte und Wirklichkeit des Vernichtungslagers* (Auschwitz: History and Reality of the Extermination Camp), Reinbek/Hamburg, 1980, pp. 155–156.

Nos. 34895–34898 are given to four female prisoners sent in a group transport.

The head of Office D-II in the WVHA, SS Lieutenant Colonel Maurer, comes to Auschwitz because the number of prisoners in the Buna auxiliary camp has decreased significantly. During a conference with the management of the Buna plant, he promises to increase the number of prisoners in the Buna A.C. to 4,000, possibly to 4,500. Owing to the small number of SS Guards available, he recommends to the management of the Buna plant that the prisoners be used only within the factory grounds.

APMO, Maurer Trial, vol. 7, p. 63.

Troubled about the imminent deadline for completion of construction work on Crematorium III, the Central Construction Office states in a letter to the Department of Labor Deployment that, of the 500 masons requested for the squad assigned to construction of Crematorium II, only 30 have been made available.

APMO, D-AuI-3a, Folder 17, pp. 250–256.

On the ramp, prisoners collect the baggage left by "new accessions" to take it to the personal effects warehouse nicknamed "Canada II."

The corpses of 33 prisoners are delivered to the morgue of the main camp; eight of the dead are from Birkenau, seven from the Buna A.C.

APMO, D-AuI-5/2, Morgue Register, p. 65.

The Commandant's Office has the first floor of the quarantine block 2a in the main camp emptied, and makes it temporarily available to the Myslowitz Investigative Detention Prison, where a typhus epidemic has broken out.

APMO, Depositions, vol. 13, p. 81, Account of Former Prisoner Mieczysław Piłat.

FEBRUARY 11

1,184 Jews, 476 men and boys and 708 women and girls, from Westerbork arrive in an RSHA transport with a shipment from Holland. Following the selection, 113 men, assigned Nos. 100852–100964, and 66 women, assigned Nos. 34899–34964, are admitted to the camp. The other 1,005 people are killed in the gas chambers.

Nos. 100965–100969 are assigned to five employees of the Weigl Institute of Lemberg: Owsiej Abramowicz (No. 100965), Ryszard Fleck (No. 100966), Ludwig Fleck (No. 100967), Jakob Seeman (No. 100968), and Bernard Umschweif (No. 100969), who arrived on February 7.

APMO, Dpr.-Hd/26, pp. 197ff.

The wives of the scientists from the Weigl Institute of Lemberg, who had likewise been brought with their children to Auschwitz, receive Nos. 34965–34967: Anna Seeman is No. 34965, Natalia Umschweif is No. 34966, and Ernestyna Fleck is No. 34967.

No. 34968 is given to a female prisoner sent from Münster on February 7.

Nos. 100970–101031 are given to 62 prisoners sent to the camp by the Sipo and SD for the Kraków District.

Nos. 101032–101042 are given to 11 prisoners sent from Kattowitz.

1,000 Jewish men, women, and children from the Drancy camp arrive in the forty-sixth RSHA transport from France. Following the selection, 77 men, given Nos. 101043–101119, and 91 women, given Nos. 34969–35059, are admitted to the camp. The other 832 deportees are killed in the gas chambers.

Nos. 35060–35066 are given to seven female prisoners sent to the camp by the Sipo and SD for the Kraków District.

The corpses of 21 prisoners are delivered to the morgue of the main camp, among them that of the Russian prisoner of war No. RKG-10400.

APMO, D-AuI-5/2, Morgue Register, p. 66.

Next to No. 72627 it is noted in the Morgue Register that this corpse was delivered from Kobior. Prisoners of Auschwitz work there in a forest labor squad that was requested by the head forestry office in Pless. The squad is housed in Kobior and, as an auxiliary camp, is under the supervision of Auschwitz.

FEBRUARY 12

The Central Construction Office requests the WVHA to intervene with the firm of J. A. Topf and Sons, as the firm is not meeting the delivery deadline of equipment for the crematoriums, and is causing significant difficulties for the Central Construction Office.

APMO, D-Z Bau/15, Inventory No. 29764.

Several transports of male and female prisoners are delivered— Communists and Socialists from Bendsburg, Bielsko, Dombrowa, Sosnowitz, Saybusch, and other Silesian towns. They are housed in the upper story of Block 2a, which has been made available to the Myslowitz Investigative Detention Prison.*

APMO, Depositions, Accounts of Former Prisoners Mieczysław Piłat, Stanisław Koprowski, and Wanda Koprowski; CA KC PZPR, 202/III-146, Documents of the Polish Government in Exile, pp. 49–52.

*The room in which approximately 200 prisoners are housed, facing the so-called Birkenallee (Birch avenue), is intended for the incarcerated women. The room facing the camp street is intended for the male prisoners; approximately 600 prisoners are housed there. The floor in the rooms is covered with a thin layer of straw. Day and night, the prisoners lie there in three rows along the wall. In the middle of the room, a path is kept free from the stoves to the exit, where an SS man armed with a carbine walks back and forth. The prisoners are permitted neither to speak with one another nor to move. They must lie on their side—the first and the third row on the right side, the second and the middle row on the left side. Every two hours the SS man gives the command to change sides. Every day 30 to 40 prisoners are brought to the Political Department, where they are interrogated by Gestapo officials from the appropriate offices, for example, from Sosnowitz or Bielsko, etc. For weeks they are interrogated, tortured, and tormented, and thus forced to make statements. Predominant among the prisoners are miners from the Upper Silesian region who have

The Polish prisoners Zygmunt Radosz (No. 91853), born on April 26, 1926, Henryk Warzecha (No. 91883), born on February 12, 1926, and Mieczysław Michałowski (No. 92154), born on May 5, 1925, all three of whom were born in Tschenstocha (Częstochowa), escape from the camp.

APMO, D-AuI-1/38, Telegrams; IZ-8/Gestapo Lodz/3/88/399; Mat.RO, vol. IV, p. 292.

Władysław Strykacz (No. 93311), Walenty Parczyński (No. 96847), the Jewish prisoner Chaim Kac (No. 89199), Józef Kocik (No. 37282), and Józef Bąk (No. 90142) are captured while escaping and delivered to the bunkers of Block 11. With the exception of Józef Bąk, all of them are shot the following day.

APMO, D-AuI-3/1b, Bunker Register, p. 120.

Nos. 101120–101725 are given to 606 prisoners sent from Lublin by the Sipo and SD.

The Polish prisoner Leopold Malarz (No. 87478) escapes from the camp.

APMO, IZ-8/Gestapo Lodz 2/88/127; Mat.RO, vol. IV, p. 292.

The numbers of 39 dead prisoners are entered in the Morgue Registry of the main camp.

APMO, D-AuI-5/2 Morgue Register, pp. 66ff.

Nos. 101726–101777 are given to 46 male prisoners and Nos. 35204–35250 to 47 female prisoners sent in a group transport.

Nos. 101772–102106 are given to 355 prisoners sent from Prague.

FEBRUARY 13

16 prisoners are shot at the execution wall in the courtyard of Block 11. They had been put in the bunkers of Block 11 on February 3, 10, 11, and 12 on the orders of the Political Department and the Camp Commander because of contacts with the civilian population, suspicion of preparing an escape, or attempted escape. The prisoners are Marian Włodek (No. 26585), Tadeusz Hrehorowicz (No. 31054), Władysław Horodelski (No. 14213), Witold Frydrychowicz (No. 63668), Bolesław Poncyliusz (No. 174), Jan Cichoń (No. 90184), Stanisław Kmiecik (No. 90342), Bolesław Zając (No. 90562), Józef Sikora (No. 87463), Stefan Noga (No. 90409), Kazimierz Rostanowski (No. 91857), Antoni Augustyniak (No. 97253), Władysław Strykacz (No. 95311), Walenty Parzyński (No. 96847), and Józef Kocik (No. 37282), as well as the Polish Jew Chaim Kac (No. 89199).

APMO, D-AuI-3/1b, Bunker Register, pp. 116, 119ff.; Höss Trial, vol. 4, pp. 37ff.

Nos. 102107–102138 are given to 32 male prisoners and Nos. 35251–35289 to 39 female prisoners sent in a group transport.

998 Jewish men, women, and children arrive from Drancy in the forty-seventh RSHA transport from France. Following the selection,

---

been arrested because of their political convictions, membership in secret organizations, and illegal possession of weapons. Some of them are shot after conclusion of the interrogations, others are imprisoned in Auschwitz. Only then are these prisoners entered in the camp registers as inmates.

143 men, given Nos. 102139–102881, and 53 women, given Nos. 35290–35342, are admitted to the camp. The other 802 people are killed in the gas chambers.

The number of prisoners ill with typhus increases. The corpses of 70 prisoners are delivered to the morgue of the main camp: 62 of the dead come from the section for infectious diseases in Block 20, and one from the Golleschau A.C. The corpse of the prisoner No. 72504 has been brought from the Kobior camp.

APMO, D-AuI-5/2, Morgue Register, pp. 67–69.

FEBRUARY 14

Because of the typhus epidemic, in Garrison Order No. 3 Höss instructs the SS members to maintain an appropriate distance from the prisoners and the prison squads in order to protect themselves from the danger of contagion.

APMO, D-AuI, Garrison Order 3/43.

FEBRUARY 15

Nos. 102282–102349 are given to 68 prisoners sent in a group transport. With this transport Polish prisoner Józef Gawel, born in Kurdwanowo on July 4, 1923, arrives in the camp for the third time and is assigned No. 102318. Probably during registration in the Political Department it is determined that on July 23, 1941, Józef Gawel had already been sent as a reeducation prisoner from Bielsko to Auschwitz by the Kattowitz Gestapo and had been given No. 18319. He must have escaped from the camp before September 15, 1941, as his name is mentioned as an escapee in the bulletin of the Gestapo of Upper Silesia on September 15, 1941. On February 2, 1943, he had been brought for the second time to Auschwitz with a transport from Kattowitz, and at that time had gotten No. 99088. Presumably he escaped again. Following his arrest, he is sent for the third time in a group transport on February 15, 1943. Following his identification, No. 102318 is canceled, and he gets the old No. 99088 and is locked in the bunker of Block 11.

APMO, D-AuI-1/2, p. 9, Bulletin of Sept. 15, 1941; D-AuI-3/1b, Bunker Register, p. 122.

Nos. 35343–35356 are given to 14 female prisoners sent in a group transport.

1,000 Jewish men, women, and children arrive from Drancy in an RSHA transport from France. Following the selection, 144 men, given Nos. 102318 and 102350–102492, and 167 women, given Nos. 35357–35523, are admitted to the camp. The other 689 people are killed in the gas chambers.

The corpses of 55 prisoners are delivered to the morgue of the main camp.

APMO, D-AuI-5/2, Morgue Register, pp. 69ff.

FEBRUARY 16

101 prisoners sent from Augsburg receive Nos. 35524–35624.

Nos. 102493–102525 are assigned to 33 male prisoners and Nos. 35625–35635 to 11 female prisoners sent from Kattowitz.

Nos. 102526–103504 are given to 979 male prisoners and Nos. 35636–35938 to 303 female prisoners. The Sipo and SD for the Kraków District has sent 1,027 prisoners from the prison in Tarnów and 252 from the Montelupich Prison in Kraków to Auschwitz.

12 prisoners who are suspected of preparing an escape are delivered to the bunker of Block 11.

APMO, D-AuI-3/1b, Bunker Register, pp. 122–124.

The corpses of 32 prisoners are delivered to the morgue of the main camp; 10 of the dead are from Birkenau and six from the Buna A.C.

APMO, D-AuI-5/2, Morgue Register, p. 71.

FEBRUARY 17

Nos. 103505–103514 are given to 10 male prisoners and Nos. 35939–35972 to 34 female prisoners sent in a group transport.

Two Polish prisoners, Władysław Szaliński (No. 91875), born in Kielce on June 13, 1919, and Leon Mróz, born in Boguchwała on August 22, 1904, who was sent to Auschwitz by the Sipo and SD for Kraków on January 28, 1943, escape from the camp.

APMO, D-AuI-1, pp. 40, 42, Telegrams; IZ-8/Gestapo Lodz/3/88/401–404.

The SS Lieutenant General and Police General Schmauser visits Auschwitz, arriving at the camp with his escort at 8:15 P.M.

APMO, Höss Trial, vol. 12, p. 220.

A female prisoner delivered from Kattowitz receives No. 36055.

The corpses of 36 prisoners are delivered to the morgue of the main camp; 17 of the dead are from Birkenau.

APMO, D-AuI-5/2, Morgue Register, pp. 71ff.

FEBRUARY 18

The Commandant's Office is ordered by the WVHA to submit a report on the deployment as labor of 5,000 Jews transferred from Theresienstadt to Auschwitz on January 20, 23, and 26, 1943.*

APMO, Höss Trial, vol. 12, p. 162, Exhibit 106.

In keeping with an earlier directive of Branch D of the WVHA, the Commandant's Office transfers 27 prisoners who are watchmakers by trade to Sachsenhausen.

APMO, D-AuI-3a/60, 66, Labor Deployment.

The Commandant's Office receives a directive from the head of Office D-II, Maurer, to assign 300 additional prisoners to the Jawischowitz coal mine. The directive states that it appears from a list of February 1 that there are still 77 prisoners in Auschwitz who are miners by trade and have not yet been deployed. These should be used in the Jawischowitz mine. At the same time, Maurer tells

APMO, D-AuI-3a/58, Labor Deployment.

*An initial request for the report is issued by telegram by WVHA on January 26, 1943.

the Commandant's Offices of Flossenbürg, Gross-Rosen, and Niederhagen to transfer the miners incarcerated there to Auschwitz so they can be used in Jawischowitz. Maurer directs the Commandant's Office of Auschwitz to reach the specified quota of 300 miners, if necessary through the commitment of unskilled workers.

1,108 Jews, 515 men and boys and 593 women and girls, arrive from Westerbork in an RSHA transport from Holland. Following the selection, 200 men, given Nos. 103515–103714, and 61 women, given Nos. 35973–36033, are admitted to the camp. The other 847 people are killed in the gas chambers.

1,000 Jews are deported from a labor camp in Chrzanów to Auschwitz. All the deportees are killed in the gas chambers.

Gilbert, *Final Solution*, p. 149, Map 193.

Nos. 36034–36053 are given to 20 female prisoners sent in a group transport. Also in this shipment is female prisoner No. 19370, probably sent back to Auschwitz from Ravensbrück.

SS Private Popp is commended by Commandant Höss because he has prevented an escape; SS Sergeant Theofil Dietrich is commended because he found a large sum of money and turned it in.

APMO, D-AuI-1/109, Commandant's Office Order 5/43.

FEBRUARY 19

14 prisoners who had been delivered to the bunker of Block 11 on February 16 are shot at the execution wall in the court of Block 11. They are Józef Gaweł (No. 99088), the Jew Maks Rudolf Sulzer (No. 85019), the Jew Hirsch Balzam (No. 63534), Józef Królikowski (No. 82647), the Jew Józef Lewin (No. 90904), Józef Mierga (No. 95268), Władysław Szczerba (No. 95312), Franciszek Nowacki (No. 95978), Hieronim Tschedel (No. 97610), Tadeusz Indrak (No. 29695), Jan Fiedko (No. 91721), Asafan Czerwieniak (No. 95236), Władysław Olszewski (No. 95300), and Józef Rywotycki (No. 96150).

APMO, D-AuI-3/1b, Bunker Register, pp. 122–124.

A female prisoner delivered from Prague receives No. 36054.

Nos. 103715–103766 are given to 52 male prisoners and Nos. 36056–36076 to 21 female prisoners sent in a group transport.

The corpses of 41 prisoners are delivered to the morgue of the main camp; 18 are from the Budy camp and three are from the Golleschau camp.

APMO, D-AuI-5/2, Morgue Register, pp. 73ff.

Nos. 103767–103795 are given to 29 male prisoners and Nos. 36067–36108 to 32 female prisoners sent in a group transport.

FEBRUARY 20

Polish prisoner Józef Lech, born in Kraków on March 19, 1910, escapes. He is killed on March 2, 1943, by gendarmes in the village of Chocznia.

APMO, IZ-10/Kripo Sieradz/2a/29, 47.

Prisoners Henryk Wrba (No. 80744) and Franciszek Różyczka (No. 84576) are captured while escaping and delivered to the bunkers of Block 11. Following a selection they are shot on March 3, 1943.

APMO, D-AuI-3/1b, Bunker Register, p. 127.

The Director of Labor Deployment in Auschwitz, SS First Lieutenant Schwarz, sends a report to Office D-II of Branch D of the WVHA about the Jews transferred from Theresienstadt. He explains that a total of 5,022 people had arrived with the transports of January 21, 24, and 27, of whom 930, 614 men and 316 women, had been added to the labor force. However, 4,092 people, including 1,422 men and 2,670 women and children, had been "lodged separately"* because of their extreme frailty. He notes that at the end of the quarantine period, on February 15, 1943,** the able-bodied prisoners had been assigned to the Construction Office for use as labor. The men were between 18 and 40 years of age, the women between 18 and 35 years of age.

APMO, D-AuI-3a/65, Labor Deployment.

Dr. Bernard Umschweif's son, Karol, born on September 4, 1937, is assigned No. 10376, and Dr. Jakób Seeman's son, Bronek, born on December 12, 1932, receives the number 103797. Both boys were sent to Auschwitz with their parents from Lemberg on February 7, 1943.

APMO, D-AuII-5/2, Prisoners' Infirmary Register in the Rajsko A.C.

1,000 Jewish men, women, and children arrive from Germany in an RSHA transport from Berlin. After the selection, 140 men, given Nos. 103798–103937, and 85 women, given Nos. 36109–36193, are admitted to the camp. The other 775 people are killed in the gas chambers.

Two female prisoners sent from Kattowitz receive Nos. 36194–36195.

The corpses of 31 prisoners are delivered to the morgue of the main camp.

APMO, D-AuI-5/2, Morgue Register, p. 74.

FEBRUARY 21

The prisoner Stanisław Haruk (No. 92025), born in Krzywowola on December 12, 1915, is captured while escaping from Birkenau and is put in the bunker of Block 11. After a selection in the bunker he is shot on March 3, 1943.

APMO, D-AuI-3/1b, Bunker Register, p. 128.

The Commandant's Office of Auschwitz is informed by the WVHA that on February 18 it has been ordered to supply Auschwitz with 93 prisoners who are miners by trade: 32 from Flossenbürg; 13 from Gross-Rosen; 28 from Niederhagen; and 20 from Ravens-

APMO, D-AuI-3a/62, Labor Deployment.

---

*One of the camouflage terms used by the SS for killing
**Schwarz does not mention how many male or female prisoners survive the quarantine. On the basis of the extant documents—which are not complete—in the Auschwitz Memorial, the author infers that from the transports mentioned a total of 42 men had died by February 15, 1943. It is not known how many women lost their lives within this period.

brück. Immediately after their arrival the prisoners should be brought to the Jawischowitz camp.

FEBRUARY 22

Two prisoners from Birkenau are delivered to the bunker of Block 11: a Pole, Jan Polański (No. 96109) and a Polish Jew, Rudolf Kaufteil (No. 90063). Both are shot on March 3, 1943, following a selection in the bunkers.

APMO, D-AuI-3/1b, Bunker Register, p. 128.

Nos. 103938–103950 and 103952–103961 are given to 23 male prisoners and Nos. 36196–36219 to 24 female prisoners sent in a group transport.

In connection with the imminent start-up of operations of Crematorium II in Birkenau, the Commandant's Office requests Office D-I of the WVHA to transfer from another concentration camp one prisoner who can be used as Capo of a labor squad for this crematorium.

APMO, D-AuI-3a/86, Labor Deployment.

A prisoner delivered from Białystok receives No. 10391.

A prisoner delivered from Kattowitz on February 20, 1943, receives No. 103962.

The Polish prisoner Stanisław Szymkowiak (No. 93254), born on May 3, 1908, escapes from the camp.

APMO, IZ-10/Gestapo Sieradz/2a/88/32; Mat.RO, vol. IV, p. 292.

Director of Labor Deployment Schwarz notifies Office D-II of the WVHA that because of the camp quarantine that was ordered, it is not possible to transfer to the Jawischowitz auxiliary camp the prisoners who are to be used there as miners.

APMO, D-AuI-3a/69, Labor Deployment.

In the evening, the prisoner Andreas Haszpurenko (No. 88356), born on June 20, 1923, escapes.

APMO, D-AuI-1/27/7, Telegrams; IZ-8/Gestapo Lodz/3/88/405; Mat.RO, vol. IV, p. 292.

The Polish prisoner Zofia Biedowa, née Baranowska (No. 30583), who was born in Warsaw on January 11, 1903, escapes from Squad 117 that is deployed in Budy. The escape is not discovered until the squad has returned from work to Birkenau. When the camp management of the women's camp checks the number and finally the names of the prisoners, irregularities are found. Therefore, general roll calls are ordered, and it is determined that in the future not only the Jewish but also the non-Jewish female prisoners must have their number tattooed on the lower left arm.

APMO, IZ-8/Gestapo Lodz/3/88/407; Depositions, vol. 8, p. 1139, Account of Former Prisoner Maria Elżbieta Jezierska.

The Commandant's Office decides that in the future not only the Jewish prisoners but all men and women assigned to the camp as prisoners should get the number tattooed on the lower left arm so they can be more easily identified. Tattooing of Jewish prisoners had already been started in 1942. Only German prisoners from the

Reich and ethnic Germans as well as reeducation prisoners and police prisoners are exempt from tattooing.

The corpses of 103 prisoners are delivered to the morgue of the main camp; 83 of the dead are from the infections department of the prisoner infirmary, Block 20; 10 were delivered from Birkenau; and one comes from the Golleschau A.C.

APMO, D-AuI-5/2, Morgue Register, pp. 75–77.

FEBRUARY 23

Nos. 103963–103974 are given to 12 prisoners sent from Kattowitz.

Nos. 103975–104026 are given to 52 prisoners sent to the camp by the Sipo and SD for the Kraków District.

Approximately 1,000 Jewish men, women, and children from the German Reich arrive with an RSHA shipment from Breslau. After the selection, six men, given Nos. 104027–104032, are admitted to the camp. The other approximately 994 deported persons are killed in the gas chambers.

Nos. 36220–36250 are given to 31 female prisoners sent in a group transport.

39 prisoners 13 to 17 years of age are brought from Birkenau to the main camp and housed there in Block 20, in a room prepared for them in the prisoners' infirmary. The boys are moved to the main camp on the pretext that they should participate in a nursing course. In the evening of this day they are killed with phenol injections. The injections are administered by SS Corporal Scherpe, the Second Medical Officer. The boys arrived with their parents on December 13 and 16 and February 5, 1943, in transports used to deport to Auschwitz Poles who had been evacuated from the Zamosc region. The boys killed with phenol injections had the following numbers: 82560, 82587, 82597, 82636, 82662, 82678, 82745, 82771, 82793, 82811, 82842, 82843, 84454, 84457, 84850, 100096, 100124, 100159, 100162, 100166, 100173, 100181, 100182, 100217, 100219, 100221, 100228, 100231, 100244, 100273, 100277, 100279, 100281, 100285, 100291, 100310, 100321, 100338, and 100343.

APMO, D-AuI-5/2, Morgue Register, pp. 77ff; Mat.RO, vol. V, p. 319; vol. VI, p. 49; vol. VII, p. 468; Höss Trial, vol. 1, p. 172; vol. 4, p. 177; vol. 5, p. 82; vol. 7, p. 155; vol. 8, p. 111, Eyewitness Testimony of Former Prisoner of Auschwitz-Birkenau.

Two Polish Jews from the Birkenau camp, Syzmon Sak (No. 92844), born in Grodno on August 16, 1916, and Honia Karelic (No. 94297), born in Wołkowysk on April 12, 1918, are suspected of preparing an escape; therefore, they are locked in the bunker of Block 11. Probably they had been assigned to the Special Squad following their arrival at Birkenau. Their corpses are delivered to the morgue; presumably they died in the bunker from the consequences of torture during their interrogation in the Political Department. Szymon Sak dies on February 24, 1943, Honia Karelic on February 26, 1943.

APMO, D-AuI-3/1b, Bunker Register, p. 128; D-AuI-5/2, Morgue Register, pp. 78, 80.

Alfred Perzyk (No. 92329), born on March 14, 1926, is captured while escaping and locked in the bunker of Block 11. Following a selection carried out in the bunkers, he is shot on March 3, 1943.

APMO, D-AuI-3/1b, Bunker Register, p. 129.

In accordance with a directive of the Political Department, the political prisoner Tomasz Czech, born on September 15, 1910, who had arrived the previous day with a group transport and had received No. 103940, is delivered to the bunker of Block 11. Following a selection in the bunkers, he is shot on March 3, 1943.

Ibid.

FEBRUARY 24

The corpses of 43 prisoners are delivered to the morgue of the main camp; seven of the dead are from Birkenau and three from the Buna A.C.

APMO, D-AuI-5/2, Morgue Register, pp. 78ff.

FEBRUARY 25

The Director of Labor Deployment, Schwarz, informs the Commandant's Offices of Ravensbrück and Flossenbürg that the transferred miners should be handed over at the Auschwitz train station, from where they will be taken by trucks to the auxiliary camp near the Jawischowitz mine.

APMO, D-AuI-3a/75, 73, Labor Deployment.

1,101 Jews, 413 men and boys and 688 women and girls, from the Westerbork camp arrive with an RSHA transport from Holland. Following the selection, 57 men, given Nos. 104033–104089, and 30 women, given Nos. 36251–36280, are admitted to the camp. The other 1,014 people are killed in the gas chambers.

SS Garrison Doctor Wirths receives from the head of Office D-III in the WVHA, Dr. Lolling, who is responsible for health and camp hygiene, a directive to announce the end of the quarantine period of the 6,000 Polish prisoners in Auschwitz, who should be moved to concentration camps in the interior of the Reich.*

Ibid.

Nos. 104090–104124 are given to 35 male prisoners and Nos. 36281–36306 to 26 female prisoners sent in a group transport.

Nos. 36308–36311 are given to four female prisoners sent in a group transport.

In Block 2a, which has been made available to the Myslowitz Investigative Detention Prison, two police prisoners die from the effects of torture.

APMO, D-AuI-5/2, Morgue Register, p. 79, Item 15; p. 80, line 29.

The corpses of 37 prisoners are delivered to the morgue of the main camp; two of the dead are from the Jawischowitz auxiliary camp;

Ibid.

*From this directive it appears that the WVHA is repeating its order of October 5, 1942, to move Polish and Ukrainian prisoners into concentration camps in the interior of the Reich in exchange for Jewish prisoners transferred from these concentration camps to Auschwitz.

Camp street in Birkenau.

among the dead are the corpses of the two police prisoners from Block 2a.

FEBRUARY 26

Nos. 104125–104152 are given to 28 prisoners, miners by trade, who were transferred from the Niederhagen concentration camp and are to be used for labor in the Jawischowitz coal mine; they are to be moved there the following day.

APMO, D-AuI-3a/72, 82, Labor Deployment.

Nos. 104153–104172 are given to 20 prisoners sent to the camp by the Sipo and SD for the Kraków District.

APMO, D-AuI-3a/79, Labor Deployment, confirmation of admission of 12 prisoners transferred from Gross-Rosen.

Nos. 104173–104188 and 104190–104235 are given to 62 prisoners sent in a group transport, including 12 miners transferred from Gross-Rosen. They are registered as prisoners in Auschwitz.

Nos. 104236–104322 are given to 87 prisoners sent from Prague.

43 female prisoners sent in a group transport receive Nos. 36312–36354.

Three prisoners sent from Kattowitz receive Nos. 104323–104325.

On the basis of the RSHA decree of January 29, 1943, the first shipment of Gypsies, several men, women, and children, from Germany is sent to Auschwitz. They are housed in the not yet completed

APMO, D-AuII-3/1/1, Register of Male Gypsies; D-AuII-3/2/1, Register of Female Gypsies.

camp in Section B-IIe of Birkenau, which gets the name Gypsy Family Camp B-IIe.*

The political prisoner Andrzej Górny (No. 85498), born in Fischersdorf on October 29, 1912, is delivered to the bunker of Block 11 on suspicion of planning an escape. Following a selection in the bunkers of Block 11, he is shot on March 3, 1943.

APMO, D-AuI-3/1b, Bunker Register, p. 130.

The WVHA notifies the Commandants of the concentration camps that civilian clothing, with appropriate identification badges, should be given only to prisoners used for labor within the camp or in closed rooms. In contrast, the striped prison clothing should be issued to prisoners who work in the outside squads (Aussenkommandos).

APMO, Höss Trial, vol. 35, pp. 112–113 (IMG, NO-1530).

The corpses of 39 prisoners are delivered to the morgue of the main camp; 20 of the dead are from Birkenau.

APMO, D-AuI-5/2, Morgue Register, pp. 80ff.

FEBRUARY 27

Nos. 36355–36408 are given to 54 female prisoners and Nos. 104326–104373 to 48 male prisoners sent in a group transport.

913 Jewish men, women, and children arrive with an RSHA transport from Berlin. Following the selection, 156 men, given Nos. 104374–104529, and 106 women, given Nos. 36409–36514, are admitted to the camp. The other 651 deportees are killed in the gas chambers.

Gilbert, *Final Solution*, p. 148, Map 192.

In the evening, seven Polish prisoners of a labor squad used in the SS kitchen escape from the camp. Involved are Kazimierz Albin (No. 118), Tadeusz Klus (No. 416), Adam Klus (No. 419), Bronisław Staszkiewicz (No. 1225), Franciszek Roman (No. 5770), Włodzimierz Turczyniak (No. 5829), and Roman Lechner (No. 3505).

APMO, D-AuI-1/1, Telegrams, Nos. 29, 30, 31; IZ-8/Gestapo Lodz/3/88/409–414; Mat.RO, vol. IV, p. 292; Kraków Auschwitz Trial, vol. 5, p. 66.

*Separate registers in which the prisoners in the Gypsy Family Camp are listed are kept for men and women. They contain a complete record of the men, who were registered with Nos. 1–10097, and for the women, who were registered with Nos. 1–10849. The register of the male Gypsies contains the following headings: number, reason for arrest—here the code "Z" is used (Zigeuner, i.e., Gypsy)—nationality, last name, first name, date of birth, place of birth, date of admission to the camp, and comments. The register for the female Gypsies has the headings number, reason for arrest (again, "Z" is noted), nationality, last name, first name, date of birth, profession, date of admission to camp, address (not filled out), and comments. Under "comments" is noted beside several names the day of transfer to a different camp or the date of death or a date with a cross, or even a date with the additional "SB" for Sonderbehandlung, meaning "special treatment," i.e., killing. In July 1944, these registers are wrapped in pieces of men's clothing and concealed in a zinc bucket with a wooden cover that has been made to fit it. When the Polish prisoners Tadeusz Joachimowki, who is record keeper in the Gypsy camp from February 1944 on, Ireneusz Pietrzyk, and Henryk Porębski find out that several thousand Gypsies still alive in the Gypsy camp are supposed to be liquidated, they bury this bucket containing the registers within the Gypsy camp near the fence. On January 13, 1949, the bucket is dug up. The books are extremely wet, so parts of the first pages are severely damaged and illegible. It is therefore impossible to determine how many Gypsies had been in each of the first transports.

In connection with the escape of the seven prisoners, 18 prisoners from the SS kitchen labor squad are delivered to the bunkers of Block 11. They are interrogated in the Political Department, and then in the course of the month released from the bunker to the camp.

APMO, D-AuI-3/1b, Bunker Register, pp. 130–132.

The prisoner Józef Pamrow (No. 22858), who escaped from the camp on June 10, 1942, is captured and, in a renewed escape attempt, is captured and shot.

APMO, IZ-8/Gestapo Lodz/3a/ 88/589.

The Polish prisoner Walenty Wiktorowicz (No. 68960) is put in the bunker of Block 11 on suspicion of planning an escape from the camp. Following a selection in the bunker of Block 11, he is shot on March 3, 1943.

APMO, D-AuI-3/1b, Bunker Register, p. 130.

The corpses of 33 prisoners are delivered to the morgue of the main camp; six of the dead are from Birkenau, one from the Jawischowitz A.C., and one from the Kobior A.C.

APMO, D-AuI-5/2, Morgue Register, pp. 81ff.

FEBRUARY 28

On this Sunday, a general roll call is ordered in the women's camp in Birkenau. Included in this roll call is the prisoners' infirmary; the sick women remain on their plank-beds, but the female prisoner doctors and orderlies as well as the assistants must line up for the roll call. The women are lined up in numerical order; then the identity of each prisoner is checked. The roll call lasts the entire day. At the same time a selection takes place at which approximately 1,000 Jewish women are selected. The selected prisoners are brought to Block 25 and wait there until they are brought to the gas chambers.

APMO, Höss Trial, vol. 3, p. 110.

The corpses of 28 prisoners are delivered to the morgue of the main camp.

APMO, D-AuI-5/2, Morgue Register, p. 82.

FEBRUARY 1–28

3,049 female prisoners have died in the women's camp in Birkenau; 1,690 of them were selected and subsequently killed in the gas chambers. Not included in the number are the female Jews who were brought from the unloading ramp directly to the gas chambers.

APMO, Mat.RO, vol. VII, p. 485.

MARCH 1

The Auschwitz II Registry Office ceases issuing death certificates for Jewish prisoners who die in the camp.

Škodowa, *Three Years*, p. 119.

Roll Call Leader Palitzsch brings 80 prisoners 13 to 17 years of age from Birkenau to the main camp. The boys are housed in a room prepared for them in the prisoners' infirmary, Block 20. They are Polish and Jewish youths who, with their families, were sent in transports from various Polish towns. In the evening of that day they are killed with phenol injections by SS Corporal Scherpe. The dead have the following numbers: 29502, 30559, 32924,

APMO, D-AuI-5/2, Morgue Register, pp. 83–85; Mat.RO, vol. V, pp. 49ff.; Höss Trial, vol. 1, p. 172; vol. 4, pp. 163, 177; vol. 5, p. 82; vol. 7, pp. 18, 155; vol. 8, p. 11, Eyewitness Testimony of Former Prisoner of Auschwitz-Birkenau.

37112, 44114, 47831, 57296, 60308, 60460, 73614, 73963,
78174, 79662, 80451, 82074, 82192, 82357, 82613, 82633,
82747, 82763, 82764, 82767, 82782, 82783, 84960, 86415,
87924, 88138, 88217, 90044, 90062, 91059, 93446, 93941,
95086, 95095, 95099, 95267, 95272, 95338, 95424, 95909,
96159, 96198, 96661, 96720, 97242, 97301, 97830, 98079,
98525, 98529, 98562, 98590, 99278, 99429, 99639, 99711,
100184, 100211, 100220, 100268, 100309, 100330, 100368,
100573, 100642, 101189, 101368, 101527, 102485, 102535,
102566, 102567, 102691, 102845, 103419, 103462, and 103504.*

The corpses of 115 prisoners are delivered to the morgue of the main camp; among them are the corpses of the 80 killed boys. Next to No. 73508 is the word "Kobior."

APMO, D-AuI-5/2, Morgue Register, pp. 83–85.

Nos. 104530–104563 are given to 34 male prisoners and Nos. 36515–36539 to 25 female prisoners sent in a group transport.

The second Gypsy transport arrives. The men, women, and children are housed in Birkenau, Section B-IIe, the so-called family camp with wooden "stable" barracks. From one end of the barracks to the other, connecting two chimneys, runs a flue that divides the barracks and at the same time forms a kind of very long table. On both sides of the flue stand three-story wooden plank-beds. One family is to be accommodated on each plank-bed. The Gypsies drape the plank-beds with covers that they have brought with them, and thus from each plank-bed is created a shelter for one family.

APMO, Depositions, vol. 13, p. 65, Account of Former Prisoner Tadeusz Joachimowski.

The prisoner Johann Leonowiec (No. 73190) who escaped on December 5, 1942, is delivered to the bunker of Block 11. He was captured in the county of Ratibor and was brought to the camp in a group transport from Heydebreck on February 25, 1943. Following a selection in the bunker of Block 11, he is shot on March 3, 1943.

APMO, IZ-8/Gestapo Lodz/2/88/145; D-AuI-3/1b, Bunker Register, p. 133.

At 3:30 P.M., 1,026 prisoners are brought from the main camp to the men's camp B-Ib in Birkenau. They are guarded by 20 SS Men from the 5th and 7th companies.

APMO, D-AuI-1/3 FvD, p. 208.

MARCH 2

Nos. 104565–104592 are given to 28 male prisoners and Nos. 36307 and 36540–36545 to seven female prisoners sent to the camp by the Sipo and SD for the Kraków District.

Nos. 104593–104597 are given to five prisoners sent from Kattowitz.

*The names of the youths are not mentioned in surviving camp documents in the archive of the Auschwitz Memorial.

Approximately 1,500 Jewish men, women, and children from the German Reich arrive in an RSHA transport from Berlin. The men worked in the Berlin armaments industry prior to deportation. Following the selection, 142 men, given Nos. 104598–104739, and 385 women, given Nos. 36546–36930, are admitted to the camp. The other approximately 973 people are killed in the gas chambers.

The Head of Office D-I in the WVHA, SS Lieutenant Colonel Liebehenschel, informs Commandant Höss that the Capo August Brück, whose services Höss requisitioned on February 22, 1943,* is being transferred immediately from Buchenwald to Auschwitz.

APMO, D-AuI-3a, vol. 86, Labor Deployment.

Nos. 36931–36933 are given to three female prisoners sent from Kattowitz.

Approximately 1,500 Jewish men, women, and children arrive with an RSHA transport from Berlin. After the selection, 150 men, given Nos. 104740–104889, are admitted to the camp. The other approximately 1,350 deportees are killed in the gas chambers.

The corpses of 19 prisoners are delivered to the morgue of the main camp; one of the dead is from the Buna A.C. and one is from Birkenau.

APMO, D-AuI-5/2, Morgue Register, p. 85.

Commandant Höss is informed at 9:40 P.M. that the deportation of the Jewish inhabitants of Berlin began on March 1, 1943. Again there is reference to the fact that with these transports approximately 15,000 able-bodied, healthy Jews will arrive who until now have been used in the Berlin armaments industry. It is stressed that they absolutely must be kept able-bodied.

APMO, D-AuI-3a/87, Labor Deployment.

MARCH 3

The Commandant of Auschwitz as well as those of Buchenwald, Gross-Rosen, Flossenbürg, Neuengamme, and Sachsenhausen concentration camps receive from the Head of Branch D in the WVHA identical radioed messages in which Auschwitz is instructed to prepare to transfer able-bodied and healthy Polish prisoners to concentration camps in the interior of the Reich. 1,000 skilled metal workers should be transferred respectively to Buchenwald, Gross-Rosen, Flossenbürg, and Sachsenhausen; and 1,000 skilled construction workers should be sent to Neuengamme. The Commandants of the concentration camps named are ordered to send commandos to Auschwitz to take charge of the Auschwitz prisoners and guard the transports.**

APMO, D-AuI-3a/89, 90, 91, 92, 99, 106, 108, 109, Labor Deployment.

Protective Custody Commander Aumeier, Grabner, and other functionaries of the Political Department carry out a selection in the

APMO, D-AuI-3/1b, Bunker Register, pp. 115, 117, 120, 125, 127, 130, 133.

*In a requisition with the file code 14/F 5/2.43./Mn./Ne, the transfer of a Capo for running the crematoriums in Birkenau is sought.
**The transfer of 5,000 young, healthy, and able-bodied Polish prisoners should also prevent even greater dangers for Auschwitz, as it is feared that political prisoners acting from patriotic motives could bring about a revolt in the camp or an uprising of the prisoners (compare the entries for March 29 and May 13, 1943).

bunkers of Block 11 where they select 26 prisoners whom they had had delivered to the bunkers and who are suspected of carrying on underground activities in the camp or preparing escape attempts or who have been captured while escaping. The prisoners selected are shot at the execution wall in the courtyard of Block 11. Among them are Eugeniusz Krzciuk (No. 76), Max Gestwiński (No. 63128), Józef Żelazny (No. 63001), Alfred Stösel (No. 435), Jaroslav Krejči (No. 63328), Josef Babička (No. 65442), the Jewish prisoners Georg Dumond (No. 27975) and Eliasz Brum (No. 86797), Józef Gronek (No. 62619), Anton Hrenčit (No. 66925), Wincenty Gawrom (No. 100214), Marian Kempiński (No. 34551), and the Jewish prisoner Lajzer Dreksler (No. 103475).

No. 36934 is given to a female prisoner sent from Kattowitz.

Approximately 1,500 Jewish men, women, and children arrive in an RSHA transport from Berlin in which there are also Norwegian Jews. Following the selection, 535 men, given Nos. 104890–105424, and 145 women, given Nos. 36935–37079, are interned in the camp as prisoners. The other approximately 820 people are killed in the gas chambers.

Approximately 1,500 Jewish men, women, and children arrive in an RSHA transport from Berlin in which there are also Norwegian Jews. Following the selection, 50 men, given Nos. 105457–105506, and 164 women, given Nos. 37080–37243, are admitted to the camp. The other approximately 1,286 people are killed in the gas chambers.

A transport of Gypsies—men, women, and children—arrives; they are housed in Camp B-IIe in Birkenau. In this shipment are 164 men.

APMO, D-AuII-3/1, Register of Male Gypsies.

The corpses of 19 prisoners are delivered to the morgue of the main camp; one of the dead is from Jawishowitz A.C., one is from the Golleschau camp, and one is from Birkenau.

APMO, D-AuI-5/2, Morgue Register, p. 86.

The Commandant's Office is again reminded by the WVHA that the Jewish armaments workers from Berlin must at all costs be kept able-bodied. At the same time, it is ordered that they be transferred directly to the Buna auxiliary camp without being quarantined in Auschwitz. The WVHA expects a significant increase within the next few days in the number of prisoners employed in the Buna plants.

Documents and Materials, p. 108.

MARCH 4

Nos. 105425 to 105456 are given to 32 miners transferred from Flossenbürg who are supposed to work in the Jawischowitz coal mine.

APMO, D-AuI-3a/93, 97.

Nos. 104189, 104564, and 105507–105570 are given to 66 prisoners sent to the camp from Radom by the Sipo and SD.

1,750 Jews arrive with an RSHA transport from Berlin of 632 men and 1,118 women and children. After the selection, 517 men, given Nos. 105571–106087, and 200 women, given Nos. 37296–37495, are admitted to the camp. The other 1,033 people, 115 men and 918 women, are killed in the gas chambers.

Documents and Materials, p. 109.

Following the selection of the 1,750 Jews deported from Berlin, the Director of Labor Deployment SS First Lieutenant Schwarz informs the WVHA that only 517 men and 200 women have been added to the labor force. He comments, "If the transports from Berlin continue to roll in with so many women and children, along with elderly Jews, I don't [promise] myself much in terms of labor. Buna needs mainly younger and stronger creatures."

1,000 Jewish men, women, and children from Drancy arrive in the forty-ninth RSHA transport from France. Following the selection, 100 men, given Nos. 106088–106187, and 19 women, given Nos. 37277–37295, are admitted to the camp. The other 881 people are killed in the gas chambers. All male prisoners selected from this transport are assigned to the Special Squad. Among them are Josef Dorębus, Jankiel Handelsman (No. 106112), Chaim Herman (No. 106113), Bela Foeldisch (No. 106099), and David Lahana; they are Polish Jews and Communists who become members of resistance groups in the camp.

Amid Unspeakable Crimes, pp. 158, 187ff., 193, 198–201.

The Capo of Crematorium I, Mieczysław Morawa (No. 5730), is transferred from the main camp to Birkenau, where the ovens in Crematorium II are to be put in operation for the first time on a trial basis. At the same time, the camp management forms a Special Squad from the just arrived Jewish prisoners for servicing Crematorium II.

APMO, D-Mau-3a/16408, Prisoner's Personal-Information Card on Mieczysław Morawa; *Amid Unspeakable Crimes*, pp. 49–51.

Nos. 37496–37535 are given to 40 female prisoners sent in a group transport.

The so-called Crematorium II Squad is transferred from the main camp to Camp B-Ib in Birkenau after having been trained in Crematorium I. 12 of the original 22 Jewish prisoners are transferred— 10 of them have died within one month—and five Poles. Among the transferred are Henryk Tauber, Władysław Biskup, Jan Agrestowski, and Władysław Tomiczek (No. 1483). Władysław Tomiczek* is on this date released from the bunker of Block 11 and assigned to the Special Squad, because it is known to the Political Department that he already worked in Crematorium I in 1941; at that time he managed to be taken off this squad and be put in the

APMO, Höss Trial, vol. 11, pp. 127ff; D-Mau-3a, Personal-Information Cards on Prisoners Władysław Biskup and Jan Agrestowski.

---

*According to a statement by Henryk Tauber, Władysław Tomiczek is summoned in August 1943 to the Political Department. The same day, SS Staff Sergeant Quakernack brings his corpse for incineration; the head is separated from the body and is wrapped in a sack. Quakernack personally monitors how the corpse of the killed man is burned. When he leaves, the prisoners bring out the sack and confirm that it contains the head of Tomiczek (APMO, Höss Trial, vol. II, p. 127ff., Statement by Former Prisoner Henryk Tauber).

camp's mill squad and, later, in the butcher squad. The Special Squad is housed in Barracks 2, a closed block in Camp B-Ib.

MARCH 5

Nos. 106188–106202 are given to 15 miners transferred from Ravensbrück who are to be used in the Jawischowitz coal mine.

APMO, D-AuI-3a/94, 98, 102.

No. 106203 is given to a Jewish prisoner sent in a group transport.

Nos. 106204–106334 are given to 131 prisoners sent in a group transport that includes August Brück, who is being transferred from Buchenwald to Auschwitz to become Capo of the crematorium in Birkenau. August Brück gets No. 106293.*

APMO, D-AuI-3a/101, Confirmation by First Lieutenant Schwarz of Brück's Arrival.

44 women who have been housed since February 12, 1943, during the interrogation proceedings, in Block 2a of the main camp, which was made available to the Myslowitz Investigative Detention Prison, are admitted to the women's camp and transferred to Camp B-Ia in Birkenau. They get Nos. 37536–37579; No. 37573 is given to Wanda Koprowska.

Nos. 37580–37646 are given to 25 female prisoners sent from Kattowitz.

An additional 34 women who during the interrogation proceedings, since February 12, 1943, have been housed in Block 2a of the main camp are admitted to the women's camp and are transferred to Camp B-Ia in Birkenau. They are given Nos. 37505–37638; No. 37625 is given to Helena Włodarska. The same day, several women against whom nothing can be proved are released from investigative detention in Block 2a.

APMO, Correspondence, K. 469/84 with the former prisoner Leokadia Pałoła of Block 2a.

Nos. 37639–37646 are given to eight female prisoners sent in a group transport.

A transport of Gypsies has arrived. They are housed in Camp B-IIe in Birkenau.

APMO, D-AuII-3/1, Register of Male Gypsies; D-AuII-3/2/1, Register of Female Gypsies.

The corpses of 18 prisoners are delivered to the morgue of the main camp; four of the dead are from the Golleschau auxiliary camp.

APMO, D-AuI-5/2, Morgue Register, p. 87.

During a test heating of the ovens in Crematorium II in Birkenau, the Capo August Brück, who has just been transferred from Buchenwald, explains the construction of the ovens to the prisoners in the Special Squads and familiarizes them with the instructions for use. The generators run from the morning until 4:00 P.M. In the course of the day, a commission arrives made up of higher-level SS people from Berlin, members of the camp management, function-

APMO, D-Mau-3a/16408, Personal-Information Card for Mieczysław Morawa; D-AuI-sa/101, Confirmation of Brück's Arrival.

---

*August Brück becomes Head Capo of the crematorium, being present at its start-up. He dies in Auschwitz on December 27, 1943.

Crematorium IV under construction, with its twin, Crematorium V, known as the "forest crematorium." Behind it was the so-called incineration pit.

aries of the camp's Political Department, as well as engineers and employees of the firm of J. A. Topf and Sons in Erfurt, which built the crematorium ovens. In their presence, the members of the Special Squad stoke the 15 retorts of the five crematorium ovens with 45 corpses. With clock in hand, the members of the commission time the cremation of the corpses, which at 40 minutes takes an unexpectedly long time. The Special Squad is therefore ordered to let the generators run constantly for several days so the ovens get heated up. Participating at the trial start-up of the crematorium ovens, which lasts from March 4 to March 6, is the Head Capo August Brück and Mieczysław Morawa (No. 5730), the Capo of Crematorium I who was ordered to Birkenau for the test. Afterward he returns to the main camp.

Nos. 106335–106368 are given to 34 prisoners brought in a group transport.

450 Gypsies from the Reich, 219 men and boys given Nos. Z-392–Z-610 and 251 women and girls given Nos. Z-438–Z-688 arrive in the camp.*

APMO, D-AuII-3/1/1, Register of Male Gypsies; D-AuII-3/2/1, Register of Female Gypsies. All further statements about the Gypsies who were sent to Auschwitz are based on these two registers as fundamental sources. Henceforth, they will be cited only in the case of a birth, a transfer to another camp, or a killing in the gas chambers.

*The numbers assigned the Gypsies on March 6, 1943, show that with the four previous transports, 828 people—391 men and boys and 437 women and girls—have been brought to the Gypsy camp. Immediately after arrival and a bath in the so-called sauna, the Gypsies are tattooed and entered in the Gypsy camp registry. Beginning around March 20, 1943, prisoners are also listed in a central registry for the use of the various administrative authorities of the camp as a whole.

MARCH 6

1,128 Jews, 540 men and 588 women and children, have arrived in an RSHA transport from Berlin. Following the selection, 389 men and 96 women, given Nos. 37647–37742, are admitted to the camp. The other 643 people, 151 men and 492 women and children, are killed in the gas chambers.

Schnabel, *Power Without Morality*, p. 514, Doc. 182.

1,405 Jewish men, women, and children arrive in an RSHA transport from Breslau, Berlin, and other German cities. Following the selection, 406 men, who with the 389 men from the previous transport get Nos. 106369–107163, and 190 women given Nos. 37743–37932 are admitted to the camp. The other 809 people, 125 men and 684 women and children, are killed in the gas chambers.

Documents and Materials, p. 110; Schnabel, *Power Without Morality*, p. 514, Doc. 182.

16 female prisoners sent in a group transport receive Nos. 37933–37948.

No. 37949 is given to a female prisoner sent by the Sipo and SD for the Kraków District. Nos. 37950–38000 are given to 51 female prisoners sent in a group transport.

The Polish prisoner Władysław Zubek (No. 96428) escapes from the camp.

APMO, IZ-8/Gestapo Lodz/2/88/164, 166.

The corpses of 13 prisoners are delivered to the morgue of the main camp; one of the dead is from the Buna A.C., one is from the Jawischowitz A.C., and one from Birkenau.

APMO, D-AuI-5/2, Morgue Register, p. 87.

MARCH 7

665 Jews have arrived in an RSHA transport from Berlin of 183 men and 482 women and children. Following the selection, 153 men, given Nos. 107164–107316, and 65 women, given Nos. 38001–38605, are admitted to the camp. The other 447 people, 30 men and 417 women and children, are killed in the gas chambers.

Documents and Materials, p. 110; Schnabel, *Power Without Morality*, p. 514, Doc. 182.

Nos. 107317–107341 are given to 25 prisoners delivered from Berlin.

Ibid., *Power Without Morality*, Doc. 182.

A group transport of Gypsies from the German Reich, Yugoslavia, Poland, and Czechoslovakia arrives. 387 men and boys get the numbers Z-611–Z-997, and 510 women and girls are given Nos. Z-689–Z-1198.

The corpses of 12 prisoners are delivered to the morgue of the main camp.

APMO, D-AuI-5/2, Morgue Register, p. 88.

MARCH 8

A conference takes place in the factory of Friedrich Krupp AG, Essen. Participants are Alfried Krupp of Bohlen and Halbach; Dr.

APMO, Maurer Trial, vol. 8, pp. 78–108; vol. 8a, p. 88.

Ewald Löser, defense economy manager (Wehrwirtschaftsführer)* and board member of Krupp AG; acting board members Professor Dr. of Engineering Eduard Houdremont, Dr. of Engineering Heinrich Korschau; Professor Dr. of Engineering Erich Müller, board member of the Krupp Steel Construction Company in Rheinhausen; Karl Pfirsich, defense economy manager and acting board member of Krupp AG; and Messrs. Hupe, Rosenbaum, and Clausnizer. During the conference it is decided quickly to move Krupp AG's manufacturing facilities for airplane parts and fuses. Negotiations with the WVHA are dragging on. The decision quickly to construct work hangars in Auschwitz and to start production there is made because of the losses suffered by the Krupp factories in Essen through the bombardment on March 5, 1943.

The political prisoner Gregor Westrikow (No. 104052), born on August 5, 1915, is captured when he attempts to escape from the Jawischowitz camp. He is locked in the bunker of Block 11. Following a selection conducted in the bunkers, he is shot on April 3, 1943.

APMO, D-AuI-3/1b, Bunker Register, p. 136.

The Jewish prisoner Max Franz Schaap (No. 86760), born on October 11, 1919, is delivered to the bunker of Block 11, because he is suspected of attempting to escape, presumably from the Kobior auxiliary camp. The same day he is transferred to the prisoners' infirmary.

Ibid.

Three prisoners escape in the morning from the Buna plants: Leonid Uriesow (No. 71738), born on July 15, 1922, Andreas Trunow (No. 72008), born on December 24, 1921, and Paweł Kaluszniyj (No. 71914), born on June 13, 1921.

APMO, D-AuI-1/1, Telegrams, pp. 60–63; IZ-8/Gestapo Lodz/ 3a/88/415; Mat.RO, vol. IV, p. 292.

Two Polish prisoners, Władysław Wojtowicz (No. 18666) and Adam Goska (No. 38109), escape from the camp.

APMO, IZ-8/Gestapo Lodz/2/88/ 161; Mat.RO, vol. IV, p. 292.

Nos. 38066–38089 are given to 24 female prisoners and Nos. 107342–107389 to 48 male prisoners sent with a group transport.

A transport of Gypsies from Czechoslovakia and the German Reich arrives. Nos. Z-998–Z-1587 are given to 590 men and boys and Nos. Z-1199–Z-1782 to 584 women and girls.

The corpses of 20 prisoners are delivered to the morgue of the main camp; three of the dead are from the Buna A.C. and one is from the Kobior A.C.

APMO, D-AuI-5/2, Morgue Register, pp. 88ff.

MARCH 9

Nos. 107390–107438 are given to 49 prisoners sent from Pawiak Prison in Warsaw by the SD.

---

*"Wehrwirtschaft" is the concept of "mobilizing the economy of the nation on the same totalitarian basis as everything else in order to properly prepare for [and conduct] total war" (Shirer, *Rise and Fall of the Third Reich*, p. 259). —ED.

Nos. 107439–107493 are given to 55 prisoners, many of whom had already been incarcerated in the Montelupich Prison in Kraków, who arrive in a group transport.

Nos. 38090–38116 are given to 27 female prisoners sent by the Sipo and SD for the Kraków District.

Polish political prisoner Jan Janota (No. 85201) is captured during an escape attempt and delivered to the bunker of Block 11. He is shot on April 3, 1943 following a selection in the bunkers.

APMO, D-AuI-3/1b, Bunker Register, p. 137.

Two Jewish prisoners escape from the Special Squad; they worked at burning the corpses in the pits in Birkenau. They are captured in a wooded area near the Vistula River. One of the two dies from a shot wound; the other, Bela Foeldisch (No. 106099), born in Budapest on May 10, 1909, is delivered to the bunker of Block 11, where he dies on March 16, 1943, probably from the effects of a bullet wound as well as the torture endured during the interrogations in the Political Department.*

APMO, D-AuI-1/20, Commandant's Office Order No. 8/43; D-AuI-3/1, Bunker Register, p. 137.

A transport with 300 Gypsies arrives from the German Reich. 147 men and boys are given Nos. Z-1588–Z-1734; 153 women and girls are given Nos. Z-1783–Z-1935.

The corpses of 18 prisoners are delivered to the morgue of the main camp; two of the dead are from the Golleschau A.C.

APMO, Morgue Register, p. 89.

MARCH 10

1,000 Polish prisoners are transferred from Auschwitz to Buchenwald. The prisoners who had been delivered to the bunkers of Block 11 on February 27, 1943, because of the escape of their seven comrades from the SS kitchen squad also leave the camp with this transport; they had been released from the bunker into the camp on March 9, 1943.

APMO, D-AuI-3a/112, 113, 118, Labor Deployment; Mat.RO, vol. VII, p. 453; D-AuI-3/1b, Bunker Register, pp. 131ff.; Dpr.-ZO/61, p. 215.

1,001 Polish prisoners are transferred from Auschwitz to Neuengamme.

APMO, D-AuI-3a/111, 112, 117, 127, Labor Deployment; Mat.RO, vol. VII, p. 453; Dpr.-ZOd/55, pp. 169, 245.

The Polish prisoner Jurko Ondicz (No. 95293), born on March 28, 1909, is delivered to the bunker of Block 11 and dies the same day. He is suspected of having wanted to escape from Birkenau.

APMO, D-AuI-3/1b, Bunker Register, p. 137; D-AuI-5/2, Morgue Register, p. 90, Item 13.

The political prisoner Jan Krynicki (No. 95797), born in Braddock on March 28, 1908, is captured while escaping from the Birkenau camp and delivered to the bunker of Block 11. Following a selection in the bunkers, he is shot on April 2, 1943.

APMO, D-AuI-3/1b, Bunker Register, p. 137.

*Bela Foeldisch (No. 106099) is entered in the Morgue Register of the main camp under the date March 16, 1943, where it is also noted that the deceased had been delivered from Block 11 (APMO, D-AuI-5/2, Morgue Register, p. 93).

Nos. 107494–107504 are given to 11 male prisoners and Nos. 38117–38127 to 11 female prisoners sent from Bielsko by the Kattowitz Gestapo. No. 38119 goes to Barbara Staszkiewicz; she is sent to the camp as a hostage for her son Bronisław, who escaped from the SS kitchen squad of the main camp on February 27, 1943. Next to the gong in the main camp Barbara Staszkiewicz is placed on a podium, above which a message written in Polish and German on a blackboard states that she has been delivered to the camp in place of her escaped son and will remain until the escapee has been found.* All prisoners must pass this podium upon return from work. The Commandant's Office hopes thereby to exert pressure to keep the prisoners from attempting escapes.

APMO, Höss Trial, vol. 4, p. 3, Statement of Former Prisoner Tadeusz Bałut.

The corpses of 13 prisoners are delivered to the morgue of the main camp.

APMO, D-AuI-5/2, Morgue Register, p. 90.

MARCH 11

Anna Malik, born in the Gypsy camp in Birkenau, is assigned No. Z-1936.

APMO, D-AuII-3/1, Register of Female Gypsies.

The political prisoner Władysław Zubek (No. 96428), who escaped from Birkenau on March 6, 1943, is captured while fleeing and locked in the bunker of Block 11.

APMO, D-AuI-3/1b, Bunker Register, p. 138.

A transport of Gypsies has arrived from Czechoslovakia. Nos. Z-1735–Z-2085 are given to 351 men and boys, and 413 women and girls are identified with the Nos. Z-1937–Z-2349.

Peter Wachler, who is born in the Gypsy camp, gets No. Z-2086.

APMO, D-AuII-3/11-3/1/1, p. 62, Register of Male Gypsies.

Commandant Höss forbids SS members to set foot on the poultry farm in Harmense because of the chicken-pest prevalent there.

APMO, D-AuI-1/14, Commandant's Office Special Order, March 11, 1943.

The corpses of 15 prisoners are delivered to the morgue of the main camp.

APMO, D-AuI-5/2, Morgue Register, p. 90.

MARCH 12

A discussion takes place in the Berlin office of Friedrich Krupp AG. Participants are Lieutenant Colonel Dr. von Wedel and Captain Hartfuss, representing the Army High Command; Director Wielan of the Special [ad hoc] Committee of the Ministry of War Economy and Production; SS Lieutenant Colonel Maurer, of the WVHA, and Messrs. Koettgen and Hoelkeskamp from the Krupp-Werke. It is decided that the WVHA will lease to the Krupp company a shop floor of 400 x 393 square feet at Auschwitz for the production of airplane parts. The administrative personnel will be provided by

APMO, Maurer Trial, vol. 8, pp. 89ff.

*Bronisław Staszkiewicz is not recaptured. His mother, Barbara Staszkiewicz, dies in the women's camp in Auschwitz-Birkenau on November 4, 1943 (APMO, D-RO/10, List of Polish Women who Died in Auschwitz).

Krupp, but the concentration camp should make available approximately 1,500 prisoners as labor. The machines and manufacturing plants will be brought to Auschwitz by Krupp.

1,000 Polish prisoners are transferred from Auschwitz to Flossenbürg.

APMO, D-AuI-3a/120, 125, 128, Labor Deployment; Mat.RO, vol. VII, p. 453.

1,000 Polish prisoners are transferred from Auschwitz to Gross-Rosen.

APMO, D-AuI-3a/114, 124, 125, 127, Labor Deployment; Mat.RO, vol. VII, p. 453.

The Ukrainian prisoner Paweł Kalusznyj (No. 71914), who escaped from the Buna plants on March 8, 1943, is captured while fleeing and locked in the bunker of Block 11. Following a selection, he is shot on April 3, 1943.

APMO, D-AuI-3/1b, Bunker Register, p. 138.

Nos. 107505–107536 are given to prisoners sent to the camp by the Sipo and SD of the Kraków District.

Nos. 107537–107558 are given to 22 prisoners sent in a group transport; one prisoner delivered from Kattowitz gets No. 107543.

Nos. 38128–38142 are given to 15 female prisoners delivered in a group transport.

A transport of Gypsies has arrived from Germany. 113 men and boys are given Nos. Z-2087–Z-2199, and 130 women and girls get Nos. Z-2350–Z-2479.

In the evening, the two prisoners Jan Sarapata (No. 300) and Aleksander Martyniec (No. 644) escape from the camp.*

APMO, D-AuI-1/1, Telegrams, p. 74; IZ-8/Gestapo Lodz/3a/88/ 417; Mat.RO, vol. IV, p. 292.

The corpses of 24 prisoners are delivered to the morgue of the main camp; two of the dead are from the Buna A.C.

APMO, D-AuI-5/2, Morgue Register, p. 91.

MARCH 13

1,000 Polish prisoners are transferred from Auschwitz to Sachsenhausen.

APMO, D-AuI-3a/119, 126, 131, Labor Deployment; Mat.RO, vol. VII, p. 453.

Nos. 107559 to 107583 are given to 25 male prisoners, and Nos. 38143–38159 to 17 female prisoners sent in a group transport.

Nos. 107585–107771 are given to 187 prisoners sent from Minsk. Two of them, the prisoners with Nos. 107627 and 107759, die on the day of arrival. This is the first transport to Auschwitz from Minsk.

APMO, D-AuI-5/2, Morgue Register, p. 91, Items 24, 25.

*In the telegram in which Commandant Höss informs the appropriate police authorities, he advises that these two prisoners had been sent to the camp on June 14, 1940, because of active participation in the resistance movement.

964 Jews, 344 men and 620 women and children, arrive in an RSHA transport from Berlin. Following the selection, 218 men, given Nos. 107772–107989, and 147 women, given Nos. 38160–38306, are admitted to the camp. The other 599 people, 126 men and 473 women and children, are killed in the gas chambers.

APMO, Höss Trial, vol. 12, p. 172, Exhibit 116; *Documents and Materials*, p. 117.

A transport of Gypsies arrives from Germany. 640 men and boys are given Nos. Z-2200–Z-2839, and 713 women and girls get Nos. Z-2480–Z-3192.

The corpses of 32 prisoners are delivered to the morgue of the main camp; two of the dead are from the Budy A.C., two are from the Golleschau A.C., one is from the Buna A.C., and three are from Birkenau.

APMO, D-AuI-5/2, Morgue Register, p. 91.

The Commandant of Ravensbrück informs the Commandant's Office in Auschwitz that, in keeping with a directive of March 1, 1943, from the Head of Branch D of the WVHA, a shipment with 42 prisoners ill with tuberculosis is departing on this day for Auschwitz.

APMO, D-AuI-3a/121, Labor Deployment.

Approximately 2,000 Jewish men, women, and children from Ghetto B in Krakau arrive with an RSHA transport. Following the selection, 484 men, given Nos. 107990–108409 and Nos. 108467–108530, and 24 women, given Nos. 38307–38330, are interned in the camp as prisoners. The other approximately 1,492 people are killed in the gas chambers of Crematorium II.*

APMO, Dpr.-Hd/64, p. 71; Dpr.-ZOd/56, p. 151.

MARCH 14

Nos. 108410–108412 are given to three male prisoners and Nos. 38331–38346 to 16 female prisoners sent in a group transport.

Nos. 108413–108454 are given to 42 prisoners ill with tuberculosis, who, under a directive of the Head of Branch D, dated March 1, 1943, have been transferred from Ravensbrück to Auschwitz.

APMO, D-AuI-3a/139, Labor Deployment.

Nos. 108455–108458 are given to four prisoners sent in a group transport.

A transport of Gypsies has arrived from Germany. 461 men and boys get Nos. Z-2840–Z-3300 and 505 women and girls get Nos. Z-3193–Z-3697.

In the evening the prisoner Stanisław Fiutowski, born in Kraków on May 3, 1916, who worked outside the actual camp area, escapes from the camp.

APMO, D-AuI-1/1/64, Telegrams; IZ-8/Gestapo Lodz/3a/88/421.

*Henryk Tauber reports that the Special Squad for the first time cremated the corpses of Jews who had been killed in the gas chamber of Crematorium II. The members of the Special Squad did not see how the gassing itself was carried out, because they were locked in the autopsy room for two hours (APMO, Höss trial, vol. 11, p. 135ff.).

The Construction Office makes the prisoners who are to complete the works buildings that the WVHA has promised to lease to the Krupp enterprises work on Sundays. These prisoners paint the building all day.

APMO, Construction Office 80/6, entry of March 15, 1943; Depositions, vol. 13, p. 170, Account of Former Prisoner Władysław Siwek.

The corpses of 17 prisoners are delivered to the morgue of the main camp.

APMO, D-AuI-5/2, Morgue Register, p. 92.

MARCH 15

Commandant Rudolf Höss makes it known that in keeping with a directive of March 9, 1943, by the Head of Branch D in the WVHA, SS First Lieutenant Ludwig Baumgartner is this day taking over as Adjutant in the Commandant's Office.

APMO, D-AuI-5/2, Commandant's Office Order 7/43, April 2, 1943.

The Commandant's Office informs all units and the Guard that the official working hours for the prisoners are from 6:00 A.M. to 5:30 P.M., with a one-hour break from 12:00 noon until 1:00 P.M.

APMO, Construction Office 80/6, communication from Commandant's Office to all SS units and the guards.

Nos. 108459–108463 are given to five prisoners sent from Kattowitz.

No. 108531 is assigned to a prisoner delivered from Oppeln.

Nos. 38347–38355 are given to nine female prisoners sent in a group transport.

A transport of Gypsies has arrived from Germany. 215 men and boys are given Nos. Z-3301–Z-3515, and 244 women and girls are given Nos. Z-3698–Z-3941.

Justina Ružička, who was born in the Gypsy camp, receives No. Z-3942.

APMO, D-AuII-3/2/2, p. 255, Register of Female Gypsies.

The resistance groups in the camp convey to Kraków a piece of information that is intended for the Polish Government in Exile; it says that "from January 15 to March 15, 1943, the number of prisoners who died, were gassed, and were killed by injections is officially given as 20,000 registered prisoners."

APMO, Mat.RO, vol. VII, p. 485; vol. II, p. 17a.

The corpses of 27 prisoners are delivered to the morgue of the main camp; four of the dead are from the Buna A.C.

APMO, D-AuI-5/2, Morgue Register, p. 92.

MARCH 16

Nos. 108532–108574 are given to 43 male prisoners and Nos. 38356–38358 to three female prisoners sent from Kattowitz.

Nos. 108575–108605 are assigned to 31 male prisoners and Nos. 38359–38413 to 55 female prisoners sent to the camp by the Sipo and SD for the Kraków District.

Nos. 108606–108663 are given to 58 police prisoners who during their investigative detention had been put in Block 2a, which was being used by the Myslowitz Investigative Detention Prison, and were waiting for a decision about their fate. Now they are admitted to the camp as prisoners. Among these is Stanisław Koprowski, who receives No. 108611.

APMO, Depositions, vol. 13, p. 132, Account of Former Prisoner Stanisław Koprowski.

Nos. 38414–38425 are given to 12 female prisoners sent in a group transport.

Approximately 1,000 Jewish men, women, and children from the dissolved Ghetto B in Kraków arrive in an RSHA transport. Following the selection, 15 men, given Nos. 108664–108678, and 26 women, given Nos. 38426–38451, are admitted to the camp. The other approximately 959 deportees are killed in the gas chambers.

Nos. 108679–108687 are given to nine prisoners sent from Kattowitz.

A transport of Gypsies from the German Reich, Hungary, and Poland arrive. 565 men and boys get Nos. Z-3116–Z-3680, and 198 women and girls get Nos. Z-3944–Z-4141.

In accordance with a March 8 directive of the WVHA, the Polish physician Józef Roszkowski (No. 64844) is transferred to Stutthof concentration camp, near Danzig, as a prisoner doctor to assist the Camp Doctor.

APMO, D-AuI-3a/110/122/135, Labor Deployment.

The corpses of 31 prisoners are delivered to the morgue of the main camp; four of the dead are from the Buna A.C. and one is from the Jawischowitz A.C.

APMO, D-AuI-5/2, Morgue Register, p. 93.

MARCH 17

Nos. 108688–108731 are given to 26 prisoners sent from Kattowitz.

Nos. 38452–38456 are given to 26 prisoners sent in a group transport.

A transport of Gypsies from Czechoslovakia, the German Reich, and Poland arrives. 332 men and boys receive Nos. Z-3681–Z-4012 and 366 women and girls receive Nos. Z-4142–Z-4505.

Prisoner No. 103918 is shot "while escaping."

Ibid., p. 93, Item 11.

The corpses of 31 prisoners are delivered to the morgue of the main camp; three of the dead are from the Buna A.C. and one is from the Budy A.C.

Ibid., pp. 92ff.

MARCH 18

The Polish prisoner Andrzej Komski (No. 102914), born in Brzozów on March 19, 1924, is suspected of preparing an escape attempt and is delivered to the bunker of Block 11. Following a selection in the bunkers, he is shot on April 3, 1943.

APMO, D-AuI-3/1b, Bunker Register, p. 141.

The Polish prisoner Eugeniusz Zdebski (No. 96422), born on April 6, 1915, is captured while escaping and delivered to the bunker of Block 11. Following a selection in the bunkers, he is shot on April 3, 1943.

Ibid.

Nos. 108714–108762 are given to 49 male prisoners and Nos. 38457–38468 to 12 female prisoners sent in a group transport.

Nos. 108763–109227 are given to 465 male prisoners and Nos. 38469–38582 to 114 female prisoners sent to the camp from Radom by the Sipo and SD.

A female prisoner sent to the camp from Kattowitz on March 9, 1943, receives No. 38583.

A transport of Gypsies has arrived from the Reich (Germany). 370 men and boys receive Nos. Z-4013–Z-4319 and 340 women and girls receive Nos. Z-4508–Z-4847.

The corpses of 32 prisoners are delivered to the morgue of the main camp; five of the dead are from the Buna A.C.

APMO, D-AuI-5/2, Morgue Register, p. 94.

MARCH 19

As the Auschwitz concentration camp is not in a position to make available the prisoners promised for work in the Buna plant, the representative of the WVHA, SS Lieutenant General Schmitt, calls on the Commandant's Office of Auschwitz to familiarize himself with the situation in person. Accompanied by the head of Office D-11, Maurer, and the Director of Labor Deployment, Schwarz, Schmitt inspects the Buna plants as well as the apprentice home, the apprentice workshops, and the camp for the prisoners.*

APMO, Maurer Trial, vol. 7, pp. 63ff.

By order of the Political Department, eight prisoners are delivered to the bunker of Block 11: the Czech political prisoner Jan Sikora (No. 96653) from the prisoners' infirmary, the reeducation prisoner Józef Łabudek (No. EH-3408) from the prisoners' infirmary, Rajmund Karwiński (No. EH-3404), and Franciszek Kajzar (No. EH-3404) from the Buna A.C., the Czech political prisoner Josef Gajdzica (No. 96649) from the prisoners' infirmary, the Polish political prisoner Konrad Zelechowski (No. 13665) from Block 6, as well as the Jewish prisoner Jozef Malmet (No. 54319) and the

APMO, D-AuI-3/1b, Bunker Register, pp. 141ff.

*As a result of this visit, 1,000 non-Polish prisoners are ordered from Mauthausen to Auschwitz so they can be used in the Buna plants.

Russian Gregor Łukaszow (No. 58551), both from Birkenau. Six of these prisoners are shot on the day of delivery to the bunkers, but the two prisoners Jozef Malmet and Gregor Łukaszow are shot on April 3, 1943, following a selection in the bunkers.

Nos. 109228–109259 are given to 32 prisoners sent by the Sipo and SD Security Service for the Kraków District.

A transport of Gypsies arrives from Czechoslovakia. 545 men and boys receive Nos. Z-4320–Z-4864 and 529 women and girls receive Nos. Z-4848–Z-5376.

Nos. 109260–109297 are given to 38 male prisoners and Nos. 38584–38644 to 61 female prisoners sent in a group transport.

A transport of Gypsies arrives from the German Reich. 31 men and boys get Nos. Z-4865–Z-4895 and 69 women and girls get Nos. Z-5377–Z-5445.

Five boys who were born in the Gypsy camp in Birkenau receive Nos. Z-4896–Z-4900.

APMO, D-AuII-3/1/1, pp. 144ff., Register of Male Gypsies.

Three girls who were born in the Gypsy camp in Birkenau are given Nos. Z-5446–Z-5448.

APMO, D-AuII-3/1/1, pp. 144ff., Register of Female Gypsies.

The corpses of 31 prisoners are delivered to the morgue of the main camp; two of the dead are from the Buna A.C.

APMO, D-AuI-5/2, Morgue Register, p. 95.

MARCH 20

No. 109298 is given to a prisoner transferred from Dachau.

Nos. 109299–109370 are given to 72 male prisoners and Nos. 38645–38720 to 76 female prisoners sent in a group transport.

2,800 Jewish men, women, and children from the ghetto in Salonika have arrived with an RSHA transport from Greece. Following the selection, 417 men, given Nos. 109371–109787, and 192 women, given Nos. 38721–38912, are admitted to the camp as prisoners. The other approximately 2,191 people are killed in the gas chambers.

The Polish reeducation prisoner Zygmunt Koper (No. EH-3692), born in Dąbrowa Górnicza on March 4, 1921, is captured during an attempted escape from the Buna plants and is delivered to the bunker of Block 11. He is shot following a selection on April 3, 1943.

APMO, D-AuI-3/1b, Bunker Register, p. 143.

Three prisoners from the main camp are ordered to the Gypsy Family Camp in Birkenau to fill out the personal-information cards of the Gypsies. Among the prisoners who are in the Gypsy camp for several days are Kazimierz Sichrawa (No. 231) and Tadeusz

APMO, Depositions, vol. 13, pp. 57–58, Account of Former Prisoner Tadeusz Joachimowski.

Joachimowski (No. 3720). The Gypsy camp is still under construction. The Gypsies are registered according to the sequence of the housing barracks used by them. The registration takes place outside, at tables set up in front of the respective barracks. Apart from the sick prisoners, allegedly from typhus fever, who are isolated in Barracks Nos. 20 and 22, all camp inmates stand in front of their barracks from morning until evening roll call. Filling out the cards lasts three days altogether.

Three Polish prisoners are captured during an attempted escape from the main camp and delivered to the bunker of Block 11. Nikodem Sałagacki (No. 97598) dies in the bunker on March 24, 1943, most probably from the injuries resulting from torture suffered during interrogations. During a selection carried out in the bunkers by the camp management on April 3, 1943, Stanisław Kołodziej (No. 102939) and Józef Dziubek (No. 102773) are condemned to death by shooting.

APMO, D-AuI-3/1b, Bunker Register, p. 143; D-AuI-5/2, Morgue Register, p. 101, Item 48.

The corpses of 58 prisoners are delivered to the morgue of the main camp; six of the dead are from the Buna A.C., three from the Kobior A.C., two from the Golleschau A.C., and one from the Jawischowitz A.C.

APMO, D-AuI-5/2, Morgue Register, pp. 96ff.

MARCH 21

Two boys who were born in the Gypsy camp in Birkenau receive Nos. Z-4901 and Z-4902.

APMO, D-AuII-3/1/1, p. 145, Register of Male Gypsies.

A transport of Gypsies has arrived from the German Reich. 29 men and boys receive Nos. Z-4903–Z-4931, and 35 women and girls get Nos. Z-5449–Z-5483.

The corpses of 44 prisoners are delivered to the morgue of the main camp.

APMO, D-AuI-5/2, Morgue Register, p. 97.

Nos. 109788–109870 are given to 83 prisoners sent from Kattowitz.

MARCH 22

Nos. 109872–109895 are given to 24 male prisoners and Nos. 38913–38960 to 48 female prisoners sent in a group transport.

A transport of Gypsies has arrived from the Reich territory. 25 men and boys receive Nos. Z-4932–Z-4956 and 35 women and girls receive Nos. Z-5484–Z-5518.

The Central Construction Administration in Auschwitz of the Waffen SS and Police hands over to the garrison administration the newly completed Crematorium IV (Project KGL-30), which is connected with gas chambers. This crematorium, whose construction is identical with that of Crematorium V, has an oven with eight

APMO, D-ZBauKGL/BW/30/25/14, Table of Construction Projects Already Turned Over to the Garrison Administration; Dpr.-Hd/11a, p. 77, Exhibit 13.

Crematorium IV in spring 1943, shortly after its completion.

combustion chambers and four fireboxes that can also be heated with gas, as well as three gas chambers—the third is divided into two smaller ones—with space for 1,500, 800, and 150 people, respectively. The gas chambers are located in an aboveground part of the building. As with the so-called bunkers, the gas intake holes are in the outside walls. They are barred on the inside and can be closed from the outside with gastight drop doors.

The corpses of 61 prisoners are delivered to the morgue of the main camp; five of the dead are from the Buna A.C.

APMO, D-AuI-5/2, Morgue Register, pp. 98ff.

MARCH 23

On the orders of the WVHA, the Polish political prisoners Tomir Gajewski (No. 18849) and Bolesław Łuczek (No. 97451) are transferred to Riga as prisoner doctors to assist the Camp Doctor in the labor camp. They arrive there on March 28, 1943.

APMO, D-AuI-3a/115, 137, 154, Labor Deployment.

No. 38962 is given to a female prisoner sent from Kattowitz.

In turning over the crematorium to the administration of Auschwitz, the prisoner Mieczsław Morawa (No. 5730), who until now was Capo of Crematorium I in the main camp, is transferred to Birkenau permanently and made Capo of Crematorium IV. The cremation of corpses in the crematorium is begun.

APMO, D-Mau-3a/16408, Personal-Information Card of Morawa; *Amid Unspeakable Crimes*, pp. 49–52.

In the evening, after curfew has been ordered in the Gypsy camp in Birkenau, the approximately 1,700 men, women, and children

APMO, Depositions, vol. 13, pp. 57ff., Account of Former Pris-

housed in barracks No. 20 and 22 who were not registered during the census of the Gypsy camp are led from their barracks, brought to the gas chambers, and killed there. These Gypsies were deported from the Białystok region and isolated in Barracks 20 and 22 on suspicion of having typhus. They were not registered in the camp, got no numbers, and were in the camp only a few days.

oner Tadeusz Joachimowski. He was at this time the "scribe" of the Gypsy camp.

Three German criminal prisoners—Reinhold Wienhold (No. 15174), the Block Senior of Block 22a; Walter Walterscheid (No. 15476), the Capo of the butcher's shop; and Franz Fichtinger (No. 15473), the Capo of the leather factory squad—are delivered to the bunkers of Block 11 because they collected and smuggled gold. Wienhold and Walterscheid commit suicide during the investigation: Walterscheid poisons himself in the guard room in Block 11, and Wienhold hangs himself in the cell. Their death dates are not entered into the Bunker Register because the camp management wants the matter to remain an open secret. Fichtinger is detained in the bunkers until May 22, 1932, and then is assigned to the Penal Company.

APMO, D-AuI-3/1b, Bunker Register, p. 144; Brol et al., "Bunker Register of Block 11," p. 36.

The corpses of 75 prisoners are delivered to the morgue of the main camp; five of the dead are from the Buna A.C. and one is from the Golleschau A.C.

APMO, D-AuI-5/2, Morgue Register, p. 100.

MARCH 24

The Head of Office D-II, Maurer, informs the Commandant's Office that it is apparent from information received the previous day that 3,204 Polish prisoners in Auschwitz were not used for labor. Maurer asks when these 3,204 Polish prisoners can be transferred, as able-bodied men are urgently needed.

APMO, D-AuI-3a/143, Labor Deployment.

Approximately 2,800 Jewish men, women, and children from the ghetto in Salonika arrive in an RSHA transport from Greece. Following the selection, 584 men receive Nos. 109896–110479 and 230 women receive Nos. 38962–39191 and are admitted to the camp. The other approximately 1,986 people are killed in the gas chambers.

No. 39192 is given to a female prisoner delivered from Kattowitz.

Nos. 110480 and 110481 are given to two prisoners sent from Kattowitz the previous day.

A transport of Gypsies arrives from the territory of the German Reich. 133 men and boys receive Nos. Z-4957–Z-5089 and 128 women and girls receive Nos. Z-5519–Z-5646.

The Czech political prisoner Wilhelm Feter (No. 25649) from the Birkenau camp, who was put in the bunker on order of the Protective Custody Commander, and the Polish prisoner Nikodem

APMO, D-AuI-3/1b, Bunker Register, pp. 141, 143; D-AuI-5/2, Morgue Register, p. 101, Items 5, 48.

Sałagacki (No. 97598) die in the bunker of Block 11 from injuries resulting from tortures suffered during their interrogations.

The corpses of 69 prisoners are delivered to the morgue of the main camp; two of the dead are from the Buna A.C. and two are from the Kobior A.C.

APMO, D-AuI-5/2, Morgue Register, p. 101.

MARCH 25

Rudolf Weiss, who was born in the Gypsy Family Camp in Birkenau on March 22, 1943, is assigned No. Z-5090.

APMO, D-AuII-3/1/1, p. 150, Register of Male Gypsies.

The free Nos. 107543 and 108464–108466 are given to four prisoners delivered from Kattowitz.

No. 110482 is given to a Jewish prisoner.

1,901 Jewish men, women, and children from the ghetto in Salonika arrive in an RSHA transport from Greece. Following the selection, 459 men, given Nos. 110483–110941, and 236 women, given Nos. 39193–39428, are admitted to the camp. The other 1,206 people are killed in the gas chambers.

Nos. 110942–110980 are given to 57 male prisoners. 35 female prisoners who had arrived in a group transport are given Nos. 39429–39453 and 39455–39464.

A transport of Gypsies arrives from the territory of the German Reich. 25 men and boys receive Nos. Z-5091–Z-5115 and 29 women and girls receive Nos. Z-5647–Z-5675.

52 Poles from the prison in Myslowitz are shot in the gas chamber of Crematorium I. The court-martial had condemned them to death for high treason and preparations for the separation of Silesia from the German Reich.*

CA KC PZPR, 202/III, Documents of the Polish Government in Exile, p. 259.

Two Polish prisoners, Stefan Koźmiński (No. 101281) and Zbigniew Fizyta (No. 101322) are captured while escaping and delivered to the bunkers of Block 11. Following a selection in the bunkers, they are shot on April 3, 1943.

APMO, D-AuI-3/1b, Bunker Register, p. 145.

The corpses of 51 prisoners are delivered to the morgue of the main camp; four of the dead are from the Jawischowitz A.C. and two from the Buna A.C.

APMO, D-AuI-5/2, Morgue Register, pp. 102ff.

MARCH 26

The prisoner Władysław Zubek (No. 96428), who was captured during an escape attempt and delivered to the bunker of Block 11

APMO, D-AuI-3/1b, Bunker Register, p. 138; D-AuI-5/2, Morgue Register, p. 103, Item 8.

*These prisoners had been housed in the main camp since February 12, 1943. The Gestapo interrogated them in the rooms of the Political Department.

on March 11, 1943, dies from injuries received during the torture he suffered during interrogation.

The reason for the arrest of a female reeducation prisoner is changed: the woman is reregistered as a political prisoner and receives No. 39454.

A prisoner delivered from Kattowitz receives the free No. 109871.

Nos. 111001–111074 are given to 74 male prisoners and Nos. 39465–39490 to 26 female prisoners sent in a group transport.

A transport of Gypsies arrives from the territory of the German Reich. 30 men and boys receive Nos. Z-5116–Z-5145, and 24 women and girls receive Nos. Z-5676–Z-5699.

The corpses of 56 prisoners are delivered to the morgue of the main camp; two of the dead are from the Kobior A.C., two are from the Buna camp, and one is from the Golleschau camp.

APMO, D-AuI-5/2, Morgue Register, pp. 103ff.

MARCH 27

Wera Malik, who is born in the Gypsy camp in Birkenau, gets No. Z-3934.

APMO, D-AuII-3/2/2, p. 255, Register of Female Gypsies.

No. 110999 goes to a prisoner sent from Sachsenhausen.

No. 111000 is given to a prisoner sent from Frankfurt an der Oder.

Nos. 111075–111131 are given to 57 male prisoners and Nos. 39491–39504 to 14 female prisoners sent with a group transport.

A transport of Gypsies arrives from the territory of the German Reich. 251 men and boys get Nos. Z-5146–Z-5396 and 263 women and girls get Nos. Z-5700–Z-5962.

Nos. 111132–111133 are given to two male prisoners and Nos. 39505–39519 to 15 female prisoners sent in a group transport.

The corpses of 68 prisoners are delivered to the morgue of the main camp; two of the dead are from the Buna A.C. and one is from the Kobior A.C.

APMO, D-AuI-5/2, Morgue Register, pp. 104ff.

A Czech political prisoner from the Camp B-Ib in Birkenau, Ladislav Walys (No. 101796), dies from injuries received during torture inflicted in the course of interrogation. He was delivered to the bunker by order of the Protective Custody Commander on March 22, 1943, because he was suspected of preparing an escape.

APMO, D-AuI-3/1b, Bunker Register, p. 144; D-AuI-5/2, Morgue Register, p. 105, Item 67.

MARCH 28

The Director of Labor Deployment, SS First Lieutenant Schwarz, advises the head of Office D-III, Maurer, in response to his inquiry

APMO, D-AuI-3a/145, Labor Deployment.

concerning able-bodied Polish prisoners, that because of the new tasks of the construction squads as well as illness, Auschwitz cannot transfer more than 2,500 Polish prisoners. These prisoners can be transferred between the fifteenth and twentieth of April, following the exchange of winter for summer clothing.

A transport of Gypsies has arrived from the German Reich. 160 men and boys receive Nos. Z-5397–Z-5458 and Z-5462–Z-5559, and 192 women and girls receive Nos. Z-5963–Z-6154.

Three boys born the previous day in the Gypsy camp in Birkenau are given Nos. Z-5459–Z-5461.

APMO, D-AuII-3/1, p. 161, Register of Male Gypsies.

The corpses of 42 prisoners are delivered to the morgue of the main camp.

APMO, D-AuI-5/2, Morgue Register, p. 106.

MARCH 29

In the afternoon, three Polish prisoners, Stefan Kubiczek (No. 85462), Władysław Kunda (No. EH-3836), and Bernard Jenczmyk* (No. EH-3838) escape from the camp.

APMO, D-AuI-1/1, p. 84, Telegrams; IZ-8/Gestapo Lodz/3a/88/425; Mat.RO, vol. IV, p. 292.

Nos. 111134–111146 are given to 13 male prisoners and Nos. 39420–39530 to 11 female prisoners sent in a group transport.

Nos. 39531–39622 are given to 92 female prisoners sent from Augsburg.

A group transport of Polish Gypsies has arrived. 14 men and boys receive Nos. Z-5560–Z-5573, and 23 women and girls receive Nos. Z-6155–Z-6177.

Two girls born in the Gypsy camp get Nos. Z-6178–Z-6179.

APMO, D-AuII-3/2/3, p. 399, Register of Female Gypsies.

Wiktoria Grabowski, who was born in the Gypsy camp on March 25, 1943, gets No. Z-6180.

Ibid.

The Commandant's Office is notified by the Head of Branch D of the WVHA that the Commandant's Office of Mauthausen-Gusen Concentration Camp will transfer as prisoners 1,000 security detainees,** who should not be kept in Auschwitz, but should be assigned immediately after arrival to the Buna plant. For security reasons, no Poles are among the prisoners transferred. Auschwitz should in turn transfer to Mauthausen by April 15, 1943, the Poles who were in quarantine.†

APMO, D-AuI-3a/151ff.

*Bernard Jenczmyk is arrested again on January 3, 1944, and delivered to the bunker. He is released from the bunker on January 19, 1944.
**Prisoners who, after completion of a court-imposed sentence, were preventively arrested and sent to the concentration camps. At Auschwitz-Birkenau, they are identified with a green triangle standing on its base.
†Prisoners who are supposed to be released from the camp or transferred to another camp go through quarantine, after which the Camp Doctor decides whether their physical condition permits them to be released or transferred.

Back view of Crematorium II in March 1943. In the background (middle) the chimney of Crematorium III under construction.

The corpses of 71 prisoners are delivered to the morgue of the main camp; five of the dead are from the Buna camp.

APMO, D-AuI-5/2, Morgue Register, p. 107.

MARCH 30

Georg Dietrich, born the previous day in the Gypsy camp, gets No. Z-5574.

APMO, D-AuII-3/1/2, p. 164, Register of Male Gypsies.

2,501 Jewish men, women, and children from the ghetto in Salonika arrive from Greece in an RSHA transport. Following the selection, 312 men, given Nos. 111147–111458, and 141 women, given Nos. 39623–39763, are admitted to the camp. The other 2,048 people are killed in the gas chambers.

Nos. 39764–39772 are given to nine female prisoners sent by the Sipo and SD for the Kraków District.

A transport of Gypsies arrives from the German Reich. 37 men and boys receive Nos. Z-5575–Z-5611 and 30 women and girls receive Nos. Z-6181–Z-6210. Commandant Höss has the previous designation, "women's concentration camp" (Frauenkonzentrationslager—FKL), changed to "women's camp" (Frauenlager—FL).* The

APMO, D-AuI-1, Garrison Order 7/43, March 30, 1943; Dpr.-Hd/12, p. 35, Exhibit 9.

*In this work, the term "women's camp" is used for the women's section of the Auschwitz-Birkenau concentration camp.

change is intended to conceal the fact that this camp is a concentration camp.

Four Jewish prisoners from the Special Squad are killed,* probably with phenol injections. The prisoners, who have been brought for this purpose from Camp BI-b to the prisoners' infirmary in the main camp, have Nos. 106106, 106143, 106154, and 106165.

APMO, D-AuI-5/2, Morgue Register, p. 108, Items 25–28.

The corpses of 58 prisoners are delivered to the morgue of the main camp. Among the dead are the prisoners from the Special Squad in Birkenau who were killed with phenol injections, as well as two prisoners from the Buna A.C.

APMO, D-AuI-5/2, Morgue Register, p. 108, Items 25–28.

MARCH 31

Nos. 111459–111488 are given to 30 prisoners sent from Kattowitz.

Nos. 111489–111546 are given to 58 prisoners sent from Kraków by the Sipo and SD.

Nos. 111547–111565 are given to 19 prisoners sent from Kattowitz.

Nos. 111566–111668 are given to 105 male prisoners and Nos. 39773–39792 to 20 female prisoners sent in a group transport.

Approximately 1,000 Jewish men, women, and children arrive from Poland with an RSHA transport from the ghetto in Sieradz. After the selection, 240 men, given Nos. 111669–111908, and 24 women, given Nos. 39793–39816, are admitted to the camp. The other approximately 736 people are killed in the gas chambers.

Nos. 111909–112107 are given to 199 prisoners sent in a group transport.

Nos. 39817–39836 are given to 20 female prisoners sent from Kattowitz and Oppeln.

A transport of Gypsies from Vienna and the Lakkenbach camp has arrived. 182 men receive Nos. Z-5612–Z-5793 and 256 women and girls receive Nos. Z-6211–Z-6466.

APMO, Depositions, vol. 13, p. 144, Account of Former Prisoner Theresa Franzl.

The SS Central Construction Administration turns over to the garrison administration Crematorium II (Project KGL-30), connected with a gas chamber, which has been completed in Birkenau. Cre-

APMO, D-ZBau/BW/30/25/14, Table of Construction Projects Already Turned Over to the Garrison Administration; Dpr.-Hd/11a, p. 77, Exhibit 13.

*This is practiced as long as the Special Squad exists (APMO, Höss Trial, vol. 1, pp. 4–28, Statement by the Former Prisoner Alter Feinsilber (a.k.a. Stanisław Jankowski); SAM, *Amid Unspeakable Crimes*, p. 52).

matorium II, whose construction is identical with that of Crematorium III, has five ovens with three combustion chambers and two fireboxes per oven. As in Crematorium III, the gas chamber of Crematorium II is intended for 3,000 people and, like the undressing space, is situated below ground. In it are floor-to-ceiling columns consisting of several layers of thick, woven wire. The gas is poured into them from above through openings in the ceiling. Next to the gas chamber is an elevator that transports the dead from the basement to the hall with the crematorium ovens, which is situated on the ground floor.

The Commandant of the Auschwitz Guard Stormtroopers (Wachsturmbann), SS Major Hartjenstein, announces that SS Second Lieutenant Lange has been appointed leader of the 8th Company (U), which is made up of Ukrainian, White Ruthenian, and other volunteers. SS Men Ruzicic, Max Schmidt, Fuchsberger, Rutschke, Alexander Wirth, Wieczorek, Jochann Rudolf Wojciechowski, Mitte Filop, and Sudarewitch are assigned to the 8th Company (U) as training personnel.

APMO, D-AuI-1, Stormtrooper Order 52/43.

The corpses of 75 prisoners are delivered to the morgue of the main hall; among them are the corpse of the prisoner who had just been registered as No. 111612 and three dead persons from the Buna A.C.

APMO, D-AuI-5/2, Morgue Register, pp. 109–111.

Approximately 3,000 Jewish men, women, and children arrive from the ghetto and labor camp in Ostrowiec-Świętokrzyski in an RSHA transport. They are all most likely killed in the gas chamber of the newly constructed Crematorium II.

AGKBZH, *Inquiry of the District Court, Province of Kielce, Camps—Ghettos*, vol. 1, pp. 118–119.

MARCH 1–31

3,391 registered prisoners have died in the women's camp in Birkenau; 1,802 women have been killed in the gas chambers.

APMO, Mat.RO, vol. VII, p. 485.

APRIL 1

A transport of Polish Gypsies has arrived. 29 men and boys receive Nos. Z-5794–Z-5822 and 38 women and girls receive Nos. Z-6467–Z-6504.

Four boys born in the Gypsy camp get Nos. Z-5823–Z-5826.

APMO, D-AuII-3/1/2, p. 172, Register of Male Gypsies.

Sonie Franz, born in the Gypsy camp, is given No. Z-6505.

APMO, D-AuII-3/2/3, Register of Female Gypsies.

25 German prisoners transferred from Dachau in accordance with a January 11, 1943, directive of the WVHA are given Nos. 112108–112132. In Dachau they worked as orderlies and should again be used as orderlies in Auschwitz.

APMO, D-AuI-3a/, pp. 153, 160, Labor Deployment.

A Jewish prisoner, Siegfried Berger (No. 107050) is captured while fleeing and is delivered to the bunker of Block 11. After a selection in the bunkers, he is shot on April 3, 1943.

APMO, D-AuI-3/2, Bunker Register, p. 1.

By order of the WVHA, Commandant Höss places Block 10 of the main camp under the command of SS Brigadier General Professor Dr. Carl Clauberg. In this block an experimental station is to be set up in which Clauberg, using women he has selected, wants to continue the sterilization experiments that he already began in the women's camp in Birkenau in December 1942.

APMO, Dpr.-ZO/5, p. 187; Dpr.-ZOd/59, p. 47; Jan Sehn, "Carl Claubergs verbrecherische Unfruchtbart machungsversuche" (Carl Clauberg's Criminal Sterilization Experiments on Female Prisoners in the Nazi Concentration Camps), *HvA*, no. 2 (1955): 3–32, documents in appendix, pp. 51–87.

The occupancy level of the women's camp in Auschwitz-Birkenau is 15,200 prisoners; of these, 2,369 are not able-bodied, 10,269 are not used for work, and 2,562 are employed in labor squads.

APMO, D-AuI-3a/370/3, p. 227, Overview of the Deployment of Prisoners in the Women's Camp of Auschwitz-Birkenau (hereafter cited as Overview). [occupancy level]

The firm of J. A. Topf und Sons submits a cost proposal for an oven for cremating corpses; including the assembly, the costs should be 25,148 RM. The oven weighs 8,899 pounds.

Schnabel, *Power Without Morality*, p. 352, Doc. 133.

The corpses of 48 prisoners are delivered to the morgue of the main camp; five of the dead are from the Buna A.C.

APMO, D-AuI-5/2, Morgue Register, pp. 111ff.

APRIL 2

The Commandant's Office is notified by the WVHA that not 1,000, but 658 security detainees will arrive from Mauthausen, and these should be taken to the Buna auxiliary camp immediately after arrival of the train.

APMO, D-AuI-3a/162, Labor Deployment.

Nos. 112133–112135 are given to three prisoners sent in a group transport.

Nos. 112136–112186 are given to 51 prisoners sent from the Radom Prison by the Sipo and SD.

Nos. 112187–112193 are given to seven prisoners delivered from Kattowitz.

No. 112194 is given to a prisoner sent from Kraków.

Nos. 112195–112271 are given to 77 male prisoners and Nos. 39840–39851 and 39853–39963 to 123 female prisoners sent in a group transport. With this transport the RSHA has sent a Jewish prisoner, No. 112272, as well as four Jewish female prisoners who get Nos. 39837–39839 and 39852.

Two boys born in the Gypsy camp in Birkenau receive Nos. Z-5827 and Z-5828.

APMO, D-AuII-3/1/2, p. 172, Register of Male Gypsies.

A transport of Gypsies has arrived from the German Reich. 27 men and boys receive Nos. Z-5829–Z-5855 and 29 women and girls receive Nos. Z-6506–Z-6534.

The corpses of 61 prisoners are delivered to the morgue of the main camp; six of the dead are from the Buna A.C.

APMO, D-AuI-5/2, Morgue Register, pp. 112ff.

12 Polish prisoners are transferred from Mauthausen.

APMO, D-AuI-3a/161, p. 199.

Commandant Höss informs all offices and factories that from April 4 to April 17, rat poison will be put out within the Auschwitz Concentration Camp's Interest Zone. Therefore all domestic animals should be locked inside in order to avoid poisonings.

APMO, D-AuI-1/16, Commandant's Office Order 7/43.

APRIL 3

Approximately 20 women of various nationalities are brought from Women's Camp B-Ia in Birkenau to Block 10, the experimental station of the main camp; they are supposed to work there as doctors and medical orderlies.*

APMO, Höss Trial, vol. 6, p. 94; Kraków Auschwitz Trial, vol. 5, p. 187.

Zdenka Daniel, born in the Gypsy camp in Birkenau, receives No. Z-6535.

APMO, D-AuII-3/2/3, p. 421, Register of Female Gypsies.

In the bunker of Block 11 a selection is carried out; the 26 prisoners selected were put in the bunker by order of the Political Department or the Camp Commander, or were captured during an escape attempt or were suspected of having planned one. They are shot the same day at the execution wall in the court of Block 11.

APMO, D-AuI-3/1b/2, Bunker Register, pp. 137ff., 141–146.

Nos. 112273–112299 are given to 27 prisoners sent in a group transport.

Nos. 112300–112306 are given to seven Jewish prisoners sent to the camp by the RSHA on April 1, 1943.

A group transport of German and Austrian Gypsies has arrived. 101 men and boys receive Nos. Z-5856–Z-5956 and 125 women and girls receive Nos. Z-6536–Z-6660.

2,800 Jewish men, women, and children from the ghetto in Salonika have arrived with an RSHA transport from Greece. After the selection, 334 men, given Nos. 112307–112640, and 258 women, given Nos. 39964–40221, are admitted to the camp as prisoners. The other 2,208 people are killed in the gas chambers.

The corpses of 57 prisoners are delivered to the morgue of the main camp; five of the dead are from the Buna A.C. and two are from the Kobior A.C.

APMO, D-AuI-5/2, Morgue Register, pp. 113ff.

*The resistance groups in the camp report in a message smuggled out to Kraków on April 3: "Block 10 will be an experimental station for castration, sterilization, and artificial insemination. . . . The women are already with us" (APMO, Mat.RO, vol. I, p. 18).

Crematorium V in Birkenau, nicknamed the "forest crematorium."

APRIL 4

The SS Central Construction Office turns over to the garrison administration the completed Crematorium V and its connected gas chambers, located in Birkenau (Building No. KGL30c). Its construction is like that of Crematorium IV, which was turned over on March 22, 1943.

APMO, D-ZBau/BW/30/25/14, Table of Construction Projects Turned Over to the Garrison Administration; Dpr.-Hd/11a, p. 77, Exhibit 13.

Two girls born in the Gypsy camp receive Nos. Z-6661 and Z-6662.

APMO, D-AuII-3/2/3, p. 429, Register of Female Gypsies.

The corpses of 28 prisoners are delivered to the morgue of the main camp.

APMO, D-AuI-5/2, Morgue Register, p. 115.

APRIL 5

Irena Janosch, born in the Gypsy camp, gets No. Z-6663.

APMO, D-AuII-3/2/3, p. 429, Register of Female Gypsies.

A transport of Austrian Gypsies arrives. 44 men and boys are given Nos. Z-5957–Z-6000 and 34 women and girls are given Nos. Z-6664–Z-6697.

Nos. 112641–112691 are given to 51 male prisoners and Nos. 40222–40241 to 20 female prisoners sent in a group transport. 10 German women in this transport have been transferred from Ravensbrück as punishment for smuggling letters via the SS Comthurey

APMO, D-AuI-3a/140, 148ff., Labor Deployment.

Above and below: Crematorium IV under construction in winter 1943.

experimental farms with the assistance of a female supervisor. Involved are the prisoners Elisabeth Schoknecht, Grete Wohlfahrt, Annemarie Baumann, Lilli Sjögreen, Maria Steinmann, Anneliese Bach, Irmgard Ludwig, Ludmilla Lassmann, Henriette Rabenschlag, and Marta Wasner. The Commandant of Ravensbrück, SS Captain Suhren, applied to the WVHA for their transfer to Auschwitz on March 23, 1943.

The Commandant's Office receives a directive from Branch D to assign immediately two Polish physicians to the Camp Doctor of the Neuengamme concentration camp. Tadeusz Kowalski (No. 93197) and Janusz Okla (No. 41698) are chosen.

APMO, D-AuI-3a/164, Labor Deployment.

Branch D announces the order for female prisoner orderlies to be transferred from Ravensbrück to Auschwitz to work in the Gypsy camp. The transferred prisoners are Luise Diener, Ursula Ginter, Margott Knesebeck, Erna Koppe, Virginia Lukans, Anna Maierhofer, Magdalene Manczek, Katarine Paquet, Irene Polewczynski, and Anna Schulz.

APMO, D-AuI-3a/165, Labor Deployment.

The Polish political prisoner Kazimierz Brenner (No. 3551), who had been sent to Auschwitz by order of the Sipo and SD for the District of Kraków, escapes from the camp.

APMO, D-AuI-1/1/96, Telegrams; IZ-8/Gestapo Lodz/3a/88/427; Mat.RO, vol. IV, p. 292.

The corpses of 36 prisoners are delivered to the morgue of the main camp; one of the dead is from the Jawischowitz A.C. and four are from the Buna A.C.

APMO, D-AuI-5/2, Morgue Register, pp. 115ff.

The WVHA directs the Commandants of Dachau and Gross-Rosen to transfer to Auschwitz the prisoners needed by SS Major Caesar in the Agricultural Department. Dachau is to transfer a blacksmith, a gardener for a tree nursery, and three shepherds; Gross-Rosen is to transfer two surveyors and three blacksmiths.

APMO, D-AuI-3a/166ff., Labor Deployment.

APRIL 6

Nos. 112692–112741 are given to 50 male prisoners and Nos. 40242–40250 to nine female prisoners sent by the Sipo and SD for the Kraków District.

Nos. 112742–112761 are given to 20 prisoners sent in a group transport. In this shipment are two Jews from Darmstadt, Pierre Braunschweig and Paul Guarien, who had been captured during their escape from the fifty-third RSHA transport of March 26, 1943, from le Bourget–Drancy to Sobibor.

The corpses of 35 prisoners are delivered to the morgue of the main camp. Among these is the corpse of the German criminal prisoner Herbert Roman (Romann), who was brought from Block 11. In the Bunker Register, however, it is not noted that this prisoner had been delivered to Block 11.

APMO, D-AuI-5/2, Morgue Register, pp. 116ff., Item 25.

APRIL 7

The Polish Gypsy Stania Ciuroń,* born on August 27, 1909, escapes from the camp. She had been delivered to Auschwitz on February 12, 1943, before the Gypsy Family Camp was set up.

APMO, D-AuI-1/1/102; IZ-8/ Gestapo Lodz/3a/88/429.

Nos. 112762–112785 are given to 24 prisoners sent from Kattowitz.

Nos. 112786–112853 are given to 68 prisoners delivered from Brünn.

Nos. 40251–40279 are given to 29 female prisoners sent in a group transport.

The corpses of 48 prisoners are delivered to the morgue of the main camp; eight of the dead are from the Buna A.C.

APMO, D-AuI-5/2, Morgue Register, pp. 117ff.

APRIL 8

Friedrich Weinlich, who was delivered to the camp on April 1, 1943, receives No. Z-6001.

Two boys born in the Gypsy camp receive Nos. Z-6002 and Z-6003.

APMO, D-AuII-3/1/2, p. 177, Register of Male Gypsies.

Herbert Franz, born in the Gypsy camp in Birkenau on April 5, 1943, is given No. Z-6004.

Ibid.

The German prisoner Zygfryd Koprowiak (No. 71343) escapes from the camp.

APMO, Mat.RO, vol. IV, p. 292; IZ-10/Kripo Sieradz/2a/88/ 62, 100.

Nos. 112854–112960 are given to 107 prisoners sent from Lodz.

Nos. 112961–112973 are given to 13 prisoners sent from Kattowitz.

The corpses of 40 prisoners are delivered to the morgue of the main camp; three of the dead are from the Kobior A.C. and four are from the Buna A.C.

APMO, D-AuI-5/2, Morgue Register, pp. 118ff.

The Commandant's Office is informed by the Commandant's Office of Mauthausen that in compliance with the order of the WVHA of March 29, 1943, a shipment of 658 prisoners, escorted by three SS officers and 53 noncommissioned officers and SS men, left for Auschwitz at 2:05 P.M.

APMO, D-AuI-3a/175, Labor Deployment.

APRIL 9

Austrian Gypsies arrive in a group transport. 52 men and boys receive Nos. Z-6005–Z-6056, and 61 women and girls receive Nos. Z-6698–Z-6758.

*Stania Ciuroń is not captured. Her fate is not known.

2,500 Jewish men, women, and children from the ghetto in Salonika arrive in an RSHA transport from Greece. After the selection, 318 men, given Nos. 112974–113291, and 161 women, given Nos. 40280–40440, are admitted to the camp. The other 2,021 people are killed in the gas chambers.

Nos. 113292–113378 are given to 87 male prisoners and Nos. 40441–40466 to 26 female prisoners sent in a group transport.

Nos. 40467–40479 are given to 13 female prisoners sent in a group transport.

No. 40480 is given to a female prisoner sent from Kattowitz.

The corpses of 39 prisoners are delivered to the morgue of the main camp; one of the dead is from the auxiliary camp in Kobior.

APMO, D-AuI-5/2, Morgue Register, pp. 119ff.

APRIL 10

Three prisoners, the German criminal prisoner Michael Eschmann (No. 15583), the camp senior in Golleschau auxiliary camp, the Polish Jew Hans Brandwein (No. 90018), and the Croatian Jew Brando Mautner (No. 62180), who escaped from the Golleschau camp, are captured in their further flight and delivered to the bunker. Brandwein and Mautner are shot on April 27; Eschmann, however, is released from the bunker into the camp on May 22, 1943.

APMO, D-AuI-3/2, Bunker Register, p. 2; Frąckiewicz, "Golleschau," p. 67.

Nos. 113379–113403 are given to 25 male prisoners and Nos. 40481–40522 to 42 female prisoners sent in a group transport.

No. 40524 is given to a female prisoner sent from Kattowitz.

Nos. 113404–113431 are given to 28 male prisoners and Nos. 40525–40535 to 11 female prisoners sent by the Sipo and SD for the Kraków District.

No. 40536 is given to a prisoner sent from Kattowitz.

Nos. 113432–114089 are given to 658 SV and BV prisoners from the Mauthausen concentration camp who are to be used for labor in the Buna plants.

APMO, D-AuI-3a/184, Labor Deployment, Confirmation of Arrival and Inclusion in the Camp Occupancy.

Nos. 114090–114093 are given to four prisoners from Gross-Rosen who have been assigned to Caesar, the Director of the Agricultural Department: surveying specialist Jan Dymitrowski, surveying assistant Karl Plöchinger, blacksmith and car mechanic Kazimierz Milan, and blacksmith Jan Sova.

APMO, D-AuI-3a/167, 177, Labor Deployment.

Approximately 2,750 Jewish men, women, and children from the ghetto in Salonika arrive in an RSHA transport from Greece. After the selection, 537 men, given Nos. 114094–114630, and 246 women, given Nos. 40537–40782, are admitted to the camp as prisoners. The other approximately 1,967 people are killed in the gas chamber.

Lisbeth Brzezinska, born in the Gypsy camp in Birkenau, is assigned No. Z-6759.

APMO, D-AuII-3/2/3, p. 437, Register of Female Gypsies.

In the Gypsy camp, five men receive Nos. Z-6057–Z-6061 and five women and girls are given Nos. Z-6760–Z-6764.

Magda Widicz, born in the Gypsy camp on April 8, 1943, is given No. Z-6765.

Ibid.

Daniela Kling, born in the Gypsy camp, is given No. Z-6766.

Ibid.

Vlasta Daniel, born in the Gypsy camp on March 22, 1943, is given No. Z-6767.

Ibid.

Two boys who were born in the Gypsy camp in Birkenau are given Nos. Z-6062 and Z-6063.

APMO, D-AuII-3/1/2, p. 179, Register of Male Gypsies.

No. Z-6768 goes to a female Gypsy.

Irini Holomek, born in the Gypsy camp in Birkenau, is given No. Z-6769.

APMO, D-AuII-3/2/3, p. 437, Register of Female Gypsies.

The corpses of 48 prisoners are delivered to the morgue of the main camp; 12 of the dead are from the Buna A.C.

APMO, D-AuI-5/2, Morgue Register, p. 120.

The camp arrest for members of the SS garrison, previously ordered because of the typhus epidemic, is moderated. Still in effect is the ban on entering the Waffen SS House, visiting restaurants, and setting foot in the town of Auschwitz. SS family members can, however, be granted leave if they have themselves disinfected beforehand. At the same time, Höss threatens that if the hygienic measures which were ordered in agreement with the Garrison Doctor are not followed, he will be forced again to withdraw leave for all members of the SS garrison.

APMO, D-AuI-1, Garrison Order 8/43 of March 10, 1943.

APRIL 11

Gustaw Lassisch, born in the Gypsy camp, is given No. Z-6064.

APMO, D-AuII-3/1/2, p. 179, Register of Male Gypsies.

Two male Gypsies are given Nos. Z-6065 and Z-6066 and two female Gypsies Nos. Z-6770 and Z-6771.

The corpses of 29 prisoners are delivered to the morgue of the main camp.

APMO, D-AuI-5/2, Morgue Register, p. 121.

APRIL 12

In compliance with an order by the WVHA of April 6, 1943, the Polish prisoner doctors Zenon Hoffman, Engelhardt, Leonard Daj-

APMO, D-AuI-3a/168, 180, Labor Deployment.

kowski, and Stanisław Wrona-Merski, as well as the German prisoner doctor Aleksander Burze from the Lublin (Majdanek) concentration camp will be transferred to Auschwitz and assigned to the First Camp Doctor. The prisoner Wrona-Merski gets his former number, 13842,* the other four get Nos. 114631–114634.

Nos. 114635–114816 are given to 182 men and Nos. 40783–40800 to 18 women who during interrogations, and before any decision about their fate had been made, had been housed in Block 2a of the main camp, which had been made available to the investigative detention prison in Myslowitz. They are now registered as prisoners of Auschwitz. Included are Mieczysław Piłat (No. 114743) and Bronisław Włodarski (No. 114793).**

APMO, Deposition, vol. 13, pp. 81–85, Account of Former Prisoner Mieczysław Piłat.

Nos. 114817–114833 are given to 17 male prisoners and Nos. 40801–40820 to 20 female prisoners sent in a group transport.

In compliance with an order by the WVHA, 1,212 Polish prisoners are transferred from Auschwitz to Mauthausen.

APMO, D-AuI-3a/143, 145, 152, 156, 182, 187, 188, 189, 197, Labor Deployment.

By order of the WVHA, the prisoner Zbigniew Nowacki (No. 37360) is transferred from Auschwitz to the Herzogenbusch concentration camp.

APMO, D-AuI-3a/174, Labor Deployment.

The corpses of 49 prisoners are delivered to the morgue of the main camp.

APMO, D-AuI-5/2, Morgue Register, p. 122.

APRIL 13

By order of the WVHA, 1,024 Polish prisoners are transferred from Auschwitz to Mauthausen.†

APMO, D-AuI-3a/152, 156, 189.

Nos. 114834–114836 are given to three prisoners sent from Kattowitz.

By order of the Political Department, two German Gypsies, Arthur Bubanick (No. Z-3343) and Georg Pompe (No. Z-3359), are de-

APMO, D-AuI-3/2, Bunker Register, p. 2.

*The prisoner Stanisław Wrona-Merski had been transferred from Auschwitz to Majdanek on February 18, 1942.
**The prisoner Bronisław Włodarski dies in the camp on June 29, 1943.
†The transfer of 5,001 Polish construction and metal workers to the Neuengamme, Buchenwald, Flossenbürg, Gross-Rosen, and Sachsenhausen concentration camps and of 2,236 Polish skilled workers to Mauthausen in April 1943 occurred mainly for security reasons, and is intended to prevent resistance actions by these prisoners as well as to impede possible contacts to the civilian population. For a short period of time, this procedure in fact leads to a situation in which the resistance groups in the camp become smaller and fewer Poles escape from the camp. But it has the added consequence that significant difficulties arise in the deployment of the prisoners' labor, particularly in the further enlargement of the main camp and of the mass killing facilities. After the Head of the Central Construction Office in Auschwitz, Bischoff, protests and the Head of Branch C (Works and Buildings) in the WVHA, Kammler, similarly uses his influence, several dozen prisoners, all trained masons, electricians, installers, etc., are finally sent back to Auschwitz in late May (APMO, D-AuI-3a/254, 255, 256, 257, 258, 259, 264, 266, 272, 273).

livered to the bunkers of Block 11. After a selection in the bunkers they are shot on April 27, 1943.

Nos. 114837–114838 are given to two prisoners sent from Zichenau.

Nos. 40821–40823 are given to three female prisoners sent in a group transport.

Nos. 114839–114868 are given to 30 male prisoners and Nos. 40824–40830 to seven female prisoners sent by the Sipo and SD for the Kraków District.

Nos. 114869–114874 are given to six prisoners sent from Kattowitz.

Nos. 40831–40840 are given to 10 female prisoners from Ravensbrück whom the WVHA has assigned to work as orderlies in the infirmary of the Gypsy camp in Birkenau.

APMO, D-AuI-3a/165, 186, 193, 198.

Marian Schmelzen, born in the Gypsy camp in Birkenau on April 11, 1943, is given Z-6067.

APMO, D-AuII-3/1/2, p. 179, Register of Male Gypsies.

Approximately 2,800 Jewish men, women, and children from the ghetto in Salonika arrive in an RSHA transport from Greece. After the selection, 500 men, given Nos. 114875–115374, and 364 women, given Nos. 40841–41204, are admitted to the camp as prisoners. The other approximately 1,936 people are killed in the gas chambers.

The corpses of 48 prisoners are delivered to the morgue of the main camp; two of the dead are from the Kobior A.C. and 23 are from the Buna A.C.

APMO, D-AuI-5/2, Morgue Register, p. 123.

APRIL 14

Anton Georg Bernhardt, born in the Gypsy camp, is given No. Z-6068.

APMO, D-AuII-3/1/2, p. 179, Register of Male Gypsies.

A seven-year-old, Robert Weiss, delivered to the camp the previous day, is given No. Z-6069.

Ibid.

Vladislav Janaček, born in the Gypsy camp on March 23, 1943, is given No. Z-6070.

Ibid.

Two girls born in the Gypsy camp are given Nos. Z-6772–Z-6773.

APMO, D-AuII-3/2/3, p. 437, Register of Female Gypsies.

A transport of Gypsies arrives from the territory of the German Reich. 20 men and boys are given No. Z-6071–Z-6090 and 15 women and girls get Nos. Z-6774–Z-6788.

Johann Weinrich, born in the Gypsy camp on March 11, 1943, is given No. Z-6091.

APMO, D-AuII-3/1/2, p. 180, Register of Male Gypsies.

Adelheid Ernst, born in the Gypsy camp, is given No. Z-6789.

APMO, D-AuII-3/2/3, p. 437, Register of Female Gypsies.

By order of the WVHA, two Polish prisoner doctors, Janusz Okla and Tadeusz Kowalski, are transferred to Neuengamme.

APMO, D-AuI-3a/179, 194, Labor Deployment.

In compliance with an order by the WVHA of March 24, 1943, four Polish prisoners are transferred and assigned to the First Camp Doctor in Ravensbrück. They are the doctor Aleksander Bugajski (No. 74503) and orderlies Jósef Bareja (No. 103758), Stanisław Mareas (No. 74598), and Jan Gniadet (No. 95573). The prisoners are guarded on the shipment by the SS Men who previously brought female orderlies from Ravensbrück to Auschwitz.

APMO, D-AuI-3a/146, 1772, 186, 191, Labor Deployment.

Nos. 115375–115377 are given to three prisoners sent from Kattowitz.

Nos. 115378–115489 are given to 112 prisoners sent to the camp from the prison in Radom by the Sipo and SD in Radom.

The corpses of 34 prisoners are delivered to the morgue of the main camp; three of the dead are from the Buna A.C.

APMO, D-AuI-5/2, Morgue Register, p. 124.

80 people who were arrested in Chełmek, in Libiąż, and in the vicinity of Auschwitz are shot in the gas chamber of Crematorium I at the main camp.

CA KC PZPR, 202/III-146, Documents of the Polish Government in Exile, pp. 61, 259.

APRIL 15

Because of a visit by SS Commander in Chief Himmler, expected within the next few days, the commanding officer of the Death's Head Unit at Auschwitz orders the company officers to make preparations, and makes them responsible for an exemplary state of order in the housing and barracks.

Documents and Materials, p. 96.

The occupancy level of the women's camp in Birkenau is 16,003; 5,332 women are not able-bodied, 6,159 are not used for work, and 4,512 are employed in labor squads.

APMO, D-AuI-3a/379/3, p. 227, Overview.

Nos. 115490–115510 are given to 21 male prisoners and Nos. 41205–41236 to 32 female prisoners sent to the camp by the Sipo and SD of Radom.

In the evening, the Czech prisoner Gottlieb Krbeček, born in Brünn on June 1, 1919, escapes from the camp.

APMO, IZ-8/Gestapo Lodz/3a/88/431; D-AuI-1/1, Telegrams, p. 110.

Three Czech political prisoners, Emil Olbrych (No. 68311), Jaroslav Nadvornik (No. 96894), and Rudolf Mrkos (No. 21094) are put in the bunkers of Block 11, probably in connection with Krbeček's

APMO, D-AuI-3/2, Bunker Register, p. 3.

escape. They are released from the bunker into the camp on April 27, 1943.

The corpses of 37 prisoners are delivered to the morgue of the main camp; five of the dead are from the Buna A.C.

APMO, D-AuI-5/2, Morgue Register, pp. 124ff.

APRIL 16

Vera Daniel, born in the Gypsy camp in Birkenau, is given No. Z-6790.

APMO, D-AuII-3/2/3, p. 439, Register of Female Gypsies.

A transport of Austrian Gypsies arrives. 909 men and boys receive Nos. Z-6092–Z-7000 and 938 women and girls receive Nos. Z-6791–Z-7728.

Nos. 115511–115515 are given to five prisoners who were assigned to Caesar, Director of the Agricultural Department, by order of the WVHA. Three shepherds, an expert on tree nurseries, and one smith were ordered on April 6.

APMO, D-AuI-3a/192, 204.

Nos. 115516–115550 are given to 35 prisoners sent to the camp by the Sipo and SD in Radom.

Nos. 115551–115573 are given to 23 male prisoners and Nos. 41237–41253 to 17 female prisoners sent in a group transport. With this transport female prisoner No. 253 is again delivered to the camp; she had previously been interned in the women's camp of Auschwitz-Birkenau.

Nos. 115574–115701 are given to 128 male prisoners and Nos. 41254–41269 to 16 female prisoners sent in a group transport.

The corpses of 22 prisoners are delivered to the morgue of the main camp.

APMO, D-AuI-5/2, Morgue Register, pp. 125ff.

APRIL 17

Commandant Höss informs the SS Guard Stormtroopers that a company made up of Ukrainians has been formed and will start service on April 18, 1943.*

APMO, D-AuI-1, ST No. 63/43.

Nos. 115702–115708 are given to seven male prisoners and Nos. 41270–41319 to 50 female prisoners sent in a group transport.

Nos. 115709–115805 are given to 97 prisoners sent to the camp by the Lodz Gestapo.

---

*As the number of available SS men is not sufficient to guard the prisoners employed in the outside labor squads as well as in the auxiliary camps and factories, there is a move to enlist volunteers for the SS among the ethnic Germans in the satellite countries, i.e., Czechoslovakia, Croatia, Hungary, and Romania, as well as in the Baltic countries—Lithuania, Latvia, and Estonia. The Ukrainians serving in this company are collaborators who work with the Nazis.

Nos. 115806–115813 are given to eight male prisoners and Nos. 41320–41353 to 34 female prisoners sent in a group transport.

Nos. 115814–115847 are given to 34 prisoners sent to the camp by the Sipo and SD for the Kraków District.

A female prisoner sent from Kraków gets the free No. 40523.

Sonia Herzensberger, born in the Gypsy camp in Birkenau, gets No. Z-7729.

APMO, D-AuII-3/2/4, p. 499, Register of Female Gypsies.

Approximately 3,000 Jewish men, women, and children from the ghetto in Salonika arrive with an RSHA transport from Greece. After the selection, 467 men, given Nos. 115848–116314, and 262 women, given Nos. 41354–41615, are admitted to the camp. The other approximately 2,271 people are killed in the gas chambers.

The Commandant's Office is informed by the WVHA that a cooking course that will last approximately 10 days will begin in Dachau on May 1, 1943. Eight prisoners should be sent to this course.

APMO, D-AuI-3a/183, Labor Deployment.

The corpses of 43 prisoners are delivered to the morgue of the main camp; nine of the dead are from the Buna A.C. and one is from the Jawischowitz A.C.

APMO, D-AuI-5/2, Morgue Register, p. 126.

APRIL 18

No. 116315 is given to a prisoner sent to the camp on April 3, 1943, from Kattowitz.

No. 116316 is given to a prisoner sent to the camp from Kattowitz on April 2, 1943.

2,501 Jewish men, women, and children from the ghetto in Salonika arrive with an RSHA transport from Greece. After the selection, 360 men, given Nos. 116317–116676, and 245 women, given Nos. 41616–41860, are admitted to the camp. The other 1,896 people are killed in the gas chambers.

The corpses of 20 prisoners are delivered to the morgue of the main camp.

Ibid., p. 127.

APRIL 19

Elfriede Kozak, born in the Gypsy camp, is given No. Z-7730.

APMO, D-AuII-3/2/4, p. 499, Register of Female Gypsies.

Nos. 116678–116727 are given to 50 male prisoners and Nos. 41861–41868 to eight female prisoners sent with a group transport.

No. 41869 is given to a female prisoner sent from Białystok.

The corpses of 47 prisoners are delivered to the morgue of the main camp; 18 of the dead are from the Buna A.C., two are from the Jawischowitz A.C., and one, the Gypsy No. Z-3124, is from the Gypsy camp in Birkenau.

APMO, D-AuI-5/2, Morgue Register, p. 128.

APRIL 20

Nos. 116728–116736 are given to nine prisoners sent from Kattowitz.

Nos. 116737–116753 are given to 17 prisoners sent by the Sipo and SD for the Kraków District.

Approximately 1,000 Jewish men, women, and children arrive with an RSHA transport from Neudorf in Lower Silesia. After the selection, 299 men, given Nos. 116754–117052, and 158 women, given Nos. 41870–42027, are admitted to the camp. The other approximately 543 deportees are killed in the gas chambers.

Marie Baranyai, born in the Gypsy camp in Birkenau, is given No. Z-7731.

APMO, D-AuII-3/2/4, p. 499, Register of Female Gypsies.

Three Gypsies receive Nos. Z-7001–Z-7003.

Jaroslauw Daniel, born in the Gypsy camp on April 19, 1943, gets the number Z-7004.

APMO, D-AuII-3/1/2, p. 206, Register of Male Gypsies.

A group transport includes some Gypsies. 35 men and boys receive Nos. Z-7005–Z-7039, and 19 women and girls receive Nos. Z-7732–Z-7750.

Nos. 117053–117112 are given to 60 prisoners sent to the camp from the prison in Tarnów by the Sipo and SD.

Two representatives of Friedrich Krupp AG, the directors Weinhold and Velten, arrive in the Commandant's Office in order to catch up on the progress of the transfer of the Krupp factories to Auschwitz. In addition, they wish to inform themselves about the housing possibilities for the management personnel and to establish direct relations between the management of the factory and the Commandant's Office.

APMO, Maurer Trial, vol. 8a, pp. 98–104.

Because of the feared spread of the typhus epidemic, Commandant Höss orders that all vehicles used for the transport of prisoners and their clothing and laundry should be disinfected immediately upon returning. Höss makes SS Technical Sergeant Weigandt responsible for the exact execution of the order.

APMO, D-AuI-1/20, Commandant's Office Order 8/43.

Commandant Höss praises SS Technical Sergeant Jochum and 10 SS members of the 2nd Guard Company, because they, despite unfavorable circumstances, captured two prisoners who had es-

Ibid.

caped from the Special Squad on March 9, 1943, and gotten as far as the forest near Jedlin.*

SS Lieutenant Colonel Karl Möckel takes over the direction of the Administrative Department (Department IV) of Auschwitz Concentration Camp. The previous director, Willi Burger, is demoted to Office D-IV in Branch D of the WVHA, which is the administrative section for all concentration camps.

APMO, D-AuI-1/20, Commandant's Office Order 8/43.

Walter Polenz, SS No. 85132, and Heinrich Schwarz, SS No. 19691, are promoted to SS Captain. Otto Brossmann, SS No. 352200, is promoted to SS First Lieutenant.**

Ibid.

32 members of the Guard Stormtroopers of Auschwitz C.C. are awarded a Distinguished Service Cross, Second Class, with Swords. Among the recipients are many SS members who personally mistreat and kill prisoners, including Roll Call Leader SS Corporal Oswald Kaduk, SS Corporal Herbert Kirschner, and Gerhard Lachmann from the Political Department as well as Medical Orderlies SS Corporal Josef Klehr and SS Staff Sergeant Herbert Scherpe, who kill prisoners with phenol injections into the heart.

Ibid.

The Distinguished Service Medal is awarded to 20 SS members of the Auschwitz Guard Stormtroopers, and the Iron Cross of World War I is awarded to 29 SS members.

Ibid.

The corpses of 20 prisoners are delivered to the morgue of the main camp; six of the dead are from the Buna A.C.

APMO, D-AuI-5/2, Morgue Register, p. 129.

APRIL 21

Branch D informs the Commandant that the cooking course for prisoners will last not 10 days but four weeks.

APMO, D-AuI-3a/211, Labor Deployment.

No. 116677 is given to a prisoner sent from Kattowitz.

Nos. 117113 and 117114 go to two prisoners sent on April 17.

Nos. 117115–117198 are given to 84 male prisoners and Nos. 42028–42037 to 10 female prisoners sent from Prague.

The corpses of 26 prisoners are delivered to the morgue of the main camp; one of the dead is from the Buna A.C.

APMO, D-AuI-5/2, Morgue Register, pp. 129ff.

APRIL 22

2,800 Jewish men, women, and children from the ghetto in Salonika arrive in an RSHA transport from Greece. After the selection, 255

*Pery Broad recalls this escape, or a comparable one, by two prisoners of the Special Squad (*Auschwitz in the Eyes of the SS*, p. 171).
**Hitler's fifty-fourth birthday: Promotions and awards are usually announced or awarded on the Führer's birthday.

men, given Nos. 117199–117453, and 413 women, given Nos. 42038–42450, are admitted to the camp. The other 2,132 deportees are killed in the gas chambers.

No. 117454 is given to a prisoner sent from Kattowitz.

1,400 Jews from the Malines camp arrive with the twentieth RSHA transport from Belgium. In it are 507 men and 121 boys, as well as 631 women and 141 girls. After the selection, 276 men, given Nos. 117455–117730, and 245 women, given Nos. 42451–42695, are admitted to the camp. The other 879 people are killed in the gas chambers.

No. 117731 is given to a prisoner sent from Kattowitz.

112 female prisoners, Nos. 42451–42562, are transferred from the women's camp in Birkenau to the research station in Block 10 of the main camp. These women were selected from the transport that arrived on this day from Malines.

APMO, Dpr.-Hd/6, p. 94.

Nos. 117732–117744 are given to 13 male prisoners and Nos. 42696–42698 to three female prisoners sent from Oppeln.

Nos. 117745–117804 are given to 60 prisoners sent from the prison in Tarnów by the Sipo and SD.

Nos. 117805–117883 are given to 79 prisoners from the prison in Radom, sent by the Sipo and SD in Radom.

The corpses of 38 prisoners are delivered to the morgue of the main camp; four of the dead are from the Buna A.C.

APMO, D-AuI-5/2, Morgue Register, p. 130.

APRIL 23

Nos. 117884–117943 are given to 60 male prisoners and Nos. 42699–42707 to nine female prisoners sent in a group transport.

Nos. 117944–118289 are given to 346 prisoners sent to the camp by the Prague Gestapo.

Nos. 42708–42811 are given to 104 female prisoners sent in a group transport.

Austrian Gypsies arrive in a transport. 57 men and boys receive Nos. Z-7040–Z-7096 and 49 women and girls receive Nos. Z-7751–Z-7799.

Manfred Rosenberg, born in the Gypsy camp on April 22, 1943, receives No. Z-7097.

APMO, D-AuII-3/1/2, p. 209, Register of Male Gypsies.

Bruno Franz, born in the Gypsy camp on April 21, 1943, receives No. Z-7098.

Ibid.

Marie Adler, born in the Gypsy camp in Birkenau on April 21, 1943, receives No. Z-7800.

Five male Gypsies receive Nos. Z-7099–Z-7103, and five female Gypsies receive Nos. Z-7801–Z-7805.

Hermann Horwath, born in the Gypsy camp, gets No. Z-7104.

Ursula Gutenberger, born in the Gypsy camp, gets No. Z-7806.

The corpses of 34 prisoners are delivered to the morgue of the main camp; one of the dead is from the Buna A.C.

APMO, D-AuII-3/2/4, p. 503, Register of Female Gypsies.

APMO, D-AuII-3/1/2, p. 209, Register of Male Gypsies.

APMO, D-AuII-3/2/4, p. 503, Register of Female Gypsies.

APMO, D-AuI-5/2, Morgue Register, p. 131.

APRIL 24

Nos. 118290–118376 are given to 87 males and Nos. 42812–42865 to 54 females sent from the prison in Tarnów by the Sipo and SD in Tarnów.

Nos. 118377–118414 are given to 38 male prisoners and Nos. 42866–42881 to 16 female prisoners sent by the Sipo and SD for the Kraków District.

Nos. 118415–118424 are given to 10 prisoners sent from Kattowitz.

Anna Horwath, born in the Gypsy camp, receives No. Z-7807.

The corpses of 24 prisoners are delivered to the morgue of the main camp. One of the dead, a reeducation prisoner with the number EH-4014, is from the Buna A.C.

APMO, D-AuII-3/2/4, p. 503, Register of Female Gypsies.

APMO, D-AuI-5/2, Morgue Register, p. 132.

APRIL 25

Easter. The resistance organization in the camp sends a message to Kraków via a secret route, in which the following occupancy levels for men in the various parts of the Auschwitz complex* are given for April 25, 1943:

Birkenau	11,671
Buna-Werke	3,301
Golleschau	289
Jawischowitz	1,194
Kobior	156
Budy	167
Harmense	91
Russian POWs	149
Auschwitz	17,037
Gypsy camp	12,000

The corpses of 17 prisoners are delivered to the morgue of the main camp.

APMO, Mat.RO, vol. 1, p. 24.

APMO, D-AuI-5/2, Morgue Register, p. 132.

*The report gives the total number of female and male Gypsies, as these are housed together in a family camp. Data for the occupancy level of the women's camp are not available.

View of section of Auschwitz main camp.

APRIL 26

Five male Gypsies receive Nos. Z-7105–Z-7109 and four female Gypsies receive Nos. Z-7808–Z-7811.

2,700 Jewish men, women, and children from the ghetto in Salonika arrive in an RSHA transport from Greece. After the selection, 445 men, given Nos. 118425–118869, and 193 women, given Nos. 42882–43074, are admitted to the camp. The other 2,062 people are killed in the gas chambers.

Nos. 118870–118887 are given to 18 male prisoners and Nos. 43075–43121 to 47 female prisoners sent in a group transport.

The corpses of 33 prisoners are delivered to the morgue of the main camp.

Ibid., p. 133.

APRIL 27

The three prisoners, Tomasz Serafiński (No. 4859), whose real name is Witold Pilecki; Jan Retko (No. 5430), actually Jan Redzej; and Edward Ciesielski (No. 12969) escape at 2:00 A.M. from the bakery squad, Landsmann Bakery, while the bread is baking.*

APMO, D-AuI-1/1, Telegrams, pp. 116–119; IZ-8/Gestapo Lodz/3a/88/433-436; Mat.RO, vol. IV, p. 292.

*The escape has been precisely planned and prepared. The prisoners cross the Soła and Vistula rivers and in this way reach Alwaria, where they find help in crossing the border to the General Government. In early May, they reach the agreed-on meeting place in Bochnia. Witold Pilecki, one of the leaders of the association of military organizations in the camp, who has been trained for an eventual possible

Three male Gypsies receive Nos. Z-7110–Z-7112 and three female Gypsies receive Nos. Z-7812–Z-7814.

Johann Narday, born in the Gypsy camp on April 26, 1943, receives No. Z-7113.

APMO, D-AuII-3/1/2, p. 210, Register of Male Gypsies.

Ursula Weiss, born in the Gypsy camp on April 26, 1943, receives No. Z-7813.

APMO, D-AuII-3/2/4, p. 505, Register of Female Gypsies.

The Head of Branch D, Glücks, informs the Commandants of the decision of the SS Commander in Chief that "in future, only mentally ill prisoners can be chosen for the '14 f 13' operation by the medical commissions intended for this purpose. All other non-able-bodied prisoners (tubercular prisoners, bedridden cripples, etc.) are basically to be excluded from this operation. Bedridden prisoners should be called upon for appropriate work that they can do even in bed."*

Mitscherlich and Mielke, *Doctors Trial*, p. 219.

The Director of Labor Deployment, SS Captain Schwarz, requests Office D-II of the WVHA to transfer 30 female Bible researchers, so-called IBV prisoners, from Ravensbrück to Auschwitz because they are needed for child care in families of SS members. In the communiqué it is stated that a large number of the female IBV prisoners incarcerated in Auschwitz are too ill to work.

APMO, D-AuI-3a/217, Labor Deployment.

The Director of the Political Department, Grabner, informs the camp management, the Camp Doctor, and Labor Deployment that in compliance with the WVHA order of April 12, 1943, the prisoners Tadeusz Lisowski (No. 329), Michał Jojczyk (No. 883), Kazimierz Szelest (No. 3454), Antoni Urbański (No. 3629), Tadeusz Chmura (No. 5633), Andrzej Patalas (No. 6671), Zygmunt Szczepański (No. 17701), and Antoni Śmierzchalski (No. 25321) are transferred in prisoner clothing to Dachau on April 29, 1943, for participation in a cooking course.

APMO, D-AuI-3a/218, Labor Deployment.

The corpses of 35 prisoners are delivered to the morgue of the main camp. Five of the dead are from the Buna A.C. and one, No. Z-

APMO, D-AuI-5/2, Morgue Register, pp. 133ff.

---

uprising in the camp in case of favorable circumstances, regards his task as fulfilled. He voluntarily undertook camp internment when he had himself smuggled into a group transport that the Warsaw Sipo and SD sent to Auschwitz from Warsaw on September 22, 1940. In mid-April he decides to escape from the camp—which is connected with significant risks—because he is of the opinion that at this stage of the resistance work he must work outside in the underground for the liberation of the concentration camp, which under certain circumstances might be possible (Garliński, *Fighting Auschwitz*, pp. 163–173; compare entry for Sept. 22, 1940).

*On the basis of this order, the treatment of patients in the blocks of the prisoners' infirmary changes. The killing of severely ill prisoners by phenol injections or by poison gas is stopped. In the following month, the number of the dead registered in the Morgue Register of the main camp falls to 30, on some days even to less than 20. The sick bays of the prisoner infirmary gradually change from a "gateway to death" into medical facilities whose purpose is the saving of human life. Starting in August 1943, Jewish prisoners are again selected (Danuta Czech, "Die Rolle des Häftlingskranken baulagers ein KL Auschwitz" (The Role of the Prisoners' Infirmary in Auschwitz Concentration Camp II), *HvA*, no. 15 (1985): pp. 5–112).

5615, is brought from the prisoners' infirmary of the main camp, Block 21a.

3,070 Jewish men, women, and children from the ghetto in Salonika arrive with an RSHA transport from Greece. After the selection, 180 men, given Nos. 118888–119067, and 361 women, given Nos. 43123–43483, are admitted to the camp. The other 2,529 deportees are killed in the gas chambers.

Nos. 43484–43486 are given to three female prisoners delivered from Bielsko.

SS Captain Schwarz informs Dachau that the eight prisoners intended for the cooking course will leave Auschwitz in the evening. Schwarz therefore requests confirmation of the arrival of the prisoners and their inclusion in the occupancy level of Dachau.

APMO, D-AuI-3a/220, Labor Deployment.

SS First Lieutenant Sommer, the acting head of Office D-II in the WVHA, orders the Commandant's Office to allot 128 Jewish female prisoners for experimental purposes.

APMO, Dpr.-Hd/8, p. 9, Telegram No. 2678.

128 Greek Jewish females from the women's camp in Birkenau, previously selected by Professor Dr. Clauberg, are transferred to the experimental station in Block 10 of the main camp.

APMO, Dpr.-Hd/8, p. 9.

The Gypsy Heinrich Klein (No. Z-5353) is captured when he attempts to escape from the DAW plant and is delivered to the bunker of Block 11. He is shot on May 25, 1943.

APMO, D-AuI-3/2, Bunker Register, p. 4.

The corpses of 37 prisoners are delivered to the morgue of the main camp; among them is No. EH-3862, who is from the Buna A.C.

APMO, D-AuI-5/2, Morgue Register, pp. 134ff.

APRIL 29

The reason for the arrest of a woman interned until now as a reeducation prisoner (EH) is changed. She remains in the camp as a political prisoner and receives No. 43122.

Nos. 119068–119111 are given to 44 prisoners sent from Kattowitz.

Nos. 119112–119122 are given to 11 prisoners sent the previous day from Kattowitz.

Nos. 119123–119126 are given to four prisoners sent from Kattowitz.

Armanda Braun, born in the Gypsy camp, receives No. Z-7816.

APMO, D-AuII-3/2/4, p. 505, Register of Female Gypsies.

Nos. 119127–119526 are given to 400 male prisoners and Nos. 43488–43593 and 43662 to 107 female prisoners sent from Warsaw. No. 119339 is given to Zygmunt Łempicki, professor of German at the University of Warsaw; No. 43530 is given to his wife, Wanda Łempicka. No. 43513 is given to film director Wanda Jakubowska.*

No. 119527 is given to a prisoner sent from Kattowitz on April 22, 1943.

APMO, D-AuI-5/2, Morgue Register, p. 135.

The corpses of 18 prisoners are delivered to the morgue of the main camp; one of the dead is from the Buna A.C.

APRIL 30

A transport of Austrian Gypsies arrives. 48 men and boys receive Nos. Z-7114–Z-7161 and 47 women and girls receive Nos. Z-7817–Z-7863.

Peter Wachter, born in the Gypsy camp on April 11, 1943, gets No. Z-7162.

APMO, D-AuII-3/1/2, p. 211, Register of Male Gypsies.

Emma Weitz, born in the Gypsy camp on April 29, 1943, gets No. Z-7864.

APMO, D-AuII-3/2/4, p. 507, Register of Female Gypsies.

Three male Gypsies receive Nos. Z-7163–Z-7165; two female Gypsies receive Nos. Z-7865 and Z-7866.

Miroslaus Strzeszczyk, born in the Gypsy camp on April 29, 1943, gets the number Z-7166.

APMO, D-AuII-3/1/2, p. 211, Register of Male Gypsies.

The Commandant's Office advises the WVHA that 242 female prisoners are earmarked for experimental purposes. This is the first report that mentions the number of women housed in the experimental station of Professor Dr. Clauberg in Block 10 of the main camp.

APMO, Dpr.-ZOd/IV, p. 27.

18,659 female prisoners are imprisoned in the women's camp of Auschwitz-Birkenau, of whom 6,119 are incapable of working. On this day, 6,968 female prisoners are deployed and 5,572 have nothing to do. Included in the number of working women are also the 242 female prisoners who have been transferred to the experimental station of Professor Clauberg and 22 female orderlies.

APMO, D-AuI-3a/370/3, Overview. In Rubric 11 under the title "Office W," the categories "Care Giver" and "Prisoner for Research Purposes" have been added. In the archive of the Auschwitz Memorial there are six overviews of prisoner deployment in the women's camp in which the daily figures are cited for April, May, June, October, November, and December, 1943.

In response to the April 27, 1943, request of the Director of Labor Deployment, Schwarz, for the transfer of 30 IBV prisoners from Ravensbrück to Auschwitz, Maurer, the Head of Office D-II, asks for a report as to which households have until now employed female IBV prisoners and which ones at present need domestic help.

APMO, D-AuI-3a/225, Labor Deployment. [transfer of 30 IBV prisoners]

The reason for the arrest of a woman until now incarcerated as a reeducation prisoner is changed to political prisoner; she receives No. 43487.

*Wanda Jakubowska made two feature films about Auschwitz: *Ostatni Etap* (The Last Stage), 1948, and *Koniec naszego Świata* (The End of Our World), 1964.

Nos. 43594–43661 are given to 68 female prisoners sent in a group transport.

No. 119528 is given to a prisoner sent from Kattowitz.

Nos. 119529–119554 are given to 26 prisoners sent to the camp by the Sipo and SD for the Kraków District.

Nos. 43663–43665 are given to three female prisoners and Nos. 119555–119653 to 99 male prisoners sent in a group transport. 13 Jews who escaped from the fifty-third RSHA transport from Drancy, which was headed for Sobibor, are transferred with this shipment to Auschwitz.

Commandant Höss advises the SS guard units that Hitler has awarded it the Distinguished Service Cross, First Class, with Swords. The Director of the crematoriums in Birkenau, SS Captain Otto Moll, also receives this award.

APMO, D-AuI-1/23, Commandant's Office Order 10/43.

The corpses of 25 prisoners are delivered to the morgue of the main camp; two of the dead are from the Buna A.C.

APMO, D-AuI-5/2, Morgue Register, pp. 135ff.

A Jewish prisoner, No. 104797, is captured during an escape attempt and delivered to the bunker of Block 11. He dies there on May 6, 1943. His corpse is delivered on this day from Block 11 to the morgue.

APMO, D-AuI-3/2, Bunker Register, p. 5; D-AuI-5/2, Morgue Register, p. 139, Item 10.

The Central Construction Office requests 250 prisoners who are needed in the construction of Crematorium III in Birkenau to be made available on Saturday, May 1 (holiday), and on Sunday. The reason for the application is the urgency of the construction work.

APMO, D-AuI-3a, Folder 17, p. 218.

APRIL 1–30

1,859 registered prisoners have died in the women's camp in Auschwitz-Birkenau; following a selection in the camp, 277 of these women were killed in the gas chambers.

APMO, Mat.RO, vol. VII, p. 485.

MAY 1

The occupancy level of the women's camp is 18,787 prisoners, of whom 6,123 are incapable of working. Since a holiday is involved, on this day 1,827 work, and 10,837 are without employment.

APMO, D-AuI-3a/370/3, p. 237, Overview.

17 female prisoners sent in a group transport receive Nos. 43666–43682, and 34 male prisoners get Nos. 119654–119687.

SS Second Lieutenant Hans Schurz, detective constable, is assigned to the Political Department.

APMO, D-AuI-1/23, Commandant's Office Order 10/43.

242 female prisoners for experimental purposes and 22 female prisoner orderlies are housed at the experimental station of Professor Dr. Clauberg in Block 10 of the main camp.

APMO, D-AuI-3a/370/3, p. 237, Overview.

The corpses of 14 prisoners are delivered to the morgue of the main camp.

APMO, D-AuI-5/2, Morgue Register, p. 136.

MAY 2

The prisoner Bolesław Leśniak (No. 3555) escapes. He had been sent to the camp by the Sipo and SD on August 30, 1940, because of his Communist activity.

APMO, D-AuI-1/1, p. 124, Telegrams; IZ-8/Gestapo Lodz/3a/88/442; Mat.RO, vol. IV, p. 292.

Of the prisoners sent from Radom by the Sipo and SD, 42 women receive Nos. 43683–43724, and 74 men receive Nos. 119688–119761.

Margot Reinhardt, born in the Gypsy camp, receives No. Z-7867.

APMO, D-AuII-3/2/4, p. 507, Register of Female Gypsies.

10 prisoners sent from Vienna receive Nos. 119762–119771.

36 female prisoners sent in a group transport receive Nos. 43725–43760.

The corpses of 20 prisoners are delivered to the morgue of the main camp.

APMO, D-AuI-5/2, Morgue Register, pp. 136ff.

MAY 3

Housed at the experimental station of Professor Dr. Clauberg in Block 10 of the main camp are 243 female prisoners for experimental purposes and 22 female prisoner orderlies.

APMO, D-AuI-3a/370/3, p. 237, Overview.

A prisoner from Auschwitz is transferred to Dachau and 12 are transferred to Mauthausen.

APMO, D-AuI-3a/216, Labor Deployment.

Ivan Stadnik (No. EH-4202) escapes from the Buna A.C. He was sent to the camp by the Kattowitz Stapo for loafing on the job.

APMO, D-AuI-1/1, p. 126, Telegrams; IZ-8/Gestapo Lodz/3a/88/444; Mat.RO, vol. IV, p. 292.

Nos. 119772–119780 are given to nine male prisoners and Nos. 43761–43778 to 18 female prisoners who arrive in a group transport.

19 corpses, including three from the Buna A.C., are delivered to the morgue of the main camp.

APMO, D-AuI-5/2, Morgue Register, p. 137.

MAY 4

Ketty Grünholz is born in the Gypsy camp and receives No. Z-7868.

APMO, D-AuII-3/2/4, p. 507, Register of Female Gypsies.

Elisabeth Scheifer, born on May 1, and Anna Holomek, born on April 29, both in the Gypsy camp, receive Nos. Z-7869 and Z-7870.

Ibid.

Of the Gypsies sent from Austria, 14 men receive Nos. Z-7167–Z-7180 and 14 women receive Nos. Z-7871–Z-7884.

2,930 Jewish men, women, and children from the ghetto in Salonika arrive with an RSHA transport from Greece. After the selection, 220 men, given Nos. 119781–120000, and 318 women, given Nos. 43779–44096, are admitted to the camp. The other 2,392 people are killed in the gas chambers.

On the initiative of the firm of Berg- und Hüttenwerksgesellschaft (Mining and Smelting Company), called Berghütte, a conference takes place in Schwientochlowitz (Świętochłowice), at which representatives of Office D-II of the WVHA and of the Oberschlesischen Maschinen- und Waggonfabrik AG (Upper Silesian Machine and Vehicle Factory), OSMAG, located in Kattowitz, participate. The conference is chaired by Emil Gömmer, director of the Eintrachthütte. The conference has been called to discuss the employment of prisoners from Auschwitz in the OSMAG factories in Schwientochlowitz. As a result of the conference, a contract is signed between the representatives of Office D-II and OSMAG to the effect that 1,000 prisoners should be made available to work in the Eintrachthütte.

Franciszek Piper, "Das Nebenlager Eintrachthütte" (Eintrachthütte Auxiliary Camp), *HvA*, no. 17 (1985): 91–155.

Nos. 120001–120023 are given to 23 prisoners sent from Troppau.

Nos. 44097–44099 are given to three female prisoners who arrive in a group transport.

Housed at the experimental station of Professor Dr. Clauberg in Block 10 of the main camp are 243 female prisoners for experimental purposes and 22 female orderlies.

APMO, D-AuI-3a/370/3, p. 237, Overview.

Two Gypsies, Józef Cerinek (No. Z-1904) and Franz Rożyczka (No. Z-2035), are locked in the bunker of Block 11 because they tried to escape from their workplace. When they distanced themselves from their workplace, they were noticed and arrested by the SS Man Alexander Horschütz of the 6th Guard Company. Both prisoners are shot on May 22, 1932, following a selection conducted in the bunkers.

APMO, D-AuI-3/2, Bunker Register, p. 5; D-AuI-1/24, Commandant's Office Order 11/43 of May 6, 1943.

The corpses of 26 prisoners are delivered to the morgue of the main camp; one of the dead is from the Buna A.C.

APMO, D-AuI-5/2, Morgue Register, p. 138.

During a night air raid on the Buna plants, nine bombs are released in the vicinity of the Buna camp. A watchtower is hit by aircraft cannon from one of the airplanes. No damage is found in the auxiliary camp.

APMO, IZ-13/89, Various Documents of the Third Reich, p. 287.

MAY 5

The occupancy level of the women's camp is 19,070, of whom 6,081 are able-bodied. On this day, 9,867 female prisoners work, and 3,122 have no employment.

APMO, D-AuI-3a/370/3, p. 237, Overview.

245 female prisoners are housed for experimental purposes at the experimental station of Professor Dr. Clauberg in Block 10 of the main camp.

Ibid.

Nos. 120024–120038 are given to 15 prisoners sent from Kattowitz.

Nos. 44106–44111 are given to six female prisoners sent in a group transport.

Nos. 120039–120072 are given to 34 prisoners sent to the camp from Radom by the Sipo and SD.

The German prisoner Wilhelm Stüber* (No. 113968), born in Bonn on February 20, 1904, who had been transferred from Mauthausen to Auschwitz on April 10, 1943, escapes from the camp.

APMO, IZ-10/Kripo Sieradz/2a/70/89; Mat.RO, vol. IV, p. 292.

The corpses of 15 prisoners are delivered to the morgue of the main camp; one of the dead is from the Buna A.C.

APMO, D-AuI-5/2, Morgue Register, p. 138.

MAY 6

The SS man Alexander Horschütz is promised three days special leave by Commandant Höss for the capture of the two Gypsies, Józef Cerinka and Franz Rożycki, on May 4.

APMO, D-AuI-1/24, Commandant's Office Order 11/43.

Nos. 120073 and 120074 are given to two prisoners delivered from Oppeln.

Nos. 120075–120353 are given to 279 male prisoners and Nos. 44112–44192 to 81 female prisoners sent from Lodz.

Nos. 120354–120355 are given to two prisoners sent from Kattowitz.

Two Gypsies, Paul Reinhardt (No. Z-4208), born in Lauffen on April 22, 1922, and Josef Reinhardt (No. Z-4210), born in Lauffen on June 15, 1924, are captured while attempting an escape and locked in the bunkers of Block 11. Both are shot on May 22, 1943, after a selection in the bunkers.

APMO, D-AuI-3/2, Bunker Register, p. 6.

Housed at the experimental station of Professor Dr. Clauberg in Block 10 of the main camp are 200 female prisoners for experimental purposes and 67 female prisoner orderlies.

APMO, D-AuI-3a/370/3, p. 237, Overview.

Police security detainee (Polizeisicherungsverwahrter—PSV) prisoner Ernst Metzner (No. 84437), born in Kattowitz on December 17, 1912, dies in the bunker of Block 11; he had been sent there

APMO, D-AuI-3/2, Bunker Register, p. 5; in the Bunker Register there is a note that this man

---

*Wilhelm Stüber is recaptured in Beuel near Bonn on May 18, 1943.

on May 4 by order of the Political Department. His corpse is delivered to the morgue of the main camp.

is a "half-breed" (Mischling); D-AuI-5/2, Morgue Register, p. 139, Item 12.

The corpses of 20 prisoners are delivered to the morgue of the main camp.

APMO, D-AuI-5/2, Morgue Register, p. 139.

MAY 7

Maurer, the Head of Office D-II in the WVHA, confirms in writing the contract between the SS and the OSMAG concerning the use of 1,000 prisoners from Auschwitz as laborers in the plants of Entrachthütte. Also clarified are the housing of the prisoners, the wages, and other questions having to do with the employment of prisoners and the organization and maintenance of the auxiliary camp. The prisoners should be housed in the barracks of the forced labor camp for Jews who are destined for liquidation. The immediate supervision of the implementation of these measures is in the hands of SS Captain Schwarz.

WAP Kattowitz, BH-2511, pp. 28ff.; Piper, "Eintrachthütte," pp. 91–97; photocopy of a communication from Maurer, ibid., pp. 92–94.

Housed at the experimental station of Professor Dr. Clauberg in Block 10 of the main camp are 200 female prisoners for experimental purposes and 67 female prisoner orderlies.

APMO, D-AuI-3a/370/3, p. 237, Overview.

Gypsies from Czechoslovakia arrive: 438 men and boys get Nos. Z-7181–Z-7618 and 425 women and girls get Nos. Z-7885–Z-8309.

No. Z-8310 is given to Sofie Stefan, born in the Gypsy camp in Birkenau.

APMO, D-AuII-3/2/4, p. 537, Register of Female Gypsies.

Two Poles, Józef Michalczyk (No. 14268) and Edward Borkowski (No. 14750),* escape from the camp.

APMO, D-AuI-1/1, p. 140, Telegrams; IZ-10/Kripo Sieradz/2a/73; Mat.RO, vol. IV, p. 292.

Six Gypsies escape from the camp. They are Jaromir Daniel (No. Z-1051), Jan Daniel (No. Z-4836), Anton Holomek (No. Z-1173), Stefan Holomek (No. Z-4808), Stanisław Holomek (No. Z-4809), and Vruzen Vrba (No. Z-4831). Except for Vruzen Vrba, five of them are captured during the pursuit and are immediately locked in the bunker of Block 11. After a selection in the bunker, they are shot on May 22, 1943.

APMO, D-AuI-3/2, Bunker Register, p. 7.

Six female prisoners sent from Kattowitz receive Nos. 44100–44105.

Nos. 120356–120487 are given to 132 men and Nos. 44193–44258 to 66 women who have been delivered to the camp in a group transport.

---

*Edward Borkowski is captured on August 12, 1943, and is shot during another escape attempt in Lublin on August 13, 1943.

Director of Labor Deployment Schwarz hands over to Office D-II of the WVHA a list of SS families that employ female IBV prisoners as domestic help, as well as a list of offices and administrative centers of the SS that employ 63 female IBV prisoners as cleaning women, maids, cooks, etc. At the same time, he notes that in the camp there are still 13 female IBV prisoners, one of whom is sick and the other too ill and too old to work. In an accompanying letter Schwarz repeats his request of April 27 to transfer to Auschwitz 30 female IBV prisoners; they are needed in households with many children where the wife is ill; the Commandant and the Garrison Doctor confirm this.

APMO, D-AuI-3a/230ff., Labor Deployment.

Approximately 1,000 Jewish men, women, and children from the ghetto in Salonika arrive in an RSHA transport from Greece. After the selection, 68 women are admitted to the camp and receive Nos. 44259–44326. The other people are killed in the gas chambers.

Nos. 44327–44371 are given to 45 female prisoners from Posen who have been sent by the Gestapo.

Approximately 1,000 Jewish men, women, and children from the ghetto in Agram arrive in an RSHA transport from Yugoslavia. After the selection 40 men are admitted to the camp; the next day they are given Nos. 120596–120635. The other people are killed in the gas chambers.

The corpses of 23 prisoners are delivered to the morgue of the main camp; among them is one from the Buna A.C. and a Gypsy, No. Z-5227, from the prisoners' infirmary, Block 19 of the main camp.

APMO, D-AuI-5/2, Morgue Register, pp. 139ff.

MAY 8

Housed at the experimental station of Professor Dr. Clauberg in Block 10 of the main camp are 228 female prisoners for experimental purposes and 39 female prisoner orderlies.

APMO, D-AuI-3a/370/3, p. 237, Overview.

Commandant Höss orders that incoming mail to female prisoners should be handed out by the newly equipped mail censor's station in the women's camp in Birkenau. Höss makes the squad leader and the Head Supervisor, Zimmer, primarily responsible for the proper and punctual distribution of mail in the auxiliary camps and other locations in which female prisoners are employed.* He also

APMO, D-AuI-1/27, Commandant's Office Special Order 14/43; Dpr.-ZOd/40.

*Female prisoners who are permanently employed at the animal-breeding farms, the agricultural enterprises in Harmense and Budy, in horticulture, or at the experimental facility in Rajsko for the development and extraction of plant caoutchouc, or india rubber, live in the auxiliary camps set up there. Starting in September 1942, female Jews who work in the offices of the Political Department, Labor Deployment, the Construction Office, and other administrative offices live in staff buildings on the grounds of the camp. Also housed there are more than 90 female IBV prisoners who work as domestic help in private households of the SS as well as in the casinos, canteens, and other facilities of the SS as waitresses (APMO, D-AuI-3a/231, Deployment List of Female IBV Prisoners, May 7, 1943).

makes clear that the address of both the recipient and the sender must be precisely noted.

Nos. Z-8311 and Z-8312 are given to Helena Murka and Angela Vasek, who were born in the Gypsy camp.

APMO, D-AuII-3/2/4, p. 537, Register of Female Gypsies.

Nos. Z-7619–Z-7635 are given to 17 Gypsies brought from Germany in a group transport.

Nos. Z-7636 and Z-7637 are given to two boys born in the Gypsy camp.

APMO, D-AuII-3/1/2, p. 225, Register of Male Gypsies.

Nos. 120488–120571 are given to 84 prisoners sent in a group transport.

Nos. 102572–120595 are given to 24 male prisoners and Nos. 31592 and 44372–44379 to nine female prisoners from Kraków who have been sent to the camp by the Sipo and SD. The free No. 31592 is given to Janina Nowak, who was sent to Auschwitz for the first time on June 12, 1942, escaped on June 24, 1942, and was arrested again in Lodz on March 12, 1943, and brought back to the camp.

APMO, IZ-8/Gestapo Lodz/2/88/20.

No. 120636 is given to a prisoner sent from Kattowitz.

No. 120637 is given to a prisoner sent from Oppeln.

Nos. 120640–120649 are given to 10 prisoners sent from Kattowitz.

2,500 Jewish men, women, and children from the ghetto in Salonika have arrived with an RSHA transport from Greece. After the selection, 568 men and 247 women are admitted to the camp and are given Nos. 120650–121217 and 44380–44626, respectively. The other 1,685 people are killed in the gas chambers.

Leopold Malarz (No. 87476), who escaped on February 12, 1943, is locked in the bunker of Block 11. He was captured on April 5 and sent back to the camp on May 4, 1943. He is shot on June 25, 1943, following a selection in the bunkers.

APMO, D-AuI-3/2, Bunker Register, p. 7; IZ-8/Gestapo Lodz/2/88/129–133.

The reeducation prisoner Kazimierz Orlikowski (No. EH-3844), who was put in the bunker of Block 11 on April 16, dies. His corpse is taken to the morgue.

APMO, D-AuI-5/2, Morgue Register, p. 140, Item 11; D-AuI-3/2, Bunker Register, p. 3.

The corpses of 24 prisoners are delivered to the morgue of the main camp; one of the dead is from the Jawischowitz A.C. and one is from the Kobior A.C.

APMO, D-AuI-5/2, Morgue Register, p. 140.

MAY 9

Housed at the experimental station of Professor Dr. Clauberg in Block 10 of the main camp are 228 female prisoners for experi-

APMO, D-AuI-3a/370/3, p. 237, Overview.

mental purposes and 39 female prisoner orderlies. This status remains unchanged until May 20, 1943.

Nos. 120638 and 120639 are given to two prisoners who have been transferred by order of Office D-II of the WVHA from Buchenwald, where they worked in the print shop, to Auschwitz. They are Józef Culik, typesetter, and Wacław Jakubcyk, printer.

APMO, D-AuI-3a/233, 234, 235, 236.

Nos. 44627 and 44628 are given to two female prisoners sent from Kattowitz.

Nos. Z-7638–Z-7645 are given to six male Gypsies and Nos. Z-8313–Z-8316 to four female Gypsies.

The corpses of 18 prisoners are delivered to the morgue of the main camp.

APMO, D-AuI-5/2, Morgue Register, p. 141.

MAY 10

The well-known French resistance fighter Danielle Casanova (No. 31655), a Communist, dies of typhus in the Auschwitz-Birkenau women's camp.

APMO, D-AuI-2/1593, Death Certificate, Inventory No. 7593.

Nos. Z-7646 and Z-7647 are given to Kurt Devis and Karl Horwath, born in the Gypsy camp.

APMO, D-AuII-3/1/2, p. 225, Register of Male Gypsies.

Nos. Z-7648–Z-7665 are given to 18 male Gypsies and Nos. Z-8317–Z-8330 to 14 female Gypsies sent from Germany in a group transport.

Nos. 121218–121233 are given to 16 male prisoners and Nos. 44629–44636 to eight female prisoners sent in a group transport.

Three Gypsies, Anton Daniel (No. 112791), Ludwig Daniel (No. 112792), and Viktor Daniel (No. 112793), attempt an escape. In the pursuit, Ludwig and Viktor Daniel are captured and locked in the bunker of Block 11. They are shot on May 22, 1943, following a selection carried out in the bunkers.

APMO, D-AuI-1/1, p. 147, Telegrams; D-AuI-3/2, Bunker Register, p. 7; IZ-10/Kripo Sieradz/2a/74, 75, 78; Mat.RO, vol. IV, p. 292.

Commandant Höss announces that starting May 10 the departure of prisoners to jobs will take place at 6:00 A.M.

APMO, D-AuI-1/24, Commandant's Office Order 11/43.

Reserve Police Sergeant Wilhelm Görlich is transferred from Breslau to Auschwitz by Superior SS and Police Commander Schmauser.

APMO, D-AuI-1/29, Commandant's Office Order 13/43.

The corpses of 14 prisoners are delivered to the morgue of the main camp. Among them are four from the Buna A.C.

APMO, D-AuI-5/2, Morgue Register, p. 141.

MAY 11

Nos. 121234 and 121235 are given to two prisoners sent from the administrative district of Kattowitz.

No. 121236 is given to a prisoner sent from Oppeln.

Nos. 121237–121245 are given to nine prisoners sent from Kattowitz.

Nos. 121246–121277 are given to 32 male prisoners and Nos. 44637–44642 to six female prisoners who have been sent to the camp from Kraków by the Sipo and SD.

Nos. 121278–121285 are given to eight prisoners sent from the Kattowitz District.

Nos. 44643–44651 are given to nine female prisoners sent in a group transport.

Nos. 121286–121323 are given to 38 male prisoners and Nos. 44652–44656 to five female prisoners who have been sent to the camp from Posen by the Gestapo.

The corpses of 25 prisoners are delivered to the morgue of the main camp.

Ibid., pp. 141ff.

MAY 12

Nos. 121324–121329 are given to six prisoners sent from Kattowitz.

Nos. 121330–121354 are given to 25 male prisoners and Nos. 44657–44666 to 10 female prisoners sent to the camp from Kraków by the Sipo and SD.

No. 121355 is given to a male prisoner and Nos. 44667–44668 to two female prisoners sent from the Kattowitz District.

Nos. Z-7666–Z-8133 are given to 468 men and boys and Nos. Z-8331–Z-8833 to 503 women and girls, Polish Gypsies who were sent from Białystok.

In connection with the request of the Commandant's Office for 30 female IBV prisoners to work as domestic help, the Head of Office D-II of the WVHA requests that a list be sent by May 15 showing the number and age of children of the SS families who employ the IBV prisoners as domestic help.

APMO, D-AuI-3a/241, Labor Deployment.

A transport of Gypsies from Austria arrives; 45 men and boys receive Nos. Z-8134–Z-8178 and 31 women and girls receive Nos. Z-8834–Z-8864.

APMO, D-AuI-5/2, Morgue Register, p. 142.

The corpses of 19 prisoners, including four from the Buna A.C., are delivered to the morgue of the main camp.

MAY 13

No. Z-8865 is given to Margarete Weiss, born in the Gypsy camp in Birkenau.

APMO, D-AuII-3/2/4, p. 571, Register of Female Gypsies.

No. Z-8866 is given to Erika Klein, who was born in the Gypsy camp in Birkenau on May 12, 1943.

Ibid.

Nos. 121356–121358 are given to three prisoners sent from Kattowitz.

No. 121359 is given to a prisoner sent from Koblenz.

Nos. 121360–121365 are given to six prisoners sent from Kattowitz.

Nos. 121366–121454 and 121456–121703 are given to 337 male prisoners and Nos. 44694–44812 to 19 female prisoners sent from Warsaw by the Sipo and SD. The prisoners arrive barefoot, for their shoes were taken away before they left Pawiak Prison. Immediately after arrival, 24 female prisoners from this transport are assigned to the Penal Company.

Dománska, *Pawiah*, p. 321.

No. 121455 is given to a prisoner sent from Kattowitz.

Approximately 1,000 Jewish men, women, and children from the ghetto in Agram arrive in an RSHA transport from Yugoslavia. After the selection, 30 men, given Nos. 121704–121733, and 25 women, given Nos. 44669–44693, are admitted to the camp as prisoners. The other approximately 945 people are killed in the gas chambers.

Nos. 44813–44829 are given to 17 female prisoners who have arrived in a group transport.

Nos. 44830–44835 are given to six female prisoners sent from Kraków.

August Frank, the Head of Branch A of the WVHA, reports to the SS Commander in Chief Himmler that the Buna auxiliary camp, which is part of Auschwitz Concentration Camp, was the target of an air raid during the night of May 4–5. Nine bombs were released in the vicinity of the camp, and one airplane opened fire on the watchtower of the camp with machine guns. No damage was found. The Commandant has been informed so that he can requisition 12 20 mm antiaircraft guns.

APMO, IZ-13/89, Various Documents of the Third Reich, p. 287.

The corpses of 22 prisoners are delivered to the morgue of the main camp.

APMO, D-AuI-5/2, Morgue Register, p. 143.

MAY 14

No. Z-8179 is given to Lothar Weis, who was born in the Gypsy camp in Birkenau on May 11, 1943.

APMO, D-AuII-3/1/2, p. 242, Register of Male Gypsies.

No. Z-8180 is given to Henryk Zdenek, who was born in the Gypsy camp.

Ibid.

Nos. Z-8181–Z-8188 are given to eight male Gypsies and No. Z-8867 goes to a female Gypsy.

Nos. 121736–121737 are given to two prisoners sent from the Kattowitz District.

Nos. 121738–121766 are given to 29 prisoners from Kraków sent by the Sipo and SD.

Nos. 121767–121769 are given to three prisoners sent from Kattowitz.

Nos. 121770–121778 are given to nine prisoners sent from Berlin.

In the name of the SS Commander in Chief, SS Lieutenant Colonel Dr. Berndorf of the RSHA addresses to the Commandants of all concentration camps the question of how many miners and explosives experts are available to them in the camps and auxiliary camps under their direction. A report must be made by May 17 at 2:00 P.M. at the latest.

APMO, D-AuI-3a, Labor Deployment.

Nos. 121780–121878 are given to 99 prisoners sent in a group transport.

The Gypsy Vruzen Vrba, who escaped from the camp on May 7, is captured and locked in the bunker of Block 11. He is shot on May 22, 1943, following a selection carried out in the bunker.

APMO, D-AuI-3/2, Bunker Register, p. 8.

The corpses of 18 prisoners, including two from the Buna A.C., are delivered to the morgue of the main camp.

APMO, D-AuI-5/2, Morgue Register, p. 143.

MAY 15

Nos. 44836–44913 are given to 78 female prisoners sent in a group transport.

No. 44914 is given to a female prisoner and No. 121734 to a male prisoner who have been sent from Halle an der Saale.

The Director of Labor Deployment sends to Office D-II of the WVHA the following list concerning number and age of children in SS families that employ female IBV prisoners as domestics.

APMO, D-AuI-3a/249, Labor Deployment.

	Number of children	Age	Number of IBV prisoners
1. SS Lt. Col. Höss	4	5, 9, 10, 12	2
2. SS Maj. Bischoff	—	—	1
3. SS Maj. Burger	2	1/4, 3 1/2	1
4. SS Maj. Hartjenstein	2	6, 7	2
5. SS Maj. Caesar	3	—	2
6. SS Capt. Aumeier	1	11	1
7. SS 1st Lt. Rieck	1	1	1
8. SS 2nd Lt. Hössler	3	1, 4, 6	1
9. SS 2nd Lt. Thomsen	2	5, 10	1
10. SS Tech. Sgt. Heider	7	1, 6, 7, 8, 10, 12, 14	1
11. SS Staff Sgt. Oester	3	1, 2, 3	1
12. SS Staff Sgt. Knittel	1	4	1
13. SS Staff Sgt. Bott	2	2, 3	1
14. SS Tech. Sgt. Remmele	2	6, 12	1
15. SS Corp. Clausen	3	1, 2, 4	1
16. SS Corp. Hoffmann	1	2	1
17. SS Corp. Markmann	1	1	1
18. SS Corp. Mesmer	3	2, 4, 6	1
19. SS Sgt. Koehler	2	1, 3	1
20. SS Sgt. Jaeger	4	1, 3, 4, 6	1
21. SS Priv. 1st Class Ludwig	4	1, 4, 13, 16	1
22. SS Priv. 1st Class Müller	4	1, 3, 5, 7	1
23. Dr. Scheer*	—	—	1
			26

*Dr. Dietholm Scheer was a former prisoner who was released from the camp but continued in his position as a civilian worker (compare the entry on July 27, 1942).

No. 121735 is given to a prisoner sent from Cologne.

Nos. 121879–121909 are given to 31 male prisoners and Nos. 44915–44933 to 19 female prisoners sent in a group transport.

No. Z-8189 is given to Gerhard Blum, born in the Gypsy camp in Birkenau. He dies on May 24, 1943.

APMO, D-AuII-3/1/2, p. 242, Register of Male Gypsies.

No. Z-8190 is given to Bruno Bock, born in the Gypsy camp on May 14, 1943.

Ibid.

Commandant Höss informs the offices that report to him that a new concentration camp with the name "Civilian Internment Camp Bergen-Belsen" has been set up in Bergen-Belsen, in the county of Celle.

APMO, D-AuI-1/31, Commandant's Office Order 14/43.

The corpses of 17 prisoners, including one from the Buna A.C., are delivered to the morgue of the main camp.

APMO, D-AuI-5/2, Morgue Register, p. 144.

MAY 16

Approximately 4,500 Jewish men, women, and children from the ghetto in Salonika arrive with an RSHA transport from Greece. Following the selection, 466 men, given Nos. 121910–122375, and 211 women, given Nos. 44934–45144, are admitted to the camp. The other more than 3,800 people are killed in the gas chambers.

The corpses of 18 prisoners are delivered to the morgue of the main camp.

Ibid.

MAY 17

No. Z-8868 is given to Gisela Ernst, born in the Gypsy camp.

APMO, D-AuII-3/2/4, p. 573, Register of Female Gypsies.

The Head of the Central Construction Office orders the managers of individual projects to make a list of prisoners from the various concentration camps—Flossenbürg, Buchenwald, Neuengamme, Sachsenhausen, and Mauthausen—who should be transferred back to Auschwitz.

APMO, D-AuI-3a, Folder 17, p. 167.

In response to the RSHA's inquiry of May 14, Labor Deployment Director Schwarz reports that in Auschwitz there are 162 miners who are being used in the mines of the Herman Göring Reich Works and who cannot be transferred to another camp.

APMO, D-AuI-3a/250, Labor Deployment.

No. 121779 is given to a prisoner sent from Kattowitz.

Nos. 122376–122398 are given to 23 male prisoners and Nos. 45145–45160 to 16 female prisoners who have arrived with a group transport.

The corpses of 20 prisoners are delivered to the morgue of the main camp; one of the dead is from the Jawischowitz A.C. and two are from the Buna A.C.

APMO, D-AuI-5/2, Morgue Register, p. 144.

MAY 18

No. Z-8191 is given to Stefan Horwath, who was born in the Gypsy camp in Birkenau.

APMO, D-AuII-3/1/2, p. 242, Register of Male Gypsies.

No. Z-8869 is given to Anna Karoly, born in the Gypsy camp.

APMO, D-AuII-3/2/4, p. 573, Register of Female Gypsies.

No. Z-8192 is given to a male Gypsy.

No. Z-8193 is given to Bolesław Balasch, who was born in the Gypsy camp on May 17, 1943.

APMO, D-AuII-3/1/2/ p. 242, Register of Male Gypsies.

The prisoner Jerzy Siwak (No. 102615) escapes from the camp.

APMO, Mat.RO, vol. IV, p. 292.

Nos. 122399–122404 are given to six prisoners sent from Kattowitz.

Nos. 122405–122475 are given to 71 prisoners who have been sent by the Sipo and SD from the prison in Radom.

Nos. 45161–45166 are given to six female prisoners who have arrived in a group transport.

No. 45167 is given to a female prisoner sent from the town of Auschwitz.

Nos. Z-8194–Z-8196 are given to three male Gypsies.

Commandant Höss forbids the SS members of the garrison to enter the towns of Szopienice, Sosnowitz, and Bendin.

APMO, D-AuI-1/30, Commandant's Office Order 14/43.

Commandant Höss introduces the following camp designations:

Ibid.

Main camp	A-I
New Building 7	A-II
Birkenau Section I—(women's camp and current men's camp with the subdivisions a and b)	B-I
Section II—(men's camp and Gypsy camp with subdivisions a, b, c, d, e, f)	B-II
Section III—(not yet occupied)	B-III

The corpses of 11 prisoners are delivered to the morgue of the main camp.

APMO, D-AuI-5/2, Morgue Register, p. 145.

MAY 19

Approximately 1,000 Jewish men, women, and children arrive with an RSHA transport. After the selection, 80 men, given Nos. 122476–122555, and 115 women, given Nos. 45168–45282, are admitted to the camp. The other more than 800 people are killed in the gas chambers.

The camp management arrests the resistance fighter Helena Płotnicka and locks her in the bunker of Block 11. Helena Płotnicka is one of the most self-sacrificing women from the vicinity of the camp, who with help of prisoners in the surveying and nursery squads in Rajsko brought food, medications, and mail into the main camp and smuggled prisoners' reports and letters out. Helena Płotnicka initially came of her own accord to help the prisoners, but later

APMO, Depositions, vol. 13, pp. 125–126, Account of Wojciech Jekiełka; Memoirs, vol. 5, pp. 1–29, Memoirs of Former Prisoner Jan Winogroński.

worked with the local unit of the peasants' battalion (Bataliony Chłopskie).

The corpses of 12 prisoners are delivered to the morgue of the main camp; three are from the Buna A.C., Nos. EH-3710, EH-3930,* and 105824.

APMO, D-AuI-5/2, Morgue Register, p. 145.

MAY 20

Three boys born in the Gypsy camp in Birkenau receive Nos. Z-8197–Z-8199.

APMO, D-AuII-3/1/2, p. 242, Register of Male Gypsies.

No. 122556 is given to a prisoner sent from Kattowitz.

Three prisoners in the surveying squad, the Poles Kazimierz Jarzębowski** (No. 115), Stanisław Chybiński (No. 6810), and Józef Rotter (No. 365), whose real name is Florian Basiński,† who had had contact with Helena Płotnicka, feel themselves particularly endangered after her arrest and incarceration in the bunker of Block 11, and decide to escape from the camp. During their surveying work in Skidzin-Wilczkowice, they offer their SS guard a drink containing a narcotic. When the SS man falls asleep, they flee from their workplace.

APMO, D-AuI-1/1, p. 145, Telegrams; IZ-8/Gestapo Lodz/3a/88/450; D-AuI-1, Stormtrooper Order 83/43; Memoirs, vol. 5, pp. 1–29, Memoirs of Former Prisoner Jan Winogroński.

228 female prisoners for experimental purposes and 30 female prisoner orderlies are still housed at the experimental station of Professor Dr. Clauberg in Block 10 of the main camp.

APMO, D-AuI-3a/370/3, p. 237, Overview.

The corpses of 15 prisoners are delivered to the morgue of the camp.

APMO, D-AuI-5/2, Morgue Register, p. 146.

The occupancy level of the women's camp of Auschwitz-Birkenau is 20,635, of whom 6,788 are incapable of working. On this day, 9,337 female prisoners are employed, and 4,510 remain without work.

APMO, D-AuI-3a/370/3, p. 237, Overview.

MAY 21

The Capo of the surveying squad, Stanisław Dorosiewicz (No. 18379), who collaborates with the Political Department as a spy, accuses the prisoners Jan Winogroński (No. 8235), from the gardening squad, and Stanisław Stawiński (No. 6569), Czesław Marcisz (no. 26891), and Edmund Hakaszewski (No. 7196), all from

APMO, D-AuI-3/2, Bunker Register, p. 9, Memoirs, vol. 5, pp. 1–29, Memoirs of Former Prisoner Jan Winogroński.

---

*Reeducation prisoners are assigned to the Buna A.C. to work in the Buna plants. Mortality among them is high.
**Jarzębowski is one of the prisoners who since 1940 had maintained clandestine contacts with the Poles living in the vicinity of Auschwitz. The surveying work done by the prisoners made possible continual contact with representatives of the resistance organizations operating near the camp.
†Józef Rotter is arrested again and is hanged in Sosnowitz in the fall of 1943.

the surveying squad, of having had contact with the resistance fighter Helena Płotnicka. The accused are locked in the bunker of Block 11.

SS Major Hartjenstein, commanding officer of the Guard Stormtroopers, advises the SS Men that the previous day an SS Man from the 4th Company who was overseeing the surveying squad accepted a beverage from them and fell asleep, whereupon the prisoners had fled. The SS Man is being punished severely, but the event should be a serious warning to all SS Guards that it is forbidden to accept anything from the prisoners. This order is to be understood in the context of the escape of Kazimierz Jarzebowski's group.

APMO, Dpr.-ZOd/40, Storm-trooper Order 83/43.

Nos. 122557–122589 are given to 33 prisoners who have been sent in a group transport.

Nos. 122590–122649 are given to 60 prisoners sent from the prison in Tarnów by the Sipo and SD.

Nos. 122650–122747 are given to 98 male prisoners and Nos. 45283–45295 and 45298–45311 to 18 female prisoners sent in a group transport.

Nos. 122748–122771 are given to 24 prisoners sent from Oppeln.

Nos. 45312–45376 are given to 65 female Jews selected from an RSHA transport from Sosnowitz of approximately 1,000 Jewish men, women, and children. The other more than 900 people are killed in the gas chambers.

Szternfinkiel, *Jews of Sosnowitz*, p. 59.

Nos. 45377–45489 are given to 113 female prisoners sent in a group transport.

Nos. Z-8200–Z-8202 are given to three male Gypsies and Nos. Z-8870–Z-8875 to six female Gypsies who have arrived in a group transport.

The occupancy level at the experimental station of Professor Dr. Clauberg in Block 10 of the main camp diminishes by one: 227 female prisoners are now housed there for experimental purposes as well as 39 female prisoner orderlies.

APMO, D-AuI-3a/370/3, p. 237, Overview.

During an escape attempt, the Pole Mieczysław Jelec (No. 121455) is captured and put in the bunker of Block 11. During interrogations in the Political Department he admits that he was already in Auschwitz Concentration Camp and had fled at the turn of the year 1941–42. At that time he was in the camp under the name Jerzy Krzy-

APMO, D-AuI-3/2, Bunker Register, p. 9; Brol et al., "Bunker Register of Block 11," p. 32.

żanoski and had the number 5715. He remains in the bunker under the special authority of the Political Department.*

The Frenchwoman Dr. Claudette Bloch (No. 7963) is locked in the dark cell in the bunker of Block 11. In the chemical laboratory of the plant-breeding facility in Rajsko, she directed the work done by the female prisoners for the botany labor squad.**

APMO, Dpr.-ZOd/7, p. 130.

The corpses of 24 prisoners are delivered to the morgue of the main camp. Among them are three from the Buna auxiliary camp with the following numbers: EH-3755, EH-4171, and 81367.

APMO, D-AuI-5/2, Morgue Register, p. 146.

MAY 22

No. 45490 is given to a female prisoner sent from Breslau.

A selection is carried out in the bunkers of Block 11 during which 26 prisoners are selected who were assigned there by order of the Political Department or the Camp Commander, or who are suspected of planning an escape attempt or have been captured while attempting to escape. They are shot the same day at the execution wall in the courtyard of Block 11. Among them are the Jewish prisoners Szlama Bursztyn (No. 88773), Wolf Jablonowski (No. 60431), Hirsch Jablonowski (No. 76334), Israel Naparstek (No. 76487), Elie Mordok (No. 109588) from Salonika, and Schmul Weinberg (No. 43664), as well as the Gypsies Józef Cerinek (No. Z-1904), Franc Rożyczka (No. Z-2035), Herman Pol (No. Z-3029), Albert Bernhardt (No. Z-247), and Rudolf Stein (No. Z-3108).

APMO, D-AuI-3/2, Bunker Register, pp. 5–9.

Three boys born in the Gypsy camp receive Nos. Z-8203–Z-8205.

APMO, D-AuII-3/1/2, p. 242, Register of Male Gypsies.

No. Z-8876 is given to a girl born in the Gypsy camp in Birkenau.

APMO, D-AuII-3/2/4, p. 573, Register of Female Gypsies.

No. Z-8206 is given to August Weiss, born in the Gypsy camp on May 20, 1943.

APMO, D-AuII-3/1/2, p. 243, Register of Male Gypsies.

No. Z-8207 is given to Franz Kosak, born in the Gypsy camp on April 20, 1943.

Ibid.

The corpses of 14 prisoners, including two from the Buna A.C., are delivered to the morgue of the main camp.

APMO, D-AuI-5/2, Morgue Register, p. 147.

MAY 23

No. Z-8208 is given to a male Gypsy and Nos. Z-8877–Z-8879 to three female Gypsies.

*By order of the new Commandant of Auschwitz, Liebehenschel, Jelec and other prisoners are released from the bunker and transferred to Flossenbürg.
**Dr. Claudette Bloch is released from the bunker on May 29, 1943.

227 female prisoners for experimental purposes and 39 female prisoner orderlies are housed at the experimental station of Professor Dr. Clauberg in Block 10 of the main camp.

APMO, D-AuI-3a/370/3, p. 237, Overview.

The corpses of 17 prisoners are delivered to the morgue of the main camp.

APMO, D-AuI-5/2, Morgue Register, p. 147.

MAY 24

Nos. 122773–122794 are given to 22 male prisoners and Nos. 45494–45502 to nine female prisoners who arrive in a group transport.

Nos. 122795–122854 are given to 60 male prisoners and Nos. 45503–45512 to 10 female prisoners sent from the prison in Tarnów by the Sipo and SD.

Nos. 44513–45519 are given to seven female prisoners sent from Kattowitz.

The corpses of 20 prisoners, including three from the Buna A.C., are delivered to the morgue of the main camp.

Ibid., pp. 147ff.

The Commandant's Office receives a letter dated May 22, 1943, from the Energieversorgung Oberschlesien AG (Upper Silesia Power Company) in Kattowitz with a request for the transfer, by July 1, 1943, of 2,000 prisoners who are to be used in the construction of a power station and the enlargement of the mine. The EVO reports in the same letter that it has provided 16 residential barracks for the prisoners and two barracks with approximately 200 places for the guard personnel, as well as an infirmary barracks, furnished as a mess barracks, two wash barracks, and five latrines. 700 prisoners are to be used in coal mining, 700 in the construction of the power station, 300 in laying railway track, and 300 in construction work in the mines.*

APMO, Jaworzno, Folder I, p. 304; Franciszek Piper, "Das Nebenlager Neu-Dachs" (The Neu-Dachs Auxiliary Camp), *HvA*, no. 12 (1971): 55–111.

MAY 25

Nos. Z-8209–Z-8216 are given to eight boys in the Gypsy camp in Birkenau.

APMO, D-AuII-3/1/2, p. 243, Register of Male Gypsies.

No. Z-8880 is given to Maria Farago, born in the Gypsy camp.

APMO, D-AuII-3/2/4, p. 573, Register of Female Gypsies.

226 female prisoners for experimental purposes and 39 female prisoner orderlies are housed at the experimental station of Professor Dr. Clauberg in Block 10 of the main camp.

APMO, D-AuI-3a/370/3, p. 237, Overview.

No. 122772 is given to a male prisoner and No. 45492 to a female prisoner sent from Kattowitz.

*The EVO sends a similar letter on May 29, 1943, to Office D-II in WVHA.

Nos. 122855–122952 are given to 98 prisoners sent to the camp by the Lodz Gestapo.

Nos. 122953–122974 are given to 22 prisoners sent from Kattowitz.

Nos. 122975–123002 are given to 28 prisoners sent from Kraków by the Sipo and SD.

Nos. 123003–123013 are given to 11 prisoners sent from Kattowitz.

No. 123014 is given to a prisoner sent the previous day from the Kattowitz District.

Two female police prisoners incarcerated in Block 11 of the main camp are entered in the camp registers of the women's camp and receive Nos. 45491 and 45493.

Czesław Warcisz, who is being held in the bunker of Block 11, is interrogated by SS functionaries of the Political Department.

APMO, Memoirs, vol. 5, pp. 1–29, Memoirs of Former Prisoner Jan Winogroński.

The SS Camp Doctor orders a quarantine for the Gypsy camp in Birkenau, in the course of which 507 male Gypsies, Nos. Z-7666–Z-8178, and 528 female Gypsies, Nos. Z-8331–Z-8864, are led to the gas chambers. Among them are several sick with typhus and several hundred suspected of having typhus. Among the killed are Polish Gypsies from Białystok and Gypsies from Austria who were delivered to the camp on May 12, 1943. The prisoner in the orderly room is commanded to enter a natural cause of death on the death certificates of the gassed Gypsies, in fact, to enter a good dozen deaths daily.*

APMO, Depositions, vol. 13, pp. 67–68; vol. 15, pp. 53–66, Account of Former Prisoners Tadeusz Joachimowski and Dr. Tadeusz Śnieszko.

The corpses of 12 prisoners are delivered to the morgue of the main camp.

APMO, D-AuI-5/2, Morgue Register, p. 148.

MAY 26

In Schwientochlowitz near Kattowitz, the Eintrachthütte auxiliary camp is set up near the Eintrachthütte armaments factories. 30 prisoners, a so-called prison advance squad, are transferred to the auxiliary camp. The squad's tasks include clearing the sites and preparing the premises for the next prisoner shipment.

APMO, D-AuI-3a, Labor Deployment Lists for Prisoners in Auschwitz.

*In the Register of Male Gypsies between May 25 and June 3 a cross and the date are entered beside the names of the male Gypsies from these two transports who were gassed. In the Register of Female Gypsies either "SB," the abbreviation for "Sonderbehandlung," "special treatment," or a cross with a date between May 26 and June 11, 1943, is entered beside the names of the women from these transports (APMO, D-AuII-3/1/2, pp. 226–242; D-AuII-3/2/4, pp. 538–572).

Nos. 123023–123037 are given to 15 male prisoners and Nos. 45528–45536 to nine female prisoners who have been sent from Kattowitz.

Nos. 123038–123081 are given to 44 male prisoners and Nos. 45537–45551 to 15 female prisoners sent from the prison in Tarnów by the Sipo and SD.

The corpses of 20 prisoners are delivered to the morgue of the main camp; among them are four from the Buna A.C. with the following numbers: EH-4160, EH-114072, and 115857.

APMO, D-AuI-5/2, Morgue Register, pp. 148ff.

13 prisoners from the surveying squad are locked in the bunker of Block 11 because they are under suspicion of being active in the resistance group of the camp and of having made contact with the civilian population during their work in the area and of having helped Kazimierz Jarzebowski and his companions to escape.

APMO, D-AuI-3/2, Bunker Register, pp. 10ff.

MAY 27

Nos. Z-8217–Z-8222 are given to six male Gypsies and Nos. Z-8881–Z-8885 to five female Gypsies who have arrived in a group transport.

Two girls born in the Gypsy camp in Birkenau receive Nos. Z-8886 and Z-8887.

APMO, D-AuII-3/2/4, p. 573, Register of Female Gypsies.

Commandant Höss orders that Sundays in the camp and the auxiliary camps are to be used for delousing and repairing underwear and clothing.

APMO, D-AuI-1, Commandant's Office Order 19/43.

Nos. 123082 and 123083 are given to two prisoners sent from Kattowitz.

11 more prisoners from the surveying squad are locked in the bunkers of Block 11, because they are under suspicion of maintaining contact with the civilian population as well as of having assisted Kazimierz Jarzebowski and the other prisoners with their escape plans.

APMO, D-AuI-3/2, Bunker Register, pp. 11ff.

No. 45552 is given to a female prisoner sent to the camp on April 5, 1943.

The WVHA orders the Commandant's Office to transfer 800 prisoners who are sick with malaria to the Lublin (Majdanek) C.C.

APMO, D-AuI-3a/283, Labor Deployment.

At the experimental station of Professor Dr. Clauberg in Block 10 of the main camp, the occupancy level decreases by one: 225 female prisoners for experimental purposes and 29 female prisoner orderlies are now housed there.

APMO, D-AuI-3a/370/3, p. 237, Overview.

The corpses of 22 prisoners are delivered to the morgue of the main camp; among them are one from the Buna A.C. and one from the Kobior A.C.

APMO, D-AuI-5/2, Morgue Register, p. 149.

MAY 28

226 female prisoners for experimental purposes as well as 39 female prisoner orderlies are housed at the experimental station of Professor Dr. Clauberg in Block 10 of the main camp.

APMO, D-AuI-3a/370/3, p. 237, Overview.

Nos. 45296 and 45297 are given to two female prisoners sent from Oppeln.

Included in the occupancy level of the men's camp are 453 Polish skilled workers who were transferred back to Auschwitz from Neuengamme the previous day.*

APMO, D-AuI-3a/281, Labor Deployment.

Nos. 123015–123022 are given to eight male prisoners and Nos. 45553–45559 to seven female prisoners who have been sent in a group transport.

Nos. 123084–123110 are given to 27 male prisoners and Nos. 45560–45601 to 42 female prisoners sent in a group transport.

Nos. 123111–123139 are given to 29 prisoners sent in a group transport.

SS Major Hartjenstein grants two SS men from the 2nd Guard Company three days' special leave: The previous day one of the men shot a prisoner who was escaping; the second one captured an escaping prisoner, a Gypsy, shortly before he attempted to cross the Vistula.

APMO, D-AuI-1/40, Stormtrooper Order 87/43; Dpr.-ZOd/40.

The prisoner Johann Winterstein (No. Z-7635), who was captured the previous day at the Vistula, is locked in the bunker of Block 11. He is shot on June 25, 1943, following a selection carried out in the bunkers.

APMO, D-AuI-3/2, Bunker Register, p. 12.

Two boys born in the Birkenau Gypsy camp receive Nos. Z-8223 and Z-8224.

APMO, D-AuII-3/1/2, p. 243, Register of Male Gypsies.

The corpses of seven prisoners are delivered to the morgue of the main camp.

APMO, D-AuI-5/2, Morgue Register, p. 150.

MAY 29

Commandant Höss confirms the order of SS Major Hartjenstein concerning the granting of three days' special leave to two SS Men.

APMO, D-AuI-1/36, Commandant's Office Order 20/43.

*These prisoners do not get a sequential number, as they were already marked with a number the first time they were sent to Auschwitz.

Nos. 123140–123203 are given to 64 male prisoners and Nos. 45602–45634 to 33 female prisoners who have been sent in a group transport.

Included in the occupancy level of the men's camp are 39 prisoners, Polish skilled workers, who at the request of the Auschwitz C.C. have been transferred back from Mauthausen.

APMO, D-AuI-3a/286, Labor Deployment.

Labor Deployment Director SS Captain Schwarz requests from the Commander of the Guard Unit an SS officer, a noncommissioned officer, and 24 SS Men as an escort for the immediate transport of 800 prisoners who are sick with malaria from Auschwitz to the Lublin (Majdanek) C.C.

APMO, D-AuI-3a/289, Labor Deployment.

Commandant Höss issues a ban forbidding the children of SS families from setting foot in the camp.

APMO, D-AuI-1/36, Commandant's Office Order 20/43.

The corpses of 19 prisoners are delivered to the morgue of the main camp.

APMO, D-AuI-5/2, Morgue Register, p. 150.

By order of the Camp Commander, five German Gypsies are locked in the bunker of Block 11. They are released into the camp on June 25, 1943.

APMO, D-AuI-3/2, Bunker Register, pp. 12 ff.

MAY 30

The position of Camp Doctor in the Gypsy Family Camp in Birkenau is taken over by SS Captain Josef Mengele, a medical doctor with a doctorate in philosophy, born on May 16, 1911. Wounded in the spring of 1943 on the Eastern Front, Mengele does not wish to return to the front and volunteers for service in the concentration camps. During selections at the ramp, he sends thousands to their death. He does service in the outpatient services of the B-IIa, B-IIb, and B-IId camps. In the Gypsy camp he conducts pseudoscientific research on twins and dwarfs, killing several of them for so-called research purposes.*

Yves Ternon and Socrate Helman, *Historia medycyny* SS *czyli mit rasizmu biologicznego* (History of SS Medicine, or the Myth of a Biological Racism), Warsaw, 1973, pp. 148–150, 230–238.

The occupancy level in the men's camp includes 31 Polish skilled workers who at the request of the Auschwitz concentration camp have been transferred back from Buchenwald.

APMO, D-AuI-3a/287, Labor Deployment.

The occupancy level in the men's camp includes 22 Polish skilled workers who at the request of the Auschwitz concentration camp have been transferred back from Sachsenhausen.

APMO, D-AuI-3a/290, Labor Deployment.

*After the war Mengele succeeds in avoiding arrest by escaping to South America. In 1962, he files an appeal before a court in Frankfurt am Main against the decision of the University of Frankfurt to revoke his medical diploma, giving a power of attorney to his former wife to conduct this trial. Josef Mengele loses the case. However, he continued to avoid prosecution for his crimes in the Auschwitz-Birkenau concentration camp.

Two boys born in the Gypsy camp receive Nos. Z-8225 and Z-8226.

APMO, D-AuII-3/1/2, p. 243, Register of Male Gypsies.

225 female prisoners for experimental purposes as well as 39 female prisoner orderlies are now housed at the experimental station of Professor Dr. Clauberg in Block 10 of the main camp, where the occupancy level has decreased by one.

APMO, D-AuI-3a/370/3, p. 237, Overview.

By order of the Camp Commander, six male Gypsies are locked in the bunkers of Block 11. Karl Devis (No. Z-5311) dies in the bunker on June 4; the other five prisoners, Stefan Horvath (Z-6303), Josef Istviann (Z-7476), Rudolf Daniel (No. Z-7843), Vincent Malik (No. 7500), and Johann Daniel (No. Z-7506), are transferred to the Penal Company on June 6, 1943.

APMO, D-AuI-3/2, Bunker Register, p. 13.

The corpses of 15 prisoners are delivered to the morgue of the main camp.

APMO, D-AuI-5/2, Morgue Register, p. 150.

Albert Speer, the Reich Minister for Armaments and Munitions, notifies SS Commander in Chief Himmler that on the basis of the reports presented to him by Desch and Sander concerning the inspection of the Auschwitz concentration camp, he is willing to make available to the camp the following construction materials: 1,000 metric tons* of iron, 1,000 metric tons of cast-iron pipes, 100 metric tons of water pipes, and 8–20 mm girders of hardened steel in the requisite number. This quantity of iron is intended only for expansion of the concentration camps, particularly Auschwitz. At the moment he is unable to grant any more iron for additional construction projects of the new SS division that is being created. The requirements can be covered from the general SS iron quota. All other allocation questions must be clarified between the SS Commander in Chief's headquarters and the office for raw materials in Speer's ministry. A request for 1,000 tons of cast-iron pipes and a delivery of water pipes is being processed.**

APMO, IZ-13/89, Various Documents of the Third Reich, pp. 288ff.

MAY 31

25 prisoners are transferred from Auschwitz to Mauthausen.

APMO, D-AuI-3a/184, Labor Deployment.

No. 123204 is given to a prisoner sent from Kattowitz.

Nos. 45635–45680 are given 46 female prisoners sent from Augsburg.

Nos. 123205–123234 are given to 30 male prisoners and Nos. 45681–45698 to 18 female prisoners sent in a group transport.

*One metric ton equals 1.102 short tons (American standard).—Ed.
**After signing the letter, Speer adds a handwritten postscript expressing his satisfaction that the inspection of another concentration camp yielded a favorable picture.

Nos. Z-8888 and Z-8889 are given to two female Gypsies sent in a group transport.

Josef Holomek, who was born in the Birkenau Gypsy camp, receives No. Z-8227.

APMO, D-AuII-3/1/2, p. 243, Register of Male Gypsies.

By order of the Camp Commander, the prisoner Johann Dytkow (No. Z-7867), a Polish Gypsy born in Radziechów on November 11, 1920, is put in the bunker of Block 11 and shot the same day.

APMO, D-AuI-3/2, Bunker Register, p. 13.

The occupancy level of the women's camp of Auschwitz-Birkenau is 20,542, of whom 6,939 are incapable of working. On this day, 9,930 female prisoners are employed, and 4,673 female prisoners remain without work.

APMO, D-AuI-3a/370/3, p. 237, Overview.

The corpse of the criminal prisoner Heinz Roman (No. 17808) is delivered to the morgue of the main camp. He was assigned to Auschwitz on July 4, 1941, and was locked in the bunker of Block 11 four times: from December 3, 1941, to January 3, 1942; on June 13, 1942; from February 12 to February 16, 1943; and from February 18 to March 31, 1943.

APMO, D-AuI-3/1/2, Bunker Register, pp. 43, 67, 121, 127.

The corpses of 22 prisoners, including 10 from the Buna A.C., are delivered to the morgue of the main camp; among the Buna dead are three reeducation prisoners with the numbers EH-4077, EH-4185, and EH-4353.*

APMO, D-AuI-5/2, Morgue Register, p. 151.

MAY 1–31

857 registered female prisoners die in the women's camp, B-Ia, in Birkenau.

APMO, Mat.RO, vol. VII, p. 485.

JUNE 1

Nos. 123235–123245, 123247, and 123248 are given to 13 male prisoners and No. 45699 to a female prisoner sent from Kattowitz.

No. 123246 is given to a prisoner sent from Oppeln.

No. Z-8229 is given to a male Gypsy.

The corpses of 18 prisoners are delivered to the morgue of the main camp; among them are one from the Kobior A.C. and one from the Buna A.C.

APMO, D-AuI-5/2, Morgue Register, p. 151.

---

*From this numbering it is apparent that the number of reeducation prisoners in Auschwitz is 4,300 men. The Morgue Register of the main camp, in which the prisoner numbers are noted, shows clearly that the mortality of this group is high.

Included in the occupancy level of the men's camp are 37 Polish skilled workers who at the request of the Auschwitz Concentration Camp have been transferred back from Flossenbürg.

APMO, D-AuI-3a/292, Labor Deployment.

JUNE 2

10 prisoners sent from Kattowitz receive Nos. 123249–123258.

Nos. 123259–123262 and 45700 are given to four male prisoners and one female prisoner who have been sent from the Kattowitz District.

Two Gypsies, Anton Delies (No. Z-5175) and Paul Steinbach (No. Z-5277), are captured during an escape attempt and sent to the bunker of Block 11. They are shot on June 25, 1943, following a selection in the bunkers.

APMO, D-AuI-3/2, Bunker Register, p. 14.

The corpses of 12 prisoners are delivered to the morgue of the main camp.

APMO, D-AuI-5/2, Morgue Register, p. 152.

JUNE 3

Commandant Höss informs the SS members of the garrison that in compliance with an order by the WVHA, female prisoners can be employed as domestic help in SS families. 25 Reichsmarks per month must be paid to the camp administration for their services.

APMO, Dpr.-ZOd/39, Garrison Order 22/43.

The occupancy rate at the experimental station of Professor Dr. Clauberg in Block 10 of the main camp decreases by 89 women. 136 women for experimental purposes and 39 female prisoner orderlies are now housed there.

APMO, D-AuI-3a/370/4, Monthly Labor Deployment List.

542 male prisoners and 302 female prisoners who are ill with malaria are transferred to the Lublin (Majdanek) C.C.

APMO, D-AuI-3a/303, 304, Labor Deployment.

Two prisoners, Stefan Siwak (No. 102627) and Johan Buriański (No. Z-5571), are captured during an escape attempt and locked in the bunkers of Block 11. They are shot on June 25, 1943, following a selection carried out in the bunkers.

APMO, D-AuI-3/2, Bunker Register, p. 14.

Two escaped prisoners are transferred to Auschwitz after their second arrest and are locked in the bunkers of Block 11. They are Władysław Wójtowicz (No. 18666) and Adam Goska (No. 38109), who escaped on March 8, 1943. They are shot on June 25, 1943, following a selection in the bunkers.

APMO, D-AuI-3/2, Bunker Register, p. 14; IZ-8/Gestapo Lodz/ 2/88/160, 162.

Nos. 123263–123790 are given to 528 male prisoners and Nos. 45520–45527 and 45701–45826 to 134 female prisoners sent from the prison in Radom by the Sipo and SD.

Nos. 45827–45828 are given to two female prisoners sent from Kattowitz.

Nos. 123791–123809 are given to 19 male prisoners and Nos. 45829–45853 to 25 female prisoners sent in a group transport.

A Pole, Maria Brandt (No. 35354), who was sent to the camp from Zichenau on February 15, 1943, escapes from the forestry squad.

APMO, D-AuI-1/1, p. 156, Telegrams; IZ-8/Gestapo Lodz/3/88/454.

The corpses of 12 prisoners are delivered to the morgue of the main camp.

APMO, D-AuI-5/2, Morgue Register, p. 152.

A Polish gypsy, Mieczysław Brzeziński (No. PSV-109320) is locked in the bunker of Block 11 on suspicion of preparing an escape. He is shot on June 25, 1943, following a selection in the bunkers.

APMO, D-AuI-3/2, Bunker Register, p. 14.

JUNE 4

At the experimental station of Professor Dr. Clauberg the occupancy level decreases by one female prisoner. 137 women for experimental purposes and 39 female prisoner orderlies are now housed there.

APMO, D-AuI-3a/370/4, Monthly Labor Deployment List.

Eight prisoners who returned the previous day from a cooking course at Dachau are included in the occupancy level of the men's camp.

APMO, D-AuI-3a/294, 394, 301, Labor Deployment.

Nos. 123810–123857 are given to 48 male prisoners and Nos. 45854–45879 to 26 female prisoners who have been sent in a group transport.

Two Russian prisoners are locked in the bunker of Block 11 on suspicion of preparing an escape. They are Ivan Ratuszny (No. 105453) and Trofim Miakinkowas (No. 107614). Following a selection carried out in the bunkers, they are shot, Ratuszny on June 25, 1943, and Miakinkowas on July 29, 1943.

APMO, D-AuI-3/2, Bunker Register, p. 14.

Nos. 123858–123911 are given to 54 male prisoners and Nos. 45882–45981 to 100 female prisoners who have been delivered in a group transport.

Included in the occupancy level of the men's camp are 19 Polish skilled workers who at the request of the Auschwitz Concentration Camp have been transferred back from Sachsenhausen.

APMO, D-AuI-3a/297, 307, Labor Deployment.

The corpses of 12 prisoners, including one from the Buna A.C., are delivered to the morgue of the main camp.

APMO, D-AuI-5/2, Morgue Register, p, 152.

JUNE 5

At the experimental station of Professor Dr. Clauberg the occupancy level decreases by two. 135 women for experimental purposes and 39 female prisoner orderlies are now housed there.

APMO, D-AuI-3a/370/4, Monthly Labor Deployment List.

The Director of the Political Department informs the individual departments in the camp that on June 7, 1943, the railway man-

APMO, D-AuI-3a/308, Labor Deployment.

agement of Oppeln will make available a train consisting of 11 freight cars and two passenger cars in order to ship 500 prisoners to Silesia.*

Nos. 123912–123927 are given to 16 prisoners from Brünn.

Nos. 123928–123994 are given to 67 prisoners sent from Prague.

Nos. 123995–124043 are given to 49 prisoners sent from Lodz.

The corpses of 15 prisoners are delivered to the morgue of the main camp; among them are three from the Buna A.C.

APMO, D-AuI-5/2, Morgue Register, p. 153.

JUNE 6

137 women for experimental purposes and 39 female prisoner orderlies are housed at the experimental station of Professor Dr. Clauberg.

APMO, D-AuI-3a/370/4, Monthly Labor Deployment List.

Approximately 1,000 Jews are delivered with an RSHA transport from labor camps that have been shut down in the so-called Wartheland Gau ("Gau" is a Nazi Party administrative district) in occupied Poland. After the selection, 238 men are admitted to the camp and given Nos. 124044–124281. The others, more than 700 people, are killed in the gas chambers.

The Director of Friedrich Krupp AG, Engineer Weinhold, arrives from Essen with a staff of 30 technicians and foremen. They are housed in the vicinity of the Auschwitz train station in a barracks intended for civilian workers at the Krupp factories.

APMO, Maurer Trial, vol. 8a, p. 120.

The corpses of 12 prisoners are delivered to the morgue of the main camp.

APMO, D-AuI-5/2, Morgue Register, p. 153.

JUNE 7

The civilian workers at the Krupp Works begin assembling machines and technical equipment in a factory hall leased from the Auschwitz camp, situated in the camp area a little more than a half mile from the train station. In addition to the technical personnel that have arrived from Essen, 80 prisoners are used in the assembly work: The Capo of this labor squad is Schulz. Prisoners of various nationalities work in this squad.

APMO, Maurer Trial, vol. 8a, pp. 120–126.

The Krupp technical personnel employed in the factory hall sign a statement obligating them to maintain silence about everything concerning Auschwitz Concentration Camp.

Ibid., p. 122.

---

*The resistance movement active in the camp reports to Kraków: "A branch of our camp was recently set up in Świętochłowice, where there is a smelting works and, we hear, a coal mine. Primarily Jews are shipped there" (APMO, Mat.RO, vol. I, p. 30).

At the experimental station of Professor Dr. Clauberg in Block 10 of the main camp, the occupancy level decreases by two: 135 women for experimental purposes and 39 female prisoner orderlies are now housed there.

APMO, D-AuI-3a/370/4/285.

No. Z-8890 is given to a female Gypsy sent from Kielce, and her son, born on April 4, 1943, receives No. Z-8230.

No. Z-8891 is given to Anita Reinhardt, born in the Gypsy camp on June 6, 1943.

APMO, D-AuII-3/2/4, p. 573, Register of Female Gypsies.

No. Z-8892 is given to Irene Kinder, born in the Gypsy camp on May 31, 1943.

Ibid.

No. Z-8231 is given to Horst Maatz, born in the Gypsy camp on June 5, 1943.

APMO, D-AuII-3/1/2, p. 243, Register of Male Gypsies.

No. Z-8232 is given to Josef Horwath, born in the Gypsy camp in Birkenau on June 6, 1943. He dies on June 26, 1943.

Ibid.

500 prisoners from the men's camps in Auschwitz and Birkenau are transferred to the newly created Eintrachthütte auxiliary camp in Schwientochlowitz.

APMO, D-AuI-3a/308, Labor Deployment; Depositions, vol. 70, p. 92; vol. 82, p. 18; Depositions of Former Prisoners Alfred Panica and a Former Worker in Eintrachthütte, Erwin Śmieja; Piper, "Eintrachthütte," pp. 91–155.

Professor Dr. Clauberg, who conducts experiments in the experimental station in Block 10, writes to Himmler:

Schnabel, *Power Without Morality*, pp. 233, 274, Doc. 103.

Trials, vol. 1, pp. 730ff. (No. 212). [conducts experiments]

> The method I thought of for achieving sterilization of the female organism without operation has been worked out to the point of being as good as finished. It takes place through a single injection at the entrance to the ovaries and can be performed by any physician at the usual gynecological examination. When I say, "The method is as good as finished," that means:
>
> 1. Only its refinements are still to be worked out.
> 2. It could already be used in our usual eugenic sterilizations in place of the operation.
>
> As for the question which you, General, posed to me almost a year ago, regarding the period of time in which it would be possible to sterilize 1,000 women in this way, I can predict this today. Namely: If the experiments conducted by me continue as thus far—and there is no reason to assume that they won't— then the moment is not far off when I can say, "With great probability, several hundred—or even 1,000—in a day by a suitably trained physician at a suitably equipped location, with a staff of perhaps 10 (the number of the staff depending upon the desired acceleration).

Nos. 45880–45881 are given to two prisoners sent from Zichenau.

Nos. 124282–124324 are given to 43 male prisoners and Nos. 45982–45994 to 13 female prisoners sent in a group transport.

The Commandant announces that SS Second Lieutenant Ganninger is taking over the function of Counterespionage Officer.

APMO, D-AuI-1/41, Commandant's Office Order 23/43.

The corpses of 12 prisoners, including four from the Buna A.C., are delivered to the morgue of the main camp.

APMO, D-AuI-5/2, Morgue Register, p. 153.

JUNE 8

No. Z-8233 is given to Johann Horwath, who was born in the Gypsy camp in Birkenau on June 4, 1943; he dies on June 26, 1943.

APMO, D-AuII-3/1/2, p. 243, Register of Male Gypsies.

No. Z-8234 is given to a boy born in the Gypsy camp on June 1, 1943; he dies on June 9, 1943.

Ibid.

No. Z-8235 is given to Franz Daniel, who was born in the Gypsy camp on June 1, 1943; he dies on June 9, 1943.

Ibid.

No. Z-8236 is given to a boy born in the Gypsy camp on June 2, 1943; he dies on September 2, 1943.

Ibid.

880 Jewish men, women, and children from the ghetto in Salonika arrive in an RSHA transport from Greece. Admitted to the camp following the selection are 220 men, given Nos. 124325–124544, and 88 women, given Nos. 45995–46082. The other 572 deportees are killed in the gas chambers.

No. 46083 is given to the physician Jadwiga Hevelka, who by order of the WVHA has been transferred to Auschwitz from Ravensbrück.

APMO, D-AuI-3a/296, 310, Labor Deployment.

Nos. 124545–124547 are given to three prisoners sent from Kattowitz.

The corpses of 18 prisoners, among them five from the Buna A.C., are delivered to the morgue of the main camp. Among the prisoners who died in the Buna camp are four reeducation prisoners, EH-3612, EH-4036, EH-4235, and EH-4282.

APMO, D-AuI-5/2, Morgue Register, p. 154.

JUNE 9

The firm of J. A. Topf and Sons confirms receipt of the order for ventilation equipment for Crematoriums IV and V and submits a cost estimate of 2,510 Reichsmarks.

APMO, D-ZBau/1, Inventory No. 29745.

The following prisoners are transferred to Buchenwald: Stefan Homme (No. 46989), Henryk Cyran (No. 35697), and Zygmunt Skibiński (No. 6763).

APMO, D-AuI-3a/311, Labor Deployment.

No. 46084 is given to a female prisoner sent from Kattowitz.

Two Russian prisoners, Nikolas Timofeyev and Paul Mariuczenko, escape at approximately 5:30 P.M.

APMO, D-AuI-1/1/158, 160, Telegrams; IZ-8/Gestapo Lodz/3/88/456.

At the experimental station of Professor Dr. Clauberg in Block 10 of the main camp, the occupancy level decreases by one: housed there now are 134 women for experimental purposes and 39 female prisoner orderlies.

APMO, D-AuI-3a/370/4, Monthly Labor Deployment List.

The corpses of 21 prisoners are delivered to the morgue of the main camp; among them are two from the Buna A.C.

APMO, D-AuI-5/2, Morgue Register, p. 154.

22 prisoners sent from Troppau are given Nos. 124548–124569. On the same day, 20 of these, Nos. 124548–124567, are locked in the bunker of Block 11.

APMO, D-AuI-3/2, Bunker Register, pp. 15–17.

JUNE 10

20 prisoners who were delivered the previous day from Troppau are shot at the execution wall in the courtyard of Block 11. They are Eugeniusz Krencjasz (No. 124548), Jan Wolak (No. 124549), Marian Romański (No. 124550), Stanisław Masiera (No. 124551), Andrzej Wieczorek (No. 124552), Marian Białek (No. 124553), Stanisław Białek (No. 124554), Marian Mendrzycki (No. 124555), Eugeniusz Kotliński (No. 124556), Leon Kęsicki (No. 124557), Władysław Kaczmarek (No. 124558), Roman Sopala (No. 124559), Julian Pawłarczyk (No. 124560), Bronisław Faligowski (No. 124561), Wenzel Wiśniewski (No. 124562), Józef Zabłocki (No. 124563), Roman Nadolski (No. 124564), Roman Parczewski (No. 124565), Tadeusz Juda (No. 124566), and Józef Szwajkowski (No. 124567).

Ibid.

Nos. 124570–124581 are given to 12 male prisoners and Nos. 46085 and 46086 to two female prisoners who have been sent from Kattowitz.

At the experimental station of Professor Dr. Clauberg the occupancy level decreases by three: there are now 135 women for experimental purposes and 35 female prisoner orderlies.

APMO, D-AuI-3a/370/4, Monthly Labor Deployment List.

The Jew Alfred Pendzel (No. 10621), born in Berlin on February 13, 1927, is captured in an escape attempt and locked in the bunker of Block 11. Following a selection carried out in the bunkers, he is shot on June 25, 1943.

APMO, D-AuI-3/2, Bunker Register, p. 17.

The corpses of 23 prisoners, including one from the Jawischowitz A.C. and one from the Buna A.C., are sent to the morgue of the main camp.

APMO, D-AuI-5/2, Morgue Register, p. 155.

JUNE 11

Nos. 124582–124632 are given to 51 male prisoners and Nos. 46087–46098 to 13 female prisoners sent in a group transport. In compliance with the WVHA order of June 1, 1943, in this shipment are five prisoner orderlies from the Neuengamme C.C. and a

APMO, D-AuI-3a/296, 315, 317, Labor Deployment.

woman, No. 13193, who is transferred back to the camp after another interrogation.

Nos. Z-8237–Z-8242 are given to six Polish Gypsies who were sent in a group transport.

Two Jewish prisoners, Wilhelm Bielschowski (No. 122481) and Rudolf Juliusberger (No. 122508), are captured during an escape attempt and locked in the bunker of Block 11. Following a selection carried out in the bunkers, Wilhelm Bielschowski is shot on June 25, 1943; Rudolf Juliusberger, however, is released from the bunker to the camp on June 23, 1943.

APMO, D-AuI-3/2, Bunker Register, p. 17.

The corpses of 12 prisoners, including one from the Kobior A.C., are delivered to the morgue of the main camp.

APMO, D-AuI-5/2, Morgue Register, p. 155.

At 4:00 P.M. a group of 17 German criminal prisoners who have declared themselves willing to serve as volunteers in the armed forces travel from Auschwitz to Sachsenhausen for a four-week military training course.* Among the transferees are several who are familiar to most of their fellow prisoners as particularly bloodthirsty Capos. The transferred prisoners are August Müller (No. 22), Karl Müller (No. 3194), Johann Klausing (No. 3200), Willi Kühne (No. 3274), Kurt Heyne (No. 3286), Karl Andörfer (No. 15488), Franz Waldhauser (No. 15532), Gerhard Drzymala (No. 15544), Reinhold Hollek (No. 39179), Robert Vogl (No. 55908), Heinrich Lange (No. 62871), Willi Pütter (No. 62882), Kurt Kranz (No. 71345), Ottomar Schubert (No. 71394), Siegfried Gschirr (No. 71892), Kurt Schultz (No. 78718), and Herbert Tschiche (No. 78828).

APMO, D-AuI-3a/316, 318, 325, Labor Deployment.

JUNE 12

Nos. 124633–124707 are given to 75 male prisoners and Nos. 46099–46149 to 51 female prisoners who have been sent in a group transport.

APMO, D-AuI-3a/370/4, Monthly Labor Deployment List.

The experimental station of Professor Dr. Clauberg obtains 100 more female prisoners; 235 women for experimental purposes and 35 female prisoner orderlies are now housed there.

Nos. 46150–46192 are given to 43 female prisoners sent in a group transport.

Gerhard Baumberger, born in the Gypsy camp in Birkenau, gets No. Z-8243.

APMO, D-AuII-3/1/2, p. 244, Register of Male Gypsies.

*On June 14, the resistance organization in the camp makes its second report on the recruitment of volunteers for the defense forces from among the "green triangles" and the political prisoners, Reich Germans as well as ethnic Germans, provided they obtain a permit from the Political Department. The first group of 17 volunteers is taken to Sachsenhausen on June 10, where they are supposed to complete a four-week training course. Additional transports will follow (APMO, Mat.RO, vol. I, pp. 30ff.).

No. Z-8244 goes to Josef Rötzen, born in the Gypsy camp in Birkenau on June 10, 1943.

Ibid.

The corpses of 17 prisoners, including four from the Buna A.C., are delivered to the morgue of the main camp.

APMO, D-AuI-5/2, Morgue Register, p. 156.

A Pole, Piotr Ziomek (No. 123624), is captured during an escape attempt and locked in the bunker of Block 11. Following a selection carried out in the bunkers, he is shot on June 25, 1943.

APMO, D-AuI-3/2, Bunker Register, p. 17.

An auxiliary camp for female prisoners is set up in Rajsko in the vicinity of the experimental facility for plant cultivation. Housed there is the gardening squad, which has been coming there daily from the women's camp in Birkenau, and the plant cultivation squad for research and development in extracting caoutchouc (india rubber) from kok-saghyz (a type of dandelion). The caoutchouc squad has until now been housed in staff buildings on the grounds of the main camp. SS men Grell and Schmidt are responsible for the work in the gardening squad, and the SS man Dr. Schattenberg is responsible for the plant cultivation squad, in which 23 female prisoners with university-level training in biology and chemistry are employed. Supervision of the greenhouses is in the hands of SS Special Officer Christophensen, who is called "Locher" ("Puncher") by the female prisoners. The director of the laboratories is the German civilian Weimann, the second wife of SS Major Dr. Joachim Caesar, the director chief of the agricultural operations in the camp. The function of supervisor in the Rajsko auxiliary camp is performed, in succession, by Flora Cichoń, Joanna Borman, and Frau Franz.

Zięba, "Rajsko," pp. 81–91.

The Commandant's Office receives from Office D-II of the WVHA a copy of the decision of June 9, 1943, in which the inquiry by the EVO is discussed. 1,000 prisoners from Auschwitz are to be made available to work in the EVO plants; for this purpose, an auxiliary camp is to be set up in Jaworzno.

APMO, Jaworzno, Folder I, p. 37; Piper, "Neu-Dachs," p. 60.

JUNE 13

216 Czech prisoners are put in quarantine prior to release from the camp.

APMO, Mat.RO, vol. I, p. 33.

The corpses of six prisoners are delivered to the morgue of the main camp.

APMO, D-AuI-5/2, Morgue Register, p. 156.

JUNE 14

Two boys born in the Gypsy camp, Josef Delis and Andreas Horwath, get Nos. Z-8245 and Z-8246.

APMO, D-AuII-3/1/2, p. 244, Register of Male Gypsies.

Franciszka Rużycka, born in the Gypsy camp, is given No. Z-8893; she dies on June 25, 1943.

APMO, D-AuII-3/2/4, p. 573, Register of Female Gypsies.

Božena Ružycka, born in the Gypsy camp in Birkenau on June 8, 1943, is given No. Z-8894; she dies on July 27, 1943.

Ibid.

Maria Wuchinger, born in the Gypsy camp on June 11, 1943, receives No. Z-8895; she dies on July 3, 1943.

Ibid.

No. Z-8896 is given to Hilda Luza, born in the Gypsy camp on June 12, 1943. She dies on July 17, 1943.

Ibid.

No. Z-8897 is given to Maria Blum-Winterstein, born in the Gypsy camp; she dies on June 17, 1943.

Ibid.

In a report to Kraków, the camp resistance movement suggests the destruction of the Friedrich Krupp factory located on the grounds of Auschwitz Concentration Camp by an Allied air aid. Author of this report is the prisoner Stanisław Klodziński (No. 20019), a physician who uses the pseudonym "Stakło" in the resistance. The report is worded as follows: "Directly beside our block, an enormous factory hall of Friedrich Krupp AG is being constructed. The machines were recently assembled. I assume that within a month it will be time for the 'birds' to fly in. No need for you to take any consideration of us. Gladly will we prove with our blood that our concern is the destruction of the enemy. . . . The factory of Friedrich Krupp AG should be destroyed and the earth leveled."

APMO, Mat.RO, vol. I, p. 32.

The corpses of nine prisoners are delivered to the morgue of the main camp.

APMO, D-AuI-5/2, Morgue Register, p. 156.

JUNE 15

Nos. 46193–46202 are given to 10 female prisoners sent in a group transport.

An auxiliary camp is set up in Jaworzno near the EVO. 100 prisoners are transferred there who are supposed to enlarge the auxiliary camp and prepare for the housing of 5,000 prisoners. Among the transferees are Poles, Germans, and Jews. SS Second Lieutenant Pfütze becomes Camp Commander. The function of Camp Senior is filled by the German criminal prisoner Bruno Brodniewitsch (No. 1), former Camp Senior in the men's camp of Auschwitz and, from May 23 to June 7, 1943, in the Gypsy camp in Birkenau.

APMO, Mat.RO, vol. I, p. 31; vol. VII, p. 484; Jaworzno, Folder I, p. 37.

Because of the danger of a typhus epidemic, SS Captain Dr. Bruno Beger, an employee of the SS teaching and research society, Ahnenerbe (literally, "forbears' legacy"), finishes his work in Auschwitz, probably sooner than planned. On the basis of his work, 115 prisoners are selected—79 male Jews, two Poles, four Asians, and 30 female Jews—who are to be transferred to the Natzweiler Concen-

APMO, Dpr.-ZOd/37, p. 27; Ternon and Helman, *History of SS Medicine*, 219ff.

tration Camp* after a quarantine period. Following their murder, the plan is to have their corpses earmarked for shipment to the Anatomical Institute in Strasbourg. The director of this institute, SS Captain Professor Dr. August Hirt, is building up a skeleton collection.

In his letter expressing gratitude to Armaments Minister Albert Speer for the allocation of an additional supply of iron for enlargement of the Auschwitz camp, Himmler closes with the formulation, "Your lines strengthened me in the conviction that there is still justice."

APMO, IZ-13/89, Various Documents of the Third Reich, p. 291.

SS Lieutenant Colonel Brandt from the personal staff of the SS Commander in Chief hands over to the Head of the WVHA, Pohl, a copy of Albert Speer's letter of May 30, 1943, to Himmler concerning the special iron allocation with the request for attention.

Ibid., p. 292.

The corpses of 15 prisoners, including two from the Buna A.C., are delivered to the morgue of the main camp.

APMO, D-AuI-5/2, Morgue Register, p. 157.

JUNE 16

Nos. 124708–124731 are given to 24 male prisoners and Nos. 46205–46211 to seven female prisoners sent in a group transport.

Nos. 124732–124760 are given to 29 prisoners sent from Kraków by the Sipo and SD.

Nos. 124761–124768 are given to eight prisoners sent from Kattowitz.

Nos. 124814–124829 are given to 16 male Jews and Nos. 46212–46219 to eight female Jews sent in an RSHA transport.

Nos. 46220–46230 are given to 11 female prisoners sent in a group transport.

The German Gypsy Gustav Weiss (No. Z-6053) is captured during an escape attempt and locked in the bunker of Block 11. Following a selection carried out in the bunkers, he is shot on June 25, 1943.

APMO, D-AuI-3/2, Bunker Register, p. 17.

---

*In mid-1943, a gas chamber for killing prisoners earmarked for Professor Dr. Hirt is constructed in the Natzweiler C.C. According to statements made before the military court in Strasbourg on July 26, 1945, by the former Commandant of Natzweiler Concentration Camp, Josef Kramer, the transport from Auschwitz arrived on July 26, 1945. He himself killed the people in the gas chamber, using chemicals obtained from Professor Dr. Hirt—hydrogen cyanide compounds—and following his instructions. The corpses of the killed were transported to the Anatomy Institute in Strasbourg. There the corpses were conserved in containers with 55 percent synthetic alcohol. The laboratory assistant Henry Henrypierre, who worked there as a forced laborer, states in the Doctors' Trial before the International Military Tribunal in Nuremberg on December 18, 1946, that 87 corpses were delivered. He secretly noted the five-digit prisoner numbers that were tattooed on the left lower arms (Ternon and Helman, *History of SS Medicine*, pp. 219ff.).

The Director of the Political Department informs the separate departments in Auschwitz that he has received from Kripo headquarters in Magdeburg a clarification dated May 6, 1943, according to which the Gypsy halfbreed Heinrich Rose (No. Z-583), born in Magdeburg on April 14, 1938, was born on February 21, 1937. The date of birth of the child must be corrected in the appropriate records.

APMO, D-AuI-3a/323, Labor Deployment.

The corpses of 13 prisoners, including one from the Buna A.C., are delivered to the morgue of the main camp.

APMO, D-AuI-5/2, Morgue Register, p. 157.

JUNE 17

Nos. 124769–124793 are given to 25 prisoners sent from Kraków by the Sipo and SC.

No. 124794 is given to a prisoner sent from Oppeln.

Nos. 124795–124813 are given to 19 prisoners sent from Kattowitz.

During the early morning hours, a Russian prisoner, Siemion Korolkov (No. 64773), escapes from the camp.

APMO, D-AuI-1/1, p. 168, Telegrams; IZ-8/Gestapo Lodz/3/88/458; Mat.RO, vol. IV, p. 292.

Hubert Bibel, born in the Gypsy camp, receives No. Z-8247.

APMO, D-AuII-3/1/2, p. 244, Register of Male Gypsies.

Ursula Adler, born in the Gypsy camp, receives No. Z-8898; she dies on June 30, 1943.

APMO, D-AuII-3/2/4, p. 575, Register of Female Gypsies.

No. Z-8899 is given to Theresia Schubert, born in the Gypsy camp; she dies on June 18, 1943.

Ibid.

The corpses of 13 prisoners are delivered to the morgue of the main camp.

APMO, D-AuI-5/2, Morgue Register, p. 157.

JUNE 18

Two female prisoners sent from Kattowitz are given Nos. 46203 and 46204.

Nos. 124830–124960 are given to 131 male prisoners and Nos. 46231–46285 to 55 female prisoners sent in a group transport.

Nos. 124961 and 124963–125150 are given to 189 prisoners who were sent from Minsk. Among them are 16 Polish policemen who have fought side by side with Soviet partisans in White Russia.

APMO, Mat.RO, vol. I, p. 33.

No. 124962 is given to a prisoner sent from Breslau.

Nine corpses are delivered to the morgue of the main camp; among them is one from the Buna A.C., No. EH-3679.

APMO, D-AuI-5/2, Morgue Register, p. 158.

JUNE 19

No. Z-8900 is given to a female Gypsy and No. Z-8248 to a son born to her on March 26, 1943. Mother and child have arrived in the camp with a group transport.

Nos. 125151–125207 are given to 57 male prisoners and Nos. 46286–46343 to 58 female prisoners who have arrived in a group transport.

Nos. 125208–125217 are given to 10 male Jews and Nos. 46344–46351 to eight female Jews sent to the camp by the RSHA in Leipzig and arrived in a group transport.

12 prisoners sent from Kattowitz receive Nos. 125218–125229.

At the experimental station of Professor Dr. Clauberg in Block 10 of the main camp, the occupancy level decreases by one: There are now 234 female prisoners for experimental purposes and 35 female prisoner orderlies.

APMO, D-AuI-3a/370/4, Monthly Labor Deployment List.

The corpses of seven prisoners are delivered to the morgue of the main camp.

APMO, D-AuI-5/2, Morgue Register, p. 158.

A Polish Jew, Jovel Gerszkorn (No. 9888), is captured during an escape attempt and locked in the bunkers of Block 11. Following a selection carried out in the bunkers, he is shot on June 25, 1943.

APMO, D-AuI-3/2, Bunker Register, p. 18.

By order of the Camp Commander, the Polish Gypsies Mieczysław Rutkowski (No. Z-8238), Stanisław Brylewicz (No. Z-8239), Ferdynand Głowatzki (No. Z-8240), Antoni Głowatzki (No. Z-8241), and Władysław Kubat (No. Z-8242) are locked in the bunkers of Block 11. They are shot on June 28, 1943.

Ibid.

JUNE 20

No. 125230 is given to a prisoner sent from Kattowitz.

After a selection, 10 male Jews receive Nos. 125231–125240, and 35 female Jews receive Nos. 46352–46386. They have arrived with an RSHA transport from Sosnowitz. Probably these are the Jews who received notification from the police presidium in Sosnowitz on June 19, 1943, that they are recognized as foreigners and as representatives of the headquarters of the Jewish congregations in East Silesia: Moniek Merin, Chaim Merin, Fania Czarna, Borensztajn, and Dr. Lewensztajn.

Szternfinkiel, *Jews of Sosnowitz*, pp. 52ff.

Six boys who were born in the Gypsy camp in Birkenau receive Nos. Z-8249–Z-8254. All die in the course of the year 1943.

APMO, D-AuII-3/1/2, p. 244, Register of Male Gypsies.

No. Z-8901 is given to a girl born in the Gypsy camp.

APMO, D-AuII-3/2/4, p. 575, Register of Female Gypsies.

The corpses of seven prisoners are delivered to the morgue of the main camp.

APMO, D-AuI-5/2, Morgue Register, p. 158.

JUNE 21

Dead of typhus is Zygmunt Łempicki, No. 119339, professor at the University of Warsaw and member of the Polish Academy of Sciences. He was sent to Auschwitz by the Sipo and SD on April 28, 1943.

APMO, D-AuI-5/2, Morgue Register, p. 159; Mat.RO, vol. I, p. 33.

59 prisoners sent from Kattowitz get Nos. 125241–125299.

14 male prisoners are given Nos. 125300–125313, and 23 female prisoners receive Nos. 46387–46409. They have arrived in a group transport.

Josef Strauss, born in the Gypsy camp in Birkenau, receives No. Z-8255.

APMO, D-AuII-3/1/2, p. 244, Register of Male Gypsies.

The corpses of 11 prisoners, including three from the Buna A.C., are delivered to the morgue of the main camp.

APMO, D-AuI-5/2, Morgue Register, p. 159.

JUNE 22

A Russian woman, Walentyna Trepaczowa, born on December 25, 1924, escapes from the camp in the evening. She had been sent to the camp from Breslau on April 24, 1943.

APMO, D-AuI-1/1, p. 170, Telegrams; IZ-8/Gestapo Lodz/4/88/460.

The 35 male prisoners sent from Kattowitz receive Nos. 125314–125348 and one female prisoner gets No. 46410.

The corpses of 20 prisoners, including two from the Buna A.C., are delivered to the morgue of the main camp.

APMO, D-AuI-5/2, Morgue Register, p. 159.

JUNE 23

Two boys born in the Gypsy camp in Birkenau receive Nos. Z-8256 and Z-8257.

APMO, D-AuII-3/1/2, p. 244, Register of Male Gypsies.

The Commandant's Office receives the news that a transport with 1,002 Jews has left le Bourget–Drancy at 10:00 A.M. for Auschwitz.

APMO, D-RF-3/55.

Two prisoners escape from the camp in the evening, a Pole, Stefan Łukasik (No. 5723), and a Russian POW, Siemion Rudenko (No. RKG-10130).

APMO, D-AuI-1/1, pp. 172, 176; IZ-8/Gestapo Lodz/3/88/462; IZ-10/Kripo Sieradz/2, 118; Mat.RO, vol. IV, p. 292.

Nos. 125349–125378 are given to 30 male prisoners and Nos. 46411–46415 to five female prisoners sent from Kraków by the Sipo and SD.

The six male prisoners sent from Kattowitz are given Nos. 125379–125384 and two female prisoners get Nos. 46416 and 46417.

The corpses of 10 prisoners, including one from the Buna A.C., are delivered to the morgue of the main camp.

APMO, D-AuI-5/2, Morgue Register, p. 160.

The prisoner Leo Hazan (No. 11436), a Greek Jew, is captured during an escape attempt and locked in the bunker of Block 11. Following a selection conducted in the bunkers, he is shot on June 25, 1943.

APMO, D-AuI-3/2, Bunker Register, p. 19.

JUNE 24

Two Russians, Michail Maslankov (No. 771100) and Michael Ponenko (No. 102297), escape from the camp.

APMO, D-AuI-1/1, p. 174, Telegrams; IZ-8/Gestapo Lodz/3/88/464; Mat.RO, vol. IV, p. 292.

SS Second Lieutenant Max Sell, Deputy Director of Labor Deployment, and the Camp Doctor, Bruno Kitt, arrive in the Lublin (Majdanek) C.C. to evaluate prisoners selected by the Lublin Camp Doctor for deployment in the Buna plants or Jaworzno. They find out after their arrival that of the 5,500 male and female prisoners made available by the WVHA, 1,700 have already been earmarked for the labor camp in Radom. Only 3,800 prisoners remain for Auschwitz. In addition, they confirm that only 30 percent of the 1,000 prisoners selected are suitable for the work in the Buna factories or Jaworzno.

Documents and Materials, pp. 138ff.

Nos. 125386–125418 are given to 33 male prisoners and Nos. 46419–46424 to six female prisoners who have been sent from Kattowitz. Among them is a prisoner from Leipzig, given No. 125400.

Approximately 1,600 Jewish men, women, and children from the ghetto in Środula, the hospital in Sosnowitz, and the Kamionka ghetto in Bendin have arrived in an RSHA transport. Following the selection, 19 men, given Nos. 125419–125437, and six women, given Nos. 46425–46430, are admittted to the camp. The other 1,575 deportees are killed in the gas chambers.

Szternfinkiel, *Jews of Sosnowitz*, pp. 52ff.; CA KC PZPR, 202/III-148, Documents of the Delegation of the Polish Government in Exile, p. 402.

Nos. 125438–125780 are given to 343 prisoners sent from Radom by the Sipo and SD.

By order of the Politcial Department, 18 political prisoners are locked in the bunkers of Block 11. The next day, five of them are released into the camp again, and 13 are shot: the ones shot are Franciszek Kocur (No. 123028), Józef Dziuk (No. 123023), Teodor Mroczek (No. 123032), Franciszek Wybrańczyk (No. 107484), Alois Siąkala (No. 109857), Archop Rudyj (No. 107758), Jan Klistalla (No. 111912), Stanisław Sobik (No. 107482), Alois Nawrath (No. 111913), Alouis Burysz (No. 108694), Franciszek Stroba (No. 108699), Piotr Kowalenko (No. 47757), and Henryk Hoffman (No. 123025).

APMO, D-AuI-3/2, Bunker Register, pp. 20ff.

Nos. 46431–46524 are given to 94 female prisoners sent from Kraków by the Sipo and SD.

During an escape attempt, three Gypsies, Josef Janacek (No. Z-7216), Emil Rozycka (No. Z-7266), and Anton Rozycka (No. Z-7388), are captured and locked in the bunker of Block 11. They are shot following a selection carried out in the bunkers on June 25, 1943.

Ibid., p. 19.

The Russian Anatoli Katuzhenko (No. 107597) is captured during an escape attempt and locked in the bunker of Block 11. He is shot the next day, on June 25, 1943.

Ibid.

The political prisoner Jan Pasterny (No. 123036) is captured during an escape attempt and locked in the bunker of Block 11. He is shot the next day, on June 25, 1943, following a selection in the bunkers.

Ibid.

The corpses of eight prisoners are delivered to the morgue of the main camp; three of the dead are from the Buna A.C.

APMO, D-AuI-5/2, Morgue Register, p. 160.

Commandant Höss orders the SS to have their clothing cleaned by civilians outside the camp, as there is danger of contagion in Auschwitz.

APMO, D-AuI-1/44, Commandant's Office Order 26/43.

JUNE 25

In the Lublin (Majdanek) C.C., SS Second Lieutenant Sell and SS First Lieutenant Dr. Kitt select 2,000 prisoners who are suited for the hardest labor. They find the others unfit for the work in the Buna plants or Jaworzno and reject them.

Documents and Materials, pp. 138ff.

With the results of the inspection conducted in the Lublin concentration camp by Sell and Kitt in hand, Labor Deployment Director Schwarz asks Office D-II of the WVHA whether it might not be possible to obtain an additional 1,000 prisoners from the Lublin C.C., for masons, carpenters, and plumbers are urgently needed in the Buna plants. SS Second Lieutenant Sell, who is still at the Lublin camp, could make the selection of the suitable prisoners.

APMO, D-AuI-3a/334, Labor Deployment.

Crematorium III in Birkenau.

Two male Gypsies delivered with a collective shipment receive Nos. Z-8258 and Z-8259, and a female Gypsy receives No. Z-8902.

Nos. 125781–125857 are given to 177 male prisoners, and Nos. 46525–46536 go 12 female prisoners sent in a group transport.

The Central Construction Administration turns over to the Auschwitz garrison administration the finished Crematorium III with gas chambers in Birkenau (Project KGL-30a). The construction is identical with that of Crematorium II, which was put into operation on March 31, 1943.

APMO, D-ZBauKGL/BW/30/25/ 14, Table of Construction Projects Turned Over to the Garrison Administration; Dpr.-Hd/ 11a, p. 77, Exhibit 13.

1,018 Jewish men, women, and children arrive from Drancy with the fifty-fifth RSHA transport from France. After the selection, 383 men, given Nos. 125858–126240, and 217 women, given Nos. 46537–46753, are admitted to the camp. The other 418 deportees are killed in the gas chambers.

No. 46754 goes to a woman sent from Frankfurt am Main.

2,500 Jewish men, women, and children from the ghetto in Bendin arrive in an RSHA transport. All are killed in the gas chambers.*

CA KC PZPR, 202/III-148, Documents of the Delegation of Polish Government in Exile, p. 402.

*A message smuggled out by Stanisław Kłodziński to Teresa Lasocka in Kraków states: "Last Friday or Thursday in Rajsko [that is what the prisoners called Birkenau at that time—Danuta Czech] 3,000 persons, including 1,200 women, were sent into the gas. It seems they were Jews and Poles. Five days ago, a smaller transport from Kraków was also sent into the gas. We don't know any more details about it"

Nos. 126241–126350 are given to 110 male prisoners and Nos. 46755–46796 to 42 female prisoners sent in a group transport.

The Camp Commander and the Director of the Political Department carry out an investigation of the prisoners incarcerated in the bunkers of Block 11, in the presence of SS functionaries, who conduct the interrogations. 55 prisoners are condemned to death, among them prisoners captured during an escape attempt, or suspected of having prepared an escape, and 13 prisoners from the surveying squad who were locked in the bunkers on May 26 and 27 on charges of being active in the resistance groups of the camp, maintaining contacts to the civilian population during their work in the area near the camp, and providing assistance in the escape of the prisoner Kazimierz Jarzębowski and his companions. Some of the condemned are Władysław Krzyżagórski (No. 7322), Wacław Jamiołkowski (No. 10058), Tadeusz Kokesz (No. 10745) Leon Wardaszko (No. 66803), Józef Dziuba (No. 74507), Władysław Ćwikliński (No. 84764), Romuald Krzywosiński (No. 6529), Jan Lisiak (No. 63808), Bogdan Zaręba-Zarębski (No. 76960), Leon Czerski (No. 19630), Marian Moskalski (No. 17219), Władysław Pierzyński (No. 27301), and Stanisław Tokarski (No. 64611). They are shot the same day at the execution wall in the courtyard of Block 11.

APMO, D-AuI-3/2, Bunker Register, pp. 7, 10–12, 14, 17–21; Höss Trial, vol. 4, p. 40, Depositions of Former Prisoner Wilhelm Wohlfahrt; Mat.RO, vol. I, p. 35.

The Police Court-martial of the Kattowitz Gestapo* meets in the barracks of the Political Department to consider the cases of 120 male and female workers from the "Paris" mine. The court sits at a table set up in front of the window in the interior of the barracks, and outside the accused walk past this window. They are asked their family and Christian name and must then walk back. All who are condemned to death are shot the same day in Crematorium I in the main camp. One of the condemned is merely wounded and during the night creeps out of the window of the crematorium. Naked and covered with blood, he wanders around the grounds of the Construction Office. In the morning he is captured by SS men on the way to work, taken back to the crematorium, and shot.

APMO, Höss Trial, vol. 4, p. 101, Statement of Former Prisoner Roman Taul. The date and the circumstances are confirmed in a report of the camp resistance movement, which however does not describe the event. Mat.RO, vol. I, p. 35; vol. VII, p. 485.

The resistance organization in the camp spreads word of the arrival of two trucks containing approximately 240 civilians, all of whom are immediately killed in the gas chambers.

APMO, Mat.RO, vol. I, p. 35; vol. VII, p. 485.

(APMO, Mat.RO, vol. I, p. 35, message of June 28, 1943). Probably the killing of this transport is related to disturbances at Crematorium III. Including the Jews selected from the RSHA transport from Drancy, approximately 3,000 people were killed in the gas chambers. The gas chambers in Crematorium III are set up for that many people.

*Police Court-martial sessions have taken place once or twice a month since January in the ground floor of Block 11. Until October 1943, the commanding officer of the Kattowitz Gestapo, Rudolf Mildner, presides. (Compare Pery Broad's comments, in SAM, Auschwitz in the Eyes of the SS, pp. 142–153.) Starting in October 1943, his successor, Johannes Thümmler, presides. (Compare Alfred Konieczny, "Uwagi o sadzie doraźnym katowickiego Gestapo pod kierownictwem SS-Obersturmbannführer Johannesa Thümmlera" ["Observations on the Court-martial by the Kattowitz Gestapo under the Leadership of SS Lieutenant Colonel Johannes Thümmler"], Bulletin GKBZHwP, vol. 24, 1972, pp. 105–168.)

At the experimental station of Professor Dr. Clauberg in Block 10 of the main camp, the occupancy level increases by six: There are now 240 women for experimental purposes and 35 female prisoner orderlies.

APMO, D-AuI-3a/370/4, Monthly Labor Deployment List.

During an escape attempt a Russian political prisoner, Simon Kirstenko (No. 55866), is captured and locked in the bunker of Block 11. He is shot on September 4, 1943.

APMO, D-AuI-3/2, Bunker Register, p. 21.

The corpses of seven prisoners are delivered to the morgue of the main camp; one of them is from the Kobior A.C.

APMO, D-AuI-5/2, Morgue Register, p. 160.

JUNE 26

Two prisoners are delivered from Oppeln: a woman, given No. 46418, and a man, given No. 125385.

24 prisoners sent in a group transport receive Nos. 126351–126374.

1,052 male and female Jews whom SS Second Lieutenant Sell and SS Camp Doctor Kitt considered fit for extremely hard labor are sent from the Lublin (Majdanek) C.C. The 426 men are given Nos. 126377–126802 and 626 women are given Nos. 46797–47422.

Nos. 126803–126826 are given to 24 prisoners sent to the camp by the Sipo and SD for the Kraków District.

Nos. 47423–47482 are given to 60 female prisoners sent in a group transport.

Labor Deployment Director Schwarz sends a second request to the RSHA for the transfer of 1,000 additional prisoners, as 1,000 laborers must be transferred to Jaworzno on July 1, 1943.

APMO, D-AuI-3a/338, Labor Deployment.

Two Rumanian Gypsies, Josef Kasperowicz (No. Z-8) and Franz Kasperowicz (No. Z-9), are captured during an escape attempt and locked in the bunkers of Block 11. They are shot on June 28, 1943.

APMO, D-AuI-3/2, Bunker Register, p. 21.

The corpses of 14 prisoners are delivered to the morgue of the main camp.

APMO, D-AuI-5/2, Morgue Register, p. 161.

JUNE 27

Three boys born in the Gypsy camp in Birkenau receive Nos. Z-8260–Z-8262.

D-AuII-3/1/2, Register of Male Gypsies.

Four girls born in the Gypsy camp receive Nos. Z-8903–Z-8906.

APMO, D-AuII-3/2/4, p. 575, Register of Female Gypsies.

The corpses of 12 prisoners are delivered to the morgue of the main camp.

APMO, D-AuI-5/2, Morgue Register, p. 161.

JUNE 28

Johann Wajtz, born in the Gypsy camp in Birkenau, receives No. Z-8263.

APMO, D-AuII-3/1/2, p. 244, Register of Male Gypsies.

The Czech BV prisoner Franz Varadinek (No. 117196) escapes from the camp.

APMO, IZ-10/Kripo Sieradz/2a, p. 92, Bulletin, vol. 3/283.

Two prisoners sent from Kattowitz get Nos. 126375 and 126376.

Nos. 126827–126901 are given to 75 male prisoners and Nos. 47483–47488 to six female prisoners sent in a group transport.

Nos. 126902–126955 are given to 28 prisoners from the prison in Tarnów and 26 prisoners from Montelupich Prison sent by the Sipo and SD for the Kraków District.

Nos. 47489–47506 are given to 18 female prisoners sent in a group transport.

30 prisoners are shot at the execution wall in the courtyard of Block 11.

APMO, Mat.RO, vol. I, p. 36.

The corpses of seven prisoners, including one from the Kobior A.C., are delivered to the morgue of the main camp.

APMO, D-AuI-5/2, Morgue Register, p. 161.

The Head of the Central Construction Office, SS Major Karl Bischoff, reports to the Head Chief of Branch C in the WVHA, Heinz Kammler, that the construction of Crematorium II was completed on June 26, 1943, and that herewith all crematoriums have been set up as commanded. From now on, the following capacity, based on 24-hour operation, can be counted on:

Committee of Antifascist Resistance Fighters in the GDR, *SS in Action*, p. 269.

1. Old Crematorium I (Auschwitz) 3 double-muffle cremation ovens	340 corpses
2. New Crematorium II (Birkenau) 5 three-muffle cremation ovens	1,440 corpses
3. New Crematorium III (Birkenau) 5 three-muffle cremation ovens	1,440 corpses
4. New Crematorium IV (Birkenau) eight-muffle cremation oven	768 corpses
5. New Crematorium V (Birkenau) eight-muffle cremation oven	768 corpses
Total	4,756 corpses

JUNE 29

Nos. 126956–126967 are given to 12 prisoners sent in a group transport.

22 prisoners sent from Kattowitz receive Nos. 126968–126989.

346 Jews arrive in the thirty-ninth RSHA transport from Berlin. After the selection, 117 men, given Nos. 126990–127106, and 93 women, given Nos. 47507–47599, are admitted to the camp. The other 136 people are killed in the gas chambers.

65 female German Jews are transferred from the women's camp, B-Ia, in Birkenau to the main camp and housed at the experimental station in Block 10. They have been selected by Professor Dr. Clauberg for sterilization.*

APMO, Mat.RO, vol. I, p. 36.

Nos. 127107–127115 are given to nine men, and one woman who was sent from Kattowitz gets No. 47601.

Ibid.

40 hostages from Warsaw are shot in the courtyard of Block 11. This operation is intended as revenge for acts of sabotage of train equipment, causing the rails to loosen,** committed by members of the resistance movement.

Commandant Höss forbids SS men access to the Krupp factory and the area of the camp in which the assembly of machines is taking place if they have no official orders to do so.

APMO, D-AuI-1/45, Commandant's Office Order 27/43.

The corpses of prisoners are delivered to the morgue of the main camp.

APMO, D-AuI-5/2, Morgue Register, p. 162.

JUNE 30

In the early morning hours, a female Russian prisoner, Natalia Cymbaliuk (Sembeluk), born in Sepetovka in 1920, escapes.

APMO, D-AuI-1/1, p. 178, Telegrams; IZ-10/Kripo Sieradz/2a, p. 104.

Eight prisoners flee from the camp. During the pursuit, probably four prisoners are shot,† the others succeed in escaping. Among the escapees are Eugen Vorobiov (No. 73101), Ivan Vorlamov (No. 58825), Ivan Jarmak (No. 58803), and Jakob Sołowjow (No. 44702).

APMO, D-AuI-1/1, p. 183, Telegrams; IZ-10/Kripo Sieradz/2a/93; Mat. RO, vol. IV, p. 293.

A woman sent from Kattowitz is admitted to the camp and receives No. 47600.

39 male prisoners sent by the Sipo and SD for the Kraków District are given Nos. 127116–127154, and nine female prisoners receive Nos. 47602–47610. Among them are 20 prisoners from the prison in Tarnów.

*In all probability Clauberg chose 65 female prisoners from the 93 female Jews who were selected from the thirty-ninth RSHA transport from Berlin.
**Operations to destroy and disrupt German transports and train lines are undertaken by partisan groups in the People's Guard (Gwardia Ludowa—GL).
†The telegram reporting the escape to the appropriate regional Stapo and Kripo headquarters refers to eight prisoners, but only four names are mentioned. It is not possible to determine the names of those who were shot.

Nos. 127155 and 127156 are given to two male prisoners and Nos. 47611–47616 to six female prisoners sent from Kattowitz.

15 women sent from Kraków as prisoners by the Sipo and SD are given Nos. 47617–47631.

65 German Jewish women selected the previous day by Professor Dr. Clauberg are taken in at the experimental station in Block 10 of the main camp; 300 female prisoners for experimental purposes and 40 female prisoner orderlies are now housed here.

APMO, D-AuI-3a/370/4, Monthly Labor Deployment List.

The commanding officer of the Guard Stormtroopers, SS Major Hartjenstein, announces that the new auxiliary camps have been given the following names.:

APMO, Dpr.-ZOd/40, Storm-trooper Order 101/43.

1. The Schwientochlowitz auxiliary camp is now called Ein-trachthütte.
2. The Jaworzno auxiliary camp is now called Neu-Dachs.

The camp resistance movement spreads the news that the camp management has opened a bordello in Block 24 of the main camp.*

APMO, Mat. RO, vol. I, p. 36.

The corpses of 11 prisoners, including one from the Golleschau A.C., are delivered to the morgue of the main camp.

APMO, D-AuI-5/2, Morgue Register, p. 162.

JUNE 1–30

In the course of the month, 1,624 female prisoners have died in the women's camp, B-Ia, in Birkenau.

APMO, Mat.RO, vol. VII, p. 485.

JULY 1

Commandant Höss informs the SS members of the garrison that the fence of Section II in Birkenau, in Camps B-IId, B-IIe, and B-IIf, is connected to the mains and carries a high-voltage charge.**

APMO, D-AuI-1, Garrison Order 25/43.

805 Jews selected by SS Second Lieutenant Sell and SS Camp Doctor Kitt are transferred from the Lublin (Majdanek) C.C. Among these are 222 men, given Nos. 127157–127378, and 583 women, given

APMO, D-AuI-1/1, p. 182, Tele-grams; IZ-8/Gestapo Lodz/3a/88/466.

---

*Such an establishment is later opened in the Buna auxiliary camp. The prisoners are permitted to visit the bordello once a week. For each visit the prisoners must pay 2 Reichsmarks, from which the prostitute gets .45 Reichsmark; the female attendant, a Capo, gets .05 Reichsmark, and the camp treasury gets 1.50 Reichs-marks. The purpose of this institution is to divert the prisoners from political interests and to goad them to greater productivity. The bordello is visited mainly by prisoner functionaries, predominantly criminals. Jewish and Russian prisoners and Russian POWs are forbidden access. The political prisoners boycott it consciously and jeer at those who go there. The bordello does not fulfill the purpose intended by the SS (APMO, Höss Trial, vol. 7, p. 7, Statement of the Former Prisoner Alfred Woycicki).
**This information constitutes a warning that any contact with the wires of the fence is life-threatening. At the time when the fence was connected to the mains, the Camps B-IId and B-IIf were still under construction. The camp management decided to use these sections for the male prisoners housed until now in Camp B-Ib, which in turn was to serve as an enlargement of the women's camp, B-Ia. In contrast, Camp B-IIe, the Gypsy Family Camp, has already been in operation since February 26, 1943.

Nos. 47632–48214. Lejbko Ponzek, born on February 1, 1914, flees during the transport.

20 prisoners sent in a group transport receive Nos. 127379–127398.

Nos. Z-8264 and Z-89265 are given to two male Gypsies and Nos. Z-8907–Z-8910 to four female Gypsies sent in a group transport.

A reeducation prisoner, Ivan Romanenko, born in Bajrak on August 25, 1925, who was sent by the Oderberg Kripo on June 23, 1943, escapes from the camp.

APMO, D-AuI-1/1, p. 185, Telegrams; IZ-8/Gestapo Lodz/3a/88/468.

Six boys born in the Gypsy camp receive Nos. Z-8266–Z-8271. All die in the course of the year 1943.

APMO, D-AuII-3/1/2, p. 244, Register of Male Gypsies.

Nos. Z-8911–Z-8913 go to three girls born in the Gypsy camp.

APMO, D-AuII-3/2/4, p. 575, Register of Female Gypsies.

Department IV, the administrative office in Auschwitz, is made into an independent administrative headquarters with the designation SS Garrison Administration. It has the following staff:

APMO, D-AuI-1/47, Commandant's Office Order 28/43.

1. Director of the SS Garrison Administration is SS Lieutenant Colonel Möckel.
2. Director of the Garrison Finance Department is SS Captain Polenz.
3. Director of the Garrison Pay Office is SS Staff Sergeant Jordan.

The corpses of 17 prisoners, including one from the Babitz (Babice)* auxiliary camp, are delivered to the morgue of the main camp.

APMO, D-AuI-5/2, Morgue Register, p. 162.

JULY 2

Nos. 127399–127470 are given to 72 male prisoners and Nos. 48215–48233 and 48235–48247 to 32 female prisoners sent in a group transport.

Five prisoners suspected of preparing an escape are locked in the bunker of Block 11. They are the Jewish prisoner Zuken Aleksandrowicz (No. 122727), the reeducation prisoner Piotr Milewski (No. EH-4837), and the Polish political prisoners Władysław Romanowski (No. 119418), Sergiusz Jarosiński (No. 125448), and Marian Piłka (No. 125463). They are shot on July 17, 1943, after a selection in the bunkers.

APMO, D-AuI-3/2, Bunker Register, p. 22.

---

*This auxiliary camp was set up near an agricultural operation in March 1943. Approximately 60 prisoners are housed there; later, 150 prisoners are used in horse breeding and crop farming and 150 female prisoners, later 180, are used in animal husbandry and growing potatoes, cabbage, beets, kohlrabi, and harvesting hay.

The corpses of nine prisoners are delivered to the morgue of the main camp.

APMO, D-AuI-5/2, Morgue Register, p. 163.

JULY 3

The Labor Deployment Department submits Invoice No. 1/43 for prisoner labor during the period June 7–30 to Friedrich Krupp AG, Essen Cast-Iron Factory, Auschwitz Plant:

APMO, Maurer Trial, vol. 8a, p. 109 (IMG, NO-2817).

1,916 day's wages for skilled workers @ 4 RM	7,664	RM
1 day's wages for an assistant @ 3 RM	3	RM
Total	7,667	RM

This sum should be transferred by August 1, 1943, to the account of the SS Garrison Administration of Auschwitz at the Reichsbank in Kattowitz, Account No. 1410, or to the Postal Savings Account in Breslau, No. 4356.

The Commandant's Office receives word from the Head of Office D-II of the WVHA, SS Lieutenant Colonel Maurer, that he personally carried out an inspection of the prisoners destined for Auschwitz in the Lublin (Majdanek) C.C. and determined that these prisoners are able-bodied, which is why he does not understand their rejection by SS Second Lieutenant Sell and Camp Doctor Kitt. For this reason, he is ordering the transfer of the other 3,000 prisoners, men and women, to Auschwitz, particularly as 1,500 men in any case will be useful in the Buna plants, and in Neu-Dachs, whereas in Lublin space for new prisoners must be created.

APMO, D-AuI-3a/344, Labor Deployment.

Three prisoners sent from Kattowitz receive Nos. 127471–127473.

Nos. 127474–127579 are given to 106 prisoners from the prison in Lodz who have been sent to the camp by the Gestapo. Between Heydebreck (Kędzierzyn) and Kattowitz, the prisoner Jósef Nowicki, born in Mieronowski on December 20, 1911, escapes by leaping from the moving train.

APMO, IZ-10/Kripo Sieradz/2a/91.

Nos. 127580–127596 are given to 17 prisoners sent from the prison in Posen.

10 prisoners delivered from Lodz get Nos. 127597–127606.

Nos. 127607–127673 are given to 67 male prisoners and Nos. 48248–48284 and 48286–48300 to 52 female prisoners sent in a group transport.

10 prisoners sent from Silesian prisons are shot at the execution wall in the courtyard of Block 11.

APMO, Mat.RO, vol. I, p. 37.

The corpses of 13 prisoners, including three from the Buna A.C., are delivered to the morgue of the main prison.

APMO, D-AuI-5/2, Morgue Register, p. 137.

15 Ukrainians from the 8th Company (U), which was assembled from Ukrainian volunteers on March 31, 1943, flee during the night, fully armed with ammunition.* During the pursuit and battle that occurs in the area of Chełm Wielki near Bieruń, eight Ukrainian men are killed and one captured. Of the pursuers three are dead, including two SS men: SS Sergeant Karl Rainicke and SS man Stephan Rachberger.**

APMO, Höss Trial, vol. 53, p. 238; D-AuI-1, Garrison Order 23/43; Mat.RO, vol. I, p. 37; vol. XVII, pp. 67–68; SAM, *Auschwitz in the Eyes of the SS,* p. 175.

JULY 4

Six prisoners sent from Kattowitz receive Nos. 127674–127679.

After a session in Block 11 of the Police Court-martial, 1,214 people including 34 women who have been sent from East Upper Silesia, are shot in Crematorium I.

CA KC PZPR, 202/III-8, Documents of the Delegation of the Polish Government in Exile, p. 211; Mat.RO, vol. III, p. 240; vol. VII, p. 485; Dpr.-ZOd/3, p. 136.

The corpses of eight prisoners are delivered to the morgue of the main camp.

APMO, D-AuI-5/2, Morgue Register, p. 163. [eight prisoners]

During the night, two prisoners, Tomasz Radecki, born on December 22, 1899, and Stefan Wieczorek, born on July 15, 1908, escape from the camp. Both had been sent to the camp from Radom by the Sipo and SD on April 15, 1943.

APMO, D-AuI-1/1, p. 195, Telegrams; IZ-8/Gestapo Lodz/3a/ 88/470.

JULY 5

Two women sent from Kattowitz are given Nos. 48234 and 48301.

Nos. 127680–127710 are given to 31 male prisoners and Nos. 48302–48320 to 19 female prisoners sent in a group transport.

Theresie Steinbach, born in the Gypsy camp in Birkenau, receives No. Z-8914.

APMO, D-AuII-3/2/4, p. 575, Register of Female Gypsies.

The corpses of eight prisoners, including one from the Buna A.C., are delivered to the morgue of the main camp.

APMO, D-AuI-5/2, Morgue Register, p. 164.

JULY 6

131 prisoners from Pawiak Prison in Warsaw, sent by the Sipo and SD, are given Nos. 127711–127841.

34 prisoners sent from Kattowitz receive Nos. 127842–127875.

---

*According to Pery Broad, the reason for the revolt came from the conviction that the guard companies, particularly the foreign units, would one day be liquidated as superfluous witnesses.
**On the basis of these events, the other Ukrainians are transferred for service to Buchenwald. Office D-I orders that in the future ethnic German and foreign SS members should not be formed into a company of their own, but should be integrated into units made up of SS men from Germany (APMO, D-RF-9, WVHA, 8/1, p. 55, Edict Collection).

24 female prisoners sent in a group transport are given Nos. 48321–48344.

A female Gypsy sent in a group transport gets No. Z-8915.

The corpses of eight prisoners, including one from the Jawischowitz A.C. and one from the Buna A.C., are delivered to the morgue of the main camp.

Ibid.

By order of the Political Department, a Russian POW, Jakow Dasz-kowski (No. RKG-10465), is locked in the bunker of Block 11. After a selection carried out in the bunkers, he is shot on September 4, 1943.

APMO, D-AuI-372, Bunker Register, p. 23.

JULY 7

Nos. 127876–127912 are given to 37 male prisoners and Nos. 48345–48348 to four female prisoners sent from Kattowitz.

Commandant Höss makes it known that in the last two days two SS men who were on duty in the Gypsy camp and the men's camp, B-Ib, have come down with typhus. In order to prevent a further spread of typhus among the SS guards and to avoid having to return to an absolute quarantine, Höss orders that the SS men doing service in the Gypsy camp, the women's camp, B-Ia, and in the men's camp, B-Ib, be isolated and that they must be examined and deloused daily after going off duty.

APMO, D-AuI-1/40, Comman-dant's Office Special Order 15/43.

The Commandant's Office receives from the Lublin (Majdanek) C.C. the news that a transport of 1,500 Jews is departing for Auschwitz.

APMO, D-AuI-3a/345, Labor Deployment.

The prisoner Michał Sałata (No. 4875) escapes from the camp.

APMO, D-AuI-1/1, p. 197, Tele-grams; IZ-10/Kripo Sieradz/2a/90; Mat.RO, vol. IV, p. 293.

The corpses of 11 prisoners are delivered to the morgue of the main camp.

APMO, D-AuI-5/2, Morgue Register, p. 164. [11 prisoners]

JULY 8

The 750 male Jews transferred from the Majdanek camp by order of Head of Office D-II Maurer are given Nos. 127913–128662 and the 750 female Jews get Nos. 48349–49098. In order to determine why Sell and Kitt rejected them, medical examinations are con-ducted that show that 49 male prisoners must be assigned to the prisoners' infirmary or the convalescent block because of significant exhaustion, severe skin and connective tissue inflammations, and hernias; 277 male prisoners must remain in the Auschwitz camp because of slight physical exhaustion; 424 male prisoners can be transferred to the Buna plants after a four-week quarantine; five female prisoners have died after arrival; two female prisoners show traces of gunshot wounds; 80 female prisoners, including 28 be-tween the ages of 15 and 17, are unable to work; two female

D-AuI-3a/348, Labor Deploy-ment; *Documents and Materials*, Documents on pp. 140ff.

prisoners have pulmonary emphysema; 44 female prisoners show traces of slight and severe wounds on their arms and legs; five female prisoners have gangrenous legs; one female prisioner has an inflammation of connective tissue, and the other female prisoners are plagued by scabies. It is further established that the general condition of the transferred prisoners does not permit their labor to be fully exploited in Auschwitz Concentration Camp.

40 prisoners sent in a group transport are given Nos. 128663–128702.

Nine female prisoners sent from Kattowitz receive Nos. 49099–49107.

The Commandant's Office receives word from Majdanek that the second transport of 1,500 prisoners will depart on July 10.

APMO, D-AuI-3a/347, Labor Deployment.

SS Corporal Josef Koch of the lst Company of the Auschwitz SS Death's Head Stormtroopers receives from Commandant Höss a commendation and three days' special leave for his conduct during the escape of an imprisoned Gypsy.

APMO, D-AuI-1, Garrison Order 24/43.

The corpses of nine prisoners are delivered to the morgue of the main camp.

APMO, D-AuI-5/2, Morgue Register, p. 165.

JULY 9

Three prisoners sent from Kattowitz receive Nos. 128703–128705.

Nos. 128706–128827 are given to 122 male prisoners and Nos. 49108–49131 and 49133–49159 to 51 female prisoners sent in a group transport.

No. 128828 is given to a prisoner sent from Vienna.

Five Jewish prisoners who arrive in an RSHA transport receive Nos. 128829–128833.

Nos. 128834–128913 are given to 80 prisoners from Posen sent to the camp by the Gestapo.

The corpses of seven prisoners, including two from the Jawischowitz A.C., are delivered to the morgue of the main camp.

Ibid.

A general delousing starts in the women's camp in Birkenau. Work in the camp is stopped and all blocks are closed and thoroughly disinfected. The female prisoners, lined up by block, step up to a large tub placed next to Block 14. Here they must remove all clothing and give the bundle to camp personnel, who throw the clothing into the tubs containing so-called blue gas dissolved in water. Then the female prisoners go to the sauna barracks, where they wait as long as several hours for delousing and a shower. The delousing

APMO, Dpr.-Hd/3, p. 111; Depositions, vol. 9, pp. 1292–1298, Account of Former Prisoner Wanda Urbańska.

operation lasts three days. During this operation, the female prisoners get no warm meals.*

JULY 10

Nos. 128914–128950 are given to 37 male prisoners and Nos. 49160–49206 to 47 female prisoners sent in a group transport.

The German Gypsy Johan Reinhardt, a PSV prisoner (No. 113572), is captured during an escape attempt and locked in the bunker of Block 11. Following a selection in the bunkers, he is shot on July 17, 1943.

APMO, D-AuI-3/2, Bunker Register, p. 24.

The corpses of 12 prisoners, including one from the Eintrachthütte A.C., are delivered to the morgue of the main camp.

APMO, D-AuI-5/2, Morgue Register, p. 165.

JULY 11

Nos. 128951–129713 are given to 763 male Jewish prisoners, including one who is already dead, and 568 female prisoners receive Nos. 49207–49774. These are the prisoners transferred from the Lublin (Majdanek) C.C. After looking over the male and female prisoners, the Camp Doctor of the men's camp, BI-b, SS Second Lieutenant Dr. Rohde, reports to the Commandant's Office that of the 763 male prisoners, one is already dead; 78 require medical treatment; 65 are suited for light work; 237 are suited for moderately heavy work; 328 prisoners are suited for heavy work. He reports that of the 568 female prisoners, 49 require medical treatment; 32 are suited for light work; 103 are suited for moderately heavy work; and 384 are suited for heavy work.

APMO, D-AuI-3a/394, 350, 351, 352, 353, Labor Deployment.

The corpses of six prisoners are delivered to the morgue of the main camp.

APMO, D-AuI-5/2, Morgue Register, p. 166.

JULY 12

The prisoners who are ranked as healthy and able-bodied by the camp administration and are used in the various labor squads inside and outside the camp area are transferred from Camp B-Ib to Camp B-IId in Birkenau. This section is called "Men's Camp B-IId," although the designation "Camp B-IId" is generally used. In Camp B-Ib, only the prisoners in the prisoners' infirmary in Barracks 7, 8, and 12 remain. The previous Camp B-Ib is intended for enlargement of the women's camp.**

APMO, Dpr.-Hd/6, p. 34, 88; Mat.RO, vol. II, p. 80; Albert Menasche, *Birkenau (Auschwitz II)*, New York 1947, p. 42.

---

*The delousing operation is related to the plan to put female prisoners to work in outside squads in Camp B-Ib, until now occupied by male prisoners, and from which male prisoners are just starting to be moved into the newly constructed Camp B-IId.

**The information about the transfer of the men to Section II and the future use of the camp section previously used by the male prisoners comes from a secret message of July 14, 1943, sent by the resistance movement in the camp.

In a cover letter sent with Camp Doctor Rohde's reports to the Commandant's Office regarding the health of the prisoners transferred the previous day from Majdanek, Labor Deployment Director Schwarz states that the health of these prisoners was in general better than that of the previous shipment.

APMO, D-AuI-3a/354, 355, Labor Deployment.

Five prisoners sent from Kattowitz receive Nos. 129714–129716, 129778, and 129779.

28 male prisoners receive Nos. 129717–129744, and 16 female prisoners receive Nos. 49775–49790. They have arrived in group transports.

Nine corpses, including one from the Buna A.C., are delivered to the morgue of the main camp.

APMO, D-AuI-5/2, Morgue Register, p. 166.

JULY 13

All Jewish prisoners with the exception of Poles and Greeks are ordered to write letters to their families requesting food packages. In these letters it must be stated that they are healthy and feeling well. The return address is "Birkenau Labor Camp, Neu-Berun Post Office."*

APMO, Mat.RO, vol. II, p. 80.

No. 129745 is given to a male prisoner, and Nos. 49791–49803 to 13 female prisoners sent from Kattowitz.

Nos. 129746–129777 are given to 32 prisoners sent in a group transport.

Nos. Z-8277 and Z-8278 are given to two Gypsies sent in a group transport.

The corpses of six prisoners are delivered to the morgue of the main camp.

APMO, D-AuI-5/2, Morgue Register, p. 166.

JULY 14

Nos. 49804–49807 are given to four female prisoners and Nos. 129780–129825 to 46 male prisoners sent from Kattowitz.

Five boys born in the Gypsy camp receive Nos. Z-8279–Z-8283. All die within the course of the year 1943.

APMO, D-AuII-3/1/2, p. 245, Register of Male Gypsies.

Eight girls born in the Gypsy camp receive Nos. Z-8920–Z-8927. All die within the course of the year 1943.

APMO, D-AuII-3/2/4, p. 575, Register of Female Gypsies.

*This letter campaign is supposed to counteract and undermine information about the extermination of the Jews. Such information had become internationally known through the resistance movement in the camp, which established contact with the delegation of the Polish Government in Exile. The delegation passed the information on to the Polish Government in Exile, which in turn informed the governments of the Allied nations.

No. Z-8928 is given to Isabella Schmidt, who was born in the Gypsy camp on June 3, 1943.

Ibid.

The corpses of eight prisoners are delivered to the morgue of the main camp.

APMO, D-AuI-5/2, Morgue Register, p. 167.

JULY 15

24 prisoners sent from Kattowitz receive Nos. 129826–129849.

A woman sent from Klagenfurt receives No. 49808.

159 Yugoslavs sent from Belgrade receive Nos. 49809–49967. The sculptress Vidosave Jocic, who is in this group, gets No. 49865.

Nos. 129850–129855 are given to six prisoners sent from the Kattowitz District.

The corpses of five prisoners, including one from the Jawischowitz A.C. and one from the Buna A. C., are delivered to the morgue of the main camp.

Ibid.

JULY 16

The Polish prisoner Zdzisław Wijas, born in Skarżysko Kamienna, who was sent from Radom by the Sipo and SD, escapes from the camp.

APMO, IZ-8/Gestapo Lodz/3a/88/473.

The Polish prisoner Stanisław Stępiński (No. 123876) escapes from the camp.

APMO, Mat.RO, vol. IV, p. 293.

Nos. 129856–129929 are given to 74 male prisoners and Nos. 49968–50032 to 65 female prisoners sent to the camp from Pawiak Prison by the Sipo and SD of Warsaw.

84 female prisoners sent in a group transport receive Nos. 50033–50116 and 84 male prisoners get Nos. 129930–130013.

The Polish political prisoner Marian Gondek (No. 62579) is captured during an escape attempt and locked in the bunker of Block 11. Following a selection carried out in the bunkers, he is shot on July 29, 1943.

APMO, D-AuI-3/2, Bunker Register, p. 25.

Nos. 130020–130035 are given to 16 prisoners sent in a group transport.

Nos. 130036–130060 are given to 25 prisoners sent from Prague.

Nos. 130061–130107 are given to 47 prisoners sent by the Lodz Gestapo.

Nos. 130108–130125 are given to 18 prisoners sent in a group transport.

On the basis of a complaint by the SS Garrison Doctor, Commandant Höss threatens the SS guards with a total ban on leaves until every single SS man has submitted to the prescribed series of vaccinations.

APMO, D-AuI-1/39, Garrison Order 26/43.

Commandant Höss informs the SS garrison that the Führer so highly rates the efforts during the war of the WVHA that he has awarded its chief, Oswald Pohl, the German Cross in Silver.

Ibid.

Commandant Höss; Herr Düllberg, a representative of the Fürstengrube AG, an I. G. Farben* representative; and Head Engineer Dürrfeld of the Buna plants conduct an inspection of Fürstengrube in Wesoła and the Janina mine in Libiąż, as well as the forced labor camp located there. During the inspection of the Janina camp, which is still filled with English prisoners of war, it is decided that these prisoners should be transferred to another camp and their place should be taken by prisoners of Auschwitz. After a fleeting inspection, the participants determine that the camp, occupied until now by 150 English prisoners, could accommodate 300 and, after enlargement, approximately 900 prisoners. From the inspection of the Fürstengrube camp, they decide that approximately 600 prisoners can be housed there. Another inspection is scheduled for mid-August, at which time the deadline for staffing the camp should be determined. The camp in which the Jews are housed is also inspected. Commandant Höss states that this camp probably will also be taken over by Auschwitz. As this one holds 600 to 700 prisoners, it will be possible to house 1,200 to 1,300 prisoners in the Fürstengrube auxiliary camp by the planned deadline.

APMO, Maurer Trial, vol. 7, pp. 86ff. (ImG, NO-12019).

The corpses of 11 prisoners, including six from the Buna A.C., are delivered to the morgue of the main camp.

APMO, D-AuI-5/2, Morgue Register, p. 167.

JULY 17

A selection is carried out in the bunkers of Block 11, in the course of which 10 prisoners are selected who had been put in the bunkers by order of the Political Department or the camp management or had been accused of preparing an escape attempt. They are shot that same day at the execution wall in the courtyard of Block 11.

APMO, D-AuI-3/2, Bunker Register, pp. 19, 22–25.

*The I. G. Farben concern is interested in coal deliveries to the Buna plants, and has consequently acquired over 51 percent of the shares of Fürstengrube GmbH in February 1941, whereby it got three seats on the six-man board of directors and hence de facto control of the company. In response to pressure by I. G. Farben, Fürstengrube GmbH tries to purchase the Janinagrube (Janina mine). In January 1943 Fürstengrube GmbH takes over the Janinagrube provisionally, and in March 1944 it takes possession. The labor shortage was one of the primary obstacles to the quick expansion of the mine and the increase in coal production. These factors explain the efforts to obtain the labor of Auschwitz prisoners. Compare T. Iwaszko, "Das Nebenlager Fürstengrube" (Fürstengrube Auxiliary Camp), *HvA*, No. 16 (1978): 5–92; E. Iwaszko, "Das Nebenlager Janinagrube" (The Janinagrube Auxiliary Camp), *HvA*, no. 10 (1976): 51–66.

Six prisoners sent from Kattowitz receive Nos. 130014–130019.

Nos. 130126–130213 are given to 88 prisoners sent from Lodz by the Gestapo.

Nos. 130214–130230 are given to 17 male prisoners and Nos. 50117–50157 to 41 female prisoners sent in a group transport.

Nos. 130231–130294 are given to 64 prisoners sent from Kraków by the Sipo and SD.

The corpses of 11 prisoners are delivered to the morgue of the main camp.

APMO, D-AuI-5/2, Morgue Register, p. 168.

JULY 18

The Commandant's Office receives the news that a transport of 1,000 Jews left the Paris-Bobigny train station for Auschwitz at 9:30 A.M.

APMO, D-RF-3/56.

The corpses of 14 prisoners, including three from the Buna A.C., are delivered to the morgue of the main camp.

APMO, D-AuI-5/2, Morgue Register, p. 168.

JULY 19

Tadeusz Mieczkowski, born in Żuromin on May 25, 1917, escapes from the camp.

APMO, D-AuI-1/1, p. 200. Telegrams; IZ-10/Kripo Sieradz/2a/103.

Nos. Z-8284–Z-8309 are given to 26 male Gypsies and Nos. Z-8929–Z-8951 to 23 female prisoners sent in a group transport from the German Reich.

Nos. 50158–50160 are given to three female prisoners sent from Potsdam.

Nos. 50163–50169 are given to seven female prisoners sent from Breslau.

No. 50172 is given to a female prisoner and Nos. 130295–130335 to 41 male prisoners sent from Kattowitz.

A woman sent from Oppeln gets No. 50173.

Nos. 50175 and 50176 are given to two female prisoners transferred from Ravensbrück.

26 prisoners sent in a group transport receive Nos. 130336–130354 and 130357–130363.

A large gallows with 12 nooses is set up on the square in front of the camp kitchen. After evening roll call, 12 prisoners, handcuffed and clad only in overalls, are taken from the surveying squad. They were locked in the bunkers on May 21, 26, and 27, 1943. They are

APMO, D-AuI-3/2, Bunker Register, pp. 9, 10–12; Höss Trial, vol. 2, pp. 36, 95; vol. 4, pp. 40–41; vol. 8, p. 112.

Stanisław Stawiński (No. 6569), Czesław Marcisz (No. 26891), Janusz Skrzetuski-Pogonowski (No. 253), Edmund Sikorski (No. 25419), Jerzy Woźniak (No. 35650), Józef Wojtyga (No. 24740), Zbigniew Foltański (No. 41664), Bogusław Ohrt (No. 367), Leon Rajzer (No. 399), Tadeusz Rapacz (No. 36043), Józef Gancarz (No. 24538), and Mieczysław Kulikowski (No. 25404). The nooses are placed around the necks of the condemned prisoners, and Commandant Höss steps forward from the group of SS men present and starts to read the sentences.* He does not finish, however; as an expression of protest, the prisoner Janusz Skrzetuski pushes away the stool on which he is standing. SS officers and subordinates then run to the condemned men, yank the stools from under their feet, and in this manner finish the execution.

14 prisoners are assigned to the Penal Company in Birkenau.**

APMO, D-AuI-3/1, p. 2, Penal Company Register.

Five boys born in the Gypsy camp get Nos. Z-8310–Z–Z-8314.

APMO, D-AuII-3/1/2, p. 246, Register of Male Gypsies.

Two girls born in the Gypsy camp get Nos. Z-8952 and Z-8953.

APMO, D-AuII-3/2/4, p. 577, Register of Female Gypsies.

The corpses of 10 prisoners are delivered to the morgue of the main camp.

APMO, D-AuI-5/2, Morgue Register, p. 168.

The Special Squad, consisting of eight prisoners that run the crematorium, is shifted from the main camp to Birkenau to run Crematorium IV. From now on, Crematorium I is not used.

APMO, D-Mau-3a/8071, 14129, Personal-Information of Józef Ilczuk and Wacław Lipka; Höss Trial, vol. 1, pp. 4–28, Statement of Former Prisoner in the Special Squad Stanisław Jankowski (a.k.a. Alter Feinsilber).

JULY 20

Nos. 130355 and 130356 are given to two prisoners sent from Kattowitz.

Nos. 130364–130387 are given to 24 male prisoners and Nos. 50177–50184 to eight female prisoners sent from Kraków by the Sipo and SD.

Nos. 130388–130418 are given to 31 prisoners sent from Kattowitz.

*During his trial, Rudolf Höss states that he recalls the escape of three prisoners from the surveying squad in mid-January 1943. They fled from their workplace in the vicinity of Skidzin and Wilczkowice. As it was determined during the investigations that other prisoners from the squad had known of the escape, he issued the order to punish them with death as a deterrent to the other prisoners. Himmler agreed and ordered several of the prisoners who had been locked in the bunkers—he no longer knew the number—to be hanged publicly. The execution took place in front of the camp kitchen; all were hung from a large gallows. Höss recalled that prior to the execution he read aloud the death sentence in the presence of prisoners from the entire camp who had come to the roll call. He justified the death penalty with the necessity of securing the camp against similar incidents (APMO, Höss Trial, vol. 21, p. 96, statement of the Accused, Höss).
**Following the transfer of prisoners from Camp B-Ib to Camp B-IId in Birkenau, the Penal Company is housed in Barracks No. 11. The Special Squad is assigned to neighboring Barracks No. 13. The courtyard between these two barracks is blocked, so the prisoners of the Penal Company and those of the Special Squad are isolated from the other prisoners in Camp B-IId.

Nos. 130419–130465 are given to 47 male prisoners and Nos. 50185–50203 to 19 female prisoners sent in a group transport.

1,000 Jewish men, women, and children from Drancy arrive with the fifty-seventh RSHA transport from France. Following the selection, 369 men, given Nos. 130466–130834, and 191 women, given Nos. 50204–50394, are admitted to the camp. The other 440 people are killed in the gas chambers. A good dozen of the selected female prisoners are assigned to the experimental station in Block 10 of the main camp.

APMO, Dpr.-Hd/6, p. 94; Schnabel, *Power Without Morality*, p. 277.

Stanisław Stepiński (No. 123876), who escaped from the camp on July 16, is captured and locked in the bunker of Block 11. Following a selection carried out in the bunkers, he is shot on July 29, 1943.

APMO, D-AuI-3/2, Bunker Register, p. 25.

152 Czech prisoners are transferred from Auschwitz to Buchenwald.

APMO, Mat.RO, vol. VII, p. 474.

Rudolf Franc (No. Z-5928), a Gypsy from Germany, is locked in the bunker of Block 11 because he is suspected of having made escape preparations. Following a selection carried out in the bunkers, he is shot on July 29, 1943.

APMO, D-AuI-3/2, Bunker Register, p. 25.

By order of the Camp Commander, the reeducation prisoner Ignacy Suchorda (No. EH-5078) is locked in the bunker of Block 11. Following a selection carried out in the bunkers, he is shot on July 29, 1943.

Ibid.

The corpses of nine prisoners, including one from the Eintrachthütte A.C. and one from the Neu-Dachs A.C., are delivered to the morgue of the main camp.

APMO, D-AuI-5/2, Morgue Register, p. 169.

JULY 21

37 men sent in a prisoner transport from Kattowitz receive Nos. 130835–130871 and four women receive Nos. 48285, 49132, 50170, and 50171.

On suspicion of attempting escape, two Polish Jews, Moses Fischsohn (No. 128006) and Elu Salzmann (No. 128312), are locked in the bunker of Block 11. Following a selection in the bunkers, both are shot on July 29, 1943.

APMO, D-AuI-3/2, Bunker Register, p. 26.

By order of the Political Department, Szymon Galpern, a Polish Jew, is locked in the bunker of Block 11. He is shot on July 29, 1943, following a selection carried out in the bunkers.

Ibid.

The corpses of seven prisoners are delivered to the morgue of the main camp.

APMO, D-AuI-5/2, Morgue Register, p. 169.

JULY 22

In the afternoon, the prisoner Stefan Kołodziejczak (No. 66442) escapes.

APMO, D-AuI-1/1, p. 202, Telegrams; IZ-8/Gestapo Lodz/3a/88/475; Mat.RO, vol. IV, p. 294.

The 22 male prisoners sent from Kattowitz receive Nos. 130872–130893, and eight female prisoners are given the free Nos. 50161, 50162, 50174, 50395, and 50399.

50 male prisoners, given Nos. 130894–130943, and four female prisoners, given Nos. 50400–50403, were sent to the camp by the Sipo and SD for the Kraków District. Among them are the parents of Tadeusz and Adam Klus (Nos. 416 and 419), who escaped on February 27, 1943. The father, Tomasz Klus, gets No. 130943 and the mother, Stefania Klus, gets No. 50401.*

APMO, Prisoners Card File.

Three prisoners sent from Kattowitz are given Nos. 130944–130946.

The Head of Office D-IV of the WVHA orders** the administrations of Dachau, Sachsenhausen, Buchenwald, Mauthausen, Flossenbürg, Natzweiler, Ravensbrück, Neuengamme, Bergen-Belsen, Stutthof, Herzogenbusch, Gross-Rosen, Lublin, and Auschwitz concentration camps to report to WVHA by August 6, 1943, about their total receipts of civilian clothing handed over by the Lublin and Auschwitz concentration camps. The following pattern must be followed:

APMO, IZ-13/89, Various Documents of the Third Reich, pp. 223ff.

> Title: Receipt of Civilian Clothing from the Secondhand Materials Processing Offices of Lublin and Auschwitz.
> Separate categories: day of receipt; place; overcoats; cardigans; jackets; pants; vests; sweaters; shirts; underwear; pajamas; work clothing; handkerchiefs
> Total:
> Usable:
> Meanwhile depreciated:
> Status as of August 1, 1943:
> Signature by the clothing specialists and by the Director of the Administration Department.

The corpses of five prisoners are delivered to the morgue of the main camp.

APMO, D-AuI-5/2, Morgue Register, p. 169.

By order of the Camp Commander the reeducation prisoner Konstanty Jęczkiewicz (No. EH-5106) is locked in the bunker of Block 11. Following a selection carried out in the bunkers, he is shot on July 29, 1943.

APMO, D-AuI-3/2, Bunker Register, p. 26.

JULY 23

The German prisoner Siegfried Koprowiak (No. BV-71343), who escaped from the camp on April 8, 1943, is arrested again, delivered to the camp, and locked in the bunker of Block 11. He is released into the camp on August 17, 1943.

Ibid., p. 27.

*The arrests and internment of family members of escaped concentration camp prisoners is supposed to deter prisoners from escape attempts.
**This order proves that in the year 1943 the Lublin and Auschwitz concentration camps sent the clothing that was stolen from the Jews who were delivered for extermination to other concentration camps via the Office for Processing Secondhand Goods.

A prisoner sent from Kattowitz receives No. 130947.

55 prisoners sent from Kattowitz receive Nos. 130948–131002.

42 male prisoners sent in a group transport are given Nos. 131003–131044 and 60 female prisoners receive Nos. 50404–50463.

Eight male Gypsies sent in a group transport receive Nos. Z-8315–Z-8322 and three female Gypsies receive Nos. Z-8954–Z-8956.

In Birkenau a separate infirmary is set up for male prisoners, which is officially called Prisoner Infirmary B-IIf. The ill prisoners left behind in Barracks Nos. 7, 8, and 12 are moved there. The camp is not yet completely finished; not until September will the street along the barracks start to be paved. In the east Camp B-IIf borders the Gypsy Family Camp, B-IIe, and in the west it borders the site of Crematorium III, the wastewater purification plant, and the warehouse of stolen objects, which officially is called the Personal Effects Camp, in camp parlance known as "Canada." Camp B-IIf is off-limits to healthy prisoners. They can enter there only on official business or by order of the Camp Doctor or a doctor authorized by the Camp Doctor.

Czech, "Role of Prisoners' Infirmary," pp. 41ff.

The Polish political prisoner Jerzy Opilka (No. 111482) and the Polish PSV prisoner Jan Zakrzewski (No. 107360) are put in the bunkers of Block 11. They are supposed to be brought before the Police Court-martial, which holds sessions in Auschwitz C.C. and which, in compliance with an RSHA order, carries out in the concentration camp executions that are not to be done publicly for deterrence purposes.

APMO, D-AuI-3/2, Bunker Register, p. 27; Depositions, vol. 35, p. 13, Account of Pelagia Bednarska; compare SAM, *Auschwitz in the Eyes of the SS*, pp. 149–157.

Two Russian prisoners, Pavel Yeraszewitz, born on June 26, 1922, and Piotr Yarovenko, born on December 8, 1923, escape in the evening.

APMO, D-AuI-1/1, pp. 206, 208, Telegrams; IZ-8/Gestapo Lodz/3a/88/477; IZ-10/Kripo Sieradz/2a/107.

The corpses of five prisoners, including one of the new arrivals bearing No. 131017, are delivered to the morgue of the main camp.

APMO, D-AuI-5/2, Morgue Register, p. 170.

JULY 24

Nos. 131045–131095 are given to 51 male prisoners and Nos. 50464–50508 to 45 female prisoners sent in a group transport.

The Polish prisoner Henryk Radomski (No. 14186) is led from the bunker to the washroom of Block 11 and shot there. He was captured during an escape attempt on November 3, 1942, at which time a pistol was found on him.* He was in the bunker more than 260 days, because the Political Department wanted to extract from him information of interest to them. His corpse is delivered to the morgue of the main camp.

APMO, D-AuI-3/2, Bunker Register, p. 27, D-AuI-5/2, Morgue Register, p. 170.

*Information based on Brol et al., "Bunker of Block 11," p. 29.

Prisoners unload "new accessions'" baggage, which has been brought to the personal effects warehouse, called "Canada."

The reeducation prisoner Franciszek Goszkowski (No. EH-4807), who is to be brought before the Police Court-martial, is delivered to the bunker of Block 11.

APMO, D-Au-I-3/2, Bunker Register, p. 27.

By order of the Camp Commander, seven prisoners are locked in the bunker of Block 11, five Jews—Alfred Grynberg (No. 128032), Feiweld Kleiner (No. 128113), Herszt Zlocist (No. 128317), Gidale Goldblat (No. 76304), and Natan Mahel (No. 110280)—and two Gypsies—Johann Betschker (No. Z-6174) and Kristian Chorwat (No. Z-6262). Following a selection carried out in the bunkers, they are shot on July 29, 1943.

Ibid.

On suspicion of planning an escape, the Jew Mathys Blumenstock (No. 58805) is locked in the bunker of Block 11. He is shot on July 29, 1943, following a selection carried out in the bunkers.

Ibid.

The bodies of eight prisoners, including one from the Jawischowitz A.C., are delivered to the morgue of the main camp.

APMO, D-AuI-5/2, Morgue Register, p. 170.

After completion of the disinfection measures in Camp B-Ib, previously occupied by men, all women who work outside the camp, mainly in the agricultural squads, are housed there. The female prisoners who work inside the camp grounds, as well as those who

APMO, Depositions, vol. 9, pp. 1292–1298, Account of Former Prisoner Wanda Urbańska.

work in the prisoners' infirmary of the women's camp, the package office, and the orderly room are housed in Camp B-Ia.

JULY 25

10 prisoners are assigned to the Penal Company in Birkenau.

APMO, D-AuI-3/1, p. 3, Penal Company Register.

The corpses of four prisoners are delivered to the morgue of the main camp.

APMO, D-AuI-5/2, Morgue Register, p. 170.

JULY 26

Nos. 50509–50510 are given to two female prisoners and No. 131096 to a male prisoner who were delivered from the Kattowitz District.

Nos. 131097–131111 are given to 15 prisoners sent from Kraków by the Sipo and SD.

Nos. 131112–131133 are given to 22 male prisoners and Nos. 50511–50525 to 15 female prisoners sent in a group transport.

Four boys born in the Gypsy camp in Birkenau get Nos. Z-8323–Z-8326.

APMO, D-AuII-3/1/2, p. 246, Register of Male Gypsies.

By order of the Political Department, the Polish political prisoner Franciszek Rybiński (No. 39865) is locked in the bunker of Block 11. He is probably* to be brought before the Police Court-martial.

APMO, D-AuI-3/2 Bunker Register, p. 28.

By order of the Camp Commander, the Polish political prisoner Zygmunt Walaszczk (No. 62064) is locked in the bunker of Block 11. He is shot on August 20, 1943, following a selection carried out in the bunker.

Ibid.

By order of the Political Department the following prisoners are locked in the bunker of Block 11: the Polish Jew Abraham Weisbaum (No. 31925), the Pole Jan Raczyński (No. BV-37988), the Jew Wilhelm Wiesen (No. 67170), the Jew and Peruvian national Feliks Leipziger (No. 68238), and the Polish political prisoner Józef Lewandowski (No. 8154). These prisoners are said to have been persuaded by Józef Lewandowski to escape from the camp through the wastewater canal. As the matter is generally known and the prisoners know about the role of Józef Lewandowski, all of them, together with Lewandowski, are shot on August 20, 1943, following a selection in the bunkers.

Ibid.; Brol et al., "Bunker Book of Block 11," pp. 36ff.

The corpses of 11 prisoners, including one from the Jawischowitz A.C. and one from the Buna A.C., are delivered to the morgue of the main camp.

APMO, D-AuI-5/2, Morgue Register, p. 171.

*He is shot following the session of the Police Court-martial.

JULY 27

Nos. 131134–131139 are given to six male prisoners and Nos. 50526–50530 to five female prisoners sent from Kattowitz.

Nos. 131140–131165 are given to 26 prisoners sent from the Kattowitz District.

Nos. 131166–131169 are given to four prisoners sent in a group transport.

At 2:00 A.M. the German police, some of them in armed units, begin the evacuation of the Poles living in Auschwitz and the surrounding area. The affected are people without paid employment but who have ration cards—women with children whose husbands are prisoners of war or have disappeared in camps or prisons, the aged and frail, and invalids.

CA KC PZPR, 202/III-146, Documents of the Delegation of the Polish Government in Exile, p. 95.

60 prisoners from Kraków sent to the camp by the Sipo and SD are given Nos. 131170–131229. In this transport are 50 Russians and 10 prisoners from the prison in Tarnów.

The corpses of eight prisoners are delivered to the morgue of the main camp.

APMO, D-AuI-5/2, Morgue Register, p. 171.

JULY 28

In Block 11 there is a session of the Police Court-martial, during which the prisoners delivered from the Silesian prisons are sentenced. Among those sentenced to death are four prisoners who were initially sent to the camp in order to be locked in the bunkers of Block 11 several days prior to the session of the court-martial. The ones condemned to death are shot the same day. Among them are Jan Zakrzewski (No. 107360), Jerzy Opiłka (No. 111482), Franciszek Goszkowski (No. EH-4807), and Franciszek Rybiński (No. 39865).

APMO, D-AuI-3/2, Bunker Register, pp. 27ff.

No. 131230 is given to a prisoner sent from the Kattowitz District.

Nos. 131231 and 131232 are given to two prisoners sent from Oppeln.

Nos. 131233–131260 are given to 28 prisoners sent from Brünn.

Nos. 131261–131312 are given to 52 prisoners sent from Prague.

Nos. 131313–131317 are given to five prisoners sent from Kattowitz.

Nos. 50531–50543 are given to 13 female prisoners sent from the prison in Tarnów by the Sipo and SD.

Of the women and children who were evacuated from Auschwitz and the vicinity, some were sent to the General Government and the rest to camps in Oderberg (Bohumin), Czechoslovakia, and Ratibor (Raciborz). The aged, feeble, and crippled whose addresses were previously determined* are picked up separately and brought to Auschwitz C.C. They are killed in the gas chambers.

CA KC PZPR, 202/III-7, Documents of the Delegation of the Polish Government in Exile, p. 170.

Tomasz Klus (No. 130943) and Stefania Klus (No. 50401), the parents of escaped prisoners Adam and Tadeusz Klus (Nos. 419 and 416), are exhibited on a podium specially set up on the main street leading to the camp gate with the sign, "Labor Makes Free." Beside them is a bulletin board with the message that they are the parents of the escapees and have been arrested in retaliation for the escape of their sons. All prisoners returning from work to the main camp must pass by the podium. Tomasz and Stefania Klus are afterward locked in the bunker of Block 11. Tomasz Klus is released from the bunker into the camp on August 18, 1943, and works in the so-called potato squad. The fellow prisoners of his escaped sons assist him a great deal. It is impossible to determine just when Stefania Klus's release from the bunker into the camp occurred.

APMO, D-AuI-3/2, Bunker Register, p. 28.

The corpses of 14 prisoners, including one from Buna A.C., are delivered to the morgue of the main camp.

APMO, D-AuI-5/2, Morgue Register, p, 171.

JULY 29

By order of the Political Department, the following four prisoners are locked in the bunker of Block 11: Marian Platek (No. EH-4289), shot on July 29, 1943; Wencel Čorman, a Gypsy (No. 39780), shot on September 28, 1943; and Kazimierz Mieżyński (No. EH-5184) and Walenty Idzi (No. 125187), both of whom were shot on August 20, 1943, following a selection carried out in the bunkers.

APMO, D-AuI-3/2, Bunker Register, p. 28.

Nos. 131318 and 50544 are given to one male and one female prisoner sent from the Kattowitz District.

At the selection carried out in the bunkers of Block 11, 26 prisoners are selected who were locked up by order of the Political Department or the Camp Commander or were captured while escaping or who are suspected of having prepared an escape. Of the selected, six prisoners are assigned to the Penal Company and 20 prisoners are shot the same day.

Ibid., pp. 14, 24–28.

Nos. 131375–131392 and 131411–131452 are given to 60 prisoners sent to the camp by the Sipo and SD for the Kraków District.

---

*One of the residents of Auschwitz who is employed by the railroad as an assistant to the locomotive driver manages to rescue his aged father by doing without the food ration cards that he gets for the father. His immediate superior, a German, helps him in this. In another instance an aged mother is ransomed from the camp in Ratibor for 3,000 Reichsmarks and the waiver of food ration cards (APMO, Depositions, vol. 84, pp. 240–243, Account of Wojciech Chowaniec; information from Józef Kojdecki, of Auschwitz).

Among them are 38 prisoners from the prison in Tarnów and 18 Russians from the prison in Kraków.

Nos. 131393–131410 are given to 18 prisoners sent from Kattowitz.

Nos. 131453–132061 are given to 609 male prisoners and Nos. 50545–50640 are given to 96 female prisoners sent by the Sipo and SD for the Radom District.

Nos. 132062 and 132063 are given to two prisoners sent from the Kattowitz District.

The corpses of 11 prisoners, including one from the Neu-Dachs A.C., are delivered to the morgue of the main camp.

APMO, D-AuI-5/2, Morgue Register, p. 172.

JULY 30

The Commandant's Office receives a permit from the WVHA to send a truck to pick up Zyklon B gas from Dessau.

APMO, Dpr.-Hd/12, p. 173, Appendix 117.

The prisoner Józef Błodziński (No. 91753), who escaped on January 23, 1943, is again brought to the camp and locked in the bunker of Block 11. He is shot on August 20, 1943, following a selection carried out in the bunkers.

APMO, D-AuI-3/2, Bunker Register, p. 29.

Motel Redak (No. 91223), a Polish Jew, is captured while escaping and locked in the bunker of Block 11. He is shot on August 20, 1943, following a selection carried out in the bunkers.

Ibid.

Nos. 131319–131374 are given to 56 male prisoners and Nos. 50641–50676 to 36 female prisoners sent in a group transport.

Nos. 132064–132182 are given to 119 male prisoners and Nos. 50677–50738 are given to 62 female prisoners sent in a group transport.

The Polish political prisoner Franciszek Balas (No. 126803) escapes from the camp.

APMO, Mat.RO, vol. IV, p. 293.

The Camp Commander orders a delousing operation, based on the new method of the Camp Doctor Dr. Wirths, in the Men's Camp B-IId in Birkenau for Saturday, July 31, and Sunday, August 1.

APMO, D-AuI-1/46, Commandant's Office Special Order 17/43.

The corpses of eight prisoners are delivered to the morgue of the main camp.

APMO, D-AuI-5/2, Morgue Register, p. 172.

JULY 31

Nos. 132183–132200 are given to 18 male prisoners and Nos. 50739–50797 to 59 female prisoners sent in a group transport.

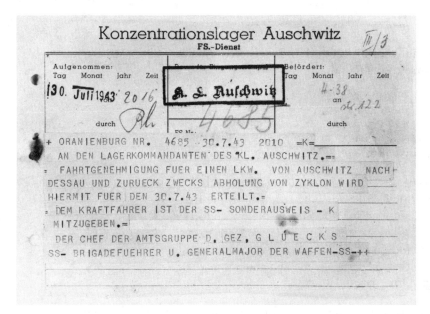

Konzentrationslager Auschwitz
FS.-Dienst

Aufgenommen:
Tag Monat Jahr Zeit
30. Juli 1943 2016

Befördert:
Tag Monat Jahr Zeit
4-38

+ ORANIENBURG NR. 4685 30.7.43 2010 =K=
AN DEN LAGERKOMMANDANTEN DES KL. AUSCHWITZ.==
: FAHRTGENEHMIGUNG FUER EINEN LKW. VON AUSCHWITZ NACH
DESSAU UND ZURUECK ZWECKS ABHOLUNG VON ZYKLON WIRD
HIERMIT FUER DEN 30.7.43 ERTEILT.=
: DEM KRAFTFAHRER IST DER SS- SONDERAUSWEIS - K
MITZUGEBEN.=
: DER CHEF DER AMTSGRUPPE D. GEZ. G L U E C K S
SS- BRIGADEFUEHRER U. GENERALMAJOR DER WAFFEN-SS-++

Armed SS Brigadier General Richard Glücks issues a travel permit for the transport of Zyklon B.

Nos. 132201–132252 are given to 52 male prisoners and Nos. 50798–50806 to nine female prisoners sent from the prison in Tarnów by the Sipo and SD.

Nos. 50807–50836 are given to 30 female prisoners who were sent from Kraków by the Sipo and SD.

The Commandant's Office is informed that a transport of 1,000 Jews left the train station of Paris-Bobigny for Auschwitz at 10:00 A.M.

APMO, D-RF-3/57/3401.

Two Russian prisoners, Gregor Karchov (No. 53812) and Kuzma Skudnov (No. 55827), are captured while escaping and locked in the bunker of Block 11. They are shot on August 20, 1943, following a selection carried out in the bunkers.

APMO, D-AuI-3/2, Bunker Register, p. 29.

Kazimierz Jarzbowski (No. 115), who escaped from the surveying squad on May 20, 1943, is arrested again and sent to the camp. He is locked in the bunker of Block 11. During interrogations by functionaries of the Political Department, he is tortured to extract information about the escape route and the escape helpers. As a consequence, he twice tries to commit suicide in the bunker. He is shot on August 20, 1943, following a selection carried out in the bunkers.

APMO, Höss Trial, vol. 4, pp. 43–44, Statement of Former Prisoner Wilhelm Wohlfahrth; D-AuI-3/2, Bunker Register, p. 29.

Two Russian prisoners, Siemion Olitzveski and Aleksander Kasperovitz, escape from the camp.

APMO, D-AuI-1/1, p. 210; IZ-10/Kripo Sieradz/2/121ff.

Owing to bad weather, the delousing operation in Men's Camp B-IId is canceled.

APMO, Dpr.-Hd/6, p. 75.

The corpses of five prisoners, Nos. 97885, 112052, 120604, 120646, and 124296, are delivered to the morgue of the main camp.

APMO, D-AuI-5/2, Morgue Register, p. 172.

In the Auschwitz-Birkenau women's camp, 1,133 registered female prisoners die in the course of the month.

APMO, Mat.RO, vol. VII, p. 485.

AUGUST 1

A so-called quarantine camp* is set up in Camp B-IIa of Birkenau for newly arrived male prisoners.

In a written inquiry to the governor of the administrative district of Kattowitz, the chief of police of Sosnowitz requisitions the free provisions to which he is entitled for 690 men in the police force from Sosnowitz, Bendin, Gleiwitz, and Kattowitz who are to be deployed in the implementation of the so-called Jewish operation in the last ghettos still existing in Silesia, i.e., Bendin and Sosnowitz. This operation is planned for August 1 to 4.

Szternfinkiel, *Jews of Sosnowitz*, pp. 55, 71.

Approximately 2,000 Jewish men, women, and children from the ghetto in Bendin arrive with an RSHA transport. Following the selection, 208 men, given Nos. 132253–132460, and 141 women, given Nos. 50837–50977, are admitted to the camp. The other people, more than 1,600, are killed in the gas chambers.

Approximately 2,000 Jewish men, women, and children arrive in an RSHA transport from the ghetto in Bendin. Following the selection, 210 men, given Nos. 132461–132670, and 260 women, given Nos. 50978–51237, are admitted to the camp. The other people, more than 1,500, are killed in the gas chambers.

Approximately 2,000 Jewish men, women, and children from the ghetto in Bendin arrive in an RSHA transport. After the selection, 183 men, given Nos. 132671–132853, and 269 women, given Nos. 51238–51506, are admitted to the camp. The others, more than 1,500 people, are killed in the gas chambers.

Approximately 2,000 Jewish men, women, and children from the ghetto in Sosnowitz arrive in an RSHA transport. After the selection, 155 men, given Nos. 132854–133008, and 263 women, given Nos. 51507–51769, are admitted to the camp. The others, more than 1,500 people, are killed in the gas chambers.

Approximately 2,000 Jewish men, women, and children from the ghetto in Sosnowitz** arrive with an RSHA transport. After the selection, 241 men, given Nos. 133009–133249, and 207 women,

*The quarantine camp consists of 16 wooden barracks in which 4,000 to 6,000 prisoners are housed. From the extant documents, it is evident that from September 1943 to November 1944, 4,012 prisoners become so ill that they are moved to the prisoners' infirmary in Camp B-IIf, 1,902 prisoners die, and 6,717 prisoners are selected and killed in the gas chambers. The several-week quarantine is supposed to accustom the prisoners to camp life and to put their physical and psychological stamina to a severe test (Sehn, *Concentration Camp*, p. 26).
**SS Men from Auschwitz C.C. also participate in the liquidation of the ghetto in Sosnowitz (APMO, Dpr.-Hd/5, p. 145).

given Nos. 51981–52187, are admitted to the camp. The others, more than 1,500 people, are killed in the gas chambers.

The corpses of 11 prisoners, including one from the Neu-Dachs auxiliary camp, No. 120843, are delivered to the morgue of the main camp.

APMO, D-AuI-5/2, Morgue Register, p. 173.

AUGUST 2

Two girls born in the Gypsy camp in Birkenau receive Nos. Z-8957 and Z-8958.

APMO, D-AuII-3/2/4, p. 577, Register of Female Gypsies.

10 male Gypsies sent in a group transport from the territory of the Reich receive Nos. Z-8959–Z-8968.

Four girls born in the Gypsy camp on July 26, 1943, receive Nos. Z-8969–Z-8972.

Ibid., p. 579.

The prisoner Franciszek Balas (No. 126803), who escaped on July 30, 1943, is captured and locked in the bunker of Block 11. He is shot on August 20, 1943, following a selection in the bunkers.

APMO, D-AuI-3/2, Bunker Register, p. 29.

1,553 Jews from the Malines camp arrive with the twenty-first RSHA transport from Belgium. In the shipment are 664 men, 117 boys, 681 women, and 91 girls. After the selection, 255 men, given Nos. 133250–133504, and 211 women, given Nos. 51770–51980, are admitted to the camp. The other 1,087 people are killed in the gas chambers.

2,000 Jewish men, women, and children from the ghetto in Bendin have arrived in an RSHA transport. After the selection, 276 men, given Nos. 133505–133780, and 109 women, given Nos. 52188–52296, are admitted to the camp. The other more than 1600 people are killed in the gas chambers.

1,000 Jewish men, women, and children from Drancy camp arrive in the fifty-eighth RSHA transport from France. After the selection, 218 men, given Nos. 133781–133998, and 55 women, given Nos. 52297–52351, are admitted to the camp. The other 727 people are killed in the gas chambers. The 55 female prisoners selected from this shipment are moved from the women's camp in Birkenau to the experimental station of Professor Dr. Clauberg in Block 10 of the main camp.

APMO, Dpr.-Hd/6, p. 94; Schnabel, *Power Without Morality*, pp. 276, 278–281.

Nos. Z-8327–Z-8332 are given to six male Gypsies and Nos. Z-8973–Z-8975 to three female Gypsies sent in a group transport.

Nos. 133999–134041 are given to 43 male prisoners and Nos. 52353–52373 to 21 female prisoners sent in a group transport.

Kurt Weiss, born in the Gypsy camp in Birkenau, receives No. Z-8333.

APMO, D-AuII-3/1/2, p. 246, Register of Male Gypsies.

Nos. 134042–134095 are given to 54 prisoners sent by the Sipo and SD for the Kraków District. In this transport are 13 prisoners from the prison in Tarnów.

The Russian prisoner Volodymir Ulyvanov, born on October 19, 1916, escapes in the evening.

APMO, D-AuI-1/1, p. 216, Telegrams; IZ-10/Kripo Sieradz/2a/105.

The corpses of six prisoners, including one from the Neu-Dachs A.C., are delivered to the morgue of the main camp.

APMO, D-AuI-5/2, Morgue Register, p. 173.

AUGUST 3

Approximately 3,000 Jewish men, women, and children from the ghetto in Sosnowitz arrive in an RSHA transport. After the selection, 404 men, given Nos. 134096–134499, and 448 women, given Nos. 52374–52821, are admitted to the camp. The others, more than 2,100 people, are killed in the gas chambers.

Approximately 3,000 Jewish men, women, and children from the ghetto in Sosnowitz arrive in an RSHA transport. After the selection, 264 men, given Nos. 134500–134763, and 390 women, given Nos. 52822–53211, are admitted to the camp. The others, more than 2,300 people, are killed in the gas chambers.

Approximately 3,000 Jewish men, women, and children from the ghetto in Sosnowitz arrive in an RSHA transport. Following the selection, 434 men, given Nos. 134764–135197, and 332 women, given Nos. 53212–53543, are admitted to the camp. The others, more than 2,200 people, are killed in the gas chambers.

No. 135202 is given to a prisoner sent from Kattowitz.

Nos. 135203–135276 are given to 74 prisoners sent to the camp by the Lodz Gestapo.

200 Jews from Berlin arrive in an RSHA transport. Following the selection, all are killed in the gas chambers.

CA KR PZPR, 202/III-146, Documents of the Delegation of the Polish Government in Exile, p. 154.

Nos. 135277–135290 are given to 14 male prisoners and Nos. 53544–53555 to 12 female prisoners sent in a group transport from Lodz.

The Labor Deployment Department submits bill No. 2/43 in the amount of 21,306 Reichsmarks to the Krupp factories in Auschwitz for prisoner labor for July 1–31, 1943.

APMO, Maurer Trial, vol. 8, p. 114.

The corpses of seven prisoners are delivered to the morgue of the main camp.

APMO, D-AuI-5/2, Morgue Register, p. 173.

AUGUST 4

The resistance movement in the camp reports in a message smuggled out to Kraków: "... large transports from Bendin and Sosnowitz

APMO, Mat.RO, vol. I, p. 39.

are arriving for gassing. A precise figure is so far hard to arrive at, approximately 20,000. Of these, hardly 10 percent are admitted to the camp."

Because of delays in the "resettlement operation" from the ghetto in Sosnowitz, the so-called Jewish operation, the Sosnowitz chief of police requests the governor of the administrative district of Kattowitz to provide the cost-free provisions that are due for the period August 5–8, 1943, for 499 men in the police forces from Sosnowitz, Gleiwitz, Kattowitz, and Maczek. At the same time, he reports that members of the Bendin cavalry school have returned to their normal service.

Szternfinkiel, Jews of Sosnowitz, p. 73.

Józef Garzala (No. 125319), born on May 10, 1923, escapes from the camp.

APMO, D-AuI-1/1, p. 214, Telegrams; IZ-10/Kripo Sieradz/2/123; Mat.RO, vol. IV, p. 293.

52 prisoners who were in the transports from Warsaw and Radom are assigned to the Penal Company until this is countermanded.

APMO, D-AuI-3/1, pp. 3–4, Penal Company Register.

Four male prisoners delivered from the Kattowitz District receive Nos. 135198–135201, and five female prisoners receive Nos. 53556–53560.

20 prisoners sent from Kattowitz receive Nos. 135291–135310.

The Jewish prisoner Moric Stawkowski (No. 126179) is locked in the bunker of Block 11 under suspicion of preparing an escape. He is shot on August 20, 1943, following a selection in the bunkers.

APMO, D-AuI-3/2, Bunker Register, p. 30.

The Czech prisoner Franz Varadinek (No. 117196), who escaped from the camp on June 28, 1943, is brought back to the camp and locked in the bunker of Block 11. He is shot on August 20, 1943, following a selection in the bunkers.

Ibid.

The corpses of six prisoners are delivered to the morgue of the main camp.

APMO, D-AuI-5/2, Morgue Register, p. 174.

AUGUST 5

A male Gypsy sent from Essen receives No. Z-8334.

Four boys born in the Gypsy camp in Birkenau receive Nos. Z-8335–Z-8338.

APMO, D-AuII-3/1/2, p. 246, Register of Male Gypsies.

Four girls born in the Gypsy camp in Birkenau receive Nos. Z-8976–Z-8979.

APMO, D-AuII-3/2/4, p. 579, Register of Female Gypsies.

Nos. 135311–135364 are given to 54 male prisoners and Nos. 53561–53571 to 11 female prisoners sent from Brünn.

Nos. 135365–135372 are given to eight prisoners sent from Kattowitz.

100 Jewish men and women arrive in the fortieth RSHA transport from Berlin, and approximately 3,000 Jewish men, women, and children arrive in an RSHA transport from the ghetto in Sosnowitz. Following the selection from both transports, 265 men, given Nos. 135373–135637, and 249 women, given Nos. 53572–53820, are admitted to the camp. The others, almost 2,600 people, are killed in the gas chambers.

APMO, D-RF-3/121/15, pp. 19–31, Gestapo Berlin, Auschwitz Transports.

Approximately 1,000 Jews—patients and nursing staff from the local Sosnowitz hospital—arrive from the ghetto in Sosnowitz in an RSHA transport. Following the selection, 26 women are admitted to the camp and given Nos. 53821–53846. The others, almost 1,000 people, are killed in the gas chambers.

Szternfinkiel, *Jews of Sosnowitz*, p. 56.

125 Jews from the prison in Dresden are sent in an RSHA transport. They are all killed in the gas chambers.

CA KC PZPR, 202/III-146, Documents of the Delegation of the Polish Government in Exile, p. 154.

The corpses of seven prisoners are delivered to the morgue of the main camp.

APMO, D-AuI-5/2, Morgue Register, p. 174.

By order of the Political Department, the Russian reeducation prisoner Rodion Ilochenko is locked in the bunker of Block 11. Following a selection carried out in the bunkers, he is shot on August 20, 1943.

APMO, D-AuI-3/2, Bunker Register, p. 30.

By order of the Camp Commander, the Jewish prisoner Georg Kaufmann (No. 97971) is locked in the bunker of Block 11. Following a selection carried out in the bunkers, he is shot on August 20, 1943.

Ibid.

During the night, three Russian prisoners, Andreas Melnyk (No. 112203), Andreas Novikov (No. 107643), and Alexander Grigoriev (No. 115694), escape from the Eintrachthütte auxiliary camp.

APMO, D-AuI-1/1, p. 217, Telegrams; IZ-10/Kripo Sieradz/2/122; Mat.RO, vol. IV, p. 293.

AUGUST 6

The Russian prisoner Yevgeni Zablovski (No. 125008) escapes from the camp during the morning hours.

APMO, D-AuI-1/1, p. 219, Telegrams; IZ-10/Kripo Sieradz/2/122; Mat.RO, vol. IV, p. 293.

74 male prisoners from Pawiak Prison in Warsaw sent by the Sipo and SD receive Nos. 135638–135711, and 59 female prisoners receive Nos. 53847–53905.

53 prisoners sent from Kattowitz get Nos. 135712–135764.

The Central Construction Administration employs 10,226 male prisoners, including 1,358 skilled workers, and 662 female prisoners, including seven skilled workers,* in the expansion of the camp. The daily wage to be paid to the account of the Auschwitz

APMO, D-AuI-3a/370/5, pp. 301, 301a, 327, 327a, Monthly Labor Deployment List.

---

*The employment level, particularly of the unskilled labor, varies. It probably depends upon the type of work to be done.

C.C. is 4 Reichsmarks for a skilled worker, 3 Reichsmarks for an unskilled worker, and 2 Reichsmarks for female prisoners for both skilled and unskilled work.

Nos. 135765–135772 are given to eight male prisoners and Nos. 53906–53922 to 17 female prisoners sent in a group transport.

Approximately 3,000 Jewish men, women, and children from the ghetto in Sosnowitz arrive in an RSHA transport. Following the selection, 211 men, given Nos. 135773–135983, and 275 women, given Nos. 53923–54197, are admitted to the camp. The others, more than 2,500 people, are killed in the gas chambers.

The 29 male prisoners sent in a group transport get Nos. 136034–136062, and the 31 female prisoners are given Nos. 54198–54228.

Five prisoners sent from Kattowitz get Nos. 136063–136067.

130 prisoners from Posen sent by the Gestapo receive Nos. 136068–136197.

The Protective Custody Commander, SS Captain Aumeier, announces to the SS members of the garrison the Commandant's order that all work will cease on Saturday, August 7, starting at 1:00 P.M., including Sunday, August 8, as recognition for the work accomplished by all SS men in recent days for the special operation.* — APMO, Dpr.-Hd/12, p. 177, Garrison Order 31/43.

250 patients suffering from tuberculosis are sent from factories connected with the Fürstenberg mill in Stettin. They are killed the same day in the gas chambers. — CA KC PZPR, 202/III-146, Documents of the Delegation of the Polish Government in Exile, p. 154.

Four prisoners sent in a group transport receive Nos. Z-8339–Z-8342.

The corpses of five prisoners are delivered to the morgue of the main camp. — APMO, D-AuI-5/2, Morgue Register, p. 174.

AUGUST 7

The chief of police in Sosnowitz reports to the police inspector in Breslau the deportation of approximately 30,000 Jews from the ghettos in Sosnowitz, Bendin, and Dąbrowa Górnicza and the shooting of almost 400 people who tried to flee or resist. — Biuletyn Żydowskiego Instytutu Historycznego (Bulletin of Jewish Historical Institute [Warsaw]), no. 43-44 (1962): 115ff. (document), (hereafter cited as BZIH).

The chief of police in Sosnowitz requests from the governor of the Kattowitz District the cost-free provisions due for 206 policemen from Sosnowitz and Maczek for the period August 8–12, as the Jewish operation begun in Sosnowitz County is not yet finished. — Szternfinkiel, Jews of Sosnowitz, p. 75.

---

*The recognition expressed in the order and the decision to have a rest break for the SS Men has to do with their active participation in the liquidation of the ghettos in Bendin and Sosnowitz.

A female prisoner sent from Graz receives No. 52352.

50 prisoners transferred from Ravensbrück receive Nos. 135984–136033.

Nos. 136198–136213 are given to 16 male prisoners and Nos. 54229–54295 to 67 female prisoners sent in a group transport.

Two German Gypsies, Robert Böhmer (No. Z-3301), born in Hamburg on February 17, 1918, and Rudolf Adler (No. Z-5639), born in Berlin on April 22, 1918, are captured while escaping and locked in the bunker of Block 11. They are shot on August 20, 1943, following a selection carried out in the bunkers.

APMO, D-AuI-3/2, Bunker Register, p. 30.

The corpses of 10 prisoners are delivered to the morgue of the main camp.

APMO, D-AuI-5/2, Morgue Register, p. 175.

By order of the Political Department, reeducation prisoner Antoni Woicik (No. EH-5068) is locked in the bunker of Block 11. Following a selection carried out in the bunkers, he is shot on August 20, 1943.

APMO, D-AuI-3/2, Bunker Register, p. 30.

AUGUST 8

A prisoner sent from Kattowitz gets No. 136302.

14 prisoners are assigned to the Penal Company in Birkenau for two to six months.

APMO, D-AuI-3/1, p. 4, Penal Company Register.

The corpses of eight prisoners are delivered to the morgue of the main camp.

APMO, D-AuI-5/2, Morgue Register, p. 175.

AUGUST 9

Five boys born in the Gypsy camp in Birkenau receive Nos. Z-8343–Z-8347.

APMO, D-AuII-3/1/2, p. 247, Register of Male Gypsies.

Nos. 136214–136286 are given to 73 male prisoners and Nos. 54296–54302 to seven female prisoners sent from Kattowitz.

Of the 11 prisoners assigned to the Penal Company, two are to remain there two months, nine until recalled, and one prisoner for life. This is Denny Blumenthal (No. 107555); he loses his life on August 20, 1943, in other words, after 11 days in the Penal Company.

APMO, D-AuI-3/1, p. 4, Penal Company Register.

15 prisoners sent in a group transport receive Nos. 136287–136301.

Nos. Z-8348–Z-8352 are given to five male Gypsies and Nos. Z-8980–Z-8984 to five female Gypsies sent in a group transport.

Two girls born in the Gypsy camp in Birkenau receive Nos. Z-8985 and Z-8986.

APMO, D-AuII-3/2/4, p. 579, Register of Female Gypsies.

25 female prisoners sent from the administrative district of Kattowitz are given Nos. 54303–54327.

Two female prisoners sent from the prison in Zichenau get Nos. 54328–54329.

A group of prisoners who are doctors, dentists, and pharmacists is shifted from Men's Camp B-IId in Birkenau to the main camp, where they are employed in the prisoners' infirmary.

APMO, Dpr.-Hd/1, p. 169.

The corpses of six prisoners, including one from the Buna A.C. and one from the Babice A.C., are delivered to the morgue of the main camp.

APMO, D-AuI-5/2, Morgue Register, p. 175.

AUGUST 10

Two female prisoners sent from Kattowitz receive Nos. 54330 and 54331.

In connection with the liquidation of the Bendin ghetto, the management of Auschwitz takes over 753 sewing machines.

APMO, D-AuI-4/29, Inventory No. 155936, p. 8, Warehouse Log.

Approximately 3,000 Jewish men, women, and children from the ghetto in Sosnowitz arrive with an RSHA transport. Following the selection, 110 men, given Nos. 136303–136412, and 195 women, given Nos. 54332–54526, are admitted to the camp. The other almost 2,700 people are killed in the gas chambers.

Four prisoners sent from the Kattowitz District are given Nos. 136413–136416.

Five prisoners sent from Kattowitz are given Nos. 136417–136421.

22 prisoners are assigned to the Penal Company in Birkenau, 20 until recalled and two for 12 months.

APMO, D-AuI-3/1, p. 5, Penal Company Register.

The German Gypsy Karl Steinbach (No. Z-5278), born in Essen on January 8, 1921, is captured while escaping and locked in the bunker of Block 11. Following a selection carried out in the bunkers, he is shot on August 20, 1943.

APMO, D-AuI-3/2, Bunker Register, p. 31.

The Russian prisoner Nikolai Zapavalov (No. 125098), born on April 30, 1918, escapes in the evening.

APMO, D-AuI-1/1, p. 229, Telegrams; IZ-10/Kripo Sieradz/2/ 132; Mat.RO, vol. IV, p. 293.

Seven corpses are delivered to the morgue of the main camp.

APMO, D-AuI-5/2, Morgue Register, p. 176.

AUGUST 11

The police chief in Sosnowitz reports to the governor of the Kattowitz Administrative District that the Jewish operation begun on April 1, 1943, is not yet finished. Some 256 policemen from Sos-

Szternfinkiel, *Jews of Sosnowitz*, p. 76; Schnabel, *Power Without Morality*, p. 455, Doc. 157.

nowitz and Maczek are still participating in it. For this reason, he requests an extension of the cost-free provisioning of 252 men for the period from August 13 to August 16, 1943.*

55 prisoners sent from Kattowitz receive Nos. 136422–136476.

24 male prisoners sent by the Kraków Sipo and SD receive Nos. 136477–136500 and 11 female prisoners receive Nos. 54527–54537.

No. 136501 is given to a male prisoner and No. 54538 to a female prisoner sent from Lemberg.

Seven female prisoners sent from Kattowitz get Nos. 54539–54545.

By order of the Camp Commander, the Russian political prisoner Ivan Presnov (No. 86399) is locked in the bunker of Block 11. Following a selection, he is shot on August 20, 1943.

APMO, D-AuI-3/2, Bunker Register, p. 31.

The Russian prisoner Gavril Horbov (No. 115609), born on April 4, 1920, is captured while escaping and locked in the bunker of Block 11. He is shot on September 21, 1943, after a selection in the bunkers.

Ibid.

By order of the Political Department, the Polish political prisoner Henryk Żukowski (No. 6478), born in Białystok on June 1, 1922, and the political prisoner Wladimir Rudzin (No. 125018), born in Minsk on October 2, 1922, are locked in the bunker of Block 11. Żukowski is shot on August 10, and Rudzin on September 4, 1943.

Ibid.

The corpses of 13 prisoners are delivered to the morgue of the main camp; among them are two from the Neu-Dachs A.C., Nos. 122184 and 125232.

APMO, D-AuI-5/2, Morgue Register, p. 176.

AUGUST 12

Nos. 136502–136509 are given to eight male prisoners and Nos. 54546–54552 to seven female prisoners sent from Kattowitz.

Approximately 1,000 Jewish men, women, and children from the ghetto in Sosnowitz arrive in an RSHA transport. Following the selection, 46 men, given Nos. 136510–136555, are admitted to the camp. The other almost 1,000 people are killed in the gas chambers.

The Polish prisoner Henryk Starziak (No. 100422), born on April 27, 1922, is locked in the bunker of Block 11 on suspicion of preparing to escape. He is shot on August 20, 1943, following a selection in the bunkers.

APMO, D-AuI-3/2, Bunker Register, p. 31.

*The approval is given the same day (Szternfinkiel, *Jews of Sosnowitz*, p. 77).

By order of the Camp Commander, the Russian political prisoner Piotr Kozniev (No. 71539), born on March 4, 1925, is locked in the bunker of Block 11. He is shot on August 20, 1943, following a selection carried out in the bunkers.

Ibid.

612 prisoners, including 52 skilled and 560 unskilled workers, are employed in the Eintrachthütte plants in Schwientochlowitz.

APMO, D-AuI-3a/370/5, p. 304a, Monthly Labor Deployment List.

The corpses of seven prisoners are delivered to the morgue of the main camp, among them No. 55525, from the Jawischowitz A.C., Nos. 125042 and 127047, from the Buna A.C.

APMO, D-AuI-5/2, Morgue Register, p. 176.

AUGUST 13

The reeducation prisoner Jaroslaw Mamczur (No. EH-5165), born on February 2, 1917, who was sent from Kattowitz by the Gestapo on July 9, 1943, escapes from the camp.

APMO, D-AuI-1/1, p. 223, Telegrams; IZ-8/Gestapo Lodz/3a/88/479; Mat.RO, vol. IV, p. 293.

Three female prisoners sent in a group transport receive Nos. 54553–54555.

38 Poles, from the prison in Myslowitz, arrested in connection with so-called Operation Oderberg* are given Nos. 136556–136593, and 186 female Poles are given Nos. 54556–54741.**

The Director of Labor Deployment, SS Second Lieutenant Sell,† notifies the camp management that the following auxiliary camps can be turned over to their control within the next weeks:

APMO, Fürstengrube GmbH, Inventory No. 72829, pp. 46–48.

*The goal of this operation is to exterminate entire Polish families in Silesia who are known for their patriotic attitude. The operation is carried out by order of the Kattowitz Gestapo during the night of August 11–12, 1943, in the following villages: Sosnowitz, Czeladź, Piaski near Bendin, Klimotów, Kłobuch, Jęzor near Krenau, Dobra near Krenau, Krenau, Siersza, Myślachowice, Jaworzno, Ilkenau, and Karwina in Czechoslovakia. In the process approximately 750 persons are arrested and put in prison in Myslowitz. No legal investigations are carried out against them. Children under age 15 are separated from their mothers. The women and men are assigned to Auschwitz, Ravensbrück, and Mauthausen. Starting in August 1943, the children arrested during the Oderberg operation are transferred to the following camps: Lyski near Rybnik, Kietrz, Gorzyce, Oderberg, and Żory near Rybnik. Their journey through a collection of camps in Silesia lasts a whole year. One group of the children was moved to the so-called U.W.Z. (Umwandererzentralstelle, or "Central Resettlement Office") Camp Potulitz-Lebrechtsdorf in August 1944. On August 4, 61 children between one and 15 years of age are moved from the camp in Kattowitz to the Potulitz camp; on August 11, 78 children between two and 15 years of age arrive in Potuliz from the camp in Zory near Rybnik. Compare Roman Hrabar, "Germanizacja dzicci polskich w swietle dokumentow" (The Germanization of Polish Children in the Light of Documents), *Bulletin GKBZHwP*, vol. 5 (1949); Roman Hrabar, "Osadzenie małotenich z tzw. Prowincji Górnośląsjkiej w obozach, Dokumenty wybrane" (The Placement in Concentration Camps of Minor Children from the so-called Upper Silesian Province), *Bulletin GKBZHwP*, vol. 19 (1968).
**The number 54573 is given to Maria Odrzywolek; she survives. Her children, Czesław, born in 1930, and Lucjan, born in 1933, are found again in Potulitz. Helena Rudek receives No. 54609. She dies in Auschwitz on January 2, 1944. Her children, Fryderyk, born 1929, Emilia, born 1930, Jadwiga, born 1932, and Franciszek, born 1937, are found again in Potulitz. The cases mentioned may serve as examples (APMO, IZ–U.W.Z. Camp Potulitz, vol. II, pp. 141–150; Prisoner Card Index and Correspondence).
†Captain Schwarz, the Director of Labor Deployment, was promoted. See entry for August 18, 1943.

Janinagrube: for 300 prisoners, later 900
Fürstengrube: for 500–600 prisoners, later 1,300
Sosnowitz: for 100 prisoners
Lagischa: for 100 prisoners, later 1,000

The takeover could take place in approximately 14 days. For this reason, the plans for supplying provisions would have to be assured.

29 prisoners sent in a group transport receive Nos. 136594–136622.

79 prisoners from Posen who were sent by the Gestapo receive Nos. 136623–136701.

16 prisoners sent from Lodz by the Gestapo get Nos. 136702–136711 and 136713–136718.

No. 136712 is given to a prisoner sent from the Kattowitz District.

Nos. 136719–136722 are given to four prisoners sent in a group transport.

Nos. Z-8353–Z-8357 are given to five male Gypsies and Nos. Z-8987 and Z-8988 to two female Gypsies sent in a group transport.

By order of the Camp Commander, the Polish Jew Benjamin Berek (No. 92575), born in Grodno on December 6, 1909, is locked in the bunker of Block 11. He is shot on August 20, 1943, following a selection in the bunkers. | APMO, D-AuI-3/2, Bunker Register, p. 32.

By order of the Political Department, the Polish Jew Heim Pilozof (No. 42408) and the Greek Jew Moses Benjamin (No. 120765) are locked in the bunker of Block 11. They are shot on August 20, 1943, following a selection in the bunkers. | Ibid.

The corpses of three prisoners, Nos. 75045, 113909, and 122906, are delivered to the morgue of the main camp. | APMO, D-AuI-5/2, Morgue Register, p. 177.

AUGUST 14

Nos. 136723–136835 are given to 113 prisoners from Lodz sent to the camp by the Gestapo.

Nos. 136836–136876 are given to 41 male prisoners and Nos. 54742–54846 to 105 female prisoners arrested in the Oderberg operation in the Kattowitz District and have been transferred from the prison in Myslowitz to Auschwitz.

A prisoner sent from Kattowitz gets No. 136877.

The general delousing operation in Men's Camp B-IId in Birkenau begins on Saturday at 1:00 P.M. | APMO, Dpr.-Hd/6, pp. 75–77.

The corpses of 12 prisoners are delivered to the morgue of the main camp; among them are one from the Buna A.C. and two from the Jawischowitz A.C.

APMO, D-AuI-5/2, Morgue Register, p. 177.

AUGUST 15

Three Polish prisoners, Feliks Sroka (No. 123872), Henryk Piontek (No. 117912), and Zygmunt Hoffman (No. 124035), escape from the camp.

APMO, D-AuI-1/1, pp. 228, 231, Telegrams; IZ-10/Kripo Sieradz/2/88/133; IZ-8/Gestapo Lodz/3a/88/481; Mat.RO, vol. IV, p. 293.

The corpses of five prisoners are delivered to the morgue of the main camp.

APMO, D-AuI-5/2, Morgue Register, p. 177.

The delousing operation in Men's Camp B-IId in Birkenau ends in the evening.

APMO, Dpr.-Hd/6, pp. 75–77.

AUGUST 16

Nos. 136878–136911 are given to 34 male prisoners and Nos. 54847–54851 to five female prisoners sent from the prison in Myslowitz. They were arrested in the Oderberg operation in the Kattowitz District.

Nos. 136912–136916 are given to five male prisoners and Nos. 54852–54872 to 21 female prisoners sent in a group transport.

The commanding officer of the SS Guard Stormtroopers, SS Major Hartjenstein, rewards SS man Edmund Waitop with three days' special leave for the capture of a prisoner who left his labor squad in the Buna plants on August 14 and hid in a canal.*

APMO, Dpr.-ZOd/40, Storm-trooper Order 126/43.

The corpses of six prisoners are delivered to the morgue of the main camp; among them are two from the Buna A.C. and two from the Neu-Dachs A.C.

APMO, D-AuI-5/2, Morgue Register, p. 178.

AUGUST 17

51 prisoners, including 39 prisoners from Radom who were sent to the camp by the Sipo and SD on July 29, 1943, are condemned to the Penal Company on August 23, 1943. Their Nos. are: 131572, 131577, 131578, 131580–131582, 131586–131588, 131592–131594, 131596–131599, 131744, 131780, 131835, 131843, 131869, 131950, 131966, 131968, 131985–131997, 131999, and 132000. Mikołaj Grzejszczak (No. 131580) dies on September 28, 1943; Stanisław Barański (No. 131987) dies on October 2, 1943; 33 prisoners are transferred to Mauthausen on November 5, 1943, and one to Buchenwald. One prisoner is released into the camp on November 18, 1943, and two others on February 2, 1944.

APMO, D-AuI-3/1, pp. 5–6, Penal Company Register.

*Probably the captured prisoner was killed, for he is not locked in the bunker of Block 11; however, in the Morgue Register under August 14 is the entry "No. 128072 Buna."

Nos. 136917 and 136918 are given to two male prisoners and Nos. 54873–54875 to three female prisoners sent from Kattowitz.

Five girls born in the Gypsy camp get Nos. Z-8989–Z-8993.

APMO, D-AuII-3/2/4, pp. 579, 581, Register of Female Gypsies.

Five boys born in the Gypsy camp get Nos. Z-8358–Z-8362.

APMO, D-AuII-3/1/2, p. 247, Register of Male Gypsies.

The Polish political prisoner Stanisław Pióro (No. 125606), born on August 5, 1918, is locked in the bunker of Block 11 on suspicion of preparing an escape. He is shot on August 20, 1943, following a selection carried out in the bunkers.

APMO, D-AuI-3/2, Bunker Register, p. 32.

The corpses of five prisoners are delivered to the morgue of the main camp.

APMO, D-AuI-5/2, Morgue Register, p. 178.

Around 10:00 A.M. three Polish political prisoners, Edward Ki-czmachowski (No. 3414), Edward Salwa (No. 5256), and Józef Szajna (No. 18729), attempt an escape from Birkenau. They seek refuge in a prepared hiding place near the SS canteen in the area of the boilerhouse. During the night they leave their hiding place to flee from the camp, but they are discovered and stopped by SS men working at the platform on a transport that has arrived. While they are being led back to the camp, Edward Kiczmachowski tries to get away by exploiting the darkness and his familiarity with the area. He does not succeed. Shot several times, he is severely wounded, captured again, and brought to Camp B-IId. All three escapees are put on show at the camp gate on August 18 during the morning hours when the prisoners are marching off to work. The severely wounded Edward Kiczachowski is put in the sick bay of Camp B-IIf and interrogated there. Barely able to move, he is locked in the bunker of Block 11 on September 14.

APMO, Depositions, vol. 3, pp. 65–68, Account of Former Prisoner Edward Kiczmachowski.

AUGUST 18

The two prisoners captured the previous day during an escape attempt, Edward Salwa, born on September 15, 1923, and Józef Szajna, born on March 13, 1922, are locked in the bunker of Block 11. They are released from the bunker into the camp on October 11.

APMO, D-AuI-3/2, Bunker Register, p. 32.

Commandant Höss makes known to the SS members of the garrison that SS Captain Schwarz has taken over the position of First Protective Custody Commander for the Auschwitz main camp and its auxiliary camps from SS Captain Aumeier, who has been transferred to Riga as Commandant. Starting August 18, 1943, SS Captain Schwarz takes over as First Protective Custody Commander in Auschwitz.

APMO, Dpr.-ZOd/39, Special Garrison Order, August 18, 1943.

The management of the Janinagrube in Libiąż sends a telegram to the Prisoner of War Camp VIII-B in Lamsdorf (Lambinowice) with the request to bring about the immediate removal of the English

APMO, Maurer Trial, vol. 7, pp. 88ff.

POWs from Camp No. 562 in Libiąż, because the prisoners from Auschwitz are supposed to be housed there.

In the Brzeszcze-Jawiloschowitz coal mine 1,326 prisoners from Auschwitz, including 99 skilled workers, are employed.

APMO, D-AuI-3a/370/5, p. 305a, Monthly Labor Deployment List.

Approximately 1,800 Jewish men, women, and children from the ghetto in Salonika arrive in an RSHA transport. Following the selection, 271 men are admitted to the camp as prisoners and get Nos. 136919–137189. The others, more than 1,500 people, are killed in the gas chambers.

33 prisoners from Kattowitz are given Nos. 137190–137222.

532 prisoners are transferred from Auschwitz to Sachsenhausen.

APMO, Mat.RO, vol. VII, p. 474.

By order of the Political Department, the reeducation prisoner Leon Melnik (No. EH-5594) is locked in the bunker of Block 11. He is shot on August 20, 1943, following a selection in the bunkers.

APMO, D-AuI-3/2, Bunker Register, p. 33.

The corpses of 12 prisoners, including two from the Buna A.C., are delivered to the morgue of the main camp.

APMO, D-AuI-5/2, Morgue Register, p. 178.

AUGUST 19

Three Polish Jews, Dawid Lieberman, born in Rekjowiec on May 21, 1923; Szmul Cymerman, born in Rekjowiec on March 12, 1921, and Srul Soroka, born in Rejkowiec on July 7, 1923,*escape from the camp.

APMO, D-AuI-1/1, p. 235, Telegrams; IZ-8/Gestapo Lodz/3a/88/483.

1,094 Czech prisoners are transferred from Auschwitz to Buchenwald.

APMO, Mat.RO, vol. VII, p. 474.

Nos. 137223–137230 are given to eight prisoners delivered from Kattowitz.

Nos. 137231–137253 are given to 23 male prisoners and Nos. 54876–54879 to four female prisoners sent from Kraków by the Sipo and SD.

Nos. 137254–137256 are given to three male prisoners and Nos. 54880–54883 to four female prisoners sent from the Kattowitz District.

A prisoner sent from Kattowitz on August 17 is given No. 137257.

The corpses of 10 prisoners are delivered to the morgue of the main camp. Among them are five from the Neu-Dachs A.C., Nos. 110037, 130618, 122177, 120943, and 116700. Probably they are prisoners employed in the Friedrich-August Pit in Neu-Dachs who

APMO, D-AuI-5/2, Morgue Register, p. 179; Depositions, vol. 5, pp. 609–617, Account of Former Prisoner Wiktor Pasikowski.

*The escaped prisoners had been transferred on June 26, 1943, from the Majdanek to Auschwitz.

tried to escape on Mostowa Street on the way back from work and were shot by the SS guards. The corpses of the killed prisoners are lined up next to the entrance gate to deter the other prisoners from escape attempts. Afterward they are taken to the morgue of the main camp.

By order of the Political Department, the Jewish prisoner Adolf Kessler (No. 68512), born in Frankfurt am Main on May 20, 1922, is locked in the bunker of Block 11. He is shot on August 20, 1943, following a selection in the bunkers.

APMO, D-AuI-3/2, Bunker Register, p. 33.

By order of the Roll Call Leader, the two Norwegian Jews Herman Feldman (No. 105273), born in Trondheim on March 1, 1918, and Willi Scherman (No. 105392), born in Oslo on November 14, 1918, are locked in the bunker of Block 11. They are shot the next day, August 20, 1943, following a selection in the bunkers.

Ibid.

AUGUST 20

1,405 prisoners of Auschwitz, including 524 skilled workers, are employed in the armaments plants of DAW—Auschwitz.

APMO, D-AuI-3a/370/5, p. 307, Monthly Labor Deployment List.

Nos. 137258–137338 are given to 81 male prisoners and Nos. 54884–54923 to 40 female prisoners sent in a group transport.

A selection is carried out in the bunkers of Block 11. 38 prisoners are selected who were locked in the bunkers by order of the Political Department, the Camp Commander, or the Roll Call Leader or were captured while escaping or are suspected of preparing an escape. That same day they are shot against the execution wall in the courtyard of Block 11.*

APMO, D-AuI-3/2, Bunker Register, pp. 15, 28–33; Memoirs, vol. 5, pp. 1–29, Memoirs of Former Prisoner Jan Winogroński.

The corpses of prisoners Nos. 106506 and 124833 are delivered to the morgue of the main camp.

APMO, D-AuI-5/2, Morgue Register, p. 179.

Jakob Weiss (No. Z-5349), a Gypsy born on March 3, 1924, is captured while escaping and locked in the bunker of Block 11. Following a selection carried out in the bunkers, he is shot on September 4, 1943.

APMO, D-AuI-3/2, Bunker Register, p. 33.

AUGUST 21

SS Private First Class Adolf Michalek, SS Private Georg Ukrainetz, and SS Private Johann Jotzkus of the 4th Guard Company are

APMO, D-AuI-1, Garrison Order 33/43.

---

*Among those shot is Kazimierz Jarzębowski (No. 115), who escaped from the camp on May 20, 1943, was arrested again on July 31, 1943, and locked in the bunker of Block 11. As a surveyor employed in the surveying squad he was one of the first prisoners to make illegal contact with the Polish people living in the Auschwitz C.C. interest zone. He was a known and esteemed underground fighter who was aware of the danger threatening him (CA KC PZPR, 202/III-205, Documents of the Delegation of the Polish Government in Exile, p. 16).

commended by the Deputy Commandant, SS Captain Schwarz, for their superior response in the capture of the escaping prisoner.

Nos. 137339–137352 are given to 14 male prisoners and Nos. 54924–54998 to 72 female prisoners sent in a group transport.

No. Z-8363 is given to a male Gypsy, and Nos. Z-8994 and Z-8995 to two female Gypsies sent in a group transport.

The camp management carries out a selection in the women's camp of Auschwitz-Birkenau. 498 female Jewish prisoners are selected who, in the opinion of the camp management and the SS Camp Doctor, cannot be used for work. They are condemned to death in the gas chambers. They are brought to Block 25, considered the waiting block for the gas chambers and also called the death block. Among those selected are 438 Greek women. The list of selected women is marked with "G.U.," which stands for "gesonderte Unterbringung," or "separate accommodation," a euphemism for the death sentence. The list is signed by Camp Commander, Head Supervisor Maria Mandel.*

APMO, Mat.RO, vol. I, p. 41; vol. IV, pp. 262–266.

Approximately 500 Jews arrive with a shipment from the Reich Autobahn Camp in Pomerania. Following the selection, 66 men are admitted to the camp and receive Nos. 137353–137418. The other more than 400 people are killed in the gas chambers.

Four boys born in the Gypsy camp receive Nos. Z-8364–Z-8367.

APMO, D-AuII-3/1/2, p. 247, Register of Male Gypsies.

A girl born in the Gypsy camp receives No. Z-8996.

APMO, D-AuII-3/2/4, p. 581, Register of Female Gypsies.

The corpses of 15 prisoners are delivered to the morgue of the camp, among them are three from the Buna A.C., Nos. EH-5140, EH-6555, and EH-5694,** and one from the Neu-Dachs A.C.

APMO, D-AuI-5/2, Morgue Register, p. 179.

By order of the Camp Commander the Jewish prisoner Oskar Fudem (No. 32218), born on January 8, 1918, is locked in the bunker of Block 11. Following a selection in the bunkers, he is shot on September 4, 1943.

APMO, D-AuI-3/2, Bunker Register, p. 33.

By order of the Political Department, two Russian political prisoners, Tichon Tserutsin (No. 125091) and Piotr Ivanov (No. 125801), are locked in the bunker of Block 11. They are shot on September 21, 1943, following a selection in the bunkers.

Ibid.

AUGUST 22

A prisoner sent from Kattowitz receives No. 137419.

---

*A carbon copy of the original list with the names of the 498 Jewish women selected and the signature of the Head Supervisor Mandel is stolen and smuggled out of the camp by a member of the resistance movement in the camp, Stanisław Kłodziński, and is brought to Teresa Lasocka in Kraków; from there the information was to be conveyed to London.
**Probably these prisoners were shot during an alleged escape attempt or died from an accident while working. Their corpses are delivered to the morgue of the main camp in order to make a proper protocol, for the crematorium in the main camp has not been in operation since July 19, 1943.

Nos. Z-8368–Z-8701 are given to 334 Gypsies, men and boys, and 434 female gypsies, women and girls, are given Nos. Z-8997–Z-9430. They were sent from Czechoslovakia.

APMO, D-AuII-3/1/2, pp. 247–257, Register of Male Gypsies; D-AuII-3/2/4, pp. 581–609, Register of Female Gypsies.

The corpses of four prisoners are delivered to the morgue of the main camp.

APMO, D-AuI-5/2, Morgue Register, p. 180.

AUGUST 23

Nos. 137420–138185 are given to 766 male prisoners and Nos. 54999–55116 to 118 female prisoners sent from the prison in Radom by the Sipo and SD.

Nos. 138186–138206 are given to 21 prisoners sent in a group transport.

Nos. 138207–138222 are given to 16 male prisoners and Nos. 55117–55120 to four female prisoners sent from Kattowitz.

Approximately 2,000 Jews arrive in an RSHA transport from the labor camp in Koło. Following the selection, 441 men, given Nos. 138223–138663, and 591 women, given Nos. 55121–55711, are admitted to the camp. The others, almost 1,000 people, are killed in the gas chambers.

14 female prisoners sent in a group transport receive Nos. 55712–55725.

The Commandant's Office informs the offices under its authority that SS men and German civilian employees will receive mosquito repellent free of charge.

APMO, D-AuI-1/52, Commandant's Office Special Order, Aug. 23, 1943.

The Deputy Commandant, SS Captain Schwarz, announces to the SS members of the garrison that the town of Auschwitz is still off limits to SS men. The command No. 17/42 of July 10, 1942, is still in effect, and is related to the spread of the typhus epidemic.

APMO, D-AuI-1, Garrison Order 34/43.

The corpses of five prisoners are delivered to the morgue of the main camp.

APMO, D-AuI-5/2, Morgue Register, p. 180.

AUGUST 24

33 prisoners from Kraków, sent to the camp by the Sipo and SD, receive Nos. 138664–138696.

Nos. 138697–138752 are given to 56 male prisoners and Nos. 55726–55757 to 32 female prisoners sent from Kattowitz.

100 ill Jews from the Markstädt labor camp near Breslau arrive in an RSHA transport. They are killed the same day in the gas chambers.

CA KC PZPR, 202/III-146, Documents of the Delegation of the Polish Government in Exile, p. 154.

By order of the Political Department, four prisoners are locked in the bunker of Block 11 and shot the same day. They are the Polish political prisoner Tadeusz Karcz (No. 120580), born in Kraków on June 8, 1904; the Polish Jew Chaim Binenstok (No. 130837), born in Sosnowitz on January 24, 1905; the Polish Jew Jakob Silbinger (No. 136468), born in Auschwitz on December 14, 1922; and the Polish Jew Wiktor Lajber (No. 136465), born in Żarki on December 10, 1916.

APMO, D-AuI-3/2, Bunker Register, p. 34.

By order of the Political Department, the following prisoners are locked in the bunker of Block 11: Jan Bartulec (No. EH-5687), Józef Bulusek (No. 117117), Gottlieb Stasny (No. 117159), Max Gompertz (No. 117544), a Dutch Jew, and Ivan Tsorefka (No. 137222), a Russian. Following a selection in the bunkers, they are shot on September 4, 1943.

Ibid.

By order of the Camp Commander, the Polish political prisoner Marian Matuga (No. 95913), born in Tarnów on October 11, 1906, is locked in the bunker of Block 11. He is shot on September 21, 1943, following a selection in the bunkers.

Ibid.

On suspicion of planning an escape, the German BV prisoner Helmuth Herfort (No. 31941), born in Oppeln on November 12, 1921, is locked in the bunker of Block 11. He is shot on September 4, 1943, following a selection in the bunkers.

Ibid.

The corpses of seven prisoners are delivered to the morgue of the main camp.

APMO, D-AuI-5/2, Morgue Register, p. 180.

AUGUST 25

Nine prisoners sent from Kattowitz receive Nos. 138753–138761.

50 Jewish men and women assigned by the Gestapo arrive with the forty-first RSHA East-transport from Berlin. Following the selection, nine men, given Nos. 138762–138770, and 18 women, given Nos. 55758–55775, are admitted to the camp. The other 23 deportees are killed in the gas chambers.

APMO, D-RF-3/121/15, Gestapo Berlin, Auschwitz Transports, pp. 32ff.

Two female prisoners sent from Kattowitz receive Nos. 55776–55777.

Nos. 138771–139645 are given to 875 male prisoners* and Nos. 55778–55918 to 141 female prisoners** from Pawiak Prison who have been sent to the camp by the Gestapo and the Warsaw SD.

60 prisoners sent in a group transport receive Nos. 139646–139705.

*No. 138907 is given to Dr. Alfred Fiderkiewicz, an outstanding figure in the labor movement and author of the camp memoirs published under the title *Brzezinka* (Birkenau), in Warsaw in 1954.
**No. 55908 is given to Krystyna Żywulska, author of the book *Przeżyłam Oświęcim* (I Survived Auschwitz), Warsaw, 1960.

Seven female prisoners sent from Lodz receive Nos. 55919–55925.

The Deputy Commandant, SS Captain Schwarz, announces to the SS members of the garrison that by order of the WVHA, SS Second Lieutenant Franz Hössler will take over the function of Camp Commander in the women's camp.*

APMO, Dpr.-ZOd/40, Special Garrison Order, Aug. 25, 1943.

500 Polish prisoners are transferred from Auschwitz to Neuengamme.

APMO, Mat.RO, vol. VII, pp. 453, 474.

By order of the Deputy Commandant, the Polish asocial prisoner Mieczysław Mierkiewicz (No. 126297), born on October 14, 1904, is locked in the bunker of Block 11. He is shot on September 4, 1943, following a selection out in the bunkers.

APMO, D-AuI-3/2, Bunker Register, p. 34.

The bodies of five prisoners, including one from the Buna A.C., No. 96625, are delivered to the morgue of the main camp.

APMO, D-AuI-5/2, Morgue Register, p. 181.

AUGUST 26

Two prisoners sent from the Kattowitz District are given Nos. 139706 and 139707.

439 prisoners, including 19 skilled workers, from the Golleschau A.C. are working in the cement factory in Golleschau.

APMO, D-AuI-3a/370/5, p. 316a, Monthly Labor Deployment List.

1,001 Jews from Westerbork arrive in an RSHA transport from Holland. In the shipment are 121 children, 233 men and 263 women up to 50 years of age, and 384 older people. After the selection, 188 men, given Nos. 139708–139885 and 141817–141826, and 48 women, given Nos. 55926–55973, are admitted to the camp. 44 additional women, given Nos. 55974–56017, are assigned to the experimental station of Professor Dr. Clauberg in Block 10 of the main camp. The other 721 deportees are killed in the gas chambers.

A prisoner sent from Kattowitz is given No. 56018.

Maurer, the Head of Office D-II of the WVHA, informs Commandant Höss that he had notified Captain Schwarz the previous day that he soon expects a transfer of Jewish prisoners from Auschwitz to other concentration camps. What is needed is completely able-bodied Jews from West European countries, so-called Western Jews. Maurer notes that he expects an answer.

APMO, D-AuI-3a/356, Labor Deployment; Maurer Trial, vol. 13, p. 171.

Approximately 1,500 Jewish men, women, and children from the ghetto in Zawierć have arrived in an RSHA transport. Following the selection, 437 men, given Nos. 139897–140333, and 501 women, given Nos. 56019–56519, are admitted to the camp. The other more than 500 people are killed in the gas chambers.

*This position previously was unofficially filled by Head Supervisor Maria Mandel (APMO, Dpr.-ZOd/56, pp. 104–114).

By order of the Political Department, two prisoners, Teodor Neczporuk (No. EH-5656) and Józef Krek (No. 119712), are locked in the bunker of Block 11. They are shot on September 4, 1943, following a selection in the bunkers.

APMO, D-AuI-3/2, Bunker Register, p. 35.

On suspicion of planning an escape, the Jewish prisoner Isaak Kac (No. 120579) is locked in the bunker of Block 11. He is shot on September 4, 1943, following a selection in the bunkers.

Ibid.

The corpses of four prisoners are delivered to the morgue of the main camp.

APMO, D-AuI-5/2, Morgue Register, p. 181.

AUGUST 27

Approximately 1,500 Jewish men, women, and children from the ghetto in Zawierć arrive in an RSHA transport. Following the selection, 387 men, given Nos. 140334–140720, and 418 women, given Nos. 56520–56937, are admitted to the camp. The other almost 700 people are killed in the gas chambers.

205 Jews from the labor camp near the Märkische Stahlform-Werke* in Eberswalde arrive in an RSHA transport. They are killed the same day in the gas chambers.

CA KC PZPR, 202/III-146, Documents of the Delegation of the Polish Government in Exile, p. 154.

1,026 Jews from the labor camp in Wolsztyn in the province of Posen arrive in an RSHA transport. Following the selection, 1,016 men, given Nos. 140721–141736, are admitted to the camp. The other 10 men are killed in the gas chambers.

Ibid.

3,542 female prisoners, including 119 skilled workers, and 2,280 male prisoners, including 433 skilled workers, are employed in agriculture in Auschwitz. On this day a total of 5,822 prisoners are working in the agricultural and animal breeding operations.**

APMO, D-AuI-3a/370/5, pp. 321ff., Monthly Labor Deployment List.

500 Polish prisoners are transferred from Auschwitz to Neuengamme.

CA KC PZPR, 202/III-146, Documents of the Delegation of the Polish Government in Exile, p. 154.

Six prisoners sent the previous day from Prague receive Nos. 141737–141742.

The Russian prisoner Afanasi Myrhorodov, born on December 26, 1916, escapes in the afternoon.

APMO, D-AuI-1/1, p. 243, Telegrams: IZ-10/Kripo Sieradz/2/88/147.

Nos. 141743–141816 are given to 74 male prisoners and Nos. 56938–56965 to 28 female prisoners sent in a group transport.

28 female prisoners sent in a group transport receive Nos. 56966–56993.

*The Mark Steel Works; "Mark" refers to the Mark Brandenburg, the province in Prussia where Eberswalde is located.—Ed.
**In the agricultural operations the employment level is subject to great day-to-day vacillations. This is probably related to changing labor requirements in agricultural and animal husbandry.

The baggage of recently arrived prisoners after the selection on the ramp.

By order of the Political Department, the Polish Jew Josef Weinstock (No. 26155), born in Radom on October 19, 1923, is locked in the bunker of Block 11. He is shot on September 4, 1943, following a selection carried out in the bunkers.

APMO, D-AuI-3/2, Bunker Register, p. 35.

On suspicion of preparing an escape, the Greek Jew Simon Salter (No. 114095) and the Polish Jew Symcha Herszman (No. 128441) are locked in the bunker of Block 11. Following a selection in the bunkers, they are shot on September 4, 1943.

Ibid.

The corpses of four prisoners are delivered to the morgue of the main camp.

APMO, D-AuI-5/2, Morgue Register, p. 181.

SS Second Lieutenant Franz Hössler takes over the function of Protective Custody Commander in the women's camp in Birkenau.

APMO, D-AuI-1/53, Special Garrison Order, Aug. 28, 1943.

AUGUST 28

SS Second Lieutenant Sell announces in a report to Office D-II of the WVHA that of the 3,581 able-bodied Jews admitted to Auschwitz, 446 came from the German Reich, 700 from France, 198 from Slovakia, 162 from Western Czechoslovakia (Bohemia and Moravia), 37 from Croatia, 127 from Holland, 184 from Belgium, five from Norway, and 1,722 from Greece. They are employed in the armaments industry.

APMO, D-AuI-3a/357, Labor Deployment.

69 prisoners are transferred from Auschwitz to Majdanek.

APMO, Mat.RO, vol. VII, p. 474.

Nos. 141827–141855 are given to 29 male prisoners and Nos. 56994–57014 to 21 female prisoners sent in a group transport.

No. 141856 is given to a prisoner sent from Kattowitz on August 23, 1943. His corpse is delivered to the morgue on the same day he is registered.

APMO, D-AuI-5/2, Morgue Register, p. 182, Item 3.

46 prisoners sent in a group transport are given Nos. 141857–141902.

800 Jews from the labor camp in Küstrin (Kostrzyń) arrive in an RSHA transport. Following the selection, 667 men, given Nos. 141903–142569, are admitted to the camp. The other 133 men are killed in the gas chambers.

CA KC PZPR, 202/III-146, Documents of the Delegation of the Polish Government in Exile, p. 154.

Two Russian prisoners of war, Jacob Szevcov (No. RKG-10398) and Nicholai Ulianov (No. RKG-10446), are locked in the bunker of Block 11 by order of the camp management. They are shot on September 4, 1943, following a selection in the bunkers.

APMO, D-AuI-3/2, Bunker Register, p. 35.

By order of the Political Department, the following Russian prisoners are locked in the bunker of Block 11: Alex Konovodchenko (No. 131429), Sergei Hunka (No. 131432), Piotr Lukasiewicz (No. 131440), Alex Neporadny (No. 132091), Dmitri Chudiakov (No. 132224), Pavel Czmyr (No. 134018), Dmitri Stechenko (No. 135294), and Akim Bielikov (No. 135728). They are shot on September 4, 1943, following a selection carried out in the bunkers.

Ibid., pp. 35 ff.

The corpses of four prisoners, including one from the Buna A.C., No. 129108, are delivered to the morgue of the main camp.

APMO, D-AuI-5/2, Morgue Register, p. 182.

By order of the Political Department, the Austrian prisoner Hermann Langbein (No. 60355), one of the leaders of the international conspiratorial task force in Auschwitz formed within the political resistance movement in the camp in May 1943, is locked in the bunker of Block 11. He is released into the camp on November 3, 1943.*

APMO, D-AuI-3/2, Bunker Register, p. 36.

By order of the Political Department, the following prisoners are locked in the bunker of Block 11: the Belgian Jew Karl Kahn (No. 63231), who is shot on September 4, 1943, following a selection carried out in the bunkers, and the German political prisoners Paul Wienhold (No. 60361) and Ludwig Wörl (No. 60363), who are Camp Seniors in the blocks of the prisoners' infirmary in the main

Ibid.

*Langbein performs the function of secretary to the Garrison Doctor SS Major Wirths. Having succeeded in exerting a certain influence on Wirths, he is able to make several suggestions to him that are favorable for the prisoners. He is transferred to Neuengamme on August 25, 1944. Langbein is the author of the following books: *Die Stärkeren* (The Stronger), 2d ed. Cologne, 1982; *Menschen in Auschwitz* (People in Auschwitz), Vienna, 1972; *Auschwitz: zeugnisse und Berichte* (Auschwitz: Testimonies and Accounts), with Hans-Günter Adler and Ella Lingens-Reiner, 3d ed. Cologne, Frankfurt/Main, 1962; *Der Auschwitz-Prozess, Eine Dokumentation* (The Auschwitz Trial: A Documentation), Vienna, 1965.

camp. Both are released from the bunker into the camp on November 23, 1943.

In Order No. 133/34 the Commanding Officer of the Guard Storm-troopers demands reports concerning experiences with the use of dogs in the pursuit of escaped prisoners.

Documents and Materials, p. 97.

AUGUST 29

An SS Camp Doctor carries out a selection in Men's Quarantine Camp B-IIa in Birkenau. He selects 462 Jewish prisoners. They are killed the same day in the gas chambers.

APMO, Dpr.-Hd/6, p. 4.

An SS Camp Doctor carries out a selection in Men's Camp B-IId in Birkenau. He selects approximately 4,000 Jewish prisoners. They are killed the same day in the gas chambers.

Ibid., pp. 51, 222.

Approximately 2,000 Jewish men, women, and children arrive from the labor camp in Rawicz in an RSHA transport. Following the selection, 1,392 men given Nos. 142570–143961, are admitted to the camp. The others, more than 600 people, are killed in the gas chambers.

CA KC PZPR, 202/III-146, Documents of the Delegation of the Polish Government in Exile, p. 154.

Approximately 1,600 Jewish men, women, and children from the ghetto in Koluszki have arrived in an RSHA transport. Following the selection, 210 men, given Nos. 143962–144171, and 17 women, given Nos. 57015–57031, are admitted to the camp as prisoners. The others, almost 1,400 people, are killed in the gas chambers.

AGKBZH, *Camps, Ghettos*, p. 9.

A prisoner delivered from Kattowitz is given No. 144172.

The corpses of two prisoners, Nos. 117664 and 107506, are delivered to the morgue of the main camp.

APMO, D-AuI-5/2, Morgue Register, p. 182.

AUGUST 30

5,541 prisoners of Auschwitz, including 1,337 skilled workers, are employed in the I. G. Farben plants.

APMO, D-AuI-3a/370/5, p. 309a, Monthly Labor Deployment List.

2,019 prisoners of Auschwitz, including 138 skilled workers, are employed in the Neu-Dachs auxiliary camp in Jaworzno.

Ibid., p. 313a.

10 prisoners sent in a group transport get Nos. 144173–144182.

A female prisoner sent from Kattowitz receives No. 57032.

Four male Gypsies sent in a group transport receive Nos. Z-8702–Z-8705, and one female Gypsy receives No. Z-9431.

Four boys born in the Gypsy camp in Birkenau get Nos. Z-8706–Z-8709.

APMO, D-AuII-3/1/2, p. 258, Register of Male Gypsies.

Six girls born in the Gypsy camp get Nos. Z-9432–Z-9437.

APMO, D-AuII-3/2/4, p. 609, Register of Female Gypsies.

By order of the Camp Commandant, the following four prisoners are locked in the bunker of Block 11: the Polish Jews Szmul Duży (No. 79684) and Baruch Hartmann (No. 127271), and the two German criminal prisoners August Pap (No. 62881) and Paul Pianchiny (No. 71281). The Jewish prisoners are shot on September 4, 1943, following a selection in the bunkers. The German criminal prisoners are released from the bunker into the camp on September 7, 1943.

APMO, D-AuI-3/2, Bunker Register, p. 36.

By order of the Political Department, the following six prisoners are locked in the bunker of Block 11: the German PSV prisoner Anton Brückelmeier (No. 113650), who is released from the bunker into the camp on November 1, 1943; the Polish Jews Abram Szafran (No. 126729), Szlama Goldstein (No. 126734), Mordka Pachciaż (No. 126739), Wolf Tempelman (No. 126743), Abraham Pachciaż (No. 128533); and the Russian political prisoner Alexander Lucienko (No. 123111). Following a selection carried out in the bunkers, they are shot on September 4, 1943.

Ibid., pp. 36ff.

The corpses of nine prisoners are delivered to the morgue of the main camp.

APMO, D-AuI-5/2, Morgue Register, p. 182.

AUGUST 31

The Head of Branch D of the WVHA orders a report from the Commandant of Auschwitz as to how many of the 3,581 able-bodied Jews are employed in the armaments industry and in which factories.

APMO, D-AuI-3a/358, Labor Deployment.

500 Jewish prisoners are transferred to the Warsaw concentration camp.

APMO, Mat.RO, vol. VII, p. 474.

Approximately 3,000 Jewish men, women, and children from the ghetto and labor camp in Bochnia, a city east of Kraków, have arrived in an RSHA transport. Following the selection, 280 men, given Nos. 144183–144462, and 795 women, given Nos. 57033–57827, are admitted to the camp. The other almost 2,000 people are killed in the gas chambers.

235 prisoners, including 230 skilled workers, are employed in the Friedrich Krupp plant in Auschwitz.

APMO, D-AuI-3a/370/5, p. 315a, Monthly Labor Deployment List.

No. 144464 is given to a prisoner sent from Kattowitz.

Nos. 144465–144489 are given to 25 prisoners from Kraków sent by the Sipo and the SD.

Nos. 57828–57844 are given to 17 female prisoners sent in a group transport.

No. Z-8710 is given to a male Gypsy and Nos. Z-9438–Z-9439 to two female Gypsies sent from Trier.

Four female Jews who arrived the previous day get Nos. 57845–57848.

By order of the Political Department, two Polish political prisoners are locked in the bunker of Block 11: Ryszard Wiśniewski (No. 9580), who dies in the bunker on September 17, 1943, and Piotr Pavelski (No. 71961), who is shot on September 21, 1943, following a selection carried out in the bunkers.

APMO, D-AuI-3/2, Bunker Register, p. 37.

By order of the Camp Commander, four Polish political prisoners are locked in the bunker of Block 11: Stanisław Fąfara (No. 11685), Stanisław Witek (No. 3660), Stefan Latak (No. 7663), and Wilhelm Kmak (No. 3456). Following a selection in the bunkers, they are shot on September 4, 1943.

Ibid.

In Sosnowitz, the auxiliary camp Sosnowitz I is set up at 12 Targowa Street, in the building previously used by the Council of Jewish Elders of Upper Silesia. Now, 100 prisoners employed in the renovation of the building are housed there—masons, joiners, carpenters, metal workers, electricians, glaziers, and stove-builders who have been transferred from Auschwitz. Initially, SS Private First Class Lehmann is head of the auxiliary camp; later, SS Corporal Czerwiński. The auxiliary camp is liquidated in February 1944.

APMO, Fürstengrube GmbH, p. 48; Franciszek Piper, "Das Nebenlager Sosnowitz (I)" (Sosnowitz [I] Auxiliary Camp), *HvA*, no. 11 (1970): 89–96.

The Political Department intensifies the terror in the camp. It orders eight prisoners locked in the bunker of Block 11. The German asocial prisoner Richard Jungnick (No. 15567) is released from the bunker into the camp on September 28, 1943. But the Polish prisoner Antoni Matusek (No. 123230) is shot on September 4, 1943, and the Polish prisoners Kazimierz Tomal (No. 99536), Jerzy Pecold (No. 114741), Kazimierz Leśniewski (No. 115458), Stanisław Kleszcz (No. 123850), Kazimierz Bogacz (No. 131815), and Stanisław Blukacz (No. 131971) are shot on October 11, 1943, following a selection in the bunkers.

APMO, D-AuI-3/2, Bunker Register, pp. 37ff.

On suspicion of preparing to escape, the Polish political prisoner Mieczyław Nowakowski (No. 120420) is locked in the bunker of Block 11. He is shot on September 4, 1943, following a selection in the bunkers.

Ibid.

The corpses of nine prisoners are delivered to the morgue of the main camp; among them are one from the Budy A.C., No. 84536, and two from the Buna A.C., Nos. 125465 and 117567.*

APMO, D-AuI-5/2, Morgue Register, p. 183.

AUGUST 1–31

1,433 female prisoners have died in the women's camp in Auschwitz-Birkenau; 498 of them were killed with gas.

APMO, Mat.RO, vol. VII, p. 585.

*This entry brings to an end the multivolume register that was compiled in the morgue of the main camp and is now in the archive of the Auschwitz Memorial.

SEPTEMBER 1

The Friedrich Krupp factory in Auschwitz notifies the Commandant's Office that, in accordance with invoices Nos. 1/43 and 2/43 of July 3 and August 3, 1943, payments for a total of 23,973 RM, reflecting the 5,000 RM paid in by Engineer Weinhold of Krupp on July 22, 1943, have been made to the account of the SS garrison administration of Auschwitz at the Reichsbank in Kattowitz.

APMO, Maurer Trial, vol. 8a, p. 114.

Four female prisoners sent from Kraków get Nos. 57849–57852.

Three prisoners escape from the camp: the Pole Eugeniusz Modrzewski (No. 132168) and the Russians Jakub Lysenko (No. 86420) and Vladimir Bessonov.

APMO, D-AuI-1/1, p. 246, Telegrams; IZ-10/Kripo Sieradz/2/88/142.

By order of the Camp Commander, the German political prisoner Oskar Lazarus (No. 119771), born in Bad Ischl on June 6, 1906, is locked in the bunker of Block 11. He is shot on September 4, 1943, following a selection in the bunkers.

APMO, D-AuI-3/2, Bunker Register, p. 38.

No. 144490 is given to a male prisoner and Nos. 57853 and 57854 to two female prisoners sent from Kattowitz.

The Russian political prisoner Dmitro Balarz (No. 121770) is captured during an escape attempt and locked in the bunker of Block 11. He is shot on September 4, 1943, following a selection in the bunkers.

Ibid., p. 32.

SS Second Lieutenant Sell of Labor Deployment informs the Head of Office D-II in the WVHA that 3,581 able-bodied Jews are being used for labor: 1,966 Jewish prisoners at Buna, 83 at the Eintrachthütte, 606 in Jaworzno, 22 in the Friedrich Krupp plant, 726 in Jawischowitz, and 148 in Golleschau.

APMO, D-AuI-3a/360, Labor Deployment.

SEPTEMBER 2

The prisoner Vladimir Bessonov, who escaped the previous day, is captured and brought back to the camp. Since he is not locked in the bunker of Block 11 following his arrest, he is probably shot.

APMO, D-AuI-1/1, p. 245, Telegrams.

100 Auschwitz prisoners are employed at the Sosnowitz I auxiliary camp in renovating a building in Targowa Street that is intended for the Gauleitung of Upper Silesia. At the end of the month there are only 94 prisoners.

APMO, D-AuI-3a/370/5, p. 336a, Monthly Labor Deployment List.

No. 144463 is given to a prisoner sent from Kattowitz.

Approximately 3,000 Jewish men, women, and children from the ghetto and labor camp in Bochnia arrive in an RSHA transport. Following the selection, 788 men, given Nos. 144491–145278, and 42 women, given Nos. 57855–57896, are admitted to the camp.

AGKBZH, vol. 5425, p. 2; vol. 4501, p. 1.

The other approximately 2,170 people are killed in the gas chambers.

1,004 Jews from Westerbork arrive in an RSHA transport from Holland. In the shipment are 160 children, 268 men, and 381 women under 50 years of age, and 195 older people. After the selection, 259 men, given Nos. 145279–145537, and 247 women, given Nos. 57897–58143, are admitted to the camp. The other 498 people are killed in the gas chambers.

Two female prisoners sent from The Hague receive Nos. 58144 and 58145.

No. 145538 is given to a prisoner transferred from Belgrade.

Nos. 145539–145544 are given to six male prisoners and Nos. 58146–58151, 58153–58155, and 58157–58160 to 13 female prisoners sent from Kattowitz.

Nos. 145545 and 145546 are given to two male prisoners and Nos. 58152 and 58156 to two female prisoners sent from Oppeln.

36 prisoners sent from Kattowitz receive Nos. 145547–145582.

Two prisoners, the Russian Konstanty Pazkovski (No. 125143) and the Czech Anton Čermak (No. 117119), are captured while escaping and locked in the bunker of Block 11. Following a selection in the bunkers, they are shot on September 4, 1943.

APMO, D-AuI-3/2, Bunker Register, p. 39.

The Russian political prisoner Vladimir Popovich (No. 107526) escapes from the camp.

APMO, IZ-10/Kripo Sieradz/2/88/150.

An auxiliary camp is set up in Wesoła near Myslowitz, in the vicinity of the Fürstengrube coal mine. The first prisoners who arrive there are used for cleanup work on the grounds and for setting up barracks for subsequent transports. The Commander of the Fürstengrube A.C. is SS Technical Sergeant Otto Moll; SS Staff Sergeant Max Schmidt succeeds him in April 1944. The prisoners are employed in coal mining, construction of a new pit, and enlargement of the camp.*

APMO, Fürstengrube GmbH, pp. 46–48; T. Iwaszko, "Fürstengrube," pp. 5–92.

Two German criminal prisoners are locked in the bunkers of Block 11: Gustav Vaupel (No. 3267)** and Alois Neumann (No. 24478).† Following a selection carried out in the bunker, they are shot on September 4, 1943.††

APMO, D-AuI-3/2, Bunker Register, p. 38.

*129 prisoners work there on September 4, 400 on September 6, and more than 600 in November.
**Gustav Vaupel is locked in the bunker of Block 11 for the sixth time.
†Alois Neuman, together with Vaupel, is delivered to the bunker of Block 11 for the second time.
††In principle, German criminal prisoners employed as functionaries are very seldom punished with death. Usually they are transferred to the Penal Company or are put under pressure to commit suicide.

In Block 11 of the main camp, the Police Court-martial of the Kattowitz Gestapo condemns to death 63 men and 30 women who have been brought from Silesian prisons.

APMO, Mat.RO, vol. IV, p. 254.

SEPTEMBER 3

Nos. 145583–145633 are given to 51 male prisoners and Nos. 58233–58299 to 67 female prisoners delivered in a group transport.

Two female Gypsies sent in a group transport get Nos. Z-9440 and Z-9441.

Nos. 145634–145748 are given to 115 prisoners sent to the camp by the Posen Gestapo.

A prisoner transferred from Paris is given No. 145749.

41 prisoners sent in a group transport receive Nos. 145750–145790.

By order of the Political Department, four prisoners are put in the bunker of Block 11. They are the Polish Jews Hersz Trop (No. 34558), born in Lodz on September 1, 1915; Izak Boczkowski (No. 99260), born in Białystok on April 25, 1914; Enach Małecki (No. 99402), born in Szczekow on June 5, 1921; and Chaim Czotkin (No. 100536), born in Białystok on December 25, 1901. They are shot the day after their arrest, on September 4, 1943, following a selection carried out in the bunkers.

APMO, D-AuI-3/2, Bunker Register, p. 39.

SS Major Hartjenstein announces to the SS Guard Stormtroopers that in compliance with an order by the WVHA, clothing that becomes available to SS Men in the so-called Jewish operation* may be neither sold nor given away.

APMO, Dpr.-ZOd/40, Stormtrooper Order 136/43.

A selection is carried out in the women's camp in Birkenau during which several female Jewish prisoners are selected. They are killed in the gas chambers the same day.

Gerald Reitlinger, *Die Endlösung: Hitler's Versuch der Ausrottung der Juden Europas 1939–1940* (The Final Solution: Hitler's Attempt to Extirpate Europe's Jews 1939–1945), Berlin, 1956, p. 131.

SEPTEMBER 4

In Libiąż, an auxiliary camp of Auschwitz is set up near the Janina mine. Approximately 300 prisoners, mostly Jews, intended for work in coal mining, are transferred to the camp, which previously housed 150 English POWs. As the majority of these prisoners arrived at Auschwitz in August in an RSHA transport, the Camp Doctor orders them placed in quarantine. SS Corporal Baumgartner is Head of the auxiliary camp at the Janina pit.

APMO, Maurer Trial, vol. 12a, p. 242 (Ni-12582), p. 250 (Ni-11654); E. Iwaszko, "Janinagrube," pp. 41–66.

Nos. Z-8711–Z-8715 are given to five male Gypsies and Nos. Z-9442–Z-9444 to three female Gypsies.

*Another camouflage term for the extermination of the Jews.

By order of the Political Department, the reeducation prisoner Ivan Zolotucha (No. EH-5016), born on September 11, 1924, is locked in the bunker of Block 11. Following a selection, he is shot on September 21, 1943.

APMO, D-AuI-3/2, Bunker Register, p. 39.

Two prisoners sent from Radom on August 24 receive Nos. 145791 and 145792.

Three prisoners transferred from Kattowitz get Nos. 145793 and 145795.

1,000 Jews from Drancy arrive in the fifty-ninth RSHA transport from France. Following the selection, 232 men, given Nos. 145796–146027, and 106 women, given Nos. 58300–58405, are admitted to the camp. The other 662 people are killed in the gas chambers.

A selection is carried out in the bunkers of Block 11. 53 prisoners who have been put there by order of the Political Department, the Roll Call Leader, or the Deputy Commandant, or who are suspected of planning an escape or who have attempted an escape are selected. That same day they are shot at the execution wall in the courtyard of Block 11.

Ibid., pp. 21, 23, 31, 33–39.

SEPTEMBER 5

Six female prisoners from Kattowitz get Nos. 58406–58411.

Six boys born in the Gypsy camp in Birkenau get Nos. Z-8716–Z-8721.

APMO, D-AuII-3/1/2, p. 258, Register of Male Gypsies.

Nos. 146028–146134 are given to 107 male prisoners and Nos. 58436–59442 to seven female prisoners sent from Oppeln.

Six girls born in the Gypsy camp get Nos. Z-9445–Z-9450.

APMO, D-AuII-3/2/5, p. 609, Register of Female Gypsies.

By order of the Camp Commander the following prisoners are locked in the bunkers of Block 11: the Gypsy Eduard Laubinger (No. Z-5147), born in Flensburg on September 30, 1924, and the German BV prisoner Paul Michna (No. 26541), born in Leobschütz on March 5, 1904. Laubinger is shot on September 28, 1943, following a selection in the bunkers, and Paul Michna is released from the bunker on October 11, 1943.

APMO, D-AuI-3/2, Bunker Register, p. 39.

SEPTEMBER 6

Commandant Höss informs the SS members of the garrison that he has again taken over the function of Commandant of Auschwitz Concentration Camp.*

APMO, Dpr.-ZOd/39, Garrison Order 37/43.

*The reason for his absence was probably his vacation, which he had to take before his transfer.

447 prisoners who have been sent to the camp by the Belgrade Gestapo get Nos. 146135–146581.

24 female prisoners from Kattowitz are given Nos. 58412–58435.

Nos. 146582–146620 are given to 39 male prisoners and Nos. 58443–58461 to 19 female prisoners sent in a group transport. 70 prisoners who have been sent to the camp by the Kraków Sipo and SD are given Nos. 146621–146690. Among them are 58 prisoners from the prison in Tarnów.

The Commander of the SS Guard Stormtroopers, SS Major Hartjenstein, expresses his gratitude to SS Staff Sergeant Spiecker, because while pursuing an escaped prisoner during the night of September 4–5 he located him in his hiding place and impeded his further flight.*

APMO, Dpr.-ZOd/40, Stormtrooper Order 137/43.

By order of the Camp Commander, Artur Lafrens (No Z-5156), a German Gypsy born in Hamburg on January 2, 1927, is locked in the bunker of Block 11. He is shot on September 28, 1943, following a selection carried in the bunkers.

APMO, D-AuI-3/2 Bunker Register, p. 39.

The Czech asocial prisoner Georg Bruzek (No. 104238), born on May 18, 1921, is locked in the bunker of Block 11. Following a selection carried out in the bunker, he is shot on September 21, 1943.

Ibid.

A female Polish prisoner, Irena Kotalski, escapes during the evening hours from the Budy auxiliary camp. She was sent to Auschwitz from Warsaw under the name Leokadia Kurek by the Sipo and SD on August 6, 1943, and given No. 58875.**

APMO, D-AuI-1/2, p. 200, Telegrams; IZ-8/Gestapo Lodz/3a/88/503.

SEPTEMBER 7

Prisoners from the Buna auxiliary camp whom the Political Department suspects of conspiratorial activity in a leftist political organization in the camp are locked in the bunkers of Block 11. An investigation is initiated by the Political Department. Several of the prisoners manage to stay alive, many are shot. The incarcerated include the Polish political prisoner Józef Niezgoda (No. 131960), who is shot on October 11, 1943; the Jew Moritz Dalicz (No. 100621), who is shot on September 28, 1943; the Polish political prisoner Bolesław Smoliński (No. 15725), who is released from the bunker into the camp on October 19, 1943; the Jewish prisoners Kurt Posener (No. 68619) and Werner Szczepansky (No. 70206), who are released from the bunker into the camp on September 15,

APMO, D-AuI-3/2, Bunker Register, pp. 39ff., Information of Former Prisoner Cass Stankiewicz-Wiśniewski, Correspondence, No. 2060/70.

---

*Probably the fleeing prisoner was shot in his hiding place, as there is no entry about the delivery to the bunkers of Block 11 on the date mentioned. Also, Spiecker receives only praise instead of additional leave.
**She succeeds in getting to Kraków, where total strangers help her; she then hides on a farm until the end of the war (APMO, Depositions, vol. 68, pp. 131ff., Account of the Former Prisoner Irena Popanda).

1943, and Walter Windmüller (No. 70270), who is shot on September 21, 1943; and the Polish political prisoner Wilhelm Karp (No. 114693), who is shot on September 9, 1943. Walter Windmüller was one of the leaders of the resistance organization in the Buna A.C.

In the evening, two Jewish prisoners escape from the Neu-Dachs auxiliary camp in Jaworzno: Charles Zussmann, born in Paris on June 17, 1912, and Icek Chaber Rosenblatt (No. 133329), born in Przedbórz on July 26, 1919.

APMO, D-AuI-1/1, p. 249, Telegrams; IZ-10/Kripo Sieradz/2/88/154; IZ-8/Gestapo Lodz/2/88/178.

The Polish prisoner Stefan Urban, born in Tarnów on January 14, 1907, who had been sent to Auschwitz by the Sipo and SD for the Kraków District, escapes from the Buna A.C.

APMO, D-AuI-1/1, p. 251, Telegrams; IZ-8/Gestapo Lodz/88/485.

Three prisoners sent in a group transport are given Nos. 146691–146693.

No. 58462 is given to a female prisoner.

Eight female prisoners sent from Kattowitz are given Nos. 58463–58470.

Nos. 61184–61215 are given to 23 women and nine girls from Bromberg (Bydgoszcz). They are killed the same day in the gas chambers. They are Helena Szydłowski (No. 61184), born in Mroczenko on December 31, 1899; Lucia Mazur (No. 61185), born in Wertheim on October 12, 1913; Zofia Rebarczyk (No. 61186), born in Neudorf on January 24, 1905; Wiktoria Wilczewski (No. 61187), born in Pruszcz on December 23, 1901; Paulina Górny (No. 61188), born in Wols Erly on January 10, 1872; Anna Górny (No. 61189), born in Kowalewo on July 21, 1905; Anastazja Górny (No. 61190), born in Schönsee on February 22, 1909; Agnes Górny (No. 61191), born in Schönsee on February 3, 1934; Barbara Górny (No. 61192), born in Thorn on March 14, 1936; Eleonora Górny (No. 61193), born in Schönsee on January 2, 1942; Stanisława Wiśniewski (No. 61194), born in Schönsee on December 20, 1902; Helene Wiśniewski (No. 61195), born in Brzesen on September 29, 1942; Hedwig Gackowski (No. 61196), born in Bischofswerder on February 23, 1915; Bronisława Dombrowski (No. 61197), born in Zwinierz on July 16, 1917; Stefania Iwicki (No. 61198), born in Zwinierz on August 28, 1928; Bronisława Lieder (No. 61199), born in Gnesen on April 27, 1903; Pelagia Wesołowski (No. 61200), born in Bromberg on January 29, 1925; Antonina Wilczewski (No. 61201), born in Nowy Jasin on May 16, 1910; Kazimiera Zastempowski (No. 61202), born in Niemcze on July 8, 1927; Apolonia Dominikowski (No. 61203), born in Rozewin on April 18, 1919; Wanda Galecki (No. 61204), born on April 11, 1936; Johanna Paske (No. 61205), born in Gutkiny on September 19, 1930; Zophie Szerszant (No. 61206), born in Derschau on April 9, 1939; Rozalia Szerszant (No. 61207), born in Derschau on May 10, 1911; Helena Gumowski (No. 61208), born in Myszkowice on October 18, 1928;

APMO, Mat.RO, vol. IV, p. 261; Dpr.-ZOd/3, p. 136.

Helena Czerwiński (No. 61209), born in Czarne Błoto on November 12, 1930; Julia Krzyżykowski (No. 61210), born in Ciche on April 13, 1910; Veronika Lukiewicz (No. 61211), born in Rosenthal on January 6, 1918; Helena Mazur (No. 61212), born in Wertheim on May 12, 1912; Helena Pietrzak (No. 61213) born in Białobrody on October 25, 1896; Stanisława Zadun (No. 61214), born on July 26, 1940; Maria Slupska (No. 61215), born in Keslen on November 20, 1923.*

Friedrich Krupp AG is notified that the Weichsel-Union-Metallwerke (Vistula Union of Metal Companies), which owns a fuse factory in Zaporož'e,** must be evacuated. The machinery and production equipment are to be shipped to Auschwitz within 10 to 12 days. The following solutions are proposed to the Krupp factories:

APMO, Maurer Trial, vol. 8a, pp. 115ff.

1. To take over Weichsel-Union's production
2. To turn over the production of the Krupp factories to Weichsel-Union
3. To form a combination (Interessengemeinschaft)

SEPTEMBER 8

Commander SS Major Hartjenstein of the SS guard troops praises SS Private First Class Spieker for discovering the hiding place on the grounds of the DAW plant of a prisoner who escaped on September 4.

APMO, Dpr.-ZOd/40, Stormtrooper Order 138/43.

5,006 Jews are transferred from Theresienstadt with an RSHA transport. In the transport are 2,293 men and boys, given Nos. 146694–148986, and 2,713 women and girls, given Nos. 58471–61183.

APMO, D-RF-3/90, 91, 92, Transport Dl-Dm of Sept. 6, 1943, List of Names; Adler, *Theresienstadt 1941–1945*, pp. 53, 127.

No. 148987 is given to a prisoner transferred the previous day from Oppeln.

A prisoner who was transferred the previous day from Kattowitz is given No. 148988.

Four prisoners sent in a group transport receive Nos. 148989–148992.

Nos. 148993–149036 are given to 44 male prisoners and Nos. 61321–61323 to four female prisoners who have been sent to the camp by the Lodz Gestapo. 33 female prisoners sent by the Posen Gestapo get Nos. 61324–61356.

---

*According to a notation the camp resistance movement makes on a copy of the list, the Commandant's Office receives the command in 1944 to release 23 women and nine children from the camp. It cannot carry out this order, as the persons named have been gassed.
**A town in the Ukrainian Soviet Republic. The tanks of the Red Army advanced as far as the Dnieper River south of Kiev on August 22, 1943.

An auxiliary camp is set up in Lagischa in a forced labor camp for Jews, taken over for this purpose. The EVO uses the prisoners to build the Walter power station in Lagischa. The prisoners are used in construction and assembly work, to work the cranes, to build the concrete foundations, and to run the factory railroad. The first few days they are used for cleanup work on the grounds of the former forced labor camp and in organizational tasks.

Jerzy Frąckiewicz, "Das Neben-lager Lagischa" (Lagischa Auxil-iary Camp), *HvA*, no. 9 (1966), pp. 109–124.

Nos. 149037–149061 are given to 25 male prisoners and Nos. 61357–61392 to 36 female prisoners sent from the prison in Tar-nów by the Kraków District Sipo and SD.

Four prisoners sent in a group transport get Nos. 149062–149065.

No. 61393 is given to a female prisoner sent from Kattowitz.

35 prisoners sent from Bromberg receive Nos. 149066–149100.*

No. 61394 is given to a female prisoner sent from Oppeln.

No. 61395 is given to a female prisoner sent from Kattowitz.

The Polish prisoner Tadeusz Czech (No. 126363), born on August 5, 1925, sent to the camp by the Posen Gestapo on June 26, 1943, escapes from the camp.

APMO, IZ-8/Gestapo Lodz/3a/88/487; Mat.RO, vol. IV, p. 293.

By order of the Camp Commander, the Gypsy Joseph Czurka (No. Z-3647), born in Graudenz on May 20, 1911, is locked in the bunker of Block 11. He is shot on September 21, 1943, following a selection in the bunkers.

APMO, D-AuI-3/2, Bunker Reg-ister, p. 40.

SEPTEMBER 9

987 Jews from Westerbork arrive in an RSHA transport from Hol-land. In the transport are 170 children, 264 men, and 338 women under 50 years of age as well as 215 older people. Following the selection, 187 men, given Nos. 149101–149287, and 105 women, who are given Nos. 61216–61320, are admitted to the camp as prisoners. The other 695 people are killed in the gas chambers.

Nos. 149288–149367 are given to 80 male prisoners and Nos. 61396–61416 to 21 female prisoners sent from Kattowitz.

Three prisoners are given Nos. 149368–149370.

Seven prisoners sent from Kattowitz are given Nos. 149371–149377.

*Probably these are the husbands and sons of the women sent to the camp the previous day from Bromberg and gassed. The further fate of the men with Nos. 149066–149100 is not known, as no documents relating to these prisoners survive. Probably they were likewise killed in the gas chambers.

459 male prisoners are given Nos. 149467–149925, and Nos. 61417–62169 are given to 753 female prisoners sent from Mobile Strike Commando (Einsatzkommando) 9 in Vitebsk in White Russia. The latter are suspected of collaborating with or helping partisans active in White Russia.

Seven female prisoners sent from Kattowitz receive Nos. 62170–62176.

Icek Chaber Rosenblatt (No. 133329), who escaped from the Neu-Dachs A.C. on September 7, is captured and locked in the bunker of Block 11. Following a selection in the bunkers, he is shot on September 21, 1943.

APMO, D-AuI-1/1a, pp. 248ff., IZ-8/Gestapo Lodz/2/88/180; D-AuI-3/2, Bunker Register, p. 40.

By order of the Political Department the Polish Jew Naftalin Tuchmann (No. 67812), born in Tyczyn on March 21, 1890, is locked in the bunker of Block 11. He is shot on October 11, 1943.

APMO, D-AuI-3/2, Bunker Register, p. 40.

Seven male Gypsies are given Nos. Z-8722–Z-8728, and one female Gypsy gets No. Z-9451.

By order of the Camp Commander, the Greek Jew Lieto Kapon (No. 116052), born in Salonika, is locked in the bunker of Block 11. Following a selection in the bunkers, he is shot on September 21, 1943.

Ibid.

The Commandant's Office receives an order dated September 4, 1943, from Office D-II in the WVHA commanding Höss to explain why only 3,581 Jewish prisoners have been used in the armaments industry and what the other approximately 25,500 Jewish prisoners are doing.

APMO, Maurer Trial, vol. 13a, Document on p. 175.

The 5,006 Jews transferred the previous day from Theresienstadt are housed in the newly opened Camp B-IIb in Birkenau. This camp is designated Theresienstadt Family Camp.*

APMO, Dpr.-Hd/6, p. 48; Dpr.-ZOd/3, p. 191.

SEPTEMBER 10

The EVO in Lagischa employs 302 prisoners, including 44 skilled laborers and 258 unskilled laborers, in the construction of the Walter power station.**

APMO, D-AuI-3a/370/5, pp. 351, 351a, Monthly Labor Deployment List.

*The Jewish prisoners housed in this camp are treated better than the others. They are permitted to keep their things, their hair is not shorn, they are permitted to write to their families every 14 days and to receive packages. A small garden is set up for the children, and at the beginning they receive better food. This serves as propaganda, to counteract the news of the extermination of the Jews that is reaching the public in the free world. Despite the better treatment, the mortality in this camp is very high. From documents preserved in the Archives of the Auschwitz memorial, it is clear that by March 1944 approximately 1,140 people from the above-mentioned shipment die. From August 8 to March 9, 1944, 3,791 people are killed in the gas chambers. Only physicians and twins, in whom Camp Doctor Mengele is particularly interested, escape death (Zdeněk and Jiři Steiner, "Zwillinge in Auschwitz" [Twins in Auschwitz], in Adler et al., eds., *Auschwitz: Testimonies*).
**By the end of the month the number of prisoners employed drops to 296.

5,470 prisoners, including 1,231 skilled workers, are employed in the Buna plants in Morowitz.*

APMO, D-AuI-3a/370/5, p. 331a, Monthly Labor Deployment List.

Nos. 149378–149466 are given to 89 male prisoners, and Nos. 62177–62256 identify 80 female prisoners sent in a group transport.

65 prisoners sent to the camp by the Sipo and SD for the Kraków District get Nos. 149930–149994. Among them are 38 prisoners from the prison in Tarnów.

64 prisoners sent to the camp in a group transport get Nos. 149995–150058.

By order of the Political Department four prisoners are locked in the bunkers of Block 11: Wasyl Weliszo (No. EH-5612) and the Polish political prisoner Władysław Jurczak (No. 115527), who are shot on September 21, 1943, following a selection in the bunkers; and the Polish political prisoners Władysław Tyczkowski (No. 114785) and Tadeusz Musiałowicz (No. 115421), who are shot after the selection on October 11, 1943.

APMO, D-AuI-3/2, Bunker Register, p. 40.

SEPTEMBER 11

Nos. Z-9452 is given to a female Gypsy delivered to the camp.

The Russian prisoner Stefan Symonenko (No. 68755) escapes from the camp.

APMO, D-AuI-1/1a, p. 256, Telegrams; IZ-10/Kripo Sieradz/2/88/143; Mat.RO, vol. IV, p. 294.

Two male prisoners sent from Kattowitz are given Nos. 150059 and 150060, and one female, also from Kattowitz, receives No. 62257.

No. 62258 is given to a female prisoner sent on September 8, 1943.

The forty-second East transport of the RSHA arrives from Berlin, oganized by the Gestapo. It includes 54 Jewish men, women, and children. Following the selection, nine women, given Nos. 62259–62267, are admitted to the camp. The other 45 people are killed in the gas chambers.

APMO, D-RF-3/121/15, pp. 37–40, Gestapo Belin, Auschwitz Transports, List of Names.

Lili Tofler (No. 4738), who works at the horticultural station in Rajsko, secretly gives a letter addressed to an acquaintance in the camp to the Jewish prisoner Abram Solarz (No. 101028), who has been sent to Rajsko with the Pole Wacław Gniazdowski (No. 102331) to pick up flowers. Solarz delivers the flowers to the Political Department and loses the letter while doing so. One of the SS Men finds it; investigations begin immediately and he and Gniaz-

APMO, Dpr.-Hd/1, p. 108; D-AuI-3/2, Bunker Register, p. 40; Škodowa, *Three Years*, pp. 131ff.

*On September 25 and 26, the prisoners from each group work only a half day; 4,939 prisoners are employed there on September 26. On September 27, the number is 5,542, including 1,347 skilled workers.

SS officers during the selection of prisoners.

dowski are locked in the bunkers of Block 11. During the investigations, Abram Solarz does not disclose the name of the prisoner to whom the letter was directed, and Gniazdowski knows nothing at all about it. The author of the letter is identified by her signature and is likewise locked in the bunker of Block 11, but she does not disclose the name of the prisoner to whom the letter was directed. All three are shot on September 21, 1943, following a selection in the bunker.

SEPTEMBER 12

Three boys born in the Gypsy camp get Nos. Z-8729–Z-8731.

APMO, D-AuII-3/1/2, p. 258, Register of Male Gypsies.

Five girls born in the Gypsy camp get Nos. Z-9453–Z-9457.

APMO, D-AuII-3/2/5, p. 609, Register of Female Gypsies.

SEPTEMBER 13

Four prisoners delivered from Kattowitz get Nos. 149926–149929.

Nos. 150061–150083 are given to 23 male prisoners and Nos. 62268–62280 to 13 women prisoners sent in a group transport.

Nos. 62281–62283 are given to three female prisoners sent from Kattowitz.

The Polish prisoner Stefan Turski (No. 131930), born on April 18, 1909, escapes from the camp in the evening.

APMO, D-AuI-1/1a, p. 257, Telegrams; IZ-8/Gestapo Lodz/3a/88/489; Mat.RO, vol. IV, p. 294.

By order of the Political Department, Franciszek Zawada (No. 145793), born in Krenau on September 25, 1919, is locked in the bunker of Block 11. The next day he is brought before a Police Court-martial session in Block 11. The fate of the prisoner is not known.

APMO, D-AuI-3/2, Bunker Register, p. 41.

SEPTEMBER 14

2,394 prisoners, including 258 skilled workers, are employed in the Neu-Dachs A.C. The management of the mines in Jaworzno and the EVO, which is constructing the power station, pay 4 RM per day for the labor of one skilled worker and 3 RM for an unskilled laborer.

APMO, D-AuI-3a/370/5, pp. 344, 344a, Monthly Labor Deployment List.

No. 62284 is given to a female prisoner sent to the camp.

Five female prisoners transferred from Ravensbrück get Nos. 62285–62289.

Nos. 150084–150430 are given to 347 male prisoners and Nos. 62290–62352 to 63 female prisoners sent from the prison in Radom by the Sipo and SD.

Nos. 150431–150562 are given to 132 prisoners sent from Pawiak Prison in Warsaw by the Sipo and SD.

No. 150563 is given to a prisoner transferred from Vitebsk on September 10, 1943.

The Polish political prisoner Edward Kizmachowski (No. 3414), born in Strasbourg on July 20, 1922, is locked in the bunker of Block 11. He is captured after an escape attempt, and having been wounded during the escape, has somewhat healed in the prisoners' infirmary. He is released from the bunker into the camp on October 11, 1943.*

APMO, D-AuI-3/2, Bunker Register, p. 41; Dpr.-ZOd/5, pp. 76–79; Dpr.-ZOd/55, p. 246.

By order of the Camp Commander, the Polish political prisoner Jan Kornaszewski (No. 127806) is locked in the bunker of Block 11. He is shot on September 21, 1943, following a selection in the bunkers.

APMO, D-AuI-3/2, Bunker Register, p. 41.

By order of the Camp Commander, four prisoners, the Greek Jews Haskiel Malloh (No. 110285), Jakes Benosilio (No. 110554), Samuel Faradgi (No. 110641), and Samuel Cohen (No. 112413), are locked in the bunkers of Block 11. They are shot on September 21, 1943, following a selection in the bunker.

Ibid.

The German political prisoner Willi Knauf (No. 112075), born in Richtenburg on August 20, 1910, is captured while escaping and

Ibid.

*Compare the entry for August 17, 1943.

locked in the bunker of Block 11. He is released from the bunker into the camp on November 23, 1943.

The Polish political prisoner Józef Kramorz (No. 20462), born in Hindenburg on February 18, 1906, is locked in the bunker of Block 11 by order of the Camp Commander and is shot on September 21, 1943, following a selection carried out in the bunkers.

Ibid.

SEPTEMBER 15

39 male prisoners and 14 female prisoners sent from Kattowitz are given Nos. 150564–150602 and 62353–62366, respectively.

The female political prisoner Stefania Uroda, a Pole born in Schieratz on December 18, 1905, escapes from the camp. She was registered on August 13, 1943.

APMO, D-AuI-1/1a, p. 263, Telegrams; IZ-8/Gestapo Lodz/3a/88/492.

The SS Garrison Senior and Commandant, Rudolf Höss, announces in a garrison command the names of 18 SS men who are being awarded the War Service Cross 2nd Class with Swords—including the Director of the Pharmacy, SS Captain Krömer, and the SS Camp Doctor, SS First Lieutenant Dr. Bruno Kitt—and of 10 SS men awarded the War Service Medal. The overseer of the women's camp, Emma Zimmer, is awarded the War Service Cross 2nd Class without Swords.

APMO, D-AuI, Garrison Order 39/43 of Sept. 15, 1943.

Following consultations with the Committee for Ammunition and the Reich Ministry for Armaments and War Production, the Army High Command decides that the firm of Weichsel-Union-Metallwerke, evacuated from Zaporož'e, will take over the production facilities of Friedrich Krupp AG that were set up in Auschwitz.

APMO, Maurer Trial, vol. 8, pp. 117ff.

SEPTEMBER 16

Two prisoners from Kattowitz receive Nos. 150603–150604.

1,005 Jews from the Westerbork camp arrive in an RSHA transport from Holland. In it are 119 children, 302 men and 330 women under age 50, and 245 older men. Following the selection, 233 men, given Nos. 150605–150837, and 194 women, given Nos. 62367–62560, are admitted to the camp as prisoners.* The other 578 people are killed in the gas chambers.

Four female prisoners transferred from The Hague get Nos. 62561–62564.

57 prisoners delivered in a group transport get Nos. 150838–150894.

---

*Several days later, 40 and then an additional 100 female prisoners from this transport are moved to the experimental station of Professor Dr. Clauberg in Block 10 of the main camp (APMO, Dpr.-Hd/6, p. 94).

Three female prisoners sent from Zichenau receive Nos. 62565–62567.

A female prisoner sent from Königsberg in East Prussia receives No. 62568.

The Political Department discovers the Union of the Military Combat Groups (Vereinigung der Militärischen Kampfgruppen) that are conspiratorially active in the main camp, in Birkenau, and in the Buna auxiliary camp. The arrests start in the Buna camp; among others, the Polish political prisoner Major Kazimierz Gilewicz (No. 71886) is locked in the bunker. Within a few days 74 prisoners from the main camp and Birkenau are delivered to the bunker. The next day Kazimierz's older brother, Colonel Juliusz Gilewicz (No. 31033), the head of the conspiratorial committee of the Union, is in the bunker. Among the arrested are army men, doctors, politicians, lawyers, and artists. The majority of them are shot on October 11, 1943; some are released from the bunker into the camp.

APMO, D-AuI-3/2, Bunker Register, pp. 42–49; Mat.RO, vol. I, p. 40; Garliński, *Fighting Auschwitz*, pp. 214–219.

SEPTEMBER 17

Nos. 150895–150897 are given to three male prisoners, and Nos. 62569–62570 to two female prisoners sent from Kattowitz.

Nos. 150898–150923 are given to 26 male prisoners and Nos. 62571–62599 to 29 female prisoners sent in a group transport.

28 prisoners sent from Brünn receive Nos. 150924–150951.

45 prisoners sent from Prague receive Nos. 150952–150996.

67 prisoners sent with a group transport get Nos. 150997–151063.

126 prisoners sent to the camp by the Lodz Gestapo get Nos. 151064–151189.

40 prisoners sent to the camp by the Posen Gestapo get Nos. 151190–151229.

Nos. 151230–151243 are given to 14 prisoners sent in a group transport.

Nos. 151244–151268 are given to 25 prisoners sent to the camp by the Sipo and SD for the Kraków District.

A prisoner from Oppeln is given No. 151269.

Nos. Z-8732–Z-8739 are given to eight male Gypsies and Nos. Z-9458–Z-9466 to nine female Gypsies sent from the interior of the Reich.

The Gypsy Erich Schmidt (No. Z-268) is captured during an escape attempt and locked in the bunker of Block 11. Following a selection in the bunkers, he is shot on September 21, 1943.

APMO, D-AuI-3/2, Bunker Register, p. 42.

SEPTEMBER 18

Nos. Z-8740–Z-8741 are given to two male Gypsies and No. Z-9467 to a female Gypsy sent in a group transport.

The Krupp factory at Auschwitz decreases the number of prisoners it employs from 239 to 100 and starts dismantling machines and factory equipment.

APMO, D-AuI-3a/370/5, p. 344a, Monthly Labor Deployment List.

95 female prisoners sent in a group transport get Nos. 62600–62694.

No. 62695 is given to a girl born to a woman transferred into the camp from Kraków. This is the first registration of a child born in the women's camp in Birkenau.

Five female prisoners sent to the camp by the Sipo and SD for the Kraków District get Nos. 62696–62700.

SEPTEMBER 19

Approximately 1,300 Jews from the ghetto in Dąbrowa Tarnowska arrive in an RSHA transport. They are killed the same day in the gas chambers.

AGKBZH, *Camps, Ghettos*, p. 70.

Nos. 62701–62703 are given to three female prisoners sent from Kattowitz.

SEPTEMBER 20

The Weichsel-Union-Metallwerke, which was evacuated from Zaporož'e, uses 137 skilled workers from Auschwitz, probably in unloading machinery and factory equipment. The following day, they employ an additional 200 unskilled workers and 21 female prisoners.*

APMO, D-AuI-3a/370/5, pp. 332a, 333a, Monthly Labor Deployment List.

Five boys born in the Gypsy camp get Nos. Z-8742–Z-8746.

APMO, D-AuII-3/1/2, p. 259, Register of Male Gypsies.

Five girls born in the Gypsy camp get Nos. Z-9468–Z-9472.

APMO, D-AuII-3/2/5, p. 611, Register of Female Gypsies.

The Jewish prisoner Judelis Vainiunskas (No. 39077) escapes from the camp.

APMO, Mat.RO, vol. IV, p. 294.

*During the final days of September there are more than 230 skilled workers and 15 female prisoners employed in the Weichsel-Union factory. The male prisoners are used for assembling machines and equipment, the female prisoners are assigned cleaning and repair tasks.

53 Polish prisoners are transferred from Auschwitz to Buchenwald.

Ibid., vol. VII, p. 453.

Nos. 151270–151298 are assigned to 29 male prisoners and Nos. 62704–62741 to 38 female prisoners sent in a group transport.

SEPTEMBER 21

A selection is carried out in the bunkers of Block 11. 29 prisoners are selected who have been incarcerated there by order of the Political Department or the Camp Commander or who have been captured while escaping or are suspected of planning an escape. That same day they are shot at the execution wall in the courtyard of Block 11.

APMO, D-AuI-3/2, Bunker Register, pp. 18, 31, 33, 34, 37, 39–43.

The Polish prisoner Franciszek Wicek (No. 125662) escapes from the Neu-Dachs A.C.; two prisoners are shot while escaping by SS Private First Class Wilhelm Reichel.

APMO, D-AuI-1/1a, p. 267, Telegrams; IZ-8/Gestapo Lodz/3a/88/494; Mat.RO, vol. IV, p. 294; Dpr.-Hd/12, p. 17, Garrison Order 43/43.

Three Polish prisoners escape from the camp: Zbigniew Wąsowicz (No. 123599), Henryk Piątkowski (No. 119396), and Zdzisław Mendygrał (No. 119361).

APMO, D-AuI-1/1a, p. 269, Telegrams; IZ-8/Gestapo Lodz/3a/88/486; Mat.RO, vol. IV, p. 294.

100 prisoners delivered with a group transport are given Nos. 151299–151398.

Nos. 151399–151401 are given to three male prisoners and Nos. 62742–62746 to five female prisoners sent from Kattowitz.

78 prisoners from Posen, sent to the camp by the Gestapo, get Nos. 151402–151479.

No. 151480 is given to a prisoner sent from Oppeln.

No. 62747 is given to a girl born to a woman in the Birkenau camp who was transferred from Vitebsk.

13 female prisoners transferred from Kattowitz get Nos. 62748–62760.

By order of SS Colonel Dr. Lolling, Head of Office D-III in the WVHA, Dr. Alina Brewda is transferred from Majdanek to Auschwitz; she is given No. 62761.

SEPTEMBER 22

Nos. 62762–62803 are given to 42 female prisoners from Posen who have been sent to the camp by the Gestapo.

A female prisoner sent from Kattowitz gets No. 62804.

1,425 Jews from Malines arrive in RSHA transports Nos. 22a and 22b from Belgium. In the transports are 586 men and 124 boys and 598 women and 117 girls. Following the selection, 371 men, given Nos. 151481–151851, and 179 women, who are given Nos. 62805–62983, are admitted to the camp. The other 875 people are killed in the gas chambers.

SEPTEMBER 23

979 Jewish men, women, and children arrive from Westerbork in an RSHA transport from Holland. In the transport are 60 children, 384 men and 394 women under age 50, and 141 older people. After the selection, 303 men, given Nos. 151852–152154, and 288 women, given Nos. 62984–63271, are admitted to the camp. The other 388 people are killed in the gas chambers.

No. 152155 is given to a male prisoner and Nos. 63272–63273 to two female prisoners sent from Kattowitz.

SEPTEMBER 24

By order of the Camp Commander, three Polish political prisoners, Władysław Węgielek (No. 150152), Władysław Zatorski (No. 150156), and Józef Augustyniak (No. 150161), are locked in the bunker of Block 11. They are shot on September 28, 1943, following a selection in the bunkers.

APMO, D-AuI-3/2, Bunker Register, p. 44.

The Jewish prisoner Gert Lemmel (No. 130030) is captured while escaping and locked in the bunker of Block 11. He is shot on September 28, 1943, following a selection carried out in the bunkers.

Ibid.

Nos. 152156–152247 are given to 92 male prisoners and Nos. 63274–63293 to 20 female prisoners sent in a group transport.

15 prisoners who have been transferred to Auschwitz from Buchenwald get Nos. 152248–152262.

Nos. 152263–152380 are given to 118 male prisoners and Nos. 63294–63380 to 87 female prisoners sent in a group transport.

22 prisoners sent from Kattowitz receive Nos. 152381–152402.

SEPTEMBER 25

Three male Gypsies, given Nos. Z-8747–Z-8749, and one female Gypsy, given No. Z-9473, are sent in a group transport.

The Czech prisoner Josef Vajdlich (No. 131258) escapes from the Buna A.C.

APMO, D-AuI-1/1a, p. 271, Telegrams; IZ-8/Gestapo Lodz/3a/88/599; Mat.RO, vol. IV, p. 294.

The German prisoner Otto Küsel (No. 2), who escaped from the camp on December 29, 1942, and hid in Warsaw, is transferred from a Warsaw prison. He is locked in the bunker of Block 11 and is released from the bunker into the camp on November 23, 1943.

APMO, D-AuI-3/2, Bunker Register, p. 45; Mat.RO, vol. I, p. 40.

Nos. 63381–63386 are given to six female prisoners sent in a group transport.

Commandant Höss orders the SS to inform the prisoners that on September 28 they must not eat any kind of food found on the ground, as rat poison is being set out on the entire grounds of the camp and the surrounding area.*

APMO, Dpr.-Hd/12, p. 137, Garrison Order 42/43.

SEPTEMBER 26

88 male prisoners given Nos. 152403–152490 and 13 female prisoners given Nos. 63387–63399 have been sent to the camp by the Lodz Gestapo.

In the Commandant's response to a directive from Head of Office D-II Maurer concerning a transfer of Jewish prisoners to the Warsaw concentration camp, he states that an escort squad of at least 150 men, including 50 SS men armed with machine pistols, and a suitable commanding officer are necessary. This is because the transport will travel through areas made insecure by outlaw bands,** necessitating increased security measures. Concerning the dispatch of the escort squad,† he will provide the authorization as soon as the transport date is set.††

APMO, D-AuI-3a/359, Labor Deployment.

No. 63400 is given to a girl born to a woman in the women's camp in Birkenau who was sent to the camp by Mobile Commando 9 from Vitebsk.

SEPTEMBER 27

No. 152491 is given to a prisoner sent to the camp on September 24, 1943, by Mobile Commando 9.

The Czech prisoner Josef Vajdlich (No. 131258), who escaped on September 25, is captured, delivered to the camp, and locked in the bunker of Block 11. Following a selection carried out in the bunkers, he is shot on September 28, 1943.

APMO, D-AuI-3/2, Bunker Register, p. 48.

The Polish prisoner Mieczysław Dziób (No. 64258), born May 22, 1922, who escaped from the camp on October 16, 1942, is captured and brought back to the camp. He is locked in the bunker of Block 11 and is shot the next day, following a selection carried out in the bunkers.

Ibid.

Nos. 152492–152594 are given to 103 male prisoners and Nos. 63401–63446 to 46 female prisoners sent in a group transport.

---

*This order shows that the Commandant is quite familiar with the prisoners' condition, which compels them to gather up leftovers from dog kennels, pigpens, and garbage pails.
**What he means is partisan units.
†It must be provided by the Commandant of the camp to which the shipment is sent.
††Compare the entries for October 7 and 8, 1943.

Five Gypsies sent in a group transport get Nos. Z-8750–Z-8754.

SEPTEMBER 28

A selection is carried out in the bunkers of Block 11.* 18 prisoners are selected who were incarcerated by order of the Political Department or who were captured while escaping or are suspected of planning an escape. Among the prisoners selected are Gypsies, Czechs, Poles, and Jews: the Gypsies Wenzel Čarmen (No. 39780), Edward Laubinger (No. Z-5147), Artur Lafrens (No. Z-5156); the Jews Moritz Dalicz (No. 100621) and Gert Lemmel (No. 130030); the Poles Władysław Węgielek (No. 150152), Władysław Zatorski (No. 150156), and Józef Augustyniak (No. 150161); the Czech Josef Vajdlich (No. 131258); the Jew Julius Kantorowitcz (No. 151642); the Pole Mieszsław Dziób (No. 64258), the Jews Scheja Mondry (No. 76426), Wolf Kaufman (No. 79792), and Rafael Goldbruch (No. 83148); the Poles Władysław Prokop (No. 122462), Aleks Jaworzek (No. 122866), Paweł Kociuk (No. 122872), and Edward Krzek (No. 126811).)** They are shot the same day at the execution wall in the courtyard of Block 11.

Ibid., pp. 28, 39, 44, 48, 49.

600 Jewish prisoners are transferred from Auschwitz to Mauthausen.

APMO, Mat.RO, vol. VII, p. 474.

30 male prisoners, given Nos. 152595–152624, and 15 female prisoners, given Nos. 63447–63461, arrive from Kattowitz.

24 male prisoners, given Nos. 152625–152648, and a female prisoner, given No. 63462, have been sent from Kraków.

Five prisoners sent from Lemberg receive Nos. 152649–152653.

SEPTEMBER 29

Friedrich Krupp AG in Auschwitz completes the dismantling of equipment for fuse production. Weichsel-Union will continue their production in the same workshops. In the end, only six skilled workers are employed in dismantling work.

APMO, D-AuI-3a/370/5, p. 334a, Monthly Labor Deployment List.

12 prisoners delivered in a group transport are given Nos. 152654–152665.

Nine female prisoners sent from Kattowitz are given Nos. 63463–63471.

*This is the third selection in the bunker carried out during September. Most probably it is in the context of the fact that the Political Department has come upon illegal organizations of the resistance movement in the camp, and further arrests are expected among the prisoners.
**The 10 last-mentioned prisoners were locked in the bunkers on the day prior to the execution. The Poles, identified with Nos. 150152, 150156, and 150161, who had been delivered to Auschwitz from Radom on September 14, 1943, by order of the Sipo and SD were probably sent to the camp for the execution of their death sentences.

Nos. 63472–63478 are given to seven girls born in the women's camp in Birkenau.

The Director of the Political Department sends a prisoner transport vehicle to pick up 25 Jews killed in Środula near Sosnowitz, where there was a ghetto from March 1943 to August 1943.*

APMO, Dpr.-Hd/12, p. 57, Exhibit 19.

Four Gypsies are given Nos. Z-8755–Z-8758.

SEPTEMBER 30

Weichsel-Union takes over from the Commandant's Office a work-hall previously leased by Friedrich Krupp AG, and from the latter also takes over some machinery and equipment. Weichsel-Union starts up the assembly of their own machines and the manufacture of fuses.

APMO, Maurer Trial, vol. 8, pp. 115–126.

No. 152666 is given to a prisoner sent from Kattowitz.

53 female prisoners sent in a group transport are given Nos. 63479–63531.

Nos. Z-8759–Z-8761 are given to three male Gypsies and Nos. Z-9474–Z-9477 to four female Gypsies who have been sent in a group transport.

698 prisoners, including 86 skilled workers, are employed** in the factories of Eintrachthütte in Schwientochlowitz.

APMO, D-AuI-370/5, p. 339a, Monthly Labor Deployment List.

423 prisoners, including eight skilled workers, are employed in the Janina mine in Libiąż.

Ibid., pp. 350, 350a.

Commandant Höss informs the RSHA and other agencies that the Polish political prisoner Mieczysław Dziób (No. 64258) who escaped October 16, 1942, was captured and again delivered to the camp on September 17, 1943. Höss withholds further information about the prisoner's fate. Mieczysław Dziób was locked in the bunker of Block 11 on September 27 and is shot the next day. This is evidence of the arbitrariness of the camp authorities and their concealment of their high-handed actions.

APMO, IZ-8/Gestapo Lodz/2/88/94; D-AuI-3/2, Bunker Register, p. 48.

SEPTEMBER 1–30

1,871 women in the Auschwitz-Birkenau women's camp who are included in the camp registers have died; 1,181 were killed with gas.

APMO, Mat.RO, vol. VII, p. 485.

---

*Following the liquidation of the ghetto in August, 1,000 Jews who were left behind to complete work in the Braun enterprise and clean up the ghetto were quartered in several houses in Środula. In this camp there are approximately 1,600 people, of whom 1,000 are there legally (Szternfinkiel, *Jews of Sosnowitz*, p. 45).
**The daily wage for one skilled worker, according to the demand for payment, is 6 RM; the daily wage for an unskilled worker was 4 RM (ibid., p. 339).

Prisoners of the Buna A.C. auxiliary camp did 33,904 days of work for the I. G. Farben companies at 4 RM/day, 3,180 half days at 2 RM/half day, 105,292 workdays at 3 RM/day, and 11,543 half days at 1.50 RM/half day. The management of Auschwitz issues a demand for payment* totaling 475,166.50 RM for the prisoners' labor.

APMO, D-AuI-3a/370/5, p. 331, Monthly Labor Deployment List.

In the camp expansion, prisoners of Auschwitz-Birkenau have provided labor as follows for the Central Construction Administration, the largest user of prisoner labor: 33,892 days of skilled-worker days at 4 RM, 1,433 half days at 2 RM, 214,709 unskilled-worker days at 3 RM, and 11,461 half days at 1.50 RM. The demand for payment issued by the Auschwitz management totals 799,752.50 RM.

Ibid., p. 335, Monthly Labor Deployment List. In *Labor Deployment*, Franciszek Piper discusses in detail the deployment of the prisoners' labor and the resulting profits.

OCTOBER 1

Weichsel-Union employs 237 male prisoners, including 235 skilled workers, and 16 female prisoners.

APMO, D-AuI-3a/370/6, pp. 369a, 370a, Monthly Labor Deployment List.

Nos. 152667–152679 are given to 13 Jewish prisoners who were selected on September 30, 1943, from the forty-third RSHA East-transport from Berlin, which included 81 males and females. The other 68 people are killed in the gas chambers.

APMO, D-RF-3/121/15, pp. 41–46, Gestapo Berlin, Auschwitz Transports.

Nos. 152680–152731 are given to 52 male prisoners and Nos. 63532–63552 to 21 female prisoners sent in a group transport.

Nos. 152732–153006 are given to 275 male prisoners and Nos. 63553–63603 to 51 female prisoners sent from Kraków by the Sipo and SD.

Nos. 153018–153107 are given to 90 male prisoners and Nos. 63604–63675 to 72 female prisoners sent in a group transport.

No. 153108 is given to a female prisoner sent from Kattowitz.

The Commander of the SS Guard Stormtroopers orders that for the duration of an air raid, the search for escaped prisoners is to cease until the all-clear signal is given.

APMO, Dpr.-Hd/12, Exhibit 80, Stormtrooper Order 149/43.

241 prisoners who are to be used in the construction of a planned auxiliary camp in Brünn are taken to the Auschwitz train station and loaded into five closed freight cars. During the trip, a police squad from Brünn sent to fetch the prisoners provides the escort.

APMO, Dpr.-ZOd/63, p. 49; D-Hyg. Inst./33, Folder 20a, p. 626, Coll. SS Hygiene Institute; Mat.RO, vol. VII, p. 453.

The occupancy level of the women's camp is 32,066, of which 6,288 women are not able-bodied. Of the 25,778 able-bodied women,

APMO, D-AuI-3a/370/6, p. 377, Monthly Labor Deployment List.

*The demand for payment is issued at the end of each month on the basis of the monthly labor deployment list to all enterprises, factories, etc., which purchase prisoner labor from the Commandant's Office of Auschwitz. Of course, the prisoners receive no wage for their work.

10,520 are deployed on this day; of this number, 2,743 women work in the camp; 2,673 in agriculture; 787 for the Central Construction Office; eight work permanently for the Deutsche Erd- und Steinwerke (DEST; German Earth- and Stoneworks) at Auschwitz; 286 prisoners for DAW; 24 prisoners in German food factories; 3,321 in various offices of the SS; 200 prisoners in private enterprises and households of SS members; and 16 prisoners in arms production for Weichsel-Union. In addition, 395 female prisoners for experimental purposes and the 67 female prisoner orderlies are still at the experimental station of Professor Dr. Clauberg and are likewise counted as working prisoners. Of the able-bodied female prisoners, 15,258 are without employment.*

The Jewish prisoner Heinz Grünfeld, born in Berlin on March 25, 1907, who was sent to Auschwitz by the RSHA on January 13, 1943, escapes from the camp during the morning.**

APMO, IZ-8/Gestapo Lodz/3a/88/501.

OCTOBER 2

22 prisoners are put in the Penal Company in Birkenau.

APMO, D-AuI-3, p. 7, Penal Company Register.

No. Z-9478 is given to a female Gypsy.

Commandant Höss orders that the prisoners should work from 6:00 A.M. to 5:00 P.M., with a half-hour break.

APMO, D-AuI, Garrison Order 44/43.

17 prisoners sent from Kattowitz receive Nos. 153109–153125.

Nos. 153126–153522 are given to 397 male prisoners and Nos. 63676–63758 to 83 female prisoners sent from the prison in Tarnów by the Sipo and SD for the Kraków District.

Nos. 153523–154391 are given to 869 male prisoners and Nos. 63759–63952 to 194 female prisoners sent to the camp from the prison in Radom by the Sipo and SD.

By order of the Political Department, the Jewish prisoner Moriz Schreiber (No. 123148), born in Zurich on November 25, 1901, is locked in the bunker of Block 11. He is shot on October 11, 1943, following a selection carried out in the bunkers.

OCTOBER 3

An SS Camp Doctor carries out a selection among the prisoners in Quarantine Camp B-IIa, during which he selects 139 prisoners. They are killed the same day in the gas chambers.

APMO, Dpr.-Hd/6, p. 4.

*The labor deployment is subject to constant fluctuations, for transports arrive daily, and every day several or several dozen female prisoners die; at a selection, often as many as several hundred die.
**Grünfeld is captured on February 24, 1944, and brought back to Auschwitz.

Nos. 154392–155121 are given to 730 male prisoners and Nos. 64085–64323 to 239 female prisoners sent from Lemberg by the Sipo and SD.

Nos. 155122–155863 are given to 742 male prisoners and Nos. 63953–64084 to 132 female prisoners sent by the Lublin Sipo and SD.

By order of the Roll Call Leader, David Pinkus (No. 135906), a Polish Jew born in Bendin on October 10, 1909, is locked in the bunker of Block 11. Following a selection carried out in the bunkers, he is shot on October 11, 1943.

APMO, D-AuI-3/2, Bunker Register, p. 50.

OCTOBER 4

This is the first workday of the 250 prisoners who have been transferred to the outside squad in Brünn for the completion of the interiors of the already constructed building of the Technical College of the SS and Police. The head of the squad is the former Roll Call Leader, SS Technical Sergeant Palitzsch. The prisoners work on the orders of the Brünn office of Branch C of the WVHA.

APMO, D-AuI-3a/370/6, p. 391a, Monthly Labor Deployment List. Emeryka Iwaszko writes in detail on the Brünn outside squad: "Podobóz Brünn" (Brünn Outside Squad), *Zeszyty Oświęcimskie* (Polish edition of *Hefte von Auschwitz*), no. 18 (1983): 223–244 (hereafter cited as ZO).

The Polish reeducation prisoner Jan Flak (No. EH-5893), born on May 10, 1922, is locked in the bunker of Block 11. Following a selection in the bunkers, he is shot on November 9, 1943.

APMO, D-AuI-3/2, Bunker Register, p. 50. [Jan Flak]

In Quarantine Camp B-IIa in Birkenau, SS guards shoot 10 prisoners who were delivered in the morning by the Lemberg Sipo and SD.

APMO, Dpr.-Hd/6, p. 52.

No. 64324 is given to a female prisoner sent from Kattowitz on October 2, 1943.

No. 64325 is given to a female prisoner sent from Oppeln.

Nos. 155868–155908 are given to 41 male and Nos. 64326–64351 to 26 female prisoners sent in a group transport.

11 boys born in the women's camp in Birkenau during the past months are entered in the register of the men's camp and are given Nos. 155909–155919. No. 155910 is given to Józef Gomez, born on April 18, 1943. According to the report by his mother, Anna Gomez, she hid the newborn with the aid of fellow prisoners. When the infant is discovered and the boy threatened with death, the mother pleads with Camp Commander Hössler, who permits her to keep the child.*

APMO, Depositions, vol. 6, pp. 917–919, Account of Former Prisoner Anna Gomez.

*Probably the permission by Hössler can be attributed to a permit of the WVHA, which results from the curtailment of "euthanasia" as well as from the fact that there are two family camps—for Gypsies and for Jews from Theresienstadt—in which children are born and housed.

In Professor Dr. Clauberg's experimental ward in Block 10 in the main camp are 67 female prisoner orderlies and 395 female prisoners for research purposes.

APMO, D-AuI-3a/370/6, p. 377, Monthly Labor Deployment List.

OCTOBER 5

The occupancy level at the experimental station of Professor Dr. Clauberg in Block 10 of the main camp decreases by four female prisoners. There are now 64 female prisoner orderlies and 394 female prisoners for research purposes.

Ibid.

Three boys born in the Gypsy camp get Nos. Z-8767–Z-8769.

APMO, D-AuII-3/1/2, pp. 259ff., Register of Male Gypsies.

Six girls born in the Gypsy camp receive Nos. Z-9480–Z-9485.

APMO, D-AuII-3/2/5, p. 611, Register of Female Gypsies.

100 prisoners are assigned to the Penal Company "until further notice."

APMO, D-AuI-3/1, pp. 7–9, Penal Company Register.

Nos. 153007–153017 are given to 11 male prisoners and Nos. 64352–64359 to seven female prisoners sent in a group transport.

Nos. 155920–156724 are given to 805 male prisoners and Nos. 64360–64552, 64554, 64555, 64557–64566, 64569–64571, and 64573–64608 to 244 female prisoners sent to the camp from Pawiak Prison in Warsaw by the Sipo and SD. Among those transferred with this transport are the prominent author Zofia Kossak-Szczucka (No. 64491), who is registered under the alias Zofia Śliwińska, and the radiologist and head of the radiology laboratory in the Polish Hospital in Warsaw, Dr. Maria Werkenthin (No. 64511). Maria Werkenthin is shot dead near the camp fence on January 22, 1944.

APMO, D-RO/10, List of Polish Women Who Died in Auschwitz.

The Russian political prisoner Vasyl Boyan (No. 154563), born on February 11, 1927, is captured while attempting to escape and is locked in the bunker of Block 11. Following a selection in the bunkers he is shot on October 11, 1943.

APMO, D-AuI-3/2, Bunker Register, p. 50.

By order of the Political Department, nine Polish prisoners, Henryk Landau (No. 44212), Izaak Ostrzega (No. 27596), Kadysz Alpern (No. 89846), Ignac Latacz (No. 69039), Hersz Kanarek (No. 79780), Naftali Kanarek (No. 79782), Josek Toborek (No. 79931), Hersz Brona (No. 82084), and Herman Braunstein (No. 105182), who was born in Budapest, are locked in the bunkers of Block 11. Landau, Ostrzega, and Alpern are shot on October 11, 1943; the others are shot on November 9, 1943.

Ibid.

By order of the Political Department, four Polish prisoners who were sent to the camp by the Lodz Gestapo on May 25, 1943, are locked in the bunkers of Block 11: Jan Kupczyk (No. 122917),

Ibid., p. 51

Stanisław Kordanowski (No. 122920), Mieczysław Lorentowicz (No. 122923), and Edward Zerkiewicz (No. 122930). They are shot on November 9, 1943, following a selection carried out in the bunkers.

By order of the Political Department, the following prisoners are delivered to the bunker of Block 11: the German political prisoner Karl Götz (No. 71310), who is released from the bunker into the camp on November 2, 1943; the Jew Julian Samuel (No. 107056), who is shot on October 11; the Polish political prisoner Franciszek Dziedzic (No. 119090), who is shot on November 9; the Austrian political prisoner Franz Kefmar (No. 20158) and the German political prisoner Josef Wiesinger (No. 39355), both of whom are released from the bunker into the camp on October 11; and the Polish Jew Joachim Lebenbaum, who is shot on October 11.

Ibid.

By order of the Camp Commander, two Russian political prisoners, Vasili Ostapenko (No. 53813) and Jakov Parfeniuk (No. 79569), are locked in the bunker of Block 11. They are shot on October 11, 1943, following a selection carried out in the bunkers.

Ibid.

OCTOBER 6

By order of the Political Department, the Jewish prisoner Mendel Pfenigstein (No. 77297), born in Richenfeld on June 29, 1918, is locked in the bunker of Block 11. He is shot on October 11, 1943, following a selection in the bunkers.

Ibid.

The Commander of the SS Guard Stormtroopers again orders the officers on duty to report immediately whether dogs are used in search operations for escaped prisoners, and if so, with what success.

APMO, D-AuI, Stormtrooper Order 152/43.

OCTOBER 7

1,260 Jewish children and their 53 care givers are transferred from Theresienstadt in an RSHA transport. They are killed the same day in the gas chambers.*

APMO, D-RF-3/93, Transport Dn/a; Adler's *Theresienstadt 1941–1945* contains a list with the names of the care givers, pp. 54, 151.

1,151 Jewish prisoners from Auschwitz are transferred to the Warsaw concentration camp.**

APMO, Mat.RO, vol. VII, p. 474.

Nos. 155864–155867 are given to four male prisoners and No. 64609 to a female prisoner sent from Kattowitz.

Two Jewish prisoners get Nos. 156725 and 156726.

---

*The children are from the ghetto in Białystok. Their parents were shot during the uprising in the ghetto August 16–20, 1943. On August 24, 1943, the authorities initially assigned 1,260 children from Białystok to the Theresienstadt ghetto.
**Compare the entry for September 26, 1943. The numerical strength of the escort squad is not known.

On the ramp in Birkenau new arrivals are separated by sex.

Nos. Z-8762–Z-8766 go to five male Gypsies and No. Z-9479 to a female Gypsy who was transferred from Bochum.

OCTOBER 8

1,032 Jewish prisoners are transferred from Auschwitz to Warsaw.   Ibid.

15 prisoners delivered in a group transport are given Nos. 156727–156741.

No. 156742 is given to a Jewish prisoner.

An SS Camp Doctor carries out a selection in the barracks of the prisoners' infirmary in Women's Camp B-Ia in Birkenau, during which he selects 156 female prisoners. They are killed in the gas chambers that same day. Afterward, the number of ill female prisoners is 6,261.   APMO, D-AuI-3a/370/6, p. 377, Monthly Labor Deployment List.

On the eve of the Jewish holiday Yom Kippur, SS Camp Doctors carry out a selection in Camps B-IId and B-IIf, the men's infirmary in Birkenau, during which they select several thousand Jewish prisoners. They are killed in the gas chambers the same day.   Alfred Fiderkiewicz, *Brzezinka: Wspomnienia z obozu* (Birkenau: Memories from the Concentration Camp), p. 77.

Nos. 156743–156913 are given to 171 male prisoners and Nos. 64610–64706 to 97 female prisoners sent in a group transport.

People on their way to the gas chambers who have been condemned to immediate death at the selection.

Nos. 156914–156920 are given to seven prisoners from Maribor sent to the camp by the Sipo and SD.

SS Private First Class Wilhelm Reichel of the guard company of the Neu-Dachs A.C. receives from the Commandant of the SS Guard Stormtroopers a commendation for shooting two prisoners during their escape attempt from the auxiliary camp on September 21, 1943.

APMO, D-AuI, Garrison Order 45/43.

By order of the Political Department, the German PSV prisoner Bernhart Schmitt (No. 113791), born in Gevelsberg on July 20, 1908, is locked in the bunker of Block 11. He is shot on October 11, 1943, following a selection carried out in the bunkers.

APMO, D-AuI-3/2, Bunker Register, p. 51.

OCTOBER 9

19 prisoners sent in a group transport get Nos. 156921–156939.

Four female prisoners transferred from Zichenau get Nos. 64707–64710.

OCTOBER 10

1,000 Jewish men, women, and children from the Drancy camp arrive in the sixtieth RSHA transport from France. After the selection, 340 men, given Nos. 156940–157279, and 169 women, given Nos. 64711–64879, are admitted to the camp. The other 491 deportees are killed in the gas chambers.

270 Russian prisoners sent to the camp by Mobile Sipo and SD Commando C are transferred from Vitebsk and brought to Quarantine Camp B-IIa in Birkenau.

APMO, Dpr.-Hd/6, p. 5.

An SS Camp Doctor carries out a selection in Quarantine Camp B-IIa, during which he selects 327 prisoners. Among them are the 270 Russian prisoners from Vitebsk.* The prisoners selected are killed the same day in the gas chambers.

APMO, Dpr.-Hd/6, pp. 4, 5.

OCTOBER 11

Two female prisoners sent from Kattowitz get Nos. 64880 and 64881.

32 female prisoners from Vitebsk assigned to the camp by Mobile Division C are given Nos. 64884–64915.

Nos. 157280–157300 are given to 21 male prisoners and Nos. 64916–64940 to 25 female prisoners sent in a group transport.

By order of the Political Department, the Polish political prisoner Józef Bartusiak (No. 87104), born on October 8, 1922, is locked in the bunker of Block 11. He is shot on November 9, 1943, following a selection in the bunkers.

APMO, D-AuI-3/2, Bunker Register, p. 52.

A selection is carried out in the bunkers of Block 11. 54 prisoners are selected who have been locked in there by order of the Political Department, the Camp Commander, or the Roll Call Leader. That same day the selected prisoners are shot in front of the execution wall in the courtyard of Block 11. Among them is a group of important Polish military men, politicians, figures from public life, and members of the conspiratorial Union of Military Combat Groups in the camp. They were arrested in the main camp, in Birkenau, and in the Buna A.C. and locked in the bunker of Block 11 between September 16 and 29, 1943, accused of plotting against the SS in the camp, and were tortured during the investigation conducted by the Political Department. They include Major Kazimierz Gilewicz (No. 71886), Tadeusz Lisowski (No. 329), First Lieutenant Teofil Dziama (No. 13578), Colonel Juliusz Gilewicz (No. 31033), Jan Chmielewski (No. 78221), Jerzy Skibiński (No. 114762), Wacław Skibiński (No. 114763), Rudolf Homa (No. 114675), Major Zygmunt Bończa (Bohdanowski) (No. 30959), First Lieutenant Kazimierz Stamirowski (No. 66786), Jan Mosdorf (No. 8230), Kazimierz Kowalczyk (No. 353), Colonel Mieczysław Dobrzański (No. 121408), Karol Karp (No. 626), Władysław Patrzałek (No. 3070), Michał Kołodziej (No. 4475), Zbigniew Koell-

Ibid., pp. 37–40, 42–51; Mat.RO, vol. I, pp. 49, 50; Dpr.-Hd/4, pp. 143, 168; Dpr.-ZOd/3, pp. 111, 189.

---

*These probably are partisans captured in White Russian territory.

In "Canada II," female prisoners—at times over 1,000—sort the baggage that has been taken from people on their arrival at Auschwitz.

ner (No. 9333), Henryk Kalinowski (No. 6395), Julian Drozda (No. 10935), Zbigniew Mossakowski (No. 135678), Hieronim Kurczewski (No. 18486), Józef Somper (No. 4118), Antoni Szczudlik (No. 11459), Wacław Szumański (No. 13540), Aleksander Szumielewicx (No. 21213), Maurycy Potocki (No. 31252), Józef Poklewski-Kozieł (No. 127776), Henryk Wacław Sokołowski (No. 13239), Kazimierz Szafrański (No. 3427), and Józef Woźniakowski (No. 52338).*

OCTOBER 12

Nos. 157301–157318 are given to 18 male prisoners and Nos. 64941–64949 to nine female prisoners sent from Kattowitz.

No. Z-9486 is given to a female Gypsy transferred from the German Reich.

OCTOBER 13

29 prisoners sent in a group transport get Nos. 157319–157344.

A male prisoner and 13 female prisoners who have been sent to the camp from the Kattowitz District are given No. 157345 and

*The names of the other prisoners shot on this day were noted when their delivery into the bunker was made.

Nos. 64951–64954, 64962, 64963, 64967, 64968, and 64970–64974.

No. 157346 is given to a prisoner who was transferred the previous day from Nuremberg.

Two Polish prisoners, Edward Łopatecki (No. 139123), born in Lemberg on July 6, 1925, and Wacław Matuszewski (No. 139164), born in Skierniewice on February 17, 1917, escape from the camp.

APMO, D-AuI-1/2, p. 286, Telegrams; IZ-8/Gestapo Lodz/3a/88/508; Mat.RO, vol. IV, p. 294.

Nos. 64950, 64955–64961, 64964–64966, and 64969 are given to 12 female prisoners sent from Oppeln.

A Russian female prisoner, Anna Yurchenko, born on May 1, 1922, who was sent to the camp in a group transport on July 31, 1943, escapes from the Budy A.C.

APMO, D-AuI-1/2, p. 288, Telegrams; IZ-10/Kripo Sieradz/1/90/289.

By order of the Political Department, the Polish prisoner Salomon Zilbertrest (No. 128243), born in Warsaw on May 5, 1908, is locked in the bunker of Block 11. He is shot on November 9, 1943, following a selection carried out in the bunkers.

APMO, D-AuI-3/2, Bunker Register, p. 52.

No. Z-8770 is given to a Gypsy brought to the camp.

OCTOBER 14

52 prisoners are assigned to the Penal Company in Birkenau "until recalled."

APMO, D-AuI-3/1, pp. 9ff., Penal Company Register.

Nos. 157347–157382 are given to 36 prisoners sent in a group transport.

Nos. Z-8771–Z-8774 are given to four Gypsies who arrive in a group transport.

Nos. 64975–64982 are given to eight female prisoners sent from the Kattowitz District.

Two political prisoners, the Poles Julian Kalasiński (No. 156230), born in Warsaw on February 15, 1890, and Antoni Szczepiński (No. 156698), born in Warsaw on August 26, 1925, are locked in the bunkers of Block 11 by order of the Political Department. Following a selection carried out in the bunkers, they are shot on November 9, 1943.

APMO, D-AuI-3/2, Bunker Register, p. 52.

OCTOBER 15

The technical personnel of Friedrich Krupp AG leave the camp and go to the Bertha plant in Breslau to start production there.

APMO, Maurer Trial, vol. 8a, p. 123.

16 prisoners are sent to the Penal Company "until recalled."

APMO, D-AuI-3/1, pp. 10ff., Penal Company Register.

Nos. 157383–157550 are given to 168 male prisoners and Nos. 64983–65108 to 126 female prisoners sent in a group transport.

Several hundred Jewish men and women from the labor camp in Posen are transferred in an RSHA transport. After the selection, 16 men, given Nos. 157551–157566, and 22 women, given Nos. 65109–65130, are admitted to the camp. The other people are killed in the gas chambers.

Nos. Z-9487 is given to a female Gypsy.

Four girls born in the Gypsy camp get Nos. Z-9488–Z-9491.

APMO, D-AuII-3/2/5, p. 163, Register of Female Gypsies.

Five boys born in the Gypsy camp get Nos. Z-8775–Z-8779.

APMO, D-AuII-3/1/2, p. 260, Register of Male Gypsies.

300 prisoners are transferred from Auschwitz to a camp in Wuppertal.

APMO, Mat.RO, vol. VII, p. 474.

300 prisoners—Czechs, Poles, and Russians—are transferred from Auschwitz to Buchenwald.

Ibid., vol. VII, p. 453.

Two female Gypsies get Nos. Z-9492 and Z-9493.

Ibid., vol. IV, p. 293.

The Polish prisoner Mieczysław Rzesza (No. 129889) escapes from the camp.

APMO, D-AuI-3/2, Bunker Register, pp. 52ff.

The Polish political prisoners Stefan Demski (No. 114659), Mieczsław Pawłowski (No. 9488), Stanisław Muszalski (No. 156338), and Stefan Polkowski (No. 156404), and the Russian political prisoner Michael Skiba (No. 127824) are locked in the bunkers of Block 11 by order of the Political Department. Following a selection in the bunkers, they are shot on November 9, 1943.

OCTOBER 16

223 male prisoners, including 305 skilled workers, and 35 female prisoners of Auschwitz are employed in the factory of the Weichsel-Union-Metallwerke.

APMO, D-AuI-3a/370/6, pp. 369a, 370a, Monthly Labor Deployment List.

23 prisoners sent in a group transport are given Nos. 157567–157589.

No. 64882 is given to a female prisoner sent from Kattowitz.

No. 64883 is given to a female prisoner sent from Zichenau.

Two Polish prisoners, Stefan Skowron (No. 125371) and Kazimierz Fita (No. 126816), escape from the Buna A.C. in the evening.

APMO, D-AuI-1/2, p. 303, Telegrams; IZ-8/Gestapo Lodz/3a/88/506; IZ-10/Gestapo Sieradz/1, p. 289; Mat.RO, vol. IV, p. 293.

Nos. Z-9494–Z-9496 are given to three female Gypsies.

APMO, D-AuI-3/2, Bunker Register, p. 53. [Gypsies]

By order of the Political Department, the Polish political prisoners Józef Gołembiowski (No. 115524), Antoni Węgrzyniak (No. 123000), Aleksander Lewiński (No. 156286), and Władysław Skoroszewski (No. 156454), as well as the Jewish prisoners Hersz Kinstler (No. 18800), Werner Prager (No. 127064), Adolf Ekman (No. 68413), Bernard Rosenberg (No. 70161), and Herszko Kranicki (No. 128104) are locked in the bunkers of Block 11. They are shot on November 9, 1943, following a selection in the bunkers.

OCTOBER 17

Six female prisoners sent from Kattowitz are given Nos. 65131–65136.

189 female prisoners transferred from Mauthausen get Nos. 65137–65325. They are the Russians from Dnepropetrovsk, who are moved to Auschwitz after a few days' stay in Mauthausen.

OCTOBER 18

Two female prisoners sent from Breslau are given the free Nos. 64553 and 64556.

A female prisoner is given the free No. 64567.

Free Nos. 64568 and 64572 are given to two female prisoners sent from Oppeln.

No. 65326 is given to a girl born to a woman who was transferred from Vitebsk to the women's camp in Birkenau on October 10, 1943.

Approximately 1,000 Jewish men and women from a labor camp in Zawiercie are transferred in an RSHA transport. Following the selection, 249 men, given No. 157590–157838, and 152 women, given Nos. 65327–65478, are admitted to the camp. The other 600 deportees are killed in the gas chambers.

Nos. 157839–157883 are given to 45 male prisoners and Nos. 65479–65490 to 12 female prisoners sent in a group transport.

Two prisoners who were transferred from Lublin on October 3 get Nos. 157884 and 157885.

A prisoner transferred from Dresden is given No. 157886.

Nos. Z-8780–Z-8781 are given to two male Gypsies and Nos. Z-9497 and Z-9498 to two female Gypsies.

1,500 prisoners are transferred from Auschwitz to Buchenwald.

APMO, Mat.RO, vol. VII, p. 474.

Following denunciations by a Capo in the Neu-Dachs auxiliary camp, 127 prisoners are arrested and locked in the bunkers of Block 11. They have secretly dug a tunnel leading from one of the barracks into the nearby forest, through which they planned to escape from the camp. Delivered to the bunker are Franz Slosarzyk (No. 7301), Ottokar Ruzička (No. 84578), Henryk Fonfara (No. 123229), Władysław Slońka (No. 123924), Franc Fok (No. 123925), Venzel Hajner (No. 123940), Władysław Vidlak (No. 123982), Franz Kurka (No. 58669), Marian Pajak (No. 119724), Edward Dulka (No. 120271), Jan Janeczek (No. 122414), Franciszek Reperowski (No. 122435), Julian Bak (No. 122595), Stefan Stawiarski (No. 123808), Stanisław Brylewski (No. 123867), Arnold Altof (No. 123900), Franz Hostusa (No. 123919), Miroslav Kubalek (No. 123921), Rudolf Rossypalek (No. 123923), Franz Bilek (No. 123930), Jan Dawid (No. 123936), Jaroslav Matousek (No. 123989), Jaroslav Starec (No. 123993), Marian Bińkowski (No. 124040), Jan Pieron (No. 125605), Jan Sokolnicki (No. 130358), and Dawid Trzemski (No. 143769). The five first-mentioned prisoners are released from the bunker on October 23 and 27 and assigned to the Penal Company. Following the investigation, the next 19 prisoners are condemned to death by hanging. The last-mentioned, Dawid Trzemski, is released from the bunker into the camp on November 23, 1943.

APMO, D-AuI-3/2, Bunker Register, p. 56; Mat.RO, vol. I, pp. 46–47; *Memoirs*, vol. 30, pp. 1–36, Antoni Siciński, "Czapki zjąć" (Hats Off).

The Polish political prisoner Stanisław Karcz (No. 152281) is locked in the bunker of Block 11 by order of the Political Department. He is shot on November 9, 1943, following a selection carried out in the bunkers.

APMO, D-AuI-3/2, Bunker Register, p. 54.

OCTOBER 19

Nos. Z-8782–Z-8833 are given to 52 Gypsies, men and boys, and Nos. Z-9499–Z-9538 to 40 Gypsies, women and girls, who have been transferred from Czechoslovakia.

The German prisoner Otto Smigulla (No. 125845) escapes from the camp.

APMO, Mat.RO, vol. IV, p. 294.

The Polish prisoner Karol Steczysńki (No. 131756), born on September 21, 1920, escapes from the Buna A.C.

APMO, D-AuI-1/2, p. 390, Telegrams; IZ-8/Gestapo Lodz/3a/88/510; Mat.RO, vol. IV, p. 294.

A prisoner from Prague is given No. 157887.

By order of the Political Department, eight prisoners under suspicion of cooperating in an escape attempt are locked in the bunker of Block 11. They are Josef Veskrna (No. 84958) and Mendel Srebrnik (No. 87638), who are released from the bunker on October 23 and assigned to the Penal Company; and Jan Kosmala (No. 115758), Edward Chmielewski (No. 117889), Jakob Bleier (No. 118251), Henryk Masiarek (No. 119156), Leon Rupala (No. 119558), and Józef Gladycz (No. 119572), who are condemned to death by hanging.

APMO, D-AuI-3/2, Bunker Register, p. 54; Mat.RO, vol. I, pp. 46–47; Paul Heller, "Das Aussenlager Jaworzno" (Jaworzno Auxiliary Camp), in Adler et al., eds., *Auschwitz: Testimonies*, p. 170.

Head of Branch D Glücks instructs all the Camp Commandants regarding the disposition of unassigned property of deceased and released prisoners, as well as of all deceased Polish and Jewish prisoners, referring to the regulations of January 7, March 22, and July 23, 1943:

APMO, Dpr.-Hd/12, pp. 183ff., Exhibit 123.

1. Cash is to be transferred quarterly on the tenth of the month at the beginning of the quarter to Account 426 of Branch D at the Stadtsparkasse (municipal savings bank) Oranienburg.
2. Foreign currency, gold, gold teeth, silver, and jewels are to be sent in double packaging every six months, on October 1 and April 1, as consignments of valuables. The inner packaging may contain only a list of the contents and no notation of the sender, as it will be forwarded to the Reichsbank without being opened.
3. Other valuables such as watches and eyeglasses of every kind are to be sent, together with a list of the contents, as consignments of valuables.

The consignments mentioned under Points 2 and 3 are to be addressed to the WVHA Branch D, Concentration Camps, Chief of Administration, Oranienburg/b. Berlin.

At the instigation of the Political Department, the following prisoners are locked in the bunkers of Block 11: the Polish Jew Hersz Wasserlauf (No. 136410), who is released from the bunker into the camp on October 23, 1943; the French Jew Maurice Darteusel (No. 157010) and the Russian prisoner of war T. Chebikin (No. RKG-10607), both of whom are shot on November 9, 1943, following a selection in the bunkers.

APMO, D-AuI-3/2, Bunker Register, p. 56.

OCTOBER 20

20 prisoners are transferred from Auschwitz to Buchenwald.

APMO, Mat.RO, vol. VII, p. 474.

An SS Camp Doctor carries out a selection in Quarantine Camp B-IIa in Birkenau, during which he selects 293 prisoners. They are killed the same day in the gas chambers.

APMO, Dpr.-Hd/6, p. 4.

No. 65491 is given to a female prisoner sent from the Kattowitz District.

No. 65492 is given to Helena Płotnicka, a courier of the camp resistance movement who has also organized and implemented illegal deliveries of food to the prisoners. She is arrested on May 19, 1943, and locked in the bunker. Płotnicka is released from the bunker and transferred to the women's camp in Birkenau. She dies there on March 17, 1944.

APMO, D-RO/10, List of Polish Women Who Died in Auschwitz.

Nine prisoners are assigned to the Penal Company in Birkenau "until recalled."

APMO, D-AuI-3/1, p. 11, Penal Company Register.

By order of the Political Department, the following prisoners are locked in the bunkers of Block 11: the Czechs Franz Volonec (No.

APMO, D-AuI-3/2, Bunker Register, pp. 56ff.

117197) and Anton Posolda (No. 131301), both of whom are shot on November 9, 1943; the Polish political prisoner Jan Wolczyński (No. 21160), who dies on December 6, 1943—probably he is hanged with the group of prisoners from the Neu-Dachs A.C., possibly for involvement with the escape attempt; the Polish Jews Moses Lenczowski (No. 100778) and Georg Gutermann (No. 125977), both of whom are shot on November 9, 1943, following a selection in the bunker.

At the instigation of the Camp Commander, two prisoners are locked in the bunker of Block 11, the Polish Jew Icek Top (No. 83473) and the Polish political prisoner Mieczysław Pochwala (No. 108862). Both are shot on November 9, 1943.

Ibid.

OCTOBER 21

No. 157888 is given to a prisoner sent from Kattowitz.

1,007 Jews from the Westerbork camp arrive with an RSHA transport from Holland. In the transport are 87 children, 407 men and 306 women under age 50, as well as 207 older people. Following the selection, 347 men, given Nos. 157889–158235, and 170 women, given Nos. 65493–65662, are admitted to the camp. The other 490 deportees are killed in the gas chambers.

Nos. 158236–158313 are given to 78 male prisoners and Nos. 65663–65671 to nine female prisoners sent from Kattowitz.

The Russian prisoner Michail Vinogradov (No. 53824) escapes from the camp.

APMO, D-AuI-1/2, p. 313, Telegrams; IZ-10/Kripo Sieradz/2/166; Mat.RO, vol. V, p. 294.

OCTOBER 22

Five male Gypsies and two female Gypsies, transferred from Magdeburg, receive Nos. Z-8834–Z-8838 and Z-9539–Z-9540.

176 male and 15 female prisoners, sent in a group transport, are given Nos. 158314–158489 and 65672–65686.

298 male and 441 female prisoners, sent by the Mobile Sipo and SD Commando 9 from Vitebsk are given Nos. 158666–158963 and 65687–66127.

44 female prisoners sent in a group transport receive Nos. 66128–66171.

Polish prisoner Józef Obrazowski (No. 139590) escapes from the camp.

APMO, Mat.RO, vol. IV, p. 293.

The occupancy level of the women's camp of Auschwitz-Birkenau, including the prisoners in the auxiliary camps, the headquarters building and the experimental station of Dr. Clauberg, is 33,649. After a selection made on this day, the number is decreased by

APMO, D-AuI-3a/370/6/377, Monthly Labor Deployment List; Reitlinger, *Final Solution*, p. 131.

1,260 female inmates, including 394 women from the prisoners' infirmary.* The selected prisoners are killed in the gas chambers the same day.

The Police Court-martial convenes in Block 11 to pass sentence of death on 76 men and 19 women previously transferred from the prison in Myslowitz. The new head of the Kattowitz Gestapo, SS Lieutenant Colonel Johannes Thümmler, probably already has taken over the chairmanship of the three-judge collegium.

APMO, Mat.RO, vol. IV, pp. 54–256, Court-martial—Death Sentences, List of Names.

By order of the Political Department, the following prisoners are locked in the bunker of Block 11: the French Jew Wolf Kurcweig (No. 65654), who is released into the camp the following day; the Pole Kazimierz Domanus (No. 55785) and the Czech Wladimir Bachurek (No. 63277), who are both released from the bunker into the camp on November 23, 1943; and the Jews Lenczner Sussman (No. 53968) and Judel Oliszewski (No. 98989), who are both shot on November 9, 1943, after a selection in the bunker.

APMO, D-AuI-3/2, Bunker Register, p. 57.

OCTOBER 23

Two female Gypsies receive Nos. Z-9541 and Z-9542.

At Professor Dr. Clauberg's experimental station in Block 10 of the main camp, the occupancy level is decreased by five women intended for experimental purposes; 67 prisoner orderlies and 389 prisoners for experimental purposes are now housed there.

APMO, D-AuI-3a/370/6/377, Monthly Labor Deployment List.

Russian prisoner Afanasi Mirharzodov (No. 58556), born July 21, 1913, is captured attempting to escape and locked in the bunker of Block 11. After a selection in the bunker, he is shot on November 9, 1943.

APMO, D-AuI-3/2, Bunker Register, p. 57.

A prisoner sent from Kattowitz receives No. 158490.

1,035 Jewish men, women, and children arrive with an RSHA transport from Rome. After the selection, 149 men and 47 women are admitted to the camp and receive Nos. 158491–158639 and 66172–66218. The remaining 839 people are killed in the gas chambers.

Centro di Dokumentazione Ebraica Contemporana di Milano (Center for Contemporary Jewish Documentation, Milan (hereafter cited as CDECM), *Ebrei in Italia: Deportazione, Resistenza* (Jews in Italy: Deportation, Resistance), Florence, 1974, p. 13.

A female prisoner sent from Oppeln the previous day receives No. 66219.

26 male and 64 female prisoners sent in a group transport, are given Nos. 158640–158665 and 66220–66283.

*On the following day, 32,389 female prisoners are accounted for; 6,210 of them are sick or incapable of working (APMO, D-AuI-3a/370/6/377).

Polish prisoner Boresław Ostrowski (No. 150128) escapes from the camp.

APMO, IZ-8/Gestapo Lodz/3a/88/513; Mat.RO, vol. IV, p. 293.

Two Jewish prisoners, Miklos Klein (No. 133311) and Hirz Kagan (No. 133467), escape from Neu-Dachs A.C.

APMO, D-AuI-1/2, p. 315, Telegrams; IZ-10/Gestapo Sieradz/1/292; Mat.RO, vol. IV, p. 293.

Prisoner Jan Kulpis (No. 155374), born December 20, 1918, in Novosibirsk, escapes in a transport en route from Auschwitz to Buchenwald.

APMO, IZ-10/Gestapo Sieradz/2/163; APMO Inquiry.

1,800 Polish Jews—men, women and children—arrive in an RSHA transport from Bergen-Belsen. They had received passports for departure to Latin American countries. Most of them paid a high price for these visas with the approval of the Gestapo in Warsaw's Hotel Polski, whence they were brought to the detention camp in Bergen-Belsen. These are the so-called exchange Jews. In Bergen-Belsen, Dr. Seidl, a representative of the RSHA, examined their documents and decided that the numerous members of the individual families were not related to one another. The only purpose of the passports with permission to depart was to protect their holders from extermination. They are ordered to prepare for departure to Bergau Camp near Dresden and informed that their baggage will be sent on to them. At the last moment, 70 Jews who had arrived in Bergen-Belsen are added to the transport. Not until they arrive at the unloading platform do they understand that they have been taken to Auschwitz, a place that is not unfamiliar to the Polish Jews. On the platform, men and women are separated from one another. The women are taken to Crematorium II and the men to Crematorium III. After an examination of travel documents and official announcement that a disinfection must first take place, the SS men lead the women to the undressing room. The order to undress causes unrest among the women. But the SS men begin to strip them of their rings and watches. Then, one woman, who realizes that she is in a hopeless situation, flings part of the clothes she has already taken off at the head of SS Staff Sergeant Schillinger, grabs his revolver and shoots him three times. She also shoots SS Sergeant Emmerich. The other women attack the SS men with their bare hands; they bite one SS man on the nose, they scratch the faces of others. The SS men call for reinforcements. After these have arrived, some of the women are shot, the rest are driven into the gas chambers and killed. SS Staff Sergeant Schillinger dies on the way to the hospital; SS Sergeant Emmerich recovers after a while but has a crippled leg.

APMO, Dpr.-Hd/1, p. 20; Dpr.-Hd/6, p. 28; D-RO/88, vol. 5a, p. 324. Manuscript of the account of escapee Jerzy Tabeau, who was registered in the camp under the name Wesołowski. The report was written at the end of 1943 and the beginning of 1944, sent to London, and published in the United States; Eberhard Kolb, *Bergen-Belsen: Vom "Aufenthaltslager" zum Konzentrationslager* (Bergen-Belsen: From "Transit" Camp to Concentration Camp), Hanover, 1962, p. 47.

OCTOBER 24

The occupancy level of Professor Dr. Clauberg's experimental station in Block 10 of the main camp is decreased by one: 388 female prisoners for experimental purposes and 67 prisoner orderlies are now housed there.

APMO, D-AuI-3a/370/6/377, Monthly Labor Deployment List.

Two boys born in the Gypsy camp in Birkenau receive Nos. Z-8839 and Z-8840.

APMO, D-AuII-3/1/2/, p. 262, Register of Male Gypsies.

Three girls born in the Gypsy camp in Birkenau receive Nos. Z-9543–Z-9545.

APMO, D-AuII-3/2/5, p. 615, Register of Female Gypsies.

In retaliation for the death of SS Staff Sergeant Schillinger the previous day, SS guards shoot machine guns at random in the Birkenau camp in the evening. 13 prisoners are killed, four are wounded severely, and 42 lightly.

APMO, Dpr.-Hd/6, pp. 28, 52.

OCTOBER 25

A female prisoner sent from Kattowitz receives No. 66284.

12 male and 17 female prisoners sent in a group transport are given Nos. 158965–158976 and 66285–66301.

Polish prisoner Izydor Żerdziński (No. 136608), born September 18, 1923, escapes from the camp.

APMO, D-AuI-1/Ia, p. 318, Telegrams; IZ-10/Gestapo Sieradz/1/290.

At the request of the Political Department, two prisoners, the Polish Jew Abraham Mondry (No. 76444), born May 15, 1925, and Feiwel Zaks (No. 81902), born May 19, 1924, are locked in the bunker of Block 11. They are shot on November 9, 1943, after a selection in the bunker.

APMO, D-AuI-3/2, Bunker Register, p. 58.

OCTOBER 26

Nine Gypsy men and 13 Gypsy women are sent from Stettin. The men receive Nos. Z-8841–Z-8849, the women, Nos. Z-9546–Z-9558.

48 prisoners sent in a group transport receive Nos. 158977–159024.

Five female prisoners sent from Zichenau receive Nos. 66302–66306.

Head of the WVHA Pohl writes a secret letter concerning increasing labor productivity to the following concentration camp Commandants:

APMO, IZ-13/89, Various Documents of the Third Reich, pp. 168–172.

1. Dachau—Lieutenant Colonel Weiter
2. Sachsenhausen—Lieutenant Colonel Kaindl
3. Buchenwald—Lieutenant Colonel Pister
4. Mauthausen—Lieutenant Colonel Ziereis
5. Flossenbürg—Lieutenant Colonel Kögel
6. Neuengamme—Major Pauly
7. Auschwitz—Lieutenant Colonel Höss
8. Gross-Rosen—Captain Hassebroek
9. Natzweiler—Captain Kramer
10. Stutthof—Major Hoppe
11. Ravensbrück—Captain Suhren
12. Lublin—Major Weiss

13. Hinzert—Lieutenant Colonel Sporrenbe
14. Riga—Major Sauer
15. Herzogenbusch—Major Grünewald
16. Bergen-Belsen—Captain Haas
17. Vaivara—Captain Aumeier
18. Kauen—Lieutenant Colonel Goecke
19. Warsaw—Captain Herber

Pohl states that, thanks to their activity and development in the course of the last two years, the concentration camps have become a significant factor in the German war effort. An armaments industry has been created out of nothing. Henceforth, it is imperative to take all care not only that previous performance be maintained but also increased. Commandants, SS Commanders and Camp and Garrison Doctors are to be concerned primarily with maintaining the health and performance capability of the prisoners. Not out of any false sentimentality but rather because their arms and legs are needed, and they must do their part so that the German people can achieve a great victory. The first goal is to decrease by one tenth the number of inmates unable to work because of illness. All those responsible must achieve this goal. Indispensable for this are:

1. Proper and appropriate nourishment
2. Proper and appropriate clothing
3. Utilization of all natural means to encourage health
4. Avoidance of every effort unnecessary for the performance of labor
5. Use of performance prizes

These points are treated in full by Pohl in three pages of instructions in which he even deals with how potatoes are to be stored, peeled, and prepared so that they are tasty and nourishing. In the closing section of the letter, Pohl orders every Commandant who receives this letter to present it immediately to the Administrative Director and the SS Garrison Doctor for strict compliance, for information and confirmation through a signature. Pohl emphasizes that he will personally supervise the execution of the orders transmitted in the letter.*

OCTOBER 27

A Gypsy man and a Gypsy woman are transferred in a group transport. The man is given No. Z-8850 and the woman, No. Z-9559.

*Four years of war, the losses suffered in Stalingrad, the stepped-up conscription into the Wehrmacht, and the shortage of labor prompt Pohl to write this letter to the Commandants. It does not change anything in the camp conditions, since no means for achieving the goals are provided; food rations are not increased and better clothing is not distributed. Only the roll calls are shortened. The behavior of the SS men trained in ruthlessness and horror cannot be changed with a single letter, and a secret one at that. The purpose of this letter is not to stop the extermination, direct or indirect. It simply leads to a more intensive exploitation of the prisoners' labor in hopes of victory.

21 prisoners transferred with a group transport receive Nos. 159025–159045.

10 prisoners released from the bunker of Block 11 are sent to the punishment company "until recalled."

APMO, D-AuI-3/1, p. 11, Penal Company Register.

Six female prisoners arrested in the Oderberg Operation are sent from the prison in Myslowitz and receive Nos. 66307–66312. One of them is Anna Olszowska, who receives No. 66311 and who dies in the camp on January 26, 1944. Her husband, Franciszek Olszowski, born January 26, 1907, who was first in the prison in Myslowitz and finally imprisoned in Block 11 of Auschwitz, where the Police Court-martial of the Kattowitz Gestapo imprisoned him and condemned him to death, is shot on November 29. Their children, Barbara Olszowska and Marian Olszowski, born in 1939 and 1942, spend the last year of the war in a children's camp in Potulitz.

APMO, Mat.RO, vol. IV, pp. 256–257; D-RO/10, List of Polish Women Who Died in Auschwitz.

Prisoner Izydor Żerdziński (No. 136608), who escaped from the camp on October 25, is captured while fleeing and sent to the bunker of Block 11. After a selection in the bunker, he is shot on November 9, 1943.

APMO, D-AuI-3/2, Bunker Register, p. 58.

OCTOBER 28

Two female prisoners sent from Kattowitz receive Nos. 66313 and 66314.

230 male and 55 female prisoners sent to the camp by the Sipo and SD from Lemberg receive Nos. 159046–159275 and 66315–66369.

29 prisoners sent in a group transport receive Nos. 159276–159304.

A prisoner sent from Bremen receives No. 158964.

348 Jews from the labor camp in Pabianice arrive in an RSHA transport. After the selection, 72 men are admitted to the camp and given Nos. 159305–159376. The remaining 276 deportees are killed in the gas chambers.

APMO, D-AuII-3/1, p. 15, Quarantine List.

OCTOBER 29

On instructions from the Roll Call Leader, the German Jew Fritz Meyer (No. 157561), born October 5, 1919, in Berlin, is locked in the bunker of Block 11. After a selection in the bunker, he is shot on November 9, 1943.

APMO, D-AuI-3/2, Bunker Register, p. 58.

By order of the Political Department, two prisoners are locked in the bunker of Block 11. They are the Polish Jew Dawid Boruchowicz (No. 127933), who is released from the bunker into the camp on November 23, 1943, and the Polish political prisoner Stanisław

Ibid.

Struzik (No. 119079), who is shot on November 9, 1943, after a selection in the bunker.

By order of the Camp Commander, the Greek Jew Salomon Chaciel (No. 114992), born December 12, 1921, in Salonika, is locked in the bunker of Block 11. After a selection in the bunker, he is shot on November 9, 1943.

Ibid.

At Professor Dr. Clauberg's experimental station in Block 10 of the main camp, the occupancy level is increased by one: 389 female prisoners for experimental purposes and 67 female prisoner orderlies are now housed there.

APMO, D-AuI-3a/370/6/377, Monthly Labor Deployment List.

164 male and 81 female prisoners sent in a group transport are given Nos. 159377–159540 and 66370–66450.

A female Gypsy sent in a group transport receives No. Z-9560.

OCTOBER 30

Five prisoners sent from Kattowitz receive Nos. 159541–159545.

1,000 Jewish men, women, and children arrive from the Drancy camp with the sixty-first RSHA transport from France. After the selection, 284 men are given Nos. 159546–159817 and 103 women receive Nos. 66451–66553, and are admitted to the camp. The remaining 613 people are killed in the gas chambers. The Jewish prisoners admitted to the camp are registered on October 30 and 31.

14 male Gypsies receive Nos. Z-8851–Z-8864 and nine female Gypsies receive Nos. Z-9561–Z-9569. They were sent from the Reich territory.

In Professor Dr. Clauberg's experimental station, the occupancy level is decreased by one: 388 women for experimental purposes and 67 prisoner orderlies are housed there.

APMO, D-AuI-3a/370/6/377, Monthly Labor Deployment List.

OCTOBER 31

In Professor Dr. Clauberg's experimental ward, the occupancy level is reduced by one: 387 women for experimental purposes and 67 prisoner orderlies are now housed there.

Ibid.

A girl born in the women's camp in Birkenau to a woman sent from Radom by the Sipo and SD receives No. 66554.

OCTOBER 1–31

2,274 female prisoners die in the women's camp of Auschwitz-Birkenau Concentration Camp; 1,545 are killed with gas.

APMO, Mat.RO, vol. VII, p. 485.

NOVEMBER 1

The occupancy level of the women's camp of Auschwitz-Birkenau is 32,943, including 6,718 women who are sick and incapable of working.

APMO, D-AuI-3a/370/7/435, Monthly Labor Deployment List.

The occupancy level of the men's camp of Auschwitz Concentration Camp, including all the auxiliary camps, is 54,630, including 7,830 who are sick and unable to work.

APMO, D-AuI-3a/370/7/424, Monthly Labor Deployment List.

The total occupancy of all the camps is 87,573 male and female prisoners.

On the recommendation of the Camp Commander, three prisoners are locked in the bunker of Block 11: two German prisoners, Karl Kritzan (No. 114028) and Nikolaus Sender (No. 114086), sent to the Penal Company on November 3, 1943; and the Czech Gypsy Vencel Holomek (No. Z-4738), born April 4, 1925, who is shot on November 9, 1943, after a selection in the bunker.

APMO, D-AuI-3/2, Bunker Register, pp. 58ff.

The Polish prisoner Andrzej Michalski (No. 153272) escapes from the camp. He is captured on November 9, 1943. After being sent back to the camp, he is sent to the Penal Company until recalled on April 2. He is transferred to Mauthausen.

APMO, D-AuI-1a, pp. 321, 323, Telegrams; IZ-10/Gestapo Sieradz/2/195; D-AuI-3/1, p. 17, Penal Company Register.

The Labor Deployment Department issues the Weichsel-Union-Metallwerke in Auschwitz demand for payment for prisoners' labor for the period October 1–October 31, 1943, of 35,781 RM; they calculate 8,236 skilled-worker days at 4 RM, 43 skilled-worker half days at 2 RM, 857 unskilled-worker days at 3 RM, and 120 unskilled-worker half days at 1.50 RM.

APMO, Dpr.-Hd/12, p. 147, Exhibit 99.

67 female prisoner orderlies and 387 prisoners for experimental purposes are housed at Professor Dr. Clauberg's experimental ward in Block 10 of the main camp.

The Labor Deployment Department issues a demand for payment to I. G. Farben for prisoners' labor for the period October 1–31, 1943, of 488,949 RM. They calculate 36,423 skilled-worker days at 4 RM, 3,855 skilled-worker half days at 2 RM, 105,254 unskilled-worker days at 3 RM, and 13,190 unskilled-worker half days at 1.50 RM.

Ibid., p. 149, Exhibit 100.

22 male and 18 female prisoners sent in a group transport are given Nos. 159830–159851 and 66555–66572.

NOVEMBER 2

By order of the Political Department, nine prisoners are locked in the bunker of Block 11. One of them is Józef Cyrankiewiecz (No. 62933), one of the leaders of the left-oriented Polish resistance

APMO, D-AuI-3/2, Bunker Register, p. 59.

movement in the camp and the international Auschwitz Combat Group.

Two prisoners sent from Kattowitz receive Nos. 159852 and 159853.

One Gypsy male receives No. Z-8865.

67 male and 16 female prisoners transferred from Brünn are given Nos. 159854–159920 and 66573–66588.

1,870 Jews from the labor camp in Szopienice arrive with an RSHA transport. After the selection, 463 men and 28 women are admitted to the camp and receive Nos. 159921–160383 and 66589–66616. The remaining 1,379 people are killed in the gas chambers.

APMO, D-AuII-3/1, p. 15, Quarantine List.

NOVEMBER 3

Three Russian prisoners escape from the camp. They are Jan Mitrochanov (No. 75198), Vasili Osipov (No. 124942) and Jan Komashenko (No. 151298).

APMO, IZ-10/Gestapo Sieradz/2/165/168/183; Mat.RO, vol. IV, p. 293.

338 female prisoners for research purposes and 55 female prisoner orderlies are housed in Professor Dr. Clauberg's experimental ward.

APMO, D-AuI-3a/370/7/435, Monthly Labor Deployment List.

1,203 Jews from the labor camp in Szopienice arrive with an RSHA transport. After the selection, 284 men and 23 women are admitted to the camp and given Nos. 160384–160667 and 66617–66639. The remaining 896 people are killed in the gas chambers.

In Men's Camp B-IId, a general delousing operation is carried out.

APMO, Dpr.-Hd/6, pp. 40ff.

NOVEMBER 4

Two prisoners of war, Vasili Zmailov (RKG-10428) and Vasili Tilikin (RKG-10422), escape from Camp B-IId in Birkenau.

APMO, Mat.RO, vol. IV, p. 293.

34 male and 19 female prisoners sent from Kattowitz are given Nos. 160668–160701 and 66640–66658.

NOVEMBER 5

1,000 Jews from Riga arrive in the camp with an RSHA transport. After the selection, 120 men and 30 women are admitted to the camp and given Nos. 160702–160821 and 66659–66688. The remaining 850 men and women are killed in the gas chambers.

APMO, D-AuII-3/1, p. 15, Quarantine List.

The occupancy level in Professor Dr. Clauberg's experimental ward changes; 56 prisoner orderlies and 387 prisoners for experimental purposes are now housed there.

APMO, D-AuI-3a/370/7/435, Monthly Labor Deployment List.

57 male and 10 female prisoners sent in a group transport are given Nos. 160822–160878 and 66689–66698.

Three female prisoners sent from Kattowitz receive Nos. 66699–66701.

4,237 Jewish men, women, and children from the Szebnie labor camp arrive in an RSHA transport. After the selection, 952 men and 396 women are admitted to the camp and given Nos. 160879–161830 and 66702–67097. The remaining 2,889 people are killed in the gas chambers.

APMO, Dpr.-Hd/6, p. 79; D-AuII-3/1, p. 15, Quarantine List.

35 male and 90 female prisoners are sent in a group transport. The men receive Nos. 161831–161865, the women, Nos. 67098–67172 and 67174–67188.

Two Jewish female prisoners sent in a group transport receive Nos. 67173 and 67189.

Three prisoners escape from the water supply squad of Birkenau. They are the Austrian Frank Kejmar (No. 26158), and the Poles Zbigniew Rupalski (No. 96117) and Edward Pasdor (Pazdroń) (No. 100419). The prisoners escape with an SS man named Michael. While escaping, they separate during a police check; then the three prisoners continue their flight toward the border of the General Government in the area near Trzebinia. They are arrested the next day near Krzeszowice.

APMO, Account of Former Prisoner Franz Kejmar of July 6, 1986; IZ-10/Gestapo Sieradz/2/165, 169.

NOVEMBER 6

Franz Kejmar, Zbigniew Rupalski and Edward Pazdroń, caught trying to escape, are locked in the bunker of Block 11. They are released from the bunker into the camp on November 23, 1943.

APMO, D-AuI-3/2, Bunker Register, p. 60.

10 prisoners sent in a group transport receive Nos. 161866–161875.

Three Gypsy men and seven Gypsy women arrive from the Reich territory. The men receive Nos. Z-8866–Z-8868 and the women, Nos. Z-9570–Z-9576.

The German prisoner Teodor Retzlar (No. PSV-113944) is caught trying to escape and locked in the bunker of Block 11. On November 23, 1943, he is released from the bunker into the camp.

Ibid.

The Jewish prisoner Zygmunt Loewenberg, born October 4, 1924, escapes from the camp. He was sent to Auschwitz from Sosnowitz with an RSHA transport on August 10, 1943.

APMO, IZ-8/Gestapo Lodz/3a/88/515.

1,500 Polish prisoners are transferred from Auschwitz to Mauthausen-Gusen. In the transport are about 150 inmates who had previously been sent to the Penal Company "until further notice."

APMO, Mat.RO, vol. VII, p. 453; D-AuI-3/1, pp. 5–11, Penal Company Register.

NOVEMBER 7

During the transport of the 1,500 prisoners from Auschwitz to Mauthausen, four prisoners escape, one on the Lundenburg-Vienna stretch, and three from the train between Vienna and Amstetten near St. Polten. Zdzisław Karnicki (No. 156212), was born May 25, 1915, in Radom, and sent to Auschwitz by the Sipo and SD of Warsaw on October 5. Kazimierz Kołodziejczyk (No. 156232), born September 24, 1925, in Moszno, was sent to Auschwitz by the Sipo and SD of Warsaw on October 5. Kołodziejczyk is arrested on November 9 by a police sentry in Maria Anzbach and taken to prison in Vienna. Kazimierz Zieliński (No. 153818), born November 20, 1926, in Warsaw, was sent to Auschwitz by the Sipo and SD of Radom on October 2. He is captured on November 8 and taken to prison in Vienna. On November 20, 1943, he is sent back to Auschwitz and locked in the bunker of Block 11. On February 2, 1944, he is released from the bunker into the camp with the order not to leave the camp grounds.* The fourth escapee is Jan Henryk Przanowski (No. 156411), born May 20, 1923, in Schakanau (Czekanów), sent to Auschwitz by the Sipo and SD of Warsaw on October 5. He is seriously wounded in the area of St. Polten, captured and taken to a hospital there. On November 19, he is sent back to Auschwitz and locked in the bunker of Block 11. On January 3, 1944, he is released from the bunker into the camp with the order not to leave the camp grounds.

APMO, Mat.RO, vol. VII, p. 453; IZ-8/Gestapo Lodz/3a/88/ 521, 522; IZ-8/Gestapo Lodz/2/ 88/172, 174, 176; D-AuI-3/2, Bunker Register, pp. 65, 67.

Two Gypsy men receive Nos. Z-8869 and Z-8870; two Gypsy women receive Nos. Z-9577 and Z-9578.

Eight boys born in the Gypsy camp in Birkenau are given Nos. Z-8871–Z-8878.

APMO, D-AuII-3/1/2, p. 263, Register of Male Gypsies.

Five girls born in the Gypsy camp are given Nos. Z-9579–Z-9583.

APMO, D-AuII-3/2/5, pp. 615, 619, Register of Female Gypsies.

NOVEMBER 8

36 prisoners sent in a group transport receive Nos. 161876–161911.

Seven female prisoners sent from Breslau receive Nos. 67190–67196.

By order of the Political Department, the following prisoners are locked in the bunker of Block 11: Polish political prisoner Teodor Kuhn (No. 32618), who is released from the bunker to the camp on November 8; the French Jew Samuel Sperber (No. 42545) and the German political prisoner Edmund Miklajewski (No. 63048),

APMO, D-AuI-3/2, Bunker Register, p. 61.

---

*Prisoners who receive the order not to leave the camp grounds must wear a red dot on a white piece of cloth sewn on the back of their jackets, or they are marked with the letters "i.L." (im Lager—"in camp"). Political prisoners considered especially dangerous or held in the camp as hostages are also marked in this way. Prisoners with this mark are the ones most frequently killed.

both released from the bunker to the camp on November 19; the Russian political prisoner Michail Lavrishchev (No. 106196) and the German political prisoner August Kaufeld (No. 39375), who are both released from the bunker to the camp on November 23.

Konstanty Kwiatkowski (No. 131919), a Polish Gypsy suspected of planning an escape, is locked in the bunker of Block 11. He is released after an inspection conducted by the new Commandant of Auschwitz, Arthur Liebehenschel, on November 23, 1943.

Ibid.

NOVEMBER 9

Several hundred young and healthy Gypsies are transferred from the Gypsy Family Camp in Birkenau to Natzweiler.

APMO, D-AuII-3/1/2, pp. 1–263, Register of Male Gypsies.

A selection is conducted in the bunker of Block 11. 50 prisoners are selected who were locked up by order of the Political Department, the Camp Commander, or the Roll Call Leader, or who were captured trying to escape from the camp. On the same day they are taken to Birkenau, where—as reported by the resistance organizations in the camp—they are shot to commemorate the anniversary of Hitler's march on Munich's Feldherrnhalle during the putsch of 1923.

APMO, D-AuI-3/2, Bunker Register, pp. 50–54, 56–59; Mat.RO, vol. I, p. 48.

87 prisoners sent in a group transport receive Nos. 161912–161998.

15 female prisoners sent in a group transport receive Nos. 67197–67211.

Two female Gypsies sent in a group transport, are given Nos. Z-9584 and Z-9585.

By order of the Political Department, the German PSV prisoner Richard Faustmann (No. 113666) is locked in the bunker of Block 11. He is released after an inspection conducted by Commandant Liebehenschel on November 23, 1943.

APMO, D-AuI-3/2, Bunker Register, p. 61.

Seven prisoners escape from the camp: the five Polish Jews Jehuda Szperling, born February 15, 1920, in Skidel; Lipa Cymbler, born April 10, 1904, in Bendin; Moszek Rotmensz, born May 4, 1905, in Bendin; Benjamin Chmielnicki, born June 23, 1917, in Łodz; Icek Boruch Apelman, born December 12, 1912, in Miechów; and the Poles Bronisław Paluch (No. 121567), born July 28, 1923, and Jan Majksner (No. 119353), born April 23, 1923.*

APMO, IZ-8/Gestapo Lodz/3a/88/517; Mat.RO, vol. IV, p. 293.

NOVEMBER 10

Four Gypsy men and seven Gypsy women are sent in a group transport. The men are given Nos. Z-8879–Z-8882 and the women Nos. Z-9586–Z-9592.

*Jan Majksner is captured on January 31, 1944, and sent to Auschwitz (APMO, IZ-10/Gestapo Sieradz/2/186).

Two Polish prisoners, Józef Koziol (No. 131979) and Jan Orlikowski (No. 132055), escape from the camp.*

APMO, IZ-10/Gestapo Sieradz/ 2/169; Mat.RO, vol. IV, p. 293.

16 Jewish men and three Jewish women arrive in an RSHA transport from the Reich territory and are selected. They receive Nos. 161999–162014 and 67212–67214.

Two girls born in the women's camp in Birkenau on November 5 and November 9 receive Nos. 67215 and 67216.

Two prisoners sent from Kattowitz receive Nos. 162015 and 162016.

59 male and eight female prisoners sent from Oppeln are given Nos. 162017–162075 and 67217–67224.

The Commandant's Office is instructed by Office D-II in the WVHA to transfer 82 skilled laborers to Buchenwald.

APMO, IZ-13/89, Various Documents of the Third Reich, p. 219.

NOVEMBER 11

The male occupancy level of the main camp, Birkenau, and the auxiliary camps of Buna, Golleschau, Jawischowitz, Eintrachthütte, Neu-Dachs, Fürstengrube, Janinagrube, Lagischa, Sosnowitz, and Brünn and in the outside squads on the farms and in the agricultural operations is 54,673, including 8,373 who are unfit for work, or are in the prisoners' infirmary or convalescent block. There are 46,300 able-bodied prisoners on this day, 34,731 of them employed; 11,569 able-bodied prisoners remain unemployed.

APMO, D-AuI-3a/370/7/424, Monthly Labor Deployment List.

The occupancy level of the women's camp in Auschwitz-Birkenau and the outside squads on the farms and in the agricultural operations is 33,179, including 6,967 sick women and those incapable of working. 11,164 female prisoners are employed, including 393 assigned for experimental uses and counted as employed in the monthly labor deployment lists. 15,048 able-bodied prisoners remain unemployed.

APMO, D-AuI-3a/370/7/435, Monthly Labor Deployment List.

SS Lieutenant Colonel Arthur Liebehenschel, former Head of Office D-I of Branch D of the WVHA, informs the SS personnel of the garrison that, by order of Himmler, he has taken over as Commandant of Auschwitz Concentration Camp from former Commandant Rudolf Höss. The classification of Auschwitz ordered by the Head of the WVHA into Camps I (main camp), II (women's camp), and III (auxiliary camps) is carried out within the next few days.

APMO, D-AuI-1, Garrison Order 50/43, Nov. 11, 1943.

34 male and 43 female prisoners sent to the camp by the Posen Gestapo are given Nos. 162076–162109 and 67225–67267.

*Jan Orlikowski is captured on December 20, 1943, sent to Auschwitz, and locked in the bunker of Block 11. He is released from the bunker on February 2, 1944, with instructions not to leave the camp grounds.

Interior view of a masonry barracks in Birkenau. Eight to 10 prisoners slept on each three-decker plank-bed.

108 prisoners sent from Pawiak Prison by the Sipo and SD of Warsaw receive Nos. 162110–162217.

Two prisoners sent from Kattowitz receive Nos. 162218 and 162219.

99 female prisoners sent to the camp by the Radom Sipo and SD receive Nos. 67268–67366.

By order of the Political Department, Polish political prisoner Emanuel Grytz (No. 102000) is locked in the bunker of Block 11. After an inspection carried out by the new Commandant, he is released into the camp on November 23, 1943.

APMO, D-AuI-3/2, Bunker Register, p. 61.

NOVEMBER 12

The Russian POW Emids Yuri Karpushev (RKG-104449), born April 4, 1922, in Moscow, escapes from Birkenau.

APMO, Mat.RO, vol. IV, p. 293; IZ-10/Gestapo Sieradz/2/165.

Interior view of wooden barracks in Birkenau.

Two Polish prisoners, Lucjan Piliński (No. 150131) and Henryk Janecki (No. 150423), escape from the camp.*

APMO, Mat.RO, vol. IV, p. 293; IZ-10/Gestapo Sieradz/2/165, 181.

362 prisoners sent to the camp by the Radom Sipo and SD receive Nos. 162220–162581.

APMO, D-AuII-3/1, p. 3, Quarantine List.

152 male and 18 female prisoners sent to the camp in a group transport are given Nos. 162582–162733 and 67367–67384.

105 female prisoners sent by the Posen Gestapo receive Nos. 67385–67489.

60 female prisoners sent in a group transport receive Nos. 67490–67549.

Jewish women arrive from a Silesian labor camp with an RSHA transport. After the selection, 191 women are admitted to the camp

---

*Lucjan Piliński is captured in Jawischowitz on November 19, 1943. On November 8, 1944, the search for Henryk Janecki, who was no doubt also captured, is called off.

and given Nos. 67550–67740. The remaining women are killed in the gas chambers.

The Polish prisoners Jan Bojarski (No. 155176), Michał Ćwiek (No. 155224), and Stanisław Kensik (No. 155372) and the German prisoner Emil Arth (No. 113636) are captured trying to escape and locked in the bunker of Block 11. After an inspection by Commandant Liebehenschel, they are released into the camp.

APMO, IZ-10/Gestapo Sieradz/ 2/165; D-AuI-3/2, Bunker Register, pp. 61ff.

NOVEMBER 13

35 prisoners sent in a group transport receive Nos. 162734–162768.

Seven female prisoners sent by the Zichenau Gestapo receive Nos. 67741–67747.

A Gypsy woman sent in a group transport receives No. Z-9593.

Jews arrive in an RSHA transport. After the selection, 100 women are admitted to the camp and given Nos. 67748–67847. The remaining people are killed in the gas chambers.

A girl born the previous day to a woman sent to the camp by the Sipo and SD of Warsaw receives No. 67848.

Two female prisoners sent from Kattowitz receive Nos. 67849 and 67850.

Two prisoners are captured trying to escape and are locked in the bunker of Block 11: the Jew Fritz Lustig (No. 100913) and German PSV prisoner Wilhelm Lamberz (No. 113716). After an inspection by Commandant Liebehenschel on November 23, 1943, they are released from the bunker into the camp.

APMO, D-AuI-3/2, Bunker Register, p. 62.

NOVEMBER 14

An SS Camp Doctor makes a selection in Quarantine Camp B-IIa in Birkenau. He selects 219 prisoners. They are killed in the gas chamber the same day.

APMO, Dpr.-Hd/6, p. 5.

75 Russian POWs transferred from Lamsdorf prisoner-of-war camp the previous day receive Nos. RKG-10632–RKG-10706.

APMO, D-AuII-3/1, pp. 3, 15, Quarantine List.

A female prisoner sent from Klagenfurt receives No. 67851.

400 Jewish men, women, and children, arrested in Florence and Bologna, arrive in an RSHA transport from Rome. After the selection, 13 men and 94 women are admitted to the camp and receive Nos. 162770–162782 and 67852–67945. The remaining 243 people are killed in the gas chambers.

APMO, D-AuII-3/1, pp. 3, 15, Quarantine List; CDECM, *Jews in Italy*, p. 13.

NOVEMBER 15

A female prisoner sent from Kattowitz receives No. 67946.

A prisoner sent from Oppeln receives the free No. 162769.

Nine male and 115 female prisoners sent in a group transport are given Nos. 162783–162791 and 67947–68061.

By order of the Political Department, three political prisoners are locked in the bunker of Block 11. They are the Pole Antoni Bujak (No. 125687), who is released from the bunker into the camp on November 19, and Ignacy Piasecki (No. 136650) and Marian Perszak (No. 145611), both of them released from the bunker into the camp on November 23, 1943.

APMO, D-AuI-3/2, Bunker Register, p. 62.

NOVEMBER 16

23 prisoners sent to the camp by the Königsberg Gestapo receive Nos. 162792–162814.

295 prisoners sent from the prison in Wiśnicz by the Sipo and SD for the Kraków District receive Nos. 162815–163109.

A female prisoner sent from Kraków receives No. 68062.

A female prisoner sent from Warsaw receives No. 68063.

Two female prisoners sent from Zichenau receive Nos. 68064 and 68065.

13 female prisoners sent from Lublin receive Nos. 68066–68078.

Commandant Liebehenschel admonishes the members of the SS garrison that the prisoners' property, whether clothing, gold, valuables, food, or personal belongings, and no matter where it is found is inviolable. The state determines the use of this property, since in special cases it is the property of the state.* Whoever misappropriates state property is committing a criminal offense and excludes himself from the ranks of the SS.**

APMO, D-AuI-1, Garrison Order 51/43.

*The property stolen from the prisoners, especially from the Jews immediately condemned to death, is turned over to the state. This illegal seizure of property is not called robbery. But an individual SS man caught attempting to appropriate some objects is treated like a thief and tried in an SS court.
**No doubt this warning is connected with the arrival in Auschwitz of a special commission of the SS assigned to investigate embezzlement in the concentration camps. The committee is headed by a judge of the SS court, SS Major Dr. Konrad Morgen. Other members are SS Lieutenant Colonel Reimers, SS Captain Bartsch, and SS Captain Dr. Fischer, all of the Gestapo. The inquiry turns up many infringements in Auschwitz, including some by the leadership of the Political Department as well as embezzlement of state property by other SS personnel. The collected proof is secured and preserved in a barracks of the Political Department in the main camp (SAM, *Auschwitz in the Eyes of the SS*, p. 187).

Polish political prisoner Antoni Garcarczyk (No. 137851) is captured trying to escape and locked in the bunker of Block 11. On November 23, 1943, he is released into the camp.

APMO, D-AuI-3/2, Bunker Register, p. 62.

NOVEMBER 17

A prisoner sent from Kattowitz receives No. 163110.

Two male and 11 female prisoners sent from Kraków are given Nos. 163111 and 163112 and 68079–68089.

Russian political prisoner Vladimir Popovich (No. 107526), who escaped from the camp on November 15, is captured and locked in the bunker of Block 11. On November 23, 1943, he is released into the camp.

Ibid.

A gypsy woman receives No. Z-9594.

Two prisoners sent from Kattowitz receive Nos. 163113 and 163114.

45 prisoners sent to the camp by the Lublin Sipo and SD receive Nos. 163115–163159.

23 prisoners sent by the Sipo and SD for the Kraków District receive Nos. 163160–163182.

18 prisoners sent from Kattowitz receive Nos. 163183–163200.

559 male and 589 female Jews transferred from Herzogenbusch are given Nos. 163201–163759 and 68090–68678.

38 prisoners sent in a group transport receive Nos. 163760–163797.

Three boys born in the Gypsy camp receive Nos. Z-8883–Z-8885.

APMO, D-AuII-3/1/2, p. 263, Register of Male Gypsies.

Three girls born in the Gypsy camp receive Nos. Z-9595–Z-9597.

APMO, D-AuII-3/2/5/, p. 619, Register of Female Gypsies.

A female prisoner sent from Bromberg receives No. 68679.

Three female prisoners sent from Lodz receive Nos. 68680–68682.

41 female prisoners sent from Posen receive Nos. 68683–68723.

A Gypsy man and five Gypsy women are sent with a group transport. The man is given No. Z-8886 and the women, Nos. Z-9598–Z-9602.

995 Jews arrive from Westerbork in an RSHA transport from Holland. In the transport are 166 children, 281 men and 291 women below the age of 50, and 257 old people. After the selection, 275

men and 189 women are admitted to the camp and receive Nos. 163798–164072 and 68724–68912. The remaining 531 people are killed in the gas chambers.

At around 9:00 A.M., on the way from Birkenau to work, one political prisoner escapes, the Polish woman Mariana Bugaj, born May 25, 1910, and sent to the camp by the Radom Sipo and SD on July 29, 1943.

APMO, IZ-8/Gestapo Lodz/3a/88/523.

NOVEMBER 18

The Commandant's Office receives instructions from the WVHA to pay performance premiums to Jewish prisoners who excel in work performance.*

APMO, Dpr.-Hd/12, p. 140, Exhibit 92.

27 male and two female prisoners sent to the camp by the Lublin Sipo and SD are given Nos. 164073–164099 and 68913 and 68914.

10 male and five female prisoners sent from Kattowitz are given Nos. 164100–164109 and 68915–68919.

Two prisoners transferred the previous day from Herzogenbusch receive Nos. 164110 and 164111.

A prisoner sent from Vienna receives No. 164112.

A prisoner sent from the Kattowitz District receives No. 164113.

NOVEMBER 19

Lucjan Piliński, who escaped from Birkenau on November 12, is captured in Jawischowitz. He is locked in the bunker of Block 11 and released into the camp on November 23, 1943.

APMO, D-AuI-3/2, Bunker Register, p. 62.

1,000 Polish and Russian prisoners are transferred from Auschwitz to Neuengamme.

APMO, Mat.RO, vol. VII, p. 453.

Two Polish prisoners, Roman Cieliczko (No. 27089) and Jerzy Wesołowski (No. 27273), escape from Camp B-IIe, the Gypsy Family Camp.**

APMO, IZ-8/Gestapo Lodz/3a/88/527; Mat.RO, vol. IV, p. 292; Martin Gilbert, *Auschwitz und die Allierten* (Auschwitz and the Allies), Munich, 1982; Account of Jerzy Wesołowski.

---

*The level of the premium depends on the kind of labor unit. On average, they amount to .50–2.00 RM. The purpose of the premiums is generally the maintenance as well as the increase of labor productivity. They are not paid consistently and one cannot buy very much with them in the camp canteen.

**Dr. Jerzy Tabeau is registered in the camp under the name Wesołowski. After a long march and a stop in Zakopane, he reaches Kraków and makes contact with Teresa Lasocka, who keeps in constant contact with Józef Cyrankiewicz and Stanisław Klodziński. At the request of the members of the Kraków underground movement, Tabeau writes a report several dozen pages long about Auschwitz at the end of 1943 and the beginning of 1944, in which he describes the mass murder of the Jews. The report is sent to England, and subsequently the resistance movement is asked to smuggle the escapee to England as an important witness. The order is carried out and Tabeau is in Hungary in March 1944. The occupation of Hungary by the German Wehrmacht makes further travel impossible and he goes back to occupied Poland on courier roads and fights in a partisan unit. The content of his report is published in spring 1944 in the United States as the report of a Polish major.

280 male and 87 female prisoners sent in a group transport are given Nos. 164114–164393, 68920–68942 and 68944–69007. A girl born to a woman transferred with this transport is registered as No. 68943.

A selection takes place in the women's camp in Birkenau and 394 Jewish prisoners are selected. As they are transported to the gas chambers in vehicles, Bina Braun (No. 62390) and Rosa Thieberger (No. 66462), who have tried to escape and hide in the camp, are shot. The rest are killed in the gas chambers. The list of the selected Jewish women includes some sent to the camp only a few days previously: Mina Kraft (No. 67111), born April 11, 1878, in Neuenhain, sent on November 5 in a group transport; Ilse Plotka (No. 67214), born March 24, 1915, in Tübingen, and sent to the camp on November 10; Aaltje Bresden (No. 68294), born February 14, 1891, in Amsterdam, transferred to the camp from Herzogenbusch on November 17; and Rachel D'Ancona (No. 68730), born November 26, 1906, in Amsterdam, transferred to the camp from Westerbork on November 17. The list of 394 selected female prisoners is signed by Camp Commander SS Second Lieutenant Hössler. A copy of the typewritten list, stolen in the women's camp and turned over to a cell of the resistance organization in the main camp, is sent by Stanisław Kłodiński to Kraków on November 21, 1943, for use and transmission of the original to London.

APMO, Mat.RO, vol. 1, p. 41, vol. IV, pp. 267–271. The date of the selection is confirmed by the enumeration in the monthly labor deployment list.

NOVEMBER 20

25 male and 26 female prisoners sent in a group transport receive Nos. 164394–164418 and 69008–69033.

Two female prisoners sent from Kattowitz receive Nos. 69034 and 69035.

By order of the Political Department, Polish political prisoner Józef Krokocki (No. 131977) is locked in the bunker of Block 11. He is released into the camp on November 23 with orders not to leave the camp grounds.

APMO, D-AuI-3/2, Bunker Register, p. 62.

Nine Poles and one Russian are captured trying to escape and locked in the bunker of Block 11. They are Leon Mokrowski (No. 15415), Aleksander Kowal (No. 154790), Józef Laszek (No. 154822), Józef Miśkow (No. 154875), Zygmunt Węgrzyn (No. 155063), Stanisław Adamczyk (No. 155128), Jan Dmowski (No. 155251), Feliks Malczewski (No. 155507), Bohdan Banasik (No. 155923), and Ivan Ivchenko (No. 155337). They are all released from the bunker after an inspection by Commandant Liebehenschel on November 23, 1943.

NOVEMBER 21

The number of prisoners who are sick and unable to work constantly increases and comes to 9,063 male and 7,656 female prisoners. A typhus epidemic spreads again in Birkenau.

APMO, D-AuI-3a/370/7/424, 435, Monthly Labor Deployment List; Mat.RO, vol. I, p. 51.

Commandant Liebehenschel divides Auschwitz into three independent concentration camps under the following management:

APMO, D-AuI-1, Garrison Order 53/43, Nov. 22, 1943; the same, Dpr.-Hd/12, pp. 36–40.

1. Auschwitz I—Main camp. The Commandant is SS Lieutenant Colonel Liebehenschel with adjutants SS Captain Zoller and First Protective Custody Commander SS First Lieutenant Hofmann.
2. Auschwitz II—Birkenau. The Commandant is SS Major Harjenstein with adjutants SS Second Lieutenant Schindler and the First Protective Custody Commander for the men's camp SS Second Lieutenant Schwarzhuber and the First Protective Custody Commander for the women's camp SS Second Lieutenant Hössler.
3. Auschwitz III—Auxiliary Camps. The Commandant is SS Captain Schwarz with an adjutant who has not yet been appointed.

At the same time, Liebehenschel leaves control of the SS Death's Head units in the hands of their commander, SS Major Hartjenstein, whom he appoints as his deputy. In issues of economics, discipline, and personnel, he puts the guard companies under the supervision of the respective Camp Commandant.

1. The 1st, 2nd, 3rd, and 4th Guard Companies and two staff units are assigned to the Commandant of Auschwitz I.
2. The 6th, 7th, and 8th Guard Companies, one staff unit, and the dog squadron are assigned to the Commandant of Auschwitz II.
3. The 5th Guard Company and the Buna Guard Company are assigned to the Commandant of Auschwitz III.

The Commandant of Auschwitz I is the senior Camp Commandant and Garrison Senior of the SS garrison of Auschwitz. The camp administration is henceforth to be directed centrally for all camps.

Eight prisoners sent in a group transport receive Nos. 164419–164426.

86 prisoners are put in the bunker of Block 11. Commandant Liebehenschel makes an inspection in the bunker of Block 11. He leaves 30 prisoners in the bunker, 26 of them for digging an escape tunnel in the Neu-Dachs auxiliary camp. The previous Commandant, Rudolf Höss, probably applied to the SS Commander in Chief for the death penalty for them. Liebehenschel orders 56 prisoners released into the camp, including Poles, several German Communists, Czechs, Russians, and Jews who were locked in the bunker by order of the Political Department or of the Camp Commander, or they were caught trying to escape or were suspected of planning an escape. Among those released are the political prisoners Jerzy Krzyżanoski alias Mieczysław Jelec, who has been held in the bunker

APMO, D-AuI-3/2, Bunker Register, pp. 9, 15, 19, 28, 36, 41, 44, 52, 56–63; Mat.RO, vol. I, pp. 42, 43.

since he was arrested on May 21, 1943, after his second escape from the camp; the Czech Emil Poupa, who has been held in the bunker since June 22, 1943; and the Pole Tadeusz Szatkowski, who has been held in the bunker since July 27, 1943. In addition, there are the German Communists Paul Wienhold and Ludwig Wörl, who have been in the bunker since August 28, 1943. Willi Knauf has been in the bunker since September 14, 1943, along with Otto Küsel (No. 2), who was arrested in Warsaw after a successful escape and locked in the bunker on September 25, 1943. The Russian Nikolai Gronov, who was put in the bunker on October 13, 1943; the Jew David Boruchowicz, who was sent to the bunker on August 29, 1943; the German Stanisław Walikowski and the Pole Józef Cyrankiewicz,* who were put in the bunker on November 2, 1943; and 34 other prisoners who were locked in the bunker between November 6 and November 20.**

1,200 Jewish men, women, and children arrive from Drancy with the sixty-second RSHA transport from France. After the selection, 241 men and 45 women are admitted to the camp and receive Nos. 164427–164667 and 69036–69080. The remaining 914 people are killed in the gas chambers.

Four female prisoners sent from Breslau receive Nos. 69081–69084.

Two female prisoners sent from Potsdam receive Nos. 69085 and 69086.

211 male and 159 female prisoners are sent to the camp from Vitebsk by Mobile Sipo and SD Commando 9.† The men are given Nos. 164668–164888 and the women, Nos. 69087–69245.

APMO, D-AuI-3/1, p. 3, Quarantine List.

Eight prisoners sent in a group transport receive Nos. 164889–164894.

11 Gypsies sent from Belgium receive Nos. Z-8887–Z-8897.

NOVEMBER 24

Three female prisoners sent from Kattowitz receive Nos. 69246–69248.

---

*Józef Cyrankiewicz is suspected of planning an escape because civilian clothing and a wig were found under the straw sack of his bunk during a block inspection. This is considered incontrovertible proof of his plan. In fact, his incarceration in the bunker takes place one day before the date of his planned escape.
**All prisoners released from the bunker are marked with red dots on the chest and back of their clothing.
†208 men from this transport are sent to quarantine in Camp B-IIa. The telegram notifying the Commandant's Office of the arrival of the transport from Vitebsk on November 17, 1943, states that there are 391 members of the Communist Party in the transport. 380 men and women altogether are admitted to the camp. 11 people probably escaped from the transport or died during the six-day trip.

Four female prisoners sent from the Kattowitz District receive Nos. 69249–69252.

Seven prisoners are sent to the Penal Company in Birkenau, three "until recalled" and the rest for six months. One of those sent "until further notice" is Izydor Dobraszkin (No. 142765), who dies on December 1, 1943, after eight days in the Penal Company.

APMO, D-AuI-3/1, p. 12, Penal Company Register.

SS Major Hartjenstein informs the members of the SS garrison that according to Garrison Command No. 53/43 of November 22, 1943, he is Commandant of Auschwitz II (Birkenau). He also states that the Protective Custody Commander for the men's camp is SS Second Lieutenant Schwarzhuber and the Protective Custody Commander for the women's camp is SS Second Lieutenant Hössler. According to the service regulations, Head Supervisor Mandel is responsible for the deployment of the female prisoners' labor.

APMO, D-AuII-1/56, Commandant's Office Order 1/43.

In a secret message addressed to Teresa Lasocka, Stanisław Klodziński reports that "Józek has [gotten] out by a miracle.* They're freeing the whole bunker, more than 100 people. It's an order from Berlin, which is carried out precisely by the Political Department and the new Commandant.** All SS Men must personally sign a form prohibiting the killing of the prisoners. The death penalty for escape and suspicion of escape is abolished. The bunker of Block 11 will be only for serving punishments and not as an interrogation prison. This is a completely new era in the camp which is clearly perceived. . . ."

APMO, Mat.RO, vol. I, p. 43.

NOVEMBER 25

Three prisoners, Jan Kosmenda (No. 115391), Bronisław Kuźnicki (No. 131959), and Adolf Kołdas (No. 131978)—escape from the camp.

APMO, IZ-8/Gestapo Lodz/3a/88/533, 534; Mat.RO, vol. IV, p. 292.

Stanisław Wierusz-Kowalski (No. 1873), a known informer and confidant (V-Man) of SS Sergeant Lachmann of the Political Department, an expert in anticonspiracy activity in the camp, comes to Józef Cyrankiewicz to congratulate him on his release from the bunker. He informs him that his friend, the foreman Stanisław Dorosiewicz, is head of the camp informers. In this way, he tries to win his trust and get necessary information for the Political Department.†

APMO, Mat.RO, Józef Cyrankiewicz File.

Following the order of Office D-II dated November 10, 82 skilled workers are transferred to Buchenwald. The transport is assembled on November 10, after an SS Camp Doctor has examined the pris-

APMO, IZ-13/89, Various Documents of the Third Reich, p. 219.

---

*I.e., Józef Cyrankiewicz.
**The freeing of the prisoners from the bunker of Block 11 caused a quarrel between the Political Department and the new Commandant, Liebehenschel.
†The Political Department operates a net of informers in the camp. The resistance movement is well informed about the working methods of the Political Department and also knows the names of their so-called V-men, or agents ("V-man" stands for "Verbindungsman," or "contact person").

oners' fitness for work. On the previous day, coats, jackets, trousers, underwear, pullovers, socks, wooden clogs, caps, earmuffs, and mittens were distributed to them. The commander of the escort, SS Sergeant Schmidt, signs for the rations for the three-day trip, and for the prisoner files, and the charge of the prisoners.*

The occupancy level in Professor Dr. Clauberg's experimental ward rises by seven. 400 female prisoners have been transferred there for experimental purposes.

APMO, D-AuI-3a/370/7/435, Monthly Labor Deployment List.

Three male and two female prisoners sent from Kattowitz are given Nos. 164895–164897 and 69253 and 69254.

APMO, Dpr.-Hd/6, p. 26.

All prisoners suffering from malaria in the prisoners' infirmary and convalescent blocks are ordered to be registered. Prisoners with malaria are transferred to Majdanek.

NOVEMBER 26

69 female prisoners sent in a group transport receive Nos. 69255–69323.

A Gypsy woman sent in a group transport receives No. Z-9603.

75 male and 33 female prisoners are sent from Pawiak Prison by the Warsaw Sipo and SD. The men are given Nos. 164898–164972 and the women, Nos. 69324–69356.

26 prisoners sent with a group transport receive Nos. 164973–164998.

Two girls born the previous day in the women's camp in Birkenau receive Nos. 69357 and 69358.

11 prisoners sent from Pawiak Prison by the Warsaw Sipo and SD receive Nos. 164999–165010.

141 prisoners sent in a group transport receive Nos. 165011–165151.

At around 11:00 P.M., Ludwig Daniel (No. Z-8810) and Waclav Ferda (No. Z-8811) escape from the Gypsy Family Camp in Birkenau. They are captured on December 2 and locked in the bunker of Block 11 the next day. Ludwig Daniel is released from the bunker on December 4 and Waclav Ferda on December 11, 1943.

APMO, D-AuI-1/2b, p. 302, Bulletin of Dec. 15, 1943; D-AuI-3/2, Bunker Register, p. 64.

*This is the procedure for a transfer of prisoners to another camp or a prison. The prisoners are deleted from the occupancy list of the original camp as soon as they are registered in the new camp or prison.

In Auschwitz I, Auschwitz II, and Auschwitz III, 2,018 registered male prisoners died.

In the women's camp of Auschwitz-Birkenau, 1,603 registered female prisoners died; 394 female prisoners were killed in the gas chambers.

APMO, D-AuI-3a/370/7/424; calculated on the basis of the Monthly Labor Deployment List, to which newly arrived prisoners are added and from which those transferred to other camps or escaped are subtracted.

APMO, Mat.RO, vol. VII, p. 486; vol. IV, pp. 267–271. [women's camp]

DECEMBER 1

SS Private Basil Malaiko of the 2nd Guard Company is rewarded by the Commandant of Auschwitz I with five days' vacation for preventing the escape of 10 prisoners on November 20. Because of his effort, the prisoners were locked in the bunker of Block 11.

APMO, D-AuI-1, Garrison Order 54/43; D-AuI-3/2, Bunker Register, p. 63.

Commandant Liebehenschel appoints SS Second Lieutenant Schurz Director of the Political Department. At the same time, he informs the SS members of the garrison that the previous director, SS Second Lieutenant Grabner, is returning to his former Gestapo post in Kattowitz. In fact, Grabner is arrested for repeated abuse of office in Auschwitz.*

APMO, D-AuI-1, Garrison Order 54/43.

427 prisoners in the Golleschau A.C. work in the cement factory of the Golleschau Portland-Zement AG. This is the highest rate of employment of prisoners reached there in December.

APMO, D-AuI-3a/370/7/469a, Monthly Labor Deployment List.

2,199 prisoners in the Neu-Dachs A.C. work in the coal mines of Jaworzno and on the construction of the power station of Wilhelm, now Jaworzno. This is the maximum employment rate of prisoners for the month of December. In the course of the month, the employment rate goes back to 1,969 prisoners by December 30.

APMO, D-AuI-3a/370/7/470, Monthly Labor Deployment List.

Commandant Liebehenschel changes the name of the Buna auxiliary camp to "Monowitz Labor Camp."

APMO, D-AuI-1, Garrison Order 54/43.

Commandant Liebehenschel warns the SS members of the garrison not to leave their pistol holsters in the wardrobe of the barber or in other rooms accessible to inmates.

Ibid.

65 male and 18 female prisoners sent to the camp by the Lodz Gestapo are given Nos. 165245–165309 and 69446–69463.

---

*Pery Broad discusses Grabner's arrest thus: "Grabner was arrested. It didn't help him that he referred to the fact that the Commandant and Mildner [head of the Gestapo of Kattowitz—D.C.] knew of these executions and would have approved of them. Mildner had meanwhile become inspector of the Sipo and SD in Denmark and was too far away to be reached. The Commandant [Höss—D.C.] got out of the matter by committing perjury. Aumeier acted the same way and so did all the SS commanders who had played prominent roles in the bunker operation in Block 11, like Captain Schwarz, later Commandant of the auxiliary camp Monowitz attached to Auschwitz [this should have been called Auschwitz III—D.C.] or SS First Lieutenant Hoffmann [Hofman—D.C.] . . ." (SAM, *Auschwitz in the Eyes of the SS*, p. 188).

DECEMBER 2

The prisoner employment rate in Sosnowitz A.C. (Auschwitz I) drops from 92 to 50 prisoners. Since the repairs are coming to an end, 42 prisoners are transferred to Lagischa A.C.

APMO, D-AuI-3a/370/7/464a, Monthly Labor Deployment List.

SS Captain Schwarz informs the SS members of the garrison that in compliance with the order of November 22, 1943, he has taken over the function of Commandant of Auschwitz III, which consists of the auxiliary camps of Monowitz, Neu-Dachs, Jawischowitz, Eintrachthütte, Lagischa, Fürstengrube, Golleschau, Janinagrube, Sosnowitz, and Brünn.

APMO, D-AuIII-1/121, Commandant's Office Order 1/43.

SS First Lieutenant Schöttl takes over the functions of First Protective Custody Commander of Auschwitz III and Deputy of Commandant Schwarz.

Ibid.

In the individual auxiliary camps the numbers of prisoners employed are: in Monowitz, in the I. G. Farben factory, 4,901; in Neu-Dachs, 2,198; in Jawischowitz, 1,264; in Eintrachthütte, 659; in Lagischa, 545; in Fürstengrube, 564; in Golleschau, 425; in Janinagrube, 396; in Sosnowitz, 50; and in Brünn, 249.*

APMO, D-AuI-3a/370/7/464, Labor Deployment Lists for December 1943.

21 male and seven female prisoners sent from the Kraków District are given Nos. 165310–165330 and 69464–69470.

Approximately 100 Jews arrive in an RSHA transport from Vienna. After the selection, 13 men and 11 women are admitted to the camp and receive Nos. 165331–165343 and 69471–69481. The more than 70 people remaining are killed in the gas chambers.

APMO, D-AuII-3/1, p. 4, Quarantine List.

30 Gypsy men and boys and 47 Gypsy women and girls are sent from Yugoslavia. The men are given Nos. Z-8923–Z-8952 and the women, Nos. Z-9620–Z-9666.

Commandant Schwarz of Auschwitz III commends SS Corporal Erich Ligoni and SS Private First Class Aristarch Dobrowolski, guards in Jawischowitz A.C., for capturing Lucjan Piliński, who escaped from Birkenau on November 19.

APMO, D-AuIII-1/121, Commandant's Office Order 1/43; D-AuI-3/2, Bunker Register, p. 62.

In the evening, Karol Polcak, born July 3, 1921, escapes from Monowitz A.C., and Leib Segal (No. 127164), born May 10, 1924, in Warsaw, escapes from Jawischowitz A.C.

APMO, IZ-8/Gestapo Lodz/3a/88/540–543; D-AuI-1/2b, p. 300, Bulletin of Dec. 15, 1943.

DECEMBER 3

162 male and 122 female prisoners sent in a group transport are given Nos. 165344–165505 and 69482–69603.

*Altogether 11,251 prisoners of Auschwitz III are working on this day. The number who are sick and unable to work and are in the infirmaries of the respective auxiliary camps is not known.

DECEMBER 4

Six Gypsy men and two Gypsy women are transferred from the territory of the German Reich. The men are given Nos. Z-8953–Z-8958 and the women, Nos. Z-9667 and Z-9668.

Five female prisoners sent from Zichenau by the Gestapo receive Nos. 69604–69608.

19 prisoners sent in a collective transport receive Nos. 165506–165524.

Two male prisoners sent from Lemberg receive Nos. 165525 and 165526.

1,477 White Russian and Polish men and women are sent in a transport of the Mobile Sipo and SD Commando 9 from Minsk. As partisans and active members of the Russian resistance movement in the occupied territory, these men and women fought against the German army. In the transport are 934 men and 543 women. The men are given Nos. 165527–166039 and 166882–167302 and the women, Nos. 69609–70151.

APMO, D-AuI-3/1, p. 4, Quarantine List.

673 prisoners of the auxiliary camp work in Eintrachthütte in Schwientochlowitz. This is the highest level of employment in the month of December. In the following days, it remains over 650.

APMO, D-AuI-3a/370/7/475a, Monthly Labor Deployment List.

DECEMBER 5

1,200 prisoners and POWs, most of them sick and invalid, are transferred from Flossenbürg. During the transport 258 prisoners die. 34 Russian POWs receive Nos. RKG-11041–RKG-11074. 827 prisoners receive Nos. 166040–166866. 81 prisoners are reassigned their previous numbers, since they were already imprisoned in Auschwitz and were transferred to Flossenbürg on March 12, 1943. The transport is to be sent to the gas chambers but is nevertheless sent to the Quarantine Camp B-IIa in Birkenau, where the 80 weakest prisoners are left lying in the ice and snow of the lumberyard by order of the Camp Commander and cold water is subsequently poured on them. In the night, the prisoner attendants manage to bring 47 of those lying in the lumberyard into a barracks. 32 prisoners die, among them one who lay buried under the bodies of the others and dies in the morning when he is carried away.*

APMO, D-AuII-3/1, p. 4, Quarantine List; Dpr.-Hd/6, pp. 25, 53.

9,407 prisoners are sick and unable to work.

APMO, D-AuI-3a/370/7/438, Monthly Labor Deployment List.

*On December 18, 1943, 799 prisoners from that transport are still alive, by January 18, 1944, 751 are still alive, and on February 18, 1944, only 393 prisoners are still alive (APMO, Dpr.-Hd/6, p. 25).

DECEMBER 6

The number of female prisoners who are sick and unable to work is reduced by 231, to 9,176 women.*

Ibid.

13 prisoners sent from Kattowitz receive Nos. 167303–167315.

11 female prisoners sent from Breslau receive Nos. 70152, 70155, and 70157–70165.

Three female prisoners sent from Kattowitz receive Nos. 70153, 70154, and 70156.

In the afternoon, Mieczysław Pogan escapes from Auschwitz I. Born on September 10, 1925, he was sent to Auschwitz by the Kraków Sipo and SD on September 18, 1943.

APMO, IZ-8/Gestapo Lodz/3a/88/543.

The Czech Emil Mlynařyk (No. 112827) is captured trying to escape and locked in the bunker of Block 11. On December 9, 1943, he is released from the bunker into the camp.

APMO, D-AuI-3/2, Bunker Register, p. 65.

32 prisoners are transferred from Auschwitz to Sachsenhausen.

APMO, Mat.RO, vol. VII, p. 474.

During evening roll call in Neu-Dachs auxiliary camp in Jaworzno, a public hanging of 26 prisoners takes place. They are brought to Neu-Dachs from the bunker of Block 11 for this purpose. They were locked in the bunker between October 18 and October 20 when an escape tunnel started by the prisoners was discovered in Neu-Dachs. Commandant Schwarz of Auschwitz III reads the sentence. Some of them shout: "Don't give up, boys" and "Long live Poland." Then Schwarz orders the tables to be pulled away and the prisoners are hanged on the mass gallows. Afterward, the prisoners gathered for roll call must pass by the executed men. Their bodies are not taken down for 24 hours. The murdered men are the Poles Jan Kosmala, Edward Chmielewski, Henryk Masiarek, Leon Rupala, Józef Gladycz, Marian Pająk, Edward Dulka, Jan Janeczek, Franciszek Reperowski, Julian Bąk, Stefan Stawiarski, Stanisław Brylewski, Arnold Altof, Marian Binkowski, Jan Pieron, Jan Sokolnicki, and Jan Wołczyński; the Czechs Franc Kurka, Franc Hostusa, Miroslav Kubalek, Rudolf Rossypalek, Franc Bilek, Jan Dawid, Jaroslav Matousek, and Jaroslav Starec; and the Jew Jakob Bleier.

APMO, D-AuI-3/2, Bunker Register, pp. 54–57; Statements, vol. 5, pp. 609–617, Account of Former Prisoner Wiktor Pasikowski; Paul Heller, "Das Aussenlager Jaworzno" (Jaworzno Auxiliary Camp), in Adler et al., eds., Auschwitz: Testimonies, p. 170.

The denouncer and informer of the Political Department, prisoner Wierusz-Kowalski, calls prisoner Józef Cyrankiewicz out of the prisoners' office to the block corridor and warns him in a provoking

APMO, Mat.RO, Józef Cyrankiewicz File.

---

*In the women's camp in Birkenau, several dozen female prisoners suffering from typhus are admitted every day to the prisoners' infirmary and patients die every day from lack of medicine or are selected and killed. The typhus epidemic prevails in all the camps in Birkenau, the quarantine camp, the family camps of the Jews from Theresienstadt and the Gypsies, and in the men's camp.

way: "A serious danger threatens the 'red dots.' Sergeant Lachmann told me that the Political Department is fighting the Commandant, they want to compromise him and his soft policy. I'm telling you this as one Pole to another. So, in the near future, before Christmas, Dorosiewicz is to escape from the camp with the knowledge of the Political Department. At the same time, something is to happen that will be such a bomb* that Berlin will be forced to take retaliatory measures against the prisoners. Moreover, Dorosiewicz will set out with the mission to expose camp contacts with the resistance." Finally, Wierusz-Kowalski proposes an escape plan to Józef Cyrankiewicz and, when the latter refuses definitively, asks him for an address in Kraków where he can find help for the escape. When he does not get this address, he asks for financial support and does not get that either. Józef Cyrankiewicz reports the conversation to the leadership of the resistance movement in the camp. They decide to send a warning out of the camp concerning Dorosiewicz.** In addition, the prisoner Hermann Langbein† is assigned to report on this conversation to SS Garrison Doctor Wirths, who maintains good relations with Commandant Liebehenschel and who is fighting against the Political Department, which also poses a threat to him.

DECEMBER 7

The occupancy level in Professor Dr. Clauberg's experimental station is increased by one: 398 female prisoners are now housed there for research purposes.

APMO, D-AuI-3a/370/7/438, Monthly Labor Deployment List.

Auschwitz I, II, and III have an occupancy level of 56,082; 10,085 of them are sick and unable to work.

APMO, D-AuI-3a/370/7/448, Monthly Labor Deployment List.

During the night, a fire breaks out in the barracks where the special committee sent to Auschwitz by SS Commander in Chief Himmler, and led by Dr. Morgen, deposited the evidence of the thievery of the SS men. Among the pieces of evidence are jewelry and valuables found on the SS men during the inquiry. The evidence of guilt is eliminated by the burning of the barracks.††

*This "bomb" is to be the murder of SS man Jarosiewitsch.
**Warnings about Dorosiewicz and Wierusz-Kowalski are sent out of the camp twice (APMO, Mat.RO, vol. I, pp. 50, 51, 53).
†After his release from the bunker, Hermann Langbein returned to his position as clerk of the Garrison Doctor, Wirths, on whom he has great influence.
††Pery Broad writes: "Diamonds, thousands of gold rings, chains and watches, mountains of fur, clothing and property of every kind could be seen in the money and valuables departments and the large sorting and storage barracks of the SS garrison administration. . . . Suitcases full of jewelry, paper money, and coins were dragged to the cellar of the administration building because they couldn't keep up with the sorting and counting. A whole staff was employed just to count enormous sums of money day after day. Sentries with machine guns guarded the trucks that went to Berlin with this treasure. . . . The deplorable state of affairs in Auschwitz had already assumed such proportions that a money bunker of the money administration was broken into. In the frightening pile of suitcases, which still contained uncounted amounts, it was never possible to determine how many suitcases, not to mention what sums, the thief had stolen" (Broad, *Memoirs*, pp. 46ff.).

DECEMBER 8

65 prisoners sent from Pawiak Prison by the Warsaw Sipo and SD receive Nos. 167316–167380.

47 prisoners sent in a group transport receive Nos. 167381–167427.

16 female prisoners sent from the Kattowitz District receive Nos. 70166–70181.

Jews from Vienna arrive in an RSHA transport. After the selection, 14 men are admitted to the camp and receive Nos. 167428–167441.

Two Polish prisoners, Jan Sławiński (No. 131865) and Franciszek Wołowiec (No. 131877), escape from Auschwitz III.

APMO, IZ-8/Gestapo Lodz/3a/88/545, 546; Mat.RO, vol. IV, p. 292.

Two boys born in the Gypsy camp in Birkenau receive Nos. Z-8959 and Z-8960.

APMO, D-AuII-3/1/2, p. 265, Register of Male Gypsies.

DECEMBER 9

A member of the resistance movement in the camp, Stanisław Kłodziński, reports in a secret message to Teresa Lasocka: "The changed course, which forbids shootings, etc., has been achieved through pressure from abroad. Our greatest murderers—Grabner, Boger, Woźnica, Palitzsch—are relieved of their duties: dismissed and transferred. They are being investigated because of thievery in Canada. On the night of the seventh-eighth, they set fire to a barracks of the Political Department where the evidence of their thievery was deposited. They destroyed this material. Lachmann did it. In this way, they want to prevent Berlin from learning of the evidence of their guilt. Publish. The new Commandant has eased tension. The Political Department has fallen from its leading position in the camp and plays only a subordinate role."

APMO, Mat.RO, vol. I, p. 44.

For fear that the burning of the barracks and the evidence of the guilt of individual accused SS men would lead to the cessation of the investigation and the acquittal of the accused, the resistance movement in the camp prepares an indictment and probably assigns the clandestine cell of the PPS in Brzeszcze to make sure that the investigation takes a proper course.* The leader of the Polish wing

APMO, Mat.RO, vol. I, p. 45.

*The letter is not completely preserved, it lacks the addressee. Pery Broad writes: "Meanwhile, the Polish resistance movement was indefatigably active to lift the cloud of secrecy surrounding Auschwitz and tell the world of the crimes taking place there. Secret messages conveyed by escaped prisoners and civilian workers employed in the camp provided a lot of material. A letter was composed, called 'The Death Camp.' While most outsiders probably interpreted these descriptions as exaggerated horror propaganda, they nonetheless contained only a fraction of the real events. The Commandant's Office of Auschwitz was sent a copy of this explanatory pamphlet by the Head of RSHA with a 'request for comment.' In Berlin, they were furious and wanted to know how so much could get out. The Poles were even informed about the murders in Block 11!" (Broad, *Memoirs*, p. 47).

of the Auschwitz brigade, Józef Cyrankiewicz, gives instructions in a secret message: "Attention! Put this letter into good German *as soon as possible* in 3 copies on a German typewriter. It is to be sent to the following addresses:

1. The director of the Special Commission in Auschwitz Concentration Camp.
2. The Commandant of Auschwitz I.
3. The Camp Commander of Auschwitz I.

The letters must be sent immediately by mail in carefully sealed envelopes. Send from *Auschwitz* (best) or from Silesia (*not so good*). *All possible speed is demanded!!!* Send an answer, how soon this will be done."

Reeducation prisoner Emil Szeliga (No. EH-5588) is caught trying to escape and is locked in the bunker of Block 11. He is released from the bunker into the camp with orders not to leave the camp grounds.

APMO, D-AuI-3/1, Bunker Register, p. 65.

The occupancy level of Professor Dr. Clauberg's experimental ward is increased by one: 399 female prisoners for research purposes are housed there.

APMO, D-AuI-3a/370/7/438, Monthly Labor Deployment List.

645 prisoners from the Fürstengrube A.C. are employed in the Fürstengrube in Wesoła extracting coal and building a new mine. This is the highest level of employment in December. At the end of December, only 483 prisoners are employed.

APMO, D-AuI-3a/370/7/476a, Monthly Labor Deployment List.

A Gypsy woman receives No. Z-9669.

Three girls born in the Gypsy camp the previous day receive Nos. Z-9670–Z-9672.

APMO, D-AuII-3/2/5, p. 623, Register of Female Gypsies.

13 Jewish prisoners transferred from Vienna on December 2 are taken out of Quarantine Camp B-IIa in Birkenau and killed in the gas chamber.

APMO, Dpr.-Hd/6, p. 24; D-AuII-3/1, p. 4, Quarantine List.

A female prisoner transferred from Ravensbrück receives No. 70182.

A prisoner sent from Prague receives No. 167709.

DECEMBER 10

28 Gypsy men and 22 Gypsy women sent in a group transport from the territory of the German Reich are given Nos. Z-8961–Z-8988 and Z-9673–Z-9694, respectively.

A female prisoner sent from Dusseldorf receives No. 70183.

1,000 Jewish men, women, and children arrive from Drancy with the sixty-fourth RSHA transport from France. In the transport are

CDECM, *Jews in Italy*, p. 14.

350 Italian Jews who were sent from Nice to Drancy. After the selection, 267 men and 72 women are admitted to the camp and receive Nos. 167442–167708 and 70184–70255. The remaining 661 people are killed in the gas chambers.

24 male and 88 female prisoners sent in a group transport are given Nos. 167710–167733 and 70256–70343.

72 prisoners sent from Pawiak Prison by the Warsaw Sipo and SD receive Nos. 167734–167805.

124 prisoners sent in a group transport receive Nos. 167806–167929.

Late in the evening, 334 Russian POWs are chosen from the Quarantine Camp B-IIa in Birkenau. These are prisoners wounded in the war and transferred from Viljandi on November 28. They are taken to the gas chambers and killed. To cover up killing the POWs, the camp administration circulates the story that the prisoners were transferred to Majdanek.

APMO, Dpr.-Hd/6, p. 24; D-AuII-3/1, p. 4, Quarantine List.

DECEMBER 11

50 female inmates, sent to the camp by the Gestapo from a prison in Munich, receive Nos. 70344–70393. There are 40 Yugoslavian women in the transport.

A female prisoner sent from Zichenau receives No. 70394.

Two female prisoners sent from Königsberg receive Nos. 70395 and 70396.

Two Gypsy women receive Nos. Z-9695 and Z-9696.

35 prisoners sent in a group transport receive Nos. 167934–167968.

The resistance movement in the camp sends the following letter to the Committee for the Assistance of Concentration Camp Prisoners (PWOK) in Kraków: "The present so-called change of course does not affect all the camps. It affects Auschwitz, where the abuse was no doubt most flagrant and numerically most significant. . . . The Commandant is carrying out an investigation in the Political Department concerning the constant illegal shootings. In the documents the cause of death is listed as of illness and the prisoners' infirmary is given as the place of death—signed by the Camp Doctor. The mysterious but unambiguous fire in the barracks of the Political Department in which what was supposed to burn indeed did burn and the arrest of the former Director of the Political Department, Grabner, and of one of his worst henchmen, Boger*—

APMO, Mat.RO, vol. I, p. 46.

*SS Staff Sergeant Wilhelm Boger.

In Auschwitz were to be found prisoners of different nationalities, religions, political convictions, and professions, from almost all the countries in Europe. Here, Soviet prisoners of war are brought to the camp.

who, in his limited mind sniffed plots everywhere and has almost all the murders of the last months on his conscience—ended the entire operation. At present, a quiet but bitter struggle between the Political Department and the Commandant is in progress. The Political Department takes pains to prove that the previous bloody Terror was necessary and that on this terrain, the Auschwitz Camp, surrounded by a hostile and organized population, this was the only method."*

600 Jews, arrested in Milan and Verona, arrive with an RSHA transport from Italy. After the selection, 61 men and 35 women are admitted to the camp and receive Nos. 167969–168029 and 70397–70431. The remaining 504 deportees are killed in the gas chambers.

Jews in Italy, p. 14.

A transport with 200 Polish and Russian prisoners is transferred from Auschwitz to Buchenwald.**

APMO, Mat.RO, vol. VII, p. 474.

Commandant Liebehenschel of Auschwitz I orders that the Commandant's Office of Buchenwald be notified by telegraph immediately that the 200 prisoners who are en route must undergo a delousing and be quarantined strictly for one week after their arrival.†

APMO, IZ-13/89, Various Documents of the Third Reich, p. 212.

---

*The original of the letter is not extant, but a carbon of the typewritten manuscript is preserved. This letter proves that the leadership of the resistance movement understood the situation clearly. This allowed the movement to participate in the struggle on the side of the Commandant, to the advantage of the political prisoners.

**The 200 prisoners are deleted from the Camp Register on December 14 and subtracted from the occupancy of Auschwitz on December 14, after confirmation of their arrival in Buchenwald.

†The reason for this order is the typhus epidemic raging in Birkenau and again in the main camp (APMO, Mat.RO, vol. I, pp. 50ff.).

DECEMBER 12

In the women's camp in Birkenau, 9,324 female prisoners are sick and unable to work. An SS Camp Doctor along with SS men and female overseers carries out a selection and selects 2,106 prisoners. They are killed in the gas chambers the same day. The next day, 7,418 female prisoners are sick and unable to work.

APMO, D-AuI-3a/370/7/438, Monthly Labor Deployment List; Mat.RO, vol. I, pp. 50ff.; Seweryna Szmaglewska, *Dymy nad Birkenau* (Smoke over Birkenau), Warsaw, 1946, p. 199.

55 prisoners of war are transferred from the Lamsdorf camp. They receive Nos. RKG-11075–RKS-11129.

DECEMBER 13

Russian prisoner Vladimir Popovich* (No. 107526) escapes a second time, from the work hall of Weichsel-Union-Metallwerke.

APMO, IZ-10/Gestapo Sieradz/2/197; D-AuI-1/2b, p. 303, Bulletin of Jan. 1, 1944.

14 male and 17 female prisoners sent in a group transport are given Nos. 168030–168043 and 70432–70448.

DECEMBER 14

Siemens-Schuckert Electric employs 40 female prisoners in its newly built plant in Bobrek near Auschwitz. They are taken to work daily in a truck. Molds for parts and electrical equipment for motors are produced there.

APMO, D-AuI-3a/370/7/449a, Monthly Labor Deployment List.

Two boys born in the women's camp in Birkenau receive Nos. 166879 and 166880.

Four Gypsy women sent from the territory of the German Reich receive Nos. Z-9697–Z-9700.

In Camp B-IIg in Birkenau, the construction of the personal effects warehouse complex is finished. It is called Canada by both prisoners and SS men. The warehouse complex, which is between Crematoriums III and IV and borders the men's prisoners' infirmary, in Camp B-IIf, consists of 30 barracks. In 25 barracks, the items taken from Jews sent to death in the camp are stored and sorted. The stolen property that can't be stored piles up, some still packed in valises, between the barracks. The prisoners who are employed in this unit live in two barracks; the three additional barracks are for the administration.

APMO, D-AuII-1/55, Commandant's Office Order 2/43; Dpr.-Hd/6, p. 35.

21 male and 13 female prisoners sent from Montelupich Prison by the Sipo and SD of Warsaw are given Nos. 168044–168064 and 70449–70461. The male prisoners are taken to the main camp.

APMO, Mat.RO, vol. 1, p. 50.

*The first time he escaped was on September 2, 1943; he was captured, locked in the bunker on November 17, and released on November 23. He is shot on January 27, 1944, while again fleeing.

DECEMBER 15

The occupancy level of Professor Dr. Clauberg's experimental ward is decreased by one: 398 female prisoners transferred for experimental purposes are now housed there.

APMO, D-AuI-3a/370/7/438, Monthly Labor Deployment List.

Two Gypsy women sent in a group transport from the territory of the German Reich receive Nos. Z-9701 and Z-9702.

A prisoner sent from Kattowitz on December 12 receives No. 168065.

Nine prisoners sent in a group transport receive Nos. 168066–168074.

The employment level in the Buna plants reaches its highest point in the month of December with 5,594 prisoners. At the end of the month, only 5,314 prisoners are still employed.

APMO, D-AuI-3a/370/7/474a, Monthly Labor Deployment List.

A female prisoner sent from Kattowitz receives No. 70462.

SS man Alois Kulovitz of the 2nd Guard Company is commended by Garrison Senior Liebehenschel and given five days' vacation for preventing the escape of Emil Mlynařyk on December 6.

APMO, D-AuI-1, Garrison Order 55/43, Dpr.-Hd/12, p. 81.

DECEMBER 16

Four prisoners sent in a group transport receive Nos. 168075–168078.

Six female prisoners sent from Kattowitz receive Nos. 70463–70468.

16 Gypsy men and two Gypsy women are sent in a group transport from the territory of the German Reich. The men are given Nos. Z-8989–Z-9004 and the women, Nos. Z-9703 and Z-9704.

One female prisoner sent from Dresden receives No. 70469.

47 male and 35 female prisoners sent to the camp by the Sipo and SD for the Kraków District are given Nos. 168079–168125 and 70470–70504.

28 prisoners sent in a group transport receive Nos. 168126–168153.

The Gestapo of Zichenau sends eight female prisoners to the camp who are given Nos. 70505–70512. Among them is Stanisława Olewnik (No. 70508), born September 27, 1917, imprisoned on October 8, 1943, and sentenced to Auschwitz on November 27,

APMO, IZ-11/Gestapo Zichenau/1/90/291-337, Trial Documents; D-RO/10, p. 13, List of Polish Women Who Died in Auschwitz.

1943, for sheltering and assisting the Jewish family Mławski.* Stanisława Olewnik dies in the camp on April 20, 1944.

11 prisoners are locked in one of the rooms of Block 11. They were released from the bunker on November 23 and marked as dangerous political prisoners with red dots and the letters "i.L." for "im Lager," "in camp." One of those again locked in Block 11 is Józef Cyrankiewicz.

APMO, Mat.RO, vol. I, p. 50.

2,491 Jews from Theresienstadt arrive in an RSHA transport of 981 men and boys and 1,510 women and girls. The men are given Nos. 168154–169134 and the women, Nos. 70513–72019 and 72028–72030. They are housed in the Theresienstadt Family Camp in Camp B-IIb in Birkenau without a selection taking place.

APMO, Dpr.-Hd/6, p. 255; D-RF-3/94, Lists of Names.

Stanisław Klodzniński smuggles a secret message out of the camp, addressed to "Borutatelladam,"** in which he reports the renewed incarceration of Józef Cyrankiewicz in Block 11. He goes on: "Moreover, a trap must be set either near Marysia in Zator or somewhere on the way for Dorosiewicz, a camp informer, a big, dark-haired man. He's wearing a black jacket and the yellow Capo's band and has long hair. The civilian workers who come here know him, he is about 35 years old. He intends to reveal the contacts of the camp to the outside world. He must either be poisoned (he drinks vodka) or shot. Without hesitation—on the spot and as fast as possible. . . . In addition, the case of Lili K.,† who is known to the camp informers, disturbs me. If there's an opportunity, get rid of the informer—Wierysz-Kowalski—poison or shoot him."

APMO, Mat.RO, vol. I, pp. 50ff.

Four prisoners sent from Prague receive Nos. 169135–169138.

Eight female prisoners sent from Vienna receive Nos. 72020–72027.

At 3:00 P.M., high-voltage current is turned on in the fence around the personal effects complex in Birkenau.

APMO, D-AuII-1/55, Commandant's Office Order 2/43.

41 prisoners are moved from Auschwitz to Majdanek.

APMO, Mat.RO, vol. VII, p. 474.

The Director of the surgical section in the prisoners' infirmary in Auschwitz I draws up a report for the period from September 15 to December 15 indicating that 106 castrations and sterilizations

APMO, Dpr.-Hd/6, p. 86.

*Ruchla Mławska, born 1887; Abraham Mławski, born 1918; Henia Mławska, born 1921; and Hanka Mławska, born 1924.
**"Boruta" is the underground alias of Edward Hałoń, one of the organizers of the clandestine PPS group in Brzeszcze, who was active in the Assistance Committee of the PWOK in Kraków from the middle of 1943; "Tell" is the alias of Teresa Lasocka; "Adam" means Adam Rysiewicz, the secretary of the local workers' committee of the PPS in Kraków and member of the PWOK.
†Irena Kuźmierzewska-Kabatowa, manager of the Section for the Welfare of Prisoners and Their Families (called the Patronat) in Kraków.

were performed in the hospital by amputation of the testicles, genital operations, ovariectomy, removal of the Fallopian tubes, etc.*

Seven Polish Gypsy women transferred in a group transport receive Nos. Z-9705–Z-9711.

DECEMBER 17

Four prisoners sent from Vienna receive Nos. 167930–167933.

800 Jewish men and women from Bendin arrive in an RSHA transport. After the selection, 92 men and 169 women are admitted to the camp and are given Nos. 169139–169230 and 72060–72228. The remaining 539 men and women are killed in the gas chambers.

Szternfinkiel, *Jews of Sosnowitz*, pp. 57, 59; APMO, Personal-Information Cards.

191 prisoners sent in a group transport receive Nos. 169231–169421.

The Czech Jaroslav Studeny (No. 67311), who escaped from the camp on November 5, is captured and locked in the bunker of Block 11. He is released from the bunker into the camp on February 2, 1944, with orders not to leave the camp grounds.

APMO, D-AuI-1/2b, p. 254, Bulletin of the Gestapo of Silesia; D-AuI-3/2, Bunker Register, p. 65.

60 Jewish prisoners are transferred from Auschwitz to Majdanek.

APMO, Mat.RO, vol. VII, p. 474.

Five Gypsy women sent from the territory of the German Reich in a group transport receive Nos. Z-9712–Z-9716.

Accompanied by Camp Commander SS First Lieutenant Hofmann and Labor Deployment Director SS Second Lieutenant Sell, Commandant Liebehenschel inspects Block 11. During the inspection, Hofmann explains that he cannot take responsibility for the prisoners isolated here who wear the red dot and the letters "i.L." for "im Lager." Józef Cyrankiewicz makes a risky decision and asks the Block Clerk to announce him to report to the Commandant,**

APMO, Mat.RO, Józef Cyrankiewicz File.

---

*The sterilizations carried out by Dr. Schumann in Women's Camp B-Ia in Birkenau on male and female prisoners are done with X rays of varying levels of radiation. The experimental ward is in Birkenau in Block 30. Castrations and surgical sterilizations, on the other hand, are performed in Block 21 in the main camp, where the surgical section of the infirmary is located. After the radiation, the young men and women are moved in groups, some after two to four weeks, others after two to eleven months, to Block 21. There, the operations are done in series; according to the experimental purpose, the men have either one or both testicles amputated. In a single-testicle castration, the second testicle is removed one to two months later. The histological preparations are sent to the Institute for Pathological Anatomy in Breslau. After the radiation, the victims of the experiment return to their work unit. Some, whose health is too bad—it depends on the radiation dose—are sent immediately to the gas chambers. Those who undergo operations spend 10 to 12 days in Block 21. If complications occur because of infection and the recent radiation, they are chosen during a selection and sent to the gas chambers. Of the total number of 1,000 victims of these experiments, only a few survive. Some of them testify at the Nuremberg Trial (Ternon and Helman, *History of SS Medicine*, pp. 183–185). **Normally, a prisoner can ask permission to report to the Commandant. The possibility of reporting to the Commandant exists only since Liebehenschel has taken over. Until then, it was dangerous for a prisoner to ask to report, since he had no rights.

since he assumes there is a connection between this statement and a provocation prepared by the Political Department to discredit the soft policy of the new Commandant and to regain influence.

DECEMBER 18

98 prisoners are moved from the Brünn auxiliary camp to Jawischowitz auxiliary camp, where they are put to work in the coal mines.

APMO, D-AuI-3a/370/7/455a, Monthly Labor Deployment List; Dpr.-ZOd/63, p. 49.

The occupancy level in Professor Dr. Clauberg's experimental ward is decreased by one: 397 female prisoners transferred for research purposes are now housed there.

APMO, D-AuI-3a/370/7/438, Monthly Labor Deployment List.

1,418 prisoners are employed in the mine in Brzeszcze-Jawischowitz for extracting coal and above-ground construction. This is the highest employment level for the month of December.

APMO, D-AuI-3a/370/7/456a, Monthly Labor Deployment List.

A prisoner transferred from Kattowitz receives free No. 166881.

Seven prisoners sent from Kattowitz receive Nos. 169422–169428.

33 female prisoners sent in a group transport receive Nos. 72229–72261.

On Saturday night, when the prisoners return from the mines, a prisoner escapes from the Fürstengrube A.C., which belongs to Auschwitz III. It is the Jew Gabriel Rothkopf, born May 16, 1919, in Brzesko, who was sent to Auschwitz on November 6, 1943, in an RSHA transport from the labor camp in Szebnie. After the prisoners' return, Camp Commander Otto Moll has all the prisoners awakened and orders them to the roll-call area. Without any investigation, he chooses a few prisoners and shoots them personally in front of the lined-up prisoners. He leaves the bodies lying on the ground until the next work shift returns.

APMO, IZ-8/Gestapo Lodz/3a/88/547; D-AuI-1/1b, p. 303, Bulletin of Jan. 1, 1944. Statements: vol. 50, p. 94; vol. 54, p. 36; vol. 60, p. 107, Accounts of Former Prisoners Józef Łabudek, Paul Halter, Jan Ławnicki.

DECEMBER 19

An SS Camp Doctor makes a selection in Quarantine Camp B-IIa in Birkenau. He chooses 338 prisoners, who are killed in the gas chambers the same day.

APMO, Dpr.-Hd/6, pp. 5, 54; D-AuI-3a/370/7/448; Monthly Labor Deployment List in which 338 prisoners are listed as deceased on this day.

151 prisoners are employed in the Brünn A.C. on the renovation of a building that Branch C of the WVHA has taken over for the Technical College of the SS and Police.

APMO, D-AuI-3a/370/7/455a, Monthly Labor Deployment List.

310 male and 61 female prisoners are sent from Radom by the Sipo and SD. The men are given Nos. 166867–166870 and 169429–169734; the women receive Nos. 72262–72322.

The Polish prisoner Eugeniusz Lachowski (No. 119331) is caught trying to escape and locked in the bunker of Block 11. He is released from the bunker on December 21, 1943.

APMO, D-AuI-3/2, Bunker Register, p. 65.

DECEMBER 20

850 Jewish men, women, and children arrive from Drancy with the sixty-third RSHA transport from France. After the selection, 233 men and 112 women are admitted to the camp and receive Nos. 169735–169967 and 72323–72434. The remaining 505 people are killed in the gas chambers.

2,473 Jews arrive from Theresienstadt in an RSHA transport. 1,137 men and boys in the transport receive Nos. 169969–171105, and 1,336 women and girls receive Nos. 72435–73700. They are housed in the so-called Theresienstadt Family Camp, in B-IIb, in Birkenau.

APMO, Dpr.-Hd/6, p. 255; D-RF-3/95, 95a, List of Names.

44 male and 33 female prisoners sent in a group transport are given Nos. 171106–171149 and 73771–73803.

509 prisoners of the Janinagrube A.C. are employed in extracting in the Janinagrube. This is the highest prisoner employment level in the mine in December.

APMO, D-AuI-3a/370/7/459, Monthly Labor Deployment List.

11 Jewish men and 15 Jewish women are selected from a transport of December 18 transferred from Stutthof. The men are given Nos. 171150–171160 and the women, Nos. 73804–73818. Approximately 600 people from this transport are killed in the gas chambers.

The Director of the Administration Department of Auschwitz I sends to the Lodz Gestapo a package with various personal documents like passes, registrations, labor and identity cards, and fingerprints of nine prisoners who died in September and had been sent to the camp by the Lodz Sipo and SD.

APMO, IZ-8/Gestapo Lodz/3a/88/656.

DECEMBER 21

A Gypsy woman transferred in a group transport receives No. Z-9717.

APMO, D-AuI-3a/370/7/438, Monthly Labor Deployment List.

38 female prisoners sent in a group transport receive Nos. 73819–73856.

The occupancy level in Professor Dr. Clauberg's experimental ward is increased by one: 400 female prisoners for research purposes are housed there.

Six prisoners are sent to the Penal Company, four for three months and two for six months. The prisoner Freibig (No. 151046) dies on January 6, 1944. Three of those sent are Russian POWs: Vladimir Potapov (No. RKG-10478), Fyodor Popov (No. RKG-10543), and Michail Sorokin (No. RKG-10543). They complete their punishment and are released from the Penal Company into the camp on March 21, 1944.

APMO, D-AuI, p. 13, Penal Company Register.

Two prisoners, so-called V men (Verbindungsmänner—informers) of the Political Department, escape from Auschwitz I. They are the Capo Stanisław Dorosiewicz (No. 18379) and the Jew Hersz Kurcweig (No. 65655) of the so-called Canada squad. The prisoners leave the camp accompanied by an SS man on the pretext of wanting to show him where the Communist resistance movement in the camp meets with outside resistance groups. They make good their escape, planned by the Political Department, and en route murder SS Private First Class Peter Jarosiewitsch, who accompanies them. The murder was planned in advance and was the operation announced in advance by the informer Wierusz-Kowalski as a "bomb."

APMO, IZ-10/Gestapo Sieradz/2/88/178; D-AuI-1, Garrison Order 3/44, Jan. 19, 1944; Mat.RO, vol. IV, p. 295, and Józef Cyrankiewicz File.

DECEMBER 22

Josef Daniel, born in the Gypsy camp, receives No. Z-9005.

APMO, D-AuII-3/1/2, p. 267, Register of Male Gypsies.

Two boys born in the women's camp in Birkenau receive the free Nos. 166871 and 166872.

A girl born to a woman transferred from Lemberg on December 19 receives No. 73857.

A girl born to a female prisoner sent to the women's camp in Birkenau on December 20, 1943, by Mobile Command 9 receives No. 73858.

Cyryl Szweda (No. 120514) is sent to the Penal Company for six months. On January 20, 1944, he dies in the Penal Company.

APMO, D-AuI-3/1, p. 13, Penal Company Register.

In the morning, the news of the escape of Stanisław Dorosiewicz and the murder of the SS man spreads through the main camp. Commandant Liebehenschel and SS Garrison Doctor Wirths set out for the place where the body of the murdered SS man was found. A resistance movement liaison in the camp informs Józef Cyrankiewicz and also communicates the declaration of Roll Call Leader Clausen that Berlin will have at least 100 prisoners shot in retaliation for such an act.

APMO, Mat.RO, Józef Cyrankiewicz File.

The prisoner Hermann Langbein is called to the office of Commandant Liebehenschel, where he takes the opportunity to repeat the comments of the informant Wierusz-Kowalski, in the presence of Dr. Wirths and after receiving a guarantee that his testimony would not become known to the Political Section. Furthermore, he is willing to describe the previous work and methods of the Political Department and to describe the provocative activity of the camp informers and the criminal prisoner functionaries in the service of the Political Department. After his return to the office of the SS sick bay, Langbein sends a secret message to Józef Cyrankiewicz in Block 11 communicating to him the content of the conversation and informing him that he will perhaps be called to the Commandant's Office.

Hermann Langbein, *Die Stärkeren* (The Stronger Ones), 2d rev. ed. Cologne, 1982, pp. 188–194; APMO, Mat.RO, Józef Cyrankiewicz File.

When Cyrankiewicz is called by Commandant Liebehenschel to his office, he finds the nine directors of the Political Department there along with the Commandant. Therefore, he limits himself to the following statement: "I declare that for fourteen days I have had knowledge that Dorosiewicz, who is known in the entire camp as chief informer, planned an escape for provocative purposes. Moreover, it is known to me—as another camp informant openly announced to me, incidentally, with a provocative intent—that an event was to be connected with the escape that would unleash repressions against the prisoners. It is not my business to find out who is behind this plan. If one relies on the hints made by the camp informants, some circles in the Political Department are behind it. Since as prisoners we have no possibility of defending ourselves against attempts to shift the responsibility for the heinous deeds of a notorious camp informant and provocateur onto us, I declare in the presence of the Commandant that the escapee is a completely official figure of the Political Department, and as such is the last person for whom the prisoners could take moral responsibility. To hold the prisoners physically responsible for this incident means simply to fulfill the wishes of the circles whose intention was revealed to me for a completely different purpose by one of the leaders of the Political Department."

In the subsequent brief discussion, Cyrankiewicz communicates to the Commandant that in the presence of SS Second Lieutenant Schurz, he can say no more. The Commandant declares that he will have him called another time.

APMO, Mat.RO, Józef Cyrankiewicz File.

64 male prisoners and 75 female prisoners sent in a group transport receive Nos. 171161–171224 and 73859–73933.

Commandant Liebehenschel reminds the SS members of the garrison of the prohibition against entering the bordello in Auschwitz I.

APMO, Dpr.-ZOd/39, Garrison Order 56/43.

Commandant Liebehenschel, the Garrison Senior, orders a prohibition, to take immediate effect, against prisoners' driving vehicles, even in the presence of sentries.

Ibid.

Garrison Senior Liebehenschel informs the SS men that guard escorts must maintain a distance of six paces from prisoners. SS men who do not follow this order are to be punished by arrest in the future.*

Ibid.

DECEMBER 23

93 prisoners sent in a group transport receive Nos. 171225–171317.

*This warning and threat of imprisonment is connected with the murder of SS Private First Class Jarosiewitsch by Dorosiewicz and Kurcweig. Liebehenschel does not yet inform the personnel of the garrison of the facts surrounding the incident, because he has not yet sent a report to Berlin. He institutes further inquiries.

Four Gypsy women transferred from the territory of the German Reich receive Nos. Z-9718–Z-9721.

DECEMBER 24

20 male and 15 female prisoners sent in a group transport are given Nos. 171318–171337 and 73934–73948.

A female prisoner transferred to the camp on December 19 receives No. 73949.

Józef Cyrankiewicz is once again ordered to Commandant Liebe-henschel. As he is led through the camp, the prisoners are gathering for roll call, held early because of Christmas Eve. In a one-to-one talk, Cyrankiewicz has an opportunity to repeat what was previ-ously said by the leaders of the Auschwitz combat group about the curtailment of the influence of the Political Department, the main-tenance of the prohibitions introduced by Liebehenschel of punish-ing prisoners with death, and the destruction of the network of informers who are in the service of the Political Department.* Cyr-ankiewicz speaks in his own name, of course, but it is clear to the Commandant that all prisoners are in agreement. The Commandant declares that he has formed his opinion on the Dorosiewicz case. He will not allow repressions against the prisoners and he will take care of men like Dorosiewicz. He orders Cyrankiewicz to compose a written statement on the questions set forth during the conver-sation and declares that no harm will come to him as a result and that the written account will be sent for after the holidays.

APMO, Mat.RO, Józef Cyran-kiewicz File.

DECEMBER 25

The first day of Christmas: The total occupancy level of Auschwitz I, II, and III is 56,596 registered male and 30,324 registered female prisoners, 86,920 prisoners in all. There are 19,081 prisoners in the prisoners' infirmary and in the convalescent blocks, 11,039 of them men and 8,042 women. 8,289 prisoners—5,811 men and 2,478 women—are employed on this date, in the camp, on the farms and in agricultural operations, in the armaments industry, and in other labor squads.

APMO, D-AuI-3a/370/7/438/448, Monthly Labor Deploy-ment List.

DECEMBER 26

The second day of Christmas: The total occupancy level of of Ausch-witz I, II, and III is 56,554 registered male and 30,346 registered female, 86,900 prisoners in all. 18,872 prisoners are in the pris-oners' infirmary and convalescent blocks, 10,841 of them men and 8,031 women. 45,713 male and 22,315 female inmates are classified as able-bodied by the SS. 27,804 prisoners, 22,345 men and 5,459

Ibid.

---

*Two hours after his talk with Commandant Liebehenschel, Cyrankiewicz gets the news from fellow prisoners that the informers of the Political Department named by him have been strictly forbidden to leave their blocks.

women,* are employed on this date, for camp purposes, on the farms and in agricultural operations, in the expansion of the camp, the SS offices, and in the armaments industry.

DECEMBER 27

28 female prisoners sent in a group transport receive Nos. 73950–73977.

Six prisoners sent from Kattowitz receive Nos. 166873–166878.

A messenger is sent by Commandant Liebehenschel to fetch a letter, written in German and dated December 24, from Józef Cyrankiewicz.**

APMO, Mat.RO, Józef Cyrankiewicz File.

DECEMBER 28

Two Gypsy women receive Nos. Z-9722 and Z-9723.

The occupancy level in Professor Dr. Clauberg's experimental ward is decreased by one. 399 female prisoners for research are now housed there.

APMO, D-AuI-3a/370/7/438, Monthly Labor Deployment List.

DECEMBER 29

Three Gypsy men and five Gypsy women are transferred from the territory of the German Reich. The men are given Nos. Z-9006–Z-9008 and the women, Nos. Z-9724–Z-9728.

One male and five female prisoners sent from Kattowitz are given Nos. 171338 and Nos. 73978–73982.

A commission consisting of Commandant Liebehenschel, Camp Commander Hofmann, SS Garrison Doctor Wirths, and Roll Call Leader Clausen comes to Block 11 to communicate the contents of the punishment orders to the prisoners who were previously released from the bunker and subsequently isolated in Block 11. Most receive a flogging of 25 blows with a stick and the notification that they are being transferred for disciplinary reasons to other camps. Liebehenschel has Cyrankiewicz called into a separate room and, holding a letter, informs him that he is to receive a punishment which was confirmed by Berlin. Nevertheless, since he has convinced him, Liebehenschel, of the reasons for his desire to escape, he excuses

APMO, Mat.RO, Józef Cyrankiewicz File.

---

*It follows from these numbers that the second day of Christmas is a workday for some of the prisoners. As a result of the permanent admission of new prisoners into the camp and the high mortality rate caused by the living conditions, the terror, and the typhus epidemic, there is constant considerable variation in the total number of male and female prisoners.
**On March 22, 1944, Cyrankiewicz sends a copy of the letter, along with an extensive report covering the period from November 23, 1943, to mid-March 1944, to Adam Rysiewicz in Kraków with instructions to Teresa Lasocka to make use of both of them.

him from the punishment. He thinks that Cyrankiewicz will not escape now.*

10 prisoners transferred from Neuengamme Camp receive Nos. 171339–171348.

The Director of the Administration Department of Auschwitz I sends to the Lodz Gestapo a package with various personal documents from six deceased prisoners who were sent to Auschwitz by the Sipo and SD.

APMO, IZ-8/Gestapo Lodz/3a/ 88/658, 659.

DECEMBER 30

The following prisoners are sent to the Penal Company: Władysław Bober (No. 102693) for six months, and transferred to Buchenwald Camp at the expiration of the punishment on April 26, 1944; for three months, Hilel Gewis (No. 128410), died January 3, 1944, Zika Zmudja (No. 146283), died January 28, 1944, and Nikolai Kotov (No. 149567) and Nikola Klufinskyj (No. 159178), both of whom complete the punishment and are released into the camp on March 30, 1944.

APMO, D-AuI-3/1, p. 14, Penal Company Register.

The occupancy level in Professor Dr. Clauberg's experimental ward is reduced by one: 398 female prisoners for research purposes are now housed there.

APMO, D-AuI-3a/370/7/438, Monthly Labor Deployment List.

SS Corporal Pfeiffer and SS Privates Gonglach and Metzger are rewarded by Commandant Liebehenschel with five days' vacation for preventing an escape by seven prisoners on December 18, 1943.

APMO, D-AuI-1, Garrison Order 57/43.

Four prisoners sent from Kattowitz receive Nos. 171349–171352. This is the last transport to enter Auschwitz in 1943.

DECEMBER 31

The total occupancy level of Auschwitz I, II, and III is 55,785 men, including 11,433 men who are sick and incapable of working. 44,352 prisoners are classified as able-bodied by the SS, and of them 12,272 are unemployed. Of the 32,080 employed prisoners, 5,524 are camp personnel, 2,480 work on the farms and in the agricultural operations, 8,436 in the expansion of the camp, 1,695 in the DAW squads, 2,975 in the offices of the SS, 10,913 in industrial plants (counting the auxiliary camps), and 57 prisoners in private workplaces.

APMO, D-AuI-3a/370/7/448, Monthly Labor Deployment List.

The occupancy level of Auschwitz II is 29,513 female prisoners, including 8,266 women who are sick and incapable of working and 21,647 who are classified as able-bodied by the SS, of whom 13,470 are unemployed. Of the 7,777 employed female prisoners, 2,980

APMO, D-AuI-3a/370/7/438, Monthly Labor Deployment List.

---

*This releases him from the flogging. However, it does not protect him from transport to another camp.

work for the camp, 1,406 on the farms and in agricultural operations, 478 in construction, 297 in the DAW squads, 1,409 in the SS offices and organizations, 503 in the Weichsel-Union-Metallwerke, 250 in private operations and in the houses of SS personnel; Professor Dr. Clauberg's experimental ward houses 56 female prisoner orderlies and 398 female prisoners for research purposes, who are counted as employed.

DECEMBER 1–31

8,931 female prisoners die in the women's camp in Auschwitz II;* 4,247 of them are killed with gas after selections in the camp and in the prisoners' infirmary.

APMO, Mat.RO, vol. VII, p. 486.

5,748 male prisoners die in Auschwitz I, II, and III.**

APMO, D-AuI-3a/370/7/448, Monthly Labor Deployment List.

*According to the calculation of the author, based on the number of female prisoners admitted to Auschwitz in December and those struck from the monthly labor deployment lists, 8,908 registered female prisoners die in December. It is likely that 23 female prisoners who died in December 1943 are included in the labor deployment lists of January 1944.
**Calculated on the basis of the monthly labor deployment and accounting for the prisoners admitted in December and the 333 prisoners who were transferred to other camps or who escaped.

1 9 4 4

Soon after the collapse of his SS state a functionary of the Political Department in Auschwitz, Pery Broad, writes:

Broad, "Memoirs," p. 46.

> Hitler's will to exterminate the Jews served not only the "ideal ideological goal" of the "Purification of Europe," but also to an enormous extent the financing and support of the German war economy. In time, millions upon millions in domestic and foreign currencies were taken from the prisoners. . . . Some will wonder how the SS, which at the beginning of the war was barely able to purchase necessary equipment, a few years later was in a position to purchase entire blocks of imposing façades and government buildings."

The destruction of millions of people and the plundering committed by the SS in the name and for the aims of the Third Reich demoralize, corrupt, and criminalize all SS members involved to such an extent that Himmler sends a special SS commission to Auschwitz. Under the direction of SS Major Dr. Konrad Morgen, its purpose is to investigate the embezzlements and reestablish discipline by making examples of some miscreants by severe punishments.

The special commission's investigations, conducted during the second half of 1943, of the embezzling, i.e., thefts, committed by individual SS men of expropriated Jewish property, which in the view of the SS was state property, coincided with Allied broadcasts about ongoing SS crimes in Auschwitz.

The publication of SS men's names and of the death sentences carried out by SS henchmen in Auschwitz; the publicizing of details of crimes committed in the camp; and finally, the Polish resistance movement's published memorandum "The Death Camp" (see footnote, p. 542), a copy of which was sent by the Reich Central Security Office (RSHA) to the Commandant of Auschwitz for comment but also reached the hands of prisoners—these are all successful results of the activities of the prisoners' resistance movement and of the Polish resistance outside the camp.

By autumn 1943, all of these circumstances had led to personnel changes in the top command of Auschwitz, and the camp had been split into three parts. Ultimately, these circumstances led to Himmler's order that the special commission's investigations should go in a new direction.

The resistance movement in the camp ascertains that the new objective is to push the responsibility for most of the murders of prisoners from the higher SS echelons on to the lower ones. The question is not "Why have you murdered?" but rather, "Why have you murdered tens of thousands more than you were ordered to?" and "Why did you arouse so much attention that the whole world knows all the details of the crimes?"

The first Commandant of Auschwitz, Rudolf Höss, an ambitious organizer and zealous executor of all orders from the SS Commander in Chief and the SS Economic and Administrative Office (WVHA), thinks of himself as the great founder of the extermination camp and the planned Himmlerstadt (Himmler City) which is to arise in place of Auschwitz. He places executive power in the hands of the Camp Commanders and the functionaries of the Political Department. His successor, SS Lieutenant Colonel Arthur Liebehenschel, has no such ambitions: Upon taking over the command he explains to the prisoners that he will exercise his function in accordance with the current camp regulations—which to the prisoners must promise a loosening of the camp regime in comparison to the administration of the past years. For the functionaries of the Political Department, on the other hand, it is not acceptable, because they thereby lose the influence and personal advantages for which they are beholden to the Commandant.

The dissension within the SS and the power struggle between the Commandant and the functionaries of the Political Department are cleverly taken advantage of by the leadership of the camp resistance group. The prisoner Hermann Langbein has with time gained influence with the SS Garrison Doctor Wirths, and in his presence passes on to Commandant Liebehenschel his opinion on the situation in the camp, which has been brought about by the provocative activities of a network of the Political Department's camp spies. Prisoner Józef Cyrankiewicz makes his report to Commandant Liebehenschel in two conversations with him about the situation and the rights of the political prisoners in Auschwitz, submitting to Liebehenschel his oral argument in written form. All this leads to a reduction of the Political Department's influence in the camp. Its members are no longer allowed to remain on the camp grounds after evening roll call; they may no longer put any prisoners into Block 11 without the consent of the Commandant or at least a Camp Commander; some of the Political Department's functionaries are now assigned to guard duty; and SS Second Lieutenant Lachmann, who is in charge of the network of spies, is reassigned to Lublin and it is made known that this network of spies is to be dissolved.

In 1944 the leaders of the Auschwitz Combat Group have greater successes: after the intervention of the prisoner Hermann Langbein with SS Garrison Doctor Wirths and Wirths's intervention with the WVHA, the WVHA's orders with respect to the number of Jewish prisoners who are to be subjected to a selection are changed. As a result, the number of Jewish prisoners in the main camp selected to be killed every day in the gas chambers is reduced from 1,000 to 220. The resistance group prepares a list with the names of the camp spies who work with the Political Department and have it sent to Commandant Liebehenschel; these spies are transferred on February 2 with a punishment transport to Flossenbürg. Furthermore, the attention of the SS Garrison Doctor and the Commandant is drawn to the meetings of the Police Court-martial in Block 11, which contributes to saving dozens of prisoners from the death penalty. Finally, they succeed in keeping prisoner Józef Cyrankiewicz permanently in Block 20, for infectious diseases, which allows the resistance conspiracy to broaden its activities, especially politically.

Naturally, these successes do not change the character of Auschwitz, because this is not in the prisoners' hands. But they do achieve an improvement in the prisoners' frame of mind. They provide them with moral satisfaction, give some prisoners hope for survival, others hope for the possibility of actively participating in an armed struggle, if an appropriate moment should arise. In connection with this the secret cells formed by the leaders of the Auschwitz Combat Group and the prisoners intensify their activities. They continue to document the crimes committed by the SS in the camp, obtain copies and summaries of camp documents, and even substitute copies for the originals. The collected materials are secretly sent together with announcements and reports to the district workers' committee of the Polish Workers' Party (PPS) and to the Kraków Committee for Assistance to Concentration Camp Prisoners (Pomoc Więźniom Obozów Koncentracyjnych—PWOK). The resistance movement in the camp helps prisoners with escape preparations, so that they will be able to make or strengthen contact with the various political groups illegally active in the countryside, and will be able to join partisan units in the area. In addition, it reconnoiters the strength and armaments of the SS in the camp and in the garrison. It works toward political education with the objective of uniting the prisoners in the struggle against the National Socialist regime, and finally it prepares the prisoners for a potential revolt in the event of a favorable development on the front.

The SS also recognizes the danger to it represented by the large number of prisoners concentrated in Auschwitz and the auxiliary camps, and takes steps to protect the camp from a possible revolt by the prisoners. It increases the strength of the stationed SS units, a police company is made available as a reserve unit, and it can count on the assistance of Wehrmacht units in the area in case of an emergency.

At the end of March the WVHA decides that investments planned for the expansion of the camp must be limited to the absolutely indispensable. At the end of April, further construction on Section III of Birkenau, called "Mexico" by the prisoners, is halted, and the order comes through to deploy these laborers in the auxiliary camps and the armaments plants. The Commandant's Office of Auschwitz takes over the forced labor camps for Jews that are still operating in Upper Silesia and sets up new auxiliary camps: Bobrek, in the town of that name not far from Auschwitz, where the auxiliary camp is placed convenient to a plant of the electrical products company Siemens-Schuckert-Werke AG; Günthergrube (a mine) in Lędziny; Laurahütte (a foundry) in Siemianowice; Blechhammer in Slawentzitz (Sławięcice), near the Oberschlesische Hydrierwerke AG (Upper Silesian Waterworks); Sosnowitz II, near the Ost-Maschinenbau-Werke (Eastern Mechanical Engineering).

There were also four new auxiliary camps in Gleiwitz: Gleiwitz I, near the Reich Railway Repair Plant; Gleiwitz II, near the Deutsche Gasrusswerke GmbH (German Gas Coke Company); Gleiwitz III, near the Gleiwitzhütte; and Gleiwitz IV, a labor squad for building barracks and repairing and building military vehicles.

Further auxiliary camps are the Hindenburg A.C., near the Donnersmarck Foundry in Hindenburg; Trzebinia, near a branch of the Oberschlesische Erdölraffinerie GmbH (Upper Silesian Oil Refinery); Tschechowitz, a bomb search commando on the grounds of the refinery in Tschechowitz-Dziedzitz (Czechowice-Dziedzice); Tschechowitz-Vacuum, a labor squad for cleanup and security work in the local refinery; the 2nd SS Railroad Construction Brigade in Karlsruhe (Pokój) in Silesia, a labor squad used for clearing up rubble in bombed cities and for repairing bombed railway tracks; the Altheimer auxiliary camp near the construction site of a heating power station in Stara Kuźnia near Halemba; Bismarckhütte in Königshütte (Chorzów), a foundry and assembly facility for tanks and cannons; Charlottengrube in Rydułtowy, a coal pit; Neustadt A.C. near the Schlesische Feinweberei AG (Silesian Fine Weaving Company) in Neustadt (Prudnik); Freudenthal A.C., near the firm of Emmerich Machold in Bruntál, Czechoslovakia; Lichtewerden, near the G. S. Buhl & Sons yarn factory in Světla, Czechoslovakia; and the last, founded in December 1944, the Hubertushütte A.C. in Hohenlinde (Łagiewniki).

In May 1944, SS Lieutenant Colonel Rudolf Höss returns to Auschwitz after his appointment by SS Commander in Chief Himmler to oversee the extermination of the Hungarian Jews. The reason for Höss's transfer back—as he explained during the trial conducted against him in 1947 by the Supreme People's Court in Warsaw— are the complaints by the RSHA to the Head of Branch D of the WVHA, by Glücks, about Commandant Liebehenschel of Auschwitz I: Through the destruction of the informer network in the camp, he has helped the prison resistance movement and given it the means for further development. The same is said to make the Commandant Hartjenstein of Auschwitz II unsuitable for his job. There are no complaints against the Commandant of Auschwitz III.

During the same period, the Director of Section IV-B4 of the RSHA, SS Major Adolf Eichmann, who begins to implement the program for the destruction of the Hungarian Jews, identifies a number of "deficiencies," during a visit to Auschwitz, among them: the shutting down of Incineration Facility V used to incinerate corpses outdoors, i.e., the pits near old Bunker 2, and the delay in the construction of a three-track railway spur from the unloading ramp to Auschwitz II. Eichmann also offers his opinion to the RSHA that he is for the appointment of Höss as director for the operation of destroying the Hungarian Jews. At the same time Höss is given responsibility for training the new Commandants, SS Technical Sergeant Richard Baer, who is taking over from Liebehenschel, and SS Captain Josef Kramer, who replaces Hartjenstein as Commandant of Auschwitz II.

Eichmann plans to send four transports of Hungarian Jews per day to their destruction in Auschwitz. Despite the expansion of all the facilities, it turns out that in practice the extermination facilities do not suffice for the killing of so many people. For this reason Höss goes to Budapest, where he reaches an agreement with railway officials that on alternate days two trains of deportees, then three trains, should be dispatched. The agreement with railway officials in Budapest provides for a total of 111 such trains.

Simultaneously with the arrival of the first transports of deported Hungarian Jews, Eichmann arrives for an inspection of the extermination facilities in Auschwitz, because Himmler is demanding an acceleration of the so-called Hungary Operation, whose eager executor Höss becomes—he gives these measures the name "Operation Höss."

To conceal the steadily growing number of prisoners who are selected from the transports for destruction, the SS introduces two new series of numerals for Jewish prisoners beginning with A-1, one each for men and women, and later a series beginning with B-1, for men only.

Hard-pressed by the advance of Allied troops on the borders of the Third Reich and the quick advance of the Red Army, the SS hastily realizes its program of destruction, deporting Jews to Auschwitz, the only extermination center remaining at its disposal in the occupied territories. From the still existing transit camps, collection camps, and ghettos in occupied Europe transports of Jews from Trieste, Drancy, Malines, Westerbork, Theresienstadt, Radom, Lodz, Płaszów, Kowno, Fossoli di Carpi, Athens, Corfu, Rhodes, Pustków, Bliżyn, and from Hungary, Slovakia, and Galicia arrive in Auschwitz.

After the unloading of a transport the Jews are sent on a path along a railroad track to the so-called baths. During the march of those condemned to death the SS doctors seek from among the crowds young Jews of both genders who are able to perform heavy physical labor and send them to the camp. Among the selected are twins of all ages, on whom SS Camp Doctor Josef Mengele conducts experiments. The remaining Jews are sent directly from the platform into the gas chambers. The murder victims are above all the sick, the invalid, the old, pregnant women, women with nursing children, and children under 14 years of age.

In mid-May 1944, when the mass transports of Hungarian Jews start arriving in Auschwitz, the young, healthy, and strong Jews of both genders are dispersed for a time as so-called depot prisoners to various barracks at Birkenau, but are not recorded in the camp registers. They are accommodated in Camp B-IIIc, where young, able-bodied female Jews are kept; in the recently vacated Gypsy Family Camp B-IIe, where young, able-bodied male and female Jewish prisoners are accommodated who eventually are taken to the other camps; in Camp B-IIb, which is empty since the liquidation of the Theresienstadt Family Camp; and finally, in Section B-III, still under construction, known as "Mexico" to the prisoners and also intended for female Jews. The Jews temporarily located in Birkenau receive no I.D. numbers and are not tattooed. Selections are conducted at specific intervals: When the camp administration has a need for laborers, it sends some prisoners from these camps to specific auxiliary camps or to the labor squads. Then they are registered and given numbers. Under the direction of the WVHA, others are transferred to armaments plants in the interior of the Reich.

Jewish twins of various ages—children and adults—and also dwarfs are sent mainly to Auschwitz, as they are of interest to SS Camp Doctor Josef Mengele, who conducts experiments on them.

The separate section of Camp B-IIe for unregistered male and female Jews, Camp B-IIc, and Section B-III (Mexico) are referred to in camp documents as the so-called Auschwitz II Transit Camp. The female Jews without numbers are referred to in the camp records as "transit Jews." Under inhuman conditions they remain for weeks in the camp and await the final decision on their fate. The young and healthy are deported to labor camps near the armaments plants. The weak and those exhausted from their stay in the camp are sent by SS Camp Doctors Mengele and Thilo to the gas chambers after the selection. The former prisoner Dr. Otto Wolken and other former prisoners testified in the trial against Rudolf Höss that in "Mexico," for two months there were approximately 50,000 naked young Hungarian Jewish women. That not only outer clothing but also underclothing was denied them cannot be attributed to a lack of clothing in the camp, since the storehouses of the Personal Effects Camp, "Canada," are bursting with the possessions stolen from the Jews deported to Auschwitz for extermination. It is most likely that the SS camp administration is concerned with psychologically terrorizing the relatively large number of young, healthy women, who represent a potential threat to camp security: Naked humans, especially women, feel defenseless and thus become unable to put up resistance.

From rebellious Warsaw the SS abducts thousands of women and children, and also men, to Auschwitz; at the same time it transfers to concentration camps in the interior of the Reich several thousand Polish and Russian prisoners who represent a potential threat to the existence and functioning of Auschwitz in its final phase. These other camps, together with their auxiliary camps, become out-and-out armaments factories. In July 1944, Russian troops, as well as Polish partisan units and advance detachments of the 1st Army of the Polish Armed Forces, who have been fighting for a long time between the Vistula and Bug rivers, march into Lublin's Majdanek Concentration Camp, where the camp administration, taken by surprise, has no time to destroy the mass destruction installations and murder all the prisoners. Although German authorities and the SS still believe in a final victory and in Providence, which supposedly saved the Führer from the failed assassination attempt by Colonel Count von Stauffenberg for the sake of this ultimate victory, they nevertheless make plans for the complete liquidation of Auschwitz Concentration Camp, of the prisoners as well as of all extermination installations, in order to obliterate the traces of the crimes perpetrated here.

In light of the approaching danger of total liquidation of the camp, the leaders of the camp resistance movement establish contact with the leadership of the Polish Home Army (Armia Krajowa— AK) in Silesia and ask for support not only in the form of weapons and explosives, but also by means of organizing the diversion of attacks from other targets to the camp, so that part of the SS forces will be tied up and escape will be made possible.

The increased activity of the camp resistance movement, the increasing number of prisoners who flee to partisan units, and the revolt of the Special Squad (Sonderkommando), whose members feel most threatened by the turn of events, all lead to an intensification of SS terror in the camp and accelerate the evacuation of Polish and Russian prisoners to concentration camps in the interior of the Reich. At the end of November, Himmler gives the command to destroy the crematoriums. Work is begun to demolish and remove them and to obliterate all traces of the crimes. At the end, only Crematorium V remains in operation.

The planned prisoner revolt never takes place, for those who would have been capable of leading it have previously been carried off; in addition there is no chance for success without help from the outside, and the SS undertakes nothing, until the middle of January 1945, that could complicate the further development of Auschwitz Concentration Camp in the event of a favorable turnabout in the war.

On January 17, 1945, the prisoners of Auschwitz assemble for the last evening roll call, a total of over 67,000 men and women. More than 31,000 come from the main camp and Birkenau, more than 10,000 from the Monowitz auxiliary camp near the Buna plants, and 25,000 from the remaining auxiliary camps. The next day the SS leads all the prisoners able to march out of the camp and forces them to walk to established assembly points. From there, they are further evacuated to the interior of the Reich on cargo trains, frequently in open freight cars. Along the evacuation routes can be seen the corpses of prisoners who have been shot; these are the bodies of those who broke under the stresses of the march and of others who risked an escape attempt.

In the main camp and in Birkenau and Monowitz auxiliary camps only the sick and those incapable of making the march remain. The SS is unable to kill everyone because on January 27 the first reconnaissance troops of the 60th Army of the 1st Ukrainian Front enter the camps and bring freedom to the more than 7,000 remaining prisoners.

JANUARY 1

Nos. 171353–171430 are given to 78 male prisoners and Nos. 73983–74039 to 57 female prisoners who are sent in a group transport.

Nos. Z-9009–Z-9019 are given to 11 male Gypsies. Nos. Z-9729–Z-9743 to 15 female Gypsies from Poland.

No. 74040 is given to a girl born in the women's camp in Birkenau to a woman brought to the camp by Mobile Command 9.

5,300 prisoners from the Monowitz auxiliary camp are employed in the Buna plants.

APMO, Maurer Trial, vol. 8, p. 173.

In the Jawischowitz A.C., 1,300 prisoners are deployed in the coal mine in Brzeszcze-Jawischowitz.

Ibid.

The occupancy level of the women's camp in Birkenau is 27,053.

APMO, Mat.RO, vol. VII, p. 485.

JANUARY 2

An SS Camp Doctor conducts a selection in Men's Quarantine Camp B-IIa in Birkenau, during which he selects 141 prisoners. They are all killed the same day in the gas chambers.

APMO, Dpr.-Hd/6, p. 5.

Because of high fever and diagnosed angina, the prisoner Józef Cyrankiewicz is transferred from Block 11 to Block 20, the prisoners' infirmary, where the section for infectious diseases is located.*

APMO, Mat.RO, Józef Cyrankiewicz File.

JANUARY 3

Nos. 171431–171451 and 74041–74053 are given to 21 male and 13 female prisoners, respectively, delivered in a group transport.

The reeducation prisoner Bernard Jenczmyk (No. EH-3838), who escaped from the camp on March 29, 1943, is captured, brought back, and locked in the bunker of Block 11. On January 19, 1944, he is released from the bunker to the camp.

APMO, D-AuI-1/1a, p. 84; IZ-10/Gestapo Sieradz/2a/88/57/183; D-AuI-3/2, Bunker Register, p. 66.

JANUARY 4

SS man Paul Korhamer prevents a prisoner from escaping from the Neu-Dachs auxiliary camp in Jaworzno, for which he gets a citation and five days' special leave from Commandant Liebehenschel.

APMO, D-AuI-1, Garrison Order 3/44, Jan. 19, 1944.

No. 171452 is given to a prisoner transferred from Ravensbrück.

SS Garrison Doctor Wirths notifies the SS men who are SS Medical Officers in the auxiliary camps belonging to Auschwitz CC III that

APMO, D-AuIII, Golleschau/9, Folder 1, p. 270.

---

*The fever is induced by an injection. This is how the leaders of the Auschwitz resistance group succeed in getting him out of Block 11. He is subsequently diagnosed with scarlet fever, which saves him from the punishment transport (see entry for Dec. 29, 1943). Finally the SS Garrison Doctor Wirths arranges for him to remain in the prisoners' infirmary permanently; he also gets the right to wear civilian clothing and to move about the camp freely (APMO, Mat.RO, Józef Cyrankiewicz File; Langbein, *The Stronger*, p. 194).

as of January 4, 1944, following identification and a number check, the corpses of prisoners should be sent every day before noon directly to the crematorium, bypassing the morgues in Auschwitz I and Auschwitz II. The death certificates of the prisoners and the protocols of the corpse viewing are to be sent, as before, to the orderly room of the prisoners' infirmary in Auschwitz CC I by noon on the day the corpses are delivered to the crematorium.

JANUARY 5

Prisoners Marian Gajewski (No. 169534), Stefan Idziak (No. 169536), Stanisław Kaleta (No. 169540), and Jan Wosik (No. 169565) have been placed in the Penal Company "until further notice."

APMO, D-AuI-3/1, p. 14, Penal Company Register.

JANUARY 6

Nos. 171453–171472 are given to 20 prisoners transferred from Flossenbürg.

Prisoner Wiktor Dorszala (No. 168153), born on October 8, 1924, escapes from Auschwitz.

APMO, IZ-8/Gestapo Lodz/4/90/2-3; Mat.RO, vol. IV, p. 293.

The Head of the WVHA, SS Lieutenant General Oswald Pohl, writes to the Commandants to say that recently another SS private has been murdered during guard duty.* He left the camp without permission with two prisoners, one of whom has been a "V-man," an informer, for the Political Department for two years,** in order to look for a cache of Communist agitation materials near the camp. This was the opportunity to murder him, and both prisoners succeeded in fleeing.† If the SS man had observed the relevant regulations appropriately, he would be alive today. This fact should be incorporated into the training of SS guards, and the following points should be noted:

Teodor Musioł, *Dachau 1933–1945*, Kattowitz, 1968, p. 367, Appendix 26.

1. No prisoner is to be trusted.
2. A guard's basic duty is to get no closer to a prisoner than six paces under any circumstances.
3. The guard of a camp squad is to carry a secured carbine and keep his right hand on the cartridge belt.

JANUARY 7

Nos. 171473–171491 are given to 19 prisoners delivered in a group transport.

*The murdered man is SS Private First Class Peter Jarosiewitsch (see entry for December 21, 1943).
**"V-man" is a term meaning "agent," from "Verbindungsmann," or "contact man" between the police and criminals. In this case they are informers who work for the Political Department, or other Departments or their Directors. Pohl means prisoner Stanisław Dorosiewicz (No. 18379), who was a Capo in the surveying squad and was a V-man for the Political Department.
†After murdering SS Private Peter Jarosiewitsch, prisoners Dorosiewicz and Kurcweig escaped on December 21, 1943.

No. 169968, which was not given out last year, is given to a boy born in the women's camp in Birkenau.

Nos. 74055–74058 are given to four female prisoners transported from Kattowitz.

Nos. 74059–74060 are given to two female prisoners sent from Troppau.

Two female prisoners sent from Breslau receive Nos. 74061 and 74062.

Three female prisoners from Kattowitz receive Nos. 74063–74065.

Commandant Liebehenschel orders an immediate organizational change in the female labor squads: Female prisoners of Aryan descent, especially Germans, should be transferred from the outside squads ("Aussenkommandos") to the regular labor squads within the camps, and Jewish prisoners should be placed in the labor squads working outside of the camps.

APMO, D-AuI-1, Garrison Order 2/44, Jan. 7, 1944.

In order to prevent the further spread of the typhus epidemic, Liebehenschel orders the immediate delousing of those SS guard detachments whose members have typhus.

Ibid.

JANUARY 8

204 male prisoners and 55 female prisoners delivered in a group transport are given Nos. 171492–171695 and 74066–74122, respectively.

JANUARY 10

No. 74121 is given to a girl born in the Birkenau women's camp to a woman brought to the camp in a transport of Mobile Strike Commando 9.

Nos. 171696–171699 are given to four prisoners brought from Kattowitz.

32 female prisoners sent in a group transport receive Nos. 74122–74153.

21 Polish and Russian prisoners are transferred from Auschwitz to Sachsenhausen.

APMO, Mat.RO, vol. VII, pp. 454, 474.

SS Corporal Johann Ratzka of the 3rd Guard Company prevents the escape of two prisoners from the camp and is granted a commendation and a five-day special leave by Commandant Liebehenschel.

APMO, Dpr.-ZOd/39, Garrison Order 3/44, Jan. 19, 1944.

JANUARY 11

12 male and three female Gypsies, transported from Germany, are given Nos. Z-9020–Z-9031 and Z-9744–Z-9746.

JANUARY 12

95 prisoners from Lodz receive Nos. 171700–171794.

Nos. 74154–74176 are given to 23 female prisoners transferred from Trieste.

Nearly 1,000 male and female Jewish prisoners are transferred from Stutthof Concentration Camp, near Danzig. After the selection, 120 men, given Nos. 171795–171914, and 134 women, Nos. 74177–74310, are admitted as prisoners to the camp. The remaining 746 people are killed in the gas chambers. Among those killed are 386 men.

APMO, D-AuII-3/1, p. 5, Quarantine List.

A female prisoner from Danzig is given No. 74311.

JANUARY 13

A female prisoner brought from Kattowitz receives No. 74312.

Approximately 2,000 Jewish men and women from Bendin and Sosnowitz arrive in an RSHA transport. After the selection, 221 men and 136 women are admitted to the camp, where they are assigned Nos. 171915–172135 and 74313–74448, respectively. The approximately 1,643 remaining people, among them 896 men, are killed in the gas chambers.

APMO, D-AuII-3/1, p. 4, Quarantine List.

Nos. 172136–172141 are given to six prisoners from Kattowitz.

73 Russian POWs transferred from the prisoner-of-war camp in Lamsdorf are given Nos. RKG-11142–RKG-11214.

APMO, D-AuII-3/11-3/1, p. 4, Quarantine List; Dpr.-Hd/6, p. 6.

Nos. 74449, 74450, and 74451 are given to three girls born in the women's camp in Birkenau.

Czech prisoners Georg Ludin (No. 131247) and Józef Marek (No. 131249) are captured while escaping and locked in the bunker of Block 11. On the same day they are released from the bunker into the camp.

APMO, D-AuI-3/2, Bunker Register, p. 67.

JANUARY 14

Nos. 172142–172164 and 74452–74457 are given to 23 male prisoners and six female prisoners, respectively, who arrive in a group transport.

10 male and five female Gypsies from Germany are given Nos. Z-9032–Z-9041 and Z-9747–Z-9751.

An Austrian, Franz Kejmar (No. 20158), is sent to the Penal Company "until further notice." He had been released from the bunker already on November 23, 1943.*

APMO, D-AuI-3/1, p. 14, Penal Company Register.

Eight reeducation prisoners are given Nos. EH-7234–EH-7241.

APMO, Prisoner Card Index.

JANUARY 15

Nos. 172165–172294 are given to 130 male and Nos. 74458–74511 to 54 female prisoners, delivered in a group transport.

A prisoner from Lemberg receives No. 172295.

No. Z-9752 is given to Karlonia Horvath, who was born in the Gypsy Family Camp in Birkenau; she dies on March 14, 1944.

APMO, D-AuII-3/2/5, pp. 629ff., Register of Female Gypsies.

In answer to a letter from SS Brigadier General Fritz Kranefuss dated January 7, 1944, concerning the need for prison labor in the chemical industry, the Head of the WVHA, Pohl, claims the following:

1. The I. G. Farben factory, Auschwitz, in Upper Silesia, has employed prisoners since April 1941 and is currently deploying 5,300 prisoners.
2. The Jawischowitz carbonizing plant in Jawischowitz, Upper Silesia, has employed prisoners since July 1942; their number is currently being increased from 1,000 to 1,300 prisoners.

Schnabel, *Power Without Morality*, p. 236.

No. Z-9753 is given to Hedwig Weiss, born in the Gypsy camp in Birkenau; she dies on February 14, 1944.

APMO, D-AuII-3/2/5, pp. 629ff., Register of Female Gypsies.

No. Z-9754 is given to Ludmila Daniel, born in the Gypsy camp in Birkenau; she dies on January 24, 1944.

Ibid.

No. Z-9555 is given to Anna Horvath, born in the Gypsy camp in Birkenau; she dies on January 19, 1944.

Ibid.

No. Z-9756 is given to Renate Pfaus, born in the Gypsy camp in Birkenau; she dies on February 18, 1944.

Ibid.

No. Z-9042 is given to Anton Peter, born in the Gypsy camp in Birkenau.

APMO, D-AuII-3/1/2, p. 268, Register of Male Gypsies.

An SS Camp Doctor conducts a selection in Men's Quarantine Camp B-IIa, and selects 363 prisoners. They are killed on the same day in the gas chambers.

APMO, Dpr.-Hd./6, p. 7.

*Franz Kejmar was caught attempting to escape and was confined to the bunker in Block 11 on November 6, 1943.

JANUARY 1–15

2,661 female prisoners die in the women's camp in Birkenau, 700 of them selected and killed in the gas chambers.

APMO, Mat.RO, vol. VII, p. 486.

JANUARY 16

Nine prisoners are sent to the Penal Company for sentences of six, nine, or 12 months. Of these, Ludwig Malycha (No. 169317) dies on May 22, 1944. The remaining prisoners are either released to the camp or transferred to Buchenwald before completing their sentences.

APMO, D-AuI-3/1, p. 14, Penal Company Register.

JANUARY 17

657 Jews from the Malines camp arrive in the twenty-third RSHA transport from Belgium. In the transport are 309 men and 37 boys and 286 women and 25 girls. After the selection, 140 men and 98 women are admitted to the camp as prisoners and receive Nos. 172296–172435 and 74512–74609. The remaining 419 people are killed in the gas chambers.

351 Gypsies also arrive with this transport from the Malines camp. 78 men and 99 boys, who are given Nos. Z-9050–Z-9226, and 99 women and 75 girls, who are given Nos. Z-9761–Z-9934. The transferred Gypsies are Belgian, French, Dutch, German, and Norwegian citizens.

15 male prisoners, given Nos. 172436–172450, and 14 female prisoners, given Nos. 74610–74623, are sent in a group transport that also includes 45 Jews from Breslau. 35 of them are sent to the gas chambers; those remaining are numbered 172439–172444, 172448, and 172449.

APMO, D-AuII-3/1, p. 4, Quarantine List.

The Polish prisoner Henryk Ropczyński, alias Kepczyński (No. 121468), born on March 24, 1921, in Warsaw, escapes from the railroad platform squad of Auschwitz II.

APMO, IZ-8/Gestapo Lodz/4/90/ 12, 13; IZ-10/Gestapo Sieradz/2/ 187; Mat.RO, vol. IV, p. 293.

A month-long training program for prisoner orderlies is set up.* The course takes place in the main camp and is officially conducted by a prisoner doctor, Dr. Franciszek Gralla (No. 21938).

*As a result of a typhus epidemic, which causes numerous complications, the women's camp in Birkenau is closed and completely isolated in November 1943. The members of the resistance organization thus lose their contact with the women's camp. In order to reestablish it, they decide to introduce a training course. The lesson plan laid out by the prisoners, Dr. Alina Brewda and Dr. Sława Kleinowa, is accepted by SS Camp Doctor Wirths and is approved by the WVHA in Berlin in January 1944. Contact is reestablished through a group of selected female prisoners. Prisoner physicians from the main camp teach the training course (APMO, Dpr.-ZOd/29, pp. 34–35).

Winter 1943–44: street in Auschwitz Concentration Camp.

In the night, two prisoners, the German Karl Ottobein (No. PSV-113744) and the Russian Boris Kravchenko, escape from the coal mine at the Jawischowitz A.C.*

APMO, IZ-10/Gestapo Sieradz/2/187, 196; D-AuI-1/2b, p. 307, Bulletin.

JANUARY 18

Nos. 172451 and 172452 are given to two prisoners from Annaberg (Góra Św. Anny).

104 Polish and Russian prisoners are transferred from Auschwitz to Buchenwald.

APMO, Documents of the International Search Service in Arolsen, Folder 12 (hereafter cited as Docs. of ISD Arolsen).

Polish prisoner Franciszek Myszka (No. 134066) escapes from the camp. He is captured on January 21, 1944, and imprisoned in the bunker of Block 11, from which he is probably released back into the camp on February 2, 1944.

APMO, D-AuI-3/2, Bunker Register, p. 67.

15 male prisoners and 16 female prisoners sent from Kattowitz are given Nos. 172453–172467 and 74624–74639.

*According to a telegram directed to the Gestapo in Sieradz, the search ended on March 15, 1944, when the prisoners were caught and delivered to Auschwitz.

JANUARY 19

Nos. 74640–74694 are given to 55 female prisoners sent to the camp by the Lodz Gestapo.

Nos. Z-9043–Z-9049 and Z-9757–Z-9760 are given to seven male and four female Gypsies sent from Germany.

Commandant Liebehenschel informs members of the SS guard units that the Head of the WVHA, SS Lieutenant General Pohl, advises them in connection with the murder of SS Private Peter Jarosiewitsch that no prisoner be trusted and reminds them that

APMO, Dpr.-ZOd/39, Garrison Order 3/44, Jan. 19, 1944.

1. It is a primary duty of the guard to maintain a distance of six paces from the prisoner.
2. An armed guard of a squad working outside the camp should carry a loaded and secured carbine and keep his right hand on his cartridge belt.

JANUARY 20

The camp's resistance organization sends a made-up address—Stephan Śliwiński (No. 71825), born on January 12, 1912, Block 25, Room 6, Auschwitz Concentration Camp, Post 2, Upper Silesia—to Kraków, for packages of medicine to be sent to. As is communicated in the secret message, these packages are delivered from the parcel service at the post office directly to the resistance organization, thus circumventing the SS check.

APMO, Mat.RO, vol. II, p. 57.

Nos. 172468–172508 are given to 41 prisoners sent in a group transport.

Five female prisoners sent from Graz are given Nos. 74695–74699.

Three female prisoners sent from Kattowitz are given Nos. 74700–74702.

Nos. 74703–74737 are given to 35 female Jewish prisoners sent in a group transport from Breslau by the RSHA.

A female prisoner sent from Kattowitz is given No. 74738.

Five prisoners are sent to the Penal Company in Birkenau, four for six months and one for nine months.

APMO, D-AuI-3/1, p. 14, Penal Company Register.

Nos. 74739–74742 are given to four girls born in the women's camp in Birkenau.

The Jewish prisoner Werner Krisch (No. 143116), born on July 14, 1919, in Berlin, escapes from the Auschwitz II Men's Camp B-IId. He is caught, brought back to Auschwitz II, and sent to the Penal Company on January 3 "until further notice."

APMO, D-AuI-1/b, Bulletin, pp. 308, 314; D-AuI-3/1, p. 15, Penal Company Register.

Two Polish prisoners—Adam Błaszczyk, born on February 20, 1917, and sent to Auschwitz on July 3, 1943, by the Lodz Gestapo, and Tadeusz Piskorowski, born on June 1, 1919, and brought to Auschwitz on July 29, 1943, by the Radom Sipo and SD—escape from squad No. 79 in the Buna plants.

APMO, IZ-8/Gestapo Lodz/4/90/14, 15; IZ-10/Gestapo Sieradz/2/193.

300 prisoners are transferred from Auschwitz to Flossenbürg.

APMO, Mat.RO, vol. VII, p. 474.

The total occupancy level in Auschwitz I, II, and III is 80,839:

APMO, Mat.RO, vol. II, p. 60.

    Auschwitz I: 18,437 male prisoners
    Auschwitz II: 22,061 male prisoners
    Auschwitz II: 27,053 female prisoners
    Auschwitz III: 13,288 male prisoners (Of these 6,571 male prisoners are in the Monowitz auxiliary camp.)

At a selection in Auschwitz I, 800 Jewish prisoners from the prisoners' infirmary are put on the list for the gas chambers. Another 200 Jewish prisoners are selected from the camp and isolated in the bath barracks. At this, the leader of the Auschwitz Combat Group prevails upon the prisoner Hermann Langbein to attempt to intervene with SS Garrison Doctor Wirths. Dr. Wirths explains that there has been a command from Berlin and asks for arguments that he could use in response. The arguments, geared to those addressed, are the following:

APMO, Mat.RO, Józef Cyrankiewicz File.

1. There could be a panic in the camp, since the Polish prisoners could assume that their turn would come after the Jews.
2. Sick prisoners would avoid the prisoners' infirmary in the future.
3. As a result, infectious diseases could spread and this would result in a decline in labor productivity.

Dr. Wirths takes these arguments to Auschwitz I Commandant Liebehenschel and receives his approval to reduce the selections to the terminally ill—however, the approval of the WVHA must first be obtained. Dr. Wirths's first telephone intervention with the WVHA is a failure. His second call, in which he relays the arguments and refers to the Commandant's agreement is successful.

JANUARY 21

In the evening 200 Jewish prisoners are released from the bath barracks where they have been isolated since the selection the previous day.

Ibid.

15 male prisoners and 10 female prisoners sent in a group transport are given Nos. 172509–172523 and 74743–74752.

An SS Camp Doctor conducts a selection in the prisoners' infirmary, B-IIf, where he looks for prisoners with typhus. They are killed on the same day in the gas chambers. Among those killed are 35 prisoners who had been transferred the day before from Men's Quar-

APMO, Dpr.-Hd/6, p. 25.

antine Camp B-IIa to the prisoners' infirmary, B-IIf, without having been positively diagnosed as having typhus.

JANUARY 22

87 prisoners who arrive in two group transports are given Nos. 172524–172610.

30 female prisoners sent by the Lodz Gestapo get Nos. 74753–74782.

APMO, Mat.RO, vol. VII, p. 485.

1,155 Jewish men, women, and children arrive from Drancy in the sixty-sixth RSHA transport from France. After the selection, 236 men, given Nos. 172611–172846, and 55 women, given Nos. 74783–74797 and 74835–74874, are admitted to the camp. The remaining 864 people are killed in the gas chambers.

Nos. 74798–74834 are given to 37 female prisoners sent to the camp by the Lodz Gestapo.

In the prisoners' infirmary in Auschwitz I, an SS Camp Doctor checks again the 800 Jewish prisoners who were selected on January 20, and registers 220 as seriously ill. They are brought to Birkenau the same day and killed in the gas chambers.

APMO, Mat.RO, Józef Cyran-kiewicz File; vol. II, p. 62.

No. Z-9227 was given to a male Gypsy and Nos. Z-9935–Z-9938 to four female Gypsies who have been transferred from Austria.

An SS Camp Doctor carries out a selection in Men's Quarantine Camp B-IIa, during which he selects 542 prisoners. They are killed the same day in the gas chambers.

APMO, Dpr.-Hd/6, p. 7.

The Russian POW Semion Yemos (No. RKG-10513) escapes from the camp.

APMO, Mat.RO, vol. IV, p. 292.

The Czech prisoner Bruno Schmidt, born on August 26, 1898, in Prossnitz (Prostějov),* who was to be transferred to Buchenwald, escapes from the unloading squad of Auschwitz II.

APMO, IZ-8/Gestapo Lodz/2-26; D-AuI-1/b, Bulletin, p. 308.

335 prisoners are transferred from Auschwitz to Mauthausen.

APMO, Mat.RO, vol. VII, p. 474.

91 prisoners are transferred from Auschwitz to Buchenwald.

Ibid.

JANUARY 23

Nos. 74875–74880 are given to six female Jewish prisoners, who have been selected from an RSHA transport.

The No. 74882 is given to a girl born in the women's camp in Birkenau.

*According to a report of the Kripo headquarters in Prague of April 15, 1944, Bruno Schmidt is arrested on April 7, 1944, in Prague.

An SS Camp Doctor conducts a selection in the Gollenschau A.C. in which he selects 26 Jewish prisoners. The selected prisoners are transferred to Birkenau. In general, the transfer of sick prisoners to Birkenau is equivalent to sending them to the gas chambers. The list of names of the selected and transferred prisoners is signed by the then Squad Leader, i.e., the Camp Commander of the auxiliary camp, SS Staff Sergeant Mirbeth.

APMO, D-AuIII, Golleschau/12, pp. 48ff.

JANUARY 24

The Lodz Gestapo informs the Commandant's Office that the documents left by prisoners who have died are to be destroyed immediately on site and are not to be sent back to the Gestapo. The families of the deceased are to be informed that the property of their relative will not be returned to them.

APMO, IZ-8/Gestapo Lodz/3a/88/657.

Six prisoners sent in a group transport are given Nos. 172847–172852.

Three female prisoners sent from Oppeln are given Nos. 74883–74885.

Nos. 74054 and 74886–74888 are given to four female prisoners sent from Breslau.

The Polish political prisoner Franciszek Wieczorkowski (No. 1359) and the German political prisoner Arnold Guse (No. 26878) escape from the protective custody camp expansion squad of Auschwitz I. They are arrested the next day and locked in the bunkers of Block 11; they are released on February 24, 1944, to the camp.

APMO, D-AuI/1b, Bulletin, p. 308; D-AuI-3/2, Bunker Register, p. 68.

JANUARY 25

The prisoner Władysław Bluza (No. 113308), who is suspected of giving aid to escaping fellow prisoners, is imprisoned in the bunker of Block 11. He is released on February 24, 1944, from the bunker to the camp.

APMO, D-AuI-3/2, Bunker Register, p. 68.

No. 172853 is given to a boy born in the Birkenau women's camp.

Nos. 172854–172859 are given to six prisoners sent in a group transport.

After his arrival in the Commandant's Office of Auschwitz I, SS Second Lieutenant Hartenberger of the RSHA goes to the Commandant's Office of Auschwitz III–Monowitz and to the Monowitz A.C. to discuss the so-called letter campaign of the RSHA Jews, in which Jewish prisoners are to write to their families. The objective of this campaign is to mislead those who closely follow the fate of the Jews held in Auschwitz.

APMO, Dpr.-Hd/12, p. 176, Exhibit 120, Vehicle Requisition of Jan. 25, 1944.

Two prisoners are sent to the Penal Company "until further notice": Władysław Pyrka (No. 139287) and Edwin Brandes (No. 172579). Brandes dies five days later, on January 29, 1944.

APMO, D-AuI-3/1, p. 14, Penal Company Register.

By order of Commandant Liebeshenschel, a camp informer, the prisoner Stanisław Wierusz-Kowalski (No. 1873), who works for the Political Department,* is imprisoned in the bunker of Block 11. He is released on February 2, 1944, to the camp and is sent to Flossenbürg in a penal transport.**

APMO, D-AuI-3/2, Bunker Register, p. 68.

JANUARY 26

13 female prisoners sent in a group transport receive Nos. 74889–74901.

APMO, Mat.RO, vol. VII, p. 454.

61 Jewish prisoners are transferred from Auschwitz to Sachsenhausen.

JANUARY 27

948 Jews from Westerbork arrive with an RSHA transport from Holland. In the transport are 391 men, 435 women, and 122 children. After the selection, 190 men, given Nos. 172860–173049, and 69 women, given Nos. 74902–74970, are admitted to the camp. The remaining 689 people are killed in the gas chambers.

In Block 11 a special session of the Police Court-martial of the Kattowitz Gestapo takes place, during which 25 Poles are sentenced to death for planning high treason, i.e., because of their membership in underground organizations, among others the PPR (Polish Workers Party), the PPS (Polish Socialist Party), and the AK (Polish Home Army—Armia Krajowa). It is determined that four of the condemned are to be shot to death on February 1, 1944, in Auschwitz, 10 are to be publicly hanged in Jeleśnia, Żywiec District, and five are to be publicly executed in Sosnowitz.

CA KC PZPR, 214/VIII-2, Documents of the Delegation of the Polish Government in Exile, pp. 66ff.; Konieczny, "Police Court-martial," pp. 153–156.

Nine male and five female Gypsies transferred from the Reich territory are given Nos. Z-9228–Z-9236 and Z-9939–Z-9943.

JANUARY 28

72 male and 26 female prisoners who arrive in a group transport are given Nos. 173050–173121 and 74971–74996.

*In clandestine messages of the camp resistance organization, that of December 16, 1943, and the next one, written by the prisoner Stanisław Kłodinski and addressed to the Kraków Committee for Aid to Concentration Camp Prisoners (PWOK), Wierusz-Kowalski was twice named as an informer; a message of January 1944 states that he was sent to Block 11, did not leave his cell, and was sent to another camp (APMO, Mat.RO, vol. I, pp. 50, 53; vol. II, p. 57).
**With this transport, the prisoners named by the Committee of the Auschwitz Combat Group and who worked as spies in the camp, among others, leave the camp.

30 male and 33 female Gypsies transferred from Czechoslovakia are given Nos. Z-9237–Z-9266 and Z-9944–Z-9976.

Iwan Mackowski (No. EH-7126) and Michail Denisov, a Russian POW (No. RKG-10525), escape from the camp.

APMO, Mat.RO, vol. IV, p. 292.

Nine prisoners are sent to the Penal Company in Birkenau, two for three months, five for six months, and two "until further notice."

APMO, D-AuI-3/1, pp. 14, 15, Penal Company Register.

JANUARY 29

16 male and 17 female prisoners who arrive with a group transport are given Nos. 173122–173137 and 74997–75013.

The Czech prisoner Józef Friz (No. 117124) is captured while escaping and is imprisoned in the bunker of Block 11. On January 31, 1944, he is released to the camp with the order not to leave the camp grounds.

APMO, D-AuI-3/2, Bunker Register, p. 68.

The Polish prisoner Tadeusz Krajzer (No. 167757) is sent to the Penal Company "until further notice." He dies there on July 25, 1944.

APMO, D-AuI-3/1, p. 15, Penal Company Register.

JANUARY 30

The SS Commander in Chief honors 20 SS members of the Auschwitz garrison with the War Service Cross 2nd Class with Swords. Among those honored is SS Captain Dr. Eduard Wirths, the SS Camp Doctor.

APMO, D-AuI-1, Garrison Order 5/44, Feb. 1, 1944.

Nurses Lotte Nitschke and Martha Mzyk of the SS sick bay and Dorothea Becker, Luise Brunner, Elfriede Kock, and Gertrud Liehr, supervisors in the women's camp at Birkenau, are awarded the War Service Metal 2nd Class without Swords, by the SS Commander in Chief.

Ibid.

Heinrich Josten, Heinz Kühler, Theodor Lange, and Johann Schwarzhuber are promoted from SS Second Lieutenant to SS First Lieutenant by the SS Commander in Chief.

Ibid.

A prisoner sent from Kattowitz receives No. 173138.

A prisoner who was sent to the camp on January 28, 1944, from Hohensalza receives No. 173139.

A boy who was born on January 29, 1944, in the Birkenau women's camp receives No. 173140.

A boy who was born in the Birkenau women's camp receives No. 173141.

Two girls who were born on January 28, 1944, in the Birkenau women's camp receive Nos. 75014 and 75015.

JANUARY 31

A prisoner sent from Kattowitz receives No. 173142.

Nos. 173143–173151 are given to nine prisoners who were sent on January 29, 1944, in a group transport.

16 female prisoners transferred in a group transport receive Nos. 75016–75031.

The Political Department asked for a prisoner transport railway car for the transfer of 10 police prisoners to Jeleśnia who were condemned to death by hanging on January 27 at a special session of the Kattowitz Gestapo Police Court-martial. The condemned are the Poles Józef Górny, Jan Bigos, Stefan Dudek, Alojzy Hamerlak, Michał Kąkol, Jósef Laszczak, Jósef Szczygliński, Franciszek Walus, Tadeusz Walus, and Władysław Walus.*

APMO, D-AuI-4/9, Vehicle Requisition of Jan. 29, 1944; IZ-20, Announcement of the Execution of 10 Prisoners in Jeleśnia on Jan. 31, 1944.

FEBRUARY 1

In Lędziny a new auxiliary camp of Auschwitz, Günthergrube, is set up. Approximately 300 prisoners are put up there to mine coal from the Piast Pit and to build the Güntherpit, today Ziemowit, which belongs to the Fürstliches Plessisches Bergwerk AG (the Royal Pless Mine Company). The coal from this pit is for I. G. Farben.

APMO, Trial Documents for the Trial of Denzinger et al., Part III, pp. 200–205; Camp Index Card of the Prisoner Menasze Wajsbrot (No. 145223); T. Iwaszko, "Günthergrube," HvA, no. 12 (1970): 113–143.

The Jewish prisoner Josef Engel (No. 159344) attempts suicide by cutting his throat during work on a secondary road near the coal pit in Jawischowitz. He is saved and claims during the investigation that he no longer wants to work underground.

APMO, D-AuI, II, III-2/285b, Punishment Report of Feb. 2, 1944; Dpr.-Hd/12, p. 222.

A male and a female prisoner transferred from Kattowitz receive Nos. 173152 and 75032.

A boy born on January 31, 1944, in the Birkenau women's camp receives No. 173153.

Three prisoners are shot and killed during their escape from the Penal Company in Birkenau. They are the Gypsies Franz Daniel (No. Z-8792), Johan Daniel (No. Z-8803), and Jaroslav Herak (No. Z-4466).

APMO, D-AuI-3/1, p. 12, 13, Penal Company Register.

Roman Frankiewicz (No. 9430) and Zosel Kossowski (No. 94397) are sent to the Penal Company in Birkenau for four months and six months, respectively.

Ibid., p. 15.

*Witnesses of the execution were the citizens of Jeleśnia, who were forced to gather at the gallows.

By order of Department III, i.e., of the Camp Commander, the following prisoners are locked in the bunker of Block 11: the German BV prisoners Günther Körlin (No. 3424) and August Laks (No. 20736) and the Russian political prisoner Nikita Zhelutko (No. 71714).*

APMO, D-AuI-3/2, Bunker Register, p. 68.

FEBRUARY 2

12 female prisoners transferred from Trieste are given Nos. 75033–75044.

Jews from Trieste arrive with an RSHA transport. After the selection, four men, given Nos. 173154–173157, and a woman, given No. 75045, are admitted to the camp. All the other deportees are killed in the gas chambers.

APMO, D-AuII-3/1, p. 4, Quarantine List; Mat.RO, vol. VII, p. 416.

Eight prisoners sent from Kattowitz receive Nos. 173158–173165.

24 female prisoners who arrived by mass transport received the numbers 75046–75069.

Two boys born in the Birkenau women's camp are given the Nos. 173166 and 173167.

303 prisoners are transferred from Auschwitz to Flossenbürg. With this transport all the camp informers who were on the list put together by the leaders of the Auschwitz Combat Team are deported and delivered via the SS Camp Doctor to the Commandant at his request.

APMO, Mat.RO, vol. VII, p. 454; Józef Cyrankiewicz File; Langbein, *The Stronger*, pp. 194ff.

A selection is conducted in the Birkenau women's camp during which 800 female prisoners are selected. Among them are older and younger women, sick and healthy. They are killed the same day in the gas chambers.

APMO, Mat.RO, vol. II, p. 66.

*This is the last entry in the second part of the Bunker Register, a copy of which was delivered to the prisoners' resistance organization. The prisoners who were active as scribes in Block 11 and kept the Bunker Register later say: "In the beginning of 1944, when the most tragic pages of the book were already written, Jan Pilecki [he took over the job of scribe on December 22, 1942—D.C.] decided to release the book from the camp. Since the existence of the Bunker Register was known to the SS functionaries and the keeping of the book by a writer from the block was de facto permitted, copies of both parts of the book had to be prepared. At the request of Jan Pilecki these copies were prepared by two prisoners, who were located at the time in the first floor of Block 11. . . . The entries up to February 1944 were copied from the second book. Upon receipt of the copies Pilecki discussed it with the prisoners Józef Cyrankiewicz and Stanisław Klodziński, who agreed with his suggestion to release the Bunker Registers from the camp, and who demanded that the books be given to them. Jan Pilecki created a special grocery package in which he packed the original of the first part as well as the copy of the second part of the book. This package, which he said had been erroneously sent to Block 11, was redirected to Klodziński in Block 20, who conveyed it to Cyrankiewicz. The copy of the first part and the original of the still used second part remained with the documents of Block 11" (Brol et al., "*Bunker Register* of Block 11," pp. 14–16). Both parts of the Bunker Register that the resistance movement smuggled out of the camp are intact; the parts left among the documents of Block 11 were in all likelihood destroyed by the SS before the evacuation of the camp.

FEBRUARY 3

247 Jewish prisoners from the Neu-Dachs A.C. are killed in the gas chambers of Birkenau. The list of those selected was put together on January 18, 1944. It contained the names and numbers of 254 prisoners.* Four prisoners died in the meantime, and three were stricken from the list.

APMO, D-AuIII, Jaworzno, Folder III, pp. 144–148.

FEBRUARY 4

21 prisoners sent in a group transport receive Nos. 173168–173188.

The prisoner Tichon Stasiuk (No. 137579) escapes from the labor squad employed at the Siemens-Schuckert-Werke in Bobrek. He is captured on February 15, delivered to the camp, and on February 16 is sent "until further notice" to the Penal Company.

APMO, D-AuI-1/1b, Bulletin, p. 311; Mat.RO, vol. IV, p. 292; D-AuI-3/1, p. 16, Penal Company Register.

FEBRUARY 5

39 male and 55 female prisoners sent in a group transport are given Nos. 173189–173227 and 75070–75124.

Jan Nikiel (No. 173053), Józef Sikora (No. 173054), Antoni Klimczyński (No. 173055), Eustachy Gałuszka (No. 173056), Rudolf Dwornik (No. 173057), Kazimierz Dwornik (No. 173058), and Antoni Szczygielsky (No. 173119) are sent to the Penal Company "until further notice." All of those named were sent to Auschwitz on January 28, 1944, in a group transport.

APMO, D-AuI-3/1, p. 15, Penal Company Register.

FEBRUARY 6

1,214 Jewish men, women, and children from Drancy arrive in the sixty-seventh RSHA transport from France. After the selection, 166 men and 49 women, given Nos. 173228–173393 and 75125–75173, are admitted to the camp. The remaining 999 people are killed in the gas chambers.

APMO, Mat.RO, vol. VII, p. 416.

700 Jewish prisoners arrested in Milan and Verona arrive in an RSHA transport from Italy. After the selection, 97 men and 31 women, given Nos. 173394–173490 and 75174–75204, are admitted to the camp. The remaining 572 people are killed in the gas chambers.

APMO, Mat.RO, vol. VII, p. 416; CDECM, *Jews in Italy*, p. 15.

Weronika Walansewicz (No. Z-9611), a female Polish Gypsy, escapes from the Gypsy camp, B-IIe. She was sent to the camp on November 28, 1943, by order of the Białystok Sipo and SD.

APMO, IZ-8/Gestapo Lodz/4/90/19; D-AuII-3/2/5, pp. 621ff., Register of Female Gypsies.

*The list of names from January 18 contains the abbreviation "SB" ("Sonderbehandlung," for "special treatment"), and crosses are placed next to the names of the prisoners.

FEBRUARY 7

40 Jews from Sosnowitz arrived on February 5 in an RSHA transport. After the selection, three men receive Nos. 173491–173493 and are admitted to the camp. All the remaining people are killed in the gas chambers.

APMO, D-AuII-3/1, p. 4, Quarantine List.

A boy born on February 5, 1944, in the Birkenau women's camp receives No. 173494.

A prisoner sent from Kattowitz receives No. 173495.

A boy born on January 27, 1944, in the Birkenau women's camp receives No. 173496.

Eight female prisoners sent from Oppeln and Breslau receive Nos. 75205–75212.

Two prisoners sent from Kattowitz receive Nos. 173497–173498.

FEBRUARY 9

Nine male prisoners and two female prisoners from Kattowitz are given Nos. 173499–173507 and 75213–75214.

112 prisoners from Auschwitz are transferred to Flossenbürg. The first name on the transport list is that of German prisoner Otto Küsel (No. 2), who, with three Polish prisoners, escaped from the camp on December 29, 1942, and hid in Warsaw. After his rearrest he was sent on September 25 to Auschwitz and locked in the bunker of Block 11; he was released on November 23, 1943, during the last selection conducted by Commandant Liebehenschel.

APMO, Mat.RO, vol. VIIIc, p. 6.

FEBRUARY 10

A male Jew and a female Jew were sent to the camp by order of the RSHA and receive Nos. 173508 and 75215.

1,015 Jews from Westerbork camp arrive in an RSHA transport from Holland. 340 men, 454 women, and 221 children are in the transport. After the selection, 142 men and 73 women, given Nos. 173509–173650 and 75216–75288, are admitted to the camp. The remaining 800 people are killed in the gas chambers.

APMO, D-AuII-3/1, p. 4, Quarantine List; Mat.RO, vol. VII, p. 416.

A female prisoner transferred from The Hague receives No. 75289.

22 prisoners sent in a group transport receive Nos. 173651–173672.

Eight prisoners are sent to the Penal Company in Birkenau, three of them for three months, four for six months, and one "until further notice."

APMO, D-AuI-3/1, p. 15, Penal Company Register.

45 prisoners are assigned to the Penal Company in Birkenau, among them are 41 prisoners sent to the camp on October 2, 1943, by order of the Radom Sipo and SD, and four incarcerated on October 5, 1943, by order of the Warsaw Sipo and SD. The prisoners are sent "until further notice" to the Penal Company; seven of them die there: Apoloniusz Grzeszczyk (No. 156161) on February 12, Bolesław Mrozik (No. 154334) on February 14, Zygmunt Abugow (No. 153871) on March 5, Feliks Gilewski (No. 153580) on March 22, Stefan Paszkowski (No. 153713) on April 9, Feliks Kopeć (No. 154269) on April 17, and Piotr Traczyk (No. 153782) on October 1. The Jewish prisoners Judka Kluss (No. 153983), Chaim Marly (No. 153987), Dawid Haberman (No. 154305), Abram Wassermann (No. 153966), and Abram Kurkowski (No. 154313) are released from the Penal Company and transferred to the Special Squad that was employed in the burning of corpses.

APMO, D-AuI-3/1, pp. 15ff., Penal Company Register.

FEBRUARY 11

A girl born in the Birkenau women's camp to a woman sent to the camp by Mobile Commando 9 receives No. 75290.

33 male and 26 female prisoners sent in a group transport were given Nos. 173673–173705 and 75292–75317.

Jan Barcik (No. 108601) and Kazimierz Gaździcki (No. 144474) escape from the camp.

APMO, Mat.RO, vol. IV, p. 292.

Nine male and 13 female Gypsies transferred from Germany are given Nos. Z-9267–Z-9275 and Z-9977–Z-9989.

The occupancy level in the Golleschau A.C. is 476.

APMO, D-AuIII, Golleschau/12, pp. 51–58.

FEBRUARY 12

60 Poles are transferred from Radom and are shot in the courtyard of Block 11. The transferees are not recorded in the camp registers, and on their death certificates "execution" is entered as cause of death.

APMO, Mat.RO, vol. VII, p. 416.

Two prisoners transferred from Kattowitz receive Nos. 173706 and 173707.

22 female prisoners sent in a group transport receive Nos. 75318–75339.

1,500 Jewish men, women, and children from Drancy arrive on the sixty-eighth RSHA transport from France. After the selection, 210 men and 61 women, given Nos. 173708–173917 and 75340–75400, are admitted to the camp. The remaining 1,229 people are killed in the gas chambers.

Ibid.

FEBRUARY 14

A female prisoner from Dresden receives No. 75291.

12 prisoners from Kattowitz receive Nos. 173918–173929.

Nine male and 26 female prisoners sent in a group transport are given Nos. 173930–173938 and 75401–75426.

Zdenek Daniel, born on February 14, 1944, in the Gypsy camp, receives No. Z-9276.

APMO, D-AuII-3/1/2, p. 275, Register of Male Gypsies.

Hedwig Klähr, born on February 14, 1944, in the Gypsy camp, receives No. Z-9990.

APMO, D-AuII-3/2/5, p. 645, Register of Female Gypsies.

Gertrude Stenka, born on February 14, 1944, in the Gypsy camp, receives No. Z-9991.

Ibid.

FEBRUARY 15

28 male and five female prisoners sent in a group transport are given Nos. 173939–173966 and 75427–75431.

1,500 prisoners are transferred from Auschwitz to Mauthausen.

FEBRUARY 16

Five Jewish prisoners sent to the camp by the RSHA receive Nos. 173967–173971.

APMO, Mat.RO, vol. VII, pp. 454, 474.

FEBRUARY 17

The Polish political prisoner Jan Radzikowski, born on March 15, 1893, and sent to Auschwitz on April 29, 1943, by order of the Warsaw Sipo and SD, escapes from the labor squad for barracks construction and carpentry of Auschwitz II.

APMO, IZ-8/Gestapo Lodz/4/90/24, 25.

FEBRUARY 18

13 prisoners are sent to the Penal Company in Birkenau, three of them "until further notice," three for six months, one for four months, and the rest for three months. Of them the prisoners, sentenced for three months, Paweł Witoszkin (No. 165732), dies on May 11, 1944, before completing his sentence.

APMO, D-AuI-3/1, p. 16, Penal Company Register.

Seven female Jewish prisoners sent to the camp by the RSHA receive Nos. 75432–75438.

28 male and seven female prisoners sent in a group transport are given Nos. 173972–173999 and 75439–75445.

The Polish prisoner Lucjan Adamiec (No. 124001), born on December 13, 1903, and sent to Auschwitz on June 5, 1943, by the Posen Kripo, escapes from Squad 157 in the Buna plant in the Monowitz auxiliary camp of Auschwitz III.

APMO, IZ-8/Gestapo Lodz/4/90/22/23; D-AuIII-5/4, 60, Death Register of Auschwitz III.

FEBRUARY 19

50 prisoners are transferred from Auschwitz III to the Golleschau A.C.; they are 33 Poles, four Polish Jews, one German, one Czech, and 11 Russians.

APMO, D-AuIII, Golleschau/12, pp. 59–61.

37 female prisoners sent in a group transport receive Nos. 75446–75482.

Seven male Gypsies and one female Gypsy transferred from Germany are given Nos. Z-9277–Z-9282 and Z-9992.

Robert Bern, born in the Gypsy camp, receives No. Z-9283.

APMO, D-AuII-3/1/2, p. 275, Register of Male Gypsies.

The following are sent to the Penal Company: Vasili Kulin (No. RKG-10594) for six months, Vasili Chichirkov (No. RKG-10695) for six months, Noe Chachibaya (No. 162286) for four months, and Alexander Rshetielski (No. 164812) for four months. Alexander Rshetielski dies on March 18, 1944, in the Penal Company before completing his sentence. The rest are released from the Penal Company after serving their sentences.

APMO, D-AuI-3/1, p. 17, Penal Company Register.

FEBRUARY 21

260 Jewish prisoners are transferred from Płaszów Concentration Camp to Auschwitz. They receive Nos. 174000–174259.

A female prisoner sent from Kattowitz receives No. 75483.

A girl born to a Jewish female prisoner in Birkenau receives No. 75484.

Six male and 22 female prisoners sent in a group transport are given Nos. 174260–174265 and 75485–75506.

Three boys born on February 18 in the Birkenau women's camp receive Nos. 174266–174268.

FEBRUARY 22

17 male and 89 female prisoners sent in a group transport are given Nos. 174269–174285 and 75507–75595.

145 prisoners are transferred from Auschwitz to Buchenwald.

APMO, Mat.RO, vol. VII, p. 474; Docs. of ISD Arolsen, Folder 12.

Commandant Schwarz of Auschwitz III directed the leaders of the secondary camps to: (1) avoid burdening the prisoners on the night shift with daytime work but rather to allow them a seven- to eight-

APMO, D-AuIII-1/59, Comman-

Barracks of the "stable" type in Section B-II of Birkenau.

Prisoners at work on the construction of a sewage system in Section B-III of Birkenau.

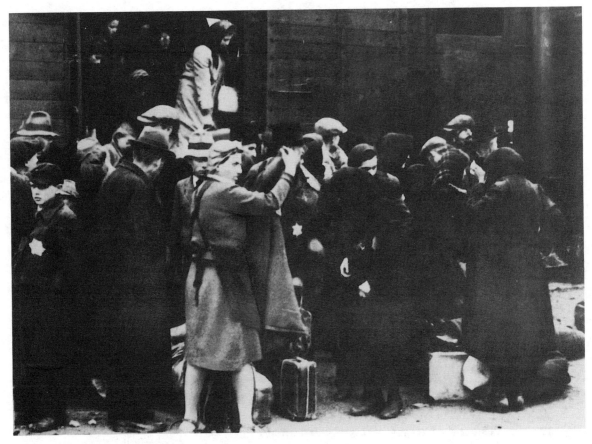

People who have been abducted to Auschwitz get off the train.

hour break to preserve their efficiency; (2) to shorten the roll call, which because of the relatively small number of prisoners in the auxiliary camps should not last longer than five to 10 minutes.*

dant's Office Order 4/44, Feb. 22, 1944; Dpr.-ZOd/40.

The total occupancy level in all the camps in Auschwitz is 73,669, distributed as follows:

APMO, Mat.RO, vol. VII, p. 475.

Auschwitz I	17,177 male prisoners
Auschwitz II	18,378 male prisoners
	24,637 female prisoners
Auschwitz III	13,477 male prisoners

The distribution of the 13,477 prisoners in the auxiliary camps of Auschwitz III is as follows:

Ibid.

Monowitz	6,603
Golleschau	526
Jawischowitz	1,646
Eintrachthütte	796
Neu-Dachs	1,708

*The goal of this directive is to raise again the sinking productivity of the prisoners who work in the armament industry's firms, so that the required production results can be achieved. The Commandants of the concentration camps were given similar directives during a meeting in the WVHA in Berlin.

Brünn	146
Lagischa	494
Fürstengrube	661
Günthergrube	300
Janinagrube	597*

FEBRUARY 23

Two prisoners sent from Kattowitz receive Nos. 174286 and 174287.

24 male and 22 female Jewish prisoners, who were selected from an RSHA transport that arrived in the morning with several hundred Jews from the Narva camp in Estonia, are given Nos. 174288–174311 and 75596–75617. 86 men are among those sent to the gas chambers. The number of women killed is unknown.

APMO, D-AuII-3/1, p. 4, Quarantine List.

A female prisoner sent from Kattowitz receives No. 75618.

18 male and three female prisoners sent in a group transport receive Nos. 174312–174329 and 75619–75621.

Two Gypsy children arrive in a group transport: Hugo Rose, born on May 17, 1938, in Gotha and Gertruda Rose, born on July 31, 1939, in Vienna; they are given Nos. Z-9284 and Z-9993.

APMO, D-AuII-3/1/2, p. 275, Register of Male Gypsies; D-AuII-3/2/5, pp. 645ff., Register of Female Gypsies.

FEBRUARY 24

The number of prisoners in the Special Squads, who work in the crematoriums in Birkenau, is reduced by half because 200 members of squads are transferred to Majdanek.**

Sałmen Lewental, and Chaim Herman, manuscripts in SAM, *Amid Unspeakable Crimes*, pp. 167, 200.

10 prisoners from Kattowitz receive Nos. 174330–174339.

Three Jewish prisoners, who were selected from an RSHA transport from Berlin that arrived in the camp on February 23 with 29 Jews, receive Nos. 174340–174342. The other 26 men from this transport are killed in the gas chambers.

APMO, D-AuII-3/1, p. 4, Quarantine List.

40 female prisoners sent in a group transport receive Nos. 75622–75661.

119 Russian POWs are transferred from the prisoner-of-war camp in Lamsdorf. They receive Nos. RKG-11222–RKG-11340.

Ibid.

*Not on the list is Sosnowitz, which was dissolved on February 20, 1944, after completion of the repair work to be done there (Piper, "Sosnowitz I," p. 96).
**According to the statement of a member of the special task force, the prisoner Stanisław Jankowski (a.k.a. Alter Feinsilber), the transfer to Majdanek was in retaliation for the—unsuccessful—escape attempt by Daniel Obstbaum and four other members of the Special Squad. They are transferred to Majdanek to be killed, and they are shot there (SAM, *Amid Unspeakable Crimes*, p. 61).

11 men and boys and 19 women and girls, German Gypsies, are given Nos. Z-9285–Z-9295 and Z-9994–Z-10012. In the transport are Erika Franz, born on January 11, 1944, in Stettin, who receives No. Z-10002, and her mother, Frante Franz, born on February 24, 1917, in Stolp (Słupsk), who is given No. Z-10001.

APMO, D-AuII-3/2/5, pp. 645ff., Register of Female Gypsies.

The Jewish prisoner, Heinz Grünfeld, who escaped from the camp on October 1, 1943, is captured and transferred to Auschwitz.*

APMO, IZ-10/Gestapo Sieradz/1/80/294.

FEBRUARY 25

Commandant Liebehenschel informs the SS members of the garrison that the SS Commander in Chief has promoted the Director of Agriculture, Dr. Joachim Caesar, from SS Major to SS Lieutenant Colonel.

APMO, D-AuI-1, Garrison Order 8/44, Feb. 25, 1944.

Commandant Liebehenschel informs the SS members of the garrison that the Director of Construction of the Waffen SS and Police in Silesia, SS Major Karl Bischoff, has been awarded the War Service Cross 1st Class with Swords, on January 30, 1944, for his contributions to victory through his work in construction.** The Führer honored him on the recommendation of the SS Commander in Chief.

Ibid.

94 prisoners sent in a group transport receive Nos. 174343–174436.

41 Jews are transferred in an RSHA transport from Vienna. After the selection, four men given Nos. 174437–174440, are admitted to the camp as prisoners. The remaining 37 men are killed in the gas chambers.

APMO, D-AuII-3/1, p. 4, Quarantine List.

Two Jewish prisoners, Moszek Weinryb and Mordka Baum,† escape from the Golleschau A.C.

APMO, D-AuI-1/1a, pp. 327ff.; IZ-10/Gestapo Sieradz/2/80/207, 193.

FEBRUARY 26

20 male and seven female prisoners sent in a group transport receive Nos. 174441–174460 and 75662–75668.

64 Jews arrive in an RSHA transport from Sosnowitz. After the selection, 10 men, given Nos. 174461–174470, are admitted to the camp. The remaining 54 men are killed in the gas chambers.

APMO, D-AuII-3/1, p. 4, Quarantine List.

650 Jewish men, women, and children from the Fossoli camp arrive in an RSHA transport from Italy. After the selection, 95 men, given

APMO, Dpr.-ZOd/28, pp. 76, 78; CDECM, *Jews in Italy*, p. 19.

*The further fate of Heinz Grünfeld is not known.
**The wooden barracks in Birkenau, the four large crematoriums complete with gas chambers, and the expansion of the main camp were constructed under his direction.
†According to a report of the Oppeln Gestapo, Moszek Weinryb is captured on March 1, 1944, in Zawiercie and sent to prison, where he allegedly hangs himself on March 7, 1944. The fate of the second escapee is unknown.

Nos. 174471–174565, and 29 women, given Nos. 75669–75697, are admitted to the camp.* The remaining 526 people are killed in the gas chambers.

84 Russian POWs are transferred from the prisoner-of-war camp in Lamsdorf to Auschwitz and are brought to the so-called sauna. The next day only 66 POWs are sent to quarantine and given Nos. RKG-11341–RKG-11406. The other 18 POWs were shot and killed in the sauna.

APMO, Dpr.-Hd./6, p. 24; D-AuII-3/1, p. 4, Quarantine List.

Two male Gypsies, who receive Nos. Z-9296 and Z-9297, and a female Gypsy, who receives No. Z-10013, are transferred from Czechoslovakia.

FEBRUARY 27

Eight Gypsies who were transferred from Germany receive Nos. Z-9298–Z-9305.

Nikolaus Gorgan, born in the Gypsy camp, receives No. Z-9306.

APMO, D-AuII-3/1/2, p. 276, Register of Male Gypsies.

Adolf Elster, born on February 26, 1944, in the Gypsy camp, receives No. Z-9307.

Ibid.

FEBRUARY 28

Two Polish political prisoners who were brought on July 29, 1943, to Auschwitz by order of the Radom Sipo and SD escape from squad 149 in the Buna plants. The escapees are Władysław Szulikowski (No. 115544), born on January 1, 1924, and Stanisław Tamulewicz, born on December 11, 1920.

APMO, IZ-8/Gestapo Lodz/4/90/26, 27; IZ-10/Gestapo Sieradz/2/194.

13 prisoners sent in a group transport receive Nos. 174566–174578.

A female prisoner sent from Lodz is given No. 75715.

APMO, Materials of the Information Section, Prisoner Card Index (hereafter cited as Mat.Ref.Inf., Prisoner Card Index).

FEBRUARY 29

The Jewish prisoner Mordka Cytryn (No. 30980), born in 1909 in Warsaw, escapes from Grading Squad 3 in Auschwitz II. He is captured during a later phase of his escape, delivered to Auschwitz II, and sent "until further notice" to the Penal Company.

APMO, D-AuI-3/1, p. 17, Penal Company Register; IZ-8/Gestapo Lodz/4/90/30, 31.

17 prisoners sent in a group transport receive Nos. 174579–174595.

*This is the last entry in the list of women's transports to Auschwitz, which was completed illegally by prisoners employed in the admissions office of the Political Department.

The Director of the Jewish Section, IV-B4, of the RSHA, SS Lieutenant Colonel Adolf Eichmann, views the Theresienstadt Family Camp during his stay in Auschwitz, in Camp B-IIb in Birkenau. Dr. Leo Janowitz, the former director of the Central Secretariat in the Theresienstadt ghetto, and Fredy Hirsch, a teacher and children's attendant in Camp B-IIb, report to him. Eichmann also converses with Miriam Edelstein, informing her that her husband, the former senior of the Jewish community in the Theresienstadt ghetto, the so-called Jewish Eldest, is most probably in Germany. Meanwhile, Jakob Edelstein, after his arrival in December 1943 in Auschwitz I, has been imprisoned in Block 11 together with his closest coworkers.

Adler, *Theresienstadt 1941–1945*, p. 730.

In Block 11 of Auschwitz a session of the Police Court-martial of the Kattowitz Gestapo takes place, during which 163 Poles who were sent to Block 11 from the prison in Myslowitz several days previously are condemned to death.* Among the condemned are also 41 people who were already in Auschwitz in autumn 1943 and received numbers. After the meeting the condemned are driven to Crematorium IV in Birkenau. In the crematorium a young woman steps forward from among the condemned and says, facing the SS men, that all those present are clear about the fact that they are about to die in the famous Auschwitz gas chambers and burned in the crematorium, but that the times in which these crimes can be committed in secret were now past. Today the entire world knows what is going on in Auschwitz, and for every person murdered here the Germans will have to pay dearly. Finally, she says she leaves this world convinced that an end to these crimes is not far away. While entering the crematorium the condemned sing "Poland is not yet lost" and "To the Barricades."

APMO, Mat.RO, vol. II, p. 71; vol. IV, pp. 258–259, List of Names; Konieczny, "Police Court-martial," pp. 131, 156–160.

MARCH 1

Two prisoners sent in a group transport receive Nos. 174596 and 174597.

Docs. of ISD Arolsen, NB-Frauen (Number Assignment in Auschwitz [Women]), p. 31 (hereafter cited as NA-Women, and for men, NA-Men).

Four female prisoners sent to the camp by the Trieste Sipo and SD receive Nos. 75740–75743.

16 prisoners sent from Kattowitz receive Nos. 174598–174613.

13 prisoners are transferred from Auschwitz to Sachsenhausen.

Mat.RO, vol. VII, p. 454.

The Jewish prisoner Szymon Lewenstein, born on November 5, 1918, in Berlin, who was sent from Bendin to Auschwitz on August 1, 1943, by the RSHA, escapes while working outside the grounds of the Günthergrube A.C.

APMO, D-AuI-1/1b, FS. 185; IZ-8/Gestapo Lodz/4/90/28, 29; IZ-10/Gestapo Sieradz/2/80/193.

---

*During this session 23 people are condemned to internment in Auschwitz. The session lasts six hours. Alerted by the Auschwitz Combat Group, Commandant Liebehenschel and the SS Camp Doctor Wirths take part in the meeting, and the latter explains apologetically the next day that more of the accused could not be saved in spite of his efforts (APMO, Mat.RO, Józef Cyrankiewicz File).

In the Theresienstadt Family Camp, B-IIb, in Birkenau, the rumor spreads that the transport of Jews who arrived on September 8, 1943, is to be deported to the labor camp in Heydebreck.

Adler et al., *Auschwitz: Testimonies*, p. 154.

MARCH 2

Seven prisoners sent from Kattowitz receive Nos. 174614–174620.

421 Czech prisoners are transferred from Auschwitz to Buchenwald.

Docs. of ISD Arolsen, Folder 12.

Four prisoners escape from Auschwitz II: the Pole Stefan Majewski (No. 131937) and the Jews Getzel Abramowicz (No. 27577), Mendel Eisenbach (No. 32704), and Kuba Balaban (No. 86794). The prisoners Abramowicz, Eisenbach, and Balaban are captured, returned to Auschwitz, and sent to the Birkenau Penal Company on March 17, 1944, "until further notice."

APMO, D-AuI-1/1b, FS. 186; IZ-8/Gestapo Lodz/4/90/35, 36; D-AuI-3/1, p. 17, Penal Company Register.

MARCH 3

24 prisoners sent in a group transport receive Nos. 174621–174644.

Three male Gypsies and two Gypsy girls, Roswitha Winter, born on April 5, 1942, and Giselle Delies, born on October 3, 1938, who were transferred from Germany, are given Nos. Z-9308–Z-9310 and Z-10014–Z-10015.

A female prisoner sent to the camp by the Stettin Stapo receives No. 75766.

Docs. of ISD Arolsen, NA-Women, p. 31.

16 prisoners sent in a group transport receive Nos. 174645–174660.

MARCH 4

17 prisoners sent in a group transport receive Nos. 174661–174677.

Seven male and seven female Gypsies transferred from Poland are given Nos. Z-9311–Z-9317 and Z-10016–Z-10022.

Six Jewish prisoners who are selected from an RSHA transport from Sosnowitz with 27 men receive Nos. 174678–174683.

APMO, D-AuII-3/1, p. 5, Quarantine List.

MARCH 5

732 Jews from Westerbork arrive in an RSHA transport from Holland. After the selection, 179 men, given Nos. 174684–174862, and 76 women, given Nos. 75816–75891, are admitted to the camp as prisoners. The remaining 477 persons are killed in the gas chambers.

APMO, D-AuII-3/1, p. 5, Quarantine List; Docs. of ISD Arolsen, NA-Women, p. 31.

The Jewish prisoners who were transferred on September 8, 1943, from the Theresienstadt ghetto in an RSHA transport and are now in the family camp, B-IIb, are given postcards, are ordered to date these March 25–27, and to write their relatives that they are healthy and that things are going well for them. It is prohibited to write about the transfer to the labor camp in Heydebreck. The completed postcards are brought to the Political Department, which sends them on to the addressees after March 25, 1944.*

APMO, Dpr.-ZO/3, p. 192; Mat.RO, vol. VII, p. 418; Adler, *Theresienstadt 1941–1945*, p. 152; Adler et al., *Auschwitz: Testimonies*, p. 154.

MARCH 6

A boy born in the Birkenau women's camp receives No. 174863.

12 prisoners sent in a group transport receive Nos. 174864–174875.

SS Private Konrad Strecker prevents a prisoner from escaping from the Monowitz A.C. As a reward he receives five days' special leave from Commandant Liebehenschel.

APMO, D-AuI-1, Garrison Order 10/44, March 22, 1944.

MARCH 7

Four prisoners sent from Kattowitz receive Nos. 174876–174879.

Eight prisoners sent in a group transport receive Nos. 174880–174887.

With the end of the six-month stay of the first group of Jews from the Theresienstadt Family Camp B-IIb and the instruction of the RSHA to kill them, it is decided to liquidate them. To prevent unrest, it should appear that the camp inmates were being transferred to labor camps in the Reich's interior. Consequently, all prisoners who are healthy and able to work are transferred to the Quarantine Camp B-IIa in Birkenau.** First the men are brought over and put up in special blocks; later the women are also brought over and put in other blocks. They are allowed to take their entire belongings with them, which they brought in boxes and suitcases from Theresienstadt. For this period the blocks in the quarantine camp are ordered closed.

APMO, Dpr.-Hd/6, pp. 48ff.; Dpr.-Hd/1, pp. 4–28; Ryszard Gert, *Trzebe głęboko oddychać, Kominy: Oswiecim 1940–1945* (Breathe Deeply, Chimneys: Auschwitz 1940–1945), Warsaw, 1962, pp. 17–64. Ryszard Gert is the pseudonym of Ryszard Kozielewski.

MARCH 8

85 Polish and Russian prisoners are transferred from Auschwitz to Buchenwald.

APMO, Mat.RO, vol. VII, p. 454; Docs. of ISD Arolsen, Folder 12.

*The Jews transferred in September 1943 were to be killed in order to make room for the next transports from Theresienstadt. The postcard action was to mislead their families and simultaneously the International Red Cross in the event that the news about their extermination should reach the international public (APMO, Mat.RO, vol. VII, p. 418).
**On September 8, 1943, the day of its arrival in Auschwitz, this transport contained 5,006 persons. By March 1944, approximately 1,140 of them had died. 3,800 deportees were still alive.

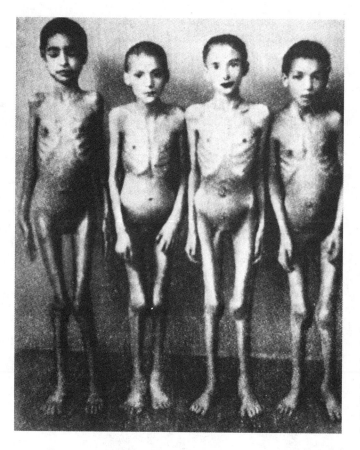

It was standard procedure in Auschwitz to kill all the children immediately in the gas chambers. Only a few were allowed to live; for example, twins, on whom the SS Doctor Josef Mengele carried out his "medical experiments."

SS Camp Doctor Mengele, who undertakes experiments on twins in the Gypsy Family Camp B-IIe, demands that approximately 70 doctors and twins be removed from the transport of Theresienstadt Jews who were moved from Camp B-IIb to Camp B-IIa. The doctors and twins are transferred again to the prisoners' infirmary in Camp B-IIb and then, in July 1944, to the prisoners' infirmary for men in Camp B-IIf. Among them are the twins Zdenek and Jiři Steiner (Nos. 147742 and 147743) and the physicians Dr. Heller (No. 146703), Dr. Bloch (No. 146737), Dr. Julius Samek (No. 147636), and Dr. Pollak (No. 148775).

APMO, Statements, vol. 71, pp. 227–241, Account of Former Prisoner Jiři Steiner; Steiner, Zdenek and Jiři, "Zwillinge in Birkenau" (Twins in Birkenau), in Adler et al., *Auschwitz: Testimonies*, pp. 154–156; Czech, "Role of Prisoners' Infirmary," pp. 48, 51, 55.

The prisoner Fredy Hirsch, teacher and care giver of the children in Camp B-IIb, commits suicide, because he cannot protect the women and children from destruction, and does not want to be a passive witness.

Ota Kraus and Erich Kulka, *Tovarna na smrt* (The Death Factory), Prague, 1957, pp. 134ff.; Adler, *Theresienstadt 1941–1945*, pp. 53ff.

The Jews held in special blocks in Quarantine Camp B-IIa, who await the alleged transport to the labor camp, begin to voice their fears ever more strongly and loudly. The Camp Commander of Auschwitz II, who is responsible for the smooth running of the operation, calls SS Camp Doctor Thilo for assistance. He selects several prisoners employed in the prisoners' infirmary, among them, Dr. Kleinberg, who has with him various medications and medical instruments. Dr. Thilo begins to make doctor's visits in the blocks,

Gert, *Breathe Deeply*, pp. 17–64.

during which he asks after the people's health and generously distributes medications. This pacifies the people waiting for the transport.

Around 8:00 P.M., Camp B-IIa is put under curfew. A large number of SS men from Auschwitz II and the Political Department arrive in the camp. Capos and Block Commanders whom the SS men trust somewhat are called for support. Half an SS company with dogs surrounds the camp. Around 10:00 P.M., 12 trucks covered with tarps drive up. The Jews are ordered to leave the heavy luggage in the barracks and are promised that it will be brought to the train. To maintain order and quiet, 40 people at a time are left on the truck loading platform and the trucks leaving Camp B-IIa do not turn left, i.e., the direct route to the crematoriums, but right, so it looks as though they are driving to the train station. This operation lasts several hours. First the men are driven to Crematorium III, then the women to Crematorium II. After waiting several hours for their departure, the Jews in one of the blocks become anxious and around 2:00 A.M. begin to sing a Czech folk song. In the next block singing also begins. Startled, the SS men begin to fire warning shots. The Jews are forbidden to sing, under the threat that the transport will be stopped. The disrobing rooms in the crematoriums have been prepared in such a manner that the waiting prisoners hope, to the end, that they are leaving for a labor camp. Only the order to disrobe makes it clear that they are in the crematorium. The women who are already in the gas chamber and are still waiting for the others sing the "Internationale," the "Hatikva," at that time the Jewish national hymn, and the Czech national anthem, and a partisans' song. Toward morning, 3,791 Jewish prisoners from Theresienstadt—men, women, and children—are killed in Crematoriums II and III.*

APMO, Dpr.-Hd/6, pp. 43, 48, 49, 50, Statement of Former Prisoner Dr. Otto Wolken; Mat.RO, vol. II, p. 68; vol. VII, p. 418; Adler, *Theresienstadt 1941–1945*, pp. 53, 124; Gert, *Breathe Deeply*, pp. 17–64.

MARCH 9

Seven prisoners sent from Kattowitz receive Nos. 174888–174894.

Seven Jewish prisoners sent by the RSHA in Bielitz receive Nos. 174895–174901.

The prisoner Walentyna Kowalenko (No. 27694), born on May 15, 1918,** escapes from the women's camp of Auschwitz II.

APMO, IZ-10/Gestapo Sieradz/ 2/193.

Two prisoners from the Kattowitz District receive Nos. 174902–174903.

10 male and six female Gypsies who were transferred from Germany are given Nos. Z-9318–Z-9327 and Z-10023–Z-10028.

---

*According to the author's calculations 3,791; according to Dr. Otto Wolken, 3,792 people.
**In the report of her escape it is stated that she escaped before March 10, 1944.

Angelika Schmidt, born on March 6, 1944, who dies on March 16, 1944, receives No. Z-10029. Her parents have French citizenship.

APMO, D-AuII-3/2/5, pp. 647, 648, Register of Female Gypsies.

The Polish prisoner Wojciech Poskuta (No. 125509), born on March 30, 1901, in Jędrzejów and sent to Auschwitz on June 24, 1943, by order of the Radom Sipo and SD, escapes from the railroad platform squad of Auschwitz II.*

APMO, IZ-8/Gestapo Lodz/4/90/ 32–34; IZ-10/Gestapo Sieradz/2/ 206, 207.

MARCH 10

1,501 Jewish men, women, and children from Drancy arrive in the sixty-ninth transport of the RSHA from France. After the selection, 110 men, given Nos. 174904–175013, and approximately 80 women are admitted to the camp as prisoners. The other more than 1,300 people are killed in the gas chambers.

Nine prisoners sent in a group transport receive Nos. 175014–175022.

Three boys and four girls, Gypsy children with the family name Franz who were probably transferred from an orphanage in Germany, are given Nos. Z-9328–Z-9330 and Z-10030–Z-10033.

The BBC "congratulates" Captain Nowotny for gassing his former wife on March 9 in Auschwitz; she was part of a transport of Czech prisoners from Theresienstadt.**

APMO, Dpr.-Hd/6, p. 32.

MARCH 11

21 prisoners sent in a group transport receive Nos. 175023–175043.

Six Jewish prisoners who were sent from Berlin and Sosnowitz by the RSHA receive Nos. 175044–175049.

A boy born in the Birkenau camp receives No. 175050.

Five men and the two boys, Harry Wollersheim, born on July 1, 1940, and Albert Wagner, born on May 10, 1942, receive Nos. Z-9331–Z-9337; Nos. Z-10034 and Z-10035 are given to two girls, Elisabeth Wollersheim, born on January 7, 1937, and Vera Wollersheim, born on January 25, 1939; Frieda Franz, born on February 18, 1929, is registered as No. Z-10036. All of them were transferred from Germany.

*He is captured, sent back to Auschwitz II, and sent on June 16, 1944, to the Penal Company. He is then transferred to Mauthausen (APMO, D-AuI-3/1, p. 22, SK Register).
**Dr. Wolken states: "In the camp we received the latest news every day from the English radio broadcasts. We knew things that the German radio didn't broadcast until a week later. This news was communicated to us by the Polish Jew Josef Kenner, who later was hanged in connection with a failed escape attempt. . . . Josef never divulged to us how this news reached his ears. . . ."

At 5:30 A.M. the Polish prisoner Edward Pawelczak escapes from Auschwitz I. Born on October 13, 1922, in Posen and sent to Auschwitz on December 2, 1943, by the Kattowitz Stapo, he was employed as a cleaner in the barracks squad. He is most probably dressed in an SS uniform and flees on a bicycle.

APMO, IZ-8/Gestapo Lodz/4/90/37–38; IZ-10/Gestapo Sieradz/2/206.

MARCH 12

In Sosnowitz a conference takes place on the deployment of prisoners in the Ost-Maschinenbau-Werke (Eastern Mechanical Engineering Works), in which representatives of the company and Branch D of the WVHA participate. A contract is drawn up for the employment of 1,400 prisoners in the departments for the production of cannon barrels for air defense artillery weapons and shells.

WAP Kattowitz, Berghütte Collection, 2511, pp. 6–8a; Franciszek Piper, "Das Nebeulager Sosnowitz II" (Sosnowitz II Auxiliary Camp), HvA, no. 11, 1970, pp. 97–128, compare the document on pp. 101–104.

MARCH 13

19 prisoners sent in a group transport receive Nos. 175051–175069.

The Degesch Company submits an invoice for 1,050 RM for the delivery of 462 pounds of the gas Zyklon B to Auschwitz March 8.

Schnabel, Power Without Morality, p. 356, Document 134.

MARCH 14

Eight Jewish prisoners who were selected from an RSHA transport of 39 Jewish prisoners from Sosnowitz receive Nos. 175070–175077. 31 men are killed in the gas chambers.

APMO, D-AuI-3/1, p. 5, Quarantine List.

Six Gypsies are sent to the Penal Company in Birkenau for periods of four to six months. Two of them die before completion of their sentences: Johann Geisler (No. Z-3287) and Zacharias Reinhardt (No. Z-9259).

APMO, D-AuII-3/1, p. 17, Penal Company Register.

34 prisoners sent in a group transport receive Nos. 175078–175111.

MARCH 15

Three female Gypsies are given Nos. Z-10037–Z-10039. Two Gypsy boys, Ernst Laudsberger, born on October 25, 1939, in Linz, who dies on July 8, 1944, in Birkenau, and Michael Horvath, born on October 9, 1943, in Engerau, who dies on April 4, 1944, in Birkenau, are given Nos. Z-9338 and Z-9339.

APMO, D-AuII-3/1/2, p. 277, Register of Male Gypsies.

MARCH 16

Two Jewish prisoners who are selected from an RSHA transport from Bielitz receive Nos. 175112–175113. Four female prisoners from this transport are admitted to the camp.

The Minister for the People's Enlightenment and Propaganda, Josef Goebbels, sends a secret document containing the government's suggestions for civil air defense in the Gau of Upper Silesia to the Minister of the Interior and SS Commander in Chief Himmler so that the offices that are in the area of responsibility of the SS Commander in Chief will receive appropriate instructions. Among the suggestions that deal with the strengthening of civil air defense is one relative to the defense of Auschwitz through the transfer to the region of a reserve battle division.

APMO, IZ-13/89, Various Documents of the Third Reich, pp. 294ff.

Three prisoners sent from Kattowitz receive Nos. 175114–175116.

A boy born in Birkenau receives No. 175117.

MARCH 17

An accounting of the accommodation costs for a concentration camp prisoner is prepared. According to it, the daily costs for clothing, room, and board per prisoner are 1,22 RM for a female prisoner and 1,34 RM for a male prisoner. The cost for women's clothing is calculated on the basis of the outfitting norm from January 19, 1944. It is .27 RM per person per day. The cost for men's clothing is calculated on the basis of the outfitting norm from January 18, 1944. It comes to .39 RM per person per day. The accommodation costs are found to be .30 RM per person per day. All maintenance costs are calculated to be .65 RM per person per day.

APMO, Dpr.-Hd/12, pp. 125ff., Exhibit 83.

16 prisoners sent in a group transport receive Nos. 175118–175133.

22 prisoners transferred from a house of correction in Mirau, Czechoslovakia, received the Nos. 175134–175155. In the transport are 21 tubercular prisoners.

APMO, D-AuII-3/1, p. 5, Quarantine List; Documents of the SS Hygiene Institute, Folder 3/435, 436.

31 prisoners sent in a group transport receive Nos. 175156–175186.

MARCH 18

Two male Gypsies are given Nos. Z-9340 and Z-9341, and a female Gypsy with German citizenship receives No. Z-10040.

A marriage between an Austrian prisoner, Rudolf Friemel (No. 25173), and a French citizen, Margarita Ferrer Rey, is performed in the registry office of Auschwitz II.* A commemorative photograph is made for them in the photo studio located in Block 26 of the main camp. For half a day the first floor of Block 24a is put at

APMO, Dpr.-Hd/7, pp. 7–8, Statement of Former Prisoner Alfred Woycicki; Dpr.-Hd/8, p. 107, Statement of Former Prisoner Jan Dziopek; Langbein, *The Stronger*, p. 210.

*Rudolf Friemel, an Austrian Socialist, had fought with the International Brigades in Spain, where he met and married the Spaniard Margarita Ferrer Rey. He had a son with her. Margarita Ferrer Rey then left Spain and lived in France. Since the

their disposal. The next day Margarita Ferrer Rey leaves the camp with her son.

MARCH 19

German troops cross the Hungarian border. The Sztójay government is formed in Budapest.

MARCH 20

10 prisoners sent from Kattowitz receive Nos. 175187–175196.

A man and two boys who were born on May 10, 1933, and December 23, 1933, are given Nos. Z-9342–Z-9344, and two women are given Nos. Z-10041 and Z-10042. This is the Polish Gypsy family Paczkowski.

APMO, D-AuII-3/1/2, p. 277, Register of Male Gypsies; D-AuII-3/2/5, pp. 647ff., Register of Female Gypsies.

Josefa Prohaska, born in the Gypsy camp, receives No. Z-10043.

APMO, D-AuII-3/2/5, p. 647, Register of Female Gypsies.

MARCH 21

30 Polish prisoners are transferred from Auschwitz to Natzweiler.

APMO, Mat.RO, vol. VII, p. 454.

16 prisoners sent in a group transport receive Nos. 175197–175212.

A female prisoner sent by the Graz Kripo receives No. 76037.

Docs. of ISD Arolsen, NA-Women, p. 31.

Associated Press reports from London that the Polish Information Ministry alleges that more than 500,000 persons, mainly Jews, have been killed in the Auschwitz Concentration Camp southwest of Kraków; in an extensive report, the ministry has proved that the camp contains three crematoriums for the daily elimination of 10,000 corpses, and gas chambers where men, women, and children have been killed within 10 to 15 minutes of their arrival in freight cars.

Mel Mermelstein, *By Bread Alone: The Story of A-4685*, Los Angeles, 1979, p. 61.

MARCH 22

A female prisoner sent from Kattowitz receives No. 175213.

31 prisoners sent in a group transport receive Nos. 175214–175244.

German authorities did not recognize their marriage; they worked for a long time for permission to have another wedding, which they finally received. According to Hermann Langbein, the parents also participate in the wedding celebration in Auschwitz. Rudolf Friemel works in the vehicle squad and belongs to the leadership of the Auschwitz resistance group. He is hanged on December 30, 1944 in Auschwitz. This marriage of a prisoner in the Auschwitz Concentration Camp is the only one in the history of the registry office in the camp. A meeting between Hitler and the regent of Hungary, Admiral Horthy, took place. The Hungarian side rejected the German demand, which sought military, police, and economical control over Hungary.

A man and three boys are given Nos. Z-9345–Z-9348 and a woman and two girls are given Nos. Z-10044–Z-10046. They are Gypsies transferred from Germany.

MARCH 23

Three men and seven boys receive Nos. Z-9349–Z-9358 and five women and five girls receive Nos. Z-10047–Z-10057; they have been transferred from the German Reich.

MARCH 24

SS Lieutenant Colonel Brandt of the personal staff of the SS Commander in Chief informs the Head of the WVHA, Pohl, that in connection with Minister Goebbels's suggestion regarding the security of the camp and the transfer of a replacement division to the area, Himmler would like a detailed account of measures taken so far for the security of such a camp expansion. Himmler is of the opinion that something must be done immediately to prevent any possible uprising.*

APMO, IZ-13/89, Various Documents of the Third Reich, p. 296.

23 prisoners sent in a group transport receive Nos. 175245–175267.

Nos. 175268–175280 are given to 13 Jewish prisoners who were selected from an RSHA transport on March 22, 1944.

11 men and youths receive Nos. Z-9359–Z-9369 and two women and three girls receive Nos. Z-10058–Z-10062. They are German and Polish Gypsies sent in a group transport.

15 prisoners of war are brought into the camp, among them two colonels, who were captured in Dubno. The eight Russians, four Poles, and three Jews are all shot in Crematorium IV in Birkenau.

APMO, Mat.RO, vol. VII, p. 423.

MARCH 25

Nos. 175281–175292 are given to 12 prisoners sent in a group transport.

30 prisoners from The Hague receive Nos. 175293–175322.

Seven female prisoners are transferred from The Hague.

184 Jews—men, women, and children—arrive in an RSHA transport from The Hague. They were hidden by Dutch citizens and arrested as a result of denunciations by informers. They are put in Block 4, which is isolated, of the so-called depot in Men's Quar-

APMO, Dpr.-Hd/6, pp. 24, 50, 55.

*The German authorities, including Himmler, fear that in a camp with so many inmates as Auschwitz, the danger exists of an armed uprising in the event of an unfavorable turn of events in the war.

Prisoners during the construction of the admissions building in winter 1944.

antine Camp B-IIa. They receive no numbers, as directives are expected from the RSHA.* Only prisoner functionaries have access to this block, among them Dr. Wolken, a prisoner doctor from the outpatient department in Camp B-IIa.

599 Jews from Westerbork—387 men, 169 women, and 43 children—arrive in an RSHA transport from Holland. After the selection, 304 men, given Nos. 175323–175626, and 56 women, given Nos. 76076–76131, are admitted to the camp. The other 239 deportees are killed in the gas chambers.

Two Polish prisoners escape from the disassembly squad of Auschwitz II: Henryk Lewandowski (No. 139108), who was sent to Auschwitz on August 25, 1943, by order of the Warsaw Sipo and SD, and Tadeusz Frydrykiewicz, born on October 30, 1924, who was sent to Auschwitz on December 19, 1943, by order of the Radom Sipo and SD.

APMO, IZ-8/Gestapo Lodz/4/90/ 59, 60; IZ-10/Gestapo Sieradz/2/ 206.

Nos. Z-9370–Z-9375 are given to six male Gypsies and Nos. Z-10063–Z-10068 to five female Gypsies and one girl who have been transferred from the German Reich.

*They are killed on April 4, 1944, in the gas chambers.

MARCH 26

443 prisoners transferred from Gross-Rosen receive Nos. 175628–176070.*

A Jewish prisoner who is transferred to the camp in the morning receives No. 176071.

MARCH 27

Eight prisoners sent in a group transport receive Nos. 176072–176079.

A female prisoner sent to the camp by the Klagenfurt Stapo receives No. 76139.

Docs. of ISD Arolsen, NA-Women, p. 31.

After a several-week retraining period the SS guard Martin Lumnitzer takes over the guard in the newly created Gleiwitz I (Gliwice I) auxiliary camp.** He finds around 100 prisoners in the camp, which belongs to Auschwitz III. The Reich railway renovation works employs the prisoners for repairing the railroads. In January 1945 there are 1,336 prisoners in the camp.

MARCH 28

14 prisoners sent in a group transport receive Nos. 176080–176093.

Two female prisoners sent to the camp by the Klagenfurt Stapo receive Nos. 76140–76143.

Ibid.

MARCH 29

Two prisoners sent from Kattowitz receive Nos. 176094 and 176095.

Johanna Kahl, born in the Birkenau Gypsy camp, receives No. Z-10069; she dies on April 5, 1944.

APMO, D-AuII-3/2/5, p. 649, Register of Female Gypsies.

The Commandant's Office of Auschwitz I is informed by the Warsaw Sipo and SD that the prisoner Karol Schornstein, who escaped from the camp on September 15, 1941, has been captured in Lemberg and is in investigative detention.

APMO, D-AuI-1b, FS.200; IZ-8/Gestapo Lodz/2/88/155.

*The freight train that transports the prisoners from Gross-Rosen to Auschwitz is first directed to the unloading ramp in the Eintrachthütte A.C. There, 161 prisoners are left and put up in the Eintrachthütte A.C. They receive Nos. 175628–175788. Then the train went to Auschwitz (APMO, Statements, vol. 50, p. 65; vol. 61, p. 49; vol. 67, p. 177, Accounts of Former Prisoners).
**The precise date of the formation of Gleiwitz I has not yet been determined. A more detailed account of the history of the camp was given by Irena Strzelecka, "Gleiwitz I Labor Camp," HvA, no. 14 (1973): 75–106.

During a discussion in the SS WVHA between the Head of Branch C, Kammler, and the Director of the Central Construction Administration of the Waffen SS and Police in Silesia, SS Major Karl Bischoff, it was decided to limit to the absolutely necessary the investments that are planned for the orderly functioning of the camp and its further development, especially the development of the main camp. Among other things it is decided to discontinue the construction of the prisoners' barracks in Section III of Birkenau, which the prisoners call "Mexico," and instead to deploy the prisoners at construction sites essential to armaments.

APMO, Construction Office, vol. 80/6, Memo, March 31, 1944.

MARCH 30

1,000 Jewish men, women, and children from the Drancy camp arrive in the seventieth RSHA transport from France. After the selection, 380 men, who receive Nos. 176096–176475, and 148 women, who are given Nos. 76162–76309, are admitted to the camp. The remaining 472 people are killed in the gas chambers.

202 Czech prisoners are transferred from Auschwitz to Buchenwald.

APMO, Mat.RO, vol. VII, p. 454; Docs. of ISD Arolsen, Folder 12.

106 Polish and Russian prisoners are transferred from Auschwitz to the Watenstedt-Drütte auxiliary camp of Neuengamme.

APMO, Mat.RO, vol. VII, p. 454. [Watenstedt-Drütte]

The Polish prisoner Józef Hanka, born on February 2, 1912, in Lodz, escapes from the dismantling squad in Auschwitz II.

APMO, D-AuI/1b, FS.196; IZ-10/Gestapo Sieradz/2/208.

13 female prisoners transferred from the POW camp Stalag VII-A (Moosburg) receive Nos. 76319–76331.

Docs. of ISD Arolsen, NA-Women.

MARCH 31

22 prisoners sent in a group transport receive Nos. 176476–176497.

A prisoner who arrives in the morning from Kattowitz receives No. 176498.

The term "KGL" (Kriegsgefangenenlager—prisoner-of-war camp) used in the construction documents to refer to the POW camp is changed in Birkenau.

APMO, Dpr.-Hd/12, p. 60, File Memo, March 31, 1944.

The documents of deceased prisoners that contained the abbreviations "SB" (Sonderbehandlung—"special treatment") and "G.U." (Gesonderte Unterbringung—"separate accommodation") are brought to the crematorium in Auschwitz II and burned in an oven designated for this purpose.

APMO, Dpr.-Hd/4, p. 85, Statement of Former Prisoner Wilibald Pająk.

The Head of Branch D in the WVHA, Glücks, directs a communiqué to the Commandants of all concentration camps informing them that it has proved indispensable and extremely important that the prisoners be watched by suitable fellow prisoners (informers). The Commandants are to devote special attention to goings-on in

Klaus Drobisch, *Widerstand in Buchenwald* (Resistance in Buchenwald), Berlin, 1985, p. 115.

the camp, so that they will not one day be surprised by unpleasant events.

APRIL 1

A boy born in Birkenau receives the free No. 175627.

12 prisoners sent in a group transport receive Nos. 176499–176510.

The Commandant's Office of Auschwitz III takes over the so-called Jews' forced-labor camp in Blechhammer, whose prisoners are employed in the construction of plants of the chemicals company, Oberschlesische Hydrierwerke AG. A small group of prisoners employed in the admissions office of the Political Department traveled with an SS escort to Blechhammer, where they were put to work preparing the personnel forms of the 3,056 male prisoners, who were given Nos. 176512–179567, and nearly 150 female prisoners, and tattooing them.* The camp received the name Blechhammer Labor Camp, and SS Captain Otto Brossmann became the Camp Commander. The camp is first mentioned as Blechhammer Labor Camp (Heydebreck Office, Heydebreck 334) in a Commandant's Office order of April 22, 1944, in which the numbers of the telephone connections were established.

APMO, D-AuIII-1/63, Commandant's Office Order 6/44, April 22, 1944; Franciszek Piper, "Das Nebenlager Blechhammer" (Auxiliary Camp Blechhammer), *HvA*, no. 10 (1967): 19–39.

24 Jewish prisoners are transferred from Auschwitz to Kraków-Płaszów.

APMO, Mat.RO, vol. VII, p. 454.

APRIL 3

Eight prisoners sent from Kattowitz receive Nos. 179568–179575.

The management of the crematoriums in Auschwitz II awards the DAW with the contract to repair 18 oven doors, to make a new grate, to weld broken spots, and to fix seven scratches.**

APMO, IZ-13/89, Various Documents of the Third Reich, p. 207, Invoice copy for bookkeeping.

184 Jewish men, women, and children who were transferred from The Hague on March 25 and are not entered in the camp registers are taken from Quarantine Camp B-IIa in Birkenau to the gas chambers.

APMO, Dpr.-Hd/6, pp. 24, 50, 55.

APRIL 4

11 prisoners from Kattowitz receive Nos. 179576–179586.

29 Jewish prisoners selected from an RSHA transport from Trieste receive Nos. 179587–179615; the remaining 103 prisoners are killed in the gas chambers.

APMO, D-AuII-3/1, p. 5, Quarantine List.

---

*Probably 132 female prisoners, who receive Nos. 76330–76461, remain in Blechhammer while the remaining women are transferred to Birkenau, where they are killed because they are unable to work.
**The repair costs run to 339.80 RM, according to the invoice of December 20, 1944.

53 female Jewish prisoners selected from an RSHA transport from Trieste and Istria receive Nos. 75460–76512.

Docs. of ISD Arolsen, NA-Women, p. 31; APMO, Mat.Ref.Inf., Prisoner Card Index.

32 prisoners sent in a group transport receive Nos. 179616–179697.

Three female prisoners sent in a group transport by the Magdeburg Stapo receive Nos. 76530–76532.

Docs. of ISD Arolsen, NA-Women, p. 31.

In connection with the efforts to check the typhus epidemic, Commandant Liebehenschel rescinds the prohibition for SS members to enter the town of Auschwitz. But he informs them that they may visit the following German entertainment spots, cinemas, and restaurants: the city hall, the new Cinema and Theater, open starting the April 16, 1944: the old Cinema Skala, on the Ring; the restaurant/hotel Ratshof on Marketplatz; Gasthofzur Burg (Restaurant at the Fort), Bohnhofstrasse; the Kaffee au Markt (Cafe at the Market), and the Deutsche Gaststätte, both on the Marktplatz; the restaurants the Gefolgschaftskasino and Grzywok, in Krakauer Strasse; as well as the Fremdenheim Hotel in the Bahnhofstrasse. For health reasons, Friedrichstrasse and Ostlandstrasse remain closed to off-duty visits.

APMO, D-AuI, Garrison Order 11/44, April 4, 1944.

Commandant Liebehenschel demands that the SS guards check all vehicles thoroughly, especially trucks in which prisoners who intend to escape from the camp could be hidden.

Ibid.

The Russian, Olga Musiyenko, who was transferred from Brünn, is not admitted to the camp, since she succeeds in escaping on the way from the train station to the camp.

APMO, D-AuI-1/1b, FS.201; IZ-10/Gestapo Sieradz/2/208.

APRIL 5

The Head of the WVHA, Pohl, informs the SS Commander in Chief on the number of individual concentration camps and labor camps. On March 31, 1944, there are the following camps:

APMO, D-RF-3/RSHA/117a, p. 54, RSHA General Orders.

Concentration Camps

In the Reich territory	13
In the Government General	3
In the East	3
In the Netherlands	1
Total	20

Labor Camps

In the Reich territory	130
In the General Government	3
In the East	30
In the Netherlands	2
	165
Total	185 camps

The female German Gypsy Anneliese Winterstein, who was born on February 25, 1924, in Würzburg and who dies in Birkenau on June 7, 1944, receives No. Z-10070.

APMO, D-AuII-3/2/5, pp. 649ff., Register of Female Gypsies.

The Jewish prisoner Siegfried Lederer, who was transferred from Theresienstadt on February 19, 1943, in an RSHA transport, flees from the Theresienstadt Family Camp, Camp B-IIb, wearing the uniform of an SS Private First Class.*

APMO, D-AuI-1/1b, FS.202; IZ-8/Gestapo Lodz/4/90/61–64; IZ-10/Gestapo Sieradz/2/208.

50 of 380 Jewish prisoners who arrived from Drancy in an RSHA transport on March 30 and were housed in Auschwitz are transferred from Auschwitz III to Golleschau A.C. They are ordered to stay in quarantine until April 27.

APMO, D-AuIII, Golleschau/12, p. 66.

In answer to a communiqué from SS First Lieutenant Brandt of March 24, 1944, regarding the security of Auschwitz, WVHA Head Pohl produces a report for the SS Commander in Chief to which he appends two plans. He gives the number of prisoners as follows:

APMO, Pohl Trial, vol. Pd 13, pp. 23–27 (NI-317); Schnabel, *Power Without Morality*, pp. 128–130.

Auschwitz I	16,000 men
Auschwitz II	15,000 men, 21,000 women
Auschwitz III	15,000 men
	46,000 men, 21,000 women
Total	67,000 prisoners

Auschwitz II has the greatest number of prisoners, with 36,000, of whom 21,000 are women.

Regarding the question of Upper Silesia's security in case of a rebellion or revolt, one must think in terms of 34,000 prisoners, since 15,000 prisoners are located in the auxiliary camps and 18,000 prisoners are sick and invalid. The 34,000 could represent a danger for Auschwitz in case of a rebellion, if security measures are insufficient.

For surveillance of the prisoners reportedly 2,300 SS members are available for Auschwitz I and II; for the auxiliary camps an additional 650 guards are available. SS Lieutenant General Schmauser will set up a police company of 130 men by the middle of the month for the additional security of Auschwitz II. In addition to the watchtowers and the electric fence, a bunker line has been created as an inner ring, which is to be manned by SS members. In the case of a rebellion an outer ring will be formed, to be manned by the Wehrmacht. In this ring will encompass the Monowitz A.C. and the entire I. G. Farben complex. The deployment of the Wehrmacht was decided upon several weeks ago in Auschwitz between SS Lieutenant General Schmauser and the Commanding General of the 8th Division, General von Koch-Erbach. Moreover, the Luftwaffe units stationed in Auschwitz, 1,000 men strong, will be

---

*Lederer reaches Czechoslovakia and as a member of the Czech resistance movement is smuggled into the Theresienstadt ghetto to inform the committee of elders of the Jewish community of the fate of the Jews in Auschwitz (Adler, *Theresienstadt 1941–1945*, p. 152).

available, assuming the alarm does not occur at the same time as an air raid.

APRIL 7

240 Jews arrive from Westerbork in an RSHA transport from Holland. 106 men, 112 women and 22 children are in the transport. After the selection, 62 men, given Nos. 179648–179709, and 67 women, given Nos. 76534–76600, are admitted to the camp. The remaining 111 people are killed in the gas chambers.

Docs. of ISD Arolsen, NA-Women, p. 4.

625 Jews—302 men, 269 women, and 54 children—arrive from Malines in the twenty-fourth RSHA transport from Belgium. After the selection, 206 men, given Nos. 179710–179915, and 146 women, given Nos. 76601–76746, are admitted to the camp. The other 273 people are killed in the gas chambers.

Ibid., p. 31.

The Central Construction Administration of the Waffen SS and Police order that the documentation of the discontinued construction projects in Auschwitz be handled in a way that they can be taken up again without difficulty, if necessary.

APMO, Construction Administration, vol. 80/6.

A female prisoner sent from Breslau receives No. 76747.

APMO, Mat.Ref.Inf., Prisoner Card Index.

A female prisoner sent by Stapo headquarters in Frankfurt an der Oder receives No. 76750.

Docs. of ISD Arolsen, NA-Women, p. 31.

Nine prisoners from The Hague receive Nos. 179916–179924.

38 prisoners sent in two group transports receive Nos. 179925–179940 and 179941–179962.

Two prisoners escape from Auschwitz II; they are the Slovak Jews Alfred Wetzler (No. 29162), born on May 10, 1918, in Tyrnau (Trnava), and Walter Rosenberg (No. 44070), who later uses the name Rudolf Vrba, born on September 11, 1924, in Tyrnau.*

APMO, D-AuI-1/1b, p. 360; IZ-8/Gestapo Lodz/4/90/65–67.

APRIL 8

11 prisoners sent in a group transport receive Nos. 179964–179973.

---

*The motive for their escape is the desire to inform the world of the truth concerning the crimes committed by the SS in Auschwitz, and their intention to warn the Hungarian Jews of their planned destruction. After an exhausting journey of several days on foot, the two reach Slovakia. On April 25, 1944, they make contact in Sillein (Žilina) with representatives of the Jewish Council, to whom they give an oral and later written account of their stay in Auschwitz. These reports are confirmed by the next two escapees, Czesław Mordowicz and Arnost Rosin, who flee at the end of May 1944 from Auschwitz II. They are able to send translated texts of their statement to the neutral nations and to the papal legate. The complete text of the report is published in November 1944 in the U.S.A. by the War Refugee Board in Washington, D.C. (APMO, Statements, vol. 40, pp. 24–49, Account of Former Prisoner Alfred Wetzler; Wetzler went under the name Jožko Lánik after his escape and published in 1946 in Czechoslovakia a pamphlet entitled *Auschwitz, the Grave of Four Million People*).

Three male Gypsies and seven female Gypsies sent in a group transport from the Reich territory are given Nos. Z-9376–Z-9378 and Z-10071–Z-10077.

A cook, the German prisoner Karl Schmied (alias Schmidt) (No. 113326), is transferred from the Eintrachthütte A.C. to the newly completed Laurahütte.* The Laurahütte auxiliary camp in Siemianowice belongs to Auschwitz III; it is located on the grounds of the foundry, and the prisoners were deployed for the production of air defense weapons. The Camp Commander is SS Staff Sergeant Walter Quackernack. In January 1945 there are 937 prisoners in the camp.

APMO, d-Hyg.Inst. 37/64; D-AuIII-3a, Questionnaire.

APRIL 9

An evacuation transport from Majdanek is transferred to Auschwitz and housed in Quarantine Camp B-IIa in Birkenau. The transport consists of sick people and contains 2,000 prisoners on departure from Lublin. It was originally taken to Sachsenhausen but was not taken in because it was overloaded. The deportees are under way eight days without any medical treatment or water, in the command of SS men who shoot and kill 20 prisoners but report that these individuals had attempted to flee. When the prisoners leave the railroad cars it is found that 99 prisoners are dead. There is not enough room in the prisoners' infirmary in Quarantine Camp B-IIa. The sick are left to lie on the ground between the infirmary barracks.

APMO, Mat.RO, vol. VII, p. 424; Dpr.-Hd/6, p. 56; Dpr.-Hd/64, p. 39.

APRIL 10

935 Jews arrested in Fossoli di Carpi, Mantua, and Verona arrive in an RSHA transport from Italy. After the selection, 154 men and 80 women, given Nos. 179974–180127 and 76776–76855, are admitted to the camp. The remaining 692 people are killed in the gas chambers.

CDECM, *Jews in Italy*, p. 19.

1,846 numbers** are planned for the prisoners who arrive in the morning from Majdanek. The recording of the personal data, the tattooing of the numbers, and other formalities last four days. 1,724 prisoners are entered into the camp registers, receiving Nos. 180128–181842, 181845, and 184036–184043. There are 38 Russian POWs in the transport, who receive Nos. RKG-11494–RKG-11531. The remaining 119 prisoners had already been in Auschwitz and receive the numbers they had been given before.

APMO, D-AuII-3/1, p. 5, Quarantine List.

86 prisoners from the evacuation transport from Majdanek die.

APMO, Dpr.-Hd/6, p. 56.

---

*This is the first mention of the Laurahütte auxiliary camp. Schmidt was transferred on November 7, 1944, to the SS Special Dirlewanger Unit (Tadeusz Iwaszko offers more detail on the Laurahütte auxiliary camp: "Das Nebenlager Laurahütte," ["Laurahütte Auxiliary Camp"], *HvA*, no. 10 [1967] 87–102).
**130 numbers too many are reserved. They are given out at a later point.

Train with deportees on Track 3 of the so-called new ramp, in Birkenau, spring 1944.

Jews arrive in an RSHA transport. After the selection, 151 men, given Nos. 181978–182128, are admitted to the camp. All remaining people are killed in the gas chambers.

Three prisoners sent in a group transport receive Nos. 182129–182131.

APRIL 11

After the selection of the Jews who arrive in an RSHA transport, 308 men, given Nos. 182132–182439, are admitted to the camp. All remaining people are killed in the gas chambers.

Approximately 2,500 Jewish men, women, and children who were arrested in Athens arrive in an RSHA transport from Greece. After the selection, 320 men, given Nos. 182440–182759, and 328 women, who probably receive Nos. 76856–77183, are admitted to the camp. The remaining people, among them 1,067 men, are killed in the gas chambers.

APMO, D-AuII-3/1, p. 5, Quarantine List.

22 prisoners sent from Kattowitz receive Nos. 182760–182781.

Two female prisoners who were transferred in a group transport and sent to the camp by order of the Klagenfurt Stapo, receive Nos. 77193 and 77199.

Docs. of ISD Arolsen, NA-Women, p. 31.

Two prisoners, the Pole Czesław Mądrzyk and the Russian Grigori Orlov-Maro (No. 64908), escape from Auschwitz II.

APMO, D-AuI-1/1a, p. 364; IZ-10/Gestapo Sieradz/2/208.

The Head of Office D-I in the WVHA directs the Commandants to order the death penalty for offenses that have the character of acts of sabotage.

APMO, D-RF-9 WVHA, 8/2, p. 47, Edict Collection.

The expansion of Section III in Birkenau, called "Mexico" by the prisoners, as well as other construction projects in Birkenau are discontinued.

APMO, D-AuI-1, Garrison Order 12/44, April 12, 1944.

APRIL 12

Two prisoners sent from Kattowitz receive Nos. 182782 and 182783.

In Quarantine Camp B-IIa in Birkenau an SS man kills the prisoner Piotr Hromojew (No. 181378), who attempted to defend his brother.

APMO, Dpr.-Hd/6, p. 56.

Two men and two boys and three women and three girls, all German Gypsies, are given Nos. Z-9379–Z-9382 and Z-10078–Z-10083.

Seven prisoners are sent to the Penal Company in Birkenau, two for three months and five for six months.

APMO, D-AuI-3/1, p. 18, Penal Company Register.

The RSHA releases a directive that German female prisoners are to be transferred from Auschwitz to Ravensbrück, because the mortality among this group has been determined to be too high.

APRIL 13

14 prisoners sent in a group transport receive Nos. 182784–182797. The 12-year-old German Gypsy, Gerhard Petermann, born in Berlin, arrives with this transport and is registered as No. Z-9383.

APRIL 14

For the first time, Allied air reconnaissance takes photographs of Auschwitz from an altitude of 15,000 to 20,000 feet. On the photos can be seen Auschwitz I, the town of Auschwitz, the I. G. Farben complex, and Auschwitz III, among other features. The Allies are interested in destroying the production installations of the petrochemical industry, which are part of the war effort of the

APMO, Analyses, vol. 64, Klein/194a, Aerial Photos, pp. 23–37, Negative Nos. 20989/1–14.

Third Reich; this is the reason for the interest in the I. G. Farben complex.

Two prisoners escape from Auschwitz II, the Poles Eugeniusz Werla, born on August 22, 1903, and Tadeusz Wolniewicz (No. 119504), born on April 27, 1922.

APMO, IZ-8/Gestapo Lodz/4/90/68, 69.

60 prisoners sent in a group transport receive Nos. 182798–182857.

Two German female Gypsies receive Nos. Z-10084 and Z-10085.

1,239 prisoners are transferred from Majdanek, of whom 52 had previously been in Auschwitz. 1,187 prisoners receive Nos. 182858–184035 and 184044–184052.

APMO, D-AuII-3/1, p. 5, Quarantine List.

APRIL 15

The Russian prisoner Ivan Potechin escapes from the Fürstengrube auxiliary camp.

APMO, D-AuI-1b, FS.211, p. 374.

The Russian prisoner Alexander Demidov escapes from the Neu-Dachs A.C. in Jaworzno.

Ibid.

38 prisoners are sent to the Penal Company in Birkenau "until further notice."

APMO, D-AuI-3/1, p. 18–19, Penal Company Register.

Seven prisoners sent in a group transport receive Nos. 184090–184096.

884 prisoners, Gypsies, are transferred from Camp B-IIe of Auschwitz II to Buchenwald.*

APMO, Mat.RO, vol. VII, p. 454; D-AuII-3/1/2, Register of Male Gypsies, pp. 1–278; Docs. of ISD Arolsen, Folder 12.

473 female Gypsies are transferred from Camp B-IIe of Auschwitz II to Ravensbrück.

APMO, Mat.RO, vol. VII, p. 454; D-AuII-3/2/5, Register of Female Gypsies, pp. 1–650. [to Ravensbrück]

Four Jewish prisoners escape from a labor squad in Auschwitz II that was deployed in the construction of a rail connection from the Auschwitz freight station to the Birkenau unloading ramp: Karol Gotkieb, born on January 1, 1913, in Włoszczowa, Saul Orenstein (No. 32196), Boruch Gajc (No. 138273), and Abram Kohn (No. 138387). Orenstein, Gajc, and Kohn are captured by the Gendarmerie on April 20 in the area of Bielitz, are delivered to Auschwitz II, and are sent on April 21, 1944, to the Penal Company.

APMO, D-AuI-1/1b, FS.210; IZ-8/Gestapo Lodz/4/90/70, 71; D-AuI-3/1, p. 19, Penal Company Register.

An SS Camp Doctor conducts a selection in Quarantine Camp B-IIa in Birkenau, during which he selects 184 prisoners. They are killed the same day in the gas chambers.

APMO, Dpr.-Hd/6, p. 7.

*883 Gypsies arrive on April 17, 1944, at Buchenwald; one prisoner probably died en route, or he succeeded in fleeing.

Prisoners from the Lublin concentration camp (Majdanek) are transferred; 988 women and 38 children were received.* They were all put up in Men's Quarantine Camp B-IIa in Birkenau, in Blocks 3–6.

APMO, D-AuII-3/1, p. 5, Quarantine List; Dpr.-Hd/6, pp. 88–89.

APRIL 16

299 female Jewish prisoners and two nursing infants are transferred from Majdanek.** They are put up in Men's Quarantine Camp B-IIa in Birkenau in Block 2. With this transport the Majdanek Special Squad arrives, which consists of 19 Russian POWs and a German prisoner who was the Capo of this squad. After their arrival they were put in the Auschwitz-Birkenau Special Squad and housed in Camp B-IId in Block 13, which is occupied at the time by the Special Squad.

APMO, D-AuI-3/1, p. 5, Quarantine list; Dpr.-Hd/6, p. 7; Dpr.-Hd/1; Statement of Former Prisoner Stanisław Jankowski (a.k.a. Alter Feinsilber); SAM, *Amid Unspeakable Crimes*, p. 61.

In connection with the transfer of evacuation transports from Majdanek, in which there were many sick prisoners, several blocks in the Men's Quarantine Camp B-IIa in Birkenau were set up as temporary infirmaries. Blocks 3, 4, 5, and 6 are planned to be the women's section, and Blocks 9 and 10 are set up for men who suffer from diarrhea, so-called starvation dysentary; Block 11 is the so-called convalescent block for convalescents and weak individuals; Blocks 12, 13, and 14 are for those with tuberculosis; Block 15 is for internal and surgical medicine; and Block 16 is for those with infectious diseases. The section for infectious diseases remains in Block 16 until the dissolution of the quarantine camp, while the other sections are dissolved within two months.

APMO, Dpr.-Hd/6, pp. 88–89, Statement of Dr. Otto Wolken.

1,500 Jewish men, women, and children arrive from Drancy with the seventy-first RSHA transport from France. After the selection, 165 men, given Nos. 184097–184261 and 223 women, who receive Nos. 78560–78782, are admitted to the camp. The remaining deportees are killed in the gas chambers.

Docs. of ISD Arolsen, NA-Women, p. 32.

407 men and boys are given Nos. Z-9384–Z-9790, and 445 women and girls are given Nos. Z-10086–Z-10530. They are German and Polish Gypsies from Prussia and Masuren who were transferred from Brest-Litovsk.

APRIL 17

15 prisoners sent in a group transport receive Nos. 181847–181861.

*The female prisoners from this transport probably receive Nos. 77235–78222 (APMO, Mat.Ref.Inf., Prisoner Card Index; Docs. of ISD Arolsen, NA-Women, p. 31).
**They probably receive Nos. 78246–78548, since these numbers are later recalled, and reassigned on June 6, 1944.

APRIL 18

20 prisoners sent in a group transport receive the free Nos. 181862–181881.

In the evening, SS men with guard dogs lead the 299 female Jewish prisoners and two nursing infants, who were transferred on April 16 from Majdanek from Block 2 of Quarantine Camp B-IIa to the gas chambers. The numbers that had been given to them are given later to other female prisoners.*

APMO, Dpr.-Hd/6, p. 7, Statement of Dr. Otto Wolken.

APRIL 19

14 prisoners sent from Kattowitz receive the free Nos. 181843 and 181882–181894.

12 Jewish prisoners who are selected from an RSHA transport from Germany receive Nos. 181895–181906.

Two Russian POWs, Michail Sadli, born 1919, and Viktor Sodorov, born 1923, escape from the disassembly plant squad of Auschwitz II.

APMO, D-AuI-1/1a, p. 380; IZ-10/Gestapo Sieradz/2/208.

Michal Liszka (No. 85114) is so severely beaten by an SS man that he dies from a kidney injury and other injuries. The reason for the beating is a poor greeting.

APMO, Dpr.-Hd/6, p. 57, Statement of Former Prisoner Dr. Otto Wolken.

APRIL 20

Six prisoners sent from Kattowitz receive Nos. 181907–181912.

20 Polish prisoners are transferred from Auschwitz to Gross-Rosen.

APMO, Mat.RO, vol. VII, p. 454.

APRIL 21

37 prisoners transferred in a group transport receive Nos. 181913–181949.

Two Polish prisoners in the Monowitz A.C. escape from Squad 156 in the Buna plants: Czesław Wleklik and Franciszek Skorzewski. Skorzewski is captured on May 1, 1944, in Gleiwitz and returned to Auschwitz III.**

APMO, IZ-8/Gestapo Lodz/2/88/21; D-AuI-1/1a, pp. 383, 385.

37 men and boys and 37 women and girls, German Gypsies, are given Nos. Z-9791–Z-9827 and Z-10531–Z-10567.

---

*The prisoner Stanisław Jankowski (a.k.a. Alter Feinsilber), a member of the Special Squad, states that the female prisoners, Polish Jews, were shot and killed that night in the crematorium. The prisoners on night shift of the Special Squad, who burned their corpses, were witnesses (SAM, *Amid Unspeakable Crimes*, p. 61).
**On August 15, 1944, he transferred to Buchenwald.

APRIL 22

Seven prisoners from Lodz receive Nos. 181950–181956.

Four prisoners from Kraków receive Nos. 181957–181960.

Nine prisoners sent from Kattowitz receive Nos. 181961–181969.

21 Jews arrive in an RSHA transport from Sosnowitz. After the selection, 3 men, given Nos. 181970–181972, are admitted to the camp; 18 men are killed in the gas chambers.

APMO, D-AuII-3/1, p. 5, Quarantine List.

500 Jewish prisoners are transferred from Auschwitz to Gross-Rosen.

APMO, Mat.RO, vol. VII, p. 454.

Josef Lagrene is born in the Gypsy camp, B-IIe, in Birkenau, and receives No. Z-9828.

APMO, D-AuII-3/1/2, p. 292, Register of Male Gypsies.

The Commandant of Auschwitz III, SS Captain Schwarz, in Commandant's Office Order No. 6/44 lists the following auxiliary camps together with their telephone numbers: Blechhammer, Bobrek in the county of Auschwitz, Brünn, Eintrachthütte, Fürstengrube, Gleiwitz I, Gleiwitz II,* Gleiwitz III,** Golleschau, Günthergrube, Janinagrube, Jawischowitz, Lagischa, Laurahütte, Neu-Dachs, Sosnowitz.†

APMO, D-AuIII-1/63, Commandant's Office Order 6/44.

APRIL 23

Heinrich Wagner is born in the Gypsy camp in Birkenau and receives No. Z-9829.

APMO, D-AuII-3/1/2, p. 292, Register of Male Gypsies.

Siegfried Ringart, who was born on April 21, 1944, receives No. Z-9830; he dies on July 6, 1944.

Ibid.

APRIL 24

Five prisoners sent from Kattowitz receive Nos. 181973–181977.

Ewa Herak, born in the Gypsy camp in Birkenau, receives No. Z-10568.

APMO, D-AuII-3/2/5, p. 681, Register of Female Gypsies.

Two male Gypsies and four female Gypsies with German citizenship are given Nos. Z-9831–Z-9832 and Z-10569–Z-10572.

30 prisoners sent in a group transport receive Nos. 184058–184087.

*The Gleiwitz II auxiliary camp is established through the takeover of a Jewish labor camp on May 3, 1944.
**The Gleiwitz III A.C. is established in July 1944.
†The Sosnowitz A.C. is established on May 4, 1944, according to the contract of March 12, 1944.

A female prisoner sent to the camp by the Magdeburg Gestapo receives No. 78875.

Docs. of ISD Arolsen, NA-Women, p. 32.

APRIL 25

The Commandant of Auschwitz II, SS Major Hartjenstein, informs the personal staff of the SS Commander in Chief that the Czech prisoner Bruno Schmidt, who escaped on January 22, 1944, has been captured on April 7, 1944, in Prague. Buchenwald Concentration Camp, where he is to be transferred, is also informed of his capture.

APMO, IZ-8/Gestapo Lodz/2/88/27.

Two prisoners sent from Kattowitz receive Nos. 184088 and 184089.

45 prisoners sent in a group transport receive Nos. 184262–184306.

The Special Squad that operates the four crematoriums and the gas chambers totals 207 prisoners.

APMO, D-AuII-3a/11a, Labor Deployment List.

The number of occupants in the Gypsy Family Camp in Auschwitz Birkenau totals 2,921 men,* 2,890 of whom were located in the Gypsy Family Camp, B-IIe. There are eight men in the Men's Camp B-IId, 22 men in the prisoners' infirmary, B-IIf, and a boy under 14 years of age, presumably a newborn, in Women's Camp B-Ia.

Ibid.

APRIL 26

A 12-year-old boy, a woman, and seven girls, all Gypsies with German citizenship, are given Nos. Z-9833 and Z-10573–Z-10580.

600 prisoners are transferred from Auschwitz to Buchenwald. In the transport are 60 prisoners from the Penal Company. The transport consists of 599 Poles and a Russian. It reaches Buchenwald the next day.

APMO, Mat.RO, vol. VII, p. 454; Docs. of ISD Arolsen, Folder 12.

Two Polish prisoners, Janusz Tusiński (No. 120257) and Kazimierz Owczarek (No. 125601), escape from the labor squad for road construction and barrack expansion in Auschwitz II.

APMO, D-AuI-1/1b, FS.225; IZ-8/Gestapo Lodz/4/90/78, 79.

APRIL 27

Five Jewish prisoners sent by the RSHA receive Nos. 184307–184311.

Five prisoners sent in a group transport receive Nos. 184312–184316.

---

*Information on the number of female Gypsies imprisoned at this time has not survived. In all probability it was approximately 3,000 women.

APRIL 28

Three prisoners and five Russian POWs are sent to the Penal Company in Birkenau, two of them are sentenced for five months, four Russian POWs "until further notice," and the rest to six months in the Penal Company.

APMO, D-AuI-3/1, p. 19, Penal Company Register.

30 prisoners sent in a group transport receive Nos. 184317–184346.

APRIL 29

Two Jewish prisoners sent to the camp by the RSHA receive Nos. 184347–184348.

295 Jews who were transferred from a forced labor camp for Jews in Upper Silesia on April 16, 1944, receive Nos. 184349–184643. They are probably transferred to Gleiwitz I.

Docs. of ISD Arolsen, NA-Men, 1944, p. 109.

248 Jews who were transferred after selection on April 23 to the forced labor camp for Jews in Silesia receive Nos. 184644–184891. Those who are sick and unable to work are killed in the gas chambers of Auschwitz II. The Jews who are admitted to the camp are probably transferred to Gleiwitz I.

Ibid.

24 prisoners sent in a group transport receive Nos. 184892–184912 and 184919–184921.

Six Jewish prisoners sent to the camp by the RSHA and delivered in a group transport receive Nos. 184913–184918.

Rosemarie Anton, born in Gypsy Family Camp B-IIe in Birkenau, receives No. Z-10581.

The Deputy Director of Department II of the Führer's Chancellery, Blankenburg, makes a written report to the SS Commander in Chief on the experiments of Dr. Schumann in Auschwitz. By order of Reich Director Bouhler he is forwarding the work by Dr. Horst Schumann on the influence of X rays on human gonads. In his report he refers primarily to the second part of the work, which demonstrates that castration of men by this method is not to be considered, as it entails too many costs. Surgical castration, as he himself has been convinced, takes six to seven minutes and is, in comparison to castration by X ray, significantly faster and more reliable. He closes his report with the hope that he will be able to report on the continuation of these experiments soon.

APMO, D-AuI-1/18, Personal-Information Files, Microfilm 132/2.

Commandant Liebehenschel orders a several-day alarm readiness, in order to increase the security of Auschwitz in light of expected subversive activities, attacks, and acts of sabotage by conspiratorial groups in the vicinity of the camp, especially by members of the PPR. He points out that the central committee of the PPR has called

APMO, D-AuI-1, Special Garrison Order, April 29, 1944; Mat.RO, vol. II, p. 75.

on its members for an intensification of actions of various sorts, including attacks on prisons, to mark the celebration of May 1 and the national holiday of May 3. Liebehenschel cancels leave for members of the SS Guard Stormtroopers and orders frequent searches of civilian personnel and, above all, greater alertness all around.

APRIL 30

13 Jewish prisoners selected from an RSHA transport, receive Nos. 181844 and 184922–184933. All remaining deportees are killed in the gas chambers.

Two male and 21 female prisoners sent to the camp by the Sipo and SD of Triest are given Nos. 184934 and 184935 and 80547–80567.

APMO, Mat.Ref.Inf., Prisoner Card Index.

1,655 prisoners who were transferred from Paris, among them intellectuals, politicians, high officials, members of the French resistance movement as well as a small group of Polish emigrés, receive Nos. 184936–186590. The healthy individuals are accommodated in the Theresienstadt Family Camp in Camp B-IIb, the sick individuals in Quarantine Camp B-IIa.

APMO, Dpr.-Hd/6, p. 16.

Maria Bertram, born in the Gypsy camp, receives No. Z-10582.

The doctors employed in the prisoners' infirmary receive the order to register the prisoners stricken with malaria. The 212 malarial prisoners are immediately put in Block 8 of Quarantine Camp B-IIa and are later placed in Block 13.

Ibid., p. 26.

MAY 1

Five prisoners sent in a group transport receive Nos. 186591–186595.

1,004 Jewish men, women, and children from Drancy arrive in the seventy-second RSHA transport from France. 48 men and 91 women, given Nos. 186596–186643 and 80569–80659, are admitted to the camp after the selection. The remaining 865 persons are killed in the gas chambers.

Docs. of ISD Arolsen, NA-Women, p. 32.

A boy who is born in Birkenau receives No. 186644.

The Russian prisoner Stepan Nyemzov, escapes from the Neu-Dachs A.C. in Jaworzno.

APMO, D-AuI-1/1a, pp. 401, 405; D-AuI-1/1b, Bulletin 3/322, May 15, 1944.

23 Jewish prisoners are transferred from Auschwitz to Gross-Rosen.

APMO, Mat.RO, vol. VII, p. 454.

118 prisoners return from the Brünn A.C. to Auschwitz III, Monowitz. 28 prisoners—all skilled workers such as cabinetmakers, locksmiths, electricians, and radio technicians, who are essential for the building renovations of the Technical School of the SS and Police—remain in Brünn.

Czesław Wincenty Jaworski, *Wspomnienia z Oświęcimia* (Memories of Auschwitz), Warsaw, 1962.

MAY 2

Two transports arrive from Hungary, the first sent from Budapest on April 29 and containing approximately 1,800 able-bodied Jewish men and women between the ages of 16 and 50, the second sent on April 30 from Topoly and containing 2,000 able-bodied prisoners. After the selection, 486 men, given Nos. 186645–187130, and 616 women, given Nos. 76385–76459 and 80000–80540, are admitted to the camp. The remaining 2,698 men and women are killed in the gas chambers.

Randolph L. Brahm, *The Destruction of Hungarian Jewry (September 1940–April 1945): A Documentary Account*, New York, 1963, p. 363.

A Jewish prisoner sent in a group transport by the RSHA receives No. 187131.

29 prisoners sent in a group transport receive Nos. 187132–187158, 187160, and 187161.

The Jewish prisoner Willi Kormes receives No. 187159 and his seven-year-old daughter, Judith Kormes, who works in Block 24 of the women's camp as messenger for the Block Senior, Greta Glaser, receives No. 78999.

APMO, Correspondence, VI/349/66.

The Polish prisoner Jan Wyroba escapes from the construction squad.

APMO, D-AuI-1/1a, p. 403; IZ-8/Gestapo Lodz/4/90/82, 83.

MAY 3

A 14-year-old German Gypsy, Otto Pfaus, receives No. Z-9834.

1,400 Polish and Russian prisoners are transferred from Auschwitz to Natzweiler.

APMO, Mat.RO, vol. II, p. 454.

The Commandant's Office of Auschwitz III takes over the forced labor camp of the Degusa Gleiwitz-Steigern Deutsche Gasrusswerke GmbH (Gas Coke Company), where 245 female Jews and 261 male Jews are located. The camp receives the name Gleiwitz II Labor Camp.

State Archive in Gliwice, Documents of the Deutsche Gasrusswerke GmbH (German Gas Coke Works), p. 11, Letter from the Commandant's Office of Auschwitz III of May 15, 1944; compare Irena Strzelecha, "Arbeitslager Gleiwitz II" (Gleiwitz II Labor Camp), *HvA*, no. 14 (1973):107–127.

MAY 4

The Polish prisoner Aleksander Kawka (No. 119292), born on April 10, 1914, is captured while escaping and sent "until further notice" to the Penal Company.

APMO, D-AuI-3/1, p. 19, Penal Company Register; IZ/Gestapo Sieradz/2/209.

261 Jewish prisoners who are acquired in the takeover of the forced labor camp for Jews in Gleiwitz receive Nos. 187162–187422. Three of the female prisoners receive Nos. 79205, 79207, and 79246. Probably the other 245 female Jews receive Nos. 79128–79372.

Docs. of ISD Arolsen, NA-Women/1986.

Ten Jewish prisoners sent by the RSHA receive Nos. 187423–187432.

Part of the Auschwitz admissions building—built by prisoners—in spring 1944.

Four prisoners sent in a group transport receive Nos. 187433–187436.

Five prisoners escape from the Monowitz A.C. of Auschwitz III: The Poles Zenon Milaczewski (No. 10433) and Jan Tomczyk (No. 126261) and the Jews Riwen Żurkowski, Karstein Peller (No. 68608), and Chaim Goslawski.*

APMO, D-AuI-1/1a, pp. 410, 407; IZ-8/Gestapo Lodz/2/88/157, 158.

Two women, four girls, and two boys who are German Gypsies are given Nos. Z-10583–Z-10588 and Z-9835 and Z-9836. Among those transferred is very likely a mother with five young children.

The Poles Józef Naporski, born on February 12, 1925, and Michał Piwowarczyk, born on August 25, 1915, escape from the reed cutters squad in Brzeszcze of Auschwitz II.

APMO, IZ-8/Gestapo Lodz/4/90/84, 85.

In accordance with a contract signed on March 12, 1944, with the WVHA, an auxiliary camp is established in Sosnowitz near the Ost-Maschinenbau-Werke, which belongs to Auschwitz III. It is called Sosnowitz Labor Camp. 600 prisoners are housed there. The

APMO, D-Mau/3a/4138, 4409, 18780, 2290, Prisoner's Personal-Information Cards; Piper, "Sosnowitz II."

*Milaczewski, Tomczyk, and Zurkowski are captured in Kraków and sent back to Auschwitz on May 26.

majority of the prisoners work in the armaments plants of Ost-Maschinenbau, in stamping operations or in the production of cannon barrels. Some work outside the factory in a series of smaller squads. The commander of the camp is SS Technical Sergeant Albin Vaupel. The camp is frequently visited by Commandant SS Captain Schwarz of Auschwitz III.

The German monitoring service of the RSHA for foreign broadcasters, the so-called Special Service Seehaus in Berlin, sends a BBC communiqué of May 3, 1944, which was transmitted in French. It says: "Dateline Poland, 7:30 A.M. London time. According to a report by the secret Polish radio station the Germans executed 1,004 Poles in Kraków between October 1943 and February 1944, because they had sheltered Jews.* The Polish armed forces** will continue to support the Jews by sending arms and food in to the ghettos."

APMO, IZ-13/89, Various Documents of the Third Reich, p. 85 (original in BA Koblenz).

At a conference in Vienna, during which a travel plan is worked out for the deportation transports of Jews from Hungary—from 10 camps in the Carpathia area (Zone 1) with approximately 200,000 Jews from the Siebenbürgen area (Zone II), where approximately 110,000 Jews were located—it is decided that in the middle of May, four transports, each with 3,000 persons, should take place daily.† The conclusion of the deportations from these zones is foreseen for the middle of June.

Brahm, *Hungarian Jewry*, pp. 366, 370, 373.

The Special Squad, which operates the four crematoriums and gas chambers in Auschwitz, has 208 prisoners.

APMO, D-AuII-3a/2a, Labor Deployment.

MAY 5

The Jewish prisoner Chaskiel Freiermaurer, born on October 31, 1918, in Tschenstochau, escapes from the Blechhammer A.C.

APMO, IZ-8/Gestapo Lodz/4/90, 91; IZ-10/Gestapo Sieradz/2/210.

26 prisoners sent in a group transport receive Nos. 187437–187462.

A female prisoner sent from Karlsruhe is given No. 74881.

The camp resistance group states in its report to the PWOK for April 20–May 5, 1944, that the Germans are concerned with eradicating all traces of their murders as quickly as possible. The so-called old crematorium in Auschwitz is being converted to an air raid shelter. The so-called black death wall, the execution wall in the courtyard of Bunker 11, which was equipped with cork plates

APMO, Mat.RO, vol. VII, pp. 433ff.

---

*Poles who were discovered helping Jews were shot and killed on the spot; those suspected of helping were sent to prison and delivered to Auschwitz after investigations by the Gestapo.
**The Polish Home Army, Armia Krajowa (AK).
†The transport route goes via Miskolc, Koszyce, Preszow, Muszyna, Tarnów, and Płaszów-Kraków to Auschwitz.

to catch bullets, has been torn down. The sand on the ground near this wall has been removed, as it was soaked with blood to a depth of two yards. The extent of the flagrant insanity of the SS soldateska is shown by the fact that they shot down six English POWs who worked in the Buna plants in Dwory. The reason they gave was the slow work pace of the phlegmatic Englishmen. The English POWs stopped work on the spot in protest.

MAY 6

36 prisoners sent in a group transport receive Nos. 187463–187498.

34 men and boys and 39 women and girls, Gypsies from Germany, are given Nos. Z-9837–Z-9870 and Z-10589–Z-10627. There are many children on the transport.

MAY 7

281 male and 111 female prisoners sent from Minsk by Mobile Strike Commando 9 are given Nos. 187499–187779 and 81351–81461.

Docs. of ISD Arolsen, NA-Women, p. 32.

Three Polish prisoners, Marceli Godlewski (No. 175783), born on June 2, 1921, Tadeusz Krupa, born on June 27, 1919, in Mielic, and Antoni Narowski, born on March 23, 1906, in Mielic, escape from the Eintrachthütte A.C. in Schwientochlowitz.

APMO, D-AuI-1/1b, FS.232; IZ-8/Gestapo Lodz/4/90/88, 89.

MAY 8

14 prisoners sent in a group transport receive Nos. 187780–187793.

SS Lieutenant Colonel Arthur Liebehenschel, the Commandant of Auschwitz I and SS Camp Senior, is transferred to the post of the Commandant of the Lublin (Majdanek) concentration camp and labor camps in Warsaw, Radom, Budzyń, and Bliżyn.*

APMO, D-AuI-1, Garrison Order 14/44, May 8, 1944.

SS Major Hartjenstein, the Commandant of Auschwitz II and Deputy Commandant of Auschwitz I, becomes Commandant of Natzweiler.**

Ibid.

*According to a statement by Höss, the RSHA had complained about Liebehenschel to Head of Branch D Glücks, charging Liebehenschel with dissolving the informer network in Auschwitz and with favoring the resistance movement in the camp, which has contributed to its further development. Therefore, it is decided to name him the Commandant of another camp (APMO, Höss Trial, vol. 26b, pp. 166–168).
**The Director of the Jewish Section, IV-B4, in the RSHA, SS Major Eichmann, complained about Hartjenstein after his last inspection of the extermination installations in Auschwitz II, saying that Hartjenstein had not fulfilled his duties. Eichmann discovered that the outdoor incineration installations of Crematorium V were not in service; it is not known whether he meant the incineration pits near Bunker 2 or the planned crematorium for outdoor incineration. He also discovered that there were delays in the construction of the three-track rail spur connecting with the unloading ramp in Birkenau. As a result of this it was decided to send Hartjenstein to Natzweiler (APMO, Höss Trial, vol. 26b, pp. 166–168).

The function of the SS Camp Senior is taken over until further notice by the Head of Office D-I in the WVHA, the former Commandant SS Lieutenant Colonel Rudolf Höss.*

Ibid.

SS Captain Josef Kramer, the Commandant of Natzweiler, takes over the post of Commandant of Auschwitz II.

Ibid.

MAY 9

In connection with the accelerated start of the destruction of Hungarian Jews, SS Camp Senior Höss announces a series of directives. He orders that the expansion of the platform and the three-track rail connection in Birkenau be sped up; that the inactive cremation ovens in Crematorium V be put in operation; that next to this crematorium five pits (three large and two smaller ones) for the incineration of corpses be dug. Furthermore, Bunker 2 is to be put back into operation, incineration trenches are to be dug next to it, barracks for use as disrobing rooms are to be built, and, finally, the Commander of Gleiwitz I, SS Master Sergeant Otto Moll, is promoted to Director of all crematoriums.** Höss orders that the Special Squad be enlarged, i.e., the prisoners who work in the crematoriums and in Canada, on the sorting of stolen property.†

APMO, Höss Trial, vol. 26b, pp. 168–170, Statement of Rudolph Höss; vol. 28a, pp. 123ff., 127, Testimony of Former Prisoner and Members of the Special Squad Szlama Dragon; vol. 29, p. 47, Testimony of Former Prisoner and Member of the Special Squad Henryk Tauber.

The camp resistance movement reports to PWOK in Kraków: "On Monday, May 8, the former, since November 1943, Commandant, SS Lieutenant Colonel Liebehenschel, was removed. At the time of his departure he made a speech to the Block Seniors in which he took leave of the prisoners and expressed his satisfaction with their behavior. The former Commandant of Auschwitz, who was responsible for all the crimes committed here, Lieutenant Colonel Höss, was named 'interim' commander. This is a transitional phase, another is to follow him. Whether it will come to that no one

APMO, Mat.RO, vol. II, p. 76, a report written by Józef Cyrankiewicz.

*As a result of the negative judgments of the Commandants of Auschwitz I and II and because SS Commander in Chief Himmler does not consider them suitable for the planned destruction of a hundred thousand people, he gives Höss full authority for the destruction of the Hungarian Jews and sends him back to Auschwitz (APMO, Höss Trial, vol. 26b, pp. 166–168).
**Henryk Tauber states: "He [Moll—D.C.] was entrusted with directing all crematoriums in connection with the preparations for dealing with the Hungarian mass transports. He prepared the entire plan for the mass destruction of the people arriving in these transports. Prior to the arrival of the Hungarian transports he ordered that pits be dug next to the crematorium and put back into operation the previously inactive Bunker 2 and its pits. In the courtyard of the crematorium he had signs put up saying that those who arrived in the transports come to a camp where work awaits them, but they must first bathe and be disinfected. . . . He repeated this personally in the speeches he directed to the people who arrived in the transports. These transports were very numerous and it happened that the gas chambers of Crematorium V could not handle everyone. The people for whom there was no more space in the gas chambers were mostly shot by him personally. In many cases he threw living people into the burning pits" (APMO, Höss Trial, vol. 29, p. 47).
†For clarification Höss explained that the time required to unload a train, people and their entire baggage, was four to five hours per transport. No transport had been processed in less than this time. The people could indeed be processed in this time, but there was such a quantity of baggage that there could be no thought of enlarging the transports, even though the sorting squads had been reinforced with 1,000 additional prisoners (APMO, Höss Trial, vol. 26b, pp. 168–170).

knows. . . . We do not consider it appropriate to sound an alarm in the press and the radio about Höss's return, as long as it is officially a transition phase of correspondingly short duration and no situations occur that indicate a change of course. A premature alarm that is not based on concrete events could strengthen his position for reasons of prestige for the SS. But we do consider it absolutely necessary to sound the alarm if anything starts up here. Then one must act decisively. They fear this attention. I add that the death penalty for 15 SS leaders from Auschwitz published recently in London made a great impression on the condemned and resulted in the collapse of several of them. That is thus a very effective method."*

16 prisoners sent in a group transport receive Nos. 187794–187809.

The Russian prisoner Piotr Voskresenski, born on August 28, 1919, in Dnepropetrovsk, escapes from the Jawischowitz A.C.

APMO, D-AuI-1/1a, p. 418; IZ-10/Gestapo Sieradz/2/212.

MAY 10

Five prisoners sent from Kattowitz receive Nos. 187810–187814.

The female Gypsy Aloisie Wolf, born on January 3, 1930, in Graz, receives No. Z-10628.

Werner Klein, born on May 8, 1944, in the Gypsy camp, receives No. Z-9871.

APMO, D-AuII-3/1/2, p. 293, Register of Male Gypsies.

MAY 11

17 prisoners sent from Kattowitz receive Nos. 187815–187831.

SS Camp Senior Höss informs the SS members of the garrison that starting May 11, 1944, SS Captain Richard Baer is taking over as Commandant of Auschwitz I.**

APMO, D-AuI-1, Garrison Order 15/44, May 11, 1944.

MAY 12

15 prisoners sent in a group transport receive Nos. 187832–187846.

Two prisoners transferred on May 10 from Lublin receive Nos. 187847 and 187848.

*In the next clandestine communiqué it was stated: "We suggest that you prepare an attack on Höss and execute it soon. Get specialists ready, we are awaiting an answer and will send directions. Since May 1 all SS leave has been canceled by order of Berlin. The reason: increasing sabotage. In the last few days there has been livelier telephone communication with Berlin than ever before. Everything 'secret.' Continuous conferences with the leadership" (APMO, Mat. RO, vol. II, p. 77, communiqué written by Cyrankiewicz).
**Before his promotion to Commandant of Auschwitz I, Baer was assistant to Pohl in the WVHA.

33 Russian prisoners are transferred from Auschwitz to Lodz.

APMO, Mat.RO, vol. VII, p. 454.

26 prisoners are transferred from Auschwitz to Flossenbürg.

APMO, Mat.RO, vol. VII, p. 454; Docs. of ISD Arolsen, Folder 6.

11 female prisoners transferred from Kattowitz receive Nos. 79388–79398.

Docs. of ISD Arolsen, NA-Women, p. 6.

No. 79399 is given to a female prisoner sent from Kleine Festung ("Little Fortress") in Theresienstadt.

Ibid.

11 female prisoners sent in a group transport receive Nos. 79400–79410.

Ibid.

1,638 prisoners, who arrived on April 30 from Paris, are transferred from Auschwitz II to Buchenwald, and 39 Polish and Russian prisoners are transferred from Auschwitz III, Monowitz, to the Dora-Mittelbau A.C., which belongs to Buchenwald.*

Docs. of ISD Arolsen, Folders 6, 12.

39 Gypsy children were transferred from the St. Josefspflege (St. Josef's Care) children's home in Mulfingen—20 boys who receive Nos. Z-9873–Z-9892 and 19 girls who receive Nos. Z-10629–Z-10647.

APMO, D-AuII-3/1/2, p. 293, 294, Register of Male Gypsies; D-AuII-3/2/5, pp. 685–688, Register of Female Gypsies; Correspondence I-3/666–671 of the German Red Cross, Search Service Hamburg.

The Polish prisoner Franciszek Dzwonkowski, born on October 29, 1915, escapes from the Jawischowitz A.C.

APMO, D-AuI-1/1b, FS.239; IZ-8/Gestapo Lodz/4/90/93, 94. [Franciszek Dzwonkowski]

The monitoring service of the RSHA for foreign broadcasters conveys the content of a May 10, 1944, broadcast by the radio transmitter in Daventry on the situation in the General Government. The names of seven additional SS functionaries on the list of German war criminals and the charges against them are given. They are (1) Ludwig Honzels (?) from Breslau, (2) Wihelm Will (?) from Sinzig, (3) Willy Gebhard from Breslau, (4) Robert Robota (?) from Kattowitz, (5) Augustin Wagner from Kattowitz-Brynów, (6) Waldhofer (?), an SS man from Kattowitz, and (7) Dietzel (?) from the SS Police Corps.

APMO, IZ-13/89, Various Documents of the Third Reich, p. 62 (original in BA Koblenz).

MAY 13

34 prisoners sent in a group transport receive Nos. 187849–187882.

The monitoring service of the RSHA for foreign broadcasters conveyed the content of a Polish-language broadcast transmitted on May 12, 1944, by the BBC: "For two years there has been an assistance organization for oppressed Polish Jews in occupied Po-

Ibid. p. 79 (original in BA Koblenz).

*On May 14, 1944, 1,677 prisoners from Auschwitz arrive in Buchenwald.

land.* The organization has been governed up till now by the Polish Government in Exile. On April 24 of this year the government called together a special . . . council for this purpose [assisting the Polish Jews]. Debates on this problem were conducted in London, and Minister Banaczek spoke about it. Polish and Jewish representatives were called to the council. The Polish government will provide significant financial support to this organization."**

14 men and boys and 10 women and girls, Gypsies from the German Reich, are given Nos. Z-9893–Z-9906 and Z-10648–Z-10657.

Three Russian POWs, Serafim Ruban, born on November 14, 1915, Piotr Korotkov, born on March 15, 1921, and Michail Busorgin, born 1920 in Kazan, escape from Auschwitz II.

APMO, D-AuI-1/1a, p. 420; IZ-10/Gestapo Sieradz/2/212.

Jews from Blechhammer are transferred in an RSHA transport. After the selection, 72 men are admitted to the camp and given Nos. A-1–A-72.† The remaining men are killed in the gas chambers.

APMO, D-RO/123, vol. 20b, vol. 20c, List of Transports of Jews, clandestinely prepared by prisoners who worked in the Admissions Office of the Political Department. It encompasses male Jewish prisoners Nos. A-1–A-20,000 and B-1–B-10481, as well as female Jewish prisoners Nos. A-1–A-25378. This is the basic information source for this group of prisoners and will not be cited specifically hereafter.

14 female prisoners sent to the camp by the border control office Zimnodol/Kattowitz in Olkusz prison receive Nos. 79411–79424.

MAY 14

Eight female prisoners sent in a group transport receive Nos. 79429–79434, 79436, and 79437.

Docs. of ISD Arolsen, NA-Women, p. 6. [14 female prisoners]

Ibid. [Eight female prisoners]

A female arrested by the police who is transferred from Block II to Birkenau receives No. 79435.

APMO, Mat.Ref.Inf., Prisoner Card Index. [A female arrested]

Jews, sick individuals, children, and old persons are transferred from the Płaszów Concentration Camp. They are killed in the gas chambers.

Léon Poliakov and Josef Wulf, *Das Dritte Reich und die Juden* (The Third Reich and the Jews: Documents and Essays), Berlin-Grünewald, 1955, pp. 285, 305.

MAY 15

400 female prisoners are housed at the experimental station of Professor Dr. Clauberg in Auschwitz I.

APMO, Höss Trial, vol. 8, p. 9.

*The first organized assistance committee for Jews, founded by the delegation of the Polish Government in Exile, was established on September 27, 1942. On December 4, 1942, the Provisional Committee formally dissolved itself and was replaced by the newly established Assistance Council for Jews (RPŻ), cover name "Zegota," in the delegation of the Polish Government in Exile in Warsaw. This is the only organization of its type in the countries of occupied Europe. The RPŻ founds branch offices in Kraków and Lemberg and numerous agencies in other cities. The assistance operation affects approximately 30,000 Jews. Forms of assistance are hiding Jews, continuous financial support, emergency aid, and organizing escapes from ghettos and labor camps. The RPŻ also provides information on the destruction of Jews to the Allies. It exists until January 1945.
**Over two years the Polish Government in Exile in London gives the RPŻ financial help with a value of more than 27 million złoty through illegal channels.
†The new number series, beginning with A-1 each for males and females and then with B-1 for male Jewish prisoners, is introduced in order to conceal the actual number of prisoners registered in Auschwitz (Škodowa, *Three Years*, p. 144).

Two boys born in Birkenau receive Nos. 187883 and 187884.

10 prisoners sent from Kattowitz receive Nos. 187888–187897.

31 female prisoners sent from a camp in Budapest receive Nos. 79438–79468.

Docs. of ISD Arolsen, NA-Women, p. 6.

10 Jewish prisoners are transferred from Auschwitz to Płaszów.

APMO, Mat.RO, vol. VII, p. 454.

The number of prisoners in the Special Squad is increased by 100. 308 prisoners are now employed in the Special Squad.

APMO, D-AuII-3a/6a, Labor Deployment List.

The Commandant's Office of Auschwitz decides to liquidate the residents of the Gypsy Family Camp, B-IIe, in Birkenau the next day. Approximately 6,000 men, women, and children are in camp B-IIe. The Director of Camp B-IIe at the time, Paul Bonigut, an opponent of this decision, secretly informs Gypsies whom he trusts so that they will not give themselves up alive.

APMO, Statements, vol. 13, pp. 56–80, Account of Former Prisoner Tadeusz Joachimowski.

MAY 16

A so-called camp arrest is announced at about 7:00 P.M. in the Gypsy Family Camp in Birkenau. Vehicles drive up in front of the camp, from which SS men armed with machine guns emerge and surround the camp. The leader of the operation orders the Gypsies to leave the barracks. Forewarned, the Gypsies, armed with knives, spades, crowbars, and stones, refuse to leave the barracks. Astonished, the SS men go to the commander of the operation in the Block Leader's room. After a conference, a whistle signals the SS men who have surrounded the barracks to retreat from their positions. The SS men leave Camp B-IIe. The first attempt to liquidate the Gypsies has failed.

Ibid.

The prisoner Stefan Wastian (No. 183208) is sent to the Penal Company in Birkenau "until further notice." He dies on May 29, 1944, in the Penal Company.

APMO, D-AuI-3/1, p. 20, Penal Company Register.

20 prisoners sent from Kattowitz receive Nos. 187898–187917.

Two German Gypsies receive Nos. Z-9907 and Z-9908.

Oskar Broschinski, born in the Gypsy camp, receives No. Z-9909.

APMO, D-AuII-3/1/2, p. 294, Register of Male Gypsies.

Edward Weiss is born in the Gypsy camp and receives No. Z-9910.

Ibid.

Two female prisoners sent from a Viennese prison receive Nos. 79469 and 79470.

Docs. of ISD Arolsen, NA-Women, p. 6.

Six female prisoners sent to the camp by the Munich Gestapo receive Nos. 79472–79477.

Ibid.

15 female prisoners sent in a group transport receive Nos. 79478–79492.

APMO, D-AuII-3a/7c, Labor Deployment Lists; Mat.RO, vol. VII, p. 454.

1,578 Polish and Russian prisoners are transferred from Auschwitz to Buchenwald.

Jews from Sosnowitz arrive in an RSHA transport. Three men who receive Nos. A-73–A-75 and 14 women who receive Nos. A-1–A-14 are admitted to the camp. The remaining people, among them 14 men, are killed in the gas chambers.

Six female prisoners transferred from the prison Kleine Festung ("Little Fortress") in Theresienstadt receive Nos. 79501–79506.

Docs. of ISD Arolsen, NA-Women, p. 6.

2,503 Jews from the Theresienstadt ghetto arrive in an RSHA transport. 707 men and boys, given Nos. A-76–A-842, and 1,736 women and girls, given Nos. A-15–A-999 and A-2000–A-2750, arrive in the transport. All are taken into the Theresienstadt Family Camp, B-IIb.

APMO, D-RF-3/RF-3/96, 96a, pp. 1–110, Transport Dz from Theresienstadt, May 15, 1944, List of Names.

The Jewish prisoner Abram Kantorowski (No. 93836) and three Russian POWs, Ivan Boiev, born on August 28, 1917; Pavel Gavrish, born on January 9, 1916; and Petro Chyrva (No. RKG-10471), born on August 19, 1915, escape from the disassembly squad of Auschwitz II.

APMO, D-AuI-1/1a, pp. 431ff.; IZ-8/Gestapo Lodz/4/90/102ff.

The first long block arrest for prisoners is ordered in Auschwitz II. Three freight trains arrive on the track connection; they are the first RSHA transports of Hungarian Jews.* The arriving Jews are ordered to unload their luggage; thereafter they are to stand in rows of five and are led in the direction of the crematoriums. From this night on the chimneys of the crematoriums begin to smoke.**

APMO, Höss Trial, vol. 5, p. 132, Statement of Former Prisoner Dr. Wanda Szaynoch; vol. 6, p. 44, Statement of Former Prisoner Dr. Otto Wolken; Mat.RO, vol. VII, p. 440.

MAY 17

46 prisoners sent from Kattowitz receive Nos. 187918–187963.

2,447 Jews from the Theresienstadt ghetto arrive in an RSHA transport. 576 men and boys and 1,871 women and girls are given Nos.

APMO, D-RF-3/97, pp. 1–43; D-RF-3/97a, pp. 44–74, Trans-

---

*A train consists of 40 to 50 freight cars. In one car are approximately 100 persons. After the selection the boys and healthy individuals, without being recorded in the camp registers, are admitted to the camp as so-called depot prisoners. The remaining people are sent to the gas chambers.
**During the trial before the Supreme People's Court in Warsaw Höss explains that Eichmann has anticipated in his plan five trains daily, but the facilities can't handle this volume, despite the expansion of the installations. For this reason Höss has to travel personally to Budapest, in order to cancel the arrangement. Then the thing is arranged so that on alternate days two trains, then three trains would be sent. He claims to have known that the program, arranged in conversation with the railroad authorities in Budapest, planned on a total of precisely 111 trains. As the first transports arrive in Auschwitz, Eichmann is also to arrive in order to determine whether it is possible to add trains, as SS Commander in Chief Himmler demands that the so-called Hungary operation be accelerated as much as possible (APMO, Höss Trial, vol. 26, pp. 166–168).

A-843–A-1418, A-1000–A-1999, and A-2751–A-3621. They are housed in the Theresienstadt Family Camp, B-IIb, in Birkenau.

port Ea from Theresienstadt, May 16, 1944, List of Names.

The number of residents in the Gypsy Family Camp in Auschwitz II is 2,830 men and boys.*

APMO, D-AuII-3a/8c, Labor Deployment List.

SS Camp Commander Bogumił assigns the prisoners employed as scribes in the office of Camp B-IIe in Birkenau to put together a list of those Gypsies and their families who, on the basis of their statements, served before their imprisonment in the German army and possess military awards; and the same for the Gypsies who continue to serve in the German defense. The registration lasts several days.

APMO, Statements, vol. 13, pp. 56–80, Account of Former Prisoner Tadeusz Joachimowski.

19 Jews—twin brothers and any boys born as a twin—are selected from the RSHA transports from Hungary and admitted to the camp; they receive Nos. A-1419–A-1437. Some young and healthy individuals are probably kept as so-called depot prisoners in the camp. The remaining people are killed in the gas chambers.

APMO, D-AuI-3/2/26, Inventory No. 148855.

A girl born in the camp in Birkenau receives No. 79496.

APMO, MAt.Ref.Inf., Prisoner Card Index.

MAY 18

Eight prisoners sent from Kattowitz receive Nos. 187964–187971.

20 female Jews from the RSHA transports from Hungary are admitted to the camp after the selection. They are twin sisters that SS Camp Doctor Mengele has selected for his experiments. They receive Nos. A-3622–A-3641. Some of the young and healthy individuals are probably kept in the camp as "depot prisoners." The remaining people are killed in the gas chambers.

Docs. of ISD Arolsen, NA-Women, p. 19; APMO, Microfilm No. 164/10–13.

10 Jewish prisoners are transferred from Auschwitz to Sachsenhausen.

APMO, Mat.RO, vol. VII, p. 454.

MAY 19

Seven Jews from the RSHA transports from Hungary—twin brothers and any boys born as a twin—are admitted to the camp after the selection and given Nos. A-1438–A-1444. Some of the young and healthy individuals are probably kept in the camp as "depot prisoners." All remaining people are killed in the gas chambers.

APMO, D-AuI-3/26, Inventory No. 148855.

2,499 Jews arrive in an RSHA transport from the Theresienstadt ghetto. 1,062 men and boys and 1,437 women and girls are given Nos. A-1445–A-2506 and A-3642–A-5078. They are sent to the Theresienstadt Family Camp in Birkenau.**

APMO, D-RF-3/98, 99, pp. 1–117, Transport Eb from Theresienstadt, May 18, 1944.

*The number of imprisoned female Gypsies is not known. It was probably in the neighborhood of 3,000 women and girls.
**In the transports from Theresienstadt of May 16, 17, and 19 there are Jews with German, Czechoslovakian, Austrian, and Dutch citizenship.

The Gypsy boy Erhard Reinhardt, born on December 10, 1938, in Ebingen, who was transferred in a group transport, receives the free No. Z-9872.

38 prisoners sent in a group transport receive Nos. 187972–188009.

Two female prisoners sent by the Metz Stapo receive Nos. 79510 and 79511.

Docs. of ISD Arolsen, NA-Women, p. 6.

MAY 20

31 prisoners from Oppeln receive Nos. 188010–188040.

19 prisoners sent in a group transport receive Nos. 188041–188059.

34 male Jews (twin brothers and any boys born as a twin), given Nos. A-2507–A-2540, and 58 female Jews (twin sisters and any girls born as a twin), given Nos. A-5079–A-5136, arrive in an RSHA transport from Hungary and are admitted to the camp. Some of the young and healthy individuals are probably admitted as "depot prisoners." The remaining people are killed in the gas chambers.

APMO, D-AuI-3/26, Inventory No. 148855, Microfilm No. 164/10–13.

Three female Gypsies who arrive in a group transport from the German Reich receive Nos. Z-10658–Z-10660.

Hilda Hartmann, who was born on May 17, 1944, in the Gypsy camp, receives No. Z-10661.

APMO, D-AuII-3/2/5, p. 693, Register of Female Gypsies.

Six female prisoners who were transferred from the Neubrandenburg Squad task force at Ravensbrück receive Nos. 79530–79535.

Docs. of ISD Arolsen, NA-Women, p. 6.

MAY 21

Five male Jews (twin brothers and any boys born as a twin) are given Nos. A-2541–A-2545 and six female Jews (twin sisters and any girls born as a twin) are given Nos. A-5137–A-5142 after the selection from the RSHA transports from Hungary and are admitted to the camp. Some of the young and healthy individuals are probably kept in the camp as "depot prisoners." The remaining people are killed in the gas chambers.

APMO, D-AuI-3/26, Inventory No. 148855; Microfilm No. 164/10–13.

507 Jews, 228 men and 29 boys and 221 women and 29 girls, from Malines arrive in the twenty-fifth RSHA transport from Belgium.*

Probably approximately 200 Jews were added to this transport en route, since after the selection 300 men—more than were trans-

*These numbers were provided by Serge Klarsfeld and Maxime Steinberg in *Mémorial of the Deportation of the Jews of Belgium.*

ferred from the Malines camp—are admitted to the camp and receive Nos. A-2546–A-2845. 99 female Jews receive Nos. A-5143–A-5241. The approximately 300 remaining are killed in the gas chambers.

453 Jewish men, women, and children from Westerbork arrive in an RSHA transport from Holland. 250 men, given Nos. A-2846–A-3095, and 100 women, given Nos. A-5242–A-5341, are admitted to the camp. The remaining 103 deportees are killed in the gas chambers.

Four Jews, given Nos. A-3096–A-3099, are admitted after the selection from the RSHA transport from Hungary. Some of the young and healthy individuals are probably kept as "depot prisoners." The remaining people are killed in the gas chambers.

122 men and boys and 124 women and girls—Dutch, German, and stateless Gypsies—who were transferred from the Vught camp in Holland, are given Nos. Z-9911–Z-10032 and Z-10662–Z-10785.

Else Ringart is born in the Gypsy camp in Birkenau and given No. Z-10786.

APMO, D-AuII-3/2/5, p. 695, Register of Female Gypsies.

Three Jewish men were chosen from among the pairs of twins during the selection from the RSHA transports from Hungary and receive Nos. A-3100–A-3102. Some of the young and healthy individuals are probably kept in the camp as "depot prisoners." The rest are killed in the gas chambers.

APMO, D-AuI-3/26, Inventory No. 148855.

A female in police custody who was transferred from Bunker 11 of Auschwitz I to Birkenau receives No. 79540.

Docs. of ISD Arolsen, NA-Women, p. 6.

12 female prisoners who were sent to the camp from Vienna and Viennese Neustadt receive Nos. 79545–79556.

Ibid.

MAY 22

29 prisoners sent in a group transport receive Nos. 188060–188088.

2,000 Jews selected from the RSHA transports from Hungary receive Nos. A-3103–A-5102.

Seven male Jews and three female Jews who were selected from an RSHA transport from Hungary are given Nos. A-5103–A-5109 and A-5342–A-5344. Probably some young and healthy individuals are admitted to the camp as "depot prisoners." The remaining people are killed in the gas chambers.

Josef Reinhardt, born in the Gypsy camp, receives No. Z-10033. He dies on June 14, 1944.

APMO, D-AuII-3/1/2, p. 298, Register of Male Gypsies.

The Jewish prisoner Abraham Katz escapes from the Jawischowitz A.C. of Auschwitz III.*

APMO, D-AuI-1/1b, Bulletin, June 1, 1944, p. 326.

Six POWs escape from Birkenau: the Pole Antoni Kasjan, born on February 5, 1906; and the Russians Alexander Moros, born on November 3, 1922; Michail Batrakov, born in 1920; Pavel Musykin, born on December 12, 1912; Prokofi Vijertshenko, born in 1912; and Viktor Nasarov, born on February 2, 1921.

APMO, D-AuI-1/1a, pp. 434ff.

Over 400 female prisoners who have been employed in the offices and agencies of Auschwitz I, i.e., in the Political Department, the Labor Deployment office, the Administration,** the Construction Office, and the DAW Office; and female IBV prisoners who work as attendants and messengers in the Commandant's villa and the residences of SS men, are transferred from the staff building, where they have lived since August 1942, to one of the newly built blocks on the grounds of the camp expansion.† The block is fenced in with barbed wire and is marked by the number "6." On the same day the female prisoners to be used for experiments are transferred from Block 10 of the main camp to the block opposite and completely fenced around. This block is designated as the future research station for Professor Dr. Clauberg.

Škodowa, *Three Years*, p. 146.

MAY 23

In Blocks 10 and 11 in the main camp, over 1,500 Gypsies—men, women, and children—are housed who have been selected from the Gypsy Family Camp, B-IIe, to be transferred to other concentration camps in the Reich interior—this after the failed attempt by the SS to liquidate the Gypsies.

APMO, Statements, vol. 13, pp. 56–80, Account of Former Prisoner Tadeusz Joachimowski.

Four female prisoners sent by the Stapo headquarters in Klagenfurt receive Nos. 79558–79561.

Docs. of ISD Arolsen; NA-Women, p. 32.

1,200 Jewish men, women, and children from Drancy arrive in the seventy-fourth RSHA transport from France. 221 men and 247 women, given Nos. A-5110–A-5330 and A-5420–A-5666, are admitted to the camp. The remaining 732 people are killed the gas chambers.

186 male Jews and 70 female Jews who were selected from an RSHA transport from Italy are given Nos. A-5343–A-5528 and A-5345–A-5414.

---

*The prisoner is captured, sent to the auxiliary camp, and publicly hanged during the roll call (APMO, Statements, vol. 47, p. 120, Account of the Former Prisoner Witold Tokarz).
**Predominantly female Jewish prisoners are employed in their offices (ibid. p. 50).
†There, prisoners have built 20 buildings in four rows of five blocks each. In the first row of blocks, garment workshops, tailor shops, and shoemaker shops are already built in May 1944, in which prisoners of the main camp were employed. According to the expansion plans for the main camp, 45 one-story blocks are planned for this area.

Five female Jews, twin sisters and any girls born as a twin, who were selected from an RSHA transport from Hungary receive Nos. A-5415–A-5419. Some of the young and healthy individuals are probably admitted as "depot prisoners." The remaining people are killed in the gas chambers.

APMO, Microfilm No. 164/13.

1,000 prisoners, Hungarian Jews, are transferred from Auschwitz to Buchenwald.*

Docs. of ISD Arolsen, Folder 12.

Josef Meinhardt is born in the Gypsy camp and receives No. Z-10034. He dies on July 9, 1944.

APMO, D-AuII-3/1/2, p. 298, Register of Male Gypsies.

Harry Franz, born on May 22, 1944, in the Gypsy camp in Birkenau, receives No. Z-10035.

Ibid.

Johanna Fröhlich is born in the Gypsy camp in Birkenau and receives No. Z-10787.

APMO, D-AuII-3/2/5, p. 695, Register of Female Gypsies.

MAY 24

188 Jews who were transferred from the forced labor camp in Ottmuch to the Blechhammer A.C. receive Nos. A-5529–A-5716.

Docs. of ISD Arolsen, NA-Men, Series A, p. 1.

57 female prisoners who were transferred from the prison in Baranowicze or the prison in Koldyszewo receive Nos. 79568–79624.

Docs. of ISD Arolsen, NA-Women, p. 6.

288 male and 202 female prisoners sent by the Minsk Sipo and SD receive Nos. 188089–188376 and Nos. 79626–79827.

APMO, D-AuII-3/1, p. 5, Quarantine List; Docs. of ISD Arolsen, NA-Women, p. 6.

13 prisoners sent in a group transport receive Nos. 188377–188389.

34 prisoners sent from Kattowitz receive Nos. 188390–188423.

2,000 Jewish prisoners selected from an RSHA transport from Hungary receive Nos. A-5729–A-7728. The remaining people are killed in the gas chambers.

82 male Gypsies are transferred to Flossenbürg and 144 female Gypsies to Ravensbrück. All transferred Gypsies are between 17 and 25 years of age.**

APMO, D-AuII-3/1; D-AuII-3/2, Register of Male Gypsies; Mat.RO, vol. VII, p. 454.

The Head of the WVHA, Pohl, informs SS Commander in Chief Himmler that the first transports of Hungarian Jews have arrived and that of those able to work 50 percent are women, for whom there is no work available that corresponds to their skills. He asks Himmler for permission to employ them in the construction projects of the Todt Organization.†

Brahm, *Destruction of Hungarian Jewry*, pp. 378ff.

*These Jews probably are not registered in the camp but are so-called depot prisoners.
**This calculation is based on the Gypsy Register.
†Fritz Todt was an engineer who directed construction of Germany's autobahns and the West Wall line of fortifications. He founded the Organization Todt, which during the war erected bunkers, air-raid shelters, etc., using slave labor and collaborating with Germany's industrial leaders. He was Albert Speer's mentor, and when he died in an airplane crash in 1942, Speer was given Todt's portfolio as Reich Minister for Armaments and Munitions.

A female prisoner sent from Kattowitz receives No. 79830.

APMO, Mat.Ref.Inf., Prisoner Card Index.

2,000 Hungarian Jews are transferred as reinforcements for the prisoners deployed in the auxiliary camps in Auschwitz III.

APMO, Mat.RO, vol. VII, p. 442.

The Polish prisoner Roman Kraśnicki, born on May 22, 1913, in Riga, escapes from the workshop and construction squad.

APMO, D-AuI-1/1a, p. 437; IZ-8/Gestapo Lodz/111.

MAY 25

The resistance movement in the camp states in its regular report that the number of Hungarian Jews killed already amounts to over 100,000 people, and the work shifts of the SS men involved in the extermination operation is 48 uninterrupted hours, followed by an eight-hour break.

APMO, Mat.RO, vol. VII, p. 442.

24 prisoners sent in a group transport receive Nos. 188424–188447.

Two German Gypsies receive Nos. Z-10036 and Z-10037.

The German ambassador and plenipotentiary for Hungary, SS Brigadier General Dr. Edmund Veesenmayer, informs the Foreign Ministry that as of May 25 nearly 150,000 Jews have been deported from Zone I (Carpathia) and Zone II (Siebenbürgen) in Hungary to the target area* and that the transports from Zone III, the area north of Budapest, should take place June 11–16 and should involve approximately 65,000 Jews.

Brahm, *Hungarian Jewry*, p. 386.

100 female Jews selected from an RSHA transport from Hungary receive Nos. A-5667–A-5766.

Three female Jewish prisoners who were selected from an RSHA transport on May 21, 1944, receive Nos. A-5767–A-5769.

253 female Jews selected from an RSHA transport from Hungary receive Nos. A-5770 to A-6022.

A female Jew selected from an RSHA transport from Hungary receives No. A-6023.

Unregistered Hungarian Jews are deported from Birkenau to Gross-Rosen.

APMO, Mat.Ref.Inf., Card 1902/85, Statistics.

The camp resistance movement states in a special addition to its periodical report for the period May 5–25, 1944: "Auschwitz—Operation Höss. Since the middle of May numerous transports of Hungarian Jews. Every night eight trains arrive; every day five. The trains consist of 48 to 50 cars each, and in each car are 100 people.

APMO, Mat.RO, vol. VI, p. 440.

*The target area is Auschwitz, whose name is mentioned two times in the correspondence.

'Settlers' arrive with these transports. Each train of 'settlers' also has two freight cars of lumber, which the 'settlers' unload on the 'death ramp', bring to another site and stack in piles . . . that are intended for them. In order to simplify the work, the people arrive already separated, for example, children in separate cars. The closed trains wait for several hours on the special track to be unloaded. They stand in the nearby small forest.''

Several dozen Jews attempt to escape from an RSHA transport from Hungary that arrives in the evening. They try to hide behind the ditches in the small forest that borders the crematorium building. The Camp Commander of the women's camp, Franz Hössler, leads the pursuit. All of the escapees are shot down in the beam of a spotlight.

APMO, Mat.RO, vol. VII, p. 445.

MAY 26

22 prisoners sent in a group transport receive Nos. 188448–188469.

In Block 11 of Auschwitz I a session of the Police Court-martial of the Kattowitz Gestapo takes place during which between 160 and 170 people are sentenced to death. Among them are members of the resistance movement of Silesia that operates near the camp, Kazimierz Jędrzejowski, Engineer Cezary Uhtke, and Professor Jan Junach. Approximately 17 to 20 of the accused are sentenced to be sent to Auschwitz Concentration Camp. Among them is Stanisław Bies, who receives No. 188478 the same day.

APMO, Mat.RO, vol. XVI, Secret Message from Kazimierz Jędrzejowski; vol. XXIX, Secret Message from Wacław Stacherski; Memoirs of the Former Prisoner Stanisław Bies; Konieczny, "Police Court-martial," p. 136.

46 prisoners sent from Kattowitz receive Nos. 188470–188515.

After the selection from an RSHA transport from Hungary, four female Jews given Nos. A-6024–A-6027, are admitted to the camp. They are the pairs of twins Judith and Andrea Silberger and Eva and Vera Weiss.

APMO, Microfilm No. 116/13.

25 female prisoners sent from the prisons in Sosnowitz, Myslowitz, and Bielitz receive Nos. 79829–79853.

Docs. of ISD Arolsen, NA-Women, p. 6.

The Commandant's Office of Auschwitz III is notified that the prisoners Zenon Milaczewski, Jan Tomczyk, and Riwen Żurkowski, who escaped on May 4, have been captured in Kraków and are to be sent to the camp in a few days.

APMO, D-AuI-1/1a, p. 407.

The Jewish prisoner Mendel Gross, born on December 2, 1921, in Miechow, escapes from the Blechhammer A.C. Auschwitz III.

APMO, D-AuI-1/1a, p. 442; IZ-8/Gestapo Lodz/4/90/116, 117.

MAY 27

31 prisoners sent in a group transport receive Nos. 188516–188546.

SS Commander in Chief Himmler gives an ironic answer to a question by the Head of the WVHA on May 25, which may be meant as a joke, since it was put in the following way: "My dear Pohl! Certainly Jewish women are to be put to work. One must in this case simply provide healthy nourishment. Here raw vegetables are important for nutrition. Do not forget to include garlic in sufficient quantities from Hungary."

Brahm, *Destruction of Hungarian Jewry*, p. 391.

A female prisoner sent to the camp by the Dessau Stapo receives No. 79864.

Docs. of ISD Arolsen, NA-Women, p. 2.

Two Jewish twin brothers who receive Nos. A-5331–A-5332 and six female Jews who receive Nos. A-6028–A-6033, are admitted to the camp after the selection from an RSHA transport from Hungary. Boys and healthy individuals are probably admitted as "depot prisoners." The remaining people are killed in the gas chambers.

APMO, D-AuI-3/26, Inventory No. 148855.

Three German Gypsies receive Nos. Z-10038–Z-10040, and nine-month-old Sigrid Heilik, who dies on June 25, 1944, in Birkenau, receives No. Z-10788.

APMO, D-AuII-3/2/5, pp. 695, 696, Register of Female Gypsies.

Two Jewish prisoners, Arnost Rosin (No. 29858) and Czesław Mordowicz (No. 84216), escape from Auschwitz II. The two reach Slovakia, where they are arrested. The news of their escape and imprisonment reaches a secret organization that succeeded in collecting 10,000 crowns and buying their freedom from prison. The escapees meet with Alfred Wetzler and Walter Rosenberg (Rudolf Vrba) and confirm these men's statements regarding the approaching destruction of the Hungarian Jews, in that they describe the actual beginning of this operation. They also write reports that together with those of Wetzler and Rosenberg go to Switzerland, England, and the U.S.A.

APMO, D-AuI-1/1a, pp. 438ff.; IZ-8/Gestapo Lodz/4/90/118ff.; Statements, vol. 40, pp. 42–44, Account of Former Prisoner Alfred Wetzler.

Two prisoners escape from Auschwitz: a Russian, Boris Semenko, born on June 24, 1907, and a Jew, Abraham Lejsman (No. 81609), born on September 29, 1924. Lejsman is captured on June 3, 1944, in Alt Berun. On June 6, 1944, he is delivered to Auschwitz, and on June 13, 1944, is sent to the Penal Company in Birkenau.

APMO, D-AuI-1/1b, FS.249, pp. 438–440; IZ-8/Gestapo Lodz/4/90/118ff.; D-AuI-3/1, p. 22, Penal Company Register.

Seven Russian POWs escape from Auschwitz II: Vasili Astachov, born on May 3, 1921; Dmitri Radionovski, born on October 15, 1914; Ivan Ilyin, born on April 29, 1919; Volodimir Masurenko, born on November 14, 1920; Anatoli Pietko, born on April 19, 1918; and Vladimir Piegow, born on December 22, 1919.

APMO, D-AuI-1/1b, FS.249, pp. 438–440; IZ-8/Gestapo Lodz/4/90/118ff.

MAY 28

The Polish POW Antoni Kasjan and the Russian POW Pavel Musykin, who escaped on May 22 with four other POWs, are shot and killed by SS men in Babice near Auschwitz. Prokofi Vijertshenko is wounded and brought to the prisoners' infirmary in Auschwitz.

APMO, D-AuI-1/1a, p. 436.

12 male Jews (twin brothers) who receive Nos. A-5717–A-5728 and two female Jews (twin sisters Rose and Helene Moszkowicz), who receive Nos. A-6034–A-6035, selected from an RSHA transport from Hungary, are admitted to the camp. Some of the young and healthy individuals are kept in Birkenau as "depot prisoners." The remaining people are killed in the gas chambers.

APMO, D-AuI-3/26; Microfilm No. 164/12.

963 Hungarian Jews, who were in the camp as "depot prisoners," are transferred to Mauthausen.

APMO, D-Mau, vol. 3, pp. 12–26, Transport List.

12 Jews (twin brothers) selected from an RSHA transport from Hungary receive Nos. A-7729–A-7740 and are admitted to the camp. Young and healthy individuals are admitted to the camp as "depot prisoners." The remaining people are killed in the gas chambers.

APMO, D-AuI-3/26.

Hungarian Jews who sense the danger as they are led to the crematorium buildings scatter and attempt to escape and to reach the small forest nearby. The SS men pursue them like hunters. All escapees are shot dead in the beam of the spotlights.

APMO, Mat.RO, vol. VII, p. 445.

MAY 29

A female prisoner in police custody who was transferred from Block 11 of Auschwitz I to Auschwitz II receives No. 79875.

Docs. of ISD Arolsen, NA-Women, p. 7.

Nine prisoners sent in a group transport receive Nos. 188547–188555.

10 prisoners sent from Sosnowitz receive Nos. A-5333–A-5342.

APMO, D-AuII-3/1, p. 5, Quarantine List.

2,000 Jews, given Nos. A-7741–A-9740, after selection from the RSHA transports from Hungary are admitted to the camp. Some of the young and healthy individuals are admitted as "depot prisoners." Women and girls are sent to Camp B-IIc. Among them are the wife and daughter of Dr. Miklos Nyiszli, who is given No. A-8450* and then transferred to the Monowitz A.C. of Auschwitz III. The remaining people are killed in the gas chambers.

Miklos Nyiszli, *Pracownia doktora Mengele* (Dr. Mengele's Laboratory), Warsaw, 1966, pp. 4–14, 105–122.

MAY 30

14 prisoners sent in a group transport receive Nos. 188556–188569.

1,000 male Jews, who receive Nos. A-9741–A-10740, and three female Jews (twins), who receive Nos. A-6036–A-6038, are admitted to the camp after selection from an RSHA transport from

---

*Dr. Miklos Nyiszli, anatomist and pathologist, is transferred at the end of June from the Monowitz camp back to Camp section B-IIf and assigned by SS Camp Doctor Mengele to work in the laboratory and the autopsy room of Crematorium III.

Hungary. Some of the young and healthy are probably admitted as "depot prisoners." The remaining people are killed in the gas chambers.

A female prisoner sent to the camp by the Klagenfurt Stapo receives No. 79880.

Docs. of ISD Arolsen, NA-Women, p. 32.

A female Gypsy from the so-called Reich Protectorate of Bohemia and Moravia receives No. Z-10789.

Five prisoners are sent "until further notice" to the Penal Company in Birkenau.

APMO, D-AuI-1/3, p. 20, Penal Company Register.

20 female prisoners who were sent in a group transport receive Nos. 81589–81608.

Docs. of ISD Arolsen, NA-Women, p. 8.

MAY 31

A prisoner from Breslau receives the free No. 176511.

Two Jewish prisoners sent from Annaberg receive Nos. 188570–188571.

100 Jews selected from an RSHA transport from Hungary receive Nos. A-10741–A-10840 and are admitted to the camp. Part of the transport is probably admitted as "depot prisoners." The remaining people are killed in the gas chambers.

Seven prisoners are sent "until further notice" to the Penal Company in Birkenau.

1,000 male Jews who receive Nos. A-10841–A-11840, and 1,000 female Jews who receive Nos. A-6039–A-7038 are admitted to the camp after the selection from an RSHA transport from Hungary. Some of the young and healthy individuals are probably admitted as "depot prisoners." The remaining people are killed in the gas chambers.

APMO, D-AuI-3/1, p. 20, Penal Company Register.

Two German Gypsies receive Nos. Z-10041 and Z-10042.

The Russian prisoner Vasili Krupin, born on March 2, 1921, and the Russian POW Avram Yanchilin, born on August 19, 1911, escape from the disassembly squad of Auschwitz II.

APMO, D-AuI-1/1a, p. 445.

The management of the crematoriums in Auschwitz II orders four shovels 8 × 10 inches from the DAW, for shoveling coke into the generators, and five cast-steel frames including the complete wooden model for the iron shield plates.

APMO, IZ-13/89, Various Documents of the Third Reich, p. 198.

The management of the Birkenau crematoriums gives the DAW a contract to make small repairs on shovels and pokers and to weld two large and five small oven doors and an iron plate.*

Ibid., p. 204, Invoice Copy for Bookkeeping.

*The repairs are done between June 20 and July 20, 1944, and cost 46.90 RM.

SS camp officials acquire 88 pounds of gold and white metal from false teeth, removed from the Jews killed between May 16 and 31.

APMO, Mat.RO, vol. VII, p. 446.

JUNE 1

17 prisoners sent from Kattowitz receive Nos. 188572–188588.

277 male prisoners and 204 female prisoners sent to the camp by the Minsk Sipo and SD and Mobile Commando 9 are given Nos. 188589–188865 and 79892–79999, 81474–81493, 81495–81561 and 81563–81571.*

APMO, D-AuII-3/1, p. 5, Quarantine List; Docs. of ISD Arolsen, NA-Women, p. 6.

26 female Jews (twin sisters and any girls born as a twin) who receive Nos. A-7039–A-7064 are admitted to the camp after the selection from the RSHA transports from Hungary. Some of the female Jews are probably sent to Camp B-IIc. The remaining people are killed in the gas chambers.

13 Polish prisoners and 1,000 Hungarian Jews are transferred from Auschwitz to Buchenwald.

APMO, Mat.RO, vol. VII, p. 454; Docs. of ISD Arolsen, Folder 12.

SS Corporal Johann Trunz from the 7th Guard Company prevents two prisoners from escaping, for which he receives a commendation from SS Camp Senior Höss.

APMO, D-AuI-1, Garrison Order 17/44, June 9, 1944.

Three prisoners, the Russians Nikolai Milayev, Nikolai Abakumov, and Stepan Staroshchuk, escape from the Lagischa A.C. Milayev is captured on the same day and sent to the auxiliary camp.

APMO, D-AuI-1/1a, pp. 448ff.

From the neutral zone squad of Auschwitz II flee the Russian POW war prisoner Nikolai Batuyev (No. RKG-10425) and the two Russian prisoners Fedor Skiba and Stepan Klechko (Klochko). Batuyev is captured on June 8, brought to Bielitz, and delivered from there to Auschwitz on June 13. On June 16, 1944, he is sent to the Penal Company. Klechko is captured and brought to Bielitz. During his next escape attempt he is shot and killed.

APMO, D-AuI-1/1a, pp. 452ff.

15 prisoners sent in a group transport receive Nos. 188866–188880.

JUNE 2

1,000 Jewish men, women, and children arrive from Drancy in the seventy-fifth RSHA transport from France. 239 men, given Nos. A-11841–A-12079, and 134 women, given Nos. A-7065–A-7198, are admitted to the camp after the selection. The remaining 627 people are killed in the gas chambers.

*Two female Hungarian Jews receive Nos. 81494 and 81563 in June (Documents of the ISD Arolsen, NB-Women, p. 75).

*Taken secretly by a prisoner, this photo shows the Special Squad burning
corpses in the pit of Crematorium V in Birkenau.*

11 Jews, twin brothers and single twins, arrive in an RSHA transport from Hungary. After the selection they receive Nos. A-12080–A-12090 and are admitted to the camp. The remaining people are killed in the gas chambers.

APMO, D-AuI-3/26.

Five female Gypsies from Czechoslovakia receive Nos. Z-10043–Z-10047.

JUNE 3

Five prisoners sent in a group transport receive Nos. 188881–188885.

Nine prisoners sent in a group transport receive Nos. 188887–188895.

Jews arrive in an RSHA transport from Italy. The men are sent to Quarantine Camp B-IIa in Birkenau and the women to the women's camp. After this it is ordered that the transport be liquidated. The women and 25 men are sent to the gas chambers. Three prisoners in this transport, from Trieste, are kept. They receive Nos. 188896–188898.

APMO, Dpr.-Hd/6, pp. 30, 31; D-AuII-3/1, p. 5, Quarantine List.

122 female prisoners sent to the camp by the Trieste Sipo and SD receive Nos. 81612–81733. The prisoners come from Gorizia, Trieste, and Fiume (Rijeka).

Docs. of ISD Arolsen, NA-Women, p. 8.

19 prisoners, among them two Russian POWs, are sent to the Penal Company in Birkenau "until further notice."

APMO, D-AuI-3/1, p. 21, Penal Company Register.

The Gypsy family Unger is sent from the German Reich: the father, Anton Unger, born on December 31, 1903, and the sons Beno, born on February 4, 1931, Arnold, born on March 1, 1933, and Heinz, born on May 28, 1936, as well as Anna Unger, born on September 20, 1928, and Maria, born on November 14, 1941. They receive Nos. Z-10043–Z-10051 and Z-10790 and Z-10791.

Rosa Franz, born on June 1, 1944, in the Gypsy camp, receives No. Z-10792.

APMO, D-AuII-3/2/5, p. 697, Register of Female Gypsies.

Heinrich Adler, born in the Gypsy camp in Birkenau, receives No. Z-10052.

APMO, D-AuII-3/1/2, p. 298, Register of Male Gypsies.

In connection with the repeated breakouts from the crematorium buildings by Hungarian Jews the practice of turning off the current in the electric fence in the daytime is discontinued, i.e., the current is left on.*

APMO, D-AuI-1, Garrison Order 17/44, June 9, 1944.

*In the daytime, the camp and the surrounding grounds on which the prisoners work are guarded by the so-called Outer Sentry Line. For that reason the current for the camp fence was turned off.

JUNE 4

Three female Jews chosen from twin pairs in an RSHA transport from Hungary receive Nos. A-7199–A-7201 and are admitted to the camp. Some of the young and healthy are admitted as "depot prisoners." The remaining people are killed in the gas chambers.

JUNE 5

413 female prisoners who are to be used for experimental purposes are housed at the experimental station of Professor Dr. Clauberg in Block 10 of the main camp.

APMO, Dpr.-Hd/8, p. 9.

Six prisoners sent in a group transport receive Nos. 188899–188904.

2,000 Hungarian Jews are transferred from Auschwitz to Buchenwald. They probably are not registered and receive no numbers.

Docs. of ISD Arolsen, Folder 13.

Emile Larze, born in the Gypsy camp in Birkenau, receives No. Z-10793.

APMO-D-AuII-3/2/5, p. 697, Register of Female Gypsies.

The two Russian prisoners, Michail Volkov and Gregor Butko, escape from the work hall squad in the Eintrachthütte A.C. of Auschwitz III.

APMO, D-AuI-1/1a, pp. 463, 464, Telegrams.

JUNE 6

Nine female prisoners from Hungary receive Nos. 78238–78246.

Docs. of ISD Arolsen, NA-Women, p. 5.

Two female prisoners sent by the Klagenfurt Stapo receive Nos. 78247 and 78248.

Ibid.

21 prisoners sent in a group transport receive Nos. 188905–188925.

496 male and female Jewish prisoners are transferred from the Herzogenbusch-Vught Concentration Camp. 99 men, who receive Nos. 188926–189024, and 397 women, who receive Nos. 78253–78533 and 81735–81850 are admitted to the camp as prisoners.

Ibid., pp. 5, 8.

100 Hungarian Jews who were given Nos. from the "A" series are transferred from Auschwitz I to the Golleschau A.C. of Auschwitz III. The lowest number in the "A" series is A-7716, the highest, A-11824.

APMO, D-AuIII, Golleschau/12, pp. 70–73.

Four female Jews, twin sisters, who receive Nos. A-7202–A-7205 after the selection from an RSHA transport from Hungary, are admitted to the camp as prisoners. Some of the people from this transport are probably admitted as "depot prisoners." The remaining deportees are killed in the gas chambers.

2,000 Hungarian Jews, so-called depot prisoners, are transferred from Auschwitz I to Mauthausen. On June 8 the transport is accounted for in the occupancy level of Mauthausen.

APMO, D-Mau, Folder 5, p. 2525, Situation Report, June 8, 1944.

Two Russian prisoners, Alex Maximchuk (No. 86349) and Vasili Drachenko (No. 99540), escape from Auschwitz II. Drachenko is captured and sent on June 27 back to the camp.*

APMO, D-AuI-1a, pp. 470ff.

Allied troops land in the region of Caen in Normandy. There is now a second front in Europe.

JUNE 7

A prisoner sent from Kattowitz receives No. 189025.

2,002 Jews from an RSHA transport from Hungary, given Nos. A-12091–A-14092, are admitted to the camp after the selection. The remaining people are killed in the gas chambers.

The Polish prisoner Stanisław Paradowski escapes from squad No. 23, Woodworkers 1; and three Russians, Vladimir Osminkin (No. 65862), Peter Polakov (No. 107736), and Jakub Yunusov (No. 151284), escape from squad No. 58, carbide works—all in Monowitz A.C. of Auschwitz III. Polakov and Yunusov are captured on June 15 in the town of Stanisław Górny.

APMO, D-AuI-1/1a, pp. 475–478.

Two male Jews from twin pairs, who receive Nos. A-14093 and A-14094, and three female Jews from twin pairs, who receive Nos. A-7206–A-7208, are admitted to the camp after the selection of an RSHA transport from Hungary. Some of the people in this transport are probably admitted as "depot prisoners." The remaining deportees are killed in the gas chambers.

Margot Friedrich and Vlasta Herak, born in the Gypsy camp, receive Nos. Z-10794 and Z-10795.

APMO, D-AuII-3/2/5, p. 697, Register of Female Gypsies.

Walter Brozinski, born in the Gypsy camp, receives No. Z-10053.

APMO, D-AuII-3/1/2, p. 298, Register of Male Gypsies.

The management of the crematoriums in Auschwitz II orders four sieves from the DAW for sifting through human ashes. The sieves are to be equipped with an iron frame. The openings of the sieve screens are to be ⅖ inch in size.**

APMO, IZ-13/89, Various Documents of the Third Reich, p. 205, Invoice Copy for Bookkeeping (original in BA Koblenz).

JUNE 8

15 prisoners and two Russian POWs are sent to the Penal Company in Birkenau. 13 of the prisoners are released to the camp in June,

APMO, D-AuI-3/1, p. 21, Penal Company Register.

---

*The prisoners escaped from the production area of Birkenau. This area is located within the Outer Sentry Line. The fate of the captured prisoner is not known; he is not sent to the Penal Company. He is most probably hanged, since at this time those who are captured while escaping are punished in this way.
**A former prisoner and member of the Special Squad, Szlama Dragon, states during the Höss Trial that the ashes of the burned corpses are taken from the pits near the crematoriums, ground fine in special mortars, and taken to the Soła River (APMO, Dpr.-ZO/28a, p. 127).

and three in July. One of the prisoners, Józef Steinberg (No. 30459), presumably remains in the Penal Company until the camp is evacuated.

Two prisoners sent from Kattowitz receive Nos. 189026 and 189027.

18 male prisoners and one female prisoner sent from the Kleine Festung ("Little Fortress") prison in Theresienstadt are given Nos. 189028–189045 and 81858.

A female Jew selected from an RSHA transport from Hungary receives No. A-7209. The young and healthy are probably admitted to the camp as "depot prisoners," and the remaining people are killed in the gas chambers.

Two Polish prisoners, Roman Gostyński (No. 123458) and Roman Muchowski (No. 138091), escape from the disassembly squad of Auschwitz II.

APMO, D-AuI-1/1a, pp. 472–474, Telegrams.

The Polish prisoner Bogustaw Dąbrowski (No. 18375) and the Russian POW Vladimir Kudriashov, who has No. RKG-10437 tattooed on his chest, escape from the grading squad in Auschwitz II.

Ibid.

Two Russian war captives, Nigmatulla Kobylov (No. RKG-9951) and Andrei Shevchenko (No. RKG-10415), escape from the gravel pit squad of Auschwitz II.

Ibid.

The Polish prisoners Bronisław Wieczorek (No. 612) and Leon Woźniak (No. 122911), escape from squad No. 200 of the Monowitz A.C. of Auschwitz III.

Ibid., pp. 483, 484; IZ-Gestapo Lodz/4/90/129ff.

JUNE 9

15 prisoners sent from Kattowitz receive Nos. 189046–189060.

Erwin Habedank, born in the Gypsy camp in Birkenau, receives No. Z-10054.

APMO, D-AuII-3/1/2, p. 299, Register of Male Gypsies.

30 prisoners sent in a group transport receive Nos. 189061–189090.

JUNE 10

The German Gypsies Saga Tritschler, born on September 21, 1917, in Magdeburg, and Udo Tritschler, born on November 2, 1943, in Bückeburg (most probably Saga's son) are given Nos. Z-10796 and Z-10055.

APMO, D-AuII-3/2/5, p. 697, Register of Female Gypsies; D-AuII-3/1/2, p. 299, Register of Male Gypsies.

JUNE 11

2,000 Hungarian Jews, so-called depot prisoners, are transferred from Auschwitz to Mauthausen. They are accounted for on June 13 in the occupancy level of Mauthausen.

APMO, D-Mau, Folder 5, p. 2531, Situation Report, June 13, 1944.

JUNE 12

Eight male and 15 female Jewish prisoners who were transferred from Bergen-Belsen are given Nos. 189091–189098 and 81869–81883.

APMO, D-AuII-3/1, p. 5, Quarantine List.

Nine prisoners sent in a group transport receive Nos. 189099–189107.

A female Jew who was selected from an RSHA transport from Hungary receives No. A-7210.

503 Polish and Russian prisoners are transferred from Auschwitz to Ravensbrück.

APMO, Mat.RO, vol. VII, p. 454; vol. VIII, List of Names.

JUNE 13

The Polish prisoner Antoni Balda (No. 126903) escapes from squad No. 99, antiaircraft construction, in the Buna plants of Auschwitz III.

APMO, IZ-8/Gestapo Lodz/4/90/135ff.

The Reich's plenipotentiary in Hungary, Dr. Veesenmayer, notifies the Foreign Ministry that the deportation of Jews from the areas of Carpathia and Siebenbürgen (Zones I and II) has been completed on June 7. A total of 289,357 Jews have been deported to the "target destination" in 92 trains, each of which consisted of 45 cars. The concentration of Jews from the area north of Budapest (Zone III) was completed on June 10. The transports are planned for June 11–16, and 21 trains. The anticipated total is approximately 67,000 deportees. It is planned to complete the concentration of Jews in Zone IV, east of the Donau except for Budapest, by June 24. The deportation of the nearly 45,000 Jews would take place June 25–28.

Brahm, *Destruction of Hungarian Jewry*, p. 399.

10 prisoners sent in a group transport receive Nos. 189108–189117.

Five female Jewish twins who were selected from an RSHA transport from Hungary receive Nos. A-7211–A-7215.

APMO, Microfilm No. 164/12.

Three prisoners who were captured in Wadowice and Bielitz while fleeing are sent to the camp: Petro Chyrva, who escaped from the camp on May 16, and Nikolai Batuyev and Stepan Klechko, who escaped on June 1. The last-named attempts another escape and is shot and killed.

APMO, D-AuI-1/1b, FS.242, 257, Telegrams.

20 Gypsies are sent to the Penal Company in Birkenau "until further notice." Georg Greis (No. 6704), born on January 24, 1903, dies while serving his sentence. The remaining people are released from the Penal Company to the Gypsy camp, Camp B-IIe, in Birkenau on June 23.

APMO, D-AuI-3/1, pp. 21ff., Penal Company Register.

Two Jewish prisoners, Lazar Anticoli (No. 15851) and Icek Czerniker (No. 79675), who are assigned to the Jawischowitz A.C., attempt to enter the pig barn to gather scraps of food there. For that they are sentenced to "10 weeks of hard labor under guard."

APMO, D-AuI, II, III-2/284, Punishment Report, June 13, 1944.

JUNE 14

Six female Jews, twin sisters, receive Nos. A-7216–A-7221 after selection from an RSHA transport from Hungary and are admitted to the camp. Some of the people in this transport are probably killed; the young and healthy are kept in the camp as "depot prisoners."

APMO, Microfilm No. 164/11.

Three prisoners sent in a group transport receive Nos. 189118–189120.

Three Polish prisoners escape from Auschwitz: Antoni Rusznica (No. 121606), from the troop hospital squad, and Zygmunt Stępień (No. 137504) and Jan Ignatowicz (No. 131975), from the disassembly squad.

APMO, IZ-8/Gestapo Lodz/4/90/138, 139.

The Polish prisoner Andrezj Gąsienica (No. 5654), born on November 18, 1906, in Poronin, escapes from the DAW squad of Auschwitz I.

APMO, IZ-8/Gestapo Lodz/4a/90/140ff.

Three female Jews, given Nos. A-7222–A-7224, are admitted to the camp after selection from an RSHA transport from Hungary. Some of the young and healthy are probably kept as "depot prisoners." The remaining people are probably killed in the gas chambers. Among those admitted to the camp are two 12-year-old twin sisters.

APMO, Microfilm No. 164/12.

JUNE 15

Two prisoners sent in a group transport receive Nos. 189121 and 189122.

203 Jews, given Nos. A-14095–A-14297, are admitted to the camp after selection from an RSHA transport from Hungary. Some of the young and healthy are kept in the camp as "depot prisoners." The remaining people are killed in the gas chambers.

Two prisoners who are members of the camp resistance movement escape from the DAW squad of Auschwitz II: Dr. Alfred Klahr, member of the Central Committee of the Communist Party of Austria, who was in the camp under the name Ludwig Lokmanis (No. 58933), and the Polish Communist Stefan Bratkowski (No. 64783), PPR member and organizer of the secret group in the DAW. The escape is organized by the prisoners' resistance movement. The escapees are given the task of establishing contact with the PPR leadership in Warsaw and Kraków and with the Red Army. They succeed in reaching Warsaw. Alfred Klahr dies in Warsaw several

APMO, IZ-8/Gestapo Lodz/4a/90/142, 143; Langbein, *The Stronger*, pp. 128, 132, 232–234, 241; Statements, vol. 37, pp. 30, 39, 44, Account of Former Prisoner Tadeusz Hołuj.

weeks after the escape, and Stefan Bratkowski dies during the Warsaw uprising.

The camp resistance movement states in its periodical report, which covers the period from May 25 until June 15, 1944, that the camp officials have received, as a result of the war situation, the order to deport the Aryan prisoners from Auschwitz. That's why a partial evacuation has already begun. A transport of 2,000 Polish and Russian prisoners destined for Buchenwald is being made ready.*

APMO, Mat.RO, vol. VII, 446.

JUNE 16

21 prisoners sent from Kattowitz receive Nos. 189123–189143.

Nine male Jews and 29 female Jews who arrive in an RSHA transport from Trieste are given Nos. A-14298–A-14306 and A-7225–A-7253.

12 Jewish prisoners who arrive in an RSHA transport from Berlin receive Nos. A-14307–A-14318.

APMO, D-AuI-3/1, p. 5, Quarantine List.

14 male and 29 female prisoners who arrive in a group transport are given Nos. 189145–189158 and 81895–81923.

Ibid.

86 female prisoners who are sent by the Trieste Sipo and SD receive Nos. 81927–82012.

Docs. of ISD Arolsen, NA-Women, p. 8.

Three female prisoners from the Kleine Festung ("Little Fortress") prison in Theresienstadt who were sent by the Prague Gestapo receive Nos. 82013–82015.

Ibid.

Three female Polish Gypsies from Bielszowice receive Nos. Z-10797–Z-10799.

Six prisoners and three Russian POWs are sent to the Penal Company in Birkenau. Among the POWs are Nikolai Batuyev and Petro Chyrva, who were captured while fleeing and brought back to the camp on June 13.

APMO, D-AuI-3/1, p. 22, Penal Company Register.

The Head of the WVHA, Pohl, visits Auschwitz. After he has familiarized himself with the progress of the construction projects, he approves the continuation of 29 of the 35 projects interrupted in April, ones that do not require a great investment of capital and labor. Among other things he orders the completion of a second complex of prisoner barracks in the main camp, 20 one-story blocks—the so-called camp expansion; the completion of the Admissions Building with disinfection rooms and a bath for the prisoners in the main camp; the construction of the SS troop hospital in Birkenau; and the erection of several barracks for the agricultural operations that belong to the camp. During his visit Pohl draws

APMO, Pohl Trial, vol. 22, pp. 44–48; Höss Trial, vol. 11, pp. 65–66.

*The transport departed on June 23 from Auschwitz.

attention to the insufficient camouflage of the extermination installations and orders that special fences of branches, field grasses, hazel twigs and mats be placed parallel to the barbed-wire fence surrounding the crematoriums and gas chambers.

The foreign broadcaster monitoring service of the RSHA, the so-called Special Service (Sonderdienst) Seehaus in Berlin, communicates the contents of a broadcast in German by the BBC on June 15, 1944:

APMO, IZ-13/89, Various Documents of the Third Reich, p. 72 (original in BA Koblenz).

> Important news! It has been reported to London that the German authorities in Czechoslovakia have ordered that the 3,000 Czechoslovak Jews who were brought to Birkenau from the Theresienstadt concentration camp on the Elbe on or around June 20 be killed in the gas chambers of Birkenau.* 4,000 Czechoslovak Jews who were transferred in December 1943 from Theresienstadt to Birkenau were murdered in the gas chambers on March 7.** The German authorities in Czechoslovakia and the officials and authorities subordinate to them have been made aware that exact reports of the mass murders in Birkenau have been filed in London. All those responsible for these mass murders, from those in authority to those who carry out the orders, will be made accountable.

JUNE 17

A prisoner sent to the camp from Munich receives No. 189144.

21 prisoners sent in a group transport receive the Nos. 189159–189179.

Two prisoners sent from Kattowitz receive Nos. 189180 and 189181.

10 male Jews, four twin pairs and two boys, each born as a twin, who receive the numbers A-14319–A-14328, and two female Jews, 19-year-old twin sisters, who receive the numbers A-7254 and A-7255, are admitted to the camp after being selected from an RSHA transport from Hungary. The young and healthy people are probably kept in the camp as "depot prisoners" and the remaining people are killed in the gas chambers.

APMO, D-AuI-3/26, Microfilm No. 164/13.

1,000 Hungarian Jews, so-called depot prisoners, are transferred from Birkenau to Buchenwald. They arrive the next day in Buchenwald.

Docs. of ISD Arolsen, Folder 13; Mat.RO, vol. VII, p. 446.

---

*A total of 4,964 Jewish men, women, and children from Theresienstadt were brought to Auschwitz in December 1943. It is possible that the public exposure of the intentions of the SS to liquidate the mentioned group of Jewish prisoners on June 20 delays their destruction; it takes place on July 11 and 12, 1944.

**Those mentioned here are 5,006 Czechoslovak Jews who were transferred on September 8, 1943, from Theresienstadt to Auschwitz and were killed on March 9, 1944, in the gas chambers. Most likely the reception at the monitoring service was poor, thus the wrong dates in the account of the broadcast.

320 Jews, given Nos. A-14329–A-14648, are admitted to the camp after being selected from an RSHA transport from Hungary. Some of the young and healthy are probably kept in the camp as "depot prisoners." The remaining people are killed in the gas chambers.

300 Jews who arrive in an RSHA transport from Hungary receive Nos. A-14649–A-14948 and are admitted to the camp after the selection. Some of the young and healthy are probably kept in the camp as "depot prisoners." All the remaining people were killed in the gas chambers.

The German plenipotentiary in Hungary, Dr. Veesenmayer, reports in a telegram to Foreign Minister von Ribbentrop that as of June 17 nearly 340,000 Jews have been deported from Hungary to the Reich territory. This number could be doubled by the end of July, according to the current estimates, without producing great traffic congestion, and later a total of approximately 900,000 could be reached.

Brahm, *Destruction of Hungarian Jewry*, p. 403.

After the selection from an RSHA transport from Hungary, 120 Jews, given Nos. A-14949–A-15068, are admitted to the camp. Some of the young and healthy are probably kept as "depot prisoners" in the camp. The remaining people are killed in the gas chambers.

13 men and boys and four women and children, German Gypsies, are given Nos. Z-10056–Z-10067 and Z-10800–Z-10803.

Nine men and boys and nine women and girls, Russian Gypsies from Vitebsk, are given Nos. Z-10068–Z-10076 and Z-10804–Z-10812.

Three female prisoners from Vitebsk receive Nos. 82022–82024.

Docs. of ISD Arolsen, NA-Women, p. 8.

1,500 Hungarian Jews, so-called depot prisoners, are transferred from Birkenau to Mauthausen. They are accounted for in the occupancy level of Mauthausen on June 19.

APMO, D-Mau/Folder 5, p. 2537, Situation Report, June 19, 1944.

Renata Ernst, born on June 13, 1944, in the Gypsy camp, receives No. Z-10813.

APMO, D-AuII-3/2/5, p. 699, Register of Female Gypsies.

The Polish prisoners Gerard Witkowski (No. 165402), Jerzy Pieńkowski (No. 121574), and Piotr Przemyski (No. 150133), escape from squad No. 73 in the Buna plants of the Monowitz A.C. of Auschwitz III.

APMO, IZ-8/Gestapo Lodz/4a/90/144ff.

JUNE 18

After the selection from an RSHA transport from Hungary, four female Jews, twin sisters, receive Nos. A-7256–A-7259* and are

APMO, Microfilm No. 164/11.

*The twins here are Elisabeth and Marie Erenthal and Izabella and Vilmas Fekete.

admitted to the camp. Young and healthy individuals are probably kept as "depot prisoners" and all remaining people are killed in the gas chambers.

A girl born in the Birkenau women's camp receives No. A-7260.

The Polish prisoner Franciszek Nowak (No. 137243) escapes from Auschwitz I.

APMO, IZ-8/Gestapo Lodz/4a/90/146.

JUNE 19

A prisoner sent from Kattowitz receives No. 188886.

Five prisoners sent in a group transport receive Nos. 189182–189186.

13 Polish prisoners are sent "until further notice" to the Penal Company in Birkenau. Antoni Witkowski (No. 153794)* dies while serving his sentence, as do Zygmunt Chyra (No. 154045), on June 25, and Franciszek Jedrzejewski, on June 27.

APMO, D-AuI-3/1, pp. 22ff., Penal Company Register.

Nine female prisoners from Lodz receive Nos. 82030–82038.

Docs. of ISD Arolsen, NA-Women, p. 8.

348 female prisoners are housed at the experimental station of Professor Dr. Clauberg for research purposes.

APMO, Höss Trial, vol. 8, p. 9.

JUNE 20

20 prisoners sent in a group transport receive Nos. 189187–189206.

Oskar Weindlich, born in the Gypsy camp, receives No. Z-10077.

APMO, D-AuII-3/1/2, p. 299, Register of Male Gypsies.

The Polish prisoner Stanisław Okrzeja (No. 119384) escapes from Auschwitz I.

APMO, IZ-8/Gestapo Lodz/4a/90/153, 154.

The Jewish elder of the ghetto in Theresienstadt, Jakob Edelstein, is shot and killed, together with his family and a group of co-workers, in Crematorium III in Birkenau.**

APMO, Mat.RO, vol. VII, p. 451; Adler, *Theresienstadt 1941–1945*, pp. 693, 730.

JUNE 21

13 prisoners sent from Kattowitz receive Nos. 189207–189219.

Three German Gypsies are given Nos. Z-10078–Z-10080.

The monitoring service of the RSHA relays a broadcast by a New York station, in Italian, from June 20, 1944: The newspaper of the Christian party, *Tempo,* which appears in Rome, writes that during

APMO, IZ-13/89, Various Documents of the Third Reich, p. 68 (original in BA Koblenz).

*No date of death is given for Antoni Witkowski.
**The documents of the camp resistance movement (Mat.RO, vol. VII, p. 451) state that this group consisted of 50 persons.

the occupation of Rome 6,000 Jews disappeared. Some of them were arrested, some were deported to other areas. It was stated further in the article that the Gestapo took 110 pounds of gold from the families of the arrested and/or deported.

JUNE 22

The German prisoner Ludwig Ligotzki, who was sent to Auschwitz on March 3, 1944, by the Kattowitz Gestapo, and the Russian prisoner Andrei Dryhailo (No. 175131) escape from Gleiwitz I A.C., which belongs to Auschwitz III.

APMO, IZ-8/Gestapo Lodz/4a/155, 156.

JUNE 23

The big summer offensive by the Red Army begins near Vitebsk; it ends on August 3 with the occupation of a bridgehead on the Vistula near Sandomir (Sandomierz).

Eight prisoners sent in a group transport receive Nos. 189220–189227.

2,000 prisoners are transferred from Auschwitz to Buchenwald. There were 1,216 Poles and 784 Russians in the transport.

APMO, Mat.RO, vol. VII, pp. 446, 454; Docs. of ISD Arolsen, Folder 13.

434 Hungarian Jews, so-called depot prisoners, are transferred from the transit camp in Birkenau to Buchenwald.

Docs. of ISD Arolsen, Folder 13.

JUNE 24

A prisoner sent from Stettin receives No. 189228.

Six prisoners who arrive in the morning in a group transport receive Nos. 189229–189234.

Two female prisoners transferred by the Prague Stapo receive Nos. 82064 and 82065.

Docs. of ISD Arolsen, NA-Women, p. 8.

Two female prisoners who were transferred from Ravensbrück receive Nos. 82074 and 82075.

49 prisoners sent in a group transport receive Nos. 189235–189283.

Tadeusz Blada (No. 169495) escapes from squad No. 132, anti-aircraft construction, in Auschwitz II.

APMO, IZ-8/Gestapo Lodz/4a/90/159/160.

Mala Zimetbaum (No. 19880), born on January 26, 1918, in Brzesko, a female Polish Jew who was sent to the camp in an RSHA transport from the Malines camp in Belgium, escapes from Auschwitz II, together with the Polish political prisoner Edward Galiński (No. 531), born on October 15, 1923, who was brought to the

APMO, IZ-8/Gestapo Lodz/2/88/184; 8/Gestapo Lodz/4/90/157–160; Krystyna Justa, *Z bagna i kamieni* (From Swamp and Stone), Warsaw, 1948, pp. 162ff.; Škodowa, *Three Years*, p. 156.

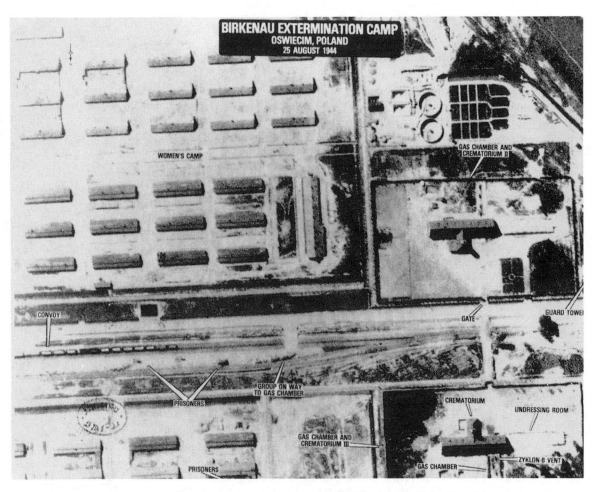

A photo taken by U.S. air reconnaissance on June 26, 1944 (photo is dated incorrectly).

camp with the first transport of Polish prisoners from the prison in Tarnów on June 14, 1940. They are captured on July 6, 1944, and brought back to Auschwitz the next day by the Bielitz Stapo. They are locked in the bunker of Block 11 and subjected to lengthy interrogation, during which neither Zimetbaum nor Galiński, who is tortured, betrayed any of those who assisted in their escape. Because of their escape they are condemned to death by hanging; the sentences are carried out publicly in the camp.

In Ryczów, at the border station between the Government General and the Reich territory, three members of the PPS in Kraków die in a fight with the Germans: Ryszard Krogulski, Józef Kornaś, and Adam Rysiewicz, pseudonym "Teodor," the secretary of the local workers' committee of the PPS and also the chairman of the Committee for Assisting Prisoners of the Concentration Camps. They stayed in Ryczów in order to take in escapees from Auschwitz. Only Władysław Denikiewicz, cover name "Romek," who jumps onto a train at the right moment, is able to save himself.

Tomasz Sobański, *Ucieczki oświecimskie* (Escapes from Auschwitz), 3d ed., Warsaw, 1974, pp. 62–64, Wroński, *Chronicle*, p. 348.

JUNE 25

A Jewish girl born in Birkenau receives No. A-7261.

Empty children's strollers are taken away from the storerooms of the personal effects camp, known as "Canada," which is located behind Camp B-IIf between Crematoriums III and IV. The strollers are pushed in rows of five along the path from the crematoriums to the train station; the removal takes an hour.

APMO, Dpr.-Hd/8, p. 133, Witness Dr. Wanda Szaynoha.

109 female prisoners sent by the Trieste Sipo and SD receive Nos. 82080–82188.

Docs. of ISD Arolsen, NA-Women, p. 9.

JUNE 26

Four prisoners sent in a group transport receive Nos. 189285–189289.

778 prisoners are transferred from Auschwitz to Buchenwald.

APMO, Mat.RO, vol. VIIIc, List of Names.

The management of the crematoriums in Auschwitz II receives four sieves from the DAW for sifting human ashes. The sieves, ordered on June 7, will serve to sift out the unburned human bones, which were taken out of the incineration trenches near the crematoriums and ground in special mortars. The sieves cost 232 RM.

APMO, IZ-13/89, Various Documents of the Third Reich, p. 205, Invoice Copy for Bookkeeping (original in BA Koblenz).

Allied air reconnaissance takes photographs of the camp from an altitude of 30,000 feet. Visible in the photographs are the town of Auschwitz, Auschwitz I, Auschwitz II, and Auschwitz III and the I. G. Farben compound, which because of the production of synthetic rubber and benzin are of greatest interest to the 15th Unit of the United States Air Force stationed in southern Italy. A sevenfold enlargement of the photographs shows in detail the features in the area of the camp—the crematoriums with the gas chambers, the connecting railroad track with the platform, and traces of extermination activities.

APMO, Analyses, vol. 64, pp. 38–49, Aerial Photos; Analyses, vol. 64, p. 87, David S. Wyman, "Why Auschwitz Wasn't Bombed" (originally published in *Commentary*, May 1978; hereafter cited as Analyses/Wyman); Analyses, vol. 64, pp. 108–125, Dino A. Brugioni and Robert G. Poirier, *The Holocaust Revisited: A Retrospective Analysis of the Auschwitz-Birkenau Extermination Complex* (originally published in Washington, D.C., 1979; hereafter cited as Analyses/Brugioni, Poirier).

JUNE 27

Nine prisoners sent in a group transport receive Nos. 189290–189298.

The prisoner Vasili Drachenko, who escaped on June 6, is returned to the camp.

APMO, D-AuI-1/1b, FS.268, Telegrams.

SS Lieutenant Colonel Höss notifies the SS members of the garrison that the barbed-wire fence around Crematoriums III and IV were electrified at 4:00 P.M. the previous day.*

APMO, D-AuI, Garrison Order 18/44, June 27, 1944.

---

*Höss was probably in Budapest June 18–26, during a several-day interruption in the preparation of the transport trains, to discuss details and accelerate the deportation operation—thus the late bulletin to SS members.

Two political prisoners, Konstanty Jagiełło (No. 4507), born on July 12, 1916, and Tomasz Sobański (No. 13609), born on September 22, 1922, escape from the roofing squad in Auschwitz II, under the direction and with the help of the camp resistance movement and with assistance from outside. The prisoners are given the task of taking camp plans and documents out of the camp and then returning to the area to organize the next escapes. They have been in Auschwitz since 1940.

APMO, IZ-8/Gestapo Lodz/4a/90/162, 163; Sobański, *Escapes from Auschwitz*, pp. 78–87.

JUNE 28

Five prisoners sent from Kattowitz receive Nos. 189299–189303.

Eight female Jews sent from Vienna by the RSHA receive Nos. A-7262–A-7269.

112 female prisoners, Greeks and Yugoslavs, who were sent from Belgrade by the Sipo and SD, receive Nos. 82211–82322.

The Polish prisoner Feliks Bielenin (No. 169398), born on May 12, 1915, in Brzeszcze, escapes from the disassembly squad of Auschwitz II.

APMO, IZ-8/Gestapo Lodz/4a/90/164, 165; D-AuI-1/1b, Bulletin, July 15, 1944.

Two Russian prisoners, Nikolai Shenin (No. 174589), of squad No. 178, power station, and Alexander Sharaniuk (No. 66907), of squad No. 32, escape from the Monowitz A.C. of Auschwitz III.

APMO, D-AuI-1/1b, Bulletin, July 15, 1944, vol. III, pp. 334ff.

1,000 female Hungarian Jews who are selected for the women's camp from the transit camp in Birkenau receive Nos. A-7270–A-8269.

Docs. of ISD Arolsen, NA-Women, Series A, p. 4.

Eight prisoners sent from Kattowitz receive Nos. 189304–189311.

JUNE 29

After the selection from an RSHA transport from Hungary, 150 Jews who receive Nos. A-15069–A-15218 are admitted to the camp. Some of the young and healthy are probably kept as "depot prisoners." The remaining people are killed in the gas chambers.

Four twins who were selected from the Hungarian female Jews by SS Camp Doctor Mengele receive Nos. A-8270–A-8273.

Ibid.

Four male and eight female Jews who were selected from an RSHA transport of 61 Jews from Sosnowitz are given Nos. A-15219–A-15222. The remaining 49 men and women are killed in the gas chambers.

APMO, D-AuII-3/1, p. 6, Quarantine List; Docs. of ISD Arolsen, NA-Women, Series A, p. 4.

Six Jews, given Nos. A-15223–A-15228, are admitted to the camp after selection from an RSHA transport of 38 Jews from Vienna.

Two twin brothers, Hungarian Jews, receive Nos. A-15675 and A-15676.

APMO, D-AuI-3/26, Inventory No. 148855.

Two prisoners, the Pole Mieczysław Paluch (No. 150498) and the Jew Abram Frydberg (No. 99288), escape from the potato squad of Auschwitz II. They are captured the following day, brought to the camp, and sent "until further notice" to the Penal Company.

APMO, IZ-8/Gestapo Lodz/4a/90/166, 167; D-AuI-3/1, p. 23, Penal Company Register.

The Russian POW Nikolai Tarasov (No. RKG-11360), who was sent to Auschwitz from Stalag 336 on February 24, 1944, escapes from the track connection squad of Auschwitz II.

APMO, IZ-8/Gestapo Lodz/4a/90/166, 167.

JUNE 30

27 prisoners sent in a group transport receive Nos. 189312–189338.

2,044 Jews arrive in an RSHA transport from Athens and the island of Corfu. After the selection, 446 men, given Nos. A-15229–A-15674, and 175 women, given Nos. A-8282–A-8456, are admitted to the camp. The remaining 1,423 people are killed in the gas chambers.

APMO, D-AuII-3/1, p. 6, Quarantine List; Dpr.-ZO/28, pp. 65, 72, Statement of Former Prisoner Enrica Jona; Docs. of ISD Arolsen, NA-Women, Series A, p. 4.

Nearly 1,000 Jews arrive in an RSHA transport from the Fossoli di Carpi transit camp. After the selection, 180 men, given Nos. A-15677–A-15856, and 51 women, who receive Nos. A-8457–A-8507, are admitted to the camp. The remaining people, among them 582 men, are killed in the gas chambers.

APMO, D-AuII-3/1, p. 6, Quarantine List; Docs. of ISD Arolsen, NA-Women, Series A, p. 4.

A female prisoner from Westerbork receives No. 82325.

Docs. of ISD Arolsen, NA-Women, p. 9.

13 female prisoners sent to the camp by the Stapo headquarters in Magdeburg and Dessau receive Nos. 82327–82339. Among them are Russian women who were employed as forced laborers and had escaped.

Ibid.

The German plenipotentiary in Hungary, Dr. Veesenmayer, notifies the Foreign Ministry that the deportation of Jews from Zone III has been completed with 50,805 persons as planned. A total of 340,162 Jews have been deported from Zones I, II, and III.

Brahm, *Hungarian Jewry*, p. 143.

The Superior SS and Police Commander in Budapest reports to Dr. Veesenmayer that the deportation of Jews from Zone IV has been completed. A total of 381,661 Jews have been deported from Zones I–IV.

Ibid., p. 617.

JULY 1

Five prisoners are sent "until further notice" to the Penal Company in Birkenau.

APMO, D-AuI-3/1, p. 23, Penal Company Register.

Five prisoners sent in a group transport receive Nos. 189339–189343.

Three prisoners from Kraków receive Nos. 189344–189346.

Nine prisoners sent in a group transport receive Nos. 189347–189355.

Nine male and three female Gypsies who were transferred from the Reich territory are given Nos. Z-10081–Z-10089 and Z-10814–Z-10816.

Four female prisoners sent to the camp on order of the Prague Gestapo from the prison Kleine Festung in Theresienstadt receive Nos. 82345–82348.

Docs. of ISD Arolsen, NA-Women, p. 9/1986.

11 female prisoners sent by the Lodz Stapo receive Nos. 82349–82359.

Ibid.

102 female prisoners sent by the Trieste Sipo and SD receive Nos. 82365–82466.

Ibid.

2,000 female Hungarian Jews, so-called depot prisoners, are transferred from the transit camp in Birkenau to Buchenwald. The train is bombed en route. 1,216 female prisoners are then transferred to the Gelsenkirchen A.C. and later to Sömmerda, and 518 to Essen. 266 female prisoners die during the bombardment.

Docs. of ISD Arolsen, Folder 15.

JULY 2

Four prisoners sent to the camp by the Trieste Sipo and SD receive Nos. 189356–189359.

Five prisoners sent from Kattowitz receive Nos. 189360–189364.

The Labor Deployment Department of Auschwitz II transfers 174 Hungarian Jews, Nos. A-15857–A-16030, to Auschwitz III. In the transfer documents it is stated that the Jewish prisoners have been examined and found healthy, have been deloused, and have received fresh laundry and clothing. But since they have been in a camp where cases of scarlet fever and measles broke out several days ago, they were in 21 days' quarantine. This statement is also signed by SS Camp Doctor Mengele.

APMO, D-AuIII, Golleschau/12, pp. 75–79.

A prisoner from Budapest receives No. 189365.

Six male and four female Jews sent from Czechoslovakia by the RSHA receive Nos. A-16031–A-16036 and A-8731–A-8734.

Four prisoners escape from the power station squad in the Jawischowitz A.C., which belongs to Auschwitz III: the Poles Jan Fischer

APMO, IZ-8/Gestapo Lodz/4a/90/172ff.

(No. 162823) and Józef Górecki (No. 162825) and Jews Bogel Jakubowicz (No. 87500) and Israel Jakubowicz (No. 42154).

The Jews Karl Fischer (No. 175199) and Simon Einhorn (No. 176185) escape from the Laurahütte A.C., which belongs to Auschwitz III. Both prisoners are again imprisoned and sent back to Auschwitz on July 15.

APMO, IZ-8/Gestapo Lodz/4a/90/168ff.; IZ-8/Gestapo Lodz/2/45.

In order to conceal the criminal plan to liquidate the Theresienstadt Family Camp, B-IIb, the camp management orders a selection. Dr. Mengele selects 3,080 young, healthy, able-bodied women, men, and youths. Among those selected, approximately 2,000 women are destined for the camps in Stutthof and Hamburg and 1,000 men for Sachsenhausen. Nearly 80 youths are sent to vocational training.*

Kraus and Kulka, *Death Factory*, p. 178.

JULY 3

Three prisoners sent in a group transport receive Nos. 189366–189368.

174 Jews selected from an RSHA transport from Hungary receive Nos. A-15857–A-16030. Some young and healthy individuals are probably kept as "depot prisoners." The remaining prisoners are killed in the gas chambers.

500 Jews selected from an RSHA transport from Hungary receive Nos. A-16037–A-16536. These 500 Jewish prisoners are destined to work in the coal mines of one of the auxiliary camps that belong to Auschwitz III. Some young and healthy individuals are probably kept as "depot prisoners." The remaining people are killed in the gas chambers.

APMO, Dpr.-Hd/6, p. 81.

Nine prisoners escape from the Eintrachthütte A.C. of Auschwitz III through an underground tunnel that has been dug for this purpose. Those involved were the Pole Władysław Rutecki (No. 175641), the Polish Jew Leib Zizmemski (a.k.a. Ziziemski, No. 98143), the Russians Luka Didenko (a.k.a. Lizniov, No. 175582), Jakob Vishnievski (No. 125038), Ivan Vasiukov (No. 175728), Sergei Michalevski (No. 175769), Nikola Titov (No. 175696), Nikolai Ivanenko (No. 129985), and Fedor Ryshynovich (a.k.a. Griszanowicz, a.k.a. Riszanowicz, No. 175681). Leib Ziziemski is rearrested in Bielsko on July 13, 1944, and transferred to Auschwitz. Sergei Michalevski is also arrested and sent to Auschwitz on August 7, 1944. Władysław Rutecki and Fedor Griszanowicz reach the

APMO, D-AuI-1/1b, Bulletin, July 15, 1944, pp. 335ff.; IZ-8/Gestapo Lodz/2/79; Depositions, vol. 50, pp. 60–65, Account of Former Prisoner Władysław Rutecki; Piper, "Eintrachthütte," pp. 131–135.

---

*The current number of occupants in Camp B-IIb is approximately 10,000: Of those who arrived with the transports of December 16 and 20, 1943, from Theresienstadt, 3,256 prisoners were alive on May 11, 1944, and on May 16, 17, and 19 another 7,449 people were delivered and sent to Camp B-IIb. 6,231 female prisoners were interned on June 10, 1944: 5,799 women and 432 girls under the age of 14 (APMO, D-AuII-3a/3–7, Documents from SU [Soviet Union]; Table from Dept. 3a, May 11, 1944; *Documents and Materials*, pp. 100, 105).

partisan units of the farmers' battalion in the area of Ryczów, and Lizniov joins a unit of the Polish Home Army in the area of Pilica.*

The foreign broadcast monitoring service of the RSHA relays the contents of a broadcast transmitted by the BBC on July 2 in Spanish: 400,000 Jews have been deported from Hungary to Germany and killed in the gas chambers. It is feared that the same fate awaits the remaining 350,000 Hungarian Jews.

APMO, IZ-13/89, Various Documents of the Third Reich, p. 130 (original in BA Koblenz).

JULY 4

28 prisoners sent in a group transport receive Nos. 189369–189396.

After the selection from the seventy-sixth RSHA transport from France, from the Drancy camp, which arrived with 1,100 men, women, and children, 398 men and 223 women, given Nos. A-16537–A-16934 and A-8508–A-8730, are admitted to the camp. The remaining 479 people are killed in the gas chambers.

Two Polish prisoners escape from Auschwitz II: Henryk Dzięgielewski (No. 121412), born on May 23, 1917, from the Headquarters squad of the Lenz Company, and his brother, Tadeusz Dzięgielewski (No. 121413), born on November 12, 1915, from the street construction squad of the Riedel Company. Tadeusz Dzięgielewski is recaptured in the town of Plazy and transferred back to Auschwitz.

APMO, IZ-8/Gestapo Lodz/4a/90/174ff.; IZ-8/Gestapo Lodz/2/45.

Three Polish prisoners escape at night from the coal mine squad in the Neu-Dachs A.C. of Auschwitz III: Jan Kura (No. 125506), Józef Karys (No. 125568), and Mieczysław Szafraniec (No. 125618).

APMO, IZ-8/Gestapo Lodz/4a/90/170ff.

JULY 5

Three prisoners sent from Kattowitz receive Nos. 187885–187887.

Four prisoners sent from Kattowitz receive Nos. 189397–189400.

After an interrogation in the Political Department, the French-woman Berta Falk (No. 14184) is sent for three months to the Women's Penal Company because she has written a short story dated July 14, 1944, in which she relates how she imagines the liberation of Paris by the Allies. Berta Falk works in the experimental plant breeding facility in Rajsko. In her and her colleagues' opinion she receives this mild punishment only because at the time she is writing the dissertation for the wife of SS First Lieutenant Caesar. During her stay in the Penal Company she is repeatedly called by Frau Caesar into the laboratory to complete the dissertation.

APMO, Dpr.-Hd/1, p. 109, Statement of Former Prisoner Eugenia Halbreich; Dpr.-ZOd/VII, pp. 125, 127, Statement of Former Prisoner Berta Falk.

*The fate of the other escapees is unknown.

Four Jews selected from an RSHA transport from Hungary receive Nos. A-16935–A-16938. Some healthy and young individuals are probably kept in the camp as "depot prisoners." The remaining people are killed in the gas chambers.

13 Jews selected from an RSHA transport from Hungary receive Nos. A-16939–A-16951. Some young and healthy individuals are probably kept in the camp as "depot prisoners." The remaining people are killed in the gas chambers.

Four female prisoners sent by the Vienna Stapo receive Nos. 82474–82477.

Docs. of ISD Arolsen, NA-Women, p. 9.

Seven female prisoners sent from Budapest receive Nos. 82479–82485.

Ibid.

30 female prisoners sent in a group transport receive Nos. 82492–82521.

JULY 6

The Polish prisoner Bolesław Limanowski (No. 130377) escapes from the DAW squad in Auschwitz.

APMO, IZ-10/Kripo Sieradz/2, p. 218.

Five prisoners are sent to the Penal Company in Birkenau "until further notice."

APMO, D-AuI-3/1, p. 23, Penal Company Register.

Two Russian prisoners escape from the potato squad in Auschwitz II: POW Genady Hashenko (No. RKG-11559), who is tattooed on the chest, and Beniamin Biriukov (No. 100382). Hashenko is recaptured and sent back to Auschwitz on August 4; he is sent to the Penal Company "until further notice" on August 7.

APMO, IZ-8/Gestapo Lodz/4a/90, pp. 181–184; D-AuI-3/1, p. 24, Penal Company Register.

Two prisoners, the Polish orderly Feliks Walentynowicz (No. 36) and the Hungarian Jew Nicolaus Sebestyen (No. A-8605), are transferred from the medical service in the Monowitz A.C. to the Gleiwitz IV A.C., completed at the end of June 1944, in order to set up a clinic in the new auxiliary camp—where Nicolaus Sebestyen eventually takes over the function of prisoner doctor. The auxiliary camp is located on the grounds of the army camp in Gleiwitz. The average number of occupants in Gleiwitz IV A.C. totals approximately 700 to 800 prisoners. They work on the expansion of the camp, on the repair and the retooling of military vehicles to run on wood-gas, and on the harbor in the Gleiwitz Canal. First Camp Commander in Gleiwitz IV is SS Corporal Otto Arthur Lätsch,* who distinguishes himself among the SS guards by his great brutality toward the prisoners.

APMO, D-AuIII-5/3, p. 587, Transfer List; Dpr.-ZO/64, pp. 51–81, 151ff.; Andrzej Strzelecki, "Arbeitslager Gleiwitz IV" (Gleiwitz IV Labor Camp), HvA, no. 14 (1972): 151–169.

*He is sentenced to death by the Supreme Court in Kraków in 1947. The sentence is carried out.

13 prisoners sent in a group transport receive Nos. 189401–189413.

1,000 female prisoners are transferred from the women's camp in Birkenau to Ravensbrück.

APMO, Mat.RO, vol. VIII, p. 47, List of Names.

Four Polish prisoners escape from the road construction squad of the Riedel Company in Auschwitz II: Marian Wójcik (No. 13122), Edward Ciesielski (No. 172571), Tadeusz Ziółkowski (No. 19521), and Aleksander Mroz (No. 138159).

APMO, IZ-8/Gestapo Lodz/4a/90/181–184.

JULY 7

Three prisoners sent from Kattowitz receive Nos. 189414–189416.

After the selection from an RSHA transport from Hungary, 283 Jews, given Nos. A-16952–A-17234, are admitted to the camp. Some young and healthy individuals are probably kept in the camp as "depot prisoners." The remaining people are killed in the gas chambers.

After the selection from an RSHA transport from Hungary, 217 Jews, given Nos. A-17235–A-17451, and six female twins, given Nos. A-8735–A-8740, are admitted to the camp. Some young and healthy individuals are probably kept in the camp as "depot prisoners." The remaining people are killed in the gas chambers.

1,000 young and healthy female Jews, who were selected on July 2 by SS Camp Doctor Mengele from the Theresienstadt Family Camp, B-IIb, are led to the so-called sauna. After the bath in the sauna their hair is shorn, they receive the striped prisoner's uniform, and are taken to a train waiting on the ramp, which brings them to Sachsenhausen. From there they are sent to the Schwarzheide A.C. to work in an airplane factory.

APMO, Mat.RO, vol. VII, p. 454; Kraus and Kulka, *Death Factory*, 178–180; Reitlinger, *Final Solution*, pp. 190–192.

Three Jews selected from an RSHA transport from Hungary receive Nos. A-17458–A-17460.

44 Russian POWs who are transferred from the prisoner-of-war camp in Lamsdorf to Auschwitz receive Nos. RKG-11574–RKG-11617. They are sent to the quarantine in Camp B-IIa.

APMO, D-AuII-3/1, p. 6, Quarantine List.

JULY 8

44 prisoners sent in a group transport receive Nos. 189417–189460.

18 female prisoners sent in a group transport receive Nos. 82526–82543.

Two Jews sent in an RSHA transport from Hungary receive Nos. A-17452–A-17453. They are the twin brothers Antal and Josef Brodt, who were born on March 12, 1930.

APMO, D-AuI-3/26, p. 7, Inventory No. 148855.

999 female Hungarian Jews, who were kept in the transit camp in Birkenau as so-called depot prisoners, receive Nos. A-8741–A-9739. They were sent to Auschwitz in RSHA transports from Hungary between May 16 and June 30, 1944.

Docs. of ISD Arolsen, NA-Women, Series A, p. 4.

The fourth Allied reconnaissance flight takes place over Monowitz. On photographs made during the flight, 16 elements in the I. G. Farben works are visible. Only on the last photograph, which is made shortly before the camera is shut off, is a part of Auschwitz I visible. This time, too, the interpreters of the photographs who put together the commentaries on the pictures concern themselves only with Monowitz and the I. G. Farben works.

Gilbert, *Auschwitz and the Allies*, p. 323.

Three Polish and two German male Gypsies receive Nos. Z-10090–Z-10094,* and a German and a Polish female Gypsy receive Nos. Z-10817 and Z-10818.**

The prisoner Marian Henryk Kałużyński, born on August 11, 1915, in Warsaw, escapes. He is captured on July 11 in Miechów and is to be delivered back to Auschwitz with the next group transport from Kraków.

APMO, IZ-8/Gestapo Lodz/2–170.

JULY 9

10 Jews selected from an RSHA transport from Hungary receive Nos. A-17500–A-17509. Some young and healthy individuals are probably kept in the camp as "depot prisoners." The remaining people are killed in the gas chambers.

Five female Jewish twins who were selected by Dr. Mengele from an RSHA transport from Hungary receive Nos. A-9740–A-9744.

Docs. of ISD Arolsen, NA-Women, Series A, p. 4.

1,000 Polish and Russian prisoners are transferred from Auschwitz to Mauthausen.

APMO, Mat.RO, vol. VII, p. 454.

1,000 female Jews from Theresienstadt are transferred from Camp B-IIb to Women's Camp B-Ia in Birkenau. They were selected on July 2 by Dr. Mengele and taken into Barracks 25, where they waited for a transport to other concentration camps. Approximately 80 youths between 14 and 16 years of age are placed in Men's Camp B-IId.

APMO, Dpr.-Hd/6, p. 49; Kraus and Kulka, *Death Factory*, pp. 178–181.

JULY 10

Four prisoners sent in a group transport receive Nos. 189461–189464.

*This is the last entry in the Register of Male Gypsies to note the number, the citizenship, the family name, the first name, and the date and place of birth. After this entry only the assigned numbers are noted, without indicating to whom and when they were given.
**In the Register of Female Gypsies no names are entered next to Nos. Z-10814 and Z-10819–Z-10827.

Two Hungarian Jews, the twin brothers Peter and Wenzel Samoggi, born on April 14, 1935, receive Nos. A-17454 and A-17455. Two Hungarian Jewish twin sisters receive Nos. A-9745 and A-9746. They were selected by Dr. Mengele from the RSHA transports from Hungary that arrived between May 15 and June 30.

Two Hungarian Jews, the twins Andrea and Karl Brichta, born on January 5, 1935, receive Nos. A-17456 and A-17457. Two Hungarian Jewish twin sisters receive Nos. A-9747 and A-9748. They were selected by Dr. Mengele from the RSHA transports that arrived between May 15 and June 30.

Four female Hungarian Jewish twins who are selected by SS Dr. Mengele from one of the RSHA transports that arrived between May 15 and June 30 receive Nos. A-9749–A-9752.

800 female Hungarian Jews are transferred from Auschwitz to Dachau. They are housed at the Allach A.C.

Docs. of ISD Arolsen, Folder 6.

The DAW in Auschwitz is given a contract to renovate and refit a passenger car and 14 freight cars that will be part of a construction train which is planned for 90 SS men and 504 prisoners. This is a so-called railroad brigade, which has the task of clearing rubble from destroyed train stations and repairing rail connections destroyed during Allied air attacks on the Third Reich. The passenger car is planned as an office. It is to be equipped with three office cupboards, three clothes closets, six desks, two typewriter desks, four chairs, 10 stools, beds with six sleeping places, and four stoves with cooking burners. Seven freight cars are to be fitted out as living space for the SS escort. Each of these wagons is to be equipped with three-tiered beds for 12 SS men, eight closets, a table, eight stools, a toilet, and a stove with cooking burners. The remaining seven freight cars are to be set up in the following manner: one as a kitchen for the SS men, one as a kitchen for the prisoners, one as a writing and infirm room, two wagons for tools, a wagon for a locksmith and blacksmith workroom, and a wagon for a woodworking and plumbing shop.*

APMO, IZ-13/89, Various Documents of the Third Reich, pp. 200ff. (original in BA Koblenz).

The St. Gallen newspaper *Die Ostschweiz* (Eastern Switzerland) publishes an article with the title "People Are Disappearing." The article cites as sources the Foreign Ministry of the Polish Government in Exile in London, news accounts by the delegation of the Polish exile government in Poland, and reports of the Reuter news agency. It reports that so far approximately 400,000 Hungarian Jews have been deported to Poland, of whom the majority have been sent to Auschwitz. The deportations, it continues, began on May 15 when 62 cars with Jewish children arrived in Poland. Since then it has been observed that daily six trains of Jews pass the train station in Płaszów near Kraków, whereby the majority are taken

APMO, IZ-13/89, Various Documents of the Third Reich, p. 101.

---

*This will leave Auschwitz on September 18, 1944, with a brigade numbering 505 prisoners.

to Auschwitz and the people are killed in the gas chambers. According to the Polish Interior Ministry, these gas chambers have a daily capacity of 6,000 persons. It has been determined further that two more death camps, in Treblinka and Rawa Ruska, were established in the second half of 1942, though it is uncertain whether gas chambers are also located there. Among the deported are children between two and eight years of age. The article mentions the warning of the Polish Government in Exile not to believe any of the letters sent from Auschwitz where it is claimed that the senders of these letters are well. The author of the article points out further that according to figures supplied by the Polish Assistance Committee for Jews, two million Polish Jews have died in the three concentration camps.*

In the Theresienstadt Family Camp in Camp B-IIb in Birkenau a camp arrest is ordered, in the course of which 3,000 women and children are transferred to the crematorium and killed in the gas chambers.

APMO, Dpr.-Hd/6, p. 49; Kraus and Kulka, *Death Factory*, p. 178.

JULY 11

Five prisoners sent from Kattowitz receive the free Nos. 181846 and 184053–184056, which had not yet been distributed.

Three prisoners from Oppeln receive Nos. 184057, 189284, and 189289, which have not yet been given out.

A prisoner sent from Breslau receives No. 189465.

The Polish Jew Adolf Krys (No. 161322), born on March 26, 1915, in Przemyśl, escapes from the Jawischowitz A.C. of Auschwitz III.

APMO, IZ-8/Gestapo Lodz/4a/90/187.

The German plenipotentiary, Veesenmayer, reports in a telegram to the Foreign Minister of the Third Reich that the deportation of 55,741 Jews from Zone V (the area west of the Danube in the suburbs of Budapest) was completed on July 9. The number of Jews deported from all five zones in Hungary reaches 437,402 persons.

Brahm, *Hungarian Jewry*, p. 443.

After the selection from an RSHA transport from Zone V in Hungary, SS Dr. Mengele probably admits a pair of twin sisters to the camp. They receive Nos. A-9753 and A-9754. Some of the deportees are probably admitted to the camp as "depot prisoners." The remaining people are killed in the gas chambers.

After the selection from an RSHA transport from Zone V in Hungary, SS Dr. Mengele probably admits a pair of twin sisters to the

*The press in neutral Switzerland is very careful not to provoke the Third Reich. It is thus revealing that in the mentioned article the National Socialist German Reich is in no way criticized. It is not obvious from the text who has established the camps, who occupies Poland, and who has deported and murdered Jews.

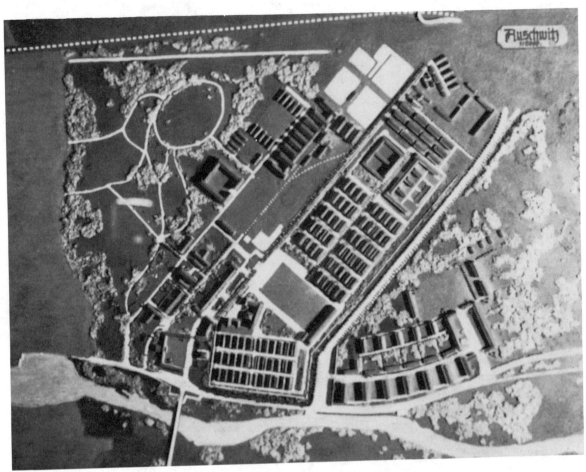

Architectural model for the expansion of the main camp at Auschwitz.

camp. They receive Nos. A-9755 and A-9756. Some of the new arrivals are probably selected as "depot prisoners." The remaining people are killed in the gas chambers.

A camp arrest in Theresienstadt Family Camp, B-IIb, in Birkenau is ordered, in the course of which all of the camp residents still alive, approximately 4,000 Jewish women and men, are led to the gas chambers.

APMO, Dpr.-Hd/6, p. 49; Kraus and Kulka, *Death Factory*, p. 178; Adler, *Theresienstadt 1941–1945*, p. 693.

JULY 12

Six prisoners sent in a group transport receive Nos. 189466–189471.

39 male and 30 female Jews who had been selected from the forced labor camp Annaberg receive Nos. A-17461–A-17499 and A-9757–A-9786. They are immediately transferred to the Blechhammer A.C. The sick and not able-bodied are brought to the gas chambers of Auschwitz II.

Docs. of ISD Arolsen, NA-Women, Series A, p. 4.

23 Jews who arrive in an RSHA transport from Sosnowitz receive Nos. A-17510–A-17532.

The camp occupancy totals:

Auschwitz I	14,386 prisoners
Auschwitz II	19,711 male prisoners
Auschwitz II	31,406 female prisoners
Auschwitz III	26,705 prisoners
Total	92,208 prisoners*

APMO, Mat.RO, vol. VII, p. 454.

Occupants of Auschwitz I by category:

Jews	8,189
Poles	3,822
Russians	632
Germans	808
Others	935
Total	14,386

Ibid.

JULY 13

16 prisoners sent in a group transport receive Nos. 189472–189487.

After the selection of the fifty-fifth East-transport from Berlin, 10 men, given Nos. A-17533–A-17542, and six women, given Nos. A-9787–A-9792, are admitted to the camp. The remaining people are killed in the gas chambers.

APMO, D-AuII-3/1, p. 6, Quarantine List; Docs. of ISD Arolsen, NA-Women, Series A, p. 4/1986.

19 female Jugoslav prisoners sent by the Graz Stapo receive Nos. 82556–82574.

Docs. of ISD Arolsen, NA-Women, p. 9/1986.

A transport with 2,500 Hungarian Jews, "depot prisoners," leaves Auschwitz for Buchenwald.

Docs. of ISD Arolsen, Folder 6a.

The Polish Jew who escaped on July 3 from the Eintrachthütte A.C., Leib Zizmemski (a.k.a. Ziziemski, No. 98143), is captured near Bielsko and brought to Auschwitz III.

APMO, IZ-8/Gestapo Lodz/2/88/80.

JULY 14

Three prisoners and two Russian POWs are sent to the Penal Company in Birkenau "until further notice." Three of them die on August 26, 1944, in the Penal Company: Ivan Drobacha (No. 59505), Vasili Rozkazov (No. RKG-10133), and Anatoli Viesielov (No. RKG-10470).

APMO, D-AuI-3/1, p. 24, Penal Company Register.

Two Czechoslovak prisoners, Franz Habetin (No. 123939) and Josef Malina (No. 123958), and a Czech Jew, Nikolaus Engel (No. 48540), escape from Auschwitz II. They are captured on July 18

APMO, IZ-8/Gestapo Lodz/2/88/81–84; IZ-8/Gestapo Lodz/4a/90/192, 193.

---

*The male and female Hungarian Jews who were not registered but were kept as so-called depot prisoners or transit Jews in Camps B-IIc, B-IIe, and Section B-III—called "Mexico"—are not included in the occupancy level of Auschwitz II. Following the selections that took place in these camps, young and healthy individuals were transferred to other labor or concentration camps; the sick and the weak, however, who were classified as unable to work by the SS Camp Doctor, were brought to the gas chambers.

(Habetin in the village of Dankowice and Malina and Engel in Międzybród) and sent back to Auschwitz.

Eight prisoners sent in a group transport receive Nos. 189488–189495.

After the selection from an RSHA transport from Trieste, two men, given Nos. A-17543 and A-17544, and seven women, given Nos. A-9793–A-9799, are admitted to the camp. The remaining people, among them nine men, are killed in the gas chambers.

APMO, D-AuII-3/1, p. 6, Quarantine List; Docs. of ISD Arolsen, NA-Women, Series A, p. 4/1986.

2,000 female Jews who were selected from the Theresienstadt Family Camp, B-IIb, on July 2 by SS Dr. Mengele are transferred from Auschwitz II to Stutthof. They wait in Barracks 25 in Women's Camp B-Ia for the transport.

Kraus and Kulka, *Death Factory*, p. 180.

Four Polish prisoners escape from Auschwitz II: Kazimierz Andrysik (No. 89), Zdzisław Michalak (No. 180), Ryszard Kordek (No. 10291), and Józef Papuga (No. 12049).*

APMO, IZ-8/Gestapo Lodz/4a/90/195, 196.

The crematorium management of Auschwitz orders another four sieves from DAW for sifting burned human bones.

APMO, IZ-13/89, Various Documents of the Third Reich, p. 205.

The Commandant of Auschwitz III, Schwarz, informs the guard troops that the following SS men have foiled escape attempts by prisoners from the camp through their prudent behavior:

APMO, D-AuIII-a, Commandant's Order 8/44; Dpr.-ZOd/40.

> On June 22, 1944: SS Staff Sergeant Fritz Frischholz of the 1st Company
> On June 23, 1944: SS Private Johann Ciener of the 2nd Company
> On June 23, 1944: SS Private Martin Kempl of the 2nd Company
> On June 24, 1944: SS Private Josef Miowitz of the 3rd Company
> On June 27, 1944: SS Private Franz Klemm of the 3rd Company
> On June 29, 1944: SS Private Adam Rausch of the 4th Company
> On July 7, 1944: SS Private Josef Berger of the 4th Company

Commandant Schwarz expressed his gratitude to those named.

39 female prisoners sent from Trieste by the Sipo and SD receive Nos. 82598–82635.

Docs. of ISD Arolsen, NA-Women, p. 10/1986.

32 female prisoners sent from Görz by the Sipo and SD receive Nos. 82637–82668.

Ibid.

---

*The prisoners hide for three days in a bunker prepared for this in "Mexico." They don't leave it until the Outer Sentry Line is lifted. On the other side of the Vistula waits someone acquainted with the area. They reach Kraków by means of the steam tugboat *Piast* and take a small passenger steamer to Nowy Korczyn. In the unit of Major Jan Panczakiewicz, pseudonym "Skala," of the Armia Krajowa (the Polish Home Army) they met another Auschwitz escapee, Henryk Dzięgielewski, who is already active with the AK in the resistance struggle (Sobański, *Escapes from Auschwitz*, pp. 103–113).

JULY 15

Five prisoners sent in a group transport receive Nos. 189496–189500.

A prisoner sent from Stettin receives No. 189502.

Two Hungarian Jews who were kept in the transit camp in Birkenau receive Nos. A-17545 and A-17546.

2,500 Hungarian Jews who were kept in the transit camp in Birkenau as so-called depot prisoners are transferred to Buchenwald.

Docs. of ISD Arolsen, Folder 13.

32 female prisoners sent in a group transport receive Nos. 82672–82704.

Two Jewish prisoners, Karl Fischer (No. 175199) and Simon Einhorn (No. 176185), who escaped on July 2 from the Laurahütte A.C. in Schwientochlowitz, are captured in Oppeln and sent back to Auschwitz III.

APMO, IZ-8/Gestapo Lodz/2/88/45.

The Jewish prisoner Robert Wolf (No. 68735) escapes from Auschwitz III, from squad No. 27 in the Buna works.

APMO, IZ-8/Gestapo Lodz/4a/90/200.

The camp resistance organization states in its report to Kraków: "From June 13 on there was a several-day pause in the transports of Hungarian Jews. Between May 16 and June 13 over 300,000 Hungarian Jews were delivered in 113 trains; in addition there was a transport of French Jews (2,500), a transport of Italian Jews (1,500), two transports of Czech Jews (50) headed by the elder of the Czech ghetto, who was immediately gassed with his entire family. Moreover, 100 English and American citizens of Jewish descent were delivered, who were separated and destroyed in particular ways. . . . The evacuation of Poles and Russians as the most dangerous elements of the camp continues. 4,500 prisoners, among them 2,900 Poles and 1,600 Russians,* were evacuated in June in three transports from Auschwitz I."

APMO, Mat.RO, vol. VII, p. 451.

JULY 16

A prisoner sent from Kattowitz receives No. 189503.

JULY 17

19 prisoners sent in a group transport receive Nos. 189504–189522.

Jane Haining (No. 79467), born on June 6, 1897, an Englishwoman, dies in Auschwitz II. She was director of the Scottish Institute in Budapest and was imprisoned at the end of April 1944 on the charge

APMO, Correspondence IV-8520-162/1995/86; Brahm, *Hungarian Jewry,* p. 555.

*The Russians were delivered to Auschwitz for the most part in group transports.

of conducting espionage for England.* On May 15 she was sent to Auschwitz.

Two children are born in the Gypsy camp in Birkenau.

APMO, D-AuI-3a, Occupancy Report, AuII-Fr.BIIe.

JULY 18

77 prisoners sent in a group transport receive Nos. 189523–189599.

Nine men, given A-17547–A-17555, are admitted to the camp. After the selection from an RSHA transport from Sosnowitz of 47 Jews. The remaining 38 people are killed in the gas chambers.

APMO, D-AuII-3/1, p. 6, Quarantine List.

Two Polish prisoners, Józef Grabowski (No. 127631) and Stanisław Trześniewski (No. 131558), escape from Auschwitz III, from squad No. 165 in the Buna works.

APMO, IZ-8/Gestapo Lodz/4a/90/217ff.

Two prisoners escape from Auschwitz II: the Pole Władysław Majewski (No. 139145) and the Russian Alex Kamkov (a.k.a. Mogilov, No. 48873).

APMO, IZ-8/Gestapo Lodz/4a/90/215ff.

JULY 19

Five prisoners sent from Kattowitz receive Nos. 189600–189604.

After the selection from an RSHA transport from Sosnowitz and Bendin, 34 men, given Nos. A-17556–A-17589, and seven women, given Nos. A-9800–A-9806, are admitted to the camp. All others from this transport, among them 276 men, are killed in the gas chambers.

APMO, D-AuII-3/1, p. 6, Quarantine List.

The Polish prisoner Lucjan Motyka (No. 136678) escapes from Auschwitz I. The escape was planned and prepared by the camp resistance movement. Motyka spends three days in the storage room of the SS kitchen before he leaves the area of the main camp.

APMO, IZ-8/Gestapo Lodz/4a/202; Sobański, *Escapes from Auschwitz*, pp. 183–190.

JULY 20

11 prisoners sent from Prague receive Nos. 189605–189615.

Colonel Claus Schenk Graf von Stauffenberg, who represents a group of officers and politicians from the conservative wing of the secret opposition, attempts an abortive bomb attack on Hitler in the Führer's main quarters, the "Wolfsschanze" (Wolf's Lair). The Gestapo punishes the resistance in an extremely brutal manner. The confusion resulting from the attack is not taken advantage of by the Allies. Hitler, by comparison, who has lost his trust in the generals of the armed forces, names Himmler the Supreme Com-

---

*The journalist Tivider Daresis, a Hungarian citizen, is imprisoned with Haining on the charge of espionage for England. Probably the real cause is assistance to Jews.

mander of the replacement army (Oberkommando des Heeres— OKH).

A prisoner sent from Kattowitz receives No. 189616.

JULY 21

10 prisoners sent in a group transport receive Nos. 189617– 189626.

A boy born in the women's camp in Birkenau receives No. 189627; the mother was sent to the camp from Minsk.

The following escape from Auschwitz I: the Polish prisoner Jerzy Bielecki (No. 243), born on March 28, 1921, who was sent from the camp in Tarnów on July 14, 1940, with the first transport of Polish prisoners by the SD; and the Polish Jewess Cyla Stawiska (No. 29558), born on December 29, 1920, who was sent to the camp in an RSHA transport from the ghetto in Zambrów on January 19, 1943. After the successful escape the two hide themselves in the area around Miechów until the end of the war.

APMO, IZ-8/Gestapo Lodz/4a/ 90/204; Depositions, vol. 16, p. 57, Account of Former Prisoner Jerzy Bielecki.

Six female prisoners sent to the camp by the Kattowitz Stapo receive Nos. 82732–82737.

Docs. of ISD Arolsen, NA-Women, p. 10/1986.

22 female Lithuanian Gypsies receive Nos. Z-10828–Z-10849.*

APMO, D-AuII-3/2/5, pp. 699– 702, Register of Female Gypsies.

A prisoner sent from Reichenau receives No. 189652.

SS Dr. Thilo conducts a selection in Men's Quarantine Camp B-IIb among the 446 male Greek Jews who were sent into quarantine on June 30 and were given Nos. A-15229–A-15674. After the selection Dr. Thilo sends 434 able-bodied prisoners to Camp B-IId. There they are put on the disassembly squad, the unloading squad, and other labor squads.

APMO, D-AuII-3/1, p. 6, Quarantine List.

JULY 22

The Camp Commander of the Golleschau A.C., SS Staff Sergeant Mirbeth, reports to the management of Auschwitz III that he transferred seven prisoners to Auschwitz the day before: Salomon Zara (No. 116310), a Greek Jew, and the Hungarians Guzna Schöhberg (No. A-11633), Hermann Eisikowits (No. A-15877), Istvan Gonda (No. A-15915), Dawid Kohn (No. A-15936), Bela Szugyi (No. A-15999), and Miklos Grünberg (No. A-16028).**

APMO, D-AuIII, Golleschau/12, p. 80.

---

*This is the last entry in the Register of Female Gypsies. Probably not only women and girls, but also men are in the transport. The relevant entries in the Gypsy register—if they were made—are not decipherable, since the last pages were destroyed by moisture, because the books were not protected sufficiently in their hiding place in the ground.
**After a selection they are probably transferred to Auschwitz II because of inability to work.

In the transport sent to Auschwitz by the Budapest Sipo and SD are 150 Poles and Polish Jews (there are possibly Hungarians and Hungarian Jews among them) who were arrested in Budapest and charged with activities directed against the Third Reich.* 21 men, who receive Nos. 189628–189646, A-17590, and A-17591; two female Jews, who receive Nos. 82739–82740; and 10 female Poles, who receive Nos. 82745–82754, after the selection are admitted to the camp. The remaining people, among them 94 men, are killed in the gas chambers. Among the Poles sent in this transport are First Lieutenant Benedykt Woynowski, Bolesław Nowak Kucharski, Michał Krzanowski (a.k.a. Krzakowski), who concerned themselves with occupied Poland as members of a contact group of the Polish exile government that was active until the middle of June 1944 in Budapest and whose acronym was "Romek." Władysław Dzięgiel, Dionizy Sokołowski, Franciszek Rybarczyk, Henryk Dąbrowski, Mieczysław Dybugiński, and Irena Lukomska are also in the transport.

APMO, D-AuII-3/1, p. 6, Quarantine List; Mat.RO, vol. II, p. 82; Brahm, *Hungarian Jewry*, pp. 554, 566, 596.

Five prisoners sent from Kaunas receive Nos. 189647–189651.

25 prisoners sent in a group transport receive Nos. 189653–189677.

998 female prisoners are transferred from Auschwitz to Ravensbrück.

APMO, Dpr.-ZOd/56, p. 156.

The Red Army is nearing Lublin. At 3:30 P.M. the last transport to evacuate Majdanek is ordered to leave.

Zofia Leszczyńska, *Kronika obozu na Majdanku* (Chronicle of the Camp at Majdanek), Lublin, 1980, p. 336.

The following escape from Auschwitz I: the Polish Jew Szymon Zajdow-Wojnarek (No. 27832), a Communist and organizer of the secret Jewish groups in the camp, and the Austrian Jew Josef (Pepi) Meisel (No. 173943), also a Communist, who is threatened with the death sentence. Both prisoners were members of the International Brigades in Spain. The escape has been planned and prepared by the directorate of the Auschwitz Combat Team.

APMO, IZ-8/Gestapo Lodz/4a/90/210, 211; Sobański, *Escapes from Auschwitz*, p. 189.

JULY 23

A prisoner sent from Klagenfurt receives No. 189678.

34 Russian POWs who were sent from Tschenstochau are given Nos. RKG-11618–RKG-11651.

85 Jews, given Nos. A-17592–A-17676, are admitted to the camp after the selection from an RSHA transport from Ludwigsdorf. The remaining 370 men are killed in the gas chambers.

APMO, D-AuII-3/1, p. 6, Quarantine List.

*After the occupation of Hungary by the Third Reich in March 1944 there were mass arrests among the Polish refugees who were active in the Hungarian-Polish institutions that existed in Hungary or in the secret liaison group "Romek." Many Polish couriers were also arrested together with the Hungarians who worked with them. The arrested were sent to Auschwitz and Mauthausen.

12 female Jews who arrive in an RSHA transport from Sosnowitz receive Nos. A-9807–A-9818.

Three Polish prisoners escape from the work hall squad in the Eintrachthütte A.C. in Schwientochlowitz: Jan Zieliński (No. 76962), Roman Symotiuk (No. 122997), and Marian Krycia (No. 169947).

APMO, IZ-8/Gestapo Lodz/4a/ 90/208, 209.

JULY 24

Two female prisoners sent from the Kleine Festung prison in Theresienstadt by the Prague Gestapo receive Nos. 82790 and 82791.

Docs. of ISD Arolsen, NA-Women, p. 10/1986.

The advance of the Red Army on Lublin leads to the first concentration camp liberation, that of Majdanek, located in Lublin's fortified castle. Found in the castle are the instruments of mass murder, which the SS was not able to destroy, as well as mountains of human bones. The castle courtyard is strewn with the corpses of the prisoners whose transport to another camp was cut short by the Red Army's advance.

A prisoner sent from Kattowitz receives No. 189680.

JULY 25

A prisoner sent from Kattowitz receives No. 189501.

Four Poles and 23 Polish Jews, given Nos. 189681–189707, are admitted to the camp after the selection from an RSHA transport with 78 prisoners sent by the Budapest Sipo and SD. The remaining 51 prisoners are killed in the gas chambers.

APMO, D-AuII-3/1, p. 6, Quarantine List.

40 prisoners sent in a group transport receive Nos. 189708–189747.

Docs. of ISD Arolsen, NA-Women, p. 10/1986.

A female prisoner sent by the Klagenfurt Stapo receives No. 82799.

11 Hungarian Jews, who are transferred from Transit Camp B-IIe to Camp B-IId receive Nos. A-17677–17687.

2,000 female Jews sent in RSHA transports from Hungary between May 15 and July 9 and who were kept in the transit camp in Birkenau as so-called depot prisoners receive Nos. A-9819–A-11818.

Docs. of ISD Arolsen, NA-Women, Series A, p. 5/1986.

Two Russian POWs whose numbers were tattooed on their chests escape from Auschwitz II: Mykola Rudenko (No. RKG-10078) and Michael Andreyev (No. RKG-10434).

APMO, IZ-8/Gestapo Lodz/4a/ 90/221, 222.

The Jewish prisoner Ajzyk Retman (No. 178450), born on February 9, 1921, in Sosnowitz, escapes from the Blechhammer A.C. of Auschwitz III.

APMO, IZ-8/Gestapo Lodz/4a/ 90/219.

JULY 26

10 prisoners sent in a group transport receive Nos. 189748–189757.

A prisoner sent from Breslau receives No. 189758.

2,008 female Jews who arrive in RSHA transports from Hungary between May 15 and July 9 and were kept in the transit camp in Birkenau as so-called depot prisoners receive Nos. A-11819–A-13826.

800 female Jews and 500 male Jews who arrive in RSHA transports from Hungary are transferred from Auschwitz II to Dachau. They are housed in the Kaufering auxiliary camp.

Docs. of ISD Arolsen, Folders 6, 7.

JULY 27

The DAW in Auschwitz is given another contract to renovate and refit 24 freight cars that are to be part of a construction train. The cars are intended for 504 prisoners. Each of the cars is to be equipped with three-tiered cots, each with 21 sleeping places, and shelves, benches, tables that fold up to the walls, clothes hooks, and toilets. The walls and the ceilings are to be lined with stiff insulation cardboard. Three small, screened windows were to be cut in each car.

APMO, IZ-13/89, Various Documents of the Third Reich, p. 201 (original in BA Koblenz).

Three prisoners sent from Kattowitz receive Nos. 189759–189761.

261 Hungarian Jews, who probably were selected in Transit Camp B-IIe, receive Nos. A-17688–A-17948.

Five Hungarian Jews receive Nos. A-17949–A-17953.

463 male Jews who were selected from an evacuation transport from the labor camp in Pustków near Dębica receive Nos. A-17954–A-18416. There were 1,700 men in the transport; 1,237 of them are killed in the gas chambers. After a quarantine period in Auschwitz II, the 463 selected individuals are transferred on August 25 to Auschwitz III.

APMO, D-AuII-3/1, p. 6, Quarantine List.

Two prisoners escape from Auschwitz II: the Pole Grzegorz Romaszewski (No. 94660) and the Russian POW Vasili Olenichev (No. RKG-11387).

APMO, D-AuI-1/1b, Bulletin, vol. 3/338ff.

JULY 28

378 male prisoners and 52 female prisoners who were sent from Radom by the Sipo and SD receive Nos. 189762–190139 and 82806–82857.

20 Russian POWs who were sent to the camp from Radom receive Nos. RKG-11652–RKG-11671.

28 prisoners sent in a group transport receive Nos. 190160–190187.

An evacuation transport with male and female prisoners from Majdanek arrives in Auschwitz II. The transport of more than 1,000 prisoners left the Lublin concentration camp on July 22. It was escorted by SS men and soldiers of the Wehrmacht. The prisoners were first led in the direction of Kraśnik. During the march on foot, which lasted some days, the weak and the sick are shot and killed. Finally the prisoners are packed into a freight train and sent to Auschwitz. Of the more than 1,000 evacuees, 681 men (among them 229 male Jews) and 156 female Jews arrive in Auschwitz. The 229 male Jews from Majdanek and a male Jew from the Pustków labor camp receive Nos. A-18417–A-18646. The following day the female Jews are given Nos. A-13827–A-13982. The remaining 452 prisoners receive Nos. 190188–190639.

APMO, Dpr.-Hd/1, p. 147; Leszczyńska, *Majdanek*, p. 336.

The Polish prisoner Jerzy Sokołowski (No. 156692) escapes from Auschwitz.

APMO, D-AuI-1/1b, Bulletin, vol. 3/344.

Two children are born in the Gypsy Family Camp, B-IIe.

APMO, D-AuI-3a, Occupancy Report, AuII F.-BIIe.

JULY 29

14 prisoners sent in a group transport receive Nos. 190640–190653.

The Polish prisoner Zbigniew Kaczanowski (No. 125727) escapes.

APMO, D-AuI-1/1b, Bulletin, vol. 3/350.

SS Lieutenant Colonel Höss, authorized to annihilate the Hungarian Jews, leaves Auschwitz. Commandant Richard Baer of Auschwitz I becomes SS Camp Senior.

APMO, D-AuI-1, Garrison Order 20/44, July 29, 1944.

A boy born in the women's camp in Birkenau receives No. 190654. The mother was sent from Minsk.

SS Staff Sergeant Lampert from the 1st Guard Company in Auschwitz I receives eight days unpaid special leave in the SS recreation center in Solahütte (Porąbka-Międzybrodzie), because he prevented the escape of a prisoner who had hidden himself in a truck.

Ibid.

1,495 male Gypsies are located in the Gypsy Family Camp, B-IIe. There is another Gypsy in Quarantine Camp B-IIa, there are six Gypsies in Men's Camp B-IId and six Gypsies in the prisoners' infirmary, Camp B-IIf. The number of female Gypsies is unknown.

APMO, D-AuII-3a/16, Labor Deployment List, vol. 11.

873 prisoners, among them three skilled workers, work in the so-called Special Squad operating the gas chambers, the four crematoriums, and the incineration pits in day and night shifts.

Ibid.

790 male prisoners from Auschwitz II work in the Canada squad, known officially as clean-up squad AuI-51-B and clean-up squad AuII, New Expropriation-52-B, which takes and sorts the property and items of value taken from Jews subjected to selection and condemned to death.

Ibid.

JULY 30

530 female Hungarian Jews are transferred from Auschwitz II to the Buchenwald Allendorf I A.C. in Lippstadt.

Docs. of ISD Arolsen, Folder 15.

349 female prisoners for research purposes are housed in the experimental station of Professor Dr. Clauberg in Block I of the camp expansion.

APMO, Dpr.-Hd/8, p. 9.

1,298 men, given Nos. A-8647–A-9944, and 409 women, given Nos. A-13983–A-14391, are admitted to the camp after the selection from an RSHA transport of Polish Jews from labor camps in the Radom District. The remaining people are killed in the gas chambers.

79 boys up to 14 years of age, among them many newborns, are located in Women's Camp B-Ia. 96 boys up to 14 years of age are housed in Men's Camp B-IId in Birkenau as prisoners.

APMO, D-AuII-3a/17, Labor Deployment List, vol. 11.

The number of men in Gypsy Family Camp B-IIe increases to 1,518 male prisoners. Besides those mentioned are 13 Gypsies in Camps B-IIa, B-IId, and B-IIf in Birkenau.

Ibid.

A boy born in Birkenau receives No. 190655. The mother was sent to the camp from Vienna.

Two Jews sent from Hungary receive Nos. A-19945 and A-19946.

Five Jews sent from Radom receive Nos. A-19947–A-19951.

Five prisoners escape from Auschwitz II: Josef Kenner (No. 37894), Franciszek Piechowiak (No. 138097), Dr. Jakow Wagschal (No. 160351), and two unknown prisoners who are shot and killed during the pursuit.

APMO, Dpr.-Hd/6, p. 59.

JULY 31

Josef Kenner, Franciszek Piechowiak, and Jakow Wagschal are captured while fleeing and are sent to Men's Camp B-IId in Birkenau. Beaten bloody, they are put on display at the entrance gate to Camp B-IId, together with the escapees shot and killed in the morning, to frighten prisoners who might be thinking of an escape attempt. After the evening assembly Josef Kenner and Franciszek Piechowiak are sent to the Penal Company with broken ribs and serious internal injuries. Dr. Jakow Wagschal is brought before the Political Department for an interrogation.

APMO, D-AuI-3/1, p. 24, Penal Company Register.

Five prisoners sent from Kattowitz receive Nos. 190140–190144.

51 prisoners sent from Radom by the Sipo and SD receive Nos. 190656–190706.

A prisoner from Majdanek who probably attempted an escape during the evacuation and was caught in the process receives No. 190707.

Two female Jews who arrive in an RSHA transport from Tarnów of approximately 3,000 Jews* are admitted to the camp and receive Nos. A-14392 and A-14393.

APMO, Dpr.-Hd/1, p. 141, Statement of Former Prisoner Lejzor Braun.

1,147 and 817 women are admitted to the camp after the selection from an RSHA transport of approximately 3,000 Jewish men and women from the forced labor camp for Jews in Pionki in the Radom District. The men receive Nos. B-1–B-1147** and the women, Nos. A-14394–A-15210. The remaining people are killed in the gas chambers.†

Docs. of ISD Arolsen, NA-Women, Series A, p. 5/1986.

1,614 male Jews, given Nos. B-1160–B-2773, and 715 female Jews, given Nos. A-15211–A-15925, are admitted to the camp after the selection from an RSHA transport from Blizyn, an auxiliary camp of Majdanek.

Ibid.

427 female Hungarian Jews selected from the so-called depot prisoners in the transit camp receive Nos. A-15926–A-16352.

Ibid.

The SS Commander in Chief Himmler, in a letter to the gauleiter and Reich governor in Sachsen, Martin Mutschmann, expresses his gratitude for the letter from July 25 and the congratulations†† as well as for various ideas that coincide completely with his own experiences. Himmler writes further that within the framework of his reorganization mission, he would take on the inspection of the armed forces,‡ as well as the question of the POW camps.‡‡ On the question of the Jews in Europe he reports that the removal of

APMO, IZ-13/89, Various Documents of the Third Reich, p. 301.

---

*Lejzor Braun states: "One day a transport came from Tarnów with Jews. There were approximately 3,000 people. Upon its arrival in Auschwitz all were dead. Maybe a few showed some weak signs of life, but only a very few. I threw the corpses from the cars.... The rumor circulated at the time that these Jews had suffocated in the cars, because the transport came in July or August; it was very hot and the journey lasted approximately four days. In each of the cars were 120 persons. They received nothing to drink."
**A new series of numbers that begins with B-1 is introduced for male Jewish prisoners.
†These are transfers necessitated by the approaching front.
††The congratulations are for Himmler's appointment as Commander in Chief of the replacement army (OKH) following the failed assassination attempt on July 20, 1944.
‡In his letter Mutschmann considers the idea that too many officers of the armed forces remain in the rear lines during various inspections.
‡‡Mutschmann assesses very critically the situation in the POW camps and characterizes the conditions that reign there as too humanitarian. For him, prisoners of war are thieves and bandits.

the Jews from France* was especially difficult because of the very tense relationship to the local Wehrmacht commander. 450,000 Jews had reportedly been deported from Hungary up to this point and the rest were resettled. In conclusion Himmler assures his correspondent that as always he possesses the necessary relentlessness during this decisive moment of war.

At the end of July the first transport of prisoners from Auschwitz III arrives at the Gleiwitz Foundry, which had originally been leased by the Luftwaffe and in the second half of 1944 was given to the Zieleniewski-Werke, which had been evacuated from Kraków. The transport is housed in a barracks near the former steel foundry. In April the newly created auxiliary camp was already named Gleiwitz III Labor Camp. On May 22, the Commandant's Office of Auschwitz III orders SS men of the 6th Guard Company to occupy the auxiliary camp. The first prisoners in Gleiwitz III A.C. come from the transports of Polish Jews at the end of July who were transferred from the Pustków labor camp and were evacuated from Majdanek. In August there are approximately 450 prisoners in the auxiliary camp. The prisoners are deployed both inside and outside the grounds of the Gleiwitzer Foundry in earth removal, drainage, and construction projects and in the renovation of work halls—for the time being, in preparation for the restartup production of railroad wheels, gun carriages for air defense weapons, sea mines, and various bullets.

APMO, D-AuIII-1, Commandant's Office Order 6/44, April, 22, 1944; D-AuIII-1, Commandant's Office Special Order, May 22, 1944; Andrzej Strzelecki, "Arbeits lager Gleiwitz III" (Gleiwitz III Labor Camp), *HVA*, no. 14 (1973): 129–150.

AUGUST 1

The Commandants of the concentration camps are given full authority by the WVHA to confiscate all packages addressed to the prisoners from abroad or from the International Red Cross. The contents of the packages end up not in the prisoner's kitchen, as planned, but in the storerooms of the SS. Probably the point of this order is to make it impossible for the prisoners to sign for the receipt of the packages and thus to confirm that they are in the concentration camp.

APMO, Dpr.-Hd/12, p. 141.

The number of prisoners in the Special Squad which operates the gas chambers, the crematoriums, and the incineration pits in day and night shifts reaches 903. 900 prisoners are employed as unskilled workers and three as specialists.

APMO, D-AuII-3a/18, Labor Deployment List, vol. 11.

82 boys under 14 years of age are located in Women's Camp B-Ia in Birkenau, including newborns. 106 boys under 14 years of age

Ibid.

---

*In his letter Mutschmann expresses his surprise that in Normandy, after the retreat of the Wehrmacht, Jews were still to be found who now—as was to be read in the press—were being promoted to high positions by Englishmen and Americans. He recommends that all Jews in Europe should be either removed or concentrated in labor camps. As long as even one Jew lives in Europe, the Führer will have partisans, criminals, and saboteurs behind the lines (APMO, IZ-13/89, Various Documents of the Third Reich, Letter of Martin Mutschmann of July 25, 1944, pp. 298–300 [original in the BA Koblenz]).

live in Men's Camp B-IId in Birkenau. A total of 188 children are housed in both camps.

108 prisoners intended to be used for research purposes are located in the prisoner's infirmary for men in Camp B-IIf. Among them are 49 twins or prisoners who came from twin pairs. The number of female prisoners and twin sisters or single female twins located in the women's camp and who are intended for research purposes or placed at the disposal of SS Camp Doctor Mengele is unknown, but is probably around 400 women and girls.

APMO, D-AuII-3a/18, Labor Deployment List, vol. 11, Photograph Collection of Josef Mengele, vol. 114, Microfilm No. 164/8–15.

12 prisoners sent in a group transport receive Nos. 190145–190156.

129 Jewish boys from the ghetto in Kaunas who were transferred from Dachau to Auschwitz in an RSHA transport receive Nos. B-2774–B-2902. The boys are between the ages of eight and 14 and left Kaunas with their parents. The mothers and sisters were retained in Stutthof. The fathers and older brothers were selected in Stettin and transferred to Dachau Concentration Camp. In a few days they were sent from there to Auschwitz. In Dachau the boys learned from the prisoners that Auschwitz is an extermination camp. Some youths succeeded in escaping during the transport.* After their arrival in Auschwitz they are sent to Men's Quarantine Camp B-IIa.

APMO, D-AuII-3/1, p. 6, Quarantine List; Dpr.-Hd/6, p. 50, Account of Former Prisoner Lazar Greis (No. B-2810).

A female prisoner sent to the camp by the Gestapo headquarters in Klagenfurt receives No. 82904.

Docs. of ISD Arolsen, NA-Women, p. 11/1986.

94 female Jews who were selected from an RSHA transport from the forced labor camp for Jews in Kielce receive Nos. A-16353–A-16447. Those who are unable to work are sent to the gas chambers.

Docs. of ISD Arolsen, NA-Women, Series A, p. 5/1986; Dpr.-ZO/58, p. 81, Statement of Former Prisoner Rozalia Sabat.

SS Private Heinrich Edelmann shoots and kills a civilian who breaks through the sentry ring at night. SS Camp Senior Baer assumes that the civilian must be an agent and gives Edelmann a five-day special leave in the SS recreation center in Solahütte (Porąbka Między-brodzie) as a reward.

APMO, D-AuI-1, Garrison Order 21/41, August 3, 1944.

The number of prisoners in the Gypsy Family Camp B-IIe in Birkenau has increased in the last two days by 1,297 and totals 2,815. This is probably the total number of men and women.

APMO, D-AuII-31/18, Labor Deployment List, vol. 11.

The Warsaw uprising begins. Units of the Polish Home Army begin the battle. All the military divisions of the resistance movement and the whole civilian population of the city participates. The surprise factor keeps the initiative on the side of the rebels from August 1 to 4. From August 4 on, police units commanded by Major General Reinefarth that were ordered up by Himmler, as well as SS Brigadier General Dirlewanger's special unit made up of criminals released

*The fate of the escapees is unknown.

from prisons and concentration camps, including Auschwitz, for this purpose, take part in the battles. The 608th Guard Regiment and the brigade of SS Brigadier General M. Kamiński, among others forming a special unit under the command of SS Lieutenant General von dem Bach-Zelewski, also participate in the battles.

AUGUST 2

The occupancy level in Gypsy Family Camp B-IIe increases by 70 prisoners and reaches 2,885. In addition to this are: a Gypsy in Quarantine Camp B-IIa, five Gypsies in Men's Camp B-IId, and seven Gypsies in the prisoners' infirmary B-IIf. 2,898 Gypsies—probably both men and women—are located in Birkenau.

APMO, D-AuII-3a/19, Labor Deployment List, vol. 11.

An empty freight train is made ready in the afternoon on the railroad ramp in Birkenau. 1,408 male and female Gypsies who were selected from Camp B-IIe and Blocks 10 and 11 of the main camp are brought here from the main camp. They are to remain alive and are, therefore, to be transferred to other camps. The deportees take their leave from the Gypsies remaining in Camp B-IIe through the wire fence. The train departs from the ramp at around 7:00 P.M.. On it are 918 men, among them 15 boys under 14 years of age, and 490 women. The destination of the train is Buchenwald. On August 3 and 4, 1,408 male and female Gypsies are still registered on the labor deployment projects lists in Auschwitz II, with the notation that they are on a transport to another camp. They were removed from the Occupancy Register after confirmation of their registration at Buchenwald is received.

APMO, D-AuII-3/a/20/21, Labor Deployment List, vol. 11; report of the Garrison Doctor in Buchenwald regarding the ages of the 918 Gypsies transferred from Auschwitz; Schnabel, *Power Without Morality*, p. 152.

During the evening roll call in Gypsy Family Camp B-IIe SS Doctor Mengele orders all Polish doctors and nurses to step forward and directs them immediately into the Penal Company in Camp B-IId in Birkenau.

APMO, Depositions, vol. 15, p. 65, Account of Former Prisoner Dr. Tadeusz Śnieszko.

After the evening roll call, a camp arrest is ordered in Auschwitz II and a block arrest in the Gypsy Family Camp, B-IIe. Camp B-IIe and other barracks where Gypsies are housed are surrounded by armed SS men. Trucks drive into the camp and 2,897 defenseless women, men, and children are driven to the gas chambers. After the gassing the corpses of the murdered are incinerated in the pit next to the crematorium, since the crematorium ovens are not operating at the time.

APMO, Dpr.-Hd/1, p. 26; Dpr.-Hd/5, p. 31; Dpr.-Hd/6, p. 63, Statements of Former Prisoners; D-AuII-3a/19/20, summary of labor deployment of prisoners in Auschwitz II of August 2, 1944, in which the number of Gypsies is still included; in later summaries these data are not present.

A prisoner sent from Prague receives the free No. 190157.

Two Polish prisoners, Jan Karpiński (No. 39572) and Eugeniusz Bachleda (No. 100379), escape from the camp. The prisoners hide themselves in a fully loaded truck. Eugeniusz Bachleda is shot and killed in Zabierzów near Kraków by the codriver. Jan Karpiński succeeds in escaping, although he is injured in the shoulder by a shot.

APMO, IZ-8/Gestapo Lodz/4a/ 90/230, 231.

The Russian prisoner Iliarion Karlash (No. 173926) escapes from the Blechhammer auxiliary camp, which belongs to Auschwitz III.

APMO, IZ-8/Gestapo Lodz/4a/90/233, 234.

Nos. B-2903–B-3449 are given to 547 Jews selected from an RSHA transport from the forced labor camp for Jews in Kielce. The weak and those unable to work are sent to the gas chambers.

Docs. of ISD Arolsen, NA-Men, Series B, p. 1/1980.

563 Jews from the Malines camp, among them 276 men, 24 boys, 240 women, and 23 girls, arrive in the twenty-sixth RSHA transport from Belgium. After the selection, 223 men, given Nos. B-3450–B-3672, and 138 women are admitted to the camp. The women are housed in the transit camp in Birkenau and do not receive a number at first; they are first registered on August 22. The remaining 202 people, among them 47 children, are killed in the gas chambers.

Four Polish prisoners escape from the Monowitz A.C., which belongs to Auschwitz III. Those involved are Tadeusz Stasik (No. 870), Henryk Roman (No. 3734), Henryk Machala (No. 8023), and Henryk Pilch (No. 13407).

APMO, IZ-8/Gestapo Lodz/4a/90/233,234.

The prisoner Dr. Jakow Wagschal (No. 160351) is sent to the Penal Company in Birkenau "until further notice," after interrogation in the Political Department after his escape attempt.

APMO, D-AuI-3/1, p. 24, Penal Company Register.

AUGUST 3

A Gypsy in Prisoners' Infirmary Camp B-IIf in Birkenau remains alive.

APMO, D-AuII-3a/20, Labor Deployment List, vol. 11.

Two prisoners sent from Kattowitz receive the free Nos. 190158 and 190159.

33 female prisoners sent from Görz (Gorizia) by the Sipo and the SD receive Nos 82910–82942.

Docs. of ISD Arolsen, NA-Womens, p. 11/1986.

38 female prisoners and six male prisoners sent from Trieste by the Sipo and SD are given Nos. 82943–82980 and 190708–190713.

APMO, D-AuII-3/1, p. 6, Quarantine List; Docs. of ISD Arolsen, NA-Women, p. 11/1986.

After the selection from an RSHA transport from Trieste, which arrives with 49 Jews, 10 men are admitted to the camp and are given Nos A-19952–A-19961. The remaining 39 men are killed in the gas chambers.

APMO, D-AuII-3/1, p. 6, Quarantine List.

The prisoner Josef Freiwald (No. Z-9967), a Swiss Gypsy, escapes from the transport from Auschwitz to Buchenwald between 2:00 and 7:00 A.M., on the Gera-Weimar stretch of track.

APMO, IZ-Gestapo Lodz/4a/90/237.

The Gypsy transport from Auschwitz II arrives at Buchenwald. 918 Gypsies are in the transport, among them 105 boys between nine and 14 years of age, 393 boys between 15 and 24 years of age, 330 men between 25 and 44 years of age, 59 men between 45

Schnabel, *Power Without Morality*, p. 152.

One of the execution areas in the main camp: the so-called group gallows.

and 54 years of age, 23 men between 55 and 64 years of age; two men over 65 years old, one man for whom no age is given, and five men whose names are not placed on the list. The women are probably sent to an auxiliary camp.

Five prisoners sent from Kattowitz receive Nos. 190714–190718.

193 female Hungarian Jews who are selected from the transit camp in Birkenau and transferred to the women's camp receive Nos. A-16459–A-16651.

Docs. of ISD Arolsen, NA-Women, Series A, p. 5/1986.

1,300 Jews from Drancy arrive in the seventy-seventh transport of the RSHA from France. 291 male Jews and 183 female Jews, given Nos. B-3673–B-3963 and A-16652–A-16834, are admitted to the camp after the selection. The remaining 826 people are killed in the gas chambers.

Ibid.

Five Polish prisoners escape from the Monowitz A.C.: Franciszek Petersile (No. 131861), Tadeusz Petrykowski (No. 131862), Władysław Tomasiak (No. 131873), Józef Toporek (No. 131873), and Antoni Lao (No. 169599).

APMO, IZ-8/Gestapo Lodz/4a/90/227–229.

Three Russian prisoners escape from the Eintrachthütte A.C., which belongs to Auschwitz III: Gregor Ivanchenko (No. 6377), Paelo Hus (No. 175633), and Jan Semykobylenko.

APMO, IZ-8/Gestapo Lodz/4a/90/228, 229, 236.

306 female Jews who were selected from an RSHA transport from the forced labor camp for Jews in Ostrowiec, in the Radom District, receive the Nos. A-16835–A-17140. The female Jews who are classified as unable to work are killed in the gas chambers.

Docs. of ISD Arolsen, NA-Women, Series E, p. 5/1986.

AUGUST 4

1,443 male Jews who were selected from an RSHA transport from the forced labor camp for Jews in Ostrowiec, in the Radom District, receive Nos. B-3964–B-5406. The male Jews classified during the selection as unable to work are killed in the gas chambers.

A prisoner sent from Bochum is given free No. 189679.

23 prisoners sent in a group transport receive Nos. 190719–190741.

AUGUST 5

23 prisoners sent in a group transport receive Nos. 190742–190764.

109 Russian POWs who are transferred from the POW camp in Lamsdorf receive Nos. RKG-11672–RKG-11780.

APMO, D-AuII-3/1, p. 6, Quarantine List.

Two Russian POWs whose numbers were tattooed on their chests escape from Auschwitz II: Timofei Anisimov (No. RKG-10499) and Nikolai Simonok. Both are captured during the escape attempt and sent on August 9 to the Penal Company "until further notice."

APMO, D-AuI-1/1b, Bulletin, vol. 3, p. 345; D-AuI-3/1, p. 24, Penal Company Register.

AUGUST 6

Commandant Schwarz of Auschwitz III halts the search for the three prisoners who escaped from the Eintrachthütte A.C., Hus, Ivanchenko, and Semykobylenko, because they are captured.

APMO, IZ-8/Gestapo Lodz/4a/90/236.

71 prisoners arrive in Auschwitz in an evacuation transport that left Majdanek two weeks previously. They receive Nos. 190765–190835. These prisoners were probably evacuated with the movable freight, e.g., office furnishings, which were transported to Auschwitz.

Four prisoners sent from Verona receive Nos. 190841–190844.

314 male Jews arrive in an RSHA transport from Fünfteichen. After the selection, 31 men, given Nos. A-19962–A-19992, and 12 prisoners who were previously in Auschwitz and were already tattooed with numbers are admitted to the camp. The remaining 271 men are killed in the gas chambers.

7,500 female Jews arrive from the Płaszów concentration camp in an RSHA transport.

Two Jews arrive on an RSHA transport from the Galicia District. After the selection they are admitted to the camp. They receive Nos. B-5407 and B-5408. The remaining people are killed in the gas chambers.

Usche. Damm Ludwig

Ich wurde heute mit dem Schreiben des Chefs des SS-Wirtschafts-
Verwaltungshauptamtes vom 29.6.44 über einen besonders krassen
Fall der fahrlässigen Preisgabe eines Staatsgeheimnisses durch
eine Fernschreiberin, die vom Volksgerichtshof zum Tode verur-
teilt wurde, bekanntgemacht und nochmals eingehend über die
Geheimhaltung im Dienstbetrieb belehrt.

Auschwitz, den 28.8.44

SS Corporal Ludwig Damm receives some stern advice.

AUGUST 7

Five prisoners sent from Kattowitz receive Nos. 190836–190840.

The occupancy level in Birkenau is 19,115 male prisoners, among them 102 boys under 14 years of age—mostly newborns, who are housed in Women's Camp B-Ia. There are still 129 boys from Kaunas in Quarantine Camp B-IIa, and 106 boys under 14 years of age are housed in Men's Camp B-IId.

APMO, D-AuII-3a/24, Labor Deployment List, vol. 11.

Heavy American bombers carry out air attacks on the area surrounding Auschwitz, in which the chemical plants of the Oberschlesische Hydrierwerke (Upper Silesian Hydration Works) in Blechhammer and the oil refinery about 12 miles northeast of Auschwitz are destroyed.

APMO, Analyses/Wyman, vol. 64, P. 88; Gilbert, *Auschwitz and the Allies*, p. 354.

In the newly created Trzebinia auxiliary camp, which belongs to Auschwitz III and is located near the O.S. oil refinery in Trzebinia, 305 prisoners begin clearing rubble and repairing the damage after the heavy bombing attack. By the end of August the occupancy level in the Trzebinia A.C. reaches 621. Most of the prisoners are borrowed by the construction and assembly firms from the management of the refinery to carry out the expansion project.

APMO, Trzebinia, vol. 3/2, pp. 4, 47; Franciszek Piper, "Das Nebenlager Trzebinia" (Trzebinia Labor Camp), *HvA*, no. 16 (1978): 93–135.

The number of prisoners employed in the so-called foodstuffs collection squad a.d.R. (an der Rampe—at the ramp) is increased by 20, to 40 prisoners. They work on the ramp of Auschwitz II and collect the food the deported Jews bring with them.*

APMO, D-AuII-3a/24, Labor Deployment List, vol. 11.

AUGUST 8

14 prisoners sent in a group transport receive Nos. 190845–190858.

*Well-packaged foodstuffs and such products as preserved meat and fish, coffee, tea, and cocoa are taken to the SS storerooms. Loose and spoilable foods go to the prisoner's kitchen, frequently mixed with various little objects. Consequently, prisoners not infrequently find buttons, razor blades, and other things in their soup.

After the selection from an RSHA transport of Jews from the forced labor camp in Pustków, 137 men are admitted to the camp. They receive Nos. B-5409–B-5545. Those Jews who are classified as unable to work are killed in the gas chambers.

In the first trial of the conspirators who planned the assassination attempt against Hitler, which takes place on August 7 and 8, General Field Marshal von Witzleben and Generals Hoeppner, Hase, and Stieff as well as other officers are condemned to death by hanging. The sentences are executed immediately after the conclusion of the trial; the condemned are hanged on meat hooks. The entire trial and the execution is filmed and shown to Hitler that evening. The presiding judge in the trials against the members of the July 20, 1944, resistance movement* is the president of the People's Court, Roland Freisler. During the trial against Field Marshal von Witzleben, Freisler explains that only criminals and felons serve time in the concentration camps. Press accounts of the trial reached Auschwitz. This explanation by Freisler has as a consequence that the leadership of the Auschwitz Combat Group draws up a resolution by the political prisoners, protesting the insulting and untrue claim. This resolution is smuggled out of the camp and sent to PWOK in Kraków so it can be further circulated and to familiarize public opinion in the free world with its contents.

Alan Bullock, *Hitler: Studium tyranni* (Hitler: A Study in Tyranny), Warsaw, 1970, p. 277; APMO, Mat.RO, vol. II, pp. 86–90, the resolution is released on August 21.

The previous day, a transport of the RSHA with 165 men from an auxiliary camp of Gross-Rosen arrived. After the selection 23 Jews are admitted to the camp as prisoners and receive Nos. B-5546–B-5568. 142 men are killed in the gas chambers.

APMO, D-AuII-3/1, p. 6, Quarantine List.

25 Hungarian Jews who were probably selected from the transit camp in Birkenau receive Nos. B-5569–B-5593.

23 female Italian Jews and 80 male Italian Jews who are selected from an RSHA transport probably receive the Nos. 83018–83040 and B-5594–B-5673. There are approximately 300 people in the transport, which arrived on August 6.

CDECM, *Jews in Italy*, p. 24.

Two Jewish prisoners sent from Radom receive Nos. A-19993 and A-19994.

1,414 female Hungarian and Polish Jews who were selected from the female Jews kept in the transit camp in Birkenau receive Nos. A-17141–A-18554. The female Hungarian Jews are from the RSHA transports that arrived between May 15 and June 30 from Hungary. The female Polish Jews were transferred on August 6 from the Płaszów concentration camp to Auschwitz.

Docs. of ISD Arolsen, NA-Women, Series A, p. 6/1986.

AUGUST 9

American air reconnaissance planes took photographs of Auschwitz. Auschwitz I, Auschwitz II, and Auschwitz III, Monowitz, are

Gilbert, *Auschwitz and the Allies*, p. 355.

*It is generally estimated that nearly 5,000 people in the Third Reich were killed in connection with the assassination attempt of July 20, 1944.

Konzentrationslager Auschwitz   Auschwitz, den 5. Januar 1943.
Der Kommandant

An den
SS-Sturmmann Ludwig D a m m,
Kdtr.-Stab, K.L. Au.,
A u s c h w i t z.

Ich bestrafe Sie gemäss D.B.O. für den mobilen Zustand
§ 8, Abs C, Ziff. 2 mit

<u>einem strengen Verweis,</u>

weil Sie während Ihres Urlaubes entgegen den bestehenden
Befehle und Vorschriften handelten.

<u>Begründung:</u> Während Ihres Urlaubes im Dezember 1942
unterhielten Sie sich mit Soldaten und
Parteigenossen über das Judenproblem und
tätigten hierbei Äusserungen über die Lösung
der Judenfrage in Auschwitz. Durch dieses
Verhalten, welches unter Umständen geeignet
war, Unruhe in die Bevölkerung zu bringen,
handelten Sie entgegen den Ihnen bekannten
Befehlen.
Ich habe lediglich auf Grund Ihrer bisher
einwandfreien Führung und einer anderweitigen
guten Beurteilung von einer strengeren Bestrafung abgesehen und erwarte, dass Ihnen
dieser Vorfall als Lehre für die Zukunft
dienen wird.

SS-Obersturmbannführer und Kommandant

Meine Bestrafung mit einem strengen Verweis, d.Kdt.
v.5.1.1943, wurde mir bekanntgegeben und mir
gehändigt.
Auschwitz, den 5, Januar 1943

Ludwig Damm

SS Private Ludwig Damm receives a severe reprimand.

to be seen in the photographs. The major part of the film is over-exposed, so the objects can be recognized only with difficulty.

Two prisoners sent from Kattowitz receive Nos. 190859 and 190860.

According to the order from July 14, 1944, the crematorium management in Auschwitz II receives four sieves for sifting burned human bones at a price of 232 RM, from the DAW.

APMO, IZ-13/89, Various Documents of the Third Reich, p. 205.

Eight female prisoners sent to the camp by the Munich Stapo receive Nos. 83041–83048.

AUGUST 10

31 prisoners sent in a group transport receive Nos. 190861–190891.

1,446 female Polish Jews receive Nos. A-18555 to A-20000. They are among the Jewish women sent from the Płaszów Concentration Camp and housed in the transit camp.

Docs. of ISD Arolsen, NA-Women, Series A, p. 6/1986.

1,000 female Hungarian Jews who were selected from the transit camp receive Nos. A-20001–A-21000. They arrived in the RSHA transports from Hungary of the period from May 15 to June 30.

Ibid.

AUGUST 11

Nine prisoners are sent to the Penal Company in Birkenau.

APMO, D-AuI-3/1, p. 24, Penal Company Register.

Four prisoners sent from Kattowitz receive Nos. 190892–190895.

Two Polish prisoners escape from Auschwitz: Edward Padkowski (No. 16366) and Wincenty Ciesielczuk (No. 16369).

APMO, IZ-8/Gestapo Lodz/4a/90/241, 242.

Four Polish prisoners attempt an escape from Auschwitz II: Tadeusz Uszyński (No. 1880), Ludwik Nowakowski (No. 5010), Jerzy Sadczykow (No. 623), and Rudolf Szymański. They hide themselves in a bunker prepared for this purpose in "Mexico."

APMO, IZ-8/Gestapo Lodz/4a/90/241, 242; Sobański, *Escapes from Auschwitz*, p. 126.·

16 Jewish prisoners transferred from Gross-Rosen receive Nos. B-5674–B-5689.

APMO, D-AuII-3a/30, Labor Deployment List, vol. 11.

1,999 female Jews who are selected from the transit camp in Birkenau receive Nos. A-21001–A-22999. There are probably Hungarians and Poles among them.

212 prisoners sick with malaria are transferred from Auschwitz to Flossenbürg.

Ibid.

There are 469 prisoners up to 14 years of age in the men's camps of Auschwitz II. Of them 186 boys are in Quarantine Camp B-IIa,

Ibid.

280 in Men's Camp B-IId, and three in Camp B-IIe, which after the liquidation of the Gypsies becomes a quarantine camp for Jewish prisoners.

AUGUST 12

16 prisoners sent in a group transport receive Nos. 190896–190911.

Allied air reconnaissance take photographs of Auschwitz for the sixth time. Auschwitz I, Auschwitz II, and Auschwitz III, Monowitz, can be seen in the photographs. This time also the quality of the pictures is not good.

Gilbert, *Auschwitz and the Allies*, p. 355.

After the Warsaw uprising breaks out there are mass arrests among the civilian population in the Polish capital. The arrested are sent to the Pruszków transit camp and are taken from there to forced labor in Germany or sent to concentration camps. The first transport from Pruszków, with 1,984 men, youths, and boys and over 3,800 women and girls reaches Auschwitz II. The men, youths, and boys receive Nos. 190912–192895 and the women and girls receive Nos. 83085–86938. The women and children are put in Women's Camp B-Ia and the men in Men's Quarantine Camp B-IIa. The numbers are not tattooed onto them. Otherwise their treatment is no different from that of other prisoners in the camp. Among those delivered by this transport were 169 boys under 14 years of age.

APMO, Mat.RO, vol. VI, p. 57; Docs. of ISD Arolsen, NA-Women, p. 11/1986.

From an RSHA transport from Hirschberg with 18 Jews, two men receive Nos. A-19995 and A-19996 after the selection and are admitted to the camp. The remaining men are killed in the gas chambers.

APMO, D-AuII-3/1, p. 7, Quarantine List.

1,020 female Hungarian and Polish Jews who are selected from the transit camp in Birkenau receive Nos. A-23000–A-24019.

Docs. of ISD Arolsen, NA-Women, Series A, p. 6/1986.

21 female Italian Jews sent to the camp from the prison in Turin receive Nos. A-24020–A-24040.

Ibid.

19 male and 12 female Jews who are selected from the fifty-sixth RSHA East-transport from Berlin receive Nos. B-5690–B-5708 and A-24179–A-24190. The remaining prisoners, among them 68 men, are killed in the gas chambers.

APMO, D-AuII-3/1, p. 7, Quarantine List.

During the evening roll call two prisoners who were captured while trying to escape and who had been sent to the Penal Company from time to time, Josef Kenner (No. 37894) and Jakow Wagschal (No. 160351), are hanged.*

APMO, D-AuI-3/1, p. 24, Penal Company Register; Dpr.-Hd/6, p. 59.

*The third escapee, Franciszek Piechowiak (No. 138097), is transferred on August 17, 1944, by penal transport to Mauthausen.

Nos. B-5709–B-5859 are given to 131 Jews who were transferred from the Kistsarcsa camp in Hungary, as political prisoners—Jews of Hungarian nationality in so-called protective custody. They are transferred the same day from Auschwitz II to the Golleschau A.C. and are to be in quarantine for 21 days.

APMO, D-AuIII, Golleschau/12, pp. 80–87.

The prisoners hidden in a bunker of the Section B-III, "Mexico"—Ludwik Nowakowski, Jerzy Sadczykow, Rudolf Szymański, and Tadeusz Uszyński—leave the bunker a second time and attempt to break through the outer sentry line. In spite of the darkness they are discovered and three of them, Nowakowski, Sadczykow, and Szymański, fall dead from the bullets of the SS. Tadeusz Uszyński succeeds in returning, wounded, to the bunker. Thanks to the assistance of the resistance movement in the camp and the solidarity of the fellow prisoners he is able to hold out until September 9, when he tries to escape again. This time he is successful.

APMO, Mat.RO, vol. II, pp. 83, 119, 127, 128, 134, 139, 142, 145, 152; Sobański, *Escapes from Auschwitz*, pp. 129–136.

1,000 female Hungarian Jews are transferred from the women's camp in Birkenau to the Allendorf auxiliary camp that belongs to Buchenwald.

Docs. of ISD Arolsen, Folder 7.

AUGUST 14

A prisoner sent from Berlin on August 4 receives No. 192908.

Nine prisoners sent from Kattowitz receive Nos. 192909–192917.

The Police Court-martial of the Kattowitz Gestapo has a session in Block 11 and condemns 58 men and some women to death. They are killed on the same day in the gas chambers in Birkenau.

APMO, Mat.RO, vol. IX, p. 5a; vol. XXIX, p. 110, Secret Message from Bernard Swierczyna and Wacław Stacherski.

350 Hungarian Jews receive Nos. B-5860–B-6209. They are probably political prisoners from the Kistsarcsa camp.

Docs. of ISD Arolsen, NA-Men, Series B, p. 1/1980.

1,999 prisoners—Poles and Russians—are transferred from Auschwitz to Buchenwald. Among those transferred are 1,134 prisoners from Auschwitz I and 865 from Auschwitz II.

APMO, D-AuII-3a/31, Labor Deployment Lists, vol. 11; Mat.RO, vol. VIII; Docs. of ISD Arolsen, Folder 13.

During the evening roll call the names of 60 Polish prisoners, primarily prisoner functionaries—so-called prominent persons—are read aloud in the main camp while all safety measures are observed, part of the guard units is placed on standby alert, and a few groups of SS men cover the area with machine guns and are positioned to attack immediately from automobiles. They are led into Block 11 under escort. This operation is an attempt to smash the leadership of the camp resistance organization. When the SS realizes that the operation has backfired it cancels interrogations. The prisoners are kept in Block 11 and finally transferred in two transports to Neuengamme camp and Sachsenhausen. According to the information of the camp resistance movement, the most important camp informer,

APMO, Mat.RO, vol. II, pp. 130ff.

the Slovak Miszutko—a successor to the prisoner Dorosiewicz—is killed in the gas chambers. He hated Poles and had lodged over 250 reports to the Political Department during his approximately half year activity.

AUGUST 15

43 prisoners sent in a group transport receive Nos. 192918–192960.

SS Major Burger, the Head of the Office D-IV, responsible for concentration camp administration, reports to the Head of Branch B in the WVHA, SS Major General Georg Lörner,

Schnabel, *Power Without Morality*, p. 200.

The occupancy level of Auschwitz on August 1, 1944, is:

1. male prisoners		379,167
2. female prisoners		145,119
	Total	524,286

New arrivals are as follows:

1. From the Hungary Program (Jewish Operation)	90,000
2. From Litzmannstadt (police prison and ghetto)	60,000
3. Poland, from the General Government	15,000
4. Criminal prisoners from the East	10,000
5. Former Polish officers	17,000
6. From Warsaw (Poland)	400,000
7. Imminent arrivals from France	ca. 15,000–20,000
Total	612,000

A large portion of the prisoners are already en route and will arrive for delivery into the concentration camp in the next few days.

Burger notes further that among the expected new arrivals are approximately 387,000 men and 225,000 women.

244 men are admitted to the camp after selection from an RSHA transport from the Lodz ghetto and receive Nos. B-6210–B-6453. Those classified as unable to work are sent to the gas chambers. Young and healthy prisoners were probably kept in the camp as "depot prisoners."

Seven women are admitted to the camp after the selection from an RSHA transport from the Galicia District and receive Nos. A-24197–A-24203. Those female Jews who are classified as unable to work are killed in the gas chambers.

AUGUST 16

11 Russian prisoners escape through a tunnel that was dug under the floor of the barracks and leads behind the camp fence.

APMO, D-AuII-2/1, vol. 4, pp. 671–673, punishment report against prisoner Hijman Bierman (No. 175337), who fell asleep while on night duty, thus facilitating the escape.

Eight prisoners sent from Kattowitz receive Nos. 192961–192968.

400 men are admitted to the camp after the selection from an RSHA transport from the Lodz ghetto and receive Nos. B-6454–B-6853. The Jews who are classified as unable to work are killed in the gas chambers. Young and healthy prisoners are probably kept in the camp as "depot prisoners."

35 men are admitted to the camp as prisoners after the selection from an RSHA transport from the Galicia District and receive Nos. B-6854–B-6888. Those Jews who are classified as unable to work are killed in the gas chambers.

270 men are admitted to the camp after the selection from an RSHA transport from the Lodz ghetto and receive Nos. B-6889–B-7158. Young and healthy prisoners are probably kept in Birkenau as "depot prisoners." The remaining prisoners are killed in the gas chambers.

After a selection in the transit camp six female Hungarian Jews are admitted to the camp and receive Nos. A-24191–A-24196.

Docs. of ISD Arolsen, NA-Women, Series A, p. 6/1986.

Approximately 2,500 Jews arrive in an RSHA transport from the island of Rhodes. 346 men, given Nos. B-7159–B-7504, and 254 women, given Nos. A-24215–A-24468, are admitted to the camp. The remaining persons, among them 1,202 men, are killed in the gas chambers.

APMO, D-AuII-3/1, p. 7, Quarantine List.

66 male Jews arrive in an RSHA transport from Trieste and Zagreb. After the selection eight men are admitted to the camp and receive Nos. B-7505–B-7512. The remaining 58 men are killed in the gas chambers.

Ibid.

The occupancy level in the Prisoners' Infirmary Camp B-IIf for men increases by 59 men and includes 82 male prisoners for research purposes. In addition 49 twins are housed in Prisoners' Infirmary Camp B-IIf.

APMO, D-AuII-3/a/33, Labor Deployment List, vol. 11

AUGUST 17

A prisoner sent from Kattowitz receives No. 192897.

A prisoner sent from Prague receives No. 192969.

Four prisoners sent from Kattowitz receive Nos. 192970–192973.

After the selection from an RSHA transport from Kattowitz, nine male Jews are admitted to the camp and receive Nos. B-7513–B-7521. The remaining prisoners, among them 84 men, are killed in the gas chambers.

APMO, D-AuII-3/1, p. 7, Quarantine List.

A male Jew who is sent to the camp by order of the RSHA receives No. B-7522.

Nine female Hungarian Jews selected from the transit camp in Birkenau receive Nos. A-24204–A-24212.

Docs. of ISD Arolsen, NA-Women, Series A, p. 7/1986.

20 female prisoners transferred from the Coroneo prison in Trieste by order of the Trieste Sipo and the SD receive Nos. 86962–86981.

Docs. of ISD Arolsen, NA-Women, p.11/1986.

21 female prisoners sent to Auschwitz by order of the Görz Sipo and SD receive Nos. 86986–87006.

Ibid.

The male Polish Jew Salam Schott (No. 70212) escapes from the Monowitz A.C.

APMO, IZ-8/Gestapo Lodz/4a/90/423.

398 prisoners are transferred from Auschwitz to Mauthausen.

APMO, Mat.RO, vol. VIIIc, pp. 75–77.

1,050 male prisoners wait in Men's Quarantine Camp B-IIa for their transfer to another camp.

APMO, D-AuII-3/a/34, Labor Deployment List, vol. 11.

AUGUST 18

The Polish male prisoner Jan Purgal (No. 101260) escapes from the Laurahütte A.C., which belongs to Auschwitz III.

APMO, IZ-8/Gestapo Lodz/4a/90/243, 244.

139 Jews from Trieste and from the Galicia District arrive in a group transport of the RSHA. 19 male Italian Jews, given Nos. B-7523–B-7541, and eight male Hungarian Jews, given Nos. B-7542–B-7549, are admitted to the camp after the selection. The remaining 112 men are killed in the gas chambers.

APMO, D-AuII-3/1b, p. 7, Quarantine List.

16 prisoners sent to Auschwitz on July 18, 1944, receive Nos. 192974–192989.

Four female prisoners who were transferred to the camp from the Kleine Festung ("Little Fortress") prison in Theresienstadt by the Prague Stapo receive Nos. 87012–87015.

Docs. of ISD Arolsen, NA-Women, p. 11/1986.

Two female Jews sent from Warsaw by the RSHA receive Nos. A-24213 and A-24214.

SS Private Johann Antoni and SS man Hans Kartusch from the 3rd Guard Company of Auschwitz II receive eight days' special leave in the SS recreation center in Solahütte as recognition for the suc-

APMO, D-AuI-1, Garrison Order 22/24, Aug. 18, 1944.

cessful use of their weapons during the escape of four prisoners,* in spite of darkness.

After completing an inspection Commandant Schwarz of Auschwitz III directs the Commanders of the auxiliary camps to eliminate the problems that have arisen from their failure to carry out his directives. He places his main emphasis on the security of the camp, on conducting daily inspections as well as on a renewed examination and thorough investigation of all escape cases. In sharp words he mentions the escape from Gleiwitz I A.C., during which—despite his instructions—11 Russian prisoners escaped through the underground tunnel under conditions similar to those earlier in the Eintrachthütte A.C. He threatens the SS men responsible for this and similar negligence with being charged before a court regardless of their rank.** In addition he orders the supplementation and identification of the prisoners' clothing.

APMO, D-AuIII-1/65, Commandant's Office Orders, vol. 5, p. 33.

AUGUST 19

A prisoner sent from Kattowitz receives No. 192896.

A Jewish prisoner receives No. 192991.

Seven prisoners sent in a group transport receive Nos. 192992–192998.

Three prisoners sent from Kattowitz receive Nos. 192999–193001.

16 Hungarian Jews receive Nos. B-7550–B-7565.

510 female Jews are admitted to the camp and receive Nos. A-24469–A-24978 after the selection of an RSHA transport from the labor camp in Radom, which belongs to the Lublin concentration camp. The remaining prisoners are killed in the gas chambers.

20 female prisoners sent in a group transport receive Nos. 87018–87037.

SS Garrison Doctor Wirths presents an assessment to the SS Camp Doctor in Birkenau, SS Captain Josef Mengele. He writes among other things that Dr. Mengele has applied his practical and theoretical knowledge in combating serious epidemics during his service

APMO, Photograph Collection of Josef Mengele, vol. 114, Microfilm No. 1613/93; Nyiszli, *Mengele's Laboratory*, pp. 42–44.

---

*The SS men shot and killed the three Polish prisoners Ludwik Nowakowski, Jerzy Sadczykow, and Rudolf Szymański during their escape attempt. (Compare the entries for August 11 and 13, 1944.)

**The inspection and the directives result from the escape of 11 Russian prisoners from Gleiwitz I A.C. on August 16, which took place in a similar manner as the escape of nine prisoners from the Eintrachthütte A.C. in Schwientochlowitz on July 3, 1944—by means of an underground tunnel.

as a physician in the Auschwitz concentration camp.* With care, perseverence, and energy, he has fulfilled all tasks assigned to him despite often difficult conditions to the full satisfaction of his superiors and showed himself to be capable of handling every situation.** In addition he has used every free moment to educate himself further as an anthropologist. He has accomplished extraordinary things in the area of anthropology by using to the fullest the scientific materials at the disposal of a person in his position.† In the conscientious fulfillment of his medical responsibilities during the fight against an epidemic he contracted typhus himself. On account of his outstanding accomplishments he was honored with the War Service Cross, Second Class, with Swords. In addition to his medical knowledge he possesses special knowledge in the area of anthropology. Thus he appeared suited for any additional mission as well as for greater tasks.

From the perspective of a witness, Dr. Miklos Nyiszli, a prisoner in Auschwitz (No. A-8450), who carried out autopsies on the corpses of twins for Dr. Mengele writes:

Immediately after the arrival of a transport one of the SS men walks down the row of new arrivals and looks for twins and dwarfs.... The twins and the dwarfs are selected and place themselves on the right side. The guards lead this group to a special barracks. In this barracks good food and comfortable sleeping areas are available, hygienic conditions are acceptable and the prisoners are treated well. This is Block 14 in Camp B-IIf. From here the prisoners are led under escort to the research block. Here all experiments that can be conducted on a living person are conducted on the prisoners: blood tests, thigh punctures, blood transfers among the twins and a multitude of various other experiments. All painful and exhausting.... Dwarfs are also experimented upon. These experiments—camouflaged as medical experiments ... conducted in vivo, that is on living persons, are far removed from the scientific examination of the problem of twins as such. They are relative and do not say much. The next stage of the experiments follows: analysis on the basis of autopsy. The comparison of normal and pathological or sick organs. For this corpses are necessary. Since the autopsy and analysis of the individual organs must proceed simultaneously, the twins must die simultaneously. Thus they die simultaneously in the experimental block of the Auschwitz Concentration Camp.... Dr. Mengele kills them.... This is the most dangerous criminal type, who in addition has an unlimited power. He sends millions to their deaths, since according to the German

---

*The use of this knowledge consisted of sending those sick with typhus to the gas chambers.
**He conducts these selections on the ramp ruthlessly and without moral qualms. Of the rightness of this behavior he persuades SS Doctor Delmotte, who nevertheless refuses to continue after the first selection.
†This scientific material is represented by twins and dwarfs whose organs and body parts are conserved after they were killed and sent to the Kaiser Wilhelm Institute for Anthropology in Berlin-Dahlem.

race theory these are not human beings, but rather beings of a lower order, who have a ruinous effect on humanity.

AUGUST 20

270 prisoners, Hungarian Jews, are transferred from Auschwitz to Buchenwald, to the Bochum A.C.

Docs. of ISD Arolsen, Folder 13.

Ludwik Ligocki (a.k.a. Ludwig Ligotzki), a Polish political prisoner, formerly a German citizen, who escaped from the camp on June 22, is captured in Istebna near Bielsko and sent back to Auschwitz III.

APMO, IZ-8/Gestapo Lodz/2/88/156.

Late Sunday afternoon, an American air squadron consisting of 127 bombers and 100 fighter jets of the Mustang type bombards the I. G. Farben chemical plants near Auschwitz for 28 minutes under the best weather conditions. The antiaircraft guns and the 19 German fighter jets are ineffectual. Only one bomber is shot down. Air photographs taken during the bombardment demonstrate the extent of the damage. In the photographs sections of Auschwitz I and Auschwitz II, five miles from the chemical plants, are visible.

APMO, Analyses/Wyman, vol. 64, p. 87.

The following are bombed in the air attack: the train station in Tschechowitz-South, which was approximately 15 miles from the Auschwitz train station, several industrial targets, among them the oil refinery, which during the war belongs to the Vacuum Oil Company AG, which belongs to Deutsche Vacuum Oil in Hamburg, and an electro-technical factory. The water pipes in Tschechowitz and the brickworks in Bestwin are damaged. As a result the Commandant's Office of Auschwitz I immediately sends a squad of prisoners to Tschechowitz, whereby the auxiliary camp called Tschechowitz—Bomb Search Squad is created. At first, 60 German prisoners, three Jews, and several Capos are housed there. Several days later the German prisoners are sent back and 100 Jews are transferred in their place. The prisoners defuse duds and clear away bombed targets. SS Staff Sergeant Wilhelm Claussen becomes the Camp Commander of the auxiliary camp. After the removal of all duds the camp is dissolved.

APMO, Kraków Auschwitz Trial, vol. 78, pp. 255–260; Irena Strzelecka, Tadeusz Szymański, "Podobózy Tschechowitz-Bombensachkommando i Tschechowitz-Vacuum" (The Tschechowitz Bomb Search Squad and Tschechowitz-Vacuum), ZO, no. 18 (1983): 187–222.

During the bomb attack the prisoner Adam Szaller (No. 126255) escapes from the Monowitz A.C., which belongs to Auschwitz III.

APMO, IZ-8/Gestapo Lodz/4a/245, 246.

AUGUST 21

The camp resistance movement responds to a query of the liaison man of the Armia Krajowa, the Polish Home Army, that it is in a position to blow up the crematorium and the gas chambers, if it is provided with explosive materials.

APMO, Mat.RO, Vol. II, p. 84.

The Auschwitz Combat Group includes in its communiqué of August 21 a resolution of political prisoners to be sent via Kraków to London and published in the press. The resolution begins with the following words:

APMO, Mat.RO, vol. II, pp. 86ff. In the original resolution, Józef Cyrankiewicz's handwriting can be recognized.

As political prisoners of the National Socialist concentration camps we denounce before the entire world the lying and cynical statement about these same concentration camps by the president of the so-called People's Court, which is presiding over the trial of the German generals in connection with the events of July 20.

After refuting the cynical thesis that only criminals and felons are incarcerated in the concentration camps, the resolution ends:

Although we are in camps of oppression, we are people of freedom and want to announce to the free world our existence and our unequal battle for our rights as political prisoners. We are behind bars as soldiers and citizens of our nations and demand recognition as soldiers, our human rights, and our rights as prisoners of war. We know that only a resolute stance on the part of the free world can secure these rights for us. We demand such determination, because it will be at the same time an expression of the common struggle for the freedom of the people and of the world and of human values. The political prisoners of the German concentration camps.

500 female prisoners are transferred from the Women's Camp in Birkenau to Natzweiler in Alsace, the Ebingen A.C.

APMO, Mat.RO, vol. VIIId, pp. 71–75, 89ff., List of Names.

1,000 prisoners are transferred from Auschwitz to Natzweiler. They are Poles who were sent to Auschwitz after the outbreak of the Warsaw uprising.

APMO, D-AuII-3a/37, Labor Deployment List, vol. 11.

Two male and 47 female prisoners sent to the camp by order of the Sipo and SD for the Adriatic coast, the region of Trieste, Fiume, and Pola/Istrian, receive Nos. 192900 and 192901, and 87047–87093.

Docs. of ISD Arolsen, NA-Women, p. 12/1986.

An RSHA transport of Jews from the Lodz ghetto arrives. After the selection 131 men are admitted to the camp and receive Nos. B-7566–B-7696. They are put in quarantine in Camp B-IIe. The remaining people are killed in the gas chambers.

APMO, D-AuII-3a/38, Labor Deployment List, vol. 11.

The camp resistance movement informs PWOK in Kraków on the number of prisoners:

APMO, Mat.RO, vol. II, p. 116.

In Auschwitz I there are 15,971 prisoners,
    of whom 3,934 are Poles and 1,711 Polish Jews.
In Auschwitz II there are 19,424 prisoners,
    of whom 5,772 are Poles and 4,386 Polish Jews.
In Auschwitz III there are 30,539 prisoners,
    of whom 1,624 are Poles and 12,031 Polish Jews.
In the women's camp of Auschwitz II, Birkenau, there are 39,234 female prisoners, of whom 7,284 are Poles and 4,902 Polish Jews.

A total of 750 boys under 14 years of age are located in Auschwitz II, of whom 171, among them newborns, are in Women's Camp

APMO, D-AuII-3a/37ff., Labor Deployment List, vol. II.

B-Ia, 384 are in Quarantine Camp B-IIa, 171 are in Men's Camp B-IId, and four are in Camp B-IIe.

AUGUST 22

Another group of 1,000 Polish prisoners is transferred from Auschwitz II to Natzweiler.

Ibid.

The number of boys under 14 years of age in Quarantine Camp B-IIa decreases by 198 and totals 186. These boys are probably killed in the gas chambers after a selection, since in the daily list of labor assignments their transfer to another camp or to a transport is not noted.

Ibid.

Three Polish prisoners sent to the camp by the Budapest Sipo and SD receive Nos. 192898, 192899, and 192902.

35 prisoners sent in a group transport receive Nos. 193002–193036.

An RSHA transport from the Lodz ghetto consisting of 40 cars* arrives at Auschwitz. 64 men, given Nos. B-7697–B-7760, and two women, given Nos. 87095 and 87096, are admitted to the camp.

APMO, Mat.RO, vol. II, p. 117.

Three Hungarian Jews sent to the camp by the Budapest Sipo and SD receive Nos. B-7761–B-7763.

A transport with 853 Jews arrives from Mauthausen. 455 Jews are from Mauthausen and 398 are from Gusen II A.C., which belongs to Mauthausen. The transport left the Mauthausen Concentration Camp on August 20. After the selection on the ramp in Birkenau 94 Jews are sent to Quarantine Camp B-IIa. Of these 93 receive the Nos. B-7764–B-7856—one of the selected has been in Auschwitz previously and thus already has a number. 759 Jews are killed in the gas chambers.

APMO, D-Mau, Folder II, pp. 1005–1037; Folder V, p. 2601; Folder VIII, p. 3689; Folder XIII, pp. 4184, 4194, Situation Report. These prisoners are stricken from the occupancy roll of Mauthausen on Aug. 26, 1944; D-AuII-3a/40, Labor Deployment List, vol. 11.

10 female prisoners who were sent from the Yugoslavian peninsula of Istrian, near Trieste, the day before receive Nos. 87097 to 87106.

Docs. of ISD Arolsen, NA-Women, p. 12/1986.

Three Slovak Jews receive Nos. B-7857–B-7859.

138 female Jews who arrived on August 2 in an RSHA transport from the Malines and had been kept in the transit camp in Birkenau receive Nos. A-24041–A-24178.

Docs. of ISD Arolsen, NA-Women, Series A, p . 6/1986.

Six female prisoners and two female Jews sent by the Gestapo from the prison in Vienna are given Nos. 87107–87112, and A-24979 and A-24980.

---

*In a clandestine message to Teresa Lasocka the prisoner Stanisław Kłodziński notes: "The gassings continue. Today, for example, 40 cars with Jews arrived from Lodz—all went in to the gas."

308 persons from Montluc-Lyon in France arrive in an RSHA transport and are put in the transit camp in Birkenau.

The secret military council in the camp (RWO)* gives Urban** a letter for the command of the Armia Krajowa (AK), the Polish Home Army, in Silesia with exact information on the number of prisoners in Auschwitz and in the I. G. Farben works; on their own ability to fight while lacking every resource such as weapons, ammunition, explosives; and on the strength of the enemy—SS, police, army: its housing, technical equipment, arms, and morale. The letter also contains an assessment of the strategic situation and related plans for an armed insurrection—depending on how the camp management proceeds. Also discussed are the possibilities of assistance from outside, i.e., from the AK in Silesia, and the effects of developments on the Eastern Front. The plans of the RWO have a provisional character and are tightly bound up with the fate of the prisoners in the main camp, in Birkenau, and in Monowitz, for whose lives the RWO feels responsible in case of an insurrection. In this letter the RWO gives the following occupancy levels in the camps:

APMO, Mat.RO, vol. II, pp. 94–115.

Auschwitz I	15,971 male prisoners
Auschwitz II	19,424 male prisoners
Auschwitz II	39,234 female prisoners
	30,000 unregistered Hungarian Jews in the transit camp
Auschwitz III	30,539 male prisoners
Total	135,168 prisoners

It is further stated that 35,000 civilian workers—Poles, Russians, Czechs, and Germans—and approximately 1,000 English POWs are employed in building installations for the production of synthetic gas and other chemical products. The number of guards is stated to be 3,250 well-armed soldiers equipped with all technical aids, including 120 officers. 70 percent of the guards are SS Men and 30 percent members of the Wehrmacht. Antiaircraft and police units, on whom the SS could rely in the case of resistance, are also available located in the vicinity.

Finally, the letter also mentions that the plans made by the Commandant's Office in agreement with Berlin call for leaving 1,100 Poles in Auschwitz I and 900 in Birkenau in the event of an early evacuation. These figures must be seen as the minimum number of Polish prisoners that would have to remain behind, naturally only until the moment of the final evacuation. This would probably mean the sending by train or on foot the 2,000 Poles together with

*In the middle of 1944 an agreement to cooperate was made between the secret military groups in the camp and the Auschwitz Combat Group; from that arose the RWO (Rada Wojskowa Obozu—Camp Military Council) (Jarosz, "Resistance Movement in the Camp," p. 153).
**Pseudonym of Stefan Jasieński, liaison officer of the Polish Home Army, who was sent to Poland by the Government in Exile in London to place himself at the disposal of the AK high command (Sobański, *Escapes from Auschwitz*, pp. 95–102; Sobański gives the name as Stefan Jasiński).

the Germans and possibly a part of the able-bodied Jewish skilled workers.

AUGUST 23

Five prisoners sent from Kattowitz receive Nos. 192903–192907.

AUGUST 24

The Camp Commander of the Golleschau A.C., SS Staff Sergeant Mirbeth, reports to the Commandant's Office of Auschwitz III that he has transferred 28 sick prisoners who are useless in the auxiliary camp to Auschwitz II that day. In the inventory of prisoners unable to work are nine Jews who were sent to the camp in 1943, and 19 Jews who arrived between January 27 and July 1, 1944.

APMO, D-AuIII, Golleschau/12, pp. 88–90.

11 prisoners sent in a group transport receive Nos. 193037–1903047.

After the selection from among the Jews delivered in an RSHA transport from the Lodz ghetto, 17 men are admitted to the camp and given Nos. B-7860–B-7876. The young and healthy individuals are probably kept as so-called depot prisoners in Birkenau. The remaining prisoners are killed in the gas chambers.

Four Jewish boys born in Auschwitz receive Nos. A-19997–A-20000.

28 Hungarian Jews who are probably selected from the Jews kept as "depot prisoners" in Birkenau receive Nos. B-7877–B-7904.

After the selection of the Jews sent in an RSHA transport from the Lodz ghetto, 222 men are admitted to the camp and given Nos. B-7905–B-8126. Some of the young and healthy individuals are probably kept as "depot prisoners" in Birkenau. The remaining prisoners are killed in the gas chambers.

Two Jewish prisoners from Borysław receive Nos. B-8127–B-8128.

A female prisoner sent from Munich receives No. 87116.

Docs. of ISD Arolsen, NA-Women, p. 12/1986.

434 prisoners are transferred from Auschwitz I to Ravensbrück.

APMO, Mat.RO, vol. VIIId, pp. 62ff., 76–79.

AUGUST 25

Two prisoners sent from Kattowitz receive Nos. 193048 and 193049.

APMO, D-AuII-3a/41, Labor Deployment List, vol. 11.

750 Polish and Russian prisoners are transferred from Auschwitz II to the Bremen A.C., which belongs to Neuengamme. Some of the prisoners sent to Block 11 on August 14 are in the transport.

People waiting to go to the gas chamber in the Birkenau (Brzezinka) woods.

The Austrian prisoner Hermann Langbein (No. 60355), a member of the leadership of the Auschwitz Combat Group who worked as secretary to SS Garrison Doctor Wirths, is placed in the transport at the last moment.*

Three prisoners who were captured while escaping are delivered to Auschwitz II.

Ibid.

Two prisoners escape from the Monowitz A.C., which belongs to Auschwitz III: the Polish Jew Natan Gringlas (No. B-4906) and the Polish reeducation prisoner Władysław Ciupek, born on July 11, 1919, in Kraków, who was sent to the camp on August 19, 1944, by the Kattowitz Stapo.

APMO, IZ-8/Gestapo Lodz/4a/90/251, 252.

American air reconnaissance takes photographs of Auschwitz from an altitude of approximately 30,000 feet. It is given the task of photographing the grounds of the I. G. Farben chemical works near Auschwitz and to determine the damages incurred during the August 20 bombing.** At the edge of the photos are Auschwitz I and II. On a tenfold enlargement of these photographs the women's camp in Auschwitz II can be seen: the fencing, the watchtowers, the main gate to the camp with the guardroom, the railroad ramp within the camp and a freight train with 33 cars, and approximately 1,500 prisoners on their way to the gas chambers and to Crematorium II, to which the gate in the fence opens. In the photograph of Auschwitz I all camp objects can be recognized, even the prisoners

APMO, Analyses, Aerial Photos, vol. 64, pp. 50–59; Gilbert, *Auschwitz and the Allies*, p. 363.

*According to information provided by the camp resistance movement, the assignment of Hermann Langbein to the transport is by order of the Political Department and is against the will of the SS Garrison Doctor (APMO, Mat.RO, vol. II, p. 131).
**The prisoner Stanisław Klodziński writes in a secret message to Teresa Lasocka, at the Committee for Assisting Concentration Camp Prisoners (PWOK) on August 30, 1944: "In our camp the bombing had no effect, but B is properly ruined, so that production is now limited to carbide. Among the prisoners were several dead and wounded" (APMO, Mat.RO, vol. II, p. 125).

standing in a row before the registration building, who are waiting to be registered and tattooed.*

AUGUST 26

A prisoner from Verona receives the free No. 192990.

41 prisoners sent in a group transport receive Nos. 193050–193090.

18 female prisoners sent in a group transport receive Nos. 87132–87149.

AUGUST 27

31 prisoners are transferred from Auschwitz to Flossenbürg.

Docs. of ISD Arolsen, Folder 7.

AUGUST 28

The Polish Jew Józef Kluger (No. 177734), born in Krenau, who was sent to the camp on April 1, 1944, escapes from the Blechhammer A.C., which belongs to Auschwitz III.

APMO, IZ-8/Gestapo Lodz/4a/90/256.

29 prisoners sent in a group transport receive Nos. 193091–193119.

Four female prisoners sent on August 22 from Montluc-Lyon receive Nos. 87160–87163.

Docs. of ISD Arolsen, NA-Women, p. 12/1986.

A female Hungarian Jew receives No. A-24981.

Five prisoners escape from a transport on the stretch of railroad between Magdeburg and Uelzen. They are Jerzy Kubicki (No. 190006),** Wiktor Korolew (No. 187885), Wiktor Poltaradnia (No. 187886), Władysław Bukowski (No. 189775), and Stanisław Gasiniec (No. 189781).

APMO, D-AuI-1/1b, Bulletin, Sept. 15, 1944, p. 349.

AUGUST 29

Three prisoners sent from Kattowitz receive Nos. 193120–193122.

807 prisoners from Auschwitz I are transferred in a penal transport to Sachsenhausen. The remaining prisoners from a group sent to Block 11 on August 14 are in this transport.

APMO, Dpr.-Hd/12, p. 153; Dpr.-ZO/59, p. 30/ Mat.RO, vol. II, pp. 125, 131, vol. VIIId, pp. 64–67.

---

*The photographs are not analyzed during the war. They are first identified and analyzed 35 years after the war in an article by Dino A. Brugioni and Robert G. Poirier (*The Holocaust Revisited: A Retrospective Analysis of the Auschwitz-Birkenau Extermination Complex*, Washington, D.C., 1979).

**He is captured on September 8 and sent to the Penal Company in Birkenau. On September 17 he is transferred in penal transport to Mauthausen.

The Reich German prisoner Paul Kozdon, born on July 11, 1924, in Chwałowice, who was sent to Auschwitz by the Kattowitz Stapo on July 23, 1943, escapes from the Monowitz A.C.

APMO, IZ-8/Gestapo Lodz/4a/90/258, 259; D-AuI-1/1b, Bulletin, vol. 3/348.

The Jewish prisoner Abraham Salamon (No. A-15983), escapes from the Golleschau A.C., which belongs to Auschwitz III.

APMO, IZ-8/Gestapo Lodz/4a/90/260; D-AuI-1/1b, Bulletin, vol. 3/347.

25 female prisoners selected from the 72 women sent the previous day from the Leipzig-Schönefeld (HASAG) squad, Buchenwald, receive Nos. 87168–87192. The remaining women and children are killed in the gas chambers. In the transport were predominantly sick and pregnant Polish women and Jewish women with children.

Docs. of ISD Arolsen, NA-Women, p. 12/1986; Docs. of ISD Arolsen, Folder 14.

536 female prisoners—Poles, Russians, and Jews—are transferred from Auschwitz II to Ravensbrück.

Andrzej Strzelecki, *Ewakuacja, likwidacja i wyzwolenie KL Auschwitz* (Evacuation, Liquidation and Liberation of Auschwitz), Oświęcim, 1982, p. 303.

619 boys between the ages of one month and 14 years are prisoners in Auschwitz II. 187 of these are in Women's Camp B-Ia, 204 are in Men's Quarantine Camp B-IIa, 175 are in Men's Camp B-IId, four are in the Jewish Men's Camp B-IIe, and 49 twins for experimental purposes are in Infirmary Camp B-IIf.

APMO, D-AuII-3a/45, Labor Deployment List, vol. 11.

The number of prisoners in the Special Squad, which operates the gas chambers and crematoriums, is:

Ibid.

Squad 57B, Crematorium II	Days	111 prisoners, among them two specialists
	Nights	104 prisoners
Squad 58B, Crematorium III	Days	110 prisoners
	Nights	110 prisoners
Squad 59B, Crematorium IV	Days	110 prisoners, among them one specialist
	Nights	109 prisoners
Squad 60B, Crematorium V	Days	110 prisoners, among them one specialist
	Nights	110 prisoners
	Total	874 prisoners

The occupancy level in the men's camp in Auschwitz II is 17,662 men and boys under 14 years of age; 10,274 of these prisoners are employed, 3,321 are sick or unable to work, and 4,067 are without work.

Ibid.

AUGUST 30

Five prisoners sent from Kattowitz receive Nos. 193123–193127.

After the selection from among the Jews who arrive in an RSHA transport from Lodz, 75 men are admitted to the camp and given

Nos. B-8129–B-8203. Some young boys and healthy prisoners are sent to the transit camp in Birkenau. The remaining prisoners are killed in the gas chambers.

The prisoner Stanisław Kłodziński writes in a secret letter to Teresa Lasocka of PWOK: "further transports with Poles and Russians leave the camp for Germany. The gassing of Jews continues. Transports from Lodz, Holland, and Italy. The pits in which the corpses of gassing victims were burned when the crematoriums could not keep up are now covered over in order to destroy the evidence." | APMO, Mat.RO, vol. II, p. 126.

500 female Hungarian Jews are transferred from the transit camp in Birkenau to Buchenwald and sent to the labor squad of the Junkers aircraft company in Markkleeberg, near Leipzig. | Docs. of ISD Arolsen, Folders 7, 15.

A female French Jew, a physician, is transferred from the women's camp in Auschwitz II to Buchenwald. | Docs. of ISD Arolsen, Folder 15.

AUGUST 31

Two prisoners sent from Kattowitz receive the Nos. 193128 and 193247.

A prisoner sent on August 29 from Lyon receives the No. 193129.

The Jewish prisoner Natan Gringlas (No. B-4906), who escaped on August 25 from Monowitz and was captured on August 29 in Wolbrom, is sent back to Auschwitz III. | APMO, IZ-8/Gestapo Lodz/2/88/182.

SEPTEMBER 1

An RSHA transport of Jews arrives from Čadcy in Slowenia. After the selection, six men, given Nos. B-8204–B-8209, and eight women, given Nos. A-24982–A-24989, are admitted to the camp. The remaining prisoners, among them 72 men, are killed in the gas chambers. | APMO, D-AuII-3/1, p. 7, Quarantine List.

An order comes from the WVHA to the Commandant's Office of Auschwitz III to dissolve the Lagischa camp because of the halt in construction work on the planned Water Electrical Station. | APMO, D-AuIII-1, Commandant's Office Order 9/44, Sept. 6, 1944.

SEPTEMBER 2

35 prisoners sent in a group transport receive Nos. 193248–193282.

From among the Jews sent by an RSHA transport from the Lodz ghetto, 393 men are admitted to the camp and given Nos. B-8210–B-8602. The young and healthy individuals are probably sent to the transit camp in Birkenau. The remaining prisoners are killed in the gas chambers.

From among the Jews sent in an RSHA transport from the Lodz ghetto, 500 men are admitted to the camp and given Nos. B-8603–B-9102. The young and healthy individuals are sent to the transit camp in Birkenau. The remaining prisoners are killed in the gas chambers. The resistance organization in the camp states in its report for the period September 1–20 that the SS currently is gassing Jews from the Lodz ghetto and in this way is liquidating the last surviving Polish Jews.

APMO, Mat.RO, vol. VII, p . 460.

14 female prisoners sent from the prison in Budapest receive Nos. 87225–87238.

From a group transport of the RSHA and from the transit camp, 70 women are admitted to the camp as prisoners and given Nos. A-24990–A-25059.

The Polish Jew Abraham Zylbersztajn (No. 17528), born on June 12, 1912, in Olkusz, escapes from the Blechhammer A.C.

APMO, D-AuI-1/1b, Bulletin, vol. 3/348.

SEPTEMBER 3

The camp resistance movement states: "Höss has returned from Berlin. Naturally he is disseminating among the SS an anti-Polish attitude, which reaches its peak in the thesis that the Poles incarcerated in the camps should also pay for Warsaw. This is, by the way, a thesis that originates in Himmler's circle, which is, therefore, significant for all camps in Germany."

APMO, Mat.RO, vol. II, p. 130.

SEPTEMBER 4

51 prisoners sent in a group transport receive Nos. 193283–193333.

A second transport arrives from the transit camp in Pruszków, where masses of the civilian population have been imprisoned after the Warsaw uprising. In it are 1,955 men and boys who receive Nos. 193334–195288, and 1,131 women and girls, who receive Nos. 87261–88391.

APMO, D-AuII-3/1, p. 7, Quarantine List; Mat.RO, vol. VII, p. 459.

A prisoner sent from Kattawitz receives No. 195430.

The camp resistance organization sends photographs from Birkenau to the Kraków PWOK; the photographs show the incineration of corpses in the open as well as a section of forest where prisoners are to disrobe, ostensibly to bathe, but really to be sent to the gas chambers. The resistance organization also reports that the possibility of making further photographs exists, for which two rolls of film in the format 6 X 9 are urgently requested.

APMO, Mat.RO, vol. II, p. 136.

From the 43 men delivered from an RSHA transport from Vienna, five Jews are admitted to the camp and are given Nos. B-9103–B-9107. 38 men are killed in the gas chambers.

APMO, D-AuII-3/1, p. 7, Quarantine List.

SEPTEMBER 5

141 prisoners from The Hague receive Nos. 195289–195429.

1,019 Jews arrive from Westerbork camp in an RSHA transport from Holland. There were 498 men, 442 women, and 79 children in the transport. After the selection, 258 men, given Nos. B-9108–B-9365, and 212 women, given Nos. A-25060–A-25271, are admitted as prisoners to the camp. The remaining 549 prisoners are killed in the gas chambers. Anne Frank (the author of the famous diaries), her mother, Edith, her father, Otto, and her sister, Margot, arrive in Birkenau with this transport. Otto Frank, who receives No. B-9174, is freed from the camp on January 27, 1945. The mother does not survive to witness the liberation and dies in January 1945 in Auschwitz. Margot and Anne Frank are transferred from Auschwitz to Bergen-Belsen. Margot dies first, and on March 31, 1945, Anne Frank dies there.

Kempner, *Edith Stein and Anne Frank*, pp. 60–63.

37 female prisoners from Westerbork receive Nos. 88397–88433.

Docs. of ISD Arolsen, NA-Women, p. 12/1986.

33 prisoners sent in a group transport receive the Nos. 195431–195463.

32 French Jews, also some Belgian citizens, who were selected from an RSHA transport from Lyon receive Nos. 195464–195495. This transport, in which there were 103 men, was probably held up in Saarbrücken. The remaining 71 men are killed in the gas chambers.

APMO, D-AuII-3/1, p. 7, Quarantine List.

Five Hungarian Jews receive Nos. B-9366–B-9370.

A male Slovak Jew receives No. B-9371 and two female Slovak Jews are given Nos. A-25272 and A-25273. They were delivered from Čadca.

18 female prisoners from France receive Nos. 88457–88474. Possibly they are part of the transport from Lyon that traveled via Saarbrücken.

Docs. of ISD Arolsen, NA-Women, p. 12/1986.

SEPTEMBER 6

With the request to direct the information to London, the camp resistance movement notifies Teresa Lasocka of PWOK that the former Commandant in Auschwitz, SS First Lieutenant Höss, who had just directed the operation for the annihilation of Hungarian Jews, has received a special new mission from Himmler. Höss had asked several SS leaders what technical possibilities exist to completely liquidate the Birkenau camp, in which the gas chambers and the crematoriums are located. He has asked the Commandant of Auschwitz II and Crematoriums Director Moll, among others, how one could conduct an operation in which all traces of persons, barracks, and, above all, of the gas chambers and crematoriums could be eliminated and the area quickly leveled. Moll has showed

APMO, Mat.RO, vol. II, p. 140. The Kraków underground publication *Kurier Powszechny* (General Courier) published this information in its Oct. 14, 1944, issue (vol. I, no. 13).

himself to be prepared to carry out such an operation, on condition that he receives motorized SS units, artillery to bombard and destroy the barracks, six bombers, and a sufficient number of people to bring the grounds into order and give him the appearance of innocence.

A Gypsy is transferred from Auschwitz I to Buchenwald.

Docs. of ISD Arolsen, Folder 13.

Commandant Schwarz of Auschwitz III informs the SS guards that in connection with the discontinuation of the construction of the Water Power Station the Lagischa auxiliary camp is to be dissolved* and the SS guard units are to take over security operations in the Neustadt auxiliary camp, which is under construction.

APMO, D-AuIII-1/66, Commandant's Office Order 9/44, Sept. 6, 1944.

The following SS men receive commendations from Commandant Schwarz of Auschwitz III: SS Corporal Wilhelm Haefner of the 1st Company, SS Private First Class Ferdinard Ohlschläger of the 3rd Company, and SS Lieutenant Stefan Hummel and SS Lieutenant Josef Kleinfelder of the 4th Company. Special thanks were expressed to the camp director of the Trzebinia secondary camp SS Corporal Wilhelm Kowol for his courageous and farsighted response during a terrorist attack on the Trzebinia auxiliary camp.**

Ibid.

The prisoner Andrei Dryhailo (No. 175131), who escaped from the Gleiwitz I A.C. on June 22, 1944, is sent to the Penal Company in Birkenau. He is transferred to Mauthausen on September 17 in a penal transport.

APMO, D-AuI-3/1, p. 25, Penal Company Register.

Four Russian prisoners escape from the Sosnowitz A.C., which belongs to Auschwitz III: Sasha Minski, Vladimir Potapov, Nikolai Korolkov (No. 179634), and Hryhori Siyev—actually, Hawrił Nikiszyn—(No. 174277). The escapees wear civilian clothing. At 11:30 P.M. Sasha Minski stumbles in front of the gate, and his cap falls off. Because of his shorn head the guard recognizes him to be a prisoner and shoots him to death. The others escape; in the area of Wolbromia and Pilica they meet a Polish-Soviet partisan group in whose ranks they fight until the arrival of the Red Army.

APMO, D-AuI-1/1b, Bulletin, vol. 3/354; here the names of only two escapees are given, Hrihoryi Siyev (No. 174277) and Nikolai Korolkov (No. 179634); Depositions, Account of Former Prisoner Hawrił Nikiszyn.

Eight Russian prisoners are sent to the Penal Company in Birkenau, most of whom were captured during escape attempts. They are transferred to Mauthausen on September 17 by penal transport.

APMO, D-AuI-3/1, p. 25, Penal Company Register.

SEPTEMBER 7

200 prisoners are transferred from Auschwitz II to Flossenbürg—Herzbruck A.C.

APMO, D-AuIII-3a/46, Labor Deployment List, vol. 11.

18,708 men are in Camps B-IIa, B-IId, B-IIe, and B-IIf of Auschwitz II. 10,356 of them are employed, 3,139 are sick and unable to

Ibid.

---

*The prisoners from the Lagischa A.C. are transferred to the Neu-Dachs A.C. in Jaworzno.
**The exact circumstances of this event have not yet been determined.

work, and 5,213 are without work. Among those unable to work, 189 boys between the ages of one month and 14 years are in Women's Camp B-Ia, 198 are in Camp B-IIa, 175 are in Camp B-IId, and four are in Camp B-IIe. Among those unable to work are also 133 invalids in Camp B-IId and 49 twins and 82 men for experimental purposes in the prisoners' infirmary for men, B-IIf.

Six prisoners sent from Kattowitz receive Nos. 193130–103135.

247 Jews from the Lodz ghetto who were kept as so-called depot prisoners in the transit camp in Birkenau receive Nos. B-9372 to B-9618.

Three Hungarian Jews who were kept as "depot prisoners" in the transit camp in Birkenau receive Nos. B-9619–B-9621.

Four female Jews sent from Vienna receive Nos. A-25274–A-25277.

117 male Jews and 63 female Jews who left Montluc-Lyon on August 11 in an RSHA transport, arrived at Auschwitz on August 22, and were sent to the transit camp are registered as occupants of Auschwitz II. The male Jews registered receive the Nos. B-9622–B-9738 and the female Jews, Nos. A-25278–A-25340.

Docs. of ISD Arolsen, NA-Women, Series A, p. 7/1986.

Of the 69 Jews who arrive in an RSHA transport from Trieste, 13 are admitted to the camp as prisoners and are given Nos. B-9739–B-9751. The remaining 56 men are killed in the gas chambers.

APMO, D-AuII-3/1, p. 7, Quarantine List.

15 male Jews, given Nos. B-9752–B-9766, and 15 female Jews, given Nos. A-25341–A-25355, were selected from the fifty-seventh RSHA East-transport from Berlin. The remaining people, among them 39 men, are killed in the gas chambers.

Ibid.

63 female prisoners sent to Auschwitz by the Trieste Sipo and SD receive Nos. 88479–88541.

38 female prisoners sent in a group transport receive Nos. 88556–88593.

Docs. of ISD Arolsen, NA-Women, p. 13/1986.

Three female prisoners—two female physicians and a nurse—are transferred from the women's camp in Auschwitz II to the Leipzig-Schönefeld (HASAG company) squad in Buchenwald.

Ibid., Folder 7.

120 prisoners, Poles and Russians, are transferred from Auschwitz I to Buchenwald.

Ibid., Folder 13.

SEPTEMBER 8

The secret Camp Military Council (RWO) answers the additional questions of the liaison man, Urban, of the Silesian unit of the AK. The information contains data on:

APMO, Mat.RO, vol. II, pp. 147–151.

1. Strength and role of the dog squadron
2. Antiaircraft strength
3. Quarters of the Wehrmacht in the vicinity
4. Alarm system
5. Air alarm—assault equipment
6. Arms of the guards
7. Patrols
8. Smoke screens
9. Depots of the SS: foodstuff and uniforms

In addition the number of SS men and the functions of the permanent SS guard units are given:

Auschwitz concentration camp I:	1,119 SS men
Auschwitz concentration camp II:	908 SS men
Auschwitz concentration camp III:	1,315 SS men
Buna:	439 SS men
Other camps:	876 SS men
Total	3,342 SS men

In conclusion it is emphasized that the source of these statistics is easy to figure out and that therefore care must be taken with them. In addition to the permanent SS guard units there are also Wehrmacht units. In case of any "action," the numbers to bear in mind are 1,119 and 908, that is, a total of 2,027 SS men, the number of guards in Auschwitz I and II, which together make up one whole entity.*

28 prisoners sent in a group transport receive Nos. 193136–193163.

Four prisoners sent from Kattowitz receive Nos. 193164–193167.

50 Jews from the Lodz ghetto who were kept as "depot prisoners" in the transit camp in Birkenau receive Nos. B-9767–B-9816.

216 Jews who were sent from the Lodz ghetto and kept as "depot prisoners" in the transit camp in Birkenau receive Nos. B-9817–B-10032.

39 Jews who were sent to Auschwitz on August 22 in an RSHA transport from Montluc-Lyon receive Nos. B-10033–B-10071

Docs. of ISD Arolsen, NA-Men, Series B.

SS men begin wildly shooting in Men's Quarantine Camp B-IIa in order to terrorize those deported from Warsaw who were delivered to the camp on September 4 from Pruszków. The following five prisoners are seriously injured in the shooting: Zenon Wierzbicki (No. 193809), Wiesław Wagner (No. 194053), Kazimierz Bor-

APMO, Dpr.-HD/6, p. 60.

*These data are related to preparations for a possible armed uprising, in case the camps are threatened by the SS, the situation on the front is favorable, and assistance from outside is guaranteed. The information is signed by "Rot," one of the pseudonyms of prisoner Józef Cyrankiewicz.

kowski (No. 193352), Wincenty Petkowicz (No. 194419), and Józef Juszcyk (No. 193539).

Nos. 88600–88952 are given to 53 female prisoners who were sent to Auschwitz by order of the Trieste Sipo and SD.

Docs. of ISD Arolsen, NA-Women, p. 13/1986.

A Russian POW and four prisoners are sent to the Penal Company in Birkenau.

APMO, D-AuI-3/1, p. 25, Penal Company Register.

SEPTEMBER 9

Five Polish prisoners escape from Auschwitz I: Stanisław Maliński (No. 69), Stanisław Furdyna (No. 193), Antoni Wykrcęt (No. 613), Henryk Kwiatkowski (No. 3002), and Stanisław Zakrzewski (No. 118410). The escaped prisoners strengthen the ranks of the Armia Krajowa fighters in the camps near Auschwitz under the command of Jan Wawrzyczka, whose pseudonyms are "Danuta" and "Marusza." They take in further prisoners from the camp.*

APMO, Depositions, vol. 4, pp. 503–507, Account of Former Prisoner Stanisław Maliński and Stanisław Zakrzewski; Mat.RO, vol. II, p. 153: The secret message, signed by Józef Cyrankiewicz, suggests that the escapees be sent to the partisans in the forest.

Nine prisoners sent in a group transport receive Nos. 193168–193176.

12 prisoners sent from Radom by the Sipo and SD receive Nos. 193177–193188.

A prisoner sent from Berlin receives No. 193189.

A prisoner sent from Cologne receives No. 193190.

SEPTEMBER 11

Two female Jews, a physician and a nurse, are transferred from Auschwitz II to the Essen auxiliary camp of Buchenwald.

Docs. of ISD Arolsen, Folder 7.

598 male and female prisoners are transferred from Stutthof. After the selection two men are admitted to the camp as prisoners and are given Nos. 193191–193192. The remaining 596 prisoners are probably killed in the gas chambers.

APMO, Mat.Ref.Inf., Prisoner Card Index.

23 prisoners sent in a group transport receive Nos. 193193–193215.

A prisoner sent from Kattowitz receives No. 193216.

Two Russian prisoners escape from the Sosnowitz A.C. of Auschwitz III. They are Ivan Terno (No. 173924) and Vasyli Lubimov (No. 174433).

APMO, D-AuI-1/1b, Bulletin, vol. 3/358.

Two Russian prisoners escape from Auschwitz III: Viktor Antonov (No. 173922) and Dmitri Podbira (No. 175135).

Ibid.

*Stanisław Furdyna dies on December 3, 1944, during a battle with the SS.

Kazimierz Szwemberg (No. 62760), who works in a mine squad, escapes from the Jawischowitz A.C. during the nightly shift change. The escape was prepared with the cooperation of the Jawischowitz A.C. resistance group and of the members of the Polish resistance in compounds near the camp.

Ibid., Sobański, *Escapes from Auschwitz*, pp. 137–142.

SEPTEMBER 12

100 female prisoners, Hungarian Jews and a Russian, are transferred from Auschwitz II to Flossenbürg.

Docs. of ISD Arolsen, Folder 7.

Three prisoners sent from Kattowitz receive Nos. 193217–193219.

16 prisoners sent to the camp by the Budapest Sipo and SD receive Nos. 193220–193235.

300 Jewish children from the area around Kaunas arrive in an RSHA transport. They are killed in the gas chambers on the same day.*

APMO, Mat.RO, vol. VII, p. 460.

The Labor Deployment Department in Auschwitz II completes a list of specialists among the prisoners who were destined for the railroad construction brigade, a kind of mobile auxiliary camp in a refitted freight train. The prisoners are to work in the interior of the Reich on repairing tracks and clearing rubble from bombed railway stations and cities. A number of prisoners from the Penal Company in Birkenau are sent to the railroad construction train.

APMO, D-AuI-3/1, Penal Company Register; Ryszard Krosnowski and Aleksander Miziewicz, "7. SS-Eisenbahnbaubrigade" (The 7th Railroad Construction Brigade), ZO, no. 5 (1961): 41–50.

The Polish political prisoner Reinhold Puchała (No. 1172), who works as an electrician in the construction of a barracks for the Silesian construction inspection office in Kattowitz, informs Kazimierz Smoleń (No. 1327), also a Polish political prisoner who is employed in the Admissions Office squad, that he has the opportunity to smuggle out of the camp a small package with documents, for example, on prisoners. On the construction compound Puchała is able to meet with his sister, who could bring the package to the given address.

APMO, Dpr.-Hd/4, p. 75; Depositions, vol. 76, p. 183, Account of Former Prisoner Kazimierz Smoleń.

SEPTEMBER 13

Five prisoners sent in a group transport receive Nos. 193236–193240.

A boy born on September 12 in the Birkenau women's camp receives No. 193241. The mother was sent from Warsaw.

The third transport arrives with civilians from the Pruszków transit camp; people are being arrested and sent there in droves since the outbreak of the Warsaw uprising. 929 men and boys, given Nos.

APMO, Mat.RO, vol. VII, p. 459; D-AuII-3/1, p. 7, Quarantine List.

*The camp resistance organization adds the following: ". . . Despite all evacuation plans, transports with Jews from the East and recently from France, Belgium, and Holland continue to arrive."

195496–196424, and approximately 900 women and girls arrive with the transport.*

The I. G. Farben works in Dwory near Auschwitz are bombed for thirteen minutes, from 11:17 to 11:30 A.M. The squadron, which consists of 96 bombers of the model Liberator, encounters no German airplanes but is met by a strong artillery defense, which shoots down three bombers. Just as in the case of the air attacks conducted previously, again no attempt is made to destroy the extermination installations in Birkenau.

APMO, Mat.RO, vol. VII, p. 460; Gilbert, *Auschwitz and the Allies*, pp. 370ff.; Škodowa, *Three Years*, pp. 159ff.; Czesław Wicenty Jaworski, *Memories of Auschwitz*, p. 258.

The airplane squadron drops 1,000 bombs from an altitude of about 23,000 feet. Several fall on the compound of Auschwitz I. In the camp expansion area, four residential blocks of the SS, the clothing workshops, and half of Block 6—where female prisoners who work in the SS offices in the main camp live—are destroyed. 15 SS men die in the SS residential blocks and 28 are seriously wounded. In Block 6, a female prisoner is killed and many are injured. 40 prisoners, 23 Jews among them, are killed in the workshops: 55 are seriously injured and 13 are still buried in the rubble. Two bombs fall in Auschwitz II. One damages the railroad embankment and the connecting track to the crematoriums; the second destroys a dugout between the tracks, killing 30 civilian workers.

The bombs cause property damage in the I. G. Farben works by destroying part of the factory installations. The number of those killed and injured is approximately 300, among them prisoners who work there.

Aerial photographs are made of Auschwitz during the bombing. For the first time high-quality photographs are made in which Auschwitz I and II can be seen. In the opinion of Brugioni and Poirier, a train consisting of 65 freight cars can be seen standing on the railroad tracks in Birkenau; there is a column of approximately 1,500 persons on the camp street that leads in a north-south direction. The gas chambers and Crematorium IV are in operation and the gate leading there is open. That is the probable destination of the newly arrived prisoners.

APMO, Analyses, vol. 64, pp. 153–154; Brugioni and Poirier, *Holocaust Revisited*.

The prisoners employed in the Admissions Office squad in the Political Department decide—on the suggestion of the prisoner Reinhold Puchała—to put together registers of the prisoner transports. This task is carried out by the prisoners Piotr Datko (No. 22312), Lucjan Rajewski (No. 4217), Kazimierz Smoleń (No. 1327), Tadeusz Szymański (No. 20034), and Tadeusz Wasowicz (No. 20035). The registers are handwritten copies of originals of the arrivals lists, which are stored in the Admissions Office. These registers contain the transport's arrival date and the number, an abbreviation of the location of the agency or office that sent the prisoner, and perhaps the type of transport, e.g., group transport, RSHA transport, etc.

APMO, Dpr.-Hd/4, p. 56, 81; Depositions, vol. 76, pp. 183ff., Account of Former Prisoner Kazimierz Smoleń.

*The men are put in Quarantine Camp B-IIa and the women in the former Theresienstadt Family Camp, B-IId.

The inventories are made secretly in the office, and strict precautions are observed so that the SS guards don't notice anything. Fellow prisoners who work in the registration office are initiated into this clandestine work.

SEPTEMBER 14

The prisoners wounded the previous day during the American air attack receive flowers, milk, a double portion of margarine, etc. during a visit by the Commandant to the prisoners' infirmary. Of course this one-time gesture has the character of propaganda and therefore takes place in the presence of many photo-reporters.

APMO, Dpr.-Hd/4, p. 146.

524 prisoners are transferred from Auschwitz to Flossenbürg.

Docs. of ISD Arolsen, Folder 7.

Five prisoners sent from Kattowitz receive Nos. 193242–193246.

The camp resistance movement states in a clandestine letter to Teresa Lasocka and Edward Hałoń, of PWOK, that 9,279 men, women, and children from the civilian population in rebellious Warsaw have been arrested and sent to Auschwitz via the Pruszków transit camp. The men are sent to the interior of the Reich to work in the armaments industry and the women are sent to work in agriculture.

APMO, Mat.RO, vol. II, p. 157.

A female Jew from Teschen receives No. A-25356.

Five prisoners sent from Kattowitz receive Nos. 196425–196429.

SEPTEMBER 15

Two prisoners sent from Kattowitz receive Nos. 196430–196431.

101 Hungarian Jews selected from among the Jews kept as "depot prisoners" in the transit camp in Birkenau receive Nos. B-10072–B-10172.

97 Jews who arrived in an RSHA transport from the Lodz ghetto and who were kept in the transit camp in Birkenau as "depot prisoners" receive Nos. B-10173–B-10269.

The Polish prisoner Józef Jasiński (No. 87026),* born on February 23, 1917, is publicly hanged in Auschwitz II in Camp B-IId. Jasiński was sent twice to the Penal Company: the first time on April 17, 1944, after which he was released again to the camp on April 22, 1944; the second time on June 8, 1944, this time for 12 months. Labor Deployment sent him to the construction train squad. The Political Department probably did not consent to this, for he was condemned to death for sending a letter in which he described the

APMO, Mat.RO, vol. II, p. 161; vol. VII, p. 477; D-AuI-3/1, pp. 19, 21, Penal Company Register; Depositions, vol. 13, p. 78, Account of Former Prisoner Tadeusz Joachimowski; IZ-8/ Gestapo Lodz/4a/90/157.

*The execution date probably applies only to Józef Jasiński, since the day of the other executions cannot be determined.

conditions in Auschwitz and Flossenbürg. The judgment was read before his execution. According to the judicial opinion the letter could damage the good reputation of the government of the German Reich if it fell into the hands of the enemy's secret service. Besides Jasiński, three other prisoners are publicly hanged.

Mieczysław Borek (No. 763) was born on March 23, 1922. In the main camp he had the function of assistant to the caretaker of Block 11, but he was also frequently employed as translator for SS men. This gave him the opportunity to listen to the radio and to pass the news so gained on to fellow prisoners. In 1944 he was transferred to Birkenau. He was interrogated by the Political Department for listening to the radio in Block 11 and disseminating the news he heard, and was sent, together with Józef Jasiński, to the Penal Company on June 8, 1944. After being released to the camp on July 22, 1944, he exercised the function in August and September of the Block Senior in Transit Camp B-IIe. Fellow prisoners wanted to help him escape from the camp, but he did not take advantage of this. In September he is sent from Camp B-IIe to Camp B-IId and hanged there for listening to radio broadcasts.

Edward Galiński (No. 531), born on October 5, 1923, is hanged in punishment for the escape from the camp with the female Jew Mala Zimetbaum (No. 19880).*

Lucjan Adamiec,** Mikolai Andreyev, and Ivan Rudenko are hanged in punishment for an escape attempt from the camp.

The Jewish prisoner Moses Jakubowitz (No. 177540) escapes from the Blechhammer A.C., which belongs to Auschwitz III.

APMO, D-AuI-1/1b, Bulletin, vol. 3/352.

A new auxiliary camp called Althammer Labor Camp, which belongs to Auschwitz III, is being constructed in Stara Kuźnia near Halemba. The first group of 30 prisoners prepares the grounds and the already existing barracks for the next prisoner transports. The average number of residents in the auxiliary camp is 500. They were deployed in the construction of the heat power works in Stara Kuźnia.

Aleksander Drozdzyński, "Mafy spokojny obóz" (A Small, Quiet Camp), ZO, no. 8 (1964): pp. 35–52; Franciszek Piper, "Das Nebenlager Althammer" (Althammer Auxiliary Camp), HvA, no. 13 (1971): 141–158.

*Edward Galiński and Mala Zimetbaum escaped from the camp in Birkenau on June 24, 1944. They were captured on July 6, 1944, sent to Auschwitz, and incarcerated in the bunker of Block 11. After a long interrogation and probably after waiting for confirmation of the judgment by Himmler, they are transferred to Birkenau to be publicly executed there. According to Tomasz Sobański and Wiesław Kielar the executions take place simultaneously, Mala Zimetbaum's in Women's Camp B-Ia and Edward Galiński's in Men's Camp B-IId. Mala Zimetbaum succeeds in preventing the execution. While the sentence is being read she slits her wrists and hits SS man Ruitters, who attempts to stop her, in the face with her bleeding hands. The execution was interrupted. Mala Zimetbaum is taken in a cart to the prisoners' infirmary to stop the bleeding so that the execution can proceed. According to reports by several female prisoners, she dies on the way to the crematorium. According to other reports she is shot to death in front of the crematorium. Edward Galiński does not succeed in spoiling the execution. He is immobilized when he kicks the stool away from under him with the words "Poland lives!" while the sentence is being read. The execution by hanging is carried out. The intended terrorization of the prisoners by means of these public executions elicits the opposite effect—admiration and respect (Justa, *From Mire and Stone*, pp. 162, 163; Kielav, *Anus Mundi*).
**Compare the entry on February 18, 1944. According to the entry in the Death Register of Auschwitz III, Lucjan Adamiec (No. 124001) is hanged on September 11, 1944.

SEPTEMBER 16

10 prisoners sent in a group transport receive Nos. 196432–196441.

A prisoner from Warsaw receives No. 196442.

Five prisoners sent in a group transport receive Nos. 196443–196447.

979 prisoners, Poles sent to the camp after the outbreak of the Warsaw uprising, are transferred from Auschwitz to Flossenbürg.

Docs. of ISD Arolsen, Folder 7.

SEPTEMBER 17

1,824 prisoners, among them 1,396 Poles, are transferred from Auschwitz to Mauthausen. In this transport are prisoners who were sent to the Penal Company in Birkenau between July and September 1944. The transport reaches Mauthausen on September 19.

APMO, D-Mau, Folder III, p. 1297, Report of Registration Change, Sept. 19, 1944.

The fourth transport of civilians arrested since the outbreak of the Warsaw uprising arrives from the Pruszków transit camp. In this transport are 3,021 men and boys, who receive Nos. 196448–199468. They are put in Quarantine Camp B-IIa.

APMO, D-AuII-3/1, p. 7, Quarantine List.

The SS guard units begin a wild shootout in Men's Quarantine Camp B-IIa in Birkenau, thus repeating their terror operation against the prisoners from Warsaw. The following Polish prisoners are seriously wounded: Jan Strinkowski (No. 196061), Leonard Kaligowski (No. 196312), Mieczysław Gawroński (No. 195644), Józef Hnick (No. 194834), Tadeusz Boliński (No. 193343), Jan Wdowiak (No. 193519), Wojciech Wojak (No. 193910), Franciszek Salorski (No. 194946), and Edward Kempiński (No. 196689). Wiktor Molak (No. 199468) is shot to death.

APMO, Dpr.-Hd/6, p. 60.

Two prisoners sent in a group transport receive Nos. 199469 and 199470.

SEPTEMBER 18

SS Camp Commander Mirbeth of Golleschau A.C. reports to the Commandant's Office of Auschwitz III that on this day he transferred 10 prisoners—nine Jews, and a Pole—to Auschwitz II. Among those transferred is the deceased Paul Gabor (No. B-5742). The occupancy level in Golleschau A.C. decreases to 886 prisoners.

APMO, D-AuIII, Golleschau/12, p. 93.

Three prisoners from Kattowitz receive Nos. 199471–199473.

A prisoner from Breslau receives No. 199474.

Three prisoners transferred from Gross-Rosen receive Nos. 199475–199477.

A good dozen prisoners are taken from Block 11 of the main camp to the gas chambers in Birkenau. The prisoners had been condemned to death by the Police Court-martial of the Kattowitz Gestapo. Among those condemned is Wacław Stacherski, pseudonym "Nowina," the AK commander in chief for Silesia who was arrested in Kattowitz on March 24, 1944.

APMO, Mat.RO, vol. IX, pp. 13a, 14, Secret Message of Former Prisoner Bernard Świerczyna.

Five prisoners sent from Kattowitz receive Nos. 199478–199482.

37 prisoners sent to the camp by the Radom Sipo and SD receive Nos. 199483–199519.

A mobile auxiliary camp, a so-called construction train called the 2nd SS Railroad Construction Brigade, is formed. 505 prisoners from Auschwitz I are destined for this train, whose commanding officer is SS First Lieutenant Schäfer. The construction train departs for Karlsruhe in Silesia with the prisoners. They are to be deployed in railroad repair projects and in clearing rubble from bombed train stations and cities. The employer is Branch C in the WVHA.

APMO, D-AuII-3/3, Inventory No. 47253, Documents of Railroad Brigade.

The leadership of the Auschwitz Combat Group develops a thesis regarding the political aims of the Nazi publicity relating to bomb attacks on concentration camps. On the one hand, they study the account of the bombing of the town of Auschwitz* published in an armed forces report and the news circulated widely in the German press of an Allied air attack on Buchenwald, during which the German labor leader, Communist, and longtime concentration camp prisoner Ernst Thälmann dies.** On the other hand, they note the denials on English radio that the Buchenwald concentration camp had ever been bombed by the Allies. The leadership of the Auschwitz Combat Group comes to the conclusion that the objective of the German reports is to mislead public opinion and to distract attention from the Nazis' plans to bomb Auschwitz-Birkenau and other extermination camps themselves in order to get rid of them. For this reason the Combat Group turns to PWOK with the request to send on to London via radio the information on German plans to liquidate Auschwitz that has already been communicated.

APMO, Mat.RO, vol. II, p. 161; Józef Cyrankiewicz and Stanisław Kłodziński signed the secret message.

An RSHA transport with 2,500 Jews arrives from the Lodz ghetto. After the selection 150 men are admitted to the camp and given Nos. B-10270–B-10419. Up to 80 percent of the transport consists of children between 13 and 16 years of age. The remaining 2,350 persons were killed in the gas chambers.

APMO, Mat.RO, vol. VII, p. 477.

468 prisoners are transferred from Auschwitz I to Flossenbürg.

APMO, Mat.RO, vol. VIII.

1,000 female prisoners, predominantly female Hungarian Jews, are transferred from the transit camp in Birkenau to the Hessisch-Lichtenau labor squad, Buchenwald.

Docs. of ISD Arolsen, Folder 15.

*The objective of the attack was not the town of Auschwitz, but rather the I. G. Farben works in Dwory, near Auschwitz.
**Ernst Thälmann was murdered on August 18, 1944.

On the second day of the Jewish celebration Rosh Hashanah the SS Doctors conduct a selection in the prisoners' infirmaries. 330 Jews from Men's Quarantine Camp B-IIa and 65 boys from Kaunas in the men's prisoners' infirmary, Camp B-IIf, who were delivered to the camp on August 1, are selected. They are killed the same day in the gas chambers.

APMO, Dpr.-Hd/6, pp. 8, 11, 50.

1,300 prisoners, among them 698 Poles, are transferred to Mauthausen. They are registered in the Camp Occupancy Register of Mauthausen on September 20, 1944.

APMO, D-Mau, Folder III, p. 1302, Report of Registration Change, Sept. 20, 1944.

SEPTEMBER 19

Approximately 200 prisoners from Auschwitz are deployed in the Charlottengrube in Rydułtowy and set up the Charlottengrube auxiliary camp, which belongs to Auschwitz III. In November the occupancy level of the Charlottengrube A.C. is more than 900 prisoners, who are deployed mining coal and constructing a mine. During the war the mine belongs to the Hermann Göring Works.*

Pszczyna State Archive, Rybnik Repository, Documents of the District Office of Mines, Rybnik, 1654, p. 316; Andrzej Strzelecki, "Das Nebenlager Charlottengrube in Rudołtowy" (Charlottengrube Auxiliary Camp in Rudołtowy), *HvA*, no. 17 (1985): 41–90.

200 female Hungarian Jews are transferred from Auschwitz II to the Lebau A.C. of Gross-Rosen. In Gross-Rosen they receive Nos. 59801–60000.

APMO, D-Gr-3/10, Correspondence IV-8522/983/82.

SEPTEMBER 20

Two prisoners are sent from Dachau. They receive Nos. 199520 and 199521.

From the 60 Jews who arrive in an RSHA transport from Budapest, eight men are admitted to the camp and are given Nos. 199522–199529. The remaining 52 men are killed in the gas chambers.

APMO, D-AuII-3/1, p. 8, Quarantine List.

From the 177 Jews who arrive in an RSHA transport from Slovakia, 31 men are admitted to the camp and given Nos. B-10423–B-10453. The remaining 146 persons are killed in the gas chambers.

Ibid.

22 female Hungarian Jews who were transferred from the transit camp in Birkenau to Women's Camp B-Ia receive Nos. A-25357–25378.**

A boy born on September 17, 1944, in Auschwitz II receives No. 199530. The mother was sent to the camp from Vienna.

A boy born on September 18, 1944, in Auschwitz II receives No. 199531.† The mother was sent to the camp from Minsk.

*A giant concern established to produce steel out of low-grade ore, as part of Göring's Four-Year Plan to make Germany economically self-sufficient.
**This is the last entry in the Register of Jewish Women's Transports, Series A, which was prepared illegally by Polish prisoners employed in the admissions office of the Political Department.
†This is the last entry in the Register of Men's Transports, which was prepared secretly by political prisoners who were employed in the admissions office of the Political Department.

A female prisoner who was transferred from Block 11 of the main camp to the women's camp of Auschwitz II receives No. 88710.

Docs. of ISD Arolsen, NA-Women, p. 13/1986.

25 female prisoners sent from the prisons in Olkusz and Tschenstochau receive Nos. 88712–88736.

Ibid.

671 prisoners, Poles and a Frenchman, are transferred from Auschwitz to Mauthausen. They are entered in the Occupancy Register of Mauthausen on September 22.

APMO, D-Mau, Folder III, p. 1308, Report of Registration Change, Sept. 22, 1944.

The crematorium management in Auschwitz II receives the shovels and fencing they ordered from the DAW on May 31. The cost for the shovels is 42.40 RM (four @ 10.60 RM) and for the fencing 210 RM (five @ 42 RM).

APMO, IZ-13/89, Various Documents of the Third Reich, p. 198.

SEPTEMBER 21

The prisoners Piotr Datko, Lucjan Rajewski, Kazimierz Smoleń, Tadeusz Szymański, and Tadeusz Wascowitz of the admissions office squad interrupt their secret work on the registers of the male and female prisoners admitted to the camp, since these registers must be given to the prisoner Reinhold Puchała, who is to leave on September 22 to work on the barracks for the construction inspection office in Kattowitz. They succeed in updating all the registers to September 21, 1944, except the one for female prisoners from the general number series.

APMO, Dpr.-Hd/4, p. 81; D-RO/123, vol. 20b, vol. 20c, Admissions Rolls.

The preparation of the technical plans for the refitting of Crematorium I (the so-called old crematorium) in Auschwitz I to an air-raid bunker for the SS hospital is completed. The plan is called "Expansion of the Old Crematorium, Air-Raid Bunker for SS Hospital with an Operating Room"* and is dated September 21, 1944.

APMO, D-AuI-Z.Bau/BW 11/5.

23 Jewish prisoners sent in an RSHA transport from Hungary and kept in the transit camp in Birkenau as "depot prisoners" receive Nos. B-10454 and B-10481.**

In the evening Kazimierz Smoleń (No. 1327) turns over to his fellow prisoner Reinhold Puchała (No. 1172) a small package containing secretly prepared registers of the male and female prisoners arriving at Auschwitz between May 20, 1940, and September 21, 1944. The package is to be given to Puchała's sister, with whom Reinhold Puchała was able to meet secretly, to Smoleń's mother, Helena Smoleń in Königshütte. The prisoners Tadeusz Wasowicz, Lucjan Rajewski, Tadeuz Szymański, and Jan Trebaczowski know the documents are being handed over and know the address of the recipient. The reason so many fellow prisoners are initiated into this operation

APMO, Dpr.-Hd/4, p. 75, 81; Depositions, vol. 75, p. 184.

*The renovation of Crematorium I was begun in April 1944 (APMO, Mat.RO, vol. VII, p. 433).
**This is the last entry in the Register of Male Jewish Transports, Series B, which was clandestinely prepared by Polish prisoners employed in the admissions office of the Political Department.

is to ensure that someone would survive the war and retrieve the documents, which verify the number of prisoners registered in the camp and the data on the transports, in order to present them as evidence in possible trials of the camp management.*

Another auxiliary camp called Tschechowitz-Vacuum Labor Camp is established in Tschechowitz and becomes part of Auschwitz III. Approximately 300 Polish Jews sent to Auschwitz III in the last RSHA transport from the Lodz ghetto are housed there. The prisoners are deployed in the breaking up of bomb targets, but also in masonry, cement, and excavation projects as well as in putting into operation the tracks and roads on the refinery grounds.

Strzelecka et al., "Tschechowitz," pp. 199–222.

SEPTEMBER 23

Some of the female Jews sent on August 6, 1944, from the Płaszów camp to Auschwitz II are transferred from the transit camp in Birkenau to Stutthof.

Documents and Materials, vol. I, p. 63.

Two Polish prisoners, Marian Batkowski (No. 428) and Stanisław Oszamniec (No. 109316), escape from the Lagischa A.C., which belongs to Auschwitz III.**

APMO, D-AuI-1/1b, Bulletin, vol. 3/356.

30 female prisoners sent to the camp by the Trieste Sipo and SD receive Nos. 88740–88769.

Docs. of ISD Arolsen, NA-Women, p. 13/1986.

At 10:15 P.M. the head of the decoding office of the Polish Government in Exile in London deciphers the telegram of September 23, which was sent over the secret Polish transmitter, and which contains the following statement: "We have received the news that the Germans plan the liquidation of Auschwitz and Buchenwald. Auschwitz Commandant Höss, a confidant of Himmler's, has asked various SS leaders for suggestions concerning the liquidation of the camp and all persons. At present there are 16,727 men and 39,125 women in Birkenau. Commandant Moll† of Birkenau has come forward with a suggestion whose realization requires motorized SS units, artillery for shelling the blocks, and bombers, as well as an appropriate number of people for grading the grounds."††

APMO, RO/21, Microfilm No. 648/21.

200 Jewish prisoners in the Special Squad who are deployed to incinerate corpses in open pits are removed—after the trenches are covered and graded—with the explanation that they are to be taken to the Gleiwitz A.C. The selected persons receive food supplies and are loaded onto freight cars that are standing on a siding in Ausch-

APMO, Salmen Lewental, handwritten manuscript published in SAM, *Amid Unspeakable Crimes*, p. 172; Mat.RO, vol. II, pp. 166ff.; vol. VII, pp. 477, 481; Committee of Antifascist

*These documents are coded NO KW 2824 in the Nuremberg trial documents and in the archives of the State Auschwitz Museum (APMO) are identified as D-RO/ 123, vols. 20b, 20c.
**These prisoners are probably deployed in breaking up the camp, which was dissolved on September 6, 1944.
†SS Technical Sergeant Otto Moll is director of the Special Squads, which operate the crematoriums and must incinerate corpses in pits and on pyres.
††This telegram is based on the information sent to the PWOK on September 6, 1944.

witz II, Birkenau. Rather than to Gleiwitz the train moves onto a siding in Auschwitz I. Here the prisoners are led to a not very large building in which clothing and other goods are disinfected. Their particulars are recorded as if they were new arrivals. In the evening the supervisor of the Special Squad, SS Technical Sergeant Moll, and the SS men who were guarding them drank schnapps, which they offered to the prisoners. As soon as the prisoners were drunk, the room they were in was locked from outside. Zyklon B was thrown in through a window, which killed them. This dénouement was overseen by the physician on duty, SS Camp Doctor Horst Paul Fischer.

Resistance Fighters in the German Democratic Republic, *Schuldig im Sinne des Rechts und des Völkerrechts* (Guilty Under National and International Law: Extracts from the Protocol of the Trial of the Concentration Camp Doctor [Horst] Fischer Before the Supreme Court of the German Democratic Republic), Berlin, 1966.

SEPTEMBER 25

The DAW sends an invoice for 37,420 RM to the SS Central Administration in Auschwitz for refitting and equipping the construction train. It is itemized as follows:

APMO, IZ-13/89, Various Documents of the Third Reich, pp. 201ff.

For refitting and equipping 24 cars for the prisoners	24 x 1,080 RM = 25,920 RM
For the seven cars of the SS men	7 x 978 RM = 6,846 RM
For the office/living car of the SS management	1,350 RM
For the seven workshop and depot cars	3,304 RM

SEPTEMBER 26

200 prisoners are transferred from Buchenwald to Auschwitz.

Docs. of ISD Arolsen, Folder 11.

The Jewish prisoner Dr. Paul Citron (No. 159985) receives 30 strokes of the rod for attempting to throw bread to a female prisoner over the fence that separates Camps B-IIa and B-IIb. He is so severely beaten that he has to be taken to the prisoners' infirmary.

APMO, Dpr.-Hd/6, p. 60.

By order of SS Staff Sergeant Kirschner most of the documents of the Political Department that relate to deceased prisoners are loaded onto a wagon and brought to Birkenau. They are burned there in the crematorium.

APMO, Dpr.-Hd/4, p. 107, Statement of Former Prisoner Jan Trebaczowski. He worked in the Admissions Office of the Political Department.

The camp resistance movement reports the following in a clandestine letter to Teresa Lasocka and Edward Hałoń of the PWOK:

APMO, Mat.RO, vol. II, pp. 166ff.; vol. VII, pp. 477, 481.

1. The Political Department has destroyed a large portion of the documents up to and including 1943 by burning them in the old crematorium. This operation will, of course, continue.
2. 200 Jews from the so-called Special Squad were gassed in a special way. They made up a closed group that was employed in Birkenau with filling in and leveling pits in which corpses were incinerated when the crematorium was overloaded. When they finished their work, they were not sent back to their squad, but rather to Auschwitz I. With a great display they were reg-

istered like newly admitted arrivals and finally were led to the baths in the so-called depersonalization chamber, where so far no gassings had taken place. They were killed there with gas. The explanation of the camp management of Auschwitz I to the director of the operation, Moll, that the 200 prisoners were guests in Auschwitz and that their "departure" from Birkenau was to be reported, was characteristic.

400 female Jews from Auschwitz II are transferred to the newly established Neustadt auxiliary camp near the textile factory of the Schlesische Feinweberei AG (Silesian Fine Weaving). They are trained and are deployed in the weaving mill. The auxiliary camp belongs to Auschwitz III.

APMO, Dpr.-ZO/50, pp. 287ff., Irena Strzelecka, "Das Nebenlager Neustadt" (Neustadt Auxiliary Camp), *HvA*, no. 13 (1971): 159–170.

SEPTEMBER 27

Camp Commander Mirbeth of the Golleschau A.C. reports to the Commandant's Office of Auschwitz III that on this day he has transferred 10 Hungarian Jewish prisoners from Golleschau to Auschwitz II. Among them are two deceased: Zoltan Földes (No. A-15888) and Abraham Salamon (No. A-15983).

APMO, D-AuIII, Golleschau/12, p. 94.

SS Lieutenant Colonel Möckel, Director of Administration of the Waffen SS in Auschwitz, signs a travel permit for a five-ton truck and a personnel truck to Oranienburg and back for the purpose of transporting personal effects.*

APMO, Dpr.-ZOd/38, pp. 130, 131, Exhibits 75, 76.

SEPTEMBER 28

Six Polish prisoners escape from Auschwitz I: Tadeusz Donimirski (No. 2033), Wacław Maliszewski (No. 59195), Leonard Zawadzki (No. 13390), Tadeusz Żaboklicki (No. 21668), Alfons Szumiński (No. 23483), and Jan Prejzner (No. 14046).

APMO, German Search Book No. 310/45; Depositions, vol. 12a, vol. 16, Accounts of Former Prisoners Jan Prejzner and Wacław Maliszewski.

SEPTEMBER 29

A session of the Police Court-martial of the Kattowitz Gestapo takes place in Block 11 of Auschwitz. 52 men and 13 women are condemned to death in the gas chamber. Another 23 men and a woman are admitted to the camp.

APMO, Mat.RO, vol. IV, pp. 252ff., List of Names; Konieczny, "Police Court-martial," pp. 131–132, 161–163.

1,500 prisoners—predominantly Poles and Russians—are transferred from Auschwitz to Buchenwald.

Docs. of ISD Arolsen, Folder 7.

500 Jewish prisoners from Gross-Rosen are transferred to Auschwitz. They are sick and invalid prisoners. All transferred prisoners are probably killed in the gas chambers.

APMO, Kor. IV-8521/2151/83, List of Names. The names on this list do not appear in the documents of Auschwitz C.C.

---

*This is for the transport of the goods that were stolen from the Jews sent to Auschwitz for extermination. Broad states that these trucks were protected on the way to Berlin by guards with machine guns (Broad, "Auschwitz Concentration Camp," pp. 46ff.).

The camp resistance movement informs former prisoner Konstanty Jagiełło,* who is active in a resistance group operating near the camp and who takes care of escapees, and Teresa Lasocka and Edward Hałoń of the PWOK in Kraków, that an active liaison man from the Armia Krajowa commando in Silesia who uses the pseudonym "Urban"** has been brought to Auschwitz I. Photographs of the plans for the prisoners' self-defense were allegedly found on him. This discovery has made the camp undefendable. Now, the only possible military concept—naturally only under favorable conditions—is an air assault. As a result of the current threat the number and names of hostages for Auschwitz Concentration Camp should be drawn up by those who bear primary responsibility for the camp: SS Lieutenant General Oswald Pohl of Berlin; SS First Lieutenant Rudolf Höss, Commandant in Auschwitz I; SS Major Baer, Commandant in Auschwitz II; SS Captain Kramer, Commandant in Auschwitz III; SS Captain Schwarz; Camp Commander Hössler; as well as the Head of the Political Department, SS Second Lieutenant Schurz and SS Technical Sergeant Kirchner, Labor Deployment Director Sell; and all who obey their immoral orders.

APMO, Mat.RO, vol. II, pp. 169ff.

2,499 Jews from the Theresienstadt ghetto arrive in an RSHA transport. During the selection SS Camp Doctor Mengele sends three male twin pairs to the camp. The brothers Hauptmann, born on October 23, 1930, receive Nos. B-10502 and B-10503; the brothers Steiner, born on June 9, 1929, receive Nos. B-10504 and B-10505; the brothers Reichenberger, born on August 11, 1928, receive Nos. B-10506 and B-10507. Of the remaining deportees approximately one fourth is sent to the transit camp in Birkenau and the rest are killed in the gas chambers.†

APMO, D-AuI-3/26, Inventory No. 148855; Docs. of ISD Arolsen, NA-Men, Series B, p. 2/1980.

A delegate of the International Committee of Red Cross (ICRC) arrives at the Commandant's Office of Auschwitz I. He concludes from the conversation with the Commandant, which is conducted in the presence of "polite but reticent" officers, that the packages personally addressed to the prisoners are all distributed to them and that there is a spokesman in the camp for each national group, as well as a so-called Senior, and they accept all the packages and distribute them, whereby each breach of trust is strictly punished.††

Comité International de la Croix Rouge (CICR), "Visite au Commandant du camp d'Auschwitz d'un délégue du CICR (Septembre 1944)" (Visit to the Commandant of Auschwitz by a Delegate of the International Committee of the Red Cross in [September 1944]), in *Documents sur l'activité du Comité International de la Croix Rouge en faveur des civils détenus dans les camps de concentration en Allemagne (1938–1945)* (Documents on the Activity of the International Committee of the Red Cross on Behalf of Civilians Detained in Concentration Camps in Germany [1938–1945]), Geneva, 1947, pp. 91ff.

---

*He escaped from the camp on June 27, 1944.
**"Urban," Stefan Jasiński, was shot at Malec, brought to Auschwitz, and put in Block 21 of the prisoners' infirmary. He was then interrogated. He later died under unspecified circumstances. Jasiński was an officer of a Polish unit in Great Britain. In the spring of 1943 he parachuted into the area of Kielce (Sobański, *Escapes from Auschwitz*, pp. 96–102).
†371 people from this transport survived the war (Adler, *Theresienstadt 1941–1945*, p. 693).
††This account indicates that the delegate of the ICRC saw prisoners on the railroad stretch between Teschen and Auschwitz working in the fields or in mines under supervision of SS men. He noticed their pale ash-gray faces. He had no opportunity to speak with the prisoners, to find out from them that the Commandant's information on the spokesman, the Senior Jew, and the distribution of packages was false. Also, he was not actually in the camp, of which he noticed six to eight large buildings. He couldn't answer the question of the main spokesman of the British POWs whom he met in Teschen, whether there was in Auschwitz a modern bathing facility equipped with showers in which prisoners were gassed.

SEPTEMBER 30

The Polish prisoners Roman Taul (No. 1108) and Józef Drożdż escape from Auschwitz I.

APMO, Dpr.-Hd/4, p. 102, German Search Book No. 310/45.

In the night SS Corporal Kaduk conducts a selection among the prisoners of Auschwitz I. He selects approximately 1,000 prisoners, whom he orders to report to Block 10 the next day.

In view of the hopeless situation in rebellious Warsaw, where there is hunger and a shortage of weapons and munitions as well as medical care for the wounded, the High Command of the Armia Krajowa opens negotiations with SS Lieutenant General von dem Bach-Zelewski.

APMO, Dpr.-Hd/5, p. 16, Account of Former Prisoner Geza Mansfeld.

Of the 1,437 men sent in an RSHA transport of the Reich from the Annaberg labor camp, 411 are admitted to the camp and are given Nos. B-10607–B-11017. They were put into Men's Quarantine Camp B-IIa on October 2. The remaining 1,026 men are killed in the gas chambers.

APMO, D-AuII-3/1, p. 8, Quarantine List.

1,500 Jewish men, women, and children arrive from the camp of the Theresienstadt ghetto in an RSHA transport. After the selection the young and the healthy individuals are sent to the transit camp and the remaining persons are killed in the gas chambers.

Adler, *Theresienstadt 1941–1945*, p. 694. Adler states that 76 people survived this transport.

OCTOBER 1

The Commandant's Office of Auschwitz I takes over a new camp for female prisoners, which arises on the adjacent grounds, the so-called protective custody camp expansion. It also takes over from Auschwitz II the agricultural operations and the breeding farms together with the auxiliary camps that belonged to them and the labor squads that worked in them, as well as the squads for tailoring, the SS laundry, the leather factory, the women's squads working in the SS offices and agencies, the IBV prisoners who work as domestic help for SS families, as well as the numerically largest squad of female prisoners, which works in two shifts at the Weichsel-Union-Metallwerke. In the camp expansion area, seven further blocks intended for female prisoners are fenced in.

APMO, D-AuI-1, Garrison Order 25/44, Sept. 30, 1944; Škodowa, *Three Years*, pp. 163–164.

Commandant Baer of Auschwitz I informs the SS members in the main camp that Supervisor Volkenrath has been appointed Director of the new women's camp in Auschwitz I.

APMO, D-AuI, Garrison Order 25/44, Sept. 30, 1944.

The occupancy level of the women's camp in Auschwitz I is 3,785.

APMO, D-AuI-3a/1, Women's Camp (FL—Frauenlager) Occupancy Report 1.

The occupancy level in the women's camp in Auschwitz II, Camps B-Ia, B-Ib, B-IIb, and B-IIc, is 26,230.

APMO, D-AuII-3a/1, FL, 399a, b. [Camps B-Ia, B-Ib]

OCTOBER 2

298 Jews from Theresienstadt who were sent to the transit camp on September 30 after the selection receive Nos. B-11105–B-11402.

APMO, D-AuIII, Golleschau/12, pp. 95ff.

949 Jews who probably arrived in RSHA transports from the Lodz and Theresienstadt ghettoes and were kept in the transit camp as "depot prisoners" receive Nos. B-11403–B-12351. From these transports 297 prisoners are selected for the Golleschau A.C., among them 295 Jews from Theresienstadt and two from Lodz. SS Camp Doctor Mengele claims that the prisoners have been deloused but not submitted to the prescribed quarantine, although infectious diseases such as measles, scarlet fever, and typhus reign. Other prisoners are sent to Gleiwitz I A.C. Among them is František Kraus (No. 11632), who was delivered from Theresienstadt.

305 Jews from an RSHA transport from Theresienstadt who were sent to the transit camp after the selection on September 30 receive Nos. B-12352–B-12656. After a week they are transferred to the Tschechowitz-Vacuum A.C.

Docs. of ISD Arolsen, NA-Men/1980.

22 female Jews selected from an RSHA transport from the Annaberg camp receive Nos. A-25417–A-25438.

Ibid., NA-Women/1986.

The SS Camp Doctor Thilo conducts a selection in the men's quarantine camp during which he choses 101 prisoners. They are killed the same day in the gas chambers.

APMO, Dpr.-Hd/6, p. 8.

30 prisoners, adolescents from Kaunas, who were delivered to Auschwitz II on August 1, 1944, are singled out, among others, during a selection in Camp B-IIf. They are killed the same day in the gas chambers. Dr. Otto Wolken reports that as they were being chased to the autos some of them cried. Then a 12-year-old ran forward and shouted, "Don't cry, children! Be brave! You have seen how your mothers and fathers were murdered. Do not have fear of death! Today we go to our deaths, but we are sure that they too"—and he pointed to the SS men—"will bite the dust." The youth was beaten bloody by the SS men.

APMO, Dpr.-Hd/6, p. 50, Statement of Former Prisoner Dr. Otto Wolken.

The workday for the outside squads is set at from 6:00 A.M. to 5:30 P.M., with a half-hour lunch break from 12:00 to 12:30.

APMO, D-AuI-1, Garrison Order 25/44, Sept. 30, 1944.

The occupancy level in the women's camp of Auschwitz I is 3,785, of whom 355 work in the Rajsko A.C., 449 in the Budy A.C., 184 in the Babice A.C., and 39 in the Harmense A.C.

APMO, D-AuI-3a/2/2b, FL Labor Deployment List.

In the experimental station of Professor Dr. Clauberg in the women's camp of Auschwitz I are 196 female prisoners for research purposes and eight prisoner orderlies.

APMO, D-AuI-3a/2b, p. 340, FL Labor Deployment List.

After exhausting all military possibilities the rebels in Warsaw see themselves forced to give up. The capitulation is signed in the staff headquarters of SS Lieutenant General von dem Bach-Zelewski in Ożarów. The rebel army is guaranteed the rights of prisoners of war according to the norms of international law. The 63-day battle has been conducted against overwhelmingly superior German forces and in an exceptionally unfavorable political situation. The losses of the rebels are 16,000 to 18,000 dead and nearly 25,000 wounded. Among the Warsaw civilian population over 150,000 dead and murdered are to be mourned. The evacuated population is sent to concentration and forced labor camps. After total evacuation German special units rage in Warsaw, blowing up and burning the surviving buildings, so that the city is 80 percent destroyed.

There are 26,230 registered female prisoners in the women's camp of Auschwitz II, of whom 11,506 are working. 7,150 female prisoners are sick and unable to work, of whom 1,508 are on their way to other concentration camps. Of these 168 are under 14 years old, some are even nursing infants. Among the sick are 42 prisoners over 60 years old and invalid; 555 female prisoners remain in quarantine suffering from mange and malaria; 44 are being interrogated in the Political Department. 2,886 female prisoners are sick, recovering, or registered with the physician; 87 await transfer to another camp; 1,860 female prisoners are in quarantine after delivery to the camp, among them were 817 women from rebellious Warsaw, who are housed in Camp B-IIb. A further 7,574 female prisoners have no work, of whom 1,020 await transfer to another camp.

APMO, D-AuII-3a/2, p. 340, Labor Deployment List.

In the daily listing of the labor deployment of female prisoners in Auschwitz II it is noted that 250 female prisoners work in the service posts of the SS in Sorting Squad I on the grounds of the DAW, i.e., the so-called Canada Squad I, and 815 female prisoners work in Sorting Squad II in Camp B-IIg, i.e., so-called Canada Squad II. They must sort the belongings that have been stolen from the people brought to Auschwitz to be destroyed.

APMO, D-AuII-3a/2b, p. 340b, vol. 1/8.

17,251 female prisoners are registered in the women's camp of Auschwitz II; of them 49 are recent arrivals and 17,202 come from the transit camp, called "Mexico," in Birkenau. Among the recent arrivals there are probably 46 female prisoners sent to the camp by the Trieste/Görz Sipo and SD. They receive Nos. 88903–88948. The female prisoners in the transit camp are not required to work.

APMO, D-AuII-3a/53a, FL Occupancy Report; Docs. of ISD Arolsen, NA-Women/1986.

19 female prisoners die in the women's camp of Auschwitz II. Eight of them are murdered on the spot.

Ibid.; the abbreviation "SB," for "Sonderbehandlung," "special treatment," meaning violent killing, was added next to the names of eight female prisoners.

OCTOBER 3

1,172 female prisoners work in the Weichsel-Union plant. 868 prisoners, of them 54 skilled workers, work during the day shift, and 304, of whom 19 are skilled workers, work the night shift.

APMO, D-AuI-3a/3b, FL Labor Deployment List, vol. 7.

1,500 Jewish men, women, and children are sent from the camp of the Theresienstadt ghetto in an RSHA transport. The young and the healthy individuals are sent to the transit camp after the selection and the remaining people are killed in the gas chambers.

Adler, *Theresienstadt 1941–1945*, p. 694. According to Adler, 293 of these people survived the war.

There are 43,462 female prisoners in the women's camp of Auschwitz II, counting the female Jews brought from the transit camp

APMO, D-AuII-3a/54a, FL Occupancy Report.

the previous day. 16 female new arrivals sent by the Sipo and SD head branch office are registered in the women's camp, as well as 488 so-called transit female Jews, who probably arrive the same day in RSHA transports and who probably also come from the Theresienstadt ghetto.

993 female prisoners die in the women's camp of Auschwitz II, of whom 989 are killed in the gas chambers after being selected by an SS Camp Doctor. There are now 42,973 female prisoners in the women's camp.

Ibid.

OCTOBER 4

500 prisoners are transferred from Auschwitz I to Buchenwald.

APMO, Mat.RO, vol. VIII, Transport List.

1,050 female prisoners are transferred from Auschwitz II to another concentration camp.

APMO, D-AuII-3a/5c, p. 343c, Labor Deployment List.

Commandant Schwartz of Auschwitz III informs the SS guard units that four prisoners have overpowered a guard who turned his back on them for a long time. They escaped after they tore his weapon from him and rendered it useless. Schwarz orders that "this unfortunate incident of negligence" be made known to all guard companies as a warning.

APMO, D-AuIII-1/67, Commandant's Office Order 10/44.

The Administration Department of Auschwitz II asks the SS Central Administration for 230 plank-beds, 6,000 blankets, and 8,000 boards for the bottom level of the beds, which are necessary to furnish the former Gypsy Family Camp B-IId, being used as an admissions and transit camp until the end of October but also as a transport camp. Prisoners are kept here who are slated for transport to concentration camps in the interior of the Reich. The reason for this request is that there are no plank-beds in some blocks and the lower boards of the beds are missing in others. Moreover, the plank-beds collapse, since instead of the prescribed five prisoners 15 are sleeping on a plank-bed. With such a burden the triple-decker plank-beds are destroyed and the prisoners are crushed. It is further claimed that the broken under-boards and also some of the plank-beds can no longer be used.

Documents and Materials, vol. I, pp. 95ff.

OCTOBER 5

15 female IBV prisoners are employed in the following SS households as domestic servants: Höss—two female prisoners, Caesar—two, Möcke—one, Wirths—one, Kramer—one, Fischer—one, Thomsen—one, Bott—one, Messner—one, Boger and Walter—one, Karmann—one, Ludwig—one, Frank—one.*

APMO, D-AuI-3a/5b, FL Labor Deployment List, vol. 7.

The occupancy level in the experimental station of Professor Dr. Clauberg in Auschwitz I increases by 10 and is 206 women for research purposes.

APMO, D-AuI-3a/5b, Labor Deployment List.

*IBV prisoners are also employed in the casinos, the kitchens, and as cleaning women in the SS offices.

Five female prisoners are transferred from the women's camp of Auschwitz II to the women's camp of Auschwitz I. There are 3,790 female prisoners in Auschwitz I.

APMO, D-AuI-3a/6, FL Occupancy Report.

1,188 prisoners are transferred from Buchenwald to Auschwitz II, among them 800 Gypsies who were already in Auschwitz. Most of the prisoners from this transport are probably killed in the gas chambers.

Docs. of ISD Arolsen, Folder 11.

160 Jewish prisoners are transferred from Auschwitz II to the Golleschau A.C. They belong to the group of 297 prisoners who were slated on October 2 for the Golleschau A.C.

APMO, D-AuIII, Golleschau/12, p. 95.

There are 42,990 female prisoners—women and girls—in the women's camp of Auschwitz II.

APMO, D-AuII-3a/6c/344c, Labor Deployment List.

OCTOBER 6

There are 38,544 female prisoners in the women's camp of Auschwitz II, a reduction of 4,446 women, of whom 2,558 are transferred to other concentration camps and 1,888 are probably killed in the gas chambers after a selection conducted in the camp.

Ibid.

Of the 297 prisoners slated for the Golleschau A.C. the remaining 137 prisoners are transferred, of whom 295 are Jews from Theresienstadt and two are Jews from Lodz. They receive Nos. B-11105–B-11404.

APMO, D-AuIII, Golleschau/12, pp. 95, 98–104.

The prisoner Józef Cyrankiewicz presents the following information in a clandestine letter to Teresa Lasocka and Edward Hałoń of PWOK:

APMO, Mat.RO, vol. III, p. 173; vol. VII, p. 480.

> Grabner was condemned to death by an SS court in Buchenwald, which was commuted to 12 years in prison, for exceeding authority and arbitrary shooting to death in approximately 40 cases (!). Apart from all the other methods of destruction, there are thousands of other such cases, so that in Auschwitz when Höss was Commandant and Grabner was leading the Political Department over 100,000 registered prisoners were murdered. In his statements Grabner strongly incriminates Commandant Höss and other "helper's helpers." Lachmann has been sent to the front. The other murderers remain undisturbed. This trial is the attempt by Grabner's employers in Berlin to distance themselves formally from the responsibility for Auschwitz. In Auschwitz there were months in which the number of those shot, beaten, and gassed to death reached 10,000 registered prisoners, not to mention the people who were sent directly to the gas chambers without being registered. In the daily reports sent to Berlin there was often news of over 500 deaths among the prisoners. Nobody asked at that time in Berlin what this horrendous death rate meant. These statistics were often considered normal reports from an extermination camp. Now they put on this comedy of a trial against one of these mass murderers—and

charge him with approximately 40 (!) deaths. The main criminal, however, Commandant Höss, and the other executors such as Bogner, Aumeier, Woznitza, and those named in the executioner's list, continue to exercise their special functions. Those responsible in Berlin attempt to elegantly wash their hands in innocence. They will not be able to escape their responsibility. . . .The bare numbers of recently gassed prisoners possess horrifying force. . . . The gassing never ends: 3,000 prisoners from Theresienstadt; 2,500 from Auschwitz I, II, and III; 6,000 female Hungarian Jews; 500 male Jews from the ghetto in Lodz; 400 prisoners from Buchenwald. Selections from among the sick and the unhealthy for gassing continue unabated.

Several hundred young and healthy individuals, among them 271 women, are sent to the transit camp after selection from the 1,500 Jewish men, women, and children who arrived on an RSHA transport from the ghetto in Theresienstadt. The remaining persons are killed in the gas chambers.*

APMO, D-AuII-3a/55a, FL Occupancy Report.

The women's transit camp "Mexico" is liquidated. The female Jews who were already registered in the women's camp on October 2 are transferred to Camp B-IIc, which is still called the transit camp, among them 943 sick female prisoners, 1,777 destined for further transport, 961 young girls, and 10,079 who remain at the "disposal" of the camp.

APMO, D-AuII-3a/6c, 344c, Labor Deployment List.

2,000 Jewish prisoners selected in the camp are killed in the gas chambers of Crematorium II.

APMO, Memoirs/148, vol. 38a, Notebook of a Member of the Special Squad.

13 female prisoners are transferred from the women's camp in Auschwitz II to the women's camp of Auschwitz I. There are now 3,803 female prisoners in the women's camp of Auschwitz I.

APMO, D-AuI-3a/7, FL Occupancy Report.

OCTOBER 7

In the Special Squads that are deployed in the incineration of corpses are:

APMO, D-AuII-3a/1, Inventory No. 29723.

Squad 57B, Crematorium II	Daily:	84 prisoners
	Nightly:	85 prisoners
Squad 58B, Crematorium III	Daily:	84 prisoners
	Nightly:	85 prisoners
Squad 59B, Crematorium IV	Daily:	84 prisoners
	Nightly:	85 prisoners
Squad 60B, Crematorium V	Daily:	72 prisoners
	Nightly:	84 prisoners
	Total	663 prisoners

*127 persons survived, according to Adler's reports in *Theresienstadt 1941–1945* (p. 694).

The occupancy level in the experimental station of Professor Dr. Clauberg declines by two and is 204 female prisoners for research purposes and eight female prisoner orderlies.

APMO, D-AuI-3a/6b, Labor Deployment List.

Two female prisoners sent to the camp by the Prague Stapo receive Nos. 88952 and 88953.

Five female prisoners sent in a group transport receive Nos. 88954–88959.

APMO, D-AuII-3a/56, FL Occupancy Report; Docs. of ISD Arolsen, NA-Women/1986.

1,150 female prisoners are transferred from Auschwitz II to Flossenbürg.

APMO, D-AuII-3a/56, FL Occupancy Report.

In Auschwitz II 1,236 female prisoners die, of whom 1,229 are killed in the gas chambers after selection.

Ibid.

The barracks in Section B-III, "Mexico," are dismantled, and the construction elements are sent to Gross-Rosen.

APMO, Dpr.-Hd/6, p. 287.

SS Camp Doctor Thilo conducts a selection in the men's quarantine camp, during which he selects 20 prisoners. They are killed the same day in the gas chambers.

Ibid., pp. 9–10.

On Saturday morning the camp resistance movement informs the leader of the Auschwitz Combat Group, who is in the Special Squad, that news has been obtained about the camp management's plans to liquidate as quickly as possible the surviving members of the Special Squad. This news probably confirms the information that the operation announced a few days ago by the SS to reduce the size of the Special Squads of Crematoriums IV and V by 300 named prisoners allegedly slated for a transport is to be carried out.

APMO, Dpr.-Hd/1, pp. 26, 27, 63; Hd/6, p. 29; Hd/11, p. 115; Dpr.-ZO/26, pp. 161ff.; Mat.RO, vol. III, p. 175; vol. VII, p. 481; Depositions, vol. 13, pp. 76ff.; Lewental, "Manuscript," pp. 178–184 (Lewental was a member of Special Squad 58B in Crematorium III whose manuscript was buried and later dug up on the grounds of the crematorium); *Za Wolność i Lud* (For Freedom and the People), no. 6, Warsaw, 1951.

The named prisoners decide to mount a resistance. At the midday break, during a conference in Crematorium IV, the staff of the Special Squad Combat Group is surprised by a German BV prisoner, who threatens to report them to the SS.* The informer is killed on the spot. At 1:25 P.M. the threatened group attacks the approaching SS guard unit with hammers, axes, and stones. They set Crematorium IV on fire and throw several self-made grenades. Afterward some of the prisoners from Squad 59B reach the small wooded area nearby. At the same time the prisoners of Squad 57B, who work in Crematorium II, become active. When they see the flames and hear the shooting, they believe that this is a sign for the general uprising of the prisoners in the camp. They overpower the Head Capo, a Reich German, and push him and an SS man whom they have disarmed into the burning crematorium oven. They beat to death a second SS man, tear up the fence that surrounds the crematorium area, and flee.

---

*The person guilty of betraying this operation is probably the orderly, called Max, of SS Squad Leader Buch, since he warned SS Sergeant Buch, who was coming to Crematorium IV by bicycle. Buch then returned to the camp and notified the block leadership. Consequently, the SS guards intervened very quickly (APMO, Depositions, vol. 13, p. 76, Account of Former Prisoner Tadeusz Joachimowski).

The prisoners of Squads 58B and 60B in Crematoriums III and IV undertake nothing because some of them are not informed about the plans, and also because the SS men there bring the situation quickly under control. The immediate intervention by the SS guards, the surrounding of the crematorium compound, and the heavy machine-gun and artillery fire in the direction of the small woods near Crematorium IV, where the prisoners mount a resistance, quickly squelches the uprising. In Rajsko pursuing SS men block the way of the fleeing prisoners of Squad 57B. The prisoners barricade themselves in a barn and prepare to resist. The SS men set the barn on fire and murder the prisoners. 250 prisoners die in this battle, among them the organizers of the uprising: Zelman Gradowski from Suwałki; Josef Warszawski from Warsaw, actually Josef Dorębus, who was sent from Drancy; Józef Deresiński from Łuny near Grodno; Ajzyk Kalniak from Łomża; Lajb Langfus from Warsaw, who was sent from Makow Mazowiecki; and Lajb Panusz (Herszko) from Łomża.

A fire-fighting squad is sent from Auschwitz I to put out the fire in Crematorium IV. These prisoners, who put out the fire under supervision by the SS, are witnesses to the suppression of the uprising by the SS and the shooting to death of the members of Squad 59B. The fire-fighting squad is then brought to Rajsko, to put out the fire in the barn. An air-raid alarm prevents the SS men from a further pursuit.

In the evening, all the prisoners who were killed are brought to the grounds of Crematorium IV and the remaining members of the Special Squad are driven together. Another 200 prisoners from the squads that took part in the uprising are shot to death. A representative of the Commandant delivers a threatening speech in which he announces that if there is a repetition of such incidents all prisoners in the camp will be shot to death. Afterward work is resumed in Crematoriums II, III, and V.

APMO, Dpr.-ZO/26, p. 162, Statements of Former Prisoner and Special Squad Member Henryk Mandelbaum (No. 181970); SAM, *Auschwitz in the Eyes of the SS*, pp. 188ff.

During the uprising three SS men are killed by the prisoners: SS Corporal Rudolf Erler, SS Corporal Willi Freese, and SS Corporal Josef Purke.*

APMO, D-AuI-1, Garrison Order 26/44, Oct. 12, 1944.

SS Brigadier General Oskar Dirlewanger suggests to SS Commander in Chief Himmler a project to enlist German prisoners, former criminals, in the concentration camps for the SS Special Unit Dirlewanger. The project is approved by Himmler and relayed on October 15 to SS Lieutenant Berger, the Head of the SS Main Office.

APMO, D-RF-9, WVHA 2, p. 33, Edict Collection.

OCTOBER 8

The Labor Deployment Department registers the same number of prisoners in the Special Squad as in the morning—663 prisoners—

APMO, D-AuII-3a/1, Inventory No. 29723.

---

*According to statements by the former prisoner and member of the Special Squad, Alter Feinsilber (a.k.a. Stanisław Jankowski), 12 SS men are injured during this uprising (APMO, Dpr.-Hd/1, pp. 26ff.).

without taking into account the prisoners murdered during the mutiny.

In an isolated block in Women's Camp B-Ia in Birkenau 370 girls between the ages of several months and 14 years are kept who were arrested in Warsaw with their families after the outbreak of the uprising and were sent to Auschwitz II.	APMO, D-AuII-3a/8b/346b, FL Labor Deployment List.
48 female prisoners are sent to Auschwitz II.	APMO, D-AuII-3a/57a, FL Occupancy Report.
100 male Czechoslovak Jews and 401 female Hungarian Jews are transferred from Auschwitz II to Buchenwald, the HASAG squad in Taucha, near Leipzig.	Ibid., Docs. of ISD Arolsen, Folders 13, 15.
Three female prisoners are killed.	APMO, D-AuII-3a/57a, FL Occupancy Report.
The SS Camp Commander of the Golleschau A.C. notifies the Commandant of Auschwitz III that he has transferred this day 108 exhausted prisoners who are unable to work to Auschwitz II. Among them is the deceased Polish Jew Jcek Bornstein (No. 157610).	APMO, D-AuIII, Golleschau/12, pp. 106–108.

OCTOBER 9

19 female prisoners are sent to Auschwitz II by Sipo and SD field headquarters.	APMO, D-AuII-3a/58a, FL Occupancy Report.
From the Jews sent in an RSHA transport from Trieste, five men are admitted to the camp and are given Nos. B-12657–B-12661. The remaining people, among them 12 men, are killed in the gas chambers.	APMO, D-AuII-3/1, p. 8, Quarantine List.
1,550 Jews arrive in an RSHA transport from the Theresienstadt ghetto. 191 women and several dozen men* are sent to the transit camp after the selection.	APMO, D-AuII-3a/58a, FL Occupancy Report.
2,000 Jewish men, women, and children sent in an RSHA transport from Theresienstadt and Trieste are killed in the gas chambers of Crematorium II.	APMO, Memoirs/148, vol. 38a, Notebook of a Member of the Special Squad.
2,000 unregistered female Jews** from Camp B-IIc are killed in the gas chambers of Crematorium V.	Ibid.
The Labor Deployment Department reports the status of the Special Squad:	APMO, D-AuII-3a/2, Inventory No. 29722.

*76 persons survive the camp, according to Adler's *Theresienstadt 1941–1945*, p. 694.
**These female prisoners are not registered in the women's camp.

Squad 57B, Crematorium II	Daily:	27 prisoners
	Nightly:	26 prisoners
Squad 58B, Crematorium III	Daily:	26 prisoners
	Nightly:	27 prisoners
Squad 59B, Crematorium IV	Daily:	27 prisoners
	Nightly:	26 prisoners
Squad 60B, Crematorium V	Daily:	26 prisoners
	Nightly:	27 prisoners
	Total	212 prisoners*

OCTOBER 10

Three female Jewish prisoners employed in the Weichsel-Union-Metallwerke, Ella Gärtner, Ester Wajsblum, and Ragina Safin, are arrested in the women's camp of Auschwitz I. They are charged with stealing explosives from the depot of the plant and giving them to the prisoners of the Special Squad. With them the prisoners fashioned primitive grenades, which they used during the uprising on October 7.

19 female prisoners are sent by various offices of the Sipo and SD to Auschwitz II.

19 female prisoners die in Auschwitz II, of whom 12 are killed (SB, for "Sonderbehandlung," or "special treatment," by their names indicates individual murders).

2,219 female prisoners who are transferred to other concentration camps—to Buchenwald, Flossenbürg and others—are stricken from the camp register of Auschwitz II. The next day 34,024 female prisoners are registered in Auschwitz II and 3,799 female prisoners in Auschwitz I.

800 Gypsies, among them children,** who had been delivered on October 5 from Buchenwald, are killed in the gas chambers of Crematorium V. Before their transfer to Buchenwald the Gypsies had been in Gypsy Family Camp B-IIe in Auschwitz II.

14 prisoners in the Special Squad are arrested and locked in the bunker of Block 11, among are them Jankiel Handelsman from

APMO, Dpr.-ZO/29, p. 107, Statements of Former Prisoner Gustawa Kinselewsk; Wsp./51, vol. 1, pp. 50–169, Dounia Ourisson; Ośw./252, vol. 10, pp. 49–60, Raya Kagan, "Frauen im Amt der Hölle" (Women in the Office of Hell); Israel Gutman, "Der Aufstand des Sonderkommandos" (The Revolt of the Special Squad), and Raya Kagan, "Die letzten Opfer des Widerstandes" (The Last Victims of the Resistance), both in Adler et al., eds., Auschwitz: Testimonies, pp. 279, 282, 284; Michał Grynberg, Zydzi w rejecnji ciechanowskiej 1939–1942 (Jews in the Zichenau Administrative District 1939–1942), Warsaw, 1984, pp. 126ff.

APMO, D-AuII-3a/59a, FL Occupancy Report. [Sipo and SD]

Ibid. ["special treatment"]

APMO, D-AuII-3a/59a; D-AuI-3a/12, FL Occupancy Report. [2,219 female prisoners]

APMO, Memoirs/148, vol. 38a, Notebook of a Member of the Special Squad.

APMO, D-AuII-3a/2, Inventory No. 29722; Memoirs/51, vol. 1.

*It can be seen from these figures that the Special Squad was reduced after the mutiny by 451 persons. A member of the Special Squad wrote in his notebook that 460 men had been shot to death on October 7. Probably this number is rounded off. On the basis of available documents and materials it is impossible to determine whether any of the prisoners succeeded in escaping during the uprising.
**During the liquidation of the Gypsy Family Camp on August 2, 1944, they were transferred from Auschwitz to Buchenwald, where they were registered on August 5, 1944.

Radom, one of the organizers of the uprising, who was sent to the camp on March 4, 1943, in an RSHA transport from Drancy; the prisoner Wróbel, a Polish Jew, who received the explosives from the female prisoners; and five Russian POWs who after being evacuated from Majdanek, together with the director of the crematorium there, SS Staff Sergeant Erich Muhsfeld, were taken into the Special Squad on April 5, 1944. The interrogation by the SS functionaries of the Political Department, among others Draser and Broch, is conducted with great harshness.* After the arrest and incarceration of the 14 prisoners in Block 11, 198 prisoners remain in the Special Squad. They are divided into three squads of 66 prisoners each and sent to Crematoriums II, III, and V. They continue to work in day and night shifts, with 33 prisoners in each shift. Crematorium IV, which was destroyed during the uprising, is no longer mentioned in the daily summaries of the deployment of the prisoners in Auschwitz II.

150, Dounia Ourisson; Ośw./ 252, vol. 10, pp. 49–60, Raya Kagan, "Women in the Office of Hell," pp. 49–60; Kagan, "Last Victims," pp. 282–284; Grynberg, *Jews in Zichenau*, pp. 126ff.

Two more female prisoners are arrested in the women's camp of Auschwitz II on the charge of having contact with the Special Squad and transporting explosives there. One of those arrested, the female Polish Jew Róża Robota, works in the personal effects camp, which borders on the compound of Crematorium IV. Róża Robota accepted from one of her fellow prisoners explosive material stolen by Ella Gärtner in the Weichsel-Union plant and passed it on to Wróbel of the Special Squad.**

APMO, D-AuII-3a/11c/349, FL Labor Deployment List; Ośw./ 252, vol. 10, pp. 49–60; Kagan, "Women."

OCTOBER 11

Two female prisoners are taken from the women's camp in Auschwitz I to the Political Department for an interrogation.†

APMO, D-AuI-3a/9c, FL Labor Deployment List.

2,000 Jewish men, women, and children who are selected from an RSHA transport from Slovakia and another transport from Buchenwald†† are killed in the gas chamber of Crematorium III.

APMO, Memoirs/148, vol. 38a, Notebook of a Member of the Special Squad.

OCTOBER 12

3,000 women, who were singled out during a selection in the women's camp of Auschwitz II, are killed in the gas chamber of Crematorium II, among them three female prisoners from the prisoners'

Ibid.; D-AuII-3a/60a, FL Occupancy Report.

---

*The interrogations, during which torture takes place, continue for several weeks. The prisoners in the bunkers of Block 11 probably die as a result of these tortures, since no record of sentences or executions can be found.
**There is no confrontation between Róża Robota and Wróbel, since she probably mentions his name only after she becomes certain that he has died during the interrogations (Kagan, "Last Victims," p. 284; Gutman, "The Uprising," p. 279).
†The interrogation is probably related to the investigations into the uprising of the Special Squad. The interrogated prisoners are presumably female Jews from the squad that works in the Weischel-Union plant. They are interrogated for three days.
††132 female Hungarian Jews who are no longer capable of working are transferred on October 11 from Buchenwald. 123 come from the Altenburg squad, and nine from the squad in Leipzig-Schönefeld (HASAG company). Neither of the two transports is entered in the camp occupancy registers (Kagan, "Last Victims," p. 284; Gutman, "Revolt," p. 279).

infirmary, 131 female Jews from the transit camp, and 2,866 female Jews from RSHA transports who were not registered in the camp.

Two female prisoners are sent to the Auschwitz concentration camp.

APMO, D-AuII-3a/60a, FL Occupancy Report.

537 female prisoners who are transferred to another concentration camp are stricken from the occupancy register of the women's camp in Auschwitz II.

Ibid.

Several hundred young and healthy persons are admitted to the transit camp from 1,600 Jews sent in an RSHA transport from the ghetto in Theresienstadt. Among them are 181 women. The remaining people are killed in the gas chambers.

Ibid. Accoridng to Adler in *Theresienstadt 1941–1945* (p. 694), 22 of these people survived the camp.

The 2nd SS Railroad Construction Brigade, which numbered 505 prisoners on the day of its departure from Auschwitz on September 18, 1944, is made part of Buchenwald. Meanwhile, 10 prisoners have escaped from the brigade, two have died, and three were sent back to Auschwitz. The brigade's name is changed to 7th SS Railroad Construction Brigade.

APMO, D-AuII-3/3, Documents of the Railroad Brigade; Ośw./1256, vol. 56, pp. 58–60, Account of Former Prisoner Aleksander Miziewicz (No. 25410).

Two more female prisoners are arrested in the women's camp in Auschwitz II who are probably suspected of helping the members of the Special Squad in acquiring the explosive material for the production of primitive grenades.

APMO, D-AuII-3a/13c/351c, FL Labor Deployment List.

Commandant Baer announces in Garrison Order No. 26/44 that on Saturday, October 7, 1944, the following died at the hands of the enemy:

APMO, D-AuI-1, Garrison Order 26/44; Broad, "Memoirs," p. 40.

SS Corporal Rudolf Erler, born on August 31, 1904, of the 5th SS Stormtroopers, Auschwitz Concentration Camp I
SS Corporal Willi Freese, born on September 30, 1921, of the 2nd SS Stormtroopers, Auschwitz Concentration Camp II
SS Corporal Josef Purka, born on February 28, 1903, of the 1st SS Stormtroopers, Auschwitz Concentration Camp II

Compare what Pery Broad writes in his memoirs: "Several days later five SS men ran around inflated with newly awarded Iron Crosses. In a speech before the troops the Commandant of Auschwitz, SS Major Baer, drew attention to the fact that this was the first case where concentration camp troops had received Iron Crosses from the General of the Army for 'heroic behavior in the prevention of a mass uprising.' "

OCTOBER 13

2,000 Jewish men, women, and children are killed in the gas chamber of Crematorium II. They arrive in an RSHA transport from Slovakia and the Theresienstadt ghetto and were selected the day before.

APMO, Memoirs/148, vol. 38a, Notebook of a Member of the Special Squad.

Two female prisoners are sent to Auschwitz II.

APMO, D-AuII-3a/61a, FL Occupancy Report.

Nine female prisoners lose their lives in Auschwitz II, of whom one dies and eight are killed. Among those killed are three female Jews from the transit camp.

Ibid.

849 female prisoners from the women's camp of Auschwitz II and 81 female Jews from the transit camp are transferred to another concentration camp.

Ibid.

3,000 women are killed in the gas chamber of Crematorium III; they were selected in Auschwitz I. Among them are five female prisoners from the prisoners' infirmary, three female Jews from the transit camp, and 2,992 female Jews not registered in the camp.

Ibid.

OCTOBER 14

30 German criminals are transferred from Auschwitz to Buchenwald.*

Docs. of ISD Arolsen, Folder 13.

A female prisoner from the women's camp of Auschwitz I is locked in the bunker of Block 11** by order of the Commandant's Office.

APMO, D-AuI-3a/11c, FL Labor Deployment List.

Of the four female prisoners arrested in Auschwitz II, two are still in command arrest, that is, in the bunker of Block 11. The two other female prisoners were probably released into the camp.

APMO, D-AuII-3a/14c, FL Labor Deployment List.

322 female prisoners are transferred from the women's camp in Auschwitz II to another concentration camp.

APMO, D-AuII-3a/62, FL Occupancy Report.

49 female Jews are transferred from the transit camp to another concentration camp.

Ibid.

477 female Jews are selected and killed in the gas chambers.

Ibid.

The Special Squad begins to break up the walls of Crematorium IV, which was destroyed during the uprising.

SAM, *Amid Unspeakable Crimes*, p. 127.

1,500 Jewish men, women, and children arrive in an RSHA transport from the Theresienstadt ghetto. Young and healthy men and women are sent to the transit camp and the remaining persons are killed in the gas chambers. Among these arrivals are three men who receive Nos. 199785, B-13300, and B-13301, and who are transferred the following day to Men's Quarantine Camp B-IIa. 242 female prisoners are sent to the transit camp. Hans-Günter Adler arrives in Auschwitz with this transport and is sent to the transit camp, B-IIe. His wife and his mother are killed in the gas chamber on the day of their arrival.†

Adler, *Theresienstadt 1941–1945*, pp. 694, 697; APMO, D-AuII-3/1, p. 8, Quarantine List; D-AuII-3a/63a, FL Occupancy Report.

---

*They arrive in Buchenwald on October 16. The Political Department probably has nothing against transferring them to the SS Special Unit Dirlewanger.
**Of the two female prisoners interrogated, one was probably released into the camp and the other locked in the bunker.
†74 persons survived the camp (Adler, *Theresienstadt 1941–1945*, pp. 694, 697).

The occupancy levels of female prisoners in the individual auxiliary camps of Auschwitz are as follows:

APMO, D-AuIII-3a/1, vol. 9, Labor Deployment List.

Blechhammer, O.S. Hydrierwerke AG	158
Gleiwitz II, Deutsche Gasrusswerke GmbH	357
Neustadt, Schlesische Feinweberei AG	401
Freudenthal,* Emmerich Machold	300
Hindenburg,** Oberhütten	371
Bobrek, Siemens-Schuckert-Werke AG	37
Total	1,624

3,000 Jewish men, women, and children are killed in the gas chamber of Crematorium III, among them Jews from Theresienstadt, who were singled out on the ramp.

APMO, Memoirs/148, vol. 38a, Notes of a Member of the Special Squad.

OCTOBER 15

There are over 3,801 female prisoners in the women's camp of Auschwitz I. By comparison there are 30,516 female prisoners in Auschwitz II.

APMO, D-AuI-3a/16; D-AuII-3a/63a, FL Occupancy Report.

The occupancy level in the experimental station of Professor Dr. Clauberg increases by two and is 206 women for research purposes and eight prisoner orderlies.

APMO, D-AuI-3a, Labor Deployment List.

3,000 female Jews who were selected in Camp B-IIc without being entered in the camp registers are killed in the gas chamber of Crematorium II.

APMO, Memoirs/148, vol. 38a, Notes of a Member of the Special Squad.

A girl born in Birkenau receives No. 88988; the mother is Polish.

Docs. of ISD Arolsen, NA-Women/1986.

OCTOBER 16

19 female prisoners are sent to Auschwitz II.

APMO, D-AuII-3a/64a, FL Occupancy Report.

From among the Jews sent in an RSHA transport from Berlin, several women and five men are admitted to the camp and are given Nos. B-13302–B-13306. The remaining 800 prisoners are killed in the gas chamber of Crematorium III.

APMO, D-AuII-3/1, p. 8, Quarantine List; Memoirs/148, vol. 38a, Notes of a Member of the Special Squad.

Another female prisoner is locked in the bunker of Block 11 and yet another is brought from the women's camp in Auschwitz I to an interrogation.

APMO, D-AuI-3a/13b, FL Labor Deployment List.

*The founding date of this camp cannot be determined. The female prisoners probably worked in mineral water production.
**The Hindenburg A.C. was founded near the Hütte Donnersmarck in Hindenburg. In the first days of August 1944, approximately 400 female prisoners were transferred from Auschwitz II to this auxiliary camp. They work in Foundry III in armaments production and in Foundry IV in welding and assembling vehicles for transporting bombs. Camp Commander of the camp is SS Corporal Adolf Taube (compare Irena Strzelecka, "Das Nebenlager Hindenburg" [The Hindenburg Auxiliary Camp], HvA, no. 11 [1970]: 127–147).

600 prisoners who were selected by an SS Camp Doctor in the men's infirmary in Camp B-IIf are killed in the gas chamber of Crematorium III.	APMO, Memoirs/148, vol. 38a, Notes of a Member of the Special Squad.
A prisoner who was transferred from Dachau receives No. 199786.	APMO, D-AuII-3/1, p. 8, Quarantine List.
255 female prisoners are transferred from the women's camp in Auschwitz II to Flossenbürg, the Dresden auxiliary camp. They are deployed there in a munitions factory.	APMO, D-AuII-3a/64a, FL Occupancy Report; Dpr.-ZO/56, p. 138.
348 female prisoners are transferred from the transit camp in Auschwitz II to another concentration camp.	APMO, D-AuII-3a/64a, FL Occupancy Report.
Seven female prisoners die in Auschwitz II, three of them on the spot.	Ibid.

OCTOBER 17

It is recorded in the daily summary of the deployment of female prisoners in Auschwitz II that 1,116 female prisoners are employed in sorting stolen property, of whom 70 are in Sorting Squad I on the grounds of the DAW plant and 1,046 are in Sorting Squad II in Camp B-IIg in Birkenau.	APMO, D-AuII-3a/17b, p. 355b, vol. 1/8.
2,000 prisoners who were selected in the Monowitz A.C. near the Buna works of Auschwitz III are killed in the gas chamber of Crematorium II.	APMO, Memoirs/148, vol. 38a, Notes of a Member of the Special Squad.
24 female prisoners are sent to Auschwitz II.	APMO, D-AuII-3a/18c, FL Labor Deployment List.
156 female prisoners selected in the women's camp of Auschwitz II are killed in the gas chambers.	Ibid.
445 prisoners are transferred from Auschwitz to Buchenwald.	APMO, IZ-13/89, Various Documents of the Third Reich, p. 216.
SS Camp Doctor Mengele and the SS members Polenz and Josten employ female IBV prisoners in their houses.	APMO, D-AuI-3a/14b, FL Labor Deployment List.

OCTOBER 18

The Polish prisoners Władysław Piłat (No. 330), Jan Stojakowski (No. 577), and Tadeusz Lach (No. 22482) escape from Section III of Auschwitz II, called "Mexico." A civilian truckdriver brings the prisoners out of the camp hidden among the rubble of the razed barracks.	APMO, Ośw./1484, vol. 68, Account of Former Prisoner Jan Stojakowski.
Two Polish prisoners, Stanisław Zygula (No. 682) and Marian Szajer (No. 17036), escape from the Budy A.C. of Auschwitz II.*	APMO, Depositions, vol. 4, Account of Former Prisoner Stanisław Zyguła.

*Marian Szajer dies on December 3, 1944, in Budy, near Auschwitz, during a battle with SS men.

There are 3,801 female prisoners in the women's camp of Auschwitz I, of whom 47 women in the camp and in the auxiliary camps are sick, 55 are recovering, 29 are registered with the doctor, two are under arrest, i.e., locked in the bunkers of Block 11, four are being interrogated, and 97 are without occupation.

APMO, D-AuII-3a/18c, 356c, FL Labor Deployment List.

Of the four female prisoners who were arrested in the women's camp of Auschwitz II, one is still in the bunker of Block 11. 69 female prisoners are taken to the Political Department for interrogation.

APMO, D-AuII-3a/18b, p. 356b, Labor Deployment List.

2,154 female prisoners from the women's camp of Auschwitz II work in the agricultural squads, which are led daily to the agricultural operations of the SS. Some of the squads carry the name of the SS Squad Leaders, e.g., Daschke squad, which has 285 female prisoners, and Dachmann squad, with 136 female prisoners, work on October 18 on the farm in Birkenau. The following squads work in Budy: the forestry squad, with 90 female prisoners; the Pöllman squad, with 79 female prisoners; the Heims squad, with 124 female prisoners, and the fruit tree nursery squad, with 45 female prisoners. The following worked in the operations in Plawy: the Sinschkowski squad, with 100 female prisoners; the Mokr squad, with 331 female prisoners; and the Haseloch squad, with 200 female prisoners. The Klein squad, with 290 female prisoners, works in the gardening operations in Rajsko. The Schoninger squad, with 145 female prisoners, works in Harmense, and the Zippenpfenning squad, with 329 female prisoners, in Babitz. In addition to the SS Squad Leader, two to three armed SS men (depending on the number of prisoners) with vicious, appropriately trained dogs guard each labor squad. The female prisoners' tasks vary with the seasons.

APMO, D-AuII-3a/18b, p. 356b, Labor Deployment List.

3,000 Jewish men, women, and children sent in an RSHA transport from Slovakia are killed in the gas chamber of Crematorium III.

APMO, Memoirs/148, vol. 38a, Notebook of a Member of the Special Squad.

218 female prisoners who were previously in Auschwitz are transferred from Buchenwald to Auschwitz II, among them 49 female Gypsies from the Altenburg squad and 168 female Gypsies from the HASAG squad in Taucha near Leipzig. Another woman is transferred from Auschwitz I to Auschwitz II.

APMO, D-AuII-3a/65a, Fl Occupancy Report; Docs. of ISD Arolsen, Folder 14.

Five female prisoners are sent to Auschwitz II.

APMO, D-AuII-3a/65a, FL Occupancy Report.

13 female prisoners are transferred from Auschwitz II to Auschwitz I.

APMO, D-AuI-3a/19, FL Occupancy Report.

1,500 Jewish men, women, and children arrive in an RSHA transport from the ghetto in Theresienstadt. The young and the healthy, among them 157 women, are sent to the transit camp after the selection.* The remaining people were killed in the gas chamber of Crematorium III.

APMO, Memoirs/148, vol. 38a, Notebook of a Member of the Special Squad.

*According to Hans-Günter Adler's reports, 110 persons survived the camp (Adler, Theresienstadt 1941–1945, p. 694).

13 Polish male and female prisoners are killed in the gas chamber of Crematorium III.

Ibid.

The occupancy level of the Golleschau A.C. is 1,060.

APMO, D-AuIII, Golleschau/12, p. 109.

18 men, given Nos. 199811–199828, and 55 women, given Nos. A-25471–A-25525, are admitted to the camp after the selection of an RSHA transport of Jews from the prison in Budapest. The remaining people, among them 79 men, are killed in the gas chambers.

APMO, D-AuII-3/1, p. 8, Quarantine List; Docs. of ISD Arolsen, NA-Men/1980, NA-Women, Series A/1986.

300 people from various transports, including probably Jews from Budapest, are killed in the gas chamber of Crematorium III.

APMO, Memoirs/148, vol. 38a, Notebook of a Member of the Special Squad.

OCTOBER 19

22 Polish prisoners, who were serving out punishments in the bunkers of Block 11 of Auschwitz I, are killed in the gas chamber of Crematorium III.

Ibid.

A Polish female prisoner receives No. 88999.

Docs. of ISD Arolsen, NA-Women/1986.

From the prisoners sent in an RSHA transport from the Sered camp in Slovakia, 113 female Jews are admitted to the camp and given Nos. A-25528–A-25640.

Docs. of ISD Arolsen, NA-Women, Series A/1986.

In the daily summary of the deployment of female prisoner labor in the women's camp of Auschwitz I, it is noted that three female prisoners are under arrest and 15 are being interrogated in the Political Department.

APMO, D-AuI-3a/16c, FL Labor Deployment List.

In the daily summary of the labor deployment of female prisoners in the women's camp of Auschwitz II, it was noted that one female prisoner is under arrest by the Commandant's Office and 33 are being interrogated in the Political Department.

APMO, D-AuII-3a/19b, 357b, FL Labor Deployment List.

Eight female prisoners, of whom three were murdered on the spot, lose their lives in the women's camp of Auschwitz II.

APMO, D-AuII-3a/66a, FL Occupancy Report.

203 female prisoners, among them 200 Polish and Hungarian female Jews, are transferred from the transit camp of Auschwitz II to the Mühlhausen labor squad of Buchenwald.

Ibid.

2,000 Jewish men, women, and children sent from the Sered camp in Slovakia are killed in the gas chamber of Crematorium II.

APMO, Memoirs/148, vol. 38a, Notebook of a Member of the Special Squad.

2,000 Jewish men, women, and children are killed in the gas chamber of Crematorium III.

Ibid.

OCTOBER 20

1,500 Jewish men, women, and children are sent in an RSHA transport from the ghetto in Theresienstadt. After the selection, 169 women are admitted to the transit camp* and 173 men as prisoners to the camp. The men receive Nos. B-13307–B-13479. The remaining 1,158 people are killed in the gas chamber of Crematorium III.

APMO, Dpr.-Hd/1, pp. 123–128; D-AuII-3a/68, FL Occupancy Report; Memoirs/148, vol. 38a, Notebook of a Member of the Special Squad.

30 female prisoners are sent to Auschwitz II by various offices of Sipo and SD.

APMO, D-AuII-3a/67a, FL Occupancy Report.

13 German female prisoners are transferred from Auschwitz II to Flossenbürg.

Ibid.; Docs. of ISD Arolsen, Folder 7.

996 female Jews are transferred from the transit camp in Birkenau to Gross-Rosen, the Hochweiler A.C.

Ibid.

Two taxis and a prisoner transport truck are used to bring prisoner documents—i.e., index files, death certificates, and written complaints—from Auschwitz I to be burned in the crematorium.

Handwritten Account by an Unknown Member of the Special Squad, in SAM, *Amid Unspeakable Crimes*, p. 127.

117 female prisoners who were selected in the prisoners' infirmary in Camp B-Ia in Birkenau, and 77 female Jews, 23 from the prisoners' infirmary and 54 from the barracks for young people in the transit camp in Camp B-IIc, are killed in the gas chamber. A total of 194 women was selected.

APMO, D-AuII-3a/20c, 21c, FL Labor Deployment List; D-AuII-3a/67a, FL Occupancy Report.

1,000 young people between the ages of 12 and 18 are killed in the gas chamber of Crematorium III, including 357 young Jews who arrived the same day from an auxiliary camp in the village of Dyherrnfurth that belonged to the Gross-Rosen camp.

APMO, Memoirs/148, vol. 38a, Notebook of a Member of the Special Squad; Correspondence IV-8521/1044/83, List of Names, analyzed by Dr. Alfred Konieczny.

110 girls remain after the selection in the barracks for youths in the so-called transit camp.

APMO, D-AuII-3a/21c, FL Labor Deployment List.

OCTOBER 21

173 Jews are transferred from Auschwitz II to Auschwitz III, Fürstengrube A.C.** They were selected the day before from an RSHA transport and were given Nos. B-13007–B-13479.

APMO, Dpr.-Hd, pp. 123–128, Statements of Former Prisoner Rudolf Ehrlich.

The Polish prisoner Józef Barcikowski escapes from Auschwitz I.

APMO, German Search Book No. 310/45, p. 85.

The Polish prisoner Zdzisław Walczak (No. 39543) escapes from Auschwitz I.

APMO, Ośw./655, vol. 30, pp. 103–109, Account of Former Prisoner Zdzisław Walczak; Correspondence IV-2/1395/59 from Stanisław Kłodziński.

---

*According to Hans-Günter Adler, of those who were sent to the transit camp, 51 survived the war (Adler, *Theresienstadt 1941–1945*, p. 694).
**The occupancy level of the auxiliary camp is 1,138 who work in three shifts in the mines. Only a few prisoners work aboveground.

10 Jewish prisoners from an RSHA transport receive Nos. B-13480–B-13489.

Docs. of ISD Arolsen, NA-Men, Series B/1980.

A girl born in the women's camp of Auschwitz II receives No. 89006; the mother is a Pole.

Docs. of ISD Arolsen, NA-Women/1986.

Four female Poles sent to the camp by the Sipo and SD offices receive Nos. 89007–89010.

Ibid.

510 female Jews are transferred from the transit camp to another concentration camp.

APMO, D-AuII-3a/68, FL Occupancy Report.

The SS Camp Doctor conducts a selection in Transit Camp B-IIc, sending 513 female Jews to the gas chambers. Among those selected are 137 sick female prisoners from the prisoners' infirmary, 110 young female prisoners, i.e., girls who were still in Camp B-IIc, and 266 physically exhausted female prisoners.

APMO, D-AuII-3a/21c/22b, FL Labor Deployment List; D-AuII-3a/68, FL Occupancy Report.

In the daily summary of the labor deployment of female prisoners in Auschwitz II it is noted that three female prisoners remain under camp arrest, i.e., in the bunkers of Block 11, and that 77 female prisoners have been taken to the Political Department to be interrogated.

APMO, D-AuII-3a/12b, p. 359b, vol. 1/8.

60 female prisoners work in Expropriation Room I, on the grounds of the DAW, sorting and packing stolen goods, and 1,064 female prisoners work in Expropriation Room II in Camp B-IIg in Auschwitz II. A total of 1,124 female prisoners do this work. SS members Schmidt and Hoppmans are Squad Leaders.

APMO, D-AuII-3a/21b, p. 359b, vol. 1/8.

After a selection conducted in the men's camps 1,000 prisoners are killed in the gas chamber of Crematorium III.

APMO, Memoirs/148, vol. 38a, Notebook of a Member of the Special Squad.

OCTOBER 22

Two female prisoners from Auschwitz I and three from Auschwitz II are under Commandant's Office arrest in the bunkers of Block 11.

APMO, D-AuI-3a/22b; D-AuII-3a/19b, Labor Deployment List.

126 girls up to 14 years of age, among them newborns, and 323 girls from the Warsaw transports are prisoners in Camp B-Ia of Auschwitz II. 30 girls up to 14 years of age and 41 girls up to 16 years of age are prisoners in Camp B-IIb. A total of 520 girls are prisoners in both camps. There are also 36 invalid female prisoners over 60 years old in the women's camp.

APMO, D-AuII-3a/22b, Labor Deployment List.

A female Pole receives No. 89007.

Docs. of ISD Arolsen, NA-Women/1986; APMO, D-AuII-3a/23c, Labor Deployment List.

Over 2,000 female Jews from the Płaszów concentration camp and a good dozen male Jews from the prisoners' infirmary are brought to Auschwitz II in the evening. They have to spend the night in the so-called sauna.

Poliakov and Wulf, *Third Reich and the Jews*, pp. 286ff.

OCTOBER 23

SS Camp Doctor Mengele conducts a two-hour selection among the female Jews sent from the Płaszów concentration camp. He sends 1,765 women to Transit Camp B-IIc. The remaining women are killed in the gas chambers. Giza Landau, who arrives with this transport, receives No. A-26098, and another female Jew is given No. A-27752.

APMO, D-AuII-3a/69a, Fl Occupancy Report; Prisoner Card Index; Poliakov and Wulf, *Third Reich and the Jews*, pp. 286ff.

28 female prisoners sent to the camp by various Sipo and SD offices are sent to Auschwitz II.

APMO, D-AuII-3a/69a, FL Occupancy Report.

Five female prisoners are transferred to Auschwitz II from another concentration camp.

Ibid.

Nine female prisoners die in Auschwitz II, four of them in the gas chamber.

Ibid.

400 prisoners sent from the Gleiwitz A.C. camp are killed in the gas chamber of Crematorium III.

APMO, Memoirs/148, vol. 38a, Notebook of a Member of the Special Squad.

1,996 female Jews are transferred from the transit camp in Auschwitz II to other concentration camps.

APMO, D-AuII-3a/69a, FL Occupancy Report.

104 female prisoners are transferred from Auschwitz II to Auschwitz I.

Ibid.; D-AuI-3a/21c FL Labor Deployment List.

OCTOBER 24

The occupancy level in the experimental station of Professor Dr. Clauberg in the women's camp of Auschwitz I increases by 95; there are 301 women for research purposes and eight female prisoner orderlies. Clauberg probably selected the 95 women from among the 104 female prisoners transferred the day before from Auschwitz II.

APMO, D-AuI-3a/21b, Labor Deployment List.

Five female prisoners are delivered to Auschwitz II.

APMO, D-AuII-3a/70a, FL Occupancy Report.

A female prisoner is killed in Auschwitz II.

Ibid.

A female prisoner is transferred from the transit camp to another camp.

Ibid.

OCTOBER 25

219 men are admitted to auxiliary camps of Auschwitz after the selection from among the 1,715 Jewish men, women, and children sent in an RSHA transport from the Theresienstadt ghetto; 215 women are sent to the transit camp in Camp B-IIc.*

APMO, D-AuII-3a/71a, FL Occupancy Report; Adler, *Theresienstadt 1941–1945*, p. 694.

*According to Hans-Günther Adler, 159 people from this transport survived the camp.

209 female prisoners are transferred from Auschwitz II to Flossenbürg.

APMO, D-AuII-3a/71a, FL Occupancy Report.

Approximately 2,000 prisoners are transferred from Auschwitz I
to Auschwitz II. They are put in Camp B-IIe, which becomes a so-
called transport camp, since the transports of people being transferred to other concentration camps are assembled here.

APMO, Dpr.-Hd/7, p. 7, Depositions, vol. 13, pp. 78, 149.

The Commandant's Office of Dachau transfers 1,024 Jewish prisoners who are sick and unable to work to Auschwitz. The fact that
four of these prisoners die while the transport is still at the Dachau
train station is evidence of the prisoners' condition. They are probably killed in the gas chambers after arriving in Auschwitz.

APMO, D-Da-3/2/2, Transport
Lists to Auschwitz.

A female prisoner is sent to Auschwitz.

APMO, D-AuII-3a/71a, FL Occupancy Report.

In the daily labor deployment summary of the female prisoners in
Auschwitz I it is noted that four female prisoners remain under
Commandant's Office arrest in the bunkers of Block 11 and 12
female prisoners are being taken to interrogations in the Political
Department.

APMO, D-AuI-3a/22c, vol. 1/7.

In the daily labor deployment summary of the female prisoners in
Auschwitz II it is noted that three female prisoners remain under
Commandant's Office arrest in the bunkers of Block 11 and that
59 female prisoners are being interrogated in the Political Department.

APMO, D-AuII-3a/25c, vol. 1/8.

OCTOBER 26

A girl born in Auschwitz II receives No. 89097; the mother is a
Pole.

Docs. of ISD Arolsen, NA-
Women, p. 15/1986.

91 female prisoners sent to the camp by offices of the Sipo and SD
arrive at Auschwitz II.

APMO, D-AuII-3a/72a, FL Occupancy Report.

Seven female prisoners lose their lives in Auschwitz II, of whom
three are killed outright.

Ibid.

A female prisoner is transferred to another camp.

Ibid.

OCTOBER 27

Three female prisoners are sent to Auschwitz II.

Ibid.

Three prisoners lose their lives in Auschwitz II, of whom two are
killed on the spot.

APMO, D-AuII-3a/73, FL Occupancy Report.

497 female prisoners are transferred from the transit camp of Auschwitz II to another camp.

Ibid.

301 Polish prisoners are transferred from Auschwitz I to Buchenwald, the Wansleben am See squad.*

Docs. of ISD Arolsen, Folder 13.

150 Jewish prisoners from Theresienstadt are transferred from the transit camp of Auschwitz II to Buchenwald, the HASAG squad in Meuselwitz.

Ibid.

The number of prisoners employed in the incineration of corpses increases by one, for a total of 199 men.

APMO, D-AuII-3a, Inventory No. 29734.

Approximately 1,500 Jewish prisoners are transferred from the transit camp of Auschwitz II to Stutthof.

APMO, Dpr.-Hd/1, pp. 136, 142.

The driver of a truck, SS Private Johannes Roth, betrays a group of prisoners who attempt to escape from Auschwitz I. Members of the group are the members of the Auschwitz Combat Group, the RWO, and the camp resistance movement, Ernst Burger (No. 23850), the Austrian Bernard Świerczyna (No. 1393), Czesław Duzel (No. 3702), Zbigniew Raynoch (No. 60746), and Piotr Piaty (No. 130380), as well as SS man Frank, who had been taken into their confidence. Roth was to have smuggled the above-mentioned people out of the camp when he drove the dirty clothes to the laundry in Bielsko and to have left the escapees along the way in the village of Łeki. Instead he informs the Political Department of the plan, and a trap is arranged. The truck with the hidden prisoners departs and is stopped at a checkpoint. Several armed SS men climb in and the truck returns to the camp and drives directly to Block 11. When the hidden prisoners grasp the changed situation, they take poison. Zbigniew Ranoch and Czesław Duzel die, the others survive. The Austrian prisoners Rudolf Friemel (No. 25173) and Ludwig Vesely (No. 38169), who arranged the escape, are taken into custody. They are locked in the bunkers of Block 11. The SS man, Frank, who made arrangements with Roth, the driver, and trusted him, is also taken into custody.

APMO, Memoirs/49, vol. 7, pp. 1–28, Account of Former Prisoner Leon Mackiewicz (No. 3618); Mat.RO, vol. III, pp. 193ff.; Sobański, *Escapes from Auschwitz*, pp. 211–224.

With the truck that was to have driven to Bielsko, armed SS men take off for Łeki, four miles from Auschwitz, where Konstanty Jagiełło,** the leader of the resistance group that operated near the camp, waits with his comrades Tomasz Sobański,† Franciszek Dusik, Kazimierz Ptasiński, and the female messenger Wanda Dusik for the escapees in Julian Dusik's inn. During the operation Konstanty Jagiełło and Jan Galoch, the 70-year-old gardener who because of his deafness does not respond to the command by the SS man, "Hands up!" are shot to death. Julian, Franciszek, and Wanda

APMO, Mat.RO, vol. III, p. 193; Sobański, *Escapes from Auschwitz*, pp. 211–224.

---

*The prisoners are employed in the firm Kalkwerk-Georgi (Georgi Chalk Works), located in Wansleben am See, Teuschental Station, Arrival Track.
**Konstanty (Kostek) Jagiełło and Tomasz Sobański escaped on June 27, 1944, from Auschwitz. They return to the area near the camp and provide assistance for prisoners escaping from the camp within the framework of their activity in the resistance organization.
†Sobański observes the operation from a distance, since Jagiełło has sent him away at that moment to obtain a sack of civilian clothing for the escapees.

Dusik are arrested. The corpses of Jagiełło and Galoch are taken to the camp. The arrested, however, are left in the building, which has been taken over by the Auschwitz Gestapo; Kazimierz Ptasiński manages to escape in the night.

OCTOBER 28

The number of prisoners in the Special Squad employed to incinerate corpses increases by one prisoner, to 200.

APMO, D-AuII-3a/4, Inventory No. 29734.

19 prisoners receive Nos. 199839–199857. A Polish political prisoner housed in Quarantine Camp B-IIa receives No. 199857.

Docs. of ISD Arolsen, NA-Men/ 1980; APMO, D-AuII-3/1, p. 8, Quarantine List.

59 men are admitted to the camp and given Nos. 199858–199883 and B-13710–B-13742 after the selection from a mixed transport of 196 men and an unknown number of women sent by the Sipo and SD as well as the RSHA from Bozen (Bolzano). The remaining 137 men are killed in the gas chambers.

APMO, D-AuII-3/1, p. 8, Quarantine List.

Two female prisoners are sent to Auschwitz II and 105 newly arrived female prisoners are delivered to Auschwitz I.*

APMO, D-AuII-3a/74; D-AuI-3a/23, FL Occupancy Report.

Two female prisoners lose their lives in Auschwitz II, of whom one was killed on the spot.

APMO, D-AuII-3a/74, FL Occupancy Reports.

504 female prisoners—Poles, Russians, and French—are transferred from the women's camp in Auschwitz II to Flossenbürg.

Ibid.

1,308 female Jews** are transferred from the transit camp in Auschwitz II to Bergen-Belsen.

Ibid.; Dpr.-ZO/56, p. 153.

283 Czech and Polish Jews are transferred from Transit Camp B-IIe in Auschwitz II to Buchenwald, the Niederorschel squad.

Docs. of ISD Arolsen, Folder 13.

Polish prisoners waiting for a transport are taken from Camp B-IIe to the so-called sauna. In front of the bath a selection is conducted, during which primarily young Russians are separated from the older prisoners. After the bath the prisoners destined for the transport are taken to the men's camp in B-IId.

APMO, Ośw./Siwek/381, p. 150, Account of Former Prisoner Władysław Siwek.

OCTOBER 29

17 female prisoners sent to the camp by the Sipo and SD are delivered to Auschwitz II.

APMO, D-AuII-3a/75a, FL Occupancy Report.

653 female prisoners—Poles, Czechs, and Yugoslavs—are transferred from Auschwitz II to Ravensbrück.

Ibid.

---

*Possibly these are the women who arrived in the transport from Bozen.
**Anne and Margot Frank are probably transferred to Bergen-Belsen with this transport.

An SS Camp Doctor conducts a selection in Men's Quarantine Camp B-IIb, during which he singles out 64 prisoners. They are taken the same day to the bath of the prisoners' infirmary and from there are driven with other selected prisoners to the crematorium, in whose gas chambers they die.

APMO, Dpr.-Hd/6, p. 10.

Seven men are admitted to the camp and receive Nos. B-13747–B-13753 after the selection from among the Jews delivered in an RSHA transport from the Sered camp in Slovakia. Some of these prisoners are sent to the transit camp. The remaining prisoners, among them 84 men, are killed in the gas chambers.

APMO, D-AuII-3/1, p. 8, Quarantine List.

Approximately 2,200 prisoners—predominantly Poles and Russians—are transferred from the men's camp in B-IId in Auschwitz to Sachsenhausen.

APMO, Dpr.-ZO/55, p. 218; Ośw./Siwek/381, vol. 13, p. 150; Ośw./Brandhuber/1708, vol. 76, p. 112.

OCTOBER 30

1,362 female prisoners are transferred from Auschwitz II to Auschwitz I. They are put in Blocks 22 and 23 of the men's camp. These blocks are separated by fences from the rest of the men's camp.

APMO, D-AuI-3a/24, FL Occupancy Report; D-AuI-3a/27c, Labor Deployment List.

33 female prisoners are delivered to Auschwitz II.

APMO, D-AuII-3a/Labor Deployment Lists.

2,038 Jews arrive in an RSHA transport from the Theresienstadt ghetto. There are 949 men and boys and 1,089 women and girls in the transport. After the selection 217 men are sent to the camp and given Nos. B-13754–B-13970. 132 are put in the transit camp. The remaining 1,689 people are killed in the gas chambers.

APMO, D-AuII-3/1, p. 8, Quarantine List; D-AuII-3a/FL Labor Deployment Lists; Adler, *Theresienstadt 1941–1945*, p. 694.

The Police Court-martial of the Kattowitz Gestapo sits in Block 11 of Auschwitz I and condemns 59 male Poles and 10 female Poles to death. Inscriptions that the condemned left on the walls in Block 11 indicate that they were executed on November 1 in a crematorium of Auschwitz II.

APMO, Mat.RO, vol. IV, pp. 242–248.

OCTOBER 31

Eight female prisoners are brought to Auschwitz II.

APMO, D-AuII-3a/76a, FL Occupancy Report.

257 female prisoners are transferred from Auschwitz II to Auschwitz I. The occupancy level in Camps B-Ia, B-Ib, B-IIb, and Transit Camp B-IIc of Auschwitz II is 23,469 female prisoners.

Ibid.

The occupancy level of the women's camp in Auschwitz II and its auxiliary camps is 5,640 female prisoners.

APMO, D-AuI-3a/25, FL Occupancy Report.

OCTOBER 1–31

3,836 registered female prisoners die in Auschwitz II. 3,758 of these die in the gas chambers.

APMO, D-AuII-3a/51-76c, FL Occupancy Report.

206 female Hungarian Jews brought in a retransfer transport from the Buchenwald Hessisch-Lichtenau labor squad are killed in the gas chambers.

Docs. of ISD Arolsen, Folder 14.

NOVEMBER 1

11 female prisoners are sent to Auschwitz II.

APMO, D-AuII-3a/77a, FL Occupancy Report.

1,717 registered female prisoners are transferred from Auschwitz II to Ravensbrück.

Ibid.

634 female Jews* are transferred from Transit Camp B-IIc of Auschwitz II to Bergen-Belsen.

Ibid.

Men's Quarantine Camp B-IIa is dissolved, whereby the healthy prisoners and some of the prisoner functionaries are transferred to Camp B-IId and the sick are transferred to Prisoners' Infirmary B-IIf.

APMO, Dpr.-Hd/1, p. 74.

81 female prisoners die in Auschwitz II, 73 of them in the gas chamber.

APMO, D-AuII-3a/77a, FL Occupancy Report.

The occupancy level in the experimental station of Professor Dr. Clauberg in the women's camp of Auschwitz I decreases by one female prisoner for research purposes and includes 300 women for research purposes and eight prisoner orderlies.

APMO, D-AuI-3a/29b, Labor Deployment List.

Four female prisoners from the women's camp of Auschwitz I are under Commandant's Office arrest in Block 11.

Ibid.

NOVEMBER 2

Killing with Zyklon B gas in the gas chambers of Auschwitz is probably discontinued. The selected prisoners are shot to death in the gas chamber or on the grounds of Crematorium V.

Adler, *Theresienstadt 1941–1945*, p. 694; Škodowa, *Three Years*, p. 168.

Three female prisoners are sent to the women's camp of Auschwitz II.

APMO, D-AuII-3a/78a, FL Occupancy Report.

Nine female Jews from the Buchenwald labor squads of Mühlhausen (four women) and five from Allendorf/Mühlhausen (five Hungarian women) are sent in a retransfer transport. The retransferred prisoners were previously in Auschwitz II.

Ibid.; Docs. of ISD Arolsen, Folder 14.

11 female prisoners from Auschwitz II are transferred to Auschwitz I.

APMO, D-AuII-3a/78a, FL Occupancy Report.

*The female prisoner Lin Jaldati is on this transport. She meets Anne and Margot Frank in Bergen-Belsen (Lin Jaldati, "Memories of Anne Frank," in Joachim Hellwig and Günther Deicke, *A Diary for Anne Frank*, Berlin, 1959, pp. 32–46).

795 female Jews are transferred from Transit Camp B-IIc of Auschwitz II to Bergen-Belsen.

Ibid.

Eight female prisoners die in Auschwitz II, of whom four were killed on the spot.

Ibid.

NOVEMBER 3

Five female prisoners are transferred from Auschwitz II to Auschwitz I.

APMO, D-AuII-3a/79a, FL Occupancy Report.

Six female prisoners die in Auschwitz II, of whom two are killed on the spot. A female prisoner dies in Auschwitz I.

APMO, D-AuII-3a/79a; D-AuI-3a/26, FL Occupancy Report.

An RSHA transport of Jews, 990 men among them, arrives from the Sered camp. Men, women, and children are registered as prisoners and admitted to the camp without a selection.

APMO, D-AuII-3/1, p. 8, Quarantine List; Docs. of ISD Arolsen, NA-Men, Series B/1980.

10 Polish Jews receive Nos. B-14431–B-14440.

Docs. of ISD Arolsen, NA-Men, Series B/1980.

The transfer of sick prisoners from Quarantine Camp B-IIa to Prisoners' Infirmary B-IIf ends. Some of the prisoner doctors and nurses are also transferred. Among them is Dr. Otto Wolken (No. 128828), who on the day of his transfer to Camp B-IIf makes the last entries in the camp documents (among them the Quarantine List) that he compiled.

APMO, D-AuII-3/1, p. 8, Quarantine List.

Office B-II in the WVHA receives from Branch D a list of 1,910 prisoners from various concentration camps who are slated for the SS Special Dirlewanger Unit. Subsequently, 400 Auschwitz prisoners are chosen to be transferred as soon as October 10 to their destination.

APMO, D-RF-9 WVHA 2, p. 35, Edict Collection.

1,156 female Jews, so-called transit Jews, are located in Transit Camp B-IIc of Auschwitz II. Of them 138 are sick, two are children, 320 await a transport to another camp, and 696 remain in the camp "until further notice."

APMO, D-AuII-3a/34c, Labor Deployment List.

NOVEMBER 4

Transit Camp B-IIc is liquidated. The female Jewish prisoners there are taken into the women's camp in Auschwitz II. The term "transit Jews" is no longer used in the documents of Section B-III, "Mexico."

APMO, D-AuII-3a/35c, Labor Deployment List.

Two female prisoners are sent to Auschwitz II.

APMO, D-AuII-3a/80, FL Occupancy Report.

Three female prisoners die in Auschwitz II, of whom one is killed on the spot.

Ibid.

Eight female prisoners are released from Auschwitz II.

Ibid.

Four female prisoners are transferred from Auschwitz II to Auschwitz I.

Ibid.

2,362 female prisoners are transferred from Auschwitz II to other concentration camps.

Ibid.

NOVEMBER 6

50 female prisoners are delivered to Auschwitz II.

APMO, D-AuII-3a, Labor Deployment List.

Seven female prisoners are transferred from Auschwitz II to Auschwitz I.

APMO, D-AuI-3a/27, FL Occupancy Report.

In the daily summary of the labor deployment of female prisoners in the women's camp of Auschwitz I it is noted for the last time that the family of the former Commandant in Auschwitz, SS Lieutenant Colonel Höss, employs two IBV prisoners. In all probability the Höss family, that is, his wife and five children, leave the villa they occupy on the periphery of the main camp and move to the area near Ravensbrück. Four freight cars are required to move the abundant furnishings of the villa and the many possessions the Höss family acquired.

APMO, D-AuI-3a/34b, Labor Deployment List; SAM, Auschwitz in the Eyes of the SS, p. 279; Statement of Former Prisoner Stanisław Dubiel.

NOVEMBER 7

German prisoners slated for the SS Special Dirlewanger Unit are transported from Auschwitz.

APMO, D-AuII-3a/1, Prisoner Card Index.

23 female prisoners are delivered to Auschwitz II.

APMO, D-AuII-3a/82a, FL Occupancy Report.

10 female prisoners die in Auschwitz II, of whom eight are killed on the spot.

Ibid.

30 female prisoners are transferred from Auschwitz II to another concentration camp and 56 to Auschwitz I.

APMO, D-AuII-3a/82a; D-AuI-3a/28/29, FL Occupancy Report.

The occupancy level at the experimental station of Professor Dr. Clauberg in the women's camp of Auschwitz I decreases by two female prisoners for research purposes, leaving a total of 298 women for experimental purposes and eight prisoner orderlies.

APMO, D-AuI-3a/35b, Labor Deployment List.

The SS Camp Senior, SS Major Baer, orders all SS men and Wehrmacht soldiers to identify themselves by means of a password, since it has been ascertained that members of the Polish resistance, the Polish Home Army (AK), have shown up in SS and Wehrmacht uniforms in the Auschwitz interest zone. Baer requires all SS men, supervisors, SS assistants, nurses, and even German civilian employees to use the password to verify their identity to each other. He informs them that the password changes every day.

APMO, D-AuI-1, Special Garrison Order, Nov. 7, 1944.

207 prisoners are transferred from Dachau to Auschwitz II. Involved are 17 Germans, eight Belgians, 158 French, an Italian, five

APMO, D-Da-3/2/2, Transport Lists to Auschwitz.

Luxembourgers, and 18 Dutch. They probably receive the Nos. 200001–200207.

NOVEMBER 8

132 female prisoners die in Auschwitz II, of whom 131 are killed.

APMO, D-AuII-3a/83a, FL Occupancy Report.

A girl is born in the women's camp of Auschwitz II and receives No. 89136.

APMO, Mat.Ref.Inf., Prisoner Card Index.

The number of prisoners at the experimental station of Professor Dr. Clauberg in the women's camp of Auschwitz I decreases by one female prisoner; the total is 297 women for research purposes and eight prisoner orderlies.

APMO, D-AuI-3a/36b, Labor Deployment List.

NOVEMBER 9

The camp resistance movement informs the resistance cells near the camp of Baer's order of November 7.

APMO, Mat.RO, vol. III, p. 197.

SS Second Lieutenant Kurt Klipp becomes Commander of the Blechhammer auxiliary camp.

APMO, D-AuIII-1/68, Commandant's Office Order 11/44, Nov. 11, 1944.

460 female prisoners are sent to Auschwitz II, among them a woman who was already in the women's camp of Auschwitz II.

APMO, D-AuII-3a/84a, FL Occupancy Report.

Eight female prisoners are released from Auschwitz II.

Ibid.

12 female prisoners die in Auschwitz II, of whom five are killed on the spot.

Ibid.

300 female Jews who are slated for the new auxiliary camp Lichtewerden in Světla in Czechoslovakia, are transferred from Auschwitz II to Auschwitz III, and three female prisoners go to Auschwitz I.

APMO, D-AuII-3a/84a, FL Occupancy Report; D-AuIII-3a/29, Labor Deployment List/9.

In the daily summary of the labor deployment of female prisoners in the women's camp of Auschwitz I it is noted that two female prisoners have escaped from the camp.* They are registered in the group of the women who are unemployed and unable to work.

APMO, D-AuI-3a/37c, Labor Deployment List.

NOVEMBER 10

The number of the female prisoners being interrogated in the Political Department increases from three to six.

APMO, D-AuI-3a/38c, Labor Deployment List.

21 female prisoners are delivered to Auschwitz II and a female prisoner is transferred out of Auschwitz I.

APMO, D-AuII-3a/85, FL Occupancy Report.

34 female prisoners are released from Auschwitz II.

Ibid.

*Neither female prisoner is stricken from the register. They are probably captured during their escape attempt.

Five female prisoners die in Auschwitz II, four from "special treatment" (SB).

APMO, D-AuII-3a/85a, FL Occupancy Report.

300 female Jews are transferred from Auschwitz II to Gross-Rosen, the Brünnlitz auxiliary camp in Czechoslovakia, and 54 to the women's camp of Auschwitz I.

APMO, D-AuII-3a/85, FL Occupancy Report.

The SS Camp Commander of the Golleschau A.C. reports to the Commandant's Office of Auschwitz III that at 3:45 P.M., SS man Martin Kempl of the 2nd Company Monowitz shot and killed the prisoner Henrik Rosner (No. B-5828), a Hungarian Jew, as he crossed the sentry line during an escape. Kempl delivered two shots.

APMO, D-AuIII, Golleschau/12, p. 3.

The number of prisoners at the experimental station of Professor Dr. Clauberg in the women's camp of Auschwitz I increases by 54, totaling 351 women for research purposes and eight prisoner orderlies.

APMO, D-AuI-3a/38b, Labor Deployment List.

NOVEMBER 11

The number of prisoners at the experimental station of Professor Dr. Clauberg in the women's camp of Auschwitz I decreases by two female prisoners, totaling 349 women for research purposes and eight prisoner orderlies.

APMO, D-AuI-3a/39b, Labor Deployment List.

The number of female prisoners doing time in the bunker of Block 11 who came from the women's camp of Auschwitz I increases by two women, probably the women who attempted the escape, and totals three.

APMO, D-AuI-3a/39c, Labor Deployment List.

12 female prisoners are delivered to the women's camp of Auschwitz II.

APMO, D-AuII-3a/86, FL Occupancy Report.

Three female prisoners die in the women's camp of Auschwitz II, of whom one is killed.

Ibid.

Commandant Baer informs the SS members of the garrison that starting November 13 the prisoners' workday is to begin at 6:30 A.M. and end at 4:00 P.M. The midday break is to last only long enough for rapid consumption of the soup.

APMO, D-AuI-2, Garrison Order 28/44, Nov. 11, 1944.

300 female Jewish prisoners are transferred to the Lichtewerden A.C., which has recently been created near the yarn factory G. S. Buhl and Sons. The new A.C. is subordinate to Auschwitz III. It consists of six barracks—four living barracks, a kitchen barracks, and a wash barracks—which are surrounded by a wire fence and watchtowers. Director of the camp is an SS Staff Sergeant, whom the female prisoners call "Schnauze" ("Snout"). There are four women among the guards in the camp. The female prisoners start work there on November 13.*

APMO, D-AuIII-3a/29-31, Labor Deployment List; *Documents and Materials*, vol. I, pp. 49ff.

*The health of the female prisoners does not appear to be good, since more become sick daily. On December 6 invalid quarters are erected in the camp, in which 17 female prisoners are accommodated. 20 female prisoners report to the outpatient clinic (APMO, D-AuIII-3a/31–54, Labor Deployment List).

The following SS men are praised by Commandant Schwarz of Auschwitz II for thwarting an escape attempt:

SS Technical Sergeant Otto Moll,* of the Commandant's Office staff
SS Private Anton Bencie, of the 2nd Company
SS man Friedrich Sehne, of the 2nd Company
SS man Bruno Petzold, of the Commandant's Office staff

APMO, D-AuIII-1, Commandant's Office Order 11/44, Nov. 11, 1944.

NOVEMBER 12

25 female prisoners, among them five female Polish Jews, are transferred from Auschwitz II to Buchenwald, the HASAG squad in Meuselwitz near Leipzig.

APMO, D-AuII-3a/87a, FL Occupancy Report.

The Commandant's Office of Auschwitz I strikes from the records of the women's camp the names of two female prisoners who were transferred on November 8 to Ravensbrück, as confirmation of their entry and registration arrive from Ravensbrück.

APMO, D-AuI-3a/36c–39c; D-AuI-3a/30, FL Occupancy Report.

NOVEMBER 13

The number of prisoners at the experimental station of Professor Dr. Clauberg increases by one, totaling 350 women for research purposes and eight prisoner orderlies.

APMO, D-AuI-3a/41b, Labor Deployment List.

15 female prisoners die in Auschwitz II, of whom 11 are killed on the spot.

APMO, D-AuII-3a/88a, FL Occupancy Report.

1,205 female prisoners are transferred from Auschwitz II to Ravensbrück.

Ibid.; APMO, Dpr.-ZO/58, p. 81, Statements of Former Female Prisoner Rozalia Sabat; D-AuII-3/4, notebook with the title "Camp Occupancy" containing figures on the occupancy level and other entries relating to the Birkenau women's camp.

50 young prisoners are transferred from Auschwitz II to Gross-Rosen, the Landshut auxiliary camp. These young prisoners, born in the years 1928 to 1931, are sent to Auschwitz after the outbreak of the Warsaw uprising. In Gross-Rosen they receive Nos. 84905–84954.

APMO, Mat.Ref.Inf., Correspondence IV-8521/931/82-KL Gross-Rosen. [Gross-Rosen]

NOVEMBER 14

Five political prisoners, Polish Jews, are transferred to Buchenwald.

APMO, D-Bu-3/1/6, KL Buchenwald Arrivals Lists, vol. 6.

12 female prisoners sent to the camp by offices of the Sipo and SD are sent to Auschwitz II.

APMO, D-AuII-3a/89a, FL Occupancy Report.

Two female prisoners are transferred from Auschwitz I to Auschwitz II.

Ibid.

---

*After completion of the operation to exterminate the Hungarian Jews and Jews in the Lodz and Theresienstadt ghettos, Otto Moll returns to his earlier position as Camp Commander of Gleiwitz I A.C. The commendation is probably in connection with an unsuccessful escape attempt from Gleiwitz I.

14 female prisoners die in Auschwitz II, four of them are killed on the spot.

Ibid.

130 female prisoners are transferred from Auschwitz II to Gross-Rosen.

Ibid; APMO, D-AuII-3/4, Notebook "Camp Occupancy."

NOVEMBER 15

Two female prisoners are sent to Auschwitz II.

APMO, D-AuII-3a/90a, FL Occupancy Report.

Five female prisoners are transferred from Auschwitz II to Auschwitz I.

APMO, D-AuI-3a/31, FL Occupancy Report.

Six female prisoners die in Auschwitz II, of whom five are killed on the spot.

APMO, D-AuII-3a/90a, FL Occupancy Report.

The number of prisoners at the experimental station of Professor Dr. Clauberg decreases by two, totaling 348 women for research purposes and eight prisoner orderlies.

APMO, D-AuI-3a/43b, Labor Deployment List.

Two female prisoners are released from Auschwitz I.

APMO, D-AuII-3a/31a, FL Occupancy Report.

The number of prisoners in the women's camp of Auschwitz II is 16,081; in the women's camp of Auschwitz I are 5,775 female prisoners, and in the auxiliary camps under Auschwitz III there are 1,921 female prisoners.

APMO, D-AuII-3a; D-AuI-3a; D-AuIII-3a, Labor Deployment List.

NOVEMBER 16

An agent of Branch Group B in the WVHA conducts a check on the management of prisoners' clothing in Auschwitz. The inspection lasts four days. The examiner is interested in the condition of the clothing, that is, its storage, repair, disinfection, and cleaning.

APMO, IZ-13/89, Various Documents of the Third Reich, pp. 158ff.

A female prisoner is delivered to Auschwitz II.

APMO, D-AuII-3a/91a, FL Occupancy Report.

The number of prisoners at the experimental station of Professor Dr. Clauberg decreases by three, totaling 345 female prisoners for research purposes and eight prisoner orderlies.

APMO, D-AuI-3a/44b, Labor Deployment List.

18 female prisoners die in Auschwitz II, of whom 13 are killed directly.

APMO, D-AuII-3a/91a, FL Occupancy Report.

105 female prisoners are transferred from Auschwitz II to Auschwitz III, the Hindenburg A.C.

Ibid.

The number of prisoners in the Hindenburg A.C. is now 471 women. 457 female prisoners work in the foundries in Oberhütte and five in the auxiliary camp; nine female prisoners are in the infirmary.

APMO, D-AuIII-3a/34, Labor Deployment List.

NOVEMBER 17

Three female prisoners are delivered to Auschwitz II.

APMO, D-AuII-3a/92a, FL Occupancy Report.

Seven prisoners are transferred from Auschwitz II to Buchenwald, the Lippstadt auxiliary camp. They are Vida Levi (No. 75035), Berta Guth (No. 82065), Elisa Sara Bollermann (No. 82474), Anna Kalecka (No. 82529), Irma Baum (No. 82556), Maria Teresa d'Amici (No. 83021), and Anna Herget (No. 89127).

APMO, IZ-13/89, Various Documents of the Third Reich, p. 217; D-AuII-3a/92b, FL Occupancy Report.

Seven female prisoners die in Auschwitz II, of whom six are killed on the spot.

APMO, D-AuII-3a/92a, FL Occupancy Report.

40 female prisoners are transferred from Auschwitz II to Flossenbürg.

Ibid.; APMO, D-AuII-3/4, Notebook "Camp Occupancy."

Two female prisoners are transferred from Auschwitz II to Gross-Rosen.

Ibid.

The number of prisoners in the women's camp of Auschwitz II is 15,959 in Camps B-Ia–b, B-IIb, and B-IIg. The camp management decides to put all male and female prisoners together in Section B-II.* First, the female prisoners who are sick and unable to work and the children are transferred from Camp B-Ia–b to Camp B-IIe, the former Gypsy Family Camp and later transit camp or transport camp.

APMO, D-ezw Transport Camps. APMO, D-AuII-3a/91a, 92a, 93a, and other reports on the number of female prisoners and daily summaries of labor deployment. In these, "Camp B-Ia–b" is no longer mentioned. The terms "Camp B-IIc" and "Camp B-IIe" start to be used. Ośw./143, Account of Former Female Prisoner Bożena Krzywobtocka-Tyrowicz.

NOVEMBER 18

Four female prisoners are delivered to Auschwitz II.

APMO, D-AuII-3a/93, FL Occupancy Report.

12 female prisoners die in Auschwitz II, of whom eight are killed directly.

Ibid.

From the women's camp of Auschwitz II two female Jews are transferred to Gross-Rosen, five to Buchenwald, and 50 to Flossenbürg, the Zschopau secondary camp.

Ibid.; D-AuII-3/4, Notebook "Camp Occupancy."

On the basis of the findings of the examiner from Branch B in the WVHA regarding the management of prisoners' clothing, the First Protective Custody Commander in Auschwitz informs Block Seniors that prisoners' clothing is to be changed within the next four weeks. The change is to take place on Sunday afternoon. Each prisoner is to possess only one set of clothing. This is to be strictly controlled by the Block Seniors. The possession of several pieces of clothing or sabotage of clothing, such as intentional tearing or damaging, are to be reported directly to the Camp Commander. The Block Seniors, who are to confirm with their signature that they are aware of the regulation, are made responsible for its execution. The an-

APMO, D-AuI-3/42/R, Inventory No. 155930.

---

*The male prisoners remain in Camp B-IId and the prisoners' infirmary, B-IIf. Men's Quarantine Camp B-IIa is converted to a depot for various types of camp equipment.

nouncement of this regulation is posted in the individual prisoners' blocks. It was signed by the Director of the Prisoner's Clothing Room of Auschwitz I and by SS First Lieutenant Hössler, the First Protective Custody Commander.

NOVEMBER 19

Four female prisoners are transferred from Auschwitz I to Auschwitz II.

APMO, D-AuI-3a/32, FL Occupancy Report.

283 Jewish prisoners are transferred from Auschwitz II to the Niederorschel squad in Buchenwald.

APMO, D-Bu-3/1/6, KL Buchenwald Arrivals Lists, vol. 6.

NOVEMBER 20

Four female prisoners are transferred from Auschwitz II to the labor camp of Gerätebau (Machinery Construction) GmbH, Mühlhausen/Thüringen, belonging to Buchenwald. Among those transferred is a female Hungarian Jew, the physician Jolan Nemedi, who is not given a number.

APMO, D-AuII-3a/95a; D-Bu-e/1/4, pp. 33ff., KL Buchenwald Arrivals Lists.

Two female prisoners are sent to Auschwitz II.

APMO, D-AuII-3a/95a, FL Occupancy Report.

15 female prisoners die in Auschwitz II, of whom five are killed directly.

Ibid.

21 female prisoners—20 nurses and a physician—are transferred from Auschwitz II to Buchenwald, the Leipzig-Schönefeld (HASAG) squad. They are Cezara Kobylańska (No. 43520), Maria Michalak (No. 44178), Apolonia Kilian (No. 44735), Keti Kowalska (No. 46245), Zofia Owsianowska (No. 46625), Jadwiga Rutyna (No. 55113), Elżbieta Panczynszyn (No. 55852), Regina Stanisławowa (No. 82384), Fajna Kuznesowa (No. 82744), Marianna Vafek (No. 82859), Jadwiga Krasnowska (No. 87132), Waleria Burczyńskaja (No. 69814), Regina Kozmińska (No. 44128), Sara Gelder (No. 76559), Elisabeth Bollasch (No. 76429), Mona Buchholz (No. A-9787), Fanny Chiel (No. A-8619), Regina Ancol (No. A-7070), Annette Karbowitz (No. A-8619), and two female Hungarian Jews, Margit Schreiber and the physician Margarete Kallosch.

APMO, IZ-18/89, Various Documents of the Third Reich, p. 217; D-Bu-3/1, pp. 29, 30, 31, KL Buchenwald Arrivals Lists, Women.

NOVEMBER 21

The number of prisoners at the experimental station of Professor Dr. Clauberg decreases by 53, totaling 292 women for research purposes and eight prisoner orderlies.

APMO, D-AuI-3a/49b, Labor Deployment List.

Three female prisoners are transferred from Auschwitz II to Auschwitz I.

APMO, D-AuII-3a/96a; D-AuII-3a/33, FL Occupancy Report.

From Auschwitz I, 235 female prisoners are transferred to Gross-Rosen and five to Flossenbürg.

APMO, D-AuII-3a/96a, FL Occupancy Report; D-AuII-3/4, Notebook "Camp Occupancy."

Five female prisoners die in Auschwitz II, of whom four are killed directly.

APMO, D-AuII-3a/96a, FL Occupancy Report.

Four Polish prisoners escape from Auschwitz I: Leszek Piwirotto (No. 380), Stanisław Pawliczek (No. 1085), Stanisław Kwiatkowski (No. 12374), and Władysław Kokosiński (No. 41766).

APMO, Mat.RO, vol. III, p. 198; Dpr.-Hd/8, p. 108; German Search Book No. 310/45, p. 328; Stanisław Pawliczek, "Droga do słońca" (Road to the Sun), ZO, no. 5 (1961), pp. 87–95.

On the authority of an order from Himmler,* the Commandant's Office of Auschwitz I requests the Central Construction Administration of the Waffen SS and Police of Auschwitz to build a special passage, the so-called lion's way,** between the camp and the DAW and Weichsel-Union workshops for the use of the male and female prisoners employed there.

APMO, Dpr.-Hd/12, p. 124, Appendix 82.

NOVEMBER 22

The number of prisoners in the experimental station of Professor Dr. Clauberg decreases by three, totaling 289 women for research purposes and eight prisoner orderlies.

APMO, D-AuI-3a/50b, Labor Deployment List.

Eight female prisoners are sent to Auschwitz II.

APMO, D-AuII-3a/54b, Labor Deployment List.

From Auschwitz II, 300 female prisoners are transferred to Buchenwald, the Lippstadt squad, and 450 female prisoners to Flossenbürg, the Zschopau squad.

APMO, D-AuII-3a/55b, Labor Deployment List; Docs. of ISD Arolsen; D-Bu-3/1/4, pp. 36–41, KL Buchenwald Arrivals Lists.

From Auschwitz II two female prisoners are transferred to Mauthausen, three Hungarian female prisoners to Buchenwald, 12 female prisoners to Neuengamme, and a female prisoner to Bergen-Belsen.

APMO, D-AuII-3a/53b, Labor Deployment List; D-AuII-3/4, Notebook "Camp Occupancy."

NOVEMBER 23

The number of prisoners at the experimental station of Professor Dr. Clauberg decreases by 20, totaling 269 women for research purposes and eight prisoner orderlies. They are probably transferred to Auschwitz II.

APMO, D-AuI-3a/51b, Labor Deployment List.

29 female prisoners are transferred from Auschwitz I to Auschwitz II.

APMO, D-AuI-3a/54b, Labor Deployment List.

49 female prisoners are transferred from Auschwitz I to Auschwitz II.

Ibid.; APMO, D-AuII-3/4, Notebook "Camp Occupancy."

NOVEMBER 24

The transfer of female prisoners from Camps B-Ia–b to B-IIa and B-IIe is ended.† Camp B-IIb is slated for working female prisoners.

APMO, Dpr.-Hd/6, p. 87, Statements of Former Prisoner Dr.

*Written communication of the Head of Branch D in the WVHA of July 23, 1944.
**The "Lion's Way" is a covered passage; the name alludes to the passage in a circus between the lion's cage and the ring.
†From November 24 the term "BIa–b" was no longer used in the documents of Section IIIa of the women's camp of Auschwitz II, i.e., in the daily summaries of the labor deployment and in the reports on the changes in the occupancy level.

The sick, exhausted, and invalid female prisoners as well as children are put in Camp B-IIe, the former Gypsy Family Camp. The barracks are divided in the following way: Barracks 16 for non-Jewish female prisoners suffering from internal diseases; Barracks 18 for female prisoners suffering from diarrhea; Barracks 20 as a surgical section; Barracks 22 for female Jews suffering from internal diseases; Barracks 24 for German female prisoners suffering from internal diseases as well as for children and functionary prisoners; Barracks 28 as an outpatient clinic and gynecological section; Barracks 30 for female prisoners with tuberculosis; Barracks 32 for female prisoners with infectious diseases; Barracks 11 and 13 are set aside for children.

Otto Wolken; Ośw./Krzywo-błocka-Tyrowicz/413, vol. 15, pp. 85ff.

The number of prisoners in the women's camp of Auschwitz II is 14,793.

APMO, D-AuII-3a/55b, Labor Deployment List.

Six female prisoners are delivered to Auschwitz II.

APMO, D-AuII-3a/97a, FL Occupancy Report.

16 female prisoners die in Auschwitz II, of whom 10 are killed on the spot.

Ibid.

From Auschwitz II, 171 female prisoners are transferred to Flossenbürg, 295 female prisoners to Buchenwald, 30 female prisoners to Gross-Rosen, eight female prisoners to Bergen-Belsen, seven female prisoners to Neuengamme, and one female prisoner to Ravensbrück.

Ibid.; APMO, D-AuII-3/4, Notebook "Camp Occupancy."

NOVEMBER 25

22 female prisoners are transferred to Gross-Rosen, 19 female prisoners to Buchenwald, four female prisoners to Auschwitz I, three female prisoners to Sachsenhausen, and one female prisoner to Neuengamme.

APMO, D-AuII-3a/57b, Labor Deployment List; D-AuII-3/4, Notebook "Camp Occupancy."

Eight female prisoners are sent to Auschwitz II.

APMO, D-AuII-3a/58b, Labor Deployment List; *Documents and Materials*, vol. 1, p. 118.

24 female prisoners die in Auschwitz II, of whom 13 are killed directly.

APMO, D-AuII-3a/57b, Labor Deployment List; *Documents and Materials*, vol. 1, p. 118. [24 female prisoners]

By order of the Head of the WVHA, Auschwitz I is renamed Auschwitz Concentration Camp and Auschwitz III is renamed Monowitz Concentration Camp. Auschwitz II, Birkenau, is made part of Auschwitz Concentration Camp, that is, of the old main camp. The Camp Senior and former Commandant of Auschwitz I, SS Major Baer, orders that starting immediately, all SS men and all female supervisors of Auschwitz II, as well as the guard company and the dog squadron become part of the command unit Auschwitz Concentration Camp (C.C.). The male and female prisoners of Auschwitz II become part of the occupancy total of Auschwitz C.C.

APMO, D-AuI-1, Garrison Order 29/44, Nov. 25, 1944.

The dismantling of the technical facilities in Crematorium II begins. First, the motor, which pumps the air out of the gas chambers, is dismantled: it is sent to Mauthausen, and the pipes to Gross-Rosen.

Handwritten record of an unknown member of the Special Squad, in SAM, *Amid Unspeakable Crimes*, p. 127.

NOVEMBER 26

1,014 prisoners are transferred from Dachau to Auschwitz: 850 French, 12 Belgians, a Dane, three Italians, two Croats, 10 people from Lorraine, seven Luxembourgers, 14 Dutch, a Serb, four Spaniards, two Slovaks, an Argentinian, a Swiss, an Arab, a Russian, a stateless person, and 103 Germans. Among the Germans are 23 PSV prisoners, 12 accused of desertion from the Wehrmacht, and one labeled a "Red Spain soldier," who had fought as member of the International Brigades in the Spanish Civil War, as well as a prisoner sent to the camp in compliance with Paragraph 175. 975 of the prisoners transferred are labeled as political prisoners, i.e., "protective custody." They probably receive Nos. 201210–201231.

APMO, D-Da-3/2/2, Transport Lists to Auschwitz; Docs. of ISD Arolsen, NA-Men/1980.

A selection is conducted among the 200 prisoners of the Special Squad who operate the crematoriums in Birkenau, during which 30 prisoners were singled out for work in Crematorium V. 170 prisoners are told that they will be taken to the so-called sauna.*

Handwritten record of an unknown member of the Special Squad, in SAM, *Amid Unspeakable Crimes*, p. 128.

The SS Commander in Chief orders the destruction of the crematoriums in Auschwitz-Birkenau.

IMG, vol. 11, p. 370; vol. 33, pp. 68–70 (Doc. No. PS-3762), Statements of Kurt Becher; Adler, *Theresienstadt 1941–1945*, p. 694; Reitlinger, *Final Solution*, p. 608.

NOVEMBER 27

The women's camp in Birkenau receives the label "Auschwitz Concentration Camp, Birkenau External Camp, Women's Camp." The occupancy level there is 14,206 women; in the women's camp in Auschwitz are 5,740 female prisoners.

APMO, D-AuII-3a/98a; D-AuI-3a/34, FL Occupancy Report.

The occupancy level in the experimental station of Professor Dr. Clauberg decreases by one, totaling 268 women for research purposes and eight prisoner orderlies.

APMO, D-AuI-3a/55b, Labor Deployment List.

Two female prisoners are delivered to Auschwitz-Birkenau.

APMO, D-AuII-3a/60b, Labor Deployment List.

Four female prisoners are transferred from the women's camp of Auschwitz-Birkenau to the women's camp of Auschwitz.

APMO, D-AuI-3a/34, FL Occupancy Report.

*An anonymous author, a member of the Special Squad, wrote in his notes, "We are now going to the zone. The 170 remaining men. We are certain that they are taking us to our deaths. They have selected 30 people to remain in Crematorium V. Today is November 26, 1944." Of the 170 prisoners of the Special Squad, 70 are probably kept in the camp and sent to the so-called demolition squad, which was employed in dismantling the crematoriums and eliminating all traces of the crimes. These two groups, the 30 prisoners who operated Crematorium V and the 70 prisoners from the demolition squad, leave the camp on January 18, 1945, together with the prisoners evacuated from Birkenau. These prisoners arrive at Mauthausen (several escape en route), where they conceal their activity in the crematoriums and thus save their lives. The rest of the approximately 100 prisoners selected on November 26 are probably shot to death in Birkenau in one of the incineration pits and their corpses burned. This is suggested by the few brief sentences in the hand of Lejb (Lajb) Langfuss (*HvA*, no. 14 [1973]: 69).

12 female prisoners are transferred from the women's camp of Auschwitz-Birkenau to Gleiwitz II, which belongs to Monowitz Concentration Camp.

APMO, D-AuIII-3a/46, Labor Deployment List.

55 prisoners are transferred from Auschwitz to Buchenwald, the Langensalza labor squad. They are prisoners who were captured while escaping and must wear a red dot, a so-called escape dot.

APMO, IZ-13/89, Various Documents of the Third Reich, p. 216.

SS Captain Kersten, the agent of Branch B, gives the WVHA an extremely critical report of his inspection, conducted November 16–19, 1944, of clothing management in Auschwitz. He claims that most of the prisoners who work in closed and heated rooms, in the tailor and shoe-repair shops, in the disinfection area, the laundry, and the kitchen, wear double under- and outerwear.* The clothing lies in the repair, disinfection, and laundry areas in great heaps disorderly and unsorted. When garments are pulled out they are only further damaged. The clothing is stuffed unsorted into the washing machines, without regard for the type of weave: synthetics, cotton, and wool are washed together at the same temperature. This understandably leads to further damage. The supervision is unsatisfactory. The removal of refuse is particularly unacceptable. The most various of textiles are brought in refuse containers to the compost piles outside of the camp, the sight of which is horrifying. It is incomprehensible and indescribable, how many pieces of clothing and blankets could be pulled out of this refuse. The inventory of what appeared here just within one month speaks for itself: 35 cloth coats, 72 blouses of cloth and canvas, 114 pairs of pants of cloth and canvas, 175 pullovers, 415 shirts, 297 underpants, 463 handkerchiefs, 2,243 socks, 387 caps, and 141 mittens. Part of this clothing could be worn, part could be made use of in the prison tailor shops. SS Captain Kersten closes his report with the conclusion that the clothing available in Auschwitz, especially in view of the high-quality civilian clothing from the Jewish resettlement, should suffice for a long time if used sensibly.

APMO, IZ-13/89, Various Documents of the Third Reich, pp. 159–163.

NOVEMBER 28

148 female prisoners, among them 115 reeducation prisoners, are transferred from the Auschwitz-Birkenau women's camp to the Auschwitz women's camp.

APMO, D-AuII-3a/99a, FL Occupancy Report; D-AuII-3a/57c, Labor Deployment List.

141 female prisoners are transferred from the Auschwitz-Birkenau women's camp to other concentration camps, 128 of them to Gross-Rosen and one to Mauthausen.

APMO, D-AuII-3a/99a, FL Occupancy Report; D-AuII-3/4, Notebook "Camp Occupancy."

Nine female prisoners die in Auschwitz-Birkenau, of whom five are killed directly.

APMO, D-AuII-3a/99a, FL Occupancy Report.

*In this manner prisoners in this labor squad bring clothing and underwear into the camp for their fellow prisoners who work outside, in construction projects, road construction, etc. Although the storerooms are stuffed with civilian clothing, in January 1945 the prisoners are forced to march away from the approaching front in their striped canvas clothing, often without coats, caps, and gloves.

NOVEMBER 29

Barbara Dziewur is born in the women's camp of Auschwitz-Birkenau; she receives No. 89325.

APMO, Mat.Ref.Inf., Prisoner Card Index; D-AuII-3a/100a, FL Occupancy Report.

Two Polish prisoners escape from the Neu-Dachs A.C. in Jaworzno: Wiktor Pasikowski (No. 745) and Włodzimierz Smigielski (No. 6916). The prisoners ride out of the auxiliary camp on the locomotive of the narrow-gauge track. The escape succeeds thanks to the help of civilian workers, their families, and friends.

APMO, Depositions, vol. 6, p. 111, Account of Former Prisoners Wiktor Pasikowski and Włodzimierz Smigielski.

11 female prisoners die in the women's camp of Auschwitz-Birkenau, of whom seven are killed on the spot.*

APMO, D-AuII-3a/100a, FL Occupancy Report.

231 female prisoners are transferred from the women's camp of Auschwitz-Birkenau to Gross-Rosen.

Ibid.; D-AuII-3/4, Notebook "Camp Occupancy."

Two female prisoners are transferred from the women's camp of Auschwitz C.C. to another concentration camp, and a female prisoner dies.

APMO, D-AuI-3a/35, FL Occupancy Report; D-AuI-3a/57b, Labor Deployment List.

The number of prisoners at the experimental station of Professor Dr. Clauberg decreases by one female prisoner for research purposes. This is probably the woman mentioned in the occupancy report as dead.

The female prisoners transferred on November 27, 1944, from Auschwitz-Birkenau to Gleiwitz II A.C. are employed in the Deutsche Gasrusswerke (Degusa). The number of prisoners in the Gleiwitz A.C. increases from 359 to 371 prisoners. Of them 356 female prisoners worked in the Deutsche Gasrusswerke (German Gas Coke Company), one in the Borsig-Koks-Werke (Borsig Coke Works), and one in the auxiliary camp itself. 12 female prisoners are in the sickroom and one is unemployed.

APMO, D-AuIII-3a/47, Labor Deployment List.

During an American air raid on the I. G. Farben works and Monowitz, photographs are made in the region of Auschwitz, in which Auschwitz I, II, and III and the I. G. Farben compound can be seen.**

APMO, Analyses, Aerial Photographs, vol. 64, pp. 60–67.

*In the occupancy report of the women's camp of Auschwitz-Birkenau of November 30, 1944, it is stated for the last time that the number of prisoners decreased on November 29, 1944, viz. four female prisoners died a natural death and seven female prisoners were killed by so-called special treatment. After the beginning of the demolition of the extermination facilities probably no more selections are conducted among the prisoners. The prisoners die a "natural death" from starvation, heavy labor, and the inconceivable living, hygiene, and sanitary conditions.
**These photographs are a by-product of the Allies' tactical air reconnaissance that had comprised Auschwitz since April 4, 1944. In the photographs from November 29 for the first time no train can be seen on the siding in Birkenau. The external appearance of the extermination facilities is unchanged, with the exception of the gas chambers and Crematorium IV, which were razed after October 7, 1944. The dissolution of Section III in Birkenau, so-called Mexico, can be seen clearly (APMO, Analyses, vol. 64, p. 122; Brugioni and Poirier, *Holocaust Revisited*; Gilbert, *Auschwitz and the Allies*, p. 388).

NOVEMBER 30

Five female prisoners are released from the women's camp of Auschwitz-Birkenau.

APMO, D-AuII-3a/101a, FL Occupancy Report.

A female Hungarian Jew is transferred from the women's camp of Auschwitz-Birkenau to Neuengamme.

APMO, D-AuII-3a/191a, FL Occupancy Report; D-AuII-3/4, Notebook "Camp Occupancy."

Because of the prevailing condition in the camp, 27 female prisoners die in the women's camp of Auschwitz-Birkenau.

APMO, D-AuII-3a/191a, FL Occupancy Report.

NOVEMBER 1–30

439 registered female prisoners die in the women's camp of Auschwitz-Birkenau, 322 by violence—the so-called special treatment.

APMO, D-AuII-3a/77a-101a.

DECEMBER 1

A female prisoner is delivered to the women's camp of Auschwitz-Birkenau.

APMO, D-AuII-3a/102a, FL Occupancy Report.

From the women's camp of Auschwitz-Birkenau 16 prisoners are transferred to another concentration camp and one prisoner to the Auschwitz women's camp.

Ibid.

10 female prisoners die as a result of the poor living conditions in the women's camp of Auschwitz-Birkenau.

Ibid.

Nine prisoners are transferred from Auschwitz to Buchenwald, the Langensalza labor squad. These prisoners are transferred on January 6, 1945, from the Langensalza squad to Buchenwald. In a written document of the Political Department in Buchenwald it is stated that these prisoners, who were also marked by a red dot, a so-called escape dot, were sent from Auschwitz to the Langensalza squad. Eight Poles and one German (also possibly an Austrian) are political prisoners. They are Jan Brummer (No. 765), Dionizy Barański (No. 127713), Stanisław Fudalej (No. 137898), Kazimierz Pejas (No. 150499), Mieczysław Armatys (No. 190656), Zygmunt Stadnicki (No. 190657), Andrzej Molenda (No. 190658), Zbigniew Stepka (No. 190660), and the German Ernst Müller (No. 58615).

APMO, Docs. of ISD Arolsen; D-Bu-3/1/6, pp. 20, 30, KL Buchenwald Arrivals Lists.

The Crematorium III demolition squad is created in Birkenau. It consists of 100 female prisoners who worked on the demolition of the crematorium.*

APMO, D-AuII-3a/62b, Labor Deployment List.

DECEMBER 2

The number of prisoners at the experimental station of Professor Dr. Clauberg decreases by one, totaling 226 women for research

APMO, D-AuI-3a/60b, Labor Deployment List; D-AuI-3a/36, FL Occupancy Report.

---

*At the same time a squad of male prisoners is put together for the demolition of the crematorium. The number of persons in it is unknown. The prisoners have to pound holes in the walls of the gas chambers for placement of dynamite charges (APMO, Dpr.-Hd/3, p. 134, Statements of Former Female Prisoner Stanisława Rachwałowa).

Crematorium IV. Prisoners are preparing the area in the foreground for the construction of the personal effects warehouse Canada II.

purposes and eight prisoner orderlies. One woman probably died, since the "departure" of a female prisoner and the delivery of two female prisoners is noted in the occupancy report.

13 female prisoners in Birkenau die of exhaustion.

APMO, D-AuII-3a/103a, FL Occupancy Report.

From Auschwitz-Birkenau 100 female prisoners are transferred to Flossenbürg, and one female prisoner, No. 9139, to Auschwitz.

APMO, D-AuII-3a/104a, FL Occupancy Report; D-AuII-3/4, Notebook "Camp Occupancy."

DECEMBER 3

Two female prisoners are transferred from Auschwitz-Birkenau to Gross-Rosen.

APMO, D-AuII-3a/104a, FL Occupancy Report; D-AuII-3/4, Notebook "Camp Occupancy."

1,120 prisoners, skillled workers, are transferred from Mauthausen to Auschwitz C.C. Among them are Belgians, Greeks, Yugoslavs, Italians, French, Germans, Hungarians, Norwegians, Lithuanians, Latvians, Slovaks, Czechs, Romanians, Luxembourgers, and Dutch. There are no Jews in the transport. The prisoners receive Nos. 201237–202356.

APMO, D-Mau, Folder 4, pp. 2154, 2176; Folder 5, p. 2704; Folder 8, pp. 3563–3584, List of Names; Docs. of ISD Arolsen, NA-Men.

A resistance group that belongs to the "Sosienka" association and that consists of prisoners who have escaped from the camp waits in the house of the Zdrowak family in Budy-Bór for a planned operation. Surrounded by SS men in an ambush, they take up the fight. Stanisław Furdyna, Stanisław Kwiatkowski, and Marian Szajer are killed in the battle. The entire Zdrowak family—Anna, her husband, and the daughers Zofia and Emilia—and the tenant Edmund Kluczny and the prisoner Antoni Wykręt are arrested. Only the youngest, a 10-year-old son, is able to save himself by hiding

APMO, Mat.RO, vol. III, pp. 204, 209; Depositions, vol. 42, p. 107, Account of Anna Zdrowak and Emilia Zdrowak-Kamińska.

at neighbors' during the fray. All the men from the neighborhood, moreover, are arrested as hostages. During the transport to Auschwitz C.C., Antoni Wykręt, after he recovers consciousness, springs from the moving truck and escapes.*

The Camp Commander of the Golleschau A.C. reports to the Commandant's Office of Monowitz C.C. that on December 3 he has transferred 33 Polish prisoners and a Polish Jew to Birkenau. The transfer of the 34 prisoners decreases the number of prisoners in the auxiliary camp from 1,045 to 1,011 prisoners.

APMO, D-AuIII, Golleschau/12, p. 114.

DECEMBER 4

The number of female prisoners at the experimental station of Professor Dr. Clauberg increases by three, totaling 269 women for research purposes and eight prisoner orderlies.

APMO, D-AuI-3a/62b, Labor Deployment List.

500 Polish prisoners are transferred from Auschwitz C.C. to Buchenwald. They arrive in Buchenwald on December 7, 1944, in very poor physical and psychological condition. Because of the Allied air raids the transport is detained at various train stations. En route the prisoners receive no nourishment whatsoever.

Docs. of ISA Arolsen; APMO, D-Bu-3/1/6, KL Buchenwald Arrivals List.

The following eight prisoners are transferred from Mauthausen to Auschwitz C.C.: the German Otto Bruder, the Frenchman Roger Decote, the Yugoslavs Svetyslaw Aleksic and Steven Cvorkov, and the Hungarians Lajos Beres, Sandor Tonogy, Joszef Urlauber, and Kalman Varga.

APMO, D-Mau, Folder 8, p. 3561.

DECEMBER 5

The women's squad employed in dismantling Crematorium III increases by 50, to 150.

APMO, D-AuII-3a/66b, Labor Deployment List.

The woodland demolition squad is created in Birkenau, to which 50 female prisoners are sent. The squad works on the grounds of the so-called big sauna and Crematorium IV. It must clear the grounds and fill in and cover with grass all the pits previously used for burning the corpses of those killed in the gas chambers. It must also sift through the human ash remains before they are strewn in the Vistula.** Little trees are planted on the leveled grounds.

APMO, D-AuII-3a/66b, Labor Deployment List.

843 prisoners work in Sorting Room II in Camp B-IIg.

Ibid.

*During the battle an SS man dies. The Zdrowak family and Edmund Kluczny are locked in the bunker until the evacuation of the camp. During the evacuation Anna Zdrowak escapes with her daughters in the neighborhood of Rybnik. Her husband, however, dies in Mauthausen. The other men are released from the bunker after a month. All are brutally treated and tortured during the interrogations.
**The male and female prisoners attempt to sabotage the orders of the SS and avoid whenever possible removing the ashes of the murdered before the pits are filled in, in the hope that these human remains—some incompletely burned bones—will in the near future prove the crime of genocide that was committed here.

A female prisoner is transferred from the women's camp of Auschwitz-Birkenau to Dachau.

APMO, D-AuII-3a/105a, FL Occupancy Report.

Nine female prisoners are delivered to the women's camp of Auschwitz C.C.

APMO, D-AuI-3a/37, FL Occupancy Report.

16 female dwarfs* on whom SS Doctor Mengele has conducted experiments, are transferred from the prisoners' infirmary for men in B-IIf to the women's camp in B-IIe.

APMO, D-AuII-3a/66b, Labor Deployment List.

Nine female prisoners die of exhaustion in the women's camp.

APMO, D-AuII-3a/105a, FL Occupancy Report.

DECEMBER 6

Six female prisoners are transferred from the women's camp of Auschwitz-Birkenau to the Auschwitz women's camp.

APMO, D-AuII-3a/106a, FL Occupancy Report.

182 "conditionally functional" female prisoners who previously were employed in the weaving squad are put in the prisoners' infirmary in Camp B-IIe in Birkenau. At first the weaving mill was in Section B-III, called "Mexico," and was moved on November 25 to Camp B-IIc. Female prisoners who are not fully able-bodied are employed in the weaving mill. They make plaits from cellophane and various textile scraps, which serve as caulking for submarines. The number of laborers totals over 2,000 female prisoners. Not only are the working conditions very difficult, but also the work itself.

APMO, D-AuII-3a/54b, 56b, 67b, Labor Deployment List.

Nine female prisoners died of exhaustion in the women's camp of Auschwitz-Birkenau.

APMO, D-AuII-3a/106a, FL Occupancy Report.

DECEMBER 7

38 female prisoners die of exhaustion in the women's camp of Auschwitz-Birkenau.

APMO, D-AuII-3a/107a, FL Occupancy Report.

Three female prisoners are released from Auschwitz-Birkenau.

Ibid.

The number of the "conditionally functional" female prisoners sent to the prisoners' infirmary in Camp B-IIe from the weaving mill squad increases to 450 women.

APMO, D-AuII-3a/68b, Labor Deployment List.

The number of prisoners at the experimental station of Professor Dr. Clauberg increases by one, totaling 270 women for research purposes and eight prisoner orderlies.

APMO, D-AuI-3a/65b, Labor Deployment List.

DECEMBER 8

The number of prisoners at the experimental station of Professor Dr. Clauberg decreases by three, totaling 267 women for research purposes and eight prisoner orderlies.

APMO, D-AuI-3a/66b, Labor Deployment List.

*For the first time the 16 dwarfs are mentioned among the female prisoners who are sick and unable to work.

A street in Section B-II of Birkenau.

10 female prisoners die of exhaustion in the women's camp of Auschwitz-Birkenau.

APMO, D-AuII-3a/108a, FL Occupancy Report.

The number of female dwarfs in prisoners' infirmary Camp B-IIe decreases by 11. Five female dwarfs remain in the camp. The fate of these 11 dwarfs is unknown. They probably died the previous day as a result of the experiments conducted on them by SS Doctor Mengele. In the occupancy report of December 7, 1944, it is noted that 38 female prisoners have died. The next day, however, the numbers are rectified and in the occupancy report of December 8, 1944, 27 female prisoners inadvertently stricken from the report are included again in the inventory; the difference in the two numbers is 11 female prisoners.

APMO, D-AuII-3a/69b, Labor Deployment List; D-AuII-3a/107a, 108a, FL Occupancy Report.

55 female prisoners are released from the women's camp of Auschwitz-Birkenau.

APMO, D-AuII-3a/108a, FL Occupancy Report.

The number of "conditionally functional" female prisoners sent to Camp B-IIe from the weaving squad increases to a total of 846 women.

APMO, D-AuII-3a/69b, Labor Deployment List.

DECEMBER 9

Two female prisoners are delivered to the women's camp in Auschwitz and one female prisoner to the camp in Auschwitz-Birkenau.

APMO, D-AuI-3a/38; D-AuII-3a/109, FL Occupancy Report.

15 female prisoners die of exhaustion in the women's camp of Auschwitz-Birkenau.

APMO, D-AuII-3a/109, FL Occupancy Report.

The number of prisoners at the experimental station of Professor Dr. Clauberg increases by two, totaling 269 females for research purposes.

APMO, D-AuI-3a/67b, Labor Deployment List.

DECEMBER 10

The occupancy level in all the women's camps in Auschwitz is 19,236, 13,333 of whom are in Birkenau.

APMO, D-AuI-3a/68c, Labor Deployment List.

DECEMBER 11

694 female prisoners were subjected to a delousing on the grounds of Camp B-IIe.

APMO, D-AuII-3a/72b, Labor Deployment List.

The Auschwitz Combat Group relays to Teresa Lasocka and Edward Hałoń of the PWOK in Kraków on this date and the next day the news, received in confidence, that the Commandant in Auschwitz again made representations by telephone to his superiors in Berlin and requested confirmation of the death sentences issued to the five prisoners locked in the bunkers of Block 11 because of an escape attempt, diversionary activity—attempting to involve SS men in the escape plan—and contact to resistance organizations. The death penalty should serve as a deterrent. The condemned are Ernst Burger, Rudolf Friemel, Ludwig Vesely, Bernard Świerczyna, and Piotr Piąty. The leaders of the Auschwitz Combat Group emphasize that the death penalty in fact is against the regulations of the German concentration camps. To save the comrades of the Auschwitz Combat Group and the RWO, it suggests sending a communiqué with the following message via the radio stations: "Several political prisoners in Auschwitz—Poles and Germans— are threatened with the death penalty. Their only crime is the attempt to escape from the concentration camp. In this they were the victims of a provocation by the SS man Wiktor Roth,* a Romanian, who persuaded them to attempt this escape, in order then to turn them over to the camp directorate as a new sacrifice to their bloody delirium." The Assistance Committee (PWOK) is to decide which form of retaliation to threaten.**

APMO, Mat.RO, vol. III, pp. 205ff.

12 female prisoners are transferred from the women's camp in Auschwitz to the women's camp in Auschwitz-Birkenau.

APMO, D-AuI-3a/39; D-AuII-3a/111a, FL Occupancy Report.

20 female prisoners die of exhaustion in Auschwitz-Birkenau.

APMO, D-AuII-3a/111a, FL Occupancy Report.

DECEMBER 12

38 female prisoners are transferred from Birkenau to Auschwitz.

APMO, D-AuII-3a/122a, FL Occupancy Report.

*It should be Johann Roth. It goes without saying that Roth was paid for the escape assistance and did not persuade them to escape. The Combat Group chooses this tactic for the defense of its comrades.
**Józef Cyrankiewicz composed and signed the clandestine communication.

The number of prisoners at the experimental station of Professor Dr. Clauberg increases by one, totaling 270 women for research purposes and eight prisoner orderlies.

APMO, D-AuI-3a/70b, Labor Deployment List.

20 female prisoners die of exhaustion in Auschwitz-Birkenau.

APMO, D-AuII-3a/112, FL Occupancy Report.

425 Polish prisoners are transferred from Auschwitz to Buchenwald. The transport doesn't arrive until December 18 because of Allied air attacks. The prisoners are completely exhausted.

APMO, IZ-13/89, Various Documents of the Third Reich, p. 216; Docs. of ISD Arolsen; Depositions, vol. 65, pp. 70–71; D-Bu-3/1/6, KL Buchenwald Arrivals Lists.

2,688 female prisoners, including the entire weaving squad, are subjected to a delousing. The delousing operation is conducted in Camp B-IIc in Birkenau.

APMO, D-AuII-3a/73b, Labor Deployment List.

12 female prisoners are delivered to Auschwitz.

APMO, D-AuI-3a/40, FL Occupancy Report.

DECEMBER 13

14 female prisoners are delivered to Auschwitz, of whom 11 are transferred from the women's camp in Birkenau.

APMO, D-AuI-3a/41; D-AuII-3a/113a, FL Occupancy Report.

10 female prisoners die of exhaustion in Auschwitz-Birkenau.

APMO, D-AuII-3a/113a, FL Occupancy Report.

The number of prisoners at the experimental station of Professor Dr. Clauberg decreases by two, totaling 268 women for research purposes and eight female prisoner orderlies.

APMO, D-AuI-3a/71c, Labor Deployment List.

1,111 female prisoners work in the Weichsel-Union-Metallwerke in Auschwitz. 726 female prisoners, among them 55 skilled workers, are in the day shift, and 370, among them 20 skilled workers, are in the night shift. 15 female prisoners were employed in the garden operations of Weichsel-Union.

Ibid.

3,004 female prisoners are employed in the weaving squad in Camp B-IIc. The two female supervisors Zlotos and Schrottke oversee the squad.

APMO, D-AuI-3a/74b, Labor Deployment List.

DECEMBER 14

Four female prisoners are sent to Auschwitz.

APMO, D-AuI-3a/42, FL Occupancy Report.

11 female prisoners are released from Auschwitz-Birkenau. Six female prisoners die of exhaustion.

APMO, D-AuII-3a/114a, FL Occupancy Report.

1,923 female prisoners work in the agricultural and stock-raising operations, in which auxiliary camps for women are set up.

APMO, D-AuI-3a/72b, Labor Deployment List.

DECEMBER 15

Seven female prisoners die of exhaustion in Auschwitz-Birkenau.

APMO, D-AuII-3a/115a, FL Occupancy Report.

28 female prisoners are released from Auschwitz-Birkenau, and six are transferred to other concentration camps.

Ibid.

The number of prisoners at the experimental station of Professor Dr. Clauberg increases by three, totaling 271 women for research purposes and eight female prisoner orderlies.

APMO, D-AuI-3a/73b, Labor Deployment List.

DECEMBER 16

Three Polish prisoners are delivered from Mauthausen to Auschwitz: Adam Kocemba, Kazimierz Krzyczman, and Wojciech Napora.

APMO, D-Mau/Folder 5, p. 2715; Folder 8, p. 3550.

Nine female prisoners are sent to Auschwitz.

APMO, D-AuI-3a/43, FL Occupancy Report.

10 female prisoners die in Auschwitz-Birkenau from exhaustion resulting from the conditions in the camp.

APMO, D-AuII-3a/116, FL Occupancy Report.

DECEMBER 17

The number of prisoners at the experimental station of Professor Dr. Clauberg increases by one, totaling 272 women for research purposes and eight female prisoner orderlies.

APMO, D-AuI-3a/76b, Labor Deployment List.

300 female prisoners who were transferred to other concentration camps in the preceding days* are removed from the occupancy total of Auschwitz-Birkenau.

APMO, D-AuII-3a/117a, FL Occupancy Report.

DECEMBER 18

27 female prisoners die of exhaustion in Auschwitz-Birkenau.

APMO, D-AuII-3a/118a, FL Occupancy Report.

A female prisoner is transferred from the Birkenau women's camp to Auschwitz.

Ibid.

29 prisoners are transferred from Auschwitz to Gross-Rosen, the Breslau-Lissa auxiliary camp, in order to establish depots there for various technical facilities and materials removed from Auschwitz.

APMO, Depositions, vol. 41, pp. 13–19, Account of Former Prisoner Zygmunt Nowacki; Dpr.-Hd/5, p. 168.

Renewed Allied air attacks on the I. G. Farben plants in Dwory near Auschwitz take place.

Gilbert, *Auschwitz and the Allies*, p. 389.

The Chief of the SD in Kattowitz submits a report with extensive information about the Silesian district of the AK. This information is based on material gathered either during arrests or during interrogations of imprisoned AK members in the period from January 1 to December 1, 1944. It is stated among other things that the Bielsko inspectorate of the AK is one of the most important inspectorates. Until recently a certain "Czysty" (pseudonym of An-

Zygmunt Walter Janke, *Armia Krajowa na Śląsku w świetle dokumentow niemieckich, Najnowsze dzieje Polski, Materiały z studia w okresu II wojny światowej* (The Home Army in Silesia in the Light of German Documents: Recent History of Poland—Materials and Studies

*200 female prisoners left Birkenau on December 13 and 100 left on December 14 (APMO, D-AuII-3a/74b, 75b, Labor Deployment List).

drzej Harat) was in command. Since he was not up to the job, however, he was relieved by a certain "Lach."* From this report is can be inferred that the pseudonyms of the commanders of the AK districts are almost completely known and recorded in an organization diagram. A special role within this inspectorate is assigned to the Auschwitz commando. The report reflects awareness that Auschwitz Concentration Camp is surrounded by the AK. The activities of the RWO within the camp are also mentioned, as is the fact that numerous persons maintain contact with the camp. This takes place primarily through the district commander, "Danuta,"** and a member of the PPS, "Kostek."† A certain "Rot," one of the pseudonyms of Józef Cyrankiewicz, has been named commander of the AK in the camp. He mainly puts together reports on the concentration camp and passes them on through a certain "Urban."†† Intercepted situation reports that contain data on delivered and transferred prisoners, camp structures, personnel in the guard companies, evaluations of individual SS men, prisoner organizations, and future plans have been handed over to the RSHA, Section IV-B2. One of the tasks of the RWO is also to prepare prisoners' escapes. After an escape, escapees are picked up by a resistance organization that has various contacts with Kraków. The liquidation of this organization is taking place. It is concluded that the Gestapo is on the trail of the resistance movement in the camp and knows the pseudonyms and activities of the leading resistance fighters.

on the Period of World War II), Vol. III, Warsaw, 1959, p. 199.

DECEMBER 19

21 female prisoners, of whom two come from Birkenau, are delivered to the women's camp of Auschwitz.

APMO, D-AuI-3a/44, FL Occupancy Report.

12 female prisoners die from exhaustion in Auschwitz-Birkenau.

APMO, D-AuII-3a/119a, FL Occupancy Report.

DECEMBER 20

1,192 female prisoners are subjected to a delousing in the women's camp of Auschwitz.

APMO, D-AuI-3a/78c, Labor Deployment List.

200 prisoners are transferred from Auschwitz to the newly constructed Hubertushütte A.C. in Hohenlinde (Lagiewniki). The secondary camp is under the Commandant's Office of Monowitz, the former Auschwitz III. The prisoners work in the Hubertushütte,

WAP Kattowitz, Berghütte, 2224, p. 5; Irena Strzelecka, "Das Nebenlager Hubertushütte (Arbeitslager Hohenlinde)" (Hubertushütte Auxiliary Camp

---

*Pseudonym of Stanisław Chybiński (No. 6810), who escaped on May 20, 1943, from Auschwitz.
**Jan Wawrzyczek, career officer and first lieutenant of the infantry, and commander of the partisan unit "Sosienka." He uses the pseudonyms "Marusza" and "Danuta."
†Pseudonym of the former prisoner and later commander of the resistance group, Konstanty Jagiełło, who died on October 27, 1944. It appears that the Gestapo do not connect this pseudonym with Jagiełło.
††Pseudonym of Stefan Jasiński, delegate of the high command of the AK and liaison officer of the Polish Government in Exile in London, who was arrested in Malec near Auschwitz and on September 29, 1944, was sent to Auschwitz.

which has belonged since 1942 to the company Königs- und Bismarckhütte AG.

[Hohenlinde Labor Camp]), *HvA*, no. 12 (1971): 161–173.

Nine female prisoners die of exhaustion in Auschwitz-Birkenau.

APMO, D-AuII-3a/120a, FL Occupancy Report.

DECEMBER 21

747 female prisoners in the Auschwitz women's camp and 320 female prisoners from the weaving squad in Auschwitz-Birkenau are deloused.

APMO, D-AuI-3a/79c; D-AuII-3a/82b, Labor Deployment List.

Eight female prisoners die of exhaustion in the women's camp of Auschwitz-Birkenau.

APMO, D-AuII-3a/121a, FL Occupancy Report.

The number of prisoners at the experimental station of Professor Dr. Clauberg decreases by two, totaling 270 women for research purposes and eight female prisoner orderlies.

APMO, D-AuI-3a/79b, Labor Deployment List.

21 female prisoners are transferred from the women's camp in Auschwitz-Birkenau to the camp in Auschwitz.

APMO, D-AuII-3a/121a, FL Occupancy Report.

38 prisoners who were transferred from Buchenwald to Auschwitz receive Nos. 202372–202409.

Docs. of ISD Arolsen, NA-Men/1980.

Three days after the bombardment of the I. G. Farben works in Dwory near Auschwitz, American air reconnaissance takes aerial photographs to determine the extent of damage. Auschwitz Concentration Camp and Auschwitz-Birkenau are to be seen near the edges of these photographs. In the enlarged photographs of Birkenau one can see that the fence and the watchtowers that surround former Section III, "Mexico," have been removed. Also removed are the roofs of the gas chamber and the changing rooms, which are underground. The roof and the chimney of Crematorium II have been demolished, and the fence around Crematorium II is gone, as is the fence around Crematorium III. The entire area is littered with rubble. The facilities of I. G. Farben and their production remain the target of the tactical air reconnaissance.*

Gilbert, *Auschwitz and the Allies*, p. 389.

DECEMBER 22

A girl is probably born in Auschwitz-Birkenau, since a "new delivery" is entered in the occupancy report under the rubric "admissions" on December 22, 1944. Such an entry appears for the first time.

APMO, D-AuII-3a/122a, FL Occupancy Report.

A female prisoner is sent to Auschwitz and the departure of five female prisoners is recorded.

APMO, D-AuI-3a/47, FL Occupancy Report.

*The roofs of the gas chamber, the disrobing room, and the crematorium as well as the crematorium's chimney were probably demolished to disassemble the technical fittings so they could be transported to Mauthausen or Gross-Rosen.

11 female prisoners die of exhaustion in Birkenau women's camp.

APMO, D-AuI-3a/122a, FL Occupancy Report.

The Commandant of the Monowitz Concentration Camp, SS Captain Schwarz, announces that the new auxiliary camp Hubertushütte in Hohenlinde has a telephone connection via the post office in Konigshütte with the number 41761, extension 51.

APMO, D-AuIII-1/69, Commandant's Office Order 12/44, Dec. 22, 1944.

Commandant Schwarz of Monowitz praises a number of his SS men for anticipatory action that prevented the escape of prisoners from the auxiliary camp. Those commended are Corporal Albrecht Geldner of the 5th Company, Corporal Hermann Stens of the 5th Company, SS Corporal Wilhelm Köhler of the 6th Company, SS Private First Class Heinrich Spalek of the 6th Company, SS Private Johann Hartelik of the 2nd Company, and SS man Martin Kempl* of the 2nd Company.

Ibid.

DECEMBER 23

Three female prisoners, one from the Birkenau women's camp, are delivered to Auschwitz.

APMO, D-AuI-3a/48; D-AuII-3a/123, FL Occupancy Report.

The number of prisoners at the experimental station of Professor Dr. Clauberg increases by two, totaling 272 women for research purposes and eight female prisoner orderlies.

APMO, D-AuI-3a/81b, Labor Deployment List.

A female prisoner is transferred from the Auschwitz women's camp to the Birkenau women's camp.

APMO, D-AuII-3a/123, FL Occupancy Report.

11 female prisoners die of exhaustion in Auschwitz-Birkenau.

Ibid.

14 female prisoners are in Commandant's Office arrest in the bunkers of Block 11—nine from Auschwitz and five from Birkenau. 17 female prisoners, five from the Auschwitz camp and 12 from the Birkenau camp, were being interrogated.

APMO, D-AuI-3a/81c; D-AuII-3a/85b, Labor Deployment List.

DECEMBER 24

300 female prisoners from the weaving squad are taken to the baths in the so-called sauna. All their clothing is taken from them for the purpose of disinfection. The return to the blocks, naked, and the wait in the unheated barracks for clothing leads to pneumonia or even death for many of them.

APMO, D-AuII-3a/85b, Labor Deployment List.

DECEMBER 25

Three girls were born in Auschwitz-Birkenau.

APMO, D-AuII-3a/125, FL Occupancy Report.

*Martin Kempl shot the prisoner Henryk Rosner to death in the Golleschau A.C. on November 10 as the latter crossed the sentry wire; this was an example of "anticipatory action."

The admission of one female prisoner and the departure of a female prisoner are recorded in the occupancy report of Auschwitz Concentration Camp.

APMO, D-AuI-3a/49, FL Occupancy Report.

DECEMBER 26

During another American air raid on the I. G. Farben works in Dwory several bombs fall on the SS sick bay, which is near Birkenau, killing five SS men. Moreover, the air-raid shelter set up for nurses working in the sick bay is destroyed. Two original registers of the prisoners in the infirmary of Auschwitz I from the year 1943 have been hidden in the shelter by an Austrian, Sister Maria Stromberger,* a Red Cross nurse and mother superior of the nurses working in the SS sick bay. They are to be given over to PWOK in Kraków. Although she herself is a patient in the SS sick bay because of a joint inflammation, Sister Maria goes to the air-raid shelter and, with the help of Mira, a 19-year-old Yugoslav prisoner, digs in the rubble until the books are found.

APMO, D-AuI-1, Garrison Order 31/44, Dec. 27, 1944; Dpr.-Ad/3, p. 135; Dpr.-ZO/29, pp. 66–70, Statements of Former Prisoner Stanisław Rachwałowa and Sister Maria Stromberger; Gilbert, *Auschwitz and the Allies*, p. 390; Stanisław Kłodziński, "Maria Stromberger," *PL*, no. 1a (1962): 102–107.

DECEMBER 27

Nine female prisoners are transferred from Birkenau to Auschwitz.

APMO, D-AuI-3a/50; D-AuII-3a/127a, FL Occupancy Report.

The number of prisoners at the experimental station of Professor Dr. Clauberg increases by two, totaling 274 women for research purposes and eight prisoner orderlies.

APMO, D-AuI-3a/85b, Labor Deployment List.

38 female prisoners die of exhaustion in Auschwitz-Birkenau.

APMO, D-AuII-3a/127a, FL Occupancy Report.

Commandant Baer of Auschwitz announces to the SS members of the garrison that SS Private First Class Johann Roth, for preventing the escape of five prisoners,** has received out of gratitude from WVHA Head Oswald Pohl, his picture with a dedication.

APMO, D-AuI-1, Garrison Order 31/44, Dec. 27, 1944.

Commandant in Auschwitz and Camp Senior Baer announces further that during the bombing the previous day the following SS men died: SS Private First Class Johann Rometsch, SS Private Albert Franke, SS Private Ferdinand Dressler, and the SS men Heinrich Schuster and Michael Putz.

Ibid.

DECEMBER 1–27

293 female prisoners die in the women's camp of Auschwitz-Birkenau.†

APMO, D-AuII-3a/102a–127a, FL Occupancy Report.

*Sister Maria Stromberger had already taken the side of the prisoners in 1942 when she began her work in Auschwitz, and helped silently where she could. In the autumn of 1944 she became a member of the camp resistance movement and took on the function of messenger.
**Compare entries of October 27 and December 11, 1944.
†Calculated on the basis of the daily occupancy report, the last of which bears the date December 28, 1944.

A camp street in Auschwitz in December 1944.

DECEMBER 28

The number of prisoners at the experimental station of Professor Dr. Clauberg decreases by one, totaling 273 women for research purposes and eight female prisoner orderlies.

APMO, D-AuI-3a/86b, Labor Deployment List.

300 female prisoners in the weaving squad are subjected to delousing.

APMO, D-AuII-3a/89b, Labor Deployment List.

DECEMBER 29

A female prisoner is delivered to Auschwitz-Birkenau.

APMO, D-AuII-3a/90b, Labor Deployment List.

The Auschwitz camp management notifies the Buchenwald Concentration Camp that the personal possessions, i.e., the civilian clothing, in which the prisoners were delivered to the camp, jewelry, documents, money, etc., of the prisoners transferred to Buchenwald on September 29, October 17, November 27, December 4, and December 12, 1944, cannot be transferred at present due to transportation problems.

APMO, IZ-13/89, Various Documents of the Third Reich, p. 216 (original in BA Koblenz).

DECEMBER 30

Three female prisoners are sent to the Birkenau women's camp.

APMO, D-AuII-3a/91b, Labor Deployment List.

150 female prisoners are employed in the demolition squad, working on the demolition of Crematorium III. 50 prisoners work in the forestry-demolition squad, which is filling in the incineration pits and covering them with grass and planting small trees on the grounds of Crematorium IV.*

APMO, D-AuII-3a/90a, Labor Deployment List.

525 girls between one week and 16 years of age are in Birkenau Camp B-IIe in the children's barracks. 297 of them were delivered with their mothers to the camp after the outbreak of the Warsaw uprising.**

APMO, D-AuII-3a/90b, Labor Deployment List.

The occupancy level in Auschwitz-Birkenau women's camp is 12,692 women who with their children occupy Camp B-IIe. 4,287 women are sick and unable to work. 1,499 female prisoners remain without work and four have been in transit since December 4 to another camp.†

Ibid.

The number of prisoners in the Auschwitz women's camp is 6,015. 840 of them are sick and unable to work, 1,913 work in the agricultural and stock breeding operations of the SS, and 1,090 work in the Weichsel-Union plant. There are 273 female prisoners for research purposes at the experimental station of Professor Dr. Clauberg.

APMO, D-AuI-3a/88a–c, Labor Deployment List.

The number of female prisoners in the auxiliary camps that belong to Monowitz is as follows:

APMO, D-AuIII-3a/78, Labor Deployment List.

Gleiwitz II, Deutsche Gasrusswerke GmbH	371
Hindenburg, Hütte Donnersmarck	470
Blechhammer, O.S. Hydrierwerke AG	157
Freudenthal, the firm Emmerich Machold	301
Lichtewerden, the firm of G. S. Buhl and Son	300
Bobrek, Siemens-Schuckert-Werke AG	38
Neustadt, Schlesische Feinweberei AG	399
Total	2,036

After the evening roll call and the reading of the sentences on Saturday, five prisoners who attempted to escape or were accomplices in the effort†† and were betrayed by SS Private First Class Johann Roth‡ are publicly hanged. The condemned prisoners do not allow their eyes to be bound. Before they are hanged they shout, "Away with Hitler!" "Away with fascism!" "Today us, tomorrow you!" "Poland lives!" The condemned are the Austrians Ernst Burger, Rudolf Friemel, and Ludwig Vesely as well as the Poles

APMO, Dpr.-Hd/8, Statement of Former Prisoner Jan Dziopka; Memoirs/Dounia Ourisson/51, vol. 1; Sobański, *Escape from Auschwitz*, pp. 221ff.

*Crematorium IV was burned down during the uprising of the Special Squad and has been called "Large Sauna" since then.
**There are also boys in these barracks, but it is not known how many there are on this date.
†Since the camp management of the other camp has not yet received confirmation of the admission of these female prisoners, they are not stricken from the occupancy report.
††Compare the entry for October 27, 1944.
‡Compare the entry of December 27, 1944; the efforts of the Auschwitz Combat Group to save them were without success.

Piotr Piąty and Bernard Świerczyna, who are members of the Auschwitz Combat Group and the RWO.

DECEMBER 31

On Sunday, nurse Maria Stromberger, the messenger of the camp resistance organization, who is called "Sister" or simply "S" in the clandestine letters, succeeds in establishing contact and in giving Natalia Szpak her final message,* which contains the two original registers of the number of prisoners in the prisoners' infirmary of the main camp.**

APMO, Dpr.-ZO/29, Statement of Sister Maria Stromberger.

---

*Maria Stromberger receives the news on January 5, 1945, that she is to report to the SS main headquarters on January 7. After examination of the illness report that Dr. Wirths has written, she is transferred to the Prague neurological clinic. SS Garrison Doctor Wirths has written that Sister Maria is a morphine addict. It is likely that with such a claim Dr. Wirths is pursuing a particular goal.
**Compare the entry for December 26, 1944.

1 9 4 5

JANUARY 1

100 male and 100 female Poles who were condemned to death by the Police Court-martial are shot to death in Crematorium V in Birkenau. The condemned are transferred in two transports in a closed prisoner wagon from Block 11 in the main camp to Birkenau—first the men, then the women. SS Camp Doctor First Lieutenant Fritz Klein hands the condemned prisoners over to the Head of Crematorium V, SS Staff Sergeant Erich Muhsfeldt, for the execution of the sentence. Among the tasks of the Camp Doctor is the determination of death after the execution of the sentence.

Nyisli, *Mengele's Laboratory*, p. 156.

JANUARY 2

Four prisoners die in the Tschechowitz A.C. According to the death certificate the prisoner Sammy Rosenberg (No. B-12562) commits suicide by hanging; the Czech Jew Bernhard Schürmann (No. B-12607) dies from general weakness, dysentery, and boils; the Polish Jew Abraham Lewkowicz (No. B-8900) succumbs to general weakness, edema, and a heart attack; and the Czech Jew Moses Coevorden (No. B-12385) dies of dysentery and general weakness.

APMO, D-AuI-5/14/22–25.

The Polish prisoner Stanisław Mioduszewski (No. 129865) escapes from the coal mine of the Jawischowitz A.C. The escape is made possible by the miners Franciszek and Julian Nikel.

APMO, Depositions, vol. 12, p. 197; vol. 20, p. 23; Accounts, Wanda Neuenschwande, Franciszek Nikel, and Julian Nikel.

JANUARY 4

Three prisoners are transferred from Mauthausen to Auschwitz. They are three physicians, the Frenchman Jacques Ballanger and the Italians Piero Cattabriga and Rino Rodondi. They receive Nos. 202412–202414.

APMO, D-Mau, Folder 5, p. 2730; Folder 8, p. 3540; Docs. of ISD Arolsen, NA-Men.

The number of prisoners in the Birkenau women's camp is 11,493 women and girls* and 220 boys.

APMO, D-AuII-3/4, Notebook "Camp Occupancy."

*Between December 31, 1944, and January 4, 1945, the number of female prisoners in the Birkenau women's camp declines by 1,202, who are probably transferred to other camps.

JANUARY 5

Three female prisoners are transferred from the Auschwitz women's camp to the Birkenau women's camp.

Ibid.

Three female prisoners and a boy are released from the Birkenau women's camp.

Ibid.

23 female prisoners and three female civilian workers as well as a boy are transferred from the Birkenau women's camp to the Auschwitz women's camp.

Ibid.

A young prisoner, a Slovak boy, dies in the Birkenau women's camp.

Ibid.

Six prisoners, so-called bearers of secrets, are transferred from the men's camp in B-IId in Birkenau to Mauthausen. The transferred are five Polish prisoners who work in the Special Squad: Wacław Lipka (No. 2520), Mieczysław Morława (No. 5730), Józef Ilczuk (No. 14916), Władysław Biskup (No. 74501), Jan Agrestowski (No. 74545); and the Czech prisoner Stanisław Slezak (No. 39340), who operated the X-ray machines in the experimental station of SS Doctor Horst Schumann in Birkenau's Camp B-Ia.* At this experimental station Dr. Schumann conducted sterilizations of male and female prisoners. The transferred prisoners receive the following numbers in Mauthausen: Agrestowski—No. 114656, Biskup—No. 114657, Ilczuk—No. 114661, Lipka—No. 114663, Morława No. 114665. Slezak's number is not known. They are shot to death on April 3, 1945, in the Mauthausen crematorium building.

APMO, Mat.RO, vol. IV, p. 49; D-Mau-3/a/142, 1469, 8071, 14139, 16408, Prisoner's Personal-Information Card.

The last session of the Police Court-martial of the Kattowitz Gestapo takes place in Block 11. 70 Poles, men and women, are condemned to death. They are shot to death the following day in Crematorium V in Birkenau. Among them are Władysław Jasiowka from Sosnowitz, Stanisław Kobylka from Rusce, Józef Łuczak from Wieluń, Kazimierz Matjasiński from Sosnowitz, Jan Strychowski from Myślachowice, and Adam Tods from Jęzory; they leave their names on the walls of Block 11 with the request that their families be informed of their condemnation and execution.

Konieczny, "Police Court-martial," pp. 132, 136, 167ff.; APMO, Materials/731a, vol. 67, Block 11.

JANUARY 6

1,004 female prisoners are transferred from the Birkenau women's camp to Bergen-Belsen; one is transferred to the Auschwitz women's camp.

APMO, D-AuII-3/4, Notebook "Camp Occupancy."

*Stanisław Slezak is in possession of the list of male and female prisoners on whom Dr. Schumann has conducted sterilization experiments with the aid of X rays. Before his departure from Birkenau Slezak tells his fellow prisoners that he is traveling by special order of Schumann and would continue to work with him (APMO, Dpr.-Hd/2, p. 85, Statements of Former Prisoner Michał Kula).

Section B-III in Birkenau, nicknamed "Mexico."

In the evening four female Jewish prisoners, Ella Gartner, Róża Robota, Regina Safir, and Estera Wajsblum, are hanged in the women's camp of Auschwitz. They were condemned to death because they assisted in the uprising that broke out on October 7, 1944, among the members of the Special Squad in the crematoriums in Birkenau. They provided the Special Squad with explosives and munitions from the depots of the Weichsel-Union-Metallwerke, where three of the women worked. The execution takes place in two stages. Two female prisoners are hanged during the evening roll call in the presence of the male and female prisoners who work the night shift at Weichsel-Union. The other two female prisoners are hanged after the return of the squad that works the day shift. The reason for the sentence is read by First Protective Custody Commander Hössler in Auschwitz; he screams that all traitors will be destroyed in this manner.

APMO, Dpr.-ZO/29, p. 107, Statements of Former Female Prisoner Gustawa Kinselewska; Škodowa, *Three Years*; Ośw./ 252, vol. 10; Kagan, "Women," p. 40; Grynberg, *Jews in Zichenau*, p. 127.

JANUARY 7

After the execution is carried out a female prisoner is stricken from the registers of the Birkenau women's camp.*

APMO, D-AuII-3/4, Notebook "Camp Occupancy."

JANUARY 8

17 female prisoners and a boy die in the women's camp.

Ibid.

*This entry probably concerned the female prisoner Róża Robota. She worked in the personal effects depot, which was near Crematorium IV. She was accused of supplying explosives to the prisoners in the Special Squad.

13 prisoners—four Belgians, two Frenchmen, five Poles, a Czech, and a Polish Jew—are transferred from Auschwitz to Mauthausen.

APMO, D-Mau, Folder V, p. 2743.

Two Hungarian prisoners are shot to death at 9:00 P.M. during an escape attempt from the Golleschau A.C. They are Lajos Bencsik-Potoy (No. 201589), in whom six gunshot wounds are found, and Josef Szabo (No. 202192), in whom three gunshot wounds are found.

APMO, D-AuIII, Golleschau/9, Folder 1, pp. 9–11.

The Head of Branch D in the WVHA, SS Major Willi Burger, reports to the SS Central Administration in Auschwitz in reference to the examination of clothing management that was conducted by a representative of the WVHA, November 16–19, 1944, that various inadequacies exist and that the supervision is deficient. He repeats the criticisms, which were presented in a several-page report. Burger orders that all deficiencies be eliminated immediately and that a report of the measures taken be made.*

APMO, IZ-13/89, Various Documents of the Third Reich, p. 158.

JANUARY 9

13 female prisoners die in Birkenau as a result of the poor conditions prevailing in the camp.

APMO, D-AuIII-3/4, Notebook "Camp Occupancy."

Two female prisoners are transferred from the Birkenau women's camp to another camp.

Ibid.

JANUARY 10

16 female prisoners die in Birkenau as a result of the poor conditions prevailing in the camp.

Ibid.

135 female prisoners and 15 boys are transferred from Women's Camp B-IIe in Birkenau to a labor camp in Berlin.**

Ibid.

JANUARY 11

Nine female prisoners die in Birkenau as a result of the poor conditions in the camp.

Ibid.

107 female prisoners and seven boys are transferred from the Birkenau women's camp to a labor camp in Berlin; two female prisoners are transferred to the Auschwitz women's camp.

Ibid.

JANUARY 12

Four female prisoners are transferred from the women's camp in Auschwitz to the women's camp in Birkenau.

Ibid.

*Compare the entries for November 18 and 27, 1944.
**There are probably women with children in this transport who were delivered to Auschwitz-Birkenau after the outbreak of the Warsaw uprising.

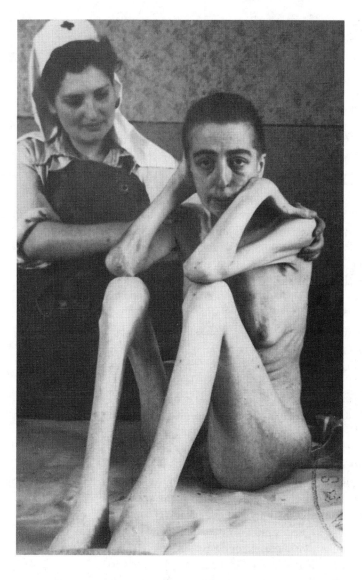

After the liberation by the Soviet Army in January 1945. This 37-year-old woman weighed just 77 pounds.

A female prisoner is transferred from Neuengamme to the Birkenau women's camp.

Ibid.

From the Birkenau women's camp 125 female prisoners are transferred to Gross-Rosen and five to the Auschwitz women's camp.

Ibid.

Seven female prisoners die in the Birkenau women's camp as a result of the poor conditions in the camp.

Ibid.

JANUARY 13

The number of prisoners in Monowitz is 9,806: 289 political prisoners—160 Germans, 68 Poles, 12 Dutch, 11 Yugoslavs, seven Russians, six Frenchmen, six Croatians, one Greek, and two Gypsies; 226 reeducation prisoners—25 Germans (BV), 30 Germans (Asoziale), two Poles (Asoziale), 168 Germans (PSV), 11 Poles (PSV), one IBV prisoner, and one Paragraph 175 prisoner; 9,054

APMO, D-AuIII-3/1, Occupancy Level of Monowitz (Auschwitz III).

Jews—3,391 Poles, 3,013 Hungarians, 1,039 Frenchmen, 598 Germans, 343 Greeks, 278 Dutch, 189 Belgians, 110 Italians, 78 Czechs, 10 Slovaks, and four Norwegians.

Three female prisoners die in the Birkenau women's camp as a result of the poor conditions in the camp.

APMO, D-AuII-3/4, Notebook "Camp Occupancy."

JANUARY 14

Three boys are born in Birkenau Women's Camp B-IIe.

Ibid.

10 German prisoners,* among them four soldiers, are transferred from Dachau to Auschwitz. They are: Hans Coljon (PSV), Johann Jaschok,** Adam Jenckel,** Heinz Juckenburg (PSV), Otto Kruh (PSV), Rudolf Märker (a Reich German in protective custody), Fritz Messer (PSV), Friedrich Neubauer,** Karl Rohrer (PSV), and Simon Wallner.**

APMO, D-Da-3/2/2, pp. 57ff.

The American air force makes the twelfth reconnaissance flight over the Auschwitz region. The objective of this reconnaissance flight is to determine the extent of the damage inflicted by the four previous bombings of the I. G. Farben works, which nevertheless continue to produce synthetic fuel. At 12:30 P.M. photographs are taken from an altitude of 5,000 feet. More than 940 bomb craters and 44 destroyed buildings are visible in these photographs. Also visible are Auschwitz I and Auschwitz-Birkenau. The analysis of the photographs by Dino A. Brugioni and Robert G. Poirier 35 years after the end of the war permit the following conclusion: Monowitz has not been abandoned at this point, since the snow on the roofs of the barracks is melted and the paths between the barracks are free of snow. Auschwitz I is also still occupied. The melted snow on the roofs of individual barracks, with the exception of Block 10, the former experimental station of Professor Dr. Clauberg,† points to the fact that prisoners are still occupying the blocks. Section III, "Mexico," in Birkenau is completely abandoned. The snow cover of the barracks of the former women camps in Camp B-Ia and B-Ib indicates that they have been abandoned.†† The partly melted snow on the roofs of the barracks in Camp B-II shows in which parts of the camp people are still present.‡ The condition of the gas chambers and Crematoriums II and III shows that these facilities are already partially demolished, since the tracks in the snow, made by persons and various vehicles in the area, point to major activity.

APMO, Opr./Klein/194a, pp. 2, 68–70; Opr./Brugioni, Poirier/187, pp. 123–125, 158–160; Gilbert, *Auschwitz and the Allies*, p. 392.

*This transport left Dachau on January 12, 1945.
**Prisoners who were arrested in the "Reich Forced Labor" operations.
†The experimental station of Professor Dr. Clauberg was relocated on May 22, 1944, from Block 10 to the so-called protective custody camp expansion. From May 23 to August 2, 1944, Gypsies who had been selected from Gypsy Family Camp B-IIe and transferred to other concentration camps were accommodated in Block 10.
††The transfer of female prisoners from Camp B-Ia–b to Camps B-IIb and B-IIe was discontinued on November, 24, 1944. The women's camp in B-Ia–b stood empty after November 24, 1944.
‡In January 1945 the male prisoners were accommodated in the prisoners' infirmary in Camps B-IId and B-IIf, and the female prisoners in Camps B-IIb and B-IIe.

JANUARY 15

At 1:50 A.M. during an American air force reconnaissance flight, Squadron Leader Friend and Officer Wheeler take eight photographs of the I. G. Farben works in Dwory near Auschwitz. These show that the repair effort is progressing and that the boiler-house for the production of synthetic fuel is probably still intact. Repair and construction projects in the Buna synthetic rubber works are being pursued.

Gilbert, *Auschwitz and the Allies*, p. 392.

The number of prisoners in Monowitz, the former Auschwitz III, and the auxiliary camps is 33,037 male prisoners and 2,044 female prisoners. The number in the SS guard units is 2,006 men and 15 women.

Docs. of ISD Arolsen.

The number of prisoners in Auschwitz-Birkenau is 15,325 male and 16,421 female prisoners. The number in the SS guard units is 2,474 men and 56 women.

Ibid.

11 female prisoners are released from the Birkenau women's camp.

APMO, D-AuII-3/4, Notebook, "Camp Occupancy."

13 female prisoners and a boy die in Birkenau as a result of the poor conditions in the camp.

Ibid.

The number of prisoners in Men's Camps B-IId and B-IIf in Birkenau is 4,482. Of them 2,102 are working, 954 are sick, 57 are convalescing, and 400 are invalids; 770 are children and youths under 18 years of age, of whom 197 children from one month to 14 years of age are in the women's camp. There are also three newborns in the women's camp, 45 prisoners registered with the doctor, two being interrogated by the Political Department, 95 in transit to other concentration camps, and 53 awaiting such a transfer transport.

APMO, D-AuII-3a/47, Labor Deployment List.

70 prisoners, former members of the Special Squad, work in Squad 104-B, the crematorium disassembly squad, which is employed in the demolition of crematorium facilities. The disassembled facilities are brought to a siding of a connecting railroad track and are transported to Gross-Rosen.* The prisoners knock holes in the walls of the crematorium buildings and the gas chambers for the placement of explosives.

APMO, D-AuII-3a/47, Labor Deployment List; Dpr.-ZO/26, pp. 155, 160; Dpr.-ZO/29, pp. 47, 48; Dpr.-Hd/6, p. 35.

210 prisoners work in the squads demolishing the barracks in the former women's camp** in B-I and B-III ("Mexico"). The squad is designated 105-B Barracks Demolition Squad B-I and B-III.

APMO, D-AuII-3a/47, Labor Deployment List.

30 prisoners work in the Special Squad that is employed in the cremation of corpses in Crematorium V.

Ibid.

---

*Part of these facilities are found after the war on the so-called construction yard in Auschwitz.
**The demolition of some of the barracks in Women's Camp B-Ia–b can be seen on the aerial photographs made on January 14, 1945.

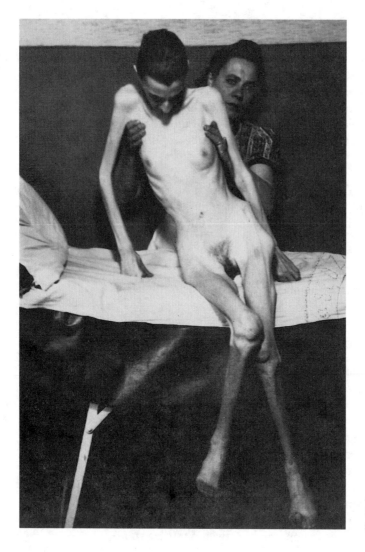

After the camp's liberation this 37-year-old woman weighed only 50 pounds.

Because of heavy fog the labor squads don't leave for work until 8:30 A.M.

Ibid.

The chancellery of the Registry II in Auschwitz receives the order to load all prisoners' documents, death certificates, and files into an auto. The female prisoners who do the packing are guarded by SS men.

Škodowa, *Three Years*, p. 169.

JANUARY 16

A female prisoner is transferred from Birkenau to Neuengamme.

APMO, D-AuII-3/4, Notebook "Camp Occupancy."

Seven prisoners die in the prisoners' infirmary in Camp B-IIf in Birkenau as a result of the bad conditions in the camp. They are the Poles Jan Rothmann (No. 4956) and Archip Shuk (Żuk—No. 182789), the Russians Ihev Picharev (Pihorov—No. 182789) and Yevgheny Shusslov (Suslov—No. 193030), and the Jews Ernst Thieberger (No. B-11370), Michal Berkovicz (No. B-13973), and Tibor Schlesinger (No. B-14785).

APMO, D-AuII-5/4, Folder 26.

10 prisoners are transferred from the prisoners' infirmary in B-IIf to Camp B-IId because they were again able to work. Among the transferred are a Polish political prisoner No. 194511, a German Jewish prisoner No. 173125, a Greek Jewish prisoner No. A-15541, a Slovak Jewish prisoner No. A-14548, three Polish Jewish prisoners Nos. B-1387, B-2109, and B-14745, two Dutch Jewish prisoners Nos. B-14771 and 14775, and a Slovak Jewish prisoner No. B-14427, who is granted an eight-day block convalescence.

APMO, D-AuII-5/4, Folder 26, HKB-BIIf. The names of the prisoners are not given in the document.

Seven female prisoners die in the Birkenau women's camp as a result of the poor conditions in the camp.

APMO, D-AuII-3/4, Notebook "Camp Occupancy."

86 female prisoners—women and children and seven youths—are transferred from the Birkenau women's camp to a labor camp in Berlin.*

Ibid.

The barracks of the camp kitchen and the foodstuffs depot are destroyed during a night-time bombing of Jaworzno. Some prisoners are killed.

APMO, Ośw./89, vol. 5, pp. 646–648; Ośw./134, vol. 5, p. 677, Accounts of Former Prisoners Aron Piernat and Borys Szojchert.

JANUARY 17

A female prisoner is released from Auschwitz-Birkenau.

APMO, D-AuII-3/4, Notebook "Camp Occupancy."

Three female prisoners die in the Birkenau women's camp from the bad conditions in the camp.

Ibid.

179 female prisoners—women and girls and 17 youths—who were sent to Auschwitz after the Warsaw uprising, are transferred in two transports from the Birkenau women's camp to a labor camp in Berlin. The first transport contains 80 women and girls and nine boys, and the second transport contains 99 women and girls and eight boys.

Ibid.

From the Birkenau women's camp, 51 female prisoners transferred to Monowitz, six to Ravensbrück, and five to Natzweiler.

Ibid.

*In this transport there were women and children who were sent to Auschwitz after the Warsaw uprising. Before the departure the adult women must sign a declaration in which they pledge to maintain silence about everything they have seen and heard in Auschwitz. An SS escort brings the transport to Berlin. At first the female prisoners and the children are housed in Henningsdorf near Berlin and must work in the AEG (Allgemeine Elektricitäts-Gesellschaft) Works. Later the transport is divided into three groups and taken to Cottbus, Linz, and the Siemensstadt (Siemens city) in Berlin. Finally the female prisoners are picked up from Cottbus and Siemensstadt and taken to the camp on Friedrich-Krause-Ufer in Berlin. In March they are transferred to Müggelheim near Berlin and in April are evacuated back to Berlin. Most of the female prisoners escape during this evacuation and hide until the arrival of the Red Army in Berlin. The entire family of the female prisoner Bóżena Krywobłocka—she and her mother, sister, and grandmother—is in this transport (APMO, Ośw./143, Account of the Former Female Prisoner Bożena Krzywobłocka-Tyrowicz).

17 girls and a boy are transferred from the Birkenau women's camp to the Lebrechtsdorf-Potulitz U.W.Z. (Umwandererzentralstelle, or "central resettlement office") camp.*

Ibid.

23 girls and five boys are transferred** from the Birkenau women's camp to the Tuchingen-Konstantinow (Konstantynów Łódzki) U.W.Z camp.†

Ibid.

Units of the Red Army advance on outlying areas of Kraków from the north and the northwest and surprise the German positions, which do not expect an attack from this flank. At 12 o'clock the last official meeting of General Governor Hans Frank takes place, in which he declares that Kraków, a German city since earliest times, could never be surrendered by the Germans. At 2:00 P.M. he leaves Kraków in the direction of Silesia. A vigorous Russian air attack on the retreating columns of the military and administrative personnel, whose departure from Kraków increasingly takes on the character of a flight, begins at 2:30 P.M.

Wroński, *Chronicle*, pp. 392–393.

178 female prisoners and two boys were transferred from the Płaszów concentration camp to the Birkenau women's camp.

Ibid.

The male and female prisoners fall in for their last roll call. The number of prisoners of the individual camps and auxiliary camps is as follows:

APMO, Mat.RO, vol. III, p. 208; D-AuII-3/4, Notebook "Camp Occupancy"; Dpr.-Hd/6, pp. 83, 84, Statements of Former Prisoner Dr. Otto Wolken.

Babitz	159 male prisoners
Budy	313 male prisoners
Plawny	138 male prisoners
Birkenau Production area	204 male prisoners
Auschwitz main camp	10,030 male prisoners
Birkenau men's camp	4,473 male prisoners
	15,317 male prisoners††

*A camp for children and young persons from the East, a so-called East youth protective camp, was founded in Potulitz November 1943. Children were sent to this camp who together with their mothers were sent to Auschwitz in transports of Mobile Commando 9 from Mińsk, Vitebsk, and Smolensk and who were registered as prisoners in Auschwitz. From August 1944 on, Polish children from Upper Silesia whose parents were sent to Auschwitz in the so-called Oderberg Operation are placed in this camp.
**In August 1943, a so-called East youth protective camp of the Tuchingen Sipo was set up in Konstantynów Łódzki. In August 1944 the children from the Potulitz camp, who came from Minsk, Vitebsk, and Smolensk, were delivered to this camp.
†The female prisoners with children, a total of 609 women and girls, who were transferred between January 10 and 17 to Berlin and other camps are still included in the occupancy of Birkenau, since the camps to which they were transferred have sent no confirmation of arrival.
††An analysis of these numbers by prisoner category and nationalities presents the following picture: three reeducation prisoners, four Gypsies, 92 Russian POWs, 1,699 Germans (among them 923 political prisoners and four members of the military), 1,208 Poles (among them 1,190 political prisoners), 396 Frenchmen, 339 Russians, 140 Yugoslavs, 81 Dutch, 37 Belgians, 24 Czechs, 22 stateless prisoners, 170 people of various nationalities, and 11,102 Jewish prisoners, among them 3,212 Polish Jews, 3,116 Hungarian Jews, 1159 French Jews, 616 Dutch Jews, 541 Slovak Jews, 536 Czech Jews, 358 Greek Jews, 269 German Jews, 268 Belgian Jews, 111 Italian Jews, 28 Croatian Jews, and 888 Jews of other citizenship (APMO, Mat.RO, vol. III, p. 208).

Auschwitz women's camp	6,196 female prisoners
Birkenau women's camp	10,381 female prisoners
Total	31,894 male and female prisoners*

In the wake of the decision to remove the prisoners from Auschwitz, Commandant Baer personally chooses the leaders of the evacuation columns from among the members of the guard companies and orders them to liquidate ruthlessly all prisoners who attempt to escape during the evacuation or drag their feet.

APMO, Dpr.Reischenbeck-P/1, vol. 12, p. 6, Certified Copy of Sentence.

The prisoners Józef Cyrankiewicz and Stanisław Klodiński write in their last report to Teresa Lasocka and Edward Hałoń of PWOK in Kraków:

APMO, Mat.RO, vol. III, p. 207.

> My Dear Ones! We are now experiencing the evacuation. Chaos. Panic among the drunken SS. We are trying with all political means to make the departure as tolerable as possible and to protect from extermination the invalids allegedly remaining behind. These objectives were—and possibly are—entirely clear. The march goes first in the direction of Bielsko. Later, a part is going toward the Sudenten (Leitmeritz), another part toward Gross-Rosen. The only train is taking the less seriously ill to Hanover. The intentions change from hour to hour, since they have no idea what orders they will receive. Radio propaganda is necessary. This type of evacuation means the extermination of at least half of the prisoners. A check by the Red Cross is necessary and, in the period of the "interregnum" in the camp is indispensable, so that some special commando of the SS doesn't simply wipe out the sick. . . . We also enclose a number of documents.

In the auxiliary camps that belong to Monowitz, formerly Auschwitz III, are the following numbers of male prisoners:

APMO, Mat.RO, vol. III, p. 208; Dpr.-Hd/6, pp. 83–84, Statement of Former Prisoner Dr. Otto Wolken.

Monowitz (Buna works)	10,223
Golleschau	1,008
Jawischowitz (Jawiszowice)	1,988
Eintrachthütte (Swiętochłowice)	1,297
Neu-Dachs (Jaworzno)	3,664
Blechhammer (Blachowina)	3,958
Fürstengrube (Wesoła)	1,283
Gute Hoffnung (Janinagrube, Libiąż	853
Güntergrube (Lędziny)	586
Brünn (Brno)	36
Gleiwitz I	1,336
Gleiwitz II	740
Gleiwitz III	609

*Actually in the camp are 31,233 prisoners, 15,265 men and 15,968 women, as 609 women and girls as well as 52 boys are in transit to other camps.

Gleiwitz IV	444
Laurahütte (Siemianowice)	937
Sosnowitz	863
Bobrek	213
Trzebinia	641
Althammer (Stara Kuźnia)	486
Tschechowitz-Dziedzitz	561
Charlottengrube (Rydułtowy)	833
Hindenburg (Zabrze)	70
Bismarckhütte (Hajduki)	192
Hubertushütte (Łagiewniki)	202
Total	33,023

2,095 female prisoners are located in the Blechhammer, Bobrek, Freudenthal, Gleiwitz II, Hindenburg, Lichtewerden (Světla), and Neustadt (Prudnik) auxiliary camps, making a total of 35,118 prisoners.

The prisoners in Sosnowitz A.C. are evacuated. Food leftovers that are found in the kitchen are divided among the prisoners, and at about 4:00 P.M. they depart on foot in the direction of Gleiwitz and continue on to Ratibor and Troppau. There they are loaded into freight cars and transported to Mauthausen. The evacuation lasts 16 days, of which 12 are on foot. The prisoners have to pull handcarts with the luggage of the SS, who zealously set about to kill the weak and those unable to march. During the deportation the prisoners each receive three potatoes and two pieces of cheese; many die during this transfer.* — Piper, "Sosnowitz II," pp. 127–128.

Approximately 3,200 prisoners who were able to march on foot are led out of the Neu-Dachs auxiliary camp. The route they must cover—with SS escort—leads to Königshütte, Beuthen, and Gleiwitz to the Blechhammer A.C. From there they go on January 21 to Gross-Rosen. Together with other prisoners who have been delivered to Gross-Rosen they are brought to Buchenwald. Over 400 prisoners remain in the Neu-Dachs A.C. — Piper, "Neu-Dachs," p. 104.

SS Camp Doctor Mengele liquidates his experimental station in Camp B-IIf and brings to safety the "material" acquired from the experiments on twins, dwarfs, and cripples. — APMO, Dpr.-Hd/3, p. 138, Statement of Former Female Prisoner Stanisława Rachwałowa.

SS Lieutenant Fischer, Camp Doctor in Auschwitz, gives the order to transport the archive of the prisoners' infirmary in the main camp up to the area in front of Block 11. All night, various camp documents are burned. Camp Doctor Fischer supervises the transport of documents himself, with the help of two SS Medical Officers. Medical Officers in the camps and secondary camps receive similar orders. — APMO, Dpr.-Hd/1, p. 175; Dpr.-Hd/5, p. 98, Statements of Former Prisoners Drs. Jakub Gordon and Jakub Wolman; Antoni Makowski, "Organisation, Entwicklung und Tätigkeit des Häftlingskrankenbaus in Monowitz (Auschwitz III)" (Organization, Development, and Activities of the Monowitz [Auschwitz III] Prisoners' Infirmary), *HvA*, no. 15 (1975): 131.

---

*On the day of the march there are 863 prisoners working in the auxiliary camp. Probably 626 prisoners reach Mauthausen on February 4, 1945 (APMO, D-Mau., Folder V, p. 2769).

In the night, SS Medical Officers come from Auschwitz to Birkenau and supervise the burning of the documents from the women's infirmary.

APMO, Dpr-Hd/3, p. 138.

The prisoner physicians in Monowitz receive the order to carefully examine the health conditions of the sick and to remove all those able to march from the hospital records. Only the seriously ill may remain behind, under the supervision of doctors who are ill and unable to march.

Jaworski, *Memories of Auschwitz*, p. 266; Makowski, "Monowitz Prisoners' Infirmary," p. 131.

JANUARY 18

At one o'clock in the morning 40 prisoners, doctors, and nurses are led from the Birkenau male prisoners' infirmary B-IIf and made to join the prisoners' column from Camp B-IId, which was waiting for the order to march. The remaining doctors receive the order to get the prisoners' files, the histories of the illnesses and fever tables from the hospital blocks. The documents are burned along with the documents from the clerical office of Camp B-IIf. SS Medical Officers supervise the burning.

APMO, Dpr.-Hd/6, p. 288.

The German BV prisoner Engelbert Marketsch, born on August 30, 1918, in Bleiberg near Villach, who is a surveyor and architect by profession, is delivered from Mauthausen. He receives No. 202499. This was the last number to be assigned to a prisoner in Auschwitz.*

APMO, D-Mau, Folder V, p. 2749, Folder VIII, p. 3529; Dpr.-Hd/4, p. 104, Statement of Former Prisoner Jan Trębaczewski.

A female prisoner is sent to the Birkenau women's camp.

APMO, D-AuII-3/4, Notebook "Camp Occupancy."

The departure of the female prisoners from the Birkenau women's camp begins toward morning. At short intervals columns of 500 women and children each leave the camp, escorted by SS men. A total of 5,345 female prisoners leave the camp on this day, among them 176 from Płaszów, 1,169 from Camp B-IIc, and 4,000 from Camps B-IIb and B-IIe. They are taken to Auschwitz and wait there for the formation of the evacuation columns. 4,428 female prisoners, women and girls, and 169 boys remain in the women's infirmary B-IIe.

APMO, D-AuII-3/4, Notebook "Camp Occupany"; Dpr.-Hd/3, p. 139.

800 prisoners are led out of the Janinagrube A.C. and are force-marched to Gross-Rosen. The prisoners have no protection against the cold. They receive small portions of dry food for the 18-day march. Of the 800 prisoners who leave Janinagrube, approximately 200 prisoners reach Gross-Rosen, in a state of complete exhaustion.

APMO, Dpr.-Mau/12, p. 247; NI 12385, Statements of Former Prisoner Dr. Erich Orlik.

During the midday period it is ordered that the physicians in Birkenau prisoners' infirmary for men, B-IIf, complete a list for each block in which they divide the sick prisoners into three groups:

APMO, Dpr.-Hd/6, p. 289.

*This prisoner was transferred to Auschwitz to incorporate him into the SS Special Unit Dirlewanger.

1. Those able to march 31 miles (50 kilometers)
2. Those able to march 1⅞ miles (three kilometers), i.e., to the train station in Auschwitz
3. Those unable to march

150 sick prisoners leave the prisoners' infirmary in Camp B-IIf at 4:00 P.M. They are to join the first group, i.e., the prisoners who were able to march 31 miles.* Only the seriously ill and a small group of physicians and nurses are to remain behind in Camp B-IIf.

APMO, Dpr.-Hd, p. 290.

Columns of prisoners leave Birkenau at specific intervals. The last column, with approximately 1,500 prisoners, leaves Camp B-IId in the afternoon. 400 prisoners join this column to escape being liquidated in the camp.** Among them are some youthful prisoners from the Penal Company, 70 prisoners from the crematorium demolition squad, and 30 prisoners from the Special Squad, who take advantage of an unguarded moment in Crematorium V to join the march. The route of this column leads through Auschwitz, Rajsko, Brzeszcze, Góra, Miedźna, Ćwiklice, Pszczyna, Kobielice, Kryry, Suszec, Rudziczka, Kleszczów, Żory, Rogoźne, Rój, Rybnik, Świerklany Dolne, and Marklowice to Wodzisław in Silesia.†

APMO, Dpr.-Hd/1, pp. 28, 65; Depositions, vol. 36, Account of Former Prisoner Jan Kupiec.

In the evening the female prisoners in the Auschwitz women's camp are formed into columns. Together with the female prisoners who have arrived from Birkenau they are driven in the direction of Rajsko. The female prisoners of the gardening and plant-breeding squads from the Rajsko A.C. join the procession of the male and female prisoners evacuated from Auschwitz-Birkenau and bring up the rear. They march through the communities of Pszczyna, Poręba Wielka, and Jastrzebie Górne to Wodzisław in Silesia. Only Eugenia Halbreich (No. 29700), who had hidden herself in the attic of an addition next to the house of SS man Grell, remains in the Rajsko A.C.††

APMO, Dpr.-Hd/1, pp. 112–113; Dpr.-Hd/3, pp. 138–141.

All the prisoners of the Monowitz A.C., the camp near the I. G. Farben works, are assembled on the parade ground in the evening. They are formed into columns of 1,000 prisoners each. Divisions of nurses are placed among the individual columns. The march leads through Bieruń, Mikołów, Mokre Śląskie, and Przyszowice to Gleiwitz.‡ 850 sick prisoners remain in the prisoners' infirmary,

Jaworski, *Memories of Auschwitz*, pp. 266, 270.

---

*In this group are also prisoners who are not strong enough for such a long march. They go voluntarily because they are afraid to remain in the camp, since they were aware of intentions of the camp management to liquidate them.
**The following prisoners of the Special Squad escape en route: Stanisław Jankowski (a.k.a. Alter Feinsilber—No. 27675), Szlama Dragon (No. 80359), Henryk Tauber (No. 90124), and Henryk Mandelbaum (No. 181970).
†172 prisoners, among them 31 women, are buried in mass graves on the stretch from Kryry to Marklowice (*Bulletin GKBZHwP*, vol. 11, Warsaw 1960, pp. 217, 219, 221, 222).
††After four days she leaves her hiding place and goes to the village of Rajsko, where she finds refuge with one of the residents.
‡On this stretch are five mass graves with 50 prisoners who were shot to death during the evacuation (*Bulletin GKBZHwP*, vol. 9, pp. 218, 221).

among them an assistant doctor and 18 doctors, including Dr. Czesław Jaworski.

The prisoners are evacuated from the Trzebinia auxiliary camp and those able to march are led to Auschwitz. Those who can go no farther remain there. Those still alive upon the arrival of the column in Rybnik are loaded into open freight cars. After four days they arrive in Gross-Rosen stiff from the cold. Because of overcrowding at the camp the transport is not accepted and is directed farther, to Sachsenhausen, but after remaining there for two weeks, it is sent to Bergen-Belsen. Arnost Tauber, Abraham Piasecki, and Karl Broszio escape during the foot march.

Piper, "Trzebinia," pp. 130ff.

Those unable to march are sent to the secondary railway track of the Trzebinia refinery, where they are crammed into four freight cars intended for coal transport over which a provisional covering is thrown, and deported in an unknown direction.

Before the march the camp management in Gleiwitz I conducts a selection, during which several dozen sick, lame, and weakened prisoners are singled out. The SS men lead them behind the barracks and shoot them to death. It is announced to the remaining prisoners that everyone will be shot to death who cannot keep up with the columns. Each of the prisoners receives a loaf of bread when they leave the camp. Some are forced to pull handcarts loaded with luggage and weapons of the supervising SS men. Weak prisoners are shot to death in small patches of forest during the march. After three days and two nights of the march, which the prisoners spend packed into barns found on their way, they arrive in the Blechhammer A.C., which is also being dissolved. Some of the prisoners from Gleiwitz I succeed in remaining in Blechhammer and thus in avoiding further deportation. Some of the prisoners die when the SS men shoot up the prisoners' barracks. Some succeed in escaping. On January 21 the remaining prisoners from Gleiwitz I are led under SS supervision from Blechhammer to Gross-Rosen, where they arrive at the beginning of February. After several days they are transported in freight cars from there to Buchenwald, Nordhausen, and Sachsenhausen.

Strzelecka, "Gleiwitz I," pp. 105ff.

After the prisoners are marched off, Gleiwitz I, like Gleiwitz II, III, and IV, becomes a temporary concentration point for thousands of prisoners from other auxiliary camps of Auschwitz, above all from Monowitz.

The male and female prisoners of Gleiwitz II receive the order to prepare themselves to leave the camp. The director of the Deutsche Gasrusswerke, Schenk, intervenes so that the female prisoners receive additional clothing. All prisoners, males and females, are given a blanket and a loaf of bread for the trip. The columns of male and female prisoners marching on foot are escorted by numerous SS guards under the direction of SS Technical Sergeant Bernhard Rackers. After a march of approximately 13 miles the columns of prisoners are driven to a barn to spend the night. The next morning three prisoners who are no longer able to march are shot and killed

Strzelecka, "Gleiwitz II," pp. 125–127.

in this barn. In view of the approach of the Red Army, the prisoners are sent back to Gleiwitz. They spend the night near the city. The next day they are led to the railroad ramp in Gleiwitz and loaded into open freight cars. The transport travels over Moravia and reaches Oranienburg approximately 10 days later. The men are sent to Sachsenhausen and the women to Ravensbrück. Several female prisoners escape from the transport, among them Anna Marko-wiecka, who clambers up the wall of the freight car, springs from the train and rolls down the slope into the undergrowth. The shots fired by the SS men do not hit her.

The prisoners of the Bismarckhütte auxiliary camp are marched off in typical prisoner clothing and in wooden clogs, some even bare-foot. They have to pull platforms behind them that are loaded with various things. SS Staff Sergeant Klemann from Hamburg is the leader of this transport. The columns reach Gleiwitz on January 20, where the prisoners wait with other prisoners from Auschwitz for further transport.

Irena Strzelecka, "Das Nebenla-ger Bismarckhütte" (Bismarck-hütte Auxiliary Camp), *HvA*, no. 12 (1971): 158ff.

The labor squads of the Günthergrube A.C. work a normal day and begin preparing for departure that evening. Approximately 20 sick prisoners are loaded into a wagon and probably brought to the neighboring Fürstengrube A.C. At about 10:00 P.M. 560 pris-oners begin the march under the supervision of 40 SS men. The march column is led toward the village of Kosztowo on side roads. In the morning hours of January 19 near the village of Mikołów the prisoners from the Günthergrube A.C. join the columns of pris-oners coming from Monowitz. A two-hour rest pause is ordered at the edge of Mikołów. After this the prisoners who are no longer able to march are shot and killed. The rest of the prisoners reach Gleiwitz in the evening and are put up in the auxiliary camp. They spend two nights there, but receive no food. On January 21 they are loaded in open freight cars with other prisoners from Auschwitz who have arrived in Gleiwitz. The train stops often, so by the next day they are only several dozen kilometers from Gleiwitz. Many prisoners die of hunger and exhaustion. On January 22 the train stops around noon next to the train station in Rzędówka. The SS guards under the direction of SS man Kurpanik order the prisoners to throw the dead out of the freight cars. Following this the re-maining prisoners must form a marching column and are led in the direction of the forest, at which point some of them attempt to escape. Some of them reach the forest, but 331 are shot and killed.* The fate of the prisoners who remain in the column is not known.**

Iwaszko, "Günthergrube," pp. 141–144.

Approximately 450 prisoners leave the Tschechowitz A.C. at 7:00 P.M., guarded by heavily armed SS men. On January 20 the prisoners reach Wodzisław in Silesia via Dziedzice, Goczałkowice, and Pszczyna. Those who cannot keep up the fast pace of the march

Strzelecka and Szymański, "Tschechowitz," pp. 218ff.

*After the war the bodies of 331 prisoners are found on the compound of the Rzędówka colony and near the train station (*Bulletin GKBZHwP*, vol. 11, p. 221).
**They are probably shot and killed in the stadium in Rybnik, since the bodies of 292 prisoners are found there after the war (ibid., p. 222).

are shot and killed. At the train station in Wodzisław they meet thousands of other prisoners from Auschwitz who had been force-marched here from the main camp and the auxiliary camps. They travel to Buchenwald in open freight cars full of snow. Of the approximately 450 prisoners who leave the Tschechowitz-Vacuum A.C., nearly 300 survive the transfer. The seriously ill, who are unable to march, and the bodies of dead prisoners are left behind in the auxiliary camps.

In the evening a column numbering several hundred prisoners from the Golleschau A.C. begins its march. A second column of equal size leaves the camp the next day. Both columns arrive by foot in Wodzisław in Silesia. From there they are taken to Sachsenhausen and Flossenbürg in open freight cars, which normally are used for transporting coal. Almost half of the prisoners die on the way of hunger, of exhaustion from the long march, and of freezing. Approximately 100 prisoners who are unable to march remain behind in Golleschau.

Frackiewicz, "Golleschau," p. 69.

In the course of the day columns of 100 prisoners each leave the Auschwitz main camp at certain time intervals. One of these columns consists of male and female civilian prisoners who have been detained in Block 11 by order of the Police Court-martial of the Kattowitz Gestapo.* They are guarded by heavily armed SS men. Books and documents are burned in all offices.

APMO, Depositions, vol. 42, p. 107; Accounts of Former Prisoners Anna Zdrowak and Emilia Zdrowak-Kamińska; Dpr.-Hd/8, p. 131, Statement of Former Prisoner Jan Dziopka.

JANUARY 19

The last large transport with 2,500 prisoners leaves the Auschwitz main camp at 1:00 A.M. under the supervision of SS First Lieutenant Wilhelm Reischenbeck. Near Rajsko the last column joins up with 1,000 prisoners from Birkenau. Behind the village of Brzeszcze the procession joins with a column of 1,948 prisoners from the Jawischowitz A.C. A good dozen prisoners who are sick and unable to march remain behind in Jawischowitz. The route of this last, very large column of prisoners is led to Wodzisław in Silesia through the following villages: Rajsko, Góra, Miedźna, Ćwiklice, Pszczyna, Poremba, Brzeszcze, Studzionka, Bzie, Pawłowice, Jastrzębie, Mszana, and Wilchwy. During the march the columns of prisoners combine to form a large unit. On the march route and at the side of the road lie the corpses of the prisoners from the preceding columns who have been shot and killed. A prisoner from Posen counts 114 corpses. After the arrival in Wodzisław the prisoners are loaded into open freight cars and transferred to Mauthausen. The transport arrives there on January 26.

APMO, Dpr.-Hd/8, p. 131; Depositions, vol. 86, pp. 125–130; Halina Wróbel, "Die Liquidation des Konzentrationslager Auschwitz-Birkenau" (The Liquidation of Auschwitz-Birkenau), HvA, no. 6 (1962): 19–29; Strelecki, "Jawischowitz," pp. 249–250; Strzelecki, Evacuation, Liquidation, pp. 165–168.

The Gendarmerie post in Miedźna, Pszczyna District, reports to the local police administrator in Ćwiklice that the corpses of 39 prisoners from an evacuation transport from the Auschwitz concentration camp have been found, 10 men and 29 women. But he

APMO, Mat./595, vol. 43, p. 45.

*Near Rybnik, Anna, Zofia, and Emilia Zdrowak escape from this transport.

supplies the numbers of only 25 prisoners, since no numbers can be found on the other prisoners.*

At 4:00 A.M. the last group with 30 prisoner functionaries leaves Auschwitz. They arrive in Wodzisław in Silesia on January 22, just as the prisoners of the last column, which had left the camp several hours before them, are being loaded into the open freight cars.

APMO, Dpr.-Hd/5, pp. 19, 98; Wróbel, "Liquidation of Auschwitz-Birkenau," p. 28.

A renewed Allied air attack on the I. G. Farben works in Dwory near Auschwitz takes place in the morning hours. As a result, the water and electric services are cut off in the town of Auschwitz and in the camps. Only prisoners unable to march and a good dozen prisoners who are caring for the sick are still in Auschwitz-Birkenau and Monowitz.

APMO, Dpr.-Hd/6, p. 290; Gilbert, *Auschwitz and the Allies*, p. 393.

The Gleiwitz III auxiliary camp is dissolved. SS men lead the prisoners westward in columns. The march lasts several days. When they reach the left bank of the Oder they turn around and are led through Cosel to the Blechhammer A.C. From there part of the column is brought to Gross-Rosen; some, however, succeed in escaping. A few return to Gleiwitz and are hidden there.

Strzelecki, "Gleiwitz III," pp. 149ff.

380 prisoners are taken from the Gleiwitz IV A.C. and led in the direction of the village of Sośnicowice. After a few miles, however, they are ordered back to Gleiwitz and taken to the Blechhammer A.C. From here some of the prisoners are transferred to Gross-Rosen and some to Buchenwald. 57 prisoners who were unable to march remain behind in the auxiliary camp itself. They are locked in the sick bay. After several hours the Commander of the Gleiwitz IV A.C., SS Corporal Otto Lätsch, returns to the camp with Gustav Günther, a member of the Todt Organization. The two men set the sick bay, in which the 57 sick and exhausted prisoners are locked up, on fire. The prisoners who jump out of the windows are shot to death by SS men, who are present during the entire operation. Only two prisoners, Dabrowski and Rosenfeld, are able to save themselves; they hide among the corpses of their comrades in suffering.

APMO, Dpr.-ZO/64, pp. 48–49, 52, 58–60; Strzelecki, "Gleiwitz IV," pp. 167–169.

In the early morning hours 202 prisoners leave the Hubertushütte A.C. under SS supervision. Before being marched off the prisoners receive bread and margarine. They are led through Chropaczów and Lipiny to Gleiwitz, where they arrive at around 3:00 P.M. They wait here with prisoners from other camps for further transport.

Strzelecka, "Hubertushütte," pp. 170–173.

In the Hindenburg A.C. Supervisor Joanna Bormann orders the women returning from work to prepare to leave. Each woman may take a blanket and dry food, mainly bread. The approximately 470 female prisoners arrive in the Gleiwitz II A.C. in the evening on foot. Here they are loaded into open coal cars and brought to Gross-

Strzelecka, "Hindenburg," pp. 145–147.

---

*His report does not say whether the numbers were found on the left lower arm or on the clothing. Numbers on the clothing could in fact have belonged to other prisoners, since during the preparations for the march, the prisoners took pains to put on civilian clothing without numbers or whichever clothing was immediately available in the hope of being able to escape.

The camp after the liberation.

Rosen. Because of overcrowding, however, the prisoners are not accommodated at Gross-Rosen. The trip to Bergen-Belsen in the open freight cars lasts two weeks. During this time the women have only dry bread to eat, and they quench their thirst with the snow that falls into the freight cars, as do all the prisoners during the transports.

833 prisoners begin the march from the Charlottengrube A.C. After one day, during which the weak who can't keep up with the column are shot to death, the prisoners reach a farm near the Oder, where they spend the night. The next day they are marched back to Ry-dułtowy and on January 22 to Wodzisław in Silesia, whence they are brought to Mauthausen in open freight cars, together with prisoners from Auschwitz.

Strzelecki, "Charlottengrube," pp. 76–78.

The liquidation of the Althammer A.C. and the evacuation of the prisoners is personally supervised by Commandant Heinrich Schwartz of Monowitz. All prisoners able to march are led at around 10:00 A.M. to Gleiwitz and are brought from here to various concentration camps. Approximately 150 prisoners remain behind in the camp. At around 4:00 P.M. an SS division arrives in the auxiliary camp. Their leader calls for a prisoner roll call, chooses a new Camp Senior and demands that everything be brought to order. Around January 25 the SS men order a new roll call. Since they themselves are leaving the camp, they take a good dozen prisoners with them. Those who remain behind are guarded by the local self-defense unit until Russian troops march in and liberate the prisoners. Among those liberated are Mieczysław Francuz, Aleksander Gelermann, and the Lejbisz brothers.

Piper, "Althammer," pp. 157ff.

The Neustadt A.C. is dissolved. The female prisoners are marched to Gross-Rosen and from here to Bergen-Belsen.

Strzelecka, "Neustadt," p. 170.

This page and right: Prisoners murdered by the SS shortly before the liberation of the camp.

Approximately 1,000 prisoners are removed from the Fürstengrube secondary camp. The liquidation of the camp and the departure of the prisoners by foot is supervised by Camp Commander Max Schmidt. In the early morning hours the columns pass through Mikołow and join the columns from Monowitz. The prisoners make it from Mikołow to Gleiwitz (15 miles) in 12 hours. In the evening the prisoners from Fürstengrube and the other auxiliary camps are put in the Gleiwitz II A.C. Over 250 sick prisoners remain behind in the Fürstengrube A.C. They are neither cared for nor fed.

Iwaszko, "Fürstengrube," pp. 81–84.

Divisions of the Red Army march into Jaworzno and liberate approximately 400 prisoners who had been left behind in the Neu-Dachs A.C. because they were unable to march.

APMO, Depositions, vol. 5, pp. 609–617, Account of Former Prisoner Wiktor Pasikowski.

In the morning hours an SS division arrives in the male prisoners' infirmary in Camp B-IIf and looks for prisoners able to work. These prisoners must carry the corpses that have been lying there for a week out of the blocks and to the compound of Crematorium V. The corpses are put in a pile, which the SS men set on fire. After this the prisoners, under the supervision of the SS men, must retrieve for them the more valuable things from the storerooms in the personal effects camp. Before leaving the SS men set a pile of suitcases on fire.

APMO, Dpr.-Hd/1, p. 77, Statement of Former Prisoner Luigi Ferri.

In the evening the prisoners in the last column from Auschwitz-Birkenau and Jawischowitz stop in the villages of Poremba and Brzeszcze, and a night camp is ordered. A few find shelter in sheds and barns; the others must spend the night outside at below zero (Fahrenheit) temperatures. On this day 71 bodies of shot and otherwise deceased prisoners remain on the road between Auschwitz and Miedzna.

Wróbel, "Liquidation of Auschwitz-Birkenau," p. 25.

JANUARY 20

At 6:00 A.M. the columns of prisoners leave Poremba and Brzeszcze. The SS men search through the straw and hay piles in the sheds and barns. They shoot to death several prisoners who attempt to hide, but nevertheless 36 prisoners succeed in escaping in Poremba.

Ibid.

During an Allied air raid on the O.S. Hydrierwerke in Upper Silesia the SS men abandon the watchtowers in Blechhammer A.C. Prisoners from Neu-Dachs A.C. who were housed in the Blechhammer A.C. take advantage of this moment to cut the wires of the camp fence, knock a hole in the wall, and escape. Some are shot to death by SS men, 42 prisoners reach the forest, where they break up into small groups and await the advance of the Red Army. Some of them join the Red Army and take part in the further course of the war.

APMO, Ośw./Piernat/89, vol. 5, pp. 646–648, Account of Former Prisoner Aron Piernat (No. 74324); Ośw./Szojchert/134, vol. 5, p. 677, Account of Former Prisoner Borys Szojchert (No. 75619).

The order to liquidate immediately all prisoners who are unable to march is received by SS Major Franz Xaver Kraus, who since December 1944 has been Head of the Auschwitz Liaison and Transition offices,* from SS Lieutenant General Schmauser, the Commander of the SS Southeast Region in Breslau.

APMO, Dpr.-ZO/52, p. 286; D-RF-3/RSHA/117/2, pp. 121–139, RSHA General Orders.

The Head of Office W-I, DEST in Oranienburg, reports to the Head of Branch W, Economic Operations (Wirtschaffsbetriebe), in the WVHA, that Auschwitz Concentration Camp was evacuated on January 18, 1945, owing to the events of the war. The most important documents, office machines, etc. of the DEST headquarters in Auschwitz were loaded onto trucks in the night of January 18–19, in order to transport them to the DEST headquarters in

APMO, IZ-13/89, Various Documents of the Third Reich, p. 155 (original in BA Koblenz).

---

*During the Auschwitz Trial in Kraków he states that he was sent to Auschwitz to "gather and analyze information." Kraus participates actively in the deportation and liquidation of the prisoners.

Gross-Rosen. With the approval of the Commandant in Auschwitz, two SS men who worked in bookkeeping and six female Jewish prisoners who worked in the DEST office have also been transferred to Gross-Rosen. Works Director Rupprecht and several ethnic German employees remain in Auschwitz. The transfer of the DEST office from Auschwitz to Gross-Rosen is the action planned to respond to case A.*

In an atmosphere of uncertainty, several SS divisions remain not far from Birkenau. In the morning one of these divisions enters Women's Camp B-IIe and orders the female prisoners to cook a midday meal for the SS men; they give the women butchered poultry and a suckling pig. Under their uniforms most of the SS men already wear civilian clothing, which they obtained from the personal effects camp, "Canada." They leave the midday meal standing because they flee when they receive the order to march. Some of the healthier male and female prisoners decide to flee too. They lift the gate to Camp B-IIe, arrive in the Block Leader's room of the SS men, and begin to demolish it. Suddenly they notice an SS division approaching from a distance. They return to the camp. An SS division under SS Corporal Perschel, the Labor Manager in the women's camp, enters the women's camp, B-IIe. Perschel orders all Jewish prisoners to leave the blocks; approximately 200 women come out. They are led in front of the camp gate and shot to death. Following this the SS division enters the prisoners' infirmary for men in Camp B-IIf. There they select a group of prisoners who must bring cases of dynamite to Crematoriums II and III.

APMO, Ośw./Kowalczyk/482, vol. 19, Account of Former Prisoner Anna Kowalczyk (No. 27658); Ośw./Matlak/894, vol. 894, Account of Former Prisoner Maria Matlak (No. 50161).

The SS division under SS Corporal Perschel blows up the already partly demolished Crematoriums II and III and abandons the camp.

Ibid.

In the night some of the female prisoners coming on foot from the women's camps in Birkenau and Auschwitz reach Wodzisław in Silesia.** They spend the night outdoors near the train station and wait to be loaded into the trains standing ready, which consist of coal cars.

APMO, Dpr.-ZO/28, Statement of Former Prisoner Enrica Jona.

At 11:55 P.M. the following male prisoners escape from the prisoners' infirmary in Camp B-IIf: Kazimierz Smoleń (No. 96238), Dr. Stanisław Zasadzki (No. 150155), Władysław Rodowicz, Jerzy

APMO, Dpr.-Hd/1, p. 96, Statement of Former Prisoner Kazimierz Smoleń.

*Case A is the cryptonym for an immediate threat to the concentration camp by enemy forces (Strzelecki, *Evacuation*, pp. 29, 31, 33–36).
**Meanwhile many female prisoners succeed in escaping, among them Anna Tytoniak, Romualda Cieślik-Ciesielska, Krystyna Żywulska, Danuta Mosiewicz-Mikusz, Walentyna Konopska, Helena Panek, Irena Głowacka-Zakrzewska, Józsefa Kaleta-Kiwałowa, Krystyna Cyankiewicz-Witek, Wanda Błachowska-Tarasiewicz, Zofia Augustyn-Pajerska, Julia Sajbner, Nadjeżda Cwietkowa, Nina Kopkowa-Małonkowa, Olga Harina, Jenny Spritzer, Jadwiga Budzińska, Danuta Figiel, Wiktoria Furman, Aniela Lasek, Stanisława Rzepka, Zdzisława Sosnowska, Maria Świeratowa, and Janina Unkiewicz (Tadeusz Iwaszko, "Ucieczki więźniarek z KL Auschwitz" (Escape Attempts by Female Prisoners from Auschwitz), ZO no. 18 (1983): 169–172; Harlina Wróbel, *Liquidation*, p. 27; Zięba, *Rajsko*, p. 89).

Bordzic, Alfons Budrowski, and the two female prisoners Władysława Kamińska and Janina Grzybowska. At 6:00 A.M. they arrive in Brzeszcze and find refuge with local Poles until August 28, that is, the day the Red Army marches in.

JANUARY 21

The dissolution of the Blechhammer A.C. camp begins. The prisoners receive 1¾ pounds of bread, a portion of margarine, and artificial honey for the trip. Approximately 4,000 prisoners from Blechhammer leave the camp, but also prisoners from the auxiliary camps of Neu-Dachs and Gleiwitz I, III, and IV who were taken to Blechhammer. During their foot march the prisoners traverse the villages of Kole, Neustadt, Głuchołazy, Neisse, Otmuchów, Ząbkowice Śląskie, Schweidnitz, and Strzegom and reach Gross-Rosen on February 2, 1945. During the march SS men murder approximately 800 prisoners.* SS Second Lieutenant Kurt Klipp directs the withdrawal. After a five-day stay in Gross-Rosen, the prisoners are loaded into a train and transferred to Buchenwald. On the way the train runs into several air raids and many lives are lost. Numerous sick prisoners, several dozen female prisoners, and those who succeed in hiding remain behind in Blechhammer. Some of these prisoners are murdered by SS men who return after the march to set it on fire. They shoot and throw grenades at the prisoners who flee from the burning barracks.

Piper, "Blechhammer," pp. 37–39.

At about 1:00 P.M. on Sunday an armed division of the Todt Organization enters the grounds of the Tschechowitz-Vacuum A.C. Approximately 100 prisoners who were left behind because of their inability to march and the corpses of dead prisoners are still in the camp. The members of the Todt Organization order the prisoners to dig a pit two yards deep and ten yards long, allegedly to bury the corpses. Some hours later several SS men appear who order the people living nearby not to leave their houses and forbids them to assist escaping prisoners under the threat of death. The SS men now go to the sick bay and shoot the bedridden prisoners to death. They order the remaining prisoners to bring those shot to the pit and to cover them with sacks of straw. Then, however, the SS men shoot at the prisoners carrying out the sacks of straw. The SS men pour an extremely flammable fluid over the heap of corpses and straw sacks and ignite it. Prisoners who succeed in escaping this inferno are shot to death by patrols who search the grounds of the camp. Probably only five prisoners are able to save themselves, among them Erwin Habal (No. B-12457) and Dr. Josef Weil (No. B-12562).

APMO, Depositions, vol. 1, p. 59, vol. 66, p. 19, Accounts of Former Prisoners Erwin Habal and Josef Weil; Strzelecka and Szymański, "Tschechowitz," pp. 219, 222.

*On March 27 and 28, 1946, by order of the district court in Neustadt, 34 corpses are exhumed of prisoners from Auschwitz who during the evacuation were murdered in Niemysłowice and buried in a bomb crater on the grounds of the village of Łaka. On April 27, 1946, the district court in Neustadt orders the exhumation of a mass grave in the Jewish cemetery in Neustadt, in which 28 corpses were buried in the typical striped prisoner clothing. 11 numbers of prisoners from Auschwitz can be deciphered. Documents in the name of Salomon Rosenzweig are found on the corpse with the number 178473 (APMO, Mat./597, 598, 599, Inventory No. 107287).

Five female prisoners attempt to escape from the women's camp in Camp B-IIe. They are detained by a drunken SS man in the so-called death gate.* He takes the youngest woman with him into the guardroom. Two shots are heard and after a while the woman runs out. She has succeeded in defending herself and in shooting the drunken SS man to death. The women prisoners conceal themselves in a railroad car loaded with feathers and pillows that stands at the ramp. After an entire day in this car they return to the women's camp.

АPMO, Ośw./Kowalczyk/428, vol. 19; Ośw./Matlak/894, vol. 43, Accounts of Former Prisoners Anna Kowalczyk and Maria Matlak.

Prisoners from the main camp arrive in Birkenau with the news that the SS storerooms are in their compound; they contain enough provisions to last for several months. The prisoners immediately form into groups who break into the storerooms equipped with wheelbarrows. They bring back two butchered hogs, cans of preserved meat, condensed milk, noodles, and other products. The salvaged provisions suffice for the prisoners in the men's and women's camps for one week. The kitchen in Birkenau is put back into operation.

APMO, Dpr.-Hd/6, p. 301.

The absence of the SS men in the camps in Birkenau leads to a lessening of tension. The Russian POWs who remain in the camp retrieve two weapons from a hiding place and shoot several times into the air. The Wehrwacht is alerted by the shots and notifies a division of the SD, which arrives and searches the barracks for guns, but without success. The German Capo Otto Schulz informs the SD that the Russian POW Andreyev had fired the shots. Andreyev, however, is not to be found.

APMO, Dpr.-Hd/1, p. 78; Dpr.-Hd/6, p. 310; Irena Perkowska-Szczypiorska, *Pamiętnik Taczniezki* (Memoires of a Courier), Warsaw, 1962, p. 277.

The next columns with female prisoners from Auschwitz-Birkenau arrive in Wodzisław in Silesia. Trains of open freight cars are assembled from the morning until late into the night, into which half-dead, unconscious, and feverish female prisoners are loaded. The individual trains are directed to Gross-Rosen,** Sachsenhausen, Ravensbrück, and Buchenwald.†

APMO, Dpr.-Hd/3, p. 141; Škodowa, *Three Years*, pp. 177–181.

The evacuation of the Golleschau A.C. camp is completed. The last group, with 96 sick and exhausted prisoners and the corpses of four prisoners who die during the transport, is put in a sealed freight car and transferred to the Freudenthal A.C. in Czechoslovakia. The stamps, with the date, of the following train stations can be seen on the bill of lading: Golleschau, January 21; Teschen, January 21;

Documents and Materials, vol. I, pp. 10ff. (reproduction of bill of lading), pp. 61, 62.

---

*This is what the entry gate to Auschwitz II, Birkenau, was called.
**Because of overcrowding the Commandant's Office of Gross-Rosen does not accept the transport. The approximately 2,000 female prisoners are transported to Ravensbrück and from there to Sachsenhausen. Since they are not accepted in Sachsenhausen, the command of the Ravensbrück concentration camp is forced to accept the transport on January 27.
†The transport with female prisoners destined for Buchenwald is detained on the other side of Breslau. The female prisoners must transfer from the open cars to closed ones, which are then sealed shut. Because of overcrowding Buchenwald does not accept the transport. Finally it is redirected to Bergen-Belsen, where it finally ends.

Oderberg, January 22; Schönbr., January 22; Freudenthal, January 25; Zwittau, Brüssen-Brünnlitz, January 29. On January 29, 1945, the station supervisor in Zwittau informs the director Oskar Schindler of the munitions factory in Brüssen-Brünnlitz that a wagon with Jewish prisoners has arrived at the station. Schindler ordered that this wagon be sent to Brüssen-Brünnlitz. There is an auxiliary camp belonging to Gross-Rosen. Since the hinges and the locks are frozen, the wagon is opened with force. Half of the prisoners have frozen or starved to death. The corpses are found in the most diverse cowering, kneeling, or standing positions. The remaining prisoners are not capable of leaving the wagon themselves. More than a dozen die after several days in the camp.

Five Polish prisoners, Tadeusz Balut (No. 1259), Alfred Barabasch (No. 62332), Wojciech Kozłowski (No. 26724), Mieczysław Zawadzki (No. 8012), and Stanisław Załęski (No. 1877), escape from the Auschwitz main camp at 5:00 P.M.

APMO, Depositions, vol. 115, Account of Former Prisoner Stanisław Załęski.

The residents along the transport route Ćwiklice, Pszczyna, Poremba, Brzeszcze, Studzionka, Bzie, Jastrzębie Górne, Mszana, Wilchwy, and Wodzisław in Silesia recover the corpses of 223 male and female prisoners* and bury them in mass graves.

Wróbel, *Liquidation of Auschwitz-Birkenau*, pp. 33–35.

In the Gleiwitz auxiliary camps, prisoners from Auschwitz who have been brought here from the Monowitz, Bismarckhütte, Hubertusburg, Althammer, Bobrek, Fürstengrube, and Günthergrube auxiliary camps wait to be transported farther. The prisoners are divided into several transport groups and taken to the ramp according to how the trains arrived. All trains consist of open freight cars. The individual transports are taken to Buchenwald, Gross-Rosen,** Sachsenhausen,† and Mauthausen.††

APMO, Dpr.-Hd/5, pp. 154–156, Statement of Former Prisoner Zygfryd Halbreich (No. 68233).

JANUARY 22

2,223 prisoners, predominantly Polish and Hungarian Jews, arrive by transport in Buchenwald. Five prisoners, Nos. 202077, 7377, 174957, 9207, 90068, and 92013 in Auschwitz, die after being

APMO, D-Bu-3/1/6, pp. 33–111.

---

*1,101 male and female prisoners die along other evacuation routes in Silesia and are buried in 29 mass graves (*Bulletin GKBZHwP*, vol. 11, pp. 209–230).
**Because of overcrowding, Gross-Rosen does not accept the transport. It is rerouted to Dachau, where it arrives on January 28, 1945. 42 of the 1,408 prisoners have died. Another 25 prisoners die after their arrival in Dachau (APMO, D-Da-3/2/2, pp. 59–87).
†Most of the prisoners in this transport come from Monowitz. Almost a quarter of the prisoners freeze to death during the transport. The prisoners who arrive in Sachsenhausen are put up in the auxiliary camp on the grounds of the Heinkel works in Oranienburg.
††Because of overcrowding, the command of Mauthausen does not accept the transport. The transport is redirected to the Nordhausen concentration camp, which it reaches on January 28, 1945. After their arrival the prisoners are taken to the Mittelbau-Dora auxiliary camp. Of the approximately 4,000 prisoners who left Gleiwitz, approximately 3,500 reach Mittelbau-Dora. The others die en route. Another 600 prisoners die in the two days after the arrival (APMO, Dpr.-Hd/5,156, 157; Mat./606a, vol. 48a, p. 177, Account of the Former Prisoner Felix Stahl).

counted in the occupancy level and given numbers in Buchenwald. More detailed data on the identity of these prisoners are not available.

In the morning a division of the SD returns in Birkenau, Camp B-IIf, and in Block 13 arrests the sleeping Andreyev and five other Russian POWs who are accused of having fired shots. They are led behind Block 14, stood up next to a water channel, and shot to death.* As soon as the SD division departs, prisoners recover one of the POWs who has only been wounded in the head. The wound is treated by a prisoner doctor, Dr. Otto Wolken. Afterward the wounded prisoner is hidden in the block. On this day SS men shoot to death many prisoners who walk about in the camp or attempt to escape.

APMO, Dpr.-Hd/1, p. 79; Dpr.-Hd/6, pp. 302, 304.

At 9:00 A.M. approximately 80 male and female prisoners attempt to break out of the Birkenau camp in the direction of the bridge in Babitz. The fire directed at them by divisions of the Wehrmacht forces them to turn back. 10 prisoners drag themselves back to the camp, the others are killed. Around midday another group of male and female prisoners with children attempts to get out of the camp. They go toward the SS barracks. There they meet an SS man who allows them to go on to the train station. The railroad workers call to the prisoners so that some of them enter a train standing ready to go to Kattowitz. The others disperse. From the large group three female prisoners from Auschwitz remain with two girls from Warsaw whose mothers died in the camp. They reach the town of Auschwitz without any problem.

APMO, Ośw./Kowalczyk/482, vol. 19; Ośw./Matlak/894, vol. 43, Accounts of Former Prisoners Anna Kowalczyk and Maria Matlak.

The last columns of prisoners reach Wodzisław in Silesia. From 11:00 A.M. on, open freight cars stand ready. 100 prisoners are loaded into each car. The prisoners spend the night in the open freight cars, guarded by SS men. The train doesn't leave until the next day and arrives in Brünn in the evening. From there the transport is directed to Mauthausen.

APMO, Depositions, vol. 86, pp. 125–130, Account of Former Prisoner Józef Ciepły.

JANUARY 23

An evacuation transport with female prisoners, including 520 Poles, from Auschwitz arrives in Ravensbrück.

Wanda Kiedrzyńska, *Ravensbrück—kobiecy obóz koncentracyjny* (Ravensbrück—A Women's Concentration Camp), Warsaw, 1961, p. 79.

A transport with 916 prisoners from Auschwitz—predominantly Polish and Hungarian Jews—arrives in Buchenwald.

APMO, D-Bu-3/1/6, p. 111; D-Bu-3/1/7, pp. 1–17. [A transport with]

The prisoners are evacuated from the Laurahütte A.C. On the railroad track near the foundry a train is prepared into which the prisoners are loaded. The civilian personnel is evacuated with the same train. A single prisoner remains behind in the camp. During

Iwaszko, "Laurahütte," p. 101.

*On January 28, 1945, one day after the liberation of the camp, the Capo Otto Schulz, a traitor who had worked together with the SS, is shot to death on this spot (APMO, Dpr.-Hd/6, p. 310; Perkowska-Szczypiorska, *Memoirs*, p. 277).

The so-called new ramp after the liberation of the camp in February 1945.

the trip through Silesia the train stops in a forest near the train station in Rzędówka. Corpses in the typical striped prison clothing lie along the track. By order of the escort unit the prisoners remove the striped clothing from the corpses, collect the scattered camp bowls, and load them into the train. The dead are probably prisoners from the Günthergrube A.C. The transport travels to Mauthausen through Kattowitz, Mährisch-Ostrau (Moravian Ostrau) in Czechoslovakia, and Vienna.* The trip lasts five days and nights. 134 prisoners die en route.

Over 1,200 prisoners are led out of the Eintrachthütte A.C. They wait the entire night on the railroad platform in Schwientochlowitz for a train to be made ready. Toward morning they are loaded into several cattle cars whose floors are thick with animal feces. A good dozen prisoners die during the transport. The trip to Mauthausen lasts several days. 1,234 prisoners are counted in the occupancy of Mauthausen on January 30, 1945. Several dozen sick prisoners remain behind in Eintrachthütte. After the liberation they are brought to hospitals in Schwientochlowitz and Kattowitz.

APMO, D-Mau, Folder V, pp. 2765, 2766; Piper, "Eintrachthütte," pp. 144ff.

*The transport arrives in Mauthausen on January 29, 1945. 968 prisoners are counted in the occupancy of Mauthausen. Prisoners from other auxiliary camps were probably added to the transport (APMO, D-Mau, Folder V, p. 2763).

An SS division arrives in the prisoners' infirmary camp in B-IIf in the afternoon and orders the prisoners to carry the corpses of the shot Russian POWs to Crematorium V. The corpses are put in a large pile, which the SS men set on fire in the evening. Following this they set 30 storeroom barracks in the personal effects camp on fire.* The prisoners in Camp B-IIf who are threatened by the fire set up a guard of healthy prisoners who watch to see that the fire does not spread to the infirmary camp, which is only a few yards away.

APMO, Dpr.-Hd/1, p. 78; Dpr.-Hd/6, p. 304, 305, Statements of Former Prisoners Luigi Ferri and Dr. Otto Wolken.

JANUARY 24

A transport with female prisoners from Auschwitz, including 166 Poles, arrives in Ravensbrück.

Kiedrzyńska, *Ravensbrück*, p. 79.

SS Major Kraus arrives in Birkenau with an SS division and shoots three prisoners to death, among them the Dutch prisoner Dr. Ackermann.

APMO, Dpr.-Hd/5, p. 9; Dpr.-Hd/6, p. 92, Statements of Former Prisoners Professor Dr. Henri Limousin and Dr. Otto Wolken.

JANUARY 25

SS Major General Richard Glücks, Head of Branch D in the WVHA, is awarded the German Cross in Silver for his contribution to the war effort, because he directed 15 large concentration camps and more than 500 auxiliary camps with 750,000 prisoners, which were guarded by 40,000 SS men.

APMO, Dpr.-Mau/10, pp. 33ff.

Libiąż is liberated. There are 60 prisoners in the Janinagrube A.C., who were left behind because of their poor health. Poles who lived near the camp provide first aid. The seriously ill are taken to the hospital. The others remain in the camp, to regain their strength slowly.

Iwaszko, "Janinagrube," p. 65.

At 2:00 P.M. an SD division arrives in the women's camp in B-IIe and the men's camp in B-IIf in Birkenau. The order is given for all Jews to leave the barracks. In Camp B-IIf Capo Schulz points to Jews and drives them out of the barracks. Some of the Jewish prisoners are able to conceal themselves under the floors in previously prepared hiding places. Approximately 150 male and 200 female Jews are taken to the gate. Several Jewish prisoners are taken behind the Block Leader's Room and shot to death, among them the Jewish prisoner Harff from Cologne. Those prisoners who cannot keep up with the march tempo are also shot to death. The transport is stopped by SS men who drive past in an automobile. The prisoners are ordered to return to the main camp. But the SD members drive away with the SS men. Some of the prisoners return to Birkenau, some of them follow the order and return to the main camp.

APMO, Dpr.-Hd/1, pp. 78, 88; Dpr.-Hd/6, pp. 306–308, Statements of Former Prisoners Luigi Ferri, Roman Goldman, and Dr. Otto Wolken.

*These barracks burn for several days. After the liberation, 1,185,345 pieces of women's and men's outerwear, 43,255 pairs of shoes, 13,694 carpets, and a large number of toothbrushes, shaving brushes, and other items such as prostheses, glasses, etc., among other things are found in the six remaining partially burned barracks.

Another SD division enters the main camp. All sick prisoners must leave the blocks and line up near the gate with the slogan "Work Makes You Free." The German Reich prisoners are to line up in front, behind them the Aryan, and the Jewish prisoners behind them. Aryan and Jewish prisoners who can no longer walk are lined up separately. The SD checks the residence and invalid blocks and drives out all prisoners. It is obvious from the SD members' behavior that the prisoners are to be shot to death. While this line-up is going on, however, an automobile with SS men drives up. After a brief exchange of words the prisoners are ordered to return to the blocks. The SD division departs with the SS men in the greatest haste.*

APMO, Dpr.-Hd/1, p. 175; Dpr.-Hd/5, pp. 9, 19, Statements of Former Prisoners Dr. Jakub Gordon, Professor Dr. Henri Limousin, and Professor Dr. Geza Mansfeld.

JANUARY 26

At 1:00 A.M. the SS squad with the task of eliminating the traces of SS crimes blows up Crematorium V, the last of the crematoriums in Birkenau.

APMO, Dpr.-Hd/1, p. 79, Statement of Former Prisoner Luigi Ferri.

Skirmishes take place in the vicinity of Auschwitz. The approaching detonations can be heard in Auschwitz and Birkenau. Numerous air raids precede the arrival of the Red Army. Scattered Wehrmacht divisions flee in panic on the only route open for them, through Rajsko in the direction of Bielsko.

APMO, Dpr.-Hd/5, p. 9.

A transport with 3,987 prisoners from Auschwitz auxiliary camps reaches Buchenwald. There are 52 dead prisoners in the transport. 115 prisoners die on the day of arrival. Their corpses are delivered to the autopsy room.

APMO, D-Bu-3/1/7, pp. 18–85, 87.

JANUARY 27

The last transports from Auschwitz-Birkenau arrive at Mauthausen. On this day 6,025 prisoners from Auschwitz are counted in the occupancy of Mauthausen.

APMO, D-Mau, Folder 5, p. 2761.

A transport with approximately 2,000 female prisoners from Auschwitz reaches Ravensbrück. In the following days another approximately 2,000 female prisoners arrive, and at the beginning of February the last transport arrives with approximately 3,000 women from Auschwitz. They traveled part of the way on foot, requiring two weeks for 185 miles.**

Kiedrzyńska, *Ravensbrück*, p. 79.

Retreating Wehrmacht troops blow up the railroad bridge over the Vistula and Soła, as well as the wooden bridge over the Soła, which the prisoners built opposite the main camp.

APMO, Dpr.-Hd/5, p. 9.

*The order to liquidate the sick prisoners in the Birkenau and Auschwitz camps is not carried out by SS Major Franz Xaver Kraus, the representative of SS Lieutenant Schmauser, for the liquidation division of the SD is threatened by encirclement by the approaching Red Army. The liberated Libiąż is less than 10 miles from Auschwitz.
**In Ravensbrück they spend 24 hours outside without food, because there is no room for them there. To quench their thirst they eat snow. The women spend the next night in tents, but only the strongest are able to provide themselves with food. After three weeks they are transported farther, to Malchów (*Bulletin GKBZHwP*, vol. 56, Statement of the Former Female Prisoner Nisla Orleańska).

The rubble of Crematorium V, which was dynamited by the SS on January 26, 1945.

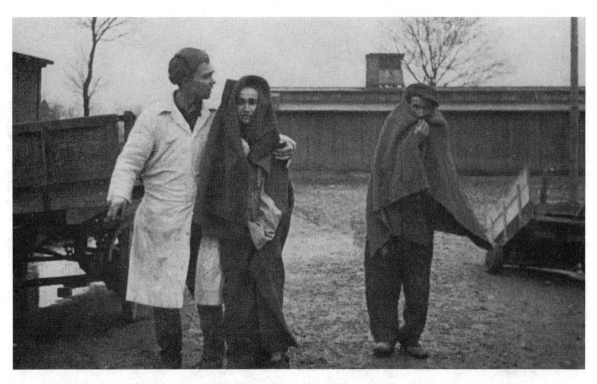

Birkenau after the liberation: a Soviet first-aid worker with two former prisoners.

An SS division arrives in Fürstengrube A.C. in which there are 250 prisoners. They order 127 prisoners, among them 40 Aryan prisoners, who can walk to leave the prisoners' infirmary and to go to the wooden barracks. There they are to position themselves at the windows. The prisoners hide themselves on the other side of the barracks. At that the SS men begin to shoot and to throw grenades inside the barracks. Since the wounded are still moving, the SS men bring up several sacks of straw, distribute them in the corners of the barracks, and set everything on fire. Prisoners who attempt to drag themselves from the burning barracks are shot to death. Afterward the SS men go to the prisoners' infirmary. They allow 10 Aryan prisoners to go into the camp kitchen, then set the barracks with all the sick on fire. All prisoners in the prisoners' infirmary barracks die in the flames.* Of the 127 prisoners who can walk, 14 are able to save themselves. After the liberation Polish miners take care of them, and after a week they are transported to the miners' hospital in Mysłowice.**

APMO, Dpr.-Hd/1, pp. 123–128, Statement of Former Prisoner Rudolf Ehrlich.

On Saturday at around 9:00 A.M. the first Russian soldier from a reconnaissance unit of the 100th Infantry Division of the 106th Corps appears on the grounds of the prisoners' infirmary in Mon-

Jaworski, *Memories of Auschwitz*, p. 281.

*One of the local people who assisted in recovering the bodies of the prisoners murdered in the Fürstengrube A.C. counts 239 bodies (Iwaszko, "Fürstengrube," p. 91).
**Among the saved is Rudolf Ehrlich (No. B-13511), who has to be treated in the hospital for gunshot wounds and burns from February 3 to April 7.

Remnants of one of the incineration units from the destroyed Crematorium V.

owitz.* The entire division arrives half an hour later. The soldiers distribute their bread among the sick. The same day, a military physician with the rank of captain arrives and begins to organize assistance. Of the 850 sick prisoners left behind during the deportations, more than 200 prisoners die by January 27.

In the afternoon soldiers of the Red Army enter the vicinity of the Auschwitz main camp and Birkenau. Near the main camp they meet resistance from retreating German units. 231 Red Army soldiers die in close combat for the liberation of Auschwitz, Birkenau, and Monowitz. Two of them die in front of the gates of the Auschwitz main camp. Among those who die is Lieutenant Gilmudin Badryyevich Baszrov.

APMO, Dpr.-Hd/5, p. 9, Statements of Former Prisoner Professor Dr. Henri Limousin; Strzelecki, "Liberation," p. 25.

*The task of liberating Auschwitz falls to the 60th Army of the 1st Ukrainian Front. By order of General Pawel Kurochkin, three divisions surround the German units in Auschwitz. The 100th Division of the 106th Corps advances the fastest, reaching Monowitz by the morning of January 27. On the same day the 148th Infantry Division of the 106th Corps, coming from the north, and the 322th Division of the 28th Corps, coming from the south, reach their goal. At midday, soldiers of the Red Army march into the center of the town of Auschwitz and are greeted joyfully by the Poles, as they emerge from rubble and hiding places (Andrzej Strzelecki, "Wyzwolenie KL Auschwitz" [The Liberation of Auschwitz], ZO Special Number III [1974]: pp. 21–35).

Part of Birkenau today.

The first Red Army reconnaissance troops arrive in Birkenau and Auschwitz at around 3:00 P.M. and are joyfully greeted by the liberated prisoners. After the removal of mines from the surrounding area, soldiers of the 60th Army of the 1st Ukrainian Front, commanded by General Pawel Kuroczkin, march into the camp and bring freedom to the prisoners who are still alive. On the grounds of the main camp are 48 corpses and in Birkenau over 600 corpses of male and female prisoners who were shot to death or died otherwise in the last few days.

APMO, Dpr.-Hd/5, p. 19; Dpr.-Hd/6, p. 89, Statements of Former Prisoners Professor Dr. Geza Mansfeld and Dr. Otto Wolken.

At the time of the Red Army's arrival there are 7,000 sick and exhausted prisoners in the Auschwitz, Birkenau, and Monowitz camps. Dr. Otto Wolken remains in the camp and is one of the organizers of the assistance measures for the prisoners. At the same time, however, he also secures the various camp documents that provide information on the crimes committed by the SS in the Auschwitz-Birkenau concentration camp. He reports the following numbers of surviving prisoners; Auschwitz—1,200 sick prisoners; Birkenau—5,800 prisoners, of whom 4,000 are women; Monowitz—600 sick prisoners.

APMO, Dpr.-Hd/6, p. 89.

SKETCHES OF SOME OF
THE PERPETRATORS

EDITED BY CHARLES SCHUDDEKOPF

Professor Dr. Otto Ambros, born in 1901 in Bavaria, went to work for I. G. Farben in 1926. He soon established himself as their expert on artificial rubber (Buna) and poison gas. In 1937, by this time a director of the concern, he became a member of the Nazi Party. In January 1941, he was sent to investigate the area around Auschwitz and advocated building a production plant there for synthetic rubber and oil. This was I. G. Farben's largest single project, with an investment capital of almost a million Reichsmarks and apparently immense opportunities for profit. Ambros, along with Heinrich Bütefisch, was appointed one of its managing directors. After 1945, Ambros was sentenced to eight years in prison in the I. G. Farben Trial. Released from prison early, he was ultimately appointed to the board of directors of several industrial enterprises and became an adviser in Konrad Adenauer's government. Bütefisch, sentenced to six years in prison but also released early, was appointed to the board of directors of Ruhrchemie, an industrial enterprise owned by the West German government.

Hans Aumeier (SS Captain), born in 1906, trained as an ironworker and was unemployed in 1924 for the first time. After joining the Nazi Party in 1931 he became a full-time employee and member of the SA and moved to the SS (No. 2700) in the same year. After several assignments in various concentration camps—in Dachau he was in charge of "special training," which Rudolf Höss underwent—he came to Auschwitz in 1942, where he was First Protective Custody Commander (Erstor Schutzhaftlagerführer). In 1943, because of various "violations," he was transferred to Vaivara C.C. in Estonia as Commandant and finally filled the same function in Grini C.C. in Norway in January 1945. He was condemned to death by the Supreme People's Court in Kraków in 1947 and was executed.

Erich von dem Bach-Zelewski (Waffen SS General), born in 1899 in Lauenburg, Pomerania, was the son of a Prussian landowner. He served in World War I as a professional soldier and joined the Friekorps after the war. In 1930 he joined the Nazi Party and, in 1931, the SS (No. 9831). He was a member of the Reichstag from 1932 to 1944 and rose rapidly in the SS. From June 1941 on, he was Superior SS and Police Commander for Central Russia; from November, SS Lieutenant General and General of the Police; and from 1942, deputy of the SS Commander in Chief responsible for Antipartisan operations ("Bandenbeckämpfung"). In 1944 he commanded the troops that put down the uprising in the Warsaw ghetto, where he was notorious for his personal cruelty. After 1945 he confessed to mass murder and appeared in Nuremberg as a witness against his fellow perpetrators; he was rewarded for this conduct by not being extradited to the Soviet Union. He was incarcerated by the Allies until 1950; in 1951 he was sentenced to 10 years in a labor camp—toward which the five years he had already spent in prison were counted—which he spent under house arrest in his own home. Arrested again in 1958 for his role in the suppression of the so-called Röhm Putsch, he received a 4½-year sentence in 1961 and a life sentence in 1962 for the murder of three Communists.

In none of the trials was there any discussion of his role in the "Final Solution" and in so-called antipartisan operations, which he had candidly described at the Nuremberg Trial as that of a mass murderer. He died in Munich in 1972.

Richard Baer (SS Major), born in 1911 in Bavaria, studied to be a pastry cook and was unemployed from 1930 until he joined the guards at Dachau C.C. in 1933. In 1960 he told the public prosecutor in Frankfurt that it was not politics but rather "the joy of playing soldier" that had led him to the SS. In 1939 he joined the SS Death's Head Division and in 1942 was named Adjutant of Neuengamme C.C. From 1943 on he was Adjutant to SS General Pohl, the Head of the WVHA, and in November 1943 he took charge of Office D-I, the central office of the Concentration Camps Inspectorate. From May 11, 1944, to the liquidation of the camp, Baer, following Liebehenschel, was the third Commandant of Auschwitz. At the end of the war he went underground and lived near Hamburg until 1960 under the name of Karl Neumann. In December of that year he was arrested, and he died in 1963, while being held for interrogation.

Stefan Baretzki (SS Sergeant) was born in 1919 in Czernowitz, Romania. Trained as a weaver, he worked as a foreman in a stocking factory. After Romania allied itself with Germany in 1941, Baretzki was designated an "ethnic German" and resettled. In 1941 he was taken into the Waffan SS and ordered to Auschwitz, where he was a Block Commander in Birkenau from 1942 to 1945. In the Frankfurt Auschwitz Trial, he described his activity thus:

> Regarding the issue of the "Moslems" from the auxiliary camps, I want to explain this clearly once and for all: There is only one "transfer" and "transmittal." Usually, the sick come on Saturday afternoon. . . . Monday they [the "transfers"] were then presented to the doctor. The prisoners who were "transmitted" didn't even come into the camp. As block commander I wasn't even allowed to open the gate. "Transmitted," that means to the gas chamber. . . . Not until Monday afternoon did they [the "transfers"] get their first meal. . . . The people who are "transmitted" don't get any food since they are to all intents and purposes already dead.*

In 1945, Baretzki moved to the Koblenz area, where he worked as a laborer in a coal business. In April 1960 he was finally arrested, accused in the Frankfurt Auschwitz Trial, and sentenced to life imprisonment on five counts of murder.

Wilhelm Boger (SS Staff Sergeant), born 1906 in Stuttgart, joined the Hitler Youth in 1922 and worked as a commercial employee until the Nazi "seizure of power" in 1933. That year he joined the Political Police, where he worked as an assistant. In 1937 he was promoted to police inspector; after the attack on Poland, in 1939, he was ordered as a member of the Gestapo to the occupied area. From 1942 to 1945 he was an SS Staff Sergeant in the Political Department in Auschwitz. There, he developed the "Boger swing," an instrument of torture that is now used internationally by torturers. It "consisted of two upright beams, in which an iron pole was laid crosswise. Boger made the victim kneel, placed the iron pole across the backs of the knees, and then chained the victim's hands to it. Then he fastened the iron pole to the beams so that the victim hung with his head down and his buttocks up." In this way Boger wrung confessions out of victims. In 1945 he was arrested but escaped from an extradition transport to Poland and lived quietly in Württemberg, legally registered as a civil servant, from 1949 on. In 1958 he was arrested, and in 1965, at the Frankfurt Auschwitz Trial, he was condemned to prison for 114 life terms on 109 counts of accessory to murder and on five counts of murder by interrogation.

Pery Broad (SS Private First Class), born 1921 in Rio de Janeiro, came to Berlin with his mother at the age of five. He studied at the technical high school and joined the Waffen SS

---

*Hermann Langbein, *Der Auschwitz-Prozess: Eine Dokumentation* (Frankfurt, 1965), p. 285.

as a foreigner in 1941. Sent to Auschwitz as a guard, in June 1942 he had himself transferred as an SS Private to the Political Department, where he carried out interrogations. He remained in Auschwitz until the closing of the camp at the beginning of 1945, and was taken a prisoner of war by the British in May 1945. In prison, he voluntarily wrote a report of his experiences in Auschwitz. In the Broad account, as it is called, he describes among other things the arrival of one of the countless trains bringing deportees:

> The leader—usually a police officer—of the escort commando, which has guarded the train during the trip, gives the SS man from the Admissions Department the transport list. Here are written the transport's place of origin, the train number, and the names and birth dates of all the Jews on the train. The SS men of the camp command make sure the deportees get off the train. On the platform all is colorful confusion: Elegant Frenchwomen wearing fur coats and silk stockings; helpless graybeards; curly-headed children; little old grannies; men in the prime of life, some in elegant business suits and some in work clothes; mothers with infants in their arms; and sick people carried by those willing to help them—all get off the train. First, men are separated from women. There are scenes of heartbreaking farewells. . . . Now the SS Camp Doctor begins to separate the able-bodied from those who, in his opinion, are incapable of work—anyone who makes a weak or sickly impression.
>
> On the platform a prisoner labor squad is busy gathering up the baggage lying around and loading it into wagons. The locomotive driver, who could easily have pulled his empty train away from the platform already, hangs around as long as possible. He makes a show of checking the cars' linkage gear while he watches for an opportunity to make a quick grab for some of the food and valuables strewn about the platform. The SS men of the Admissions Department compare the results of their count with the information on the transport list. Small discrepancies are ignored. The next morning a little note lies under the glass plate on [SS Second Lieutenant Maximilian] Grabner's desk. The laconic message reads, "Accessions on [date], Transport No. ———: 4,722, 612 of these able-bodied, 4,110 not able-bodied." Every SS man receives a voucher for schnapps—a fifth of a liter for every transport—and extra food. . . . After a short while the platform is once again empty, except for the wooden steps on which hundreds of thousands of people have trodden who had only minutes to live.

Released in 1947, he was arrested again in April 1959, freed in December 1960 on DM 50,000 bail, and was arrested again in November 1964 as a defendant in the Frankfurt Auschwitz Trial. He was convicted of supervising selections, of torturing during interrogations, and of participating in executions. In 1965, he was sentenced to four years in prison.

Dr. Joachim Caesar (SS Lieutenant Colonel), born in 1901, studied natural sciences and received a degree in agriculture. A member of the Nazi Party and the SS (No. 74704), he became mayor of Holstein in 1933 and, from 1934 on, worked in the SS training office in the RSHA, which he later headed. In March 1942, Caesar was appointed head of all agricultural activities in Auschwitz, which gained prominence because of their importance to the war effort; Himmler followed these enterprises with particular interest. After the war, Dr. Caesar went into the laundry business and wasn't troubled by any investigations into his past until his death in 1974.

Professor Dr. Carl Clauberg (Reserve SS Major General) was born in 1898 into an artisan family in Wupperhof. An infantryman in World War I, he later studied medicine and advanced to head doctor at the women's university clinic in Kiel. In 1933 he joined the Nazi Party and was quickly considered a fanatical representative of its Weltanschauung. The same year he was appointed professor of gynecology at the University of Königsberg. In 1942 he approached Heinrich Himmler, who was already interested in Clauberg's "research," and he asked Himmler for an opportunity to perform sterilization experiments on a broad scale (see entry for May 30, 1942). In December 1942, Clauberg came to Auschwitz and in April 1943 obtained Block

10 for his experiments. Looking for a "cheap and efficient method" of making women sterile, he injected corrosive liquid into the uterus, without using anesthesia. A Czech Jewess later reported how he proceeded:

> Dr. Clauberg ordered me to lie down on the gynecological table. I was able to observe Sylvia Friedmann [a prisoner orderly] preparing an injection syringe with a long needle. Dr. Clauberg used this needle to give me an injection in my womb. I felt that my belly would burst with the pain. I began to scream so that I could be heard throughout the entire block. Dr. Clauberg told me roughly to stop screaming immediately, otherwise I'd be returned at once to the camp, to Birkenau [i.e., the gas chamber]. . . . After this experiment I had an inflammation of the ovaries.*

Clauberg fled from the advancing Red Army to Ravensbrück, where he continued his experiments. It is estimated that he conducted sterilization experiments on about 700 women. In 1948 he was tried in the Soviet Union and sentenced to 25 years in prison. Freed in an amnesty in 1955, he returned to Kiel in the German Federal Republic, boasting of his "scientific achievements." Only after the Central Council of Jews denounced him was he arrested, in November 1955; he died in August 1957, shortly before his trial was to begin.

Dr. Walter Dürrfeld was born 1889 in Saarbrücken. As one of the directors of I. G. Farben, he managed the factory in Monowitz and as chief engineer and building manager supervised the general operations of the plant near Auschwitz. He and Bütefisch (see entry under "Otto Ambros") negotiated with the SS concerning the deployment of the prisoners' labor, insisting on appointing criminals as Capos and on immediately replacing prisoners who were no longer fully fit for work. In the Nuremberg I. G. Farben Trial, the former member of the board of I. G. Farben, Christian Schneider, said: "You could see the chimneys of the Auschwitz camp from I. G. [Farben] Auschwitz. I heard that I. G. people in Auschwitz, namely Walter Dürrfeld and other visiting engineers, even smelled the burning. Those gentlemen told me it was an awful smell." At this trial Walter Dürrfeld was sentenced to eight years in prison. Released early, he became managing director of Scholven-Chemic in Gelsenkirchen and sat on the board of other industrial enterprises.

Adolf Eichmann (SS Major) was born in 1906 in Solingen, moved with his family to Linz (Austria) and later studied engineering. He didn't complete his studies, but became a laborer, a salesman, and a representative for a mineral oil company. In 1932 he joined the Austrian Nazi Party and came to Berlin in 1934 to work in the so-called Jewish Section II-112 of the SD. By 1938 he was considered a specialist in the "Jewish question" and returned to Austria, where he set up the Central Office for Jewish Emigration, the only office authorized to issue exit visas to the Jews of Austria, later of Czechoslovakia, and then of the entire German Reich. In December 1939, Eichmann was transferred to the RSHA, where he took charge of Section IV-D-4 (after 1941, IV-B-4) for Jewish and Evacuation Affairs. From 1941 on his office organized the mass transports of European Jews to the extermination camps. In carrying out the deportations, as Robert Wistrich writes in *Who's Who in Nazi Germany*,

> . . . Eichmann proved to be a model of bureaucratic industriousness and icy determination even though he had never been a fanatical anti-Semite and always claimed that "personally" he had nothing against Jews. His zeal expressed itself in his constant complaints about obstacles in the fulfillment of death-camp quotas. . . . When even Himmler became more moderate toward the end of the war, Eichmann ignored his "no gassing" order, as long as he was covered by immediate superiors.**

Interned after the war, Eichmann was able to escape from the American internment camp and flee to Argentina. In 1960 he was discovered in a suburb of Buenos Aires by the Israeli secret

*Robert J. Lifton, *The Nazi Doctors* (New York: Basic Books, 1986), p. 273.
**Robert Wistrich, *Who's Who in Nazi Germany* (New York: Macmillan, 1982), p. 63.

service and abducted to Jerusalem, where he was tried. In December 1961, Eichmann was condemned to death; he was executed in June 1962.

Dr. Friedrich Entress (SS Captain) was born in 1914 in Posen (Poznań), Poland, where his father worked in the university library. Immediately after completing his university studies in Posen, where he had already committed himself to National Socialism, he came to Gross-Rosen C.C. in 1941 as an "ethnic German" and to Auschwitz in December of the same year. Against the background of a "euthanasia order," he organized the mass killing of prisoners with phenol injections directly into the heart. In this "work," as in all other "operations," he was concerned with the perfection and efficiency of the killing machinery; he later entrusted it to SS Medical Officers (like Josef Klehr), while he himself determined who was to be killed. Witnesses later described him as especially "radical" concerning selections. One prisoner doctor said of the Polish "ethnic German" Entress:

> In camp he came face to face with former friends—Poles who were now prisoners. He would not help them or talk to them in Polish . . . he pretended he did not know Polish. He was even aloof from former colleagues who graduated from the same university. He wanted to have his friends finished off as soon as possible.*

In August 1944, Entress was transferred as first camp doctor to Gross-Rosen C.C. Accused in Dachau in 1946 in an American military court, he was sentenced to death and executed in Landsberg in May 1947.

August Frank (SS Major General) occasionally functioned as a deputy for Gerhardt Pohl, Head of the WVHA (see calendar entry for Oct. 8, 1942), which administered all the concentration camps. As head of Branch A in the WVHA Frank was responsible for the storage and processing of objects taken from the victims of the concentraton camps (see entry for Sept. 26, 1942). In July 1943, for example, there were 127,000 wristwatches, 8,000 fountain pens, and four cases of stamp collections. After the war, he was sentenced to life imprisonment by an American military court, and later pardoned.

Dr. Roland Freisler was born 1893 in Celle, the son of an engineer. He began the study of law in Jena, and in World War I he served on the Eastern Front. In 1915 he was taken prisoner by the Russians and spent several years in Siberia, where he learned perfect Russian and became a Bolshevik commissar and a staunch Communist. In 1920 he returned to Germany, completed his studies, and settled down as a lawyer. In 1925 he joined the Nazi Party, serving as a deputy in the Prussian parliament in 1932 and in the Reichstag in 1933. At this time, he also began his career in the courts, succeeding Otto Thierack as president of the People's Court in 1942. In the same year, he participated as a representative of the ministry of justice in the Wannsee Conference to create "clarity in the fundamental question" of the "Final Solution" (see entry for Jan. 20, 1942). His role as president of the People's Court was marked by show trials and by the personal sadistic fanaticism with which he sent those accused of high treason to death. Freisler died in February 1945 when an Allied bomb hit the courthouse during a trial.

Karl Fritzsch (SS Captain), born in 1903 in Nassengrub, joined the Nazi Party (No. 261,135) and later the SS. From 1940 to the end of 1941, as SS Captain, he was a Protective Custody Commander in Auschwitz. Polish prisoner Tadeusz Paczuła has transmitted one of his harangues to "new accessions" on the parade ground: "You are in a German concentration camp. The entrance is through the main gate with the inscription 'Work Makes Free' on it. Here, there is only one exit: through the chimney of the crematorium. . . ." From 1942, Fritzsch was Commandant of Flossenbürg C.C. He allegedly died in May 1945.

Odilo Globocnik was born in 1904 in Trieste, the son of an official. He worked as a building engineer and joined the Nazi Party in Carinthia, Austria, in 1922, becoming by 1933 the

*Lifton, *Nazi Doctors*, p. 263.

deputy Gauleiter for Carinthia. After the annexation (Anschluss) of Austria, Globocnik was appointed Gauleiter of Vienna but was removed from office less than a year later for embezzlement. Supported by Heinrich Himmler—Globocnik had joined the SS in 1932—he was made Superior SS and Police Commander for the Lublin District (Poland) in 1939. In connection with "Operation Reinhard," the code name for the extermination of the Polish Jews, Globocnik, who was subordinate only to Himmler, was responsible for building the extermination camps of Bełzec, Sobibór, and Treblinka; by November 3, 1943, almost three million people had been murdered in these camps. Since he had a little too openly enriched himself from the valuables taken from the victims during this time—"Operation Reinhard" funneled 178.7 million Reichsmarks from victims to the German state—he was transferred to Trieste as Superior SS and Police Commander for the Adriatic Coast. When he was arrested in May 1945 by the British in Carinthia, he committed suicide.

Richard Glücks (SS Major General), born 1889, served as an officer in World War I and joined the Nazi Party relatively late. Nevertheless, he was an SS Brigadier General before the start of World War II and was appointed Inspector of Concentration Camps in autumn 1939. From 1942 on, the Concentration Camps Inspectorate formed one of the four large divisions of the WVHA with a broad purview. Glücks had authority over all the Camp Commandants and was the person who gave the monthly orders for carrying out the "Final Solution" and "extermination through labor." Thus, Glücks was one of the key figures of the concentraton camp system. Together with Himmler and Pohl, he decided how many of the deported Jews were to be killed and determined that the hair of the murdered people was to be collected and made into "hair-yarn stockings for U-boat crews and hair-felt stockings for the railroad" (see entry for Aug. 6, 1942). In 1943, Glücks was promoted to Major General of the Waffen SS. After the end of the war, in May 1945, he is thought to have committed suicide in the Flensburg Naval Hospital, where he was supposedly being treated for a shock he had suffered in a bombing.

Maximilian Grabner (SS Second Lieutenant), born in 1905 in Vienna, came from a modest rural background. He was director of the Political Department in Auschwitz until October 1943. At the Frankfurt Auschwitz Trial, the Political Department was described as the "arm of the Gestapo" and Grabner as a man of particular "bestiality" and "cruelty." In 1943, Dr. Konrad Morgen, an SS judge, investigated Grabner, who was accused of being responsible for the killing of 2,000 prisoners "beyond the general [guide] lines." A trial against him began in October 1944 in Weimar but was never concluded. After the war Grabner was indicted in Poland and, while in prison, wrote a self-justification in which he said:

> I could do nothing against this secret and ruthless regime; I was protrayed in black on black. Threat upon threat with the SS and Police Court for refusal to obey orders, insubordination, sabotage, etc. and the way the people were simply made to disappear, I had to bear the consequences.

In 1947, Grabner was condemned by the Supreme War Tribunal in Kraków and executed.

Reinhard Tristan Heydrich was born in 1904 in Halle, the son of a musician. Early on, Heydrich was associated with radical right, *voelkisch*, groups and became a partisan of their race ideology. In 1922 he joined the German Navy in Kiel and was discharged in 1931 for "dishonorable conduct"—he had an affair with the daughter of a shipyard director. In the same year, he joined the Nazi Party and the SS and became a favorite of Heinrich Himmler. By July 1932 he was an SS Colonel, and from 1933 on, as an SS Brigadier General, he was director of the Political Department of the police directorate of Munich. Between 1933 and 1934, as Himmler's henchman, Heydrich coordinated the Political Police and, in 1936, became head of the Sipo and SD for the entire German Reich. In 1939, Heydrich took over the direction of the Reich Central Security Office (RSHA), which had been created on Himmler's orders by amalgamating the Kripo (Kriminalpolizei) and the Gestapo, and the Party's Security Office. It was subordinate to the SS and supervised all official and secret police and security organs of the German Reich. Substantially involved in the "Final Solution" after the conquest of Poland in 1939, Heydrich ordered the "concentration" of Polish Jews in ghettos and the organization of mass deportation from Germany, Austria, and the parts of Poland annexed to Germany and to the General Government. On July 31, 1941, after the Wehrmacht attack on the Soviet Union, Göring commissioned Heydrich to carry out "all necessary preparations . . . for a total solution of the Jewish question in the territories of Europe in the German sphere of influence."[*] Thus occurred the Wannsee Conference, led by Heydrich, on January 20, 1942, where measures for the "Final Solution" were "discussed" by high Nazi officials. In May 1942, Heydrich, who had been deputy Reich Protector of Bohemia and Moravia since September 1941, was seriously wounded by exiled Czech partisans in an attempt on his life. A few days after his death the SS occupied the Czech village of Lidice and murdered all male inhabitants over the age of 16, while in Prague, 1,331 Czechs, including more than 200 women, were executed.

Heinrich Himmler was born in 1900 in Munich, the son of a Catholic gymnasium director. After World War I, in which he was a candidate for officer and was not at the front, he received a degree in agriculture. He joined the Nazi Party in 1922 (No. 14303) and the SS in 1925 (No. 168). After the Hitler Beer Hall Putsch of 1923, in which he took part, he became Gregor Strasser's secretary and rose to be deputy Gauleiter of Lower Bavaria. In 1929, after an unfortunate intermezzo as a poultry farmer, he was appointed Commander in Chief of the SS, which comprised 280 men and was subordinate to the SA. In 1930, Himmler was elected to the Reichstag as a deputy; in 1931 he created the Security Service (SD) within the SS, at first as an internal party secret service. In 1933 he was appointed chief of police of Munich and a bit later commander of the Political Police in Bavaria. That autumn, he was already head commissioner of the Political Police in Mecklenburg, Lübeck, Bad Württemberg, Hesse, Bremen, and Anhalt. In 1934 he took over the Gestapo from Hermann Göring and in February 1936 became SS Commander in Chief and Chief of the German Police in the Ministry of the Interior. Eight years later were added the posts of

> . . . Reich Commissioner for the Strengthening of the German *Volk* (October 1939), Reich Minister of the Interior and General Authority for the Reich Administration (August 1943), Supreme Commander of the Replacement Army and Head of Armaments (July 1944), as well as temporary commander of two units. He was in charge of the entire SS, the Waffen SS, the resettlement of ethnic Germans, and the evacuation of the occupied areas . . . the trust fund of the SS economic enterprises, the entire administrative bureaucracy of the Reich, the provinces and the new "Reichsgaue," the military and "civilian" intelligence service with an army of informers, the replacement and training units of the army in the homeland, and the armaments of the army as well in a few military interests of the Volkssturm.

With this apparatus Himmler used terror and force against the opponents of the Third Reich and transformed his fanatical race ideology into concrete politics and organization—like the system of the concentration camps. A "Syllabus for the Ideological Education of the SS and Police" put out by the SS Central Office states:

> The disintegrative influence of miscegenation [*Rassenvermischung*] with the Jews was particularly abominable in Europe. These parasites of humanity understand very well how to avoid a complete interbreeding with their hosts. . . . Furthermore there was an acute danger that Judaism had begun systematically to undermine the modes of thought and action appropriate to *Volk* groups, using the tools of moral degeneration. Their purpose was to make themselves political and economic lords and masters everywhere. To make matters worse, this crossbreeding gained ground principally among the intellectual leaders of Europe's *Volk* groups. The Jews made very genuine emotion con-

temptible, and their whole propaganda effort was aimed consciously at destroying and fragmenting the inner wholeness of the Volk-body. The consequences of this decade-long infection, this decay that gnawed at the Volk before 1933, can still be seen today. Strenuous effort is required to eradicate the last traces of this plague and to lead Europe back to the natural and one proper way of life. Thus, the solution of the Jewish question beyond the borders of the Reich has become a vital question for the people of Europe. . . .

At the end of the war, Himmler tried to escape capture disguised as an army private; after his discovery and arrest, he committed suicide on May 23, 1945.

Franz Johann Hofmann (SS Captain) was born in 1906, the son of a butcher in Hof on the Saale River. He was trained as a wallpaper hanger and, interrupted by periods of unemployment, worked as a waiter, a hotel servant, and a salesman. In 1932 he joined the Nazi Party and the SS, was trained in a course for auxiliary police, and was assigned to this position in Hoff in 1934. In the same year he was transferred to the guard troops of Dachau C.C. and was rapidly promoted to SS Captain (1939) and later to SS First Lieutenant (1942). He came to Auschwitz in 1942 as Second Camp Commander of the main camp. Later promoted to Protective Custody Commander of the Gypsy camp, in December 1943 he became Camp Commander of the main camp. Promoted again in 1944 to SS Captain, he was transferred to Natzweiler C.C. After the war he went underground, working as a farmhand and stoker before he was arrested 14 years later in April 1959 and sentenced to life imprisonment in Munich in 1961 for his crimes in Dachau. In 1965, in Frankfurt, Hofmann was sentenced again to life imprisonment, this time on 34 counts of murder and complicity in Auschwitz.

Rudolf Höss (SS Lieutenant Colonel) was born in 1900 in Baden-Baden to a strict Catholic family. At the age of 15 he joined the army as a volunteer serving in the Turkish theater of war, where he became a noncommissioned officer and received several medals. After the defeat, he was a member of the Freikorps in the Baltic region, Upper Silesia, and the Ruhr. In 1923 he was involved in the so-called Parchim Feme* murder and was sentenced to 10 years in prison. But in 1928 he was released in an amnesty. In 1934 he joined the SS and was assigned to Dachau C.C. He was named a Block Commander in 1935 and continued to be promoted thereafter, until he was transferred to Sachsenhausen C.C. as an adjutant in 1938, a function that gave him authority over a staff. He was named Commandant of Auschwitz in 1940.

Characterized as an assiduous, petit bourgeois executive, he organized mass murder with technical and administrative meticulousness. Arrested in 1946, he testified at the Nuremberg Trial as a witness for Kaltenbrunner and in the trials against Gerhard Pohl and I. G. Farben and was extradited to Poland in May of that year. In prison, he voluntarily wrote a "report" of the camp and of his function. In April 1947 he was sentenced to be hanged and was executed on the grounds of the camp.

Oswald Kaduk (SS Corporal) was born in 1906 in Königshütte in Upper Silesia the son of a blacksmith. He apprenticed as a butcher and became a municipal fireman in Königshütte in 1927. He joined the SS in 1939, was inducted into the Waffen SS in 1940, and was sent to the Eastern Front. After several illnesses and hospital stays, he was sent to the guards at Auschwitz in 1942. He soon became Block Commander and, as an SS Corporal, Rapportführer (Roll Call Leader); he remained in Auschwitz until January 1945. Later, as a defendant in the Frankfurt Auschwitz Trial, he complained that he wasn't considered reliable and that more was read into his testimony than just the facts:

Twelve prisoners were hanged in retribution. I don't know who selected them. The order probably came from Berlin, Commandant Baer gave the order. I told the Camp Senior, "Twelve will be hanged today." A platoon of the fourth company marched into

---

*"Feme murders" refers to assassinations of moderate and left-wing politicians carried out by right-wing vigilante groups in Germany between 1919 and 1923. Parchim is a city in the Baltic region.

the camp. I went to Block 11 with two Block Commanders and fetched the twelve. They went to the gallows one after another. Nobody was whipped. I had a submachine gun. It went like this: one—to the stool; two—on the stool; three—read the sentence; they had to put their own head in the noose; four—stool pulled out. I pulled out one stool. A doctor was there; he made the determination of death. There was unrest in the camp at that time, something like a mutiny. I don't know if I'm reliable today. But you should stay with the truth and not exaggerate.*

After the war, in December 1946, he was recognized by one of the survivors of Auschwitz and arrested. The following year, a Soviet military court sentenced him to 25 years of hard labor. In 1956 he was pardoned, went to West Berlin, and worked there as a hospital orderly, described by his patients as devoted; they called him "Papi." He was arrested again in 1959, charged with several murders in the Frankfurt Auschwitz Trial, found guilty, and sentenced to life imprisonment.

Josef Klehr (SS Staff Sergeant), born in 1904 in Langenau in Upper Silesia, studied cabinet-making and worked at this profession until 1934, when he became an orderly in a clinic. He had joined the SS in 1932. In 1938 he became the assistant warden in Wohlau Prison. In August 1939 he was taken into the Waffen SS, became a guard at Buchenwald, was transferred to Dachau as an SS Medical Officer in 1940, was promoted to SS Corporal in 1941 and was posted to Auschwitz the same year. First he was a Head Medical Officer in the prisoners' infirmary of the main camp, where he participated in the killing of prisoners with phenol injections, which were considered "cheap, easy to use, and absolutely reliable" when "large injections" were injected directly into the heart "with a long needle" (compare entry for early August 1941). At the Frankfurt Auschwitz Trial in November 1964, on the 110th day of hearings, the following exchange took place between witness Jean Weiss and the presiding judge:

WEISS: From the beginning of 1943 to July or August of that year I was in the corpse-bearer squad. I was there for a bit more than half a year.

PRESIDING JUDGE: During this time, did you come to know Klehr as a Medical Officer in the main camp of Auschwitz?

WEISS: Yes. He was there until maybe a month before I left the squad. Maybe until July 1943.

PRESIDING JUDGE: Did you see Klehr give injections?

WEISS: Yes. I was an eyewitness. I had to take the murdered people away. The victim was selected in Block 28 and then brought to Block 20. I had to remove the dead from the room where they were injected and bring them past the entrance to the washroom. . . . I often stood half a meter away from Klehr when he gave the injection.

PRESIDING JUDGE: How many people did Klehr kill in your presence?

WEISS: I didn't count the victims. But maybe 700 to 1,000 were killed in my presence. Sometimes he injected daily, sometimes twice or three times a week. On September 20, 1942, Klehr murdered my father right before my eyes.

PRESIDING JUDGE: Please describe this incident if it is not too hard for you.

WEISS: I request a moment's pause. Klehr was injecting daily. I went to Block 20 with Leo Sfagar [a prisoner]. A quarter of an hour later those who were selected to die came in. My father was then in Block 21, he had a boil on his left hand. I had often gone to visit him. That day, my father suddenly appeared in Block 20. Two were taken into the room at the same time, one of them was my father. Klehr spoke to both of them. He said, "Sit down. You are now going to get an injection so that you don't get typhus." I began to cry. He gave my father the injection and I carried

*Langbein, *Der Auschwitz-Prozess*, p. 265.

my father to the washroom. A week later, he asked me why I didn't tell him that was my father, he wouldn't have killed him. An attendant told him that when I was crying, my father was being injected. I didn't say anything because I was afraid he would tell me that I would be next.

In 1943, Klehr was director of the disinfection department and from July 1944, director of the prisoners' infirmary in the auxiliary camp Gleiwitz I, where he took part in selections and mass gassings. In May 1945 he was taken prisoner by the Americans and was sentenced to three years in a labor camp by a camp tribunal. Released in 1948, he worked as a cabinetmaker in Braunschweig until his arrest in September 1960. At the Frankfurt Auschwitz Trial, Klehr was sentenced to life imprisonment in 1965 for the murder of "at least 475 people."

Josef Kramer (SS Captain), born in 1906, joined the Nazi Party in 1931 and the SS in 1932. Employed in the concentration camps since 1934, he was in Dachau, Sachsenhausen, and Mauthausen before being sent to Auschwitz in May 1940 as Adjutant to Rudolf Höss. In November of that year he became Camp Commander in Dachau and later in Natzweiler, becoming Commandant of that camp in 1942. In 1944 he returned to Auschwitz as Commander of Birkenau but was transferred in November of that year to Bergen-Belsen in the same function. In 1945 he was arrested by the British and gave detailed statements at the Nuremberg Doctors Trial of how he had thrown Zyklon B into the gas chamber to kill the victims, for he had been brought up to be obedient. Indicted that year and described in the international press as the "beast of Belsen," he was sentenced to death by a British military court and executed in Hamelin.

Dr. Johann P. Kremer (SS Lieutenant Colonel), born in 1883, was associate professor of anatomy at the Univeristy of Münster and had qualified for a professorship with a work called "The Alteration of Muscle Tissue under Conditions of Hunger." In August 1942 he went to Auschwitz to carry out his "research on hunger." For this purpose he selected so-called Moslems, people who suffered from malnutrition and were extremely weakened both spiritually and physically. Later, when Kremer was in a Polish prison, he said:

> When somebody interested me because of an advanced state of starvation, I gave the orderly instructions to reserve the patient for me and to notify me of the date on which he was to be killed by injection. At that time, those patients selected by me were taken to the block and put on the dissecting table while they were still alive. I approached the table and asked the patient about details of interest to my research: for example, his weight before imprisonment, weight loss during imprisonment, if he had taken medication recently and such things. After I had obtained this information, the orderly came in and killed the patient with an injection to the heart. I myself never gave a lethal injection.

During his stay in Auschwitz, Kremer kept a journal, which was later published and in which the following entries are found:

> September 5, 1942: At noon today at a special operation from the F.K.L. [women's concentration camp]. [Moslems], the most terrible of the terrible.
> September 6, 1942: Today Sunday excellent lunch: tomato soup, ½ chicken, potatoes with red cabbage (20g fat), sweet pudding and splendid vanilla ice cream.
> October 10, 1942: Fresh material of liver, spleen and pancreas, taken and preserved.
> October 11, 1942: Today road rabbit for lunch—a very thick haunch—with dumplings and red cabbage for RM1.25.*

After the war, Kremer was sentenced to 10 years in prison. Returned to the Federal Republic of Germany, he was charged again and sentenced to another 10-year prison term but it was already considered completed. He died in 1965.

*Lifton, *Nazi Doctors*, p. 292.

Alfried Krupp von Bohlen und Halbach, born in 1907, in 1936 was a member of the board of his father Gustav Krupp's company. The Essen mining and steel enterprise was an essential part of the military rearmament and war preparations. After the beginning of World War II, Krupp took care to enrich the companies of the fatherland during the war by dismantling and taking over industrial plants in the occupied areas. From 1943 on, he employed inmates of the concentration camps, prisoner-of-war camps, and forced labor camps, almost 200,000 men, in his factories. They were forced to work under inhumane conditions that were often fatal. In the same year, Krupp, the sole owner of the Krupp concern, was rewarded by the Third Reich with an exemption from the inheritance tax and an appointment as Director of the Defense Economy (Wehrwirtschaft) for his previous service. When the defeat of the German Reich began to be evident and his economic empire was strongly affected by Allied bombardments, Krupp began to press for indemnity and repayment of debts. After the war, at Nuremberg in 1948, he was sentenced as a major war criminal to 12 years' imprisonment and confiscation of all his property. Nevertheless, through an American general amnesty for condemned industrialists, after three years Krupp was a free man again and received his personal property, then estimated at 500 million Deutschmarks (after the currency reform), as well as the confiscated business property.

Arthur Liebehenschel (SS Lieutenant Colonel), born in 1901, became a member of the Nazi Party and the SS (No. 39254). From 1934 on, he was Adjutant in Lichtenburg C.C., then transferred to the Concentraton Camps Inspectorate in Berlin. After the WVHA was created in 1942, he took over in the newly formed Branch D, the so-called Central Office for Concentration Camps, Office D-I. In November 1943 he succeeded Höss in Auschwitz as Commandant of the main camp and Garrison Senior. In his book *Menschen in Auschwitz* (People in Auschwitz), Hermann Langbein writes of the new Commandant:

> Liebehenschel introduced a new epoch in the history of Auschwitz. His reforms first applied to Block 11 [the Political Police], but the arbitrary shootings in this block initiated all changes [the replacement of Höss and Mildner and the arrest of Grabner]. He discontinued periodical selections with subsequent shootings in the bunker. Although executions were carried out later, they were farther away from the [main] camp, in the crematorium at Birkenau. He removed the standing cells, which offered no place to sit or lie and in which inmates were locked as punishment. He ordered a general bunker amnesty and later had the black wall removed. Furthermore, he canceled the order to shoot everyone caught attempting to escape; under cover of this order, disagreeable people could be gotten rid of easily. . . . From now on, captured prisoners were to be transferred to another concentration camp. . . . Then something blossomed in Auschwitz that was unknown before: hope. The selection of "Moslems" was stopped. Of course, as before, transports were selected on the platform day after day, the crematoria burned constantly. But the hope emerged that Auschwitz could lose the character of an extermination camp, at least for those who were already in the camp. All this changed the mood, along with good news from the front [late 1943, early 1944]. The appearance was deceptive.

Selections in the camp went on under Liebehenschel, who was removed in May 1944 and sent to Lublin Concentration Camp as Commandant. After the evacuation of this camp in July 1944, he was sent to Trieste in Globocnik's function of Supreme SS and Police Commander. In 1947, Liebehenschel was sentenced to death in Kraków by the Supreme People's Court and executed.

Enno Lolling, M.D. (SS Colonel), born 1888, was a member of the Nazi Party and the SS. After the outbreak of World War II he was inducted into the Waffen SS and went to Dachau as Camp Doctor. From there he became head physician in the Concentration Camps Inspectorate in Berlin. In 1942, as an SS Colonel, he became head of Office D-III for Sanitation and Camp Hygiene in the WVHA and in this capacity made several inspection tours of the concentration camps. "Professionally incompetent," according to later testimony of SS doctors, in May 1942 he is supposed to have given the order to kill prisoners who were not considered able-bodied. Lolling committed suicide in 1945 before he could be tried in a court.

Maria Mandel (SS Head Supervisor), born 1912 in Upper Austria, was a Protective Custody Commander in Auschwitz. As a "great music lover," she promoted the female orchestra in Birkenau, described by prisoner Lucie Adelsberger:

> Music was like a lapdog of the camp administration and the performers were obviously protected. The block was better tended than those of the clerks or the cooks, the food more abundant, and the girls of the women's orchestra were nicely dressed in blue cloth dresses and caps. The musicians had a lot to do. They played at roll call and the women who came back from work exhausted had to march in time to the music. Music was ordered for all official occasions, for the addresses of the Camp Commanders, for the transports and whenever anybody was hanged. . . .*

Because of her "merit" to her superiors, Female Camp Commander Mandel, considered "intelligent" and "convinced of her cause," was dreaded at selections for her personal brutality and enthusiasm. In December 1947 she was sentenced to death by the Supreme People's Court in Kraków and executed.

Gerhard Maurer (SS Colonel), born in 1907, was a member of the Nazi Party and the SS (No. 12129) and, from 1934, a colleague of Oswald Pohl, later the Head of the WVHA. In 1942 as an SS Colonel Maurer took over Office D-II, which was responsible for the deployment of prisoner labor in the concentration camps. Maurer worked closely with the leaders of the armaments industry and created the administrative basis for the rigorous exploitation of the prisoners, for example, appointing in every camp a director responsible for the problems encountered in optimizing the productivity of the forced labor deployed in the armaments industry (see calendar entries for July 3 and Aug. 26, 1943). In 1943 he became deputy to Richard Glücks, Inspector of Concentration Camps, whom he soon almost replaced in serious matters. In December 1951, Maurer was condemned to death by the District Court in Kraków and executed.

Josef Mengele, M.D., Ph.D. (philosophy), born in 1911 in Günzburg, Bavaria, came from a local industrial family and, at the age of 20, joined the *Stahlhelm* (Steel Helmet), a militant nationalist organization formed by World War I soldiers. In 1934 he switched to the SA and, in 1937, applied for membership in the Nazi Party and later in the SS. A staunch representative of the Nazi Weltanschauung while still a university student, he studied in Munich, Bonn, Frankfurt, and Vienna. He completed his doctoral dissertation in 1935 at the Anthropology Institute of the philosophy department of the University of Munich; the title was "The Racial Morphological Investigation of the Front Submaxilla Section in Four Racial Groups." In 1938 he did work for his medical doctorate on geneological research in lip, jaw, and gum fissures, which, as Robert Jay Lifton puts it in his book *The Nazi Doctors,* sounds "like a precursor of his later work in Auschwitz," and in which Mengele already refers "to the significance of research on twins."

As a member of the Nazi-founded Institute for Hereditary Biology and Race Hygiene, Mengele volunteered for the Waffen SS at the beginning of World War II and was sent as a medical officer to France and Russia, where he achieved high honors before he was declared unfit for front-line service because of a wound. In 1943 he volunteered to go to Auschwitz to carry out medical and anthropological experiments, financed by the German Research Society. In a request for extradition made by the West German courts at the end of the 1950s, Mengele was "accused of selections, fatal injections (phenol), shootings, beatings, and other

*Lucie Adelsberger, *Auschwitz: Ein Tatsachenbericht*, 3d ed. (Berlin, 1960), pp. 98ff.

forms of deliberate killing" and the suspicion was raised that "he threw newborn infants directly into the crematoriums and into open fires." An incriminating document consisting of an assessment of Mengele by SS Garrison Doctor Eduard Wirths, written in August 1944, states:

> Dr. Mengele has an open, honest character. He is absolutely reliable, upright and direct. . . . With discretion, persistence and energy he has carried out all tasks assigned him, often under difficult conditions, to the fullest satisfaction of his superiors and has shown himself equal to every situation. Moreover, . . . in his work on the analysis of the scientific materials available to him by virtue of his position, he has made a valuable contribution to anthropological science.

Mengele's "contribution" consisted of fanatically pursued research on twins with which he probably wanted to prove "a completely reliable determination of heredity in men" and "the extent of damage by unfavorable hereditary influences." Every pair of twins could be observed under the same conditions of life and, as a prisoner physician who worked for him later said, "in the best health . . . sent together to death"—an ideal circumstance for comparative post mortem research. Other "areas of research" for Mengele were dwarfism as an exemplary expression of the "abnormal" and a gangrenous necrosis of the cheeks (noma) resulting from complete physical and emotional exhaustion, which he tried to establish as a racial predisposition. Highly qualified medically, his fanatic "research interest" was aimed at a biological and medical clean-up of society and its preventive hygiene. With his "scientific" work built unshakably into Nazi ideology, he would "in normal times have become a slightly sadistic German professor," one of the former prisoner physicians in Auschwitz later said. Shortly before the evacuation of Auschwitz, Mengele returned to Günzburg, where, unhampered by the law, he turned his attention to once more building up the Carl Mengele and Sons agricultural machinery factory, the largest employer in the area. In the mid-1950s the writer Ernst Schnabel with his publications on Anne Frank called attention to Josef Mengele, who by this time had already relocated to South America. For over 20 years Mengele was able to evade all extradition attempts; he died in a swimming accident in Brazil in 1979.

Konrad Morgen, J.D. (SS Major), born in 1908, was a judge in the SS court and chairman of a special committee to investigate embezzlement and theft among SS members in the concentration camps. In this investigation the director of the Auschwitz Political Department, Maximilian Grabner, was accused by Morgen of "arbitrary killings," but, in contrast to other proceedings carried out against lower-ranking staff, Grabner was removed from his position but not sentenced. After the war, Morgen testified as a witness in the trial against the major war criminals at the International War Crimes Tribunal in Nuremberg and later at the so-called Frankfurt Auschwitz Trial in 1965. He stated:

> The investigation of the SS members of Auschwitz Concentration Camp was brought about by an army mail package. Because of its noticeably heavy weight, it was confiscated and found to contain three lumps of gold, one the size of two fists and two smaller ones. It was high-carat dental gold sent by an orderly serving in Auschwitz to his wife. According to my estimates, this quantity of gold corresponded to about 100,000 corpses, if you take into account that not everyone had gold fillings. It was inconceivable that the perpetrators could hide such quantities unnoticed. Clearly, I had to take a look at Auschwitz. . . . An SS officer took me through the whole camp and explained the death machinery in all its details. The crematoriums weren't really noticeable: The ground was hollowed on an incline, and an outsider would only see that the wagons disappeared into a depression in the ground. A big door led to the so-called undressing room, where there were numbered places and cloakroom tickets. Arrows on the wall pointed to the showers. The signs were in six or seven languages. In the enormous crematorium everything was spick and span. Nothing suggested that thousands of people had been gassed and burned the previous night. Nothing was left of them, not even a speck of dust on the oven fittings.

I wanted to meet the SS people and went to the SS guardroom in Birkenau. There I got my first real shock. While guardrooms were generally of Spartan simplicity, here SS men lay on couches and dozed, staring ahead glassy-eyed. Instead of a desk, there was a hotel kitchen stove in the room and four or five young Jewesses of Oriental beauty were making potato pancakes and feeding the SS men, who had themselves waited on like pashas. The SS men and the female prisoners used the familiar form, "Du," with one another.

At my horrified questioning look, my escort simply shrugged his shoulders and said that the men had a hard night behind them, they had to process several transports. At a final locker check, it turned out that in a few lockers, a wealth of gold, pearls, rings, and currency of all countries was piled up. In one or two lockers there were genitals of freshly slaughtered bulls, which were supposed to enhance potency.

I had never seen anything like it.

Heinrich Müller (SS Major General), born in 1900 in Munich to a Catholic family, served in World War I as a highly decorated noncommissioned officer and then joined Department IV (Political Police) of the Bavarian Police. In 1933 he was promoted to police inspector and, in 1937, to superior state councilor and police superintendent. In 1937, Reinhard Heydrich, Head of the Sipo and SD, promoted him to SS Colonel. In 1939 he became an SS Brigadier General and a police lieutenant general. As Head of Office IV in the RSHA, the Gestapo, Müller was directly involved as one of the executors in the "Final Solution"; it was he who made mass murder into a bureaucratic administrative act (see calendar entry of Dec. 16, 1942). After the War, Müller was last seen in May 1945 in the Salzburg region. Later his death was reported and a corpse was exhumed but could not be identified.

Oswald Pohl (SS Lieutenant General), born 1892 in Duisburg, served in World War I as a navy paymaster and joined the Nazi Party in 1926 (No. 30842). After a career in the administration of the SA and the SS advanced by Heinrich Himmler, Pohl was appointed SS Colonel and head of the administration in the SS Central Office. In 1942 he became an SS General and took over the direction of the WVHA, which was responsible inter alia for deploying the labor of the concentration camp prisoners, who, in Pohl's words, were to be "exhausted in the most literal sense of the word in order to obtain the highest possible output." The "valuables" taken from the prisoners in the concentration camps also were in Pohl's area, the economic processing and utilization of resources related to the "Final Solution." "Valuables" included prisoners' hair and clothes as well as watches, eyeglasses, jewelry, and foreign currency, along with gold from their teeth, which was melted down with other precious metals and deposited in the Deutsche Bank, which credited the booty to a special SS account in the name of "Max Heiliger." In May 1945, Pohl was arrested and indicted at Nuremberg. He testified that the "Final Solution" had not been a secret. He was condemned to death in November 1947 as one of those principally responsible for mass murder, but was not executed until June 1951. Until then he was imprisoned in Landsberg am Lech and was the object of the most petitions for clemency, even including intervention by representatives of the German Bundestag (parliament).

Herbert Scherpe (SS Staff Sergeant) was born in 1907 in Gleiwitz in Upper Silesia, the son of an electrician. He was a trained butcher but worked mostly as an unskilled laborer and was unemployed between 1930 and 1933, until he was hired as an auxiliary policeman by the customs service. In 1931 he joined the Nazi Party and was in an SS guard company in 1936 as SS Sergeant. At the beginning of the war, he went to Dachau as part of the SS Death's Head unit and later to the office of the Inspector of Concentration Camps. After training as an orderly, he was posted to Auschwitz in 1940. Working first in the SS sick bay, from 1941 to 1943 he worked in the prisoner's infirmary of the main camp, where, according to testimony, he attracted attention because of his friendliness and as a murderer of children and adults, whom he killed with a phenol injection in the heart. One attendant, Stanisław Kłodziński, who worked in Block 20, recalled:

> Children were brought into Block 20 through a side entrance, they had to undress and line up in a row. Then came Scherpe. Deadly silence reigned in the block, the only thing you heard was the bodies falling on the floor in the lavatory. After a few such dull blows, Scherpe came out of the room. He said "I can't do any more," and went away.

After this incident, Scherpe refused to kill children and was transferred to the auxiliary camp Golleschau, without incurring any punishment. After the war, Scherpe managed to get himself released unrecognized from an internment camp and lived in Mannheim until his arrest in 1961. At the Frankfurt Auschwitz Trial he was sentenced to 4½ years in prison.

Josef Schillinger (SS Staff Sergeant) was successively Roll Call Leader, commander of an outside squad and head of the kitchen in the men's camp in Birkenau. Simultaneously employed also in guarding the transports of Jews from the platform to the crematoriums, he was shot in October 1943 by a Jewess with a pistol in the dressing room of one of the gas chambers, and died a short time later. In his autobiography, *Commandant in Auschwitz,* Höss described the experience:

> A transport had arrived from Belsen and after about two-thirds, mostly men [were in the gas chamber], a mutiny broke out among the last third who were still in the dressing room. Three or four of the SS officers entered the room with their weapons to hurry the undressing, since the inmates of the incineration squad couldn't finish. The lighting wires was torn out, the SS men were attacked, one of them was stabbed and all of them were robbed of their weapons. Since the room was now dark, a wild shooting started between the guards at the doors and the prisoners inside. When I arrived I had the doors shut, the gassing of the first two-thirds finished and went with flashlights and the guards into the room; we forced the prisoners into a corner where they were then taken out one by one and shot on my orders in a side room of the crematorium with small-caliber weapons. [This account appears only in the German edition.]

Horst Schumann, M.D. (First Lieutenant of the Luftwaffe and SS Major), was born in 1906, the son of a general practitioner in Halle on the Saale. A member of the Nazi Party since 1930 (No. 190,002) and in the SA since 1932, Schumann received his medical degree in Halle in 1933 and was employed in the health office in Halle in 1934; in 1939, when the war began, he was conscripted as a subordinate physician in the Luftwaffe. Summoned in 1935 by Victor Brack, department head of Operation T-4 (for euthanasia of the mentally ill, the chronically ill, Jews, and so-called asocials, to which more than 50,000 citizens of the Third Reich fell victim prior to 1941) to participate in the euthanasia program as a doctor, Schumann accepted after a short period of reflection. In January 1940 he became director of the Euthanasia Institute of Grafeneck in Württemberg, where people were killed by engine exhaust (carbon monoxide). In the summer of 1940 he became director of the Sonnenstein Institute near Pirma. As a member of Secret Operation 14f-13, Schumann belonged to a committee of doctors who selected prisoners in Auschwitz, Buchenwald, Dachau, Flossenbürg, Gross-Rosen, Mauthausen, Neuengamme, and Niederhangen who were especially weak and incapable of working and "transmitted" them to death by gas in the euthanasia institutes. On July 28, 1941, Schumann went to Auschwitz for the first time, where he selected 575 prisoners to be taken to Sonnenstein and killed. A year and a half later (see entry for Nov. 2, 1942) he returned to Auschwitz to test a "cheap and rapid" mass sterilization method for men and women using X rays. He carried out his "experiments" on "young, healthy, good-looking" Jewish men, women, and girls whom he chose himself. Hardly any of his numerous victims survived; the people died from burns, from additional surgical procedures (removal of the ovaries and testicles), exhaustion, or psychic shock. In 1944, before he left Auschwitz—most likely to deal with the "special treatment" of Polish and Russian forced laborers—Schumann reported to SS Commander in Chief Himmler that "castration of men in this way is pretty much ruled out, or an expense is required that is not worthwhile." In October 1945 he surfaced in Gladbeck, where he registered with the police and was made municipal sport physician. With a refugee grant he opened his own practice in 1949 and did not attract the attention of the authorities as a wanted Nazi criminal until 1951. Since 21 days elapsed between his identification and the attempt to arrest him—and in addition he was probably warned by the Gladbeck municipal physician's council—Schumann had already escaped when the police showed up at his house. According to his own account, in subsequent years he served as a ship's doctor and worked in the Sudan after 1955, escaping from there in 1959 through Nigeria and Libya to Ghana. Not until 1966, after the fall of Nkrumah, did Ghana extradite Schumann to West Germany. In September 1970 the trial against Schumann began, but meanwhile 54 of the 115 witnesses had died. In April of the following year the trial was interrupted because of the defendant's high blood pressure. As Ernst Klee writes in his book, *What They Did—What They Were*:

> Very quietly, Schumann was released from prison. All the expert medical opinions based on "subjective complaints" like headache, vertigo, and weak concentration, confirmed his illness. Noteworthy here is that the expert opinions refer to "Doctor of Medicine" Schumann even though he had been deprived of his academic rank in 1961. Schumann spends the rest of his life in the Seckbach section of Frankfurt. . . . Horst Schumann, sought by the police for 15 years, six years of imprisonment for interrogation, died on May 5, 1983, eleven years after being released from prison. Medical certificates had protected him from judgment and punishment.[*]

Albert Speer (Minister of Armaments and War Production) was born in 1905, the son of an architect; he studied architecture and joined the SA in 1931 and the Nazi Party in 1932. As a protégé of Adolf Hitler, Speer received his first party assignment in 1932 and from 1933 on was responsible for planning and organizing Nazi mass rallies, which he conceived as an aestheticization of politics. As an architect Speer designed the new Reich Chancellery in Berlin and the party parade grounds in Nuremberg. In 1937, Hitler made him general building inspector for Berlin; in 1938 he received the title of professor and was appointed to the Prussian state council. In 1942 he succeeded Fritz Todt as Minister of Armaments and Munitions and General Inspector for Water and Energy; after September 1943 he became Minister of Armaments and War Production. Under his direction, there was a significant increase in war production, for which he employed a host of foreign laborers and concentration camp prisoners. It has been estimated that the rise in production effected by Speer prolonged the war by at least a year. After 1945, indicted as a major war criminal by the International Military Tribunal in Nuremberg, Speer appeared to be aware of his guilt and was sentenced to 20 years in prison for crimes against humanity. He was released in 1966 and in 1969 published his memoirs describing his close relationship with Adolf Hitler, the power struggles and rivalries within the Third Reich, and his own opposition to the "scorched earth" policy at the end of the war. Even before his death in September 1981, skepticism was growing regarding many historians' assessment of Speer as "a man of integrity and honor in comparison with the criminal leaders who were his associates."[**]

Hans Stark (SS Second Lieutenant) was born in 1921 in Darmstadt, the son of a police chief. In 1937 (allegedly under pressure from his father) he joined an SS Death's Head group as a 16½-year-old recruit and from January 1938 was a guard at Oranienburg C.C. After tours of duty in Buchenwald and Dachau, Stark was sent to Auschwitz at the end of 1940 as a Block Commander; soon he was employed in the Political Department. He remained in Auschwitz until 1943; during this time he was granted leave to prepare for the Abitur (secondary-school

*Klee, *What They Did—What They Were* (Frankfurt, 1986).
**Wistrich, *Who's Who in Nazi Germany*, p. 292.

examination) and to study law for three months. In 1943, clearly in connection with additional "leadership training," he was sent to the front; in 1945 as an SS officer, he ended up in a prison camp, from which he escaped. In 1950, classified as a nominal party member by a denazification court, he became a teacher in an agricultural school near Cologne. In 1959 he was arrested and was indicted in 1963 in the so-called Frankfurt Auschwitz Trial. Several witnesses testified against him for numerous murders and other crimes, some of which he confessed to. In August 1965 he was sentenced to the maximum punishment, 10 years, allowable under juvenile criminal law (since with a few exceptions he had been a minor at the time of his crimes).

Otto Thierack, J.D. (president of the People's Court and Minister of Justice), was born 1889 in Wurzen, near Leipzig, grew up in a middle-class family, and received a degree as doctor of laws in 1914. After World War I, in which he served as a lieutenant, he became district attorney in Leipzig and Dresden, joining the Nazi Party in 1932. With Adolf Hitler's seizure of power in 1933 he became provisional minister of justice in Saxony and, in 1935, vice president of the Reich Court in Leipzig and president of the People's Court in Berlin from 1936 to 1942. From 1942 to the end of the war Thierack was the Minister of Justice; he contributed substantially to the realization of "extermination through labor"—which applied to Jews, prisoners of war, so-called asocials, Gypsies, and some foreign workers (see entry for Dec. 31, 1942)—by giving it the support of the legal system. After the defeat and surrender of the Third Reich, Thierack was arrested; he committed suicide in a British internment camp in October 1946.

Heinz Thilo, M.D. (SS First Lieutenant), born in 1911, went to Auschwitz in October 1942 as Camp Doctor. He carried out selections on the platform and in the prisoners' infirmary, where he sent, among others, Schumann's victims—whose "sexual organs gradually rotted away," according to the testimony of one of the attendants—to the gas chambers. It was Thilo who dubbed Auschwitz *"anus mundi,"* and thus gave precise expression to the perpetrators' idea that they were "called upon by necessity to cleanse the world." At the end of 1944, Thilo was transferred to Gross-Rosen C.C. and is thought to have died either in Hohenelbe in May 1945 or in Berlin in October 1947.

Kurt Uhlenbrok, M.D. (SS Major), born in 1908, went to Auschwitz in 1942 as the result of a court-martial in which he was accused of not caring properly for wounded soldiers in a field hospital. At first he served in Economic Office D-III of the WVHA, which oversaw the deployment of doctors in the concentration camps. From August 17 to September 16, 1943, he functioned as SS Garrison Doctor. When he had, as a proposal for this promotion, dated September 19, 1943, says, "demonstrated his medical knowledge and put his reliability to the test in Auschwitz," Uhlenbrok was transferred out of Auschwitz. After the war he continued to work quietly in Hamburg in his own practice. It was not until the Frankfurt Auschwitz Trial that he was indicted and charged by witnesses of taking part in the selection of sick prisoners who were then put to death. But in the middle of the trial the investigation of Uhlenbrok was dropped. He returned to his practice in Hamburg and appeared in further proceedings only as an unsworn witness.

Dr. Edmund Veesenmayer (SS Brigadier General) was born in 1904. He studied economics and, after working as a lecturer at the Munich Technical College and at the Berlin School of Economics, received through the SS a position in the Foreign Ministry. In 1941 he moved to the German Legation in Zagreb, where he directed the "Final Solution" of the "Jewish question" in Serbia. In 1944 he went to Hungary as plenipotentiary of the Third Reich to carry out the deportation of the Hungarian Jews. After he had successfully planned and carried out "Enterprise Margarete," a putsch against Admiral Horthy, he created the preconditions for cooperation among the SS, the German police, and the regular Hungarian authorities. As a result, between April and August 1944, 437,000 people were sent to Auschwitz, very few of whom survived. Indicted by the International Military Tribunal in Nuremberg, on May 14 Veesenmayer, according to Jörg Friedrich's book, *Die Kalte Amnesty* (The Cold Amensty), surrendered trustingly to the American troops in order, as he declared under cross-examination when brought to trial at Nuremberg, to practice "fair play." According to Veesenmayer, he had "previously had dealings with American businessmen" and had gained the impression, "with these men, at least from the point of view—because I was personally aware of having fought a clean, fair, clear, and consistent fight—that I had carried on a fight, I do not deny. On the contrary." In 1949, Veesenmayer was sentenced to 20 years in prison as a war criminal. But three years later, in December 1951, he was released from prison under an American amnesty and subsequently became a millionaire businessman in West Germany.

Helmuth Vetter, M.D. (SS First Lieutenant), was born in 1910. He worked as a Camp Doctor in Dachau, Auschwitz, and Mauthausen. A former employee of the Bayer Company, which was a member of I. G. Farben, Vetter organized in various concentration camps "series of pharmacological experiments," working "closely" with his former employer. In these experiments he used Sulfonamide, a nitrous acid compound, Rutenol, and a combination formula containing an unknown substance labeled "Secret Sign 3582" and prussic acid (see entries of Jan. 27 and Feb. 8, 1943). In 1947 he was indicted by an American military court, which established that "in one of his series of experiments on 75 persons, who were treated experimentally with a new medication [made available by Bayer], 40 died." Vetter was sentenced to death and was executed in February 1949.

Bruno Weber, M.D. (SS Captain), was director of the SS Hygiene Institute in Rajsko near Auschwitz and head of its annex in Birkenau, Block 10, where numerous bacteriological and hematological research activities and experiments were carried out. Thus, "Weber determined prisoners' blood groups and injected some with blood from different blood groups to test the cell agglutination"*—with catastrophic results. In Block 10, blood was also taken from prisoners to supply serum for German personnel. As Robert Jay Lifton wrote: "Not only was the blood at times collected from very weakened prisoners, but it was done cruelly or even murderously by puncturing the carotid artery so that the prisoners bled to death."** The fatal injections of phenol were also Weber's responsibility in Block 10, as were the experiments with hallucinogenic drugs ordered by the Gestapo to get information from Polish prisoners about the resistance movement in the camp. In January 1945 the Hygiene Institute was evacuated, to be rebuilt in Dachau by Weber and his close colleague SS Second Lieutenant Dr. Hans Münch. Nothing is known about legal action against Weber. He died in September 1956 in Homburg on the Saar.

Eduard Wirths, M.D. (SS First Lieutenant), born in 1909 in Würzburg, came from a Catholic family associated with Democratic Socialism and worked as a rural doctor after he completed his medical studies. In 1933 he joined the Nazi Party and the SA, and undertook official health-related assignments as well as maintaining his practice. He became a member of the Waffen SS in 1939 and served with troops in Norway and the Soviet Union. Because of a heart ailment, he was designated unfit for front-line service in April 1942 and was sent briefly to the Dachau and Neuengamme camps and, in September 1942, was sent to Auschwitz as Garrison Doctor. All SS Camp Doctors were subordinate to him; he deployed them on the selection platform according to a hierarchical principle—he himself regularly participated in selections—so as to cultivate the discipline and self-image of his subordinates. Wirths himself was subordinate to Office D-III for Sanitation and Camp Hygiene in the WVHA in Berlin, which was directed after 1942 by the physician Enno Lolling. But he was also subordinate to the Commandant of Auschwitz, with whom he dealt daily. It was Wirths who, within the camp hierarchy, insisted that an order from Berlin be followed that only doctors should carry out selections.

*Lifton, *Nazi Doctors*, p. 289.
**Ibid.

Hence, Wirths had "not only control over selections, he organized the system. . . ."* Wirths's "scientific experiments" were aimed at the early detection of cervical cancer. He himself never appeared personally at the experiments, which were frequently fatal to the subjects. One female witness said, "He never operated himself . . . never did . . . anything . . . not injections, nothing." In 1945, Wirths was arrested by the British army and committed suicide. Before his death, he presented a written justification of his activity in Auschwitz, which he had written during his flight. In it he wrote, "I took pains to help sick prisoners, according to my Christian and medical conscience. . . ."

*Lifton, *Nazi Doctors*, p. 394.

GLOSSARY OF GENERAL
AND CAMP TERMS

A.C. Auxiliary camp.

AG (Aktiengesellschaft) Publicly traded corporation.

AK (Armia Krajowa) Polish Home Army.

Bauhof The so-called lumberyard, a storage site for building materials, and also the name of a labor squad. Occasionally called the "Industriehof."

Bearers of secrets (Geheiminsträger) Prisoners whose work made them witnesses of extermination activities, such as the members of the Special Squad. Most of them were subsequently murdered.

Block Prisoners' housing. In the main camp the blocks were one-story brick buildings. In Birkenau and most of the auxiliary camps they were brick or wood.

Block arrest (Blocksperre) Prohibition to leave the block.

Block Commander (Blockführer) An SS man responsible for one or more blocks.

Block Commanders' room (Blockführerstube) Block Commanders' guard house.

Block Senior (Blockältester) A prisoner functionary appointed by the SS to be responsible for a block.

Buna Trade name for synthetic unvulcanized rubber and synthetic fuel produced by I. G. Farben in its Auschwitz plants. Also the name of the factory, the labor squad that worked there, and the auxiliary camp that belonged to it. The Buna plant was in the village of Monowitz (Monowice), about a mile east of the town of Auschwitz. The camp was called both Buna and Monowitz and, ultimately, Auschwitz III.

Bunker The cellar of Block 11 in the main camp, where there were cells in which prisoners were locked up for punishment. Also the name for the gas chambers in Birkenau.

BV (Befristeter Vorbeugungshäftling) A prisoner who was incarcerated for "limited preventive detention"—a specific period of time. Later the term referred to professional criminals (Berufsverbrecher).

Camp curfew (Lagersperre) Prohibition against leaving the camp.

Camp Senior Prisoner functionary appointed by the SS to be a camp representative—but answering to the SS.

Capo An SS-appointed prisoner who was foreman of a labor squad. He worked under the SS Squad Leader.

C.C. Concentration camp.

DAW (Deutsche Ausrüstungswerke) **GmbH** German Armaments Works, Ltd., a commercial enterprise of the SS that had plants in other camps beside Auschwitz.

Death wall, also "black wall" A bullet-stopping wall at the end of the enclosed courtyard between Blocks 10 and 11 in the punishment camp, where executions by shooting were carried out.

DEST (Deutsche Erd- und Steinwerke) **GmbH** German Earth and Stone Works, Ltd.

Dog squadron (Hundestaffel) An SS kennel of wolfhounds and bloodhounds trained specifically to guard people wearing striped clothing. They were mainly used for guarding labor squads working outside the outer sentry line.

EH (Erziehungshäftling) "Reeducation" prisoner. In theory, these prisoners were incarcerated for a definite period of time.

EVO (Energieversorgung Oberschlesien) **AG** Upper Silesia Power Company, Inc.

FKL (Frauenkonzentrationslager) Women's concentration camp; collectively, the sections of Auschwitz-Birkenau housing women.

FL (Frauenlager) Women's camp (term used after March 30, 1943).

Garrison Doctor An SS officer and head doctor in the camp, to whom the troop doctors, who took care of the SS members, and the Camp Doctors, who dealt with the prisoners, were subordinate.

Gestapo (geheime Staatspolizei) Secret State Police.

GmbH (Gesellschaft mit beschränkter Haftung) Private limited liability company.

G.U. (gesonderte Unterbringung) "Separate accommodation" (code term for liquidation).

HASAG A company with three squads, in Meuselwitz, Tancha, and Leipzig-Schonefeld.

HKB (Häftlingskrankenbau) Prisoners' infirmary.

IBV (Internationale Bibelforschervereinigung) **prisoners** Jehovah's Witnesses; literally, International Bible Students, as the sect is called in non-English-speaking countries.

Interest Zone The 25-square-mile area in the fork between the Vistula and Soła rivers, controlled by the camp and off-limits to unauthorized persons.

KGL (Kriegsgefangenenlager) Prisoner-of-war camp.

KL, KZ (Konzentrationslager) Concentration camp.

Königsgraben The main drainage ditch in Birkenau, dug by the Penal Company. It was notorious for the numerous bestial murders committed there by the SS.

Kripo (Kriminalpolizei) Criminal Police.

"Mexico" Never completed Section B-III of Birkenau.

"Moslems" Prisoners who were at the absolute end of their physical and psychological resources—the living dead.

NN (Nacht und Nebel) "Night and Fog" operation, whereby citizens in the occupied countries of Western Europe whom the Nazis considered dangerous were made to disappear without a trace.

"Old crematorium" Also called the "small crematorium," this was the first crematorium, located next to the main camp, for executions by gassing or shooting. It was shut down in 1943 after the construction of the large crematoriums in Birkenau.

Orderly rooms (Schreibstuben) Literally, "writing chambers," these offices regulated and recorded all the internal activities of the camp: admissions, assignment to residential blocks, maintaining files and card indexes, etc. They were run entirely by prisoners.

Orpo (Ordnungspolizei) Regular police, literally, "order" police.

O.S. (Oberschlesien) Upper Silesia.

OSMAG (Oberschlesische Maschinen- und Waggonfabrik AG) Upper Silesia Machine and Vehicle Factory, Inc.

Penal Company Prisoners who were punished by being sent to the Penal Company were housed separately, and were not allowed to have any contact with other prisoners or to send or receive letters. The conditions in the Penal Company were significantly worse than in the camp itself, and despite the fact that the heaviest work was done, usually at a forced run, the food was particularly bad.

Personal Effects Depot or Camp Called "Canada" because to the Poles Canada represented unlimited abundance, this was the complex where possessions stolen from deportees were sorted, processed, and stored. Initially the goods were stored in five barracks; ultimately there were 30 such barracks.

Police Court-martial (of the Kattowitz Gestapo) At irregular intervals, sessions of the Police Court-martial were held in Block 11, where prisoners who had been brutally tortured during interrogations were sentenced.

Police prisoners Prisoners who were locked up in Block 11 but were not formally prisoners of Auschwitz but rather of the Kattowitz Gestapo; most were condemned to death by the Police Court-martial of the Kattowitz Gestapo.

Political Department The camp Gestapo office, which was partially independent of the camp management. This led to frequent tensions. Admissions to and releases from the camp as well as all correspondence from and to the Gestapo outside the camp were handled by the Political Department.

PPR (Polska Partia Robotnicza) Polish Labor Party.

PPS (Polska Partia Socjalistyczna) Polish Socialist Party.

Prisoner functionaries (Funktionshäftlinge) Prisoners chosen by the SS to fill certain positions such as Block Senior, Camp Senior, or Capo. They wore a special identifying armband.

Prisoner identification badges In addition to the number tattooed onto the left forearm, prisoners were identified by means of a fabric triangle sewn onto the left shirt front and right trouser leg. A red triangle signified a political prisoner; a green triangle was a criminal; purple was for Jehovah's Witnesses (IBV prisoners); black was for "asocials"; pink for homosexuals; brown for Gypsies. Those who had escaped and been returned, so-called recidivists, wore a diagonal stripe of the same color above the triangle. Jews wore in addition a yellow triangle sewn on under the colored triangle, so that a six-pointed star resulted. The nationality was indicated by an initial stamped on the triangle, thus T for Czechs (Tschechen), F for French, P for Poles, etc. Members of the Penal Company had a black dot between the lower triangle and the number; suspected escapees had a red-and-white bull's-eye painted or sewn on the chest and back of their shirts.

Prisoner orderly Prisoner who worked as a nurse in a prisoners' infirmary or in one of the medical "research" stations.

Prisoner physician Imprisoned doctors giving medical care to other prisoners.

Protective Custody Commander (Schutzhaftlagerführer) SS officer responsible to the Commandant for the camp or, in Birkenau, a camp section. The title stems from the original cover-up term for incarceration in a concentration camp, "protective custody."

PSV (Polizeisicherheitsverwahrung) Police security detention.

PWOK (Pomoc Więźniom Obozów Koncentracyjnych) Committee for Assistance to Concentration Camp Prisoners (Kraków).

Quarantine Isolation of newly arrived prisoners, ostensibly for the purpose of preventing the spread of infectious diseases. Actually, its purpose was to introduce new arrivals to the "laws" of the camp, through drills and "sport" lasting many hours in the roll-call area, and to break their spirit and will to resist.

Ramp Platform where deportees were unloaded and selected. The "old ramp" was located near the railroad facilities between the main camp and Birkenau. The "new ramp" was in the Birkenau camp between Sections B-I and B-II and led to Crematoriums II and III.

RKG (russischer Kriegsgefangener) Russian prisoner of war.

Roll Call Clerk A prisoner functionary who prepared the reports for the SS regarding the camp occupancy level.

Roll Call Leader (Rapportführer) A noncommissioned SS officer who was the immediate superior of the camp's Block Commanders or, in Birkenau, the Block Commanders in one camp section.

RSHA (Reichssicherheitszentralstelle) **transports** Transports of Jews organized by Eichmann's office, Jewish Section IV-B4, of the Reich Central Security Office.

RWO (Rada Wojskowa Obozu) Camp Military Council.

SA (Sturmabteilung) Literally, "assault department"; until 1934, the elite, left-oriented paramilitary corps of the Nazi Party.

SB (Sonderbehandlung) "Special treatment," a camouflage term for liquidation.

SD (Sicherheitsdienst) Security service within the SS.

Sentry lines The securing of the camp's borders by means of fences and sentries. The *inner sentry line* (kleine Postenkette) consisted of concrete piers connected by electrically charged barbed wire, the whole thing illuminated at night. There were watchtowers at 265-foot intervals. The inner sentry line literally enclosed the camp. The *outer sentry line* coincided with the border of the so-called off-limits zone. The watchtowers were ca. 220 yards apart. Usually guards were in the watchtowers in the daytime only, until the labor squads returned to the camp. But if a prisoner escaped the towers of the outer sentry line were occupied for three days around the clock. The outer perimeter was not secured by any fencing.

Sipo (Sicherheitspolizei) Security Police; combined Kripo and Gestapo.

SS (Schutzstaffel) Nazi Party elite guards.

SS sick bay Building right next to the main camp, across from the "old crematorium," where slightly ill SS members were treated. In the same building were also the offices of the SS Garrison Doctor, the SS dental office, the SS drug dispensary, and other offices at various times.

Standing cells Cells in the bunker of Block 11 measuring 35 × 35 inches, with one window measuring 2 × 2 inches. Four prisoners were locked in one cell. After standing all night they were led off with the other prisoners to work.

Theresienstadt Family Camp Family camp in Camps B-IIb and B-IIe (the Gypsy Family Camp) in Birkenau, where Jews deported from the Theresienstadt ghetto and Gypsies (Sinti and Roma) lived as families (not separated by sex, as in the rest of the camp), until their liquidation in March 1944.

V-Man (Verbindungsmann) Camp informer for the SS, literally "contact man." The term originally came from the world of professional crime.

WVHA (Wirtschafts- und Verwaltungshauptamt) Economic and Administrative Office, an SS "ministry." Branch D was responsible for running the concentration camps, though Branch C (Works and Buildings) and Branch W (Economic Enterprises) also had direct interests in the camps.

Z (Zigeuner) Gypsy.

Zyklon B A poisonous gas used by the SS for mass exterminations in the gas chambers. Made from hydrogen cyanide crystals, it was originally manufactured as a strong disinfectant and for pest control.

BIBLIOGRAPHY

Abbreviations Used in Footnotes, Source Notes, and Bibliography
(*Abbreviations whose use is not confined to the notes and Bibliography can be found in the Glossary on page 827.*)

AGKBZH (Archiwum Głównej Komisji Badania Zbrodni Hitlerowskich w Polsce) = Archive of the High Commission for the Investigation of Nazi Crimes in Poland

APMO (Archiwum Panstwowego Muzeum w Oświęcimiu) = Archive of the State Auschwitz Museum

BA (Bundesarchiv) **Koblenz** = Archive of the Federal Republic of Germany, Coblenz

CA KC PZPR (Centralne Archiwum Komitetu Centralnego Polskiej Zjednoczonej Partii Robotniczej) = Central Archive of the Central Committee of the United Polish Workers' Party

CDECM (Centro di Documentazione Ebraica Contemporana di Milano) = Center for Jewish Contemporary Documentation, Milan

Docs. of ISD (Internationaler Suchdienst) **Arolsen** = Documents of the International Red Cross Search Service in Arolsen, Federal Republic of Germany

Docs. ZBL (Zentralbauleitung) = Documents of the Central Construction Administration

FL (Frauenlager) = women's camp

FvD (Führer vom Dienst) = the log of the commander on duty

GKBZHP (Głównej Komisji Badania Zbrodni Hitlerowskich w Polsce) = High Commission for the Investigation of Nazi Crimes in Poland

HKB (Häftlingskrankenbau) = prisoners' infirmary

HvA (*Hefte von Auschwitz*) = *Notebooks of Auschwitz*, the journal of the State Auschwitz Museum (Oświęcim)

IMG (Internationaler Militärgerichtshof) = International Military Tribunal

KGL (Kriegsgefangenenlager) = prisoner-of-war camp

Mat.Ref.Inf. (Materiał Referatu Informacji) = Materials of the Information Section

Mat.RO (Materiały Ruchu Oporu) = Materials of the Camp Resistance Movement

NA = number assignment

Ośw. = Oświęcim

PAP (Powiatowe Archiwum Państwowe) **Pszczyna** = State Archive, Pszczyna District

PL (*Przeglad Lekạrski*) = *Medical Survey*, journal of the Medical Society of Kraków.

q.v. (quod vide) = work mentioned has a separate bibliographical entry

SAM = State Auschwitz Museum (Oświęcim)

WAP (Wojewódzkie Archiwum Państwowe) **Kattowitz** = State Archive of the Katowice District

Wsp. (Wspomnienia) = Memoirs

ZO (*Zeszyty Oświęcimskie*) = Polish edition of *Hefte von Auschwitz*

Adelsberger, Lucie. *Auschwitz: Ein Tatsachenbericht.* 3d ed. Berlin, 1960.

Adler, H. -G. *Theresienstadt 1941–1945: Das Antlitz einer Zwangsgemeinschaft—Geschichte, Soziologie, Psychologie* (Theresienstadt 1941–1945: The Face of an Involuntary Community—History, Sociology, Psychology). Tübingen, 1955.

Adler, H. -G.; Langbein, Hermann; Lingens-Reiner, Ella; eds. *Auschwitz: Zeugnisse und Berichte* (Auschwitz: Testimonies and Reports). 3d rev. ed. Cologne, Frankfurt, 1984.

Akten zur Deutschen Auswärtigen Politik 1918–1945 (Documents of German Foreign Policy 1918–1945). Series D, vol. VII. Baden-Baden, 1956.

August, Jocher, ed. *Die Auschwitz-Hefte: Texte der polnischen Zeitschrift "Przegląd Lekarski" über historische, psychische und medizinische Aspekte des Lebens und Sterbens in Auschwitz* (The Auschwitz Notebooks: Texts of the Polish Journal *Przegąld Lekarski* on Historical, Psychological and Medical Aspects of Life and Death in Auschwitz). Published by the Hamburg Institute of Social Research. Weinheim, Basel, 1987.

Biuletyn Głównej Komisji Badania Zbrodni Hitlerowskich w Polsce (Bulletin of the High Commission for the Investigation of Nazi Crimes in Poland). Vols. 1–24. Warsaw, 1946–1974.

Blumenthal et al., eds. *Dokumenty i materiały do dziejów okupacji niemieckiej w Polsce* (Documents and Materials on the German Occupation of Poland). Vol. I, *Obozy* (Camps). Lodz, 1946.

Brahm, Randolph L. *The Destruction of Hungarian Jewry (September 1940–April 1945): A Documentary Account.* New York, 1963.

Brandhuber, Jerzy Adam. "Die sowjetischen Kriegsgefangenen im Konzentrationslager Auschwitz" (Soviet Prisoners of War in Auschwitz Concentration Camp). *HvA*, no. 4 (1961): 5–45.

———. "Vergessene Erde" (Forgotten Ground). *HvA* (q.v.), no. 5 (1962): 83–95.

Broad, Pery, "KZ-Auschwitz: Erinnerungen eines SS-Mannes der Politischen Abteilung in dem Konzentrationslager Auschwitz" (Auschwitz: Memoirs of an SS Man of the Political Department in Auschwitz Concentration Camp). *HvA*, no. 9 (1966): pp. 7–48.

Brol, Franciszek; Wloch, Gerard; Pilecki, Jan. "Das Bunkerbuch des Blocks 11 im Nazi-Konzentrationslager Auschwitz" (The Bunker Register of Block 11 in the Nazi Concentration Camp Auschwitz). *HvA*, no. 1 (1959): 7–42.

Brugioni, Dino A., and Poirier, Robert G. *The Holocaust Revisited: A Retrospective Analysis of the Auschwitz-Birkenau Extermination Complex.* Washington, D.C., 1979.

Bullock, Alan. *Hitler: A Study in Tyranny.* New York, 1958.

Cegłowska, Teresa. "Strafkompanien im KL Auschwitz" (Penal Companies in Auschwitz Concentration Camp). *HvA*, no. 17 (1985): 157–203.

Centro di Dokumentazione Ebraica Contemporana di Milano (Center for Contemporary Jewish Documentation, Milan (CDECM). *Ebrei in Italia: Deportazione, Resistenza* (Jews in Italy: Deportation, Resistance). Florence, 1974.

Churchill, Winston S. *The Grand Alliance.* World War II, Memoirs, vol. III. Boston: Houghton Mifflin, 1986.

Comité International de la Croix Rouge (CICR). "Visite au Commandant du camp d'Auschwitz d'un délégue du CICR (Septembre 1944)" (Visit to the Commandant of Auschwitz by a Delegate of the International Committee of the Red Cross in September 1944), in *Documents sur l'activité du Comité International de la Croix Rouge en faveur des civils détenus dans les camps de concentration en Allemagne (1938–1945)* (Documents on the Activity of the International Committee of the Red Cross on Behalf of Civilians Detained in Concentration Camps in Germany [1938–1945]). Geneva, 1947.

Committee of Antifascist Resistance Fighters in the German Democratic Republic. *Schuldig im Sinne des Rechts und des Völkerrechts: Auszüge aus dem Protokoll des Prozesses gegen den KZ-Arzt [Horst] Fischer vor dem Obersten Gericht der DDR* (Guilty Under National and International Law: Extracts from the Protocol of the Trial of Concentration Camp Doctor [Horst] Fischer Before the Supreme Court of the German Democratic Republic). Published by the Committee's Working Group of Former Prisoners of Auschwitz, and the National Council of the National Front of Democratic Germany. Berlin, 1966.

————. *SS im Einsatz: Eine Dokumentation über die Verbrechen der SS* (The SS in Action: A Documentation of the Crimes of the SS). Berlin, 1957.

Cyprian, Tadeusz, and Sawicki, Jerzy, *Materiały Norymberskie* (The Nuremberg Materials). Warsaw, 1948.

Czech, Danuta. "Die Rolle des Häftlingskrankenbaulagers im KL Auschwitz II" (The Role of Prisoners' Infirmaries in Auschwitz II). *HvA*, no. 15 (1975): 5–112.

Domańska, Regina. *Pawiak, Więzienie Gestapo: Kronika 1939–1944* (Pawiak, a Gestapo Prison: Chronicle, 1939–1944). Warsaw, 1978.

Döring, Hans-Joachim. *Die Zigeuner im Nationalsozialistischen Staat* (Gypsies in the Nazi State). Hamburg, 1964.

Drobisch, Klaus. *Widerstand in Buchenwald* (Resistance in Buchenwald). Berlin, 1977.

Droździński, Aleksander. "Maly spokojny obóz" (A Small Quiet Camp). *ZO*, no. 8 (1964): 35–52.

Encyklopedia II wojny światowej (Encyclopedia of World War II). Warsaw, 1975.

Eschwege, Helmut, ed. *Kennzeichen J: Bilder, Dokumente, Berichte zur Geschichte der Verbrechen des Hitlerfaschismus an den deutschen Juden 1933–1945* (The Letter J: Photographs, Documents, Reports on the History of the Crimes of Hitler's Fascism Against the German Jews, 1933–1945). Berlin, 1966.

Fejkiel, Władysław. "Eksperymenty sanitariatu SS w Ościwięcimiu" (Experiments of SS Medical Officers in Auschwitz). In *Okupacja i medycyna* (The Occupation and Medicine). Vol. I (q.v.), pp. 40–44.

Fiderkiewicz, Alfred. *Brzezinka: Wspomnienia z obozu* (Birkenau, Memories of the Concentration Camp). Warsaw, 1954.

Frackiewicz, Jerzy. "Das Nebenlager Golleschau" (The Golleschau Auxiliary Camp). *HvA*, no. 9 (1966): 57–74.

————. "Das Nebenlager Lagischa" (The Lagischa Auxiliary Camp). *HvA*, no. 9 (1966): 19–124.

Garliński, Jósef. *Óświęcim walczący* (Fighting Auschwitz: The Resistance Movement in the Concentration Camp). London, 1975.

Gilbert, Martin. *Auschwitz und die Allierten* (Auschwitz and the Allies). Munich, 1982. *Auschwitz and the Allies* was originally published in the U.S. (New York: Henry Holt, 1982).

————. *Endlösung: Die Vertreibung und Vernichtung der Juden—Ein Atlas* (The Final Solution: The Expulsion and Destruction of the Jews—An Atlas), Reinbek/Hamburg, 1982. Originally published in the U.S. as *Atlas of the Holocaust* (New York: Macmillan, 1982).

Grynberg Michał. *Żydzi w rejencji ciechanowskiej 1939–1942* (Jews in the Zichenau Administrative District 1939–1942). Warsaw, 1984.

Gutman, Israel. "Der Aufstand des Sonderkommandos" (The Uprising of the Special Squad). In Adler et al., eds. *Auschwitz: Testimonies and Reports* (q.v.), pp. 273–279.

Hefte von Auschwitz (Auschwitz Notebooks, edited by Kazimierz Smoleń. Journal published by the State Auschwitz Museum, Oświęcim (cited as *HvA*). Published in Polish as *Zeszyty Oświęcimskie* (*ZO*).

Heller, Paul. "Das Aussenlager Jaworzno" (The Jaworzno Auxiliary Camp). In Adler et al., eds. *Auschwitz: Zeugnisse und Berichte* (q.v.), pp. 169–171.

Herman, Chaim. Manuscript in *Amid Unspeakable Crimes* (q.v.), pp. 193–203.

Hilberg, Raul. *Sondazüge nach Auschwitz* (Special Trains to Auschwitz). Documents on Railroad History, vol. 18. Mainz, 1981.

Höss, Rudolf. *Kommandant in Auschwitz: Autobiographische Aufzeichnungen des Rudolf*

Höss (Commandant in Auschwitz: Autobiography of Rudolf Höss). Edited by Martin Broszat. Munich, 1963. An English-language edition was published in Cleveland, 1959.

Internationaler Militärgerichtshof Nürnberg (International Military Tribunal, Nuremberg). *Der Prozess gegen die Hauptkriegsverbrecher vor dem Internationalen Militärgerichtshof* (The Trial of the Principal War Criminals Before the International Military Tribunal). Vols. 1–42. Nuremberg, 1947–1949 (cited as IMG). *Trials of War Criminals Before the Nuremberg Military Tribunals* (15 vols.) was published in the U.S. in Washington, D.C., 1949–1954.

Iswaszko, Emeryka. "Das 'Aussenkommando Chełmek,' Innenkommando Chełmek" ("Chełmek Outside Squad," Chełmek Inside Squad). *HvA*, no. 12 (1970): 45–54.

———. "Das Nebenlager Janinagrube" (Janinagrube Auxiliary Camp). *HvA*, no. 10 (1967): 41–66.

———. "Podoboź Brünn" (Brünn Outside Squad). *ZO*, no. 18 (1983): 223–244.

Iwaszko, Tadeusz. "Häftlingsfluchten aus dem KL Auschwitz" (Escapes from Auschwitz). *HvA*, no. 7 (1964): 3–57.

———. "Das Nebenlager Fürstengrube" (Fürstengrube Auxiliary Camp). *HvA*, no. 16 (1978): 5–92.

———. "Das Nebenlager Günthergrube" (Günthergrube Auxiliary Camp). *HvA*, no. 12 (1970): 113–144.

———. "Das Nebenlager Laurahütte" (Laurahütte Auxiliary Camp). *HvA*, no. 10 (1967): 87–102.

———. "Ucieczki więźniarek z KL Auschwitz" (Escape Attempts of Female Prisoners from Auschwitz). *ZO*, no. 18 (1983): 145–185.

Jaldati, Lin. "Erinnerungen an Anne Frank" (Memories of Anne Frank). In Joachim Hellwig and Günther Deicke, *Ein Tagebuch für Anne Frank* (A Diary for Anne Frank), Berlin, 1959, pp. 32–46.

Janke, Zygmunt Walter. *Armia Krajowa na Śląsku w świetle dokumentów niemieckich: Najnowsze dzieje Polski—Materiały ż studia z okresu II wojny światowej* (The Home Army in Silesia in Light of German Documents: Recent History of Poland—Material and Studies of the Period of World War II). Vol. III. Warsaw, 1959.

Jarosz, Barbara. "Widerstandsbewegung im Lager und in der Umgebung" (Resistance Movement in the Camp and the Vicinity). In Jozef Buszko, Danuta Czech, Tadeusz Iwaszko, Franciszo Piper, Barbara Jarosz, Andrzej Strzelecki, and Kazimierz Smolén, eds., *Auschwitz: Geschichte und Wirklichkeit des Vernichtungslagers* (Auschwitz: History and Reality of the Extermination Camp) Reinbek/Hamburg, 1980, pp. 143–168.

Jaworski, Czesław Wincenty. *Wspomnienia z Oświęcimia* (Memories of Auschwitz), Warsaw, 1962.

Jewish Historical Institute (Warsaw). *Biuletyn Żydowskiego Instytutu Historycznego* (Bulletin of the Jewish Historical Institute), no. 43–44 (1962).

———. *Faschismus, Getto, Massenmord: Dokumentation über Ausrottung und Widerstand der Juden in Polen während des Zweiten Weltkrieges* (Fascism, Ghetto, Mass Murder: Documentation of the Extermination and Resistance of the Jews in Poland During World War II). 2d ed. Berlin, 1961.

Justa, Krystyna. *Z bagna i kamieni* (From Swamp and Stone), Warsaw, 1948.

Kagan, Raya. "Die letzten Opfer des Widerstands" (The Last Victims of the Resistance). In Adler et al., eds., *Auschwitz: Testimonies and Reports* (q.v.), pp. 280–286.

Kaul, Friedrich Karl. *Ärtzte in Auschwitz* (Doctors in Auschwitz). Berlin, 1968.

Kempner, Robert M. W. *Edith Stein und Anne Frank, Zwei von Hunderttausend: Die Enthüllungen über die NS-Verbrechen in Holland vor dem Schwurgericht in München—Die Ermordung der nichtarischen Mönche und Nonnen* (Edith Stein and Anne Frank, Two Out of a Hundred Thousand: The Revelations Regarding Nazi Crimes in Holland in the General Court in Munich—the Murder of non-Aryan Monks and Nuns). Freiburg, Basel, Vienna, 1968.

Kiedrzyńska, Wanda. *Ravensbrück: Kobiecy obóz koncentracyjny* (Ravensbrück: A Women's Concentration Camp). Warsaw, 1961.

Kielar, Wiesław. *Anus Mundi: Fünf Jahre Auschwitz* (Anus Mundi: Five Years of Auschwitz). Frankfurt, 1979.

Klarsfeld, Serge. *Memorial to the Jews Deported from France 1942–1944: A Documentation of the Deportation of the Victims of the Final Solution in France.* New York, 1983.

Klarsfeld, Serge, and Steinberg, Maxime. *Mémorial de la déportation des juifs de Belgigue* (Memorial of the Deportation of the Jews of Belgium). Brussels, 1982.

Klee. *What They Did.* Frankfurt, 1986.

Klodziński, Stanisław. "Esemani z oświęcimskiej 'służby zdrowia' " (The SS Men of the "Health Service" in Auschwitz). In *Okupacja i medycyna* (The Occupation and Medicine). Vol. I (q.v.), pp. 339–345.

———. "Maria Stromberger." *PL*, no. 1a (1962): 102–107.

———. "Rola kryminalistów niemieckich w początkach obozu oświęcimskiego" (The Role of German Criminal Prisoners in the Origins of Auschwitz. *PL* (1974): 113–126. Also in *Okupacja i medycyna* (The Occupation and Medicine). Vol III (q.v.), pp. 45–70.

Kolb, Eberhard. *Bergen-Belsen: Vom "Aufenthaltslager" zum Konzentrationslager, 1943–1945* (Bergen-Belsen: From "Transit Camp" to Concentration Camp, 1943–1945). Hanover, 1962.

Konieczny, Alfred. "Bemerkungen über die Anfänge des Konzentrationslagers Auschwitz" (Notes on the Beginnings of Auschwitz Concentration Camp). *HvA,* no. 12 (1971): 5–44.

———. "Uwagi o sądzie doraźnym katowickiego Gestapo pod kierownictwem SS-Obersturmbannführera Johannesa Thümmlera" (Notes on the Police Court-martial of the Kattowitz Gestapo under the Direction of SS Lieutenant Colonel Johannes Thümmler). *Biuletyn GKBZHwP,* vol. 24 (1972): 105–168.

Kowalski, Stanisław. *Numer 4410 opowiada* (Number 4410 Speaks). Milwaukee, 1985.

Kozłowiecki, Adam. *Ucisk i strapienie: Pamiętnik więźnia 1939–1945* (Affliction and Anguish: Memoirs of a Prisoner, 1939–1945). Kraków, 1967.

Kraus, Ota, and Kulka, Erich. *Tovarna na smrt* (The Death Factory). Prague, 1957.

Kret, Józef. "Ein Tag in der Strafkompagnie (Erinnerung)" (A Day in the Punishment Company [Memoirs]. *HvA,* no. 1 (1959): 87–124.

———. *Ostatni krąg* (The Last Circle). Kraków, 1973.

Krosnowski, Ryszard, and Miziewicz, Aleksander. "7. SS-Eisenbahnbaubrigade" (The 7th Railroad Construction Brigade). *ZO,* no. 5 (1961): 41–50.

Kursbuch für die Gefangenenwagen, gültig vom 6. Oktober 1941 an. Mit einem Anhang: Nummernplan und Übersichtszeichnungen der eingesetzten Gefangenwagen (Timetable for Prisoner Cars, valid from October 6, 1941. With an Appendix: Numbering Plan and a Summary of Drawings of Prison Cars in Use). Documents on Railroad History. Vol. 10. Reprint. Mainz, 1979.

Langbein, Hermann. *Der Auschwitz-Prozess: Eine Dokumentation* (The Auschwitz Trial: A Documentation). Frankfurt, 1965.

———. *Menschen in Auschwitz* (People in Auschwitz). Vienna, 1972.

———. *Die Stärkeren: Ein Bericht aus Auschwitz und anderen Konzentrationslagern* (The Stronger: A Report from Auschwitz and Other Concentration Camps). 2d rev. ed. Cologne, 1982.

Lánik, Jožko. *Oświęcim, hrobka štyroch milionov ľudi* (Auschwitz, the Grave of Four Million People). Bratislava, n.d. Joško Lanik is a pseudonym for Alfred Wetzler.

Laqueur, Walter, and Breitman, Richard. *Der Mann, der das Schweigen brach: Wie die Welt vom Holocaust erfuhr* (The Man Who Broke the Silence: How the World Learned of the Holocaust). Frankfurt, Berlin, Vienna, 1986.

Lejb, ( ). Manuscript in *HvA,* no. 14 (1973): 17–71.

Leszczyńska, Zofia. *Kronika obozu na Majdanku* (Chronicle of the Camp in Majdanek). Lublin, 1980.

Lewental, Sałmen. Handwritten manuscript. In SAM, *Inmitten des grauenvollen Verbrechens* (Amid Unspeakable Crimes), q.v., pp. 131–189.

Lifton, Robert Jay. *The Nazi Doctors*. New York: Basic Books, 1986.

Madajczyka, Czesława, ed. *Zamojszczyzna—Sonderlaboratorium SS: Zbiór dokumentów polskich i niemieckich z okresu okupacji hitlerowskiej* (The Zamość Region—Special Laboratory of the SS: A Collection of Polish and German Documents from the Nazi Occupation). Vols. I and II. Warsaw, 1977.

Makowski, Antoni. "Organisation, Entwicklung und Tätigkeit des Häftlings-Krankenbaus in Monowitz (KL Auschwitz III)" (Organization, Development and Activities of the Prisoners' Infirmary in Monowitz [Auschwitz III]). *HvA*, no. 15 (1975): 113–181.

Menasche, Albert. *Birkenau (Auschwitz II)*. New York, 1947.

Mermelstein, Mel. *By Bread Alone: The Story of A-4685*. Los Angeles, 1979.

Mikulski, Jan. "Pharmakologische Experimente im Konzentrationslager Auschwitz-Birkenau" (Pharmacological Experiments in Auschwitz-Birkenau Concentration Camp). *HvA*, no. 10, (1967): 3–18.

Mitscherlich, Alexander, and Mielke, Fred, eds. *Medizin ohne Menschlichkeit: Dokumente des Nürnberger Ärzteprozesses* (Medicine Without Humanity: Documents of the Nuremberg Doctors Trial). Frankfurt, 1960.

Musioł, Teodor. *Dachau 1933–1945*. Katowice, 1968.

Nyiszli, Miklós. *Pracownia doktora Mengele, Wspomnienia lekarza z Oświęcimia* (The Laboratory of Dr. Mengele: Memoirs of a Physician at Auschwitz). Warsaw, 1966.

"Obóz koncentracyny Oświęcim w świetle akt Delegatury Rządu R.P. na Kraj" (Auschwitz Concentration Camp in Light of Documents of the Delegation of the Polish Government in Exile). *ZO*, special issue I (1968).

Okupacja i medycyna (The Occupation and Medicine). A selection of essays from *Przegląd Lekarski—Oświęcim* (Medical Overview—Oswięcim). Vol. I, 1961–1970. Warsaw, 1971. Vol. III, 1963–1976. Warsaw, 1977.

Olbrycht, Jan. "Sprawy zdrowotne w obozie koncentracyjnym w Oświęcimiu: Orzeczenie wygłoszone na rozprawie sądowej przed Najwyzszym Trybunałem Narodowym w dniu 10 grudnia 1947" (Questions of Health in Auschwitz Concentration Camp: Statements Made During the Trial at the Supreme People's Court, December 10, 1947). *PL*, no. 1a (1962): 37–49.

Ostańkowicz, Czesław, "Isolierstation—'Letzter' Block" (Isolation Ward—"Last" Block). *HvA*, no. 16 (1978): 159–187.

Paczuła, Tadeusz. "Organizacja i administracja szpitala obozowego KL Auschwitz I" (The Organization and Administration of the Prisoners' Infirmary in Auschwitz I). *PL*, no. 1a (1962): 61–68.

Pawliczek, Stanisław. "Droga do słońca" (The Road to the Sun). *ZO*, no. 5 (1961): 87–95.

Perkowska-Szczypiorska, Irena. *Pamiętnhik łączniczki* (Memoirs of a Courier). Warsaw, 1962.

Piątkowska, Antonina. *Wspomnienia oświęcimskie* (Auschwitz Memoirs). Kraków, 1977.

Piper, Franciszek. "Das Nebenlager Althammer" (Althammer Auxiliary Camp). *HvA*, no. 13 (1971): 141–158.

———. "Das Nebenlager Blechhammer" (Blechhammer Auxiliary Camp). *HvA*, no. 10 (1967): 19–39.

———. "Das Nebenlager Eintrachthütte" (Eintrachthütte Auxiliary Camp). *HvA*, no. 17 (1985): 91–155.

———. "Das Nebenlager Neu-Dachs" (Neu-Dachs Auxiliary Camp). *HvA*, no. 12 (1971) 55–111.

———. "Das Nebenlager Sosnowitz (I)" (Sosnowitz [I] Auxiliary Camp). *HvA*, no. 11 (1970): 89–96.

———. "Das Nebenlager Sosnowitz (II)" (Sosnowitz [II] Auxiliary Camp). *HvA*, no. 11 (1970): 97–128.

———. "Das Nebenlager Trzebinia" (Trzebinia Auxiliary Camp). *HvA*, no. 16 (1978): 93–135.

———. *Żatrudnienie więźniów KL Auschwitz: Organizacja pracy i methody eksploatacji sily roboczej* (Labor Deployment of Prisoners in Auschwitz Concentration Camp: Organization of Labor and Methods of Exploitation of Manpower). Oświęcim, 1981.

Poliakov, Léon, and Wulf, Josef. *Das Dritte Reich und die Juden: Documente und Aufsatze* (The Third Reich and the Jews: Documents and Essays). Berlin-Grünewald, 1955.

Przegląd Lekarski (Medical Survey). Journal of the Medical Society of Kraków.

Reitlinger, Gerald. *Die Endlösung: Hitlers Versuch der Ausrottung der Juden* (The Final Solution: Hitler's Attempt to Extirpate the Jews). Berlin, 1956. Published in the U.S. as *The Final Solution* (New York, 1961).

Schnabel, Reimund. *Macht ohne Moral: Eine Dokumentation über die SS* (Power Without Morality: Documentation on the SS). Frankfurt, 1957.

Sehn, Jan. "Carl Claubergs verbrecherische Unfruchtbarmachungs-Versuche an Häftlings-Frauen in den Nazi-Konzentrationslagern" (Carl Clauberg's Criminal Sterilization Experiments on Female Prisoners in the Nazi Concentration Camps). *HvA*, no. 2 (1959): 3–32, 51–87 (document appendix).

———. *Konzentrationslager Oświęcim-Brzezinka* (Auschwitz-Birkenau Concentration Camp). Published by the Central Committee for the Investigation of Nazi Crimes in Poland. Warsaw, 1957.

———. Introduction to *Wspomnienia Rudolfa Hössa, komndanta obozu oświęcimskiego* (Polish edition of Rudolf Höss's Autobiography). Warsaw, 1956.

Škodowa, Julia. *Tri roky bez mena* (Three Years Without a Name). Bratislava, 1962.

Smoleń, Kazimierz. "Sprawa Nr. 13" ("Case No. 13"). In *Wolni ludzie* (Free Men), no. 11 (June 1948).

Sobański, Tomasz. *Ucieczki oświęcimskie* (Escapes from Auschwitz). 3d ed. Warsaw, 1974.

State Auschwitz Museum (SAM). *Inmitten des grauenvollen Verbrechens* (Amid Unspeakable Crimes). Handwritten manuscripts of members of the Special Squad. *HvA*, special issue no. I (1972). Published in Polish as *Wśród koszmarnej zbrodni*, ZO, special issue no. I (1971).

———. *KL Auschwitz in den Augen der SS: Höss, Broad, Kremer* (Auschwitz Concentration Camp in the Eyes of the SS: Höss, Broad, Kremer). Oświęcim, 1973.

Strzelecka, Irena. "Arbeitslager Gleiwitz I" (Gleiwitz I Labor Camp). *HvA*, no. 14 (1973): 75–106.

———. "Arbeitslager Gleiwitz II" (Gleiwitz II Labor Camp). *HvA*, no. 14 (1973): 107–127.

———. "Das Nebenlager Bismarckhütte" (Bismarckhütte Auxiliary Camp). *HvA*, no. 12 (1971): 145–159.

———. "Das Nebenlager Hindenburg" (Hindenburg Auxiliary Camp). *HvA*, no. 11 (1970): 129–147.

———. "Das Nebenlager Hubertushütte (Arbeitslager Hohenlinde)" (Hubertushütte Auxiliary Camp [Hohenlinde Labor Camp]). *HvA*, no. 12 (1971): 161–173.

———. "Das Nebenlager Neustadt" (Neustadt Auxiliary Camp). *HvA*, no. 13 (1971): 159–170.

———. "Pierwsi: Polacy w KL Auschwitz" (The First Poles in Auschwitz). ZO, no. 18 (1983): 5–144.

Strzelecka, Irena, and Szymański, Tadeusz. "Podobozy Tschechowitz-Bombensuchkommando i Tschechowitz—Vacuum (Tschechowitz Bomb Search Squad Auxiliary Camp and Tschechowitz—Vacuum). ZO, no. 18 (1983): 187–222.

Strzelecki, Andrzej. "Arbeitslager Gleiwitz III" (Gleiwitz III Labor Camp). *HvA*, no. 14 (1973): 129–150.

———. "Arbeitslager Gleiwitz IV" (Gleiwitz IV Labor Camp). *HvA*, no. 14 (1972): 151–169.

———. "Das Nebenlager Charlottengrube in Rydułtowy" (Charlottengrube Auxiliary Camp in Rydułtowy). *HvA*, no. 17 (1985): 41–90.

———. "Das Nebenlager Jawischowitz" (Jawischowitz Auxiliary Camp). *HvA*, no. 15 (1975): 183–250.

——. *Ewakuacja, likwidacja i wyzwolenie KL Auschwitz* (Evacuation, Liquidation and Liberation of Auschwitz Concentration Camp). Oświęcim, 1982.

——. "Wyzwolenie KL Auschwitz" (The Liberation of Auschwitz Concentration Camp). *ZO*, special issue no. III (1974).

Szmaglewska, Seweryna. *Smoke over Birkenau.* New York, 1947.

Szternfinkiel, Natan Eliasz. *Zaglada Żydów Sosnowca* (The Extermination of the Jews of Sosnowitz). Katowice, 1946.

Szweda, Konrad. "Katakumby XX wieku" (Catacombs of the Twentieth Century). *Gość Niedzielny* (The Sunday Guest), Sept. 22, 1946.

Ternon, Yves, and Helman, Socrate. *Historia medycyny SS czyli mit rasizmu biologiecznego* (The History of SS Medicine, or the Myth of Biological Racism). Warsaw, 1973.

Tymiński, Kazimierz. *Uspokoić sen* (To Quiet Sleep). Katowice, 1985.

Veble-Hodnikova, Jažica. *Preživela sem taborišče smrti* (I Survived the Death Camp). Liubliana, 1960.

Wistrich, Robert. *Who's Who in Nazi Germany.* New York: Macmillan, 1982.

Wnuk, Włodzimierz. *Walka podziemna na szczytach* (The Underground Struggle on the Peaks). Poznań, 1948.

Wróbel, Halina. "Die Liquidation des Konzentrationslagers Auschwitz-Birkenau" (The Liquidation of Auschwitz-Birkenau Concentration Camp). *HvA*, no. 6 (1962): 3–41.

Wroński, Tadeusz. *Kronika okupowanego Krakowa* (Chronicle of Occupied Kraków). Kraków, 1974.

Wyman, David S. "Why Auschwitz Was Never Bombed." *Commentary*, May 1978.

Za Wolność i lud (For Freedom and the People), no. 6, Warsaw, 1951.

Zieba, Anna. "Die Geflügelfarm Harmense" (The Harmense Poultry Farm). *HvA*, no. 11 (1970): 39–72.

——. "Das Nebenlager Rajsko" (Rajsko Auxiliary Camp). *HvA*, no. 9 (1966): 75–108.

Zywulska, Krystyna. *Przeżyłam Oświęcim* (I Survived Auschwitz). Warsaw, 1960.

INDEX OF NAMES